THE STRUCTURE OF ECONOMICS
A Mathematical Analysis

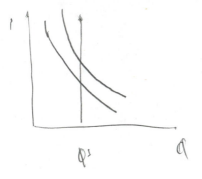

Q^s Q

$Q = 50 - 2p$ $Q = 60 - 3p$

$2p = 50 - Q$ $3p = 60 - Q$

$p = 25 - Q/2$ $p = 20 - Q/3$

$$P_s = 45 - \frac{Q}{2} - \frac{Q}{3}$$

$$P_s = 45 - \frac{5Q}{6}$$

$2p = 20$ $p = 10$ $45 - \frac{150}{6}$

$p = 10$ $p = 10$ $45 - 25$

$Q_{s} = 20$ $\boxed{20}$

THE STRUCTURE OF ECONOMICS
A Mathematical Analysis

Second Edition

Eugene Silberberg
University of Washington

McGraw-Hill Publishing Company

New York   St. Louis   San Francisco   Auckland   Bogotá   Caracas   Hamburg
Lisbon   London   Madrid   Mexico   Milan   Montreal   New Delhi   Oklahoma City
Paris   San Juan   São Paulo   Singapore   Sydney   Tokyo   Toronto

THE STRUCTURE OF ECONOMICS
A Mathematical Analysis
INTERNATIONAL EDITION 1990

Exclusive rights by McGraw-Hill Book Co. – Singapore
for manufacture and export. This book cannot be re-exported
from the country to which it is consigned by McGraw-Hill.

4 5 6 7 8 9 0 CMO UPE 9 5 4

This book was set in Times Roman by Publication Services.
the editors was Scott D. Stratford;
the production supervisor was Louise Karam.
The cover was designed by Joseph Gillians.
Project supervision was done by Publication Services.

When ordering this title use ISBN 0-07-100930-2

Printed in Singapore

To two magnificent structures:

VI_7 II_7 V_7 I, and

$I \times 4$ $IV_7 \times 2$ $I \times 2$ $V_7 \times 2$ $I \times 2$

AND TO THE FOLKS WHO DELIVERED THEM SO WELL:

Joe, Louis, Bix, Jelly, Gertrude, Bessie and their
FRIENDS.

CONTENTS

Preface   **xv**

1   Comparative Statics and the Paradigm of Economics   **1**

1.1   Introduction   1
1.2   The Marginalist Paradigm   3
1.3   Theories and Refutable Propositions   9
        The Structure of Theories   10
        Refutable Propositions   12
1.4   Theories versus Models; Comparative Statics   14
1.5   Examples of Comparative Statics   16
        Problems   23
        Bibliography   25

2   Review of Calculus (One Variable)   **26**

2.1   Functions, Limits, Continuity   26
        Limits, Continuity   28
        Problems   30
2.2   Derivatives   31
        Differentiation of Polynomials   32
        Problems   34
2.3   Differentials   34
        Problems   36
2.4   The Chain Rule   36
2.5   The Product and Quotient Rules   38
        The Product Rule   38
        The Quotient Rule   39
2.6   Implicit Functions   39

vii

2.7 Elasticity 40
2.8 Maxima and Minima 41
Problems 45
2.9 Two Important Functions: $y = e^x$; $y = \log_e x$ 46
1. The Function $y = e^x$ 46
2. The Function $y = \log_e x$ 50
Problems 52
2.10 The Mean Value Theorem 53
2.11 Taylor's Series 54
Applications of Taylor's Series: Derivation of the First- and Second-Order Conditions for a Maximum; Concavity and Convexity 56
2.12 Integration 58
Indefinite Integrals 58
The Integral as the Area under a Curve 60
Problems 64
2.13 Differential Equations 65
Problems 67
Selected References 67

3 **Functions of Several Variables** 68

3.1 Functions of Several Variables 68
3.2 Level Curves: I 69
3.3 Partial Derivatives 70
3.4 The Total Differential of a Function of Several Variables 76
Problems 78
3.5 The Chain Rule 79
Monotonic Transformations 82
Second Derivatives by the Chain Rule 84
3.6 Level Curves: II 86
Convexity of the Level Curves 89
Problems 91
3.7 Homogeneous Functions and Euler's Theorem 92
Problems 101
Appendix 101
Selected References 106

4 **Profit Maximization** 107

4.1 Unconstrained Maxima and Minima: First-Order Necessary Conditions 107
4.2 Sufficient Conditions for Maxima and Minima: Two Variables 109
Problems 112
4.3 An Extended Footnote 113
4.4 An Application of Maximizing Behavior: The Profit-Maximizing Firm 114
The Supply Function 121
4.5 Homogeneity of the Demand and Supply Functions; Elasticities 122
Elasticities 123
4.6 The Long Run and the Short Run: An Example of the Le Châtelier Principle 124
A More Fundamental Look at the Le Châtelier Principle 126
Problems 128

4.7	Analysis of Finite Changes: A Digression	130
	Appendix	131
	Taylor Series for Functions of Several Variables	131
	Concavity and the Maximum Conditions	132
	Selected References	133

5   Matrices and Determinants 135

5.1	Matrices	135
5.2	Determinants, Cramer's Rule	137
5.3	The Implicit Function Theorem	144
	Problems	149
	Appendix	149
	Simple Matrix Operations	149
	The Rank of a Matrix	151
	The Inverse of a Matrix	153
	Orthogonality	154
	Problems	155
	Selected References	155

6   Comparative Statics: The Traditional Methodology 156

6.1	Introduction; Profit Maximization Once More	156
6.2	Generalizations to n Variables	160
	First-Order Necessary Conditions	160
	Second-Order Sufficient Conditions	160
	Profit Maximization: n Factors	163
6.3	The Theory of Constrained Maxima and Minima: First-Order Necessary Conditions	166
6.4	Constrained Maximization with More than One Constraint: A Digression	171
6.5	Second-Order Conditions	173
	The Geometry of Constrained Maximization	176
6.6	General Methodology	180
	Problems	187
	Selected References	189

7   The Envelope Theorem and Duality 190

7.1	History of the Problem	190
7.2	The Profit Function	192
7.3	General Comparative Statics Analysis: Unconstrained Models	195
7.4	Models with Constraints	198
	Comparative Statics: Primal-Dual Analysis	200
	An Important Special Case	203
	Interpretation of the Lagrange Multiplier	204
	Problems	207
7.5	The Comparative Statics of Maximization Systems	210
	Reciprocity Relations	214
	Qualitative Results	215
	Le Châtelier Effects	216
	Bibliography	222

8 The Derivation of Cost Functions   223

8.1   The Cost Function   223
8.2   Marginal Cost   226
8.3   Average Cost   227
8.4   A General Relationship between Average and Marginal Costs   229
8.5   The Cost Minimization Problem   230
8.6   The Factor Demand Curves   236
      Interpretation of the Lagrange Multiplier   237
8.7   Comparative Statics Relations: The Traditional Methodology   241
8.8   Comparative Statics Relations Using Duality Theory   249
      Reciprocity Conditions   250
      Cost Curves in the Short and Long Run   252
      Factor Demands in the Short and Long Run   254
      Relation to Profit Maximization   256
8.9   Elasticities; Further Properties of the Factor-Demand Curves   258
      Homogeneity   259
      Output Elasticities   262
8.10 The Average Cost Curve   263
8.11 Analysis of Firms in Long-Run Competitive Equilibrium   265
      Analysis of Factor Demands in the Long Run   267
      Problems   269
      Selected References   271

9 Cost and Production Functions: Special Topics   272

9.1   Homogeneous and Homothetic Production Functions   272
9.2   The Cost Function: Further Properties   275
      Homothetic Functions   279
9.3   The Duality of Cost and Production Functions   281
      The Importance of Duality   285
9.4   Elasticity of Substitution; the Constant-Elasticity-of-Substitution
      (CES) Production Function   285
      Generalizations to n Factors   296
      The Generalized Leontief Cost Function   297
      Problems   297
      Bibliography   298

10 The Derivation of Consumer Demand Functions   299

10.1 Introductory Remarks: The Behavioral Postulates   299
10.2 Utility Maximization   308
      Interpretation of the Lagrange Multiplier   313
      Roy's Identity   315
10.3 The Relationship between the Utility Maximization Model and the
      Cost Minimization Model   319
10.4 The Comparative Statics of the Utility Maximization Model; the
      Traditional Derivation of the Slutsky Equation   323
10.5 The Modern Derivation of the Slutsky Equation   329
      Conditional Demands   333
      The Addition of a New Commodity   335

10.6 Elasticity Formulas for Money-Income-Held-Constant and
      Real-Income-Held-Constant Demand Curves   338
      The Slutsky Equation in Elasticity Form   338
      Compensated Demand Curves   341
10.7 Special Topics   344
      Separable Utility Functions   344
      The Labor-Leisure Choice   346
      Slutsky versus Hicks Compensations   351
      The Division of Labor Is Limited by the Extent of the Market   353
      Problems   357
      Selected References   360

11   Special Topics in Consumer Theory   **362**

11.1 Revealed Preference and Exchange   362
11.2 The Strong Axiom of Revealed Preference and Integrability   370
      Integrability   373
11.3 The Composite Commodity Theorem   381
      Shipping the Good Apples Out   384
11.4 Household Production Functions   389
      Comparative Statics   393
11.5 Consumer's Surplus   396
      Example   402
      Empirical Approximation   403
11.6 Empirical Estimation and Functional Forms   405
      Linear Expenditure System   406
      CES Utility Function   407
      Indirect Addilog Utility Function   408
      Translog Specifications   409
      Almost Ideal Demand System   411
      Problems   412
      References on Theory   414
      References on Functional Forms   415

12   Intertemporal Choice   **416**

12.1 n-Period Utility Maximization   416
      Time Preference   419
      The Fisher Separation Theorem   426
      Real versus Nominal Interest Rates   428
12.2 The Determination of the Interest Rate   430
12.3 Stocks and Flows   433
      Problems   437
      Selected References   438

13   Behavior under Uncertainty   **440**

13.1 Uncertainty and Probability   440
      Random Variables and Probability Distributions   441
      Mean and Variance   442

13.2 Specification of Preferences   445
    State Preference Approach   445
    The Expected Utility Hypothesis   446
    Cardinal and Ordinal Utility   447
13.3 Risk Aversion   449
    Measures of Risk Aversion   451
    Gambling, Insurance and Diversification   452
    Problems   454
13.4 Comparative Statics   455
    Allocation of Wealth to Risky Assets   455
    Problems   456
    Output Decisions under Price Uncertainty   456
    Increases in Riskiness   458
    References   460

14 Maximization with Inequality and Nonnegativity Constraints   462

14.1 Nonnegativity   462
    Functions of Two or More Variables   467
14.2 Inequality Constraints   470
14.3 The Saddlepoint Theorem   476
14.4 Nonlinear Programming   480
14.5 An "Adding-Up" Theorem   483
    Problems   485
    Appendix   487
    Bibliography   490

15 General Equilibrium I: Linear Models   491

15.1 Introduction: Fixed-Coefficient Technology   491
15.2 The Linear Activity Analysis Model: A Specific Example   500
15.3 The Rybczynski Theorem   507
15.4 The Stolper-Samuelson Theorem   509
15.5 The Dual Problem   510
15.6 The Simplex Algorithm   520
    Mathematical Prerequisites   520
    The Simplex Algorithm: Example   524
    Problems   528
    Bibliography   530

16 General Equilibrium II: Nonlinear Models   531

16.1 Tangency Conditions   531
16.2 General Comparative Statics Results   539
16.3 The Factor Price Equalization and Related Theorems   544
    The Four-Equation Model   550
    The Factor Price Equalization Theorem   553
    The Stolper-Samuelson Theorems   554
    The Rybczynski Theorem   561

16.4   Applications of the Two-Good, Two-Factor Model   563
       Summary and Conclusions   567
       Problems   570
       Bibliography   571

17   Welfare Economics   **573**

17.1   Social Welfare Functions   573
17.2   The Pareto Conditions   577
       Pure Exchange   578
       Production   581
17.3   The Classical "Theorems" of Welfare Economics   587
17.4   A "Nontheorem" about Taxation   589
17.5   The Theory of the Second Best   591
17.6   Public Goods   593
17.7   Consumer's Surplus as a Measure of Welfare Gains and Losses   596
17.8   Property Rights and Transactions Costs   600
       Private Property   602
       Common Property   603
       The Coase Theorem   604
       The Theory of Share Tenancy: An Application of the Coase
          Theorem   607
       Problems   611
       Bibliography   612

18   Resource Allocation over Time: Optimal Control Theory   **613**

18.1   The Meaning of Dynamics   613
       Brief History   617
18.2   Solution to the Problem   617
       The Calculus of Variations   622
       Endpoint (Transversality) Conditions   624
       Autonomous Problems   625
       Sufficient Conditions   627
18.3   Solutions to Differential Equations   628
       Simultaneous Differential Equations   631
18.4   Interpretations and Solutions   632
       Intertemporal Choice   632
       Harvesting a Renewable Resource   635
       Capital Utilization   639
       Problems   644
       Selected References   645

19   Equilibrium, Disequilibrium, and the Stability of Markets   **647**

19.1   Three Sources of Refutable Hypotheses   647
19.2   Equilibrium and Stability   651
       Walrasian Stability   652
       Marshallian Stability   655

19.3 Multimarket Equilibrium and Stability   656
      Open Systems: Stability   657
      Closed Economics   661
19.4 Game Theory   662
19.5 Overview and Conclusions   666
      Problems   669
      Bibliography   669

Hints and Answers   **671**

Index   **681**

PREFACE

Although I am flattered by the shelf-life of the first edition of this book, it is apparent that the once-esoteric tools of duality theory have now become standard issue in graduate (and some undergraduate) price theory courses. This is of course not surprising, given the economy of algebra and added clarity the new methods provide. Although the duality results—all derivations or applications of the envelope theorem—were evident in the first edition, that text adhered mainly to the older implicit function theorem approach. By way of illustration, the section entitled "Instant Slutsky Equation" in Chapter 8 of the first edition was so named because at the time, I perceived that derivation as a "trick," rather than as the fundamental basis for that classic result (and many others of a similar nature).

This second edition therefore places much greater emphasis on the methods of duality, by introducing the material earlier (in a simplified form), and deriving later propositions with those tools. The traditional approach, however, has not been abandoned. While the envelope theorem provides greater clarity and perhaps vast simplification of the traditional models, it remains the case that for some more complex models, in which specialized assumptions or specific functional forms might be incorporated, or in models not involving a specific maximization hypothesis, the older methodology may be the only available tool. Thus that methodology is preserved in the new edition, and used to derive the prominent results in a parallel fashion. This edition remains fiercely devoted to the premise that the purpose of developing this apparatus is to facilitate the derivation of refutable propositions, which, in economics, consist of predictions about the responses of decision variables to changes in constraints, assuming unchanging behavioral hypotheses.

The technique of "conditional demands" is used throughout the new edition to elucidate the relationships between the demand and other choice functions derived from related models. New applications of comparative statics models, e.g., in the theory of labor-leisure choice and household production, have been added, as well as analyses of specialization, consumption over time, and international trade. Lastly, two new chapters, control theory and behavior under risk, have been added, plus a new discussion of game theory and duoploy in the last chapter.

I have striven to use the most elementary mathematics with which the results can be reasonably demonstrated. As I indicated in the preface to the first edition, mathematicians study math for its beauty and elegance; scientists study it because it is useful. Most useful math in economics is fairly elementary. If one reviews the papers published by our Nobel Laureates, it seems apparent that with the exception of the work on the existence of general equilibrium, their lingering importance derives mainly from their creative applications and extensions of models involving fairly elementary mathematics, rather than from explorations of mathematical generality and rigor.

I have continued to benefit from associating with various smart people. In my first preface, I regrettably omitted R. T. Rockafellar's assistance in developing the primal-dual approach to comparative statics. I appreciate the help of Richard Hartman, J. Alan Hynes, Levis Kochin, Robert Pollak, Frank Rusco, and Kar-yiu Wong. Christopher Curran, Emory University; Jack Meyer, Michigan State University; John Pomeroy, Purdue University; Gerard Russo, University of Hawaii; Susan Vroman, Georgetown University; and especially Todd Sandler, Iowa State University; provided helpful constructive criticism on earlier drafts. Major assistance came from Michael Caputo on control theory, and from Wing Suen on behavior under uncertainty and the sections on specific functional forms. In addition, Professor Eiji Ohsumi, Darlene Chisholm, Michael Dueker, Bong-Ho Shin, and Kiyoun Sohn provided invaluable (well, highly valued) assistance in the tedious task of proofreading.

Because I may never get to do this in print again, allow me the following additional acknowledgments. My life was never the same after I met Bobby Berk and Gary Popkin, who showed me that the distributive law was actually useful, using the example $20 \times 22 = 20 \times 20 + 20 \times 2 = 400 + 40$. I learned my fundamental math skills through their friendship and the stimulating atmosphere at Stuyvesant High School and the City College of New York. The second and third miracles occurred in my senior year, when Morty Kamien, the only non-math major in mathematical statistics, happened to sit next to me, became my friend, and convinced me to apply for a fellowship in economics (economics?) at Purdue—which, to my astonishment, was offered. Upon our arrival, we met our lamented friend Nancy Schwartz, and the rest, as they say, is history.

Eugene Silberberg

THE STRUCTURE OF ECONOMICS
A Mathematical Analysis

CHAPTER
1

COMPARATIVE STATICS AND THE PARADIGM OF ECONOMICS

1.1 INTRODUCTION

Suppose we are in a conversation about social changes that have taken place in the past generation. We might discuss, for example, the substantial increase in the rate of participation of women in the competitive labor market, especially in "nontraditional" occupations such as engineering, law, and medicine, the increasing prominence of the "two-earner" family, the increase in the age of first marriage, the rise of "women's liberation," and the like. Suppose now that some-one says, "Let me give you an 'economic explanation' of these events." What do you expect to hear? What is meant by the phrase "economic explanation," and what would distinguish it from, say, a sociological or political explanation? For that matter, what do we mean by the term "explanation"?

A list of facts, for example, is not an explanation. Compilations of changes in the weather as seasons pass, or changes in various stock market indices, are not explanations of those events. The stylized data presented in the preceding paragraph are not an explanation of anything; they are only a collection of economic (and sociological) facts, which we typically call "data." The data may be interesting, but they are not "explanations." The term "explanation" means that there is some more general proposition than the observed data for which these facts are special cases. We interpret or understand these facts by applying some general laws or rules by which these events are supposedly guided. For example, physicists "explain" the motion of ordinary objects on the basis of Newton's

1

classical laws of mechanics. An explanation of the previous socioeconomic data would mean an interpretation of these events in terms of a framework of systematic human behavior, not merely a documentation that these events happened to occur at a particular time. Moreover, we would want to apply that same framework to different sets of facts, allowing the investigator to interpret these other data sets using the same guiding principles. The development of the framework and the specific models employed by economists to explain social phenomena is the subject of this book.

Students who have come this far in economics will undoubtedly have encountered the standard textbook definition of economics that goes something like, "Economics is the science that studies human behavior as a relationship between ends and scarce means which have alternative uses."[†] This is indeed the substantive content of economics in terms of the class of phenomena generally studied. To many economists (including the author), however, the most striking aspect of economics is not the subject matter itself, but rather the conceptual framework within which the previously mentioned phenomena are analyzed. After all, sociologists and political scientists are also interested in how scarce resources are allocated and how the decisions of individuals are related to that process. What economists have in common with each other is a methodology, or paradigm, in which *all* problems are analyzed. In fact, what most economists would classify as *noneconomic* problems are precisely those problems that are incapable of being analyzed with what has come to be called the *neoclassical* or *marginalist* paradigm.

The history of science includes many paradigms or schools of thought. The Ptolemaic explanation for planetary motion, in which the earth was placed at the center of the coordinate system (perhaps for theological reasons), was replaced by the Copernican paradigm which moved the origin to the sun. When this was done, the equations of planetary motion were so vastly simplified that the older school was soon replaced (though the Ptolemaic paradigm is essentially maintained in problems of navigation). The Newtonian paradigm of classical mechanics served admirably well in physics, and still does, in fact, in most everyday problems. For study of fundamental processes of nature, however, it has been found to be inadequate and has been replaced by the Einsteinian paradigm of relativity theory.

In economics, the classical school of Smith, Ricardo, and Marx provided explanations of the growth of productive capacity, the gains from specialization and trade (comparative advantage), and the like. One outstanding puzzle persisted: the diamond-water paradox. The classical paradigm, dependent largely on a theory of value based on inputs, was incapable of explaining why water, which is essential to life, is generally available at modest cost, while diamonds, an obvious frivolity, are expensive, even if dug up accidentally in one's backyard

---

[†]Taken from Lionel Robbins' classic monograph, *An Essay on the Nature and Significance of Economic Science,* Macmillan & Co., Ltd., London, 1932, p. 15.

(considering the opportunity cost of withholding one from sale).[†] With the advent of marginal analysis, beginning in the 1870s and continuing in later decades by Jevons, Walras, Marshall, Pareto, and others, the older paradigm was supplanted. Economic problems came to be analyzed more explicitly in terms of individual choice. Values were perceived to be determined by consumers' tastes as well as production costs, and the value placed on goods by consumers was not considered to be "intrinsic," but rather depended on the quantities of that good and other goods available.

The structure of this new paradigm was explored further by Hicks, Allen, Samuelson, and others. As this was done, the usefulness and limitations of the new paradigm became more apparent. It is with these properties that this book is concerned.

1.2 THE MARGINALIST PARADIGM

Let us consider the definition of economics in more depth. Economics, first and foremost, is an *empirical science. Positive* economics is concerned with questions of *fact,* which are in principle either true or false. What *ought* to be, as opposed to what *is,* is a normative study, based on the observer's value judgments. In this text, we shall be concerned only with positive economics, the determination of what *is.* (For expositional ease the term *positive* will generally be dropped.) Two economists, one favoring, say, more transfers of income to the poor, and the other favoring less, should still come to the same conclusions regarding the effects of such transfers. Positive economics consists of propositions that are to be tested against facts, and either confirmed or refuted.

But what *is* economics, and what distinguishes it from other aspects of social science? For that matter, what is social science? *Social science is the study of human behavior.* One particular paradigm of social science, i.e., the conceptual framework under which human behavior is studied, is known as the *theory of choice.* This is the framework that will be adopted throughout this book. Its basic postulate is that individual behavior is fundamentally characterized by individual choices, or decisions.[‡]

This fundamental attribute distinguishes social science from the physical sciences. The atoms and molecular structures of physics, chemistry, biology, etc., are not perceived to possess conscious thought. They are, rather, passive adherents to the laws of nature. The choices humans make may be pleasant (e.g., whether to buy a Porsche or a Jaguar) or dismal (e.g., whether to eat navy beans or potatoes for subsistence), but the aspect of choice is asserted to be pervasive.

[†] Of course, being different commodities with different "quantity" measurements, it is not possible to say that diamonds are *more* expensive than water.

[‡] A complicating feature, not relevant to the present discussion but also peculiar to the social sciences, is that the participants often have a vested interest in the results of the analysis.

Decisions, i.e., choices, are a consequence of the scarcity of goods and services. Without scarcity, whatever social science might exist would be vastly different than the present variety. That goods and services are scarce is a second, though not independent postulate of the theory of choice. Scarcity is an "idea" in our minds. It is not in itself observable. However, we *assert* scarcity because to say that certain goods or services are *not* scarce is to say that we can all— you, me, everybody—have as much as we want of that good at any time, at zero sacrifice to us all. It is hard to imagine such goods. Even air, if it is taken to mean *fresh* air, is not free in this sense; society must in fact sacrifice consumption of other goods, through increased production costs, if the air is to be less polluted.

Scarcity, in turn, depends upon postulates about individual preferences, in particular that people prefer more goods to less. If such were not the case, then goods, though *limited* in supply, would not necessarily be *scarce*.

The fact that goods are scarce means that choices will have to be made somehow regarding both the goods to be produced in the first place and the system for rationing these final goods to consumers, each of whom would in general prefer to have more of those goods rather than less. This problem, which is often taken as the definition of economics, has many aspects. How are consumers' tastes formed, and are those tastes dependent on ("endogenous to") or independent of ("exogenous to") the allocative process? How are decisions made with regard to whether goods shall be allocated via a market process or through the political system? What system of *rules,* i.e., *property rights,* is to be used in constraining individual choices? The issues generated by the scarcity of goods involve all the social sciences. All are concerned with different aspects of the problem of choice.

We now come to the fundamental conceptualization of the determinants of choice upon which the neoclassical, or marginalist, paradigm is based. We assert that for a wide range of problems, individual choice can be conceived to be determined by the interaction of two distinct classifications of phenomena:

1. Tastes, or preferences
2. Opportunities, or constraints

Suppose we were to list all variables that were measurable and that we believed affected individual choices; this would constitute the set of constraints on behavior. What sorts of things would appear?

Certainly, the money prices of goods and the money incomes of individuals play a major part. In most everyday decisions to exchange goods and services, prices and income are the major constraints. More fundamental, however, are the constraints imposed by the system of laws and the property rights in a given society. Without these rights, prices and money income would be largely irrelevant. Ordinary exchange is difficult or impossible if the traders have not previously agreed upon who owns what in the first place, and whether contracts entered into are enforceable. Laws also determine various restrictions on trading. During the winter of 1973–1974, gasoline was quoted at a certain price, but in many parts of the country, it was unavailable for exchange. The *price* of the good loses meaning if the good is unavailable at that price. The same situation existed during World War II when goods were price controlled. Then, the property rights individuals enjoyed over their goods no longer included the right to sell the good at a mutually satisfactory price with the buyer. Hence, the system of laws and the property rights endowed to the participants in a given society are a fundamental part of their opportunity set.

In addition to the preceding, technology and the law of diminishing returns constitute the other important constraints in economic analysis. Together with the system of laws and the property rights, technology determines the production possibilities of a society, i.e., the limits on total consumption.

Suppose now that we had available complete data on the preceding variables for a given individual. Would this be enough information to enable us to predict the choices the person would make, e.g., whether he or she would eat meat or be a vegetarian, or attend classical rather than rock concerts? It is apparent that no matter how complete a listing of constraints we could contemplate, there would still be other *unmeasured* variables that would influence behavior. These other variables are what we refer to as *tastes,* or *preferences.* Typically, they comprise the hypothetical exchanges a person is willing to make at various terms of trade. These hypothetical offers are our subjective evaluations of the relative desirability of goods.

Furthermore, these unmeasured taste variables seem to vary from individual to individual. Some people, for example, would gladly exchange two pounds of coffee for one of tea; others, in the same circumstances, would do the reverse. Even when the constraints facing two individuals are largely the same, i.e., the individuals have equal incomes, shop at the same stores, and are equal under the law, they will usually purchase different bundles of goods and services. Some people live in small houses and drive big cars; others in similar circumstances buy large houses and drive small cars.

We have thus classified the variables affecting choice as being either *con- straints,* which are in principle, at least, observable and measurable, or *tastes,* which are not. Prices, for example, are generally posted, or otherwise available; incomes are usually known to people; laws and property rights can be compli- cated but are at least on the books, and their enforceability can be determined. In contrast, tastes are not in general observable. It is in fact precisely for this reason that we make *assertions,* or *postulates,* about individual tastes. If tastes were observable, assertions about their nature would not be needed.

Observations of a person's consumption habits, i.e., the baskets of goods purchased, do not constitute observations of tastes. Actual consumption depends on opportunities as well as tastes. The generally nonobservable nature of the preferences of individuals requires that they be postulated, or asserted.

Here, then, is the central puzzle. We have seen that tastes apparently vary, and constraints clearly also vary from individual to individual. (U.S. census figures attest to large differences in incomes among individuals in the United States; the same seems to be true in most societies.) How then can any systematic analysis of choice be made under these horrendously complicated circumstances?

The answer to this important question to a large extent defines the field of economics.

To answer all questions of choice, even about a well-defined situation, both tastes and opportunities must be included. Unfortunately, this situation cannot be realized in actual practice. However, it is still often possible to analyze problems of choice in a narrower but still fruitful manner. Suppose we assume that whatever people's tastes are, they do not change very much, if at all, during the course of investigation of some problem in social science. Certain decisions will be made by individuals, given those tastes and the opportunities they face. If, now, the *opportunities* faced by those individuals *change, in an observable fashion,* then we can expect the decisions of individuals to somehow *change,* and those *changes in decisions, or choices, can be attributed to the changes in opportunities.* Moreover, if the unmeasured taste variables can be characterized in a systematic way, so that individuals display regularities in behavior, then while it may not be possible to predict the original choices made by individuals, it may still be possible to predict how those choices *change,* when opportunities or constraints *change.*

We therefore impose structure on individual preferences in order to be able to predict responses to changes in constraints. Subject, as always, to possible refutation by empirical testing, economists assert universal postulates of behavior. In particular, we construe individual behavior to be "purposeful." We assert, for example, that all individuals prefer "more" to "less," and that *they attempt to "mitigate the damages" imposed by constraints, i.e., to reduce rather than reinforce the impact of restrictions on their opportunities.* We give operational content to the behavioral postulates typically by expressing the theory (or parts of it) mathematically as a problem of maximizing (or, if convenient, minimizing) some specified objective function subject to specified constraints.[†]

In terms of methodology, therefore, *economics is that discipline within social science that seeks refutable explanations of changes in human events on the basis of changes in observable constraints, utilizing universal postulates of behavior and technology, and the simplifying assumption that the unmeasured variables ("tastes") remain constant.*[‡] This is the paradigm of economics, a paradigm that at present distinguishes economics from other social sciences.

Notice that economics does *not* thereby assert either that tastes do not matter or that they remain constant for all time. Preferences are, in fact, asserted to affect individual choices, as previously discussed. What the paradigm of economics recognizes is that it is possible to obtain answers regarding *marginal* quantities,

---

[†] Because minimizing some function is equivalent to maximizing its negative, no generality is lost by using the term "maximizing behavior."

[‡] Strictly speaking, all that is necessary for testing theories is that the unmeasured variables be *uncorrelated* with the observed data.

i.e., how total quantities *change,* without a specific investigation of individual preferences or how such preferences might be formed.

Constancy of tastes is a *simplifying assumption,* not an article of faith. It is invoked because it allows investigation of responses to changes in constraints. It is of course impossible to be certain that unmeasured variables remain constant. Tastes may change. But to accept that as an explanation of observed events is to abandon the search for an explanation based on systematic, and therefore testable, behavior. Any observation whatsoever is consistent with a theory that asserts that some unmeasured taste variables suddenly, for no apparent reason, changed. The challenge of economics is always to search for explanations based on changes in constraints; explanations based on changes in tastes are to be viewed with skepticism and as indicative of inadequate insight. We leave such explanations to those who, for example, would "explain" the prevalence of relatively large cars in the United States as a peculiar American "love affair" for big cars, rather than as a consequence of a relatively low retail price of gasoline (generally one-third to one-half of the European price) for most of the twentieth century. The switch to economy cars in the 1970s and the return of "high-performance" cars in the 1980s could be random taste changes, but these observations confirm a more general proposition, the law of demand, because the relative price of gasoline rose in the mid 1970s and fell in the 1980s. We prefer the more general theory based on responses to changes in the constraints faced by consumers of cars to *ad hoc* assertions about changes in tastes.[†]

How would we apply the neoclassical economic paradigm to the data presented in the opening paragraphs of this chapter? We reject out-of-hand any explanation based on changes in tastes. The assertion that these events occurred because the young adults of the late sixties and early seventies were more radical

---

[†] George Stigler and Gary Becker analyzed "fads and fashions," a subject seemingly not amenable to an analysis in which tastes are assumed constant. They argued that the desire to be "fashionable" is constant. Because consumption of fashion takes place over time, the axiom of diminishing marginal values suggests that fashions will change over time. Moreover, the less costly it is to be fashionable, the more frequent the changes will be. This may explain why fashions may change more quickly for clothing than for automobiles. See George Stigler and Gary Becker, "De Gustibus non est Disputandum," *American Economic Review,* **66:**76–90, March 1977.

An additional example of the power of the paradigm is provided by Corry Azzi and Ron Ehrenberg, who showed that participation in religion varied in accordance with the law of demand. The relatively higher participation of women, for example, is what would be predicted on the basis of relatively lower wages for women than for men. Relatively low church attendance in the young adult years, followed by increasing attendance with age, is an implication of young adults' typically heavy time investment in human capital, and increasing present value of possible benefits after death. Higher attendance in rural vs. urban areas is easily related to the higher opportunity costs in urban areas due to the greater variety of recreational services available. See Corry Azzi and Ron Ehrenberg, "Household Allocation of Time and Church Attendance," *Journal of Political Economy,* **83:**27–56, February 1975.

than their predecessors is an *ad hoc* hypothesis, i.e., a theory made up simply to suit a particular set of facts, with no capability for application beyond that immediate data set. Such theories are no better than asserting that people do certain things because they do them. Why should the preferences of large numbers of people suddenly have shifted in unison at that time?

In order to provide an economic explanation, we need to look for a wide-ranging constraint that changed during the 1960s, and explain the events that took place in terms of the movement of that constraint. An economic basis for explaining these events is in fact provided by the World War II "baby boom," the unprecedented increase in births that took place in North America after the war. [†] Altogether, one-third more children were born between 1946 and 1950 than between 1941 and 1945. (Births continued at a high level until the 1960s.)

Consider first how this would affect marriage prospects 20 years later, i.e., in the late sixties. The baby boomers were, of course, about equally divided by sex. However, women have always tended to marry men slightly older than themselves. When the baby boomers reached young adulthood, the women were faced with a very different constraint than the slightly older generation: There were vastly fewer men in their middle or late twenties (i.e., those born in the early 1940s) than women in their early twenties (i.e., those born in the late 1940s). In fact, for about 20 percent of the young female population, the traditional marriage pattern simply could not be sustained.[‡] Is it any wonder, therefore, that "women's liberation" flourished at this time?[§] The old plan of simply getting married and raising children was arithmetically impossible for a large portion of the young female population. Pursuing a career became relatively more attractive than in the past.

In addition to this "marriage squeeze," because there was an unusually large cohort of young adults available in the labor market, entry level wages fell.[‖] Is it surprising that this generation was somewhat disenchanted? Moreover, with earnings levels lowered, it would not be surprising that two-earner families would become more common. Because having babies raised the cost of working outside the home, these couples put off childbearing, causing birth rates to plummet in the 1970s.

Those low birth rates mean that young adults in the 1990s, being part of a *small* cohort, will experience relatively *high* entry-level wages. Also, young women will find a relatively abundant supply of slightly older young men. We should therefore expect a return to more traditional lifestyles during this decade.

[†] I am grateful to Lee Edlefsen for introducing me to these issues and analyses.

[‡] See Richard Easterlin, *Birth and Fortune,* Basic Books, New York, 1980.

[§] Similar *demographics* (population structure) took place in the late 1920s, another period in which women shocked their parents.

[‖] See Finis Welch, "Effects of Cohort Size on Earnings: The Baby Boom Babies' Financial Bust," *Journal of Political Economy,* Part II, **87**(5):S65–S98, October 1979.

This discussion is of course intended only as an illustration of economic methodology, not as a complete theory of these events. It is, however, meant to suggest the powerful nature of the economic paradigm. In addition to the usual analyses of market phenomena, events traditionally investigated by noneconomists, perhaps, eventually, even that subtle human capital we tend to call "tastes" may be amenable to analysis with the economic paradigm. Changes in events are explained on the basis of changes in constraints, assuming the unmeasured variables remain constant, and utilizing an assertion of maximizing behavior.

1.3 THEORIES AND REFUTABLE PROPOSITIONS

In the past several pages we have used the terms *theory, propositions,* and *confirm,* as well as other phrases that warrant a closer look. In particular, what is a theory, and what is the role of theories in scientific explanations?

It is sometimes suggested that the way to attack any given problem is to "let the facts speak for themselves." Suppose one wanted to discover why motorists were suddenly waiting in line for gasoline, often for several hours, during the winter of 1973–1974, the so-called energy crisis. The first thing to do, perhaps, is to get some facts. Where will they be found? Perhaps the government documents section of the local university library will be useful. A problem arises. Once there, one suddenly finds oneself up to the ears in facts. The data collected by the United States federal government and other governments fill many rooms. Where should one start? Consider, perhaps, the following list of "facts."

1. Many oil-producing nations embargoed oil to the United States in the fall of 1973.
2. The gross national product of the United States rose, in money terms, by 11.5 percent from 1972 to 1973.
3. Gasoline and heating oils are petroleum distillates.
4. Wage and price controls were in effect on the oil industry during that time.
5. The average miles per gallon achieved by cars in the United States has decreased due to the growing use of antipollution devices.
6. The price of food rose dramatically in this period.
7. Rents rose during this time, but not as fast as food prices.
8. The price of tomatoes in Lincoln, Nebraska was 39 cents per pound on September 14, 1968.
9. Most of the pollution in the New York metropolitan area is due to fixed, rather than moving, sources.

The list goes on indefinitely. There are an infinite number of facts. Most readers will have already decided that, e.g., fact 8 is irrelevant; and most of the infinite number of facts that might have been listed are irrelevant. But why? How was this conclusion reached? Can fact 8 be rejected solely on the basis that *most* of us would agree to reject it? What about facts 4 and 5? There may be less than perfect agreement on the relevance of some of these facts.

Facts, by themselves, do not explain events. Without some set of axioms, propositions, etc., about the nature of the phenomena we are seeking to explain, there is simply no way in which to sort out the relevant from the irrelevant facts. The reader who summarily dismissed fact 8 as irrelevant to the events occurring during the energy crisis must have had some behavioral relations in mind that suggested that the tomato market in 1968 was not a determining factor. Such a notion, however rudimentary, is the start of a *theory*.

The Structure of Theories

A theory, in an empirical science, is a set of explanations or predictions about various objects in the real world. Theories consist of three parts:

1. A set of *assertions,* or postulates, denoted $A = \{A_1, \ldots, A_n\}$, concerning the behavior of various *theoretical constructs,* i.e., idealized (perhaps mathematical) concepts, which are ultimately to be related to real-world objects. These postulates are generally universal-type statements, i.e., propositions of the form: all x have the property p. Examples of such propositions in economics are the statements that "firms maximize wealth (or profits)," "consumers maximize utility," and the like. At this point, terms such as *firms, consumers, prices, quantities,* etc., mentioned in these behavioral assertions, or postulates, are ideas yet to be identified. They are thus referred to as theoretical constructs.

2. If behavioral assertions about theoretical constructs are to be useful in empirical science, these postulates must be related to real objects. The second part of a theory is therefore a set of *assumptions,* or *test conditions,* denoted $C = \{C_1, \ldots, C_n\}$, under which the behavioral postulates are to be tested. These assumptions include statements to the effect that "such-and-such variable p, called the *price of bread* in the theoretical assertions, in fact corresponds to the price of bread posted at xyz supermarket on such-and-such date."

   Note that we are distinguishing the terms *assertions* and *assumptions.* There has been a protracted debate in economics over the need for realism of assumptions. The confusion can be largely eliminated by clearly distinguishing the behavioral postulates of a theory (the assertions) from the specific test conditions (the assumptions) under which the theory is tested.

   If the theory is to be at all useful, the assumptions, or test conditions, must be *observable.* It is impossible to tell whether a theory is performing well or badly if it is not possible to tell whether the theory is even relevant to the objects in question. The postulates A are universal statements about the behavior of abstract objects. They are not observable; therefore, debate as to their realism is irrelevant. Assumptions, on the other hand, are the link between the theoretical constructs and real objects. Assumptions *must* be *realistic,* i.e., if the theory is to be validly tested against a given set of data, the data must conform in essential ways to the theoretical constructs.

Suppose, for example, we wish to test whether a rise in the price of gasoline reduces the quantity of gasoline demanded. It will be observed that until the 1980s, the money price of gasoline has been rising generally since World War II and that gasoline consumption has also been rising. Does this refute the behavioral proposition that higher prices lead to less quantity demanded? Perhaps the data, specifically the assumptions about prices, are not realistic. Does the reported series of prices really reflect the intended characteristics of the theoretical construct: price of gasoline? A careful statement of the law of demand involves changes in *relative* prices, not absolute money prices, and other things, e.g., incomes and other prices, are supposed to be held fixed. When compensated by price-level changes, the *real* price of gasoline, i.e., the price of gasoline relative to other goods, has indeed been falling, except for the periods of supply interruption, 1973–1974 and 1979–1980, thus tending to *confirm* the law of demand. But in order to test the law of demand with this datum, the assumptions about income, prices of closely related goods, etc., must also be realistic, i.e., conform to the essential aspects of the theoretical constructs.

We say *essential aspects* of the theoretical constructs because it is impossible to describe, in a finite amount of time and space, every attribute of a given real object. The importance of *realism* of assumptions is to make sure that the unspecified attributes do not significantly affect the test of the theory. In the foregoing example, money prices were an *unrealistic* measure of gasoline prices; i.e., they did not contain the attributes intended by the theory. The assumptions, or test conditions, of a theory *must,* therefore, be realistic; the assertions, or behavioral postulates, are never realistic because they are unobservable.

3. The third part of a theory comprises the events $E = \{E_1, \ldots, E_n\}$ that are predicted by the theory. The theory says that the behavioral assertions A imply that if the test conditions C are valid (realistic), then certain events E will occur. For example, the usual postulates of consumer behavior (utility maximization with diminishing marginal rates of substitution between commodities), which we shall denote A, imply that if the test conditions C hold, where C includes decreasing relative price of gasoline with real incomes and other prices to be held fixed—that is, these assumptions are in fact *observed* to be true—then the event E, *higher gasoline consumption,* will be observed. Note that *both* the assumptions or test conditions C and the events E must be observable. Otherwise, we can't tell whether the theory is applicable.

The logical structure of theories is thus that the assertions A imply that if C is true, then E will be true. In symbols, this is written

$$A \rightarrow (C \rightarrow E)$$

where the symbol → means *implies*. By simple logic, the symbolic statement can also be written

$$(A \cdot C) \rightarrow E$$

That is, the postulates *A and* assumptions *C* together imply that the events *E* will be observed.

Refutable Propositions

We have spoken casually of *testing theories*. What is it that is being tested, and how does one go about it? In the first place, there is no way to test the postulates *A* directly. Suppose, to take a classic example, one wished to test whether a given firm maximized profits. How would you do it? Suppose the accountants supplied income statements for this year and past years together with the corporate balance sheets. Suppose you found that the firm made $1 million this year. Could you infer from this that the firm made *maximum* profits? Perhaps it could have made $2 million, or $10 million. How would you know?

Maybe we should ask an easier question. Is the firm *minimizing* profits? Certainly not, you say. After all, it made a million dollars. Well, maybe it was in such a good business that there was simply no way not to make less than a million dollars. No, you insist, if the owners of this firm were out to minimize profits, we should expect to see them giving away their goods free, hiring workers at astronomical salaries, throwing sand into the machinery, and indulging in a host of other bizarre behaviors. Precisely. The way one would *infer* that profits were being minimized would be to predict that if such behavior were present, then the given firm would engage in certain predicted events, specified in advance, such as the actions named. Since the object in question is undoubtedly a firm, i.e., the test conditions or assumptions *C* are realistic, and the events predicted by profit-minimization do not occur, the behavioral assertion *A*, that the firm minimizes profits, is refuted. *But the postulates are refutable only through making logically valid predictions about real, observable events based on those postulates, under assumed test conditions, and then discovering that the predictions are false.* The postulates are not testable in a vacuum. They can only be tested against real facts (events) under assumed, observable test conditions.

We have not, however, shown that firms maximize profits. But, we do know something. It will not be possible to determine whether firms maximize profits on the basis of whether we think that this is a sensible or achievable goal. The way to test the postulate of profit maximization is to derive from that postulate certain behavior that should be observed under certain assumptions. Then, if the events predicted do indeed occur, we shall have evidence as to the validity of the postulate. The theory will be confirmed. But will it be *proved?* Alas, no. The nature of logic forbids us to conclude that the postulates *A* are true, even if *C* and *E* are known to be true. This is such a classic error it has a name: It is called the fallacy of *affirming the consequent*. If *A* implies *B*, then if *B* is true, one cannot conclude that *A* is true. For example, "If two triangles are congruent, then

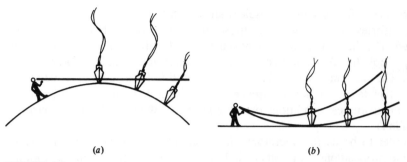

(a)   *(b)*

FIGURE 1-1

Two Theories of the Shape of the Earth. In Fig. 1-1*a*, a round earth is postulated. Under the assumption that light waves travel in straight lines, ships coming in from afar become visible from the top down, as they approach the shore. This is confirmed by actual observation. However, this does not *prove* that the earth is round. In Fig. 1-1*b*, a flat earth is postulated. However, under the assumption that light waves travel in curves convex to the surface of the earth, the same events are predicted. Therefore, on the basis of this experiment alone, no conclusion can be reached concerning the shape of the earth!

they are similar," is a valid proposition. However, if two triangles are known to be similar, one cannot conclude that they are also congruent, as counterexamples are easily demonstrated.

A striking example of why theories cannot be proved is presented in Fig. 1-1. The theory that the earth is round is to be tested by having an observer on the seashore note that when ships come in from afar, first the smoke from the smokestacks is visible, then the stacks, and so on, from the top of the ship on down. Panel *a* shows why this is to be expected. It does, in fact, occur every time. However, panel *b* shows that an alternative theory leads to the same events. Here, the earth is flat, but light waves travel in curves convex to the surface of the earth. The same events are predicted. There is no way, on the basis of this experiment, to determine which theory is correct. It is always possible that a new theory will be developed that will explain a given set of events. Hence, theories are in principle, as a matter of logic, unprovable. They can only be confirmed, i.e., found to be consistent with the facts. The more times a theory is confirmed, the more strongly we shall believe in its postulates, but we can never be *sure* that it is true.[†]

What types of theories are useful in empirical science, then? The only theories that are useful are those that might be wrong, i.e., might be refuted, but are not refuted. A theory that says that it will either rain or not rain tomorrow is no theory at all. It is incapable of being falsified, since the predicted "event" is logically true. A theory that says that if the price of gasoline rises, consumption

---

[†] See Irving M. Copi, *Introduction to Logic,* 4th ed., Macmillan, New York, 1972.

will either rise or fall is similarly useless and uninteresting, for the same reason. The only theories that are useful are those from which *refutable hypotheses* can be inferred. The theory must assert that some event E will occur and, moreover, it must be possible that E will *not* occur. Such a proposition is, at least in principle, refutable. The facts may refute the theory; for if E is false, then as a matter of logic $(A \cdot C)$ is false. (If nonoccurrence of the event E is always attributed to false or unrealistic test conditions or assumptions C, then the theory is likewise nonrefutable.)

In order to be useful, therefore, the paradigm of economics must consist of refutable propositions. Any other kind of statement is useless. In the various chapters of this book, we shall demonstrate how such refutable hypotheses are derived from behavioral postulates in economics. Perhaps nothing is more readily distinctive about economics than the insistence on a unifying behavioral basis for explanations, in particular, a postulate of maximizing behavior. The need for such a theoretical basis is not controversial; to reject it is to reject economics. The reason such importance is placed on a theoretical basis is that without it, any outcome is admissible; propositions can therefore never be refuted. Economists insist that some events are *not possible,* in the same way that physicists insist that water will never run uphill. Other things constant, a lower price will never induce less consumption of any good; holding other productive inputs constant, marginal products eventually decline. There are to be no exceptions.

1.4 THEORIES VERSUS MODELS; COMPARATIVE STATICS

The testing of a theory usually involves two fairly distinct processes. First, the purely logical aspects of the theory are drawn out. That is, it is shown that the behavioral postulates imply certain behavior for the variables of the theory. Then, at a later stage, the theoretical constructs are applied to real data, and the theory is tested empirically. The first stage of this analysis is what we shall be concerned with in this book. To distinguish the two phases of theorizing, we shall employ a distinction introduced by A. Papandreou[†] and amplified by M. Bronfenbrenner.[‡] The purely logical aspect of theories will be called a *model.* A model becomes a theory when assumptions relating the theoretical constructs to real objects are added. Models are thus logical systems. They cannot be true or false empirically; rather, they are either logically valid or invalid. A theory can be false either because the underlying model is logically unsound or because the empirical facts refute the theory (or both occur).

[†] Andreas Papandreou, *Economics as a Science,* J. B. Lippincott Company, Philadelphia, 1958.

[‡] Martin Bronfenbrenner, "A Middlebrow Introduction to Economic Methodology," in S. Krupp (ed.), *The Structure of Economic Science,* Prentice-Hall, Inc., Englewood Cliffs, NJ, 1966.

The notion of a refutable proposition is preserved, however, even in models. A refutable proposition in a logical system means that when certain *conceptual* test conditions occur, the theoretical variables will have restricted values. Suppose that in a certain model, if a variable denoted p, ultimately to mean the price of some good, increases, then another variable x, ultimately to mean the quantity of that good demanded, can validly be inferred to, say, decrease, as a matter of the logic of the model, then a refutable proposition is said to be asserted. The critical thing is that the variable x is to respond in a given manner, and it must be possible for x not to respond in that manner.

The logical simulation, usually with mathematics, of the testing of theories in economics is called the *theory of comparative statics*. The word *statics* is an unfortunate misnomer. Nothing really static is implied in the testing of theories. Recall that, in economics, theories are tested on the basis of *changes* in variables, when certain test conditions or assumptions change. The use of the term comparative statics refers to the absence of a prediction about the *rate* of change of variables over time, as opposed to the *direction* of change.

The testing of theories is simulated by dividing the variables into two classes:

1. Decision, or choice, variables.
2. Parameters, or variables exogenous to the model, i.e., not determined by the actions of the decision maker. The parameters represent the *test conditions* of the theory.

Let us denote the decision or choice variable (or variables) as x, and the parameters of the model as α. To be useful, the theory must postulate a certain set of choices x as a function of the test conditions α

$$x = f(\alpha) \tag{1-1}$$

That is, given the behavioral postulates A, if certain test conditions C, represented in the model by α, hold, then certain choices x will be made. Hence, x is functionally dependent on α, as denoted in Eq. (1-1).

As an empirical matter, economists will rarely, if ever, be able to test relations of the form (1-1) directly, i.e., formulate hypotheses about the actual amount of x chosen for given α. As mentioned earlier, to do this would require full knowledge of tastes as well as opportunities. The neoclassical economic paradigm is therefore based on observations of *marginal* quantities only. These marginal quantities are the responses of x to *changes* in α.

Mathematically, for "well-behaved" (differentiable) choice functions, it is the properties of the derivative of x with respect to α, or

$$\frac{dx}{d\alpha} = f'(\alpha) \tag{1-2}$$

that represent the potentially refutable hypotheses in economics. Most frequently, all that is asserted is a sign for this derivative. For example, in demand theory, prices p are exogenous, i.e., parameters, while quantities demanded x are choice variables. The law of demand asserts (under the usual qualifications) that $dx/dp < 0$. Because it is possible that $dx/dp > 0$, and since this would contradict the assertions of the model, the statement $dx/dp < 0$ is a potentially refutable hypothesis. *Comparative statics is that mathematical technique by which an economic model is investigated to determine if refutable hypotheses are forthcoming.* If not, then actual empirical testing is a waste of time, because no data could ever refute the theory.

1.5 EXAMPLES OF COMPARATIVE STATICS[†]

To illustrate the preceding principles, let us consider three alternative hypotheses about the behavior of firms. Specifically, suppose we were to postulate that

1. Firms maximize profits π, where π equals total revenue minus cost.
2. Firms maximize some utility function of profits $U(\pi)$, where $U'(\pi) > 0$, so that higher profits mean higher utility. Thus, profits are desired not for their own sake, but rather for the utility they provide the firm owner.
3. Firms maximize total sales, i.e., total revenue only.

By what means shall these three theories be tested and compared? It is not possible to test theories by introspection. Contemplating whether these postulates sound to us like "reasonable" behavior is not an empirically reliable test. Also, asking firm owners if they behave in these particular ways is similarly unreliable. The only way to test such postulates is to derive from them potentially refutable hypotheses and ultimately to see if actual firms conform to the predictions of the theory.

What sorts of refutable hypotheses emerge from these behavioral assertions? Among the logical implications of profit maximization is the refutable hypothesis that if a per-unit tax is applied to a firm's output, the amount of goods offered for sale will decrease. This hypothesis is refutable because the reverse can be true. We therefore begin our first example by *asserting* that firms n..aximize profits in order to derive this implication.

Example 1. Let

$$R(x) = \text{total revenue function (depending on output } x)$$

$$C(x) = \text{total cost function}$$

[†] The material in this section requires some knowledge of elementary calculus techniques. The student should review parts of Chap. 2 first if these tools are unfamiliar.

tx = total tax revenue collected, where the

per-unit tax rate t is a parameter

determined by forces beyond the firm's control

If the firm sells its output in a perfectly competitive market, i.e., it is a *price taker,* then

$$R(x) = px$$

where p is the parametrically determined market price of x. If the firm is not a perfect competitor, then p is determined, along with x, via the demand curve, and revenue is simply some function of output, $R(x)$.

In the general case, the tax rate t represents the only parameter, or test condition, of the model. The first model thus becomes

maximize

$$\pi(x) = R(x) - C(x) - tx \qquad (1\text{-}3)$$

By simple calculus, the first-order condition for a maximum is

$$R'(x) - C'(x) - t = 0 \qquad (1\text{-}4)$$

the prime denoting first derivative.

For a maximum, the sufficient second-order condition is

$$R'' - C'' < 0 \qquad (1\text{-}5)$$

Condition (1-4) is·the choice function for this firm in implicit form. It states that the firm will choose that level of output such that marginal revenue (MR) equals marginal cost (MC) plus the tax (t). If the firm is a perfect competitor, then $R'(x) = p$, and $R''(x) = 0$. Equations (1-4) and (1-5) then become, respectively,

$$p - C'(x) - t = 0 \qquad (1\text{-}4')$$

$$-C''(x) < 0 \qquad (1\text{-}5')$$

We shall pursue the model from the standpoint of a firm with an unspecified revenue function $R(x)$. Application of the model to the perfectly competitive case will be left as a problem for the student.

Equation (1-4) is a well-known application of "marginal" reasoning. Equation (1-4) states that a firm will produce at a level such that the incremental (marginal) gain in revenues is exactly offset by the incremental cost (including, of course, the tax). This condition, however, does not guarantee a maximum of profits. It is also perfectly consistent with minimizing profits with the same cost and revenue functions, since the same first-order conditions are implied. What we mean to express is that as long as marginal receipts exceed marginal cost, the firm will produce at a higher rate, and if marginal receipts are less than marginal costs, the output will be reduced. This idea is given a precise statement by Eq.(1-5), which says that receipts are increasing at a slower rate than costs. Or, in terms of the marginal-revenue and marginal-cost curves, Eq.(1-5) says that the marginal-cost curve cuts the marginal-revenue curve from below.

Notice that we do not assert that the "optimum" output for a firm is where marginal revenue equals marginal cost; this is a value judgment, not a statement about behavior. Likewise, Eq.(1-4) does not represent what this firm does *in equilibrium*. Equation (1-4) is a *necessary* event, logically deduced from the assertion of maximization of profits. If Eq.(1-4) is not observed, it constitutes a refutation of the model, not *disequilibrium* or *nonoptimal* behavior. Thus, we *assert* that firms act as if they are obeying Eqs.(1-4) and (1-5), and on that account we make predictions about their behavior.

To simply assert MR = MC + t, however, is not likely to be useful. One is not likely to observe these marginal relationships. Just as tastes are difficult to observe, the total revenue and total cost functions and, hence, their derivatives, will likely not be known. However, a prediction about the response of the firm to a change in the economic environment, i.e., some test condition—in this case, a change in the tax rate—*is*, nonetheless, possible. Even if profit-maximization, marginal revenue, and marginal cost are not directly observable, tax rates and quantities sold *are* potentially observable. And profit maximization contains implications about these observable quantities.

How can Eqs.(1-4) and (1-5) be used to obtain predictions about marginal responses? Upon closer observation we notice that Eq.(1-4) is an implicit relationship between x and t. Under certain mathematical conditions this implicit relationship between the variable x and the parameter t can be solved for the explicit choice function:

$$x = x^*(t) \tag{1-6}$$

That is, if we knew the equations of the MR and MC curves, *then as long as the firm can be counted on to always obey the appropriate marginal relations,* no matter what tax rate prevails, we can, in principle, solve for the explicit relationship that states how much output will be produced at each tax rate. Again, although it would be desirable to know the exact form of Eq.(1-6), the economist will not typically have this much information. Hence, predictions about *total* quantities will not generally be forthcoming. We can, nonetheless, make predictions about *marginal* quantities.

If Eq.(1-6) is substituted into Eq.(1-4), the *identity*

$$R'(x^*(t)) - C'(x^*(t)) - t \equiv 0 \tag{1-7}$$

results. This is an identity because the left-hand side is 0 for all values of t. It is 0 for all values of t precisely because $x^*(t)$ is that level of output that the firm chooses in order to *make* the left-hand side of (1-7) always equal 0. That is, the firm, by always equating MR to MC plus the tax, for any tax rate, transforms the Eq.(1-4) into the identity (1-7). Because we are interested in what happens to x as t *changes*, the indicated mathematical operation is the differentiation of identity (1-7) with respect to t, keeping Eq.(1-6) in mind. The student must observe that this differentiation makes sense *only if x is a function of t.* Otherwise, the symbol dx/dt has no meaning. It is premature to simply differentiate Eq.(1-4) with respect to t until such functional dependence is formally implied. It is the assertion that the firm will *always* equate at the margin, i.e., obey Eq.(1-4) *for any tax rate* that allows the specification of Eq.(1-6): the functional dependence of x upon t. The resulting identity, (1-7), *can* be validly differentiated on both sides; Eq.(1-4) cannot be. This step is often left out, yet it is critical from the standpoint of clearly understanding the implied economic relationships as well as mathematical validity.[†]

Performing the indicated differentiation of identity (1-7),

$$R''(x)\frac{dx^*}{dt} - C''(x)\frac{dx^*}{dt} - 1 \equiv 0 \tag{1-8}$$

Equivalently, assuming $(R'' - C'') \neq 0$,

$$\frac{dx^*}{dt} \equiv \frac{1}{R'' - C''} \tag{1-9}$$

Since $R'' - C'' < 0$ by the sufficient second-order condition for profit maximization, this implies

$$\frac{dx^*}{dt} < 0$$

Note well what has been accomplished here. The postulate of profit-maximization (not observable), as specified in Eq. (1-3), has led to the refutable proposition that output will decline as the tax rate the firm faces increases. In addition, nothing has been assumed as to the specific functional form of the demand or cost curves, and hence the result holds for all specifications of those functions. A prediction about *changes* in the choice variable, that is, marginal adjustment of output when the parameter facing the decision maker changes, has been rather easily derived, i.e., shown to be implied by a single behavioral assertion. This is the goal of comparative statics; the limitations and abilities of the methodology to accomplish that goal are the subject of this book.

Example 2. Consider now the second previously mentioned behavioral postulate. Let us suppose that profits are desired not for their own sake, but rather for the utility derived from them. Thus, let us now assert that the firm owner maximizes $U(\pi)$, where $U'(\pi) > 0$, so that increased profits mean increased utility. The function $U(\pi)$ is some unspecified ordinal measure of the "satisfaction" that this firm owner gains from earning profits. It might seem that since we have replaced a potentially observable quantity, profits, with an unobservable variable, utility, that this theory will be devoid of refutable implications. Let us see.

The objective function is now

maximize

$$U(R(x) - C(x) - tx) = U(\pi) \tag{1-10}$$

The firm's choice function, as before, is found by setting the derivative of $U(\pi)$ with respect to x equal to 0. Using the chain rule

---

[†] As an example of the latter, differentiation of both sides of the identity $(x + 1)^2 \equiv x^2 + 2x + 1$ is valid; differentiation of both sides of the equation $x^2 + 3x - 4 = 0$ yields nonsense. The difference is that the former holds for *all* x, whereas the latter holds only for $x = -4$ and $x = +1$.

$$\frac{dU}{d\pi}\frac{d\pi}{dx} = 0$$

or

$$U'(\pi)[R'(x) - C'(x) - t] = 0 \tag{1-11}$$

Since $U'(\pi) > 0$, the choice function (1-11) is equivalent to the previous one for simple profit-maximization:

$$R'(x) - C'(x) - t = 0 \tag{1-4}$$

Since the implicit functions (1-4) and (1-11) are equivalent, their solutions

$$x = x^*(t) \tag{1-12}$$

are identical. Thus, these firms will act identically; they have the same explicit choice functions (1-6) and (1-12) governing the response of output to tax rates. One technicality must not be overlooked, however. We must check that the point of maximum profits is also *maximum*, rather than minimum, utility; i.e., we have to check the second-order conditions for this problem. Otherwise we might be discussing two entirely different points, and the derivatives dx/dt at those points would in general differ. The second-order conditions for the two problems are, however, identical: we have, for the first-order condition

$$\frac{dU(\pi)}{dx} = U'(\pi)[\pi'(x)] = 0$$

Thus, using the product rule

$$\frac{d^2U(\pi)}{dx^2} = U'(\pi)[\pi''(x)] + [\pi'(x)]\{[U''(\pi)][\pi'(x)]\}$$

Since $\pi'(x)$ by the first-order conditions

$$\frac{d^2U(\pi)}{dx^2} = U'(\pi)\pi''(x) \tag{1-13}$$

Since $U'(\pi > 0$, $d^2U(\pi)/dx^2 < 0$ if and only if $d^2\pi/dx^2 < 0$, that is, the second-order conditions for the two models are identical.

These two theories of behavior are equivalent in the sense that they yield the same refutable hypotheses. Even if more parameters are introduced into $\pi(x)$, the first- and second-order equations will be identical. Thus, no set of data could even distinguish whether a firm was maximizing profits, or some arbitrary increasing function of profits, $U(\pi)$. We shall never know if the firm is really maximizing π, or e^π, or π^3 (*not* π^2; why?), or whatever. These behavioral postulates all yield the same refutable hypotheses. One is as good as the other.

Example 3. Consider now the last of the three hypotheses about firm behavior, the maximization of total sales. If such a firm were taxed at rate t, the objective function would be

maximize

$$\phi(x) = R(x) - tx \tag{1-14}$$

The implicit choice function of this firm is the first-order condition for a maximum

$$\phi'(x) = R'(x) - t = 0 \tag{1-15}$$

The sufficient second-order condition for maximizing $\phi(x)$ is

$$\phi''(x) = R''(x) < 0 \tag{1-16}$$

The *explicit* choice function of this firm is the solution of (1-15) for output as a function of the tax rate, or

$$x = x^{**}(t) \tag{1-17}$$

This choice function will in general indicate a different level of output for any given tax rate than the choice function (1-6) or (1-12). If the revenue function $R(x)$ were actually known, then this theory (sales maximization) would be operationally distinguishable from the prior two theories, since different choices are implied. However, if it turns out that $R(x)$ is not directly observable (indeed, this is the empirically likely situation), then the only refutable proposition will concern the sign of dx^{**}/dt. This model, like the previous ones, implies a negative sign for this derivative. Substituting (1-17) into (1-15) and differentiating with respect to t

$$R''(x)\frac{dx^{**}}{dt} \equiv 1$$

or

$$\frac{dx^{**}}{dt} \equiv \frac{1}{R''(x)} < 0 \tag{1-18}$$

using the sufficient second-order condition (1-16). Hence, *unless the revenue and cost functions are somehow known, the sales-maximization and profit-maximization postulates are equivalent, in the sense that no observation of* **changes** *in tax rates and* **changes** *in quantities sold will ever distinguish these two theories.* If $R(x)$ and $C(x)$ are unobservable, and $dx^*/dt < 0$ is implied for *any* $R(x)$ and $C(x)$ which satisfy the second-order conditions, then the same observations are implied for $C(x) \equiv 0$, i.e., sales maximization. The reader is cautioned against assuming that there is *no* test that could separate these hypotheses. There may be, for example, reasons why the long-term survivability might differ for firms that maximized profits as opposed to sales.

Example 4. Suppose the owner of a firm maximizes "net karma," i.e., karma less taxes, where karma has been reliably (at last) estimated with bivernal data, using generalized five-stage least-squares regression, with of course the usual adjustments for semi-truncation and hypercolinearity of the data set, as the function

$$K(x) = \frac{\alpha \log[\tan(e^{\beta x} + e^{\sin x}) + \cot(\beta x + \log(1 + e^{\beta x}))]}{\log(\alpha + \beta x)}$$

where α and β are positive K parameters. How will this firm react to an increase in the tax rate?

The objective function is

maximize

$$K(x) - tx$$

Assuming the first- and second-order conditions hold (don't ask), an explicit choice function $x = x^*(t)$ is implied. The structure of this model is formally identical to the model in Example 3; the results must be identical. It doesn't matter what specific functional form is used in the objective function. The only crucial elements are that

1. The first and second-order conditions hold
2. The tax parameter t enters in such a way that when the first-order identity is differentiated with respect to t, it produces a negative value on the left-hand side of that identity, and thus a positive entry when it is brought over to the right-hand side. (When taxes enter the objective function as $-tx$, this procedure yields $+1$ on the right-hand side.)

The resulting expression for dx^*/dt will then always consist of a positive term divided by an expression representing the second derivative of the objective function, which is assumed negative by the sufficient second-order conditions. Thus in every such case, we will derive $dx^*/dt < 0$. We don't have to bother differentiating a perhaps messy objective function to get this result.

Example 5. There is nothing in the previous examples that restricts the analysis to noncompetitive firms. For competitive firms, output price p is taken as given. The firm is a price taker; it cannot influence output price by its own choices regarding output levels. The revenue function, $R(x)$, for a competitive firm is simply px, price times quantity. Since this is a special case of $R(x)$, the previous analysis applies to competitive firms as well: a tax on output will lead to decreases in total output produced.

   In this model, however, a new parameter p appears. Does the postulate of profit-maximization imply a refutable hypothesis regarding changes in p? The objective function is

maximize

$$\pi(x) = px - C(x) \tag{1-19}$$

The first-order condition for maximization yields the implicit choice function

$$p - C'(x) = 0 \tag{1-20}$$

Here, marginal revenue = price p. Hence, this relation says that the firm will set marginal cost equal to price. However, unless we know the cost function, this information will not be very useful.

   The sufficient second-order condition for maximizing π is

$$\frac{d^2\pi}{dx^2} = -C''(x) = -\text{MC}'(x) < 0 \tag{1-21}$$

That is, the marginal cost function of the firm must be upward-sloping.

The explicit choice function is found by solving (in principle) Eq. (1-20) for the choice variable x in terms of the parameter p

$$x = x^*(p) \tag{1-22}$$

This function is the firm's supply function. It tells how much x will be offered for sale at any given price p. Strictly speaking, the marginal cost function is *not* the supply function of the firm. In the MC function, output x is the *independent* variable, marginal cost (which equals price at the chosen point) is the *dependent* variable. For the supply function, output is the dependent variable, dependent upon price. Thus, the supply function is really the *inverse* of the MC function. How will x *change* when p *changes*? Substituting (1-22) back into (1-20), the identity

$$p - C'(x^*(p)) \equiv 0 \tag{1-23}$$

results. The left-hand side is *always* zero, because we are now postulating that the firm will *always* set price equal to marginal cost *for any price*. Hence, this is an identity—the left-hand side vanishes completely. Since the derivative dx^*/dp is desired, differentiate identity (1-23) with respect to p, using the chain rule for $C'(x^*(p))$

$$\frac{dp}{dp} - \frac{dC'(x)}{dx}\frac{dx^*}{dp} \equiv 0$$

or

$$-C''(x)\frac{dx^*}{dp} \equiv -1$$

and thus, since $C'' \neq 0$

$$\frac{dx^*}{dp} \equiv \frac{1}{C''(x)} > 0 \tag{1-24}$$

since $C''(x) > 0$ by the sufficient second-order condition for a maximum (1-21). Thus, the behavioral postulate of profit maximization yields the refutable hypothesis that if the output price to competitive firms is somehow raised, output levels will increase. The supply function is upward-sloping. Given this mathematical property of the model, the theory can be tested using real data on the assumption that the firms in question correspond to the theoretical construct of the firm used in the model. But empirical testing is worthwhile only because the model yields refutable implications.

PROBLEMS

1. Consider the following alleged exception to the law of demand: "As the price of diamonds falls, the quantity of diamonds demanded will also fall since the prestige of owning diamonds will similarly fall." Why is this not an exception to the law of demand? What test condition is being violated? How would one test the law of demand for diamonds? (*Hint:* Do jewelry stores ever lower prices on diamonds? What results?)

2. What is the difference between an assertion and an assumption? Which is observable, which is not? Which must be "realistic"?

3. Many young people regard their parents and grandparents as rigid and conservative. Recognizing that investment and experimentation in new procedures are costly, explain why one would expect the young to be more likely than the old to adopt new methods (or, why young dogs are more apt to learn new tricks, and why old dogs will more likely perfect the old ones.)

4. Why do economists limit their analyses to marginal rather than total quantities? Do economists believe that marginal quantities are more useful than the corresponding total quantities?

5. What is the difference between a theory and a model?

6. Is there a trade-off between the realism of the assumptions of a theory and the *tractability*, i.e., the empirical usefulness, of the theory?

7. In regard to Prob. 6, is it necessary to have the latest theory of molecular action to make penicillin and other "wonder drugs"? How detailed a theory of the firm is necessary to predict the effects of tariffs on a given industry?

8. Consider a monopolist whose total cost function is $C = kx^2$ and who faces the demand curve $x = a - bp$.

   (a) What restrictions on the values of the parameters a, b, and k would you be inclined to assert, a priori?

   (b) Find the explicit function $x = x^*(t)$. Confirm that for the restricted values of a, b, and k placed in part (a) that $x^{*\prime}(t) < 0$, i.e., output decreases as the tax increases.

   (c) What restrictions does the hypothesis of profit maximization place on the parameters a, b, and k? Are these weaker or stronger than your a priori restrictions?

   (d) Substitute your $x^*(t)$ function into the first-order relation for maximization and confirm that an identity in t results.

   (e) Confirm that, for this specification of the model, profit maximization alone implies $x^{*\prime}(t) < 0$.

   (f) What is the effect on output and output price of a parallel shift in the demand curve?

9. Show that an increase of a per-unit tax on a perfect competitor will lower that firm's output.

10. Show why a monopolist has no supply function. (*Hint:* In Example 1 in this chapter, how would $x = x^*(p)$ be defined?)

11. Consider a firm that has as its behavioral postulate the minimization of total costs, irrespective of revenues. How will this theory of the firm differ from those discussed in Examples 1 through 3 in this chapter?

12. Consider a firm with "gross profits" $R(y) - C(y)$ and "net profits" $R(y) - C(y) - ty$, where t is a per unit tax. Prove under profit maximization if the tax rate rises, both net profits and gross profits will fall.

13. Tin (aluminum) cans are manufactured in the shape of right cylindrical cylinders of diameter D and height h. Assume there is no waste cutting out the rectangular piece for the side, but when the circular ends are cut from squares, the corner pieces are discarded.

   (a) Show that the shape of the can that minimizes the (cost of the) metal used for any given volume is $h/D = 4/\pi \approx 1.27$.

   (b) Run to your local supermarket and see if manufacturers utilize this result.

(c) There seem to be some outstanding anomalies, e.g., tuna fish (too short), soda pop (too long). What factors might explain these anomalies and others you might observe?

(d) Assume now that the corner pieces for the ends can be recycled at some cost, effectively reducing the amount of metal used by $k \times waste$, where $0 \le k \le 1$. Show that as the waste is reduced, the size of the can approaches $h/D = 1$.

(e) We of course pay for the item itself plus the packaging. How does the value of the item inside the can affect the preceding cost considerations? (See the discussion of the "Alchian and Allen substitution theorem," in Chap. 11.)

BIBLIOGRAPHY

Alchian, Armen A.: "Uncertainty, Evolution and Economic Theory," *Journal of Political Economy*, **58:**211–221, 1950.

Bronfenbrenner, Martin: "A Middle-brow Introduction to Economic Methodology," in S. Krupp (ed.), *The Structure of Economic Science*, Prentice-Hall, Inc., Englewood Cliffs, NJ, 1966.

Friedman, Milton: "The Methodology of Positive Economics," from *Essays in Positive Economics*, The University of Chicago Press, Chicago, 1953, pp. 3–43. The provocative essay that started the current debates on methodology.

Gordon, Donald: "Operational Propositions in Economic Theory," *Journal of Political Economy*, **63:**150–161, 1955.

Hempel, Carl: *The Philosophy of Natural Science*, Prentice-Hall, Inc., Englewood Cliffs, NJ, 1966. An extremely lucid discussion of theories and theoretical testing.

Kuhn, Thomas S.: *The Structure of Scientific Revolutions*, The University of Chicago Press, Chicago, 1962.

Nagel, Ernst: "Assumptions in Economic Theory," *American Economic Review*, pp. 211–219, May 1963.

Papandreou, Andreas: *Economics as a Science*, J. B. Lippincott Company, Philadelphia, 1958.

Robbins, Lionel: *An Essay on the Nature and Significance of Economic Science*, Macmillan & Co., Ltd., London, 1932.

Samuelson, Paul A.: *Foundations of Economic Analysis*, Harvard University Press, Cambridge, MA, 1947.

CHAPTER
2

REVIEW OF
CALCULUS
(ONE VARIABLE)

2.1 FUNCTIONS, LIMITS, CONTINUITY

Consider a *variable x*. By the term *variable,* we mean that x is a number that can take on a whole range of values. In economics, two common variables are price and quantity of a good. Most often, these variables are restricted to nonnegative values, though occasionally inputs in a production process are referred to as "negative outputs." Occasionally in economics the variable x is a *complex number* of the form $a + bi$, where $i = \sqrt{-1}$. We shall not deal with complex numbers in this chapter. In general, we shall allow x to range over any real number. The set of points between two numbers a, b, with $b > a$, is called an *interval*. If both endpoints are included, it is called a *closed* interval; if neither endpoint is included, it is an *open* interval. That is, the set of x such that $1 \leq x \leq 5$ is a closed interval; the set of x such that $-1 < x < 4$ is an open interval. In general, a set that includes all its boundary points is called *closed;* a set with no boundary points is called *open*.

By a *function,* we mean a *rule* by which a variable x is transformed into some *unique* (single-valued) number, y. For example, consider

$$y = x^2$$

This function means: "Take any value of x and square it. The resulting value is y." This rule, or function, associates with every point along the real axis some number along the nonnegative real axis. The function $y = x^2$ represents the geometric shape of a parabola and is represented in Fig. 2-1a. An especially simple, though

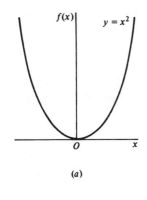

(a)

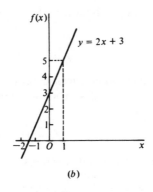

(b)

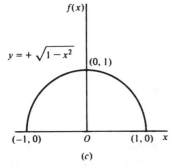

(c)

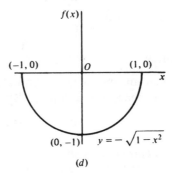

(d)

FIGURE 2-1
Four functions in x and y.

important, function comprises the equations of the form $y = mx + b$. Geometrically, these are straight lines with a vertical intercept (y intercept) b. The slopes of these lines are constant and equal to m. Consider, for example,

$$y = 2x + 3$$

When $x = 0$, $y = 3$. For each unit increase in x, y will increase by 2 units. Hence, the slope of this function is constant at $m = 2$. This function is plotted on Fig. 2-1b.

An important class of functions comprises the polynomials,

$$y = a_0 + a_1 x + a_2 x^2 + \cdots + a_n x^n$$

Functions of this type are called polynomials even if some of the a_i's are zero; for example, $y = x^n$ is still called a polynomial even though it has but one term. These functions in general wiggle around up to $n - 1$ times and then depart for plus or minus infinity. We shall explore their behavior in a while.

In contrast, consider the relationship

$$x^2 + y^2 = 1$$

The set of values of x and y which satisfies this equation corresponds to the boundary of a circle in the xy plane with center at the origin and with radius 1.

It is called the unit circle. However, this *implicit* function in x and y may not be written as

$$y = \pm \sqrt{1 - x^2}$$

and preserve the single-valuedness criterion that is part of the definition of a function. That is, for each $-1 < x < +1$, there are *two* values of y. The implicit function

$$x^2 + y^2 = 1$$

is equivalent to the *two* explicit functions,

$$y = +\sqrt{1 - x^2} \quad \text{and} \quad y = -\sqrt{1 - x^2}$$

as shown in Fig. 2-1c and *d*.

Limits, Continuity

At one time, mathematicians spoke of "infinitesimals." This nomenclature has been replaced by the concept of a "limit." By the symbol

$$\lim_{x \to x_0} f(x) = A$$

we mean that as x *approaches* some value x_0, $f(x)$ becomes arbitrarily close to the value A. No matter how close to A, say within 0.0001, or 0.000001, you wish the function to be, it can be made to be that close or closer by selecting an x near x_0. This concept is expressed rigorously as

"For any $\epsilon > 0$, there exists a $\delta > 0$ such that if $|x - x_0| < \delta$, $|f(x) - A| < \epsilon$."

The *limit* of a function as $x \to x_0$ has no necessary connection with the value of the function *at* $x = x_0$. That is, it is one thing to assert that $\lim_{x \to x_0} f(x) = A$ and quite another to say that $f(x_0) = A$. The function need not even be defined at x_0; yet it may still have a limit as x *approaches* x_0.

When the *limit* of a function as $x \to x_0$ in fact *equals* the value of the function at x_0, the function is said to be *continuous at* x_0. That is, the function is continuous if

$$\lim_{x \to x_0} f(x) = f(x_0) \tag{2-1}$$

A formal definition of continuity is obtained by using the formal definition of a limit:

"The function $f(x)$ is continuous at x_0 if for every $\epsilon > 0$, there exists a $\delta > 0$ such that if $|x - x_0| < \delta$, $|f(x) - f(x_0)| < \epsilon$."

Example 1. Consider the function $y = 2x + 1$. As $x \to 1$, $y \to 3$. That is, the *limit* of $f(x) = 3$, as $x \to 1$. This can also be shown by demonstrating that $|f(x) - 3| < \epsilon$, for *any* ϵ, if $|x - 1|$ is sufficiently small. We note that

$$|f(x) - 3| = |2x - 2| = 2|x - 1|$$

If we choose $\delta = \epsilon/2$, then if $|(x - 1)| < \delta$,

$$2|x - 1| = |2x - 2| = |f(x) - 3| < 2\delta = \epsilon$$

Hence, no matter how small ϵ is made, by choosing $\delta = \epsilon/2$, $|x - 1| < \delta$ guarantees $|f(x) - 3| < \epsilon$. Thus, by definition

$$\lim_{x \to 1}(2x + 1) = 3$$

Another matter entirely is that $f(1) = 2(1) + 1 = 3$. In this case

$$\lim_{x \to 1} f(x) = f(1)$$

Because of this, the function $f(x) = 2x + 1$ is *continuous* at $x = 1$.

Example 2. Show that the function $y = x^2$ is continuous at $x = 2$. We first note that $f(2) = 2^2 = 4$. For any $\epsilon > 0$, $|f(x) - 4| < \epsilon$ is equivalent to $|x^2 - 4| < \epsilon$, or $|x + 2||x - 2| < \epsilon$. At points near $x = 2$, $|x + 2| \to 4$. Certainly, then, $|x + 2| < 5$. Then let $\delta = \epsilon/5$. Then $|x - 2| < \delta$ implies $\epsilon > 5|x - 2| > |x + 2||x - 2| = |f(x) - 4|$. Hence, there exists a $\delta > 0$ (in this case, say, $\delta = \epsilon/5$), such that if x is within δ of $x_0 = 2$, $(|x - 2| < \delta)$, then $f(x)$ is within ϵ of the value $4 = f(x)$, $(|f(x) - 4| < \epsilon)$, *and this holds for any $\epsilon > 0$ whatsoever.* Hence,

$$\lim_{x \to 2} x^2 = 4 = f(2)$$

and thus x^2 is continuous at $x = 2$.

Example 3. In fact, the functions in the two examples above are continuous everywhere. As an example of a function that is not continuous everywhere, consider the step function depicted in Fig. 2-2*a*. This function is defined as

$$f(x) = \text{greatest integer in } x$$

For example, for $0 \le x < 1, f(x) = 0$ (note carefully the strict or weak inequalities); for $1 \le x < 2, f(x) = 1$; for $2 \le x < 3, f(x) = 2$; etc. Notice the "holes" on the

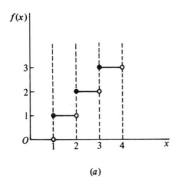

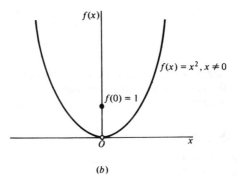

(a)   (b)

FIGURE 2-2
(a) The step function: $f(x) = $ greatest integer in x. (b) A graph of function that is discontinuous at the origin.

right-hand side of each step: At the integer values $x = 1, 2, 3, \ldots$, the function jumps to the next integer value. The function is *defined* at $x = 1, 2, 3, \ldots$; for example, $f(1) = 1, f(2) = 2$, etc. However, if one approaches the integer values $x = 1, 2, 3$, from the left (denoted $x \to x_0^-$)

$$\lim_{x \to 1^-} f(x) = 0$$

$$\lim_{x \to 2^-} f(x) = 1$$

$$\vdots$$

From the right (denoted $x \to x_0^+$),

$$\lim_{x \to 1^+} f(x) = 1$$

$$\lim_{x \to 2^+} f(x) = 2$$

$$\vdots$$

In general, for integral values of x_0, $\lim_{x \to x_0} f(x) = f(x_0)$ only when x_0 is approached from the right. In this case, no unique number for $\lim_{x \to x_0} f(x)$ exists; hence, $f(x)$ is discontinuous at integral values of x.

Example 4. Consider the function $f(x)$ defined as

$$f(x) = \begin{cases} x^2 & \text{if } x \neq 0 \\ 1 & \text{if } x = 0 \end{cases}$$

This function is depicted in Fig. 2-2b. For all points except $x = 0$, $f(x)$ is the usual parabolic shape. For no particular reason, $f(0)$ is defined to be unity. Hence, the parabola has a hole at $x = 0$. In this case

$$\lim_{x \to 0} f(x) = 0$$

from either side of the origin. Since $f(0) = 1$,

$$\lim_{x \to 0} f(x) \neq f(0)$$

Hence, this function is discontinuous at the origin.

Example 5. Consider the hyperbolas defined by $y = 1/x$. This function exists in the strictly positive first quadrant and strictly negative third quadrant. Since $f(0)$ is undefined, this function cannot be continuous at $x = 0$.

PROBLEMS

1. Sketch the following functions:
   (a) $y = -2x + 1$
   (b) $y = 1/x$
   (c) $y = \sqrt{1 - x}$ (For what values of x is this function defined?)
   (d) $y = |x|$ (absolute value of x)

(e) $y = (x + 1)/(x - 1)$

(f) $y = x$, if $x \geq 0$, $y = -x + 1$ if $x < 0$.

2. Show that the functions 1(a)–1(e) are continuous for all values of x for which the function is defined. Show that the function in 1(f) is discontinuous at $x = 0$.

3. Does the existence of a "kink" or corner in a function (such as occurs in Prob. 1(d) at $x = 0$) imply that the function is discontinuous there?

4. For the function in Prob. 1(e), what is $\lim_{x \to \infty} f(x)$? (*Hint:* divide numerator and denominator through by x.)

2.2 DERIVATIVES

One of the most important mathematical concepts is the rate of change of a function. In economics, this concept shows up under the name "marginal." Marginal cost is the rate of change of total cost per increment of output. Marginal revenue is similarly the rate of change of total revenue. Geometrically, the marginal quantities are the slopes of the total quantities.

Consider any function $y = f(x)$, as depicted in Fig. 2-3. At some point $x = x_0$, $f(x) = f(x_0)$. Suppose now that x is changed to $(x_0 + \Delta x)$. (Here, Δx is positive, but this is not a necessary restriction.) The new value of the function is given by $y + \Delta y = f(x_0 + \Delta x)$. The change in the functional value Δy is

$$\Delta y = f(x_0 + \Delta x) - f(x_0)$$

The *rate* of change of $f(x)$ per change in x is

$$\frac{\Delta y}{\Delta x} = \frac{f(x_0 + \Delta x) - f(x_0)}{\Delta x} \tag{2-2}$$

Geometrically, $\Delta y/\Delta x$ is the slope of the chord CC passing through $f(x_0)$ and $f(x_0 + \Delta x)$, as seen in Fig. 2-3. Now, as Δx becomes smaller and smaller, the

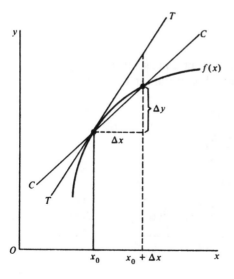

FIGURE 2-3
The derivative of a function.

slope of the chord CC approaches the slope of the line TT which is tangent to the function at $f(x_0)$. The slope of this tangent line (if it exists) is written dy/dx. Therefore, assuming the limit exists (and is thus unique),

$$\frac{dy}{dx} = \lim_{\Delta x \to x_0} \frac{f(x_0 + \Delta x) - f(x_0)}{\Delta x} \tag{2-3}$$

This important limit, the limit of a *difference quotient,* is called the *derivative* of $f(x)$ at x_0. It represents the slope of the curve at x_0.

Before investigating the rules by which derivatives are found, let us investigate cases in which these limits do not exist. Consider the function $y = |x|$. For $x > 0$, this function is simply $y = x$; it has a constant slope of unity. For $x < 0$, the function is given by $y = -x$; it has constant slope of *minus* one. At $x = 0$, the slope is undefined. The function has a "corner" there. It is *continuous,* but it is not *differentiable* there. If a function is to be differentiable at a point, it must be well defined there, and it must at least be continuous. However, these conditions alone are insufficient, as $y = |x|$ reveals. Simply stated, the difference quotient (2-3) must in fact possess a limit.

Differentiation of Polynomials

Let us find the derivative of $f(x) = x^2$. The difference quotient at any value of x is

$$\frac{\Delta y}{\Delta x} = \frac{f(x + \Delta x) - f(x)}{\Delta x} = \frac{(x + \Delta x)^2 - x^2}{\Delta x}$$

$$= \frac{2x\Delta x + (\Delta x)^2}{\Delta x} = 2x + \Delta x$$

Clearly, $\lim_{\Delta x \to 0}(\Delta y/\Delta x) = 2x$, hence

$$\frac{dy}{dx} = 2x$$

The slope of the parabola $y = x^2$ at any point equals twice the value of x. At $x = 0$, $dy/dx = 0$; that is, the function is horizontal; at $x = -2$, $dy/dx = -4$, etc.

Now consider the polynomial $y = x^n$.

$$\frac{\Delta y}{\Delta x} = \frac{(x + \Delta x)^n - x^n}{\Delta x}$$

Expanding the numerator using the binomial theorem

$$\frac{\Delta y}{\Delta x} = \frac{\left[x^n + nx^{n-1}\Delta x + \dfrac{n(n - 1)}{2}x^{n-2}(\Delta x)^2 + \ldots \right] - x^n}{\Delta x}$$

$$= nx^{n-1} + \frac{n(n-1)}{2}x^{n-2}\Delta x$$

$$+ [\text{terms in } (\Delta x)^2 \text{ and higher powers of } \Delta x]$$

As $\Delta x \to 0$, all terms except the first tend to 0. Thus

$$\frac{dy}{dx} = nx^{n-1} \tag{2-4}$$

It can be quickly verified that if $y = kx^n$ where k is any constant,

$$\frac{dy}{dx} = knx^{n-1} \tag{2-5}$$

Also, let $y = k_1x^n + k_2x^m$ where k_1 and k_2 are arbitrary constants. Then

$$\frac{dy}{dx} = k_1nx^{n-1} + k_2mx^{m-1}$$

The derivative of a sum is the sum of the derivatives. This property holds for any functions. Let us denote the derivative of functions $f(x), g(x)$, and $h(x)$ as $f'(x)$ (read "f prime of x"), $g'(x)$, $h'(x)$. Suppose

$$y = f(x) \equiv g(x) + h(x)$$

Then

$$\frac{dy}{dx} = f'(x) \equiv g'(x) + h'(x)$$

The theorem extends to sums or differences of arbitrarily many terms.

The binomial theorem used in the above proof that for $y = x^n$, $dy/dx = nx^{n-1}$ in fact holds for *all* values of n, not merely positive integers. The value of n can be any real number. Thus, for example, if

$$y = \sqrt{x} = x^{1/2}$$

$$\frac{dy}{dx} = \frac{1}{2}x^{-1/2}$$

Likewise, for

$$y = \frac{1}{x^3} = x^{-3}$$

$$\frac{dy}{dx} = -3x^{-4}$$

When any function $y = f(x)$ is differentiated, its derivative, $f'(x)$, will again be some function of x. If $f'(x)$ is sufficiently "smooth" (i.e., differentiable), it too can be differentiated with respect to x. We write

$$f''(x) = \frac{df'(x)}{dx} = \frac{d}{dx}\frac{dy}{dx} = \frac{d^2y}{dx^2}$$

In fact, as long as succeeding derivatives are differentiable, they can be successively differentiated, producing higher-order derivatives.

The second derivative of $f(x)$ is the first derivative, or the rate of change, of the first derivative of $f(x)$. That is, just as $f'(x)$ indicates the slope of $f(x)$, $f''(x)$ gives the slope of $f'(x)$. Likewise, $f'''(x)$ gives the slope of $f''(x)$, $f^{(n)}(x)$ is the slope of $f^{(n-1)}(x)$, where $f^{(n)}(x)$ is the nth derivative of $f(x)$.

Example 1. Let $y = x^2$. Then $f'(x) = 2x, f''(x) = 2, f'''(x) = \ldots = f^{(n)}(x) = 0$. All derivatives of third order and higher are 0. The fact that $f''(x) > 0$ means that $f'(x)$ is always increasing; i.e., the slope of $y = x^2$ is always increasing. The student should check this against Fig. 2-1a.

Example 2. Let $y = 1/x = x^{-1}$. Then $dy/dx = -1/x^2 = -x^{-2}, d^2y/dx^2 = f''(x) = +2x^{-3}, f'''(x) = -6x^{-4}$, etc. Note that $f'(x) = dy/dx < 0$ always. This function is always *falling*, i.e., negatively sloped. From the expression for $f''(x)$, we can infer that for $x > 0$, the slope increases with increasing x, whereas for $x < 0$, the slope decreases as x increases.

PROBLEMS

1. Find the derivatives of the following functions by taking the limit of a difference quotient:
   (a) $y = 3x^2$
   (b) $y = x^3$
   (c) $y = mx + b$
   (d) $y = 1/x$
2. For each function, find dy/dx and d^2y/dx^2:
   (a) $y = 37x^4$
   (b) $y = x^{a/b}$
   (c) $y = -x^{-2}$
   (d) $y = x^3 - 1/x^2$
3. Sketch each of the functions in Probs. 1 and 2, indicating when the *functions* are rising or falling, and when the *slopes* are rising or falling, with increasing x.
4. Show that the circumference of a circle may be regarded as the rate of change of the area with respect to the radius. Interpret geometrically.

2.3 DIFFERENTIALS

Consider Fig. 2-4, largely a reproduction of Fig. 2-3. For any change in the variable x, Δx, the actual change in the functional value of $f(x)$, is, by definition, Δy. We may distinguish this from the change in y *measured up to the tangent line*. This latter distance is defined to be dy. If dx is *any* change in x, then if $f'(x)$ represents the slope of the curve at the initial point,

$$dy = f'(x)dx = \frac{dy}{dx}dx$$

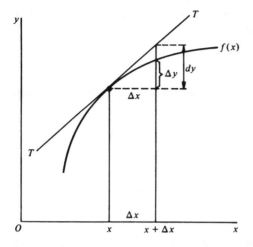

FIGURE 2-4
The distinction between the *actual* change in the function Δy and the differential change dy measured by the change in the height of the tangent line.

When we write $\lim(\Delta y/\Delta x) = dy/dx$, we are asserting that the difference ϵ where

$$\frac{\Delta y}{\Delta x} - \frac{dy}{dx} = \epsilon$$

tends to 0 as $\Delta x \to 0$. Multiplying both sides of this equation by Δx yields

$$\Delta y = \frac{dy}{dx}\Delta x + \epsilon\Delta x$$

If we let $\Delta x = dx$,

$$\Delta y = dy + \epsilon\Delta x \qquad (2\text{-}6)$$

This equation says that Δy and dy differ by an amount that is of "second-order smallness." The difference $dy - \Delta y = \epsilon\Delta x$ tends to 0 much faster than Δx, since as Δx tends to 0, ϵ tends to 0.

Example. Let $y = x^2$. Then

$$\Delta y = (x + \Delta x)^2 - x^2 = 2x\Delta x + \Delta x^2$$

However, if $dx = \Delta x$,

$$dy = f'(x)dx = 2x\Delta x$$

Hence

$$\Delta y - dy = (\Delta x)^2$$

When Δx is small (in particular, less than one in absolute value), $(\Delta x)^2$ is smaller than $|\Delta x|$. If, for example, $x = 2$, $\Delta x = 0.1$, $\Delta y - dy = 0.01$, one-tenth the amount of the change in x.

In general, the differential quantities dy are easier to calculate than the actual Δy. Hence, dy is often used as an empirical approximation to Δy. In an analytic sense, however, there is no need for dx or dy to be small, or infinitesimal. The dx's may range over any values whatsoever.

PROBLEMS

1. For each function below, find dy and Δy. Show that $\Delta y - dy$ is of second-order smallness:

   (a) $y = x^3$
   (b) $y = 2x^2 + 3x$
   (c) $y = 1/x$
   (d) $y = x^n$ (use the binomial theorem)
   (e) $y = \sqrt{x}$

2.4 THE CHAIN RULE

Suppose now that in addition to the functional dependence $y = f(x)$, x is dependent upon some other variable t, say, $x = g(t)$. Then if t varies, x will in general vary and therefore so will y. Hence, y is functionally dependent upon t by the relation

$$y = f(x) = f(g(t)) = F(t) \tag{2-7}$$

The function $F(t)$ represents the "composite function" $f(g(t))$. Assuming that $f(x)$ and $g(t)$ are differentiable, the derivative $dy/dt = F'(t)$ is well defined. How is $F'(t)$ related to the derivatives of the original functions $f(x)$ and $g(t)$? The answer is given by the *chain rule:*

$$\frac{dy}{dt} = F'(t) = \frac{dy}{dx}\frac{dx}{dt} = f'(x)g'(t) \tag{2-8}$$

There is a suggestion of canceling the dx's in the term

$$\frac{dy}{dx}\frac{dx}{dt}$$

It should remain a suggestion only. That procedure is as logically valid as cancelling the 6s in

$$\frac{\cancel{6}4}{1\cancel{6}} = 4$$

Although it gives the correct result, the procedure is invalid because it is devoid of the implied functional dependencies.

The chain rule is shown as follows. Changing t by Δt, x changes by Δx, y by Δy. Then

$$\Delta y = \frac{dy}{dx}\Delta x + \epsilon \Delta x$$

However, using the same reasoning

$$\Delta x = \frac{dx}{dt}\Delta t + \zeta \Delta t$$

where $\zeta \to 0$ as $\Delta t \to 0$. Substituting this expression into the preceding one,

$$\Delta y = \frac{dy}{dx}\frac{dx}{dt}\Delta t + \frac{dy}{dx}\zeta \Delta t + \epsilon \Delta x$$

Dividing by Δt,

$$\frac{\Delta y}{\Delta t} = \frac{dy}{dx}\frac{dx}{dt} + \frac{dy}{dx}\zeta + \epsilon \frac{\Delta x}{\Delta t}$$

If we now let $\Delta t \to 0$, $\Delta y/\Delta t \to dy/dt$, and since $\zeta \to 0$ and $\epsilon \to 0$ as $\Delta t \to 0$,

$$\frac{dy}{dt} = \frac{dy}{dx}\frac{dx}{dt}$$

Example 1. Let $y = x^2$, $x = t + t^3$. Find dy/dt. This particular problem can be solved by direct substitution:

$$y = x^2 = (t + t^3)^2 = t^2 + 2t^4 + t^6$$

Therefore

$$\frac{dy}{dt} = 2t + 8t^3 + 6t^5$$

Using the chain rule to find dy/dt, we note

$$\frac{dy}{dx} = 2x \qquad \frac{dx}{dt} = 1 + 3t^2$$

Therefore

$$\frac{dy}{dt} = 2x(1 + 3t^2) = 2(t + t^3)(1 + 3t^2)$$

$$= 2t + 8t^3 + 6t^5$$

as before.

Example 2. Let $y = (ax + b)^n$. Find dy/dx. Suppose we let $u = ax + b$. Then $y = u^n$. Therefore,

$$\frac{dy}{dx} = \frac{dy}{du}\frac{du}{dx} = (nu^{n-1})a = an(ax + b)^{n-1}$$

The foregoing example shows a powerful use of the chain rule. Often very complicated expressions can be easily differentiated by a clever substitution and subsequent use of the chain rule.

Example 3. Let $y = \sqrt{1 - 3x^2}$. Find dy/dx. Here, we let $u = 1 - 3x^2$, noting that $du/dx = -6x$. Therefore, $y = u^{1/2}$, and

$$\frac{dy}{dx} = \frac{dy}{du}\frac{du}{dx} = \frac{1}{2}u^{-1/2}(-6x)$$

$$= \frac{-3x}{(1 - 3x^2)^{1/2}}$$

2.5 THE PRODUCT AND QUOTIENT RULES

The Product Rule

Consider a function such as $y = x^2(1 + x)^{1/2}$. This function cannot yet be differentiated with the tools at hand; it is the product of two functions. Here

$$f(x) = g(x)h(x) \qquad (2\text{-}9)$$

where in this case $g(x) = x^2$, $h(x) = (1 + x)^{1/2}$. Fortunately, an easy rule is available for derivatives of functions of the type (2-9). Let $y = f(x)$, $u = g(x)$, $v = h(x)$. Then

$$y = uv$$

If x changes by an amount Δx, by definition, u changes by Δu, v changes by Δv, and y changes by Δy. We have

$$y + \Delta y = (u + \Delta u)(v + \Delta v)$$

and thus

$$\Delta y = (u + \Delta u)(v + \Delta v) - uv$$

$$= u\Delta v + v\Delta u + \Delta u\Delta v$$

Dividing through by Δx,

$$\frac{\Delta y}{\Delta x} = u\frac{\Delta v}{\Delta x} + v\frac{\Delta u}{\Delta x} + \Delta u\frac{\Delta v}{\Delta x}$$

Taking limits as $\Delta x \to 0$, the last term tends to 0. Therefore,

$$\frac{dy}{dx} = u\frac{dv}{dx} + v\frac{du}{dx} \qquad (2\text{-}10)$$

The derivative of a product of two functions of x is the first times the derivative of the second, plus the second times the derivative of the first.

Example 1. Let $y = x^2(1 + x)^{1/2}$. Here, $u = x^2, v = (1 + x)^{1/2}$. Therefore

$$\frac{dy}{dx} = x^2\frac{1}{2}(1 + x)^{-1/2} + (1 + x)^{1/2}(2x)$$

The Quotient Rule

Suppose $y = f(x) = g(x)/h(x) = u/v$. The derivative of this quotient can be found by taking a difference quotient as in the product rule derivation. However, note that

$$y = \frac{u}{v} = uv^{-1}$$

Now we can use the product rule directly:

$$\frac{dy}{dx} = u\frac{dv^{-1}}{dx} + v^{-1}\frac{du}{dx}$$

$$= -uv^{-2}\frac{dv}{dx} + \frac{1}{v}\frac{du}{dx}$$

$$= \left(v\frac{du}{dx} - u\frac{dv}{dx}\right) / v^2 \tag{2-11}$$

Equation (2-11) is the most common form of this rule. The derivative of a quotient is the denominator times the derivative of the numerator, *minus* the numerator times the derivative of the denominator, all divided by the denominator squared.

Any student who has not already learned these rules must, unfortunately, memorize them. They are extremely useful and should be readily available.

Example 2. Let $y = x^2/\sqrt{1 + x^2}$. Find dy/dx. Here, $u = x^2$, $v = (1 + x^2)^{1/2}$. Hence,

$$\frac{dy}{dx} = \frac{(1 + x^2)^{1/2}(2x) - x^2\frac{1}{2}(1 + x^2)^{-1/2}(2x)}{(1 + x^2)}$$

The student should check that he or she understands where each term comes from.

2.6 IMPLICIT FUNCTIONS

Often, functions are encountered in which y is *not* written explicitly as a function of x, but is combined with x in various terms. For example, the unit circle is defined as $x^2 + y^2 = 1$. The slope is well defined at every point except $(1,0)$ and $(-1,0)$, where $dy/dx \rightarrow +\infty$. How can the slope be determined directly, without solving for x explicitly?

If we assume that there is *some* explicit function $y = f(x)$ associated with $x^2 + y^2 = 1$ (so that the expression dy/dx makes sense), the relation $x^2 + y^2 = 1$ can simply be differentiated term by term. (A more rigorous discussion of this process follows in Chap. 3.) The derivative of x^2 is $2x$; to differentiate y^2 with respect to x, let $z = y^2$ and use the chain rule

$$\frac{dz}{dx} = \frac{dy^2}{dx} = \frac{dz}{dy}\frac{dy}{dx} = 2y\frac{dy}{dx}$$

Hence, for $x^2 + y^2 = 1$, we have

$$2x + 2y\frac{dy}{dx} = 0$$

and thus

$$\frac{dy}{dx} = -\frac{x}{y} \quad \text{for } y \neq 0$$

Example. Suppose $y^3 x^2 = 1$. Find dy/dx. We must use the product rule:

$$y^3 2x + x^2\left(3y^2\frac{dy}{dx}\right) = 0$$

$$\frac{dy}{dx} = -\frac{2y}{3x}$$

Notice that the derivatives of implicit functions will likely themselves be implicit functions.

2.7 ELASTICITY

A dimensionless variant of slope is the *percentage* change in the dependent variable due to a percentage change in the independent variable. This quantity is called the *elasticity* of the curve. Suppose $x = f(p)$ is a demand (or supply) curve, where p = price and x = quantity demanded. The elasticity of demand (or supply) is defined as

$$\epsilon = \lim_{\Delta p \to 0} \frac{\Delta x/x}{\Delta p/p} = \lim_{\Delta p \to 0} \frac{p}{x}\frac{\Delta x}{\Delta p} = \frac{p}{x}\frac{dx}{dp} \tag{2-12}$$

If $|\epsilon| > 1$, the curve is called *elastic;* if $0 < |\epsilon| < 1$, the curve is called *inelastic.* Note that supply and demand curves are usually plotted with the *dependent* variable x on the *horizontal* axis. The "slope" dx/dp is thus the reciprocal of the usual slope.

Example 1. Let $x = ap^b$. Show that these functions exhibit constant elasticity $\epsilon = b$. Using the definition (2-12),

$$\epsilon = \frac{p}{x}\frac{dx}{dp} = \frac{pbap^{b-1}}{ap^b} = b$$

These curves are either always elastic or always inelastic. If $b < 0$, these curves are downward-sloping for all p, and are used to represent demand curves. They belong to the class of functions called hyperbolas. If $b > 0$, these curves are upward-sloping and may represent supply curves.

Example 2. Consider the linear demand curves $x = a - bp$. Price varies between 0 and a/b. The elasticity at any point is

$$\epsilon = \frac{p}{a - bp}(-b) = \frac{-bp}{a - bp} = \frac{-p}{a/b - p}$$

Clearly, when $p = 0$, $\epsilon = 0$. As $p \to a/b$, $\epsilon \to -\infty$. Also, $\epsilon = -1$ when $p = a/2b$, the midpoint of the demand curve.

The elasticity of demand is related to the marginal revenue curve. Total revenue is simply price times quantity, or

$$\text{TR} = px$$

Let us write the demand curve as $p = p(x)$, that is, price as a function of quantity. Then marginal revenue MR is defined as the rate of change in total revenue with respect to quantity, or

$$\text{MR} = \frac{d(\text{TR})}{dx}$$

Using the product rule

$$\text{MR} = p \cdot 1 + x\frac{dp}{dx} = p\left(1 + \frac{x}{p}\frac{dp}{dx}\right)$$

$$= p\left(1 + \frac{1}{\epsilon}\right)$$

For demand curves, $\epsilon < 0$. Hence, MR > 0 when $\epsilon < -1$. Hence, for elastic demand curves, total revenue rises when quantity increases, i.e., when price falls. When demand is inelastic, i.e., when $-1 < \epsilon < 0$, MR < 0. Total revenue falls when quantity increases, i.e., when price falls.

2.8 MAXIMA AND MINIMA

Probably the single most important application of the calculus in economics is its application to finding the maximum or minimum of functions. Most frequently, some postulate of maximizing behavior is made in economics—e.g., firms maximize "profits," consumers maximize "utility," etc. The calculus allows a detailed description of such points of "extrema."

Consider the rather squiggly function depicted in Fig. 2-5. Points A, B, C, D, E, and F are all points of *relative extrema*. In some neighborhood around these points, they all represent maximum or minimum values of $f(x)$. The adjective "relative" means that these are *local* extrema only, not the "global" maxima or minima over the whole range of x. These points all have one thing in common: the slope of $f(x)$ is 0, i.e., the function is horizontal at all these extrema. *A necessary condition for $f(x)$ to have a local maximum or minimum is that $dy/dx = f'(x) = 0$.*

Now consider a relative maximum, say point C. Immediately to the left of C, the function is rising; that is, $f'(x) > 0$, whereas to the right of C, $f'(x) < 0$. It is for this reason that we know $f'(x) = 0$ at point C. Moreover, we also know that the slope, $f'(x)$, is continually falling (going from $+$ to $-$) as we

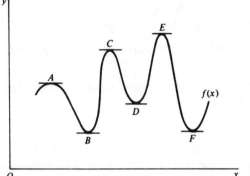

FIGURE 2-5
Relative minima and maxima (extrema).

pass through C. Hence, $f''(x) \le 0$ at C. We cannot be sure that $f''(x) < 0$ at C; $f''(x) = 0$ is a possibility. However, *if* $f'(x) = 0$ *at* $x = x_0$ *and if* $f''(x_0) < 0$, *then* $f(x)$ *has a relative maximum at* $x = x_0$. *If* $f'(x_0) = 0$ *and* $f''(x_0) > 0$, $f(x)$ *has a relative minimum.* If $f'(x_0) = 0$, $f''(x_0) = 0$, then the function may have either a maximum, minimum, or neither at that point.

Around the maximum points A, C, and E in Fig. 2-5, the function is said to be *concave downward*, or simply *concave*. Around the minimum points B, D, and F, the function is said to be *convex* (i.e., concave *upward*). For differentiable functions, concavity implies $f''(x) \le 0$; that is, the slope, $f'(x)$ is continually nonincreasing. If $f''(x) < 0$, then concavity is implied, but concavity allows the possibility that $f''(x) = 0$. Similar remarks hold for convexity. If $f''(x) > 0$, then $f(x)$ is convex, but convexity also allows the possibility of $f''(x) = 0$. Example 2 illustrates the possibilities allowed by $f''(x) = 0$.

Example 1. Consider $y = x^2$. Then $f'(x) = 2x$, $f''(x) = 2$. At $x = 0$, $f'(x) = 0$, $f''(x) > 0$. This function has a relative minimum at $x = 0$. (Check Fig. 2-1*a*.)

Example 2. Let $y = -x^4$. Then $f'(x) = -4x^3$, $f''(x) = -12x^2$. At $x = 0$, $f'(x) = f''(x) = 0$. However, this function *has* a relative maximum at $x = 0$, as a sketch of the curve quickly reveals. Likewise, $y = +x^4$ has a relative minimum at $x = 0$, with $f''(0) = 0$.

Example 3. Let $y = x^3$. Then $f'(0) = f''(0) = 0$. This function, the "cubic" function, is horizontal at $x = 0$, but it has neither a maximum nor a minimum at $x = 0$. The condition $f'(x) = 0$ is a *necessary* condition for a maximum or a minimum (a stationary value); however, $f''(x) < 0$, $f''(x) > 0$ (note the strict inequalities) are *sufficient* conditions for a relative maximum or minimum, respectively. But these strict inequalities for $f''(x)$ are not *implied by*, i.e., not necessary conditions for a maximum or minimum.

Example 4. Consider a firm with a revenue function $R(x)$ and a cost function $C(x)$, both functions of output. If the firm maximizes profits,

$$\pi(x) = R(x) - C(x)$$

the first-order necessary condition is

$$\pi'(x) = R'(x) - C'(x) = 0$$

This is the condition that the firm sets marginal revenue (MR) equal to marginal cost (MC). If the firm is a perfect competitor, it faces a fixed output price p. In that case, $R(x) = px$, and thus $R'(x) = p$. The first-order condition above therefore becomes

$$p - C'(x) = 0$$

That is, marginal revenue equals price here, which in turn equals marginal cost, $C'(x)$.

The condition that MR = MC is also consistent with *minimization* of profits. If we are to be sure that this is indeed a maximum and not a minimum, we need the sufficient second-order condition

$$\pi''(x) = R''(x) - C''(x) = MR'(x) - MC'(x) < 0$$

This second-order condition says that the marginal revenue curve must have a lower slope than the marginal cost curve. In the usual case, MR is downward-sloping; that is, $MR' < 0$, and MC is rising; that is, $MC' > 0$, and hence this sufficient condition is satisfied under these conditions. The "economic reasoning" behind this maximum condition is that as long as an addition to output will increase revenue (MR) by an amount greater than the cost of that additional output (MC), a profit-maximizing firm will produce that additional output. This process will terminate at a finite output only if, as output increases, the "marginal profitability," MR − MC, eventually falls to 0. Hence, at the profit maximum, MR = MC, and, if profits are to decrease with still more output, $\pi''(x) = MR'(x) - MC'(x) < 0$ around the profit maximum.

Example 5. Suppose the consumers' demand curve is $x = 150 - p$, and the (total) cost function is $C = x^2/2$. Find the profit-maximizing price and quantity.

The profit function is

$$\pi(x) = px - \frac{x^2}{2} = (150 - x)x - \frac{x^2}{2} = 150x - \frac{3x^2}{2}$$

Therefore

$$\pi'(x) = 150 - 3x = 0$$

$$x = 50$$

Notice that we must express profits in terms of a single variable, in this case, x. The demand curve $x = 150 - p$ was used to write p in terms of x, or $p = 150 - x$. This is indeed a point of *maximum* profits, as the second-order conditions imply:

$$\pi''(x) = -3 < 0$$

The profit-maximizing *price* is derived from the demand curve:

$$p = 150 - 50 = 100$$

The analysis could have been carried out in terms of price:

$$\pi(p) = px - \frac{x^2}{2} = p(150 - p) - \frac{(150 - p)^2}{2}$$

$$= 150p - p^2 - \frac{(150 - p)^2}{2}$$

$$\pi'(p) = 150 - 2p - \frac{2(150 - p)(-1)}{2} = 0$$

$$= 300 - 3p = 0$$

Thus

$$p = 100$$

as before.

Example 6. A farmer has a length of fence P (perimeter) and wishes to enclose the largest rectangular area with it. Find the dimensions of the rectangle.

Let x = length of the rectangle. The width is therefore

$$w = \frac{P - 2x}{2}$$

The total area, $A(x)$, is thus

$$A(x) = \frac{x(P - 2x)}{2} = \frac{Px}{2} - x^2$$

Therefore,

$$A'(x) = \frac{P}{2} - 2x = 0$$

or

$$x = \frac{P}{4}$$

The width w is

$$w = \frac{[P - 2(P/4)]}{2} = \frac{P}{4} = x$$

For any given perimeter P the rectangle enclosing the largest area is a square, with each side = $P/4$.

Example 7. Let $A(x)$ be the average cost curve of a firm, and $M(x)$ = marginal cost. Find the relation between these two important curves in economic theory.

The total cost curve $T(x)$, by definition, is

$$T(x) \equiv A(x)x$$

Marginal cost is the rate of change of total cost with respect to output, or $T'(x)$. Thus, using the product rule,

$$M(x) = T'(x) = A(x) + xA'(x) \qquad (2\text{-}13)$$

This can be written

$$A'(x) = \frac{1}{x}[M(x) - A(x)]$$

If the average cost curve has a minimum, $A'(x) = 0$. At that point, necessarily (assuming $x > 0$), $M(x) = A(x)$; that is, marginal cost equals average cost. Also, if $A(x)$ is *falling* [$A'(x) < 0$], then $M(x) < A(x)$, and if $A(x)$ is *rising*, $M(x) > A(x)$.

The relation written as

$$M(x) = A(x) + xA'(x)$$

shows the precise relation between the marginal and average curves, be they cost, product, or any other values.

PROBLEMS

1. Find the relative maxima (if any) and relative minima (if any) of the following functions. Identify each stationary value as one or the other, or neither.
   (a) $y = 2x^2 - 3x + 5$
   (b) $y = -3x^2 + 4x - 2$
   (c) $y = 3$
   (d) $y = 4x - 1/x$
   (e) $y = x^3 - 12x^2 + 5$
2. A farmer's land is bordered on one side by a straight river. Find the dimensions of the largest plot that can be enclosed on three sides by a fence of length P, the fourth side being the river.
3. Consider the linear demand curves $x = a - bp$. Show that the maximum total expenditure occurs at the midpoint of this demand curve. What are the values of x, p, and MR there?
4. (a) A monopolist faces the demand curve $x = 100 - p/2$. The cost function is $C = x^2$. Find the output that maximizes this monopolist's profits. What are prices and profits at that output?
   (b) Find the elasticity of demand at the profit-maximizing output.
5. (a) Now consider the monopolist of the previous question and suppose that a per-unit tax t is levied on output x. Find the profit-maximizing level of output, in terms of arbitrary levels of t.
   (b) How will output change when t increases?
   (c) What level of tax t should the government choose if it wishes to extract the maximum tax revenue from this monopolist?
6. Show that if the average cost curve has a minimum, marginal cost must be rising in some neighborhood of that point.
7. Show that if the average product curve for a factor of production has a maximum, it equals marginal product there. Show that at this maximum point, marginal product must be falling in some neighborhood of that point.

2.9 TWO IMPORTANT FUNCTIONS: $y = e^x$; $y = \log_e x$

1. The Function $y = e^x$

Suppose you put \$1 in a bank account that pays x percent interest over the year. At the end of the year, you will have an amount

$$y = (1 + x)$$

in the account. Suppose now the bank account pays x percent per year, *compounded semiannually*. In this case, the bank pays $(x/2)$ percent interest in the first half of the year, and $(x/2)$ percent on the increased amount in the second half. Therefore, after six months, the account would have

$$\left(1 + \frac{x}{2}\right)$$

and, with $(x/2)$ percent paid on this amount, after one year the account would have in it

$$y = \left(1 + \frac{x}{2}\right) + \left(1 + \frac{x}{2}\right)\frac{x}{2} = \left(1 + \frac{x}{2}\right)^2$$

Using similar reasoning, if interest is compounded *quarterly*, after one year the account will have

$$y = \left(1 + \frac{x}{4}\right)^4$$

If the account is compounded n times during the year ($n = 365$ is common nowadays), the account will grow to

$$y = \left(1 + \frac{x}{n}\right)^n$$

What is the limit of this expression as $n \to \infty$? Let us approach the problem in two stages.

(a) Let $x = 1$. We then inquire as to

$$y = \lim_{n\to\infty} \left(1 + \frac{1}{n}\right)^n \tag{2-14}$$

Let us expand $(1 + 1/n)^n$ by the binomial theorem:

$$y_n = \left(1 + \frac{1}{n}\right)^n = 1^n + \frac{n \cdot 1^{n-1}(1/n)^1}{1!} + \frac{n(n-1)}{2!}1^{n-2}\left(\frac{1}{n}\right)^2$$

$$+ \frac{n(n-1)(n-2)}{3!}1^{n-3}\left(\frac{1}{n}\right)^3 + \cdots$$

$$= 1 + \frac{1}{1!} + \frac{1}{2!}\left(\frac{n-1}{n}\right) + \frac{1}{3!}\left(\frac{n-1}{n}\right)\left(\frac{n-2}{n}\right) + \cdots$$

Consider the limit of the terms $(n - k)/n$ as $n \to \infty$. Dividing numerator and denominator by n,

$$\frac{n - k}{n} = 1 - \frac{k}{n}$$

Clearly

$$\lim_{n \to \infty} \left(\frac{n - k}{n} \right) = 1 - \lim_{n \to \infty} \frac{k}{n} = 1$$

Moreover, any finite product of such terms tends to 1 as $n \to \infty$. Therefore,

$$y = \lim_{n \to \infty} y_n = \lim_{n \to \infty} \left(1 + \frac{1}{n} \right)^n = 1 + \frac{1}{1!} + \frac{1}{2!} + \frac{1}{3!} + \cdots$$

This infinite series converges to an important irrational number, known as e. To five decimal places,

$$e = 2.71828 \cdots$$

(b) Now let us return to the more general case of

$$\lim_{n \to \infty} \left(1 + \frac{x}{n} \right)^n$$

Make the substitution $m = n/x$. For fixed x, as $n \to \infty$, $m \to \infty$. Thus, the preceding expression becomes

$$\lim_{m \to \infty} \left(1 + \frac{1}{m} \right)^{mx} = \left[\lim_{m \to \infty} \left(1 + \frac{1}{m} \right)^m \right]^x = e^x$$

using the previous result and the algebra of exponents. Thus,

$$e^x = \lim_{n \to \infty} \left(1 + \frac{x}{n} \right)^n$$

Letting $z_n = [1 + (x/n)]^n$, expanding this expression by the binomial theorem, as before, yields

$$z_n = 1 + n\frac{x}{n} + \frac{n(n - 1)}{2!} \left(\frac{x}{n} \right)^2 + \cdots$$

Using the same reasoning as in the case where $x = 1$,

$$\lim_{n \to \infty} z_n = e^x = 1 + x + \frac{x^2}{2!} + \frac{x^3}{3!} + \cdots \tag{2-15}$$

Thus, the exponent e^x is representable by an infinite series. The *convergence* of infinite series to a finite sum is a much-explored aspect of mathematics. That the series (2-15) converges to the number e^x is evident from the derivation. Series that do not converge to finite sums (i.e., do not have a unique finite limit) are called *divergent*.

The function $y = e^x$ has an important property that will now be demonstrated. If we differentiate $y = e^x$, term by term (the reader will have to take our word that differentiating this particular series term by term is a valid procedure),

$$\frac{d}{dx}e^x = 0 + 1 + \frac{2x}{2!} + \frac{3x^2}{3!} + \frac{4x^3}{4!} + \cdots$$

$$= 1 + x + \frac{x^2}{2!} + \frac{x^3}{3!} + \cdots = e^x$$

This function is unchanged by differentiation; because of this feature, it occurs frequently in many applications of mathematics. The function $y = e^x$ is shown graphically in Fig. 2-6.

Consider now the derivative of

$$y = e^{ax}$$

where a is a constant. Letting $u = ax$ and using the chain rule,

$$\frac{dy}{dx} = \frac{dy}{du}\frac{du}{dx} = e^u(a) = ae^{ax}$$

Consider also

$$y = e^{x^n}$$

Letting $u = x^n$,

$$\frac{dy}{dx} = \frac{dy}{du}\frac{du}{dx} = e^{x^n}(nx^{n-1})$$

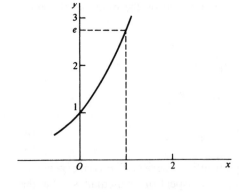

FIGURE 2-6
The function $y = e^x$. Note that at $x = 0$, $dy/dx = e^0 = 1$.

Let us now return to the original question of compound interest rates. Suppose $1 is placed in an account that pays, say, 5 percent interest compounded every instant of the day. (Actually, daily compounding is minutely close to this limit.) After one year, the account will have in it

$$e^{.05} = 1 + 0.05 + \frac{(0.05)^2}{2!} + \frac{(0.05)^3}{3!} + \cdots$$

$$= 1.0513$$

Daily (continuous) compounding will convert 5 percent annual interest to the yearly equivalent of approximately 5.13 percent.

Suppose an amount P is invested at interest rate r, continuously compounded, for a period of t years. The future value FV is

$$FV = P(e^r)^t = Pe^{rt} \qquad (2\text{-}16)$$

Also, the *present value* of an amount FV, at r percent, is by multiplying through by e^{-rt}

$$P = (FV)e^{-rt} \qquad (2\text{-}17)$$

These formulas provide an analytically easy method of incorporating discounting into problems where time intervals are significant.

Example 1: Fisherian Investment[†] Suppose a crop is planted at time $t = 0$ and grows in *value* to $g(t)$ at time t. Suppose $g'(t) > 0$ and $g''(t) < 0$ so that the crop grows at a decreasing rate. What harvest time will maximize the present value of the crop?

The present value, assuming continuous discounting, is

$$P = g(t)e^{-rt}$$

To maximize P (wealth), set $dP/dt = 0$:

$$\frac{dP}{dt} = g(t)(-re^{-rt}) + g'(t)e^{-rt} = 0$$

Dividing by e^{-rt}

$$g'(t) = rg(t)$$

or

$$r = \frac{g'(t)}{g(t)} \qquad (2\text{-}18)$$

[†] Irving Fisher, *The Theory of Interest,* Augustus M. Kelley, New York, 1970. (First edition, The Macmillan Co., New York, 1930.)

The term $g'(t)/g(t)$ can be interpreted as the percent rate of growth. Wealth maximization therefore says that the crop should be harvested when the percentage rate of growth of crop value equals the alternative earnings, measured by the interest rate. If $g(t)$ is known, the wealth-maximizing t can be obtained.

Example 2: The "Faustmann" Solution. Suppose the crop in Example 1 can be replanted immediately after each harvest. What harvest time maximizes the value of the land? Assuming complete replication, after the first harvest, the present value of the land will be its current present value, but discounted for t years:

$$P = g(t)e^{-rt} + Pe^{-rt}$$

Solving for P

$$P = \frac{g(t)e^{-rt}}{1 - e^{-rt}}$$

Using the quotient rule

$$\frac{dP}{dt} = \frac{(1 - e^{-rt})[-rg(t)e^{-rt} + e^{-rt}g'(t)] - g(t)e^{-rt}(+re^{-rt})}{(1 - e^{-rt})^2} = 0$$

Dividing by e^{-rt}, this is equivalent to

$$g'(t) = rg(t) + r\frac{g(t)e^{-rt}}{1 - e^{-rt}} \tag{2-19}$$

This equation says that the crop should be harvested when the growth in value of the crop equals the sum of the foregone annuity from the standing value of the crop and the annuity from the maximum value of the land, i.e., the annual land rent. This is the Fisherian solution with the addition of the opportunity cost of the land, expressed in terms of crop replanting.

This completes our brief discussion of $y = e^x$. We now turn to the inverse of the exponential function, the *logarithm*.

2. The Function $y = \log_e x$

The logarithm of a number a to the base b is defined as the number that, when b is raised to that power, results in a:

$$b^{\log_b a} = a$$

Before the age of computers, logarithms to the base 10 had wide empirical use. We shall be concerned here only with *logarithms to the base e*, called *natural logarithms*. The $\log_e x$ is sometimes denoted $\ln x$; we shall, however, stick to $\log x$. Throughout this book, $\log x$ *means* $\log_e x$, that is, natural log of x. Thus, $\log x$ means

$$e^{\log x} = x$$

The rules of logarithms are easily derived using the laws of exponents. Letting $e^{\log a} = a$, $e^{\log b} = b$,

$$e^{\log a} \cdot e^{\log b} = e^{\log a + \log b} = ab$$

But by definition,

$$ab = e^{\log ab}$$

Hence,

$$\log ab = \log a + \log b$$

Also

$$a^x = (e^{\log a})^x = e^{x \log a}$$

But again, by definition,

$$a^x = e^{\log a^x}$$

Hence

$$\log a^x = x \log a$$

The equation $y = \log x$ means the same thing as $x = e^y$. (See Fig. 2-7.) If we differentiate $x = e^y$ implicitly with respect to x,

$$1 = e^y \frac{dy}{dx}$$

or

$$\frac{dy}{dx} = \frac{1}{e^y} = \frac{1}{x} \qquad (2\text{-}20)$$

Thus, for $y = \log x$, $dy/dx = 1/x$.

Example 3. Let $y = \log ax$. Find dy/dx. By the laws of logarithms

$$y = \log ax = \log a + \log x$$

Since $\log a$ is a constant,

$$\frac{dy}{dx} = \frac{1}{x}$$

Example 4. Let $y = \log(a + bx)$. Find dy/dx. Using the chain rule, let $u = a + bx$.

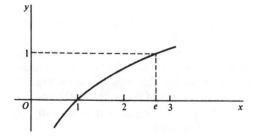

FIGURE 2-7
The function $y = \log x$. Note that at $x = 1$, $dy/dx = 1$. How is this curve related to $y = e^x$?

Then

$$\frac{dy}{dx} = \frac{dy}{du}\frac{du}{dx} = \left(\frac{1}{a + bx}\right)b = \frac{b}{a + bx}$$

Example 5. Let $y = a^x$. Find dy/dx. Take the log of both sides:

$$\log y = x \log a$$

Differentiating implicitly with respect to x,

$$\frac{1}{y}\frac{dy}{dx} = \log a$$

Thus

$$\frac{dy}{dx} = y \log a = a^x \log a$$

Example 6. Consider the demand curves $x = p^k$, $k < 0$. We previously showed that these curves exhibited constant elasticity. This can be demonstrated more quickly using logs:

$$\log x = \log(p^k) = k \log p$$

Taking the *differential* of both sides,

$$\frac{dx}{x} = k\frac{dp}{p}$$

Thus, the *percent* change in x is k times the *percent* change in price, i.e., k is the elasticity of demand. If the curve $x = p^k$ is plotted on log-log paper (graph paper with logarithmic intervals), the slope of the graph will be k, the elasticity.

PROBLEMS

1. Sketch the curve $y = e^{-x}$. What is the relationship of this curve to $y = e^x$, to $y = \log x$?
2. For each of the following functions, find dy/dx.
   (a) $y = e^{-x}$
   (b) $y = x \log x - x$
   (c) $y = xe^x$
   (d) $y = e^{(a+bx)}$
   (e) $y = e^x \log x$
   (f) $y = \log x^2$
   (g) $y = (\log x)^2$ (*Hint:* Let $u = \log x$)
   (h) $y = \log (\log x), x > 1$
3. Use the power series expansion of e^x to show that 6 percent interest compounded continuously is approximately 6.18 percent per annum.
4. Consider the wealth-maximizing times to harvest crops with or without replanting. Suppose seasonal factors do not permit replanting until after winter. Show that formulas (2-18) and (2-19) indicate that with replanting impossible, the crops will be left to grow larger than when replanting is possible. Explain in terms of opportunities forgone.
5. Consider the formula for the sum of geometric series. Letting $S_n = a + ar + ar^2 + \cdots + ar^{n-1}$, show that $S_n - rS_n = a - ar^n$, and, hence,

$$S_n = \frac{a - ar^n}{1 - r}$$

Show that if $|r| < 1$, the $\lim_{n \to \infty} S_n = a/(1 - r)$.

6. Consider an amount of money P invested at r percent annual interest, compounded continuously. Show that the number of years n it will take to double the initial investment, leaving the money in the account to accumulate compound interest, is approximately given by the formula

$$n = \frac{72}{r\%}$$

2.10 THE MEAN VALUE THEOREM

Consider Fig. 2-8a. A differentiable function $y = f(x)$ is shown between the values $x = a$ and $x = b$. Consider the chord joining the two points $(a, f(a))$, and $(b, f(b))$. The slope of this chord is

$$\frac{f(b) - f(a)}{b - a}$$

It is geometrically obvious (though it is not a proof) that at some point x^* between a and b, the slope of $f(x)$ is the same as the slope of this chord, or

$$f'(x^*) = \frac{f(b) - f(a)}{b - a}$$

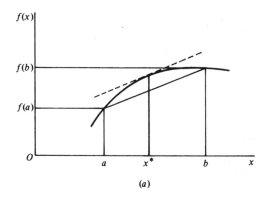

(a)

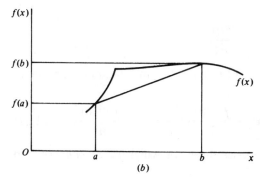

(b)

FIGURE 2-8
(a) The mean value theorem. (b) If $f(x)$ is not differentiable, the existence of x_0, $a < x_0 < b$, such that $f'(x_0) = [f(b) - f(a)]/(b - a)$ is not guaranteed.

This statement or the following equivalent one is called the *law of the mean,* or *the mean value theorem:* If $f(x)$ is differentiable on the interval $a \leq x \leq b$, then there exists an x^*, $a < x^* < b$, such that

$$f(b) = f(a) + (b - a)f'(x^*) \tag{2-21}$$

The reason why $f(x)$ has to be differentiable over the interval is exhibited in Fig. 2-8*b*. The mean value theorem is actually a special case of the more general result known as Taylor's theorem. It is to this more general problem that we now turn.

2.11   TAYLOR'S SERIES

It is often of great analytical convenience to approximate a function $f(x)$ by polynomials of the form

$$f(x) \approx f_n(x) = a_0 + a_1x + a_2x^2 + a_3x^3 + \cdots + a_nx^n$$

In particular, let us approximate $f(x)$ around the point $x = 0$. What values of the coefficients $a_0, \ldots, a_n$ will best do this? To begin, we should require $f_n(x) = f(x)$ at $x = 0$. Hence, we need to set

$$a_0 = f_n(0) = f(0)$$

Thus, the coefficient a_0 is determined in this fashion to be $f(0)$.

To approximate $f(x)$ even better, let us make the derivatives of $f(x)$ and $f_n(x)$ equal, at $x = 0$. We have

$$f_n'(x) = a_1 + 2a_2x + 3a_3x^2 + \cdots + na_nx^{n-1}$$

$$f_n''(x) = 2a_2 + 3 \cdot 2a_3x + \cdots + n(n-1)a_nx^{n-2}$$

$$\vdots$$

$$f_n^{(n)}(x) = n! \, a_n$$

Clearly, when $x = 0$, we get

$$a_1 = f'(0)$$

$$a_2 = \frac{f''(0)}{2!}$$

$$\vdots$$

$$a_n = \frac{f^{(n)}(0)}{n!}$$

Having thus determined the coefficients of $f_n(x)$ in this fashion, our approximating polynomial is

$$f_n(x) = f(0) + f'(0)x + \frac{f''(0)}{2!}x^2 + \frac{f'''(0)}{3!}x^3 + \cdots + \frac{f^{(n)}(0)}{n!}x^n \tag{2-22}$$

An important class of functions comprises those for which $f_n(x)$ *converges* to $f(x)$, as $n \to \infty$, that is,

$$f(x) = f(0) + f'(0)x + \frac{f''(0)}{2!}x^2 + \cdots \qquad (2\text{-}23)$$

These functions are called *analytic functions*. The power series representation (2-23) is called Maclaurin's series.

Suppose now we wish to approximate $f(x)$ at some arbitrary point $x = x_0$. In that case, write $f_n(x)$ in terms of powers of $(x - x_0)$:

$$f_n(x) = a_0 + a_1(x - x_0) + a_2(x - x_0)^2 + \cdots + a_n(x - x_0)^n$$

Using the same procedure as before, setting the derivatives of $f(x)$ equal to those of $f_n(x)$ at $x = x_0$, we determine

$$f(x) = f(x_0) + f'(x_0)(x - x_0) + \frac{f''(x_0)}{2!}(x - x_0)^2 + \cdots \qquad (2\text{-}24)$$

In this form, the power series is known as *Taylor's series*, or simply as a Taylor series. The Maclaurin series is a special case, where $x_0 = 0$.

Example 1. The series developed before, for e^x, is a convergent Taylor series expansion:

$$e^x = 1 + x + \frac{x^2}{2!} + \frac{x^3}{3!} + \cdots$$

Example 2. Find a Taylor series expansion for $\log(1 + x)$, around $x = 0$. (Assume convergence.)

We note:

$$f(0) = \log 1 = 0$$

$$f'(0) = \frac{1}{(1 + x)} = 1 \text{ at } x = 0$$

$$f''(0) = -(1 + x)^{-2} = -1 \text{ at } x = 0$$

$$f'''(0) = +2(1 + x)^{-3} = +2 \text{ at } x = 0$$

$$f^{iv}(0) = -3 \cdot 2(1 + x)^{-4} = -3! \text{ at } x = 0$$

$$\vdots$$

Hence

$$\log(1 + x) = x - \frac{x^2}{2} + \frac{x^3}{3} - \frac{x^4}{4} + \cdots$$

A most useful form of a Taylor series expansion for a finite power n is a Taylor series with Lagrange's form of the remainder. The finite power series can be made exact (under suitable continuity assumptions) if the last term is evaluated not at x_0, but at some point x^* between x and x_0:

$$f(x) = f(x_0) + f'(x_0)(x - x_0) + \frac{f''(x_0)}{2!}(x - x_0)^2 + \cdots + \frac{f^{(n)}(x^*)}{n!}(x - x_0)^n$$

$$(2\text{-}25)$$

where $x^* = x_0 + \theta(x - x_0), 0 \leq \theta \leq 1$.

Such an x^* between x and x_0 must exist, if $f^{(n+1)}(x)$ is continuous. Equation 2-25 is one variant of what is known as Taylor's theorem. (The variant is the particular form of the remainder, or last, term.) In this form, Eq. (2-25), the Taylor series expansion, is seen to be a generalization of the mean value theorem. To obtain the mean value theorem, merely terminate (2-25) at $f'(x^*)$.

Applications of Taylor's Series: Derivation of the First- and Second-Order Conditions for a Maximum; Concavity and Convexity

Suppose $f(x)$ has a maximum at x_0. By definition

$$f(x_0) \geq f(x)$$

for all x in some neighborhood of x_0. Using the mean value theorem, i.e., a Taylor series terminated at the first-order term,

$$f(x_0) - f(x) = (x_0 - x)f'(x^*) \tag{2-26}$$

for some x^* between x_0 and x. The left-hand side of (2-26) is nonnegative for x near x_0. Therefore, if x is to the left of x_0 (i.e., $x < x_0$), $f'(x^*) \geq 0$ necessarily, to make the product $(x_0 - x)f'(x^*) \geq 0$. For $x > x_0$, $f'(x^*) \leq 0$. Hence, $f'(x)$ is *positive* (or 0) to the left of x_0 and *negative* (or 0) to the right of x_0. If $f'(x)$ is continuous at x_0, then necessarily it passes through the value 0 at x_0; i.e.,

$$f'(x_0) = 0$$

Similar reasoning shows that $f'(x_0) = 0$ is also implied by a minimum at x_0. Let us now investigate the second-order conditions for a maximum. Consider a Taylor series expansion of $f(x)$ to the second-order term

$$f(x) = f(x_0) + f'(x_0)(x - x_0) + \frac{f''(x^*)}{2!}(x - x_0)^2$$

where, again, $x^* = x_0 + \theta(x - x_0)$, $0 \leq \theta \leq 1$. If $f(x)$ has a maximum at $x = x_0$, then $f'(x_0) = 0$. Hence, the preceding equation can be written

$$f(x) - f(x_0) = \frac{1}{2}f''(x^*)(x - x_0)^2 \tag{2-27}$$

If $f(x)$ has a maximum at x_0, the left-hand side of (2-27), by definition, is nonpositive. Since $(x - x_0)^2 > 0$,

$$f''(x^*) \leq 0$$

By "squeezing" x closer and closer to x_0, we see that $f''(x) \leq 0$ for all points in some neighborhood of x_0; hence, at $x = x_0$

$$f''(x_0) \leq 0$$

A maximum point therefore implies $f''(x_0) \leq 0$. If, however, $f''(x_0) < 0$, then necessarily $f(x_0) > f(x)$. Thus, together with $f'(x_0) = 0$, $f''(x_0) < 0$ is sufficient for a maximum. Similar reasoning shows that at a *minimum* of $f(x)$, $f''(x_0) \geq 0$; if $f''(x_0) > 0$, then a minimum is assured.

Concave and convex functions. Consider the function depicted in Fig. 2-9a. This shape is called *strictly concave*. It can be described by indicating that for any two points $x = x_0$ and $x = x_1$, say $x_0 < x_1$, the function always lies above the chord joining $f(x_0)$ and $f(x_1)$. That is, suppose x is some intermediate point

$$x = \theta x_0 + (1 - \theta)x_1 \qquad 0 < \theta < 1$$

Then $f(x)$ is strictly concave if

$$f(x) > \theta f(x_0) + (1 - \theta)f(x_1)$$

If $0 \leq \theta \leq 1$ and

$$f(x) \geq \theta f(x_0) + (1 - \theta)f(x_1)$$

the function is called *weakly concave,* or simply concave. Convex functions are functions for which the chord connecting any two points on the function lies above the function; an example is shown in Fig. 2-9b. The terms *strictly* convex and *weakly* convex apply as for concave functions. The weak inequalities allow for straight-line segments in the function. The linear functions $f(x) = a + bx$ are both (weakly) concave *and* convex.

For differentiable functions, strict concavity can be described by saying that $f(x)$ always lies below the tangent line at any point. Consider Fig. 2-9a. Concavity can be interpreted as saying the slope of the tangent line is greater than that of the chord joining $f(x_0)$ and $f(x_1)$, if $x_1 > x_0$, i.e.,

$$f'(x_0) > \frac{f(x_1) - f(x_0)}{x_1 - x_0} \quad \text{for } x_1 > x_0$$

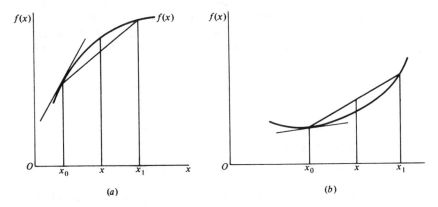

FIGURE 2-9
(a) A concave function. *(b)* A convex function.

If $x_1 < x_0$, the tangent line is less steep, or

$$f'(x_0) < \frac{f(x_1) - f(x_0)}{x_1 - x_0} \quad \text{for } x_1 < x_0$$

In either case, if both sides are multiplied by $(x_1 - x_0)$ we get, for any $x = x_1$ (if $x_1 - x_0 < 0$, the inequality reverses sign),

$$f(x) < f(x_0) + f'(x_0)(x - x_0) \tag{2-28a}$$

or

$$f(x) - f(x_0) - f'(x_0)(x - x_0) < 0 \tag{2-28b}$$

For concavity (not *strict* concavity), a weak inequality is used in statements (2-28).

Using a Taylor series expansion of $f(x)$ to two terms,

$$f(x) = f(x_0) + f'(x_0)(x - x_0) + \frac{1}{2}f''(x^*)(x - x_0)^2$$

Bringing the first two terms on the right to the other side, and using Eq. (2-28b), for concave functions

$$f''(x^*) < 0$$

since $(x - x_0)^2 > 0$. If x is squeezed toward x_0, we see that $f''(x_0) \leq 0$, but $f''(x_0) < 0$ is not implied. If, however, $f''(x_0) < 0$, the function must be concave. Similarly, convexity of $f(x)$ at $x = x_0$ implies $f''(x_0) \geq 0$; if $f''(x_0) > 0$, then $f(x)$ is convex.

2.12 INTEGRATION

Indefinite Integrals

Up to now, we have been concerned with the *differential* calculus. That is, starting with some function $y = f(x)$, we inquired as to the properties of the derivatives of $f(x)$, and applied those properties to certain outstanding problems, e.g., the theory of maxima and minima. We now ask a different question: Suppose we are *given* the derivative $dy/dx = f'(x)$. What function $y = f(x)$ has $f'(x)$ as its derivative?

For example, suppose we are told

$$\frac{dy}{dx} = 2x \tag{2-29}$$

From experience, we would know that

$$y = x^2 \quad y = x^2 + 2 \quad y = x^2 - 50,000$$

are all solutions to (2-29). The general "solution" to Eq. (2-29) is the class of equations

$$y = x^2 + c$$

where c is an arbitrary constant.

Equations of the form (2-29) in which dy/dx is a function of x (or is a function of x and y) are called *differential equations*. The process of solving these equations is called *integration*. We now turn our attention to this new technique, the *integral* calculus.

If $y = F(x)$ is a solution to $dy/dx = f(x)$, i.e.,

$$\frac{dF(x)}{dx} = f(x)$$

$y = F(x)$ is called the *integral* of $f(x)$ with respect to x. If $F(x)$ is any solution to $dy/dx = f(x)$, the general solution is given by

$$y = F(x) + c$$

where c is an arbitrary *constant of integration*. Since $dy/dx = f(x)$

$$dy = f(x)\,dx \tag{2-30}$$

We now *integrate* both sides of this equation. This is written

$$\int dy = \int f(x)\,dx$$

The integral of the differential dy is, by definition, y. The integral of $f(x)\,dx$ is $F(x) + c$. Hence, we write the solution to Eq. (2-30) as

$$y = \int f(x)\,dx + c = F(x) + c$$

The term $\int f(x)\,dx + c$ is called an *indefinite* integral, since an arbitrary constant is used.

Although differentiation is usually straightforward (though possibly tedious), integration can be difficult or impossible with analytical methods. For example, the formula

$$\int x^n\,dx = \frac{x^{n+1}}{n+1} + c$$

might readily occur to the student, since

$$\frac{d\left(\dfrac{x^{n+1}}{n+1}\right)}{dx} = \frac{(n+1)x^n}{n+1} = x^n$$

However, it might take one some time to figure out that

$$\int \log x\,dx = x \log x - x + c$$

or that

$$\int x^2 e^x dx = x^2 e^x - 2xe^x + 2e^x + c$$

Some functions, in fact, do not even possess an analytic integral function. For example

$$\int e^{x^2} dx$$

cannot be written in terms of elementary functions (although note that $\int xe^{x^2}dx = \frac{1}{2}e^{x^2} + c$, as can be verified by differentiation of the latter term).

The Integral as the Area under a Curve

An important application of integration stems from its interpretation as the area under a curve. Consider Fig. 2-10, in which a marginal-cost function, $MC(x)$, is drawn. Consider the area beneath $MC(x)$ (down to the x axis), between $x = a$ and $x = b$. For any x between a and b, let us denote the area from a to x as

$$A_a^x$$

This is shown as the shaded area in Fig. 2-10.

If x is increased to $x + \Delta x$, the area increases by an amount ΔA, where

$$\Delta A = A_a^{x+\Delta x} - A_a^x$$

In the interval from x to $x + \Delta x$, there is some minimum value of $MC(x)$, MC_m, and some maximum value, MC_M. (In general, these do not have to be at the

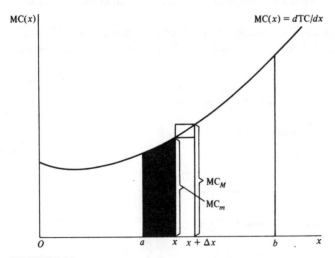

FIGURE 2-10
The integral of a function (marginal cost) as the area under the curve.

endpoints of the interval.) Clearly, therefore,

$$MC_m \Delta x \leq \Delta A \leq MC_M \Delta x$$

Dividing by Δx

$$MC_m \leq \frac{\Delta A}{\Delta x} \leq MC_M$$

If we now take a limit as $\Delta x \to 0$, MC_m and MC_M squeeze together to the limiting value, $MC(x)$. (Actually, Δx can be any interval that includes the value x.) Hence,

$$\lim_{\Delta x \to 0} \frac{\Delta A}{\Delta x} = \frac{dA}{dx} = MC(x)$$

But marginal cost, by definition, is the rate of change of total cost, $TC(x)$, as x changes; that is

$$MC(x) = \frac{dTC(x)}{dx}$$

Since A_a^x and $TC(x)$ have the same derivative, they can differ by at most an arbitrary constant:

$$A_a^x = TC(x) + c \qquad (2\text{-}31)$$

Here, the arbitrary constant of integration represents "fixed" costs, i.e., costs that do not change with output. Thus, $A(x)$ represents total *variable* costs.

Now consider the area *between* $x = a$ and $x = b$. When $x = a$,

$$A_a^x = A_a^a = 0$$

Then from (2-31),

$$A_a^a = 0 = TC(a) + c$$

and thus

$$c = -TC(a)$$

We can thus interpret A_a^x as the *change* in total costs by increasing output from a to x. In this calculation, fixed costs (the constant of integration) are irrelevant; the quantity cancels itself out in calculating total cost at x and subtracting total cost at a.

Total cost from a to b is

$$A_a^b = \int_a^b MC(x)\, dx \qquad (2\text{-}32)$$

where the term $\int_a^b MC(x)\, dx$ means

1. Find the integral function $TC(x)$ of $MC(x)$.
2. Substitute the value $x = b$ in $TC(x)$, then subtract TC evaluated at $x = a$.

The term (2-32) is called a *definite integral*. In general,

$$\int_a^b f(x)\, dx$$

gives the area under the curve $y = f(x)$ (to the x axis) between $x = a$ and $x = b$. Viewed in this manner, the area is an "infinite sum" of vertical strips of area of height $y = f(x)$. For this reason, an elongated "S" is the symbol for integration. Note that if $a > b$ and $f(x) > 0$, this integral will be negative.

Example 1. Find $\int_1^2 x^2\, dx$. This integral represents the area under the parabola $y = x^2$, from $x = 1$ to $x = 2$. Performing the indicated operations

$$\int_1^2 x^2\, dx = \left.\frac{x^3}{3}\right|_1^2 = \frac{8}{3} - \frac{1}{3} = \frac{7}{3}$$

Example 2. Find $\int_{-2}^1 4x^3 dx$.

$$\int_{-2}^1 4x^3 dx = \left. x^4 \right|_{-2}^1 = 1 - 16 = -15$$

This area is negative because for $x < 0$, $y = 4x^3$ is negative.

Example 3. Suppose a person receives a constant annual stream of income I. Find the present value of this *annuity*, at r percent annual interest, compounded continuously, from the present to T years in the future.

At any time t, the present value of the income stream is

$$I e^{-rt}$$

Integrating (summing) this income stream from $t = 0$ to $t = T$

$$\int_0^T I e^{-rt} dt$$

Performing the indicated operations

$$PV = \int_0^T I e^{-rt} dt = I \int_0^T e^{-rt} dt = \left.\left(\frac{-I}{r}\right) e^{-rt}\right|_0^T = \frac{I}{r} - \left(\frac{I}{r}\right) e^{-rT}$$

Example 4. In the previous example, suppose the annuity lasts forever. What is its present value?

In the previous example, let $T \to \infty$. Then

$$PV = \frac{I}{r} - \lim_{T \to \infty} \frac{I}{r} e^{-rT} = \frac{I}{r}$$

since the exponential term tends to zero.

The chain rule is often useful for performing integration, as shown in Example 5.

Example 5. Find $\int x \sqrt{1 + x^2}\, dx$.

Let $u = (1 + x^2)$. Then $du = 2x\, dx$. The integral can thus be written

$$\frac{1}{2}\int (1 + x^2)^{1/2}(2x\, dx) = \frac{1}{2}\int u^{1/2} du = \frac{\frac{1}{2}u^{3/2}}{\frac{3}{2}}$$

$$= \frac{1}{3}(1 + x^2)^{3/2} + c$$

Example 6. Find $\int (1/x) \log x\, dx$.

Let $u = \log x$. Then $du = (1/x)dx$. Then

$$\int \frac{1}{x} \log x\, dx = \int u\, du = \frac{u^2}{2} = \frac{(\log x)^2}{2} + c$$

It can be appreciated that a certain amount of guesswork and fortuitous circumstances are needed for evaluating integrals. For this reason, tables of integrals are published. As previously mentioned, some integrals are extremely difficult or impossible to evaluate.

Because economists infrequently work with specific functional forms, an elaborate discussion of methods of integration is not in order. However, one technique that appears in the economics literature and is useful to know about is called *integration by parts*.

Recall the formula for the derivative of the product of two functions, $u(x) \cdot v(x)$, expressed in differential form:

$$d(uv) = u\, dv + v\, du$$

Rearranging

$$u\, dv = d(uv) - v\, du$$

Integrating both sides of this equation yields

$$\int u\, dv = uv - \int v\, du \tag{2-33}$$

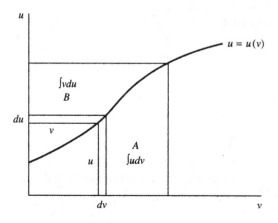

FIGURE 2-11

Integration by parts.

This formula has an intuitive geometrical explanation. In Fig. 2-11, it simply says that the area A below the function $u = u(v)$ equals the entire rectangle minus the area B to the left of the function.

It sometimes turns out that an integral can be cast into the form $\int u\,dv$, with the integral $\int v\,du$ a simpler form to integrate. Using the formula (2-33), the answer may be obtainable by performing the latter integration instead of the former.

Example 7. Find $\int \log x\,dx$.
Let us try $u = \log x$, $dv = dx$. Then $v = x$, $du = dx/x$. Using (2-33),

$$\int \log x\,dx = (\log x)x - \int (x)\,(dx/x) + K$$

$$= x \log x - \int dx + K = x \log x - x + K$$

Example 8. Find $\int_0^1 xe^x\,dx$.
Let us try $u = x$, $dv = e^x dx$. Then $du = dx$, and $v = e^x$. (The constant of integration is not needed because this is a *definite* integral.) Integrating by parts

$$\int_0^1 xe^x\,dx = xe^x \Big|_0^1 - \int_0^1 e^x\,dx = (e - 0) - e^x \Big|_0^1 = e - (e - 1) = 1$$

Example 9. Suppose $p = p(x)$ is a demand curve, and let $p = p_0$ when $x = x_0$, $p = p_1$ when $x = x_1$. The integral

$$\int_{x_0}^{x_1} p\,dx$$

represents the area under the demand curve between x_0 and x_1. Integrating by parts, letting $u = p$, $dv = dx$,

$$\int_{x_0}^{x_1} p\,dx = px \Big|_{x_0}^{x_1} - \int_{p_0}^{p_1} x\,dp$$

The area *under* the demand curve equals the change in total expenditure minus the (negative, if $p_1 < p_0$) area to the *left* of the demand curve. (Note that if $x_1 > x_0$, then $p_1 < p_0$ for downward-sloping demand curves, and, hence, $-\int_{p_0}^{p_1} x\,dp > 0$.)

PROBLEMS

1. Evaluate the following integrals:
   (a) $\int xe^{x^2}\,dx$
   (b) $\int x^2 e^{x^3}\,dx$
   (c) $\int x^{n-1} e^{x^n}\,dx$
   (d) $\int x \log x\,dx$
   (e) $\int \log x^2\,dx$
2. Consider the demand curve $x = p^{-2}$. Find the area under the demand curve and to the left of the demand curve, between $x = 2$ and $x = 4$.

3. Suppose an annuity lasts five years at 6 percent interest, compounded continuously:
   (a) Find the present value if the annuity starts immediately.
   (b) Find the present value if the annuity starts four years from now.
   (c) Find the present value if the annuity starts T years from now and ends $T + 5$ years from now.
4. Suppose the marginal cost function is $MC(x) = 10 + 2x$. Find the total (variable?) costs of producing 100 units. Find the average cost curve, $AC(x)$, and discuss the relation of this $AC(x)$ to $MC(x)$.

2.13 DIFFERENTIAL EQUATIONS

In the preceding section we explored the problems of integrating expressions of the general form

$$\frac{dy}{dx} = f(x)$$

In general, however, the right-hand side will be a function not only of x, but also of y. For example, on the unit circle, $x^2 + y^2 = 1$, the slope can be expressed as

$$\frac{dy}{dx} = \frac{-x}{y}$$

We can express this dependence of dy/dx upon both x and y by writing

$$\frac{dy}{dx} = f(x, y) \tag{2-34}$$

Functions of two variables will be explored in the next chapter. We wish here to merely indicate how certain equations of the form (2-34) are solved, i.e., integrated.

Let us begin the discussion by considering the differential equation above, that is,

$$\frac{dy}{dx} = \frac{-x}{y} \tag{2-35}$$

This equation can be solved by separating the variables. We write

$$y \, dy = -x \, dx$$

Integrating both sides yields

$$\int y \, dy = -\int x \, dx + c$$

or

$$\frac{y^2}{2} = \frac{-x^2}{2} + c$$

In terms of a new constant r^2 where $r^2 = 2c$,

$$x^2 + y^2 = r^2 \qquad (2\text{-}36)$$

is the solution to the differential Eq. (2-35). (The constant of integration must be positive in this case, since $x^2 \geq 0$, $y^2 \geq 0$, hence, we can designate it as r^2.) Equation (2-36) represents all circles of radius r with center at the origin.

In this section we will merely indicate some special cases in which differential equations can be solved by separation of variables. These differential equations occasionally appear in economic models.

Example 1. Suppose $dy/dx = y/x$. Solve for the integral function, $y = F(x)$.
Separating variables, we have

$$\frac{dy}{y} = \frac{dx}{x}$$

Integrating both sides yields

$$\log y = \log x + \log c$$

Notice that we have written the constant of integration as "$\log c$." This loses no generality since $\log c$ takes on all real values. Then, using the rules of logarithms, the solution above can be written

$$\log y = \log cx$$

or

$$y = cx$$

Example 2. Suppose $dy/dx = -y/x$. Find $y = F(x)$.
Separating variables

$$\frac{dy}{y} = \frac{-dx}{x}$$

Integrating

$$\log y = -\log x + \log c = \log \frac{1}{x} + \log c$$

or

$$y = \frac{c}{x}$$

Example 3. Suppose $dy/dx = x^a y^b$. Find $y = F(x)$. Then,

$$y^{-b}\, dy = x^a\, dx$$

If $b \neq 1$ and $a \neq -1$, these terms integrate to powers of x or y:

$$\frac{y^{-b+1}}{-b+1} = \frac{x^{a+1}}{a+1} + c$$

One can solve for y by taking the $(-b + 1)$st root of each side.

PROBLEMS

For each of the following equations, find the integral function $y = F(x)$.

1. $dy/dx = 2x/y$
2. $dy/dx = 1/y$
3. $dy/dx = -1/y$
4. $dy/dx = y/x^n$, $n \neq 1$
5. $dy/dx = x/y$
6. $dy/dx = ye^x$
7. $dy/dx = y^2xe^{x^2}$
8. $dy/dx = y \log x$

SELECTED REFERENCES

Students should have any of the usual basic calculus texts available to them.

CHAPTER
3

FUNCTIONS OF SEVERAL VARIABLES

3.1 FUNCTIONS OF SEVERAL VARIABLES

The mathematical examples in Chap. 1 involved only one decision variable. Most often, however, in economic theories, several decision variables are present, all of which simultaneously determine the value of some objective function. Consider, for example, the fundamental proposition in consumer theory that individuals desire many goods simultaneously. This postulate asserts that the satisfaction, or *utility,* derived from consuming some bundle of goods is some function of the consumption levels for each and every good in question. This is denoted mathematically as

$$U = f(x_1, x_2, \ldots, x_n)$$

where $x_1, x_2, \ldots, x_n$ are the levels of consumption of the n goods. In the theory of production, a function $y = f(L, K)$ is typically written (called the *production function*) which indicates that the level of output depends upon the levels of both labor and capital applied to production. The mathematical notation $y = f(x_1, \ldots, x_n)$ is simply a convenient shorthand to denote the inference of a unique value of some dependent variable y from the knowledge of the values of n *independent* variables, denoted $x_1, \ldots, x_n$. It is a generalization of the notion of a function of one variable, $y = f(x)$.

3.2 LEVEL CURVES: I

Consider a production function $y = f(L, K)$, where y = output, L = labor, and K = capital services. The function f is the numerical rule by which levels of inputs are translated into a level of output. With only two independent variables, geometric representation of this function is possible. In Fig. 3-1, all points in the positive quadrant (i.e., points in the Cartesian plane which correspond to positive values of L and K) represent possible input combinations. At each point in the plane, some unique value of the function $f(L, K)$ is implied. For example, at the points A, B, C, and D, output y is, say, 5, whereas at E, $y = 10$, and at F, $y = 15$.

Economists often have occasion to connect up points for which the functional values are equal. For example, in Fig. 3-1, the smooth line drawn through the points A, B, C, and D represents the locus of all points, i.e., the locus of all combinations of labor and capital, for which five units of output result. This curve, called an *isoquant* by economists, is called a *level curve* (in higher dimensions, a level *surface*) by mathematicians. It is a level curve because along such loci, the function (output, here) is neither increasing nor decreasing.[†] Another geometric representation of a function of two variables is given in Fig. 3-2.

This is a two-dimensional drawing of a three-dimensional picture. The L axis is perpendicular to the plane of this page. In this diagram, the value of the function y is plotted as the vertical distance above the LK plane. This generates a surface in three-dimensional space, whose height represents here the level of output produced. Constant output points of, say, five units would all lie in a horizontal plane (parallel to the LK plane) five units above the LK plane. The intersection of such a plane with the production surface would yield a curve in that surface all of whose points were five units above the LK axes. This level curve, or contour, would be another representation of the five-unit isoquant pictures in Fig. 3-1. In fact, the isoquants in Fig. 3-1 are really projections of the level curves of

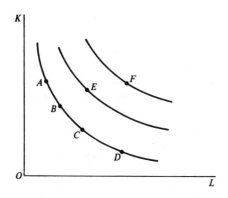

FIGURE 3-1
Level Curves for a Production Function. In this diagram, three separate level curves are drawn (out of the infinity of such curves that exist). Points A, B, C, and D all represent combinations of labor and capital which yield the same output. They are therefore all on the same level curve, called, in production theory, an *isoquant*. Point E represents a higher level of output; point F a still higher output level.

[†]Those of you familiar with "contour maps" used in geological surveys (and hiking) will recognize those contours as the level curves of a function denoting the altitude of the terrain.

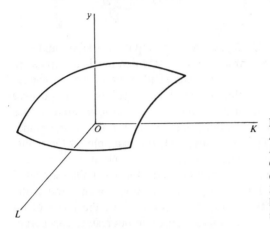

FIGURE 3-2
A Three-Dimensional Representation of a Function of Two Variables. This figure depicts a two-dimensional surface in three-dimensional space. The level curves of Fig. 3-1 are projections of the intersection of horizontal planes (at some value of y) and this surface.

the surface depicted in Fig. 3-2 into the LK plane. Similar level curves are drawn for the theory of consumer behavior. In this context, the level curves represent loci of constant utilities and are called indifference curves. Since these curves play a central role in economic theory, we will have much to say about them in the course of this book.

This three-dimensional representation of a function of two variables, although difficult to draw, provides a useful visualization of the situation. The function is increasing, say, if it is rising vertically as one moves in a given direction, and a maximum of such a function is easily pictured as the "top of the hill." But needless to say, for more than two independent variables, such visual geometry becomes impossible, and, hence, algebraic methods become necessary.

3.3 PARTIAL DERIVATIVES

Consider a consumer's utility function, $U = f(x_1, \ldots, x_n)$, where, again, $x_1, \ldots, x_n$ represent the levels of consumption of n goods. If these x_i's are indeed "goods," i.e., they contribute positively to the consumer's welfare at the margin, then it would be convenient to be able to denote and analyze this effect mathematically. The statement that the *marginal utility* of some good x_i is positive means that if x_i is increased by some amount Δx_i, *holding the other goods* (the other x_i's) *constant*, the resulting change in total utility will be positive. This is exactly the same idea as taking derivatives in the calculus of one variable, with one important qualification: Since there are other variables present, we must specify in addition that these other variables are being held fixed at their previous levels. This type of derivative is called a *partial* derivative since it refers to changes in the function with respect to changes in only one of several variables. Partial derivatives are denoted with curled d's: $\partial y/\partial x_i$, instead of the ordinary d's used in the calculus of one variable.

As another example, consider a production function $y = f(L, K)$. The marginal product of, say, labor is the rate of change of output when the labor input is adjusted incrementally, for a specified, constant level of capital input.

The marginal product of labor is thus the partial derivative of output with respect to labor (L). Likewise, the marginal product of capital is the partial derivative of $f(L, K)$ with respect to K.

Proceeding more formally, consider some function, $y = f(x_1, \ldots, x_n)$, evaluated at the point $x_1 = x_1^0, \ldots, x_n = x_n^0$. Consider how this function changes with adjustments in x_1 alone. We define the partial derivative of $f(x_1, \ldots, x_n)$ with respect to x_1 as

$$\frac{\partial y}{\partial x_1} = \lim_{\Delta x_1 \to 0} \frac{\Delta f}{\Delta x_1}$$

$$= \lim_{\Delta x_1 \to 0} \frac{f(x_1^0 + \Delta x_1, x_2^0, \ldots, x_n^0) - f(x_1^0, \ldots, x_n^0)}{\Delta x_1} \qquad (3\text{-}1)$$

The partial derivative, $(\partial f/\partial x_1)$, is evaluated at $x_1 = x_1^0, \ldots, x_n = x_n^0$ provided the limit exists. The student should note that the foregoing difference quotient is really an intuitive generalization from the difference quotient used to define the ordinary derivatives of functions of one variable. Analogously, we define:

$$\frac{\partial y}{\partial x_i} = \lim_{\Delta x_i \to 0} \frac{f(x_1^0, \ldots, x_i^0 + \Delta x_i, \ldots, x_n^0) - f(x_1^0, \ldots, x_n^0)}{\Delta x_i}$$

$$\text{where } i = 1, \ldots, n \qquad (3\text{-}2)$$

We will use the notation $\partial y/\partial x_i$ and $\partial f/\partial x_i$ interchangeably.

When taking partial derivatives, the rule is simply to treat all other variables as constants. The ordinary rules of differentiation are then applied.

Example 1. Suppose a consumer's utility is given by the function

$$U(x_1, x_2) = x_1 \log x_2$$

The marginal utilities are the partial derivatives $\partial U/\partial x_1$, $\partial U/\partial x_2$. To find $\partial U/\partial x_1$, treat x_2 as constant:

$$\frac{\partial U}{\partial x_1} = \log x_2$$

Similarly, to find $\partial U/\partial x_2$, treat x_1 as a constant:

$$\frac{\partial U}{\partial x_2} = x_1 \frac{1}{x_2} = \frac{x_1}{x_2}$$

Example 2. Suppose a firm's production function is

$$y = L^\alpha K^\beta$$

where $\alpha, \beta > 0$ are constants. The marginal products of labor and capital are, respectively,

$$\mathrm{MP}_L = \frac{\partial y}{\partial L} = \alpha L^{\alpha - 1} K^\beta$$

$$\text{MP}_K = \frac{\partial y}{\partial K} = L^\alpha \beta K^{\beta-1} = \beta L^\alpha K^{\beta-1}$$

The ordinary rules of differentiation, e.g., the product and quotient rules, apply to partial derivatives as well.

Example 3. Let $y = x_1 e^{x_1 + x_2^2}$.
Using the product rule,

$$\frac{\partial y}{\partial x_1} = x_1 e^{x_1 + x_2^2} + e^{x_1 + x_2^2} = e^{x_1 + x_2^2}(1 + x_1)$$

Also, using the chain rule as in differentiating e^{a+x^2},

$$\frac{\partial y}{\partial x_2} = x_1 e^{x_1 + x_2^2}(2x_2) = 2x_1 x_2 e^{x_1 + x_2^2}$$

As with the case of ordinary derivatives, partial derivatives can be differentiated (partially!) again yielding *second partials*. However, a richer set of second derivatives exists for functions of several variables than for functions of one variable, because partials such as $\partial f/\partial x_1$ can be differentiated with respect to any of the n variables x_1 through x_n. We can denote "the partial derivative of $\partial f/\partial x_i$ with respect to x_j" as $\partial(\partial f/\partial x_i)/\partial x_j$, or $\partial^2 f/\partial x_j \partial x_i$. Often, however, it is convenient to simply use subscripts to denote differentiation with respect to a variable. Following this tradition, we will write $\partial f/\partial x_i = f_i$, and for higher-order partials, subscripts read from left to right reflect the order of differentiation. That is, $f_{ij} = \partial^2 f/\partial x_j \partial x_i$, which, for utility functions, can be interpreted as the rate of change of the marginal utility of good i when the quantity of good j increases.

Example 4. Consider $U(x_1, x_2) = x_1 \log x_2$ again. We previously found

$$U_1 = \log x_2$$

$$U_2 = \frac{x_1}{x_2}$$

Therefore

$$U_{11} = \frac{\partial U_1}{\partial x_1} = 0$$

$$U_{12} = \frac{\partial U_1}{\partial x_2} = \frac{1}{x_2}$$

$$U_{21} = \frac{\partial U_2}{\partial x_1} = \frac{1}{x_2}$$

$$U_{22} = \frac{\partial U_2}{\partial x_2} = \frac{-x_1}{x_2^2}$$

Example 5. For the function $y = f(L, K) = L^\alpha K^\beta$, the first partials were found to be

$$f_L = \frac{\partial y}{\partial L} = \alpha L^{\alpha-1} K^\beta$$

$$f_K = \frac{\partial y}{\partial K} = \beta L^\alpha K^{\beta-1}$$

Hence

$$f_{LL} = \frac{\partial f_L}{\partial L} = \alpha(\alpha - 1)L^{\alpha-2} K^\beta$$

$$f_{LK} = \frac{\partial f_L}{\partial K} = \alpha L^{\alpha-1}\beta K^{\beta-1} = \alpha\beta L^{\alpha-1} K^{\beta-1}$$

$$f_{KL} = \frac{\partial f_K}{\partial L} = \beta(\alpha L^{\alpha-1}) K^{\beta-1} = \alpha\beta L^{\alpha-1} K^{\beta-1}$$

$$f_{KK} = \frac{\partial f_K}{\partial K} = \beta L^\alpha(\beta - 1)K^{\beta-2} = \beta(\beta - 1)L^\alpha K^{\beta-2}$$

Example 6. For $y = f(x_1, x_2) = x_1 e^{x_1 + x_2^2}$, we found

$$\frac{\partial y}{\partial x_1} = f_1 = e^{x_1 + x_2^2}(1 + x_1)$$

$$\frac{\partial y}{\partial x_2} = f_2 = 2x_1 x_2 e^{x_1 + x_2^2}$$

Thus

$$f_{11} = e^{x_1 + x_2^2} + (1 + x_1)e^{x_1 + x_2^2} = e^{x_1 + x_2^2}(2 + x_1)$$

$$f_{12} = e^{x_1 + x_2^2}(1 + x_1)2x_2 = 2(1 + x_1)x_2 e^{x_1 + x_2^2}$$

$$f_{21} = 2x_2(x_1 e^{x_1 + x_2^2} + e^{x_1 + x_2^2}) = 2(1 + x_1)x_2 e^{x_1 + x_2^2}$$

$$f_{22} = 2x_1[x_2 e^{x_1 + x_2^2}(2x_2) + e^{x_1 + x_2^2}] = 2x_1(1 + 2x_2^2)e^{x_1 + x_2^2}$$

Curiously enough, for each of these functions, $f_{12} = f_{21}$ (or, in the notation of Example 6, $f_{LK} = f_{KL}$). The same "cross partial" derivative results no matter in which order the variables are differentiated. This occurrence in fact is general for all functions of several variables whose second partials are themselves continuous.

This invariance to the order of differentiation is one of the least intuitive theorems in elementary mathematics. It is sometimes known as Young's theorem.[†] (Try asking some of your mathematician friends for an intuitive explanation of it!) The result accounts for some surprising relationships that appear in economics. Provided below is, in the author's opinion, the simplest explanation of invariance to the order of differentiation, for the case of functions in two variables. The generalization to n variables is routine. A rigorous discussion of the limit process is not given; hence, what follows is not a formal proof of the matter. It will do for our purposes, however.

Theorem. Let $y = f(x_1, x_2)$ have second-order partials that exist and are continuous. Then $f_{12} = f_{21}$.

Discussion. Consider a production function $y = f(L, K)$, where L and K are, respectively, the quantity of labor and capital used in the production process. If the theorem is to hold, then the answers to the following two questions should be identical:

1. How much, in the limit, does the marginal product of labor change when an extra unit of capital is added?
2. How much, in the limit, does the marginal product of capital change when one adds an extra unit of labor?

(Of course, both of these measurements must be made at the same point.) In Fig. 3-3, let

$$a = f(L^0, K^0)$$
$$b = f(L^0 + \Delta L, K^0)$$
$$c = f(L^0 + \Delta L, K^0 + \Delta K)$$
$$d = f(L^0, K^0 + \Delta K)$$

That is, a, b, c, and d are the *values* of the function f (here, the levels of output) at the corners of the rectangle in the LK plane formed by the initial point L^0, K^0, and then changing L and K by amounts ΔL and ΔK, respectively, separately and then together.

[†]The reference apparently is to W. H. Young, who published a rigorous proof of the theorem in 1909 using the modern mathematical theory of limits. (See Cambridge Tract No. 11, "The Fundamental Theorems of the Differential Calculus," Cambridge University Press, reprinted in 1971 by Hafner Press.) In fact, the result was published by Euler in 1734; ("De Infinitis Curvis Eiusdem Generis . . . ," Commentatio 44 indicis Enestroemiani). It really should be called "Euler's theorem," but that title is reserved for a famous result discussed later in this chapter. I am grateful to Joel Holmes and Neil Theobold for these tidbits.

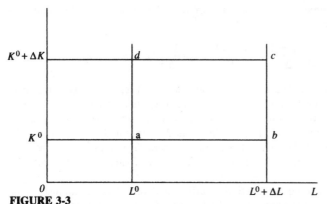

FIGURE 3-3
Young's Theorem. In this diagram, *a*, *b*, *c*, and *d* represent the *values* of $f(L, K)$ at the four corners of the rectangle.

Let us approximate the second-order partial derivatives by their second differences and see how they compare before any limits are taken. The marginal product of labor L evaluated at (L^0, K^0) is approximately

$$f_L(L^0, K^0) \approx \frac{f(L^0 + \Delta L, K^0) - f(L^0, K^0)}{\Delta L} = \frac{b - a}{\Delta L} \qquad (3\text{-}3)$$

If the amount of capital K is now increased by some amount ΔK, the marginal product of labor, evaluated at $(L^0, K^0 + \Delta K)$ is

$$f_L(L^0, K^0 + \Delta K) \approx \frac{f(L^0 + \Delta L, K^0 + \Delta K) - f(L^0, K^0 + \Delta K)}{\Delta L}$$

$$= \frac{c - d}{\Delta L} \qquad (3\text{-}4)$$

Then, f_{LK}, which measures the *change* in the marginal product of labor when an incremental amount of capital is added, can be found by taking the difference, per increment of capital, between the two marginal products of labor (3-3) and (3-4):

$$f_{LK} \approx \frac{1}{\Delta K}\left(\frac{c - d}{\Delta L} - \frac{b - a}{\Delta L}\right) = \frac{1}{\Delta K \, \Delta L}(c - d - b + a) \qquad (3\text{-}5)$$

To find the other cross-partial f_{KL} we begin the process by first finding the marginal product of capital, and then asking how that value changes when the quantity of labor changes. Proceeding as before, the marginal product of capital evaluated at (L^0, K^0) is

$$f_K(L^0, K^0) \approx \frac{f(L^0, K^0 + \Delta K) - f(L^0, K^0)}{\Delta K} = \frac{d - a}{\Delta K} \qquad (3\text{-}6)$$

Increasing the amount of labor to $L^0 + \Delta L$, the marginal product of capital is

$$f_K(L^0 + \Delta L, K^0) \approx \frac{f(L^0 + \Delta L, K^0 + \Delta K) - f(L^0 + \Delta L, K^0)}{\Delta K} = \frac{c - b}{\Delta K} \qquad (3\text{-}7)$$

Hence, the *change* in the marginal product of capital due to the change in labor is approximately

$$f_{KL} \approx \frac{1}{\Delta L}\left(\frac{c-b}{\Delta K} - \frac{d-a}{\Delta K}\right) = \frac{1}{\Delta L\,\Delta K}(c-b-d+a) \qquad (3\text{-}8)$$

Notice that Eqs. (3-5) and (3-8) are identical! That is, the second differences are the same, whether L or K is changed first. The remaining step (and it is a big step) in proving the theorem is to show that, under appropriate mathematical conditions on the function $f(L, K)$, the *limits* as $\Delta L \to 0$ and $\Delta K \to 0$, are the same, taken in either order. This step is omitted here. The argument is based on an application of the mean value theorem, and can be found in most elementary calculus texts.

In general, assuming the function is sufficiently well-behaved (no discontinuities in higher-order derivatives, etc.), the higher-order partial derivatives are also invariant to the order of differentiation. This is derived by simply applying Young's theorem over and over.

Example 7. Consider $y = f(x_1, x_2, x_3)$. Show that $f_{123} = f_{312} = f_{321}$, etc.
Applying Young's theorem to $f_1(x_1, x_2, x_3)$

$$f_{123} = f_{1(23)} = f_{1(32)} = f_{132}$$

However, $f_{13} = f_{31}$. Hence

$$f_{132} = f_{312}$$

Thus, $f_{123} = f_{312}$. Also, since $f_{3(12)} = f_{3(21)}$

$$f_{123} = f_{312} = f_{321}$$

In a similar fashion, for $y = f(x_1, \ldots, x_n)$

$$f_{ijk} = f_{jki} = \cdots$$

3.4   THE TOTAL DIFFERENTIAL OF A FUNCTION OF SEVERAL VARIABLES[†]

In the case of one variable, $y = f(x)$, one can write the *differential* expression

$$dy = f'(x)\,dx$$

The differential element dy measures the movement in y, measured along the line tangent to the function at some point x. The actual change in y, for some change in x, Δx, is given by

$$\Delta y = f(x + \Delta x) - f(x)$$

[†]The student should review the section on total differentials in Chap. 2 if this concept is unfamiliar.

However, the difference between dy and Δy is of second-order smallness, i.e.,

$$\Delta y = f'(x)\Delta x + \epsilon \Delta x$$

where $\epsilon \to 0$ as $\Delta x \to 0$.

How does the concept of a total derivative generalize to the case of two variables? For $y = f(x_1, x_2)$, the generalization is

$$dy = f_1 \, dx_1 + f_2 \, dx_2 \tag{3-9}$$

where $f_i = \partial f / \partial x_i$, $i = 1, 2$. The change dy is simply the sum of the movements in y due to changes in both x_1 and x_2.

As in the case of functions of one variable, a geometric interpretation can be given to the total differential (3-9). The function $f(x_1, x_2)$ can be thought of as ascribing a value to every point in the Cartesian coordinate plane (x_1, x_2). If this plane is thought of as laid out horizontally (parallel to the earth's surface), and if the values of the function are plotted vertically above each point in that plane, then the function will be represented by a surface suspended in three-dimensional space. Assuming this surface has the requisite smoothness, at each point one can imagine a tangent *plane*. The dy measures movements in y *measured up to the tangent plane*, due to changes in both x_1 and x_2. It does not reflect changes in the value of the *function* for changes in the independent variables. As before, Δy will denote changes in the function itself, while dy measures changes in y as we move along the plane tangent to the surface at some point.

Although Eq. (3-9) can be regarded simply as a *definition* of a total derivative, the expression can be motivated as follows. For finite changes Δx_1 and Δx_2 in x_1 and x_2, respectively, the change in the value of the function, Δy, is

$$\Delta y = f(x_1 + \Delta x_1, x_2 + \Delta x_2) - f(x_1, x_2) \tag{3-10}$$

We are now going to add 0 to this equation by both adding and subtracting the same term. (The reason for this contrivance will become clear shortly.) Hence,

$$\Delta y = f(x_1 + \Delta x_1, x_2 + \Delta x_2) - f(x_1, x_2 + \Delta x_2) + f(x_1, x_2 + \Delta x_2) - f(x_1, x_2)$$

The expression is similarly unchanged if the terms are grouped in pairs and each pair is multiplied by 1:

$$\Delta y = \frac{f(x_1 + \Delta x_1, x_2 + \Delta x_2) - f(x_1, x_2 + \Delta x_2)}{\Delta x_1} \Delta x_1$$

$$+ \frac{f(x_1, x_2 + \Delta x_2) - f(x_1, x_2)}{\Delta x_2} \Delta x_2 \tag{3-11}$$

The expression (3–11) for Δy is now a weighted sum of two difference quotients. In the first term, x_2 is held constant (at the level $x_2 + \Delta x_2$) and x_1 is varied, whereas in the second term, x_1 is held constant and x_2 is varied. This is precisely the type of difference quotient used to define partial derivatives. Hence, assuming that all the appropriate limits exist, then as $\Delta x_1 \to 0$ and $\Delta x_2 \to 0$, the first difference quotient approaches f_1 while the second approaches f_2. As in the case of functions of one variable, the difference between y, as given by Eq. (3-10) or (3-11), and dy, as defined by (3-9), is of second-order smallness. That is,

$$\Delta y = f_1 \, \Delta x_1 + f_2 \, \Delta x_2 + \epsilon_1 \, \Delta x_1 + \epsilon_2 \, \Delta x_2$$

where $\epsilon_1, \epsilon_2 \to 0$ as $\Delta x_1, \Delta x_2 \to 0$. For movements *along* the tangent plane itself,

$$dy = f_1 \, dx_1 + f_2 \, dx_2$$

where dx_1 and dx_2 are arbitrary changes (not necessarily "small") in x_1 and x_2, respectively.

The generalization of Eq. (3-9) to the case of functions of several variables is straightforward. Using the same reasoning, the formula for the total differential of $y = f(x_1, \ldots, x_n)$ is[†]

$$dy = f_1 \, dx_1 + \cdots + f_n \, dx_n = \sum_{i=1}^{n} f_i \, dx_i \qquad (3\text{-}12)$$

Geometrically, Eq. (3-12) represents movements along a "hyperplane" tangent to an n-dimensional "surface" suspended in $(n + 1)$ space. The reason why algebraic analysis eventually supplants geometric reasoning is thus obvious.

The preceding analysis of the total differential is necessary for deriving the chain rule for functions of several variables. This is done in the next section; the chain rule is a tool of critical importance and, hence, must be thoroughly understood by the student.

PROBLEMS

1. For each of the following functions, find f_1, f_2, f_{12}, and f_{21}. Verify that $f_{12} = f_{21}$ for these functions.
   (a) $f(x_1, x_2) = x_1^2 x_2^3$
   (b) $f(x_1, x_2) = (x_1 + x_2^2)/(x_1 + x_2)$
   (c) $f(x_1, x_2) = x_2 \log x_1$
   (d) $f(x_1, x_2) = x_1^2 e^{x_2}$
   (e) $f(x_1, x_2) = x_1^{x_2}$
2. Find the total differential of the functions in Prob. 1.
3. Consider the function $y = x_1^2 + x_1 x_2 - x_2^2$. Show that the difference between dy and Δy is of second-order smallness, i.e., the difference involves the increment Δx raised to powers 2 and above.
4. Consider the production function $y = L^{1/3} K^{2/3}$, where $L =$ labor, $K =$ capital, and $y =$ output. Suppose initially $L = 64$, $K = 27$. Suppose one unit of labor and two units of capital are added. By how much, approximately, will output increase? How

---

[†]The summation sign $\sum_{i=1}^{n}$ means substitute successively the values 1 through n for i in the terms to the right of the summation sign, and then add up all n terms. It is a very useful, and hence very common, shorthand.

much exactly? Which is an easier number to compute? Do you think it matters much which you use?

5. Let $y = L^\alpha K^{1-\alpha}$, where $0 < \alpha < 1$. Let $y' = \log y$, $L' = \log L$, $K' = \log K$.
   (a) Show that this production function is linear in the logs of output, labor, and capital.
   (b) Using logarithmic differentiation, show that for this production function, the percentage change in output due to small changes in the inputs is equal to the weighted sum of the percentage changes in labor and capital, the weights being α and $(1 - \alpha)$, respectively. In what sense is the relation you derive valid only for *small* changes?

3.5 THE CHAIN RULE[‡]

In economics, as well as most sciences, one often encounters a sequence of functional relationships. For example, the output of a firm depends upon the input levels chosen by the firm, as specified in the production function. However, the input levels are determined, i.e., functionally related to the factor and output prices. Hence, output is related, indirectly, to factor and output prices. It is therefore meaningful to inquire as to the changes in output that would follow a change in some price, i.e., a partial derivative of output with respect to that price. The chain rule is the mathematical device that expresses the partial derivative of the composite function in terms of the various partial derivatives of the individual functions in the functional sequence. We will now develop this idea more formally, for functions of several variables.

For functions of one variable, if

$$y = f(x) \text{ and } x = g(t)$$

then the functional dependence of y on t can be written

$$y = f(g(t)) = h(t)$$

Now

$$\Delta y = f'(x) \Delta x + \epsilon \Delta x$$

and

$$\Delta x = g'(t) \Delta t + \zeta \Delta t$$

where $\epsilon \to 0$ as $\Delta x \to 0$ and $\zeta \to 0$ as $\Delta t \to 0$. Combining these two expressions,

$$\Delta y = [f'(x) + \epsilon][g'(t)\Delta t + \zeta \Delta t]$$

or

$$\Delta y = f'(x)g'(t) \Delta t + f'(x)\zeta \Delta t + g'(t)\epsilon \Delta t + \epsilon \zeta \Delta t$$

[‡]The student should review the section on the chain rule in Chap. 2, if this concept is unfamiliar.

Dividing by Δt

$$\frac{\Delta y}{\Delta t} = f'(x)g'(t) + f'(x)\zeta + g'(t)\epsilon + \epsilon\zeta$$

Taking limits as $\Delta t \to 0$

$$\frac{dy}{dt} = f'(x)g'(t) = \frac{dy}{dx}\frac{dx}{dt} \tag{3-13}$$

since ϵ, $\zeta \to 0$ as $\Delta t \to 0$.

Suppose now that y is a function of two variables, $y = f(x_1, x_2)$. Suppose x_1 and x_2 are in turn functions of some other variable t. Let $x_1 = x_1(t)$, $x_2 = x_2(t)$.[†] Then if t changes, so will, in general, x_1 and x_2 and, hence, also y. To express this functional dependence of y on t, we write $y = f(x_1(t), x_2(t)) = y(t)$. How can $y'(t)$ be expressed in terms of $f_1, f_2, x'_1(t)$ and $x'_2(t)$?

For given changes Δx_1 and Δx_2

$$\Delta y = f_1 \Delta x_1 + f_2 \Delta x_2 + \epsilon_1 \Delta x_1 + \epsilon_2 \Delta x_2 \tag{3-14}$$

where ϵ_1, $\epsilon_2 \to 0$ as Δx_1, $\Delta x_2 \to 0$. However,

$$\Delta x_1 = x'_1(t) \Delta t + \zeta_1 \Delta t$$

$$\Delta x_2 = x'_2(t) \Delta t + \zeta_2 \Delta t$$

Substituting these relations into (3-14) yields

$$\Delta y = f_1 x'_1(t) \Delta t + f_2 x'_2(t) \Delta t + (f_1\zeta_1 + f_2\zeta_2 + \epsilon_1 x'_1 + \epsilon_1\zeta_1 + \epsilon_2 x'_2 + \epsilon_2\zeta_2)\Delta t$$

Dividing by Δt and taking limits,

$$\frac{dy}{dt} = f_1 x'_1(t) + f_2 x'_2(t) = \frac{\partial f}{\partial x_1}\frac{dx_1}{dt} + \frac{\partial f}{\partial x_2}\frac{dx_2}{dt} \tag{3-15}$$

Suppose now that x_1 and x_2 are themselves functions of several variables. For example, let $x_1 = g(r, s)$, $x_2 = h(r, s)$. In this case, $y = f(g(r, s), h(r, s)) = F(r, s)$, and we can only speak meaningfully of the *partial* derivatives of y with respect to r and s. The chain rule here is

$$\frac{\partial y}{\partial r} = f_1 \frac{\partial g}{\partial r} + f_2 \frac{\partial h}{\partial r} \tag{3-16}$$

with a similar expression holding with respect to the variable s. The only difference between (3-15) and (3-16) is that since r is one of several variables, the appropriate partial notation must be used.

The chain rule generalizes in a straightforward manner to the case where each independent variable is in turn a function of m other independent variables.

[†]Mathematicians frown on the use of the same symbol to denote a function and the value of that function. It will not get us into trouble, however, and it will reduce the number of symbols that the reader has to keep in mind.

Let

$$y = f(x_1, \ldots, x_n)$$

and let

$$x_i = g^i(t_1, \ldots, t_m) \quad i = 1, \ldots, n$$

Then the chain rule is

$$\frac{\partial y}{\partial t_k} = \frac{\partial f}{\partial x_1} \frac{\partial x_1}{\partial t_k} + \cdots + \frac{\partial f}{\partial x_n} \frac{\partial x_n}{\partial t_k} \quad k = 1, \ldots, m \qquad (3\text{-}17)$$

This can also be written as

$$\frac{\partial y}{\partial t_k} = f_1 g_k^1 + \cdots + f_n g_k^n = \sum_{i=1}^{n} f_i g_k^i \quad k = 1, \ldots, m \qquad (3\text{-}18)$$

where the symbol g_k^i means $\partial g^i / \partial t_k$.

Example 1. Let $y = f(x_1, x_2)$, and let

$$x_1 = x_1^0 + h_1 t$$

$$x_2 = x_2^0 + h_2 t \qquad (3\text{-}19)$$

where h_1 and h_2 are arbitrary constants. When $t = 0$, $x_1 = x_1^0$, $x_2 = x_2^0$. As t changes, x_1 and x_2 move along a straight line in the $x_1 x_2$ plane. This can be seen by eliminating t from these equations:

$$x_2 = x_2^0 + \frac{h_2(x_1 - x_1^0)}{h_1} = \frac{h_2}{h_1} x_1 + \left(x_2^0 - x_1^0 \frac{h_2}{h_1} \right) \quad h_1 \neq 0 \qquad (3\text{-}20)$$

This is the equation of a straight line with slope h_2/h_1, passing through the point (x_1^0, x_2^0).

Writing

$$y(t) = f(x_1^0 + h_1 t, x_2^0 + h_2 t)$$

is equivalent to saying that $f(x_1, x_2)$ is evaluated along the straight line (3-19), or, equivalently, (3-20). Using the chain rule,

$$y'(t) = f_1 h_1 + f_2 h_2 \qquad (3\text{-}21)$$

Example 2. Suppose $y = \log(x_1 + x_2)$, where $x_1 = t$, $x_2 = t^2$. This is equivalent to evaluating $\log(x_1 + x_2)$ along the parabola $x_2 = x_1^2$. Let us find dy/dt by direct substitution and by the chain rule.

(i) By direct substitution

$$y = \log(t + t^2)$$

Therefore

$$\frac{dy}{dt} = \frac{1}{t + t^2}(1 + 2t)$$

(ii) Using the chain rule,

$$\frac{dy}{dt} = f_1 \frac{dx_1}{dt} + f_2 \frac{dx_2}{dt}$$

$$= \frac{1}{x_1 + x_2} 1 + \frac{1}{x_1 + x_2} 2t$$

$$= \frac{1}{t + t^2}(1 + 2t)$$

as before.

Example 3. Suppose $y = x_1^2 e^{x_2}$, with $x_1 = \log t$, $x_2 = t^2$. Find dy/dt by *(i)* direct substitution, and by *(ii)* the chain rule.

(i) Substituting the expressions for x_1 and x_2, $y = (\log t)^2 e^{t^2}$. Using the product rule for differentiation

$$\frac{dy}{dt} = e^{t^2}(2 \log t)\frac{1}{t} + (\log t)^2(2te^{t^2})$$

(ii) Using the chain rule

$$\frac{dy}{dt} = f_1 \frac{dx_1}{dt} + f_2 \frac{dx_2}{dt} = 2x_1 e^{x_2}\frac{1}{t} + x_1^2 e^{x_2}(2t)$$

$$= 2(\log t)e^{t^2}\frac{1}{t} + (\log t)^2 e^{t^2}(2t)$$

The final expressions are, as they must be, identical by either method.

Monotonic Transformations

A particular sequence of functional relationships which plays a prominent part in the theory of the consumer is a transformation of the *dependent* variable. Suppose a consumer's utility function is given by

$$U = U(x_1, x_2)$$

In the modern theory of the consumer, this utility, or preference, function is meant to merely *rank* various options, (x_1, x_2). The value of the function itself at some point is relevant only in regard to whether it is *greater* or *less* than at some other consumption point. The amount greater is of no significance unless one proposes to actually measure "utility" or happiness. We say that $U(x_1, x_2)$ is an *ordinal* ranking, not a cardinal function of alternatives.

This ordinality is given precise expression by saying that the utility function $V(x_1, x_2)$ given by

$$V(x_1, x_2) = F(U) = F(U(x_1, x_2))$$

where $F'(U) > 0$, conveys as much information as $U(x_1, x_2)$. The condition that $F'(U) > 0$ means that U and V always move in the same direction. The function

V is called a *montonically increasing* function of U. [If $F'(U) < 0$, V would be called monotonically decreasing.] Most often, the single term *monotonic* is used to mean *monotonically increasing*.

What the function F does is relabel the level curves of U, giving them new numbers, V. This is a different situation than previously where the independent variables were dependent on some other variable or variables. Here, the dependent variable U (in this case) is given a new value, $F(U) = V$. The function V is a function of the one variable U which in turn is a function of two variables, x_1 and x_2. We can thus ask, since V ultimately depends on *both* x_1 and x_2, how is $\partial V / \partial x_i$ related to $F(U)$ and $U(x_1, x_2)$? The answer is given in the following chain rule.

We have

$$\Delta V = F'(U)\Delta U + \epsilon \Delta U \qquad (3\text{-}22)$$

where $\epsilon \to 0$ as $\Delta U \to 0$. However,

$$\Delta U = U_1 \Delta x_1 + U_2 \Delta x_2 + \epsilon_1 \Delta x_1 + \epsilon_2 \Delta x_2$$

Substituting this into (3-22) yields

$$\Delta V = F'(U)U_1 \Delta x_1 + F'(U)U_2 \Delta x_2 + [F'(U)](\epsilon_1 \Delta x_1 + \epsilon_2 \Delta x_2) + \epsilon \Delta U$$

If only x_1 changes, that is, $\Delta x_2 = 0$, then dividing by Δx_1 and taking limits gives

$$\frac{\partial V}{\partial x_1} = F'(U)U_1 = \frac{dV}{dU}\frac{\partial U}{\partial x_1}$$

Similarly,

$$\frac{\partial V}{\partial x_2} = F'(U)U_2 = \frac{dV}{dU}\frac{\partial U}{\partial x_2}$$

In general, suppose

$$y = f(x_1, \ldots, x_n)$$

and

$$z = F(y) = F(f(x_1, \ldots, x_n))$$

Then

$$\frac{\partial z}{\partial x_i} = F'(y)f_i \qquad (3\text{-}23)$$

Example 4. Suppose $y = x_1 x_2$, and let $z = \log y$. Then applying (3-23),

$$\frac{\partial z}{\partial x_1} = \frac{1}{y}x_2 = \frac{1}{x_1}$$

and

$$\frac{\partial z}{\partial x_2} = \frac{1}{y}x_1 = \frac{1}{x_2}$$

These results can be checked by direct substitution. We have

$$z = \log y = \log (x_1 x_2) = \log x_1 + \log x_2$$

Thus

$$\frac{\partial z}{\partial x_1} = \frac{1}{x_1} \qquad \frac{\partial z}{\partial x_2} = \frac{1}{x_2}$$

Example 5. Let $y = x_2 + \log x_1$, $z = e^y$. Then applying (3-23),

$$\frac{\partial z}{\partial x_1} = e^y \frac{1}{x_1} = e^{x_2 + \log x_1} \frac{1}{x_1}$$

Using the definition of logs and rules of exponents

$$\frac{\partial z}{\partial x_1} = e^{x_2} e^{\log x_1} \frac{1}{x_1} = e^{x_2} x_1 \frac{1}{x_1} = e^{x_2}$$

Similarly,

$$\frac{\partial z}{\partial x_2} = e^y(1) = e^{x_2 + \log x_1} = x_1 e^{x_2}$$

By direct substitution,

$$z = e^{x_2 + \log x_1} = e^{x_2} e^{\log x_1} = x_1 e^{x_2}$$

from which the above partials directly follow.

Second Derivatives by the Chain Rule

Suppose that $y = f(x_1, x_2)$ and $x_1 = x_1(t)$, $x_2 = x_2(t)$. We need to find an expression for $d^2 y/dt^2$, as this second derivative is important for analyzing the sufficient conditions under which a function of several variables achieves a maximum or a minimum position. Using the chain rule,

$$\frac{dy}{dt} = f_1 \frac{dx_1}{dt} + f_2 \frac{dx_2}{dt}$$

Then, to find $d^2 y/dt^2$, we have to differentiate this expression again. Do not forget, however, that f_1 and f_2 are themselves functions of x_1 and x_2, and, hence, functions of t. Then, using the product rule,

$$\frac{d^2 y}{dt^2} = \frac{d}{dt} \frac{dy}{dt} = f_1 \frac{d}{dt} \frac{dx_1}{dt} + \frac{dx_1}{dt} \frac{d}{dt} f_1(x_1(t), x_2(t)) + f_2 \frac{d}{dt} \frac{dx_2}{dt}$$

$$+ \frac{dx_2}{dt} \frac{d}{dt} f_2(x_1(t), x_2(t))$$

Now use the chain rule to differentiate $f_1(x_1(t), x_2(t))$, et cetera, with respect to t. Noting that $\partial f_1/\partial x_1 = f_{11}$, et cetera,

$$\frac{d^2y}{dt^2} = f_1\frac{d^2x_1}{dt^2} + \frac{dx_1}{dt}\left(f_{11}\frac{dx_1}{dt} + f_{12}\frac{dx_2}{dt}\right)$$

$$+f_2\frac{d^2x_2}{dt^2} + \frac{dx_2}{dt}\left(f_{21}\frac{dx_1}{dt} + f_{22}\frac{dx_2}{dt}\right)$$

Regrouping terms, and noting that $f_{12} = f_{21}$,

$$\frac{d^2y}{dt^2} = f_1\frac{d^2x_1}{dt^2} + f_2\frac{d^2x_2}{dt^2} + f_{11}\left(\frac{dx_1}{dt}\right)^2$$

$$+ 2f_{12}\frac{dx_1}{dt}\frac{dx_2}{dt} + f_{22}\left(\frac{dx_2}{dt}\right)^2$$

(3-24)

Note that this expression is linear in the second derivatives of x_1 and x_2 with respect to t, and *quadratic* in the first derivatives of x_1 and x_2. The appropriate generalization to n variables, with $y = f(x_1, \ldots, x_n)$ and $x_i = x_i(t), i = 1, \ldots, n$ is obtained in the same manner:

$$\frac{d^2y}{dt^2} = \sum_{i=1}^{n} f_i\frac{d^2x_i}{dt^2} + \sum_{i=1}^{n}\sum_{j=1}^{n} f_{ij}\frac{dx_i}{dt}\frac{dx_j}{dt}$$

(3-25)

Example 6. Let $y = f(x_1, x_2)$ and consider the straight lines $x_1 = x_1^0 + h_1t$, $x_2 = x_2^0 + h_2t$ once more. From Eq. (3-21),

$$y'(t) = f_1h_1 + f_2h_2$$

Therefore

$$y''(t) = \left(\frac{\partial f_1}{\partial x_1}\frac{dx_1}{dt} + \frac{\partial f_1}{\partial x_2}\frac{dx_2}{dt}\right)h_1 + \left(\frac{\partial f_2}{\partial x_1}\frac{dx_1}{dt} + \frac{\partial f_2}{\partial x_2}\frac{dx_2}{dt}\right)h_2$$

Since $\partial f_1/\partial x_1 = f_{11}$, et cetera, and $dx_i/dt = h_i$, this expression reduces to

$$y''(t) = f_{11}h_1^2 + 2f_{12}h_1h_2 + f_{22}h_2^2$$

(3-26)

For this "parameterization" of x_1 and x_2 in terms of t, $y''(t)$ is a "quadratic form" in h_1 and h_2.

Example 7. Let $y = f(x_1, x_2)$, and consider a monotonic transformation of y, $z = F(y) = F(f(x_1, x_2)) = g(x_1, x_2)$, with $F'(y) > 0$. How do the *second* partials of g compare with those of f?
From Eq. (3-23),

$$g_i = F'(y)f_i$$

Let us now differentiate this again, partially, with respect to x_j. Using the product rule for the right-hand side,

$$g_{ij} = F'(y)f_{ij} + f_i\frac{\partial F'(y)}{\partial x_j}$$

To evaluate this last term, keep in mind that $F'(y)$ is just some function of y, where $y = f(x_1, x_2)$ as before. Applying Eq. (3-23) to this last term,

$$\frac{\partial F'(y)}{\partial x_j} = F''(y)f_j$$

Thus,

$$g_{ij} = F'(y)f_{ij} + f_i f_j F''(y) \tag{3-27}$$

Notice that g_{ij} and f_{ij} need not have the same sign. Although $F'(y) > 0$ is assumed, $F''(y) \gtrless 0$. Suppose $y = f(x_1, x_2) = x_1^2 x_2^2$, and let $z = g(x_1, x_2) = \log y$. Then, for example,

$$f_{11} = 2x_2^2 > 0$$

However

$$g(x_1, x_2) = \log (x_1^2 x_2^2) = 2 \log x_1 + 2 \log x_2$$

Then

$$g_{11} = \frac{-2}{x_1^2} < 0$$

Also

$$f_{12} = 4x_1 x_2$$

and

$$g_{12} \equiv 0$$

This result is important in understanding the modern theory of the consumer. Let $y = f(x_1, x_2)$ be some *ordinal* utility function and $z = g(x_1, x_2)$ be a relabeling of the indifference curves through the monotonic transformation $z = F(y)$. For the above functions, the level (indifference) curves have all the usual requisite properties. We would express "diminishing marginal utility of x_1" as $f_{11} < 0$; however, utility as measured by f exhibits *increasing* marginal utility of x_1 (and x_2 also), while g exhibits *decreasing* marginal utility. Yet these two utility functions must imply the same behavior, since the indifference curves themselves are unaffected (just relabeled). The phrase "diminishing marginal utility" therefore can have no empirical meaning or content in the context of ordinal utility theory; that is, the observed behavior of consumers cannot be correlated with the sign of the second partial of the utility function with respect to some good. We shall return to this in Chap. 10.

3.6 LEVEL CURVES: II

Consider again the representation of a function of two variables as presented in Fig. 3-1, with $y = f(L, K)$, a production function. The level curve representing, say, five units of output is simply $f(L, K) = 5$. In general, the level curves of some function $y = f(x_1, x_2)$ are defined by $f(x_1, x_2) = y_0$, where y_0 is some constant. How do we determine the curvature properties, such as the slope in the x_1, x_2 plane, or the convexity of that level curve?

The equation $f(x_1, x_2) = y_0$ represents one equation in two *unknowns*, x_1 and x_2. Under certain mathematical conditions (to be determined below) this equation can be solved for one of the unknowns in terms of the other, say

$$x_2 = x_2(x_1)$$

When this solution is substituted back into the equation from which it was derived, the *identity*

$$f(x_1, x_2(x_1)) \equiv y_0$$

results, by definition of a solution. In this identity, x_2 always adjusts to any value of x_1 so as to keep $f(x_1, x_2(x_1))$ always equal to y_0.

The slope of any level curve is simply the derivative dx_2/dx_1. But it is important to understand that this symbol, dx_2/dx_1, makes sense only if we have explicitly defined x_2 as a function of x_1, as we have, in fact, done previously. It is nonsense to speak of derivatives unless one knows what function it is that is being differentiated. Since our function $x_2 = x_2(x_1)$ is well defined, dx_2/dx_1 can be found by differentiating the identity $f(x_1, x_2(x_1)) \equiv y_0$ with respect to x_1, using the chain rule. We therefore get

$$\frac{\partial f}{\partial x_1}\frac{dx_1}{dx_1} + \frac{\partial f}{\partial x_2}\frac{dx_2}{dx_1} \equiv \frac{\partial y_0}{\partial x_1} \equiv 0$$

or

$$f_1 + f_2\frac{dx_2}{dx_1} \equiv 0$$

Now assuming that $f_2 \neq 0$

$$\frac{dx_2}{dx_1} \equiv \frac{-f_1}{f_2} \tag{3-28}$$

The slope of a level curve at any point is the ratio of the first partials of the function $y = f(x_1, x_2)$, evaluated, of course, at some particular point on the level curve in question. The condition alluded to previously which allows solution of $f(x_1, x_2) = y_0$ for $x_2 = x_2(x_1)$ can be seen to be simply that $f_2 \neq 0$. When $f_2 \neq 0$, at some point the derivative dx_2/dx_1 can be expressed in terms of the partials of the original function, and, hence, the equations $f(x_1, x_2) = y_0$ and $x_2 = x_2(x_1)$ are equivalent at such points. When $f_2 = 0$, the level curve becomes vertical and its derivative does not exist.

What is the meaning of $dx_2/dx_1 = -f_1/f_2$? Consider the production function $y = f(L, K)$ again. The level curves are the isoquants of this production function. In Fig. 3-4, consider a movement along an isoquant y_0, from A to B. This movement can be conceptually broken down into a vertical movement down to C, in which case only K is changed by an amount ΔK, and then a horizontal

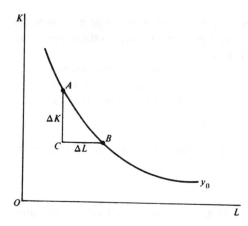

FIGURE 3-4
Movement Along an Isoquant. The move from *A* to *B* can be broken down into a decrease in *K* (*A* to *C*), then an increase in *L* (*C* to *B*) to achieve the same production level. Since *y* is constant, the *decrease* in output going from *A* to *C* ($-MP_K \Delta K$) equals the *increase* in output going from *C* to *B* ($MP_L \Delta L$). Thus $\Delta y = MP_L \Delta L + MP_K \Delta K = 0$.

movement from *C* to *B*, in which only *L* changes by an amount ΔL. The output change from *A* to *C* is approximately the marginal product of capital, evaluated at *A*, times the loss of capital, ΔK, or $f_K \Delta K$ In going from *C* to *B*, since labor is being added, the gain in output is approximately the marginal product of labor (evaluated at *B*) times the gain in labor, or $f_L \Delta L$. Since output is unchanged, by definition of an isoquant, from *A* to *B*, these quantities must add to 0, or

$$f_L \Delta L + f_K \Delta K = 0 \qquad (3\text{-}29)$$

In the limit, as points *A* and *B* are brought closer and closer together, so that ΔL and $\Delta K \to 0$, Eq. (3-29) is simply an expression that the total differential of $y = f(L, K)$ equals 0, since *y* is unchanged, or

$$dy = f_L \, dL + f_K \, dK = 0 \qquad (3\text{-}30)$$

Now if and only if *K* can be expressed as a function of *L* or $K = K(L)$, as it always can if the isoquant is not vertical, then the total differential may be divided through by dL, yielding

$$f_L + f_K \frac{dK}{dL} = 0$$

or

$$\frac{dK}{dL} = -\frac{f_L}{f_K}$$

Thus Eq. (3-28), for production functions, measures the willingness of firms to substitute labor for capital, since it measures the ratio of the benefits of the additional labor, f_L, to the output lost due to using less capital, f_K.

   In the theory of the consumer, the level curves of a utility function $U = U(x_1, x_2)$, the indifference curves, can be similarly analyzed. The slope of an indifference curve, which expresses the willingness of a consumer to make exchanges, is based on the ratio of perceived gains and losses from such an exchange. Following the above analysis, this slope, or exchange rate, dx_2/dx_1, is equal to $-U_1/U_2$, the ratio of marginal utility of good 1 to good 2. This ratio, since it expresses an evaluation of giving up some x_2 (a loss of $U_2 dx_2$) in order to obtain some x_1 (a gain of $U_1 dx_1$) is called the marginal rate of substitution of x_1 for x_2. Since along an indifference curve $dU = 0$, $U_2 dx_2 = -U_1 dx_1$. Assuming $x_2 = x_2(x_1)$ is well defined, $dx_2/dx_1 = -U_1/U_2$, the ratio of perceived gains to losses, at the margin.

Convexity of the Level Curves

From the formula $dx_2/dx_1 = -f_1/f_2$, if the first partials are both positive, the level curves must be negatively sloped. In production theory, if the marginal products of each factor input are positive, then the isoquants will have a negative slope. An analogous statement concerning the marginal utilities and indifference curves holds for the consumer. Simply stated, a movement to the "northeast" from any factor input combination, say, involves more of both factors. If the marginal products are positive, this must yield an increase in output, and, hence, the new point cannot lie along the same isoquant as the old. The willingness of consumers to make trade-offs—that is, to give up some of one good in order to get more of another good—is evidence that the level curves of utility function (the indifference curves) are negatively sloped. If they were positively sloped, consumers would have to be bribed by one good in order to consume some other good; indeed, one of the "goods" would really be a "bad," yielding negative utility at the margin.

However, in addition to asserting a negative slope of these level curves, economists also insist that these curves are "convex to the origin," as shown in Fig. 3-1.[†] Why do economists believe this, and how can we represent this convexity mathematically? Strict convexity of these level curves to the origin is a statement that the marginal value of either good (or factor) declines along that curve, as more of that good or factor is obtained, relative to the other. As x_1 is increased, say, the ratio $-f_1/f_2$ declines in absolute value, meaning that the benefits associated with having greater x_1, that is, f_1, are declining relative to the benefits of having some more x_2, measured by f_2 at the margin. The reason why economists believe this to be empirically correct is that the opposite assumption would imply that consumers would spend all of their income on one good, or that firms would hire only one factor of production. After all, if the marginal benefits of having x_1 rose the more x_1 one had, why would a person ever stop purchasing x_1 in favor of x_2 (assuming it was worthwhile to purchase some x_1 in the first place)? We are assuming that the consumer or firm is a sufficiently small part of the market to have a negligible effect on the price of x_1. Convexity

---

[†]The phrase "convex to the origin" is imprecise; the correct characterization is that the utility function is strictly increasing and *quasi-concave*. In two dimensions, this yields the familiar shape described previously. We shall define and explore such functions in Chap. 6.

of the level curves is asserted because it is the only assertion about preferences or technology that is consistent with the simultaneous use of several goods or inputs, i.e., with the decision to *stop* utilizing some economic good at some point short of exhaustion of one's entire wealth.

Mathematically, convexity of the level curves can be represented, in two-dimensional space, by considering the curve $x_2 = x_2(x_1)$, the explicit function of the level curve. The negative slope of this curve is indicated by $dx_2/dx_1 < 0$; convexity by $d^2x_2/dx_1^2 > 0$. The positive second derivative means that the slope dx_2/dx_1 is increasing as x_1 increases, and this is precisely what is indicated by the level curves in Fig. 3-1. As x_1 (or L, there) increases, the slope becomes less and less negative, i.e., it increases. How do we express d^2x_2/dx_1^2 in terms of the partials of $f(x_1,x_2)$, from which the level curve is derived? As was seen before,

$$\frac{dx_2}{dx_1} = -\frac{f_1(x_1,x_2(x_1))}{f_2(x_1,x_2(x_1))} \tag{3-31}$$

Note, however, that we have explicitly indicated the independent variables x_1 and x_2 with the functional dependence of x_2 on x_1 also explicitly shown. To find d^2x_2/dx_1^2, we must differentiate the right-hand side of (3–31), using the quotient rule, and using the chain rule in the numerator and denominator. Hence,

$$\frac{d^2x_2}{dx_1^2} = -\left\{ f_2\frac{d}{dx_1}[f_1(x_1,x_2(x_1))] - f_1\frac{d}{dx_1}[f_2(x_1,x_2(x_1))] \right\}\frac{1}{f_2^2}$$

$$= -\left[f_2\left(\frac{\partial f_1}{\partial x_1}\frac{dx_1}{dx_1} + \frac{\partial f_1}{\partial x_2}\frac{dx_2}{dx_1}\right) - f_1\left(\frac{\partial f_2}{\partial x_1}\frac{dx_1}{dx_1} + \frac{\partial f_2}{\partial x_2}\frac{dx_2}{dx_1}\right) \right]\frac{1}{f_2^2}$$

$$= -\left[f_2\left(f_{11} + f_{12}\frac{dx_2}{dx_1}\right) - f_1\left(f_{21} + f_{22}\frac{dx_2}{dx_1}\right) \right]\frac{1}{f_2^2}$$

However, $dx_2/dx_1 = -f_1/f_2$. Substituting this into the last expression, and noting that $f_{12} = f_{21}$,

$$\frac{d^2x_2}{dx_1^2} = \left(-f_2 f_{11} + 2f_1 f_{12} - \frac{f_1^2 f_{22}}{f_2} \right)\frac{1}{f_2^2}$$

or

$$\frac{d^2x_2}{dx_1^2} = (-f_2^2 f_{11} + 2f_1 f_2 f_{12} - f_1^2 f_{22})\frac{1}{f_2^3} \tag{3-32}$$

Note that convexity of the level curve depends in a rather complicated manner on the first and second partials of $f(x_1,x_2)$. We shall have more to say about this expression and how it is generalized to more than two variables in Chap. 6. But note the following: Suppose $y = f(x_1,x_2)$ is a utility function. Then convexity of the indifference curves in no way implies, or is implied by, "diminishing marginal utility," that is, $f_{11} < 0$, $f_{22} < 0$. There is a cross effect f_{12} that must also be considered, and which can outweigh the effects, positive or negative, of the second partials f_{11} and f_{22}. Hence, diminishing marginal utility and convexity of indifference curves are two entirely independent concepts. And that is how it must be: Convexity of an indifference curve relates to how marginal evaluations change *holding utility* (the dependent variable) *constant*. The concept of diminishing marginal utility refers to changes in total utilities, i.e., movements from one indifference level to another. In addition, these changes in utility from one level curve to another have no *quantitative* significance; they merely ordinally rank the desirability of consumption bundles. We shall defer further discussions of these matters to Chap. 10, Utility Theory; it is hoped, however, that the student will understand the motivations for considering the mathematical tools developed.

PROBLEMS

1. Consider the following three utility functions:
   (i) $U = x_1 x_2$ (ii) $V = x_1^2 x_2^2$ (iii) $W = \log x_1 + \log x_2$
   (a) Find the marginal utilities of x_1 and x_2 for each utility function.
   (b) Find the rates of change of marginal utility of one good with respect to a change in consumption of the other good for each utility function. Verify that, for these functions, the change in the marginal utility of one good due to a change in the other good is the same, no matter which good is chosen first.
   (c) Find the marginal rate of substitution of x_1 for x_2 for each utility function, and show that they are all identical.
   (d) From the preceding parts of this problem, which value, that derived in (b) or in (c), would you expect to play a positive role in the theory of consumer behavior?
2. Consider the two utility functions
   (i) $U = x_1 e^{x_2}$ (ii) $V = x_2 + \log x_1$
   (a) Answer the same questions as in Prob. 1.
   (b) Verify that three of the four second partials of V are identically 0, whereas for U, those three are all $\neq 0$. Can it be that these two utility functions nonetheless imply identical behavior on the part of the consumer? (*Answer:* Yes! *Moral:* Beware of rate of change of marginal utilities.)
3. Consider the production function $y = L^\alpha K^{1-\alpha}$; where L = labor, K = capital, y = output, and α is restricted to the values $0 < \alpha < 1$. (This type of production function is called *Cobb-Douglas.*)
   (a) Find the marginal products of labor and capital, MP_L and MP_K, respectively.
   (b) Find the rates of change of these marginal products due to changes in both labor and capital. Verify that the rate of change of MP_L with respect to K is the same as that of MP_K with respect to L.
   (c) Does the law of diminishing marginal productivity hold for this production function?
4. For the production function in Prob. 3, show that $f_L L + f_K K \equiv y$. (This is an example of Euler's theorem, which will be explored later.)
5. The theorem on invariance of second partials to the order of differentiation breaks down when the second partials are not continuous. Those students who know what *continuous* means to a mathematician should try to make up a function whose second partials *exist* but are not continuous.

6. Let $y = L^\alpha K^{1-\alpha}$ represent society's production function. Suppose L and K both grow at constant, though different, rates, i.e., let $L = L_0 e^{nt}$, $K = K_0 e^{mt}$, where t represents "time." Find dy/dt by direct substitution and by the chain rule.

7. Let $U = f(x_1, x_2)$ be a utility function, and let $V(x_1, x_2) = F(U)$, where $F'(U) > 0$. (V is a monotonic transformation of U.)
   (a) Show that $V_1/V_2 = U_1/U_2$.
   (b) Find V_{ij} in terms of U_{ij}, $i, j = 1, 2$. Show that in general U_{ij} and V_{ij} need not have the same sign.

8. Consider the utility function $U = x_1^{1/3} x_2^{2/3}$. The demand curves associated with U are $x_1 = M/3p_1$, $x_2 = 2M/3p_2$, as will be shown later. Find the rates of change of U with respect to changes in each price and money income. Do the signs of these expressions agree with your intuition?

9. Let $y = f(x_1, x_2) \equiv g(x_1 - x_2)$. Let $u = x_1 - x_2$. Show that

$$\partial y/\partial u \equiv \partial y/\partial x_1 \equiv -\partial y/\partial x_2, \partial^2 y/\partial u^2 \equiv \partial^2 y/\partial x_1^2 \equiv \partial^2 y/\partial x_2^2.$$

3.7 HOMOGENEOUS FUNCTIONS AND EULER'S THEOREM

In order to efficiently study the structure of many important economic models, it is necessary to first discuss an important class of functions known as *homogeneous* functions. The interest in these functions arose from a problem in the economic theory of distribution. The development of marginal productivity theory by Marshall and others led to the conclusion that factors of production would be paid the value of their marginal products. (This will be studied in the next and subsequent chapters in more detail.) Roughly speaking, factors would be hired until their contribution to the output of the firm just equaled the cost of acquiring additional units of that factor. Letting $y = f(x_1, x_2)$ be the firm's production function, and letting w_i denote the wage of factor x_i and p the price of the firm's output, the rule developed was that

$$p\text{MP}_i = pf_i = w_i$$

where $f_i = \partial f/\partial x_i$. But this analysis was developed in a "partial equilibrium" framework; that is, each factor was analyzed independently. The question then arose, how is it possible to be sure that the firm was capable of making these payments to both factors? All factor payments had to be derived from the output produced by the firm. Would enough output be produced (or perhaps would too much be produced, leaving the excess unclaimed) to be able to pay each unit of each factor the value of its marginal product?

A theorem developed by the great Swiss mathematician Euler (pronounced "Oiler") came to the rescue of this analysis. (It leads to other problems, but those will be deferred.) It turns out that if the production function exhibits constant returns to scale, then the sum of the factor payments will identically equal total output. Mathematically, if each factor x_i is paid $w_i = pf_i$, then the total payment to all x_i is $w_i x_i = pf_i x_i$. Total payment to both factors is thus

$$pf_1 x_1 + pf_2 x_2 = p(f_1 x_1 + f_2 x_2)$$

But, as we shall see, constant returns to scale production functions have the convenient property that, identically,

$$f_1 x_1 + f_2 x_2 \equiv y = f(x_1, x_2)$$

Hence, in this case,

$$w_1 x_1 + w_2 x_2 = p f_1 x_1 + p f_2 x_2 = p(f_1 x_1 + f_2 x_2) = py$$

or, total costs identically equal total revenues, and the product of the firm is exactly "exhausted" in making payments to all the factors.

How is the feature of *constant returns to scale* characterized? This means that if each factor is increased by the same proportion, output will increase by a like proportion. Mathematically, a production function $y = f(x_1, \ldots, x_n)$ exhibits constant returns to scale if

$$f(tx_1, \ldots, tx_n) \equiv tf(x_1, \ldots, x_n) \tag{3-33}$$

Note the identity sign: this proportionality of output and inputs must hold for all x_i's and all t. If, for example, all inputs are doubled, output will double, starting at any input combination.

The relation (3-33) is a special case of the more general mathematical notion of homogeneity of functions.

> **Definition.** A function $f(x_1, \ldots, x_n)$ is said to be homogeneous of degree r if, and only if
>
> $$f(tx_1, \ldots, tx_n) \equiv t^r f(x_1, \ldots, x_n) \tag{3-34}$$

That is, changing all arguments of the function by the same proportion t results in a change in the value of the function by an amount t^r, identically. Note again the identity sign—this is not an equation that holds only at one or a few points; the above relation is to hold for all t, $x_1, \ldots, x_n$. Constant returns to scale is the special case where a production function is homogeneous of degree one. Homogeneity of degree one is often called *linear homogeneity*.

> **Example 1.** Consider the very famous Cobb-Douglas production function, $y = L^\alpha K^{1-\alpha} = f(L, K)$, where $L = $ labor, $K = $ capital. This production function is homogeneous of degree one; i.e., it exhibits constant returns to scale. Suppose labor and capital are changed by some factor t. Then,
>
> $$f(tL, tK) \equiv (tL)^\alpha (tK)^{1-\alpha} \equiv t^\alpha L^\alpha t^{1-\alpha} K^{1-\alpha}$$
>
> $$\equiv t^{\alpha + (1-\alpha)} L^\alpha K^{1-\alpha} \equiv tL^\alpha K^{1-\alpha} \equiv tf(L, K)$$

Output $f(L, K)$ is affected in exactly the same proportion, t, as are both inputs.

Consider now another important area in which the notion of homogeneity arises. In the theory of the consumer (also to be discussed later), individuals are presumed to possess demand functions for the goods and services they consume. If $p_1, \ldots, p_n$ represents the money prices of the goods $x_1, \ldots, x_n$ that a person actually consumes, and if M represents the consumer's money income, the ordinary demand curves are representable as

$$x_i = x_i^*(p_1, \ldots, p_n, M) \tag{3-35}$$

That is, the quantity consumed of any good x_i depends on its price p_i, all other relevant prices, and money income, M.

How would we expect the consumer to react to a proportionate change in *all* prices, with the same proportionate change in his or her money income? Although a formal proof must wait until a later chapter, we should expect *no change* in consumption under these conditions. Economists (for good reason) in general assert that only *relative* price changes, not absolute price changes matter in consumers' decisions.

What is being asserted here, mathematically? We are asserting homogeneity of degree zero of the above demand equations, i.e.,

$$x_i^*(tp_1, \ldots, tp_n, tM) \equiv t^0 x_i^*(p_1, \ldots, p_n, M) \equiv x_i^*(p_1, \ldots, p_n, M)$$

The functional value is to be unchanged by proportionate change in all the independent variables; this is precisely homogeneity of degree zero. The demands for goods and services are not to depend on the *absolute* levels of prices and income.[†] The theoretical reasons for asserting this proposition will become clearer in later chapters; our purpose here is only to illustrate and motivate the usefulness of the concept of homogeneity of functions.

Consider now the Cobb-Douglas production function again, $y = L^\alpha K^{1-\alpha} \equiv f(L, K)$. The marginal products of labor and capital are, respectively,

$$\mathrm{MP}_L = f_L = \alpha L^{\alpha-1} K^{1-\alpha} = \alpha \left(\frac{K}{L}\right)^{1-\alpha}$$

$$\mathrm{MP}_K = f_K = (1-\alpha) L^\alpha K^{-\alpha} = (1-\alpha)\left(\frac{K}{L}\right)^{-\alpha}$$

These marginal products exhibit a feature worth noting: They can be written as functions of the *ratios* of the two inputs. They are independent of the absolute value of either input. Only their proportion to one another counts.

Because of this dependence only on ratios, the marginal products of the Cobb-Douglas function are homogeneous of degree zero:

$$\mathrm{MP}_L(tL, tK) = \alpha \left(\frac{tK}{tL}\right)^{1-\alpha} = \alpha \left(\frac{K}{L}\right)^{1-\alpha} = \mathrm{MP}_L(L, K)$$

[†]There was a time, in the macroeconomics literature, when this homogeneity of demand functions was denied, under the name "money illusion." It was asserted that a completely neutral inflation would lead an economy out of depression; that even though people were not in fact richer, a higher money income (together with proportionately higher money prices) would somehow make people "feel" richer, increasing their consumption expenditures. This line of argument has been largely abandoned.

Similarly,

$$\text{MP}_K(tL,tK) = (1-\alpha)\left(\frac{tK}{tL}\right)^{-\alpha} = (1-\alpha)\left(\frac{K}{L}\right)^{-\alpha} = \text{MP}_K(L,K)$$

If labor and capital are changed, by the same proportion, say they are both doubled, the marginal products of labor and capital will be unaffected. Geometrically, changing each input by the same proportion means moving along a ray out of the origin, through the original point. At every point along any such ray, the marginal products of the Cobb-Douglas production function (and others?) are the same.

To what extent, if any, are these results peculiar to the Cobb-Douglas functions; i.e., to what extent do other functions exhibit the same or similar properties? Consider first any function $f(x_1, \ldots, x_n)$ that is homogeneous of degree zero. By definition,

$$f(tx_1, tx_2, \ldots, tx_n) \equiv f(x_1, x_2, \ldots, x_n)$$

Since this holds for *any* t, let $t = 1/x_1$. Then we have

$$f(x_1, x_2, \ldots, x_n) \equiv f\left(1, \frac{x_2}{x_1}, \ldots, \frac{x_n}{x_1}\right) \equiv g\left(\frac{x_2}{x_1}, \ldots, \frac{x_n}{x_1}\right)$$

Similarly, we could let $t = 1/x_i$. What the above shows is that *any* function that is homogeneous of degree zero is representable as a function of the *ratios* of the independent variables to any one such variable. Hence, that the marginal products of the Cobb-Douglas function were representable as functions of the capital-labor ratios is *not* peculiar to that production function; it will hold for any marginal product functions that are homogeneous of degree zero.

What, then, are the conditions that the marginal products be homogeneous of degree zero? The answer is given, in a more general form, by the following theorem:

Theorem 1. If $f(x_1, x_2, \ldots, x_n)$ is homogeneous of degree r, then the first partials $f_1, \ldots, f_n$ are homogeneous of degree $r-1$.

Proof. By assumption, $f(tx_1, \ldots, tx_n) \equiv t^r f(x_1, \ldots, x_n)$. Since this is an identity, it is valid to differentiate both sides with respect to x_i:

$$\frac{\partial f}{\partial(tx_i)}\frac{\partial(tx_i)}{\partial x_i} \equiv t^r \frac{\partial f}{\partial x_i}$$

However, $\partial(tx_i)/\partial x_i = t$. Dividing both sides of the identity by t therefore yields

$$\frac{\partial f}{\partial(tx_i)} \equiv t^{r-1}\frac{\partial f}{\partial x_i}$$

But this says that the function f_i, evaluated at $(tx_1, \ldots, tx_n)$ equals $t^{r-1}f_i(x_1, \ldots, x_n)$. Hence, f_i is homogeneous of degree $r-1$.

If $y = f(x_1, \ldots, x_n)$ is any production function exhibiting constant returns to scale, the marginal products are homogeneous of degree zero. That is, the marginal products are the same at every point along any ray through the origin. The Cobb-Douglas function is thus only a special case of this theorem.

Homogeneity of any degree implies that the slopes of the level curves of the function are unchanged along any ray through the origin. This can be shown as follows: Let $y = f(x_1, \ldots, x_n)$ be a production function, for example, that is homogeneous of degree r. The slope of an isoquant in the x_i, x_j plane is

$$\frac{dx_j}{dx_i} = \frac{-f_i}{f_j}$$

But

$$\frac{f_i(tx_1, \ldots, tx_n)}{f_j(tx_1, \ldots, tx_n)} \equiv \frac{t^{r-1}f_i(x_1, \ldots, x_n)}{t^{r-1}f_j(x_1, \ldots, x_n)}$$

$$\equiv \frac{f_i(x_1, \ldots, x_n)}{f_j(x_1, \ldots, x_n)}$$

Thus, the slope of any isoquant evaluated along a radial expansion of an initial point is identical to the slope at the original point. In other words, the ratios of the marginal products along any ray from the origin remain unchanged for homogeneous functions. The level curves are thus radial blowups or reductions of each other. This situation is depicted in Fig. 3-5.

The following describes a related class of production functions. Let $y = f(x_1, \ldots, x_n)$ be homogeneous of degree r, and let $z = F(y)$, where $F'(y) > 0$.

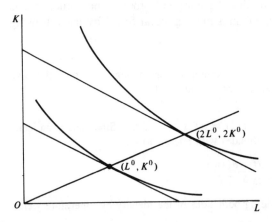

FIGURE 3-5
Invariance of the Slope of Isoquants to a Proportionate Increase in Each Factor. Consider any point (L°, K°). Suppose each input is doubled. If the production function is homogenous of any degree, the slope of the isoquant, $-f_L/f_K$, will be the same at $(2L^\circ, 2K^\circ)$ as at (L°, K°). This property is known as *homotheticity*. The most general functions that exhibit this property can be written $F(f(x_1, \ldots, x_n))$ where $f(x_1, \ldots, x_n)$ is homogenous of any degree and $F' \neq 0$.

[$F(y)$ is a monotonic transformation of y.] The function $z(x_1, \ldots, x_n)$ is called a *homothetic* function. It is easy to show that homothetic functions also preserve the property that slopes along a radial blowup remain unchanged; i.e., that the slopes of isoquants $z(tx_1, \ldots, tx_n)$ are the same as at $z(x_1, \ldots, x_n)$, and this is left to the student as an exercise. It is less than easy to show, but nonetheless true, that this is the most general class of production functions that have this property.[†]

Example 2. Consider the function $z = g(L, K) = F(y)$, where $y = L^\alpha K^{1-\alpha}$, and $F(y) = \log y$. Then

$$z = F(L^\alpha K^{1-\alpha}) \equiv \log L^\alpha K^{1-\alpha} \equiv \alpha \log L + (1 - a) \log K$$

That is, the original function $L^\alpha K^{1-\alpha}$ is transformed by the function "F," in this case "log." We note that $F'(y) = 1/y > 0$, for positive L, K. Now $L^\alpha K^{1-\alpha}$ is homogeneous of degree 1, as noted before, but $\log(L^\alpha K^{1-\alpha})$ is *not* a homogeneous function:

$$g(tL, tK) \equiv \alpha \log tL + (1 - \alpha) \log tK$$

$$\equiv \alpha(\log t + \log L) + (1 - \alpha)(\log t + \log K)$$

$$\equiv \log t + \log L^\alpha K^{1-\alpha} \neq t^r g(L, K)$$

However, $g(L, K) = \alpha \log L + (1 - \alpha) \log K$ is homothetic: The slope of a level curve is

$$\frac{-g_L}{g_K} = \frac{-\alpha/L}{(1 - \alpha)/K} = \frac{-\alpha}{1 - \alpha} \frac{K}{L}$$

As before, $-g_L/g_K$ is unaffected by changing K and L by a factor of t; the t's cancel in the expression K/L and, hence, the slope of the level curves of $\log L^\alpha K^{1-\alpha}$ are the same along any ray out of the origin. This function is *not* homogeneous but it *is* homothetic.

Suppose that instead of defining homothetic functions as $F(f(x_1, \ldots, x_n))$, where f is homogeneous of degree r, that instead we restrict f to be linearly homogeneous; i.e., homogeneous of degree 1. Though it might not seem so at first, this latter definition is just as general as the first definition; i.e., no functions are left out by so doing. The reason is that any homogeneous function of degree r can be converted to a linear homogeneous function by taking the rth root of $f(x_1, \ldots, x_n)$. Then, $[f(x_1, \ldots, x_n)]^{1/r}$ can be transformed by some function, F. Thus, since we can always consider F to be a composite of two transformations, the first of which takes the rth root of f, and the second, which operates on that, no generality is lost by defining homothetic functions as transformations of *linear* homogeneous functions.

[†]See, e.g., F. W. McElroy, "Returns to Scale, Euler's Theorem, and the Form of Production Functions," *Econometrica*, **37**(2):275–279, 1969.

Example 3. Let $y = f(x_1, x_2) = x_1 x_2$. Here, $f(x_1, x_2)$ is homogeneous of degree 2. Let

$$g(x_1, x_2) = F(f(x_1, x_2)) = \log(x_1 x_2) = \log x_1 + \log x_2$$

This function is homothetic but not homogeneous. How could $g(x_1, x_2)$ be constructed out of a *linear* homogeneous function? Let

$$g(x_1, x_2) = 2 \log(x_1 x_2)^{1/2}$$

Thus,

$$g(x_1, x_2) = 2F(\phi(f(x_1, x_2)))$$

where ϕ means "take square root" and F is log, as before. Then the same function

$$g(x_1, x_2) = \log x_1 + \log x_2$$

is constructed as a transformation of the linear homogeneous function $(x_1 x_2)^{1/2}$.

We now prove the main theorem of this section.

Theorem 2 (Euler's theorem). Suppose $f(x_1, \ldots, x_n)$ is homogeneous of degree r. Then

$$\frac{\partial f}{\partial x_1} x_1 + \cdots + \frac{\partial f}{\partial x_n} x_n \equiv r f(x_1, \ldots, x_n)$$

Note the identity sign: this is not an equation; rather, it holds for all $x_1, \ldots, x_n$. The two sides are algebraically identical.

Proof. By the definition of homogeneity,

$$f(tx_1, \ldots, tx_n) \equiv t^r f(x_1, \ldots, x_n)$$

Since this identity holds for all values of $x_1, \ldots, x_n$, and t, differentiate both sides with respect to t, using the chain rule:

$$\frac{\partial f}{\partial(tx_1)} \frac{\partial(tx_1)}{\partial t} + \cdots + \frac{\partial f}{\partial(tx_n)} \frac{\partial(tx_n)}{\partial t} \equiv r t^{r-1} f(x_1, \ldots, x_n)$$

However, $\partial(tx_i)/\partial t = x_i$, thus

$$\frac{\partial f}{\partial tx_1} x_1 + \cdots + \frac{\partial f}{\partial tx_n} x_n \equiv r t^{r-1} f(x_1, \ldots, x_n)$$

This relation is also an identity that holds for all t and all $x_1, \ldots, x_n$; in particular, it must hold for $t = 1$. Putting $t = 1$ in the preceding identity results in Euler's theorem.

An important special case of homogeneity is that of homogeneity of degree 1, also called *linear homogeneity*. In this case, $r = 1$, and thus the Euler identity yields $\sum f_i x_i \equiv f(x_1, \ldots, x_n)$. This is precisely the property that was alluded to in the beginning of this section, concerning constant returns to scale and exhaustion of the product. When $r = 1$ (linear homogeneity), Euler's theorem says that the sum of the marginal products of each factor times the level of use of that factor exactly and identically adds up to total output. Thus, marginal productivity theory is consistent with itself in that case.

Another interesting case is when $f(x_1, \ldots, x_n)$ is homogeneous of degree zero. Then, Euler's theorem yields

$$\sum f_i x_i \equiv 0$$

This formula will be used in deriving some properties of demand functions for consumers and firms, both of which exhibit this type of homogeneity.

Example 4. Consider again the Cobb-Douglas function $y = L^\alpha K^{1-\alpha} = f(L, K)$. This function is homogeneous of degree 1, i.e., $r = 1$. We have $f_L = \alpha L^{\alpha-1} K^{1-\alpha}$, $f_K = (1 - \alpha) L^\alpha K^{-\alpha}$. Then the left-hand side of the Euler identity becomes

$$f_L L + f_K K \equiv \alpha L^{\alpha-1} K^{1-\alpha} L + (1 - \alpha) L^\alpha K^{-\alpha} K$$

$$\equiv \alpha L^\alpha K^{1-\alpha} + (1 - \alpha) L^\alpha K^{1-\alpha}$$

$$\equiv (\alpha + 1 - \alpha) L^\alpha K^{1-\alpha} \equiv f(L, K)$$

Thus, $f_L L + f_K K$ is identically $L^\alpha K^{1-\alpha}$, the original production function.

Example 5. Let $y = x_1^{\alpha_1} x_2^{\alpha_2} = f(x_1, x_2)$. Then

$$f_1 = \alpha_1 x_1^{\alpha_1-1} x_2^{\alpha_2} \quad f_2 = \alpha_2 x_1^{\alpha_1} x_2^{\alpha_2-1}$$

Then

$$f_1 x_1 + f_2 x_2 \equiv \alpha_1 x_1^{\alpha_1-1} x_2^{\alpha_2} x_1 + \alpha_2 x_1^{\alpha_1} x_2^{\alpha_2-1} x_2$$

$$\equiv \alpha_1 x_1^{\alpha_1} x_2^{\alpha_2} + \alpha_2 x_1^{\alpha_1} x_2^{\alpha_2}$$

$$\equiv (\alpha_1 + \alpha_2) x_1^{\alpha_1} x_2^{\alpha_2} \equiv (\alpha_1 + \alpha_2) f(x_1, x_2)$$

This function is homogeneous of degree $\alpha_1 + \alpha_2$; hence, that multiple appears on the right-hand side of the Euler identity.

Example 6. Consider a firm with a linear homogeneous production function, $y = f(L, K)$. By Euler's theorem,

$$f_L L + f_K K \equiv y$$

Dividing by L and rearranging terms gives

$$f_K \frac{K}{L} \equiv \frac{y}{L} - f_L = \text{AP}_L - \text{MP}_L$$

Recall that if an average curve $A(x)$ is rising, then the associated marginal curve $M(x)$ lies *above* the average, i.e., $M(x) > A(x)$. Likewise, $A(x)$ is falling if and only if $M(x) < A(x)$. The equation thus says that if the average product of labor is *rising*, the marginal product of capital f_K must be *negative*. Similar manipulation shows that if the average product of capital is rising, the marginal product of labor is negative. The stage of production where AP_L is rising is called *stage I; stage II* occurs when AP_L is falling but $MP_L > 0$; $MP_L < 0$ characterizes *stage III*. The equation shows that for *linear homogeneous* production functions, stage I for labor is stage III for capital, and *vice versa*.

Example 7. Consider a two-good world with goods x_1 and x_2 which sell at prices p_1, p_2, respectively. Suppose that a consumer with money income M has the following demand function for x_1:

$$x_1 = \frac{Mp_2}{p_1^2}$$

Show that the demand for this good is unaffected by a "balanced" or neutral inflation. Show also that Euler's theorem holds for this function.

   Suppose money income M and both prices increase by the same proportion t. Then $x_1(tp_1, tp_2, tM) \equiv tM(tp_2/t^2p_1^2) \equiv Mp_2/p_1^2 \equiv x_1(p_1, p_2, M)$. Hence, the consumer is unaffected by a change in absolute prices alone; i.e., this demand function is homogeneous of degree zero. Now,

$$\frac{\partial x_1}{\partial p_1} = \frac{-2Mp_2}{p_1^3}$$

$$\frac{\partial x_1}{\partial p_2} = \frac{M}{p_1^2}$$

$$\frac{\partial x_1}{\partial M} = \frac{p_2}{p_1^2}$$

Hence,

$$\frac{\partial x_1}{\partial p_1}p_1 + \frac{\partial x_1}{\partial p_2}p_2 + \frac{\partial x_1}{\partial M}M \equiv \frac{-2Mp_2}{p_1^2} + \frac{Mp_2}{p_1^2} + \frac{Mp_2}{p_1^2} \equiv 0$$

   In many instances of dealing with homogeneous functions, what is desired is not Euler's theorem per se, but rather its converse. Suppose, for example, the product of a firm was exhausted for any input combination, i.e., we somehow knew that $\sum f_i x_i \equiv f(x_1, \ldots, x_n)$. Would this imply that the function is linear homogeneous? The answer is in the affirmative.

Theorem 3 (The converse of Euler's theorem). Suppose

$$f_1 x_1 + \cdots + f_n x_n \equiv rf(x_1, \ldots, x_n)$$

for all $x_1, \ldots, x_n$. Then

$$f(tx_1, \ldots, tx_n) \equiv t^r f(x_1, \ldots, x_n)$$

that is, $f(x_1, \ldots, x_n)$ is homogeneous of degree r.
The proof of this theorem is given in the appendix to this chapter.

PROBLEMS

1. Show that the following functions are homogeneous and verify that Euler's theorem holds.

   (a) $f(x_1, x_2) = x_1 x_2^2$

   (b) $f(x_1, x_2) = x_1 x_2 + x_2^2$

   (c) $f(x_1, x_2) = (x_1 + x_2)/(x_1^2 - 2x_2^2)$

   (d) $f(x_1, x_2) = x_1^2/(x_1 x_2 - x_2^2)$

   (e) $f(x_1, x_2) = x_1$

2. Show that the following functions are *homothetic*.

   (a) $y = \log x_1 + \log x_2$

   (b) $y = e^{x_1 x_2}$

   (c) $y = (x_1 x_2)^2 - x_1 x_2$

   (d) $y = \log (x_1 x_2) + e^{x_1 x_2}$

   (e) $y = \log (x_1^2 + x_1 x_2)^2$

3. Let $f(x_1, x_2) = A(\alpha x_1^\rho + (1 - \alpha)x_2^\rho)^{1/\rho}$. Show that $f(x_1, x_2)$ is homogeneous of degree 1. (This production function is called a constant elasticity of substitution, or CES, production function.) Its properties will be investigated in Chap. 9.

4. Let $f(x_1, x_2) = F(h(x_1, x_2))$ where h is homogeneous of degree r and $F' > 0$ (f is a homothetic function). Show that the expansion paths of f are straight lines; i.e., that the level curves of f have the same slope along any ray out of the origin.

5. Let $f(x_1, x_2)$ be homogeneous of degree 1. Show that $f_{11}x_1 + f_{12}x_2 \equiv 0$ [by considering the homogeneity of $f_1(x_1, x_2)$].

6. Let $f(x_1, \ldots, x_n)$ be homogeneous of degree r *in the first k variables only*, i.e., $f(tx_1, \ldots, tx_k, x_{k+1}, \ldots, x_n) \equiv t^r f(x_1, \ldots, x_n)$. Show that

$$\sum_{i=1}^{k} f_i x_i \equiv rf(x_1, \ldots, x_n)$$

APPENDIX

We now present some additional theorems on homogeneous functions. We begin with the converse of Euler's theorem.

Theorem 3 (The Converse of Euler's Theorem). Suppose

$$f_1 x_1 + f_2 x_2 + \cdots + f_n x_n \equiv rf(x_1, \ldots, x_n)$$

for all $x_1, \ldots, x_n$. Then $f(tx_1, \ldots, tx_n) = t^r f(x_1, \ldots, x_n)$; that is, $f(x_1, \ldots, x_n)$ is homogeneous of degree r.[†]

[†]This theorem technically holds only for positive values of t. Consider the function $f(x_1, x_2) = (x_1^2 + x_2^2)^{3/2}$. Then $f(tx_1, tx_2) = |t|^3 f(x_1, x_2)$ since the square root is always taken as positive. This type of function would satisfy the proof of Theorem 3; it however is not homogeneous for all values of t, but rather just for $t > 0$.

Proof (To save notational clutter, we shall prove the case for a function of only two independent variables, x_1, x_2. The generalization to n variables is routine.) Consider any arbitrary point (x_1^0, x_2^0). Construct the function

$$z = \phi(t) = f(tx_1^0, tx_2^0)$$

Differentiating with respect to t yields, using the chain rule,

$$\frac{dz}{dt} = \phi'(t) = x_1^0 f_1(tx_1^0, tx_2^0) + x_2^0 f_2(tx_1^0, tx_2^0) \tag{3A-1}$$

By assumption, however, applying $f_1 x_1 + f_2 x_2 \equiv rf(x_1, x_2)$ at the point (tx_1^0, tx_2^0)

$$f_1(tx_1^0, tx_2^0) tx_1^0 + f_2(tx_1^0, tx_2^0) tx_2^0 \equiv rf(tx_1^0, tx_2^0) \tag{3A-2}$$

By inspection of Eqs. (3A-1) and (3A-2)

$$t\phi'(t) \equiv rf(tx_1^0, tx_2^0) \equiv r\phi(t) \tag{3A-3}$$

Equation (3A-3) is a differential equation that is easy to solve:[†] We have $z = \phi(t)$, $\phi'(t) = dz/dt$; hence (3A-3) is equivalent to

$$t\frac{dz}{dt} \equiv rz$$

Grouping each variable,

$$\frac{dz}{z} \equiv r\frac{dt}{t}$$

Integrating both sides yields

$$\int \frac{dz}{z} \equiv r \int \frac{dt}{t} + C'$$

where C' is the constant of integration. But $\int (dz/z) \equiv \log z$, $\int (dt/t) \equiv \log t$, and letting $C' \equiv \log C$ for convenience, the solution to (3A-3) is

$$\log z \equiv r \log t + \log C$$

or

$$\equiv \log Ct^r$$

Taking antilogs, the solution of the differential Eq. (3A-3) is

$$z \equiv \phi(t) \equiv Ct^r \tag{3A-4}$$

That this is a solution to Eq. (3A-3) can be verified by substituting this expression into that differential equation. The constant of integration can be evaluated by setting $t = 1$:

[†]The interested student can review Sec. 2.13 for a review of these methods.

$$C \cdot 1^r = C = \phi(1) = f(x_1^0, x_2^0)$$

Hence, $\phi(t) = f(tx_1^0, tx_2^0) \equiv t^r f(x_1^0, x_2^0)$. But this is precisely the definition of homogeneity of degree r! Since (x_1^0, x_2^0) was any point in the $x_1 x_2$ plane, the theorem (the converse of Euler's theorem) is proven.

The following theorem discusses an easy but sometimes important special case of homogeneity—that of homogeneity of functions of only one variable.

Theorem 4. Suppose $y = f(x)$ is a function of one variable only, x. If $f(x)$ is homogeneous of degree r, then $f(x) = kx^r$. That is, the simple polynomial x^r is the only possible functional form, for one variable, which is homogeneous of degree r.

Proof. From Euler's theorem

$$f'(x)x = rf(x)$$

or

$$\frac{dy}{dx} x = ry$$

That is, all such homogeneous functions must satisfy this differential equation. We can therefore discover this class of functions by solving that equation and, it turns out, this is an easy differential equation to solve.

Collecting variables and integrating,

$$\frac{dy}{y} = r \frac{dx}{x}$$

$$\int \frac{dy}{y} = \log y, \int r \frac{dx}{x} = r \log x = \log x^r$$

Therefore,

$$\log y = \log x^r + \log k = \log k x^r$$

or, taking antilogs,

$$y = kx^r \quad \text{Q.E.D.}$$

Consider again the definition of homogeneity

$$f(tx_1, \ldots, tx_n) \equiv t^r f(x_1, \ldots, x_n)$$

Is it possible to generalize this definition, replacing t^r by some more general function of t, say $\phi(t)$? That is, are there nonhomogeneous functions $f(x_1, \ldots, x_n)$ that satisfy

$$f(tx_1, \ldots, tx_n) \equiv \phi(t) f(x_1, \ldots, x_n) \tag{3A-5}$$

In fact, there are no such functions. That is, any function $f(x_1, \ldots, x_n)$ that satisfies Eq. (3A-5) is homogeneous of some degree, as the following *lemma* shows. We will have occasion to use this result in the next theorem, which is used in a later chapter.

Lemma. Consider the class of functions $f(x_1, \ldots, x_n)$ such that

$$f(tx_1, \ldots, tx_n) \equiv \phi(t)f(x_1, \ldots, x_n) \tag{3A-5}$$

Then $\phi(t) = t^r$, for some value of r.

We will prove this for the case of two variables; the generalization to n variables is straightforward.

Proof. Differentiate equation (3A-5) with respect to t:

$$f_1(tx_1, tx_2)x_1 + f_2(tx_1, tx_2)x_2 \equiv \phi'(t)f(x_1, x_2) \tag{3A-6}$$

In fact, $\phi(t)$ can be given by setting x_1 and x_2 equal to some arbitrary numbers, e.g., $x_1 = x_2 = 1$. Then from Eq. (3A-5)

$$\phi(t) = \frac{f(t,t)}{f(1,1)}$$

and from Eq. (3A-6)

$$\phi'(t) = \frac{f_1(t,t) + f_2(t,t)}{f(1,1)}$$

Setting $t = 1$, one obtains

$$f_1x_1 + f_2x_2 \equiv \phi'(1)f \tag{3A-7}$$

Now $\phi'(1)$ is merely some constant. Whatever $\phi(t)$ is, its derivative, evaluated at $t = 1$, is some real number. But, using the converse of Euler's theorem (Theorem 3), Eq. (3A-7) says that $f(x_1, x_2)$ is homogeneous of degree $\phi'(1)$, or, $f(tx_1, tx_2) \equiv t^{\phi'(1)}f(x_1, x_2)$. Thus, no such generalization of the notion of homogeneity as indicated by Eq. (3A-5) is possible.

Consider now functions that are separable into the product of two functions, each a function of different variables:

Let $f(x_2, \ldots, x_n, y_1, \ldots, y_m) \equiv g(x_1, \ldots, x_n)h(y_1, \ldots, y_m)$. (The different variable names x and y are merely to aid in identification of the variables and the functions. There is no other significance to the distinction of x_i's and y_i's.) It will be convenient to simply designate the variables $x_1, \ldots, x_n$ simply as **x**, and $y_1, \ldots, y_m$ as **y**. This type of *vector* notation will be used occasionally throughout the book. Suppose $f(\mathbf{x}, \mathbf{y}) = g(\mathbf{x})h(\mathbf{y})$ is homogeneous of some degree r. What can be inferred about the functions $g(\mathbf{x})$ and $h(\mathbf{y})$?

Theorem 5. Let $f(\mathbf{x}, \mathbf{y}) \equiv g(\mathbf{x})h(\mathbf{y})$, where $\mathbf{x} = (x_1, \ldots, x_n)$ and $\mathbf{y} = (y_1, \ldots, y_m)$. The $f(\mathbf{x}, \mathbf{y})$ is homogeneous of degree r in $(\mathbf{x}, \mathbf{y})$ if and only if $g(\mathbf{x})$ is homogeneous of some degree p and $h(\mathbf{y})$ is homogeneous of some degree $r - p$.

Proof If $g(\mathbf{x})$ and $h(\mathbf{y})$ are homogeneous of degree p and $r - p$, respectively, then $g(t\mathbf{x}) = t^p g(\mathbf{x})$, $h(t\mathbf{y}) = t^{r-p}h(\mathbf{y})$. Then

$$f(t\mathbf{x}, t\mathbf{y}) \equiv g(t\mathbf{x})h(t\mathbf{y}) \equiv t^p g(\mathbf{x})t^{r-p}h(\mathbf{y}) \equiv t^r g(\mathbf{x})h(\mathbf{y})$$

Thus, the "if" part of the theorem is proven. Now consider the converse part. Let $f(\mathbf{x}, \mathbf{y})$ be homogeneous of some degree r. Then

$$g(t\mathbf{x})h(t\mathbf{y}) \equiv t^r g(\mathbf{x})h(\mathbf{y})$$

Rearranging,

$$\frac{g(t\mathbf{x})}{g(\mathbf{x})} \equiv t^r \frac{h(\mathbf{y})}{h(t\mathbf{y})} \tag{3A-8}$$

Now the left-hand side of Eq. (3A-8) is a function of $\mathbf{x}$ and t only; it is independent of $\mathbf{y}$. The right-hand side, similarly, is independent of $\mathbf{x}$. But then the value of $g(t\mathbf{x})/g(\mathbf{x})$ cannot depend on $\mathbf{x}$ either, for if it did, the right-hand side would change value when $\mathbf{x}$ changed, which is impossible. Hence, $g(t\mathbf{x})/g(\mathbf{x})$ is a function of t only, i.e.,

$$\frac{g(t\mathbf{x})}{g(\mathbf{x})} \equiv \phi(t)$$

Or

$$g(t\mathbf{x}) \equiv \phi(t)g(\mathbf{x}) \tag{3A-9}$$

However, by the previous lemma, Eq. (3A-9) implies that $g(\mathbf{x})$ is homogeneous of some degree p. Using the same reasoning, $h(\mathbf{y})$ must also be homogeneous of some degree q. If $g(\mathbf{x})$ and $h(\mathbf{y})$ are both homogeneous, however, and $f(\mathbf{x}, \mathbf{y})$ is homogeneous of degree r, then clearly $q = r - p$, since

$$t^r f(\mathbf{x}, \mathbf{y}) \equiv f(t\mathbf{x}, t\mathbf{y}) \equiv g(t\mathbf{x})h(t\mathbf{y}) \equiv t^p g(\mathbf{x})t^q h(\mathbf{y})$$

$$\equiv t^{p+q} g(\mathbf{x})h(\mathbf{y}) \equiv t^{p+q} f(\mathbf{x}, \mathbf{y})$$

Hence

$$r = p + q \quad \text{Q.E.D.}$$

Suppose now we are given some function $y = f(x_1, \ldots, x_n)$ that is homogeneous of degree r. Suppose some monotonic transformation is applied to $f(x_1, \ldots, x_n)$ yielding a new function $z = F(y) = F(f(x_1, \ldots, x_n)) = g(x_1, \ldots, x_n)$. Suppose this new function g is also homogeneous, of some degree s. What kinds of transformations F will produce this situation, i.e., what types of transformations will convert homogeneous functions into other homogeneous functions? The answer is given in the following theorem, a result we will have occasion to use in the sections on production functions.

Theorem 6. Let $z = g(x_1, \ldots, x_n) = F(f(x_1, \ldots, x_n)) = F(y)$, where f is homogeneous of degree r, g is homogeneous of degree s, and $F' \neq 0$. Then $F(y) = ky^{s/r}$ where k is an arbitrary constant. That is, f and g are simple powers of one another; no other transformation of a homogeneous function will result in another homogeneous function.

Proof. Clearly, if $F(y) = ky^{s/r}$, the theorem is satisfied. To show that this is the *only* functional form possible, apply Euler's theorem (again, for notational simplicity, we shall do the two-variable case only. The generalization to n variables is immediate):

$$sz = g_1x_1 + g_2x_2 = F'f_1x_1 + F'f_2x_2 = F'(y)ry$$

Rewriting,

$$\frac{s}{r}z = \frac{dz}{dy}y$$

The most general functional form, $z = F(y)$, allowed by the conditions of the theorem is the solution to this differential equation. Grouping variables,

$$\frac{dz}{z} = \frac{s}{r}\frac{dy}{y}$$

Integrating both sides yields

$$\int \frac{dz}{z} = \frac{s}{r}\int \frac{dy}{y} + \log k$$

or

$$\log z = \log y^{s/r} + \log k = \log k y^{s/r}$$

where $\log k$ is the arbitrary constant of integration. Hence, taking antilogs,

$$z = F(y) = ky^{s/r}$$

is the most general functional form of F which transforms one homogeneous function into another.

SELECTED REFERENCES

In addition to a basic calculus text, students might find the following works useful:

Allen, R. G. D.: *Mathematical Analysis for Economists,* Macmillan & Co., Ltd., London, 1938. Reprinted by St. Martin's Press.

Courant, R.: *Differential and Integral Calculus,* 2d ed., Vols. 1 and 2, Interscience Publishers, Inc., New York, 1936. This is a classic work.

CHAPTER
4

PROFIT
MAXIMIZATION

4.1 UNCONSTRAINED MAXIMA AND MINIMA: FIRST-ORDER NECESSARY CONDITIONS

Postulates of purposeful behavior lead naturally to the specification of mathematical models that involve the maximization of some function of several variables. Most often, this maximization takes place subject to test conditions specifying constraints on the movements of the variables in addition to the specifications of values of parameters. The well-known model of utility maximization is an example of such a model: the consumer is asserted to maximize a utility function subject to the condition that he or she not exceed a given budgetary expenditure. There are some important examples, however, of *unconstrained* maximization, such as the model of a profit-maximizing firm (which will be dealt with below). Since the unconstrained case is simpler, we begin the analysis there.

In models with just one independent variable, the first-order condition necessary for $y = f(x)$ to attain a stationary value is $dy/dx = f'(x) = 0$. That is, the line tangent to the curve $f(x)$ must be horizontal at the stationary point. The term *stationary point* rather than *maximum* or *minimum* is appropriate at this juncture. The property of having a horizontal tangent line is common to the functions $y = x^2$, $y = -x^2$ and $y = x^3$ at the point $x = 0$, $y = 0$. The first function has a minimum at the origin, the second, a maximum, and the third, neither. However, it is clear that if the slope of the tangent line is *not* 0 (horizontal), then the function certainly cannot have either a maximum or a minimum. Hence

$f'(x) = 0$ is a *necessary* but not sufficient condition for $y = f(x)$ to have a maximum (or minimum) value.

Suppose now that y is a function of two variables, that is, $y = f(x_1, x_2)$. What are the analogous necessary conditions for a maximum of this function? Proceeding intuitively from the case of one variable, it must necessarily be the case that at the point in question, the tangent *plane* must be horizontal. In order for the tangent plane to be horizontal, the first partials $\partial f/\partial x_1$, $\partial f/\partial x_2$ must be 0; that is, the function must be level in the x_1 and x_2 directions.

Because intuition, especially about the second-order conditions for maximization, is often unreliable, the preceding argument will now be developed more rigorously. Let $y = f(x_1, x_2)$, and suppose we wish to consider the behavior of this function at some point $\mathbf{x}^0 = (x_1^0, x_2^0)$.[†] Instead of working with the whole function, however, consider the function evaluated along any (differentiable) curve that passes through the point $\mathbf{x}^0$. The reason for doing this is that it will enable us to convert a problem in two variables to one involving one variable only, a problem we already know how to solve. All such curves can be represented parametrically by $x_1 = x_1(t)$, $x_2 = x_2(t)$, with $x_1 = x_1^0$, $x_2 = x_2^0$ at $t = 0$. That is, as t varies in value, x_1 and x_2 vary, and hence the pair $[x_1(t), x_2(t)]$, denoted $\mathbf{x}(t)$, traces out the locus of some curve in the $x_1 x_2$ plane. [Setting $x_1(0) = x_1^0$, $x_2(0) = x_2^0$ merely ensures that the curve passes through (x_1^0, x_2^0) for *some* value of t.]

Example 1. This parametric representation of a curve in the $x_1 x_2$ plane was developed in Chap. 3. Again, suppose

$$x_1 = x_1^0 + h_1 t$$

$$x_2 = x_2^0 + h_2 t$$

where h_1 and h_2 are arbitrary constants. Then these equations represent the straight lines in the $x_1 x_2$ plane which pass through (x_1^0, x_2^0). Any such line can be generated by appropriate choice of h_1 and h_2.

Example 2. Let

$$x_1 = x_1^0 + t$$

$$x_2 = x_2^0 e^t$$

This parameterization represents an exponential curve. When $t = 0$, $x_1 = x_1^0$, $x_2 = x_2^0$; hence the curve passes through (x_1^0, x_2^0).

Example 3. A parameterization that occurs frequently in the physical sciences is

$$x = a \cos \theta$$

$$y = a \sin \theta$$

[†]We will often find it convenient to use the vector notation $\mathbf{x} = (x_1, \ldots, x_n)$ wherein the single symbol $\mathbf{x}$ denotes multidimensional value.

where $0 \leq \theta \leq 2\pi$. This represents the equation of a circle in the xy plane, with radius a and center at the origin.

The function $f(x_1, x_2)$ evaluated along some differentiable curve $\mathbf{x}(t) = (x_1(t), x_2(t))$ is $y(t) = f(x_1(t), x_2(t))$. If $f(x_1, x_2)$ is to achieve a maximum value at $\mathbf{x} = \mathbf{x}^0$, the function evaluated along all such curves must necessarily have a maximum. Hence $y(t)$ must have a maximum (at $t = 0$) for all curves $\mathbf{x}(t)$. But the condition for this is simply $y'(t) = 0$. Using this chain rule the first-order conditions for a maximum are therefore

$$\frac{dy}{dt} = y'(t) = f_1 \frac{dx_1}{dt} + f_2 \frac{dx_2}{dt} = 0 \qquad (4\text{-}1)$$

However, dy/dt must be 0 for *all* curves $(x_1(t), x_2(t))$ passing through $\mathbf{x}^0$; i.e., for *all* values of dx_1/dt and dx_2/dt. That is, it must be possible to put any values of dx_1/dt, dx_2/dt into this relationship and still obtain $dy/dt = 0$. The only way this can be guaranteed is if $f_1 = f_2 = 0$. Hence a necessary condition for $f(x_1, x_2)$ to be maximized at x_1^0, x_2^0 is that the first partials of that function must be 0 at this point. The preceding conditions are, of course, only necessary conditions for y to achieve a stationary point; only the second derivative of $y(t)$ reveals whether (x_1^0, x_2^0) is in fact a maximum, a minimum, or neither.

The generalization to the n variable case is direct, and the derivation is identical to the preceding. For $y = f(x_1, x_2, \ldots, x_n)$ to be maximized at $\mathbf{x}^0 = (x_1^0, \ldots, x_n^0)$ it is necessary that all the first partial derivatives equal 0; that is, $f_i = 0$, $i = 1, \ldots, n$.

4.2 SUFFICIENT CONDITIONS FOR MAXIMA AND MINIMA: TWO VARIABLES

For functions of one variable, $y = f(x)$, a sufficient condition for $f(x)$ to have a maximum at $x = x^0$ is that, together with $f'(x^0) = 0$, $f''(x^0) < 0$. The condition $f''(x^0) < 0$ expresses the notion that the slope is decreasing, e.g., as one walked over the top of a hill, the ground would be first rising, then level at the top, then falling. Alternatively, the function is called "concave downward," or simply, concave, if $f''(x) \leq 0$. If $f(x_1, x_2)$ has a maximum at $\mathbf{x}^0$, then $y(t) = f(x_1(t), x_2(t))$ has a maximum for all curves $\mathbf{x}(t)$. Hence it must be the case that at the maximum point, $d^2y/dt^2 = y''(t) \leq 0$ for all such curves.

The issues here are considerably more subtle than the student may perceive at this point, as the next section will demonstrate. Although $y''(t) \leq 0$ is *necessary* for a maximum, it is not sufficient. By expanding $f(x_1, x_2)$ by a Taylor series for functions of two (or, more generally, n variables), it can be shown that if $y''(t) < 0$ at $t = 0$ (the maximum point), then the function $f(x_1, x_2)$ is strictly concave at (x_1^0, x_2^0). Thus, in that case, a maximum will be achieved if $f_1 = f_2 = 0$. This analysis will be presented in the appendix to this chapter.

Let us then evaluate $y''(t)$. Using the chain and product rules on Eq. (4-1),

$$y'(t) = f_1 x_1'(t) + f_2 x_2'(t)$$

one obtains (this was derived explicitly in Chap. 3)

$$\frac{d^2 y}{dt^2} = f_1 \frac{d^2 x_1}{dt^2} + f_2 \frac{d^2 x_2}{dt^2} + f_{11}\left(\frac{dx_1}{dt}\right)^2 + 2f_{12}\frac{dx_1}{dt}\frac{dx_2}{dt} + f_{22}\left(\frac{dx_2}{dt}\right)^2 \quad (4\text{-}2)$$

However, this is evaluated at $(x_1, x_2) = (x_1^0, x_2^0)$, a stationary point; hence $f_1 = f_2 = 0$. Letting $h_1 = dx_1/dt$, $h_2 = dx_2/dt$ for notational convenience, the condition that $d^2 y/dt^2 < 0$ for all curves passing through (x_1^0, x_2^0) means that

$$f_{11} h_1^2 + 2f_{12} h_1 h_2 + f_{22} h_2^2 < 0 \quad (4\text{-}3)$$

for all values of h_1 and h_2 (except $h_1 = h_2 = 0$). This inequality, since it must hold for all nontrivial h_1, h_2 (i.e., not both equal to 0), imposes restrictions on the signs and relative magnitudes of the second-order partials.

It is apparent from expression (4-3) that both f_{11} and f_{22} must be negative: Let $h_2 = 0$ and h_1 be any number and suppose f_{11} is positive. Then $d^2 y/dt^2 = f_{11} h_1^2 > 0$, violating the sufficient conditions for a maximum. Interchanging all the subscripts gives the desired restriction on f_{22}, as the formulation is completely symmetrical. Thus, in order to have $d^2 y/dt^2 < 0$ at $\mathbf{x}^0 = (x_1^0, x_2^0)$, it is necessary that

$$f_{11}(\mathbf{x}^0) < 0 \text{ and } f_{22}(\mathbf{x}^0) < 0$$

However, these conditions, which the student might have guessed at by considering the one-variable case, are *not,* by themselves, sufficient for $f(x_1, x_2)$ to have a maximum. We have yet to consider the role of the cross-partial f_{12} in this analysis. An additional restriction on the f_{ij}'s is required to ensure $d^2 y/dt^2 < 0$ for all nontrivial h_1 and h_2. It can be derived by using the technique known as *completing the square.*

Consider the expression $x^2 + 2bx$. If the term b^2 is both added and subtracted, the identity $x^2 + 2bx \equiv (x + b)^2 - b^2$ results. Take Eq. (4-3) and factor out f_{11}:

$$f_{11}\left(h_1^2 + \frac{2f_{12}h_2}{f_{11}}h_1 + \frac{f_{22}}{f_{11}}h_2^2\right) < 0$$

The first two terms in parentheses are quadratic in h_1 in the same sense as the preceding algebraic example. Completing the square in h_1 is accomplished by adding and subtracting $(f_{12}h_2/f_{11})^2$ in the parentheses. This yields

$$f_{11}\left[\left(h_1 + \frac{f_{12}h_2}{f_{11}}\right)^2 + \left(\frac{h_2}{f_{11}}\right)^2 (f_{11}f_{22} - f_{12}^2)\right] < 0 \quad (4\text{-}4)$$

Since $f_{11} < 0$, in order to guarantee $d^2 y/dt^2 < 0$, the square-bracketed term must be positive. However, the first term in the bracket is a squared term and hence is always positive anyway. In order to guarantee that $d^2 y/dt^2 < 0$ *for* *all values of h_1 and h_2*, we must also require that the second term, in particular $f_{11}f_{22} - f_{12}^2$, be positive.

To sum up, then, suppose $f(x_1, x_2)$ has a stationary point $\mathbf{x} = \mathbf{x}^0$, that is, the first-order necessary conditions for an extremum occur:

$$f_1(\mathbf{x}^0) = f_2(\mathbf{x}^0) = 0 \qquad (4\text{-}5)$$

If, in addition,

$$f_{11} < 0 \text{ and } f_{11}f_{22} - f_{12}^2 > 0 \text{ evaluated at } \mathbf{x}^0 \qquad (4\text{-}6)$$

a maximum position is assured. Note that if (4-6) is satisfied, $f_{22} < 0$ is implied. It is also important to note that condition (4-6) imposes a restriction only on the relative magnitude of f_{12}; it does not imply anything about the sign of this second partial. The sign of f_{12} is thus irrelevant in determining whether a function has a maximum or minimum.

For $f(x_1(t), x_2(t))$ to achieve a *minimum* at $\mathbf{x}^0 = (x_1^0, x_2^0)$ the same first-order conditions (4-5) must, of course, be met. The analogous sufficient second-order conditions, i.e., guaranteeing $d^2y/dt^2 > 0$, are

$$f_{11} > 0, f_{22} > 0 \text{ and } f_{11}f_{22} - f_{12}^2 > 0 \qquad (4\text{-}7)$$

where all partials are evaluated at $\mathbf{x}^0$. *Note that the term $f_{11}f_{22} - f_{12}^2$ is positive for both minima and maxima.* If this term is found to be negative, then the surface has a "saddle" shape at $\mathbf{x}^0$: it rises in one direction and falls in another, similar to the point in the center of a saddle.

One last precautionary note must be mentioned. These second-order conditions are *sufficient* conditions for a maximum or minimum; the strict inequalities (4-6) and (4-7) are *not* implied by maxima and minima. For example, the function $y = -x^4$ has a maximum at the origin, yet its second derivative is 0 there. Likewise $y = x^3$ has neither a maximum nor a minimum at $x = 0$, yet its second derivative is also 0 there. Hence, if one or more of the relations in (4-6) or (4-7) hold as *equalities*, the observer is unable at that juncture to determine the shape of the function at that point. The general rule, which will not be proved here, is if $d^2y/dt^2 = 0$ for some $\mathbf{x}(t)$, one must calculate the higher-order derivatives d^3y/dt^3, d^4y/dt^4, et cetera. Then if the first occurrence of $d^ny/dt^n < 0$ for all curves $x(t)$ is an *even* order n, then the function has a maximum (minimum, if > 0), whereas if that first occurrence happens for an odd number n, neither a maximum nor a minimum is achieved. To make matters worse, however, there are functions, for example, $y = e^{-1/x^2}$, which have a minimum, say, at some point (here, $x = 0$), and yet the derivatives of all finite orders are 0 at that point (for this function, at $x = 0$). We shall ignore all such "nonregular" situations in which the ordinary sufficient conditions for an extremum do not hold; we will confine our attention only to "regular" extrema.

It can be shown that the second-order conditions (4-6) are sufficient for a function to be concave (downward) at points other than a stationary value. Likewise, (4-7) guarantees that the function is convex (i.e., concave upward) at any point. Proof of these propositions will be deferred to the appendix.

Example 1. Suppose $f(x_1, x_2)$ has a maximum at some point. Then the sufficient second-order conditions are, again,

$$f_{11}h_1^2 + 2f_{12}h_1h_2 + f_{22}h_2^2 < 0 \tag{4-3}$$

for all nontrivial values of h_1 and h_2. Since this holds for *all* values of h_1 and h_2, suppose we let $h_1 = 1$, $h_2 = \pm 1$. Then this condition implies

$$f_{11} + f_{22} \pm 2f_{12} < 0 \tag{4-8}$$

or

$$f_{11} + f_{22} < \mp 2f_{12}$$

Since f_{11} and f_{22} are both negative,

$$|f_{11} + f_{22}| > 2|f_{12}| \tag{4-9}$$

is implied by the sufficient second-order conditions for a maximum.

Example 2. Suppose $f(x_1, x_2)$ is strictly concave at some point. The sufficient condition for concavity is again Eq. (4-3),

$$f_{11}h_1^2 + 2f_{12}h_1h_2 + f_{22}h_2^2 < 0 \tag{4-3}$$

Now let $h_1 = f_2$, $h_2 = -f_1$. Then (4-3) implies

$$f_{11}f_2^2 - 2f_{12}f_1f_2 + f_{22}f_1^2 < 0 \tag{4-10}$$

This was the condition developed in Chap. 3 [Eq. (3-32)] for the level curves to be convex to the origin. Hence concavity implies level curves having this property. The converse, however, is false.

PROBLEMS

1. For each of the following functions, find the stationary point and determine whether that point is a relative maximum, minimum, or saddle point of $f(x_1, x_2)$.
   (a) $f(x_1, x_2) = x_1^2 - 4x_1x_2 + 2x_2^2$
   (b) $f(x_1, x_2) = -4x_1 - 6x_2 + x_1^2 - x_1x_2 + 2x_2^2$
   (c) $f(x_1, x_2) = 12x_1 - 4x_2 - 2x_1^2 + 2x_1x_2 - x_2^2$
2. Using Eq. (4-3), show that the sufficient conditions for $f(x_1, x_2)$ to achieve a minimum at x^0 are the relations (4-7).
3. Consider the production function $y = L^\alpha K^\beta$. Show that this function is strictly concave (downward) for all values of L and K if $0 < \alpha < 1$, $0 < \beta < 1$ and if $\alpha + \beta < 1$. What shape does the function have for $\alpha + \beta = 1$?
4. Show that the production function $y = \log L^\alpha K^\beta$ is concave for all α, $\beta > 0$.
5. Let $y = f(x_1, x_2)$ and let $z = F(y) = F(f(x_1, x_2)) = g(x_1, x_2)$. Show that if $F' > 0$, then g has a stationary point at (x_1^0, x_2^0) when and only when f is stationary there. Under what conditions will f have a maximum when and only when g has a maximum?
6. A monopolist produces y at cost $C(y)$, and sells this output in two separated markets, producing total revenues $\text{TR}(y) = \text{TR}^1(y_1) + \text{TR}^2(y_2)$, where $y = y_1 + y_2$.
   (a) Show that the profit-maximizing monopolist will equate the marginal cost of production to the marginal revenues in each market.

(b) Assuming a regular maximum position, what conditions on the slopes of the marginal-revenue and marginal-cost curves are implied by profit-maximization?

(c) Using the equation MR $= p(1 + 1/\epsilon)$ developed in Sec. 2.7, show that a discriminating monopolist will charge a higher price in the market whose demand is less elastic.

4.3 AN EXTENDED FOOTNOTE

In the previous section, sufficient conditions for the maximization of a function of two variables were derived via an artifice that reduced the problem to one dimension, or one variable. It is true that if a function has a maximum at some point, then all curves lying in the surface depicted by that function and passing through the maximum point must themselves have a maximum at that point. In that case, therefore, $y''(t) \leq 0$ for all such curves. Various plausible-sounding converses of this proposition, however, are *not*, in general, true. For example, suppose the function $f(x_1, x_2)$ possesses a maximum when evaluated along all possible polynomial curves, for any values of the coefficients $a_1, \ldots, a_n, b_1, \ldots, b_n$, for any finite n:

$$x_1 = x_1^0 + a_1 t + a_2 t^2 + \cdots + a_n t^n$$
$$x_2 = x_2^0 + b_1 t + b_2 t^2 + \cdots + b_n t^n$$

Even if $(x_1(t), x_2(t))$ has a maximum at $t = 0$ when evaluated along this wide range of curves, the function $f(x_1, x_2)$ itself need *not* have a maximum at x_1^0, x_2^0.

To illustrate this phenomenon, suppose the curves $(x_1(t), x_2(t))$ are limited to *straight lines* passing through (x_1^0, x_2^0). That is, consider the curves in the surface $y = f(x_1, x_2)$ formed by the intersection of that surface and vertical (perpendicular to the $x_1 x_2$ plane) planes. Then it is *not* the case that if all those curves have a maximum, then the function itself has a maximum, as the following counterexample, developed by the mathematician Peano, shows: Consider the function

$$y = (x_2 - x_1^2)(x_2 - 2x_1^2)$$

depicted graphically in Fig. 4-1. This function has the value 0 along the curves $x_2 = x_1^2$, and along $x_2 = 2x_1^2$, both of which are parabolas in the $x_1 x_2$ space. In particular, $y = 0$ at the origin. The pluses and minuses shown in the diagram reflect the value of the function in the given section of the $x_1 x_2$ space. For any point below the lower parabola, $x_2 < x_1^2$ and hence $x_2 < 2x_1^2$ (the point is also below the upper parabola). Hence y is the product of two negative numbers and is thus positive. Likewise, above the upper parabola, $x_2 > 2x_1^2$, hence $x_2 > x_1^2$ and therefore $y = (+)(+) > 0$. In between the two parabolas, $x_2 > x_1^2$ but $x_2 < 2x_1^2$, hence $y = (+)(-) < 0$. Note how that any neighborhood containing the origin possesses both positive and negative values of y. Therefore, the function cannot attain either a maximum or minimum at the origin. That is, since some values are greater than 0 and some less than 0 around the origin, neither a maximum nor minimum can be achieved there. Rather, something analogous to a saddle

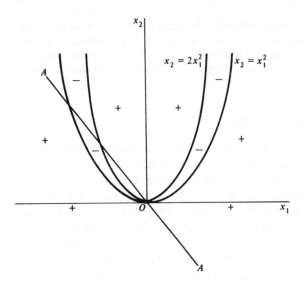

The function $y = (x_2 - 2x_1{}^2)(x_2 - x_1{}^2)$. This function exhibits the interesting property that when evaluated along all straight lines through the origin, the function has a minimum (of 0). However, the function itself clearly does *not* have either a minimum or a maximum at the origin since in any neighborhood of the origin, this function takes on both positive and negative values.

point occurs. However, consider the function evaluated along any straight line through the origin, e.g., line *AA* in Fig. 4-1. After passing through the upper parabola, the function, along this line, changes from positive to 0 (at the origin) to positive again, implying that the origin is a minimum value of y, *evaluated along this* or any such line. However, the function itself, as we just have shown, does *not* have a minimum at the origin. Thus it is *not* the case that if a function attains a maximum (or minimum) evaluated along all straight lines going through some point that the function necessarily attains a maximum (minimum) there. It is possible to construct functions such that even if $y(t)$ has a maximum for all polynomial curves in the $x_1 x_2$ plane, the function itself does not have a maximum.[†] Exactly what class of functions $\mathbf{x}(t)$ for which a valid converse is obtainable seems to be unresolved.

4.4 AN APPLICATION OF MAXIMIZING BEHAVIOR: THE PROFIT-MAXIMIZING FIRM

The tools developed in the previous sections will now be applied to analyze the comparative statics of a profit-maximizing firm that sells its output y at constant unit price p, and purchases two inputs x_1 and x_2 at constant unit factor prices

---

[†]See H. Hancock, *Theory of Maxima and Minima,* Dover Publications, Inc., New York, 1960.

w_1 and w_2, respectively. That is, the firm in question is the textbook prototype, facing competitive input and output markets. The production process of the firm will be summarized by the *production function,* $y = f(x_1, x_2)$. The production function will be interpreted here as a technological statement of the maximum output that can be obtained through the combining of two inputs, or factors, x_1 and x_2. The objective function of this firm is total revenue minus total cost *(profits)*.[†]

We assert that the firm maximizes this function, i.e.,
maximize

$$\pi = pf(x_1, x_2) - w_1 x_1 - w_2 x_2 \tag{4-11}$$

The test conditions of this model are the particular values of the input prices w_1, w_2, and output price p. The objective of the model is to be able to state refutable propositions concerning observable behavior, e.g., changes in the levels of inputs used, as the test conditions change, i.e., as factor or output prices change.

The first-order conditions for profit-maximization are

$$\pi_1 = \frac{\partial \pi}{\partial x_1} = pf_1 - w_1 = 0 \tag{4-12a}$$

and

$$\pi_2 = \frac{\partial \pi}{\partial x_2} = pf_2 - w_2 = 0 \tag{4-12b}$$

Sufficient conditions for a maximum position are

$$\pi_{11} < 0 \quad \pi_{22} < 0 \quad \text{and} \quad \pi_{11}\pi_{22} - \pi_{12}^2 > 0 \tag{4-13}$$

Since $\pi_{ij} = pf_{ij}$, these second-order conditions reduce to

$$f_{11} < 0 \quad f_{22} < 0 \tag{4-14}$$

and

$$f_{11}f_{22} - f_{12}^2 > 0 \tag{4-15}$$

What is the economic interpretation of these conditions? Equations (4-12) say that a profit-maximizing firm will employ resources up to the point where the marginal contribution of each factor to producing revenues, pf_i, the value of the marginal

---

[†]The student should be wary of the terms *firm* and *profits*. With regard to the former, the concept has not been defined here, and there is in fact, considerable debate in the profession as to exactly what firms are, why they exist at all, and what their boundaries are. With regard to profits, the model leaves unspecified who has claims to the supposed excess of revenues over cost. Alternatively, if x_1 and x_2 are indeed the only two factors, in whose interest is it to maximize the expression in Eq. (4-11)? In spite of these shortcomings, since the model does yield refutable hypotheses, as we shall see shortly, it is potentially interesting. It might be referred to as a "black box" theory of the firm.

product of factor i, is equal to the cost of acquiring additional units of that factor, w_i. These are *necessarily* implied by profit-maximization; however to ensure that the resulting factor employment pertains to *maximum* rather than minimum profits, conditions (4-14) and (4-15) are needed. Conditions (4-14) are statements of the law of diminishing returns. That such a law is involved is easily seen. [Remember, though, conditions (4-13) are sufficient, not necessary—a maximum position is consistent with these relations holding as equalities.] Assuming it was worthwhile to hire one unit of that factor in the first place, if the value of the marginal product of that factor was increasing, the firm would hire that factor without bound, since the input would be generating more income than it was getting paid. Hence a finite maximum position is inconsistent with increasing marginal productivity.

However, diminishing marginal productivity in each factor does *not*, by itself, guarantee that a maximum profit position will be achieved. Condition (4-15) is also required. This relation, though less intuitive than diminishing marginal productivity, arises from the fact that changes in one factor affect the marginal products of the other factors as well as its own marginal product, and the overall effect on all marginal products must be akin to diminishing marginal productivity. Suppose, for example, that $f_{12} = f_{21} = \partial MP_1/\partial x_2 = \partial MP_2/\partial x_1$ is very large, in absolute terms, relative to $f_{11} = \partial MP_1/\partial x_1$ and $f_{22} = \partial MP_2/\partial x_2$. That is, suppose a change in x_1, say, affects the marginal product of factor 2 much more than the marginal product of factor 1. Then consider the consequences of an increase of one unit of x_1. In Fig. 4-2, if $f_{12} = f_{21} > 0$, MP_1 initially declines; however MP_2 shifts upward by a considerable amount, causing the firm to purchase many additional units of x_2. However, these additional units of x_2 have an effect on MP_1. Since $f_{12} = \partial MP_1/\partial x_2 > 0$, MP_1 also shifts up, by a relatively large amount. The final result, then, is that an increase in x_1 can lead to an *increase* in MP_1, if the cross-effects are large enough. Hence the original factor

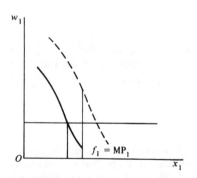
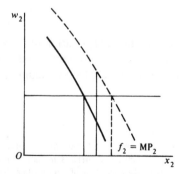

FIGURE 4-2

The law of diminishing returns. The fact that $f_{11} < 0$, $f_{22} < 0$ alone is *not* sufficient to guarantee a finite profit-maximum position. The cross-effects between the two factors must be considered. If x_1 is increased, MP_2 might shift out, say, a great deal, shifting MP_1 out resulting in a net *increase* in MP_1 even though $f_{11} = \partial MP_1/\partial x_1 < 0$. This will occur if f_{12} is large. Hence the condition $f_{11}f_{12} - f_{22}^2 \geq 0$ is also needed to achieve a finite profit maximum.

employment levels, though characterized by diminishing marginal productivity in each factor, do not nonetheless describe a profit-maximum position, since it is clearly profitable in this case to increase the usage of both x_1 and x_2 together. In the case where f_{12} is negative and large relative to f_{11} and f_{22}, the analysis is similar. An increase in x_1 causes a relatively large fall in MP_2, a fall in x_2 and hence a relatively large *increase* in MP_1. (Remember, $\partial MP_1 / \partial x_2 < 0$!) In this case, increasing one factor and decreasing the other (together) will increase profits.

Let us return now to the marginal relations (4-12). The purpose of formulating this model is not simply to assert the implied marginal reasoning; that is a rather sterile endeavor. The purpose of this analysis is to be able to formulate refutable hypotheses as to how firms react to changes in the parameters they face; in particular, in this case, to changes in factor and output prices. To this end, we now consider the comparative statics of this model.

The first-order conditions in complete form are

$$pf_1(x_1, x_2) - w_1 = 0$$

$$pf_2(x_1, x_2) - w_2 = 0$$

These are two implicit relations in essentially five unknowns: x_1, x_2, w_1, w_2, and p. Under the "right" conditions (to be discussed in what follows) it is possible to solve for two of these values in terms of the other three. In particular, we can solve for the choice functions

$$x_1 = x_1^*(w_1, w_2, p) \tag{4-16a}$$

and

$$x_2 = x_2^*(w_1, w_2, p) \tag{4-16b}$$

Equations (4-16) represent the factor demand curves. These relations indicate the amount of each factor that will be hired, according to this model, as a function of the factor prices and product price; they are the choice functions of this model. Assuming that it is possible to solve for Eqs. (4-16), it becomes meaningful to ask questions regarding the signs of the following six partial derivatives, which comprise the comparative statics of the profit-maximizing model:

$$\frac{\partial x_1^*}{\partial w_1} \quad \frac{\partial x_1^*}{\partial w_2} \quad \frac{\partial x_1^*}{\partial p} \quad \frac{\partial x_2^*}{\partial w_1} \quad \frac{\partial x_2^*}{\partial w_2} \quad \frac{\partial x_2^*}{\partial p} \tag{4-17}$$

These partials indicate the marginal changes in factor employment due to given price changes. It is important to keep in mind that in order to write down these relations and interpret them in some meaningful fashion, the explicit functions x_i^* must be well defined. Also note that the preceding factor demand curves are not the marginal product curves. The marginal product functions f_1 and f_2 are expressed in terms of the factor inputs, while the factor demand curves are expressed in terms of prices, and dependent upon the behavioral assertion of the model.

Substituting Eqs. (4-16) back into Eqs. (4-12) produces the following *identities:*

$$pf_1(x_1^*(w_1, w_2, p), x_2^*(w_1, w_2, p)) - w_1 \equiv 0 \qquad (4\text{-}18a)$$

and

$$pf_2(x_1^*(w_1, w_2, p), x_2^*(w_1, w_2, p)) - w_2 \equiv 0 \qquad (4\text{-}18b)$$

Recall the monopolist tax example of Chap. 1, where the solution $x = x^*(t)$ of the first-order relation (which set marginal revenue equal to marginal cost plus the tax) was then substituted back into that relation, yielding an *identity* in the tax rate t. For the same reasons, the relations (4-18) are identities in the prices w_1, w_2, and p. The factor demand functions x_1^* and x_2^* are precisely those levels of x_1 and x_2 that the entrepreneur employs to keep the value of the marginal products of each factor equal to the wage of each factor, for any prices.

Hence, the assertion that the firm *always* obeys Eqs. (4-12), for any prices converts those equations to the identities (4-18). Being identities, the relations (4-18) can be differentiated implicitly with respect to the various prices, producing relations that allow solutions for the partial derivatives (4-17). The general procedure is exactly the same as in the monopolist example. However, in this example, two first-order relations are present instead of only one, and that fact makes the algebra more difficult.

Before we do the differentiation, note that if the firm's production functions were in fact known, then one could actually solve for the factor-demand curves explicitly. In that case we could know the *total* quantities involved in this model, a happy state of affairs. The factor-demand curves (4-16) could be differentiated directly to yield the partial derivatives (4-17). However, the economist is not likely to have this much information. Nonetheless, it is still possible to state refutable hypotheses concerning *marginal* quantities, through implicit differentiation of the identities (4-18).

Differentiating (4-18a) and (4-18b) partially, with respect to w_1, using the chain rule (remembering that f_1 is a function of x_1 and x_2, which are in turn functions of w_1, w_2, and p, etc.),

$$p\frac{\partial f_1}{\partial x_1}\frac{\partial x_1^*}{\partial w_1} + p\frac{\partial f_1}{\partial x_2}\frac{\partial x_2^*}{\partial w_1} - 1 \equiv 0$$

$$p\frac{\partial f_2}{\partial x_1}\frac{\partial x_1^*}{\partial w_1} + p\frac{\partial f_2}{\partial x_2}\frac{\partial x_2^*}{\partial w_1} \equiv 0$$

Using subscript notation, these can be written

$$pf_{11}\frac{\partial x_1^*}{\partial w_1} + pf_{12}\frac{\partial x_2^*}{\partial w_1} \equiv 1 \qquad (4\text{-}19a)$$

$$pf_{21}\frac{\partial x_1^*}{\partial w_1} + pf_{22}\frac{\partial x_2^*}{\partial w_1} \equiv 0 \qquad (4\text{-}19b)$$

Although the identities (4-19) look complicated, they are a good deal simpler in form than (4-18). Whereas the first-order relations (4-18) are in general complicated algebraic expressions, (4-19a) and (4-19b) are simple *linear* relations in the unknowns $\partial x_1^*/\partial w_1$ and $\partial x_2^*/\partial w_1$. That is, (4-19a) and (4-19b) are of the same form as the elementary system of two simultaneous linear equations in two unknowns. The coefficients of the unknowns are the functions pf_{11}, pf_{12}, et cetera, but the system is still simple in that no products, or squares, of the terms $\partial x_1^*/\partial w_1$, et cetera, are involved. And this is fortunate, since the goal of this analysis is to solve for those terms, i.e., find expressions for the partials of the form $\partial x_i^*/\partial w_j$.

To solve for $\partial x_1^*/\partial w_1$, for example, multiply (4-19a) by f_{22} and (4-19b) by f_{12}, and subtract (4-19b) from (4-19a). This yields, after some factoring (remember that $f_{12} = f_{21}$),[†]

$$p(f_{11}f_{22} - f_{12}^2)\frac{\partial x_1^*}{\partial w_1} = f_{22}$$

Now, if $f_{11}f_{22} - f_{12}^2 \neq 0$, that term can be divided on both sides, yielding

$$\frac{\partial x_1^*}{\partial w_1} = \frac{f_{22}}{p(f_{11}f_{22} - f_{12}^2)} \qquad (4\text{-}20a)$$

In like fashion, one obtains

$$\frac{\partial x_2^*}{\partial w_1} = \frac{-f_{21}}{p(f_{11}f_{22} - f_{12}^2)} \qquad (4\text{-}20b)$$

To obtain the responses of the firm to changes in w_2, differentiate Eqs. (4-18) with respect to w_2. Noting that w_2 enters only the second equation explicitly, the system of comparative statics relations becomes

$$pf_{11}\frac{\partial x_1^*}{\partial w_2} + pf_{12}\frac{\partial x_2^*}{\partial w_2} \equiv 0$$

$$pf_{21}\frac{\partial x_1^*}{\partial w_2} + pf_{22}\frac{\partial x_2^*}{\partial w_2} \equiv 1$$

Solving these equations as before yields

$$\frac{\partial x_1^*}{\partial w_2} = \frac{-f_{12}}{p(f_{11}f_{22} - f_{12}^2)} \qquad (4\text{-}20c)$$

$$\frac{\partial x_2^*}{\partial w_2} = \frac{f_{11}}{p(f_{11}f_{22} - f_{12}^2)} \qquad (4\text{-}20d)$$

Note that sufficient condition (4-15), $f_{11}f_{22} - f_{12}^2 > 0$, is enough to guarantee $f_{11}f_{22} - f_{12}^2 \neq 0$ and hence allow solution for these partials (4-20a–d).

[†]In accordance with general custom, we will use the equality rather than the identity sign when the special emphasis is not required.

This is not mere coincidence; it is in fact an application of the "implicit function theorem" in mathematics, to be dealt with more generally in Chap. 5. The condition $f_{11}f_{22} - f_{12}^2 \neq 0$ is precisely the mathematical condition to allow solution (*locally*, not everywhere) for the factor demand curves $x_i^*(w_1, w_2, p)$ in the first place. The relevance of that term is brought out in the situation for the partial derivatives.

What refutable hypotheses emerge from this analysis? Condition (4-15) implies that the denominators of (4-20a–d) are all positive. Condition (4-14), $f_{11}, f_{22} < 0$, (diminishing marginal productivity) makes the numerators of (4-20a) and (4-20d) negative. Hence, *the regular (sufficient) conditions for maximum profits imply that the factor-demand curves must be downward sloping in their respective factor prices.* The model implies that changes in a factor price will result in a change in the usage of that factor in the opposite direction.

What about the cross-effects $\partial x_1^*/\partial w_2$, $\partial x_2^*/\partial w_1$? The most remarkable aspect of these two expressions is that they are always equal, by inspection of (4-20b) and (4-20c), noting that $f_{12} = f_{21}$. This *reciprocity relation,*

$$\frac{\partial x_1^*}{\partial w_2} = \frac{\partial x_2^*}{\partial w_1}$$

is representative of a number of such relations that appear in economics, as well as in the physical sciences, when maximizing principles are involved. As is obvious from the forms of these expressions, however, the reciprocity relations are no less intuitive than the mathematical theorem from which they originate — the invariance of cross-partial derivations to the order of differentiation.

Beyond the equality of these cross-effects, there is little else to say about them. The sign of f_{12} is not implied by the maximization hypothesis; hence the sign of $\partial x_i^*/\partial w_j$, $i \neq j$ is similarly not implied. No refutable proposition emerges about these terms from the profit-maximization model. All observed events relating, say, to the change in labor employment when the rental rate on capital increases are consistent with the previous model.

Suppose now it is desired to find expressions relating to the effects of changes in the output price p. The procedure here is identical up through relations (4-18). Then, we differentiate those identities partially with respect to p, producing

$$pf_{11}\frac{\partial x_1^*}{\partial p} + pf_{12}\frac{\partial x_2^*}{\partial p} \equiv -f_1 \tag{4-21a}$$

$$pf_{21}\frac{\partial x_1^*}{\partial p} + pf_{22}\frac{\partial x_2^*}{\partial p} \equiv -f_2 \tag{4-21b}$$

remembering that the product rule is called for in differentiating the terms pf_1, pf_2. Solving these equations for $\partial x_1^*/\partial p$ and $\partial x_2^*/\partial p$ yields

$$\frac{\partial x_1^*}{\partial p} = \frac{-f_1 f_{22} + f_2 f_{12}}{p(f_{11}f_{22} - f_{12}^2)} \tag{4-22a}$$

$$\frac{\partial x_2^*}{\partial p} = \frac{-f_2 f_{11} + f_1 f_{12}}{p(f_{11}f_{22} - f_{12}^2)} \tag{4-22b}$$

It can be seen that no refutable implications emerge from these expressions. An increase in output price can lead to an increase or a decrease in the use of either factor, since the sign of f_{12} is unknown. (Note that if $f_{12} > 0$ is assumed, $\partial x_1^*/\partial p > 0$ and $\partial x_2^*/\partial p > 0$.) It is possible to show, however, that it cannot be the case that *both* $\partial x_1^*/\partial p < 0$ *and* $\partial x_2^*/\partial p < 0$ simultaneously. An increase in output price cannot lead to less use of both factors. The proof of this is left as an exercise.

The Supply Function

It is also possible to ask how *output* varies when a parameter changes. Since $y = f(x_1, x_2)$,

$$y^* = f(x_1^*, x_2^*)$$

where y^* is the profit-maximizing level of output.

The factor demand curves are functions of the prices,

$$x_i = x_i^*(w_1, w_2, p) \quad i = 1, 2$$

Substituting these functions into $f(x_1^*, x_2^*)$ yields

$$y^* \equiv f(x_1^*(w_1, w_2, p), x_2^*(w_1, w_2, p)) \equiv y^*(w_1, w_2, p) \tag{4-23}$$

Equation (4-23) represents the supply function of this firm. It shows how output is related (1) to output price p, and (2) to the factor prices. Though the supply curve is commonly drawn only against output price p, factor prices must also enter the function, since factor costs obviously affect the level of output a firm will choose to produce.

How will output be affected by an increase in output price? To answer this, differentiate (4-23) with respect to p, using the chain rule

$$\frac{\partial y^*}{\partial p} \equiv \frac{\partial f}{\partial x_1}\frac{\partial x_1^*}{\partial p} + \frac{\partial f}{\partial x_2}\frac{\partial x_2^*}{\partial p}$$

or

$$\frac{\partial y^*}{\partial p} \equiv f_1 \frac{\partial x_1^*}{\partial p} + f_2 \frac{\partial x_2^*}{\partial p} \tag{4-24}$$

Now, substitute Eqs. (4-22) into this expression. This yields

$$\frac{\partial y^*}{\partial p} = \frac{-f_1^2 f_{22} + 2f_{12}f_1 f_2 - f_2^2 f_{11}}{p(f_{11}f_{22} - f_{12}^2)} \tag{4-25}$$

The denominator of this expression is positive by the sufficient second-order conditions. We also can infer, from Eq. (4-10), that the numerator is also positive. Therefore,

$$\frac{\partial y^*}{\partial p} > 0 \qquad (4\text{-}26)$$

This says that the sufficient second-order conditions for profit maximization imply that the supply curve, as usually drawn, must be upward-sloping. It also provides an explanation as to why it cannot be the case that both $\partial x_1^*/\partial p$ and $\partial x_2^*/\partial p$ are negative. If p increases, output will increase. It is impossible, with positive marginal products, to produce more output with less of both factors.

It is also possible to derive some *reciprocity* relationships with regard to the output supply and factor demand functions. In particular, one can show

$$\frac{\partial y^*}{\partial w_i} \equiv \frac{-\partial x_i^*}{\partial p} \quad i = 1, 2 \qquad (4\text{-}27)$$

The signs of these expressions are indeterminate; however, this curious reciprocity result is valid. Its proof is left as an exercise.

The tools used in this analysis include the solution of simultaneous linear equations. For this reason, the next chapter is on the theory of matrices and determinants. It will be of great advantage to be able to have a general way of expressing the solutions of such equation systems, instead of laboriously working through each expression separately.

4.5 HOMOGENEITY OF THE DEMAND AND SUPPLY FUNCTIONS; ELASTICITIES

Suppose the economy were to experience a perfectly neutral inflation, i.e., input and output prices all increasing in the same proportion, say 10 percent. Since relative prices would not have changed, it would be important that the model predict that no decisions would be changed in response to this. In other words, the factor demand functions and the supply function should be homogeneous of degree zero in all prices. Is this the case?

The factor demand functions are the simultaneous solutions to the first-order conditions

$$pf_1(x_1, x_2) - w_1 = 0$$

$$pf_2(x_1, x_2) - w_2 = 0$$

Suppose w_1, w_2, and p all change in the same proportion, i.e., these prices become tw_1, tw_2, and tp, where t is some scalar factor. The factor demand functions are now evaluated at these new prices: $x_1^*(tw_1, tw_2, tp)$, $x_2^*(tw_1, tw_2, tp)$. These functions are the solutions to the first-order equations at the new prices:

$$(tp)f_1(x_1, x_2) - (tw_1) = 0$$

$$(tp)f_2(x_1, x_2) - (tw_2) = 0$$

But these equations are clearly equivalent to the original ones; all that has happened algebraically is that the equations have been multiplied through by t.

Since the equations from which the two solutions are derived are algebraically identical, the solutions must also be identical. That is,

$$x_i^*(tw_1, tw_2, tp) \equiv x_i^*(w_1, w_2, p) \quad i = 1, 2$$

In this model, therefore, the factor-demand functions are necessarily homogeneous of degree zero. (It quickly follows that the supply function $y^*(w_1, w_2, p)$ must also be homogeneous of degree zero; its proof is left as an exercise.)

Notice that the preceding proof in no way depends on any assumption about the functional form of the production function. In particular, to head off a frequently made error, it is not the case that the production function must be homogeneous of some degree. The demand functions are not the partial derivatives of the production function. They are the simultaneous solutions to the first-order equations. The result follows because those first-order equations are linear in w_1, w_2, and p. When each of those parameters is increased in the same proportion, the factor of proportionality cancels out of the first-order equations, leaving the system unchanged.

Elasticities

The properties of the factor demand functions $x_i^*(w_1, w_2, p)$ are often stated in terms of dimensionless elasticity expressions, instead of the slopes (partial derivatives). These elasticities are defined as

$$\epsilon_{ij} = \lim_{\Delta w_j \to 0} \frac{\Delta x_i / x_i}{\Delta w_j / w_j} \tag{4-28}$$

The elasticity ϵ_{ij} represents the (limit of the) percentage change in the use of factor x_i per percent change in price of factor j. When $i = j$, this is called the *own elasticity* of factor demand; when $i \neq j$, it is called a *cross elasticity*.

Taking limits, and simplifying the compound fraction,

$$\epsilon_{ij} = \frac{w_j \partial x_i^*}{x_i^* \partial w_j} \tag{4-29}$$

This is the definition we shall use throughout. In like fashion, one can define the *output price elasticity* of factor demand as the percentage change in the utilization of a factor per percent change in output price (holding factor prices constant), or

$$\epsilon_{ip} = \lim_{\Delta p \to 0} \frac{\Delta x_i / x_i}{\Delta p / p} = \frac{p \partial x_i^*}{x_i^* \partial p} \tag{4-30}$$

Elasticities are dimensionless expressions, as can be seen by inspection: the units all cancel. To a mathematician, they are logarithmic derivatives. For example, letting $u_i = \log x_i$, $v_j = \log w_j$,

$$\frac{du_i}{dv_j} = \frac{dx_i / x_i}{dw_j / w_j} = \frac{w_j dx_i}{x_i dw_j}$$

The notation changes appropriately for partial derivatives. Many economists prefer to deal with elasticities; others prefer the slopes (unadorned partial derivatives). It is mainly a matter of taste.

By applying Euler's theorem to the factor demand functions (x_1 in the example that follows), we can derive some relationships concerning the elasticities and cross-elasticities of demand:

$$\left(\frac{\partial x_1^*}{\partial w_1}\right)w_1 + \left(\frac{\partial x_1^*}{\partial w_2}\right)w_2 + \left(\frac{\partial x_1^*}{\partial p}\right)p \equiv 0$$

Dividing through by x_1 yields

$$\epsilon_{11} + \epsilon_{12} + \epsilon_{1p} \equiv 0$$

with a similar expression holding for x_2. In general, for models with n factors of production,

$$\sum_j \epsilon_{ij} + \epsilon_{ip} \equiv 0, \quad i = 1, \ldots, n \tag{4-31}$$

4.6 THE LONG RUN AND THE SHORT RUN: AN EXAMPLE OF THE LE CHÂTELIER PRINCIPLE

It is commonplace to assert that certain factors of production are "fixed" over certain time intervals, e.g., that capital inputs cannot be varied over the short run. In fact, of course, these statements are incorrect; virtually anything can be changed, even quickly, if the benefits of doing so are great enough. Yet it does seem that certain inputs are more easily varied, i.e., less costly to vary than others. The extreme abstraction of this is to simply assert that for all intents and purposes, one factor is fixed. (A government edict fixing some level of input would suffice, if ignoring such edict carried with it a sufficiently long jail sentence.) How would a profit-maximizing firm react to changes in the wage of one factor x_1 when it found that it could not vary the level of x_2 employed? Would the factor demand curve for x_1 be more elastic or less elastic than previously?

Suppose x_2 is held fixed at $x_2 = x_2^0$. The profit function then becomes

$$\max \pi = pf(x_1, x_2^0) - w_1 x_1 - w_2 x_2^0.$$

In this case, there is only one decision variable: x_1. Hence the first-order condition for maximization is simply

$$\pi_1 = pf_1(x_1, x_2^0) - w_1 = 0 \tag{4-32}$$

and the sufficient second-order condition is

$$\pi_{11} = pf_{11} < 0 \tag{4-33}$$

We are dealing with a one-variable problem with, now, *four* parameters, w_1, w_2, p, and x_2^0. The factor demand curve, obtained from Eq. (4-32), is

$$x_1 = x_1^s(w_1, p, x_2^0) \tag{4-34}$$

where x_1^s stands for short-run demand. Note, however, that w_2 does not enter this factor demand curve. With x_2 fixed, $w_2 x_2^0$ is a fixed cost, and thus w_2 is irrelevant for the choice of x_1 in the short run. The slope of the short-run factor demand curve is $\partial x_1^s / \partial w_1$. To obtain an expression for this partial, substitute, as before, x_1^s into Eq. (4-32), yielding the identity

$$pf_1(x_1^s, x_2^0) - w_1 \equiv 0$$

Differentiating this identity with respect to w_1 yields

$$pf_{11} \frac{\partial x_1^s}{\partial w_1} \equiv 1$$

or

$$\frac{\partial x_1^s}{\partial w_1} \equiv \frac{1}{pf_{11}} < 0 \tag{4-35}$$

Thus, the short-run factor demand curve is downward-sloping. How does this slope compare with $\partial x_1^* / \partial w_1 = \partial x_1^L / \partial w_1$ (x_1^L for long-run demand) derived in (4-20a)? Taking the difference,

$$\frac{\partial x_1^L}{\partial w_1} - \frac{\partial x_1^s}{\partial w_1} = \frac{f_{22}}{p(f_{11}f_{22} - f_{12}^2)} - \frac{1}{pf_{11}}$$

Combining terms yields

$$\frac{\partial x_1^L}{\partial w_1} - \frac{\partial x_1^s}{\partial w_1} = \frac{f_{12}^2}{pf_{11}(f_{11}f_{22} - f_{12}^2)} < 0 \tag{4-36}$$

a determinately *negative* expression due to the second-order conditions (4-15) and (4-33). Since both $\partial x_1^L / \partial w_1$ and $\partial x_1^s / \partial w_1$ are negative, (4-36) says that the change in x_1 due to a change in its price is larger, in absolute value, when x_2 is variable (the long run) than when x_2 is fixed (the short run). This result is sometimes referred to as the "second law of demand." It is in agreement with intuition—if the price of labor, say, were to increase relative to capital's price, the firm would attempt to substitute out of labor. The degree to which it could do this, however, would be impaired if it could not at the same time increase the amount of capital employed. Hence the model implies that over longer periods of time, as the other factor becomes "unstuck," the demand for the less-costly-to-change factor will become more elastic. Incidently, the usual factor demand diagrams are drawn with the dependent variable x_1 on the *horizontal* axis; in that case the long-run factor demand curves appear flatter than the short-run curves. Also note that this comparison makes sense only if the level of x_2 employed is the same in both cases. That is, the preceding is a local theorem, holding only at the point where the short- and long-run demand curves intersect, i.e., at the common values of x_2. It is not the case that all short-run factor demand curves are less elastic than all long-run demands.

The result contained in this section is commonly believed to be empirically true, simply as a matter of assertion. It is interesting and noteworthy that this type of behavior is in fact mathematically implied by a maximization hypothesis. These types of relations are sometimes referred to as Le Châtelier effects, after the similar tendency of thermodynamic systems to exhibit the same types of responses. Some generalizations of this phenomenon and its relation to "envelope" theorems will be presented in Chap. 7.

A More Fundamental Look
at the Le Châtelier Principle

Although the above algebra proves that when the level of one factor, say, x_2, is held fixed at its profit-maximizing level, the resulting short-run factor demand curve is less elastic than the long-run curve at that point, the proof provides no insight into the fundamental relationship between the long- and short-run factor demands. *If a consistent relationship exists between the partial derivatives of two separate demand functions, it must be the case that some fundamental identity exists that relates the two demands to each other.*

In the instant case, consider what would convert the short-run demand to the long-run demand. We would accomplish this by letting x_2 adjust to the change in w_1 instead of holding it fixed. In fact, we can *define* the long-run factor demand in terms of the short-run demand by letting x_2 (the "fixed" factor) adjust to its profit-maximizing levels as w_1 changes:

$$x_1^*(w_1, w_2, p) \equiv x_1^s(w_1, p, x_2^*(w_1, w_2, p)) \qquad (4\text{-}37)$$

This identity is the fundamental relationship between the short- and long-run factor demands. Using this identity, we can demonstrate and explain the Le Châtelier results with much greater clarity. The right-hand side of Eq. (4-37) is known as a "conditional demand."[†]

The relation (4-37) is an identity; it holds for all w_1, w_2, and p. We can therefore validly differentiate it with respect to any of those arguments. In particular, differentiate with respect to w_1, noting that on the right-hand side of (4-37), w_1 enters once explicitly by itself, and another time as an argument of x_2^*:

$$\frac{\partial x_1^*}{\partial w_1} \equiv \frac{\partial x_1^s}{\partial w_1} + \left(\frac{\partial x_1^s}{\partial x_2^0}\right)\left(\frac{\partial x_2^*}{\partial w_1}\right) \qquad (4\text{-}38)$$

Inspect the notation in the chain rule part of the right-hand side of (4-38) carefully: x_1^s is a function of x_2^0 (not x_2^*); the functional dependence of x_2 on w_2 is defined by the long-run demand x_2^*.

[†] This approach was first developed by Robert Pollak, for the case of consumer demands. See his "Conditional Demand Functions and Consumption Theory," *Quarterly Journal of Economics*, **83**: 60–78, February 1969.

Equation (4-38) reveals that the slopes of the short- and long-run factor demand functions differ by a term representing the product of two effects: the change in x_2 resulting from a change in w_1, and the change in x_1 that would be induced by a (parametric) change in x_2. This product is easily seen to represent the marginal effect on x_1 of allowing x_2 to vary as w_1 changes. The important question is, can this latter term be signed?

It should seem plausible that $\partial x_1^s / \partial x_2^0$ and $\partial x_2^* / \partial w_1$ have opposite signs. From reciprocity, $\partial x_2^* / \partial w_1 = \partial x_1^* / \partial w_2$. Increasing x_2^0 parametrically accomplishes directly what a *decrease* in w_2 would induce. We can verify this algebraically as follows. Differentiating (4-37) with respect to w_2

$$\frac{\partial x_1^*}{\partial w_2} \equiv \left(\frac{\partial x_1^s}{\partial x_2^0} \right)\left(\frac{\partial x_2^*}{\partial w_2} \right) \tag{4-39}$$

Since $\partial x_2^* / \partial w_2 < 0$, $\partial x_1^* / \partial w_2$ and $\partial x_1^s / \partial x_2^0$ are of opposite sign. Using Eq. (4-39) to eliminate $\partial x_1^s / \partial x_2^0$ from Eq. (4-38), and using reciprocity,

$$\frac{\partial x_1^*}{\partial w_1} \equiv \frac{\partial x_1^s}{\partial w_1} + \frac{(\partial x_2^* / \partial w_1)^2}{\partial x_2^* / \partial w_2} \tag{4-40}$$

Since the last term must be negative, Eq. (4-40) says that $\partial x_1^* / \partial w_1$ is more negative than $\partial x_1^s / \partial w_1$, the Le Châtelier result. More importantly, it illuminates the fundamental relationship between the long- and short-run factor demand functions.

A similar analysis can be used to show that the long-run output supply function is more elastic than the short-run function. The fundamental identity is

$$y^*(w_1, w_2, p) \equiv y^s(w_1, p, x_2^*(w_1, w_2, p)) \tag{4-41}$$

Differentiating with respect to p,

$$\frac{\partial y^*}{\partial p} \equiv \frac{\partial y^s}{\partial p} + \left(\frac{\partial y^s}{\partial x_2^0} \right)\left(\frac{\partial x_2^*}{\partial p} \right) \tag{4-42}$$

By differentiating (4-41) with respect to w_2 and using a reciprocity condition, it can be shown that $\partial y^* / \partial p > \partial y^s / \partial p$. The proof is left as an exercise.

We shall employ this technique throughout this book. In so doing, many expressions that were once difficult to prove become transparently simple.

To sum up, it has again been possible to state refutable propositions about some *marginal* quantities, in spite of the scarcity of information contained in the model. Should further information be used, e.g., the specific functional form of the production function, or, less grandiosely, independent measures of the sign of the cross-effect f_{12}, additional restrictions can be placed on the signs of the partial derivatives of the factor demand functions.

PROBLEMS

1. Show that no refutable implications emerge from the profit-maximization model with regard to the effects of changes in output price on factor inputs. Show, however, that it cannot be the case that both factors decrease when output price is increased.

2. Show that the rate of change of output with respect to a factor price change is equal to the negative of the rate of change of that factor with respect to output price, i.e., Eq. (4-27).

3. (Very messy, but you should probably do this once in your life.) Consider the production function $y = x_1^{\alpha_1} x_2^{\alpha_2}$. Find the factor demand curves and the comparative statics of a profit-maximizing firm with this production function. Be sure to review Prob. 3, Sec. 4.2, first. Show that for this firm, the sign of the cross-effect term, $\partial x_2^* / \partial w_1$, is negative.

4. There are several definitions of complementary and substitute factors in the literature, among which are
   (i) "Factor 1 is a substitute (complement) for factor 2 if the marginal product of factor 1 decreases (increases) as factor 2 is increased."
   (ii) "Factor 1 is a substitute (complement) for factor 2 if the quantity of factor 1 employed increases when the price of factor 2 increases (decreases)."
   (a) Show that both of these definitions are *symmetric,* i.e., if factor 1 is a substitute for factor 2, then factor 2 can't be a complement to factor 1.
   (b) Show that these two definitions are equivalent in the two-factor, profit maximization model.
   (c) Do you think that these two definitions will be equivalent in a model with three or more factors? Why?

5. Consider again Prob. 6, Sec. 4.2, wherein a monopolist sells his or her output in two separate markets. Suppose a per-unit tax t is placed on output sold in the first market.
   (a) Show that an increase in t will reduce the output sold in market 1.
   (b) What does the maximization hypothesis *alone* imply about the response of output in the second market to an increase in t?
   (c) Suppose the output in market 2 were held fixed at the previously profit-maximizing level, by government regulation. Show that the response in output in market 1 to a tax increase is less in absolute terms in the regulated situation than in the unregulated situation. Provide an intuitive explanation for this.

6. The Le Châtelier results of Sec. 4.4 (also Prob. 5) hold, regardless of whether the two factors are complementary or substitutes. Explain the phenomenon intuitively for the case of complementary factors.

7. A monopolist sells his or her output in two markets, with revenue functions $R_1(y_1)$, $R_2(y_2)$, respectively. Total cost is a function of total output, $y = y_1 + y_2$. The same per-unit tax, t, is levied on output sold in *both* markets.
   (a) Find $\partial y_1^* / \partial t$, $\partial y_2^* / \partial t$, and $\partial y^* / \partial t$ where y_i^* is the profit-maximizing level of output in market i, and $y^* = y_1^* + y_2^*$. Which, if any, of these partials have a sign implied by profit-maximization?
   (b) Suppose output y_2 is held fixed. Find $(dy_1^*/dt)_{y_2}$. Does $(dy_1^*/dt)_{y_2}$ have a determinate sign?

8. Consider the following two models of a discriminating monopolist subject to a tax in one market:
   (i) $\max R_1(x_1) + R_2(x_2) - C(x_1 + x_2) - tx_1$
   (ii) $\max R(x_1, x_2) - C(x_1, x_2) - tx_1$

In model *(i)*, cost is a function only of total output, whereas in *(ii)*, cost and revenue are more complicated (and general) functions of both outputs. The tax rate t is a parameter. What are the observable similarities and differences between these two models?

9. Consider a profit-maximizing firm with the production function $y = f(x_1, x_2)$, facing output price p and factor prices w_1 and w_2. Suppose this firm is taxed according to the total cost of factor 2, i.e., tax $= tw_2x_2$.
    (a) Derive the factor demand functions, i.e., show where they come from, etc. Are these choice functions homogeneous of any degree in any of the parameters?
    (b) Show that if the tax rate rises, the firm will use less of factor 2.
    (c) Show that $\dfrac{\partial x_1^*}{\partial t} = w_2 \dfrac{\partial x_2^*}{\partial w_1}$
    (d) Suppose that factor 1 is held fixed at its profit-maximizing level. Show that the response of factor 2 to a change in the tax rate is less in absolute value than before.

10. Consider a monopolistic firm that hires two inputs, x_1 and x_2, in competitive factor markets at wages w_1 and w_2, respectively. The firm's revenue function is expressible in terms of the inputs as $R(x_1, x_2)$. Assuming profit maximization,
    (a) Indicate the derivation of the factor demand functions. Are these factor demands homogeneous of some degree in wages?
    (b) Show that the factor demand curves are downward-sloping in their own prices.
    (c) Is a refutable hypothesis forthcoming as to how the total revenue of this firm would change with regard to a change in a factor price?

11. Consider a profit-maximizing U.S. monopolistic firm which produces some good y at two different plants, with (total) cost functions $C_1(y_1)$, $C_2(y_2)$. The total revenue function of this firm is $R(y)$, where $y = y_1 + y_2$. Plant 2 is located in Canada and output from that plant is subject to a U.S. tariff (tax) in the amount of t per unit produced.
    (a) What is implied, if anything, about the slopes of the marginal revenue and marginal cost curves in this model?
    (b) What refutable comparative statics implications are forthcoming, if any?
    (c) Suppose this firm was not a monopolist, but rather, sold its total output in a competitive market at price p. What differences would exist in the observable implications of the model in the competitive versus the monopolistic case?
    (d) Suppose this competitive output price rose. Will the output in each plant increase?
    (e) Returning now to the monopolistic case, suppose this monopolist decided to raise the price charged to consumers. What effect would this have on the output of each plant . . . hey, wait a minute . . . does this make any sense?
    (f) Suppose the total revenue received by this (monopolistic) firm depends in some complicated way on outputs in both plants, rather than simply on the sum of those two outputs. What observable differences, if any, are implied by this change in assumptions?
    (g) Suppose output at the U.S. plant (y_1) is held fixed at the previously profit maximizing level, and the tax on Canadian output is increased. How does the resulting magnitude of the response in production at the Canadian plant compare with the response when U.S. output is unconstrained? (Again, assume the monopoly case.)

12. Prove, using Eq. (4-42), that the long-run supply curve of a competitive firm is more elastic than the supply curve in which one factor is held fixed at a previously profit-maximizing level.

4.7 ANALYSIS OF FINITE CHANGES: A DIGRESSION

The downward slope of the factor demand curves can be derived without the use of calculus, on the basis of simple algebra. Suppose that at some factor-price vector (w_1^0, w_2^0), the input vector that maximizes profits is (x_1^0, x_2^0). This means that if some other input levels (x_1^1, x_2^2) were employed at the factor prices (w_1^0, w_2^0), profits would not be as high. Algebraically, then,

$$pf(x_1^0, x_2^0) - w_1^0 x_1^0 - w_2^0 x_2^0 \geq pf(x_1^1, x_2^1) - w_1^0 x_1^1 - w_2^0 x_2^1$$

However, there must be *some* factor price vector (w_1^1, w_2^1) at which the input levels (x_1^1, x_2^1) would be the profit-maximizing levels to employ. Since (x_1^1, x_2^1) leads to maximum profits at (w_1^1, w_2^1), any other level of inputs, in particular (x_1^0, x_2^0), will not do as well. Hence,

$$pf(x_1^1, x_2^1) - w_1^1 x_1^1 - w_2^1 x_2^1 \geq pf(x_1^0, x_2^0) - w_1^1 x_1^0 - w_2^1 x_2^0$$

If these two inequalities are added together, all the production function terms cancel, leaving (after multiplication through by -1):

$$w_1^0 x_1^0 + w_2^0 x_2^0 + w_1^1 x_1^1 + w_2^1 x_2^1 \leq w_1^0 x_1^1 + w_2^0 x_2^1 + w_1^1 x_1^0 + w_2^1 x_2^0$$

If the terms on the right-hand side are brought over to the left, and the w_i's factored, the result is

$$w_1^0(x_1^0 - x_1^1) + w_2^0(x_2^0 - x_2^1) + w_1^1(x_1^1 - x_1^0) + w_2^1(x_2^1 - x_2^0) \leq 0$$

However, this can be factored again, using the terms $(x_1^0 - x_1^1)$, et cetera [Note that $(x_1^0 - x_1^1) = -(x_1^1 - x_1^0)$], yielding

$$(w_1^0 - w_1^1)(x_1^0 - x_1^1) + (w_2^0 - w_2^1)(x_2^0 - x_2^1) \leq 0 \qquad (4\text{-}43)$$

Suppose now that only one factor-price, say w_1, changed. Then Eq. (4-43) becomes

$$(w_1^0 - w_1^1)(x_1^0 - x_1^1) \leq 0$$

or

$$(\Delta w_1)(\Delta x_1) \leq 0 \qquad (4\text{-}44)$$

Equation (4-44) says that the changes in factor utilization will move oppositely to changes in factor price, i.e., the law of demand applies to these factors. Note that if the profit-maximization point is unique, the weak inequalities can be replaced with strict inequalities.

This is the type of algebra which underlies the theory of revealed preference, to be discussed later. Curiously enough, this analysis cannot be used to show the second law of demand, that (factor) demands will become more elastic as more factors are allowed to vary. As was stated in Sec. 4.4, that theorem was a strictly local phenomenon, holding only at a point. The previous analysis, which makes use of finite changes, turns out to be insufficiently powerful to analyze the Le Châtelier effects, i.e., the *second* law of demand.

APPENDIX

TAYLOR SERIES FOR FUNCTIONS OF SEVERAL VARIABLES

In Chap. 2, we indicated that it is sometimes possible to represent a function of one variable x by an infinite power series

$$f(x) = f(x_0) + f'(x_0)(x - x_0) + \frac{f''(x_0)(x - x_0)^2}{2!} + \cdots \tag{4A-1}$$

It is, however, always possible to represent a function in a finite power series:

$$f(x) = f(x_0) + f'(x_0)(x - x_0) + \cdots + \frac{f^{(n)}(x^*)(x - x_0)^n}{n!} \tag{4A-2}$$

where x^* lies between x_0 and x, that is; $x^* = x_0 + \theta(x - x_0)$ where $0 \le \theta \le 1$. These formulas were used to derive the necessary and sufficient conditions for a maximum (or minimum) at $y = f(x)$.

Let us generalize these formulas to the case of, first, two independent variables; that is, $y = f(x_1, x_2)$. This is accomplished by an artifice similar to the derivation of the maximum conditions in the text. Consider $f(x_1, x_2)$ evaluated at some point $\mathbf{x}^0 = (x_1^0, x_2^0)$, that is, $f(x_1^0, x_2^0)$. Let us now move to a new point, $(x_1^0 + h_1, x_2^0 + h_2)$, where we can consider $h_1 = \Delta x_1$, $h_2 = \Delta x_2$. If we let

$$y(t) = f(x_1^0 + h_1 t, x_2^0 + h_2 t) \tag{4A-3}$$

then when $t = 0$, $f(x_1, x_2) = f(x_1^0, x_2^0)$, and when $t = 1$, $f(x_1, x_2) = f(x_1^0 + h_1, x_2^0 + h_2)$. If h_1 and h_2 take on arbitrary values, any point in the $x_1 x_2$ plane can be reached. We can therefore derive a Taylor series for $f(x_1, x_2)$ by writing one for $y(t)$, around the point $t = 0$. In terms of finite sums,

$$y(t) = y(0) + y'(0)t + \frac{y''(0)t^2}{2!} + \cdots + \frac{y^{(m)}(t^*)t^m}{m!} \tag{4A-4}$$

where $0 \le |t^*| \le |t|$. Setting $t = 1$, we have

$$y(1) = f(x_1^0 + h_1, x_2^0 + h_2)$$

$$y(0) = f(x_1^0, x_2^0)$$

$$y'(0) = f_1(x_1^0, x_2^0)h_1 + f_2(x_1^0, x_2^0)h_2$$

$$y''(0) = \sum_{i=1}^{2} \sum_{j=1}^{2} f_{ij}(x_1^0, x_2^0)h_i h_j$$

$$\vdots$$

Therefore, Eq. (4A-4) becomes

$$f(x_1^0 + h_1, x_2^0 + h_2) = f(x_1^0, x_2^0) + \sum f_i h_i + \frac{\sum \sum f_{ij} h_i h_j}{2!} + \cdots$$

$$+ \frac{\sum \cdots \sum f_{ij} \ldots (x_1^*, x_2^*) h_i h_j \cdots}{m!} \qquad (4A\text{-}5)$$

where the last term is an m-sum of mth partials times a product of the appropriate m h_i's. The value of $\mathbf{x} = (x_1, x_2)$ at which the last term is evaluated is some $\mathbf{x}^*$ between $\mathbf{x}$ and $\mathbf{x}^0$, i.e., where

$$x_i^* = x_i^0 + \theta(x_i - x_i^0) \qquad i = 1, 2 \qquad (4A\text{-}6)$$

with $0 \le \theta \le 1$. Formula (4A-5) generalizes in an obvious fashion to functions of n variables. Then the sums run from 1 through n instead of merely from 1 to 2.

Concavity and the Maximum Conditions

FIRST-ORDER NECESSARY CONDITIONS. We can derive the first-order conditions for maximizing $y = f(x_1, x_2)$ at x_1^0, x_2^0, by considering (4A-5) with the last term being the linear term. In that case, we have the mean value theorem for $f(x_1, x_2)$:

$$f(x_1^0 + h_1, x_2^0 + h_2) - f(x_1^0, x_2^0) = f_1(\mathbf{x}^*)h_1 + f_2(\mathbf{x}^*)h_2 \qquad (4A\text{-}7)$$

If $f(x_1, x_2)$ has a maximum at $f(x_1^0, x_2^0)$, then the left-hand side of Eq. (4A-7) is necessarily nonpositive (negative for a unique maximum) for all h_1, h_2 (not both 0). Letting $h_2 = 0$ first, we see that

$$f_1(x_1^*, x_2^*) \le 0 \quad h_1 > 0$$

and

$$f_1(x_1^*, x_2^*) \ge 0 \quad h_1 < 0$$

This can happen (if f_1 is continuous) only if $f_1(x_1^0, x_2^0) = 0$. Similarly, we deduce $f_2 = 0$. This procedure generalizes to the case of n variables in an obvious fashion.

THE SECOND-ORDER CONDITIONS; CONCAVITY. If $f(x_1, x_2)$ is a *concave* function at a stationary value, then $f(x_1, x_2)$ has a maximum there. A concave function of two (or n) variables is defined as in Chap. 2 for one variable. A function $f(x_1, x_2)$ is concave if it lies above (or on) the chord joining any two points.

If $x^0 = (x_1^0, x_2^0)$ and $x^1 = (x_1^1, x_2^1)$ are any two points in the x_1, x_2 plane, $x^t = tx^0 + (1 - t)x^1$, $0 \le t \le 1$ represents all points on the straight line joining x^0 and x^1. Algebraically, then, $f(x_1, x_2)$ is concave if *for any x^0, x^1,*

$$f(tx^0 + (1 - t)x^1) \ge tf(x^0) + (1 - t)f(x^1), \quad 0 \le t \le 1$$

If the strict inequality holds (for $0 < t < 1$), implying no "flat" sections, the function is said to be *strictly concave. Convex* and *strictly convex* functions are defined analogously, with the direction of the inequality sign reversed. These definitions all generalize in an obvious way for functions of n variables; simply let x^0 and x^1 represent vectors in n-space.

For differentiable functions, concave functions lie below (or on) the tangent plane. Letting

$$y(t) = f(x_1^0 + h_1 t, x_2^0 + h_2 t) \qquad (4A\text{-}3)$$

as before, and recalling Eq. (2-28) in Chap. 2, strict concavity implies

$$y(t) - y(0) - y'(0)t < 0 \qquad (4A\text{-}8)$$

for all nontrivial h_1, h_2. Applying (4A-8) with $t = 1$, $x_i = x_i^0 + h_i$, $i = 1, 2$,

$$f(x_1, x_2) - f(x_1^0, x_2^0) - f_1(x_1^0, x_2^0)h_1 - f_2(x_1^0, x_2^0)h_2 < 0 \qquad (4A\text{-}9)$$

Taking the Taylor series expansion (4A-5) to the second-order term and rearranging slightly yields

$$f(x_1, x_2) - f(x_1^0, x_2^0) - f_1(x_1^0, x_2^0)h_1 - f_2(x_1^0, x_2^0)h_2$$

$$= \frac{1}{2} \sum_{i=1}^{2} \sum_{j=1}^{2} f_{ij}(x_1^*, x_2^*)h_i h_j \qquad (4A\text{-}10)$$

From (4A-9)

$$\sum_{i=1}^{2} \sum_{j=1}^{2} f_{ij}(x_1^*, x_2^*)h_i h_j < 0 \qquad (4A\text{-}11)$$

for all h_i, h_j not both 0. Hence, strict concavity implies (4A-11). If the h_i's are made smaller and smaller, $f_{ij}(x_1^*, x_2^*)$ converges towards $f_{ij}(x_1^0, x_2^0)$. We can deduce that concavity at x_1^0, x_2^0 implies that

$$\sum_{i=1}^{2} \sum_{j=1}^{2} f_{ij}(x_1^0, x_2^0)h_i h_j \leq 0 \qquad (4A\text{-}12)$$

for all h_i, h_j, but *not* that this expression is *strictly* negative at (x_1^0, x_2^0). If this double sum is strictly negative, then $f(x_1, x_2)$ must be strictly concave. Similar remarks hold for *convex* functions.

If $f(x_1, x_2)$ has an extremum at (x_1^0, x_2^0), then $f_1 = f_2 = 0$ there. Equation (4A-10) then reveals how the second partials are related to a maximum or minimum position. Again, all the results of this section generalize to functions of n variables by simply having the sums in expressions (4A-5), (4A-9), (4A-10), etc., run from 1 to n, instead of just from 1 to 2.

SELECTED REFERENCES

Allen, R. G. D.: *Mathematical Analysis for Economists*, Macmillan & Co., Ltd., London, 1938. Reprinted by St. Martin's Press, Inc., New York.

Apostol, T.: *Mathematical Analysis,* Addison-Wesley Publishing Co., Inc., Reading, MA, 1957. A standard reference. Advanced.

Courant, R.: *Differential and Integral Calculus,* 2d ed., Vol. 1 and 2, Interscience Publishers, Inc., New York, 1936.

Hancock, H.: *Theory of Maxima and Minima,* Ginn and Company, Boston, 1917. Reprinted by Dover Publications, Inc., New York, 1960. Difficult.

Panik, M. J.: *Classical Optimization: Foundations and Extensions,* North-Holland Publishing Company, Amsterdam, 1976.

Samuelson, P. A.: *Foundations of Economic Analysis,* Harvard University Press, Cambridge, MA, 1947. The seminal work on comparative statics methodology.

CHAPTER

5

MATRICES AND DETERMINANTS

5.1 MATRICES

Most economic models involve the simultaneous interaction of several variables. We have seen, for the case of the profit-maximizing firm with two inputs, that the comparative statics of the model depended on solving two simultaneous linear equations. This occurrence is indeed general; for models with n variables, systems of n simultaneous linear equations need to be solved. For this reason, we shall take a short departure in this chapter and study the algebra of such systems. We will then show how this algebra can simplify the comparative statics of economic models.

Let us begin with the simplest system of simultaneous equations, two equations in two unknowns. Denote these equations as

$$a_{11}x_1 + a_{12}x_2 = b_1$$
$$a_{21}x_1 + a_{22}x_2 = b_2 \tag{5-1}$$

Notice the double-subscript notation for the coefficients. This permits easy identification of these numbers. The element a_{ij} appears in the ith *row* (horizontal) and jth *column* (vertical). Here, i and j take on the values 1, 2; in general, they will run from 1 through n.

A very convenient notation that is extensively used in virtually all sciences involves separating out the coefficients (the a_{ij}'s) from the unknowns (the x_i's) and writing Eqs. (5-1) thus:

$$\begin{pmatrix} a_{11} & a_{12} \\ a_{21} & a_{22} \end{pmatrix} \begin{pmatrix} x_1 \\ x_2 \end{pmatrix} = \begin{pmatrix} b_1 \\ b_2 \end{pmatrix} \tag{5-2}$$

This is known as *matrix notation;* the rectangular arrays of numbers are called *matrices* (plural of matrix). In general, the system of m equations in n unknowns

$$a_{11}x_1 + a_{12}x_2 + \cdots + a_{1n}x_n = b_1$$
$$a_{21}x_1 + a_{22}x_2 + \cdots + a_{2n}x_n = b_2 \tag{5-3}$$
$$\vdots$$
$$a_{m1}x_1 + a_{m2}x_2 + \cdots + a_{mn}x_n = b_m$$

is written in matrix form as

$$\begin{pmatrix} a_{11} & a_{12} & \cdots & a_{1n} \\ a_{21} & a_{22} & & a_{2n} \\ \vdots & & & \\ a_{m1} & a_{m2} & & a_{mn} \end{pmatrix} \begin{pmatrix} x_1 \\ x_2 \\ \vdots \\ x_n \end{pmatrix} = \begin{pmatrix} b_1 \\ b_2 \\ \vdots \\ b_m \end{pmatrix} \tag{5-4}$$

The system (5-4) is just another way of writing Eqs. (5-3). This system involves "multiplication" of an $m \times n$ (m rows, n columns) matrix by an $n \times 1$ matrix, forming another $m \times 1$ matrix on the right-hand side. In general for any coefficient b_i from (5-3),

$$\sum_{j=1}^{n} a_{ij}x_j = b_i \quad i = 1, \ldots, m \tag{5-5}$$

Notice that to arrive at any particular b_i, the elements of the ith row of the (a_{ij}) matrix are multiplied, term by term, with the elements of the (x_j) matrix, which consists of only one column, and those products are then summed. In this manner, general matrix multiplication is defined. Consider the matrix "product"

$$\begin{pmatrix} a_{11} & \cdots & a_{1n} \\ \vdots & & \\ a_{m1} & & a_{mn} \end{pmatrix} \begin{pmatrix} b_{11} & \cdots & b_{1r} \\ \vdots & & \\ b_{nr} & & b_{nr} \end{pmatrix} = \begin{pmatrix} c_{11} & \cdots & c_{1r} \\ \vdots & & \\ c_{m1} & & c_{mr} \end{pmatrix} \tag{5-6}$$

or, simply,

$$\mathbf{AB} = \mathbf{C}$$

Any element c_{ij} of the $\mathbf{C}$ matrix is defined to be

$$\sum_{k=1}^{n} a_{ik}b_{kj} = c_{ij} \quad i = 1, \ldots, m, j = 1, \ldots, r \tag{5-7}$$

That is, the element in the ith row and jth column of $\mathbf{C}$ is defined to be the sum of the products, term by term, of the elements in the ith row of $\mathbf{A}$ and the jth column of $\mathbf{B}$. This definition is therefore valid only if the number of *columns* of $\mathbf{A}$ equals the number of *rows* of $\mathbf{B}$. Otherwise, the definition yields nonsense.

Example 1.

$$\begin{pmatrix} 2 & 1 & 0 \\ 3 & -1 & 1 \end{pmatrix} \begin{pmatrix} 1 & -1 \\ 2 & 0 \\ 0 & 2 \end{pmatrix} = \begin{pmatrix} 4 & -2 \\ 1 & -1 \end{pmatrix}$$

Here, a 2×3 matrix is multiplied by a 3×2 matrix. It results in a 2×2 matrix.

Example 2.

$$\begin{pmatrix} 2 & 1 \\ -1 & 1 \end{pmatrix} \begin{pmatrix} 1 \\ 4 \end{pmatrix} = \begin{pmatrix} 6 \\ 3 \end{pmatrix}$$

A matrix with only one column is sometimes called a column vector or column matrix; a matrix with only one row is sometimes called a row vector or row matrix.

Example 3.

$$(1 \quad 4) \begin{pmatrix} 2 & 1 \\ -1 & 1 \end{pmatrix} = (-2 \quad 5)$$

Notice that it *matters* if matrices are multiplied on the left or on the right; different matrices result.

Consider any two n vectors,

$$\mathbf{a} = (a_1, \ldots, a_n)$$

$$\mathbf{b} = (b_1, \ldots, b_n)$$

The scalar product $\mathbf{ab}$ (variously called the *dot product* or *inner product,* sometimes written $\mathbf{a} \cdot \mathbf{b}$) is defined to be

$$\mathbf{ab} = \sum_{i=1}^{n} a_i b_i$$

The matrix product $\mathbf{AB}$ can be seen to be defined in terms of the scalar product of the *row* vectors of $\mathbf{A}$ and *column* vectors of $\mathbf{B}$.

The algebra of matrices will be relegated to the appendix of this chapter. We are concerned here only with a way of systematically representing the solution of simultaneous equations.

5.2 DETERMINANTS, CRAMER'S RULE

Let us return to the two equation, two unknown system (5-1):

$$a_{11}x_1 + a_{12}x_2 = b_1$$

$$a_{21}x_1 + a_{22}x_2 = b_2 \tag{5-1}$$

To solve these equations for x_1, we multiply the first equation by a_{22} and the second equation by a_{12}, and subtract the second equation from the first:

$$(a_{11}a_{22} - a_{12}a_{21})x_1 = b_1a_{22} - b_2a_{12}$$

If

$$a_{11}a_{22} - a_{12}a_{21} \neq 0$$

then

$$x_1 = \frac{b_1a_{22} - b_2a_{12}}{a_{11}a_{22} - a_{12}a_{21}} \tag{5-8}$$

Similarly, to solve for x_2, multiply the first equation by a_{21} and the second by a_{11}, then subtract the first equation from the second:

$$(a_{11}a_{22} - a_{12}a_{21})x_2 = b_2a_{11} - b_1a_{21}$$

If, again

$$a_{11}a_{22} - a_{12}a_{21} \neq 0$$

then

$$x_2 = \frac{b_2a_{11} - b_1a_{21}}{a_{11}a_{22} - a_{12}a_{21}} \tag{5-9}$$

Let us now define something called a 2×2 *determinant*, or a *determinant of order* 2. Suppose

$$\begin{pmatrix} a & b \\ c & d \end{pmatrix}$$

is any *square*, 2×2 matrix. The determinant of this square matrix, written with straight vertical lines around the matrix, is defined to be

$$D_2 = \begin{vmatrix} a & b \\ c & d \end{vmatrix} = ad - bc \tag{5-10}$$

That is, the product of the upper right and lower left elements is subtracted from the product of the upper left and lower right elements.[†]

In terms of determinants, the solutions (5-8) and (5-9) can be written

$$x_1 = \frac{\begin{vmatrix} b_1 & a_{12} \\ b_2 & a_{22} \end{vmatrix}}{\begin{vmatrix} a_{11} & a_{12} \\ a_{21} & a_{22} \end{vmatrix}} \qquad x_2 = \frac{\begin{vmatrix} a_{11} & b_1 \\ a_{21} & b_2 \end{vmatrix}}{\begin{vmatrix} a_{11} & a_{12} \\ a_{21} & a_{22} \end{vmatrix}}$$

Notice that the determinant in the denominator of these expressions is the determinant of the matrix of coefficients, (a_{ij}). In the numerators, for the solution for

---

[†]Throughout this text, matrices and vectors will be indicated by boldface type. The determinant of a square matrix **A** will be indicated by the symbol $|\mathbf{A}|$ or A.

x_1, the *first* column of the $|a_{ij}|$ determinant is replaced with the b_i's, whereas for x_2, the *second* column is replaced by the b_i's. This formula is known as *Cramer's rule*. It is the generalization of this rule to n variables that we shall investigate.

Notice that the solutions for x_1 and x_2 exist only if

$$|\mathbf{A}| = \begin{vmatrix} a_{11} & a_{12} \\ a_{21} & a_{22} \end{vmatrix} \neq 0$$

What is the geometric significance of this condition? Equations (5-1) represent two straight lines in the x_1x_2 plane. These equations will not have any solution at all if the lines are parallel; if the lines are not only parallel but coincident, an infinity (all points on the common line) of solutions results.

These two lines will be parallel if they have the same slope. Solving each equation for x_2, Eqs. (5-1) are equivalent to

$$x_2 = -\frac{a_{11}}{a_{12}}x_1 + \frac{b_1}{a_{12}}$$

$$x_2 = -\frac{a_{21}}{a_{22}}x_1 + \frac{b_2}{a_{22}}$$

If the slopes are the same, then

$$\frac{a_{11}}{a_{12}} = \frac{a_{21}}{a_{22}}$$

or

$$|\mathbf{A}| = \begin{vmatrix} a_{11} & a_{12} \\ a_{21} & a_{22} \end{vmatrix} = a_{11}a_{22} - a_{12}a_{21} = 0$$

Hence the inability to solve Eqs. (5-1) because $|\mathbf{A}| = 0$ occurs because the lines are parallel or coincident.

Consider now a system of three equations in three unknowns:

$$\begin{pmatrix} a_{11} & a_{12} & a_{13} \\ a_{21} & a_{22} & a_{23} \\ a_{31} & a_{32} & a_{33} \end{pmatrix} \begin{pmatrix} x_1 \\ x_2 \\ x_3 \end{pmatrix} = \begin{pmatrix} b_1 \\ b_2 \\ b_3 \end{pmatrix} \tag{5-11}$$

Define the determinant of order 3 as

$$D_3 = \begin{vmatrix} a_{11} & a_{12} & a_{13} \\ a_{21} & a_{22} & a_{23} \\ a_{31} & a_{32} & a_{33} \end{vmatrix} = a_{11} \begin{vmatrix} a_{22} & a_{23} \\ a_{32} & a_{33} \end{vmatrix} - a_{12} \begin{vmatrix} a_{21} & a_{23} \\ a_{31} & a_{33} \end{vmatrix}$$

$$+ a_{13} \begin{vmatrix} a_{21} & a_{22} \\ a_{31} & a_{32} \end{vmatrix} \tag{5-12}$$

The determinant D_3 is defined in terms of certain second-order determinants. All in all, six terms involving the products of three elements are involved, with particular signs. Notice that the determinant multiplied by a_{11} is the determinant that remains from D_3 when row 1 and column 1 are deleted. In like fashion, the determinant multiplied by a_{12} is the determinant that remains from D_3 when row 1 and column 2 are deleted (the row and column that a_{12} appears in), and similarly for the last determinant.

We define the *minor of a_{ij}* as that determinant that remains when row i and column j are deleted from the original determinant.

In the above definition of D_3, the elements of the first row are multiplied by their respective minors, but one such minor comes in with a negative sign.

Define the *cofactor of a_{ij}*, written A_{ij}, as $(-1)^{i+j}$ times the minor of a_{ij}. (Sometimes the term *signed cofactor* is used. This is redundant, though perhaps useful to emphasize the signing element $(-1)^{i+j}$.) In terms of cofactors, D_3 can be written

$$D_3 = a_{11}A_{11} + a_{12}A_{12} + a_{13}A_{13} \tag{5-13}$$

Expanding this expression, i.e., Eq. (5-12),

$$D_3 = a_{11}a_{22}a_{33} - a_{11}a_{23}a_{32} - a_{12}a_{21}a_{33} + a_{12}a_{23}a_{31} + a_{13}a_{21}a_{32}$$

$$-a_{13}a_{22}a_{31} \tag{5-14}$$

In each triple, the three elements come from different rows and columns. No row or column is ever repeated. (If you are a chess player, the triples represent all possible ways three castles, or rooks, can be placed on a 3×3 chessboard such that they cannot capture one another.) Equation (5-14) can be factored in another way, e.g.,

$$D_3 = -a_{12}(a_{21}a_{33} - a_{23}a_{31}) + a_{22}(a_{11}a_{33} - a_{13}a_{31})$$

$$-a_{32}(a_{11}a_{23} - a_{13}a_{21}) \tag{5-15}$$

But this factorization can be written in terms of the elements and cofactors of column 2. By inspection, from (5-15)

$$D_3 = a_{12}A_{12} + a_{22}A_{22} + a_{32}A_{32} \tag{5-16}$$

(Notice that A_{12} and A_{32} both have negative signing factors, since $(-1)^{1+2} = (-1)^{3+2} = -1$. This doesn't mean that A_{12} or A_{32} are necessarily negative; just that the *minors* of a_{12} and a_{32} are multiplied by -1.)

This algebra indicates that D_3 can be defined as the sum of the products of the elements of *any* row or *any* column times their respective cofactors. That is, D_3 can be written as

$$D_3 = \sum_{j=1}^{3} a_{ij}A_{ij} = \sum_{i=1}^{3} a_{ij}A_{ij} \tag{5-17}$$

In the first sum, the determinant is expanded using the elements and cofactors of row i; in the second sum, column j is used. Either way, the same number results. This result can be proved for determinants of order 3 by simply finding all six sums and verifying the result. More importantly, it is the generality of this result that is useful.

Determinants of higher order can be defined in terms of lower-order ones. That is,

$$D_4 = \begin{vmatrix} a_{11} & a_{12} & a_{13} & a_{14} \\ a_{21} & a_{22} & a_{23} & a_{24} \\ a_{31} & a_{32} & a_{33} & a_{34} \\ a_{41} & a_{42} & a_{43} & a_{44} \end{vmatrix} = a_{11}A_{11} + a_{12}A_{12} + a_{13}A_{13} + a_{14}A_{14}$$

where A_{ij} is the (signed) cofactor of element a_{ij}, that is, $(-1)^{i+j}$ times the third-order determinant that remains when row i and column j are deleted from D_4. The generalization of Eq. (5-17) will be stated now, without proof.

Theorem 1. Let D_n be any nth-order determinant of a square matrix $\mathbf{A} = (a_{ij})$. Then

$$D_n = \sum_{j=1}^{n} a_{ij}A_{ij} = \sum_{i=1}^{n} a_{ij}A_{ij} \tag{5-18}$$

where A_{ij} is the cofactor of element a_{ij}.

We shall now state and briefly sketch the proofs of the important elementary properties of determinants, culminating in Cramer's rule.

Theorem 2. If all the elements in any row (column) of D_n are 0, then $D_n = 0$.

Proof. Expand D_n by that given row (column), and the sum of many 0's is 0.

Theorem 3. If D_n' is obtained from D_n by interchanging any two rows (columns), then $D_n' = -D_n$. A rigorous proof will not be given. However, it is clear that the same terms are involved in D_n' as in D_n since all the n-tuples are chosen with one element from each row and column, with no repeats. Only the signing factor $(-1)^{i+j}$ can be affected. If row 1 is interchanged, say, with row 2, then expanding D_n by the second row means that the signing factor will be $(-1)^{2+j}$ instead of $(-1)^{1+j}$. Hence, the sign of D_n will reverse. If row 1 and row 3 are interchanged, we can consider this as three separate steps: interchange rows 1 and 2, then 1 and 3, and then 3 and 2. This *odd* number of reversals changes the sign of D_n. The result in fact follows, as the theorem indicates, for an arbitrary interchange of rows, or an arbitrary interchange of columns.

Theorem 4. If D_n' is obtained from D_n by multiplying any row (column) by some scalar (number) k, then $D_n' = kD_n$.

Proof. Take that given row (column) and expand D_n by the cofactors of that row or column. Then k appears in each term, and, by factoring it out, the result is obtained.

Theorem 5. If D_n has 2 rows (columns) that are identical, then $D_n = 0$.

Proof. If any two rows, in particular the two identical ones, are interchanged, then by Theorem 3 the value of the resulting determinant is opposite in sign but has the same absolute value as the original determinant. But since the determinant has exactly the same elements after interchange as before, the value of the determinant must be identical. The only value that satisfies this relationship of $D_n = -D_n$ is $D_n = 0$.

Corollary. If one row (column) is proportional to another row (column), then $D_n = 0$.

Proof. Factor out the constant of proportionality and then use Theorem 5.

Theorem 6. Suppose each element of the kth row, a_{kj}, is equal to $a_{kj} = b_{kj} + c_{kj}$, the sum of two terms. Then let D'_n be the determinant formed by using the elements b_{kj} in the kth row and D''_n be the determinant formed using c_{kj} as elements in row k. Then $D_n = D'_n + D''_n$.

Proof. Expanding D_n by the elements and cofactors of row k,

$$D_n = (b_{k1} + c_{k1})A_{k1} + \cdots + (b_{kn} + c_{kn})A_{kn}$$

$$= \sum_{j=1}^{n} b_{kj}A_{kj} + \sum_{j=1}^{n} c_{kj}A_{kj} = D'_n + D''_n$$

Theorem 7. If D'_n is formed by adding, term by term, a multiple of any row (column) of D_n to another row (column) of D_n, then $D'_n = D_n$.

Proof. Consider for example the 3×3 determinant

$$D_3 = \begin{vmatrix} a_{11} & a_{12} & a_{13} \\ a_{21} & a_{22} & a_{23} \\ a_{31} & a_{32} & a_{33} \end{vmatrix}$$

Multiply the elements in row 1 by some number k and add this product, term by term, to row 2. Then

$$D'_3 = \begin{vmatrix} a_{11} & a_{12} & a_{13} \\ a_{21} + ka_{11} & a_{22} + ka_{12} & a_{23} + ka_{13} \\ a_{31} & a_{32} & a_{33} \end{vmatrix}$$

By Theorem 6

$$D'_3 = \begin{vmatrix} a_{11} & a_{12} & a_{13} \\ a_{21} & a_{22} & a_{23} \\ a_{31} & a_{32} & a_{33} \end{vmatrix} + k\begin{vmatrix} a_{11} & a_{12} & a_{13} \\ a_{11} & a_{12} & a_{13} \\ a_{31} & a_{32} & a_{33} \end{vmatrix}$$

By Theorem 5, this latter determinant equals 0. Thus $D'_3 = D_3$. The proof is general, of course, for any two rows (or columns), for any size determinant.

Theorem 8. If the elements of any row (column) are multiplied by the respective cofactors of some other row (column), the resulting sum is zero. This process is called *expansion by alien cofactors*.

Proof. This is equivalent to expanding a determinant that has two identical rows. Consider again the 3×3 determinant of the previous theorem. The theorem asserts, for example, that

$$a_{21}A_{11} + a_{22}A_{12} + a_{23}A_{13} = 0$$

This is the expansion of the determinant

$$\begin{vmatrix} a_{21} & a_{22} & a_{23} \\ a_{21} & a_{22} & a_{23} \\ a_{31} & a_{32} & a_{33} \end{vmatrix}$$

by row 1 or row 2. But this determinant is 0 by Theorem 5. The generalization to any D_n is straightforward.

Theorem 9 (Cramer's rule). Consider a system of n linear equations in n unknowns,

$$\begin{pmatrix} a_{11} & \cdots & a_{1n} \\ \vdots & & \\ a_{n1} & & a_{nn} \end{pmatrix}\begin{pmatrix} x_1 \\ \vdots \\ x_n \end{pmatrix} = \begin{pmatrix} b_1 \\ \vdots \\ b_n \end{pmatrix}$$

If the determinant $|\mathbf{A}|$ of the coefficient matrix $|\mathbf{A}| = (a_{ij})$ is nonzero, then a unique solution exists for each x_i. In particular, the solution for each x_i may be expressed as the quotient of two determinants: the denominator is always the determinant $|\mathbf{A}|$, while the numerator is that determinant formed when column i in $|\mathbf{A}|$ is replaced by the column of b_i's. For example,

$$x_1 = \frac{\begin{vmatrix} b_1 & a_{12} & \cdots & a_{1n} \\ \vdots & & & \\ b_n & a_{n2} & & a_{nn} \end{vmatrix}}{|\mathbf{A}|}$$

$$x_2 = \frac{\begin{vmatrix} a_{11} & b_1 & \cdots & a_{1n} \\ \vdots & & & \\ a_{n1} & b_n & & a_{nn} \end{vmatrix}}{|\mathbf{A}|}$$

Proof. We shall demonstrate Cramer's rule for the three-equation case only. Consider such a system:

$$a_{11}x_1 + a_{12}x_2 + a_{13}x_3 = b_1$$

$$a_{21}x_1 + a_{22}x_2 + a_{23}x_3 = b_2 \tag{5-19}$$

$$a_{31}x_1 + a_{32}x_2 + a_{33}x_3 = b_3$$

In general, these equations are solved by multiplying through by various numbers, adding or subtracting one equation from another, etc. The theory of determinants gives us some handy numbers to work with.

Let us solve for x_1. Multiply the first equation through by A_{11}, the cofactor of a_{11}; multiply the second and third equations, respectively, by A_{21} and A_{31}. Then add the three resulting equations together. After factoring out the x_i's, this yields

$$(a_{11}A_{11} + a_{21}A_{21} + a_{31}A_{31})x_1 + (a_{12}A_{11} + a_{22}A_{21} + a_{32}A_{31})x_2$$

$$+ (a_{13}A_{11} + a_{23}A_{21} + a_{33}A_{31})x_3 = b_1A_{11} + b_2A_{21} + b_3A_{31} \qquad (5\text{-}20)$$

The first set of parentheses in (5-20) equals the determinant $|\mathbf{A}|$, since it is the sum of the elements of the first column of $|\mathbf{A}|$ times their respective cofactors. The second and third sets of parentheses, however, represent an expansion by alien cofactors. There, the elements of the second or third column are multiplied by the cofactors of the first column, and summed. By Theorem 8, these terms sum to 0. Hence Eq. (5-20) reduces to

$$|\mathbf{A}|x_1 = b_1A_{11} + b_2A_{21} + b_3A_{31}$$

If $|\mathbf{A}| \neq 0$,

$$x_1 = \frac{\begin{vmatrix} b_1 & a_{12} & a_{13} \\ b_2 & a_{22} & a_{23} \\ b_3 & a_{32} & a_{33} \end{vmatrix}}{|\mathbf{A}|} \qquad (5\text{-}21)$$

In like fashion, x_2 is obtained by multiplying equations 1, 2, and 3 in (5-19) by A_{12}, A_{22}, and A_{32}, respectively, and summing. Then the coefficients of x_1 and x_3 are 0, and the b_i's multiply the respective cofactors of the second column. The same procedure obtains the general result, as stated in the theorem.

5.3   THE IMPLICIT FUNCTION THEOREM

We have referred at several instances to the problem of "solving" the implicit first-order equations

$$f_1(x_1, x_2, \alpha) = 0$$
$$f_2(x_1, x_2, \alpha) = 0 \qquad (5\text{-}22)$$

for the explicit relations

$$x_1 = x_1^*(\alpha)$$
$$x_2 = x_2^*(\alpha) \qquad (5\text{-}23)$$

where x_1 and x_2 are the choice variables and α represents the parameters of the model.

Sufficient conditions under which this procedure is valid are known as the *implicit function theorem*. One should be wary, incidently, of a "nontheorem" that appears every now and then. This nontheorem asserts that if there are n equations and n unknowns, a unique solution results. This proposition is valid only in the case of *linear* equations whose coefficient matrix has a nonzero determinant. Figures 5-1*a*, *b*, and *c* demonstrate why the theorem cannot be applied to nonlinear functions.

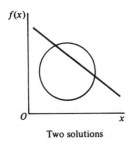
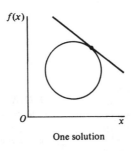
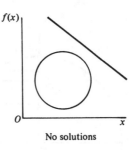

Two solutions   One solution   No solutions

FIGURE 5-1
In general, with nonlinear functions, no general assertions are possible regarding the number of solutions to n equations and n unknowns.

The implicit function theorem is narrower in scope than the above nontheorem. Suppose Eqs. (5-22) have a unique simultaneous solution at some point (x_1^0, x_2^0, α^0). Under what conditions can the implicit relations (5-22) be written as the explicit relations (5-23)?

To answer this, consider first the simplest case of one equation in two unknowns, e.g., the unit circle, depicted in Fig. 5-2,

$$x^2 + y^2 = 1 \qquad (5\text{-}24)$$

For this function to be written as some explicit function, $y = f(x)$, *a unique y* must be associated with any x, around a certain point. Of course, (5-24) can be solved for y as

$$y = \pm(1 - x^2)^{1/2}$$

The function as written here is technically not a function at all; for each x, *two* values of y are given, instead of a unique y. However, such is not the case for solutions around individual points on the unit circle. Consider some point, A, $x = 1/\sqrt{2}$, $y = 1/\sqrt{2}$. In some *neighborhood* around $x = 1/\sqrt{2}$, a unique value of y is associated. That is, *around $x = 1/\sqrt{2}$, $y = 1/\sqrt{2}$*, the explicit functional relation

$$y = +(1 - x^2)^{1/2} \qquad (5\text{-}25)$$

is valid. The implicit function (5-24) admits an explicit solution *around the point A*, not necessarily for all x.

The situation is different, however, at the intercepts of the unit circle and the x axis, the points $(-1,0)$ and $(1,0)$. At either of these two points, no matter how small the interval is made around the point, any value of x will be associated with *two* values of y. The implicit relation (5-24) does *not* admit of an explicit solution $y = f(x)$. An explicit solution of x on y, that is, $x = g(y)$, does exist—for any value of y around $(1,0)$ or $(-1,0)$, a unique value of x is implied [however, not at the points $(0,1)$ and $(0,-1)$].

It can be seen that the reason why the implicit equation $x^2 + y^2 = 1$ does not admit of a unique solution $y = f(x)$ at $(1,0)$ and $(-1,0)$ is that at these points, the function *turns back* on itself. Moving counterclockwise around the circle, as y increases through the value 0, on the right semicircle, x first increases

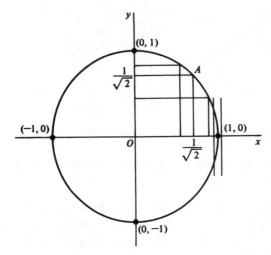

FIGURE 5-2

The implicit function theorem. Around any point where the circle is not vertical, a unique y exists for any x. However, around $x = +1$ or $x = -1$, *two* values of y are associated with any x, no matter how small the interval is made around that x value. If the function is *not* vertical, an explicit solution $y = f(x)$ exists for an explicit relation $g(x, y) = 0$. However, $\partial g/\partial y \neq 0$, while sufficient, is not necessary.

and then decreases. (On the left semicircle, moving clockwise, x decreases and then increases.) At the points $(1,0)$ and $(-1,0)$ the implicit function $x^2 + y^2 = 1$ is *vertical*, that is, $dy/dx \rightarrow \pm\infty$. As long as the function is not vertical, the implicit relation yields a well-defined explicit solution $y = f(x)$.

We can see how the preceding analysis relates to the ability to do comparative statics, in one-variable models. Consider one implicit choice equation, which might be the first-order equation of some objective function:

$$h(y, \alpha) = 0 \tag{5-26}$$

To find $\partial y/\partial \alpha$, an explicit solution of (5-26) must be assumed:

$$y = y^*(\alpha) \tag{5-27}$$

Substituting (5-27) into (5-26), the identity

$$h(y^*(\alpha), \alpha) \equiv 0 \tag{5-28}$$

results. Differentiating with respect to α,

$$h_y \frac{\partial y^*}{\partial \alpha} + h_\alpha \equiv 0 \tag{5-29}$$

In order to solve (5-29) for $\partial y^*/\partial \alpha$,

$$h_y \neq 0 \tag{5-30}$$

must be assumed. This amounts to assuming that the function $h(y, \alpha)$ is not vertical (α plotted horizontally, y vertically).

In maximization models, the *sufficient* second-order conditions guarantee the existence of the explicit solutions (5-27). In these models, the implicit relation (5-26) is already the first partial of some objective function, $f(y, \alpha)$. That is, (5-26) is

$$f_y(y, \alpha) \equiv h(y, \alpha) = 0$$

The condition that $h_y \neq 0$ is guaranteed by the *sufficient* second-order condition for a maximum,

$$f_{yy} \equiv h_y < 0$$

It should be noted that whereas $h_y \neq 0$ is sufficient to be able to write $y = y^*(\alpha)$, it is not necessary. There are some functions for which $h_y = 0$ at some point, and it is still possible to write $y = y^*(\alpha)$. For example, consider the function

$$y^3 - \alpha = 0$$

The solution to this equation, depicted in Fig. 5-3, is

$$y = \alpha^{1/3}$$

Although $dy/d\alpha \to \infty$ as $\alpha \to 0$, it is still the case that a unique y is associated with any α around $\alpha = 0$; the function, while vertical at $\alpha = 0$, does not turn back on itself there.

In models with two equations and two choice variables, the situation is algebraically more complicated, but conceptually similar. Consider the system (5-22) again, but let us just assume that these are just two equations in three unknowns, x_1, x_2, and α, without assuming for the moment that there exists an $f(x_1, x_2, \alpha)$ for which $f_1 = \partial f / \partial x_1, f_2 = \partial f / \partial x_2$. A *sufficient* condition that Eqs. (5-22) admit the explicit solution (5-23) at some point is that neither of the explicit functions (5-23) become vertical, for any α, if α is one of many parameters. Let us try to solve for $\partial x_1^* / \partial \alpha$ and $\partial x_2^* / \partial \alpha$.

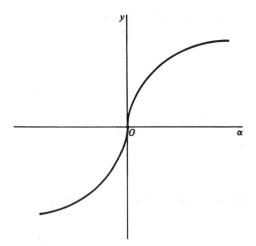

FIGURE 5-3
The function $y = \alpha^{1/3}$. This function illustrates why the condition $h_y \neq 0$ is sufficient but not necessary for writing an implicit function in explicit form. This function becomes vertical at the origin, yet it is still possible to define y as a single-valued function of α, because $\alpha^{1/3}$ does not turn back on itself. If $h_y \neq 0$, the explicit formulation is *always* possible; if $h_y = 0$, it *may* not be.

Differentiating Eqs. (5-22), we get

$$\begin{pmatrix} \dfrac{\partial f_1}{\partial x_1} & \dfrac{\partial f_1}{\partial x_2} \\ \dfrac{\partial f_2}{\partial x_1} & \dfrac{\partial f_2}{\partial x_2} \end{pmatrix} \begin{pmatrix} \dfrac{\partial x_1^*}{\partial \alpha} \\ \dfrac{\partial x_2^*}{\partial \alpha} \end{pmatrix} = \begin{pmatrix} -f_{1\alpha} \\ -f_{2\alpha} \end{pmatrix} \tag{5-31}$$

A necessary and sufficient condition for solving for $\partial x_1^*/\partial \alpha$ and $\partial x_2^*/\partial \alpha$ uniquely is that the determinant

$$J = \begin{vmatrix} \dfrac{\partial f_1}{\partial x_1} & \dfrac{\partial f_1}{\partial x_2} \\ \dfrac{\partial f_2}{\partial x_1} & \dfrac{\partial f_2}{\partial x_2} \end{vmatrix} \neq 0 \tag{5-32}$$

This determinant, whose rows are the first partials of the equations to be solved, is called a *Jacobian* determinant. If $J \neq 0$, the partials $\partial x_i^*/\partial \alpha$ are well defined, and in fact are so because the explicit equations $x_i = x_i^*(\alpha)$ are well defined. That is, $J \neq 0$ is precisely the sufficient condition that allows solution of the simultaneous equations (5-22) for the explicit equations (5-23). This is the generalization of relation (5-30) for one equation.

Condition (5-32) is implied by the *sufficient* second-order conditions for a maximum. In maximization models, $f_1(x_1, x_2, \alpha)$ and $f_2(x_1, x_2, \alpha)$ are $\partial f/\partial x_1$, $\partial f/\partial x_2$. Therefore, $\partial f_1/\partial x_1 = f_{11}$, etc., and the Jacobian is

$$J = \begin{vmatrix} f_{11} & f_{12} \\ f_{12} & f_{22} \end{vmatrix}$$

From the sufficient second-order conditions, $J \neq 0$, since $J > 0$.

For models with n equations

$$f_1(x_1, \ldots, x_n, \alpha) = 0$$

$$\vdots \tag{5-33}$$

$$f_n(x_1, \ldots, x_n, \alpha) = 0$$

a sufficient condition for explicit solutions

$$x_i = x_i^*(\alpha) \tag{5-34}$$

to exist at some point is that the Jacobian of (5-33) be nonvanishing there:

$$J = \begin{vmatrix} \dfrac{\partial f_1}{\partial x_1} & \cdots & \dfrac{\partial f_1}{\partial x_n} \\ \vdots & & \\ \dfrac{\partial f_n}{\partial x_1} & & \dfrac{\partial f_n}{\partial x_n} \end{vmatrix} \neq 0 \tag{5-35}$$

PROBLEMS

1. Evaluate the following determinants

(a) $\begin{vmatrix} 1 & 2 \\ -1 & -3 \end{vmatrix}$

(b) $\begin{vmatrix} -2 & -1 \\ -4 & -3 \end{vmatrix}$

(c) $\begin{vmatrix} 1 & 2 & -1 \\ 0 & 1 & 1 \\ -1 & 0 & 1 \end{vmatrix}$

(d) $\begin{vmatrix} 0 & 1 & 1 \\ 1 & 0 & 1 \\ 1 & 1 & 0 \end{vmatrix}$

2. Suppose a square matrix is *triangular*, i,e., all elements below the diagonal are 0:

$$\mathbf{A} = \begin{pmatrix} a_{11} & a_{12} & \cdots & a_{1n} \\ 0 & a_{22} & & a_{2n} \\ \vdots & & & \\ 0 & 0 & & a_{nn} \end{pmatrix}$$

Show that $|\mathbf{A}| = a_{11}a_{22}\cdots a_{nn}$, the product of the diagonal elements.

3. Consider the system of n equations in n unknowns

$$\mathbf{Ax} = \mathbf{b}$$

where the vector $\mathbf{b}$ consists of 0's in all entries except a 1 in some row j. Assuming $|\mathbf{A}| \neq 0$, show that the solutions can be represented as

$$x_i = \frac{A_{ji}}{|\mathbf{A}|} \quad i,j = 1, \ldots, n$$

where A_{ji} is the cofactor of element a_{ji}.

APPENDIX

SIMPLE MATRIX OPERATIONS

A matrix, again, is any rectangular array of numbers:

$$\mathbf{A} = \begin{pmatrix} a_{11} & \cdots & a_{1n} \\ \vdots & & \\ a_{m1} & & a_{mn} \end{pmatrix}$$

This matrix has m rows and n columns. Suppose some other matrix $\mathbf{B}$ has n rows and r columns ($\mathbf{B}$ must have the same number of rows as $\mathbf{A}$ has columns):

$$\mathbf{B} = \begin{pmatrix} b_{11} & \cdots & b_{1r} \\ \vdots & & \\ b_{n1} & & b_{nr} \end{pmatrix}$$

The matrix product $\mathbf{C} = \mathbf{AB}$ is defined to be the $m \times r$ matrix

$$\begin{pmatrix} c_{11} & \cdots & c_{1r} \\ \vdots & & \\ c_{m1} & & c_{mr} \end{pmatrix} = \begin{pmatrix} a_{11} & \cdots & a_{1n} \\ \vdots & & \\ a_{m1} & & a_{mn} \end{pmatrix} \rightarrow \begin{pmatrix} b_{11} & \cdots & b_{1r} \\ \vdots & \downarrow & \\ b_{n1} & & b_{nr} \end{pmatrix}$$

where any element c_{ij} of $\mathbf{C}$ is defined to be

$$c_{ij} = \sum_{k=1}^{n} a_{ik} b_{kj}$$

Schematically, each element of any *row* of $\mathbf{A}$ is multiplied, term by term, by the elements of some *column* of $\mathbf{B}$ (as shown by the direction of the arrows above) and the result is summed. Note that while the product $\mathbf{AB}$ may be well defined, $\mathbf{BA}$ may not be, since the number of columns in the left-hand matrix must equal the number of rows in the right-hand matrix in a matrix product. In general, even for square matrices, *matrix multiplication is not commutative*, i.e., in general,

$$\mathbf{AB} \neq \mathbf{BA}$$

The associative and distributive laws do hold, however. If $\mathbf{A}$ is $m \times n$, $\mathbf{B}$ is $n \times r$, and $\mathbf{C}$ is $r \times p$, then $\mathbf{ABC}$ is $m \times p$ and the following laws are valid:

Associative Law (AB)C = A(BC)

If $\mathbf{A}$ is $m \times n$, $\mathbf{B}$ and $\mathbf{C}$ are $n \times p$, then:

Distributive Law A(B + C) = AB + AC

For the associative law, we simply note

$$\sum_{h=1}^{r} \sum_{k=1}^{n} (a_{ik} b_{kh}) c_{hj} = \sum_{k=1}^{n} \sum_{h=1}^{r} a_{ik} (b_{kh} c_{hj})$$

For the distributive law,

$$\sum_{k=1}^{n} a_{ik} (b_{kj} + c_{kj}) = \sum_{k=1}^{n} a_{ik} b_{kj} + \sum_{k=1}^{n} a_{ik} c_{kj}$$

The *transpose* of any matrix, $\mathbf{A}'$, is the matrix $\mathbf{A}$ with its rows and columns interchanged. That is,

$$(a_{ij})' = (a_{ji})$$

The transpose of a product is the product of the transposed matrices, in the reverse order:

$$(\mathbf{AB})' = \mathbf{B}'\mathbf{A}'$$

To prove this, let c_{ij} be an element of $(\mathbf{AB})'$. By definition,

$$c_{ij} = \sum_{k=1}^{n} a_{jk} b_{ki}$$

An element of $\mathbf{B}'\mathbf{A}'$ is

$$\sum_{k=1}^{n} b_{ki} a_{jk}$$

identical to the former sum.

A matrix is called *symmetric* if it equals its transpose, that is,

$$\mathbf{A} = \mathbf{A}'$$

That is, for every element a_{ij}, $a_{ij} = a_{ji}$. The rows and columns can be interchanged leaving the same matrix. This is a very important class of matrices in economics. The matrices encountered in maximization models are the second partials of some objective function, $f(x_1, \ldots, x_n)$. By Young's theorem, $f_{ij} = f_{ji}$. Hence, these matrices are symmetric.

The Rank of a Matrix

Consider an $m \times n$ matrix (a_{ij}) and consider each of its rows, $\mathbf{A}_1, \ldots, \mathbf{A}_m$, separately. Each row i,

$$\mathbf{A}_i = (a_{i1}, \ldots, a_{in}) \quad i = 1, \ldots, m$$

represents a point in Euclidean n-space. It is important to discuss the "dimensionality" of these m points; i.e., do they all lie on a single line (one dimension), a plane (two dimensions), etc.? Algebraically, if these m vectors lie in an m-dimensional space, then it is not possible to write any vector $\mathbf{A}$ as a linear combination of the others. In other words, if

$$k_1 \mathbf{A}_1 + \cdots + k_m \mathbf{A}_m = 0$$

where the k_i are scalars (ordinary numbers), then all the k_i's must be zero. In this case, $\mathbf{A}_1, \ldots, \mathbf{A}_m$ are said to be *linearly independent*.

For any given matrix $\mathbf{A}$, the maximum number of linearly independent row vectors in $\mathbf{A}$ is called the *rank* of $\mathbf{A}$. If $\mathbf{A}$ has m rows and n columns, and $n > m$, then the maximum possible rank of $\mathbf{A}$ is m. It is not obvious, but true that the number of linearly independent *column* vectors of $\mathbf{A}$ equals the number of linearly independent *row* vectors. Thus the rank of a matrix is the maximum number of linear independent vectors in $\mathbf{A}$, formed from either the rows or the columns of $\mathbf{A}$.

Example 1. The vectors $A_1 = (1, 0, 0)$, $A_2 = (0, 1, 0)$, $A_3 = (0, 0, 1)$ are linearly independent.

$$k_1 A_1 + k_2 A_2 + k_3 A_3 = (k_1, k_2, k_3) = 0$$

if and only if $k_1 = k_2 = k_3 = 0$. The matrix

$$A = \begin{pmatrix} 1 & 0 & 0 \\ 0 & 1 & 0 \\ 0 & 0 & 1 \end{pmatrix}$$

therefore has rank 3.

Example 2. Let $A_1 = (1, 1, 0)$, $A_2 = (1, 0, 1)$, $A_3 = (1, -1, 2)$. These vectors are linearly *dependent*. Here, $A_3 = 2A_2 - A_1$, or

$$A_1 - 2A_2 + A_3 = 0$$

Any one of these vectors can be written as a linear combination of the other two, but not less than two. The matrix

$$A = \begin{pmatrix} 1 & 1 & 0 \\ 1 & 0 & 1 \\ 1 & -1 & 2 \end{pmatrix}$$

therefore has rank 2.

A set of m linearly independent vectors $A_1, \ldots, A_m$ is said to form a *basis* for Euclidean m-space. Any vector b in that space can be written as a linear combination of $A_1, \ldots, A_m$, that is,

$$b = \sum_{i=1}^{m} k_i A_i$$

where the k_i's are scalars.

Consider a system of n equations in n unknowns,

$$\begin{pmatrix} a_{11} & \cdots & a_{1n} \\ \vdots & & \vdots \\ a_{n1} & & a_{nn} \end{pmatrix} \begin{pmatrix} x_1 \\ \vdots \\ x_n \end{pmatrix} = \begin{pmatrix} b_1 \\ \vdots \\ b_n \end{pmatrix}$$

or, in matrix notation, $Ax = b$. If the rank of A is less than n, then some row of A is a linear combination of other rows. But this is the procedure for solving the above system for the x's. If rank $(A) < n$, then at least one equation is derivable from the others, i.e., there are really less than n independent equations in n unknowns. In this case, no unique solution exists. We saw in the chapter that simultaneous equations admitted a unique solution if the determinant of A, $|A|$, was nonzero. An important result of matrix theory is thus:

Theorem. If A is a square $n \times n$ matrix, then the rank of A is n if and only if $|A| \neq 0$.

This algebra is the basis of the nonvanishing Jacobian determinant of the implicit function theorem. Briefly, if rank $(\mathbf{A}) < n$, then some row (or column) is a linear combination of the other rows (columns). By repeated application of the corollary to Theorem 5 in the chapter proper, $|\mathbf{A}| = 0$. Conversely, if $|\mathbf{A}| = 0$, some row of $\mathbf{A}$ is either 0 or a linear combination of the other rows, and hence $\mathbf{A}_1, \ldots, \mathbf{A}_n$ are linearly dependent. A more formal proof of this part can be found in any standard linear algebra text.

A square $n \times n$ matrix $\mathbf{A}$ that has a rank n is called *nonsingular*. If rank $(\mathbf{A}) < n$, $\mathbf{A}$ is called *singular*.

The Inverse of a Matrix

In ordinary arithmetic, the inverse of a number x is its reciprocal, $1/x$. The inverse of a number x is that number y which makes the product $xy = 1$. In matrix algebra, the unity element for square $n \times n$ matrices is the *identity matrix* $\mathbf{I}$ where,

$$\mathbf{I} = \begin{pmatrix} 1 & 0 & \cdots & 0 \\ 0 & 1 & & 0 \\ \vdots & & & \\ 0 & & & 1 \end{pmatrix}$$

That is, $\mathbf{I}$ is a square $n \times n$ matrix with 1's on the main diagonal, and 0's elsewhere. Formally, if (a_{ij}) is the identity matrix, then $a_{ij} = 1$ if $i = j$, $a_{ij} = 0$ if $i \neq j$. It can be verified that for any square matrix $\mathbf{A}$,

$$\mathbf{AI} = \mathbf{IA} = \mathbf{A}$$

Thus the identity matrix $\mathbf{I}$ corresponds to the number 1 in ordinary arithmetic.

Is there a *reciprocal* matrix $\mathbf{B}$, for some matrix $\mathbf{A}$ such that

$$\mathbf{AB} = \mathbf{I}$$

If so, we call $\mathbf{B}$ the *inverse* of $\mathbf{A}$, denoted $\mathbf{A}^{-1}$.

The problem of finding the inverse of a matrix is equivalent to solving

$$\mathbf{Ax} = \mathbf{b}$$

for a unique $\mathbf{x}$, where $\mathbf{A}$ is an $n \times n$ square matrix. If $\mathbf{A}^{-1}$ exists, premultiply the equation by $\mathbf{A}^{-1}$, yielding

$$\mathbf{x} = \mathbf{A}^{-1}\mathbf{b}$$

This is the simultaneous solution for $\mathbf{x}$. This solution exists if and only if $|\mathbf{A}| \neq 0$. This is correspondingly the condition that $\mathbf{A}^{-1}$ exists, that is, $\mathbf{A}$ must be nonsingular, or have rank n.

Assuming $|\mathbf{A}| \neq 0$, consider the following matrix, $\mathbf{A}^*$, called the *adjoint* of $\mathbf{A}$:

$$\mathbf{A}^* = \begin{pmatrix} A_{11} & A_{21} & \cdots & A_{n1} \\ A_{12} & A_{22} & & A_{n2} \\ \vdots & & & \\ A_{1n} & A_{2n} & & A_{nn} \end{pmatrix}$$

The adjoint, $\mathbf{A}^*$, is formed from the cofactors of the a_{ij}'s, *transposed*. Consider the matrix product $\mathbf{AA}^*$:

$$\begin{pmatrix} a_{11} & \cdots & a_{1n} \\ \vdots & & \\ a_{n1} & & a_{nn} \end{pmatrix} \begin{pmatrix} A_{11} & \cdots & A_{n1} \\ \vdots & & \\ A_{1n} & & A_{nn} \end{pmatrix} = \begin{pmatrix} |\mathbf{A}| & \cdots & 0 \\ \vdots & \ddots & |\mathbf{A}| \\ 0 & & |\mathbf{A}| \end{pmatrix} = |\mathbf{A}|\mathbf{I}$$

Any element of $\mathbf{AA}^*$ off the main diagonal is formed by the product of the elements of some row of $\mathbf{A}$ and the cofactors of some other row; these products sum to zero by the theorem on alien cofactors. The diagonal elements of $\mathbf{AA}^*$, however, are formed from the sums of products of a row of $\mathbf{A}$ and the cofactors of that row; this sums to $|\mathbf{A}|$. Hence

$$\mathbf{AA}^* = |\mathbf{A}|\mathbf{I}$$

The inverse of $\mathbf{A}$, $\mathbf{A}^{-1}$, is thus $(1/|\mathbf{A}|)\mathbf{A}^*$, or

$$\mathbf{A}^{-1} = \begin{pmatrix} \dfrac{A_{11}}{|\mathbf{A}|} & \cdots & \dfrac{A_{n1}}{|\mathbf{A}|} \\ \vdots & & \\ \dfrac{A_{1n}}{|\mathbf{A}|} & & \dfrac{A_{nn}}{|\mathbf{A}|} \end{pmatrix}$$

By inspection, it can be seen that if $\mathbf{AA}^{-1} = \mathbf{I}$, then $\mathbf{A}^{-1}\mathbf{A} = \mathbf{I}$ also; that is, the left or right inverse of $\mathbf{A}$ is the same $\mathbf{A}^{-1}$. Also, $\mathbf{A}^{-1}$ is unique. Suppose there exists some $\mathbf{B}$ such that

$$\mathbf{AB} = \mathbf{I}$$

Premultiplying by $\mathbf{A}^{-1}$,

$$\mathbf{A}^{-1}\mathbf{AB} = \mathbf{IB} = \mathbf{B} = \mathbf{A}^{-1}$$

It is also true that

$$(\mathbf{AB})^{-1} = \mathbf{B}^{-1}\mathbf{A}^{-1}$$

The proof of this is left as an exercise.

Orthogonality

Two vectors are called orthogonal if their scalar product is 0.

Example 1. The vectors $\mathbf{E}_1 = (1,0,0)$, $\mathbf{E}_2 = (0,1,0)$, and $\mathbf{E}_3 = (0,0,1)$ are all mutually orthogonal.

Example 2. Let $\mathbf{a} = (2,-1,1)$, $\mathbf{b} = (-1,-1,1)$. Then $\mathbf{ab} = 0$; thus $\mathbf{a}$ and $\mathbf{b}$ are orthogonal.

Orthogonal vectors must be linearly independent. Suppose a square matrix **A** is made up of row vectors $\mathbf{a}_1, \ldots, \mathbf{a}_n$ which are mutually orthogonal, and whose Euclidean "length" is unity:

$$\|a_i\| = \sum_{j=1}^{n} a_{ij}^2 = 1$$

A is called an *orthogonal* matrix. It can be quickly verified that the transpose of **A**, **A′**, is the inverse of **A**, i.e.,

$$\mathbf{A'A} = \mathbf{I}$$

PROBLEMS

1. Find the rank of the following matrices. For which does $|\mathbf{A}| \neq 0$?

$$\mathbf{A} = \begin{pmatrix} -1 & 1 & 2 \\ 1 & -1 & -2 \\ -2 & 2 & 4 \end{pmatrix} \quad \mathbf{B} = \begin{pmatrix} 1 & 0 & -1 \\ -1 & 1 & 1 \\ 1 & -1 & -1 \end{pmatrix} \quad \mathbf{C} = \begin{pmatrix} -1 & 0 & 1 \\ 1 & -1 & 1 \\ 0 & -1 & 3 \end{pmatrix}$$

2. Prove that $(\mathbf{AB})^{-1} = \mathbf{B}^{-1}\mathbf{A}^{-1}$, if **A** and **B** are two square nonsingular matrices.

3. Prove that $(\mathbf{A}^{-1})^{-1} = \mathbf{A}$, that is, the inverse of the inverse is the original matrix.

4. Show that $(\mathbf{A'})^{-1} = (\mathbf{A}^{-1})'$, i.e., the transpose of the inverse is the inverse of the transpose.

5. Show that if **A** is $n \times n$, and **h** is an $n \times 1$ column vector, then

$$\mathbf{h'Ah} = \sum_{j=1}^{n} \sum_{i=1}^{n} a_{ij} h_i h_j$$

The expression **h′Ah** is called a quadratic form. These expressions appear in the theory of maxima and minima.

6. Show that if $\mathbf{h'Ah} < 0$ for any vectors $\mathbf{h} \neq \mathbf{0}$, then (among other things) the diagonal elements of **A** are all negative; that is, $a_{ii} < 0$, $i = 1, \ldots, n$.

7. Prove that if **A** is an orthogonal matrix, $\mathbf{A'A} = \mathbf{I}$; that is, $\mathbf{A'} = \mathbf{A}^{-1}$.

8. Prove that if the rows of a square matrix **A** are orthogonal and have unit length, the columns likewise have these properties.

SELECTED REFERENCES

The implicit function theorem can be found in any advanced calculus text. Classic references are:

Apostol, T.: *Mathematical Analysis,* Addison-Wesley Publishing Co., Inc., Reading, MA, 1957.

Courant, R.: *Differential and Integral Calculus,* 2d ed., Vols. 1 and 2, Interscience Publishers, Inc., New York, 1936.

Matrices and determinants are the subject of any linear, or matrix, algebra text. Perhaps the clearest and most useful for economists is:

Hadley, G.: *Linear Algebra,* Addison-Wesley Publishing Co., Inc. Reading, MA, 1961.

Samuelson, P. A.: *Foundations of Economic Analysis,* Harvard University Press, Cambridge, MA, 1947. The first systematic exposition of the application of the implicit function theorem in economic methodology.

CHAPTER
6

COMPARATIVE STATICS: THE TRADITIONAL METHODOLOGY

6.1 INTRODUCTION; PROFIT MAXIMIZATION ONCE MORE

In this chapter we shall begin the general comparative statics analysis of economic models that contain an explicit maximization hypothesis. The focus, as always, will be on discovering the structure that must be imposed on the models so that useful, i.e., refutable, hypotheses are implied. A very powerful methodology, *duality theory,* has been developed for some important models such as profit maximization, constrained cost minimization, and utility maximization subject to a budget constraint. These new methods provide a vast simplification and clarification of the traditional methodology for those models; we shall explore them in the next chapter. In order to analyze models other than the three just mentioned, however, and to better appreciate the newer methods, it is still necessary to understand the traditional methodology. It is to that task that we now turn.

Comparative statics of economic models involving more than one variable requires the solution to simultaneous linear equations in the partial derivatives of the choice variables with respect to the parameters. We shall employ elementary matrix manipulations and Cramer's rule in order to systematically write down the solutions to the first-order equations. In that way, the structure of these models can be most efficiently explored.

Consider again the profit-maximizing firm analyzed in Chap. 4, and recall Eqs. (4-19):

$$pf_{11}\frac{\partial x_1^*}{\partial w_1} + pf_{12}\frac{\partial x_2^*}{\partial w_1} \equiv 1$$

$$pf_{21}\frac{\partial x_1^*}{\partial w_1} + pf_{22}\frac{\partial x_2^*}{\partial w_1} \equiv 0 \tag{4-19}$$

In matrix form these equations appear as

$$\begin{pmatrix} pf_{11} & pf_{12} \\ pf_{21} & pf_{22} \end{pmatrix} \begin{pmatrix} \dfrac{\partial x_1^*}{\partial w_1} \\ \dfrac{\partial x_2^*}{\partial w_1} \end{pmatrix} \equiv \begin{pmatrix} 1 \\ 0 \end{pmatrix} \tag{6-1}$$

Using Cramer's rule,

$$\frac{\partial x_1^*}{\partial w_1} = \frac{\begin{vmatrix} 1 & pf_{12} \\ 0 & pf_{22} \end{vmatrix}}{H} = \frac{pf_{22}}{H} \tag{6-2}$$

$$\text{where } H = \begin{vmatrix} pf_{11} & pf_{12} \\ pf_{21} & pf_{22} \end{vmatrix}$$

This is Eq. (4-20a), which was derived by algebraic manipulations. Notice that the term 1 on the right-hand side of (6-1) will always appear in column i, in the solution for $\partial x_i^*/\partial w_j$. If the numerator is expanded by that column, it is immediately apparent that Eqs. (4-20a–d) can be written as

$$\frac{\partial x_i^*}{\partial w_j} = \frac{H_{ji}}{H} \quad i,j = 1,2 \tag{6-3}$$

where H_{ji} is the cofactor (signed, of course) of the element in the jth row and ith column. In this model, $H_{11} = pf_{22}$, $H_{22} = pf_{11}$, $H_{12} = H_{21} = -pf_{12}$. Notice, too, that $H = p^2(f_{11}f_{22} - f_{12}^2)$, and that $H > 0$, from the second-order conditions (4-15). This is in fact indicative of a trend; determinants will play a crucial role in the theory of maxima and minima.

In like fashion, Eqs. (4-21), dealing with changes in the factor utilizations due to output price changes, can be written

$$(pf_{ij}) \begin{pmatrix} \dfrac{\partial x_1^*}{\partial p} \\ \dfrac{\partial x_2^*}{\partial p} \end{pmatrix} \equiv \begin{pmatrix} -f_1 \\ -f_2 \end{pmatrix} \tag{6-4}$$

where the expression (pf_{ij}) stands for the 2×2 matrix in the left-hand side of (6-1). It is obvious from Cramer's rule that the solutions for $\partial x_1^*/\partial p$ and $\partial x_2^*/\partial p$ will involve the "off-diagonal" terms of pf_{12} and pf_{21}. Since the sign of these (equal) terms is not implied by maximization, we immediately suspect that no sign will emerge for $\partial x_1^*/\partial p$, etc., and hence no refutable hypotheses concerning the responses of inputs to output price changes will emerge.

The two-factor, profit-maximizing firm is an example of a maximization model with two choice variables. The most general form of such models is[†]

maximize

$$f(x_1, x_2, \alpha) \tag{6-5}$$

where the choice variables are x_1 and x_2 and α is a parameter, or perhaps a vector of parameters, $\boldsymbol{\alpha} = (\alpha_1, \ldots, \alpha_m)$. The first-order necessary conditions implied by (6-5), usually called the *equilibrium conditions*, are

$$f_1(x_1, x_2, \alpha) = 0$$
$$f_2(x_1, x_2, \alpha) = 0 \tag{6-6}$$

The second-order sufficient conditions are

$$f_{11} < 0 \quad f_{22} < 0 \quad f_{11}f_{22} - f_{12}^2 > 0 \tag{6-7}$$

Equations (6-6) are two equations in three variables, x_1, x_2, and α. The sufficient second-order conditions imply, by the implicit function theorem, that these equations can be solved for the explicit choice functions

$$x_1 = x_1^*(\alpha)$$
$$x_2 = x_2^*(\alpha) \tag{6-8}$$

It should always be remembered that Eqs. (6-8) are the *simultaneous* solutions of (6-6). As the parameter α changes, *both* x_1 and x_2 will in general change. Substituting (6-8) back into (6-6), the identities from which the comparative statics are derivable are obtained:

$$f_1(x_1^*(\alpha), x_2^*(\alpha), \alpha) \equiv 0$$
$$f_2(x_1^*(\alpha), x_2^*(\alpha), \alpha) \equiv 0 \tag{6-9}$$

Differentiating this system with respect to α, the following system is obtained.

$$f_{11}\frac{\partial x_1^*}{\partial \alpha} + f_{12}\frac{\partial x_2^*}{\partial \alpha} + f_{1\alpha} \equiv 0$$

$$f_{21}\frac{\partial x_1^*}{\partial \alpha} + f_{22}\frac{\partial x_2^*}{\partial \alpha} + f_{2\alpha} \equiv 0 \tag{6-10}$$

In matrix form, this system is

[†]The function f here refers to the whole maximand, not just the production function part of the previous objective function.

$$\begin{pmatrix} f_{11} & f_{12} \\ f_{21} & f_{22} \end{pmatrix} \begin{pmatrix} \dfrac{\partial x_1^*}{\partial \alpha} \\ \dfrac{\partial x_2^*}{\partial \alpha} \end{pmatrix} \equiv \begin{pmatrix} -f_{1\alpha} \\ -f_{2\alpha} \end{pmatrix} \tag{6-11}$$

Solving by Cramer's rule,

$$\frac{\partial x_1^*}{\partial \alpha} = \frac{\begin{vmatrix} -f_{1\alpha} & f_{12} \\ -f_{2\alpha} & f_{22} \end{vmatrix}}{H} = \frac{-f_{1\alpha}f_{22}}{H} + \frac{f_{2\alpha}f_{12}}{H} \tag{6-12a}$$

and

$$\frac{\partial x_2^*}{\partial \alpha} = \frac{\begin{vmatrix} f_{11} & -f_{1\alpha} \\ f_{21} & -f_{2\alpha} \end{vmatrix}}{H} = \frac{-f_{2\alpha}f_{11}}{H} + \frac{f_{1\alpha}f_{21}}{H} \tag{6-12b}$$

where H is the determinant

$$H = \begin{vmatrix} f_{11} & f_{12} \\ f_{21} & f_{22} \end{vmatrix} = f_{11}f_{22} - f_{12}^2 > 0 \tag{6-13}$$

Equations (6-12) represent the most general comparative statics relations for unconstrained maximization models with two choice variables. Not surprisingly at this level of generality, no refutable hypotheses are implied. Certain information is available, though. The denominators H in Eqs. (6-12) are positive. In addition, f_{11}, f_{22} are negative. This information is provided by the sufficient conditions for a maximum.

The other information that is available is provided by the actual structure of the model. Specifically, to be useful, a model must be constructed so that the effects of the parameters on the objective function, and hence the first-order equations, will in general be known. That is, $f_{1\alpha}$ and $f_{2\alpha}$ will have an assumed sign, or else the model is simply not specified well enough to yield any results. In the preceding profit maximization model, for the factor prices, (recall, f in that model designates only the production function, not the whole objective function)

$$f_{i\alpha} = \pi_{iw_i} = -1 \quad i = 1, 2 \tag{6-14}$$

and

$$\pi_{1w_2} = \pi_{2w_1} = 0$$

The parameter w_1, for example, appears only in the first first-order equation, $\pi_1 = 0$. That is, $f_{2\alpha} \equiv 0$, in Eqs. (6-10). For that reason, the term involving the cross-partial f_{12} in Eq. (6-12a) is 0. Since $\pi_{1w_1} = -1$, the result $\partial x_1^*/\partial w_1 < 0$ is obtained, for the profit maximization model.

Similarly, for w_2, $f_{2\alpha} \equiv -1$, $f_{1\alpha} \equiv 0$. Hence, in Eq. (6-12b), the only remaining term on the right-hand side is $-f_{2\alpha}f_{11}/H$. From the second-order conditions, $\partial x_2^*/\partial w_2 < 0$ is implied.

The situation is different for the parameter p, output price. Output price enters *both* first-order equations (6-10). Therefore, the indeterminate cross-term f_{12} appears in the expressions for $\partial x_1^*/\partial p$ and $\partial x_2^*/\partial p$. As a result, no refutable hypotheses emerge for this parameter, with regard to each input.

The preceding analysis suggests that refutable comparative statics theorems will be forthcoming in a maximization model only if a given parameter enters one and only one first-order equation. This result, known as the *conjugate pairs theorem,* will be shown in greater generality in the succeeding sections. From Eqs. (6-12), if some parameter, α_i, enters only the ith first-order equation, then $\partial x_i^*/\partial \alpha_i$ and $f_{i\alpha_i}$ must have the same sign. This can be expressed as

$$f_{i\alpha_i} \frac{\partial x_i^*}{\partial \alpha_i} > 0 \qquad (6\text{-}15)$$

Virtually all of the comparative statics results in economics are specific instances of Eq. (6-15), where some parameter α_i enters only the ith first-order equation.

6.2 GENERALIZATION TO n VARIABLES

Let us now investigate how the two-factor, profit maximization model is generalized to n factors. We must first derive the first- and second-order conditions for an unconstrained maximum (and minimum). We will then use the profit maximization model to motivate and illustrate the general methodology of comparative statics.

First-Order Necessary Conditions

As we noted in Chap. 4, the necessary first-order conditions for $y = f(x_1, \ldots, x_n)$ to have a stationary value is that all the first partials of f equal zero; that is, $f_i = 0$, $i = 1, \ldots, n$. This is a straightforward and intuitive generalization of the two-variable case. The second-order conditions, however, are a bit more complex.

Second-Order Sufficient Conditions

Using a Taylor series approach, as was done in the Appendix to Chap. 4, it can be shown that a sufficient condition for $y = f(x_1, \ldots, x_n)$ to have a maximum at some stationary value is that for all curves, $y(t) = f(x_1(t), \ldots, x_n(t))$, $y''(t) < 0$. Using the chain rule, this sufficient condition is

$$\frac{d^2 y}{dt^2} = \sum_{i=1}^{n} \sum_{j=1}^{n} f_{ij} \frac{dx_i}{dt} \frac{dx_j}{dt} < 0 \qquad (6\text{-}16)$$

for all dx_i/dt, dx_j/dt not all equal to 0.

A square matrix (a_{ij}) which has the property that

$$\sum_{i=1}^{n}\sum_{j=1}^{n} a_{ij}h_i h_j < 0 \tag{6-17}$$

for all nontrivial (not all 0) h_i, h_j is said to be *negative definite*. (If the strict inequality is replaced by "≤ 0," the matrix is called *negative semidefinite*.) Similarly, (a_{ij}) positive definite (semidefinite) means that the sum in (6-17) is strictly positive (nonnegative) for all nontrivial h_i, h_j. Thus, if at a point where $f_i = 0$, $i = 1, \ldots, n$, the matrix of second partials of f (called the *Hessian* matrix) is negative definite, then $f(x_1, \ldots, x_n)$ has a maximum there. If the Hessian matrix is positive definite there, a minimum exists. If the Hessian is negative semidefinite, then f definitely does *not* have a minimum, but it is not possible to say whether f has a maximum or some sort of saddle point at the stationary value. An expression of the form (6-17), in matrix form $\mathbf{h'Ah}$, is called a *quadratic form*.

Geometrically, negative definiteness of the Hessian matrix

$$\mathbf{H} = \begin{pmatrix} f_{11} & \cdots & f_{1n} \\ \vdots & & \\ f_{n1} & & f_{nn} \end{pmatrix}$$

ensures that the function f will be *strictly concave* (downward). If $\mathbf{H}$ is positive definite, f is strictly convex.

Example. Consider the function $y = (x_2 - x_1^2)(x_2 - 2x_1^2)$ depicted in Fig. 4-1 of Chap. 4. This is a function that has a minimum at the origin when evaluated along all straight lines through the origin, yet the function itself does *not* have a minimum there. The Hessian matrix of second partials is

$$\mathbf{H} = \begin{pmatrix} 24x_1^2 - 6x_2 & -6x_1 \\ -6x_1 & 2 \end{pmatrix}$$

At the origin, this matrix is

$$\mathbf{H} = \begin{pmatrix} 0 & 0 \\ 0 & 2 \end{pmatrix}$$

This matrix is clearly positive *semidefinite*:

$$Q = \sum_{j=1}^{2}\sum_{i=1}^{2} f_{ij}h_i h_j = 2h_2^2 \geq 0$$

When $h_1 = $ anything, $h_2 = 0$, this quadratic form $Q = 0$; when $h_2 \neq 0$, $Q > 0$.

In the two-variable case, $y = f(x_1, x_2)$, the sufficient second-order conditions for a maximum, (6-16), imply that $f_{11} < 0$, $f_{22} < 0$, and $f_{11}f_{22} - f_{12}^2 > 0$, as was shown in Chap. 4. Note that this last expression can be stated as the determinant of the cross-partials of the objective function,

$$\begin{vmatrix} f_{11} & f_{12} \\ f_{21} & f_{22} \end{vmatrix} > 0$$

Note also that the conditions $f_{11}, f_{22} < 0$ relate to the diagonal elements of that determinant. The theory of determinants allows a very simple statement of the sufficient second-order conditions for $y = f(x_1, \ldots, x_n)$ to have a maximum. First, consider the following construction:

Definition. Let A_n be some nth-order determinant. By a "principal minor of order k" of A_n we mean that determinant that remains of A_n when any $n - k$ rows and the *same numbered columns* are eliminated from A_n.

For example, if some row, row i, is eliminated, then to form a principal minor of order $n - 1$, *column i* must be eliminated. Since there are n choices of rows (and their corresponding columns) to eliminate, there are clearly n principal minors of order $n - 1$ of A_n. If, say, rows 1 and 3 and columns 1 and 3 are eliminated, then a principal minor or order $n - 2$ remains. There are $\binom{n}{2} = n(n - 1)/2!$ of these, and in general $\binom{n}{k} = n!/k!(n - k)!$ principal minors of order k [or order $(n - k)$]. Note that the first-order principal minors of A_n are simply the diagonal elements of A_n, and the second-order principal minors are the set of 2×2 determinants that look like

$$\begin{vmatrix} a_{ii} & a_{ij} \\ a_{ji} & a_{jj} \end{vmatrix}$$

The resemblance of this determinant to the 2×2 determinant of cross-partials of a function $f(x_1, x_2)$ provides the motivation for the following theorem.

Theorem. Consider a function $y = f(x_1, \ldots, x_n)$ which has a stationary value at $x = x^0$. Consider the Hessian matrix of cross-partials of f, (f_{ij}). Then if all of the principal minors of $|(f_{ij})|$ of order k have sign $(-1)^k$, for all $k = 1, \ldots, n$ ($k = n$ yields the whole determinant, $|(f_{ij})|$) at $x = x^0$, then $f(x_1, \ldots, x_n)$ has a maximum at $x = x^0$. If all the principal minors of $|(f_{ij})|$ are positive, for all $k = 1, \ldots, n$, at $x = x^0$, then $f(x_1, \ldots, x_n)$ has a minimum value at $x = x^0$. If any of the principal minors has a sign strictly opposite to that stated above, the function has a saddle point at $x = x^0$. If some or all of the principal minors are 0 and the rest have the appropriate sign given in the preceding conditions, then it is not possible to indicate the shape of the function at $x = x^0$. (This corresponds to the 0 second-derivative situation in the calculus of functions of one variable.)

The theorem as stated is the form in which we shall actually use the result. However, it is somewhat overstated. Consider the "naturally ordered" principal minors of an $n \times n$ Hessian,

$$|f_{11}| \quad \begin{vmatrix} f_{11} & f_{12} \\ f_{21} & f_{22} \end{vmatrix} \quad \begin{vmatrix} f_{11} & f_{12} & f_{13} \\ f_{21} & f_{22} & f_{23} \\ f_{31} & f_{32} & f_{33} \end{vmatrix} \quad \cdots$$

Recall that in the two-variable case, $f_{11} < 0$ and $f_{11}f_{22} - f_{12}^2 > 0$ implies $f_{22} < 0$. In fact, if all of these naturally ordered principal minors have the appropriate sign for a maximum or minimum of $f(x_1, \ldots, x_n)$, then all of the other principal minors have the appropriate sign. Thus, the theorem as stated is in some sense "too strong;" i.e., more is assumed than is necessary, but we shall need the sufficient condition that *all* principal minors of order k have sign $(-1)^k$ for a maximum, or that they are *all* positive for a minimum.

There are several inelegant proofs of this theorem, one by completing a rather gigantic square *à la* the proof used in Chap. 4, and an elegant proof based on matrix theory, a proof that is beyond the level of this book.[†] Hence, no proof will be offered. It is hoped that the discussion of the two-variable case will have at least made the theorem not implausible.

Profit Maximization: n Factors

Consider the profit-maximizing firm with n factors of production. The objective function, again, is

maximize

$$\pi = pf(x_1, \ldots, x_n) - \sum w_i x_i$$

The first-order conditions, again, are

$$\pi_i = pf_i - w_i = 0 \qquad i = 1, \ldots, n \tag{6-18}$$

The firm equates the value of marginal product to the wage at every margin, i.e., for every factor input. This is a straightforward generalization of the two-variable case. These equations represent n equations in the n decision variables $x_1, \ldots, x_n$ and $n + 1$ parameters $w_1, \ldots, w_n, p$. If the Jacobian determinant is nonzero, i.e.,

$$J = \left| \frac{\partial \pi_i}{\partial x_j} \right| \neq 0 \tag{6-19}$$

then at this stationary value, these equations can be solved for the explicit choice functions, i.e., the factor-demand curves,

$$x_i = x_i^*(w_1, \ldots, w_n, p) \qquad i = 1, \ldots, n \tag{6-20}$$

The sufficient conditions for a maximum are that the principal minors of $(\pi_{ij}) = (pf_{ij})$ alternate in sign, i.e., have sign $(-1)^k$, $k = 1, \ldots, n$. Since $p > 0$, this is equivalent to saying that the principal minors of the matrix of second partials of the production function,

---

[†] See George Hadley, *Linear Algebra*, Addison-Wesley Publishing Co., Inc., Reading, MA, 1961.

$$
\begin{vmatrix}
f_{11} & f_{12} & \cdots & f_{1n} \\
f_{21} & f_{22} & & f_{2n} \\
\vdots & & & \\
f_{n1} & f_{n2} & & f_{nn}
\end{vmatrix}
$$

alternate in sign. Specifically, this means that, among other things, the diagonal terms are all negative, that is, $f_{ii} < 0$, $i = 1, \ldots, n$. This says that there is diminishing marginal productivity in each factor. In addition, all $n(n-1)/2$ second-order determinants

$$
\begin{vmatrix}
f_{ii} & f_{ij} \\
f_{ji} & f_{jj}
\end{vmatrix} > 0 \quad i,j = 1, \ldots, n, \quad i \neq j
$$

The "own-effects" dominate cross-effects in the sense that $f_{ii}f_{jj} - f_{ij}^2 > 0$, i, $j = 1, \ldots, n$, $i \neq j$. Then there are all the remaining principal minors to consider; these are not easily given intuitive explanations.

The sufficient second-order conditions say that in a neighborhood of a maximum point, the objective function (in this example, this is equivalent to the production function) must be strictly concave (downward). The conditions $f_{ii} < 0$ ensure that the function is concave in all the two-dimensional planes whose axes are y and some x_i. The second-order principal minors relate to concavity in all possible three-dimensional subspaces y, x_i, x_j. But concavity in all of these lower-order dimensions is not sufficient to guarantee concavity in higher dimensions; hence, all the orders of principal minors, including the whole Hessian determinant itself, must be checked for the appropriate sign.

In terms of solving for the factor-demand curves, the *sufficient* second-order conditions guarantee that this is possible. The nth-order principal minor, i.e., the determinant of the entire (π_{ij}) matrix, has sign $(-1)^n \neq 0$ by these sufficient conditions. But this determinant is precisely the Jacobian of the system (6-18); hence, applying the implicit function theorem, the choice functions (6-20) are derivable from (6-18).

Substituting the choice functions (6-20) back into (6-18) yields the identities:

$$
pf_i(x_1^*, \ldots, x_n^*) - w_i \equiv 0, \quad i = 1, \ldots, n \tag{6-21}
$$

To find the responses of the system to a change in some factor price w_j, differentiate (6-21) with respect to w_j. This yields the system of equations:

$$
pf_{11}\frac{\partial x_1^*}{\partial w_j} + \cdots + pf_{1n}\frac{\partial x_n^*}{\partial w_j} \equiv 0
$$

$$
\vdots
$$

$$
pf_{j1}\frac{\partial x_1^*}{\partial w_j} + \cdots + pf_{jn}\frac{\partial x_n^*}{\partial w_j} \equiv 1
$$

$$
\vdots
$$

$$
pf_{n1}\frac{\partial x_1^*}{\partial w_j} + \cdots + pf_{nn}\frac{\partial x_n^*}{\partial w_j} \equiv 0
$$

In matrix notation, this system is written

$$
\begin{pmatrix} pf_{11} & \cdots & pf_{1n} \\ \vdots & & \\ pf_{n1} & & pf_{nn} \end{pmatrix}
\begin{pmatrix} \dfrac{\partial x_1^*}{\partial w_j} \\ \vdots \\ \dfrac{\partial x_n^*}{\partial w_j} \end{pmatrix}
\equiv
\begin{pmatrix} 0 \\ \vdots \\ 1 \\ \vdots \\ 0 \end{pmatrix}
\tag{6-22}
$$

where the 1 on the right-hand side appears in row j. Solving for $\partial x_i^*/\partial w_j$ by Cramer's rule involves putting the right-hand column in column i of the $|(pf_{ij})|$ determinant, in the numerator, i.e.,

$$
\frac{\partial x_i^*}{\partial w_j} = \frac{\begin{vmatrix} pf_{11} & 0 & pf_{1n} \\ \vdots & 1 & \vdots \\ pf_{n1} & 0 & pf_{nn} \end{vmatrix}}{H}
\tag{6-23}
$$

where $H = |pf_{ij}|$, the Jacobian determinant of second partials of π. Expanding the numerator by the cofactors of column i,

$$
\frac{\partial x_i^*}{\partial w_j} = \frac{H_{ji}}{H}
\tag{6-24}
$$

where H_{ji} is the cofactor of the element in row j and column i of H.

In general, H has sign $(-1)^n$ by the sufficient second-order conditions for a maximum. For $i \neq j$, however, the sign of H_{ij} is not implied by the maximum conditions. Thus, in general, no refutable implications emerge for the response of any factor to a change in the price of some *other* factor. However, when $i = j$,

$$
\frac{\partial x_i^*}{\partial w_i} = \frac{H_{ii}}{H}
\tag{6-25}
$$

The cofactor H_{ii} is a principal minor; by the maximum conditions it has sign $(-1)^{n-1}$, i.e., opposite to the sign of H. Thus,

$$
\frac{\partial x_i^*}{\partial w_i} = \frac{H_{ii}}{H} < 0 \quad i = 1, \ldots, n
\tag{6-26}
$$

As in the two-factor case, the model does yield a refutable hypothesis concerning the slope of each factor-demand curve. The response of any factor to a change in its *own* price is in the opposite direction to the change in its price.

Finally, from the symmetry of H, using Eq. (6-24),

$$
\frac{\partial x_i^*}{\partial w_j} = \frac{H_{ji}}{H} = \frac{H_{ij}}{H} = \frac{\partial x_j^*}{\partial w_i}
\tag{6-27}
$$

The reciprocity conditions thus generalize in a straightforward fashion to the n-factor case. Since the parameter p enters each first-order equation (6-18), no refutable hypotheses emerge for the responses of factor inputs to output price changes. The matrix system of comparative statics relations obtained from differentiating (6-18) with respect to p are (compare Eqs. (4-21), Chap. 4):

$$
\begin{pmatrix} pf_{11} & \cdots & pf_{1n} \\ \vdots & & \\ pf_{n1} & & pf_{nn} \end{pmatrix} \begin{pmatrix} \dfrac{\partial x_1^*}{\partial p} \\ \vdots \\ \dfrac{\partial x_n^*}{\partial p} \end{pmatrix} = \begin{pmatrix} -f_1 \\ \vdots \\ -f_n \end{pmatrix}
\tag{6-28}
$$

Solving by Cramer's rule for $\partial x_i^*/\partial p$,

$$
\frac{\partial x_i^*}{\partial p} = -\sum_{j=1}^{n} \frac{f_j H_{ji}}{H} \gtrless 0
\tag{6-29}
$$

It can be shown that if p increases, then at least one factor must increase, but this is precious little information.

Finally, the supply function of this competitive firm is defined as

$$
y = f(x_1^*(\mathbf{w}, p), \ldots, x_n^*(\mathbf{w}, p)) = y^*(w_1, \ldots, w_n, p)
$$

where $\mathbf{w}$ is the vector of factor prices $(w_1, \ldots, w_n)$. It can be shown that

$$
\frac{\partial y^*}{\partial p} > 0
\tag{6-30}
$$

and

$$
\frac{\partial y^*}{\partial w_i} = -\frac{\partial x_i^*}{\partial p} \quad i = 1, \ldots, n
\tag{6-31}
$$

We shall leave these results to a later chapter, as they are difficult to obtain by the present methods and outrageously simple by methods involving what is known as the *envelope theorem*, which will be discussed later.

6.3 THE THEORY OF CONSTRAINED MAXIMA AND MINIMA: FIRST-ORDER NECESSARY CONDITIONS

In most of the maximization problems encountered in economics, a separate, additional equation appears which constrains the values of the decision variables to some subspace of all real values, i.e., some subspace of what is referred to as Euclidean n-space. For example, in the theory of the consumer, individuals are posited to maximize a utility function, $U(x_1, x_2)$, subject to a constraint that dictates that the consumer not exceed a certain total budgetary expenditure. This problem can be stated more formally as

maximize

$$U(x_1, x_2) = U \tag{6-32}$$

subject to

$$p_1 x_1 + p_2 x_2 = M \tag{6-33}$$

where x_1 and x_2 are the amounts of two goods consumed, p_1 and p_2 their respective prices, and M is total money income. This problem can be solved simply by solving for one of the decision variables, say x_2, from the constraint, and inserting that solution into the objective function. In that case, an unconstrained problem of one less dimension results: From (6-33),

$$x_2(x_1) = \frac{-p_1}{p_2} x_1 + \frac{M}{p_2} \tag{6-34}$$

Since once x_1 is known, x_2 is known also from the preceding, the problem reduces to maximizing $U(x_1, x_2(x_1))$ over the one decision variable x_1. This yields

$$\frac{dU}{dx_1} = \frac{\partial U}{\partial x_1} + \frac{\partial U}{\partial x_2}\frac{dx_2}{dx_1}$$

$$= U_1 + U_2\frac{-p_1}{p_2} = 0$$

or

$$\frac{U_1}{U_2} = \frac{p_1}{p_2} \tag{6-35}$$

This is the familiar tangency condition that the marginal rate of substitution $(-U_1/U_2$, the rate at which a consumer is *willing* to trade off x_2 for x_1) is equal to the opportunity to do so in the market $(-p_1/p_2$, the slope of the budget line). The condition is illustrated in Fig. 6-1. Under the right curvature conditions on the utility function (to be guaranteed by the appropriate second-order conditions), point A clearly represents the maximum achievable utility if the consumer is constrained to consume some consumption bundle along the budget line MM.

The more general constrained maximum problem,

maximize

$$f(x_1, \ldots, x_n) = y$$

subject to

$$g(x_1, \ldots, x_n) = 0$$

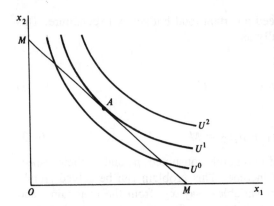

FIGURE 6-1
Utility maximization. In this diagram, three indifference levels are drawn, with $U^2 > U^1 > U^0$. The line *MM* represents a consumer's budget constraint. The constrained utility maximum occurs at point *A*, where the indifference curve is tangent to (has the same slope as) the budget constraint. The second-order conditions for a maximum say that the level curves of the utility function, i.e., the indifference curves, must be convex to the origin; i.e., the utility function must be "quasi-concave" (in addition to strictly increasing).

can be solved in the same way, i.e., by direct substitution, reducing the problem to an unconstrained one in $n - 1$ dimensions. However, a highly elegant solution that preserves the symmetry of the problem, known as the method of Lagrange multipliers (after the French mathematician Lagrange), will be given instead. The proof proceeds along the lines developed earlier for unconstrained maxima.

Consider the behavior of the function $f(x_1, \ldots, x_n)$ along some differentiable curve $\mathbf{x}(t) = (x_1(t), \ldots, x_n(t))$; that is, consider $y(t) = f(x_1(t), \ldots, x_n(t))$. If $y'(t) = 0$ and $y''(t) < 0$ for every feasible curve $\mathbf{x}(t)$, then $f(x_1, \ldots, x_n)$ has a maximum at that point. However, in this case, $\mathbf{x}(t)$ cannot represent *all* curves in n-space. Only those curves that lie in the constraint are admissible. This smaller family of curves comprises those curves for which $g(x_1(t), \ldots, x_n(t)) \equiv 0$. Notice the identity sign—we mean to ensure that $g(x_1, \ldots, x_n)$ is 0 *for every point along a given curve* $\mathbf{x}(t)$, not just for some points. The problem can be stated as follows:

maximize

$$f(x_1(t), \ldots, x_n(t)) = y(t) \tag{6-36}$$

subject to

$$g(x_1(t), \ldots, x_n(t)) \equiv 0 \tag{6-37}$$

Setting $y'(t) = 0$ yields

$$f_1 \frac{dx_1}{dt} + \cdots + f_n \frac{dx_n}{dt} = 0 \tag{6-38}$$

for all values of the dx_i/dt which satisfy the constraint. What restriction does $g(x_1(t), \ldots, x_n(t)) \equiv 0$ place on these values? Differentiating g with respect to t yields

$$g_1 \frac{dx_1}{dt} + \cdots + g_n \frac{dx_n}{dt} \equiv 0 \tag{6-39}$$

In the unconstrained case, the expression (6-38) was zero for *all* dx_i/dt; thus, in that case $f_i = 0$, $i = 1, \ldots, n$, was necessary for a maximum. Here, however, (6-38) *and* (6-39) must hold simultaneously. Hence, the values of dx_i/dt are not completely unrestricted. However, assuming $f_1 \neq 0$, we can write, from (6-38),

$$\frac{dx_1}{dt} = -\frac{f_2}{f_1}\frac{dx_2}{dt} - \cdots - \frac{f_n}{f_1}\frac{dx_n}{dt} \tag{6-40}$$

Similarly, from (6-39), if $g_1 \neq 0$,

$$\frac{dx_1}{dt} = -\frac{g_2}{g_1}\frac{dx_2}{dt} - \cdots - \frac{g_n}{g_1}\frac{dx_n}{dt} \tag{6-41}$$

Subtracting (6-40) from (6-41) yields, after factoring,

$$\left(\frac{f_2}{f_1} - \frac{g_2}{g_1}\right)\frac{dx_2}{dt} + \cdots + \left(\frac{f_n}{f_1} - \frac{g_n}{g_1}\right)\frac{dx_n}{dt} = 0 \tag{6-42}$$

and, what is more, this expression must be 0 for *all* $dx_2/dt, \ldots, dx_n/dt$. By eliminating one of the dx_i/dt's, the remaining dx_i/dt's can have unrestricted values. If $f_1 \neq 0$, $g_1 \neq 0$, then for any values whatsoever of $dx_2/dt, \ldots, dx_n/dt$, a judicious choice of dx_1/dt will allow (6-38) and (6-39) to hold. But since (6-42) holds for any values at all of $dx_2/dt, \ldots, dx_n/dt$, it must be true that the coefficients in parentheses are all 0; i.e., $f_i/f_1 = g_i/g_1$, $i = 2, \ldots, n$. In the case where all of the f_i, g_i are not 0, these conditions can be expressed simply as

$$\frac{f_i}{f_j} = \frac{g_i}{g_j} \quad i,j = 1, \ldots, n \tag{6-43}$$

These $n - 1$ conditions say that the level curves of the objective function have to be parallel to the level curves of the constraint. This is the familiar tangency condition, illustrated by the preceding utility maximization problem. The $n - 1$ conditions (6-43) and the constraint (6-37) itself constitute the complete set of first-order conditions for a constrained maximum problem with one constraint. Of course, these first-order conditions are necessary for any stationary value— maximum, minimum, or saddle shape.

The above conditions can be given an elegant and useful formulation by constructing a new function $\mathcal{L}$ called a Lagrangian, where

$$\mathcal{L} = f(x_1, \ldots, x_n) + \lambda g(x_1, \ldots, x_n)$$

The variable λ is simply a new, independent variable and is called a Lagrange multiplier.[†] Note that $\mathcal{L}$ always equals f for values of $x_1, \ldots, x_n$ that satisfy

---

[†] It is of no consequence whether one writes $\mathcal{L} = f + \lambda g$ or $\mathcal{L} = f - \lambda g$; this merely changes the sign of the Lagrange multiplier.

the constraint. Thus, $\mathcal{L}$ can be expected to have a stationary value when f does. Indeed, taking the partials of $\mathcal{L}$ with respect to $x_1, \ldots, x_n$ and λ and setting them equal to 0 yields

$$\mathcal{L}_1 = f_1 + \lambda g_1 = 0$$
$$\vdots$$
$$\mathcal{L}_n = f_n + \lambda g_n = 0$$
$$\mathcal{L}_\lambda = g(x_1, \ldots, x_n) = 0 \tag{6-44}$$

Eliminating λ from the first n equations of (6-44) (by bringing λg_i over to the right-hand side and dividing one equation by another) yields

$$\frac{f_i}{f_j} = \frac{g_i}{g_j}$$

precisely the first-order conditions for a constrained maximum. Hence, the Lagrangian function provides an easy mnemonic for writing the first-order conditions for constrained maximum problems. However, we shall see that this is a most useful construction for the second-order conditions also, and, in the theory of comparative statics, the Lagrange multiplier λ often has an interesting economic interpretation.

Example. Consider again the utility-maximization problem analyzed at the beginning of this section. The Lagrangian for this problem is

$$\mathcal{L} = U(x_1, x_2) + \lambda(M - p_1 x_1 - p_2 x_2)$$

Differentiating $\mathcal{L}$ with respect to x_1, x_2, and λ yields

$$\mathcal{L}_1 = U_1 - \lambda p_1 = 0 \tag{6-45a}$$
$$\mathcal{L}_2 = U_2 - \lambda p_2 = 0 \tag{6-45b}$$
$$\mathcal{L}_\lambda = M - p_1 x_1 - p_2 x_2 = 0 \tag{6-45c}$$

The partial $\mathcal{L}_\lambda$ is simply the budget constraint again since $\mathcal{L}$ is linear in λ. The variable λ can be eliminated from (6-45a) and (6-45b) by bringing λp_1, λp_2 over to the right-hand side and then dividing one equation by the other. This yields $U_1/U_2 = p_1/p_2$, the tangency conditions (6-35) arrived at by direct substitution.

There are many problems in economics in which more than one constraint appears. For example, a famous general-equilibrium model is that of the "small country" that maximizes the value of its output with fixed world prices, subject to constraints that say that the amount of each of several factors of production used cannot exceed a given amount. The general mathematical structure of maximization problems with r constraints is

maximize

$$f(x_1, \ldots, x_n) = y \qquad (6\text{-}46)$$

subject to

$$g^1(x_1, \ldots, x_n) = 0$$

$$\vdots$$

$$g^r(x_1, \ldots, x_n) = 0 \qquad (6\text{-}47)$$

These are r equations where, of necessity, $r < n$. (Why?)

The first-order conditions for this problem can be found by generalizing the Lagrange multiplier method previously derived. Multiplying each constraint by its own Lagrange multiplier λ^j, form the Lagrangian

$$\mathcal{L} = f(x_1, \ldots, x_n) + \lambda^1 g^1(x_1, \ldots, x_n) + \cdots + \lambda^r g^r(x_1, \ldots, x_n) \quad (6\text{-}48)$$

Then the first partials of $\mathcal{L}$ with respect to the $n + r$ variables x_i, λ^j give the correct first-order conditions:

$$\mathcal{L}_i = f_i + \lambda^1 g_i^1 + \cdots + \lambda^r g_i^r = 0 \quad i = 1, \ldots, n \qquad (6\text{-}49)$$

$$\mathcal{L}_j = g^j = 0 \quad j = 1, \ldots, r \qquad (6\text{-}50)$$

where g_i^j means $\partial g^j / \partial x_i$. The proof of this can be obtained only by more advanced methods; it is given in the next section.

6.4 CONSTRAINED MAXIMIZATION WITH MORE THAN ONE CONSTRAINT: A DIGRESSION[†]

Consider the maximization problem

maximize

$$f(x_1, \ldots, x_n) = y$$

subject to

$$g^1(x_1, \ldots, x_n) = 0$$

$$\vdots$$

$$g^r(x_1, \ldots, x_n) = 0$$

Letting $x_i = x_i(t)$, $i = 1, \ldots, n$, as before, the first-order conditions for a maximum (or any stationary value) are

$$\frac{dy}{dt} = f_1 \frac{dx_1}{dt} + \cdots + f_n \frac{dx_n}{dt} = 0 \qquad (6\text{-}51)$$

[†] In order to understand this section, the student must be familiar with some concepts of linear algebra, such as rank of a matrix, etc., developed in the Appendix to Chapter 5. I am indebted to Ron Heiner for demonstrating this approach to the problem to me.

for any $dx_1/dt, \ldots, dx_n/dt$ satisfying

$$g_1^1 \frac{dx_1}{dt} + \cdots + g_n^1 \frac{dx_n}{dt} = 0$$

$$\vdots$$

$$g_1^r \frac{dx_1}{dt} + \cdots + g_n^r \frac{dx_n}{dt} = 0 \qquad (6\text{-}52)$$

where $g_i^j = \partial g^j / \partial x_i$.

For any function $y = f(x_1, \ldots, x_n)$, the *gradient* of f, written $\nabla \mathbf{f}$, is a vector composed of the first partials of f:

$$\nabla \mathbf{f} = (f_1, \ldots, f_n)$$

The differential of f can be written

$$dy = \nabla \mathbf{f} \, d\mathbf{x}$$

where $d\mathbf{x} = (dx_1, \ldots, dx_n)$. Along a level surface, $dy = 0$, and hence $\nabla \mathbf{f}$ is orthogonal to the direction of the tangent hyperplane. The gradient of f, $\nabla \mathbf{f}$, thus represents the direction of maximum increase of $f(x_1, \ldots, x_n)$.

Note that Eq. (6-51) is the scalar product of the gradient of f, $\nabla \mathbf{f}$, and the vector $\mathbf{h} = (h_1, \ldots, h_n) = (dx_1/dt, \ldots, dx_n/dt)$. Likewise, Eqs. (6-52) are the scalar products of the gradients of the g^j functions, $\nabla \mathbf{g}^j$, and $\mathbf{h}$. Let $\nabla \mathbf{g}$ denote the $r \times n$ matrix whose rows are, respectively, $\nabla \mathbf{g}^1, \ldots, \nabla \mathbf{g}^r$. Then Eqs. (6-51) and (6-52) can be written, respectively,

$$\nabla \mathbf{f} \cdot \mathbf{h} = 0 \qquad (6\text{-}53)$$

for all $\mathbf{h} \neq 0$ satisfying

$$(\nabla \mathbf{g})\mathbf{h} = \mathbf{0} \qquad (6\text{-}54)$$

Assume now that the matrix $\nabla \mathbf{g}$ has rank r, equal to the number of constraints. This says that the constraints are independent, i.e., there are no redundant constraints. If the rank of $\nabla \mathbf{g}$ was less than r, say $r - 1$, then one constraint could be dropped and the subspace in which the dx_i/dt could range would not be affected. It is as if a ration-point constraint were imposed with the ration prices proportional to the original money prices. In that case, the additional rationing constraint would either be redundant to or inconsistent with the original budget constraint.

Assuming rank $\nabla \mathbf{g} = r$, the rows of $\nabla \mathbf{g}$, that is, the gradient vectors $\nabla \mathbf{g}^j = (g_1^j, \ldots, g_n^j)$, $j = 1, \ldots, r$, form a basis for an r-dimensional subspace E_r of E_n, Euclidean n-space. From (6-54), the admissible vectors $\mathbf{h}$ are all orthogonal to E_r; hence, they must all lie in the remaining $n - r$ dimensional space, E_r'. However, from (6-53), $\nabla \mathbf{f}$ is orthogonal to all those $\mathbf{h}$'s, and hence to E_r'. Hence, $\nabla \mathbf{f}$ must lie in E_r. Since the vectors $\nabla \mathbf{g}^j$ form a basis for E_r, $\nabla \mathbf{f}$ can be written as a unique linear combination of those vectors, or

$$\nabla \mathbf{f} = \lambda^1 \nabla \mathbf{g}^1 + \cdots + \lambda^r \nabla \mathbf{g}^r \qquad (6\text{-}55)$$

However, this is equivalent to setting the partial derivatives of the Lagrangian expression $\mathcal{L} = f - \sum \lambda^j g^j$ with respect to $x_1, \ldots, x_n$ equal to 0.

6.5 SECOND-ORDER CONDITIONS

In the past two sections, the first-order necessary conditions for a function to achieve a stationary value subject to constraints were derived. Those conditions are implied whenever the function has a maximum, a minimum, or a saddle shape (a minimum in some directions and a maximum in others). We now seek to state sufficient conditions under which the type of stationary position can be specified. The discussion will be largely limited to the two-variable case, with the general theorems stated at the end of this section.

Consider the two-variable problem,

maximize

$$f(x_1, x_2) = y$$

subject to

$$g(x_1, x_2) = 0$$

The Lagrangian function is $\mathcal{L}(x_1, x_2, \lambda) = f(x_1, x_2) + \lambda g(x_1, x_2)$. The first-order conditions are, again,

$$\frac{dy}{dt} = f_1 \frac{dx_1}{dt} + f_2 \frac{dx_2}{dt} = 0 \qquad (6\text{-}56)$$

for all dx_1/dt, dx_2/dt satisfying

$$g_1 \frac{dx_1}{dt} + g_2 \frac{dx_2}{dt} \equiv 0 \qquad (6\text{-}57)$$

These conditions imply that $\mathcal{L}_1 = f_1 + \lambda g_1 = 0$, $\mathcal{L}_2 = f_2 + \lambda g_2 = 0$. Sufficient conditions for these equations to represent a relative *maximum* are that $d^2y/dt^2 < 0$, for all dx_1/dt, dx_2/dt satisfying (6-57). Similarly, $d^2y/dt^2 > 0$, under those conditions implies a *minimum*. How can these conditions be put into a more useful form? Differentiating (6-56) again with respect to t, the sufficient second-order condition is

$$\frac{d^2y}{dt^2} = f_1 \frac{d^2x_1}{dt^2} + f_2 \frac{d^2x_2}{dt^2} + f_{11}\left(\frac{dx_1}{dt}\right)^2$$

$$+ 2f_{12}\frac{dx_1}{dt}\frac{dx_2}{dt} + f_{22}\left(\frac{dx_2}{dt}\right)^2 < 0 \qquad (6\text{-}58)$$

subject to

$$g_1 \frac{dx_1}{dt} + g_2 \frac{dx_2}{dt} \equiv 0 \qquad (6\text{-}57)$$

Since (6-57) is an identity, differentiate it again with respect to t, remembering that g_1 and g_2 are functions of $x_1(t)$, $x_2(t)$. This yields

$$g_1 \frac{d^2x_1}{dt^2} + g_2 \frac{d^2x_2}{dt^2} + g_{11}\left(\frac{dx_1}{dt}\right)^2 + 2g_{12}\frac{dx_1}{dt}\frac{dx_2}{dt} + g_{22}\left(\frac{dx_2}{dt}\right)^2 \equiv 0 \quad (6\text{-}59)$$

Now multiply (6-59) through by λ, the Lagrange multiplier, and add to Eq. (6-58). Since this amounts to adding 0,

$$\frac{d^2y}{dt^2} = (f_1 + \lambda g_1)\frac{d^2x_1}{dt^2} + (f_2 + \lambda g_2)\frac{d^2x_2}{dt^2} + (f_{11} + \lambda g_{11})\left(\frac{dx_1}{dt}\right)^2$$

$$+ 2(f_{12} + \lambda g_{12})\frac{dx_1}{dt}\frac{dx_2}{dt} + (f_{22} + \lambda g_{22})\left(\frac{dx_2}{dt}\right)^2 < 0 \quad (6\text{-}60)$$

subject to (6-57). However, from the first-order conditions, $\mathcal{L}_1 = f_1 + \lambda g_1 = 0$, $\mathcal{L}_2 = f_2 + \lambda g_2 = 0$. Also, $f_{11} + \lambda g_{11}$ is simply $\mathcal{L}_{11}$, and likewise $\mathcal{L}_{12} = f_{12} + \lambda g_{12}$, et cetera. If we simplify the notation a bit and write $h_1 = dx_1/dt$, $h_2 = dx_2/dt$, then the sufficient second-order conditions for a maximum are that

$$\mathcal{L}_{11}h_1^2 + 2\mathcal{L}_{12}h_1h_2 + \mathcal{L}_{22}h_2^2 < 0 \quad (6\text{-}61)$$

for all h_1, h_2 not both equal to 0, such that

$$g_1h_1 + g_2h_2 \equiv 0 \quad (6\text{-}62)$$

For the case of n variables and one constraint, the derivations proceed along similar lines, producing

$$\sum_{i=1}^{n}\sum_{j=1}^{n} \mathcal{L}_{ij}h_i h_j < 0 \quad (6\text{-}63)$$

for all h_i, h_j such that

$$\sum_{i=1}^{n} g_i h_i \equiv 0 \cdot \quad (6\text{-}64)$$

In this case the matrix of terms $(\mathcal{L}_{ij})$ is said to be *negative definite subject to constraint*.

Equations (6-61) and (6-62) can be combined into one useful expression: From (6-62),

$$h_2 = -h_1\frac{g_1}{g_2}$$

Substituting this into (6-61) yields

$$\mathcal{L}_{11}h_1^2 + 2\mathcal{L}_{12}h_1\left(-h_1\frac{g_1}{g_2}\right) + \mathcal{L}_{22}\left(-h_1\frac{g_1}{g_2}\right)^2 < 0$$

Or, by multiplying by g_2^2,

$$(\mathscr{L}_{11}g_2^2 - 2\mathscr{L}_{12}g_1g_2 + \mathscr{L}_{22}g_1^2)h_1^2 < 0 \qquad (6\text{-}65)$$

for any value of $h_1 \neq 0$. This implies that the expression in the parentheses must itself be < 0. How can that expression be conveniently remembered? It turns out, fortuitously, that the expression in parentheses in (6-65) is precisely the negative of the determinant

$$H = \begin{vmatrix} \mathscr{L}_{11} & \mathscr{L}_{12} & g_1 \\ \mathscr{L}_{21} & \mathscr{L}_{22} & g_2 \\ g_1 & g_2 & 0 \end{vmatrix} \qquad (6\text{-}66)$$

as can be immediately verified by expansion of H. *Hence, a sufficient condition for $f(x_1, x_2)$ to have a maximum subject to $g(x_1, x_2) \equiv 0$ is, together with the first-order relations, that $H > 0$.* Likewise, for a minimum subject to constraint, the sufficient second-order condition is that $H < 0$. Also, $H = 0$ corresponds to the case where the second derivatives $d^2y/dt^2 = 0$, hence no statement can be made regarding the type of stationary value in question. Note that $\partial^2 \mathscr{L}/\partial x_1 \partial \lambda \equiv \mathscr{L}_{1\lambda} \equiv g_1 \equiv \mathscr{L}_{\lambda 1}$ and $\mathscr{L}_{2\lambda} \equiv \mathscr{L}_{\lambda 2} \equiv g_2$, and $\mathscr{L}_{\lambda\lambda} = 0$, since λ enters the Lagrangian $\mathscr{L} = f + \lambda g$ linearly. Hence, H is simply the determinant of the matrix of cross-partials of $\mathscr{L}$ with respect to x_1, x_2, and λ, that is,

$$H = \begin{vmatrix} \mathscr{L}_{11} & \mathscr{L}_{12} & \mathscr{L}_{1\lambda} \\ \mathscr{L}_{21} & \mathscr{L}_{22} & \mathscr{L}_{2\lambda} \\ \mathscr{L}_{\lambda 1} & \mathscr{L}_{\lambda 2} & \mathscr{L}_{\lambda\lambda} \end{vmatrix}$$

For the n-variable case, the situation is more complicated, but the rules are analogous to the unconstrained case. The Lagrangian is $\mathscr{L} = f(x_1, \ldots, x_n) + \lambda g(x_1, \ldots, x_n)$. Consider the matrix of cross-partials of $\mathscr{L}$ with respect to $x_1, \ldots, x_n$ and λ, noting, as before, that $\mathscr{L}_{i\lambda} = g_i$, $\mathscr{L}_{\lambda\lambda} = 0$:

$$\mathbf{H} = \begin{pmatrix} \mathscr{L}_{11} & \cdots & \mathscr{L}_{1n} & g_1 \\ \vdots & & & \\ \mathscr{L}_{n1} & & \mathscr{L}_{nn} & g_n \\ g_1 & & g_n & 0 \end{pmatrix}$$

This matrix is commonly referred to as a "bordered Hessian" matrix, noting how the first partials of the constraint function g *border* the cross-partials of $\mathscr{L}$ with respect to $x_1, \ldots, x_n$.

Consider the following construction: By a "*border-preserving* principal minor of order k" of the preceding matrix, we mean that determinant that remains when any $n - k$ rows and the same numbered columns are deleted, *with the special added proviso that the border itself not be deleted.* Hence, the deletions that can occur must only come from rows 1 through n, not row or column $n + 1$. (Note that a border-preserving principal minor of order k is a $(k + 1) \times (k + 1)$ determinant.)

The second-order sufficient conditions are then:

Theorem. Together with the first-order conditions $\mathcal{L}_i = 0$, $i = 1, \ldots, n$ and $\mathcal{L}_\lambda = g = 0$, if all the border-preserving principal minors of H of order k have sign $(-1)^k$, $k = 2, \ldots, n$, then a maximum position is obtained. If all the border-preserving principal minors are negative, $k = 2, \ldots, n$, then a minimum is obtained.[†]

Suppose, even more generally, that there are r constraints involved. The Lagrangian function is $\mathcal{L} = f(x_1, \ldots, x_n) + \sum_{j=1}^{r} \lambda_j g^j(x_1, \ldots, x_n)$. The bordered Hessian matrix of this Langrangian is

$$
\mathbf{H} = \begin{pmatrix}
\mathcal{L}_{11} & \cdots & \mathcal{L}_{1n} & g_1^1 & \cdots & g_1^r \\
\vdots & & & & & \\
\mathcal{L}_{n1} & & \mathcal{L}_{nn} & g_n^1 & & g_n^r \\
g_1^1 & & g_n^1 & 0 & & 0 \\
\vdots & & & & & \\
g_1^r & & g_n^r & 0 & & 0
\end{pmatrix}
$$

The sufficient conditions here state that for a *minimum,* the border-preserving principal minors of order $k > r$ (which again must involve deletions only from rows 1 through n) have sign $(-1)^r$, where r is the number of (independent) constraints. For a *maximum,* the border-preserving principal minors of order $k > r$ alternate in sign, beginning with $(-1)^{r+1}$, the second of opposite sign, etc. These principal minors must be of order greater than r, because, as inspection of H reveals (note the $r \times r$ matrix of 0's in the lower right), a determinant involving fewer than r rows and columns from rows and columns 1 through n must equal 0. Note again that with r bordering rows, a border-preserving principal minor of order k has $k + r$ rows and columns. An alternative presentation of the second-order conditions is given in Table 6-1. In this table, $m \geq 2r + 1$ is the size of the whole determinant.

The Geometry of Constrained Maximization

We visualize an unconstrained maximization in three dimensions as the top of a hill; the surface must be concave there. Constrained maxima (or minima) are somewhat more subtle. Consider the problem in two variables:

maximize

$$f(x_1, x_2) = y$$

subject to

$$g(x_1, x_2) = k$$

[†]In fact, if only the "naturally ordered" principal minors have this property, then *all* of the border-preserving principal minors have that property.

TABLE 6.1
Second-order conditions: Sign of all size $m \times m$ (border-preserving) principal minors

Condition	Constraints 0	1	r
Maximum	$(-1)^m$	$(-1)^{m-1}$	$(-1)^{m-r}$
	$m = 1, \ldots, n$	$m = 3, \ldots, n + 1$	$m = 1 + 2r, \ldots, n + r$
Minimum	$(-1)^0 = +1$	$(-1)^1 = -1$	$(-1)^r$

The constraint $g(x_1, x_2) = k$ represents a curve in the x_1, x_2 plane; we typically think of it as a "frontier," i.e., some sort of boundary that constrains consumption or production. Assume that the first partials g_1 and g_2 are positive, so that the frontier has a negative slope $(-g_1/g_2)$, and increases in k move the frontier "northeast" in the x_1, x_2 plane. Three such frontiers are represented in Fig. 6-2: in panel (a), the frontier is concave, in panel (b) it is linear, and in panel (c) it is convex.

Assume that the first partials of $f(x_1, x_2)$ are also positive, so that the level curves of f are likewise negatively sloping $(-f_1/f_2)$, and increasing values of f are associated with level curves that are increasingly distant from the origin. It is visually obvious that if the constrained maximum occurs at some interior point along the frontier (i.e., not at a corner, where the constraint intersects an axis), the maximum occurs where a level curve of $f(x_1, x_2)$ is tangent to the frontier. This is the algebraic condition $-f_1/f_2 = -g_1/g_2$, derived earlier. However, this tangency condition is implied by both a maximum and a minimum. If this condition is to represent a maximum, the level curves of the objective function must be either less concave than the constraint frontier, as shown in panel (a), or more convex than the frontier, as shown in panels (b) and (c).

If the constraint is linear, the level curves must appear "convex to the origin," the classic shape attributed to consumer's indifference curves and production isoquants. However, this characterization is in fact imprecise. The essential property required of the objective function to guarantee a constrained maximum subject to a linear constraint is that $f(x_1, x_2)$ be strictly increasing and *quasi-concave*. This latter characteristic is defined as follows.

Consider a typical indifference curve U^0 as shown in Fig. 6-3. Consider the set, call it S, of points that are at least as preferred as a point on U^0, shown as the shaded area. This set has the property that if any two points in S are connected by a straight line, the entire line also lies in S. A set with this property is called a *convex set* (not to be confused with a convex function). (As an example of a set that is not convex, consider the set of consumption bundles that are *less* preferred than those on U^0.) Algebraically, if $\mathbf{x}^0 = (x_1^0, x_2^0)$ and $\mathbf{x}^1 = (x_1^1, x_2^1)$ are any two points in the x_1, x_2 plane, $\mathbf{x}^t = t\mathbf{x}^0 + (1 - t)\mathbf{x}^1$, $0 \le t \le 1$ represents all points on the straight line joining $\mathbf{x}^0$ and $\mathbf{x}^1$. *A function is called quasi-concave if the set of points for which the function takes on values greater than or equal*

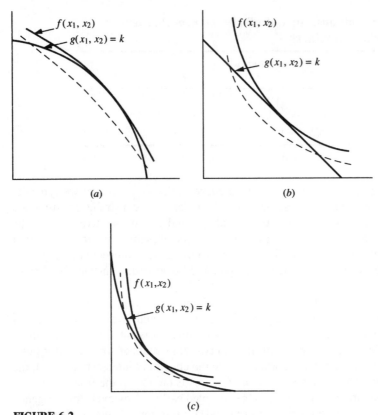

FIGURE 6-2
Constrained Maximization Constrained maximization requires, for increasing functions, than the
level curves of the objective function be either less concave or more convex than the level curves of
the constraint. If the constraint is linear, as in panel (b), or convex, as in (c), the level curves of the
objective function must be "convex to the origin," i.e., the objective function must quasi-concave.

to some arbitrary value comprises a convex set. That is, $U(x_1, x_2)$ is quasi-
concave if $U(\mathbf{x}^1) \geq U(\mathbf{x}^0)$ implies $U(t\mathbf{x}^0 + (1-t)\mathbf{x}^1) \geq U(\mathbf{x}^0)$, $0 \leq t \leq 1$.
(The definition is generalized in an obvious way for functions of n variables.)
We note in passing that if the function *decreases* as the distance from the origin
increases, quasi-concavity produces level curves that are "concave to the origin."
     Recall from Chap. 2 that a concave function is one for which $f(t\mathbf{x}^0 +$
$(1-t)\mathbf{x}^1) \geq tf(\mathbf{x}^0) + (1-t)f(\mathbf{x}^1)$, $0 \leq t \leq 1$. Concavity clearly implies
quasi-concavity: assuming $f(\mathbf{x}^1) \geq f(\mathbf{x}^0)$, $f(t\mathbf{x}^0 + (1-t)\mathbf{x}^1) \geq tf(\mathbf{x}^0) +$
$(1-t)f(\mathbf{x}^1) \geq tf(\mathbf{x}^0) + (1-t)f(\mathbf{x}^0) = f(\mathbf{x}^0)$. The converse, however, is
not true. Quasi-concavity is a weaker restriction than concavity. Concavity is
required for an unconstrained maximum; quasi-concavity is all that is required
for maximization subject to a linear constraint. In the preceding theorem, the
second-order conditions dealing with the signs of the border-preserving principal

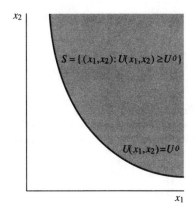

FIGURE 6-3
Quasi-concavity A function is said to be quasi-concave if the set of points for which the function takes on values greater that or equal to some arbitrary amount, say, U^0, is a convex set. These points are represented by the shaded area. This is the property generally assumed for utility and production functions.

minors define algebraically the geometric properties of the objective and constraint functions required for a constrained maximum (or minimum). If the constraint is linear, these second-order conditions for a maximum can be used to define algebraically the property of quasi-concavity of the objective function. (This requires the additional step of using the first-order conditions to replace the first partials of g with those of f in the bordering row and column.) If a linear objective function is *minimized* subject to constraint, these second-order conditions likewise describe quasi-concavity of the constraint function. This situation is encountered in Chap. 8, dealing with the minimization of cost subject to an output constraint. These concepts will be applied in the following chapters. Lastly, it is true, but not easy to prove, that if a function $f(\mathbf{x})$, $\mathbf{x} = (x_1, \ldots, x_n)$ is quasi-concave and linear homogeneous, it is (weakly) concave. Also, if f is strictly quasi-concave and homogeneous of degree r, $0 < r < 1$, it is strictly concave. The proofs are left as exercises.

Example. Consider again the basic consumer theory model, maximize $U(x_1, x_2)$ subject to $p_1x_1 + p_2x_2 = M$. (See Fig. 6-1 again.) Assuming more is preferred to less, the ordinal indifference levels must be indexed such that $U^2 > U^1 > U^0$. The condition that a point of tangency of an indifference curve and the budget constraint actually represents a maximum rather than a minimum of utility subject to a linear budget constraint is that the utility function be strictly increasing and quasi-concave. In this two-variable model, these conditions imply the usual shape, "convex to the origin." These assumptions comprise the law of diminishing marginal rate of substitution, i.e., in two dimensions, that the slope of the level (indifference) curve increases (becomes less negative) as x_1 increases. We showed in Chap. 3 that the algebraic expression of this shape is [see Sec. 3.6, Eq. (3-32)]

$$\frac{d^2x_2}{dx_1^2} \equiv [-U_2^2 U_{11} + 2U_{12}U_1U_2 - U_1^2 U_{22}]\frac{1}{U_2^3} > 0 \qquad (6\text{-}67)$$

If this is to be positive, the square-bracketed term must be positive, assuming that $U_2 > 0$, i.e., the consumer is not sated in good 2. But by inspection, the term in brackets is equal to the following determinant, which must therefore itself be positive:

$$H' = \begin{vmatrix} U_{11} & U_{12} & -U_1 \\ U_{21} & U_{22} & -U_2 \\ -U_1 & -U_2 & 0 \end{vmatrix} > 0 \tag{6-68}$$

However, from the first-order conditions for utility maximization (6-45), $U_1 = \lambda p_1$, $U_2 = \lambda p_2$. Substituting this into H' and then dividing the last row and column by λ (and, hence, H' by λ^2, which is positive), the condition $H' > 0$ is equivalent to

$$H = \begin{vmatrix} U_{11} & U_{12} & -p_1 \\ U_{21} & U_{22} & -p_2 \\ -p_1 & -p_2 & 0 \end{vmatrix} > 0 \tag{6-69}$$

But H is seen to be the determinant of the bordered Hessian matrix, the cross-partials of $\mathscr{L}$ with respect to x_1, x_2, and λ. This is in accordance with the general theorem of this section.

6.6 GENERAL METHODOLOGY

At the beginning of this chapter, we considered the general economic model which was characterized by being an *unconstrained* maximization. Let us now explore models that have a constraint as an added feature.

Consider some economic agent that behaves in accordance with the following general model.

maximize

$$f(x_1, x_2, \alpha) = y \tag{6-70}$$

subject to

$$g(x_1, x_2, \alpha) = 0 \tag{6-71}$$

where x_1 and x_2 are the decision variables and α is some parameter (or vector of parameters) over which the agent has no control. What will be the response to autonomous changes in the environment, i.e., to changes in the parameter α?

The first-order conditions for a maximum are derived by setting the partials of the Lagrangian function $\mathscr{L} = f(x_1, x_2, \alpha) + \lambda g(x_1, x_2, \alpha)$, with respect to x_1, x_2, and λ, equal to zero:

$$\begin{aligned} \mathscr{L}_1 &= f_1(x_1, x_2, \alpha) + \lambda g_1(x_1, x_2, \alpha) = 0 \\ \mathscr{L}_2 &= f_2(x_1, x_2, \alpha) + \lambda g_2(x_1, x_2, \alpha) = 0 \\ \mathscr{L}_\lambda &= g(x_1, x_2, \alpha) = 0 \end{aligned} \tag{6-72}$$

Equations (6-72) represent three equations in the four unknowns x_1, x_2, λ, and α. Assuming the implicit function theorem (as was discussed previously) is applicable, these equations can be solved, in principle at least, for the choice functions

$$x_1 = x_1^*(\alpha)$$
$$x_2 = x_2^*(\alpha) \tag{6-73}$$
$$\lambda = \lambda^*(\alpha)$$

Substituting these values back into Eqs. (6-72) from which they were derived yields the *identities*

$$f_1(x_1^*, x_2^*, \alpha) + \lambda^* g_1(x_1^*, x_2^*, \alpha) \equiv 0$$
$$f_2(x_1^*, x_2^*, \alpha) + \lambda^* g_2(x_1^*, x_2^*, \alpha) \equiv 0 \tag{6-74}$$
$$g(x_1^*, x_2^*, \alpha) \equiv 0$$

Since we are interested in *changes* in the x_i^*'s (i.e., marginal values) as α changes, we differentiate (6-74) with respect to α, using the chain rule. The first equation then yields

$$f_{11}\frac{\partial x_1^*}{\partial \alpha} + f_{12}\frac{\partial x_2^*}{\partial \alpha} + f_{1\alpha} + \lambda^* g_{11}\frac{\partial x_1^*}{\partial \alpha} + \lambda^* g_{12}\frac{\partial x_2^*}{\partial \alpha} + \lambda^* g_{1\alpha} + g_1\frac{\partial \lambda^*}{\partial \alpha} \equiv 0$$

However, noting that $\mathcal{L}_{11} = f_{11} + \lambda^* g_{11}, \ldots$, this equation can be more conveniently written

$$\mathcal{L}_{11}\frac{\partial x_1^*}{\partial \alpha} + \mathcal{L}_{12}\frac{\partial x_2^*}{\partial \alpha} + g_1\frac{\partial \lambda^*}{\partial \alpha} \equiv -\mathcal{L}_{1\alpha} \tag{6-75}$$

Similarly, differentiating the second and third equations of (6-74) yields

$$\mathcal{L}_{21}\frac{\partial x_1^*}{\partial \alpha} + \mathcal{L}_{22}\frac{\partial x_2^*}{\partial \alpha} + g_2\frac{\partial \lambda^*}{\partial \alpha} \equiv -\mathcal{L}_{2\alpha} \tag{6-76}$$

$$g_1\frac{\partial x_1^*}{\partial \alpha} + g_2\frac{\partial x_2^*}{\partial \alpha} \equiv -g_\alpha \tag{6-77}$$

In matrix notation, this system of three linear equations can be written

$$\begin{pmatrix} \mathcal{L}_{11} & \mathcal{L}_{12} & g_1 \\ \mathcal{L}_{21} & \mathcal{L}_{22} & g_2 \\ g_1 & g_2 & 0 \end{pmatrix} \begin{pmatrix} \dfrac{\partial x_1^*}{\partial \alpha} \\ \dfrac{\partial x_2^*}{\partial \alpha} \\ \dfrac{\partial \lambda^*}{\partial \alpha} \end{pmatrix} = \begin{pmatrix} -\mathcal{L}_{1\alpha} \\ -\mathcal{L}_{2\alpha} \\ -g_\alpha \end{pmatrix} \tag{6-78}$$

Notice that the coefficient matrix on the left of (6-78) is the matrix of second partials of the Lagrangian function. In unconstrained maximization models, this coefficient matrix was the matrix of second partials of the objective function.

The manipulation of the model is formally identical in the constrained and unconstrained cases; the only difference is the conditions imposed on the principal minors of the coefficient matrix by the sufficient second-order conditions.

The reason why the coefficient matrix comes out to be the second partials of $\mathscr{L}$ is that identities (6-74) are precisely the first partials of $\mathscr{L}$,

$$\mathscr{L}_1(x_1^*, x_2^*, \lambda^*, \alpha) \equiv 0$$

$$\mathscr{L}_2(x_1^*, x_2^*, \lambda^*, \alpha) \equiv 0 \tag{6-79}$$

$$\mathscr{L}_\lambda(x_1^*, x_2^*, \alpha) \equiv 0$$

(Notice that λ^* does not appear in $\mathscr{L}_\lambda = g(x_1^*, x_2^*, \alpha) \equiv 0$.) Differentiating the first identity with respect to α yields

$$\mathscr{L}_{11}\frac{\partial x_1^*}{\partial \alpha} + \mathscr{L}_{12}\frac{\partial x_2^*}{\partial \alpha} + \mathscr{L}_{1\lambda}\frac{\partial \lambda^*}{\partial \alpha} + \mathscr{L}_{1\alpha} \equiv 0$$

This is precisely Eq. (6-75), noting again that $\mathscr{L}_{1\lambda} = g_1$. In like fashion, Eqs. (6-76) and (6-77) are derivable directly from $\mathscr{L}_2 \equiv 0$, $\mathscr{L}_\lambda \equiv 0$.

Since the Jacobian determinant J needed to ensure solution of Eqs. (6-72) for the explicit choice functions (6-73) is formed from the matrix of first partials of (6-72), J is in fact the determinant of second partials of the Lagrangian $\mathscr{L}$ with respect to x_1, x_2, and λ, that is, the determinant of the coefficient matrix in (6-78). This determinant is denoted by H below. The *sufficient* second-order conditions imply, among other things, that this determinant is nonzero, and thus the explicit relations (6-73) are valid. And this determinant forms the denominator in the solution by Cramer's rule for $\partial x_i^*/\partial \alpha$ and $\partial \lambda^*/\partial \alpha$. Let us now proceed, in the same manner as for the unconstrained models.

Solving for $\partial x_1^*/\partial \alpha$ by Cramer's rule,

$$\frac{\partial x_1^*}{\partial \alpha} = \frac{\begin{vmatrix} -\mathscr{L}_{1\alpha} & \mathscr{L}_{12} & g_1 \\ -\mathscr{L}_{2\alpha} & \mathscr{L}_{22} & g_2 \\ -g_\alpha & g_2 & 0 \end{vmatrix}}{H} = \frac{-\mathscr{L}_{1\alpha}H_{11}}{H} - \frac{\mathscr{L}_{2\alpha}H_{21}}{H} - \frac{g_\alpha H_{31}}{H} \tag{6-80}$$

where H is the bordered Hessian determinant of the coefficient matrix. Solutions for $\partial x_2^*/\partial \alpha$ and $\partial \lambda^*/\partial \alpha$ are, likewise,

$$\frac{\partial x_2^*}{\partial \alpha} = \frac{\begin{vmatrix} \mathscr{L}_{11} & -\mathscr{L}_{1\alpha} & g_1 \\ \mathscr{L}_{21} & -\mathscr{L}_{2\alpha} & g_2 \\ g_1 & -g_\alpha & 0 \end{vmatrix}}{H} = \frac{-\mathscr{L}_{1\alpha}H_{12}}{H} - \frac{\mathscr{L}_{2\alpha}H_{22}}{H} - \frac{g_\alpha H_{32}}{H} \tag{6-81}$$

$$\frac{\partial \lambda^*}{\partial \alpha} = \frac{\begin{vmatrix} \mathscr{L}_{11} & \mathscr{L}_{12} & -\mathscr{L}_{1\alpha} \\ \mathscr{L}_{21} & \mathscr{L}_{22} & -\mathscr{L}_{2\alpha} \\ g_1 & g_2 & -g_\alpha \end{vmatrix}}{H} = \frac{-\mathscr{L}_{1\alpha}H_{13}}{H} - \frac{\mathscr{L}_{2\alpha}H_{23}}{H} - \frac{g_\alpha H_{33}}{H} \tag{6-82}$$

It is clear that at this level of generality, no prediction as to the sign of $\partial x_i^*/\partial \alpha$ or $\partial \lambda^*/\partial \alpha$ is forthcoming. There simply is not enough information in the system. All we know is that the denominators in these expressions are positive, but we have no information regarding the numerators. The signs of the off-diagonal cofactors are not implied by the maximum conditions.

Suppose now that the parameter α did not appear in either the second or third first-order relations (6-72). Then $\mathcal{L}_{2\alpha} = 0$ and $g_\alpha = 0$, and

$$\frac{\partial x_1^*}{\partial \alpha} = \frac{-\mathcal{L}_{1\alpha} \begin{vmatrix} \mathcal{L}_{22} & g_2 \\ g_2 & 0 \end{vmatrix}}{H} = \frac{+\mathcal{L}_{1\alpha} g_2^2}{H} \qquad (6\text{-}83)$$

The partial $\partial x_1^*/\partial \alpha$ now has a predictable sign: Since $H > 0$ and $H_{11} < 0$, by the second-order conditions (here, $H_{11} = -g_2^2 < 0$ always), $\partial x_1^*/\partial \alpha$ will have the same sign as the direction of "disturbance" of the first equation. That is, if an increase in α has the effect of shifting the marginal curve $\mathcal{L}_1$ to the right ($\mathcal{L}_{1\alpha} > 0$), then the response will be to increase the utilization of x_1. Hence, if it is possible to make statements like, "an increase in income will *shift* a demand curve to the right," or "a change in technology will lower (shift down) such and such marginal cost curve," then if that income or technology parameter enters only one first-order relation, it will in general be possible to predict the direction of change of the associated variable (the one for which that first-order equation is the first partial of the Lagrangian). More succinctly, if α enters the ith first-order equation only, then $\partial x_i^*/\partial \alpha$ and $\mathcal{L}_{i\alpha}$ have the same sign, or

$$\frac{\partial x_i^*}{\partial \alpha} \mathcal{L}_{i\alpha} > 0 \qquad (6\text{-}84)$$

This result holds for the case of n variables as well as for just two variables; its precise statement is given in the problems following. The result follows because of the conditions on the principal minors imposed by the second-order conditions for a constrained maximum.

In the case of $\partial \lambda^*/\partial \alpha$, however, a sign is *never* implied by the sufficient second-order conditions alone, no matter how the parameter α enters the first-order equations. Suppose, for example, α enters only the constraint, i.e., the third first-order equation. Then $-\mathcal{L}_{1\alpha} = -\mathcal{L}_{2\alpha} = 0$, and

$$\frac{\partial \lambda^*}{\partial \alpha} = \frac{-g_\alpha H_{33}}{H} = \frac{-g_\alpha}{H}(\mathcal{L}_{11}\mathcal{L}_{22} - \mathcal{L}_{12}^2) \gtrless 0 \qquad (6\text{-}85)$$

The cofactor H_{33}, while a principal minor, is not a *border-preserving* principal minor. The border row and column of H are deleted when forming H_{33}. Hence, no sign is implied for $\partial \lambda^*/\partial \alpha$. If α enters any of the other equations, then the off-diagonal cofactors H_{31} and H_{32} will enter the expressions. These expressions are likewise not signed by the maximum conditions.

Example. To illustrate the principles just developed, let us return to the profit maximization model, slightly modified. Consider a firm with production $y =$

$f(x_1, x_2)$ selling output y at price p. The firm hires input x_1 at wage w_1; x_2, however, represents the entrepreneur's input, and is fixed at some level x_2^0. The firm seeks to maximize net rents R, the difference between total revenue and the total factor cost of x_1. Algebraically, the model is

maximize x_1, x_2

$$R = pf(x_1, x_2) - w_1 x_1$$

subject to

$$x_2 = x_2^0$$

Although we have essentially solved this model in Chap. 4, by directly substituting the constraint into the objective function, we shall analyze it here as a constrained maximization model. Even though in this particular example the constraint says that x_2 is fixed, we treat x_2 as a variable, maintaining the structure of the Lagrangian analysis.

Using the Lagrangian

$$\mathcal{L} = pf(x_1, x_2) - w_1 x_1 + \lambda(x_2^0 - x_2)$$

the first-order conditions are

$$\mathcal{L}_1 = pf_1(x_1, x_2) - w_1 = 0 \tag{6-86a}$$

$$\mathcal{L}_2 = pf_2(x_1, x_2) - \lambda = 0 \tag{6-86b}$$

$$\mathcal{L}_\lambda = x_2^0 - x_2 = 0 \tag{6-86c}$$

Equation (6-86a) says that the firm will hire x_1 until the value of its marginal product of that factor equals its wage, as previously derived. Equation (6-86b) identifies the Lagrange multiplier λ as the value of the marginal product of the entrepreneurial input. Whereas the wage of factor 1 is exogenously set by the competitive labor market, the wage of factor 2 is endogenously "imputed." If a competitive market existed for entrepreneurial services, another firm would be willing to pay λ for this owner's services.

The sufficient second-order condition is that the bordered Hessian determinant formed from the second partials of $\mathcal{L}$ is positive:

$$H = \begin{vmatrix} pf_{11} & pf_{12} & 0 \\ pf_{21} & pf_{22} & -1 \\ 0 & -1 & 0 \end{vmatrix} > 0 \tag{6-87}$$

Evaluating this determinant (say, by the third row, which has two zeros in it) yields $pf_{11} < 0$. Note that no restriction is placed on f_{22}; since only x_1 is really variable (even though we treat x_2 as variable in the constrained model), the only margin on which the firm adjusts is how much x_1 to hire. Only diminishing marginal product of x_1 is thus required for an interior maximum.

Assuming the sufficient second-order condition holds, the first-order equations can be solved simultaneously for the explicit choice functions:

$$x_1 = x_1^*(w_1, p, x_2^0)$$

$$x_2 = x_2^*(w_1, p, x_2^0) \qquad (6\text{-}88)$$

$$\lambda = \lambda^*(w_1, p, x_2^0)$$

These choice functions represent the factor demands for x_1 and x_2 (trivial, in the case of x_2; $x_2^* = x_2^0$) and the profit-maximizing imputed value of entrepreneurial input.

Multiplying Eq. (6-86a) by x_1^*, (6-86b) by x_2^*, and adding,

$$p(f_1 x_1^* + f_2 x_2^*) \equiv w_1 x_1^* + \lambda^* x_2^* \qquad (6\text{-}89)$$

If the production function is homogeneous of degree one (constant returns to scale), then from Euler's theorem, the left-hand side of this identity is y^*. In that case, (6-89) can be interpreted as Total Revenue = Total Cost, where the total factor cost of x_2 is its imputed opportunity cost $\lambda^* x_2^*$. Thus with constant returns to scale, the product is "exhausted;" i.e., the revenue received by the firm is exactly accounted for by the total factor cost. Incidentally, (6-89) is an identity in w_1, x_2^0, and p, not in x_1 and x_2. This relation holds only for values of the factors satisfying the first-order equations, assuming the sufficient second-order conditions are also satisfied.

Let us now investigate the comparative statics of this model. Note that the parameter w_1 enters only the objective function, whereas x_2^0 enters the constraint. Substituting the solutions (6-88) back into the first-order equations yields the identities

$$pf_1(x_1^*, x_2^*) - w_1 \equiv 0$$

$$pf_2(x_1^*, x_2^*) - \lambda^* \equiv 0 \qquad (6\text{-}90)$$

$$x_2^0 - x_2^* \equiv 0$$

Since the parameter w_1 enters only the first first-order equation, we expect therefore to be able to derive a refutable implication for this parameter. The parameter x_2^0, on the other hand, appears in the constraint; we expect no refutable implication for this parameter. Differentiating these identities first with respect to w_1 produces the matrix equation

$$\begin{pmatrix} pf_{11} & pf_{12} & 0 \\ pf_{21} & pf_{22} & -1 \\ 0 & -1 & 0 \end{pmatrix} \begin{pmatrix} \dfrac{\partial x_1^*}{\partial w_1} \\[2ex] \dfrac{\partial x_2^*}{\partial w_1} \\[2ex] \dfrac{\partial \lambda^*}{\partial w_1} \end{pmatrix} = \begin{pmatrix} 1 \\ 0 \\ 0 \end{pmatrix} \qquad (6\text{-}91)$$

Solving for $\partial x_1^* / \partial w_1$,

$$\frac{\partial x_1^*}{\partial w_1} = \frac{H_{11}}{H} = \frac{-1}{-pf_{11}} < 0 \qquad (6\text{-}92a)$$

Also, as expected, since x_2 is fixed,

$$\frac{\partial x_2^*}{\partial w_1} = \frac{H_{12}}{H} = \frac{0}{-pf_{11}} = 0 \tag{6-92b}$$

and

$$\frac{\partial \lambda^*}{\partial w_1} = \frac{H_{13}}{H} = \frac{-pf_{21}}{-pf_{11}} \gtrless 0 \tag{6-92c}$$

As we showed earlier, a sign is never implied for rates of change of the Lagrange multiplier with respect to any parameter. However, Eq. (6-92c) shows that if the marginal product of x_1 increases with an increase in the entrepreneurial input (meaning, in the two-factor case, that the two factors are complements), the imputed marginal value of the entrepreneurial input moves in the opposite direction as the wage of x_1. (If elevators are fixed in supply, an increase in the wages of elevator operators will lower the imputed marginal value of elevators.)

Differentiating Eqs. (6-90) with respect to x_2^0 produces the matrix equation

$$\begin{pmatrix} pf_{11} & pf_{12} & 0 \\ pf_{21} & pf_{22} & -1 \\ 0 & -1 & 0 \end{pmatrix} \begin{pmatrix} \dfrac{\partial x_1^*}{\partial x_2^0} \\ \dfrac{\partial x_2^*}{\partial x_2^0} \\ \dfrac{\partial \lambda^*}{\partial x_2^0} \end{pmatrix} = \begin{pmatrix} 0 \\ 0 \\ -1 \end{pmatrix} \tag{6-93}$$

Solving,

$$\frac{\partial x_1^*}{\partial x_2^0} = \frac{-H_{31}}{H} = \frac{pf_{12}}{-pf_{11}} \gtrless 0 \tag{6-94a}$$

Also, since $x_2 = x_2^0$,

$$\frac{\partial x_2^*}{\partial x_2^0} = \frac{-H_{32}}{H} = \frac{-pf_{11}}{-pf_{11}} = 1 \tag{6-94b}$$

and

$$\frac{\partial \lambda^*}{\partial x_2^0} = \frac{-H_{33}}{H} = \frac{-p^2(f_{11}f_{22} - f_{12}^2)}{-pf_{11}} \gtrless 0 \tag{6-94c}$$

Note the curious "reciprocity" result $\partial x_1^*/\partial x_2^0 = -\partial \lambda^*/\partial w_1$, since $H_{13} = H_{31}$. We shall have more to say about these types of relations in the next chapter. Note also from Eq. (6-94c) that an increase in the parametric entrepreneurial input level has an unpredictable effect on the imputed marginal value of the entrepreneurial input. Only if we assume, additionally, that the production function is concave, so that $f_{11}f_{22} - f_{12}^2 > 0$ is $\partial \lambda^*/\partial x_2^0 < 0$. In that case, as in ordinary profit maximization, x_2 exhibits diminishing marginal product, lowering its marginal value as more x_2 is utilized. Thus, assuming information in addition to the maximization hypothesis leads to additional results.

To sum up, for parameters entering only the objective function, refutable implications are possible. Because such a parameter, w_1, enters one and only one first-order condition, a sign can be determined for $\partial x_1^*/\partial w_1$. For parameters entering the constraint, such as x_2^0 in this model, refutable implications are not possible on the basis of the maximization hypothesis alone, though additional assumptions may yield useful propositions.

PROBLEMS

1. Consider the constrained maximum problem

maximize

$$f(x_1, \ldots, x_n, \alpha_1, \ldots, \alpha_m) = y$$

subject to

$$g(x_1, \ldots, x_n, \alpha_1, \ldots, \alpha_m) = 0$$

Prove that if some parameter α_i enters the ith first-order relation and that equation only, then

$$\mathscr{L}_{i\alpha_i}(\partial x_i^*/\partial \alpha_i) > 0$$

2. Prove the same result if there is more than one constraint.
3. Show that diminishing marginal utility in each good neither implies nor is implied by convexity of the indifference curves.
4. Find the maximum or minimum values of the following functions $f(x_1, x_2)$ subject to the constraints $g(x_1, x_2) = 0$, by the method of direct substitution and by Lagrange multipliers. Be sure to check the second-order conditions to see if a maximum or minimum (if either) is achieved.
   (a) $f(x_1, x_2) = x_1 x_2$; $g(x_1, x_2) = 2 - (x_1 + x_2)$.
   (b) $f(x_1, x_2) = x_1 + x_2$; $g(x_1, x_2) = 1 - x_1 x_2$.
   (c) $f(x_1, x_2) = x_1 x_2$; $g(x_1, x_2) = M - p_1 x_1 - p_2 x_2$, where p_1, p_2, and M are parameters.
   (d) $f(x_1, x_2) = p_1 x_1 + p_2 x_2$; $g(x_1, x_2) = U^0 - x_1 x_2$.
5. Show that the second-order conditions for Probs. 4(a) and 4(b) are equivalent; also that the second-order conditions for Probs. 4(c) and 4(d) are equivalent.
6. Consider the class of models

maximize

$$y = f(x_1, x_2) + \alpha x_1$$

subject to

$$g(x_1, x_2) + \beta x_2 = 0$$

where x_1 and x_2 are choice variables and α and β are parameters. Using the Lagrangian

$$\mathscr{L} = f(x_1, x_2) + \alpha x_1 + \lambda(g(x_1, x_2) + \beta x_2)$$

   (a) Prove that $\partial x_1^*/\partial \alpha > 0$ but that no refutable comparative statics result is available for β.
   (b) Prove that $\partial x_1^*/\partial \beta = \lambda^*(\partial x_2^*/\partial \alpha) + x_2^*(\partial \lambda^*/\partial \alpha)$.

7. Consider a general maximization problem

   maximize

   $$y = f(x_1, x_2, \alpha)$$

   subject to

   $$g(x_1, x_2) = k$$

   where x_1 and x_2 are choice variables, and α and k are parameters. Using the Lagrangian

   $$\mathcal{L} = f(x_1, x_2, \alpha) + \lambda(k - g(x_1, x_2))$$

   (a) Prove that $f_{1\alpha}(\partial x_1^*/\partial k) + f_{2\alpha}(\partial x_2^*/\partial k) = \partial\lambda^*/\partial\alpha$.
   (b) What functional forms of the objective function and constraint would lead to the simple reciprocity result $\partial x_1^*/\partial k = \partial\lambda^*/\partial\alpha$?

8. Consider a firm that hires two inputs x_1 and x_2 at factor prices w_1 and w_2 respectively. If this firm is one of many identical firms, then in the long run, the profit-maximizing position will be at the minimum of its average cost curve. Analyze the comparative statics of this firm in the long run by asserting the behavioral postulate

   minimize

   $$AC = \frac{w_1 x_1 + w_2 x_2}{f(x_1, x_2)}$$

   where $y = f(x_1, x_2)$ is the firm's production function.
   (a) Show that the first-order necessary conditions for min AC are $w_i - AC^* f_i = 0$, $i = 1, 2$, where AC* is min AC. Interpret.
   (b) Show that the sufficient second-order conditions for min AC are the same as for profit-maximization in the short-run (fixed-output price), that is,

   $$f_{11} < 0 \quad f_{22} < 0 \quad f_{11}f_{22} - f_{12}^2 > 0$$

   (*Hint:* in differentiating the product $AC^* f_i$, remember that $\partial AC^*/\partial x_i = 0$ by the first-order conditions.)
   (c) Find all partials of the form $\partial x_i^*/\partial w_j$. (Remember that w_1 and w_2 appear in AC.) Show that $\partial x_i^*/\partial w_i < 0$ is *not* implied by this model, nor is $\partial x_i^*/\partial w_j = \partial x_j^*/\partial w_i$.
   (d) Show that $f_1 x_1^* + f_2 x_2^* \equiv y^*$. Is this Euler's theorem? (If it is, you have just proved that all production functions are linear homogeneous!)

9. Consider a firm with the production function $y = f(x_1, x_2)$, which sells its output in a competitive output market at price p. It is, however, a monopsonist in the input market, i.e., it faces rising factor-supply curves, in which the unit factor prices w_1 and w_2 rise with increasing factor usage, that is, $w_1 = k_1 x_1$, $w_2 = k_2 x_2$. The firm is asserted to be a profit-maximizer.
   (a) How might one represent algebraically a decrease in the supply of factor 1?
   (b) If the supply of x_1 decreases, will the use of factor one decrease? Demonstrate.
   (c) What will happen to the usage of factor 2 if the supply of x_1 decreases?
   (d) Explain, in about one sentence, why factor-demand curves for this firm do *not* exist.

(e) Suppose the government holds the firm's use of x_2 constant, at the previous profit-maximizing level. If the supply of x_1 decreases, will the use of x_1 change by more or less, absolutely, than previously?

10. Prove the propositions stated at the end of Sec. 6.5, that if a function $f(\mathbf{x})$, $\mathbf{x} = (x_1, \ldots, x_n)$ is quasi-concave and linear homogeneous, it is (weakly) concave, and if f is strictly quasi-concave and homogeneous of degree r, $0 < r < 1$, it is strictly concave.

SELECTED REFERENCES

Allen, R. G. D.: *Mathematical Analysis for Economists,* Macmillan & Co., Ltd., London, 1938.

Apostol, T.: *Mathematical Analysis,* Addison-Wesley Publishing Company Inc., Reading, MA, 1957.

Courant, R.: *Differential and Integral Calculus* (Trans.), Interscience Publishers, Inc., New York, 1947.

Hadley, G.: *Nonlinear and Dynamic Programming,* Addison-Wesley Publishing Company, Inc., Reading, MA, 1964.

Hancock, H.: *Theory of Maxima and Minima,* Ginn and Company, Boston, MA, 1917. Reprinted by Dover Publications, Inc., New York, 1960.

Panik, M. J.: *Classical Optimization: Foundations and Extensions,* North-Holland Publishing Company, Amsterdam, 1976.

Samuelson, P. A.: *Foundations of Economic Analysis,* Harvard University Press, Cambridge, MA, 1947.

CHAPTER

7

THE ENVELOPE THEOREM AND DUALITY

7.1 HISTORY OF THE PROBLEM

In the early 1930s, a very distinguished economist, Jacob Viner, was analyzing the behavior of firms in the short and long run. Viner defined the "short run" as a time period in which one factor of production, presumably capital, was fixed, while the other factor, labor, was variable. He posited a series of short-run cost curves, whose minimum points (for successively larger capital inputs) first fall and then rise. Viner reasoned that if both inputs were variable, the resulting "long-run" average cost would always be less than or equal to the corresponding short-run cost. He therefore concluded that the long-run average cost curve should be drawn as an "envelope" to all the short-run curves. The eventual diagram, pictured in Fig. 7-1, now appears in virtually all intermediate price theory texts.

However, Viner also was puzzled by the fact that the resulting long-run curve did not pass through the minimum points of the short-run curves, since reducing unit costs seemed to increase available profits. Moreover, at the points of tangency, the slopes of the long-run and short-run curves were the same, indicating that average cost was falling (or rising) at the same rate, irrespective of whether capital was being held constant. Viner therefore apparently asked his draftsman, Wong, to draw a long-run average cost curve that was both an envelope curve to the short-run curves, and which also passed through the

190

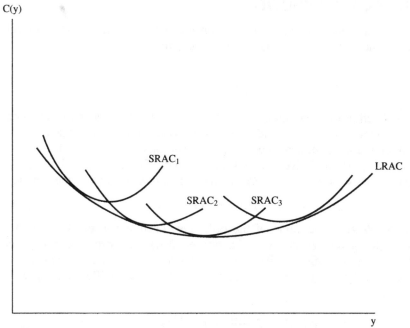

FIGURE 7-1
The modern Viner-Wong diagram showing the long-run average cost curve as an *envelope* to the short-run average cost curves.

minimum points of the short-run curves. When Wong indicated the impossibility of this joint occurrence, Viner opted to draw the long-run average cost curve through the minimum points of the short-run average cost curves, rather than as an envelope curve.[†] The egos of many succeeding economists have been soothed by that decision.

The problem was soon analyzed algebraically by Paul Samuelson, who demonstrated the correctness of the tangency of such long- and short-run curves.[‡] However, it remained somewhat of a puzzle that the rate of change of an objective function should be the same whether or not one variable is held constant. Perhaps most surprising, as economists investigated this puzzle further, was the discovery that the relationships that underlie this "envelope theorem" also reveal the basic theorems about the existence of refutable comparative statics theorems. It is to this larger issue that we now turn.

[†] See Jacob Viner, "Cost Curves and Supply Curves," *Zeitschrift fur Nationalokonomie,* **3:**1931. Reprinted in *AEA Readings in Price Theory,* Irwin, Homewood, IL, 1952.

[‡] See Paul Samuelson, *Foundations of Economic Analysis,* Harvard University Press, Cambridge, MA, 1947.

7.2 THE PROFIT FUNCTION

Samuelson began his analysis as follows. Consider a general maximization model with two decision variables, x_1 and x_2, and one parameter, α:

maximize

$$y = f(x_1, x_2, \alpha)$$

(The generalization to n variables is trivial; we will later consider models with multiple parameters.) The first-order necessary conditions are, of course, $f_1 = f_2 = 0$; assuming the sufficient second-order conditions hold, the explicit choice functions $x_i = x_i^*(\alpha)$ are derived as the solutions to the first-order equations. If we now substitute these solutions *into the objective function,* we obtain the function

$$\phi(\alpha) = f(x_1^*(\alpha), x_2^*(\alpha), \alpha) \tag{7-1}$$

The function $\phi(\alpha)$ is the value of the objective function f when the x_i's that maximize f (for given α) are used. Therefore, $\phi(\alpha)$ represents the maximum value of f, for any specified α. We call $\phi(\alpha)$ *the indirect objective function.*

How does ϕ vary (as compared to f) when α varies? Differentiating with respect to α,

$$\phi_\alpha(\alpha) = f_1 \frac{\partial x_1^*}{\partial \alpha} + f_2 \frac{\partial x_2^*}{\partial \alpha} + f_\alpha$$

However, from the first-order conditions, $f_1 = f_2 = 0$; hence the first two terms on the right-hand side vanish. Therefore,

$$\phi_\alpha(\alpha) = f_\alpha \tag{7-2}$$

Equation (7-2) says that as α changes, the rate of change of *the maximum value of f,* where x_1 and x_2 vary optimally as α varies, equals the rate of change of f as α varies, holding x_1 and x_2 constant! This result has puzzled many economists long after the publication of Viner's original article.

Before we study the geometry of Eq. (7-2), let us verify the result for the profit maximization model. The explicit choice functions (factor demand functions) that result from the hypothesis, maximize $\pi = pf(x_1, x_2) - w_1 x_1 - w_2 x_2$ are, again, $x_1 = x_1^*(w_1, w_2, p)$, $x_2 = x_2^*(w_1, w_2, p)$. If these profit-maximizing levels of input are substituted into the objective function, the resulting profit level, by definition, must be the maximum profits attainable at those factor and output prices. Algebraically,

$$\pi^*(w_1, w_2, p) = pf(x_1^*, x_2^*) - w_1 x_1^* - w_2 x_2^* \tag{7-3}$$

The function $\pi^*(w_1, w_2, p)$ is called the *profit function;* it is the indirect objective function for this model. Its value is always the maximum value of profits for given w_1, w_2, and p.

How do profits vary when, say, w_1 changes? One could simply differentiate the objective function with respect to w_1, holding not only other prices constant, but the input levels x_1 and x_2 constant as well. In that case, we would find

$$\frac{\partial \pi}{\partial w_1} = -x_1$$

No assumption of profit maximization is invoked here. This relation simply says, for example, that if a firm employed 100 workers, and if wages increased by, say, $1, profits would start to decrease (note the minus sign) by $100 (100 workers times $1, the change in the wage rate). However, a profit-maximizing firm would start to reduce the number of its workers as wages increased. If we want to evaluate how *maximum* profit varies when w_1 changes, we must differentiate the *indirect* profit function. Differentiating (7-3) with respect to w_1,

$$\frac{\partial \pi^*}{\partial w_1} = p\left(f_1\frac{\partial x_1^*}{\partial w_1} + f_2\frac{\partial x_2^*}{\partial w_1}\right) - w_1\frac{\partial x_1^*}{\partial w_1} - x_1^* - w_2\frac{\partial x_2^*}{\partial w_1}$$

Combining the terms involving $\partial x_1^*/\partial w_1$, et cetera, yields

$$\frac{\partial \pi^*}{\partial w_1} = (pf_1 - w_1)\left(\frac{\partial x_1^*}{\partial w_1}\right) + (pf_2 - w_2)\left(\frac{\partial x_2^*}{\partial w_1}\right) - x_1^*$$

However, the terms in parentheses on the right-hand side are zero at profit-maximizing values of x_1 and x_2. Therefore,

$$\frac{\partial \pi^*}{\partial w_1} = -x_1^* = \frac{\partial \pi}{\partial w_1} \tag{7-4}$$

where the latter term must be evaluated at x_1^*. Equation (7-4) says that starting at some profit-maximizing input levels, the *instantaneous* rate of change of profits with respect to a change in a factor price is the same whether or not the factors are held fixed or whether they in principle can vary as that factor price changes. Moreover, the value of this instantaneous rate of change is simply the negative of the factor demand function for x_1, $x_1 = x_1^*(w_1, w_2, p)$, evaluated at the particular prices for which the input levels are in fact profit-maximizing.

We can get a better understanding of what is going on here by considering the geometry more closely. Suppose the factor and output prices have the specific values w_1^0, w_2^0, p^0. Some values of x_1^* and x_2^* are implied:

$$x_1^0 = x_1^*(w_1^0, w_2^0, p^0) \quad x_2^0 = x_2^*(w_1^0, w_2^0, p^0)$$

Let us vary w_1 only, holding w_2 and p fixed at the above values, and observe how the level of profit varies. In particular, we shall initially hold x_1 and x_2 fixed at x_1^0 and x_2^0. In Fig. 7-2, the "constrained" profit function

$$\pi(w_1, w_2^0, p^0, x_1^0, x_2^0) = p^0 f(x_1^0 x_2^0) - w_1 x_1^0 - w_2^0 x_2^0 \tag{7-5}$$

shows the level of profits as w_1 varies, holding everything else constant, i.e., for given w_2^0 and p^0, with $x_1 = x_1^0$, $x_2 = x_2^0$. (Note that every variable in Eq. (7-5) has a superscript 0 except w_1.) Note also that $\pi(w_1, w_2^0, p^0, x_1^0, x_2^0)$ is a linear function in w_1. Its slope is $\partial \pi/\partial w_1 = -x_1^0$.

Now consider where the profit function $\pi^*(w_1, w_2^0, p^0)$ lies in relation to this line. Since $\pi^*(w_1, w_2^0, p^0)$ is by definition the *maximum* profits for given

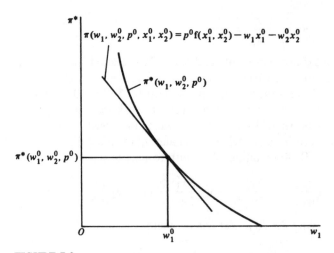

FIGURE 7-2
The profit function $\pi^*(w_1, w_2^0, p^0)$ and the profit function $\pi(w_1, w_2^0, p^0, x_1^0, x_2^0)$, where x_1^0 and x_2^0 are those levels that maximize profits when $w_1 = w_1^0$.

factor and output prices, it must in general lie above the straight line defined by $\pi(w_1, w_2^0, p^0, x_1^0, x_2^0)$. However, when $w_1 = w_1^0$, exactly the correct input levels are used, since x_1^0 and x_2^0 were *defined* as the profit-maximizing input levels when $w_1 = w_1^0$. Thus, at $w_1 = w_1^0$, $\pi^*(w_1, w_2^0, p^0) = \pi(w_1, w_2^0, p^0, x_1^0, x_2^0)$. When $w_1 \neq w_1^0$, the input levels x_1^0 and x_2^0 are "wrong," i.e., non–profit maximizing. Hence $\pi^*(w_1, w_2^0, p^0) > \pi(w_1, w_2^0, p^0, x_1^0, x_2^0)$ *on both sides* of w_1^0. But observe the geometric consequences of this in Fig. 7-2. Assuming π^* and π are both differentiable, π^* and π must be tangent to each other at w_1^0. Tangency means that π^* and π have the same slope at w_1^0. This is precisely Eq. (7-4), $\partial \pi^*/\partial w_1 = \partial \pi/\partial w_1 = -x_1^*$.

Suppose we had started at some other level of w_1, say w_1^1. In that case we would have held x_1 and x_2 fixed at the levels implied by that wage, $x_1^1 = x_1^*(w_1^1, w_2^0, p^0)$, $x_2^1 = x_2^*(w_1^1, w_2^0, p^0)$. The resulting constrained profit function would be some other straight line tangent to π^* at this different value of w_1; their common slope at this point would be $-x_1^*(w_1^1, w_2^0, p^0)$. We can see the reason for the name "envelope" theorem: the profit function $\pi^*(w_1, w_2, p)$ is the envelope of all the possible constrained profit lines as w_1 is varied.

However, we have more information than just the equality of slope of π and π^*. Since π^* lies above π on both sides of w_1^0, $\pi^*(w_1, w_2^0, p^0)$ must be more convex (or less concave) than $\pi(w_1, w_2^0, p^0, x_1^0, x_2^0)$. But in this model, π is linear, and therefore $\pi^*(w_1, w_2^0, p^0)$ must be convex in w_1, as shown in Fig. 7-2. That the indirect function is convex (we assume *strictly* convex) has major consequences for the comparative statics of this model. Convexity in w_1 means $\partial^2 \pi^*/\partial w_1^2 \geq 0$. But from Eq. (7-4), $\partial \pi^*/\partial w_1 = -x_1^*(w_1, w_2, p)$.

Differentiating both sides therefore yields

$$\frac{\partial^2 \pi^*}{\partial w_1^2} = -\frac{\partial x_1^*}{\partial w_1} \geq 0 \qquad (7\text{-}6)$$

Since in this model the factor demand function $x_1^*(w_1, w_2, p)$ is in fact the negative of the first partial of $\pi^*(w_1, w_2, p)$ with respect to w_1, the slope of the factor demand function (its first partial with respect to w_1) is the negative second partial derivative of π^* with respect to w_1. Since this second partial of π^* is positive (nonnegative), the slope of the factor demand function must be negative. Thus (in this model at least), the curvature of the indirect objective function (the profit function, here) directly implies an important comparative statics result.

By symmetry, it follows obviously that $\pi^*(w_1, w_2, p)$ is convex in w_2, yielding the same comparative statics result for that factor. It is also the case that $\pi^*(w_1, w_2, p)$ is convex in output price p, and that therefore $\partial^2 \pi^* / \partial p^2 = \partial y^* / \partial p \geq 0$. The proof and geometrical explanation of this are left as an exercise. We now turn to an examination of the general maximization model. Can the preceding results be derived without resort to visual geometry?

7.3 GENERAL COMPARATIVE STATICS ANALYSIS: UNCONSTRAINED MODELS

Consider any two-variable model, maximize $y = f(x_1, x_2, \alpha)$, where x_1 and x_2 are the choice variables and, for the moment, α is a single parameter representing some constraint on the maximizing agent's behavior. The first-order equations are $f_1 = f_2 = 0$. By solving the first-order equations simultaneously, assuming unique solutions, explicit choice functions $x_1 = x_1^*(\alpha)$, $x_2 = x_2^*(\alpha)$ are implied. Again, the refutable propositions consist of the implications of maximization regarding the directions of change in some or all x_i's as α changes. The "indirect objective function" is, again, $\phi(\alpha) = f(x_1^*(\alpha), x_2^*(\alpha), \alpha)$. By definition, $\phi(\alpha)$ gives the maximum value of f for given α. At what rates do $\phi(\alpha)$ and $f(x, \alpha)$ vary (both first- and second-order rates of change) as α changes?

In Fig. 7-3, $\phi(\alpha)$ is plotted for various α's. For an arbitrary α^0 some $x_1^0 = x_1^*(\alpha^0)$ and $x_2^0 = x_2^*(\alpha^0)$ are implied. Consider the behavior of $f(x_1, x_2, \alpha)$ when x_1 and x_2 are held fixed at x_1^0 and x_2^0 as opposed to when they are variable. Since $\phi(\alpha)$ is the *maximum* value of f for given α, in general, $f \leq \phi$. When $\alpha = \alpha^0$, the "correct" x_i's are chosen, and therefore $\phi(\alpha) = f(x_1, x_2, \alpha)$ at that one point. On both sides of α^0, the "wrong" (i.e., nonmaximizing) x_i's are used, and thus by definition, $f(x_1^0, x_2^0, \alpha) < \phi(\alpha)$ in any neighborhood around α^0. Unless f has some sort of nondifferentiable corner at α^0, ϕ and f must be tangent at α^0, and, moreover, f must be either more concave or less convex than ϕ there. Since this must happen for arbitrary α, similar tangencies occur at other values of α. It is apparent from the diagram that $\phi(\alpha)$ is the *envelope* of the $f(x_1, x_2, \alpha)$'s for each α. How do we derive these properties algebraically?

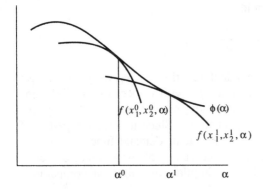

FIGURE 7-3
The indirect objective function, $\phi(\alpha)$, is an envelope curve to the direct objective functions for various α's.

Consider a new function, the difference between the actual and the maximum value of f for given α,

$$F(x_1, x_2, \alpha) = f(x_1, x_2, \alpha) - \phi(\alpha)$$

called the "primal-dual" objective function. Since $f \leq \phi$ for $x \neq x^*$ and $f = \phi$ for $x_i = x_i^*$, F has a maximum (of zero) when $x_i = x_i^*(\alpha)$.[†] Moreover, we can consider $F(x_1, x_2, \alpha)$ as a function of *three* independent variables, x_1, x_2, and α. That is, just as for a given α there are values of x_1 and x_2 that maximize f, for *given* x_1 and x_2, there is some value of α which makes those x_i's the "correct" (i.e., maximizing) values. For example, for a given amount of labor and capital, there is some set of factor and output prices for which those input levels would be the profit-maximizing values.

This maximum position of $F(x_1, x_2, \alpha)$ can be described by the usual first- and second-order conditions. The first-order conditions are that $f(x_1, x_2, \alpha) - \phi(\alpha)$ has zero partial derivatives with respect to the original choice variables x_1 and x_2, *and also* α:

$$F_i = f_i = 0, \quad i = 1, 2 \tag{7-7}$$

and

$$F_\alpha = f_\alpha - \phi_\alpha = 0 \tag{7-8}$$

Equations (7-7) are simply the original maximum conditions. Equation (7-8) is the "envelope" result, $\phi_\alpha = f_\alpha$. These first-order conditions hold whenever $x_i = x_i^*(\alpha)$, $i = 1, 2$.

The sufficient second-order conditions state that the Hessian matrix of second partials of $F(x_1, x_2, \alpha)$ (with respect to x_1, x_2, *and* α) is negative definite, or that its principal minors alternate in sign. By inspection, $F_{11} = f_{11}$, et cetera,

---

[†] If we think of x_1^* and x_2^* as an "efficient" allocation of resources, and x_1 and x_2 as any other allocation, then this says that efficient allocation occurs when "waste" equals zero.

and $F_{\alpha\alpha} = f_{\alpha\alpha} - \phi_{\alpha\alpha}$. Thus,

$$H = \begin{vmatrix} F_{11} & F_{12} & F_{1\alpha} \\ F_{21} & F_{22} & F_{2\alpha} \\ F_{\alpha 1} & F_{\alpha 2} & F_{\alpha\alpha} \end{vmatrix} = \begin{vmatrix} f_{11} & f_{12} & f_{1\alpha} \\ f_{21} & f_{22} & f_{2\alpha} \\ f_{\alpha 1} & f_{\alpha 2} & f_{\alpha\alpha} - \phi_{\alpha\alpha} \end{vmatrix} \qquad (7\text{-}9)$$

These second-order conditions include the original ones ($f_{11} < 0$, $f_{11}f_{22} - f_{12}^2 > 0$, etc.) in the top left corner. In addition, the sufficient second-order conditions also imply $F_{\alpha\alpha} < 0$, or $f_{\alpha\alpha} - \phi_{\alpha\alpha} < 0$. *Moreover, it is from this inequality that all known comparative statics results (in maximization models) flow.*

The first-order envelope result (7-8), with the functional dependence noted, is $\phi_\alpha(\alpha) \equiv f_\alpha(x_1^*(\alpha), x_2^*(\alpha), \alpha)$. Differentiating both sides with respect to α yields

$$\phi_{\alpha\alpha} \equiv f_{\alpha x_1}\frac{\partial x_1^*}{\partial \alpha} + f_{\alpha x_2}\frac{\partial x_2^*}{\partial \alpha} + f_{\alpha\alpha}$$

From the sufficient second-order conditions, therefore, and using Young's theorem,

$$\phi_{\alpha\alpha} - f_{\alpha\alpha} = f_{1\alpha}\frac{\partial x_1^*}{\partial \alpha} + f_{2\alpha}\frac{\partial x_2^*}{\partial \alpha} > 0$$

This analysis is readily generalized to the n-variable case producing the condition

$$\sum_{i=1}^{n} f_{i\alpha}\frac{\partial x_i^*}{\partial \alpha} > 0 \qquad (7\text{-}10)$$

Equation (7-10) is the general and fundamental comparative statics equation for all unconstrained maximization models. As it stands, however, it is too general to be of much use. In order for a model to have refutable implications, it must contain more structure than just a general maximization problem. Suppose therefore that some α enters only one first-order condition $f_i = 0$, i.e., $f_{j\alpha} = 0$ for $j \neq i$. Then Eq. (7-10) reduces to a single term,

$$f_{i\alpha}\frac{\partial x_i^*}{\partial \alpha} > 0 \qquad (7\text{-}11)$$

This is Samuelson's famous "conjugate pairs" result. In maximization models, if some parameter α enters only the ith first-order equation, the response of the ith choice variable x_i, to a change in that parameter is in the same direction as the effect α has on the first-order equation.

The significance of this theorem lies in its application to some important models. For example, in the profit maximization model, the parameter w_1 enters only the first first-order equation $\pi_1 = pf_1 - w_1 = 0$; it enters with a negative sign: $\partial \pi_1/\partial w_1 = -1$. Thus, the conjugate pairs theorem states that the response of x_1^* to an increase in w_1 will be negative, and similarly for x_2^*. The theorem also applies to the constrained cost minimization model, as we shall presently see.

In the more general case where x is a vector of decision variables $(x_1, \ldots, x_n)$, and α is a vector of parameters $\alpha = (\alpha_1, \ldots, \alpha_m)$, the second-order conditions for maximizing $F(x, \alpha) = f(x, \alpha) - \phi(\alpha)$ with respect to α are that the matrix $F_{\alpha\alpha} = f_{\alpha\alpha} - \phi_{\alpha\alpha}$ is negative semidefinite. The usual comparative statics results follow from the negativity of the diagonal elements of this matrix. However, a richer set of theorems is also available from the other properties of negative semidefinite matrices: the principal minors of the terms in $f_{\alpha\alpha} - \phi_{\alpha\alpha}$ alternate in sign.

The envelope theorem also reveals the origins of the nonintuitive "reciprocity" conditions that appear in maximization models. Recall that in the profit maximization model, we derived $\partial x_1^*/\partial w_2 = \partial x_2^*/\partial w_1$. This result can be more clearly shown by first noting that each factor demand is the negative first partial of π^* with respect to its factor price, i.e., $\pi_1^* = x_1^*(w_1, w_2, p)$, $\pi_2^* = x_2^*(w_1, w_2, p)$. Applying Young's theorem on invariance of cross-partials to the order of differentiation to $\pi^*(w_1, w_2, p)$ therefore yields $\pi_{12}^* = \partial x_1^*/\partial w_2 = \partial x_2^*/\partial w_1 = \pi_{21}^*$. Thus this curious result is no more curious than Young's theorem itself.

All reciprocity theorems are in fact simply the application of Young's theorem to the indirect objective function. Suppose there are two parameters α and β, so that the model is maximize $y = f(x_1, x_2, \alpha, \beta)$. The implied choice functions are then $x_i = x_i^*(\alpha, \beta)$, $i = 1, 2$, and the indirect objective function is $\phi(\alpha, \beta) = f(x_1^*(\alpha, \beta), x_2^*(\alpha, \beta), \alpha, \beta)$. Then noting that $\phi_\alpha(\alpha, \beta) = f_\alpha$,

$$\phi_{\alpha\beta}(\alpha, \beta) = f_{\alpha 1}\frac{\partial x_1^*}{\partial \beta} + f_{\alpha 2}\frac{\partial x_2^*}{\partial \beta} + f_{\alpha\beta}$$

Similarly,

$$\phi_{\beta\alpha}(\alpha, \beta) = f_{\beta 1}\frac{\partial x_1^*}{\partial \alpha} + f_{\beta 2}\frac{\partial x_2^*}{\partial \alpha} + f_{\beta\alpha}$$

Since $\phi_{\alpha\beta} = \phi_{\beta\alpha}$,

$$f_{1\alpha}\frac{\partial x_1^*}{\partial \beta} + f_{2\alpha}\frac{\partial x_2^*}{\partial \beta} = f_{1\beta}\frac{\partial x_1^*}{\partial \alpha} + f_{2\beta}\frac{\partial x_2^*}{\partial \alpha} \tag{7-12}$$

For the general case of n decision variables,

$$\sum f_{i\alpha}\frac{\partial x_i^*}{\partial \beta} = \sum f_{i\beta}\frac{\partial x_i^*}{\partial \alpha} \tag{7-13}$$

However, these relations are most interesting when each parameter enters only one first-order equation. In that case, Eq. (7-13) reduces to one term on each side, as in the profit maximization model.

7.4 MODELS WITH CONSTRAINTS

Most models in economics involve one or more side constraints. A particularly important model, for example, is minimize

$$C = \sum w_i x_i$$

subject to

$$f(x_1, \ldots, x_n) = y^0$$

If f is a production function of n inputs, $x_1, \ldots, x_n$, and the w_i's are factor prices, this famous model, which we shall presently analyze in detail, describes achieving some output level y^0 at minimum cost.

The extension of the results for unconstrained maximization models to models involving one or more side conditions (constraints) depends critically on whether the parameters enter only the objective function or whether they enter the constraints also (or exclusively). Note that in the preceding cost minimization model, the prices enter only the objective function, whereas the specified output level enters only the constraint. We shall show that if the parameters enter only the objective function, the comparative statics results are the same as for unconstrained models. However, if a parameter enters a constraint, as that parameter changes, the constraint space also changes, destroying the relation $\phi_{\alpha\alpha} \geq f_{\alpha\alpha}$. Let us investigate these more general models.

The traditional derivation of the envelope theorem for models with one constraint proceeds as follows.

Consider ·

maximize

$$f(x_1, \ldots, x_n, \alpha) = y$$

subject to

$$g(x_1, \ldots, x_n, \alpha) = 0$$

The Lagrangian is $\mathcal{L} = f + \lambda g$. Setting the first partials of $\mathcal{L}$ equal to 0,

$$\mathcal{L}_i = f_i + \lambda g_i = 0 \quad i = 1, \ldots, n \qquad (7\text{-}14)$$

$$\mathcal{L}_\lambda = g = 0 \qquad (7\text{-}15)$$

Solving these equations for

$$x_i = x_i^*(\alpha) \quad i = 1, \ldots, n$$

$$\lambda = \lambda^*(\alpha)$$

we define

$$y^* = f(x_1^*, \ldots, x_n^*, \alpha) = \phi(\alpha) \qquad (7\text{-}16)$$

as before. Here, $\phi(\alpha)$ is the maximum value of y for any α, for x_i's that satisfy the constraint.

How does $\phi(\alpha)$ change when α changes? Differentiating (7-16) with respect to α

$$\frac{\partial \phi}{\partial \alpha} = \sum f_i \frac{\partial x_i^*}{\partial \alpha} + f_\alpha \qquad (7\text{-}17)$$

Here, however, $f_i \neq 0$. Differentiating the constraint

$$g(x_1^*(\alpha), \ldots, x_n^*(\alpha), \alpha) \equiv 0$$

with respect to α,

$$\sum g_i \frac{\partial x_i^*}{\partial \alpha} + g_\alpha \equiv 0 \qquad (7\text{-}18)$$

Multiply Eq. (7-18) by λ, and add to Eq. (7-17). (This adds zero to that expression.) Then

$$\frac{\partial \phi}{\partial \alpha} = \sum f_i \frac{\partial x_i^*}{\partial \alpha} + f_\alpha + \sum \lambda g_i \frac{\partial x_i^*}{\partial \alpha} + \lambda g_\alpha$$

$$= \sum (f_i + \lambda g_i) \frac{\partial x_i^*}{\partial \alpha} + f_\alpha + \lambda g_\alpha$$

Using the first-order conditions (7-14),

$$\frac{\partial \phi}{\partial \alpha} = f_\alpha + \lambda g_\alpha = \mathcal{L}_\alpha \qquad (7\text{-}19)$$

where $\mathcal{L}_\alpha$ is the partial derivative of the Lagrangian function with respect to α, holding the x_i's fixed. Thus, in evaluating the response of the indirect objective function to a change in a parameter in a *constrained* maximization model, the Lagrangian function plays an analogous role to the objective function in an unconstrained model.

The primal-dual formulation for constrained maximization models is,

maximize $\qquad\qquad f(x_1, \ldots, x_n, \alpha) - \phi(\alpha)$

subject to $\qquad\qquad g^j(x_1, \ldots, x_n, \alpha) = 0,$

treating α as a decision variable as well as the x_i's. The Langrangian is

$$\mathcal{L} = f(x_1, \ldots, x_n, \alpha) - \phi(\alpha) + \lambda g(x_1, \ldots, x_n, \alpha) \qquad (7\text{-}20)$$

Differentiating with respect to the x_i's yields the ordinary first-order conditions for a constrained maximum; setting $\mathcal{L}_\alpha = 0$ produces the envelope result (7-19).

Comparative Statics: Primal-Dual Analysis

A more modern derivation of the envelope theorem based on the primal-dual objective function used previously for unconstrained models can be used also for models with constraints. As before, this procedure is in fact more illuminating with regard to the appearance of refutable comparative statics propositions in these models.

The simplest of all constrained maximization models is sufficient to display the nature of the results available in models with side constraints. Consider

maximize

$$f(x_1, x_2, \alpha) = y$$

subject to

$$g(x_1, x_2, \beta) = 0$$

In this model, a single parameter α enters the objective function only, and another parameter, β, enters the constraint only. Using Lagrangian techniques, the first-order equations are solved for the explicit choice equations

$$x_1 = x_1^*(\alpha, \beta)$$

$$x_2 = x_2^*(\alpha, \beta) \tag{7-21}$$

Substituting these solutions into the objective function yields the maximum value of $f(x_1, x_2, \alpha)$ for given α and β, for x_1 and x_2 that satisfy the constraint:

$$\phi(\alpha, \beta) = f(x_1^*(\alpha, \beta), x_2^*(\alpha, \beta), \alpha) \tag{7-22}$$

Since $\phi(\alpha, \beta)$ is the maximum value of f for given α and β, $\phi(\alpha, \beta) \geq f(x_1, x_2, \alpha)$ for any x_i's that satisfy the constraint. Thus, the function $F(x_1, x_2, \alpha, \beta) = f(x_1, x_2, \alpha) - \phi(\alpha, \beta)$ has a maximum (of zero) for any x_i's that satisfy the constraint. However, $F(x_1, x_2, \alpha, \beta)$ is a function of four independent variables, one of which, α, does not enter the constraint. Therefore, starting with values of x_1, x_2, and β which satisfy the constraint, and holding them fixed at those values, the constraint does not further impinge on the choice of α that maximizes $F(x_1, x_2, \alpha, \beta)$. The constraint affects the values of x_1 and x_2 that can be chosen, but not the maximizing value of α. *In the α dimension(s), therefore, $F(x_1, x_2, \alpha, \beta)$ has an unconstrained maximum.* (Consider, for example, what happens when some good, say, air, enters a person's utility function, but not the budget constraint, there being no price paid for breathing. In that case, we breathe until the marginal utility of air is zero, i.e., we consume in the manner of an unconstrained maximum in that dimension.)

Therefore, just as in the unconstrained maximization models, $F_{\alpha\alpha} = f_{\alpha\alpha} - \phi_{\alpha\alpha} < 0$ assuming, as always, the sufficient second-order conditions. The fundamental comparative statics result (7-10) follows as before:

$$f_{1\alpha} \frac{\partial x_1^*}{\partial \alpha} + f_{2\alpha} \frac{\partial x_2^*}{\partial \alpha} > 0 \tag{7-10}$$

If α represents a vector of parameters that enter the objective function only, then the matrix of terms $(f_{\alpha\alpha} - \phi_{\alpha\alpha})$ must be negative semidefinite; Eq. (7-10) then follows from the fact that the diagonal elements are nonpositive.

No such easy relationships exist with regard to changes in β. To best see this, try to construct a diagram like Fig. 7-3 for the parameter β. Plot β on the horizontal axis, and f and $\phi(\alpha, \beta)$ on the vertical axis. Hold α constant throughout. At some value β^0, $x_1^0 = x_1^*(\alpha^0, \beta^0)$, $x_2^0 = x_2^*(\alpha^0, \beta^0)$ are implied. The next step is to vary the parameter in question, holding x_1 and x_2 constant. However, it is impossible to do that for β. If x_1 and x_2 are held constant, β cannot be changed without violating the constraint! Thus the procedure for showing the greater relative concavity of f versus ϕ breaks down for parameters entering the constraint: one cannot change only one variable in an equation without destroying the equality. As a result, no refutable hypotheses are implied by the maximization hypothesis alone, for parameters that enter the constraint.

In the case where β is a vector of two or more parameters $(\beta_1, \ldots, \beta_m)$, it is possible to hold x_1, x_2 and α constant, and characterize the β_j's that solve the primal-dual problem. Since the original objective function does not contain any of the β_j's, the primal-dual problem reduces to

$$\underset{\beta}{\text{maximize}} \qquad\qquad -\phi(\alpha, \beta)$$

subject to $\qquad\qquad g(x, \beta) = 0$

where $x = (x_1, x_2)$ (or, for that matter, a general n-dimensional vector of decision variables). Of course, maximizing $-\phi(\alpha, \beta)$ is the same as minimizing $\phi(\alpha, \beta)$; thus in this case, the indirect objective function is *convex in the β parameters, subject to constraint,* i.e., in the parameters that enter the constraint exclusively. If the constraint is linear in the β_j's, then the indirect objective function must be *quasi-convex* in these parameters (though linearity is not a necessary condition for quasi-convexity.)

> **Example.** In the important consumer model, utility of goods is maximized subject to a linear budget constraint:
>
> maximize
>
> $$U(x_1, x_2)$$
>
> subject to
>
> $$p_1 x_1 + p_2 x_2 = M$$
>
> Using Lagrangian methods, the implied choice functions are the Marshallian demands $x_i = x_i^*(p_1, p_2, M)$, $i = 1, 2$. Substituting these functions into the objective function yields the *indirect utility function* $U^*(p_1, p_2, M) = U(x_1^*(p_1, p_2, M), x_2^*(p_1, p_2, M))$. The primal-dual problem is thus
>
> maximize
>
> $$U(x_1, x_2) - U^*(p_1, p_2, M)$$
>
> subject to
>
> $$p_1 x_1 + p_2 x_2 = M$$
>
> where the maximization runs over x_1, x_2, *and* the parameters p_1, p_2, and M. Since

all of the parameters are in the constraint exclusively, the maximization problem with respect to the prices and money income is simply

maximize

$$-U^*(p_1, p_2, M)$$

subject to

$$p_1 x_1 + p_2 x_2 = M$$

This says that choosing goods x_1 and x_2 so as to maximize utility (subject to the budget constraint) is equivalent to choosing prices and money income so as to minimize the indirect utility function, also, of course, subject to the budget constraint. Since the budget constraint is *linear* in prices and money income, this implies that the indirect utility function is quasi-convex in prices and money income. The result generalizes immediately to the case of n goods.

An Important Special Case

Most of the useful models encountered in economics involve expressions that are linear in at least some of the parameters, typically the prices of goods or factors. Consider, therefore, models in which the objective function involves the expression $\sum \alpha_i x_i$:

maximize

$$y = f(x, \alpha) = \theta(x_1, \ldots, x_n) + \sum \alpha_i x_i \qquad (7\text{-}23)$$

subject to

$$g(x_1, \ldots, x_n, \beta) = 0 \qquad (7\text{-}24)$$

where $x = (x_1, \ldots, x_n)$, the vector of decision variables, $\alpha = (\alpha_1, \ldots, \alpha_n)$, and β is any vector of parameters entering the constraint only. Parameters that enter the constraint are assumed to be absent from the objective function.

Denote the indirect objective function $\phi(\alpha, \beta)$. We know from the preceding analysis that the function $f(x, \alpha) - \phi(\alpha)$ must be concave in α, and that the matrix $(f_{\alpha\alpha} - \phi_{\alpha\alpha})$ must therefore be negative semidefinite. The parameters β and the functional form of g are irrelevant, as long as the first- and second-order conditions are satisfied. However, since f is linear in the α_i's, $f_{\alpha\alpha} \equiv 0$ and thus f has no effect on the curvature of the primal-dual function. Therefore, for these models, $-\phi(\alpha)$ is concave (or, alternatively, $\phi(\alpha)$ is convex), and the matrix $[-\phi_{\alpha\alpha}]$ must be symmetric (by Young's theorem) and negative semidefinite (or, $[\phi_{\alpha\alpha}]$ is positive semidefinite). In the case of *minimization* models with these properties, $\phi(\alpha)$ is *concave,* and $[\phi_{\alpha\alpha}]$ is a negative semidefinite matrix.

Even more important than these curvature properties are the implications for deriving useful comparative statics theorems. By the envelope theorem, $\phi_{\alpha_i} = f_{\alpha_i} = x_i^*$ in these models. Therefore, the matrix $[\phi_{\alpha\alpha}]$ consists of the terms $\partial x_i^*/\partial \alpha_j$. From symmetry, $\partial x_i^*/\partial \alpha_j = \partial x_j^*/\partial \alpha_i$. The properties of positive semidefinite matrices include nonnegative diagonal terms, i.e., $\partial x_i^*/\partial \alpha_i \geq 0$, and positive principal minors of higher order. These results comprise the useful theorems in economics.

The profit function derived above exhibited these properties (but note that the α_i's are the negative prices). In the next chapter we will study the cost minimization model, which has a similar structure. We shall show that the cost function associated with production functions with the usual properties must be concave, and the demand functions implied by that model are negatively sloped.

Interpretation of the Lagrange Multiplier

The Lagrange multiplier λ has been carried along thus far mainly as a convenient way of stating the first- and second-order conditions for maximization. In fact, the main reason for the use of Lagrangian techniques in economics (and also other sciences) is that λ often has an interesting interpretation of its own.

Consider the constrained maximization model

maximize

$$f(x_1, x_2) = y$$

subject to

$$g(x_1, x_2) = k$$

Usually we set the constraint equation equal to zero; here, it equals some arbitrary value k. By stating the constraint in this manner, we can consider parametric changes in the value of the g function. Using the Lagrangian

$$\mathcal{L} = f(x_1, x_2) + \lambda(k - g(x_1, x_2))$$

the usual first-order equations are

$$\mathcal{L}_1 = f_1(x_1, x_2) - \lambda g_1(x_1, x_2) = 0 \qquad (7\text{-}25a)$$

$$\mathcal{L}_2 = f_2(x_1, x_2) - \lambda g_2(x_1, x_2) = 0 \qquad (7\text{-}25b)$$

$$\mathcal{L}_\lambda = k - g(x_1, x_2) = 0 \qquad (7\text{-}25c)$$

From Eqs. (7-25a) and (7-25b),

$$\lambda = \frac{f_1}{g_1} = \frac{f_2}{g_2} \qquad (7\text{-}26)$$

However, a more revealing expression for λ can be obtained using the envelope theorem.

By solving Eqs. (7-25) simultaneously, we obtain the explicit choice functions $x_1^*(k)$, $x_2^*(k)$, and $\lambda^*(k)$. Substituting these solutions into $f(x_1, x_2)$ yields the indirect objective function

$$\phi(k) = f(x_1^*(k), x_2^*(k))$$

By the envelope theorem for constrained maximization models, Eq. (7-19),

$$\phi_k(k) = \frac{\partial \mathscr{L}}{\partial k} = \lambda^*(k) \tag{7-27}$$

That is, the Lagrange multiplier λ equals the rate of change of the maximum (or minimum, as the case may be) value of the objective function with respect to parametric changes in the value of the constraint.

Consider Eq. (7-19) again, $\phi_\alpha(\alpha) = f_\alpha + \lambda g_\alpha$. We can understand this relation by using (7-27). Think of (7-19) as

$$\frac{\partial \phi}{\partial \alpha} = \frac{\partial f}{\partial \alpha} + \frac{\partial f}{\partial g} \frac{\partial g}{\partial \alpha}$$

When a parameter that enters both the objective function and the constraint changes, it produces two separate effects. First, the objective function is affected directly, as indicated by the term $\partial f / \partial \alpha$. In addition, the value of the constraint is affected, by the amount $\partial g / \partial \alpha$. This is then converted to units of the objective function f by multiplying by $\lambda (= \partial f / \partial g)$. The sum of these two effects is the total impact of a change in α on the maximum value of y.

A common application of Eq. (7-27) concerns models in which the objective function is some sort of value of output function, which is maximized subject to a resource constrained to some level k. If an additional increment of resource, Δk, became available, output would increase by some amount $\Delta y^* \approx \lambda^* \Delta k$; in other words, λ^* *is the marginal value of that resource*. In a competitive economy, firms would be willing to pay λ^* for each increment in the resource. In the mathematical programming literature, λ^* is called a "shadow price" of the resource. In a model in which output of society is maximized subject to constraints of parametric labor and capital constraints, the Lagrange multipliers associated with those constraints impute shadow factor prices, i.e., a wage and rental rate to labor and capital. In the next chapter, in a model in which total cost is minimized subject to producing some parametric output level, λ^* measures the change in total cost if output is changed, i.e., marginal cost. We shall explore these relationships in the chapters following.

Consider again the model

maximize

$$f(x_1, x_2) = y$$

subject to

$$g(x_1, x_2) = k$$

Since the parameter k enters the constraint, we know that in general, the sign of $\partial \lambda^* / \partial k$ is indeterminate. However, in some important models, additional assumptions provide a sign for this term. Differentiating Eqs. (7-25) with respect to k,

$$
\begin{pmatrix}
\mathcal{L}_{11} & \mathcal{L}_{12} & -g_1 \\
\mathcal{L}_{21} & \mathcal{L}_{22} & -g_2 \\
-g_1 & -g_2 & 0
\end{pmatrix}
\begin{pmatrix}
\dfrac{\partial x_1^*}{\partial k} \\[2mm]
\dfrac{\partial x_2^*}{\partial k} \\[2mm]
\dfrac{\partial \lambda^*}{\partial k}
\end{pmatrix}
=
\begin{pmatrix}
0 \\
0 \\
-1
\end{pmatrix}
\tag{7-28}
$$

Solving for $\partial \lambda^*/\partial k$,

$$
\frac{\partial \lambda^*}{\partial k} = -\frac{H_{33}}{H}
$$

where H is the bordered Hessian determinant of the Lagrangian $\mathcal{L}$. From the sufficient second-order conditions, $H > 0$. Suppose now that f and g are strictly increasing functions, so that $\lambda^* > 0$ (why?). Suppose in addition that f is a concave and g is a convex function. Then $-g$ must be concave, and thus $\mathcal{L}$ is concave. In this case, then, $H_{33} = \mathcal{L}_{11}\mathcal{L}_{22} - \mathcal{L}_{12}^2 \geq 0$, and thus $\partial \lambda^*/\partial k \leq 0$. If g is linear, these conditions are met as long as f is concave. It is also possible to show, via primal-dual methods, that if $\partial \lambda^*/\partial k < 0$, $\mathcal{L}$ must be a strictly concave function; the proof is left as an exercise.

These results generalize in a straightforward manner to maximization models with multiple constraints,

maximize

$$
f(x) = y
$$

subject to

$$
g(x) \leq k
$$

where $x = (x_1, \ldots, x_n)$, $g(x) = g^j(x_1, \ldots, x_n)$, and $k = (k_1, \ldots, k_m)$, $j = 1, \ldots, m$. The choice functions $x = x^*(k)$ and the Lagrange multipliers $\lambda^*(k)$ implied by this model are obtained by simultaneous solution of the first-order Lagrangian conditions, assuming the sufficient second-order conditions hold. The indirect objective function is $\phi(k) = f(x^*(k))$. By the envelope theorem, $\lambda^{j*}(k) = \partial \phi/\partial k^j$, the marginal value of relaxing the jth "resource constraint" k^j, measured by the resulting increase in the value of the objective function. If $f(x)$ is concave and $g^j(x)$ is convex for $j = 1, \ldots, m$, $\phi(k)$ is concave in k, and thus $(\phi_{kk}) = (\partial \lambda^*/\partial k)$ is negative semidefinite. Since the diagonal elements of (ϕ_{kk}) would then be nonpositive, this implies that $\partial \lambda^*/\partial k \leq 0$. In many important models, the constraints are linear; such a specification satisfies the conditions of this theorem.

The proof relies on the definitions of concave and convex functions. Let k^1 and k^2 be two arbitrary values of the k vectors, and denote the implied choice vectors as $x^1 = x^*(k^1)$, $x^2 = x^*(k^2)$. Let $k^t = tk^1 + (1-t)k^2$, $x^t = tx^1 + (1-t)x^2$, $0 \leq t \leq 1$. By convexity of the constraints,

$$g(x^t) \leq tg(x^1) + (1 - t)g(x^2) \leq tk^1 + (1 - t)k^2 = k^t$$

Therefore, x^t is a feasible choice for, or solution to, this model; it satisfies the constraints when $k = k^t$.

Since $f(x)$ is concave,

$$f(x^t) \geq tf(x^1) + (1 - t)f(x^2) = t\phi(k^1) + (1 - t)\phi(k^2)$$

But by the definition of ϕ, $\phi(k^t) \geq f(x^t)$. Therefore,

$$\phi(k^t) \geq t\phi(k^1) + (1 - t)\phi(k^2)$$

Therefore, $\phi(k)$ is concave in k. Assuming differentiability, the Hessian matrix ϕ_{kk} is of course negative semidefinite, yielding the usual comparative statics results in those cases. An important application of this result occurs in the "small country" models of international trade, where total output of an economy is maximized subject to endowment constraints. The factor prices are the associated Lagrange multipliers of those endowment constraints. If the production functions are concave, this theorem implies that an increase in the endowment of some factor cannot increase that factor's price. This model will be developed more fully in the chapters on general equilibrium.

PROBLEMS

1. Consider maximization models with the specification

   maximize

   $$y = f(x_1, x_2, \alpha)$$

   subject to

   $$g(x_1, x_2) = k$$

   with Lagrangian $\mathcal{L} = f(x_1, x_2, \alpha) + \lambda[k - g(x_1, x_2)]$, where x_1 and x_2 are choice variables and α and k are parameters.
   (a) Define $\phi(\alpha, k) = $ maximum value of y for given α and k in this model. On a graph with α on the horizontal axis and ϕ and f on the vertical axis, explain *geometrically* the envelope results $\phi_\alpha = f_\alpha$ and $\phi_{\alpha\alpha} > f_{\alpha\alpha}$.
   (b) On a similar graph, explain why it is *not* possible to carry out a similar procedure for the parameter k. How does this result relate to the appearance of refutable comparative statics theorems in economics?
   (c) Using the results of (a), prove that

   $$f_{1\alpha}\frac{\partial x_1}{\partial \alpha} + f_{2\alpha}\frac{\partial x_2}{\partial \alpha} > 0$$

   (d) Using the primal-dual methodology, prove algebraically the envelope theorem results:

   1. $\phi_\alpha = f_\alpha$
   2. $\phi_{\alpha\alpha} > f_{\alpha\alpha}$
   3. $\phi_k = \lambda^*$

(e) Prove that $f_{1\alpha}\partial x_1^*/\partial k + f_{2\alpha}\partial x_2^*/\partial k = \partial\lambda^*/\partial\alpha$.
(f) Assume that the objective function f measures the net value of some activity, and the constraint represents a restriction on some resource. Using result 3 in part (d), explain why the Lagrange multiplier imputes a "shadow price" to the resource, i.e., a marginal value of that resource in terms of the objective specified in the model. Also, in these models, what can be said, if anything, about how this marginal evaluation of the resource changes as the constraint eases, i.e., as k increases?
(g) Suppose now that the objective function is linear in α, i.e., $f(x_1, x_2, \alpha) = h(x_1, x_2) + \alpha x_1$. Prove that $\phi(\alpha)$ is convex in α, and, assuming the sufficient second-order conditions hold, $\phi_{\alpha\alpha} > 0$.

2. Consider models with the specification

maximize

$$y = f(x_1, x_2) + h(x_1, \alpha)$$

subject to

$$g(x_1, x_2, \beta) = 0$$

where x_1 and x_2 are choice variables and α and β are parameters that enter only the functions shown.
(a) Derive a refutable comparative statics result for α, and show that no such result exists for β.
(b) Let $\phi(\alpha, \beta) = $ maximum value of y for given α and β in this model. Using the primal-dual methodology, prove the envelope theorem results:

i. $\phi_\alpha = h_\alpha(x_1^*, \alpha)$
ii. $\phi_\beta = \lambda^* g_\beta(x_1^*, x_2^*, \beta)$ where λ^* is the Lagrange multiplier.

(c) Prove the "reciprocity" theorem

$$h_{1\alpha}\left(\frac{\partial x_1^*}{\partial\beta}\right) = \lambda^*\left[g_{1\beta}\left(\frac{\partial x_1^*}{\partial\alpha}\right) + g_{2\beta}\left(\frac{\partial x_2^*}{\partial\alpha}\right)\right] + g_\beta\left(\frac{\partial\lambda^*}{\partial\alpha}\right)$$

(d) On a graph with y on the vertical axis and α on the horizontal axis, sketch possible curves $\phi(\alpha, \beta)$ and $f(x_1^0, x_2^0) + h(x_1^0, \alpha)$ where x_1^0, x_2^0 and β^0 are some fixed values of those variables. Demonstrate graphically that $\phi_\alpha = h_\alpha$ and also that $\phi_{\alpha\alpha} > h_{\alpha\alpha}$.
(e) Explain why it is not possible to carry out a similar procedure for the parameter β, and thus why no refutable comparative statics theorems are available for this parameter from maximization alone.

3. Consider the model,

minimize

$$AC = \frac{w_1 x_1 + w_2 x_2}{y}$$

where x_1 and x_2 are factor inputs, w_1 and w_2 are factor prices, and $y = g(x_1, x_2)$ is a production function. Let AC*(w_1, w_2) be the minimum average cost for given factor prices.

(a) Explain how the factor demands $x_i^*(w_1, w_2)$ and the indirect objective function are derived. Prove that the factor demands are homogeneous of degree 0 and that AC* is homogeneous of degree 1 in the factor prices.

(b) On a graph with AC and AC* on the vertical axis, and w_1 on the horizontal axis, plot a typical AC and AC*. Show graphically that AC* is necessarily concave in w_1 (and, of course, w_2 also.)

(c) What is the slope of AC* at any given w_1?

(d) Using this graphical analysis, show that $\partial(x_i^*/y^*)/\partial w_i < 0$.

(e) Show that the elasticity of demand for factor 1 is less than the elasticity of output supply with respect to w_1.

(f) Set up the primal-dual model, minimize AC − AC*, and derive the above results algebraically.

(g) Contrast the factor demands derived from this model, $x_i^*(w_1, w_2)$, with the factor demands $x_i^p(w_1, w_2, p)$ derived from, maximize $pf(x_1, x_2) - w_1 x_1 - w_2 x_2$, where output price p is parametric. Display the first-order conditions for both models, and explain the relation between the models by explaining the following identity, where $p^* = $ AC*(w_1, w_2):

$$x_1^*(w_1, w_1) \equiv x_1^p(w_1, w_2, p^*(w_1, w_2))$$

(h) From this identity, show that the elasticity of demand for x_1 derived from min AC, $[(w_1/x_1^*)/(\partial x_1^*/\partial w_1)]$ is equal to the elasticity of demand derived from profit maximization, plus an output effect which equals the share spent on x_1 times the output price elasticity of x_1.

4. Consider a profit-maximizing firm employing two factors. Define the short run as the condition where the firm behaves as if it were under a total expenditure constraint; i.e., in the short run, *total expenditures are fixed* (at the long-run profit-maximizing level). The long run is the situation where no additional constraints are placed on the firm.

(a) Are these short-run demands necessarily downward-sloping?

(b) Show that the short-run factor demand curves for this model are not necessarily less elastic than the long-run factor demand curves. Why does this anomalous result arise for this model?

(c) Show that if a factor is *inferior* in terms of its response to a change in total expenditure, the slope of the long-run factor demand is necessarily more negative than the short-run demand for that factor.

5. Consider models with the specification

maximize

$$y = f(x_1, \ldots, x_n)$$

subject to

$$g(x_1, \ldots, x_n) = k$$

Let $\phi(k) = $ maximum value of f for given k. Assuming an interior solution exists, prove that if f and g are both homogeneous of the same degree r, then $\phi(k)$ is linear in k, i.e., $\phi(k) = ak$, where a is an arbitrary constant, and thus the Lagrange multiplier for such models is a constant.

7.5[†] THE COMPARATIVE STATICS OF MAXIMIZATION SYSTEMS

We now examine the general structure of these maximization models in order to discover the structures that allow the derivation of refutable hypotheses in such models. We shall perform the analysis for models involving n decision variables $x_1, \ldots, x_n$, denoted simply as $\mathbf{x}$, and m parameters $\alpha_1, \ldots, \alpha_m$, denoted simply as α. A single side constraint will be imposed on these variables. This will allow sufficient generality to derive all results.

The general model is

maximize

$$y = f(\mathbf{x}, \alpha)$$

subject to

$$g(\mathbf{x}, \alpha) = 0 \tag{7-29}$$

The first-order conditions are found by differentiating the implied Lagrangian with respect to the x_i's and λ:

$$\mathscr{L} = f(\mathbf{x}, \alpha) + \lambda g(\mathbf{x}, \alpha)$$

$$\mathscr{L}_1 = f_1 + \lambda g_1 = 0$$

$$\vdots$$

$$\mathscr{L}_n = f_n + \lambda g_n = 0 \tag{7-30a}$$

$$\mathscr{L}_\lambda = g = 0 \tag{7-30b}$$

The sufficient second-order conditions for a constrained maximum are that the principal minors of the bordered Hessian matrix of second partials of $\mathscr{L}$ have sign $(-1)^k$, where $k =$ number of $\mathbf{x}$ rows and columns (1 less than the size of the whole determinant, here); $k = 2, \ldots, n$.

$$H = \begin{vmatrix} \mathbf{f_{xx}} + \lambda \mathbf{g_{xx}} & \mathbf{g_x} \\ \mathbf{g_x} & 0 \end{vmatrix} \tag{7-31}$$

This determinant H has $n + 1$ rows and columns. The first n rows and columns, denoted by $\mathbf{f_{xx}} + \lambda \mathbf{g_{xx}}$, consist of the second partial derivatives of the Lagrangian $\mathscr{L}$. That is, the element in the ith row and jth column is $\mathscr{L}_{ij} = f_{ij} + \lambda g_{ij}$. Bordering this matrix is the row (and column) of first partials $g_1, \ldots, g_n$ of the constraint $g(\mathbf{x}, \alpha)$ with respect to the x_i's. These elements can also be viewed as $\mathscr{L}_{i\lambda} = \mathscr{L}_{\lambda i} = g_i$. Thus, e.g., the border-preserving principal minors of order 2, formed by striking $n - 2$ of rows 1 to n and the same numbered column, are all positive, etc.

[†]This section is somewhat more difficult and may be skipped on first reading.

The choice functions which indicate the responses of the system to changes in the test conditions or environment, i.e., the parameters, are found, in principle, by simultaneous solution of Eqs. (7-30), yielding

$$x_i = x_i^*(\boldsymbol{\alpha}) \quad i = 1, \ldots, n \tag{7-32}$$

and

$$\lambda = \lambda^*(\boldsymbol{\alpha}) \tag{7-33}$$

Relations (7-32) and (7-33) are all potentially interesting, assuming that the parameters $\boldsymbol{\alpha}$ are observable. The Lagrange multiplier λ will not in general be an observable variable, though its value may be derivable, e.g., as an imputed marginal value or cost.

The indirect objective function $\phi(\boldsymbol{\alpha})$ is defined as the maximum value of $f(\mathbf{x}, \boldsymbol{\alpha})$ for given values of the parameters $\boldsymbol{\alpha}$ for values of $\mathbf{x}$ which also satisfy the constraint $g(\mathbf{x}, \boldsymbol{\alpha}) = 0$. Mathematically,

$$\phi(\boldsymbol{\alpha}) \equiv f(\mathbf{x}^*(\boldsymbol{\alpha}), \boldsymbol{\alpha}) \tag{7-34}$$

where the $\mathbf{x}^*(\boldsymbol{\alpha})$ are given by Eqs. (7-32). Consider now a new objective function,

$$z = F(\mathbf{x}, \boldsymbol{\alpha}) = f(\mathbf{x}, \boldsymbol{\alpha}) - \phi(\boldsymbol{\alpha}) \tag{7-35}$$

defined over the $n + m$ variables $x_1, \ldots, x_n, \alpha_1, \ldots, \alpha_m$. Since $\phi(\boldsymbol{\alpha})$ is the maximum value of $f(\mathbf{x}, \boldsymbol{\alpha})$ for given $\boldsymbol{\alpha}$, $f(\mathbf{x}, \boldsymbol{\alpha}) \leq \phi(\boldsymbol{\alpha})$. And when $\mathbf{x} = \mathbf{x}^*(\boldsymbol{\alpha})$, $\phi(\boldsymbol{\alpha}) = f(\mathbf{x}, \boldsymbol{\alpha})$, by definition. Thus, assuming the maximum is unique, when $\mathbf{x} \neq \mathbf{x}^*(\boldsymbol{\alpha})$, $F(\mathbf{x}, \boldsymbol{\alpha}) < 0$ and when $\mathbf{x} = \mathbf{x}^*(\boldsymbol{\alpha})$, $F(\mathbf{x}, \boldsymbol{\alpha}) = 0$. This means that $F(\mathbf{x}, \boldsymbol{\alpha})$ has a maximum value (of 0) when $\mathbf{x} = \mathbf{x}^*(\boldsymbol{\alpha})$, subject to the constraint $g(\mathbf{x}, \boldsymbol{\alpha}) = 0$.

We can thus state this new primal-dual problem as

maximize
$\mathbf{x}, \boldsymbol{\alpha}$
$$z = F(\mathbf{x}, \boldsymbol{\alpha}) = f(\mathbf{x}, \boldsymbol{\alpha}) - \phi(\boldsymbol{\alpha}) \tag{7-36}$$

subject to $\qquad\qquad g(\mathbf{x}, \boldsymbol{\alpha}) = 0$

As indicated, this maximization is to take place over the $n + m$ variables $(\mathbf{x}, \boldsymbol{\alpha})$. Here, the $\boldsymbol{\alpha}$'s are not treated as parameters but as independent variables. The Lagrangian for this problem is

$$\mathscr{L}^* = f(\mathbf{x}, \boldsymbol{\alpha}) - \phi(\boldsymbol{\alpha}) + \lambda g(\mathbf{x}, \boldsymbol{\alpha}) \tag{7-37}$$

When (7-37) is differentiated with respect to the x_i's, λ_j's and α_j's, the first-order conditions for the problem (7-36) are

$$\mathscr{L}_{x_i}^* = f_{x_i} + \lambda g_{x_i} = 0 \quad i = 1, \ldots, n \tag{7-38a}$$

$$\mathscr{L}_{\alpha_j}^* = f_{\alpha_j} + \lambda g_{\alpha_j} - \phi_{\alpha_j} = 0 \quad j = 1, \ldots, m \tag{7-38b}$$

$$\mathscr{L}_{\lambda}^* = g(\mathbf{x}, \boldsymbol{\alpha}) = 0 \tag{7-38c}$$

These conditions hold when $\mathbf{x} = \mathbf{x}^*(\boldsymbol{\alpha})$. Equations (7-38a) and (7-38c) are simply the first-order conditions for the original, or primal, problem; these conditions must hold if $f(\mathbf{x}, \boldsymbol{\alpha})$ is to have a constrained maximum. Equations (7-38b), on the other hand, represent the envelope theorem. At $\mathbf{x} = \mathbf{x}^*(\boldsymbol{\alpha})$, the rate of change of the indirect objective function $\phi(\boldsymbol{\alpha})$ with respect to some parameter α_j, that is, ϕ_{α_j}, in which the x_i's are allowed to adjust to the changes in α_j, is equal to the rate of change of the original Lagrangian $\mathscr{L} = f + \lambda g$ with respect to that α_j, holding the x_i's constant. The indirect objective function $\phi(\boldsymbol{\alpha})$ is an envelope curve to all possible direct Lagrangian functions. The tangency of $\phi(\boldsymbol{\alpha})$ and $\mathscr{L}(\mathbf{x}, \boldsymbol{\alpha})$ implies that $\phi_{\alpha_j} = \mathscr{L}_{\alpha_j} = f_{\alpha_j} + \lambda g_{\alpha_j}$. Equations (7-38$b$), the envelope theorem, are in fact derivable from Eqs. (7-38a) and (7-38c); hence, the $n + m + 1$ Eqs. (7-38) cannot in fact have dimensionality exceeding $n + 1$.

The second-order conditions for this primal-dual problem (7-36) are that the matrix of second partials of $\mathscr{L}^*$ with respect to $\mathbf{x}$ and $\boldsymbol{\alpha}$,

$$\mathscr{L}^* = \begin{pmatrix} \mathscr{L}^*_{xx} & \mathscr{L}^*_{x\alpha} \\ \mathscr{L}^*_{\alpha x} & \mathscr{L}^*_{\alpha\alpha} \end{pmatrix}$$

is negative (semi) definite subject to constraint, i.e., that

$$\sum_{i=1}^{n+m} \sum_{j=1}^{n+m} \mathscr{L}^*_{ij} h_i h_j \leq 0 \qquad (7\text{-}39a)$$

for all values of $h_1, \ldots, h_{n+m}$ which satisfy

$$\sum_{i=1}^{n+m} g_i h_i = 0 \qquad (7\text{-}39b)$$

In these expressions, the subscripts refer to partial differentiation with respect to the x_i's and α_j's; the sum runs from 1 to $n + m$ to indicate that [in (7-39a), for example] all $(n + m)^2$ second partials of $\mathscr{L}^*$ are involved.

Since the whole matrix $\mathscr{L}^*$ is negative (semi) definite subject to constraint, the square portion $\mathscr{L}^*_{\mathbf{xx}}$ in the upper left corner must be so also, the constraint being that part of $g(\mathbf{x}, \boldsymbol{\alpha}) = 0$ which applies only to the x_i's. Even more interestingly, the matrix in the lower right of $\mathscr{L}^*$, $\mathscr{L}^*_{\alpha\alpha}$, the matrix of second partials of $\mathscr{L}^*$ with respect to the α_i's only, must similarly be negative (semi) definite subject to constraint. If we let $\mathbf{h} = (h_1, \ldots, h_n, h_{n+1}, \ldots, h_{n+m}) = (0, \ldots, 0, h_{n+1}, \ldots, h_{n+m})$, that is, set the h_i's that are attached to any second partial of $\mathscr{L}^*$ involving an x_i equal to 0, Eqs. (7-39) become

$$\sum_{j=1}^{m} \sum_{i=1}^{m} \mathscr{L}^*_{\alpha_i \alpha_j} h_{n+i} h_{n+j} \leq 0 \qquad (7\text{-}40a)$$

for all h_{n+i}, h_{n+j} satisfying

$$\sum_{i=1}^{m} g_{\alpha_i} h_{n+i} = 0 \qquad (7\text{-}40b)$$

In determinant form, Eqs. (7-40) say that the border-preserving principal minors of order k of the following bordered Hessian determinant have sign $(-1)^k$ or 0:

$$H_{\alpha\alpha} = \begin{vmatrix} \mathscr{L}^*_{\alpha\alpha} & \mathbf{g}_\alpha \\ \mathbf{g}_\alpha & 0 \end{vmatrix} \tag{7-41}$$

where $\mathscr{L}^*_{\alpha\alpha}$ is the $m \times m$ matrix of second partials of $\mathscr{L}^*$ with respect to the α_i's, and $\mathbf{g}_\alpha = (g_{\alpha_1}, \ldots, g_{\alpha_m})$.

These conditions place restrictions on the comparative-statics choice functions (7-32) and (7-33). Let us evaluate the terms in $\mathscr{L}^*_{\alpha\alpha}$.

Differentiating Eq. (7-38b) with respect to some α_i gives

$$\mathscr{L}^*_{\alpha_i \alpha_j} = f_{\alpha_i \alpha_j} + \lambda g_{\alpha_i \alpha_j} - \phi_{\alpha_i \alpha_j} \tag{7-42}$$

However, when $\mathbf{x} = \mathbf{x}^*(\boldsymbol{\alpha})$, $\lambda = \lambda^*(\boldsymbol{\alpha})$,

$$\mathscr{L}^*_{\alpha_i} \equiv f_{\alpha_i}(\mathbf{x}^*, \boldsymbol{\alpha}) + \lambda^*(\boldsymbol{\alpha}) g_{\alpha_i}(\mathbf{x}^*, \boldsymbol{\alpha}) - \phi_{\alpha_i}(\boldsymbol{\alpha}) \equiv 0$$

Differentiating this identity with respect to some α_j yields

$$\sum_{k=1}^{n} \frac{\partial f_{\alpha_i}}{\partial x_k} \frac{\partial x_k^*}{\partial \alpha_j} + f_{\alpha_i \alpha_j} + \lambda^* \sum_{k=1}^{n} \frac{\partial g_{\alpha_i}}{\partial x_k} \frac{\partial x_k^*}{\partial \alpha_j} + \lambda^* g_{\alpha_i \alpha_j} + g_{\alpha_i} \frac{\partial \lambda^*}{\partial \alpha_j} - \phi_{\alpha_i \alpha_j} \equiv 0$$

Notice that three of these terms constitute exactly $\mathscr{L}^*_{\alpha_i \alpha_j}$ in Eq. (7-42). Therefore,

$$\mathscr{L}^*_{\alpha_i \alpha_j} = -\left[\sum_{k=1}^{n} \left(\frac{\partial f_{\alpha_i}}{\partial x_k} + \lambda^* \frac{\partial g_{\alpha_i}}{\partial x_k} \right) \frac{\partial x_k^*}{\partial \alpha_j} + g_{\alpha_i} \frac{\partial \lambda^*}{\partial \alpha_j} \right]$$

or, more simply,

$$\mathscr{L}^*_{\alpha_i \alpha_j} = -\sum_{k=1}^{n} \mathscr{L}_{\alpha_i x_k} \frac{\partial x_k^*}{\partial \alpha_j} - g_{\alpha_i} \frac{\partial \lambda^*}{\partial \alpha_j} \qquad i,j = 1, \ldots, m \tag{7-43}$$

Equations (7-43) are expressions involving the partial derivatives of the choice functions (7-32) and (7-33). The conditions on the bordered Hessian determinants of these terms, (7-41), place restrictions on the size and sign of these terms and constitute the known implications of the maximization hypothesis.

It is obvious from the complexity of the expressions (7-43) that at this level of generality, no refutable implications of the maximization hypothesis will be forthcoming. It is thus apparent that, at the very least, refutable comparative-statics theorems are likely to be derivable from maximization models only if the $\mathscr{L}^*_{\alpha_i \alpha_j}$ expressions boil down to exactly one term. If two terms are left in $\mathscr{L}^*_{\alpha_i \alpha_j}$, the model will at best imply a sign for the sum of two partial derivatives of the choice functions. This may be useful information, but economists are most often concerned with the effects on a single variable when a parameter changes, not, for example, with the fact that the sum of the demands for capital and labor will be reduced when wages increase, etc. Let us investigate these matters in greater detail.

Reciprocity Relations

Due to the invariance of second partials to the order of differentiation, $\mathcal{L}^*_{\alpha_i \alpha_j} = \mathcal{L}^*_{\alpha_j \alpha_i}$. From Eq. (7-43), then, the general form of all reciprocity relations in these models is

$$\sum_{k=1}^{n} \mathcal{L}_{\alpha_i x_k} \frac{\partial x_k^*}{\partial \alpha_j} + g_{\alpha_i} \frac{\partial \lambda^*}{\partial \alpha_j} = \sum_{k=1}^{n} \mathcal{L}_{\alpha_j x_k} \frac{\partial x_k^*}{\partial \alpha_i} + g_{\alpha_j} \frac{\partial \lambda^*}{\partial \alpha_i} \qquad (7\text{-}44)$$

In models with no constraints, i.e., unconstrained maximization problems like the profit maximization model, preceding Eq. (7-44) becomes

$$\sum_{k=1}^{n} f_{\alpha_i x_k} \frac{\partial x_k^*}{\partial \alpha_j} = \sum_{k=1}^{n} f_{\alpha_j x_k} \frac{\partial x_k^*}{\partial \alpha_i} \qquad (7\text{-}45)$$

In the case where each parameter α_k enters one and only one first-order equation (the kth, by definition of α_k), $f_{\alpha_i x_i} = 0$ for $i \neq k$, and thus Eq. (7-45) becomes

$$f_{\alpha_i x_i} \frac{\partial x_i^*}{\partial \alpha_j} = f_{\alpha_j x_j} \frac{\partial x_j^*}{\partial \alpha_i} \qquad (7\text{-}46)$$

In models where the parameters enter in the form of a linear expression $\sum_{i=1}^{n} \alpha_i x_i$, $f_{\alpha_i x_i} \equiv 1$, $i = 1, \ldots, n$, and then

$$\frac{\partial x_i^*}{\partial \alpha_j} = \frac{\partial x_j^*}{\partial \alpha_i} \qquad (7\text{-}47)$$

A relation like (7-47) will occur in unconstrained problems only when each parameter enters one and only one first-order relation and when those parameters shift those first-order relations at the same rate, i.e., when $f_{\alpha_i x_i} = f_{\alpha_j x_j}$, since $f_{\alpha_i x_i} = \partial f_{x_i} / \partial \alpha_i$, et cetera.

Suppose now that some parameter α_i appears in the objective function only and in only one first-order relation $\mathcal{L}^*_{x_i} = \mathcal{L}_{x_i} = 0$. And suppose a parameter α_j enters the constraint equation only. Then Eq. (7-44) becomes

$$f_{\alpha_i x_i} \frac{\partial x_i^*}{\partial \alpha_j} = \sum_{k=1}^{n} \lambda^* g_{\alpha_j x_k} \frac{\partial x_k^*}{\partial \alpha_i} + g_{\alpha_j} \frac{\partial \lambda^*}{\partial \alpha_i}$$

Suppose, in addition, g is linear in α_j, so that $g_{\alpha_j} = $ constant. Then $g_{\alpha_j x_k} = 0$, $k = 1, \ldots, n$, and the preceding equation becomes

$$f_{\alpha_i x_i} \frac{\partial x_i^*}{\partial \alpha_j} = g_{\alpha_j} \frac{\partial \lambda^*}{\partial \alpha_i} \qquad (7\text{-}48)$$

What emerges from this analysis is that the reciprocity conditions encountered in some of the elementary economic models occur only because of some highly unusual functional forms. Unusual or not from a mathematical standpoint, in the empirical process of building scientific models, these functional forms are often formulated precisely because they are so useful.

Qualitative Results

The determinantal conditions (7-41), in conjunction with Eqs. (7-42), are, again, too general to be usefully applied, even though they are in principle refutable, since they imply restrictions on observable quantities. To accomplish this, however, would require knowledge of the values of the various cross-partials of f and g, information that is not generally available. When can refutable hypotheses be derived without such detailed information on the functions in the model?

In models with no constraints, the second-order conditions state that the matrix of terms $\mathscr{L}^*_{\alpha_i\alpha_j} = -\sum_{k=1}^{n} f_{\alpha_i x_k}(\partial x^*_k/\partial \alpha_j)$ is negative semidefinite. In particular, this implies that the diagonal terms of that matrix are nonpositive, i.e.,

$$-\sum_{k=1}^{n} f_{\alpha_i x_k}\frac{\partial x^*_k}{\partial \alpha_i} \leq 0 \tag{7-49}$$

If, however, a given parameter α_i enters only one first-order relation $f_{x_i} = 0$, then all but one term in Eq. (7-49) is 0, yielding,

$$f_{\alpha_i x_i}\frac{\partial x^*_i}{\partial \alpha_i} \geq 0 \tag{7-50}$$

In this case, the decision variable will move in the same direction as the effect on the first-order relation of that parameter. For example, in the profit maximization model with $\pi = pf(x_1, \ldots, x_n) - \sum w_i x_i$, $\pi_{x_i} = pf_i - w_i$, and increasing the wage w_i tends to decrease π_{x_i}, since $\pi_{x_i w_i} = \pi_{w_i x_i} = -1$. Hence, the partial derivative $\partial x^*_i/\partial w_i \leq 0$, that is, the law of factor demand for profit-maximizing firms.

In addition to the implications of the negativity of the diagonal terms of $\mathscr{L}^*_{\alpha\alpha}$, the other determinantal conditions, e.g., that the second-order principal minors be positive, or $\mathscr{L}^*_{\alpha_i\alpha_i}\mathscr{L}^*_{\alpha_j\alpha_j} - (\mathscr{L}^*_{\alpha_i\alpha_j})^2 \geq 0$, also imply restrictions on the choice functions. However, these restrictions will be very difficult to observe directly, even in models as simple as the profit maximization model. In that model, for example, this condition says that $(\partial x^*_i/\partial w_i)(\partial x^*_j/\partial w_j) - (\partial x^*_i/\partial w_j)^2 \geq 0$, or that direct effects outweigh, in the preceding sense, the cross-effects. But such propositions in fact have limited empirical applicability.

A similar, though more complex, analysis applies to constrained maximization problems. The determinantal conditions (7-40) are, again,

$$\sum_{j=1}^{m}\sum_{i=1}^{m} \mathscr{L}^*_{\alpha_i\alpha_j}h_{n+i}h_{n+j} \leq 0 \tag{7-40a}$$

for all h_{n+i}, h_{n+j} satisfying

$$\sum_{i=1}^{m} g_{\alpha_i}h_{n+i} = 0 \tag{7-40b}$$

where $\mathscr{L}^*_{\alpha_i\alpha_j}$ is given as

$$\mathscr{L}^*_{\alpha_i \alpha_j} = -\sum_{k=1}^{n} \mathscr{L}_{\alpha_i x_k} \frac{\partial x_k^*}{\partial \alpha_j} - g_{\alpha_i} \frac{\partial \lambda^*}{\partial \alpha_j} \tag{7-43}$$

Suppose now that the parameters can be divided into two groups, $\alpha_1, \ldots, \alpha_r$, which appear only in the objective function $f(\mathbf{x}, \boldsymbol{\alpha})$, and $\alpha_{r+1}, \ldots, \alpha_m$, which appear only in the constraint $g(\mathbf{x}, \boldsymbol{\alpha})$. Then, if $h_{n+r+1}, \ldots, h_{n+m}$ are all set equal to 0, Eq. (7-40b) will be satisfied and Eq. (7-40a) will become

$$\sum_{i=1}^{r} \sum_{j=1}^{r} \mathscr{L}^*_{\alpha_i \alpha_j} h_{n+i} h_{n+j} \leq 0 \tag{7-51}$$

for *all* values h_{n+i}, h_{n+j}, $i, j = 1, \ldots, r$. That is, if this type of partitioning of the parameters is possible, the model will behave in the same manner as an unconstrained maximum: the matrix of terms $\mathscr{L}^*_{\alpha_i \alpha_j}$ with respect to those parameters appearing in the objective function only will be negative semidefinite. In fact, notice the effect of this partition on $\mathscr{L}^*_{\alpha_i \alpha_j}$, $i, j = 1, \ldots, r$. Since α_i, $i = 1, \ldots, r$, does not appear in the constraint equation, $g_{\alpha_i} \equiv 0$, $i = 1, \ldots, r$, and likewise $\partial g_{\alpha_i}/\partial x_k \equiv 0$, $i = 1, \ldots, r$. Hence,

$$\mathscr{L}^*_{\alpha_i \alpha_j} = -\sum_{k=1}^{n} f_{\alpha_i x_k} \frac{\partial x_k^*}{\partial \alpha_j} \quad i, j = 1, \ldots, r \tag{7-52}$$

an expression exactly like Eq. (7-49) for unconstrained maximization models.

A similar analysis follows. The diagonal terms of this $r \times r$ matrix are nonpositive, i.e.,

$$-\sum_{k=1}^{n} f_{\alpha_i x_k} \frac{\partial x_k^*}{\partial \alpha_i} \leq 0 \quad i = 1, \ldots, r \tag{7-53}$$

and the principal minors alternate in sign. If a parameter α_i appears only in the ith first-order relation, that is, $\mathscr{L}_{x_i} = f_{x_i}(\mathbf{x}, \alpha_i) + \lambda g_{x_i}(\mathbf{x}) = 0$, so that $f_{x_i \alpha_k} = 0$, $k \neq i$, then Eq. (7-53) becomes

$$f_{\alpha_i x_i} \frac{\partial x_i^*}{\partial \alpha_i} \geq 0 \tag{7-54}$$

the same as Eq. (7-50) for unconstrained models. Useful comparative-statics relations concerning the parameters appearing in the constraint will not in general be available.

Le Châtelier Effects

We shall finish this chapter with a discussion of the general structure of effects due to the imposition of additional constraints on the variables. These Le Châtelier effects, named after Le Châtelier, who analyzed the effects of additional constraints on thermodynamic systems, state that long-run demands in certain models are more elastic than the corresponding short-run demands. The short run is defined as a situation in which one or more variables are held constant at the level appropriate to some maximum point, as the parameters, prices, change from those values that produced the maximum point.

Consider Fig. 7-4. The indirect objective function to our constrained maximization problem is now denoted $^1\phi(\boldsymbol{\alpha})$, the preceding superscript indicating that there is one constraint, in this case the original binding constraint, on the decision variables, for illustration only. Since only one variable can be plotted on a given axis, $^1\phi(\boldsymbol{\alpha})$ is plotted against some α_i, a representative parameter. At the vector of parameter values $\boldsymbol{\alpha} = \boldsymbol{\alpha}^0$ (where $\alpha_i = \alpha_i^0$), the objective function takes on the values $^1\phi(\boldsymbol{\alpha}^0) = f(x^*(\boldsymbol{\alpha}^0), \boldsymbol{\alpha}^0)$. The function $^1\phi(\boldsymbol{\alpha})$ has no determinate shape at this level of generality; it has been drawn concave around $\alpha_i = \alpha_i^0$ for illustration only.

Suppose now another, *just binding* constraint $h(\mathbf{x}, \boldsymbol{\alpha}) = 0$ is added to the model. The phrase *just binding* means that the addition of this constraint does not displace the original solution $\mathbf{x}^0 = \mathbf{x}^*(\boldsymbol{\alpha}^0)$. An example of this is holding one factor of production fixed at the previously determined profit-maximizing or cost-minimizing level. Then, when the other factor's price varies, the response of the variable factors is different. But it is impossible to compare a short-run factor demand curve at one value of x_i and its long-run demand at some other value. These comparisons are valid only at a given point, e.g., the intersection of the short- and long-run curves in Fig. 7-4. It is not the case that all long-run factor demands are more elastic than all short-run demand curves; the Le Châtelier effects are local relations holding only at one point. Hence, in our general discussion, the original model, maximize $f(\mathbf{x}, \boldsymbol{\alpha}^0)$ subject to $g(\mathbf{x}, \boldsymbol{\alpha}^0) = 0$, is solved, resulting in the solution values $\mathbf{x}^0 = \mathbf{x}^*(\boldsymbol{\alpha}^0)$. Now, a new constraint, $h(\mathbf{x}, \boldsymbol{\alpha}) = 0$, is added to the problem, *such that* $h(\mathbf{x}^0, \boldsymbol{\alpha}^0) = 0$. By requiring $h(\mathbf{x}^0, \boldsymbol{\alpha}^0) = 0$, we know that the addition of this constraint does not alter the original solution of the model since that solution value is not constrained at all by $h(\mathbf{x}, \boldsymbol{\alpha}) = 0$. However, the comparative statics of the model *does* change. As any α_i moves away from α_i^0, the new constraint will in general become binding. Thus, for example, if capital is held fixed at some previously profit-maximizing level, then as the wage of labor changes, the response in terms of labor utilized will be different (smaller, in absolute terms) than if capital were allowed to vary, for profit-maximizing firms.

In Fig. 7-4, in addition to the original indirect objective function $^1\phi(\boldsymbol{\alpha})$, the indirect objective function $^2\phi(\boldsymbol{\alpha})$ for the amended model

maximize

$$f(\mathbf{x}, \boldsymbol{\alpha})$$

subject to

$$g(\mathbf{x}, \boldsymbol{\alpha}) = 0 \quad h(\mathbf{x}, \boldsymbol{\alpha}) = 0 \tag{7-55}$$

has been plotted. This indirect objective function is labeled $^2\phi(\boldsymbol{\alpha})$ to indicate that there are now *two* constraints in the model. Since $h(\mathbf{x}^0, \boldsymbol{\alpha}^0) = 0$, $^1\phi(\mathbf{x}^0, \boldsymbol{\alpha}^0) = {}^2\phi(\mathbf{x}^0, \boldsymbol{\alpha}^0)$; that is, the two objective functions have the same value at $\boldsymbol{\alpha} = \boldsymbol{\alpha}^0$.

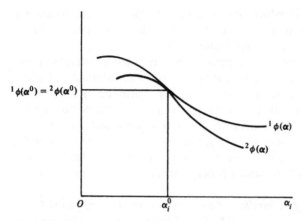

FIGURE 7-4
The indirect objective functions $^1\phi(\alpha)$, and $^2\phi(\alpha)$, the latter being the maximum value of $f(\mathbf{x}, \alpha)$ when an additional constraint $h(\mathbf{x}, \alpha)$ is added to the model, maximize $f(\mathbf{x}, \alpha)$ subject to $g(\mathbf{x}, \alpha) = 0$. The new constraint $h(\mathbf{x}, \alpha)$ is added to avoid disturbing the orignal solution $\mathbf{x}^0 = \mathbf{x}^*(\alpha^0)$, that is, by requiring $h(\mathbf{x}^0, \alpha^0) = 0$. This is akin to holding capital fixed at the previously determined profit-maximizing level and *then* changing a factor price. By this construction, $^1\phi(\alpha^0) = {}^2\phi(\alpha^0)$. However, for $\alpha \neq \alpha^0$, $^2\phi(\alpha) \leq {}^1\phi(\alpha)$ since additional restraints on the decision variables can only lower the maximum value of the objective function. Since $^2\phi(\alpha^0) = {}^1\phi(\alpha^0)$ and $^2\phi(\alpha_i) \leq {}^1\phi(\alpha_i)$ to either side of α_i^0, $^2\phi(\alpha)$ must be tangent to $^1\phi(\alpha)$ but must also be more concave in α_i (and the other parameters) than $^1\phi(\alpha)$. Since the slopes are equal, $^2\phi_{\alpha_i}(\alpha^0) = {}^1\phi_{\alpha_i}(\alpha^0)$, and from concavity $^2\phi_{\alpha_i\alpha_i}(\alpha^0) \leq {}^1\phi_{\alpha_i\alpha_i}(\alpha^0)$, among the other conditions for concavity in all the remaining parameters.

However, if $\alpha \neq \alpha^0$, $^2\phi(\alpha) \leq {}^1\phi(\alpha)$. The addition of a constraint on the x_i's can only reduce the maximum value of $f(\mathbf{x}, \alpha)$, since fewer choices are available for the values of the decision variables. If both $^1\phi(\alpha)$ and $^2\phi(\alpha)$ are differentiable, the situation $^2\phi(\alpha^0) = {}^1\phi(\alpha^0)$ and $^2\phi(\alpha) \leq {}^1\phi(\alpha)$ for $\alpha \neq \alpha^0$ must result in a tangency of $^2\phi(\alpha)$ and $^1\phi(\alpha)$ at $\alpha = \alpha^0$, as depicted in Fig. 7-4. The consequences of this tangency are:

1. $^2\phi(\alpha^0) = {}^1\phi(\alpha^0)$ [by construction: the additional constraint is just binding, that is, $h(\mathbf{x}^0, \alpha^0) = 0$].
2. $^2\phi_{\alpha_i}(\alpha^0) = {}^1\phi_{\alpha_i}(\alpha^0)$, $i = 1, \ldots, m$ [the slopes of $^1\phi(\alpha)$ and $^2\phi(\alpha)$ are equal in all directions at $\alpha = \alpha^0$, since the surfaces $^1\phi(\alpha)$ and $^2\phi(\alpha)$ are tangent].
3. $^2\phi_{\alpha_i\alpha_i} \leq {}^1\phi_{\alpha_i\alpha_i}$. In any given α_i direction, the function $^2\phi(\alpha)$ is more concave, as depicted in Fig. 7-4, or less convex than $^1\phi(\alpha)$.

Condition 3 in fact only partially characterizes this increased concavity of $^2\phi(\alpha)$ compared with $^1\phi(\alpha)$. In m dimensions, concavity is a statement that the matrix of second partials is negative semidefinite. Condition 3 is part of a statement that $^2\phi(\alpha)$ is more concave than $^1\phi(\alpha)$, subject to constraint, i.e., that $^2\phi(\alpha) - {}^1\phi(\alpha)$

is itself concave. The Le Châtelier effects are consequences of the concavity of $^2\phi(\boldsymbol{\alpha}) - {}^1\phi(\boldsymbol{\alpha})$. Let us now demonstrate these conditions analytically.

The first-order conditions for the model with two constraints, (7-55), are found by differentiating the Lagrangian $^2\mathscr{L} = f(\mathbf{x}, \boldsymbol{\alpha}) + \lambda_1 g(\mathbf{x}, \boldsymbol{\alpha}) + \lambda_2 h(\mathbf{x}, \boldsymbol{\alpha})$ with respect to the x_i's and λ's, yielding

$$f_i + \lambda_1 g_i + \lambda_2 h_i = 0 \qquad i = 1, \ldots, n$$

$$g(\mathbf{x}, \boldsymbol{\alpha}) = 0 \qquad h(\mathbf{x}, \boldsymbol{\alpha}) = 0 \qquad (7\text{-}56)$$

The solutions of (7-56) are

$$x_i = {}^2x_i^*(\boldsymbol{\alpha}) \qquad i = 1, \ldots, n$$

$$\lambda_1 = {}^2\lambda_1^*(\boldsymbol{\alpha}) \qquad \lambda_2 = {}^2\lambda_2^*(\boldsymbol{\alpha}) \qquad (7\text{-}57)$$

where, again, the preceding superscript indicates the number of constraints in the model. At this point, we shall drop the asterisks from the variables to save notational clutter. All values of the x_i's will be presumed to satisfy the respective models. The partial derivatives of these choice functions will be denoted $^2(\partial x_i / \partial \alpha_j)$; those relating to the original model will be denoted $^1(\partial x_i / \partial \alpha_j)$, etc.

Let us investigate this solution, (7-57), more closely. The solution of the model without $h(\mathbf{x}, \boldsymbol{\alpha}) = 0$, Eqs. (7-32), will be denoted $x_i = {}^1x_i(\boldsymbol{\alpha})$, $i = 1, \ldots, n$, and $\lambda = \lambda_1 = {}^1\lambda_1(\boldsymbol{\alpha})$. At $\boldsymbol{\alpha} = \boldsymbol{\alpha}^0$, $\mathbf{x} = \mathbf{x}^0 = {}^1\mathbf{x}(\boldsymbol{\alpha}^0)$, $\lambda = {}^1\lambda = {}^1\lambda^0$. These values were derived from Eqs. (7-29),

$$f_i + \lambda_1 g_i = 0 \qquad i = 1, \ldots, n$$

$$g(\mathbf{x}, \boldsymbol{\alpha}) = 0$$

But the same values of $\mathbf{x}$ and λ_1 result from the first-order Eqs. (7-56) by construction, i.e., because we have constructed $h(\mathbf{x}, \boldsymbol{\alpha}) = 0$ such that $h(\mathbf{x}^0, \boldsymbol{\alpha}^0) = 0$. Since $f_i + \lambda_1 g_i + \lambda_2 h_i = 0$, and $f_i + \lambda_1 g_i = 0$, $i = 1, \ldots, n$, it must be the case that $\lambda_2 = 0$ at the solution point, that is, $\lambda_2(\boldsymbol{\alpha}^0) = 0$. This is in accordance with our understanding of the meaning of Lagrange multipliers: these multipliers measure the marginal cost in terms of the restrictions on attainable values of the objective function due to the imposition of a constraint. Since the constraint $h(\mathbf{x}, \boldsymbol{\alpha})$ is nonbinding at $\boldsymbol{\alpha} = \boldsymbol{\alpha}^0$, that is, $^2\phi(\boldsymbol{\alpha}^0) = {}^1\phi(\boldsymbol{\alpha}^0)$, the marginal cost of this constraint, in terms of units of $f(\mathbf{x}, \boldsymbol{\alpha})$ forgone, is 0 at that one point. What, then, is the rate of change of $^2\phi(\boldsymbol{\alpha})$ with respect to a change in some α_i? By the envelope theorem,

$$^2\phi_{\alpha_i} = {}^2\mathscr{L}_{\alpha_i} = f_{\alpha_i} + \lambda_1 g_{\alpha_i} + \lambda_2 h_{\alpha_i} = f_{\alpha_i} + \lambda_1 g_{\alpha_i} = {}^1\phi_{\alpha_i} \qquad (7\text{-}58)$$

since $\lambda_2 = 0$. Hence, $^2\phi(\boldsymbol{\alpha})$ and $^1\phi(\boldsymbol{\alpha})$ have the same slope at $\boldsymbol{\alpha} = \boldsymbol{\alpha}^0$, as depicted by the tangency point in Fig. 7-4.

Now consider the second-order changes. When $\boldsymbol{\alpha} \neq \boldsymbol{\alpha}^0$, $^2\phi(\boldsymbol{\alpha}) \leq {}^1\phi(\boldsymbol{\alpha})$. In some neighborhood around $\boldsymbol{\alpha}^0$, these functions can be approximated by a Taylor series carried to second-order terms, yielding

$$^2\phi(\boldsymbol{\alpha}^0) + \sum_{i=1}^{m} {}^2\phi_{\alpha_i}(\boldsymbol{\alpha}^0)h_i + \frac{1}{2}\sum_{i=1}^{m}\sum_{j=1}^{m} {}^2\phi_{\alpha_i\alpha_j}(\boldsymbol{\alpha}^0)h_ih_j \leq$$

$$^1\phi(\boldsymbol{\alpha}^0) + \sum_{i=1}^{m} {}^1\phi_{\alpha_i}(\boldsymbol{\alpha}^0)h_i + \frac{1}{2}\sum_{i=1}^{m}\sum_{j=1}^{m} {}^1\phi_{\alpha_i\alpha_j}(\boldsymbol{\alpha}^0)h_ih_j \qquad (7\text{-}59)$$

where $h_i = \alpha_i - \alpha_i^0$. However, $^2\phi(\boldsymbol{\alpha}^0) = {}^1\phi(\boldsymbol{\alpha}^0)$ by construction, and, from Eq. (7-58), since $\lambda_2 = 0$, $^2\phi_{\alpha_i}(\boldsymbol{\alpha}^0) = {}^1\phi_{\alpha_i}(\boldsymbol{\alpha}^0)$. Relation (7-59) can thus be written

$$\sum\sum({}^2\phi_{\alpha_i\alpha_j} - {}^1\phi_{\alpha_i\alpha_j})h_ih_j \leq 0 \qquad (7\text{-}60)$$

for all values of h_i, h_j. This is condition 3 above: the Hessian matrix of second partials of $^2\phi(\boldsymbol{\alpha}) - {}^1\phi(\boldsymbol{\alpha})$ is negative semidefinite, or since $^2\phi(\boldsymbol{\alpha}) \leq {}^1\phi(\boldsymbol{\alpha})$, $^2\phi(\boldsymbol{\alpha}) - {}^1\phi(\boldsymbol{\alpha})$ is a concave (perhaps only weakly concave) function of the α_i's. This is a rather surprising result. The functions $^2\phi(\boldsymbol{\alpha}) - f(\mathbf{x}, \boldsymbol{\alpha})$ and $^1\phi(\boldsymbol{\alpha}) - f(\mathbf{x}, \boldsymbol{\alpha})$ are not concave; their difference, however, is concave.

Let us now apply Eq. (7-60) to the comparative statics of the two models. Note first that from the definitions of the Lagrangians for the primal-dual problems,

$$^1\mathcal{L}^*(\mathbf{x}, \boldsymbol{\alpha}) = f(\mathbf{x}, \boldsymbol{\alpha}) - {}^1\phi(\boldsymbol{\alpha}) + \lambda_1 g(\mathbf{x}, \boldsymbol{\alpha}) \qquad (7\text{-}37)$$

and

$$^2\mathcal{L}^*(\mathbf{x}, \boldsymbol{\alpha}) = f(\mathbf{x}, \boldsymbol{\alpha}) - {}^2\phi(\boldsymbol{\alpha})$$

$$+ \lambda_1 g(\mathbf{x}, \boldsymbol{\alpha}) + \lambda_2 h(\mathbf{x}, \boldsymbol{\alpha}) \qquad (7\text{-}61)$$

$$^1\mathcal{L}^*(\mathbf{x}, \boldsymbol{\alpha}) - {}^2\mathcal{L}^*(\mathbf{x}, \boldsymbol{\alpha}) = {}^2\phi(\boldsymbol{\alpha}) - {}^1\phi(\boldsymbol{\alpha}) - \lambda_2 h(\mathbf{x}, \boldsymbol{\alpha})$$

When $\mathbf{x} = \mathbf{x}^*$,

$$^1\mathcal{L}^*(\mathbf{x}, \boldsymbol{\alpha}) - {}^2\mathcal{L}^*(\mathbf{x}, \boldsymbol{\alpha}) \equiv {}^2\phi(\boldsymbol{\alpha}) - {}^1\phi(\boldsymbol{\alpha}) \qquad (7\text{-}62)$$

Thus, $^2\phi_{\alpha_i\alpha_j} - {}^1\phi_{\alpha_i\alpha_j}$ can be calculated from the primal-dual Lagrangians. From Eq. (7-43),

$$^1\mathcal{L}^*_{\alpha_i\alpha_j} = -\sum_{k=1}^{n} {}^1\mathcal{L}_{\alpha_i x_k}\left(\frac{\partial x_k}{\partial\alpha_j}\right)^1 - g_{\alpha_i}\left(\frac{\partial\lambda_1}{\partial\alpha_j}\right)^1 \qquad (7\text{-}63)$$

In like fashion, for the model with two constraints, one finds

$$^2\mathcal{L}^*_{\alpha_i\alpha_j} = -\sum_{k=1}^{n} {}^2\mathcal{L}_{\alpha_i x_k}\left(\frac{\partial x_k}{\partial\alpha_j}\right)^2 - g_{\alpha_i}\left(\frac{\partial\lambda_1}{\partial\alpha_j}\right)^2 - h_{\alpha_i}\left(\frac{\partial\lambda_2}{\partial\alpha_j}\right)^2 \qquad (7\text{-}64)$$

Now

$$^2\mathcal{L}_{\alpha_i x_k} = \frac{\partial f_{\alpha_i}}{\partial x_k} + \lambda_1\frac{\partial g_{\alpha_i}}{\partial x_k} + \lambda_2\frac{\partial h_{\alpha_i}}{\partial x_k}$$

However, $\lambda_2 = 0$, since $h(\mathbf{x}, \boldsymbol{\alpha})$ is just binding. Therefore,

$$^2\mathscr{L}_{\alpha_i x_k} = \frac{\partial f_{\alpha_i}}{\partial x_k} + \lambda_1 \frac{\partial g_{\alpha_i}}{\partial x_k} = {}^1\mathscr{L}_{\alpha_i x_k} \tag{7-65}$$

Although $\lambda_2 = 0$, $\partial \lambda_2 / \partial \alpha_j \neq 0$ in general. When $\boldsymbol{\alpha}$ departs from $\boldsymbol{\alpha}^0$, the constraint $h(\mathbf{x}, \boldsymbol{\alpha})$ becomes binding and then $\lambda_2 \neq 0$. Thus, λ_2 is not constant at zero; that is, $\partial \lambda_2 / \partial \alpha_j \neq 0$. Equation (7-60) now becomes, using Eqs. (7-62) to (7-65),

$$\sum_{i=1}^{m} \sum_{j=1}^{m} \left(\sum_{k=1}^{n} \left\{ \left(\frac{\partial f_{\alpha_i}}{\partial x_k} + \lambda_1 \frac{\partial g_{\alpha_i}}{\partial x_k} \right) \left[{}^2\!\left(\frac{\partial x_k}{\partial \alpha_j}\right) - {}^1\!\left(\frac{\partial x_k}{\partial \alpha_j}\right) \right] \right\} \right.$$

$$\left. + g_{\alpha_i} \left[{}^2\!\left(\frac{\partial \lambda_1}{\partial \alpha_j}\right) - {}^1\!\left(\frac{\partial \lambda_1}{\partial \alpha_j}\right) \right] + h_{\alpha_i} {}^2\!\left(\frac{\partial \lambda_2}{\partial \alpha_j}\right) \right) h_i h_j \leq 0 \tag{7-66}$$

for any values of h_i, h_j.

Equation (7-66) gives the general structure of the change in the choice functions due to the imposition of an additional, just binding constraint for differentiable maximization systems. Again, it is nothing more than the statement that the matrix of differences $({}^1\mathscr{L}^*_{\alpha_i \alpha_j} - {}^2\mathscr{L}^*_{\alpha_i \alpha_j})$ is negative semidefinite. The usual Le Châtelier effects are consequences of the negativity of the diagonal terms of this matrix, that is, ${}^1\mathscr{L}^*_{\alpha_i \alpha_i} \leq {}^2\mathscr{L}^*_{\alpha_i \alpha_i}$, with the strict inequality generally assumed. For example, for the profit-maximizing firm, if the new (and only) constraint is $x_n = x_n^0$ (note that $\partial f_{\alpha_i} / \partial x_k = 0$, $i \neq k$, and $\partial f_i / \partial \alpha_i = -1$) and $h_{\alpha_i} \equiv 0$ (prices don't enter the new constraint), a diagonal term of (7-66) is $-[{}^1(\partial x_i / \partial w_i) - {}^0(\partial x_i / \partial w_i)] \leq 0$, precisely the statement that long-run factor demands are more elastic than short-run demands. The same analysis applies to the cost minimization model, though the inequality in (7-66) must be reversed since this is a minimization rather than a maximization model. Since the prices there do not enter the constraint, and since $-\partial f_{\alpha_i} / \partial x_k = 1$ if $i = k$ and 0 otherwise, the same result follows. In addition, however, a definite result emerges for the slope of the marginal cost function. Although it is not possible to state, from cost minimization alone, whether marginal cost rises or falls with increased output, the term $\partial \lambda_1 / \partial y$ is a diagonal term of $\mathscr{L}^*_{\alpha_i \alpha_j}$; the preceding analysis therefore shows that marginal cost must be rising faster or falling slower when additional constraints are placed on the decision variables. We will derive this result directly in the next chapter. The remaining Le Châtelier effects are those relating to the alternation in sign of the principal minors of $({}^1\mathscr{L}^*_{\alpha_i \alpha_j} - {}^2\mathscr{L}^*_{\alpha_i \alpha_j})$. For example, for the profit-maximizing firm,

$$\left[{}^1\!\left(\frac{\partial x_i}{\partial w_i}\right) - {}^0\!\left(\frac{\partial x_i}{\partial w_i}\right) \right] \left[{}^1\!\left(\frac{\partial x_j}{\partial w_j}\right) - {}^0\!\left(\frac{\partial x_j}{\partial w_j}\right) \right] \geq \left[{}^1\!\left(\frac{\partial x_i}{\partial w_j}\right) - {}^0\!\left(\frac{\partial x_i}{\partial w_j}\right) \right]^2$$

with a similar result holding for the constant output demands.

Although we have derived these results for a model with one constraint and then added a second, the results are perfectly general. It is possible to start with r constraints ($r < n$, the number of decision variables) (why?) and add an $(r + 1)$st. The identical results emerge with the appropriate changes in some of the functions. If the constraints are denoted $g^1(\mathbf{x}, \alpha) = 0, \ldots, g^r(\mathbf{x}, \alpha) = 0$, then

$$r\mathcal{L}_{\alpha_i x_k} = \frac{\partial f_{\alpha_i}}{\partial x_k} + \sum_{j=1}^{r} \lambda_j \frac{\partial g_{\alpha_i}^{\,j}}{\partial x_k}$$

and the same analysis follows.

BIBLIOGRAPHY

Samuelson, P. A.: "The Le Châtelier Principle in Linear Programming," *RAND Corporation Monograph*, August 4, 1949 (Chap. 43 in *Scientific Papers*).

Samuelson, P. A.: "An Extension of the Le Châtelier Principle," *Econometrica*, pp. 368–379, April 1960 (Chap 42 in *Scientific Papers*).

Samuelson, P. A.: "Structure of a Minimum Equilibrium System," In R. W. Pfouts (ed.), *Essays in Economics and Econometrics: A Volume in Honor of Harold Hotelling*, The University of North Carolina Press, Chapel Hill, 1960 (Chap. 44 in *Scientific Papers*).

These three articles have all been reprinted in J. Stiglitz (ed.): *The Collected Scientific Papers of Paul A. Samuelson*, The M.I.T. Press, Cambridge, MA, 1966.

Samuelson, P. A.: *Foundations of Economic Analysis*, Harvard University Press, Cambridge, MA, 1947.

Silberberg, E.: "A Revision of Comparative Statics Methodology in Economics, or, How to Do Economics on the Back of an Envelope," *Journal of Economic Theory*, 7:159–172, February 1974.

Silberberg, E.: "The Le Châtelier Principle as a Corollary to a Generalized Envelope Theorem," *Journal of Economic Theory*, 3:146–155, June 1971.

Viner, J.: "Cost Curves and Supply Curves," *Zeitschrift fur nationalokonomie*, 3:1932. Reprinted in *Readings in Price Theory* (AEA).

CHAPTER
8

THE DERIVATION OF COST FUNCTIONS

8.1 THE COST FUNCTION

We begin this chapter with a discussion of a mathematical construct that has been an important part of the economics literature relating to firm and industry behavior, the *cost function* of a profit- (wealth-) maximizing firm. Specifically, we would like to determine the properties of a function that specifies the total cost of producing any given level of output. Since total costs will obviously be affected by the prices of the inputs that the firm hires, the cost function must be written

$$C = C^*(y, w_1, \ldots, w_n) \qquad (8\text{-}1)$$

where y is the output level and $w_1, \ldots, w_n$ are the prices of the factors $x_1, \ldots, x_n$, respectively. (The factor prices are assumed here to be constant, for convenience.)

The existence of a function as just specified, however, must be predicated on assertions concerning the behavior of firms. If, for example, firms acted randomly, then there would be no unique cost associated with a given output level and factor-price vector. Even without the assumption of randomness, there are multiple ways in which a firm could combine given inputs, many of which would produce different levels of output. Each of these different input arrangements would produce a different level of cost, and hence a function such as Eq. (8-1) would not be well defined. Thus, in order to be able to assert the existence of a well-defined cost function, it is necessary, at the very least, to have previously asserted a *theory* of the firm. In doing so, we explicitly recognize that the cost of production depends on what the firm's owners or managers intend to do (the theoretical assertions) and what their constraints are, such as the production function itself, the rules of contracting, and, in some contexts, the factor prices. A wealth-maximizing firm is apt to have a different cost function than a "socialist cooperative" type of firm, which seeks to maximize, say, output per laborer in the firm. Not only are the objective functions of these two firm types different (different behavioral assertions), but if the latter firm is located, say, in Yugoslavia and the former in the United States, the property rights and contracting rules are likely to differ. Thus, even with identical production functions, the cost functions of these firms would differ. And even though production functions might be regarded as strictly technological relationships (hardly likely, since legal frameworks and contracting costs affect output levels), the cost function can never be so regarded. The cost function always depends on the objectives of the firm.

We assert that the predominant firm behavior can be characterized as *wealth-maximizing,* and we derive the cost functions of a firm on this basis. Wealth-maximization and the implied resulting cost function are merely assertions. Their usefulness depends on the degree to which refutable propositions emerge from this theory. Even if confirmed, those refutable propositions may also be derivable from other hypotheses about firm behavior, and hence we should not expect to be able to "prove" that firms maximize wealth.

Consider, then, the assertion that firms maximize the quantity π, where

$$\pi = pf(x_1, \ldots, x_n) - \sum_{i=1}^{n} w_i x_i \qquad (8\text{-}2)$$

This quantity, π, is of course not *wealth,* which is a stock concept. Rather, π is the *flow* quantity *profits.* The present, or capitalized, value of π is wealth. In our present model, in which costs of adjustment do not appear, maximizing π necessarily maximizes wealth. How is the cost function (8-1), $C = C^*(y, w_1, \ldots, w_n)$ to be derived? Note that output y is entered as a *parameter* in the cost function. However, the profit-maximizing firm treats y as a decision variable, not as a parameter. That is, output is jointly determined along with inputs as a function of factor and output prices. The factor-demand curves for the profit-maximizing firm are $x_i = x_i^*(w_1, \ldots, w_n, p)$. Nowhere does y enter as an argument in these functions. Rather, $y = y^*(w_1, \ldots, w_n, p)$ defines the *supply curve* of such a firm. This latter function shows how much output will be produced for various output (and also input) prices. The cost function specified in Eq. (8-1) implies that we can observe changes in cost C when an experimental condition, output, is varied autonomously, *holding factor prices constant.* But a profit-maximizing firm never varies output autonomously; output y is changed only when some factor price or output price changes. Hence, the model specified as Eq. (8-2), maximization of profits, cannot be directly used to derive the cost function of a firm.

Cost functions must be derived from models in which output y enters as a parameter. That is, we have to assert that a firm is behaving in a particular way, with regard to the production of some arbitrary level of output y^0, where the superscript is added to indicate that this is a parametric value. If, however, it is asserted that the firm in question is a wealth or profit maximizer, then it necessarily follows that such a firm must produce output at the *minimum possible cost*. For any given output, total revenue, py, is fixed. The difference between total revenue and total cost can be a maximum only if the total cost of producing that output level is as small as possible. Hence, the only assertion concerning cost which is consistent with profit-maximizing behavior is

minimize

$$C = \sum_{i=1}^{n} w_i x_i \qquad (8\text{-}3a)$$

subject to

$$f(x_1, \ldots, x_n) = y^0 \qquad (8\text{-}3b)$$

where, again, y^0 is a parametrically assigned output level. Assuming that $f(x_1, \ldots, x_n)$ is sufficiently well behaved mathematically so that the first- and second-order conditions for a constrained minimum are valid, this model yields, by solution of the first-order Lagrangian equations, the *observable* relations

$$x_i = x_i^*(w_1, \ldots, w_n, y^0) \quad i = 1, \ldots, n \qquad (8\text{-}4)$$

Equations (8-4) would be the factor-demand curves of a profit-maximizing firm only if that firm were really operating under a constraint that held output constant. It must be noted that these demand curves are *not* the same relations derived in Chap. 4 for a profit-maximizing firm, that is, $x_i = x_i^*(w_1, \ldots, w_n, p)$. Those factor demands are functions of output *price* in addition to factor prices; the factor-demand relations (8-4) are functions of output *level* (and factor prices). They are different functions, since they involve different independent variables. It must always be kept in mind which function—i.e., which underlying model—is being considered.

The purpose of specifying these relations is to define the *indirect cost function* (generally referred to as simply the *cost function*)

$$C = \sum_{i=1}^{n} w_i x_i^*(w_1, \ldots, w_n, y^0) = C^*(w_1, \ldots, w_n, y^0) \qquad (8\text{-}5)$$

The cost function $C^*(w_1, \ldots, w_n, y^0)$ is constructed by substituting those values of the inputs at which the cost of producing y^0 is minimized into the general expression for total cost, $\sum w_i x_i$. Hence, C^* must be the minimum cost associated with the parametric values $w_1, \ldots, w_n, y^0$ (see Fig. 8-1). To reduce notational clutter, we will now drop the superscript 0 from the parameter y.

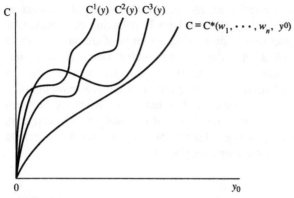

FIGURE 8-1
The cost function is the minimum cost associated with an output level y^0 and factor prices $w_1, \ldots, w_n$. It is the only cost that is relevant to the behavior of the wealth-maximizing firms. Other behavioral postulates might imply differing cost structures, such as the functions $C^1(y)$, $C^2(y)$, and $C^3(y)$ illustrated above.

8.2 MARGINAL COST

The marginal cost of a given output level is, loosely speaking, the rate of change of total cost with respect to a change in output. That is, marginal cost is the response of the firm measured by total cost (an event) to a change in a constraint (the level of output). It is tempting to define marginal cost MC as simply

$$MC = \frac{\partial C}{\partial y} = \frac{\partial(\sum w_i x_i)}{\partial y}$$

To do so, however, would be to ignore the discussion of the previous section on the meaning of a cost function.

As written, $cost = C = \sum w_i x_i$, is *not* a function of output y. It is a function of the inputs $x_1, \ldots, x_n$ and factor prices $w_1, \ldots, w_n$ only. It makes no sense mathematically to differentiate a function with respect to a nonexistent argument. The mathematics is telling us something: The cost function has not yet been adequately defined.

As indicated in the last section, there are many ways of combining inputs, and only one of those ways is relevant to us here. Only the *cost-minimizing* combination of inputs that produces a given level of output y is relevant. Additionally, marginal cost is not just some arbitrary increase in total cost that results from an increase in output level; it is the *minimum* increase in cost associated with an increase in output level. Since the function $C^*(w_1, \ldots, w_n, y)$ defined in Eq. (8-5) gives these minimum costs at any output (and factor price) levels, marginal cost is properly defined in terms of C^* as

$$MC = \frac{\partial C^*(w_1, \ldots, w_n, y)}{\partial y} \qquad (8\text{-}6)$$

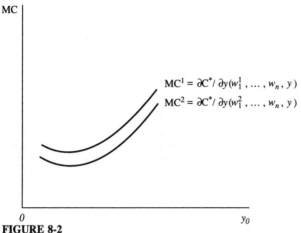

FIGURE 8-2

The Marginal Cost Function. The marginal cost function, being the partial derivative of $C^*(w_1, \ldots, w_n, y)$ with respect to output y, is itself a function of those same arguments $w_1, \ldots, w_n, y$. Shown above are two marginal cost functions, for two different values of w_1^1. It is not possible to determine from the above graph whether $w_1^1 \lessgtr w_1^2$.

This partial derivative, being well defined, also shows what is being held constant—the *ceteris paribus* conditions—when a marginal-cost schedule is drawn. As commonly drawn (see Fig. 8-2) in two dimensions, the marginal-cost function depends on the values of the factor prices, i.e., MC can shift up or down when a factor price changes. A change in factor price represents a shift in the MC curve in Fig. 8-2 only because MC there has been drawn as a function of y only, holding all the w_i's constant. It is also possible to draw MC as a function of, say, w_1, holding $y, w_2, \ldots, w_n$ constant, resulting in such a curve as is drawn in Fig. 8-3. This curve has no common name, but, as we shall see later, its slope, $\partial MC/\partial w_1$, can be either positive or negative, i.e., its sign is not implied by wealth maximization. On this graph, changes in y, as well as the other factor prices, would *shift* the curve. In the next few sections we will explore the implications of wealth maximization and cost minimization on these marginal cost functions. In addition, we shall discuss the relationships between marginal and average cost.

8.3 AVERAGE COST

A frequently discussed function, the *average cost function* AC is defined as

$$AC = \frac{C^*(w_1, \ldots, w_n, y)}{y} = AC^*(w_1, \ldots, w_n, y) \qquad (8\text{-}7)$$

Again, AC must be defined in terms of the *minimum* cost achievable at any output and factor price level, as given by $C^*(w_1, \ldots, w_n, y)$. As with the

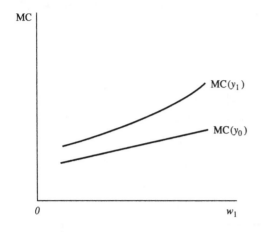

FIGURE 8-3
Marginal Cost as a Function of a Factor Price for specific levels of output. This curve, which has no common name, is drawn simply to illustrate the many-dimensional aspect of marginal cost. Its slope, $\partial MC/\partial w_1$, shown as positive here, is in fact indeterminate.

marginal cost function, a behavioral postulate is a logical necessity for a proper definition of the average cost functions. Since AC* is a function of factor prices and output, the partial derivatives $\partial AC^*/\partial w_i, i = 1, \ldots, n$ and $\partial AC^*/\partial y$ are well defined. That is, we can meaningfully inquire as to the changes in average cost when output and factor prices vary. In the usual diagram, Fig. 8-4, average cost is plotted against output y. Its familiar U shape is *not* implied solely by cost minimization, as we shall see later. Changes in factor price will shift the average cost as drawn in Fig. 8-4. As will be shown later, an increase in a factor price can only increase a firm's average costs (though this is not true for marginal costs!), as a moment's reflection clearly reveals. Otherwise, a firm could always make a larger profit by agreeing to pay more to some factors of production, say, labor. This would be readily agreed upon. Clearly, all empirical evidence refutes this particular harmony of interests. At some point, firms must begin to run short of revenues and regard increasing factor costs as profit-lowering.

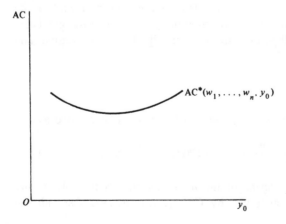

FIGURE 8-4
The average cost function. The average cost function is drawn in its usually assumed U-shaped form. Since y_0 is the only parameter allowed to vary, changes in factor prices will shift this curve. In fact, $\partial AC^*/\partial w_i > 0$, for all factor prices, i.e., an increase in a factor price must increase a firm's average cost at that output level. It would be possible to plot AC* explicitly against, say, w_1 holding $w_2, \ldots, w_n$ and y_0 constant. That curve would necessarily have a positive slope.

8.4 A GENERAL RELATIONSHIP BETWEEN AVERAGE AND MARGINAL COSTS

By definition

$$AC^* \equiv \frac{C^*(w_1, \ldots, w_n, y)}{y} \tag{8-8}$$

Since this is a mathematical identity, it is valid to differentiate both sides with respect to any of the arguments. Differentiating with respect to y yields (using the quotient rule on the right-hand side)

$$\frac{\partial AC^*}{\partial y} \equiv \frac{[y(\partial C^*/\partial y) - C^*]}{y^2} \tag{8-9}$$

Noting that $\partial C^*/\partial y \equiv MC^*$, and rearranging terms slightly, gives

$$MC^* \equiv AC^* + \frac{\partial AC^*}{\partial y} y \tag{8-9}$$

This is a general relation between marginal and average quantities. (It holds as well for average and marginal products, etc.) It is useful for understanding the nature of these magnitudes.

Marginal cost is *not* the cost of producing the "last" unit of output. The cost of producing the last unit of output is the same as the cost of producing the first or any other unit of output and is, in fact, the *average* cost of output. Marginal cost (in the finite sense) is the increase (or decrease) in cost resulting from the production of an extra increment of output, which is not the same thing as the "cost of the last unit." The decision to produce additional output entails the greater utilization of factor inputs. In most cases (the exception being firms whose productive process is characterized by constant returns to scale, i.e., linear homogeneity), this greater utilization will involve losses (or possibly gains) in input efficiency. When factor proportions and intensities are changed, the marginal productivities of the factors change because of the law of diminishing returns, therefore affecting the per unit cost of output. The effects of these complicated interrelationships are summarized in Eq. (8-9). Note what the equation says: Marginal cost is equal to average cost plus an adjustment factor. This latter effect is the *damage* (or gain, in the case of falling marginal costs) to all the factors of production caused by the increase in output, which causes the cost for each unit of output to increase (or decrease, for falling MC). This total "external" damage equals $\partial AC^*/\partial y$, multiplied by the number of units involved, y. That is to say, marginal cost differs from average cost by the per-unit effect on costs of higher output, multiplied by the number of units so affected (total output). The very reason why marginal quantities are usually more useful concepts than average quantitites is that the average quantities ignore, whereas the marginal quantities have incorporated within them, the interrelationships of all the relevant economic variables, in this case, the factor inputs.

The distinction between average and marginal cost is perhaps most clearly seen by considering a famous problem in economics, that of road congestion, first analyzed in 1924 by a distinguished theorist at the University of Chicago, Frank Knight. If a freeway is uncongested, then when an additional car enters, there is no effect on the average speed, or travel time, of the other cars already on the freeway. Suppose all trips on an uncrowded freeway take one-half hour; in this case, the average time and the marginal time both equal 30 minutes. Suppose, however, there are already 10 cars on a section of the freeway, and when the eleventh car enters the roadway, some congestion occurs, slowing everyone's travel time by 2 minutes. Then, although the *average* travel time is now 32 minutes, this is not the marginal time cost imposed by the eleventh car. The marginal time cost of adding the eleventh car is its own 32 minutes of travel time, *plus* the 2 extra minutes imposed on each of the previous 10 cars, or $32 + 10(2) = 52$ minutes. Equation (8-9) expresses this relation in continuous time.

The "economic problem" of freeway congestion exists because consumers of the freeway are unable to pay for the full consequences of using the freeway— freeways are called "freeways" because no fee is charged for their use. Since the marginal cost of using a congested freeway exceeds the price charged, we have "too much" freeway use. Frank Knight pointed out that if the road were privately owned, profit maximization would lead to efficient use. The toll that can be collected is the difference between the time value of using the (presumably slower) sidestreets and the freeway. If sidestreet travel is constant at some level whose value is p, then the private owner will maximize $T = x(p - AC(x))$, where $AC(x)$ is the average cost, in dollars, of the time spent on the freeway. The first-order condition for this model is simply $p = MC(x)$, as in ordinary profit maximization. However, in this model, this equation means that the freeway will then be utilized efficiently, since cars do not take the freeway when their marginal opportunity cost to society exceeds the marginal value of using their alternative transport mode.

8.5   THE COST MINIMIZATION PROBLEM

We now turn explicitly to the mathematical model from which all cost curves for wealth-maximizing firms are derived:

minimize

$$C = \sum_{i=1}^{n} w_i x_i \tag{8-10}$$

subject to

$$f(x_1, \ldots, x_n) = y \tag{8-11}$$

where the w_i's are unit (constant) factor prices, $f(x_1, \ldots, x_n)$ is the production function of the firm, and y is a parametric value of output. This model, referred to as the cost minimization model, asserts that firms will minimize the total cost, $\sum w_i x_i$, of producing any arbitrarily specified output level. Let us develop the empirical implications of this assertion.

To keep things manageable, we will develop the two-variable case of this model first. That is, assume that the firm employs two factors, x_1 and x_2, only. Since this is a problem of constrained minimization, form the Lagrangian function

$$\mathcal{L} = w_1 x_1 + w_2 x_2 + \lambda [y - f(x_1, x_2)] \tag{8-12}$$

where the λ is the Langrange multiplier. Differentiating $\mathcal{L}$ with respect to x_1, x_2, and λ yields the first-order conditions for a minimum:

$$\mathcal{L}_1 = w_1 - \lambda f_1 = 0 \tag{8-13a}$$

$$\mathcal{L}_2 = w_2 - \lambda f_2 = 0 \tag{8-13b}$$

$$\mathcal{L}_\lambda = y - f(x_1, x_2) = 0 \tag{8-13c}$$

The sufficient second-order condition for an interior minimum is that the following bordered Hessian determinant be *negative* (this determinant is, of course, simply the determinant of the matrix formed by the second partials of the Lagrangian $\mathcal{L}$ with respect to x_1, x_2, and λ):

$$H = \begin{vmatrix} -\lambda f_{11} & -\lambda f_{12} & -f_1 \\ -\lambda f_{21} & -\lambda f_{22} & -f_2 \\ -f_1 & -f_2 & 0 \end{vmatrix} < 0 \tag{8-14}$$

The elements of this determinant are, row by row, the *first* partials of the first-order equations (8-13), which makes them the second partials of the Lagrangian function $\mathcal{L}$.

These algebraic conditions for a minimum can be interpreted geometrically. In Fig. 8-5, the level curve $f(x_1, x_2) = y$, the constraint in the cost minimization problem, defines a locus of input combinations which yield the output y. Economists call these level curves *isoquants*. (See Chap. 3 for additional review.) The slope of these isoquants at any point is, again, found by differentiating the identity $f(x_1, x_2(x_1)) \equiv y$ implicitly with respect to x_1. This yields

$$f_1 + f_2 \frac{dx_2}{dx_1} \equiv 0$$

or

$$\frac{dx_2}{dx_1} \equiv -\frac{f_1}{f_2} \tag{8-15}$$

assuming $f_2 \neq 0$, i.e., that the isoquant is not vertical at this point. The slope of the isoquant is the negative ratio of the marginal products of input 1 to input 2. Thus, $-f_1/f_2$ defines a particular *direction* in the x_1, x_2 plane.

On the other hand, the objective function $C = w_1 x_1 + w_2 x_2$ also defines a direction. For any specific value of C, say C^0, the objective function is a linear curve, i.e., a straight line in the $x_1 x_2$ plane. Its slope is $dx_2/dx_1 = -w_1/w_2$.

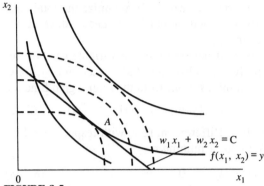

FIGURE 8-5

The Tangency Solution to the Cost Minimization Problem. Assuming that marginal products are positive, i.e., that output increases as one increases either input (movement in a "northeasterly" direction), production isoquants must be convex-to-the-origin in order that a tangency point be a *minimum* cost for a specified output. If the isoquants were shaped like the dotted curves here, A would clearly represent a maximum cost, i.e., the most inefficient way to product output y.

If λ is eliminated from Eqs. (8-13a) and (8-13b), by moving λf_1 and λf_2 to the right-hand side and dividing one equation by the other, one gets

$$\frac{w_1}{w_2} = \frac{f_1}{f_2} \tag{8-16}$$

That is, the ratio of wages equals the ratio of marginal products for the two factors. This is a straightforward application of the maximization theorems presented in Chap. 6. That this tangency is necessary for a minimum-cost solution is evident from Fig. 8-5. Lower costs are associated with *isocost* lines (i.e., curves of equal cost, $C = w_1x_1 + w_2x_2$) that are closer to the origin. The minimum-cost problem says: Pick the isocost line closest to the origin, but that still allows output y to be achieved. The furthest point toward the origin that $C = w_1x_1 + w_2x_2$ can be pushed and still make contact with the isoquant $f(x_1, x_2) = y$ is clearly the tangency point A.

The second-order conditions (8-14) say that production function is quasi-concave; i.e., in this two-dimensional case, the isoquants are "convex to the origin." If the isoquants were shaped like the broken curves in Fig. 8-5, i.e., concave-to-the-origin, or quasi-convex, the tangency would clearly not represent a minimum-cost solution. Costs could be lowered by proceeding to where such an isoquant intersected one of the axes. This would not be a tangency solution, but, rather a "corner solution."

There is a major empirical reason for believing that production isoquants are not shaped like the broken curves in Fig. 8-5, but rather are convex to the origin as originally drawn, and as implied by the second-order conditions (8-14). The empirical reason for believing in such convexity of the isoquants is that if they were otherwise, we would observe firms employing only one factor of production. With isoquants concave to the origin in all dimensions, the

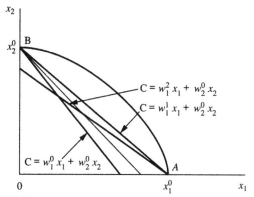

FIGURE 8-6

The Empirical Implications of Quasi-convex Production Functions. With the isoquants concave-to-the-origin and wages given by w_1^0 and w_2^0, the minimum-cost solution is at point B, where only x_2 is hired. The demand for x_1 is 0. As w_1 is lowered, the cost line pivots around B, the intersection with x_1 axis moving outward toward A. When A is reached, a multiple solution exists; the firm is indifferent between hiring x_1^0 of x_1, or x_2^0 of x_2. When w_1 is now made arbitrarily smaller, the demand for x_2 falls to 0, and the demand for x_1 jumps discontinuously to x_1^0. The demand for x_1 remains constant at x_1^0 for all further lowering of its wage, w_1. The demand curve for x_1 is thus vertical at that level.

minimum cost solution would be at the intersection of the isoquant with one axis. (In an unlikely case, two or more such intersections could occur at the same cost, providing multiple solutions.) Since wealth-maximizing firms are cost-minimizers, only one factor, that which gave the minimum solution, would be hired. Additionally, consider how the solution would change if a factor price changed. In Fig. 8-6, as the factor price w_1 is lowered from its original value of w_1^0, the minimum cost solution remains at corner B, with the firm showing no response to the decreased factor price. It hires x_2^0 amount of x_2. Then, at some critical value of w_1, say w_1^1, the isocost line would cut through both corners; i.e., both intersections of the isoquant with the axes. The firm would then be indifferent to hiring x_2^0 of x_2 or x_1^0 of x_1; i.e., the firm's costs are identical with corner A and corner B. As soon as w_1 is lowered below w_1^1, even just a trifle, the firm would suddenly switch over completely to x_1 at the level x_1^0 given by the intersection at A. The firm would show no response to further lowering of w_1. This scenario implies that the demand curves for the two factors will be in vertical sections as depicted in Fig. 8-7. There will be no response to some factor price changes, and violent responses (when the firm switches corners) to others. Now we simply do not see this combined intransigence and discontinuous hiring of factors in the real world. Rather, firms respond gradually to factor price changes, with larger responses accompanying larger price changes. This observed behavior is inconsistent with isoquants concave to the origin and hence we can assert with confidence the quasi-concavity of production functions. Indeed, as mentally changing the slope of the isocost line in Fig. 8-5 will indicate, factor price changes imply continuous, or smooth responses in factor hiring for the case of convex-to-the-origin isoquants.

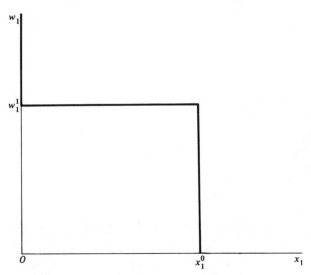

FIGURE 8-7

The Demand for x_1, if isoquants were concave to the origin. The reason for rejecting concave-to-the-origin isoquants is that they imply empirical behavior inconsistent with the facts. In particular, such firms would show no response to factor-price changes except as critical wage levels (here, w_1^1). The demand curve would consist of two vertical sections. This behavior is not observed by real-world firms.

One might believe on *intuitive* or *introspective* grounds that isoquants are convex to the origin. It may seem plausible that along any isoquant, the slope $-f_1/f_2$ decreases in absolute value as more x_1 is hired. That is, the marginal product of x_1 relative to that of x_2 falls as more x_1 is hired. This is often called the "law of diminishing marginal technical rate of substitution." It is not the same as the law of diminishing returns, discussed earlier in Chap. 3, which asserts $f_{ii} < 0$. *Neither one of these two "laws" implies the other.*

If all this is plausible to you, all well and good. But intuition is *not* a good enough reason for believing in the convexity of isoquants. None of us has ever seen an isoquant, and we are not ever likely to do so. The only reason for believing, with some confidence, in such convexity is that the reverse situation implies firm behavior that is inconsistent with the facts of the empirical world, i.e., the situation of intransigence and discontinuous response to factor price changes.

Having established that an interior tangency point is the only sensible solution to the cost minimization problem; i.e., not in contradiction with the facts, and obvious as it may be from the geometry of Fig. 8-5 that the tangency point A is the minimum cost solution, it is still interesting and useful to go on to ask: what is it about the decision-making process of the firm that leads to this type of solution? That is, what does such a solution (a tangency) imply about the nature of minimum cost decision making? To answer this question, it is necessary to

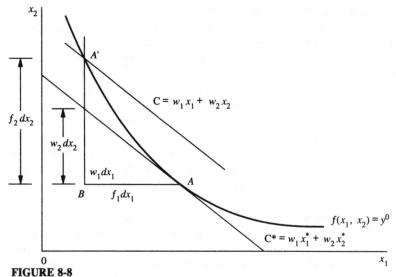

FIGURE 8-8

Tangency and Nontangency Points. It is obvious from the geometry that A' cannot be a minimum cost solution. In terms of the economics of cost-minimizing firms, however, point A' indicates that the firm's *willingness* to trade away some x_2 to get some x_1, as measured by the slope of the isoquant at A', is unequal to the firm's *opportunities* for doing so, as measured by the isocost line $C = w_1x_1 + w_2x_2$. At point A', the value, internally, to the firm of additional units of x_1 is measured by f_1/f_2, the slope of the isoquant at A'. This internal value is greater than the market cost of exchanging some x_2 to get more x_1, or w_1/w_2. It therefore is cost-saving to move from A' to A. Similar reasoning would apply if A' were to the right of A; then, x_2 would be the desirable factor at market prices.

examine again the meanings of the slopes of level curves, in this case $-f_1/f_2$ and $-w_1/w_2$. (The reader should review, if necessary, the sections of Chap. 3 dealing with level curves and surfaces.)

In Fig. 8-8, consider point A' on the isoquant $f(x_1, x_2) = y$. The cost lines $C = w_1x_1 + w_2x_2$ have a slope $-w_1/w_2$ which is less in absolute value than the slope of $f(x_1, x_2) = y$ at A', $(-f_1/f_2)$. Suppose the firm decided to produce the same output y at point A, hiring more x_1 by an amount dx_1, and less x_2 by an amount dx_2. We can view the move from A' to A conceptually as one from A' to B, and then B to A. The decrease in output caused by hiring less x_2 is the marginal product of x_2, MP_2, which is approximately f_2 evaluated at A, multiplied by the decrease in x_2, or $f_2 dx_2$. In Fig. 8-8, this is the decline in output due to a movement from A' to B. In moving from B to A, x_1 is increased by an amount dx_1, and that extra x_1 has a marginal product approximately equal to f_1 evaluated at A, and hence the gain in output going from B to A is $f_1 dx_1$. Since the output at A is the same as the output at A', both being y, it must be the case that $f_1 dx_1 + f_2 dx_2 = 0$. If the point A' is moved arbitrarily close to A, so that the approximation becomes better and better, this simply becomes the statement that along any level curve, the total differential $dy = f_1 dx_1 + f_2 dx_2$ equals 0.

Assuming x_2 can be written as a function of x_1, the slope of the isoquant again is $dx_2/dx_1 = -f_1/f_2$. But we can now understand what this relationship means to a firm. The slope of an isoquant represents how much x_2 can be given up, per unit x_1 added, in order to keep output constant. This output-preserving ratio of inputs must equal the ratio of the gain in output ($MP_1 = f_1$) to the loss in output ($MP_2 = f_2$) that occurs per unit changes in the inputs. This slope, f_1/f_2, therefore measures the values of x_1 to the firm, internally, in terms of x_2.

Suppose, for example, that the marginal product of x_1 is 10, while the marginal product of x_2 is 5. Then $f_1/f_2 = 2$. Then clearly for "small" changes at least, it will be possible to decrease x_2 by 2 units for every unit of increased x_1. The ratio f_1/f_2, equal to 2 here, measures the rate at which one factor x_2 can be displaced by additions of the other factor x_1 keeping output constant. It is the marginal technical rate of substitution.

Now consider point A' again in Fig. 8-8. Suppose that $w_1/w_2 = 1$; that is, the slope of the isocost line equals -1. This means that the factor market allows input x_1 to be substituted for input x_2 at equal cost. That is, for every added unit of x_1, exactly one unit of x_2 has to be given up in order to maintain the same expenditure level. But we have seen, in our numerical example, that the firm can give up *two* units of x_2, add one unit of x_1, and have the same output. Therefore, a savings of the cost of one unit of x_2 is obtained by moving toward A. Hence, A' cannot be a minimum cost solution.

In general, the slope of the isoquant measures the firm's *willingness* to trade one input for the other (substitute x_1 for x_2). The slope of the isocost lines represents the *opportunities* afforded by the factor market for doing so. When the firm is willing to trade one factor for another at terms of trade different from the factor market, cost saving is possible. This is the meaning of a tangency solution. It doesn't matter if the original point is to the left or right of A on the isoquant $f(x_1, x_2) = y^0$. In a more general sense, the gains from exchange (exchange with a general market at fixed prices as well as exchange with other individuals) are not exhausted unless one's *willingness* to trade, e.g., as measured by a firm's output-preserving marginal rate of factor substitution, equals the available *opportunities* for such trading, e.g., as measured by the cost of exchanging one factor for another. For firms, such efficient factor combinations are summarized by the condition that $f_1/f_2 = w_1/w_2$.

8.6 THE FACTOR DEMAND CURVES

Let us now return to the first-order Eqs. (8-13), which are, again

$$w_1 - \lambda f_1 = 0 \tag{8-13a}$$

$$w_2 - \lambda f_2 = 0 \tag{8-13b}$$

$$y - f(x_1, x_2) = 0 \tag{8-13c}$$

The sufficient second-order condition is that the determinant of the matrix of second partials of $\mathcal{L}$ with respect to x_1, x_2 and λ, which is in fact the matrix formed by the first partials of (8-13a), (8-13b), and (8-13c) with respect to those variables (these equations already being the first partials of $\mathcal{L}$), be negative.

This determinant, again, is

$$H = \begin{vmatrix} -\lambda f_{11} & -\lambda f_{12} & -f_1 \\ -\lambda f_{21} & -\lambda f_{22} & -f_2 \\ -f_1 & -f_2 & 0 \end{vmatrix} < 0 \tag{8-14}$$

The implicit function theorem, discussed in Chap. 5, says that if the determinant of the first partials of a system of equations is nonzero, those equations can be solved, locally (in principle—not, perhaps, easily) for those variables being differentiated as explicit functions of the remaining variables (here the parameters) of the system. The determinant H is such a determinant and is nonzero, in fact negative, by the sufficient second-order conditions. Hence, Eqs. (8-13) can be solved for x_1, x_2, and λ in terms of the parameters w_1, w_2, and y, yielding

$$x_1 = x_1^*(w_1, w_2, y) \tag{8-17a}$$

$$x_2 = x_2^*(w_1, w_2, y) \tag{8-17b}$$

$$\lambda = \lambda^*(w_1, w_2, y) \tag{8-17c}$$

Equations (8-17a) and (8-17b) represent the factor demand curves *when output is held constant,* previously discussed as Eqs. (8-4). Note the parameter y in these equations. If, say, x_1 is plotted on a two-dimensional graph with its wage represented on the other axis, the resulting plot will be a curve [actually, a one-dimensional projection of Eq. (8-17a)] along which w_2 and y are constant. These curves, therefore, do not represent the factor demand curves of a firm engaged in unrestricted profit maximization, in which case output would be variable, and output *price* (for the competitive case) would be parametric.

Interpretation of the Lagrange Multiplier

Equation (8-17c) gives λ as a function of w_1, w_2, and y. But what is λ? This new variable was concocted as an artifice—as a convenient way of stating a constrained minimization problem. Does λ have any meaningful economic interpretation? Indeed, we can show that λ, or more correctly $\lambda^*(w_1, w_2, y)$ is identically the marginal cost function of the firm!

The first clue to this interpretation of λ^* can be gleaned from the first-order Eq. (8-13). Solving for λ^* yields

$$\lambda^* = \frac{w_1}{f_1} = \frac{w_2}{f_2} \tag{8-18}$$

Also, by multiplying (8-13a) by x_1, (8-13b) by x_2, and adding, one obtains

$$\lambda^* f_1 x_1^* + \lambda^* f_2 x_2^* = w_1 x_1^* + w_2 x_2^*$$

Factoring out λ^*, and noting that $w_1 x_1^* + w_2 x_2^* = C^*$,

$$\lambda^* = \frac{C^*}{f_1 x_1^* + f_2 x_2^*}$$

Note the "units" of w_1/f_1 and w_2/f_2. Say that, for example, x_1 is "labor," x_2 is "capital." The wage rate w_1 is measured in dollars per laborer; the marginal product of labor has units output per laborer. Hence, the expression w_1/f_1 has the units dollars per output, since the labor units cancel. The measure dollars per output in fact comprises the units of marginal cost, though it also comprises the units of average cost.

What, then, is the meaning of the following extending equality?

$$\lambda^* = \frac{w_1}{f_1} = \frac{w_2}{f_2} = \frac{C^*}{f_1 x_1^* + f_2 x_2^*} \tag{8-19}$$

The firm is at its cost-minimizing input mix. Suppose it were to increase its input of x_1, say, labor, by a small amount Δx_1. The total cost would rise by an amount $(w_1)(\Delta x_1)$. Output would also rise, by an amount $(MP_1)(\Delta x_1) = (f_1)(\Delta x_1)$. Hence, $\lambda = w_1/f_1 = (w_1)(\Delta x_1)/(f_1)(\Delta x_1)$ represents the incremental cost of increasing output through the use of one input, here x_1, or labor. Similarly, $\lambda = w_2/f_2 = (w_2)(\Delta x_2)/(f_2)(\Delta x_2)$ represents the incremental cost of additional output when the other input, x_2, say capital, is increased. The equality of these two incremental costs, as indicated by Eq. (8-18) means that a necessary condition for cost minimization is that the incremental cost of additional output must be the same *at all margins*, i.e., for each independent decision variable. This common incremental cost of output is the *marginal cost of output*. Equation (8-18) says that the firm is indifferent, at the margin, to hiring additional labor or capital — the net costs of doing so are identical for each input.

This is, of course, what must be true at a minimum cost point. For suppose that the firm could achieve a lower incremental cost of output by hiring labor, say, rather than capital. In that case, total costs could clearly be lowered by shifting resources away from capital and toward labor. Only when costs are equalized at all the margins can a minimum cost solution be achieved. And this common marginal cost is equal to λ^*.

What about the last equality in Eq. (8-19), $\lambda^* = C^*/(f_1 x_1^* + f_2 x_2^*)$? This is a more difficult expression to interpret. Consider that $\lambda^* = w_1/f_1 = w_1 x_1^*/f_1 x_1^*$. Whereas w_1/f_1 refers explicitly to *per-unit* changes in input 1, $w_1 x_1^*/f_1 x_1^*$ applies that marginal factor cost $(w_1 x_1^*)$ and benefits $(f_1 x_1^*)$ to the total input level. Likewise, $\lambda = w_2 x_2^*/f_2 x_2^*$, the cost of all units of factor 2 per marginal contribution of that factor multiplied by the total factor usage, is also marginal cost, since the incremental costs must be the same at every margin. Then, by elementary algebra[†]

[†] It is valid to add the numerators and denominators, respectively, of fractions that are equal. Thus, if $a/b = c/d$ (implying $ad = bc$), then $a/b = c/d = (a + c)/(b + d)$, as can be quickly verified.

$$\lambda^* = \frac{w_1 x_1^*}{f_1 x_1^*} = \frac{w_2 x_2^*}{f_2 x_2^*} = \frac{w_1 x_1^* + w_2 x_2^*}{f_1 x_1^* + f_2 x_2^*}$$

This expression says that not only is marginal cost the same at every margin, it is also the same if a combination of *both* (*every*, in the multifactor case) factors is changed. Marginal cost is the same at "either or both" margins.

The foregoing was intended as an intuitive explanation of why the function $\lambda = \lambda^*(w_1, w_2, y)$ might reasonably be regarded as the marginal cost function. While intuitively plausible (and ultimately sound), the approach is deficient in terms of our original definition of marginal cost. Specifically

$$MC = \frac{\partial C^*}{\partial y}$$

where $C^*(w_1, w_2, y)$ is the (indirect) cost function. It remains to be proved explicitly that $\lambda^* \equiv \partial C^*/\partial y$. We shall now do so.

By definition

$$C^* = w_1 x_1^* (w_1, w_2, y) + w_2 x_2^* (w_1, w_2, y) \tag{8-20}$$

That is, the minimum cost for any output level y (and factor prices w_1, w_2) is obtained by substituting into the expression for total cost, $C = w_1 x_1 + w_2 x_2$, the values of the inputs that are derived from the cost minimization problem. These are the relations $x_i = x_i^*(w_1, w_2, y), i = 1, 2$ (Eqs. 8-17a,b). Thus, differentiating C^* partially with respect to y,

$$\frac{\partial C^*}{\partial y} = w_1 \frac{\partial x_1^*}{\partial y} + w_2 \frac{\partial x_2^*}{\partial y} \tag{8-21}$$

However, from the first-order relations, $w_1 = \lambda^* f_1, w_2 = \lambda^* f_2$. Substituting these values into Eq. (8-21), and factoring out λ^*,

$$\frac{\partial C^*}{\partial y} = \lambda^* \left(f_1 \frac{\partial x_1^*}{\partial y} + f_2 \frac{\partial x_2^*}{\partial y} \right) \tag{8-22}$$

If in fact $\lambda^* = \partial C^*/\partial y$, the term in parentheses in Eq. (8-22) must equal 1. How can this be shown? Consider the last equation of the first-order conditions (actually the constraint):

$$y - f(x_1, x_2) = 0$$

When the solutions to the first-order relations, the factor demand curves holding output constant, Eqs. (8-17 a,b) are substituted back into those first-order conditions, Eqs. (8-13) become identities. In particular,

$$y - f(x_1^*(w_1, w_2, y), x_2^*(w_1, w_2, y)) \equiv 0$$

That is, x_1^* and x_2^* *always* lie on the isoquant of output level y for any w_1, w_2 and any y, precisely because x_1^* and x_2^* are the solutions of equations that say, among other things: output is held to y.

Hence, we can differentiate this identity with respect to y:

$$1 - f_1 \frac{\partial x_1^*}{\partial y} - f_2 \frac{\partial x_2^*}{\partial y} \equiv 0$$

or

$$f_1 \frac{\partial x_1^*}{\partial y} + f_2 \frac{\partial x_2^*}{\partial y} \equiv 1$$

This is precisely what was needed. The term in the parentheses in Eq. (8-22) equals 1, and therefore,

$$\lambda^* \equiv \frac{\partial C^*}{\partial y} \tag{8-23}$$

That $\lambda^* \equiv \partial C^*/\partial y$ is in fact a simple consequence of the envelope theorem derived in the last chapter. Recall the general maximum problem with, for simplicity here, one constraint:

maximize

$$f(x_1, \ldots, x_n, \alpha_1, \ldots, \alpha_m) = z$$

subject to

$$g(x_1, \ldots, x_n, \alpha_1, \ldots, \alpha_m) = 0$$

The Lagrangian for this problem is

$$\mathcal{L} = f(\mathbf{x}, \boldsymbol{\alpha}) + \lambda g(\mathbf{x}, \boldsymbol{\alpha})$$

The envelope theorem says that

$$\frac{\partial z^*}{\partial \alpha_i} = \frac{\partial \mathcal{L}}{\partial \alpha_i} = f_{\alpha_i} + \lambda^* g_{\alpha_i}$$

That is, the rate of change of the indirect objective function in which all the x_i's can adjust to changes in a parameter is in fact equal to the rate of change of the Lagrangian function (which numerically equals the objective function since the constraint equals 0) with respect to that parameter, *holding all the x_i's fixed.*

Applying this theorem to the problem at hand,
minimize

$$C = w_1 x_1 + w_2 x_2$$

subject to

$$y - f(x_1, x_2) = 0$$

we have

$$\mathcal{L} = w_1 x_1 + w_2 x_2 + \lambda(y - f(x_1, x_2))$$

Here, the parameter y enters only the constraint, hence

$$\frac{\partial C^*}{\partial y} = \frac{\partial \mathscr{L}}{\partial y} = \lambda = \lambda^*$$

The Lagrange multiplier was introduced as an artifice for writing, in a convenient manner, the first- and second-order conditions for a constrained maximum problem. We see here, however, that the Lagrange multiplier can have interesting economic interpretations. This fact greatly enhances the value of Lagrangian methods. As we shall see, these multipliers, more often than not, provide useful formulas and insights for analyzing economic problems.

8.7 COMPARATIVE STATICS RELATIONS: THE TRADITIONAL METHODOLOGY

We now investigate the responses of cost-minimizing firms to changes in the parameters they face. In the next section, we will derive these results using the new and more powerful methodology of duality theory. However, we proceed first using the traditional procedure as outlined in Chap. 6, so that this important procedure can be illustrated and understood. As stated previously, for other than the basic models, and for nonmaximization models, this is likely to be the only available technique for investigating the responses of the decision variables to changes in the parameters.

The questions we ask are, how do cost-minimizing firms react to an increase or decrease in a factor price? Will more or less input be used when its own or some other input's price increases? How will marginal and average cost be affected? Will the firm increase or decrease its output if competitive pressures force it to remain at the minimum point on its average cost curve?

The format for investigating these questions is, again,

minimize

$$C = w_1 x_1 + w_2 x_2$$

subject to

$$f(x_1, x_2) = y$$

where w_1 and w_2 are the factor prices and y is a parametrically determined level of output. The Lagrangian is

$$\mathscr{L} = w_1 x_1 + w_2 x_2 + \lambda(y - f(x_1, x_2))$$

Differentiating with respect to x_1, x_2, and λ yields the first-order conditions for constrained minimization:

$$w_1 - \lambda f_1 = 0 \tag{8-13a}$$

$$w_2 - \lambda f_2 = 0 \tag{8-13b}$$

$$y - f(x_1, x_2) = 0 \tag{8-13c}$$

The sufficient second-order conditions are, again

$$H = \begin{vmatrix} -\lambda f_{11} & -\lambda f_{12} & -f_1 \\ -\lambda f_{21} & -\lambda f_{22} & -f_2 \\ -f_1 & -f_2 & 0 \end{vmatrix} < 0 \qquad (8\text{-}14)$$

These relations were given verbal interpretation in the previous sections.

If the production function $y = f(x_1, x_2)$ were actually known, then Eq. (8-13) could be used directly to characterize the least-cost solution. Everything about the firm would be completely known, including the *total* amounts of each factor that would be used at any input level, and all the changes that might come about because of a change in a parameter. However, economists are not generally blessed with this kind of information. Rather, we *assert* that some sort of production relationship $y = f(x_1, x_2)$ exists, with quasi-concave properties [summarized as the inequality $H < 0$, Eq. (8-14)]. We then inquire as to *changes* in response to parameter changes, i.e., we limit the analysis to *marginal quantitites*. This is accomplished by using the methodology of comparative statics outlined earlier.

Equations (8-13) represent three equations in six variables $x_1, x_2, \lambda, w_1, w_2$, and y. As long as certain mathematical conditions exist, namely that $H \neq 0$, these equations can be solved, in principle yielding the relations already discussed:

$$x_1 = x_1^*(w_1, w_2, y) \qquad (8\text{-}17a)$$

$$x_2 = x_2^*(w_1, w_2, y) \qquad (8\text{-}17b)$$

$$\lambda = \lambda^*(w_1, w_2, y) \qquad (8\text{-}17c)$$

The new variable λ is identified as marginal cost.

The comparative statics of this model can be summarized as the determination of the signs of the nine partial derivatives:

$$\frac{\partial x_i^*}{\partial w_j} \quad i, j = 1, 2$$

$$\frac{\partial x_i^*}{\partial y} \quad i = 1, 2$$

$$\frac{\partial \lambda^*}{\partial w_i} \quad i = 1, 2$$

$$\frac{\partial \lambda^*}{\partial y} \qquad (8\text{-}24)$$

We seek to determine, first, the extent to which the constrained minimum hypothesis generates (qualitative) information about these marginal quantities. It will also be shown that some relationships exist among these partials, and that expressions can be derived which may be useful if empirical information is used in addition to the minimization hypothesis.

The first step in comparative statics analysis, of course, is to substitute the solutions (8-17) into the first-order Eq. (8-13), from which they were solved. This yields the *identities*

$$w_1 - \lambda^*(w_1, w_2, y) f_1(x_1^*(w_1, w_2, y), x_2^*(w_1, w_2, y)) \equiv 0 \qquad (8\text{-}25a)$$

$$w_2 - \lambda^*(w_1, w_2, y) f_2(x_1^*(w_1, w_2, y), x_2^*(w_1, w_2, y)) \equiv 0 \qquad (8\text{-}25b)$$

$$y - f(x_1^*(w_1, w_2, y), x_2^*(w_1, w_2, y)) \equiv 0 \qquad (8\text{-}25c)$$

These are identities because the solutions to Eqs. (8-13) are substituted into the equations from which they were solved. The economic significance of this step is that now it is being asserted that whatever the factor prices and output level may be, the firm will always instantaneously adjust the factor inputs (its decision variables) to those levels that will minimize the total cost of that output level. The *identities* (8-25) tell us that we have asserted that we will never observe the firm to be in any other than a cost-minimizing configuration. Having built in this strong assertion, it is then possible to alter the parameters and observe the resulting changes in the x_i's. These changes are observed mathematically by differentiating the identities (8-25) with respect to a parameter and solving for the relevant partial derivatives contained in the list (8-24).

Let us begin the formal analysis by observing the cost-minimizing reaction to a change in w_1, the price of factor 1. Differentiating the identities (8-25) with respect to w_1 yields, using the product rule for $\lambda^* f_1$, and $\lambda^* f_2$, along with the chain rule,

$$1 - \lambda^* f_{11} \frac{\partial x_1^*}{\partial w_1} - \lambda^* f_{12} \frac{\partial x_2^*}{\partial w_1} - f_1 \frac{\partial \lambda^*}{\partial w_1} \equiv 0 \qquad (8\text{-}26a)$$

$$- \lambda^* f_{21} \frac{\partial x_1^*}{\partial w_1} - \lambda^* f_{22} \frac{\partial x_2^*}{\partial w_1} - f_2 \frac{\partial \lambda^*}{\partial w_1} \equiv 0 \qquad (8\text{-}26b)$$

$$- f_1 \frac{\partial x_1^*}{\partial w_1} - f_2 \frac{\partial x_2^*}{\partial w_1} \equiv 0 \qquad (8\text{-}26b)$$

These relations can be more clearly summarized using matrix notation. Since (8-26) represents three *linear* equations (actually, identities) in the three unknowns $\partial x_1^*/\partial w_1$, $\partial x_2^*/\partial w_1$, and $\partial \lambda^*/\partial w_1$, (8-26) becomes

$$\begin{pmatrix} -\lambda^* f_{11} & -\lambda^* f_{12} & -f_1 \\ -\lambda^* f_{21} & -\lambda^* f_{22} & -f_2 \\ -f_1 & -f_2 & 0 \end{pmatrix} \begin{pmatrix} \dfrac{\partial x_1^*}{\partial w_1} \\ \dfrac{\partial x_2^*}{\partial w_1} \\ \dfrac{\partial \lambda^*}{\partial w_1} \end{pmatrix} = \begin{pmatrix} -1 \\ 0 \\ 0 \end{pmatrix} \qquad (8\text{-}27)$$

One need only solve (8-27) for the marginal quantities. Using Cramer's rule,

$$\frac{\partial x_1^*}{\partial w_1} = \frac{\begin{vmatrix} -1 & -\lambda^* f_{12} & -f_1 \\ 0 & -\lambda^* f_{22} & -f_2 \\ 0 & -f_2 & 0 \end{vmatrix}}{H} = -\frac{H_{11}}{H} \qquad (8\text{-}28a)$$

In like fashion, replacing the second and third column of H with the right-hand column vector $(-1,0,0)$ for the numerator of Cramer's rule, one gets

$$\frac{\partial x_2^*}{\partial w_1} = \frac{-H_{12}}{H} \tag{8-28b}$$

$$\frac{\partial \lambda^*}{\partial w_1} = \frac{-H_{13}}{H} \tag{8-28c}$$

where H_{ij} is the (signed) cofactor of the element in row i and column j of the determinant H.

These solutions are only valid if $H \neq 0$. Otherwise, the preceding partials are undefined. The mathematics indicates that in order for these partials to exist, the solutions (8-17) must first be well defined. The implicit function theorem of Chap. 5 indicates that these solutions are valid if the determinant of first partials of (8-13) is nonzero. This determinant is exactly H, and the *sufficient* second-order condition for constrained minimization says that in fact $H < 0$. Hence, under these assumptions, the solutions (8-28) are valid expressions.

What can be said of the sign of these partials? As just noted, the denominators of these expressions, H, are all negative. The cofactor H_{11} is a border-preserving principle minor and is negative under the minimization hypothesis. Indeed, by inspection,

$$H_{11} = \begin{vmatrix} -\lambda^* f_{22} & -f_2 \\ -f_2 & 0 \end{vmatrix} = -f_2^2 < 0$$

Hence, the qualitative result $\partial x_1^* / \partial w_1 < 0$, is demonstrable.

The cofactor H_{12} is *not* a border-preserving principle minor; in general, its sign will not be known, and, hence, the sign of $\partial x_2^* / \partial w_1$ will not be determinate. However, in the *two-variable case only, assuming positive marginal products,*

$$H_{12} = (-1)^{1+2} \begin{vmatrix} -\lambda^* f_{21} & -f_2 \\ -f_1 & 0 \end{vmatrix} = +f_1 f_2 > 0$$

Hence, *for the two-variable case only,*

$$\frac{\partial x_2^*}{\partial w_1} > 0$$

The fact that it must happen that $\partial x_2^* / \partial w_1 > 0$ for the two-factor case is easily explainable. Suppose w_1 falls. The firm will then hire more x_1. If the firm also hired more x_2, then output would have to rise, given the assumption of positive marginal products. And marginal products will be positive as long as factor prices w_1 and w_2 are positive. If x_1 increases, then if output is to be held constant, x_2 must decrease. This relationship, however, need not hold for more than two factors. Some other factor (or both) must decline, but not necessarily one or the other.

Finally,

$$H_{13} = \begin{vmatrix} -\lambda^*f_{21} & -\lambda^*f_{22} \\ -f_1 & -f_2 \end{vmatrix} = \lambda^*(f_{21}f_2 - f_{22}f_1) \gtrless 0$$

Hence, $\partial \lambda^*/\partial w_1 \gtrless 0$.

Similar relationships can be derived for the responses to a change in w_2. In that case, the minus one appears in the *second* row of the right-hand side of the matrix equation, since w_2 appears only in the second first-order relation:

$$\begin{pmatrix} -\lambda^*f_{11} & -\lambda^*f_{12} & -f_1 \\ -\lambda^*f_{21} & -\lambda^*f_{22} & -f_2 \\ -f_1 & -f_2 & 0 \end{pmatrix} \begin{pmatrix} \dfrac{\partial x_1^*}{\partial w_2} \\ \dfrac{\partial x_2^*}{\partial w_2} \\ \dfrac{\partial \lambda^*}{\partial w_2} \end{pmatrix} = \begin{pmatrix} 0 \\ -1 \\ 0 \end{pmatrix} \qquad (8\text{-}29)$$

Again solving by Cramer's rule,

$$\frac{\partial x_1^*}{\partial w_2} = \frac{-H_{21}}{H} \qquad (8\text{-}30a)$$

$$\frac{\partial x_2^*}{\partial w_2} = \frac{-H_{22}}{H} \qquad (8\text{-}30b)$$

$$\frac{\partial \lambda^*}{\partial w_2} = \frac{-H_{23}}{H} \qquad (8\text{-}30c)$$

The cofactor H_{22} is a border-preserving principle minor; it must be negative by the sufficient second-order conditions. In fact, by inspection, $H_{22} = -f_1^2 < 0$. Hence, the refutable hypothesis, $\partial x_2^*/\partial w_2 < 0$, can be asserted for these relations. The cofactor H_{12} on inspection also has a determinate sign. In fact, by the symmetry of the determinant H, $H_{12} = H_{21} = f_1 f_2 > 0$. Again, that $\partial x_1^*/\partial w_2 > 0$ for this model is *not* generalizable to the n-factor case. With more than two factors present, the numerator for $\partial x_2^*/\partial w_1$, or $\partial x_1^*/\partial w_2$, will be an $n \times n$ off-diagonal cofactor. Its sign will be indeterminate.

What is curious, however, is that like the profit maximization model, the reciprocity relation

$$\frac{\partial x_1^*}{\partial w_2} = \frac{\partial x_2^*}{\partial w_1} \qquad (8\text{-}31)$$

is valid, since on comparing Eqs. (8-28b) and (8-30a) we note that $H_{12} = H_{21}$. This is a different result than that obtained for unconstrained profit maximization. In that earlier model, the x_i's were functions of factor prices and output *price;*

that is, $x_i = x_i^*(w_1, w_2, p)$. Here, the factors are functions of the output level, $y: x_i = x_i^*(w_1, w_2, y)$. These are two different functions. (We have used the same notation "x_i^*" for both in spite of this to avoid notational clutter.) The results are therefore different.

Finally, we have $\partial \lambda^*/\partial w_2 \gtrless 0$, as we had before, since $H_{23} \gtrless 0$, being an off-diagonal (and non–border-preserving) cofactor. We shall defer explanation of this sign indeterminacy until after the following discussion with respect to parametric output level changes.

How does the firm react to an autonomous shift in output? We know, from the analysis of the previous chapters, that since y enters the constraint, no refutable implication can be derived for this parameter. Differentiating the identities (8-25) with respect to y, noting that y appears only in the third identity (8-25c),

$$
\begin{pmatrix}
-\lambda^* f_{11} & -\lambda^* f_{12} & -f_1 \\
-\lambda^* f_{21} & -\lambda^* f_{22} & -f_2 \\
-f_1 & -f_2 & 0
\end{pmatrix}
\begin{pmatrix}
\dfrac{\partial x_1^*}{\partial y} \\[2ex]
\dfrac{\partial x_2^*}{\partial y} \\[2ex]
\dfrac{\partial \lambda^*}{\partial y}
\end{pmatrix}
=
\begin{pmatrix}
0 \\
0 \\
-1
\end{pmatrix}
\tag{8-32}
$$

Solving via Cramer's rule yields

$$
\frac{\partial x_1^*}{\partial y} = \frac{
\begin{vmatrix}
0 & -\lambda^* f_{12} & -f_1 \\
0 & -\lambda^* f_{22} & -f_2 \\
-1 & -f_2 & 0
\end{vmatrix}
}{H} = -\frac{H_{31}}{H} \lessgtr 0
\tag{8-33a}
$$

Similarly

$$
\frac{\partial x_2^*}{\partial y} = \frac{-H_{32}}{H} \lessgtr 0
\tag{8-33b}
$$

$$
\frac{\partial \lambda^*}{\partial y} = \frac{-H_{33}}{H} \lessgtr 0
\tag{8-33c}
$$

Consider this last relationship, $\partial \lambda^*/\partial y$, that is, $\partial \text{MC}/\partial y$. This expression gives the slope of the marginal cost function. The numerator, H_{33}, is the determinant

$$
H_{33} = \begin{vmatrix} -\lambda^* f_{11} & -\lambda^* f_{12} \\ -\lambda^* f_{12} & -\lambda^* f_{22} \end{vmatrix}
$$

(noting that $f_{12} = f_{21}$). Hence, $H_{33} = \lambda^{*2}(f_{11}f_{22} - f_{12}^2)$. This looks like an expression we have encountered previously: to be exact, in the profit maximization model. There, the term $(f_{11}f_{22} - f_{12}^2)$ appeared in the denominator of the comparative statics relations. The sign of this expression was asserted to be positive by the sufficient second-order relations for profit-maximization. Why, then,

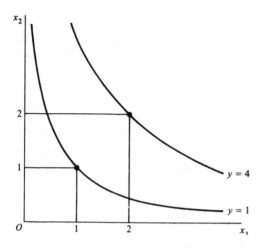

FIGURE 8-9

The Production Function $y = x_1x_2$. The level curves of this production function are clearly convex, being rectangular hyperbolas. A cost minimization solution will necessarily exist for all factor price combinations. However, for example, when $x_1 = x_2 = 2$, $y = 4$, whereas when $x_1 = x_2 = 4$, $y = 16$. Revenues will always increase twice as fast as costs, and hence no profit maximum point can exist. The marginal and average cost functions are always falling here. Profit maximization is a much stronger assertion than cost minimization, i.e., the former places much stronger restrictions on the shape of the production function than does cost minimization.

can we not assert from Eq. (8-33c) that $\partial MC/\partial y > 0$, i.e., the marginal cost curve is upward-sloping, since it appears that $H_{33} > 0$?

In fact, in the case where these cost curves refer to a firm that is also achieving maximum profits (i.e., the firm is reaching an interior solution to the profit maximization problem), the marginal cost function is indeed upward-sloping. However, profit maximization is *not* implied by cost minimization. Cost minimization is a much weaker hypothesis, both in terms of the implied behavior of firms, and, equivalently, from the mathematical conditions the cost minimization hypothesis entails on the curvature properties of the production function. For profit maximization, the production function must be strictly concave (downwards). Strict concavity, while sufficient for cost minimization, is not necessary. The second-order conditions for cost minimization require only *quasi-concavity,* i.e., convexity of the level curves (the isoquants, here) to the origin.

That this is a weaker condition can be readily seen. Consider the production function $y = x_1x_2$, shown in Fig. 8-9. This production function is homogeneous of degree 2. Its level curves are rectangular hyperbolas, and clearly, a cost minimization solution will exist for all factor prices. But will a finite profit maximum point ever be achieved (with constant factor profits)? When both input levels are doubled, output will increase by a factor of four. Costs, $C = w_1x_1 + w_2x_2$, will only double, however. Hence, this firm's marginal and average cost functions must always be declining (this will be given a rigorous proof later). Therefore, a profit-maximizing point cannot ever be achieved. This firm would make ever-increasing profits, the larger the output it produced. The second-order conditions for profit maximization immediately reveal this situation:

$$f_{11}f_{22} - f_{12}^2 = 0 \cdot 0 - 1^2 = -1 < 0$$

The profit maximization hypothesis places much stronger restrictions on the shape of the production function than does cost minimization. Quasi-concavity, while implied by concavity, does not itself imply concavity.

Consider now expressions (8-33a) and (8-33b). These expressions say that if the output level is raised, the factor input levels can either increase or decrease. The situation is analogous to the somewhat more familiar case of inferior goods in consumer theory (to be discussed formally in Chap. 10). There, when income rises, it is commonly believed that for many individuals, the quantity of hamburger, for example, will *decrease*, not increase. Hamburger is often regarded as an "inferior good." In the same manner, factors of production can be inferior.

Consider the case, perhaps, of unskilled labor. Suppose a firm wished to dig one or two ditches. In all likelihood, it would hire a worker or two and some shovels. However, if the firm intended to dig several city blocks' worth of drainage ditches, it would undoubtedly hire some mechanical diggers (backhoes) and some skilled operators. It might reduce its demand for unskilled labor, perhaps to 0.

Thus, it is reasonable to be unable to predict the sign of $\partial x_i^* / \partial y$. No refutable hypothesis concerning output effects emerges strictly from the minimization hypothesis. A negative or a positive sign for $\partial x_i^* / \partial y$ is consistent with the model.

It should be pointed out, however, that a factor in use cannot be inferior over the whole range of output. That is, it must have been the case that $\partial x_i^* / \partial y > 0$ at some lower levels of output, else the factor would not ever be employed in the first place. Remember that these comparative statics relations are *local*, not global, results.

There is one set of relationships concerning output effects that are not intuitively, or even geometrically, obvious. Note again the equations

$$\frac{\partial \lambda^*}{\partial w_1} = \frac{-H_{13}}{H} \tag{8-28c}$$

$$\frac{\partial x_1^*}{\partial y} = \frac{-H_{31}}{H} \tag{8-33a}$$

$$\frac{\partial \lambda^*}{\partial w_2} = \frac{-H_{23}}{H} \tag{8-30c}$$

$$\frac{\partial x_2^*}{\partial y} = \frac{-H_{32}}{H} \tag{8-33b}$$

The symmetry of the determinant H immediately indicates that

$$\frac{\partial \lambda^*}{\partial w_i} \equiv \frac{\partial x_i^*}{\partial y} \qquad i = 1, 2 \tag{8-34}$$

That is, the rate of change of the marginal cost function with respect to a factor price is equal to (and therefore of the same sign as) the magnitude of the output effect for that factor. But output effects can be negative as well as positive. This leads to the strange result that the marginal cost curve, as commonly drawn (see

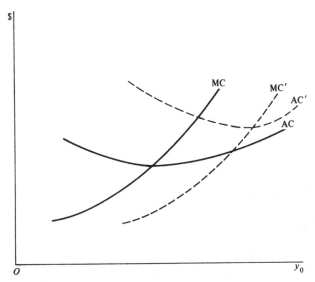

FIGURE 8-10
Changes in the Marginal and Average Cost Curves when the Price of an Inferior Factor Changes.
When the price of an inferior factor increases, the marginal cost curve of the firm shifts *down,* the average cost curve shifts up. With any increase in factor costs, unit cost of production must increase. The firm will never regard an increase in factor costs as beneficial. However, if the factor is inferior, the *marginal* cost of output declines.

Fig. 8-10) against output, will shift *down* when the wage of an inferior factor *increases.* If, say, $\partial x_1^*/\partial y < 0$, then x_1 is an inferior factor (less is used as output rises). If w_1 increases, the marginal cost curve will actually *fall,* i.e., shift down along the whole range where x_1 is inferior.

How can we explain this result? Consider Fig. 8-11. What happens when a cost minimizing firm experiences an increase in a factor price (holding output constant)? The firm, of course, substitutes away from that factor. However, if x_1 is inferior, then for any level of x_1, increases in x_2 will result in new isoquant levels that are flatter than the previous, lower one at that level of x_1. That is, since parallel shifts in the isocost line result in tangencies to the left of the original one, then the isoquants directly vertical from the original tangency must have a lower absolute slope. This means that the distance between isoquants representing successive output levels *narrows* as x_1 is reduced. Hence, an increase in w_1, which reduces x_1, *reduces* the cost of additional output.

8.8 COMPARATIVE STATICS RELATIONS USING DUALITY THEORY

We now investigate the properties of this important model using duality theory, as developed in Chap. 7.

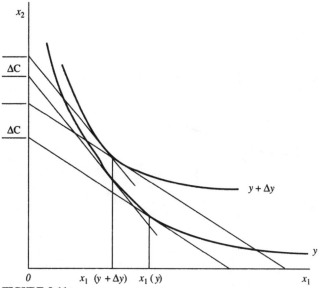

FIGURE 8-11

The Effects of an Increase in the Unit Cost of an Inferior Factor. The factor x_1 is inferior, as an increase in output from y to $y + \Delta y$ reduces the demand for x_1. At any level of x_1, as amounts of x_2 are increased (vertical movements), the isoquants become flatter. We can arbitrarily define the units such that $w_2 = 1$. Then vertical movements can be identified as marginal costs, since the intercepts of the isocost lines with the vertical axis are $x_2 = C/w_2 = C$. Since the isoquants converge as x_1 is decreased, when x_1 is inferior, the marginal cost of expanding output from y to $y + \Delta y$ is less when less x_1 is used, that is, as w_1 is raised.

Reciprocity Conditions

The reciprocity conditions $\partial x_i^*/\partial w_j = \partial x_j^*/\partial w_i$ and $\partial \lambda^*/\partial w_i = \partial x_i^*/\partial y$ can be given a simpler and more powerful proof and interpretation by use of the envelope theorem. Recall again that for the general constrained maximum (or minimum) problem,

maximize

$$f(x_1, x_2, \alpha) = y$$

subject to

$$g(x_1, x_2, \alpha) = 0$$

where α represents one or more parameters, that $\partial y^*/\partial \alpha = \partial \mathcal{L}/\partial \alpha$; that is, the rate of change of the maximum value of f for any α, with respect to α, allowing the decision variables x_1 and x_2 to "adjust" via $x_1 = x_1^*(\alpha)$, $x_2 = x_2^*(\alpha)$, is the same as the partial derivative of the Lagrangian $\mathcal{L} = f(x_1, x_2, \alpha) + \lambda g(x_1, x_2, \alpha)$ with respect to α, *holding the x_i's fixed*. We have already used this theorem to show that λ is interpretable as marginal cost [see Eq. (8-23)].

The cost minimization problem

minimize

$$C = w_1 x_1 + w_2 x_2$$

subject to

$$f(x_1, x_2) = y$$

has as its Lagrangian

$$\mathscr{L} = w_1 x_1 + w_2 x_2 + \lambda(y - f(x_1, x_2))$$

The envelope theorem thus says that

$$\frac{\partial C^*}{\partial w_1} = \frac{\partial \mathscr{L}}{\partial w_1} = x_1 = x_1^*(w_1, w_2, y) \qquad (8\text{-}35)$$

and similarly for x_2. Also, as was shown before, Eq. (8-23), $\partial C^*/\partial y = \partial \mathscr{L}/\partial y = \lambda^*(w_1, w_2, y)$. Equation (8-35) is often referred to as *Shephard's lemma;* it is an important part of the duality theory of cost and production functions. We also showed previously that

$$\frac{\partial C^*}{\partial y} \equiv \lambda^*(w_1, w_2, y) \qquad (8\text{-}23)$$

Now $C^*(w_1, w_2, y)$ is twice differentiable, assuming the production function is well-behaved, i.e., that a smooth interior solution to the cost minimization problem obtains. But observe the cross-partials of $C^*(w_1, w_2, y)$: Since $C_{w_1}^* \equiv x_1^*(w_1, w_2, y)$, $C_{w_1 w_2}^*$ is simply $\partial x_1^*/\partial w_2$, that is,

$$C_{w_1 w_2}^* \equiv \frac{\partial x_1^*}{\partial w_2}$$

However, $C_{w_1 w_2}^* \equiv C_{w_2 w_1}^*$, since partial derivatives can be taken without regard to order. But $C_{w_2 w_1}^* \equiv \partial x_2^*/\partial w_1$. Hence (almost) trivially,

$$C_{w_2 w_1}^* \equiv \frac{\partial x_2^*}{\partial w_1} \equiv \frac{\partial x_1^*}{\partial w_2} \equiv C_{w_1 w_2}^*$$

which was Eq. (8-31).

Likewise, since $\partial C^*/\partial y \equiv C_y^* = \lambda^*(w_1, w_2, y)$,

$$C_{y w_1}^* \equiv \frac{\partial \lambda^*}{\partial w_1}$$

But $C_{y w_1}^* \equiv C_{w_1 y}^* \equiv \partial x_1^*/\partial y$. Thus,

$$\frac{\partial \lambda^*}{\partial w_1} \equiv \frac{\partial x_1^*}{\partial y}$$

which was Eq. (8-34). Similar reasoning of course shows that $\partial \lambda^*/\partial w_2 \equiv \partial x_2^*/\partial y$.

This is a very powerful, yet simple, way of regarding reciprocity conditions. (Perhaps it is powerful precisely because of its simplicity.) Reciprocity conditions are simply the statement that the cross-partials of the cost function are invariant to the order of differentiation. The reciprocity conditions appear, however, only because the first partials of $C^*(w_1, w_2, y)$ have the peculiarly simple forms $\partial C^*/\partial w_i = x_i^*$, $\partial C^*/\partial y \equiv \lambda^*$. These simple first partials occur because the Lagrangian $\mathcal{L} = w_1 x_1 + w_2 x_2 + \lambda(y - f(x_1, x_2))$ is in fact *linear* in the parameters w_1, w_2, y. When such linearity of the Lagrangian occurs, reciprocity conditions will appear.

The modern development of the envelope theorem allows an easy derivation of the refutable implications of the cost minimization model. The comparative statics relations implied by this model are consequences of the curvature properties, in particular the concavity, of the (indirect) cost function. We proceed in an analogous manner to the analysis of the profit maximization model. For given values of factor prices and output, certain factor levels are implied:

$$x_1^0 = x_1^*(w_1^0, w_2^0, y^0)$$
$$x_2^0 = x_2^*(w_1^0, w_2^0, y^0)$$

In Fig. 8-12, cost is plotted vertically against w_1. As a "reference" line, the "constrained" cost function $C = w_1 x_1^0 + w_2^0 x_2^0$ is plotted. Note that the only "variable" is w_1; everything else is held fixed at the specified values. This function is clearly linear, with positive slope x_1^0.

Consider now where $C^*(w_1, w_2^0, y^0)$ has to appear in this diagram. Since by definition C^* is the *minimum* cost for given output and wages, $C^*(w_1, w_2^0, y^0)$ cannot at any time be above the constrained cost line. However, when $w_1 = w_1^0$, exactly the correct, i.e., cost-minimizing, input levels are employed; hence at $w_1 = w_1^0$, $C^*(w_1, w_2^0, y^0) = w_1 x_1^0 + w_2^0 x_2^0 = C$. Moreover, to either side of w_1^0, assuming unique solutions, $C^* < C$. It is clear from the geometry that $C^*(w_1, w_2^0, y^0)$ must be concave in w_1 (and obviously w_2 also, by symmetry). (In fact, as the algebra of Chap. 7 shows, the Hessian matrix $C^*_{w_i w_j}$ must be negative semidefinite.) The consequences of this concavity include $C^*_{w_1 w_1} \leq 0$; however, by the envelope theorem, $C^*_{w_1} = x_1^*$, and consequently, $C^*_{w_1 w_1} = \partial x_1^*/\partial w_1 \leq 0$. A similar analysis of course follows for x_2^*. These results are derived algebraically, without recourse to visual geometry, in Chap. 7. The results generalize in an obvious way for n-factor models.

Cost Curves in the Short and Long Run

In the famous Viner-Wong cost diagram (see Fig. 7-1), at any specified output level, the short- and long-run marginal cost functions are equal; however, the short-run curve either rises faster or falls slower than the long-run marginal cost function. We can show this result rigorously by the conditional demand approach.

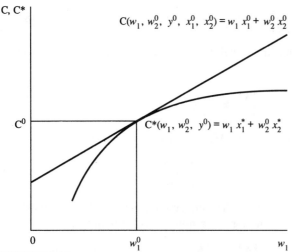

FIGURE 8-12
The cost function $C^*(w_1, w_2^0, y^0)$ for varying w_1 holding w_2 and y fixed, and the cost function $C(w_1, w_2^0, y^0, x_1^0, x_2^0)$, in which x_1 and x_2 are held fixed at $x_1^0 = x_1^*(w_1^0, w_2^0, y^0)$ and $x_2^0 = x_2^*(w_1^0, w_2^0, y_0)$. $C(w_1, w_2^0, y^0, x_1^0, x_2^0) = w_1 x_1^0 + w_2^0 x_2^0$ is clearly linear in w_1; that is, geometrically it is a straight line. At $w_1 = w_1^0$, $C = C^*$ since x_1^0 and x_2^0 are precisely those quantities which minimize total cost subject to constraint. For $w_1 \neq w_1^0$, $C^* < C$, since then the "wrong" x_i's are employed for C, whereas C^* is the *minimum* cost, calculated by using whatever x_1^* and x_2^* are appropriate. But since $C^* = C$ at $w_1 = w_1^0$ and $C^* < C$ in the neighborhood around w_1^0, C^* must be tangent to C at w_1^0; also, C^* must be concave in w_1, since $C = w_1 x_1^0 + w_2^0 x_2^0$ is linear in w_1. We therefore have, from tangency, $C_{w_1} = C_{w_1}^* = x_1^* = x_1^0$ and, from concavity in w_1, $C_{w_1 w_1}^* = \partial x_1^* / \partial w_1^* \le 0$.

Since in the short run, a factor is held fixed, we must consider models with more than two factors. There is already one constraint, $f(x_1, x_2) = y^0$; adding another would completely specify the solution at some particular point on the isoquant y^0, leaving no further degrees of freedom for the minimization hypothesis. Let us therefore consider the general n-factor model. Using vector notation, let $x = (x_1, \ldots, x_n)$, $w = (w_1, \ldots, w_n)$ represent the factor and wage levels, respectively. The fundamental identity relating the short- and long-run marginal cost functions is

$$\lambda^*(w, y) \equiv \lambda^s(w_1, \ldots, w_{n-1}, x_n^*(w, y), y) \qquad (8\text{-}36)$$

where λ^s is the appropriately defined short-run marginal cost function derived from cost minimization when x_n is parametric, and where output y is of course a parameter.

Differentiating the fundamental identity with respect to output y yields

$$\frac{\partial \lambda^*}{\partial y} \equiv \frac{\partial \lambda^s}{\partial y} + \left(\frac{\partial \lambda^s}{\partial x_n^0} \right) \left(\frac{\partial x_n^*}{\partial y} \right) \qquad (8\text{-}37)$$

Differentiating the identity with respect to w_n,

$$\frac{\partial \lambda^*}{\partial w_n} \equiv \left(\frac{\partial \lambda^s}{\partial x_n^0} \right) \left(\frac{\partial x_n^*}{\partial w_n} \right) \tag{8-38}$$

Applying Young's theorem and the envelope theorem to the cost function yields the reciprocity condition

$$\frac{\partial \lambda^*}{\partial w_n} \equiv \frac{\partial x_n^*}{\partial y}$$

Using this and (8-38) to substitute for $\partial \lambda^s / \partial x_n^0$ in Eq. (8-37),

$$\frac{\partial \lambda^*}{\partial y} \equiv \frac{\partial \lambda^s}{\partial y} + \frac{(\partial x_n^* / \partial y)^2}{(\partial x_n^* / \partial w_n)} \tag{8-39}$$

Equation (8-39) shows that the slope of the long-run marginal cost function differs from the slope of the short-run function by a nonpositive amount; thus

$$\frac{\partial \lambda^*}{\partial y} \leq \frac{\partial \lambda^s}{\partial y} \tag{8-40}$$

Equation (8-39) also shows that the difference between the elasticities of the short and long-run marginal cost functions varies directly with the size of the output effect, and inversely with the slope of the factor demand.

Factor Demands in the Short and Long Run

A similar procedure can be used to show the effect of holding a factor constant on the slope of the constant-output factor demands. Assuming x_n is the parametrically fixed factor, the fundamental identity is, for factors 1 through $n-1$,

$$x_i^*(w, y) \equiv x_i^s(w_1, \ldots, w_{n-1}, x_n^*(w, y), y) \tag{8-41}$$

Differentiating with respect to w_i,

$$\frac{\partial x_i^*}{\partial w_i} \equiv \frac{\partial x_i^s}{\partial w_i} + \frac{\partial x_i^s}{\partial x_n^0} \frac{\partial x_n^*}{\partial w_i} \tag{8-42}$$

Differentiating the fundamental identity with respect to w_n,

$$\frac{\partial x_i^*}{\partial w_n} \equiv \frac{\partial x_i^s}{\partial x_n^0} \frac{\partial x_n^*}{\partial w_n} \tag{8-43}$$

However, $\partial x_i^* / \partial w_n \equiv \partial x_n^* / \partial w_i$; using this along with (8-43) yields

$$\frac{\partial x_i^*}{\partial w_i} \equiv \frac{\partial x_i^s}{\partial w_i} + \frac{(\partial x_n^* / \partial w_i)^2}{(\partial x_n^* / \partial w_n)} \tag{8-44}$$

an expression analogous to Eq. (8-39) for the marginal cost functions. Again, since the second term on the right-hand side is necessarily nonpositive, we have

$$\frac{\partial x_i^*}{\partial w_i} \leq \frac{\partial x_i^s}{\partial w_i} \leq 0 \tag{8-45}$$

The larger the cross-effect between x_n and w_i, and the smaller the slope of x_n, $\partial x_n^*/\partial w_n$, the larger the difference in slope of the short- and long-run factor demand curves.

Similar expressions exist for the short- and long-run cross-effects; however, qualitative results depend on other assumptions about complementarity or substitutability of the factors. These relationships are left as exercises.

Example. Consider the production function $y = x_1 x_2^2$. This function exhibits increasing returns to scale and thus a finite profit maximum would not be reached with constant prices. However, there is still a cost-minimizing input combination for any given output level y. Let us find the constant-output factor demand curves.

minimize
$$C = w_1 x_1 + w_2 x_2$$

subject to
$$x_1 x_2^2 = y$$

The Lagrangian is
$$\mathcal{L} = w_1 x_1 + w_2 x_2 + \lambda(y - x_1 x_2^2)$$

Differentiating with respect to x_1, x_2, and λ,
$$\mathcal{L}_1 = w_1 - \lambda x_2^2 = 0$$
$$\mathcal{L}_2 = w_2 - 2\lambda x_1 x_2 = 0$$
$$\mathcal{L}_\lambda = y - x_1 x_2^2 = 0$$

Combining the first two expressions,
$$\frac{w_1}{w_2} = \frac{x_2}{2x_1}$$

or
$$x_2 = \frac{2w_1 x_1}{w_2}$$

Now substitute this expression for x_2 into the production function:
$$x_1 \left(\frac{2w_1 x_1}{w_2} \right)^2 = y$$

or
$$\frac{4x_1^3 w_1^2}{w_2^2} = y$$

Solving for x_1

$$x_1^* = 4^{-1/3}w_1^{-2/3}w_2^{2/3}y^{1/3}$$

In like fashion one obtains, from the first-order tangency condition,

$$x_1 = \frac{w_2 x_2}{2w_1}$$

Substituting this into the production function yields

$$\frac{w_2 x_2}{2w_1}x_2^2 = y$$

or

$$x_2^* = 2^{1/3}w_1^{1/3}w_2^{-1/3}y^{1/3}$$

Note that x_1^* and x_2^* are multiplicatively separable in the factor prices and output. Also, x_1^* and x_2^* are homogeneous of degree zero in w_1 and w_2. The cost function is obtained by substituting x_1^* and x_2^* into $C = w_1 x_1 + w_2 x_2$:

$$C^* = w_1 4^{-1/3}w_1^{-2/3}w_2^{2/3}y^{1/3} + w_2 2^{1/3}w_1^{1/3}w_2^{-1/3}y^{1/3}$$

$$= kw_1^{1/3}w_2^{2/3}y^{1/3}$$

where $k = 4^{-1/3} + 2^{1/3} = 2^{-2/3} + 2^{1/3} = 2^{1/3}(2^{-1} + 2^0) = \frac{3}{2}(2^{1/3})$. Note that C^* is homogeneous of degree 1 in w_1 and w_2, a general property of cost functions. Note also that

$$\frac{\partial C^*}{\partial w_1} = \tfrac{1}{3}kw_1^{-2/3}w_2^{2/3}y^{1/3} \equiv x_1^*$$

and

$$\frac{\partial C^*}{\partial w_2} = \tfrac{2}{3}kw_1^{1/3}w_2^{-1/3}y^{1/3} \equiv x_2^*$$

These envelope properties are shown for the general case in Eq. (8-35).

Relation to Profit Maximization

We said earlier that the main reason to consider the cost-minimization model is its relation to a firm's behavior under profit maximization. At the point of profit maximization, the firm must be minimizing the cost of that particular output level. In other words, if the parametric value y in $x_i^*(w_1, w_2, y)$ is replaced with y^*, the profit-maximizing level of output, the result must be the factor demand function derived from profit maximization, $x_i^*(w_1, w_2, p)$. In the n variable cases, the profit maximization and cost minimization models share $n-1$ first-order conditions, $f_i/f_j = w_i/w_j$. The difference between the models has to do only with the output level: in the cost minimization model, output is parametric, whereas in the profit maximization model, output is determined endogenously, by the profit maximization hypothesis.

Since the symbol "x^*" is being used to denote two different functions, denote the factor demands derived from profit maximization by $x_i^p(w_1, w_2, p)$, and those derived from cost minimization by $x_i^y(w_1, w_2, y)$. Then the above reasoning can be summarized by the *identity*

$$x_1^p(w_1, w_2, p) \equiv x_1^y(w_1, w_2, y^*(w_1, w_2, p)) \tag{8-46}$$

with a similar expression for x_2. This fundamental relation can be used to derive relationships between the slopes of these two demand functions.

Suppose a profit-maximizing firm faces a decrease in some factor price, say, w_1. Then we can imagine the response in terms of factor demand as taking place in two conceptual stages. First, a "pure substitution" effect takes place. The firm stays on the same isoquant, but slides along it to a new cost-minimizing choice of x_1 and x_2. In other words, it first responds according to the cost-minimizing demand function $x_1^y(w_1, w_2, y)$. Unambiguously, the firm chooses to hire more x_1. Next, however, an "output effect" takes place in which the firm chooses the profit-maximizing output level. The output effect, unlike the pure substitution effect, is ambiguous. Output could either increase or decrease in response to the decrease in w_1. Which demand function, $x_1^y(w_1, w_2, y)$ or $x_1^p(w_1, w_2, p)$, is more elastic?

If it seems that the ability to choose some sort of "maximizing" output level would lead the firm to choose a larger absolute factor response when that option is available, that reasoning is correct in these two models. (But be careful—such intuition is not always correct, and it is not correct in an important sense in the theory of the consumer.) This result can be shown rigorously by differentiating identity (8-46) with respect to w_1, using the chain rule on the right-hand side:

$$\frac{\partial x_1^p}{\partial w_1} \equiv \frac{\partial x_1^y}{\partial w_1} + \frac{\partial x_1^y}{\partial y} \frac{\partial y^*}{\partial w_1} \tag{8-47}$$

Inspect the notation carefully on the right-hand side: x_1^y is a function of the parametric output level y, hence the notation in the first part of the chain-rule term. However, output is then chosen according to profit maximization, hence the notation y^* in the second part of the term.

Equation (8-47) shows that the difference in the slopes between the two demand functions differs by a compound term relating to an output effect, involving the rate of change of x_1 with respect to a change in output, y. Can this second term be signed? Indeed it can—recall the reciprocity condition $\partial x_1^*/\partial p = -\partial y^*/\partial w_1$, derived by applying Young's theorem to the indirect profit function. (See Prob. 1, Chap. 4.) Substituting this in Eq. (8-47) yields

$$\frac{\partial x_1^p}{\partial w_1} \equiv \frac{\partial x_1^y}{\partial w_1} - \frac{\partial x_1^y}{\partial y} \frac{\partial x_1^p}{\partial p} \tag{8-48}$$

It should be clear that the last two terms on the right have the same sign, since p and y move in the same direction. This can be shown rigorously by differentiating the fundamental identity with respect to p:

$$\frac{\partial x_1^p}{\partial p} \equiv \frac{\partial x_1^y}{\partial y} \frac{\partial y^*}{\partial p}$$

Using this and Eq. (8-47),

$$\frac{\partial x_1^p}{\partial w_1} \equiv \frac{\partial x_1^y}{\partial w_1} - \left(\frac{\partial y^*}{\partial p}\right)\left(\frac{\partial x_1^y}{\partial y}\right)^2 \tag{8-49}$$

Since supply curves are upward-sloping, $(\partial y^*/\partial p) \geq 0$; thus

$$\frac{\partial x_1^p}{\partial w_1} \leq \frac{\partial x_1^y}{\partial w_1} \leq 0 \tag{8-50}$$

A similar procedure can be used to analyze the relative magnitudes of the cross-effects $\partial x_1^*/\partial w_2$ in the two models. For these changes, a determinate sign is not available; further assumptions regarding the output effects are required. This analysis is left as an exercise.

8.9 ELASTICITIES; FURTHER PROPERTIES OF THE FACTOR-DEMAND CURVES

The properties of the factor demand curves $x_i = x_i^*(w_1, w_2, y)$ and the marginal cost curve $\lambda = \lambda^*(w_1, w_2, y)$ are often stated in terms of dimensionless elasticity expressions, instead of using the slopes (partial derivatives) directly. The elasticities of demand are defined as

$$\epsilon_{ij} = \lim_{\Delta w_j \to 0} \frac{\dfrac{\Delta x_i}{x_i}}{\dfrac{\Delta w_j}{w_j}}$$

where ϵ_{ij} thus represents the (limit of the) percentage change in a factor usage x_i (holding output constant) due to a given percentage change in some factor price w_j. When $i = j$, this is called the *own elasticity* of factor demand; when $i \neq j$, this is called a *cross-elasticity*.

Taking limits, and simplifying the compound fraction,

$$\epsilon_{ij} = \frac{w_j}{x_i^*} \frac{\partial x_i^*}{\partial w_j} \qquad i, j, = 1, 2 \tag{8-51}$$

In like fashion, one can define the *output elasticity* of factor demand as the percentage change in the utilization of a factor per percentage change in output[†] (holding factor prices constant),

---

[†]Note that the output elasticity is *not* $[(\Delta y/y)/(\Delta x_i/x_i)]$, or $(x_i/y)(\partial y/\partial x_i) = (1/AP_i)MP_i$. This latter expression, though well-defined, is not a measure of the responsiveness of factor demand to output changes. And it is most certainly *not* the reciprocal of ε_{iy} above: ε_{iy} can be positive or negative (for the case of inferior factors); $(x_i/y)(\partial y/\partial x_i)$ is necessarily positive as long as the marginal product of x_i is positive.

$$\epsilon_{iy} = \lim_{\Delta y_i \to 0} \frac{\Delta x_i}{x_i} \Big/ \frac{\Delta y}{y} = \frac{y}{x_i^*} \frac{\partial x_i^*}{\partial y} \qquad (8\text{-}52)$$

Homogeneity

The demand curves $x_i = x_i^*(w_1, w_2, y)$ are homogeneous of degree zero in factor prices, or, for the two-factor case, in w_1 and w_2. That is $x_i^*(tw_1, tw_2, y) \equiv x_1^*(w_1, w_2, y)$. Holding output y constant, a proportional change in all factor prices leaves the input combination unchanged. This is really another way of saying that only changes in *relative* prices, not absolute prices, affect behavior.

If the cost-minimizing firm faced factor prices tw_1, tw_2, the problem would be to

minimize

$$tw_1 x_1 + tw_2 x_2$$

subject to

$$f(x_1, x_2) = y$$

Since $tw_1 x_1 + tw_2 x_2 = t(w_1 x_1 + w_2 x_2)$ is a very simple monotonic transformation of the objective function, we should expect no substantial changes in the first-order equations. Forming the Lagrangian $\mathscr{L} = t(w_1 x_1 + w_2 x_2) + \lambda(y - f(x_1, x_2))$, the first-order equations for a constrained minimum are

$$\mathscr{L}_1 = tw_1 - \lambda f_1 = 0 \qquad (8\text{-}53a)$$

$$\mathscr{L}_2 = tw_2 - \lambda f_2 = 0 \qquad (8\text{-}53b)$$

$$\mathscr{L}_\lambda = y - f(x_1, x_2) = 0 \qquad (8\text{-}53c)$$

Eliminating the Lagrange multiplier from (8-53a) and (8-53b),

$$\frac{tw_1}{tw_2} = \frac{w_1}{w_2} = \frac{f_1}{f_2}$$

Thus the same tangency condition emerges for factor prices (tw_1, tw_2) as for (w_1, w_2). The isoquant must have slope w_1/w_2, for any value of t. And output, meanwhile, is still constrained to be at level y. Hence the identical solution to the cost minimization problem (in terms of the x_i's) emerges for factor prices (tw_1, tw_2) as for (w_1, w_2); hence the solutions $x_i = x_i^*(w_1, w_2, y)$ are unchanged when (w_1, w_2) are replaced by (tw_1, tw_2). Thus $x_i^*(w_1, w_2, y) \equiv x_i^*(tw_1, tw_2, y)$, or the factor-demand curves (holding output constant) are homogeneous of degree zero in the factor prices. This result is perfectly general for the n-factor case; $x_i^*(w_1, \ldots, w_n, y) \equiv x_i^*(tw_1, \ldots, tw_n, y)$, $i = 1, \ldots, n$.

Clearly, however, *something* must be changed when factor prices are multiplied by some common scalar. What *is* changed is total cost, and therefore marginal and average costs also. If factor prices are doubled, the input combination will remain the same, but the nominal cost of purchasing that input combination will clearly double. Total cost $C \equiv C^*(w_1, w_2, y)$ is homogeneous of degree one in factor prices. Total cost $C^*(w_1, w_2, y) \equiv w_1 x_1^* + w_2 x_2^*$, a linear function of the x_i^*'s. When factor prices are changed by some multiple t, the x_i^*'s are unchanged, and hence

$$C^*(tw_1, tw_2, y) \equiv tw_1 x_1^*(tw_1, tw_2, y) + tw_2 x_2^*(tw_1, tw_2, y)$$

$$\equiv tw_1 x_1^*(w_1, w_2, y) + tw_2 x_2^*(w_1, w_2, y)$$

$$\equiv t[w_1 x_1^*(w_1, w_2, y) + w_2 x_2^*(w_1, w_2, y)]$$

$$\equiv tC^*(w_1, w_2, y)$$

Again, this result is perfectly general for the n-factor case; the cost function is homogeneous of degree one in factor prices.

Since total costs increase or decrease by whatever scalar multiple factor prices are changed, marginal and average costs are similarly affected. Since

$$AC \equiv \frac{C^*(w_1, w_2, y)}{y} \tag{8-54}$$

$$AC(tw_1, tw_2, y) \equiv C^*(tw_1, tw_2, y) \frac{1}{y}$$

$$\equiv tC^*(w_1, w_2, y) \frac{1}{y}$$

$$\equiv tAC(w_1, w_2, y)$$

Similarly, since $MC \equiv \lambda^*(w_1, w_2, y)$, from the first-order equations

$$\lambda^*(tw_1, tw_2, y) \equiv \frac{tw_i}{f_i(x_1^*, x_2^*)} \qquad i = 1, 2$$

The factor inputs x_i^* are unchanged by the multiplication of factor prices by t. Hence only the numerator of the above fraction is affected, in a simple linear fashion, and hence

$$\lambda^*(tw_1, tw_2, y) \equiv t\lambda^*(w_1, w_2, y) \tag{8-55}$$

or the marginal cost function is homogeneous of degree one in factor prices.

It should be carefully noted that all of the preceding homogeneity results are completely independent of any homogeneity of the production function itself. These results are derivable for any cost-minimizing firm. Nowhere was any assumption about the homogeneity of the production function implied or used; therefore these results hold for *any* production function for which a cost-minimizing tangency solution is achieved.

Euler relations. Since the factor-demand curve $x_i = x_i^*(w_1, w_2, y)$ is homogeneous of degree zero in w_1, w_2, by Euler's theorem

$$\frac{\partial x_i^*}{\partial w_1} w_1 + \frac{\partial x_i^*}{\partial w_2} w_2 \equiv 0 \cdot x_i^* \equiv 0 \quad i = 1, 2 \qquad (8\text{-}56)$$

This relation can be stated neatly in terms of elasticities. Dividing (8-56) by x_i^*,

$$\frac{w_1}{x_i^*} \frac{\partial x_i^*}{\partial w_1} + \frac{w_2}{x_i^*} \frac{\partial x_i^*}{\partial w_2} \equiv 0 \quad i = 1, 2$$

or

$$\epsilon_{i1} + \epsilon_{i2} \equiv 0 \quad i = 1, 2 \qquad (8\text{-}57)$$

using the definitions of elasticities and cross-elasticities given in Eq. (8-51). More generally, for the n-factor case, the factor demands $x_i^*(w_1, \ldots, w_n, y)$ are homogeneous of degree zero in $w_1, \ldots, w_n$. Similar reasoning yields

$$\epsilon_{i1} + \epsilon_{i2} + , \ldots, + \epsilon_{in} \equiv 0 \quad i = 1, \ldots, n$$

or

$$\sum_{j=1}^{n} \epsilon_{ij} \equiv 0 \quad i = 1, \ldots, n \qquad (8\text{-}58)$$

For any factor, holding output constant, the sum of its own elasticity of demand plus its cross-elasticities with respect to all other factor prices sums identically to zero.

Another relationship concerning cross-elasticities can be derived using the reciprocity relations $\partial x_i^* / \partial w_j \equiv \partial x_j^* / \partial w_i$. This reciprocity relation can be converted into elasticities as follows. Each side will be multiplied by 1 in a complicated way (the asterisks are omitted to save notational clutter):

$$\frac{x_i w_j}{x_i w_j} \frac{\partial x_i}{\partial w_j} \equiv \frac{x_j w_i}{x_j w_i} \frac{\partial x_j}{\partial w_i}$$

Rearranging terms yields

$$\frac{x_i}{w_j} \left(\frac{w_j}{x_i} \frac{\partial x_i}{\partial w_j} \right) \equiv \frac{x_j}{w_i} \left(\frac{w_i}{x_j} \frac{\partial x_j}{\partial w_i} \right)$$

or

$$(w_i x_i) \epsilon_{ij} \equiv (w_j x_j) \epsilon_{ji}$$

Dividing through by total cost $C = \sum w_i x_i$,

$$\kappa_i \epsilon_{ij} \equiv \kappa_j \epsilon_{ji} \qquad i,j = 1, \ldots, n \qquad (8\text{-}59)$$

where $\kappa_i = w_i x_i / C$ represents the share of total cost accounted for by factor x_i.

Never forget, incidentally, what is being held constant here. These elasticities and shares refer to constrained cost minimization, i.e., output-held constant factor curves. Slightly different relationships are derivable for, e.g., the profit-maximizing (unconstrained) firm.

The reciprocity relations in terms of elasticities, Eqs. (8-59), can be substituted into Eqs. (8-58) to yield new interdependencies of the cross-elasticities. Substituting (8-58) into (8-59),

$$\sum_{j=1}^{n} \epsilon_{ij} \equiv \sum_{j=1}^{n} \frac{\kappa_j}{\kappa_i} \epsilon_{ji} \equiv 0$$

Multiplying through by κ_i yields

$$\sum_{j=1}^{n} \kappa_j \epsilon_{ji} \equiv \kappa_1 \epsilon_{1i} + \kappa_2 \epsilon_{2i} + \cdots + \kappa_n \epsilon_{ni} \equiv 0 \qquad i = 1, \cdots, n \qquad (8\text{-}60)$$

The difference between (8-58) and (8-60) is that in this last relation (8-60), the elasticities being considered are those between the various factors and *one particular factor price*, whereas in Eq. (8-58), the elasticities all pertain to the relationship of one particular factor x_i to all factor prices. In the former case, the shares are not involved, the relationship being derived directly from Euler's equation; in the latter case of how all factors relate to a given price change, the shares of cost allocated to those factors do play a part.

Equation (8-60) can also be derived by a different route. Consider the production function constraint $f(x_1^*, x_2^*) \equiv y$. Differentiating with respect to some factor price w_i,

$$f_1 \frac{\partial x_1^*}{\partial w_i} + f_2 \frac{\partial x_2^*}{\partial w_i} \equiv 0$$

From the first-order relations $w_j = \lambda f_j$, this is equivalent to

$$w_1 \frac{\partial x_1^*}{\partial w_i} + w_2 \frac{\partial x_2^*}{\partial w_i} \equiv 0 \qquad (8\text{-}61)$$

Note in Eq. (8-61) that the terms refer to the change in the various factors with respect to the same factor price, w_i. If this expression is now manipulated in a manner similar to the derivation of Eq. (8-59), Eq. (8-60) results.

Output Elasticities

The output elasticities are related to one another also, as can be seen by differentiating the production constraint $f(x_1^*, x_2^*) \equiv y$ with respect to y:

$$f_1 \frac{\partial x_1^*}{\partial y} + f_2 \frac{\partial x_2^*}{\partial y} \equiv 1$$

Again using the first-order relations $w_i = \lambda^* f_i$,

$$\frac{w_1}{\lambda^*} \frac{\partial x_1^*}{\partial y} + \frac{w_2}{\lambda^*} \frac{\partial x_2^*}{\partial y} \equiv 1$$

To convert these terms to elasticities, multiply the first by $(y/y)(x_1^*/x_1^*)$, that is, by unity, in that fashion. Do the same for the second term, using x_2^* instead of x_1^*. This yields

$$\frac{w_1 x_1^*}{\lambda^* y}\left(\frac{y}{x_1^*} \frac{\partial x_1^*}{\partial y}\right) + \frac{w_2 x_2^*}{\lambda^* y}\left(\frac{y}{x_2^*} \frac{\partial x_2^*}{\partial y}\right) \equiv 1$$

or

$$\kappa_1' \epsilon_{1y} + \kappa_2' \epsilon_{2y} \equiv 1 \tag{8-62}$$

where the "weights" κ_i' are the total cost of each factor divided by marginal cost times output. This result generalizes easily to the n-factor case:

$$\sum \kappa_i' \epsilon_{iy} \equiv 1 \tag{8-63}$$

where $\kappa_i' = w_i x_i / \lambda^* y$.

It should be noted that these weights, κ_i', do not themselves sum to unity, and hence Eq. (8-63) should not properly be called a *weighted average* of the output elasticities. In fact, $\sum \kappa_i' = (\sum w_i x_i)/\lambda^* y = (1/\lambda^*)(C^*/y) = AC/MC$. In a special case, the weights do sum to 1—when marginal cost λ equals average cost. This situation will occur when a firm is operating at the minimum point on its average cost curve, i.e., where marginal cost intersects average cost. Thus we could say that for a firm in long-run competitive equilibrium, the weighted average of the output elasticities of all factors sums to unity, where the weights are the share of total cost spent on that particular factor.

8.10 THE AVERAGE COST CURVE

Consider now the average cost curve (AC) of a firm employing two variable inputs x_1 and x_2, at factor prices w_1 and w_2, respectively. By definition,

$$AC = \frac{C^*(w_1, w_2, y)}{y} = \frac{1}{y}(w_1 x_1^* + w_2 x_2^*) \tag{8-64}$$

How is average cost affected by a change in a factor price, say w_1? Can average cost ever fall in response to an increase in factor price? In this case, intuition proves correct—increased factor costs can only increase overall average cost. If this were otherwise, firms could always make larger profits by contracting for higher wage payments. This behavior is not commonly observed.

We can demonstrate the positive relationship between AC and w_1 as follows. Differentiating (8-64) with respect to w_1 yields

$$\frac{\partial \text{AC}}{\partial w_1} = \frac{1}{y}\left(x_1^* + w_1\frac{\partial x_1^*}{\partial w_1} + w_2\frac{\partial x_2^*}{\partial w_1}\right)$$

noting the use of the product rule on the term $w_1 x_1^*$. Using the first-order relations, $w_i = \lambda^* f_i$

$$\frac{\partial \text{AC}}{\partial w_1} = \frac{x_1^*}{y} + \frac{\lambda^*}{y}\left(f_1\frac{\partial x_1^*}{\partial w_1} + f_2\frac{\partial x_2^*}{\partial w_1}\right)$$

However, differentiation of the constraint identity, $f(x_1^*, x_2^*) \equiv y$, with respect to w_1 [see Eq. (8-26c)] yields $f_1(\partial x_1^*/\partial w_1) + f_2(\partial x_2^*/\partial w_1) \equiv 0$. Hence, the expression in parentheses vanishes, leaving

$$\frac{\partial \text{AC}}{\partial w_1} = \frac{x_i^*}{y} > 0$$

In general, by similar reasoning

$$\frac{\partial \text{AC}}{\partial w_i} = \frac{x_i^*}{y} \qquad i = 1, \ldots, n \tag{8-65}$$

for firms with any number of factors. For positive input and output levels (the only relevant ones), therefore, average cost must move in the same direction as factor prices.

Equation (8-65) is intuitively sensible from the definition of AC directly. Average cost is a linear function of the w_i's: $\text{AC} = (x_1^*/y)w_1 + (x_2^*/y)w_2$. If w_1 changes to $w_1 + \Delta w_1$, at the margin, the change in AC will just be the multiple of $w_1, (x_1^*/y)$, that is, $(x_1^*/y)\Delta w_1$. For finite movements, x_1^*/y and x_2^*/y also change, but *at the margin*, the instantaneous rate of change of AC is simply x_1^*/y (before x_1^* can change).

This is actually another simple application of the envelope theorem. Since $\text{AC} = C^*/y$,

$$\frac{\partial \text{AC}}{\partial w_1} = \frac{1}{y}\frac{\partial C^*}{\partial w_1}$$

However, by the envelope theorem, recalling the Lagrangian $\mathscr{L}' = w_1 x_1 + w_2 x_2 + \lambda(y - f(x_1, x_2))$,

$$\frac{\partial C^*}{\partial w_1} = \frac{\partial \mathscr{L}}{\partial w_1} = x_1^*$$

Hence

$$\frac{\partial \text{AC}}{\partial w_1} = \frac{x_1^*}{y}$$

8.11 ANALYSIS OF FIRMS IN LONG-RUN COMPETITIVE EQUILIBRIUM

The foregoing analysis can be modified and extended to analyze a well-known situation in economics. Consider a price-taking firm in a competitive industry composed of a large number of identical firms. Suppose also that entry into this industry is very easy, i.e., the costs of entry are low. What will the behavior of firms in this industry be, i.e., how will such firms respond to changes in factor prices or other parameters that might appear? (See also Chap. 6, Prob. 8.)

Under conditions of immediate entry of new firms into an industry in which positive profits appear, output price must immediately be driven down to the point of minimum average cost for all firms. Any response the firm makes to some parameter change must take into account the prospect of instantaneous adjustment of output price to minimum average cost. In this case, profit-maximizing behavior will be equivalent to each firm minimizing its average cost, since at any other point, the firm would cease to exist.

Let us now investigate how the location of the minimum AC point is affected by a change in a factor price. The point of minimum average cost occurs when

$$MC(w_1, w_2, y) = AC(w_1, w_2, y) \qquad (8\text{-}66)$$

The question being asked is, how does the output level y associated with minimum average cost change, when a factor price changes? A functional dependence of y on factor prices w_1, w_2 is being asserted. Where does this functional relationship come from? Equation (8-66) represents an implicit function of y, w_1, and w_2. Assuming the sufficient conditions for the implicit function theorem are valid, (8-66) can be solved for one variable in terms of the remaining two; in particular

$$y = y^*(w_1, w_2) \qquad (8\text{-}67)$$

We can now derive $\partial y^*/\partial w_i$ by implicit differentiation. Substituting (8-67) back into (8-66), one gets the *identity*

$$MC(w_1, w_2, y^*(w_1, w_2)) \equiv AC(w_1, w_2, y^*(w_1, w_2)) \qquad (8\text{-}68)$$

This relation is an identity because output level y is posited to always adjust via Eq. (8-67) to any change in w_1 or w_2 so as to keep the firm at minimum average cost. Differentiating this identity with respect to, say, w_1,

$$\frac{\partial MC}{\partial w_1} + \frac{\partial MC}{\partial y}\frac{\partial y^*}{\partial w_1} \equiv \frac{\partial AC}{\partial w_1} + \frac{\partial AC}{\partial y}\frac{\partial y^*}{\partial w_1}$$

However, at minimum average cost, $\partial AC/\partial y = 0$, from the first-order conditions for a minimum. Hence, solving for $\partial y^*/\partial w_1$

$$\frac{\partial y^*}{\partial w_1} = \frac{1}{\partial MC/\partial y}\left[\frac{\partial AC}{\partial w_1} - \frac{\partial MC}{\partial w_1}\right] \qquad (8\text{-}69)$$

with a similar expression holding for $\partial y^*/\partial w_2$.

Equation (8-69) admits of an easy interpretation. It says that if, say, w_1 increases, the minimum average cost point will shift to the right (i.e., the mini-

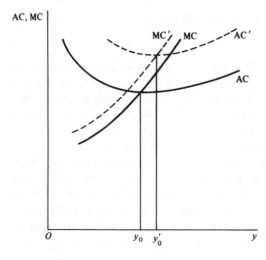

FIGURE 8-13
Shifts in the MC and AC curves when a factor price changes.

mum AC output level will increase) if the AC curve shifts up by more than the marginal cost curve. (Note that we know that $\partial \text{MC}/\partial y > 0$ at minimum AC.) This is geometrically obvious. Consider Fig. 8-13. The marginal cost curve always cuts through the AC curve from below, at the point of minimum average cost. When w_1, say, increases, average cost must shift up by some amount [Eq. (8-65)]. If marginal cost shifts by less than the shift in average cost, the point of minimum average cost will clearly move to the right. And, of course, if marginal cost actually shifts down when w_1 increases (indicating that x_1 is an inferior factor), then the new MC curve must necessarily intersect the new (raised) AC curve to the right of, i.e., at a higher output level than, the old minimum AC point.

Equation (8-69) can be used to relate the output level changes directly to the output elasticities of factor demand. From Eq. (8-65),

$$\frac{\partial \text{AC}}{\partial w_1} = \frac{x_1^*}{y}$$

and from (8-34),

$$\frac{\partial \text{MC}}{\partial w_1} = \frac{\partial x_1^*}{\partial y}$$

Substituting these values into Eq. (8-69),

$$\frac{\partial y^*}{\partial w_1} = \frac{1}{\partial \text{MC}/\partial y} \left(\frac{x_1^*}{y} - \frac{\partial x_1^*}{\partial y} \right)$$

Factoring out x_1^*/y,

$$\frac{\partial y^*}{\partial w_1} = \frac{x_1^*/y}{\partial \text{MC}/\partial y} (1 - \varepsilon_{1y})$$

where $\epsilon_{iy} = (y/x_i)(\partial x_i/\partial y)$ is the output elasticity of factor i, as defined in Eq. (8-52).

The output effects of changing factor prices on firms in long-run competitive equilibrium can be read out of Eqs. (8-69) and (8-70). If a factor price, say, w_1, rises, then if factor 1 is output elastic ($\epsilon_{1y} > 1$), all the firms will wind up producing less output. Minimum average costs (and thus the product price) increase, but the marginal cost curve shifts up even more. Hence, less total output is sold, since the product demand curve is downward-sloping. If factor 1 is output inelastic (but not inferior) ($0 \leq \epsilon_{1y} < 1$), the marginal cost curve will shift up by less than the average curve, since by Eq. (8-70), $\partial y^*/\partial w_1 > 0$. Finally, if factor 1 is inferior ($\epsilon_{1y} < 0$), then the marginal cost curve shifts *down* when w_1 increases, average cost still shifts upward, and hence $\partial y^*/\partial w_1 > 0$.

Analysis of Factor Demands in the Long Run

The combined effects of profit maximization and entry or exit of new firms leads firms to *de facto* pursue a strategy of average cost minimization. We can thus investigate the behavior of firms in the long run by explicitly considering the comparative statics implications of the model

minimize

$$\text{AC} = \frac{w_1 x_1 + w_2 x_2}{f(x_1, x_2)} \tag{8-71}$$

Denote the factor demands implied by this model $x_i^L(w_1, w_2)$, $i = 1, 2$. Since output price p is endogenous, the factor demands are functions only of the factor prices. The average cost function, $\text{AC}^*(w_1, w_2)$, is the indirect objective function associated with this model. This model can be analyzed using the traditional methods of comparative statics (see Chap. 6, Prob. 8; we shall do it here using duality theory). Consider Fig. 8-14, in which AC is plotted vertically against w_1. For given values of w_1 and w_2, say, w_1^0 and w_2^0, certain factor usages are implied: $x_1^0 = x_1^L(w_1, w_2), x_2^0 = x_2^L(w_1, w_2)$. Also, $y^0 = f(x_1^0, x_2^0)$. Holding x_1, x_2, and w_2 constant at these values, the restricted average cost function $\text{AC} = (w_1 x_1^0 + w_2^0 x_2^0)/y^0$ is a straight line with positive slope x_1^0/y^0. The *minimum* AC, $\text{AC}^*(w_1, w_2^0)$ must in general lie below this line, by definition of a minimum. However, when $w_1 = w_1^0$, exactly the correct (i.e., average cost minimizing) levels of x_1 and x_2 are used, hence $\text{AC}^* = \text{AC}$ at that point, and $\text{AC}^* \leq \text{AC}$ to both sides of w_1^0. It is clear geometrically that AC^* is concave in w_1. (We leave it as an exercise to prove algebraically, using the primal-dual methods of Chap. 7, that AC^* is in general concave in all factor prices.) We therefore have the following "envelope" results:

$$\text{AC}^*_{w_1} = \frac{x_1^L}{y^L} \tag{8-72}$$

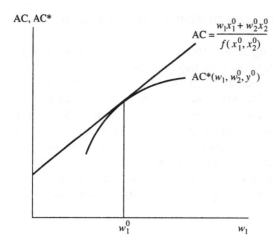

AC, AC*

$$AC = \frac{w_1 x_1^0 + w_2^0 x_2^0}{f(x_1^0, x_2^0)}$$

$AC^*(w_1, w_2^0, y^0)$

w_1^0

w_1

FIGURE 8-14
Concavity of the Long-Run Average Cost Function. The constrained AC function, in which all variables except w_1 are constant, is linear in w_1, with slope x_1^0/y^0. At w_1^0, the "correct" values of x_1 and x_2 are used; for $w_1 \neq w_1^0$, other than the average-cost minimizing values are used. Thus, $AC^* = AC$ at w_1^0, and $AC^* < AC$ to both sides of w_1^0. Since AC is linear in w_1, AC^* must be concave in w_1 and, by symmetry, in w_2 also. Therefore, $AC^*_{w_1} = x_1^*/y^*$; $AC^*_{w_1 w_1} = \partial(x_1^*/y^*)/\partial w_1 \leq 0$.

$$AC^*_{w_1 w_1} = \frac{\partial(x_1^L/y^L)}{\partial w_1} \leq 0 \tag{8-73}$$

In this model, the factor demands x_i^L are *not* the first partials of the indirect objective function; therefore, refutable comparative statics relations are not forthcoming with regard to these factor demands. However, the ratios of the factor inputs to output (the "relative" inputs) *are* such first partials; concavity of the indirect objective function therefore yields refutable implications for these relative input functions, as shown by Eq. (8-73). Using the quotient rule, we get

$$\frac{w_1}{x_1^L} \frac{\partial x_1^L}{\partial w_1} \leq \frac{w_1}{y^L} \frac{\partial y^L}{\partial w_1} \tag{8-74}$$

If, say, the price of factor 1 increases, the percent change in the use of factor 1 must be less than the resulting long-run percent change in the output of the firm. However, that output effect is not necessarily negative; thus negatively sloping long-run factor demands are not implied for competitive firms in the long run.

We can again gain greater insights into these matters by using a conditional demand procedure to analyze the relationship between the demand for factors in the short and long run. In the short run, output price is parametric; we have denoted it with the symbol p. In the long run, entry and exit of firms into an industry drives the price down to the minimum average cost of the marginal firm. If all firms are identical, except perhaps for scale, i.e., they all have the same minimum average cost level, competition will force the price down to this minimum average cost level. Instead of being parametric, output price will be determined by the equation $p = \min AC^*(w_1, w_2)$. The fundamental identity relating the short- and long-run demands is, therefore, for factor 1,

$$x_1^L(w_1, w_2) \equiv x_1^p(w_1, w_2, p^*(w_1, w_2)) \tag{8-75}$$

where $p^*(w_1, w_2)$ is simply AC*. Differentiating with respect to w_1,

$$\frac{\partial x_1^L}{\partial w_1} \equiv \frac{\partial x_1^p}{\partial w_1} + \frac{\partial x_1^p}{\partial p}\frac{\partial p^*}{\partial w_1} \tag{8-76}$$

Using the envelope theorem, $\partial p^*/\partial w_1 = x_1/y$; also, for the standard (short-run) profit maximization model, we have $\partial x_1^p/\partial p = (\partial x_1^y/\partial y)(\partial y^*/\partial p)$. Thus, (8-76) can be written

$$\frac{\partial x_1^L}{\partial w_1} \equiv \frac{\partial x_1^p}{\partial w_1} + \frac{x_1}{y}\frac{\partial x_1^y}{\partial y}\frac{\partial y^*}{\partial p} \tag{8-77}$$

We know that $\partial x_1^p/\partial w_1 < 0$ and $\partial y^*/\partial p > 0$; x_1 and y are assumed positive. Therefore, if x_1 is a normal factor, that is, $\partial x_1^y/\partial y > 0$, $\partial x_1^L/\partial w_1$ must be less negative than $\partial x_1^p/\partial w_1$. Moreover, it is possible that the second term on the right-hand side of (8-77) might be absolutely larger than the first term; in that case the long-run curve would have a positive slope.

Do not misinterpret this result—this is a compound effect. If, say, w_1 increases, the firm will hire less x_1 in the short run. However, this increase in w_1 causes the minimum level of average cost, and thus output price, to rise as well. The firm may expand in response to this. If the firm becomes sufficiently larger after the factor price increase, this "expansion effect" might outweigh the short-run response to contract the use of x_1. However, *this is a description of the response of a single firm.* Since output price has increased, then assuming a downward-sloping *industry* demand curve, less total output is demanded. On the industry level, therefore, less x_1 will be hired, in accordance with the law of demand, but this might occur via the mechanism of many fewer firms each hiring more of that factor than prior to the factor price increase. (Curiously, the increase in w_1 and thus p can actually lead to *entry* of firms, each much smaller than the previous ones!)

PROBLEMS

1. Explain why cost functions are not just technological data. Why does cost depend on the objectives of the firm and the system of laws under which the firm operates?
2. Are convex (to the origin) isoquants postulated because of empirical reasons or because they make the second-order conditions for constrained cost minimization valid for interior solutions?
3. What is the difference between the factor demand curves obtained in this chapter, i.e. from cost minimization, and those obtained earlier from the profit maximization model? What observable (in principle) differences are there between the two?
4. Discuss the relationships between the following definitions of complementary factors:
   (i) $f_{ij} > 0$
   (ii) $(\partial x_i/\partial w_i)_{w_i,p} < 0$
   (iii) $(\partial x_i/\partial w_j)_{w_i,y} < 0$
   where $f(x_1, x_2)$ is a production function for a competitive firm, and where the parameters outside the parentheses indicate that those parameters are to be held constant.
5. Consider the profit-maximizing firm with two inputs. This model can be treated as the *constrained* maximum problem,

maximize

$$py - w_1x_1 - w_2x_2$$

subject to

$$y = f(x_1, x_2)$$

Using the Lagrangian

$$\mathcal{L} = py - w_1x_1 - w_2x_2 + \lambda[f(x_1, x_2) - y]$$

(a) Show that if the profit maximum is conceived to be achieved in two steps: first hold y constant and maximize over x_1 and x_2 (as functions of y), and then maximize over the variable y, the model can be stated as

$$\mathcal{L} = \max_y \left(py - \min_{x_1, x_2}\{(w_1x_1 + w_2x_2) + \lambda[y - f(x_1, x_2)]\} \right)$$

(b) Show, therefore, that profit maximization implies cost minimization at the profit-maximizing level of output.

(c) Derive the comparative statics of this model treating y, x_1, and x_2 as independent variables subject to a constraint. Note that the reciprocity condition $\partial y^*/\partial w_i = -\partial x_i^*/\partial p$ and the supply slope $\partial y^*/\partial p > 0$ are more easily derived than in the original unconstrained format.

6. Consider the production function $y = x_1^{\alpha_1}x_2^{\alpha_2}$. Show that the constant-output factor demand functions have the form

$$x_i^* = k_i w_i^{-\alpha_j/(\alpha_1 + \alpha_2)} w_j^{\alpha_j/(\alpha_1 + \alpha_2)} y^{1/(\alpha_1 + \alpha_2)} \qquad i \neq j$$

Show that the cost function has the form

$$C^* = (k_1 + k_2) w_1^{\alpha_1/(\alpha_1 + \alpha_2)} w_2^{\alpha_2/(\alpha_1 + \alpha_2)} y^{1/(\alpha_1 + \alpha_2)}$$

and that $\partial C^*/\partial w_i \neq x_i^*$.

7. Suppose a production function $y = f(L, K)$ is linear homogeneous.
   (a) Show that

$$f_{LL}L + f_{LK}K \equiv 0$$

$$f_{KL}L + f_{KK}K \equiv 0$$

   (b) Show that

$$f_{LL}L^2 = f_{KK}K^2$$

   (c) If the law of diminishing returns applies to both factors, show that the factors are technical complements; i.e., the marginal product of either factor rises when more of the other factor is applied.

   (d) Show that if the marginal products are positive, the isoquants must be downward-sloping.

   (e) Show that

$$H = -\lambda \begin{vmatrix} f_{LL} & f_{LK} & f_L \\ f_{KL} & f_{KK} & f_K \\ f_L & f_K & 0 \end{vmatrix}$$

where H is defined as in Eq. (8-14), and λ is marginal cost.

(f) Show that $H = \lambda(y^2/K^2)f_{LL} = \lambda(y^2/L^2)f_{KK}$ if $f(L,K)$ is homogeneous of degree one. Show, therefore, that there can be no "stage I" or "stage III" of the production process if the isoquants are convex to the origin.

8. Derive an expression analogous to Eq. (8-44) for the cross-effects $\partial x_i*/\partial w_j$ and $\partial x_i^s/\partial w_j, i \neq j$. Show that if x_i and x_j are either both substitutes or both complements to x_n, then $\partial x_i^*/\partial w_j \leq \partial x_i^s/\partial w_j$.

9. Derive an expression analogous to Eq. (8-49) showing the relationship between the profit-maximizing and cost-minimizing cross-effects $\partial x_i^p/\partial w_j$ and $\partial x_i^y/\partial w_j, i \neq j$. If x_i and x_j are both normal factors, which cross-effect is larger? Can these short- and long-run cross-effects have different signs?

SELECTED REFERENCES

Alchian, A. A.:"Costs and Outputs," in M. Abramovitz (ed.), *The Allocation of Economic Resources,* Stanford University Press, Stanford, 1959.

Allen, R. G. D.: *Mathematical Economics,* MacMillan & Co., Ltd., London, 1956.

Coase, R. H.: "The Nature of the Firm," *Economica,* (N.S.), **4**:331–351, 1937. Reprinted in American Economic Association, *Readings in Price Theory,* Richard D. Irwin, Chicago, 1952.

Fuss, M., and D. McFadden.: *Production Economics: A Dual Approach to Theory and Applications,* North Holland, Amsterdam, 1978.

Hicks, J. R.: *Value and Capital,* 2d ed., Clarendon Press, Oxford, 1946.

Samuelson, Paul A.: *Foundations of Economic Analysis,* Harvard University Press, Cambridge, Ma., 1947.

Shephard, Ronald W.: *Cost and Production Functions,* Princeton University Press, Princeton NJ, 1953; also the revised version of this book which has become a classic, *The Theory of Cost and Production Functions,* Princeton University Press, Princeton, NJ., 1970.

CHAPTER
9

COST AND PRODUCTION FUNCTIONS: SPECIAL TOPICS

9.1 HOMOGENEOUS AND HOMOTHETIC PRODUCTION FUNCTIONS[†]

An interesting and important class of production functions is the homothetic production functions, of which the homogeneous functions are a subset. A production function is homogeneous of degree r if when all inputs are increased (decreased) by the same proportion, output increases (decreases) by the rth power of that increase. Formally, if $f(x_1, \ldots, x_n)$ is homogeneous of degree r,

$$f(tx_1, \ldots, tx_n) \equiv t^r f(x_1, \ldots, x_n)$$

Several properties of homogeneous functions in general were noted in an earlier chapter, especially Euler's theorem, already used extensively in other contexts. In addition, the geometric property that

$$\frac{f_i(tx_1, \ldots, tx_n)}{f_j(tx_1, \ldots, tx_n)} \equiv \frac{f_i(x_1, \ldots, x_n)}{f_j(x_1, \ldots, x_n)}$$

[†]The student may wish to review the sections in Chap. 3 on homogeneity.

i.e., that the slopes of the level curves are the same along every point of a given ray out of the origin, was proved using the homogeneity of degree $r - 1$ of the first partials f_i and f_j.

However, homogeneous functions are not the only functions with this geometric property. Consider any monotonic transformation $F(z)$ of a homogeneous production function $z = f(x_1, \ldots, x_n)$. That is, consider $y = H(x_1, \ldots, x_n) = F(f(x_1, \ldots, x_n))$, where $F'(z) > 0$. The requirement $F'(z) > 0$ ensures that z and y move in the same direction; e.g., when z increases, y must increase. The slope of a level curve $H(x_1, \ldots, x_n) = y$ in the $x_i x_j$ plane is

$$\frac{H_i}{H_j} = \frac{F'(z)f_i}{F'(z)f_j} = \frac{f_i}{f_j}$$

But we already know that f_i/f_j is invariant under a radial expansion. Hence the function $H(x_1, \ldots, x_n) = F(f(x_1, \ldots, x_n))$ also exhibits this property.

The class of functions $y = H(x_1, \ldots, x_n) = F(f(x_1, \ldots, x_n))$ where $F' \neq 0$ and $f(x_1, \ldots, x_n)$ is a homogeneous function is called the *homothetic functions*. In fact, no generality is lost if $f(x_1, \ldots, x_n)$ is restricted to *linear homogeneous functions*, i.e., functions homogeneous of degree 1. The reason is that if $f(x_1, \ldots, x_n)$ is homogeneous of degree r, then $[f(x_1, \ldots, x_n)]^{1/r}$ is homogeneous of degree 1:

$$[f(tx_1, \ldots, tx_n)]^{1/r} \equiv [t^r f(x_1, \ldots, x_n)]^{1/r} \equiv t[f(x_1, \ldots, x_n)]^{1/r}$$

Taking the rth root of f can be incorporated into the monotonic transformation $y = F(z)$. That is, $F(z)$ can be itself thought of as a composite function, the first part of which is taking the rth root of $f(x_1, \ldots, x_n)$ and the second part whatever transformation yields $H(x_1, \ldots, x_n)$. Hence we can define as the class of homothetic functions all functions $H(x_1, \ldots, x_n) \equiv F(f(x_1, \ldots, x_n))$ where $f(x_1, \ldots, x_n)$ is homogeneous of degree 1 and $F' \neq 0$.

The statement that the slopes of the level curves are invariant under radial expansion or contraction of the original point, i.e., when $x_1, \ldots, x_n$ is replaced by $tx_1, \ldots, tx_n$, can be expressed another way. The slope of the level curve (surface) at any point is H_i/H_j. This is just another function of the x_i's; that is, define

$$\frac{H_i}{H_j} \equiv h_{ij}(x_1, \ldots, x_n)$$

The function $h_{ij}(x_1, \ldots, x_n)$ designates the (negative) slope of the level surface of H in the $x_i x_j$ plane. This slope is unchanged under $x_1, \ldots, x_n \to tx_1, \ldots, tx_n$. But this is simply a statement that $h_{ij}(x_1, \ldots, x_n)$ is homogeneous of degree zero, that is, that $h_{ij}(tx_1, \ldots, tx_n) \equiv h_{ij}(x_1, \ldots, x_n)$. It can in fact be shown by more advanced methods that homotheticity can be defined in this manner also; i.e., if $h_{ij}(x_1, \ldots, x_n)$ is homogeneous of degree zero for all $x_i x_j$ planes, then $H(x_1, \ldots, x_n)$ must have the form $H(x_1, \ldots, x_n) \equiv F(f(x_1, \ldots, x_n))$, where $f(x_1, \ldots, x_n)$ is homogeneous of degree 1 and $F' \neq 0$.

Example. Consider the production function $y = H(x_1, x_2) = x_1 x_2 + x_1^2 x_2^2$. This function is not homogeneous, as can readily be verified. It is homothetic, however, since $H(x_1, x_2) \equiv z + z^2$, where $z = x_1 x_2$. That is, $H(x_1, x_2) \equiv F(f(x_1, x_2))$, where $F(z) = z + z^2$. Note that $F'(z) = 1 + 2z \neq 0$, since production is presumed to be nonnegative. The slope of a level curve of $H(x_1, x_2)$ is

$$-\frac{H_1}{H_2} = -\frac{x_2 + 2x_1 x_2^2}{x_1 + 2x_1^2 x_2}$$

$$= -\frac{x_2(1 + 2x_1 x_2)}{x_1(1 + 2x_1 x_2)} = -\frac{x_2}{x_1}$$

Note that $F'(z) = 1 + 2x_1 x_2$ appears in the numerator and denominator. Hence, $H_1/H_2 = h_{12}(x_1, x_2) = x_2/x_1$. The function h_{12} is clearly homogeneous of degree zero: $h_{12}(tx_1, tx_2) \equiv tx_2/tx_1 \equiv x_2/x_1 \equiv h_{12}(x_1, x_2)$. Thus, the level curves of $x_1 x_2 + x_1^2 x_2^2$ have the same slope at all points along any given ray out of the origin.

Still another way to express homotheticity is to state that the output elasticities for all factors are equal at any given point. That is, $\varepsilon_{1y} = \varepsilon_{2y} = \cdots = \varepsilon_{ny}$. This is clear from the geometry of straight-line expansion paths. Consider Fig. 9-1. Any increase, say, in output from y to y' will result in a new tangency point B along a straight line through the origin and the former tangency point A. The triangles OAx_1^0 and $OB(tx_1^0)$ are similar; hence, x_1 increases by $OB/OA \equiv t$. But, clearly, x_2 increases by $OB/OA \equiv t$ also, for the same reason. Hence for homothetic production functions, output elasticities are equal in all factors.

This result can be shown algebraically by noting that a straight-line expansion path implies that the ratio x_j/x_i, the slope of the ray out to that point in the $x_i x_j$ plane, is the same for any output level as long as factor prices are held constant. That is,

$$\frac{\partial(x_j^*/x_i^*)}{\partial y} \equiv 0$$

Using the quotient rule and multiplying through by x_i^2 yields

$$x_i^* \frac{\partial x_j^*}{\partial y} - x_j^* \frac{\partial x_i^*}{\partial y} \equiv 0$$

After multiplication by y and division by $x_i^* x_j^*$ this leads to

$$\frac{y}{x_j^*} \frac{\partial x_j^*}{\partial y} \equiv \frac{y}{x_i^*} \frac{\partial x_i^*}{\partial y}$$

or

$$\varepsilon_{jy} \equiv \varepsilon_{iy} \quad i, j = 1, \ldots, n \tag{9-1}$$

The value of this common output elasticity can be found by applying Eq. (8-63). Since $\varepsilon_{iy} = \varepsilon_{jy} = \varepsilon_y$, say, this constant can be removed from the

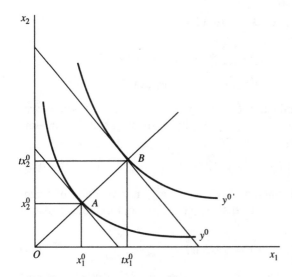

FIGURE 9-1
Homothetic production functions. The level curves of homothetic production functions are all radial expansions of one another; i.e., at the intersections of any ray out of the origin and the level curves, the slopes are all the same. Put another way, if output is increased autonomously, i.e., holding factor prices constant, the new tangency point will lie along the ray projecting the old tangency point from the origin. By similar triangles, it is clear that x_1 increases in the same proportion t as x_2 does when y is increased.

summation, yielding

$$\varepsilon_y \sum \kappa'_i = 1$$

However,

$$\sum \kappa'_i = \frac{\sum w_i x_i}{(MC)y} = \frac{AC}{MC}$$

Thus

$$\varepsilon_y = \frac{MC}{AC} \tag{9-2}$$

The common value of output elasticity, for homothetic functions, is the ratio of marginal to average cost. Therefore, for firms with increasing average costs, the factors are all output elastic; that is, $\varepsilon_y = \varepsilon_{iy} > 1$ for all factors; for firms with declining (average) cost, factors are all output inelastic. Also, if the firm is at the minimum point of its AC curve, the output elasticities of its factors are all unity if the production function is homothetic.

9.2 THE COST FUNCTION: FURTHER PROPERTIES

We have already shown that $C^*(w_1, w_2, y)$ is homogeneous of degree 1 in w_1 and w_2, or, more generally, for the n-factor firm, $C^*(w_1, \ldots, w_n, y)$ is homogeneous of degree 1 in $w_1, \ldots, w_n$. Again, since $C^* = \sum w_i x_i^*(w_1, \ldots, w_n, y)$, and since the $x_i^*(w_1, \ldots, w_n, y)$'s are homogeneous of degree zero in $w_1, \ldots, w_n$,

$$C^*(tw_1, \ldots, tw_n, y) \equiv \sum tw_i x_i^*(tw_1, \ldots tw_n, y)$$

$$\equiv t \sum w_i x_i^*(w_1, \ldots, w_n, y)$$

$$\equiv tC^*(w_1, \ldots, w_n, y)$$

Suppose in addition that the production function $y = f(x_1, \ldots, x_n)$ is homogeneous of some degree $r > 0$ in $x_1, \ldots, x_n$. In this case, we shall demonstrate that the cost function can be partitioned into

$$C^*(w_1, \ldots, w_n, y) \equiv y^{1/r} A(w_1, \ldots, w_n) \tag{9-3}$$

where it is to be noted that the function $A(w_1, \ldots, w_n)$ is a function of factor prices only. In the case where $r = 1$, that is, $f(x_1 \ldots, x_n)$ exhibits constant returns to scale,

$$C^*(w_1, \ldots, w_n, y) \equiv y\,AC(w_1, \ldots, w_n) \tag{9-4}$$

where $A(w_1, \ldots, w_n)$ becomes the average cost function AC. But average cost AC $(w_1, \ldots, w_n)$ is a function of factor prices only, i.e., independent of output level. This is of course as it must be; if a firm exhibits constant returns to scale, AC = MC = constant, i.e., a function of factor prices only at every level of output.

We shall prove some of these results for the case of differentiable functions. For simplicity, we shall deal with functions of only two variables, i.e., the two-factor case. The generalizations to n factors are straightforward and are left as exercises for the student. Remember, as always, that y is a parameter in the cost minimization model.

Equation (9-3) is intuitively plausible. Consider Fig. 9-2. Suppose the firm is initially at point $\mathbf{x}^0$ utilizing inputs $\mathbf{x}^0 = (x_1^0, x_2^0)$. Some level of cost $C(\mathbf{x}^0)$ would exist. Suppose now both inputs were doubled, to $(2x_1^0, 2x_2^0) = \mathbf{x}^1$. Then since the production function is homothetic (indeed, homogeneous), the new cost-minimizing tangency will lie on a ray from the origin extending past the original point $\mathbf{x}^0$ to point $\mathbf{x}^1$ at twice the input levels. At $\mathbf{x}^1$, the cost $C(\mathbf{x}^1)$ is clearly twice $C(\mathbf{x}^0)$ since both inputs have exactly doubled while factor prices remain the same. Hence, $C(\mathbf{x}^1) = 2\,C(\mathbf{x}^0)$. However, y^0, output at $\mathbf{x}^0$, has grown only to $2^{1/2}y^0 = \sqrt{2y^0}$, since the production function is homogeneous of degree 1/2. This means that, holding factor prices constant, cost and output are related in the proportion $C = Ay^2$, since a doubling, say, of cost is accompanied by an increase of output of the factors of $\sqrt{2}$. The proportionality constant A, in fact, must be dependent on factor prices; that is, $A = A(w_1, w_2)$. For a different slope of the isocost line, the proportionality constant will be different; however, cost and output will still have the general relation (9-3).

The preceding reasoning cannot be applied to general nonhomogeneous functions. (It can be applied in a more complicated fashion, and we shall do so, to general homothetic functions.) If the production function is nonhomothetic, a given increase in output is not related to a simple proportionate expansion of

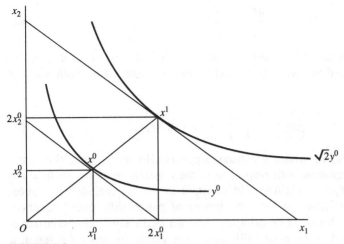

FIGURE 9-2

A production function homogeneous of degree 1/2. When input levels x_1^0, x_2^0 are doubled, say, output increases by the factor $2^{1/2} = \sqrt{2}$. However, since $C = w_1 x_1 + w_2 x_2$, cost doubles; that is, $C(x^0) = \frac{1}{2}C(x^1)$. This means that a doubling of cost is accompanied by a $\sqrt{2}$-fold increase in y, that is, cost and output are related as $C = Ay^2$. The constant of proportionality is constant only in that it does not involve y output. It *is* a function of factor prices; that is, $A = A(w_1, w_2)$.

all inputs. Instead, the ratios of one factor to another will change. Hence, the cost function will necessarily be a more complicated function than (9-3), wherein factor prices and output are all mixed together and not separable into two parts, one related to output and the other to factor prices.

In proving (9-3), we shall use the following relationship, already discussed in the first discussion of interpreting λ, the Lagrange multiplier of the constrained cost minimization problem, as marginal cost. Since $C^* \equiv w_1 x_1^* + w_2 x_2^*$, then since $w_1 = \lambda^* f_1$, $w_2 = \lambda^* f_2$,

$$C^* \equiv \lambda^*(f_1 x_1^* + f_2 x_2^*)$$

However, for homogeneous functions, $f_1 x_1 + f_2 x_2 \equiv ry$, where r is the degree of homogeneity. Hence for homogeneous functions,

$$C^* \equiv \lambda^* ry \tag{9-5a}$$

or

$$\frac{C^*}{y} \equiv r \frac{\partial C^*}{\partial y} \tag{9-5b}$$

The question now is: What general functional form $C^*(w_1, w_2, y)$ has the property of obeying Eqs. (9-5), which says that average cost C^*/y is proportional to marginal cost, the factor of proportionality being the constant r. This question is answered by integrating the partial differential Eq. (9-5).

Rearranging the terms in (9-5b) yields

$$\frac{\partial C^*}{C^*} \equiv \frac{1}{r}\frac{\partial y}{y} \tag{9-6}$$

The differential notation ∂C^* is used rather than dC^* to remind us that in that differentiation, w_1 and w_2 were being held constant. Integrating both sides of (9-6) gives

$$\int \frac{\partial C^*}{C^*} \equiv \frac{1}{r}\left(\int \frac{\partial y}{y}\right) + K(w_1, w_2) \tag{9-7}$$

As in all integrations, an arbitrary constant appears. However, since this was a *partial* differential equation with respect to y, the constant term can include any arbitrary function of the variables held constant in the original differentiation, i.e., the factor prices here. In fact, the theory of partial differential equations assures us that the inclusion of an arbitrary function in the integration constant of the variable held fixed in the partial differentiation yields the general solution to the partial differential equation.

Performing the indicated integration in Eq. (9-7) yields

$$\log C^* = \frac{1}{r} \log y + \log A(w_1, w_2) \tag{9-8}$$

Here, we have written the constant term $K(w_1, w_2)$ as $\log A(w_1, w_2)$. There is no loss of generality involved, since any real number is the logarithm of some positive number. This manipulation, however, permits us to rewrite (9-8) as

$$\log C^* \equiv \log [y^{(1/r)}A(w_1, w_2)] \tag{9-9}$$

since the logarithm of a product is the sum of the individual logarithms, and $\log a^b \equiv b \log a$. Since the logarithms (9-8) and (9-9) are equal (identical, in fact), their antilogarithms are equal, i.e.,

$$C^* \equiv y^{(1/r)}A(w_1, w_2) \tag{9-10}$$

which was to be proved.

That (9-10) is a solution of the partial differential Eq. (9-5) can be seen by substitution:

$$\lambda^* = \frac{\partial C^*}{\partial y} = \frac{1}{r}y^{[(1/r)-1]}A(w_1, w_2)$$

Substituting this into the right-hand side of Eq. (9-5a) yields

$$\frac{1}{r}y^{[(1/r)-1]}Ary \quad \text{or} \quad y^{(1/r)}A$$

But this is identically the left-hand side, C^*. By definition, since the substitution of the form $C^* = y^{(1/r)}A(w_1, w_2)$ into the equation $C^* = \lambda^* ry$ makes that equation an identity, $C^* = y^{(1/r)}A(w_1, w_2)$ is a solution of (9-5). And, it is the most general solution of (9-5) because of the inclusion of the arbitrary *function* $A(w_1, w_2)$ as the constant of integration. It is also clear that the integration constant must be positive; otherwise positive outputs would be associated with imaginary (involving $\sqrt{-1}$) costs.

To recapitulate, what has been shown is that if the production function is homogeneous of any degree r ($r > 0$), then costs, output, and factor prices are related in the multiplicatively separable fashion $C^* = y^{(1/r)}A(w_1, w_2)$. Equivalently, for homogeneous production functions, average costs are always proportional to marginal costs, the factor of proportionality being the degree of homogeneity r; that is, $C^*/y \equiv r\partial C^*/\partial y$.

Either Eq. (9-5) or (9-10) can be used to show the relationship of the degree of homogeneity to the slope of the marginal and average cost functions. From (9-10),

$$\text{MC} = \frac{\partial C^*}{\partial y} = \frac{1}{r}y^{[(1/r)-1]}A(w_1, w_2)$$

and thus

$$\frac{\partial \text{MC}}{\partial y} = \frac{1}{r}\left(\frac{1}{r} - 1\right)y^{[(1/r)-2]}A(w_1, w_2)$$

By inspection, if $r < 1$, $\partial \text{MC}/\partial y > 0$; that is, for a homogeneous production function exhibiting decreasing returns to scale, marginal costs (not surprisingly) are always increasing. Similarly, if $r > 1$, $\partial \text{MC}/\partial y < 0$; that is, falling marginal costs are associated with homogeneous production functions exhibiting increasing returns to scale. Lastly, if $r = 1$, the constant-returns-to-scale case, marginal cost is constant and equal to $A(w_1, w_2)$ for all levels of output.

Alternatively, from (9-5b), if $r > 1$, say, AC > MC. Since marginal cost is always below average cost, AC must always be falling, with similar reasoning holding for $r < 1$ and $r = 1$. Also, differentiating (9-5a) partially with respect to y yields

$$\frac{\partial C^*}{\partial y} \equiv \lambda^* \equiv r\left(\lambda^* + y\frac{\partial \lambda^*}{\partial y}\right)$$

Solving for $\partial \lambda^*/\partial y$, that is, $\partial \text{MC}/\partial y$, gives

$$\frac{\partial \text{MC}}{\partial y} \equiv \frac{1}{ry}\text{MC}(1 - r) \tag{9-11}$$

from which the preceding results can be read directly.

Homothetic Functions

Let us now consider the functional form of the cost function associated with the general class of homothetic production functions, $y = F(f(x_1, x_2))$, where $f(x_1, x_2)$ is homogeneous of degree 1, and $F'(z) > 0$, where $z = f(x_1, x_2)$. Proceeding as before, we have

$$C^* \equiv w_1 x_1^* + w_2 x_2^*$$
$$\equiv \lambda^*(F'(z)f_1)x_1^* + \lambda^*(F'(z)f_2)x_2^*$$
$$\equiv \lambda^* F'(z)(f_1 x_1^* + f_2 x_2^*)$$

or

$$C^* \equiv \lambda^* F'(z)z \qquad\qquad (9\text{-}12)$$

using Euler's theorem. Now y is a monotonic transformation of z; that is, $F'(z) > 0$. This means that if z were plotted against y, the resulting curve would always be upward-sloping. Under these conditions, a unique value of z will be associated with any value of y; that is, the function $y = F(z)$ is "invertible" to $z = F^{-1}(y)$. The situation is the same as expressing demand curves as $p = p(x)$ (price as a function of quantity) instead of the more common $x = x(p)$ (quantity as a function of price). Thus we can write

$$C^* \equiv \lambda^* F'(F^{-1}(y))[F^{-1}(y)]$$

or, combining all the separate functions of y,

$$C^* \equiv \lambda^* G(y) \qquad\qquad (9\text{-}13)$$

That is, for homothetic functions, the cost function can be written as marginal cost times some function of y only, $G(y)$. If the homothetic function were in fact homogeneous of some degree r, then $G(y) = ry$, a particularly simple form, as indicated in Eq. (9-5a). As before, the question is: What general functional form of $C^*(w_1, w_2, y)$ satisfies the partial differential Eq. (9-13)? That is, what restrictions on the form of $C^*(w_1, w_2, y)$ are imposed by the structure (9-13)?

This question is answered as before by integrating the differential Eq. (9-13). Separating the y terms and remembering that $\lambda^* = \partial C^*/\partial y$, we have

$$\frac{\partial C^*}{C^*} \equiv \frac{\partial y}{G(y)} \qquad\qquad (9\text{-}14)$$

The critical thing to notice about (9-14) is that the right-hand side is a function of y only. We shall assume that some integral function of $1/G(y)$ exists, and we shall designate that integral function as $\log J(y)$. Also, an arbitrary constant of integration must appear, and, as in the homogeneous case, this constant is not really a constant but an arbitrary *function* of the remaining variables, w_1 and w_2, which are treated as constants when the cost function is differentiated partially with respect to y. This constant function will be designated $\log A(w_1, w_2)$. Thus, integrating (9-14) gives

$$\int \frac{\partial C^*}{C^*} \equiv \int \frac{\partial y}{G(y)} + \log A(w_1, w_2)$$

which yields

$$\log C^* \equiv \log J(y) + \log A(w_1, w_2)$$

Using the rules of logarithms and taking antilogarithms, we have

$$C^* \equiv J(y)A(w_1, w_2) \tag{9-15}$$

What Eq. (9-15) says is that for homothetic productions, the cost function can be written as the product of two functions: a function of output y and another function of factors prices only. $C^*(w_1, w_2, y)$ is said to be multiplicately separable in y and the factor prices.

That C^* should have this form is entirely reasonable. Recall that a homothetic function is simply a monotonic function of a linear homogeneous function. It is as if the isoquants of a linear homogeneous (constant-returns-to-scale) production function were relabeled through some technological transformation, represented by $F(z)$. But it is only a transformation of output values, not a change in the shapes of the isoquants themselves. Since the cost function for a linear homogeneous production function can be written $C^* = yA(w_1, w_2)$, and one gets a homothetic function by operating on output y alone, not surprisingly the only change induced in the cost function is the replacement of y by some more complicated function of y, designated $J(y)$ in Eq. (9-15).

The correctness of (9-15) as a solution to (9-13) can be checked heuristically as follows. When this form, $C^* = J(y)A(w_1, w_2)$, is substituted into (9-13), the right-hand side must be identically C^*. Performing the indicated operations gives $\lambda^* = J'(y)A(w_1, w_2)$, and thus

$$C^* = J'(y)A(w_1, w_2) \times \text{some function of } y$$

and (9-15) is therefore of the requisite form.

9.3 THE DUALITY OF COST AND PRODUCTION FUNCTIONS

At this juncture let us recapitulate the analysis of production and cost functions. The starting point of the analysis was the assumption of a well-defined quasi-concave production function, i.e., one whose isoquants are convex to the origin. We asserted that the firm would always minimize the total factor cost of producing any given output level, as this was the only postulate consistent with wealth or profit maximization. The first-order conditions of the implied constrained minimization problem were then solved, in principle, for the factor demand relations $x_i = x_i^*(w_1, w_2, y)$, along with the Lagrange multiplier (identified as marginal cost) $\lambda = \lambda^*(w_1, w_2, y)$. The comparative statics relations were developed yielding certain sign restrictions on some of the partial derivatives of the previous demand relations, namely, $\partial x_i^*/\partial w_i < 0$.

These demand relations were then substituted into the expression for total cost, $C = w_1 x_1 + w_2 x_2$, yielding the total cost function

$$C^*(w_1, w_2, y) = w_1 x_1^* + w_2 x_2^*$$

It was shown via the envelope theorem that $\partial C^*/\partial w_i = x_i^*$, $\partial C^*/\partial y = \lambda^*$. Also, certain properties of the cost function regarding homogeneity and functional form were derivable from assumptions about the production function.

We now pose a new question. We have seen how it is possible to derive cost functions from production functions. Is it possible, and if so, how, to derive production functions from cost functions? That is, suppose one were given a cost function that satisfied the properties implied by the usual analysis of production functions. Is it possible to identify with that cost function some unique production function that would generate that cost function? The answer in general is yes; there is, in fact, a duality between production and cost functions: the existence of one implies, for well-behaved functions, the unique existence of the other. We shall now investigate these matters.

A critical step in the construction of the cost function was inverting the solution of the first-order relations $w_i - \lambda f_i = 0$, $y - f(x_1, x_2) = 0$ to obtain the demand relations $x_i = x_i^*(w_1, w_2, y)$. The uniqueness of these solutions is guaranteed by the sufficient second-order conditions for constrained minimum, which in turn guarantees that the Jacobian matrix of the first-order equations, i.e., the cross-partials of the Lagrangian $\mathcal{L}$, has a nonzero determinant. These sufficient second-order conditions also imply that $\partial x_i^*/\partial w_i < 0$, $i = 1, 2$. However, $x_i^* = \partial C^*/\partial w_i$. Hence,

$$\frac{\partial x_i^*}{\partial w_i} = \frac{\partial^2 C^*}{\partial w_i^2} < 0 \tag{9-16}$$

That is, the cost function has the property that the second partials with respect to the factor prices are negative. As was shown in the previous chapter, the cost functions for any well-behaved production function are weakly concave in the factor prices. Again, for the two-factor case, $C^*(w_1, w_2, y)$ is linear homogeneous in w_1, w_2. Thus, as shown earlier in a different manner, since $x_i^*(w_1, w_2, y)$ is a first partial of C^* with respect to a factor price, x_i^* is homogeneous of degree zero in w_1, w_2. Hence by Euler's theorem,

$$\frac{\partial x_1^*}{\partial w_1} w_1 + \frac{\partial x_1^*}{\partial w_2} w_2 \equiv 0$$

Similarly

$$\frac{\partial x_2^*}{\partial w_1} w_1 + \frac{\partial x_2^*}{\partial w_2} w_2 \equiv 0$$

Eliminating w_1 and w_2 (noting that $\partial x_1^*/\partial w_2 = \partial x_2^*/\partial w_1 = C_{12}^*$, $C_{ii}^* = \partial x_i^*/\partial w_i$) reveals that

$$C_{11}^* C_{22}^* - C_{12}^{*2} = 0 \tag{9-17}$$

The determinant of the cross-partials of C^* with respect to the factor prices equals 0. In fact, C^* cannot be strictly concave in w_1 and w_2 because it is linearly homogeneous in w_1 and w_2; that is, radial expansions of w_1 and w_2 produce *linear* expansions of C^*. This result easily generalizes to the case of n factors using the methodology of Chap. 7.

Consider now the problem of constructing a production function from a cost function. Before proceeding, we would check to see whether in fact the given

$C^*(w_1, w_2, y)$ exhibited "weak" concavity in w_1 and w_2 and linear homogeneity in w_1 and w_2. Assume that these conditions are met. Then the implied factor demands are

$$x_1^*(w_1, w_2, y) = \frac{\partial C^*}{\partial w_1}$$

$$x_2^*(w_1, w_2, y) = \frac{\partial C^*}{\partial w_2}$$

However, x_1^* and x_2^* are homogeneous of degree zero in w_1 and w_2; hence they can be written

$$x_1^*(w_1, w_2, y) \equiv x_1^*\left(1, \frac{w_2}{w_1}, y\right) \equiv g_1(w, y)$$

$$x_2^*(w_1, w_2, y) \equiv x_2^*\left(1, \frac{w_2}{w_1}, y\right) \equiv g_2(w, y) \qquad (9\text{-}18)$$

where $w = w_2/w_1$. But (9-18) represents two equations in the four variables x_1, x_2, w, and y. Under the mathematical conditions that the Jacobian of these equations is nonzero, i.e., that

$$J = \begin{vmatrix} g_{1w} & g_{1y} \\ g_{2w} & g_{2y} \end{vmatrix} \neq 0$$

these equations can be used to eliminate the variable w. This will leave one equation in x_1, x_2, and y, say

$$h(x_1, x_2, y) = 0$$

Solving this equation for $y = f(x_1, x_2)$ yields the production function.

How stringent is the assumption that the above Jacobian determinant be nonzero? The partials g_{1w} and g_{2w} are essentially the slopes of the factor demand relations (a reciprocal slope in the case of g_{1w}) with respect to changes in *relative* prices. In particular, using the chain rule leads to

$$\frac{\partial x_1^*}{\partial w_1} = \frac{\partial x_1^*}{\partial w} \frac{\partial w}{\partial w_1} = \frac{\partial g_1}{\partial w}\left(-\frac{w_2}{w_1^2}\right) < 0$$

and hence $g_{1w} = -(w_1^2/w_2)(\partial x_1^*/\partial w_1) > 0$. Similarly,

$$\frac{\partial x_2^*}{\partial w_2} = \frac{\partial x_2^*}{\partial w} \frac{\partial w}{\partial w_2} = g_{2w}\frac{1}{w_1}$$

and hence

$$g_{2w} = w_1 \frac{\partial x_2^*}{\partial w_2^*} < 0$$

If both factors are normal, as would be the case for homothetic production functions, then $g_{1y}, g_{2y} > 0$ and J has the sign pattern

$$\begin{vmatrix} + & + \\ - & + \end{vmatrix} > 0$$

implying that $J > 0$, and thus $J \neq 0$. In the nonhomothetic case, it would be pure coincidence if $J = 0$; hence it is not implausible to assert $J \neq 0$. Hence in general we shall expect to find a unique production function associated with any well-specified cost function. This is not to say that it will be *easy* to find either the production function or the cost function from the other. In general, the equations to be solved, i.e., the first-order relations in the case of deriving the cost functions or Eq. (9-18) in the case of deriving the production function, will be complicated nonlinear functions. But we can be assured that the functions exist, in principle, and that they are unique.

Example. We previously have found the cost function associated with a Cobb-Douglas production function. It had the same multiplicatively separable form. Let us see how Eq. (9-18) can be used to reverse the process. Suppose C^* is given to us or estimated econometrically as

$$C^* = y^k w_1^\alpha w_2^{1-\alpha} \tag{9-19}$$

where $0 < \alpha < 1$ (to ensure that $C_1^* = x_1^* > 0, C_2^* = x_2^* > 0, C_{11}^*, C_{22}^* < 0$) and the exponents of w_1 and w_2 sum to unity (to ensure C^* homogeneous of degree 1 in w_1 and w_2). The parameter k can take on unrestricted positive values. What production function will generate this cost function?

By the envelope theorem (Shephard's lemma) $\partial C^* / \partial w_i = x_i^*$. Hence

$$x_1^* = y^k \alpha w_1^{\alpha-1} w_2^{1-\alpha} = \alpha y^k \left(\frac{w_2}{w_1}\right)^{1-\alpha}$$

Similarly,

$$x_2^* = y^k (1 - \alpha) w_1^\alpha w_2^{-\alpha} = (1 - \alpha) y^k \left(\frac{w_2}{w_1}\right)^{-\alpha}$$

Letting $w = w_2/w_1$, let us eliminate this variable. The asterisks are redundant here and will be dropped to save notational clutter. It will be easiest if we take logarithms of both sides of the equation. Then

$$\log x_1 = \log \alpha + k \log y + (1 - \alpha)\log w$$

$$\log x_2 = \log(1 - \alpha) + k \log y - \alpha \log w$$

Multiply the first equation by α and the second by $1 - \alpha$, and add:

$$\alpha \log x_1 + (1 - \alpha)\log x_2 = \alpha \log \alpha + (1 - \alpha)\log(1 - \alpha) + k \log y$$

or

$$\log x_1^\alpha x_2^{1-\alpha} = \log \alpha^\alpha (1 - \alpha)^{1-\alpha} y^k$$

Taking antilogarithms and rearranging slightly, we get

$$y = K x_1^{\alpha/k} x_2^{(1-\alpha)/k} \tag{9-20}$$

where $K = [1/\alpha^\alpha(1-\alpha)^{1-\alpha}]^{1/k}$. Equation (9-20) is the production function associated with the cost function (9-19). As expected, it is of the Cobb-Douglas, or multiplicatively separable, type, and is homogeneous of degree $1/k$, since C^* was homogeneous of degree k in y.

The Importance of Duality

The duality of cost and production functions is important for reasons other than mathematical elegance. Economists will have occasion to estimate factor demand and cost functions. There are basically two ways to approach this problem. One way is to estimate, by some procedure, the underlying production function for some activity and to then calculate, by inverting the implied first-order relations, the factor demand curves (holding output constant). The cost function can then be calculated also. This, however, is a very arduous procedure. Production functions are largely unobservable. The data points will represent a sampling of input and output levels that will have taken place at different times, as factor or output prices changed. And of what use is knowledge of the production function itself? Largely, it is to derive implications regarding factor usage and cost considerations when various parameters, e.g., factor and output prices, change.

It would seem to make more sense to start with estimating the cost functions or the factor demand curves directly; i.e., some functional form of the cost function could be asserted, say a logarithmic linear function, and costs could be estimated directly. However, this procedure would always be subject to the criticism that the estimated cost or demand functions were beasts without parents, i.e., they were derived from fictitious, or nonexistent, production processes. And that would be a serious criticism indeed.

However, the duality results of the previous sections rescue this simpler approach. We can be assured that if a cost function satisfies some elementary properties, i.e., linear homogeneity and concavity in the factor prices, then there in fact is some real, unique underlying production function. Thus, the cost function will be more plausible.

Moreover, the cost function may be easier to estimate, econometrically, than the production function. The cost function is a function of factor prices and output levels, all of which are potentially observable, possibly easily so. What is more, once estimated, the cost function can be used to derive directly the constant output factor demand curves using the relation $x_i^* = \partial C^*/\partial w_i$. Thus, the simpler approach of estimating cost functions is apt to be more useful than the more complicated procedure of estimating production functions. The duality results assure us that procedure is in fact theoretically sound.

9.4 ELASTICITY OF SUBSTITUTION; THE CONSTANT-ELASTICITY-OF-SUBSTITUTION (CES) PRODUCTION FUNCTION

Neoclassical production theory recognizes the possibility of substituting one factor of production for another. The existence of more than one point on an isoquant is equivalent to such an assertion. However, we have not yet considered any quantitative measurement of the degree to which one factor can in fact be so substituted for another.

Consider a production function with L-shaped isoquants, represented in Fig. 9-3. This function can be written algebraically as $y = \min[(x_1/a_1), (x_2/a_2)]$, where a_1 and a_2 are constants. This function describes an activity for which no effective substitution is possible. For any wage ratio, the cost-minimizing firm will always operate at the elbow of the isoquants. The marginal product of each factor is 0 unless it is combined in a fixed proportion with the other input. (For this reason, this production function is described as one of *fixed coefficients*.)

How shall the degree of substitutability of one factor for another be described? Consider the Cobb-Douglas production function $y = x_1^{\alpha} x_2^{1-\alpha}$, where, say, x_1 is labor and x_2 is capital. A cost-minimizing firm satisfies the first-order conditions of the Lagrangian

$$\mathscr{L} = w_1 x_1 + w_2 x_2 + \lambda(y - (x_1^{\alpha} x_2^{1-\alpha}))$$

or, in this case,

$$w_1 - \lambda \alpha x_1^{\alpha-1} x_2^{1-\alpha} = 0 \qquad (9\text{-}21a)$$

$$w_2 - \lambda(1 - \alpha) x_1^{\alpha} x_2^{-\alpha} = 0 \qquad (9\text{-}21b)$$

$$y - x_1^{\alpha} x_2^{1-\alpha} = 0 \qquad (9\text{-}21c)$$

Upon division, Eqs. (9-21a) and (9-21b) yield

$$\frac{x_2}{x_1} = \frac{(1 - \alpha)w_1}{\alpha w_2} \qquad (9\text{-}22)$$

This expression can also be derived from the constant-output factor demand curves derived earlier:

$$x_1^* = \left(\frac{\alpha}{1 - \alpha}\right)^{1-\alpha} \left(\frac{w_2}{w_1}\right)^{1-\alpha} y \qquad (9\text{-}23a)$$

$$x_2^* = \left(\frac{\alpha}{1 - \alpha}\right)^{-\alpha} \left(\frac{w_2}{w_1}\right)^{-\alpha} y \qquad (9\text{-}23b)$$

Equation (9-22) says that for this production function, the capital-labor ratio is (1) independent of the level of output, and (2) a function only of the *ratio* of the wage rates (rental rate on capital to the labor wage rate). We shall shortly consider the generality of this situation.

We can therefore conceive of the capital-labor ratio as a simple function of the wage ratio. If we let $u = x_2/x_1$, $w = w_2/w_1$ for notational ease, Eq. (9-22) becomes

$$u = \frac{k}{w} \qquad (9\text{-}24)$$

where $k = (1 - \alpha)/\alpha$. How does x_2/x_1 vary when w_2/w_1 varies? From Eq. (9-24),

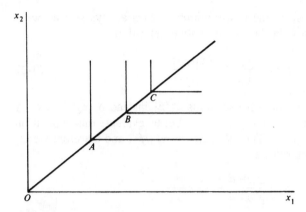

FIGURE 9-3
The fixed-coefficient production function. This production function is given by $y = \min(x_1/a_1, x_2/a_2)$, where a_1 and a_2 are parameters. No substitution among the factors is worthwhile; the marginal products of x_1 or x_2 are 0 at all points except along the corners of the production function. Although extensively used in input-output analysis and short-term forecasting models, it is doubtful that this is a useful way to look at the real world.

$$\frac{du}{dw} = -\frac{k}{w^2} \tag{9-25}$$

where the expression is negative, as expected. Although this actual rate of change in the capital-labor ratio is a measure of substitutability, a more frequent measure is the dimensionless elasticity analog,

$$\sigma = -\frac{du/u}{dw/w} = -\frac{w}{u}\frac{du}{dw} \tag{9-26}$$

the (approximate) percentage change in the input ratio per percentage change in factor prices. A minus sign is added to make the measure positive. This measure σ is called the *elasticity of substitution*. Applying Eq. (9-26) to the Cobb-Douglas case gives

$$\sigma = \frac{w}{u}\frac{k}{w^2} = \frac{w^2}{k}\frac{k}{w^2} = 1$$

Thus, the elasticity of substitution for a Cobb-Douglas production function is constant along the whole range of any isoquant and equal to 1.

The Cobb-Douglas production function $y = x_1^{\alpha}x_2^{1-\alpha}$ is a special case of production functions that exhibit constant elasticity of substitution (CES) along any isoquant. We shall investigate these important functions, deriving their functional form and other properties. These functions have wide application in empirical work on production processes.

The concept of the elasticity of substitution is not dependent on the behavioral assertion of cost-minimization. The concept can as easily be described as the percentage change in the input ratio per percentage change in the marginal rate of substitution (MRS) since the cost-minimizing firm always sets $w_1/w_2 = f_1/f_2 = $ MRS. Thus we can write, as an alternative definition,

$$\sigma = -\frac{f_1/f_2}{x_1/x_2}\frac{d(x_1/x_2)}{d(f_1/f_2)} \tag{9-27}$$

(Note that we are considering the inverse ratios x_1/x_2 instead of x_2/x_1, etc. As we shall shortly see, this is of no consequence.) Let us evaluate this expression. Along any isoquant, $x_2 = x_2(x_1)$. Then $dx_2/dx_1 = -f_1/f_2$, and therefore we can write (9-27) (using the chain rule) as

$$\sigma = -\frac{f_1 x_2}{f_2 x_1}\frac{d(x_1/x_2)/dx_1}{d(f_1/f_2)/dx_1}$$

Evaluating the terms in the second fraction yields

$$\frac{d(x_1/x_2)}{dx_1} = \left(x_2 - x_1\frac{dx_2}{dx_1}\right)\frac{1}{x_2^2}$$

$$= \left(x_2 + x_1\frac{f_1}{f_2}\right)\frac{1}{x_2^2}$$

$$= \frac{1}{f_2 x_2^2}(f_1 x_1 + f_2 x_2)$$

Similarly, $d(f_1/f_2)/dx_1$ is simply $-d^2 x_2/dx_1^2$, since $dx_2/dx_1 = -f_1/f_2$. From Chap. 3,

$$-\frac{d^2 x_2}{dx_1^2} = \frac{1}{f_2^3}(f_2^2 f_{11} - 2f_1 f_2 f_{12} + f_1^2 f_{22})$$

Combining these expressions leads to

$$\sigma = -\frac{f_1 x_2}{f_2 x_1}\frac{f_2^3}{f_2 x_2^2}\frac{f_1 x_1 + f_2 x_2}{(f_2^2 f_{11} - 2f_1 f_2 f_{12} + f_1^2 f_{22})}$$

or

$$\sigma = -\frac{f_1 f_2(f_1 x_1 + f_2 x_2)}{x_1 x_2(f_2^2 f_{11} - 2f_1 f_2 f_{12} + f_1^2 f_{22})} \tag{9-28}$$

This rather cumbersome expression for σ can be drastically simplified in the important special case of linear homogeneous production functions. First, the numerator immediately becomes $f_1 f_2 y$, upon application of Euler's theorem. For the denominator, since $f(x_1, x_2)$ is homogeneous of degree 1, f_1 and f_2 are homogeneous of degree zero. Hence, applying Euler's theorem to f_1 and f_2, we have

$$f_{11} x_1 + f_{12} x_2 \equiv 0 \quad \text{or} \quad f_{11} = -f_{12}\frac{x_2}{x_1}$$

Similarly,

$$f_{22} = -f_{12}\frac{x_1}{x_2}$$

Making these substitutions leads to

$$x_1 x_2 (f_2^2 f_{11} - 2f_1 f_2 f_{12} + f_1^2 f_{22})$$

$$= -x_1 x_2 f_{12}\left(f_2^2\frac{x_2}{x_1} + 2f_1 f_2 + f_1^2\frac{x_1}{x_2}\right)$$

$$= -f_{12}(f_2^2 x_2^2 + 2f_1 f_2 x_1 x_2 + f_1^2 x_1^2)$$

$$= -f_{12}(f_1 x_1 + f_2 x_2)^2 = -f_{12}y^2$$

Therefore, for linear homogeneous production functions

$$\sigma = -\frac{f_1 f_2 y}{-f_{12}y^2} = \frac{f_1 f_2}{y f_{12}} \tag{9-29}$$

a drastic simplification of Eq. (9-28) indeed.

A curiosity concerning Eqs. (9-28) and (9-29) is that they are symmetric between x_1 and x_2. That is, the identical expression results when the subscripts are interchanged. Thus we can speak of the elasticity of substitution between x_1 and x_2 rather than the elasticity of substitution of x_2 for x_1, or of x_1 for x_2. It does not matter whether x_2/x_1 is related to f_2/f_1 or x_1/x_2 is related to f_1/f_2 by derivatives in σ. The formula is the same either way.

Formula (9-29) can be related to the expression for the rate of change of one factor with respect to another. Recalling Eq. (8-28b) on the comparative statics of cost minimization, we have

$$\frac{\partial x_2^*}{\partial w_1} = -\frac{H_{12}}{H}$$

where

$$H = \begin{vmatrix} -\lambda^* f_{11} & -\lambda^* f_{12} & -f_1 \\ -\lambda^* f_{21} & -\lambda^* f_{22} & -f_2 \\ -f_1 & -f_2 & 0 \end{vmatrix}$$

Thus

$$\frac{\partial x_1^*}{\partial w_2} = \frac{-f_1 f_2}{\lambda^*(f_{11}f_2^2 - 2f_{12}f_1 f_2 + f_{22}f_1^2)}$$

which, for linear homogeneous production functions, becomes (as before, dropping the asterisks to remove clutter)

$$\frac{\partial x_1}{\partial w_2} = \frac{f_1 f_2 x_1 x_2}{\lambda y^2 f_{12}}$$

or

$$\frac{y\lambda}{x_1 x_2}\frac{\partial x_1}{\partial w_2} = \frac{f_1 f_2}{y f_{12}} = \sigma$$

Noting that $\lambda = w_2/f_2$, we can write this as

$$\frac{y}{f_2 x_2}\frac{w_2}{x_1}\frac{\partial x_1}{\partial w_2} = \sigma$$

Letting $\kappa_i = f_i x_i/y$ ($\kappa_1 + \kappa_2 = 1$, by Euler's theorem) and denoting the cross-elasticity of demand by ε_{12},

$$\varepsilon_{12} = \kappa_2 \sigma \qquad (9\text{-}30)$$

Thus, the elasticity of substitution is related in this simple fashion to the cross-elasticity of (constant-output) factor demand. And, of course,

$$\sigma = \frac{1}{\kappa_2}\,\varepsilon_{12} = \frac{1}{\kappa_1}\,\varepsilon_{21}$$

Knowledge of σ at any point would undoubtedly be a useful technological datum for empirical work. Beyond the strictly qualitative results of comparative statics, measurement of the degree of responsiveness to changes in parameters is an essential part of any science. Hence, it would be useful to be able to estimate a quantity like σ. A useful first approximation in so doing is to assume that the production process is linear homogeneous and exhibits *constant* elasticity of substitution everywhere. That is, σ is the same at all factor combinations. What would such production functions look like? We have already shown that the Cobb-Douglas function has the property $\sigma = 1$ everywhere. What about other values of σ?

Return to Eq. (9-26), $\sigma = -(w/u)(du/dw)$, where $u = x_2/x_1, w = w_2/w_1$. Strictly speaking, we should in general write

$$\sigma = -\frac{w}{u}\frac{\partial u}{\partial w}$$

since in general $u = x_2/x_1$ will not be a function of the wage ratio w_2/w_1 only but will also depend on the output level y. However, consider the case first of homothetic production functions. The cost function for all homothetic production functions can be written

$$C^* = J(y)A(w_1, w_2) \qquad (9\text{-}31)$$

where $A(w_1, w_2)$ is linear homogeneous. (Any cost function is linear homogeneous in the factor prices.) Using the envelope theorem (Shephard's lemma), we have

$$x_1 = J(y)A_1(w_1, w_2) \qquad (9\text{-}32a)$$

$$x_2 = J(y)A_2(w_1, w_2) \qquad (9\text{-}32b)$$

where $A_1 = \partial A/\partial w_1$, etc. Since A_1 and A_2 are first partials of a linear homogeneous function, they are homogeneous of degree zero in w_1 and w_2. But then

$$A_1(w_1, w_2) = A_1\left(1, \frac{w_2}{w_1}\right) = B_1(w)$$

and so forth, and therefore we can write

$$x_1 = J(y)B_1(w) \qquad (9\text{-}33a)$$

$$x_2 = J(y)B_2(w) \qquad (9\text{-}33b)$$

(In fact, only the factor demands of homothetic production functions have this functional form.) Dividing Eq. (9-33b) by (9-33a) gives

$$u = \frac{x_2}{x_1} = \frac{B_2(w)}{B_1(w)} = B(w)$$

That is, for all homothetic production functions, the ratio of factor inputs is a function of the ratio of wage rates only, not at all a function of output y. This of course is geometrically obvious, since the isoquants of homothetic production functions are merely radial blowups of each other. Hence, in formula (9-26) it is valid, for homothetic production functions, to write $\sigma = -(w/u)(du/dw)$ since u is indeed some well-defined function of w only.

Suppose now, maintaining the assumption of homotheticity, that σ is constant everywhere. The class of homothetic functions having constant elasticity of substitution consists of those which satisfy the differential equation

$$-\frac{w}{u}\frac{du}{dw} = \sigma = \text{constant}$$

Let us solve this differential equation. Rearranging variables gives

$$\frac{du}{u} = -\sigma\frac{dw}{w}$$

Integrating both sides and denoting the arbitrary constant of integration as $\log c$, we have

$$\log u = -\sigma \log w + \log c = \log cw^{-\sigma}$$

or

$$u = cw^{-\sigma} = c\left(\frac{1}{w}\right)^{\sigma} \qquad (9\text{-}34)$$

where, of necessity, $c > 0$. Thus, all such production functions must have the property that the capital-labor ratio is proportional to the wage ratio raised to some power, that power being the negative of the elasticity of substitution. What production functions satisfy (9-34)? For cost-minimizing firms, $1/w = w_1/w_2 = f_1/f_2 = -\partial x_2/\partial x_1$, the slope of an isoquant at some arbitrary output level y. Rewriting (9-34) in terms of the original variables yields

$$\frac{x_2}{x_1} = c\left(\frac{f_1}{f_2}\right)^\sigma$$

or, taking roots, ($k = c^{1/\sigma}$)

$$\left(\frac{x_2}{x_1}\right)^{1/\sigma} = -k\frac{\partial x_2}{\partial x_1}$$

Now k is any positive number. We can, for convenience, write $k = (1 - \alpha)/\alpha$, where $0 < \alpha < 1$. As α varies between 0 and 1, k varies from 0 to ∞, so no generality is lost. Separating variables gives

$$\alpha\frac{\partial x_1}{x_1^{1/\sigma}} = -\frac{(1 - \alpha)\partial x_2}{x_2^{1/\sigma}} \qquad (9\text{-}35)$$

We have to distinguish two cases now when integrating this expression. When $\sigma = 1$, logarithms will be involved, whereas when $\sigma \neq 1$, the integrals will be simple polynomials.

Case 1. Let $\sigma = 1$. Integrating both sides of (9-35) yields

$$\alpha\int\frac{\partial x_1}{x_1} = -(1 - \alpha)\left(\int\frac{\partial x_2}{x_2}\right) + \log g(y)$$

The arbitrary constant of integration can in general be any function of y, since y was held constant in determining the slope $\partial x_2/\partial x_1$. Again, since Eq. (9-35) is really a *partial* differential equation, the arbitrary constant of integration can involve any function of the variable or variables held constant, in this case output y. For convenience, we have denoted this constant of integration $\log g(y)$. Performing the indicated operations, we have

$$\alpha \log x_1 = -(1 - \alpha)\log x_2 + \log g(y)$$

or

$$g(y) = x_1^\alpha x_2^{1-\alpha}$$

Up to this point, the only assumption about the form of the production function we have made is that it is homothetic. Indeed, assuming $g(y)$ is monotonic, we can write

$$y = F(x_1^\alpha x_2^{1-\alpha}) \qquad (9\text{-}36)$$

where F is the inverse function of g; that is, if $z = g(y), y = g^{-1}(z) = F(z) = F(x_1^\alpha x_2^{1-\alpha})$. Equation (9-36) has the required form for homotheticity, being a function of a linear homogeneous function. If now we insist that $y = f(x_1, x_2) = F(x_1^\alpha x_2^{1-\alpha})$ be homogeneous of some degree s, then by Theorem 6 of Chap. 3, $F(z) = kz^s$, or

$$f(x_1, x_2) = kx_1^{\alpha_1}x_2^{\alpha_2} \qquad (9\text{-}37)$$

where $\alpha_1 = \alpha s$, $\alpha_2 = (1 - \alpha)s$, and thus $\alpha_1 + \alpha_2 = s$. If $f(x_1, x_2)$ is to be linear homogeneous, with $\sigma = 1$, then

$$f(x_1, x_2) = kx_1^\alpha x_2^{1-\alpha} \tag{9-38}$$

Equations (9-36) to (9-38) represent the general functional forms of production functions which exhibit constant elasticity of substitution equal to unity everywhere ($\sigma = 1$) and, in addition, are, respectively, homothetic, homogeneous of degree s, and linear homogeneous. Consider now the second case, $\sigma \neq 1$.

Case 2. If $\sigma \neq 1$, integrating both sides of Eq. (9-35) yields

$$\alpha \int \frac{\partial x_1}{x_1^{1/\sigma}} = -(1 - \alpha) \int \frac{\partial x_2}{x_2^{1/\sigma}} + g(y)$$

where again, the arbitrary constant of integration is some function of output y, designated $g(y)$, since y is held constant in finding the slope $\partial x_2/\partial x_1$ of an isoquant. Performing the indicated operations and rearranging yields, incorporating the factor $(-1/\sigma) + 1$ into $g(y)$,

$$g(y) = \alpha x_1^{(-1/\sigma)+1} + (1 - \alpha)x_2^{(-1/\sigma)+1} \tag{9-39}$$

It will simplify matters if we let $\rho = 1 - (1/\sigma)$; that is, $\sigma = 1/(1 - \rho)$; then

$$g(y) = \alpha x_1^\rho + (1 - \alpha)x_2^\rho \tag{9-40}$$

Assuming again that $g(y)$ is monotonic, (9-40) can be written

$$y = F(\alpha x_1^\rho + (1 - \alpha)x_2^\rho) \tag{9-41}$$

Equation (9-41) is the most general form of homothetic production functions exhibiting constant elasticity of substitution. As before, again using Theorem 6 of Chap. 3, if we wish $y = f(x_1, x_2)$ to be homogeneous of degree 1, then, of necessity, $F = kz^{1/\rho}$ and

$$y = k(\alpha x_1^\rho + (1 - \alpha)x_2^\rho)^{1/\rho} \tag{9-42}$$

Equation (9-42) is what is commonly referred to as the CES production function. It assumes linear homogeneity. The elasticity of substitution, of course, varies between 0 and ∞. When $\sigma \to 0$, $\rho \to -\infty$; when $\sigma = 1$, $\rho = 0$, and when $\sigma \to +\infty$, $\rho \to +1$. Hence the range of values for ρ is $-\infty < \rho < 1$. When $\sigma \to 0$ ($\rho \to -\infty$), the isoquants become L-shaped; i.e., the function becomes a fixed-proportions production function. When $\sigma \to \infty$ ($\rho \to +1$), the isoquants become straight lines, as inspection of (9-42) reveals.

Although we have proved that when $\sigma = 1$ ($\rho = 0$), the CES production function becomes Cobb-Douglas, that fact is not obvious from Eq. (9-42). In order to show this result directly, we need a mathematical theorem known as L'Hôpital's rule.

L'Hôpital's rule. Suppose that $f(x)$ and $g(x)$ both tend to 0 (have a limit of 0) as $x \to 0$. Then if the ratio $f'(x)/g'(x)$ exists,

$$\lim_{x \to 0} \frac{f(x)}{g(x)} = \lim_{x \to 0} \frac{f'(x)}{g'(x)} \tag{9-43}$$

The limit of the ratio of the functions, if it exists, equals the ratio of the derivatives of $f(x)$ and $g(x)$, respectively.

The formal proof of this theorem can be found in any advanced calculus text; we shall not present it here.

Consider the CES function (9-42) again, and take the logarithms of both sides:

$$\log y = \log k + \frac{\log(\alpha x_1^\rho + (1 - \alpha)x_2^\rho)}{\rho} \tag{9-44}$$

The right-hand side of (9-44) consists, aside from the constant, of a ratio of two functions, each of which tends to 0 as $\rho \to 0$. We find the limit as $\rho \to 0$, letting $f(\rho) =$ numerator, remembering that if $y = a^t, dy/dt = a^t \log a$:

$$f'(\rho) = \frac{1}{\alpha x_1^\rho + (1 - \alpha)x_2^\rho}[x_1^\rho \alpha \log x_1 + x_2^\rho(1 - \alpha)\log x_2]$$

$$\lim_{\rho \to 0} f'(\rho) = \frac{1}{1}[\alpha \log x_1 + (1 - \alpha) \log x_2]$$

$$= \log x_1^\alpha x_2^{1-\alpha}$$

The denominator of (9-44) is simply ρ, and thus $g'(\rho) = 1$; hence, $\lim_{\rho \to 0} g'(\rho) = 1$. Therefore, as $\rho \to 0$,

$$\log y = \log k + \log x_1^\alpha x_2^{1-\alpha}$$

or

$$y = k x_1^\alpha x_2^{1-\alpha}$$

the Cobb-Douglas function, as expected.

The factor demands and the cost functions associated with the CES production function can be derived using the cost minimization hypothesis. Formally, the problem is

minimize

$$w_1 x_1 + w_2 x_2 = C$$

subject to

$$\alpha_1 x_1^\rho + \alpha_2 x_2^\rho = y^\rho$$

where $\alpha_1 + \alpha_2 = 1$.

The Lagrangian is $\mathcal{L} = w_1 x_1 + w_2 x_2 + \lambda(y^\rho - (\alpha_1 x_1^\rho + \alpha_2 x_2^\rho))$; differentiating with respect to x_1, x_2, and eliminating λ yields (eliminating the *'s to save notational clutter)

$$\frac{w_1}{w_2} = \frac{\alpha_1 x_1^{\rho-1}}{\alpha_2 x_2^{\rho-1}}$$

Multiplying through by (x_1/x_2),

$$\frac{w_1 x_1}{w_2 x_2} = \frac{\alpha_1 x_1^{\rho}}{\alpha_2 x_2^{\rho}}$$

Now add 1 to both sides of this equation (which adds the denominator of each side to the respective numerator):

$$\frac{C}{w_2 x_2} = \frac{y^{\rho}}{\alpha_2 x_2^{\rho}}$$

Solving for x_2,

$$x_2 = C^{1/(1-\rho)} y^{-\rho/(1-\rho)} w_2^{-1/(1-\rho)} \alpha_2^{1/(1-\rho)}$$

and by symmetry,

$$x_1 = C^{1/(1-\rho)} y^{-\rho/(1-\rho)} w_1^{-1/(1-\rho)} \alpha_1^{1/(1-\rho)}$$

Therefore

$$w_2 x_2 = C^{1/(1-\rho)} y^{-\rho/(1-\rho)} w_2^{-\rho/(1-\rho)} \alpha_2^{1/(1-\rho)}$$

and

$$w_1 x_1 = C^{1/(1-\rho)} y^{-\rho/(1-\rho)} w_1^{-\rho/(1-\rho)} \alpha_1^{1/(1-\rho)}$$

Adding produces total cost; therefore

$$C = C^{1/(1-\rho)} y^{-\rho/(1-\rho)} [\alpha_1^{1/(1-\rho)} w_1^{-\rho/(1-\rho)} + \alpha_2^{1/(1-\rho)} w_2^{-\rho/(1-\rho)}]$$

and thus

$$C = y[\alpha_1^{1/(1-\rho)} w_1^{-\rho/(1-\rho)} + \alpha_2^{1/(1-\rho)} w_2^{-\rho/(1-\rho)}]^{(1-\rho)/-\rho} \tag{9-45}$$

We can derive the constant output factor demands using the envelope theorem result $\partial C^*/\partial w_i = x_i^*$:

$$\frac{\partial C^*}{\partial w_1} = y\left(\frac{1-\rho}{-\rho}\right)\left[\alpha_1^{1/(1-\rho)} w_1^{-\rho/(1-\rho)} + \alpha_2^{1/(1-\rho)} w_2^{-\rho/(1-\rho)}\right]^{1/-\rho}$$
$$\left(\alpha_1^{1/(1-\rho)} w_1^{-1/(1-\rho)}\right)\left(\frac{-\rho}{1-\rho}\right)$$

or

$$\frac{\partial C^*}{\partial w_1} = x_1^* = y\left[\alpha_1^{1/(1-\rho)} w_1^{-\rho/(1-\rho)} + \alpha_2^{1/(1-\rho)} w_2^{-\rho/(1-\rho)}\right]^{1/-\rho} \alpha_1^{1/(1-\rho)} w_1^{-1/(1-\rho)}$$

$$\tag{9-46}$$

with a similar expression for x_2^*.

Generalizations to n Factors

Consider again the definition of elasticity of substitution given in Eq. (9-27) but now assuming that the two factors in question are two of n factors that enter the production function:

$$\sigma_{ij} = -\frac{f_i/f_j}{x_i/x_j}\frac{d(x_i/x_j)}{d(f_i/f_j)} \tag{9-47}$$

This number is a measure of how fast the ratio of two inputs changes when the marginal rate of substitution between them changes. In order for this definition to make sense, the other factors must be held constant at some parametric levels $x_k = x_k^0, k \neq i,j$. When more than two factors are involved, a marginal rate of substitution of one variable for another can only be defined in some two-dimensional subspace of the original space, i.e., along a plane (hyperplane) parallel to the x_i, x_j axes, in which the other variables are held constant. Thus definitions of elasticity of substitution analogous to Eq. (9-27), for the n-factor case, are "partial" elasticities of substitution. By holding the other factors constant, they do not represent the full degree of substitution possibilities present in the production function. These partial measures would be especially deceptive if one or more of the factors held constant were either close substitutes or highly complementary to the variable factors.

As an alternative, one could develop elasticities of substitution based on Eq. (9-26):

$$\sigma_{ij}^* = -\frac{w_{ij}}{u_{ij}}\frac{\partial u_{ij}}{\partial w_{ij}} \tag{9-48}$$

where $w_{ij} = w_i/w_j, u_{ij} = x_i/x_j$. In this definition, all other *wages* are to be held constant with the other factors allowed to vary. This definition overcomes most of the objections stated above for the fixed-input definition (9-47). Clearly, σ_{ij}^* will relate to the cross-elasticities of factor demand. As such, they are less of a technological datum of the production function but most likely a more useful concept since in reality it will be unlikely that the other factors will remain constant.

The obvious generalization of the CES functional form to many factors

$$y = A(\alpha_1 x_1^\rho + \cdots + \alpha_n x_n^\rho)^{1/\rho} \tag{9-49}$$

has been shown to yield constant elasticities of the type given in (9-48); that is, the other factor *prices* are held fixed.[†] They are also called the *Allen elasticities*.[‡] However, all the partial elasticities are equal to each other and to $1/(1-\rho)$. Also,

---

[†] See H. Uzawa, "Production Functions with Constant Elasticities of Substitution," *The Review of Economic Studies*, 29:291–299, October 1962.

[‡] See R. G. D. Allen, *Mathematical Analysis for Economists*, MacMillan & Co., Ltd., London, 1938; reprinted by St. Martin's Press, New York.

when $\rho = 0$ ($\sigma_{ij} = 1$), the form reduces, as in the two-factor case, to a Cobb-Douglas or multiplicatively separable function

$$y = Ax_1^{\alpha_1}x_2^{\alpha_2} \cdots x_n^{\alpha_n}$$

where $\sum_1 \alpha_i = 1$ to preserve linear homogeneity.

The Generalized Leontief Cost Function

A cost function developed by Erwin Diewert[†] has been found to be useful in empirical analysis. This functional form is

$$C^* = y \sum \sum \beta_{ij}w_i^{1/2}w_j^{1/2} \qquad i,j = 1, \ldots, n \qquad (9\text{-}50)$$

In order for this function to satisfy the requirements of a cost function, it must display symmetry, i.e., $\beta_{ij} = \beta_{ji}$. The constant output factor demands can be obtained by differentiation with respect to the wages:

$$x_i^* = \frac{\partial C^*}{\partial w_i} = y \sum_k \beta_{ik}\left(\frac{w_k}{w_i}\right)^{1/2} \qquad i = 1, \ldots, n \qquad (9\text{-}51)$$

Differentiating further,

$$\frac{\partial x_i^*}{\partial w_j} = \frac{1}{2}y\beta_{ij}\left(\frac{1}{w_iw_j}\right)^{1/2}$$

Note that $\beta_{ij} = \beta_{ji}$ is required in order that $\partial x_i^*/\partial w_j = \partial x_j^*/\partial w_i$.

The reason this function is called a generalized Leontief function is that input-output analysis, as developed by Wassily Leontief, utilizes "fixed coefficient" technology, i.e., L-shaped isoquants, indicating an absence of substitution possibilities among factors of production. In the special case where $\beta_{ij} = 0, i \neq j$, $x_i = y\beta_{ii}$. In that case, therefore,

$$\frac{x_i}{x_j} = \frac{\beta_{ii}}{\beta_{jj}}$$

That is, the ratio of inputs is independent of output level and factor prices. This describes the Leontief-style technology. We shall further explore models of this nature in the chapter on linear programming (General Equilibrium I).

Additional functional forms will be analyzed in the context of utility theory, though some functions have been useful in both production and consumer theory.

PROBLEMS

1. If a production function is homogeneous of degree $r > 1$ ($r < 1$), it exhibits increasing (decreasing) returns to scale. The converse, however, is false. Explain.

[†]W. Erwin Diewert, "An Application of the Shephard Duality Theorem: A Generalized Leontief Production Function," *Journal of Political Economy,* **79**:481–507, June 1971.

2. Suppose all firms in a competitive industry have the same production function, $y = f(x_1, x_2)$, where $f(x_1, x_2)$ is homogeneous of degree $r < 1$. Show that all firms in this industry will be receiving "rents," i.e., positive accounting profits. To which factor of production do these rents accrue? In the long run, if entry is free in this industry, what will be the industry price, output, and number of firms?

3. Find the production function associated with each of the following cost functions:
   (a) $C = \sqrt{w_1 w_2}\ e^{y/2}$
   (b) $C = w_2[1 + y + \log(w_1/w_2)]$
   (c) $C = y(w_1^2 + w_2^2)^{1/2}$

4. It is often said that the reason for U-shaped average cost curves is indivisibility of some factors. However, indivisibility does not necessarily lead to such properties. Suppose a firm's production function is homogeneous of some degree. Suppose the production function is also homogeneous in any $n-1$ factors when the nth factor is held fixed at some level. Show that the only function with these properties is the multiplicatively separable form, $y = kx_1^{\alpha_1} x_2^{\alpha_2} \cdots x_n^{\alpha_n}$.

5. What class of *homothetic* functions $y = f(x_1, \ldots, x_n)$ is also homothetic in any $n-1$ factors, with the nth factor held fixed at some level?

6. Show that for homothetic production functions, the output at which average cost is a minimum is independent of factor prices.

7. Suppose a production function $y = f(x_1, x_2)$ is homothetic, that is, $f(x_1, x_2) = F(h(x_1, x_2))$, where $h(x_1, x_2)$ is linear homogeneous. Show that the elasticity of substitution is given by $\sigma = (h_1 h_2)/h_{12} h$.

BIBLIOGRAPHY

Allen, R. G. D.: *Mathematical Analysis for Economists*, MacMillan & Co., Ltd., London, 1938; reprinted by St. Martin's Press, New York.

Arrow, K. J., H. Chenery, B. Minhas, and R. M. Solow: "Capital-Labor Substitution and Economic Efficiency," *The Review of Economics and Statistics*, **43**:225–250, 1961. The seminal paper on CES production functions.

Blackorby, Charles, and R. Robert Russell: "Will the Real Elasticity of Substitution Please Stand Up? (A Comparison of the Allen/Uzawa and Morishima Elasticities," *American Economic Review*, **79**:882–888, September 1989.

Carlson, Sune: *A Study on the Theory of Production*, Kelley & Millman, New York, 1956.

Diewert, W. E.: "Applications of Duality Theory," Department of Manpower and Immigration, Canada, 1973.

Frisch, Ragnar: *Theory of Production*, Rand McNally & Company, Chicago, 1965.

Hicks, J. R.: *Value and Capital*, 2d ed., Clarendon Press, Oxford, 1946.

Jorgenson, D. W., L. R. Christensen, and L. J. Lau: "Transcendental Logarithmic Production Frontiers," *Review of Economics and Statistics*, **55**:28–45, February 1973.

McFadden, Daniel: "Constant Elasticity of Substitution Production Functions," *Review of Economic Studies*, **30**:73–83, June 1963.

Samuelson, Paul A.: *Foundations of Economic Analysis*, Harvard University Press, Cambridge, Mass., 1947.

Shephard, Ronald W.: *Cost and Production Functions*, Princeton University Press, Princeton, N.J., 1953; also the revised version of this book, 1970, which has become a classic.

Uzawa, H.: "Production Functions with Constant Elasticities of Substitution," *The Review of Economic Studies*, **29**:291–299, October 1962.

CHAPTER
10

THE DERIVATION OF CONSUMER DEMAND FUNCTIONS

10.1 INTRODUCTORY REMARKS: THE BEHAVIORAL POSTULATES

In this chapter we shall analyze a fundamental problem in economics, that of the derivation of a consumer's demand function from the behavioral postulate of maximizing utility. The central theme of this discussion will be to study the structure of models of consumer behavior in order to discover what, if any, refutable hypotheses can be derived. Thus, our analysis is mainly methodological: we wish to find out, in particular, what it is about the postulate of utility maximization subject to constraints that either leads to or fails to generate refutable hypotheses.

The behavioral assertion we shall study is that a consumer engages in some sort of constrained maximizing behavior, the objective of which is to

maximize

$$U(x_1, x_2, \ldots, x_n) \tag{10-1}$$

where $x_1, \ldots, x_n$ represents the goods that the consumer actually consumes, and $U(x_1, \ldots, x_n)$ represents the consumer's own subjective evaluation of the satisfaction, or utility, derived from consuming those commodities. However, we live in a world of scarcity, and consumers are faced with making choices concerning the levels of consumption they will undertake. The consequences of scarcity can be summarized by saying that consumers face a budget constraint, assumed to be linear:

Budget constraint

$$\sum p_i x_i = M \tag{10-2}$$

where p_i represents the unit price of commodity x_i, and M is the total budget per time period of the consumer. The classical problem in the theory of the consumer is thus stated as

maximize

$$U(x_1, \ldots, x_n)$$

subject to

$$\sum p_i x_i = M \tag{10-3}$$

The hypothesis (10-3) is often referred to as *rational* behavior, or as what a rational consumer would do. If this were so, then another theory would have to be developed for *irrational* consumers, i.e., consumers who did not obey (10-3). (The question of how these irrational consumers might behave has never been seriously studied, probably for good reason.) Also, utility maximization has been attacked on various introspective grounds, largely having to do with whether people are capable of performing the intricate calculations necessary to achieve a maximum of utility. And, finally, it might be argued by some that since utility is largely unmeasurable, any analysis based on maximizing some unmeasurable quantity is doomed to failure.

All the above criticisms are largely irrelevant. The purpose of formulating these models is to derive refutable hypotheses. In this context, behavior indicated by (10-3) is *asserted* to be true, for all consumers. That is, (10-3) is our basic behavioral postulate. Refutation of (10-3) can come about only if the theorems derived from it are demonstrably shown to be false, on the basis of empirical evidence. This is not a postulate for rational consumers; it is for *all* consumers. If some consumers are found whose actions clearly contradict the implications of (10-3), the proper response is not to accuse them of being irrational; rather, it is our theory which must be accused of being false.[†]

This admittedly extreme view of the role of theorizing is not lightly taken. The reason is that the *stupidity* hypothesis, and the *disequilibrium* or *slow adjustment* hypotheses are consistent with all observable behavior, and therefore are unable to generate refutable implications. Anything in the world can be explained

---

[†] A study of chronic psychotics at a New York State mental institution, people whom society has pronounced *irrational* in some sense, showed that psychotics obey the law of demand, i.e., they too buy less when prices are raised, etc. See Battalio, et al., "A Test of Consumer Demand Theory Using Observations of Individual Purchases," *Western Economic Journal,* 411–428, December 1973.

on the basis that the participants are stupid, or ill-informed, or slow to react, or are somehow in disequilibrium, without theories to describe the alleged phenomena. These terms are metaphors for a lack of useful theory or the failure to adequately specify the additional constraints on consumers' behavior. We therefore stick our necks out and assert, boldly, that all consumers maximize some utility function subject to constraints, most commonly (though not exclusively, especially if non-price or rationing conditions are imposed) a linear budget constraint of the form (10-2) above. The theory is to be rejected only on the basis of its having been falsified by facts.

We have alluded to the concept of a utility function in earlier chapters; let us now investigate such functions more closely. A utility function is a summary of some aspects of a given individual's tastes, or preferences, regarding the consumption of various bundles of goods. The early marginalists perceived this function as indicating a *cardinal* measure of satisfaction, or utility, received by a consumer upon consumption of goods and services. That is, a steak might have yielded some consumer 10 "utiles," a potato 5 utiles, and hence one steak gave twice the satisfaction of one potato. The total of utiles for all goods consumed was a measure of the overall welfare of the individual.

Toward the end of the nineteenth century, perhaps initially from introspection, the concept of utility as a *cardinal* measure of some inner level of satisfaction was discarded. More importantly, though, economists, particularly Pareto, became aware that no refutable implications of cardinality were derivable that were not also derivable from the concept of utility as a strictly *ordinal* index of preferences. As we shall see presently, all of the known implications of the utility maximization hypothesis are derivable from the assumption that consumers are merely able to *rank* all commodity bundles, without regard to the intensity of satisfaction gained by consuming a particular commodity bundle. This is by no means a trivial assumption. We assert that all consumers, when faced with a choice of consuming two or more bundles of goods, $\mathbf{x}^1 = (x_1^1, \ldots, x_n^1), \ldots, \mathbf{x}^k = (x_1^k, \ldots, x_n^k)$, can rank all of these bundles of goods in terms of their desirability to that consumer. More specifically, for any two bundles of goods $\mathbf{x}^i$ and $\mathbf{x}^j$, we assert that any consumer can decide among the following three mutually exclusive situations:

1. $\mathbf{x}^i$ is preferred to $\mathbf{x}^j$
2. $\mathbf{x}^j$ is preferred to $\mathbf{x}^i$
3. $\mathbf{x}^i$ and $\mathbf{x}^j$ are equally preferred

Only one category can apply at any one time; if that category should change, we would say that the consumer's tastes, or preferences, have changed. In the important case 3, above, we say that the consumer is indifferent between $\mathbf{x}^i$ and $\mathbf{x}^j$.

The cardinalists wanted to go much farther than this. They wanted to be able to place some psychological measure of the degree to which the consumer was better off if he or she consumed $\mathbf{x}^i$ rather than $\mathbf{x}^j$, in situation 1, above. Such a measure might be useful to, say, psychologists studying human motivation; to economists, it turns out that no additional refutable implications are forthcoming from such knowledge. Hence, cardinality as a feature of utility has been discarded.

The utility function is thus constructed simply as an index. The utility index is to become larger when a more preferred bundle of goods is consumed. Letting $U(\mathbf{x}) = U(x_1, \ldots, x_n)$ designate such an index, for cases 1, 2, and 3, above, $U(\mathbf{x})$ must have the properties, respectively,

1. $U(\mathbf{x}^i) > U(\mathbf{x}^j)$
2. $U(\mathbf{x}^j) > U(\mathbf{x}^i)$
3. $U(\mathbf{x}^i) = U(\mathbf{x}^j)$

How is the ordinality of $U(x_1, \ldots, x_n)$ expressed? Consider Fig. 10-1, in which two level curves, or indifference surfaces, are drawn for $U = U(x_1, x_2)$. The inner curve is defined as $U(x_1, x_2) = 1$; the other indifference curve is the locus $U(x_1, x_2) = 2$. Suppose, now, instead of this U index, we decided to label these two loci by the square of U or, by $V = U^2$. Then these two indifference curves, in terms of V units, would have utilities of one and four, respectively. Or, one could consider a third index $W = \log U$, in which the "W-utiles" would be 0 and log 2, respectively. Ordinality means that any one of these utility functions is as good as the other, i.e., they all contain the same information, since they all preserve the *ranking*, though not the cardinal difference, between different indifference levels. In general, starting with any given utility function $U = U(x_1, \ldots, x_n)$, consider any monotonic transformation

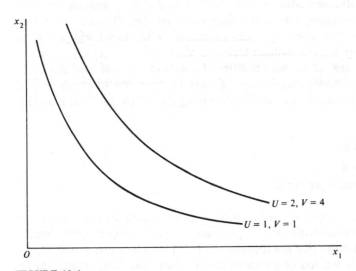

FIGURE 10-1
Ordinal Utility Levels (Indifference Curves). The ordinality of utility functions is expressed by asserting that relabeling the values of the indifference contours of utility functions has no effect on the behavior of consumers.

of U, that is, let $V = F(U(x_1, \ldots, x_n))$ where $dV/dU = F'(U) > 0$. Then V and U always move in the same direction; the V index is merely a relabeling of the U index which preserves the rank ordering of the indifference levels. To say that utility is an ordinal concept is therefore to say that the utility function is arbitrary up to any monotonic (i.e., monotonically increasing) transformation. We shall check and see that all implications regarding observable phenomena that are derivable from asserting the existence of $U(x_1, \ldots, x_n)$ are also derivable from $V = F(U(x_1, \ldots, x_n))$ where $F' > 0$ and vice versa. Ordinality means that $F(U(x_1, \ldots, x_n))$ conveys the identical information concerning a consumer's preferences as does $U(x_1, \ldots, x_n)$.

The assertion that consumers possess utility functions is a statement that people do in fact have preferences.[†] How these preferences come to be, and why they might differ among people of different countries or ethnic groups, is a discipline outside of economics. These are certainly interesting questions. They are also exceedingly difficult to grapple with. The specialty of economics arose precisely because it was fruitful in many problems to ignore the origins of individuals' tastes and explain certain events on the basis of changes in opportunities, assuming that individuals' tastes remained constant in the interim.

Merely to assert that individuals have tastes or preferences is, however, to assert very little. In order to derive refutable implications from utility analysis, certain other restrictions must be placed on the utility function. To begin with, we shall assume that the utility function is mathematically well behaved, that is, it is sufficiently smooth to be differentiated as often as necessary. This postulate is questioned by some who note that commodity bundles invariably come in discrete packages (except perhaps for liquids, such as water or gasoline), and also, for the case of services, such as visits to the doctor, the units are often difficult to define. We note these objections and then ask, what is to be gained in our analysis by explicitly recognizing the discrete nature of many goods? In most problems, very little is gained, and it is costly in terms of complexity to fully account for discreteness. Again recall the role of assumptions in economic analysis: assumptions are made because there is a trade-off between precision and tractability, or usefulness of theories. It is nearly always impossible to fully characterize any real-world object; simplifying assumptions are therefore a necessary ingredient in any useful theory. Hence, differentiability of utility functions is simply assumed.

In what class of problems is differentiability least likely to be a critical assumption? When consumers either singly or in groups make repeated purchases of a given item, we can convert the analysis from the discrete items to time (flow) rates of consumption. Instead of, say, noting that a consumer purchased one loaf of bread on Monday, another on Friday and another the following Tuesday (i.e., one loaf every four days), we can speak of an average rate of consumption of

---

[†]The mere existence of preferences, however, may not be enough to guarantee the existence of utility functions. See Chap. 11.

bread of seven-fourths loaves per week. There is no reason why the average consumption per week, or other time unit, cannot be any real number, thus allowing differentiability of the consumer's utility function. We can speak of continuous *services of goods,* even if the goods themselves are purchased in discrete units.

Assuming consumers possess differentiable utility functions $U = U(x_1, \ldots, x_n)$, the following properties of those functions are asserted. These are not intended to represent a minimum set of mutually exclusive properties; rather, they are the important features of utility functions which are the basis of the neoclassical paradigm of consumer-choice theory.

I. NONSATIATION, OR "MORE IS PREFERRED TO LESS." All goods that the consumer chooses to consume at positive prices have the property that, other things being equal, more of any good is preferred to less of it. The mathematical translation of this postulate is that if $x_1, \ldots, x_n$ are the goods consumed, the marginal utility of any good x_i is positive, or $U_i = \partial U / \partial x_i > 0$. Increasing any x_i, holding the other goods constant, always leads to a preferred position, i.e., the utility index increases.

II. SUBSTITUTION. The consumer, at any point, is willing to give up some of one good to get an additional increment of some other good. This postulate is related to postulate I. The notion of trade-offs is perhaps the most critical concept in all of economics. How do we describe the notion of trade-offs mathematically? The reasoning is analogous to that used in the definition of isoquants in the chapter on costs. Consider Fig. 10-2.

The *maximum* amount a consumer will give up of one commodity, say, x_2, to get one unit of x_1, is that amount which will leave the consumer indifferent between the new and the old situation. Starting at point A, the consumer is willing to give up a maximum of two units of x_2, say, to get one unit of x_1. The trade-offs for any consumer are hence defined by the loci of points which are indifferent to the initial point. These curves are the consumer's *indifference curves;* since the consumer is indifferent to all points on the curve, $U(x_1, \ldots, x_n) = U^0 = $ constant.

The slope of the indifference curve represents the trade-offs a consumer is willing to make. In Fig. 10-2, the slope $= -2$ (approximately) at point A; at point B the slope $= -1$, indicating that the consumer will swap x_2 and x_1 one-for-one at that point.

For the case of two commodities, the indifference curves are the level curves of the utility function $U = U(x_1, x_2)$, defined as $U(x_1, x_2) = U^0$. Defining $x_2 = x_2(x_1, U^0)$ from this relation as before, the slope of the indifference curves at any point, using the chain rule, is found by differentiating the identity $U(x_1, x_2(x_1, U^0)) \equiv U^0$ with respect to x_1:

$$U_1 + U_2 \frac{\partial x_2}{\partial x_1} \equiv 0$$

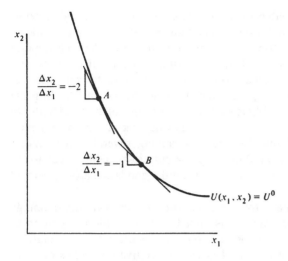

FIGURE 10-2
Value, in Economics, Means Exchange Value. The value of any commodity is the maximum amount of some other good that an individual is willing to part with in order to gain an extra unit of the good in question. In the limit (i.e., at the margin) the value of x_1 is therefore given by the slope of the indifference curve through that point. At point A, the marginal value of x_1 is the absolute slope of the level curve [indifference curve $U(x_1, x_2) = U^0$], called the marginal rate of substitution of x_1 for x_2, and is equal to two units of x_2 there. At point B, the marginal value of x_1 is one unit of x_2.

and thus

$$\frac{\partial x_2}{\partial x_1} \equiv \frac{-U_1}{U_2}$$

By postulate I, U_1 and U_2 are both positive. Hence, $\partial x_2/\partial x_1 < 0$, or the slope of the indifference curves is negative. For the n-good case,

$$\frac{\partial x_i}{\partial x_j} = \frac{-U_j}{U_i} < 0$$

A negative slope means precisely that the consumer is willing to make trade-offs. The substitution postulate means that the indifference curves are negatively sloped, a situation implied by the postulate that "more is preferred to less." If the indifference curves were positively sloped, consumers would not be trading off one good to get some of another; rather, the situation would be better characterized by that of bribing the consumer with more of one good in order to accept more of the other. One of the goods must actually be a "bad," with negative marginal utility. Only then can $-U_j/U_i$ be positive; only then would a consumer be indifferent between two consumption bundles, one of which contained more of each item than the other.

The substitution postulate is an explicit denial of the "priority of needs" fallacy. Politicians and pressure groups are forever urging that we "rearrange our priorities," i.e., devote more resources to the goods they value more highly than others. While it is useful for such groups to talk of "needs" and "priorities," it is fallacious for economists to do so. The notion of a trade-off is inconsistent with one good being "prior" to another in consumption.

The ultimate reason for rejecting the notion of priority of some goods over others is by appeal to the empirical facts, however, and not from logic. "Nonpriority" is an empirical assertion. How could one test for it? Consider a consumer who, by all reasonable measures, is considered to be rather poor. Suppose he or she is made even poorer by taxation or appropriation of some of his or her income. As income is lowered, if this consumer held the consumption of all goods except one constant and reduced some other good to zero, and then repeated the process for the other goods, we would have to conclude that such behavior indicated that some goods were prior to others, in fulfilling the person's desires. However, it is unlikely that we should find such individuals. In all likelihood, all people, even very poor people, when faced with a reduction of income will tend to spread out the reduction among several goods, rather than merely consuming only less clothing, say, or only less shelter. Real-world behavior is consistent with $U_i > 0, i = 1, \ldots, n$ for the goods actually consumed by a given individual.

The notion of substitution and trade-offs provides the critical underpinnings of the concept of *value* in economics. It is only by what people are willing to give up in order to get more of some other good that value can be meaningfully measured. In Fig. 10-2, the consumer at A is willing to give up 2 units of x_2 to get 1 unit of x_1; we conclude from this that the consumer *values* x_1 at 2 units of x_2, or that he or she values x_2 at $\frac{1}{2}$ unit of x_1. This value, indicated by the slope of the indifference curve at some point, is called the marginal rate of substitution (MRS) of x_1 for x_2; it is the marginal value of x_1 in terms of x_2.

The last postulate economists make regarding utility functions is a restriction on the behavior of these marginal values. Specifically, it is asserted that:

III. ALONG ANY INDIFFERENCE SURFACE, THE MARGINAL VALUE OF ANY GOOD DECREASES AS MORE OF THAT GOOD IS CONSUMED. This says that

$$\left(\frac{\partial^2 x_j}{\partial x_i^2} \right)_{U^0} > 0 \qquad i, j = 1, \ldots, n, \ i \neq j$$

We shall show, however, that this generalization of diminishing marginal rate of substitution, while implied by the second-order conditions for maximization of utility subject to a budget constraint, is insufficient in itself to guarantee an interior constrained maximum. The condition required is that the indifference surfaces (actually, "hypersurfaces" in n-dimensions) be convex to the origin, analogous to the convexity of the two-dimensional indifference curves. Mathematically, this is the condition of "quasi-concavity" of the utility function explored in Chap. 6. Its algebraic formulation, none too intuitive, is that the border-preserving principal minors of the following bordered Hessian alternate in sign:

$$H = \begin{vmatrix} U_{11} & \cdots & U_{1n} & U_1 \\ U_{21} & & U_{2n} & U_2 \\ \vdots & & & \\ U_{n1} & & U_{nn} & U_n \\ U_1 & & U_n & 0 \end{vmatrix} \tag{10-4}$$

The border-preserving principal minors of order 2 in H above have the form

$$H_2^{ij} = \begin{vmatrix} U_{ii} & U_{ij} & U_i \\ U_{ji} & U_{jj} & U_j \\ U_i & U_j & 0 \end{vmatrix} = -(U_{ii}U_j^2 - 2U_{ij}U_iU_j + U_{jj}U_i^2)$$

In Chaps. 3 and 6 we found

$$\frac{d^2x_2}{dx_1^2} = \frac{d(-U_1/U_2)}{dx_1}$$

$$= \frac{-1}{U_2^3}(U_{11}U_2^2 - 2U_{12}U_1U_2 + U_{22}U_1^2)$$

The bordered Hessian H_2^{ij} is precisely a generalization of this to the case of n goods, wherein all goods except x_i and x_j are held constant. $H_2^{ij} > 0$ then says that in the x_i, x_j (hyper)plane, at stipulated values of the x_k's, $k \neq i,j$, the MRS of x_i for x_j decreases, or $\partial^2 x_j/\partial x_i^2 > 0$. If this diminishing MRS holds for *every* pair of goods x_i and $x_j, i,j = 1, \ldots, n$, this says only that all the border-preserving principal minors of order two are positive; this is insufficient information from which to infer anything about the higher-order minors or H itself. Hence the notion that the indifference hypersurface is convex to the origin is a much stronger assumption, in an n-good world, than simply diminishing MRS between any pair of goods, other goods held constant. Only in the case of only two goods, wherein there are no other goods to be held constant, is quasi-concavity equivalent to diminishing MRS.

All the preceding postulates can be summarized as saying that we assert that all consumers possess utility functions $U = U(x_1, \ldots, x_n)$ which are differentiable everywhere, and which are strictly increasing ($U_i > 0, i = 1, \ldots, n$) and strictly quasi-concave. The adjective "strictly" is used to denote that there are no flat portions of the indifference curves anywhere; this guarantees uniqueness of all our solutions.

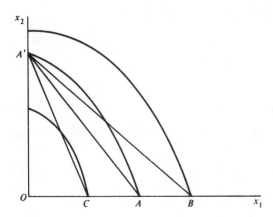

FIGURE 10-3

Nonquasi-concave Utility Functions. As p_1 increases, the budget line shifts from $A'B$ to $A'A$ to $A'C$. The maximum utility point will change suddenly from lying on the x_1 axis, to lying on the x_2 axis at A'. This behavior is not observed; for that reason it is asserted that indifference surfaces are convex to the origin, i.e., the utility function is quasi-concave.

These mathematical restrictions are asserted not merely because they guarantee an interior solution to the constrained utility-maximization problem, which they do, but more fundamentally, because such restrictions are believed to be confirmed by data involving real people. To deny these postulates is to assert strange behavior. As in the case of factor demands discussed in an earlier chapter, the assumption that, for example, indifference curves are concave to the origin implies that consumers will spend all of their budget on one good. A corner solution is achieved, point B in Fig. 10-3. At certain prices, only x_1 will be consumed. Then, as p_1 is increased past a certain level, the consumer suddenly switches over entirely to x_2. This inflexible and then erratic behavior is hard (impossible?) to find in the real world; it is for that reason and that reason only that the assumption of quasi-concavity is made.

10.2 UTILITY MAXIMIZATION

Let us now begin our analysis of the problem at hand, stated in relations (10-3),

maximize

$$U(x_1, \ldots, x_n)$$

subject to

$$\sum p_i x_i = M$$

We will, for simplicity, consider the two-variable case only, in the formal analysis, and briefly sketch the generalizations to n variables.

Suppose, then, the consumer consumes two goods, x_1 and x_2, in positive amounts. These goods are purchased in a competitive market at constant unit prices p_1 and p_2, respectively. The consumer comes to the market with an amount of money income, M. Under the assumption of nonsatiation, the consumer will spend all of his or her income M on x_1 and x_2, since M itself does not appear in the utility function. Income M is useful only for the purchase of x_1 and x_2, as expressed by writing the utility function as $U = U(x_1, x_2)$.

We assert that the consumer (i.e., all consumers) act to

maximize

$$U = U(x_1, x_2)$$

subject to

$$p_1 x_1 + p_2 x_2 = M \tag{10-5}$$

A necessary consequence of this behavior is that the first partials of the following Lagrangian equal zero:

$$\mathscr{L} = U(x_1, x_2) + \lambda(M - p_1 x_1 - p_2 x_2) \tag{10-6}$$

where λ is the Lagrange multiplier. Hence

$$\mathscr{L}_1 = U_1 - \lambda p_1 = 0 \tag{10-7a}$$

$$\mathcal{L}_2 = U_2 - \lambda p_2 = 0 \tag{10-7b}$$

$$\mathcal{L}_\lambda = M - p_1 x_1 - p_2 x_2 = 0 \tag{10-7c}$$

The sufficient second-order condition for this constrained maximum is that the bordered Hessian determinant of the second partials of $\mathcal{L}$ be positive:

$$D = \begin{vmatrix} \mathcal{L}_{11} & \mathcal{L}_{12} & \mathcal{L}_{1\lambda} \\ \mathcal{L}_{21} & \mathcal{L}_{22} & \mathcal{L}_{2\lambda} \\ \mathcal{L}_{\lambda 1} & \mathcal{L}_{\lambda 2} & \mathcal{L}_{\lambda\lambda} \end{vmatrix} = \begin{vmatrix} U_{11} & U_{12} & -p_1 \\ U_{21} & U_{22} & -p_2 \\ -p_1 & -p_2 & 0 \end{vmatrix} > 0 \tag{10-8}$$

We will, of course, assume that D is strictly greater than zero; only $D \geq 0$ is implied by the maximization hypothesis.

Thus far we have accomplished little. Most of the terms in Eqs. (10-7) and (10-8) are unobservable, containing the derivatives of an ordinal utility function. As we have repeatedly emphasized, the only propositions of interest are those which may lead to refutable hypotheses; in order to do so, all terms must be capable of being observed. Thus the objects of our inquiry are the demand functions implied by the system of Eqs. (10-7). These three equations contain six separate terms: $x_1, x_2, \lambda, p_1, p_2$, and M. Under the conditions specified by the implicit function theorem, that the Jacobian determinant formed by the first partials of these equations ($\mathcal{L}_1 = 0, \mathcal{L}_2 = 0$ and $\mathcal{L}_\lambda = 0$) is not equal to zero, this system can be solved, in principal, for the variables x_1, x_2, and λ in terms of the remaining three, p_1, p_2, and M. In fact, this Jacobian is simply the determinant D in Eq. (10-8). Each row of D consists of the first partials of the corresponding first-order equation in (10-7). Since the system of Eqs. (10-7) is itself the first partials of $\mathcal{L}$, the Jacobian determinant consists of the second partials of $\mathcal{L}$, with respect to x_1, x_2, and λ. The *sufficient* second-order conditions guarantee that $D \neq 0$ (in fact, $D > 0$), hence in this case we can write,

$$x_1 = x_1^M(p_1, p_2, M) \tag{10-9a}$$

$$x_2 = x_2^M(p_1, p_2, M) \tag{10-9b}$$

$$\lambda = \lambda^M(p_1, p_2, M) \tag{10-9c}$$

Equations (10-9) are the *simultaneous* solution of Eqs. (10-7). Note the parameters involved: prices and money income. Equations (10-9a) and (10-9b) indicate the chosen levels of consumption for any given set of prices and money income. Hence, these equations represent what are commonly referred to as the *money-income-held-constant* demand curves. These functions are also commonly referred to as the "Marshallian" demands, after the great English economist Alfred Marshall.[†] The superscript M in these functions is a mnemonic for either "money" or "Marshall."

The phrase "money income held constant" is somewhat of a misnomer. Money income M is simply one of the three parameters upon which demand

---

[†] Marshall's *Principles*, first published in 1890, is the seminal synthesis of the neoclassical paradigm of economics. In it, Marshall recognized demand as a schedule of prices and quantities.

depends. The phrase arose from the usual graphical treatment of these demand curves in which p_1, say, is plotted vertically and x_1 is plotted on the horizontal axis, as in Fig. 10-4. In this usual graph, since only two dimensions are available, only the parameter p_1 is varied, and p_2 and M are held fixed at some levels p_2^0 and M^0. Thus this graph really represents a projection of the function $x_1 = x_1^M(p_1, p_2, M)$ onto a plane parallel to the x_1, p_1 axes, at some fixed levels of p_2 and M. Because these two-dimensional graphs obscure the other variables in the demand curve, one has to specify what they are; e.g., in this case they are p_2 and M. These *ceteris paribus* (other things held fixed) conditions are simply another way of indicating exactly what variables are present in the demand function. "Movements along" the demand curve $x_1 = x_1^M(p_1, p_2, M)$ simply refer to the response of quantity x_1 to changes in its own price p_1 where "shifts in the demand curve" represent responses to either p_2 or M. But it all depends on which variables are chosen to be graphed.

Although the marginal relations from which they are solved are not observable, the demand relations (10-9a) and (10-9b) relate to observable variables, and hence are potentially interesting.

If the demand functions (10-9a) and (10-9b) are substituted into $U(x_1, x_2)$, one obtains the *indirect utility function*

$$U^*(p_1, p_2, M) \equiv U(x_1^M(p_1, p_2, M), x_2^M(p_1, p_2, M)) \qquad (10\text{-}10)$$

Note that U^* is a function only of the parameters: prices and money income. The function $U^*(p_1, p_2, M)$ gives the maximum value of utility for any given prices and money income p_1, p_2, M, since it is precisely those quantities x_1 and x_2 that maximize utility subject to the budget constraint that are substituted into $U(x_1, x_2)$.

Let us now investigate the first-order marginal relations (10-7). In so doing, we can discover some aspects of the nature of maximizing behavior and some of

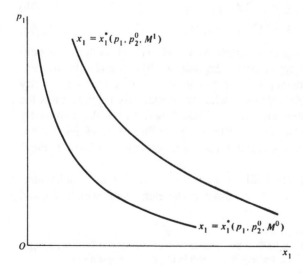

FIGURE 10-4

The Money-income-held-constant Demand Curve. The notion that "money income is held constant" is simply a way of stating that in fact x_1 is a function not only of p_1, against which it is plotted, but also p_2 and M. What is being held constant is merely a convention as to which variables are chosen to be plotted. In the usual case, depicted here, where x_1 is plotted against its price p_1, changes in M result in a different projection of the demand curve $x_1^*(p_1, p_2, M)$, and hence the drawn demand curve in the figure shifts.

the properties of the demand relations (10-9a) and (10-9b). The first proposition is one alluded to earlier, that no assumption of cardinality is necessary for the derivation of the demand curves $x_i^M(p_1,p_2,M)$; the same demand curves will occur if the indifference levels are relabeled by some monotonic transformation of $U(x_1,x_2)$.

Proposition 1. The demand curves implied by the assertion

maximize

$$U(x_1,x_2)$$

subject to

$$p_1x_1 + p_2x_2 = M$$

are identical to those derived when $U(x_1,x_2)$ is replaced by $V(x_1,x_2) = F(U(x_1,x_2))$, where $F'(U) > 0$.

Proof. Consider how the demand curves are in fact derived. The two demand curves $x_1^M(p_1,p_2,M)$ and $x_2^M(p_1,p_2,M)$ are derived from a tangency condition and the budget constraint. The tangency condition is obtained by eliminating the Lagrange multiplier λ from Eqs. (10-7a) and (10-7b), or

$$\frac{U_1}{U_2} = \frac{p_1}{p_2} \tag{10-11}$$

(This is the condition that would be obtained without the use of Lagrangian methods.) This equation, and the budget constraint

$$M - p_1x_1 - p_2x_2 = 0$$

are the two equations whose solutions are the demand curves above. How are these equations affected by replacing $U(x_1,x_2)$ by $V(x_1,x_2) = F(U(x_1,x_2))$, that is, by relabeling the indifference map, but preserving the rank ordering? Instead of (10-11) we get

$$\frac{V_1}{V_2} = \frac{p_1}{p_2} \tag{10-12}$$

However, $V_1 = F'(U)U_1, V_2 = F'(U)U_2$, and therefore

$$\frac{V_1}{V_2} = \frac{F'U_1}{F'U_2} = \frac{U_1}{U_2} = \frac{p_1}{p_2}$$

Since V_1/V_2 is identically U_1/U_2 everywhere, the equations used to solve for the demand curves are unchanged by such a transformation of U. That is, the solutions of (10-11) and the budget constraint are identical to the solutions of (10-12) and the budget constraint.

We must of course show that $V_1/V_2 = p_1/p_2$ is indeed a point of *maximum*, rather than minimum utility subject to constraint. That is, one must check that the consumer will actually set $V_1/V_2 = p_1/p_2$. If $F' < 0$, then V_1/V_2 would still equal U_1/U_2, but $V_1/V_2 = p_1/p_2$ would not be a tangency relating to *maximum* utility, since with $F' < 0$, increases in both x_1 and x_2, which would increase U, will *decrease V*. Since $V = F(U)$ and $F'(U) > 0$, V and U necessarily move in the same direction; thus U achieves a maximum if and only if V does likewise.

The demand curves are independent of any monotonic transformation of the utility function; i.e., they are independent of any relabeling of the indifference map. This proposition simply reinforces the notion that it is only *exchange values* that matter. Along any indifference curve, the slope measures the trade-offs a consumer is willing to make with regard to giving up one commodity to get more of another. These marginal evaluations of goods are the only operational measures of value; it matters not one whit whether that indifference curve is labeled as 10 utiles or 10,000 or 10^{10} utiles. It is the *slope,* and only the slope, of that level curve that matters for value and exchange, not some index of "satisfaction" associated with any given consumption bundle. In fact, it is impossible to tell whether a consumer is pleased or displeased to consume a given commodity bundle. If those are the only goods over which he or she has to make decisions, the *exchange* values do not in any way reflect whether the consumer is ecstatic or miserable with his or her lot.

The preceding derivation also makes clear why the concept of *diminishing marginal utility* is irrelevant in modern economics. With strictly ordinal utility, the rate at which marginal utility changes with respect to commodity changes depends on the particular index ranking used. Since $V_1 = F'(U)U_1$, using the product and chain rules, $V_{11} = F'U_{11} + U_1F''U_1$, and in general

$$V_{ij} = F'U_{ij} + F''U_iU_j \tag{10-13}$$

Now $F' > 0$ is assumed, and U_i and U_j are positive by nonsatiation. However, F'' can be positive or negative; for example, if $F(U) = \log U, F' > 0$ and $F'' < 0$; if $F(U) = e^U$, $F' > 0, F'' > 0$. Suppose $U_{ij} < 0$. Then if V is chosen so that $F'' > 0$, it is possible that $V_{ij} > 0$. Similarly, if $U_{ij} > 0$, there is some monotonic transformation which would make $V_{ij} < 0$, by having F'' sufficiently negative. Hence U_{ij} and V_{ij} (which include the case U_{ii} and V_{ii}) need not have the same sign, and yet identical demand curves are implied for each utility function. Thus a given set of observable demand relations is consistent with a utility function exhibiting diminishing marginal utility and some monotonic transformation of it exhibiting increasing marginal utility. Hence, the rate of increase or decrease of marginal utility carries no observable implications.

In a similar way, economists once defined complementary or substitute goods in terms of marginal utilities as follows: Two goods were called complements if consuming more of one raised the marginal utility of the other; and vice versa for substitutes. For example, it was argued that increasing one's consumption of pretzels raised the marginal utility of beer, hence beer and pretzels were complements. The algebra above shows why this reasoning is fallacious. The term being considered in this definition is $\partial U_i/\partial x_j = U_{ij} = U_{ji}$. But if $U_{ij} > 0$, say, some monotonic transformation of U, $F(U)$, with $F'' < 0$ can produce a new utility function with $\partial V_i/\partial x_j = V_{ij} < 0$, opposite to U_{ij}, and yet imply the same *observable* behavior, summarized in the demand relations. Hence this definition is incapable of categorizing observable behavior and is thus useless.

We now come to the second proposition concerning the demand curves which can be inferred directly from the first-order relations (10-7):

Proposition 2. The demand curves $x_i = x_i^M(p_1, p_2, M)$ are homogeneous of degree zero in p_1, p_2, and M. That is $x_i^M(tp_1, tp_2, tM) \equiv x_i^M(p_1, p_2, M)$.

Proof. Suppose all prices and money income are multiplied by some factor t. Then the utility maximum problem becomes

maximize

$$U(x_1, x_2)$$

subject to

$$tp_1 x_1 + tp_2 x_2 = tM$$

But this "new" budget constraint is clearly equivalent to the old one, $p_1 x_1 + p_2 x_2 = M$. Hence the first- and second-order equations are identical for these two problems, and thus the demand curves derived from this one, being solutions of those same first-order equations, are unchanged.

The meaning of this proposition is that it is only *relative* prices that matter to consumers, not absolute prices, or absolute money-income levels. This simply reinforces the tangency condition $U_1/U_2 = p_1/p_2$. It is the price *ratios* and the ratios of income to prices which determine marginal values and exchanges. Again, as mentioned earlier, some economists in the 1930s argued that consumers and producers would react to changes in nominal price levels even if real (relative) price levels remained unchanged. This concept, called money illusion, has been largely discarded. It was a denial of the homogeneity of demand curves.

Interpretation of the Lagrange Multiplier

Let us now consider the meaning of the Lagrange multiplier λ. From the first-order relations

$$\lambda^M = \frac{U_1}{p_1} = \frac{U_2}{p_2}$$

Also, by multiplying (10-7a) by x_1^M, (10-7b) by x_2^M and adding,

$$U_1 x_1^M + U_2 x_2^M = \lambda^M(p_1 x_1^M + p_2 x_2^M) = \lambda^M M$$

Hence

$$\lambda^M = \frac{U_1}{p_1} = \frac{U_2}{p_2} = \frac{U_1 x_1^M + U_2 x_2^M}{M} \tag{10-14}$$

These relations provide an important clue to the interpretation of λ^M. At any given consumption point, a certain amount of additional utility U_1 can be gained by consuming an additional increment of x_1. However, the marginal cost of this extra x_1 is p_1. Hence the marginal utility per dollar expenditure on x_1 is U_1/p_1.

Similarly, the marginal utility per dollar expenditure on x_2 is U_2/p_2. What the first equalities in (10-14) therefore say is that at a constrained maximum, the marginal utility per dollar must be the same at "both margins," i.e., for x_1 and x_2. If $U_1/p_1 > U_2/p_2$, say, the consumer could increase his or her utility with the same budget expenditure simply by reallocating expenditures from x_2 to x_1.

What of the third equality in (10-14)? This relation says that the same marginal utility per dollar must occur when the incremental expenditure is spread out over both commodities, as when it is spent at either margin. It is an envelope-related phenomenon, exhibiting the property that the rate of change of the objective function with respect to a parameter is the same, whether or not the decision variables adjust to that change. The rate of change of utility with respect to income is the same at each margin, and at all margins simultaneously.

Thus far, however, we have not shown mathematically what has been inferred on the basis of intuition. To say that λ^M is the marginal utility of money income is to say that $\lambda^M = \partial U^*/\partial M$, where again

$$U^*(p_1, p_2, M) = U(x_1^M(p_1, p_2, M), x_2^M(p_1, p_2, M)) \tag{10-10}$$

This can be shown directly. Differentiating (10-10),

$$\frac{\partial U^*}{\partial M} \equiv \frac{\partial U}{\partial x_1}\frac{\partial x_1^M}{\partial M} + \frac{\partial U}{\partial x_2}\frac{\partial x_2^M}{\partial M}$$

$$\equiv U_1\frac{\partial x_1^M}{\partial M} + U_2\frac{\partial x_2^M}{\partial M} \tag{10-15}$$

Using the first-order relations (10-7), $U_1 = \lambda^M p_1$, $U_2 = \lambda^M p_2$,

$$\frac{\partial U^*}{\partial M} \equiv \lambda^M\left(p_1\frac{\partial x_1^M}{\partial M} + p_2\frac{\partial x_2^M}{\partial M}\right) \tag{10-16}$$

Now consider the budget constraint $p_1 x_1 + p_2 x_2 = M$. When the demand curves are substituted back into this equation, one gets the identity

$$p_1 x_1^M + p_2 x_2^M \equiv M$$

Differentiating with respect to M yields

$$p_1\frac{\partial x_1^M}{\partial M} + p_2\frac{\partial x_2^M}{\partial M} \equiv 1 \tag{10-17}$$

But this is precisely the expression in parentheses in Eq. (10-16). Hence, substituting (10-17) into (10-16) yields

$$\lambda^M \equiv \frac{\partial U^*}{\partial M} \tag{10-18}$$

What we have just done is in fact merely a rederivation of the envelope theorem for the utility maximization problem. Using the envelope theorem, recalling that the Lagrangian $\mathcal{L} = U(x_1, x_2) + \lambda(M - p_1 x_1 - p_2 x_2)$,

$$\frac{\partial U^*}{\partial M} = \frac{\partial \mathscr{L}}{\partial M} = \lambda^M$$

Nonsatiation implies that $\lambda^M = \partial U^*/\partial M > 0$.

Roy's Identity

A similar procedure yields an important relation regarding the rate of change of maximum utility with respect to a price, that is, $\partial U^*/\partial p_i$. Using the envelope theorem,

$$\frac{\partial U^*}{\partial p_i} = \frac{\partial \mathscr{L}}{\partial p_i} = -\lambda^M x_i^M \qquad (10\text{-}19)$$

This result is known as Roy's identity, after the French economist René Roy, who first published it in 1931.[†] Moreover, solving for x_i^M and using (10-18),

$$x_i^M = -\frac{\partial U^*/\partial p_i}{\partial U^*/\partial M} \qquad (10\text{-}20)$$

Note that in the case of the demands derived from profit maximization, and those derived from constrained cost minimization, the choice functions are the partial derivatives of the indirect objective function, with respect to the prices. In the utility maximization model, the implied choice functions, i.e., the Marshallian demand functions, do *not* have this simple property; rather, they are the (negative) partials with respect to prices divided by the partial derivative with respect to money income.

By applying Young's theorem to the indirect utility function, we can derive reciprocity relations for the utility maximization model. From Roy's identity,

$$U_{p_1}^* = -\lambda^M x_1^M$$
$$U_{p_2}^* = -\lambda^M x_2^M$$

Therefore,

$$-U_{p_1 p_2}^* = \frac{\partial(\lambda^M x_1^M)}{\partial p_2} = \frac{\partial(\lambda^M x_2^M)}{\partial p_1} = -U_{p_2 p_1}^*$$

Applying the product rule yields

$$\lambda^M \frac{\partial x_1^M}{\partial p_2} + x_1^M \frac{\partial \lambda^M}{\partial p_2} = \lambda^M \frac{\partial x_2^M}{\partial p_1} + x_2^M \frac{\partial \lambda^M}{\partial p_1} \qquad (10\text{-}21)$$

In the profit maximization and constrained cost minimization models, the simple reciprocity results $\partial x_i^*/\partial p_j = \partial x_j^*/\partial p_i$ were derived. Since in the utility maxi-

---

[†] René Roy, *De L'Utilité, Contribution à la Théorie de Choix*, Dunod, 1931. More accessible is "La Distribution du Revenu Entre Les Divers Biens," *Econometrica*, **15**:205–225, 1947.

mization model, the explicit choice functions are not the first partial derivatives of the indirect objective function, the reciprocity conditions take on a more complicated form. It can be seen from (10-21), however, that if $\partial \lambda^M / \partial p_i = 0$ for all prices, then $\partial x_i^M / \partial p_j = \partial x_j^M / \partial p_i$. This condition implies that the utility function is homothetic, or, equivalently, the income elasticities are all unity. We will return to this at the end of the chapter.

Another reciprocity relation is available regarding responses to changes in income. Since $U_M^* = \lambda^M$, $U_{Mp_i}^* = \partial \lambda^M / \partial p_i$. However, $U_{p_iM}^* = \partial(-\lambda^M x_i^M)/\partial M = -[x_i^M (\partial \lambda^M / \partial M) + \lambda^M (\partial x_i^M / \partial M)]$. From Young's theorem, therefore,

$$\frac{\partial \lambda^M}{\partial p_i} = -x_i^M \frac{\partial \lambda^M}{\partial M} - \lambda^M \frac{\partial x_i^M}{\partial M} \tag{10-22}$$

This expression is used, among other places, in the analysis of consumer's surplus.

Example. Consider the utility function $U = x_1 x_2$. The level curves of this utility function are the rectangular hyperbolas $x_1 x_2 = U^0 = $ constant. What are the money income demand curves associated with this utility function? The Lagrangian for this problem is

$$\mathcal{L} = x_1 x_2 + \lambda(M - p_1 x_1 - p_2 x_2)$$

The first-order equations are thus

$$\mathcal{L}_1 = x_2 - \lambda p_1 = 0$$

$$\mathcal{L}_2 = x_1 - \lambda p_2 = 0$$

$$\mathcal{L}_\lambda = M - p_1 x_1 - p_2 x_2 = 0$$

The demand curves are the simultaneous solutions of these equations. Before proceeding, let us check the second-order determinant. Noting that $U_{11} = U_{22} = 0$, $U_{12} = U_{21} = 1$,

$$D = \begin{vmatrix} 0 & 1 & -p_1 \\ 1 & 0 & -p_2 \\ -p_1 & -p_2 & 0 \end{vmatrix} = 2p_1 p_2 > 0$$

The second-order condition is satisfied since both prices are assumed to be positive. Returning to the first-order equations, eliminate λ from the first two equations:

$$x_2 = \lambda p_1, \quad x_1 = \lambda p_2$$

Dividing

$$\frac{x_2}{x_1} = \frac{p_1}{p_2}$$

or

$$p_2 x_2 = p_1 x_1$$

This equation says, incidentally, that the total amount spent on $x_1, (p_1x_1)$, always equals the amount spent on $x_2, (p_2x_2)$, at any set of prices. We should thus expect the demand curves to be unitary elastic. (Why?)

The relation $p_2x_2 = p_1x_1$ is derived solely from the tangency condition $U_1/U_2 = p_1/p_2$, not at all from the budget constraint. This equation therefore holds for all possible income levels. It is the locus of all points (x_1, x_2) where the slopes of the level curves are equal to $-p_1/p_2$. Hence, $p_2x_2 = p_1x_1$ represents what is called the *income-consumption* path, shown in Fig. 10-5. The income-consumption path, one of the so-called Engel curves, illustrates how a consumer would respond to changes in income, holding prices constant. Rewriting the present equation slightly as $x_2 = (p_1/p_2)x_1$, we see that the income-consumption path is a straight line, or ray, emanating from the origin. [The point $(0,0)$ obviously satisfies the equation, and x_2 is a linear function of x_1.] The slope of this line is p_1/p_2. Since the income-consumption path is a straight line, by an easy exercise in similar triangles, a given percentage increase in money income M leads to that same percentage increase in the consumption of both commodities (see Fig. 10-6). We therefore expect to find that the demand curves derived from this utility function ($U = x_1x_2$) possess unitary income elasticity as well as unitary price elasticity. In order to derive the demand curves, the budget constraint must be brought in. The demand curves, we recall, are the simultaneous solutions of the tangency condition $U_1/U_2 = p_1/p_2$ and the budget constraint $p_1x_1 + p_2x_2 = M$. Since the former gives $p_2x_2 = p_1x_1$, substitute this into the budget equation, yielding

$$p_1x_1 + (p_1x_1) = M$$

or

$$2p_1x_1 = M$$

Therefore

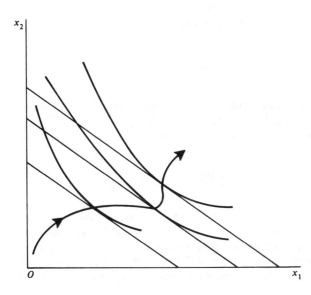

FIGURE 10-5

The Income-Consumption Path. The income-consumption path is the locus of all tangencies of the indifference curves to various budget constraints. That is, it is the locus of points (x_1, x_2) such that $U_1/U_2 = p_1/p_2$, where the slope of the indifference curve equals the slope of the budget constraint. This equation is independent of money income M; hence it represents the solutions of the first-order equations that correspond to all values of M. As M is increased, the implied consumption bundle moves in the direction of the arrow along the curve, reaching higher indifference levels for higher M.

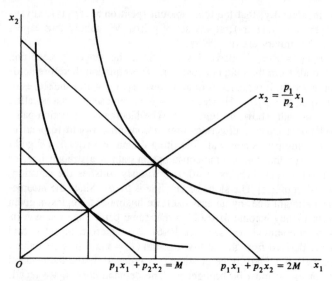

FIGURE 10-6

The Income-Consumption Path for the Utility Function $U = x_1x_2$. The income-consumption path is the solution of the tangency condition $U_1/U_2 = p_1/p_2$. For the utility function $U = x_1x_2$, $U_1 = x_2$, $U_2 = x_1$, thus the income-consumption path is $x_2/x_1 = p_1/p_2$, or $x_2 = (p_1/p_2)x_1$. This is represented geometrically as a straight line emanating from the origin. Doubling M will move the budget constraint twice as far from the origin as previously; when this is done for this utility function, clearly the consumption of x_1 and x_2 will exactly double. Hence, we expect to find demand curves with unitary income elasticities for this utility function.

$$x_1^M = \frac{M}{2p_1}$$

is the implied demand curve for x_1. In similar fashion,

$$x_2^M = \frac{M}{2p_2}$$

is the implied demand curve for x_2.

Let us check the envelope result for λ^M and Roy's equality. The indirect utility function is $U^*(p_1, p_2, M) = x_1^M x_2^M = (M/2p_1)(M/2p_2) = M^2/4p_1p_2$. Differentiating with respect to M, we find, as expected, $\lambda^M = \partial U^*/\partial M = M/2p_1p_2$. Also

$$\frac{\partial U^*/\partial p_1}{\partial U^*/\partial M} = \frac{-M^2/(4p_1^2p_2)}{M/(2p_1p_2)} = \frac{-M}{2p_1} = -x_1^M$$

Let us check the properties of these demand curves. We note, first, $\partial x_1^M/\partial p_1 = -M/2p_1^2 < 0$, $\partial x_2^M/\partial p_2 = -M/2p_2^2 < 0$; the demand curves are downward-sloping. The cross-effects are both 0; since x_1^M is not a function of p_2, and x_2^M is not a function of p_1, $\partial x_1^M/\partial p_2 = \partial x_2^M/\partial p_1 = 0$. This is a very unusual property for the money income demand curves. In general, $\partial x_i^M/\partial p_j \neq \partial x_j^M/\partial p_i \neq 0$, $i \neq j$.

The price elasticity of each demand curve is given by

$$\epsilon_{ii} = \frac{p_i}{x_i^M} \frac{\partial x_i^M}{\partial p_i}$$

Thus, for $x_1^M = M/2p_1$, $\partial x_1^M / \partial p_1 = -M/2p_1^2$.

Hence,

$$\epsilon_{11} = \frac{p_1}{x_1^M} \frac{\partial x_1^M}{\partial p_1} = \frac{2p_1^2}{M} \frac{-M}{2p_1^2} = -1$$

with a similar result for ϵ_{22}. As indicated earlier, the price elasticities of demand are indeed equal to -1, as expected, since total expenditures $p_1 x_1$ and $p_2 x_2$ are the same for all prices.

Regarding the income elasticities,

$$\epsilon_{1M} = \frac{M}{x_1^M} \frac{\partial x_1^M}{\partial M}$$

Here, $\partial x_1^M / \partial M = 1/2p_1$, $M/x_1^M = M/(M/2p_1) = 2p_1$. Hence, $\epsilon_{1M} = 1$ as expected from the linearity of the income-consumption path. Similar algebra shows that $\epsilon_{2M} = 1$ also.

10.3 THE RELATIONSHIP BETWEEN THE UTILITY MAXIMIZATION MODEL AND THE COST MINIMIZATION MODEL

In Chap. 8 we studied the problem,

minimize

$$C = w_1 x_1 + w_2 x_2$$

subject to

$$f(x_1, x_2) = y^0$$

where $y = f(x_1, x_2)$ was a production function, and w_1 and w_2 were the factor prices. Consider now a problem mathematically identical to this, that of minimizing the cost, or expenditure, of achieving a given utility level U^0, or
minimize

$$M = p_1 x_1 + p_2 x_2$$

subject to

$$U(x_1, x_2) = U^0 \tag{10-23}$$

where p_1 and p_2 are the prices of the two consumer goods x_1 and x_2, respectively, and $U = U(x_1, x_2)$ is a utility function. The entire analysis of Chap. 8 applies to this cost minimization problem. The only changes are in the interpretation of the variables; the mathematical structure is the same.

The first-order conditions for this problem are given by setting the partials of the appropriate Lagrangian equal to 0:

$$\mathcal{L} = p_1 x_1 + p_2 x_2 + \lambda(U^0 - U(x_1, x_2))$$

$$\mathcal{L}_1 = p_1 - \lambda U_1 = 0 \tag{10-24a}$$

$$\mathcal{L}_2 = p_2 - \lambda U_2 = 0 \tag{10-24b}$$

$$\mathcal{L}_\lambda = U^0 - U(x_1, x_2) = 0 \tag{10-24c}$$

The sufficient second-order condition for a constrained minimum is:

$$H = \begin{vmatrix} -\lambda U_{11} & -\lambda U_{12} & -U_1 \\ -\lambda U_{21} & -\lambda U_{22} & -U_2 \\ -U_1 & -U_2 & 0 \end{vmatrix} < 0 \tag{10-25}$$

Assuming (10-24) and (10-25) hold, choice functions of the following type are implied, as simultaneous solutions to the first-order relations (10-24):

$$x_1 = x_1^U(p_1, p_2, U^0) \tag{10-26a}$$

$$x_2 = x_2^U(p_1, p_2, U^0) \tag{10-26b}$$

$$\lambda = \lambda^U(p_1, p_2, U^0) \tag{10-26c}$$

Whereas the demand curves (10-9), $x_i = x_i^M(p_1, p_2, M)$ are called the "*money income* held constant" demand curves, the demand curves (10-26), $x_i = x_i^U(p_1, p_2, U^0)$ are called the "*real income* held constant," or "income-compensated" demand curves. These latter curves hold utility, or "real" income, constant; they are mathematically equivalent to the "output held constant" factor demands of the previous chapter. The functions $x_i^U(p_1, p_2, U^0)$ are also commonly referred to as "Hicksian" demands, after Sir John R. Hicks, the British Nobel Laureate in Economics. The partial derivatives of the Hicksian demand functions with respect to the prices represent *pure substitution effects*, since, utility being held constant, the consumer remains on the same indifference level. Substituting the Hicksian demands into the objective function yields the *expenditure function*, $M^*(p_1, p_2, U^0) = p_1 x_1^U(p_1, p_2, U^0) + p_2 x_2^U(p_1, p_2, U^0)$, indicating the minimum expenditure needed to achieve utility U^0 at prices p_1 and p_2.

What is the relation between the demand curves (10-26), derived from cost minimization, $x_i = x_i^U(p_1, p_2, U^0)$, $i = 1, 2$, and the demand curves (10-9), derived from utility maximization, $x_i = x_i^U(p_1, p_2, M)$, $i = 1, 2$? Consider the first-order relations (10-24a) and (10-24b). Eliminating λ yields

$$\frac{p_1}{p_2} = \frac{U_1}{U_2}$$

This is the same tangency condition as that derived in the utility maximization problem. In both cases, the budget line must be tangent to the indifference curve. In fact, consider Fig. 10-7. In the utility maximization problem, given parametric prices and money income M, some maximum level of utility U^* will be achieved,

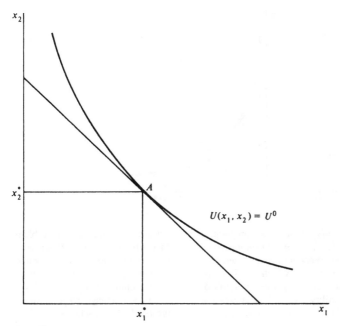

FIGURE 10-7
The Tangency Solution to the Cost-minimization and Utility-maximization Problems. If $U(x_1, x_2)$ is maximized subject to $p_1 x_1 + p_2 x_2 = M$, some level of utility U^* will be achieved at point A. If now U^* is set equal to U^0, and the consumer minimizes the cost of achieving $U^* = U^0$, the point A will again be achieved. However, the comparative statics of the two problems differs, because the parameters of the problems are not identical (see Fig. 10-8a and b).

at, say, point A, where the consumer will consume x_1^* and x_2^* amounts of x_1 and x_2, respectively.

Suppose now the indifference level U^* were specified in advance; that is, $U^* = U^0$, and the consumer minimized the cost of achieving $U^* = U^0$, with the same prices. Then, clearly, the consumer would wind up at the same A, consuming the package (x_1^*, x_2^*). *But the comparative statics of the two problems are not the same!* The adjustments to price changes are different because different things are being held constant. Consider Fig. 10-8. In the case $x_i = x_i^M(p_1, p_2, M)$, as p_1, say, is lowered, the budget line MM' swings out along the x_1 axis to MM'' to a new, higher intercept, as depicted in panel (a). This increases the achieved utility level to U^{**}. However, in the cost minimization problem [panel (b)], if p_1 is lowered, the level of U is parametric: it is held fixed at U^0. It is the achieved minimum budget M^* that decreases, as the new tangency at A'' is reached, at the new expenditure level M^{**}.

Finally, we note from (10-7a) and (10-7b),

$$\lambda^M = \frac{U_1}{p_1} = \frac{U_2}{p_2}$$

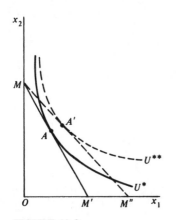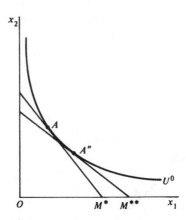

FIGURE 10-8

Utility maximization; Cost minimization. The comparative statics of the cost minimization problem differs from the statics of the utility maximization problem in that different parameters are held constant when a price changes. When p_1 changes, say, decreases, in the utility maximization problem (Fig. 10-8a), the horizontal intercept, which equals M/p_1, shifts to the right, to keep M constant. A new tangency, A', on a higher utility level, is implied. In the cost minimization problem (Fig. 10-8b), as p_1 decreases, the utility level is held constant at U^0, and hence, the tangency point slides along $U(x_1, x_2) = U^0$ to point A'', where a new, lower expenditure level M^{**} is achieved.

However, from (10-24a) and (10-24b),

$$\lambda^U = \frac{p_1}{U_1} = \frac{p_2}{U_2}$$

Hence, at any tangency point, for the proper U^* and M^*,

$$\lambda^M = \frac{1}{\lambda^U} \qquad (10\text{-}27)$$

In the production scenario, λ^U is the marginal cost of *output*. Here, in utility analysis, it is the (unobservable) marginal cost of *utility*. It is the reciprocal of λ^M, the marginal utility of money income, as the units of each term would indicate.

The student is warned, however, not to simply regard $\partial M^*/\partial U^0 = 1/(\partial U^*/\partial M)$ as trivial. These partials cannot simply be inverted; $\partial M^*/\partial U^0$ and $\partial U^*/\partial M$ refer to two separate problems. It is a matter of some curiosity that the simple relation (10-27) holds.

The fundamental contribution to the theory of the consumer, known as the Slutsky equation (developed by E. Slutsky in 1915), relates the rates of change of consumption with respect to price changes when money income is held constant, to the corresponding change when real income, or utility, is held constant. That is, a relationship is given between $\partial x_i^M/\partial p_j$ and $\partial x_i^U/\partial p_j$. This relationship will be derived in the next two sections.

We must check that the second-order conditions for the utility maximization and cost minimization problems are identical. This fact is visually obvious from

Fig. 10-7. Clearly, interior solutions to both problems require that the indifference curves be convex to the origin, at all levels. Therefore, we should be able to show that the determinant D given in (10-8) is positive if and only if H, given in (10-25), is negative. We leave it as an exercise in determinants that in fact $H = -\lambda^M D$. By nonsatiation, $\lambda^M > 0$ and thus $H < 0$ if and only if $D > 0$. For either cost minimization or utility maximization, the utility functions must be quasiconcave.

Let us recall the comparative statics of the cost minimization problem. As was shown in Chap. 8, differentiating the first-order conditions (10-24) with respect to p_1 yields the comparative statics equations

$$
\begin{pmatrix}
-\lambda U_{11} & -\lambda U_{12} & -U_1 \\
-\lambda U_{21} & -\lambda U_{22} & -U_2 \\
-U_1 & -U_2 & 0
\end{pmatrix}
\begin{pmatrix}
\dfrac{\partial x_1^U}{\partial p_1} \\[2ex]
\dfrac{\partial x_2^U}{\partial p_1} \\[2ex]
\dfrac{\partial \lambda^U}{\partial p_1}
\end{pmatrix}
=
\begin{pmatrix}
-1 \\
0 \\
0
\end{pmatrix}
$$

Differentiating with respect to p_2 would place the -1 in row 2 on the right-hand side. In general, we find, again,

$$
\frac{\partial x_i^U}{\partial p_j} = \frac{-H_{ji}}{H} \tag{10-27}
$$

Inspection of H and D quickly reveals that $H_{ij} = (\lambda^M)^2 D_{ij}$; thus

$$
\frac{\partial x_i^U}{\partial p_j} = \frac{-H_{ji}}{H} = \frac{\lambda^M D_{ji}}{D} \tag{10-28}
$$

Lastly, $\partial x_i^U / \partial p_i < 0$; when $i \neq j$, however, $\partial x_i^U / \partial p_j \gtrless 0$ (except in the two-variable case).

10.4 THE COMPARATIVE STATICS OF THE UTILITY MAXIMIZATION MODEL; THE TRADITIONAL DERIVATION OF THE SLUTSKY EQUATION

It is apparent from the structure of the utility maximization model that no refutable hypotheses are strictly implied, on the basis of the maximization hypothesis alone. All of the parameters appear in the constraint. As the general analyses of Chaps. 6 and 7 show, no testable implications appear in any model for any parameter appearing in the constraint function.

The interest in this model stems from the analysis of E. Slutsky in 1915, and expanded by John R. Hicks in 1937, in which the response to a change in price was conceptually partitioned into two separate effects; a pure substitution effect, in which "real" income (utility, in Hicks' formulation) is held constant, and a pure income effect, in which prices are held fixed, and the budget line shifts parallel to itself to the final maximum utility level. As we shall presently show, whereas the income effect is indeterminate in sign, the pure substitution effect, which is precisely the response derived from the minimum expenditure model, is always negative.

We can illustrate this analysis graphically as follows. Suppose a consumer with preferences given by the indifference curves shown in Fig. 10-9 initially faces the budget constraint MM, and achieves maximum utility at point A, consuming x_1^0 amount of x_1. Suppose p_1 is lowered. The budget line will pivot to the right, producing a new utility maximum at point B. The total change in consumption of x_1 is $x_1^M - x_1^0$. This amount, however, is partitionable into

$$x_1^M - x_1^0 = (x_1^U - x_1^0) + (x_1^M - x_1^U)$$

The first term, $x_1^U - x_1^0$, is a change in x_1, holding utility constant. The tangency point C occurs at the new, lower, p_1, but at a reduced budget level represented by the budget constraint $M''M''$. Point C is the combination of x_1 and x_2 that minimizes the cost of achieving the old utility level at the new prices (i.e., new price p_1 of x_1). Hence, the change $x_1^U - x_1^0$ is a pure substitution effect, and would be generated by the cost minimization problem.

The remaining part of the total change, $x_1^M - x_1^U$, is generated by a parallel shift of the budget equation from $M''M''$ to MM'. Since prices are held constant, this is a pure income effect.

The preceding graphical analysis, while a useful aid to understanding this model, does not correspond exactly to the comparative statics analysis. Comparative statics relations are the instantaneous rates of change of choice variables with respect to parameter changes; they are partial derivatives evaluated at a particular point. Let us now proceed with the traditional analysis of the utility maximization model, even though, as we shall see, a more powerful technique, using modern duality theory, is available for deriving the main result. However, the traditional technique is still important for nonstandard models, and so we apply it here to illustrate its use.

The first-order equations of the utility maximization problem, in identity form, are, again,

$$U_1(x_1^M, x_2^M) - \lambda^M p_1 \equiv 0$$
$$U_2(x_1^M, x_2^M) - \lambda^M p_2 \equiv 0$$
$$M - p_1 x_1^M - p_2 x_2^M \equiv 0 \qquad (10\text{-}7)$$

How will the consumer react, first, to a change in his or her money income M, prices being held constant? Differentiating these identities with respect to M, noting that M itself appears only in the third equation, the following system of equations is found:

$$U_{11}\frac{\partial x_1^M}{\partial M} + U_{12}\frac{\partial x_2^M}{\partial M} - p_1\frac{\partial \lambda^M}{\partial M} \equiv 0 \qquad (10\text{-}29a)$$

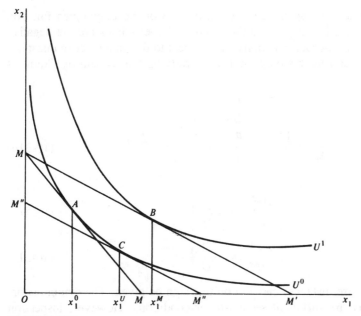

FIGURE 10-9

The Substitution and Income Effects of a Price Change. This diagram relates to finite movements in the consumption of x_1 due to a finite change in p_1. It is therefore not directly comparable with the Slutsky equation, which deals with instantaneous rates of change. However, the income and substitution effects of a price change are easily seen in the above well-known diagram. The original tangency is at A, on budget line MM. When p_1 is lowered, the horizontal intercept increases, and the budget line pivots to MM', yielding a new tangency at B. The total change in consumption of x_1 is $x_1^M - x_1^0$. This amount can be partly attributed to $x_1^U - x_1^0$, a pure substitution effect obtained by sliding the budget line around the indifference curve U^0 until it is parallel to the budget line MM', reflecting the new prices. Since utility is held constant, this is indeed a pure substitution effect. The remaining part of the total change in x_1, $x_1^M - x_1^U$, is attributable to a parallel shift in the budget line from $M''M''$ to MM'. This is a pure income effect since prices are held constant.

$$U_{21}\frac{\partial x_1^M}{\partial M} + U_{22}\frac{\partial x_2^M}{\partial M} - p_2\frac{\partial \lambda^M}{\partial M} \equiv 0 \qquad (10\text{-}29b)$$

$$1 - p_1\frac{\partial x_1^M}{\partial M} - p_2\frac{\partial x_2^M}{\partial M} \equiv 0 \qquad (10\text{-}29c)$$

In matrix form, this system of equations is

$$\begin{pmatrix} U_{11} & U_{12} & -p_1 \\ U_{21} & U_{22} & -p_2 \\ -p_1 & -p_2 & 0 \end{pmatrix} \begin{pmatrix} \dfrac{\partial x_1^M}{\partial M} \\ \dfrac{\partial x_2^M}{\partial M} \\ \dfrac{\partial \lambda^M}{\partial M} \end{pmatrix} = \begin{pmatrix} 0 \\ 0 \\ -1 \end{pmatrix} \qquad (10\text{-}30)$$

The coefficient matrix is, again, the second partials of the Lagrangian function $\mathscr{L} = U + \lambda(M - p_1x_1 - p_2x_2)$ and the right-hand coefficients are the negative first partials of the first-order equations with respect to the parameter in question, here M, as the general methodology indicates. Solving this system by Cramer's rule yields

$$\frac{\partial x_1^M}{\partial M} = \frac{\begin{vmatrix} 0 & U_{12} & -p_1 \\ 0 & U_{22} & -p_2 \\ -1 & -p_2 & 0 \end{vmatrix}}{D} = \frac{-D_{31}}{D} \tag{10-31a}$$

and similarly

$$\frac{\partial x_2^M}{\partial M} = \frac{-D_{32}}{D} \tag{10-31b}$$

$$\frac{\partial \lambda^M}{\partial M} = \frac{-D_{33}}{D} \tag{10-31c}$$

In none of these instances can a definitive sign be given. The denominators D are positive, by the sufficient second-order conditions. However, inspection reveals

$$D_{31} = -p_2U_{12} + p_1U_{22} \gtrless 0$$

and likewise

$$D_{32} = p_2U_{11} - p_1U_{21} \gtrless 0$$

Also,

$$D_{33} = U_{11}U_{22} - U_{12}^2 \gtrless 0$$

because D_{33} is not a *border-preserving* principal minor.

What Eqs. (10-31a) and (10-31b) say, not surprisingly, is that convexity of the indifference curves is insufficiently strong to rule out the possibility of inferior goods. That is, it is entirely possible to have $\partial x_1^M/\partial M < 0$ or $\partial x_2^M/\partial M < 0$, as Fig. 10-10 shows. It is *not* possible, however, for both x_1 and x_2 to be inferior. If that were so, more income would result in reduced purchases of both x_1 and x_2, violating the postulate that more is preferred to less. On a more formal level, the third equation in the comparative statics system, Eq. (10-29c), the differentiated budget constraint, says that $p_1\partial x_1^M/\partial M + p_2\partial x_2^M/\partial M = 1 > 0$. Since the prices p_1 and p_2 are both positive, it cannot be that $\partial x_1^M/\partial M < 0$ *and* $\partial x_2^M/\partial M < 0$. Also, inferiority is of necessity a *local* concept. Goods cannot be inferior over the whole range of consumption, or else they would never be consumed in positive amounts in the first place!

Let us now differentiate the first-order Eqs. (10-7) with respect to the prices, in particular, p_1. This operation will yield the rates of change of consumption of any good with respect to a change in one price, holding all other prices and money income constant. Performing the indicated operation,

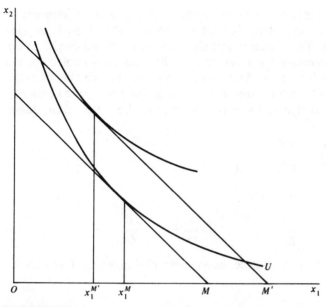

FIGURE 10-10
Convexity of the Indifference Curves Allows Inferior Goods. If money income is raised from M to M', the consumption of one good, say x_1, can decrease. A common example is the case of hamburger. As incomes rise, say, as students leave college and acquire jobs, hamburger is often replaced by steak. A word of warning: inferiority is a "local" concept. A good cannot be inferior over the whole range of consumption, or else it would never have been consumed in positive amounts in the first place!

$$U_{11}\frac{\partial x_1^M}{\partial p_1} + U_{12}\frac{\partial x_2^M}{\partial p_1} - p_1\frac{\partial \lambda^M}{\partial p_1} - \lambda^M \equiv 0 \qquad (10\text{-}32a)$$

$$U_{21}\frac{\partial x_1^M}{\partial p_1} + U_{22}\frac{\partial x_2^M}{\partial p_1} - p_2\frac{\partial \lambda^M}{\partial p_1} \equiv 0 \qquad (10\text{-}32b)$$

$$-p_1\frac{\partial x_1^M}{\partial p_1} - x_1^M - p_2\frac{\partial x_2^M}{\partial p_1} \equiv 0 \qquad (10\text{-}32c)$$

where the product rule has been used to differentiate $-\lambda^M p_1$ and $-p_1 x_1^M$ (partially) with respect to p_1. In matrix form, this system of equations is

$$\begin{pmatrix} U_{11} & U_{12} & -p_1 \\ U_{21} & U_{22} & -p_2 \\ -p_1 & -p_2 & 0 \end{pmatrix} \begin{pmatrix} \dfrac{\partial x_1^M}{\partial p_1} \\ \dfrac{\partial x_2^M}{\partial p_1} \\ \dfrac{\partial \lambda^M}{\partial p_1} \end{pmatrix} = \begin{pmatrix} \lambda^M \\ 0 \\ x_1^M \end{pmatrix}$$

It is apparent right here that no comparative statics results will be forthcoming from this model; i.e., no definitive sign for $\partial x_i^M / \partial p_1$ or $\partial \lambda^M / \partial p_1$ is implied by utility maximization. The reason is that there are two nonzero entries in the right-hand column. This means that knowledge of the signs of *two* cofactors in a given column of D will have to be determined; since only one can be a border-preserving principal minor (whose sign *is* known), at least one must be an off-diagonal cofactor, whose sign and size is indeterminate from the maximization hypothesis alone.

Solving via Cramer's rule,

$$\frac{\partial x_1^M}{\partial p_1} = \frac{\begin{vmatrix} \lambda^M & U_{12} & -p_1 \\ 0 & U_{22} & -p_2 \\ x_1^M & -p_2 & 0 \end{vmatrix}}{D} = \frac{\lambda^M D_{11}}{D} + \frac{x_1^M D_{31}}{D} \tag{10-33a}$$

Likewise, putting $(\lambda^M, 0, x_1^M)$ into the second and third columns, respectively, in the numerator,

$$\frac{\partial x_2^M}{\partial p_1} = \frac{\lambda^M D_{12}}{D} + \frac{x_1^M D_{32}}{D} \tag{10-33b}$$

$$\frac{\partial \lambda^M}{\partial p_1} = \frac{\lambda^M D_{13}}{D} + \frac{x_1^M D_{33}}{D} \tag{10-33c}$$

The determinant D_{11} is a border-preserving principal minor and is negative by the second-order conditions. Actually, by inspection, $D_{11} = -p_2^2 < 0$, quite apart from the second-order conditions. The determinant D_{33} is on-diagonal; however, it is not border-preserving; hence its sign is unknown. All the other cofactors are off-diagonal and are thus of indeterminate sign.

As expected, no sign is implied for either $\partial x_i^M / \partial p_j$ or $\partial x_i^U / \partial p_j$ $(i \neq j)$. We define consumer goods as *substitutes* if an increase in the price of one good *increases* the demand for the other, and as *complements* if an increase in the price of one good *decreases* the demand for the other good. For example, an increase in the price of gasoline would likely decrease the demand for cars (a complement) and increase the demand for coal (a substitute). Substitutes and complements can be defined to either include or exclude the income effects, i.e., by using either the Marshallian or Hicksian demand functions. If the income effects are included, then the goods are called "gross" substitutes or complements; otherwise they are termed "net" substitutes or complements. Thus, $\partial x_i^M / \partial p_j > 0$ means that x_i and x_j are gross substitutes; $\partial x_i^U / \partial p_j < 0$ means x_i and x_j are net complements. Convex indifference curves (i.e., strictly increasing, quasi-concave utility functions) allow both substitutes and complements (by either definition), except in the two-good case, where the goods must be net substitutes (why?).

The interest in Eqs. (10-33a) and (10-33b) stems from the interpretation of the individual terms in the expression. Recall Eq. (10-28). In fact, the first terms on the right-hand side of Eqs. (10-33a) and (10-33b) are the pure substitution effects of a change in price, as derived from the cost minimization model. Consider also Eqs. (10-31a) and (10-31b), relating to the income effects. These expressions are, respectively, precisely the second terms of the preceding equations when multiplied by the term $-x_1^M$. Hence, Eqs. (10-33a) and (10-33b) can be written

$$\frac{\partial x_1^M}{\partial p_1} = \frac{\partial x_1^U}{\partial p_1} - x_1^M \frac{\partial x_1^M}{\partial M} \qquad (10\text{-}34a)$$

$$\frac{\partial x_2^M}{\partial p_1} = \frac{\partial x_2^U}{\partial p_1} - x_1^M \frac{\partial x_2^M}{\partial M} \qquad (10\text{-}34b)$$

The equations for the response of the money-income-held-constant demand curves to price changes, when written in this form, are known as the *Slutsky equations*. Similar expressions can be written with respect to changes in p_2, and are left as an exercise for the student:

$$\frac{\partial x_1^M}{\partial p_2} = \frac{\partial x_1^U}{\partial p_2} - x_2^M \frac{\partial x_1^M}{\partial M} \qquad (10\text{-}34c)$$

$$\frac{\partial x_2^M}{\partial p_2} = \frac{\partial x_2^U}{\partial p_2} - x_2^M \frac{\partial x_2^M}{\partial M} \qquad (10\text{-}34d)$$

In general (and this result is, in fact, a general result for the case of n goods),

$$\frac{\partial x_i^M}{\partial p_j} = \frac{\partial x_i^U}{\partial p_j} - x_j^M \frac{\partial x_i^M}{\partial M} \qquad i,j = 1, \ldots, n \qquad (10\text{-}34)$$

The Slutsky equation shows that the response of a utility-maximizing consumer to a change in price can be split up, conceptually, into two parts: first, a pure substitution effect, or a response to a price change holding the consumer on the original indifference surface, and second, a pure income effect, wherein income is changed, holding prices constant, to reach a tangency on the new indifference curve.

10.5 THE MODERN DERIVATION OF THE SLUTSKY EQUATION

In the previous section, the Slutsky equation was derived via the traditional methods of comparative statics. The procedure is somewhat tedious and long, an unfortunate requisite for doing that derivation correctly. However, a much shorter route is available by way of the more modern envelope analysis. The new method is much more revealing than the old.

We start off with a money income demand curve, $x_1 = x_1^M(p_1, p_2, M)$. When p_1 changes, p_2 and M are held constant, producing a change in utility, since, by Roy's identity, $\partial U^*/\partial p_i = -\lambda^M x_i^M < 0$. (When p_1, for example, is lowered, the opportunity set of the consumer expands, hence the attained utility increases.) Suppose, now, when p_1 changes, M is also changed to the minimum amount necessary to keep utility constant. That is, define the function $M = M^*(p_1, p_2, U^0)$ such that M^* is exactly that minimum money income level that keeps $U = U^0$ when p_1 (or any other price) changes. Then, by definition, if $x_1^U(p_1, p_2, U^0)$ is the utility-held-constant demand curve,

$$x_1^U(p_1, p_2, U^0) \equiv x_1^M(p_1, p_2, M^*(p_1, p_2, U^0)) \tag{10-35}$$

This is an identity—it defines $x_1^U(p_1, p_2, U^0)$. Differentiate both sides with respect to p_1, say, using the chain rule on the right-hand side:

$$\frac{\partial x_1^U}{\partial p_1} \equiv \frac{\partial x_1^M}{\partial p_1} + \frac{\partial x_1^M}{\partial M} \frac{\partial M^*}{\partial p_1}$$

What is $\partial M^*/\partial p_1$? The function $M^*(p_1, p_2, U^0)$ is the minimum cost, or expenditure, of achieving utility level U^0 (at given prices). M^* is therefore simply the (indirect) cost or expenditure function from the cost minimization problem

minimize

$$M = p_1 x_1 + p_2 x_2$$

subject to

$$U^0 - U(x_1, x_2) = 0$$

the Lagrangian of which is $\mathcal{L} = p_1 x_1 + p_2 x_2 + \lambda(U^0 - U(x_1, x_2))$. By the envelope theorem,

$$\frac{\partial M^*}{\partial p_1} = \frac{\partial \mathcal{L}}{\partial p_1} = x_1^U = x_1^M$$

at any given point. Substituting this into the preceding equation yields

$$\frac{\partial x_1^U}{\partial p_1} \equiv \frac{\partial x_1^M}{\partial p_1} + x_1^M \frac{\partial x_1^M}{\partial M}$$

This is precisely the Slutsky Eq. (10-34a)! (Note that here $\partial x_1^U/\partial p_1$ appears alone on the left-hand side; we have merely rearranged the terms).

This proof is perfectly general. For n goods,

$$x_i^U(p_1, \ldots, p_n, U^0) \equiv x_i^M(p_1, \ldots, p_n, M^*(p_1, \ldots, p_n, U^0))$$

where $M^*(p_1, \ldots, p_n, U^0)$ is the minimum cost of achieving utility level U^0 at given prices. By the envelope theorem from the cost minimization problem, $\partial M^*/\partial p_j = x_j^U = x_j^M$ at a given point. Thus

$$\frac{\partial x_i^U}{\partial p_j} \equiv \frac{\partial x_i^M}{\partial p_j} + \frac{\partial x_i^M}{\partial M} \frac{\partial M^*}{\partial p_j}$$

$$\equiv \frac{\partial x_i^M}{\partial p_j} + x_j^M \frac{\partial x_i^M}{\partial M}$$

The Slutsky equation can be derived in this fashion by starting with the compensated demand curve $x_i^U(p_1, \ldots, p_n, U^0)$ and using it to derive the uncompensated demand curve $x_i^M(p_1, \ldots, p_n, M)$. Specifically, if some p_j changes, change U^0 also by that *maximum* amount consistent with holding money income M constant. That is, define $U^0 = U^*(p_1, \ldots, p_n, M)$ to be the maximum achievable utility level for a given budget M, at given prices. Then U^* is simply the indirect utility function of the utility maximization problem: max $U(x_1, \ldots, x_n)$ subject to $\sum p_i x_i = M$. The associated Lagrangian is $\mathcal{L} = U(x_1, \ldots, x_n) + \lambda(M - \sum p_i x_i)$. By the envelope theorem, $\partial U^*/\partial p_j = \partial \mathcal{L}/\partial p_j = -\lambda^M x_j^M$.

By definition, then,

$$x_i^M(p_1, \ldots, p_n, M) \equiv x_i^U(p_1, \ldots, p_n, U^*(p_1, \ldots, p_n, M))$$

A similar procedure to the preceding, together with an extra step, yields the Slutsky equation. This derivation is left to the student as an exercise.

The Slutsky equations are sometimes written

$$\left(\frac{\partial x_i}{\partial p_j}\right)_M = \left(\frac{\partial x_i}{\partial p_j}\right)_U - x_j\left(\frac{\partial x_i}{\partial M}\right)_p$$

where the parameters outside the parentheses indicate the *ceteris paribus* conditions, i.e., what is being held constant. This representation is satisfactory, but it obscures the source of these partial derivatives. As has been constantly stressed, the notation $dy/dx, \partial f/\partial x_1$, etc., makes sense only if well-specified functions $y = f(x), y = f(x_1, x_2, \ldots)$ etc., exist (and are differentiable). It is nonsense to write derivative-type expressions when the implied functional dependence is lacking. The Slutsky equation should be regarded as a relationship between two different conceptions of a demand function:

$$x_i = x_i^M(p_1, p_2, M) \tag{10-9}$$

and

$$x_i = x_i^U(p_1, p_2, U) \tag{10-26}$$

Each equation is a solution of a well-defined system of equations stemming from an optimization hypothesis; in the case of Eq. (10-9), from utility maximization, and in the case of Eq. (10-26), from cost minimization. The Slutsky equation shows that these two equations are related in an interesting manner.

Let us examine the Slutsky equation again and see why it makes sense. We have

$$\frac{\partial x_i^M}{\partial p_j} = \frac{\partial x_i^U}{\partial p_j} - x_j^M \frac{\partial x_i^M}{\partial M}$$

When a price changes, the consumer begins to substitute away from the good becoming relatively higher-priced. However, the price change also changes the opportunity set of the consumer. If the price p_j falls, the consumer can achieve certain consumption levels previously outside his or her former budget constraint.

This is like a gain in income. However, what determines the size and sign of this income effect? If p_j *decreases,* an effect similar to an *increase* in income is produced. Both produce larger opportunities. Price increases and income decreases are similarly related. Hence, it is plausible that the income term in the Slutsky equation be entered with a negative sign. The negative sign indicates that the implied change in income is in the opposite direction to the price change.

What about the multiplier x_j^M in the income term? What is its meaning and/or function? Suppose the commodity whose price has changed is salt. Salt is a very minor part of most people's budget. Hence, the income effect of a price change in salt should be small, even for large price changes. Suppose, however, the price of petroleum changes. Petroleum products may occupy a large part of our budgets, especially of those people who commute by car, or heat their homes with oil. These income effects can be expected to be large. It is plausible, therefore, to "weight" the income effect $\partial x_i^M / \partial M$ by the amount of the good x_j whose price has changed. If the price of Rolls Royces increases, the effect on my consumption of that and other goods is negligible. Change the price of something I consume intensively and my *real* income, or utility, is apt to change considerably.

In the case where $i = j$, the Slutsky equation takes the form

$$\frac{\partial x_i^M}{\partial p_i} = \frac{\partial x_i^U}{\partial p_i} - x_i^M \frac{\partial x_i^M}{\partial M} \tag{10-36}$$

The important question, again, is, what refutable hypothesis emerges from this analysis? Can anything be said of the sign of $\partial x_i^M / \partial p_i$? Strictly speaking, no. However, we know that $\partial x_i^U / \partial p_i < 0$. If x_i is not an inferior good, that is, if $\partial x_i^M / \partial M \geq 0$, then $\partial x_i^M / \partial p_i < 0$ necessarily. This proposition is nontautological only if an independent measure of inferiority (i.e., not based on the Slutsky equation) is available.

It is conceivable, though not likely, that $\partial x_i^M / \partial p_i > 0$, the so-called *Giffen good* case. Do not make the mistaken assumption that because something is mathematically possible, it is therefore likely to be observed in the real world. The refutable proposition $\partial x_i^M / \partial p_i < 0$ cannot be inferred from utility maximization alone; it is not on that account less usable. Utility maximization is a hypothesis concerning individual preferences for more rather than less, and provides probably the most successful framework for analyzing economic problems.[†]

A similar analysis can be applied to the Lagrange multiplier λ^M, the marginal utility of income. A "compensated" or "Hicksian" marginal utility of income, λ^H, would show responses in this value as one moved along a single indifference curve. Proceeding in exactly the same manner,

---

[†] There are "general equilibrium" reasons for not believing that $\partial x_i^M / \partial p_i > 0$. If p_i falls, the consumers of x_i experience a gain in wealth; however, the current owners and sellers of x_i experience a wealth loss. Since at any time the quantity bought equals the quantity sold, the overall income effects of price changes are apt to be small.

$$\lambda^H(p_1, p_2, U^0) \equiv \lambda^M(p_1, p_2, M^*(p_1, p_2, U^0)) \qquad (10\text{-}37)$$

Differentiating with respect to, say, p_1,

$$\frac{\partial \lambda^H}{\partial p_1} \equiv \frac{\partial \lambda^M}{\partial p_1} + \left(\frac{\partial \lambda^M}{\partial M}\right)\left(\frac{\partial M^*}{\partial p_1}\right) \qquad (10\text{-}38)$$

Substituting $x_1^M = x_1^U = \partial M^*/\partial p_1$, we obtain a "Slutsky" equation for the marginal utility of income:

$$\frac{\partial \lambda^H}{\partial p_1} = \frac{\partial \lambda^M}{\partial p_1} + x_1^M \frac{\partial \lambda^M}{\partial M} \qquad (10\text{-}39)$$

The result is of course valid for any price p_i, and for models involving n goods. Applying Eq. (10-22) to the right-hand side of (10-39), for any good i,

$$\frac{\partial \lambda^H}{\partial p_i} \equiv -\lambda^M \frac{\partial x_i^M}{\partial M} \qquad (10\text{-}40)$$

This equation says that along a given indifference curve, as some price changes, the change in the marginal utility of income is related in a very simple manner to the income effect of the good whose price has changed: it always has the opposite sign. We would in general expect that a lower price increases the purchasing power (measured in utility received) of additional income. If a good is inferior, however, increases in income lead to decreases in consumption of the good. This must mean that the marginal utility of income is relatively greater, if less rather than more of the good is consumed. Therefore, if the good whose price decreases is inferior, the greater consumption (along an indifference curve) leads to a fall in the marginal utility of income.

Conditional Demands[†]

In Chapter 8, we investigated the effect on the constant output factor demands when one input was held constant (see Sec. 8-8). As we have already noted, the algebra of the cost minimization model is identical to the model in which expenditure is minimized subject to a utility-held-constant constraint. Restating this analysis in the context of consumer theory, the fundamental identity relating the Hicksian demand for x_i with a "short-run" Hicksian demand when, say, x_n is held constant at its expenditure-minimizing value, is

$$x_i^U(p_1, \ldots, p_n, U^0) \equiv x_i^s(p_1, \ldots, p_{n-1}, x_n^U, U^0) \qquad (10\text{-}41)$$

Differentiating both sides of this identity first with respect to p_1 and then with respect to p_n, we obtain (see the derivation of Eq. (8-44))

[†] The short- and long-run results for the Hicksian and Marshallian demands were first developed by Robert Pollak, "Conditional Demand Functions and Consumption Theory," *Quarterly Journal of Economics*, **83**:60–78, February 1969.

$$\frac{\partial x_i^U}{\partial p_i} - \frac{\partial x_i^s}{\partial p_i} = \frac{(\partial x_i^U/\partial p_n)^2}{\partial x_n^U/\partial p_n} < 0 \tag{10-42}$$

A similar expression is obtained for the differences in the Hicksian responses of x_i with respect to p_j, except that the numerator on the right-hand side becomes $(\partial x_i^U/\partial p_n)(\partial x_j^U/\partial p_n)$ and is unsigned. (The derivation of this expression is left as an exercise.)

The analysis of the conditional Marshallian demands is somewhat more complicated, because the reciprocity results used in the derivation of (10-42) are not available for the uncompensated demand functions, and because p_n, the price of the good held constant, appears explicitly in the short-run demand. If x_n is held constant at its utility-maximizing level, the fundamental identity relating the Marshallian demand for some x_i $(i \neq n)$ is

$$x_i^M(p, M) \equiv x_i^n(p, x_n^M(p, M), M) \tag{10-43}$$

where $p = (p_1, \ldots, p_n,)$, the price vector consisting of *all* n prices. In the case of the Hicksian demands, when x_n is held constant, the price p_n drops out of the first-order equations, so that x_i^s is not a function of p_n. However, in the derivation of the Marshallian demands, p_n is in the budget constraint, and does not drop out of the first-order equations. Thus the "short-run" Marshallian demand x_i^n is a function of all n prices, $p_1, \ldots, p_n$.

Differentiating the fundamental identity (10-43) with respect to p_i and then with respect to M,

$$\frac{\partial x_i^M}{\partial p_i} \equiv \frac{\partial x_i^n}{\partial p_i} + \left(\frac{\partial x_i^n}{\partial x_n^0}\right)\left(\frac{\partial x_n^M}{\partial p_i}\right) \tag{10-44}$$

$$\frac{\partial x_i^M}{\partial M} \equiv \frac{\partial x_i^n}{\partial M} + \left(\frac{\partial x_i^n}{\partial x_n^0}\right)\left(\frac{\partial x_n^M}{\partial M}\right) \tag{10-45}$$

If we now multiply (10-45) by x_i and add the two identities together, we create pure substitution terms, for example, $\partial x_i^M/\partial p_i + x_i(\partial x_i^M/\partial M)$ on the left, and similar terms on the right:

$$\frac{\partial x_i^U}{\partial p_i} \equiv \frac{\partial x_i^s}{\partial p_i} + \left(\frac{\partial x_i^n}{\partial x_n^0}\right)\left(\frac{\partial x_n^U}{\partial p_i}\right) \tag{10-46}$$

The function x_i^s is the Hicksian demand for x_i holding x_n constant, as defined in Eq. (10-41). Combining this with Eq. (10-46) yields

$$\frac{\partial x_i^U}{\partial p_i} - \frac{\partial x_i^s}{\partial p_i} = \frac{(\partial x_i^U/\partial p_n)^2}{\partial x_n^U/\partial p_n} = \left(\frac{\partial x_i^n}{\partial x_n^0}\right)\left(\frac{\partial x_n^U}{\partial p_i}\right)$$

Therefore,

$$\frac{\partial x_i^n}{\partial x_n^0} = (\partial x_i^U/\partial p_n)/(\partial x_n^U/\partial p_n)$$

Using this to eliminate $\partial x_i^n/\partial x_n^0$ in Eq. (10-44),

$$\frac{\partial x_i^M}{\partial p_i} - \frac{\partial x_i^n}{\partial p_i} = \frac{(\partial x_n^U/\partial p_i)(\partial x_n^M/\partial p_i)}{(\partial x_n^U/\partial p_n)} \tag{10-47}$$

The denominator in (10-47) is negative; however, the numerator could be negative, if x_n were a Giffen good. Of course, we expect $\partial x_n^M/\partial p_n < 0$, making the numerator of (10-47) positive. Therefore, as in the case of the Hicksian demands, the Marshallian demand curve is more elastic than its associated "short-run" curve, except for the pathological case where the good held constant is a Giffen good.

The Addition of a New Commodity

As a last example of this technique, let us examine the situation in which a consumer, as a result of an increase in income, decides to consume some new good, x_{n+1}, offered at price p_{n+1}. In most of traditional consumer theory, the problem of choosing the bundle of goods to be consumed at positive levels is not analyzed. It is in fact a very complicated problem of the type known as *nonlinear programming,* and would require detailed knowledge of the utility function for its execution. Comparative statics techniques can only analyze the signs of partial derivatives in the neighborhood of some point. However, we can gain some insight by considering the conditional demand for some good already consumed at a positive level, x_i, $i = 1, \ldots, n$, in terms of the new good, x_{n+1}, fixed initially at $x_{n+1}^0 = 0$. The Hicksian demand for any of the previously consumed goods is

$$x_i^U(p_1, \ldots, p_n, p_{n+1}, U^0) \equiv$$
$$x_i^s(p_1, \ldots, p_n, U^0, x_{n+1}^U(p_1, \ldots, p_{n+1}, U^0)) \tag{10-48}$$

This fundamental identity establishes the relationship between the demand for x_i when x_{n+1} is absent (fixed initially at zero) and when x_{n+1} is present. Suppose now that the consumer's income increases. We can analyze the effect of this on the Hicksian demands by increasing the parametric indifference level U^0. Differentiating the fundamental identity (10-48) with respect to U^0,

$$\frac{\partial x_i^U}{\partial U^0} \equiv \frac{\partial x_i^s}{\partial U^0} + \left(\frac{\partial x_i^s}{\partial x_{n+1}^0}\right)\left(\frac{\partial x_{n+1}^U}{\partial U^0}\right) \tag{10-49}$$

Differentiating the fundamental identity with respect to p_{n+1},

$$\frac{\partial x_i^U}{\partial p_{n+1}} \equiv \left(\frac{\partial x_i^s}{\partial x_{n+1}^0}\right)\left(\frac{\partial x_{n+1}^U}{\partial p_{n+1}}\right) \tag{10-50}$$

Using this in (10-49) and reciprocity yields

$$\frac{\partial x_i^U}{\partial U^0} \equiv \frac{\partial x_i^s}{\partial U^0} + \frac{(\partial x_{n+1}^U/\partial p_i)(\partial x_{n+1}^U/\partial U^0)}{(\partial x_{n+1}^U/\partial p_{n+1})} \tag{10-51}$$

The denominator of the latter term in (10-51) is negative, and since we are assuming that x_{n+1} is initially zero and becomes positive due to the increase in income, $\partial x_{n+1}^U / \partial U^0 > 0$ at that margin. Thus, the latter term has sign opposite that of $\partial x_{n+1}^U / \partial p_i$. We therefore see that if the new good is a substitute for x_i, so that $\partial x_{n+1}^U / \partial p_i > 0$, an increase in income will produce a smaller income effect on x_i than if x_{n+1} were not present, and vice versa for complements. Consider, for example, a person who experiences an increase in current income, due, say, to completing an advanced degree and commencing gainful employment. Having been a student for most of his or her life, the individual will likely have good information on the goods available for those on low incomes, and probably less information regarding more momentous purchases. As the information on these new items is acquired, the income elasticities of the goods the items tend to replace (substitute) will fall, and the opposite holds true for complements. Conversely, people who experience a fall in income may have a more difficult time of it than people whom are always at that lower income level, since acquiring the knowledge of how to be poor, i.e., which goods to give up, may take some time.

Example. We previously showed that the money income demand curves implied by the utility function $U = x_1 x_2$ were $x_1^M = M/2p_1$, $x_2^M = M/2p_2$. Let us find the compensated demand curves $x_1^U(p_1, p_2, U^0)$, $x_2^U(p_1, p_2, U^0)$ and show that the relationship between x_1^M and x_1^U, etc., is as given by the Slutsky equation.

The compensated demand curves are solutions to the model,

minimize

$$M = p_1 x_1 + p_2 x_2$$

subject to

$$U(x_1, x_2) = x_1 x_2 = U^0$$

The Lagrangian is

$$\mathcal{L} = p_1 x_1 + p_2 x_2 + \lambda(U^0 - x_1 x_2)$$

producing the first-order equations

$$\mathcal{L}_1 = p_1 - \lambda x_2 = 0$$

$$\mathcal{L}_2 = p_2 - \lambda x_1 = 0$$

$$\mathcal{L}_\lambda = U^0 - x_1 x_2 = 0$$

The conditions $\mathcal{L}_1 = \mathcal{L}_2 = 0$ yield the tangency condition $U_1/U_2 = \lambda x_2 / \lambda x_1 = p_1/p_2$, or

$$p_1 x_1 = p_2 x_2$$

The same tangency condition is obtained for the cost minimization model as for utility maximization. The constraint, however, is not the budget equation, but rather the constant utility equation $x_1 x_2 = U^0$. Combining the tangency and constant utility conditions yields

$$x_1 \frac{p_1 x_1}{p_2} = U^0$$

or

$$x_1^U = \left(\frac{p_2 U^0}{p_1}\right)^{1/2}$$

Similarly

$$x_2^U = \left(\frac{p_1 U^0}{p_2}\right)^{1/2}$$

We note in passing that, as required by the second-order conditions,

$$\frac{\partial x_1^U}{\partial p_1} = -\frac{1}{2}(p_2 U^0)^{1/2} p_1^{-3/2} < 0$$

$$\frac{\partial x_2^U}{\partial p_2} = -\frac{1}{2}(p_1 U^0)^{1/2} (p_2)^{-3/2} < 0$$

Also, the reciprocity condition $\partial x_1^U/\partial p_2 = \partial x_2^U/\partial p_1$ holds:

$$\frac{\partial x_1^U}{\partial p_2} = \frac{1}{2}(U^0)^{1/2}(p_1 p_2)^{-1/2} = \frac{\partial x_2^U}{\partial p_1}$$

The cost, or expenditure function, is given by $M^* = p_1 x_1^U + p_2 x_2^U = 2(p_1 p_2 U^0)^{1/2}$. The Slutsky equation is a relationship that holds at any particular point of tangency with a budget line and an indifference curve. Thus, the terms $\partial x_i^M/\partial p_j$ and $\partial x_i^U/\partial p_j$ must be evaluated at the same point. Since x_i^M and x_i^U are functions of different variables, M and U, respectively, we have to make sure the same point is being considered, such that $x_i^M(p_1, p_2, M) = x_1^U(p_1, p_2, U^0)$, and $x_2^M(p_1, p_2, M) = x_2^U(p_1, p_2, U^0)$. This is most easily handled via the indirect utility function $U^* = x_1^M x_2^M = M^2/4p_1 p_2$. This can be viewed as relating, at given prices, the utility levels to money income levels. If utility is maximized subject to a given budget M, then minimizing cost subject to being on the indifference level $U^0 = M^2/4p_1 p_2$ will lead to the same consumption bundle for this utility function. We also note that this is the same relationship as was given by the expenditure function $M^* = 2(p_1 p_2 U^0)^{1/2}$.

Let us now evaluate the partial derivatives in a Slutsky equation:

$$\frac{\partial x_1^M}{\partial p_1} = \frac{\partial x_1^U}{\partial p_1} - x_1 \frac{\partial x_1^M}{\partial M}$$

Here, $\partial x_1^M/\partial p_1 = -M/2p_1^2$,

$$\frac{\partial x_1^M}{\partial M} = \frac{1}{2p_1}$$

$$x_1 \frac{\partial x_1^M}{\partial M} = \frac{M}{2p_1}\frac{1}{2p_1} = \frac{M}{4p_1^2}$$

and $\partial x_1^U/\partial p_1 = -\frac{1}{2}(p_2 U^0)^{1/2} p_1^{-3/2}$. The money income level M corresponding to U^0 is given by either the expenditure or indirect utility function, as $U^0 = M^2/4p_1 p_2$. Thus, at any given point,

$$\frac{\partial x_1^U}{\partial p_1} = -\frac{1}{2}p_2^{1/2}p_1^{-3/2}\frac{M}{2}p_1^{-1/2}p_2^{-1/2}$$

$$= \frac{-M}{4p_1^2}$$

Hence

$$\frac{-M}{2p_1^2} \equiv \frac{-M}{4p_1^2} - \frac{M}{4p_1^2}$$

$$\equiv \frac{-M}{2p_1^2}$$

as required.

10.6 ELASTICITY FORMULAS FOR MONEY-INCOME-HELD-CONSTANT AND REAL-INCOME-HELD-CONSTANT DEMAND CURVES

The Slutsky Equation in Elasticity Form

The Slutsky equation can be written in terms of dimensionless elasticity coefficients.[†] First, multiply the entire equation through by p_j/x_i. Then we have

$$\frac{p_j}{x_i}\frac{\partial x_i^M}{\partial p_j} = \frac{p_j}{x_i}\frac{\partial x_i^U}{\partial p_j} - \frac{p_j x_j}{x_i}\frac{\partial x_i^M}{\partial M}$$

The first two expressions are already elasticities; the income term can be made one by multiplying it by M/M, that is, by 1, yielding

$$\epsilon_{ij}^M = \epsilon_{ij}^U - \kappa_j \epsilon_{iM} \tag{10-52}$$

where ϵ_{ij}^M = elasticity of response of x_i to change in p_j, holding money income constant

ϵ_{ij}^U = elasticity of response of x_i to change in p_j, holding utility constant

$\kappa_j = p_j x_j/M$, the share of the consumer's budget spent on good j

ϵ_{iM} = income elasticity of good i

The difference between the (cross) elasticities of the uncompensated and compensated demand curves depends on the size of the income elasticity of the good and the importance of the good whose price has changed, measured by the share of the consumer's budget spent on the good whose price has changed.

[†] To reduce notational clutter, we will leave off the superscripts for x_i when it is not needed.

Certain useful relations concerning the various elasticities of demand are derivable from the utility maximization model. In general, they stem from either of two sources:

1. The homogeneity of the demand curves in prices and money income
2. The budget constraint

Homogeneity. We know that $x_1^M(p_1, p_2, M)$ and $x_2^M(p_1, p_2, M)$ are homogeneous of degree zero in prices and money income. Thus, by Euler's theorem, for x_1^M,

$$\frac{\partial x_1^M}{\partial p_1}p_1 + \frac{\partial x_1^M}{\partial p_2}p_2 + \frac{\partial x_1^M}{\partial M}M \equiv 0$$

Dividing this expression by x_1^M yields

$$\epsilon_{11}^M + \epsilon_{12}^M + \epsilon_{1M} \equiv 0$$

Similarly

$$\epsilon_{21}^M + \epsilon_{22}^M + \epsilon_{2M} \equiv 0$$

In general, for the case of n goods, with $x_i = x_i^M(p_1, \ldots, p_n, M)$,

$$\epsilon_{i1}^M + \epsilon_{i2}^M + \cdots + \epsilon_{in}^M + \epsilon_{iM} \equiv 0 \tag{10-53}$$

The budget constraint.
(a) Income elasticities   Differentiate the budget constraint with respect to M:

$$p_1\frac{\partial x_1^M}{\partial M} + p_2\frac{\partial x_2^M}{\partial M} \equiv 1$$

This expression is equivalent to

$$\frac{p_1 x_1}{M}\left(\frac{M}{x_1}\frac{\partial x_1^M}{\partial M}\right) + \frac{p_2 x_2}{M}\left(\frac{M}{x_2}\frac{\partial x_2^M}{\partial M}\right) \equiv 1$$

or

$$\kappa_1\epsilon_{1M} + \kappa_2\epsilon_{2M} \equiv 1$$

In general, for the case of n goods,

$$\kappa_1\epsilon_{1M} + \cdots + \kappa_n\epsilon_{nM} \equiv 1 \tag{10-54}$$

The weighted sum of the income elasticities of all goods equals one. The weights are the shares of income spent on each good; the shares themselves sum to one.

If income, say, increases by a certain percentage, and consumption of some good x_i increases by some greater percentage, we say the good is *income elastic*; if consumption of that good increases by a smaller percentage, it is *income inelastic.* If a good is income elastic, then obviously, the share of income spent on that good must rise as income rises. Algebraically, letting $\eta_i = \epsilon_{iM}$ to reduce clutter, we leave it as an exercise to show that

$$\frac{\partial \kappa_i}{\partial M} = \left(\frac{1}{M}\right)(\kappa_i \eta_i - \kappa_i) = \left(\frac{\kappa_i}{M}\right)(\eta_i - 1) \tag{10-55}$$

Clearly, $\partial \kappa_i/\partial M \gtrless 0$ as $\eta_i \gtrless 1$. Also note that homotheticity of the utility function, meaning unitary income elasticities of all goods, can also be described by the condition of unchanging shares of income spent on each good, as income changes.

It also follows that as income continues to increase, goods that remain income elastic will eventually take over the entire budget, (and would, in fact, eventually exceed it). It must be the case, therefore, that the income elasticities of income elastic goods must eventually fall. This might take the form of substitution toward higher-quality goods.[†]

There is an algebraic statement of this reasoning. Differentiating the identity $\sum \kappa_i \eta_i \equiv 1$ with respect to income,

$$\sum \kappa_i \left(\frac{\partial \eta_i}{\partial M}\right) + \sum \eta_i \left(\frac{\partial \kappa_i}{\partial M}\right) \equiv 0 \tag{10-56}$$

Substituting (10-55) into this expression yields

$$\sum \kappa_i \left(\frac{\partial \eta_i}{\partial M}\right) + \sum \eta_i \left(\frac{\kappa_i}{M}\right)(\eta_i - 1) \equiv 0$$

or

$$\sum \kappa_i \left(\frac{\partial \eta_i}{\partial M}\right) + \left(\frac{1}{M}\right)\left[\sum \kappa_i \eta_i^2 - \sum \kappa_i \eta_i\right] \equiv 0$$

Since the last term on the right-hand side is unity,

$$\sum \kappa_i \left(\frac{\partial \eta_i}{\partial M}\right) = \left(\frac{1}{M}\right)\left[1 - \sum \kappa_i \eta_i^2\right] \tag{10-57}$$

If the utility function is homothetic, so that all income elasticities are unity, then the right-hand side of (10-57) vanishes, since $\sum \kappa_i = 1$. In that case, the sum of the weighted rates of change of the income elasticities with respect to income changes, is zero, i.e., this weighted sum does not change as income changes. For all nonhomothetic utility functions, however (and this is the empirically important case), $\sum \kappa_i \eta_i^2 > 1$. This relation follows from the fact that η_i^2 is a strictly convex function (think of the shape of $y = x^2$). Therefore, any convex combination of

---

[†] Levis Kochin and Yoram Barzel enlightened me about this intriguing argument.

these squared income elasticities, $\sum \kappa_i \eta_i^2$, must be greater than $\sum \kappa_i \eta_i = 1$. For this general case, therefore,

$$\sum \kappa_i \left(\frac{\partial \eta_i}{\partial M} \right) < 0 \tag{10-58}$$

In other words, for general (nonhomothetic) utility functions, the sum of the weighted rates of change of the income elasticities, with respect to income, falls as income rises. Could it be, as a general proposition, that all income elasticities must eventually fall?

(b) Price elasticities Now differentiate the budget identity $p_1 x_1^M + p_2 x_2^M \equiv M$ with respect to p_1:

$$x_1^M + p_1 \frac{\partial x_1^M}{\partial p_1} + p_2 \frac{\partial x_2^M}{\partial p_1} \equiv 0$$

This is equivalent to

$$\frac{p_1 x_1^M}{M} \left(\frac{p_1}{x_1^M} \frac{\partial x_1^M}{\partial p_1} \right) + \frac{p_2 x_2^M}{M} \left(\frac{p_1}{x_2^M} \frac{\partial x_2^M}{\partial p_1} \right) \equiv - \frac{p_1 x_1^M}{M}$$

or

$$\kappa_1 \epsilon_{11}^M + \kappa_2 \epsilon_{21}^M = -\kappa_1$$

In general, for n goods, using the same technique,

$$\kappa_1 \epsilon_{1j}^M + \cdots + \kappa_n \epsilon_{nj}^M \equiv -\kappa_j \tag{10-59}$$

The weighted sum of the elasticities for all goods with respect to the price of a certain good sums to the negative of the share of the budget spent on the good in question. The weights are again the shares of the budget spent on each good. Note a difference between (10-53) and (10-59): Eq. (10-53) relates to *one* good and *all* prices (and income), whereas Eq. (10-59) relates to *all* goods and *one* price change.

Compensated Demand Curves

The compensated demand curves $x_i^U(p_1, p_2, U^0)$ have slightly different elasticity properties. These properties are again derived from two sources: homogeneity and the constraint equation, in this case $U(x_1, x_2) = U^0$.

Homogeneity. The demand curves $x_1^U(p_1, p_2, U^0)$, $x_2^U(p_1, p_2, U^0)$ are homogeneous of degree zero in the prices only. If prices are both doubled, say, since relative prices are unaffected, the tangency point remains the same. Hence, for x_1^U, by Euler's theorem,

$$\frac{\partial x_1^U}{\partial p_1} p_1 + \frac{\partial x_1^U}{\partial p_2} p_2 \equiv 0$$

Dividing by x_1^U yields

$$\epsilon_{11}^U + \epsilon_{12}^U \equiv 0$$

where

$$\epsilon_{ij}^U = \frac{p_j}{x_i^U} \frac{\partial x_i^U}{\partial p_j}$$

is the (cross) elasticity of compensated demand of good i with respect to the price p_j of good j. For the case of n goods, using the same technique, one finds

$$\epsilon_{i1}^U + \epsilon_{i2}^U + \cdots + \epsilon_{in}^U \equiv 0 \tag{10-60}$$

The constraint $U(x_1^U, x_2^U) \equiv U^0$. Differentiating this identity with respect to p_1, say:

$$U_1 \frac{\partial x_1^U}{\partial p_1} + U_2 \frac{\partial x_2^U}{\partial p_1} \equiv 0$$

From the first-order conditions for cost minimization, $U_1 = p_1/\lambda, U_2 = p_2/\lambda$, hence (after multiplying by λ),

$$p_1 \frac{\partial x_1^U}{\partial p_1} + p_2 \frac{\partial x_2^U}{\partial p_1} \equiv 0$$

This is almost the same relation as derived previously in Eq. (10-60); it in fact is derivable from that equation by noting that for compensated demand curves, $\partial x_i^U / \partial p_j = \partial x_j^U / \partial p_i$. Converting this expression to elasticities gives

$$\frac{p_1 x_1^U}{M} \left(\frac{p_1}{x_1^U} \frac{\partial x_1^U}{\partial p_1} \right) + \frac{p_2 x_2^U}{M} \left(\frac{p_1}{x_2^U} \frac{\partial x_2^U}{\partial p_1} \right) \equiv 0$$

or

$$\kappa_1 \epsilon_{11}^U + \kappa_2 \epsilon_{21}^U \equiv 0$$

In general, for the n-good case $x_i^U(p_1, p_2, \ldots, p_n, U^0)$,

$$\kappa_1 \epsilon_{1j}^U + \kappa_2 \epsilon_{2j}^U + \cdots + \kappa_n \epsilon_{nj}^U \equiv 0 \tag{10-61}$$

Note the difference between (10-60) and (10-61): In Eq. (10-60), only one demand relationship $x_i^U(p_1, \ldots, p_n, U^0)$ is being considered, and the cross-effects of that good and all other prices are related. In (10-61), the responses of all goods to a given price change are related. These identities are the elasticity formulas commonly encountered in the theory of the consumer.

Return a moment to the derivation of Eq. (10-60) or (10-61). From the homogeneity of degree zero of the compensated demand curves $x_i = x_i^U(p_1, \ldots, p_n, U^0)$ with respect to prices, from Euler's theorem,

$$p_1 \frac{\partial x_i^U}{\partial p_1} + \cdots + p_n \frac{\partial x_i^U}{\partial p_n} \equiv 0$$

Letting $s_{ij} = \partial x_i^U / \partial p_j$, the pure substitution effect on x_i of a change in p_j, we have

$$p_1 s_{i1} + p_2 s_{i2} + \cdots + p_n s_{in} \equiv 0$$

However, for compensated changes $s_{ij} = s_{ji}$. Hence,

$$p_1 s_{1i} + p_2 s_{2i} + \cdots + p_n s_{ni} \equiv 0$$

These results are known as Hicks' *third law*. (The first two are, respectively, $s_{ij} = s_{ji}$, $s_{ii} < 0$). The law can be stated succinctly as

$$\sum_{i=1}^{n} p_i s_{ij} = \sum_{j=1}^{n} p_j s_{ij} = 0 \tag{10-62}$$

We have shown how the behavioral assertion of utility maximization leads to certain propositions which are, at least in principle, refutable. Specifically, the proposition that if a good is noninferior, and if its price is lowered, more will be consumed, is implied by utility maximization. In addition, the income-compensated demands $x_i^U(p_1, \ldots, p_n, U^0)$ have the property of negative slope in their own price, and also possess the reciprocity properties $\partial x_i^U / \partial p_j = \partial x_j^U / \partial p_i$. In addition, the preceding elasticity properties are implied.

In the example worked out earlier for the utility function $U = x_1 x_2$, certain special results were obtained, in particular, $\partial x_i^M / \partial p_j = \partial x_j^M / \partial p_i = 0$, together with unitary price and income elasticities. In general, what types of utility functions yield these properties?

Consider the unusual case $\partial x_i^M / \partial p_j = \partial x_j^M / \partial p_i$. This condition always holds for the *compensated* demands, but not generally for the *uncompensated* demands x_i^M. If this does hold, then using the Slutsky equation,

$$\frac{\partial x_i^M}{\partial p_j} = \frac{\partial x_i^U}{\partial p_j} - x_j^M \frac{\partial x_i^M}{\partial M} = \frac{\partial x_j^U}{\partial p_i} - x_i^M \frac{\partial x_j^M}{\partial M} = \frac{\partial x_j^M}{\partial p_i}$$

However, $\partial x_i^U / \partial p_j = \partial x_j^U / \partial p_i$ always. Hence, we are left with

$$x_j^M \frac{\partial x_i^M}{\partial M} = x_i^M \frac{\partial x_j^M}{\partial M} \tag{10-63}$$

Multiplying this equation through by $M/(x_i^M x_j^M)$ yields

$$\epsilon_{iM} = \frac{M}{x_i^M} \frac{\partial x_i^M}{\partial M} = \frac{M}{x_j^M} \frac{\partial x_j^M}{\partial M} = \epsilon_{jM}$$

Thus, all pairs of goods for which $\partial x_i^M / \partial p_j = \partial x_j^M / \partial p_i$ have equal income elasticities. Suppose this is true of all commodities consumed. Then, using Eq. (10-54) that the weighted sum of income elasticities sums to unity, denoting the common value of the income elasticities as ϵ_M,

$$\kappa_1 \epsilon_M + \cdots + \kappa_n \epsilon_M = \epsilon_M (\kappa_1 + \cdots + \kappa_n) = 1$$

Thus, $\epsilon_{1M} = \cdots = \epsilon_{nM} = \epsilon_M = 1$, since the shares $\kappa_i = p_i x_i / M$ sum to unity.

What types of utility functions possess unitary income elasticities for all goods? Recall Fig. 10-6 for the specific case of $U = x_1 x_2$. The income elasticities were unity because the income consumption paths, the locus of all possible tangency points, was a straight line out of the origin. This is the property of homotheticity, of which the homogeneous function $U = x_1 x_2$ is a particular case.

Mathematically, consider Eq. (10-63) once more. This equation is equivalent to

$$\frac{\partial (x_j^M / x_i^M)}{\partial M} = 0 \tag{10-64}$$

For, using the quotient rule,

$$\left(x_i^M \frac{\partial x_j^M}{\partial M} - x_j^M \frac{\partial x_i^M}{\partial M} \right) \left(\frac{1}{x_i^M} \right)^2 = 0$$

Since x_i^M is presumed positive, Eq. (10-63) results. Equation (10-64) says that the ratio of consumption of x_j to x_i is the same at all income levels. This ratio, x_j / x_i, is simply the slope of the ray from the origin through (x_i, x_j). To say that this ray has constant slope in the x_i, x_j plane, for all pairs of goods, is to say that the utility function is homothetic. The reasoning can be reversed, using Eq. (10-64) as a definition of homotheticity to show that homothetic utility functions imply demand curves that have unitary income elasticities and exhibit the property that $\partial x_i^M / \partial p_j = \partial x_j^M / \partial p_i$. Any one of these three statements implies the other two; they are all equivalent.

10.7 SPECIAL TOPICS

Separable Utility Functions

In the early development of utility theory, utility was conceived as an *additive* function of utilities received from the consumption of separate goods, i.e.,

$$U(x_1, \ldots, x_n) = U_1(x_1) + U_2(x_2) + \cdots + U_n(x_n)$$

Such a function is called *additively* or *strongly separable*.[†] (If a utility function were multiplicatively separable, i.e., $V = U_1(x_1) \cdot U_2(x_2) \cdots U_n(x_n)$, the same implications for the demand system would occur, since taking the logarithm of V (a monotonic transformation) would produce an additively separable form, and leave the demand functions unchanged.) In the additive case, the marginal utility derived from consuming some good, x_i, is a function of x_i only, $U_i'(x_i)$. The marginal utility would be unaffected by changes in consumption of some other good x_j, since $\partial U_i'(x_i)/\partial x_j \equiv 0$. It is tempting to conclude from this that separability of the utility function implies independence of the demand for x_i on

[†] A slightly more general formulation would specify utility as a sum of functions of *groups* of commodities.

the prices of other goods, that is, $\partial x_i^M / \partial p_j = 0$, $j \neq i$. Such a conclusion is false. We leave it as an exercise to show that in the two-variable case, neither $\partial x_i^M / \partial p_j = 0$ nor $\partial x_i^U / \partial p_j = 0$ is implied. It can, however, be shown that $\partial x_i^M / \partial p_j = 0$, $j \neq i$ implies that the utility function is Cobb-Douglas (or a monotonic transformation thereof). This is a more advanced exercise, involving solutions to partial differential equations. Furthermore, it follows immediately from Hicks' third law, $\sum p_i s_{ij} = 0$ (Eq. (10-62)), that it can never be the case that $s_{ij} = \partial x_i^U / \partial p_j = 0$ for all $j \neq i$, since $s_{ii} < 0$.

Strong separability does, not surprisingly, place restrictions on observable behavior. For example, either all goods are noninferior and net substitutes for each other ($\partial x_i^U / \partial p_j \geq 0$, $j \neq i$), or all goods but one are inferior, and the noninferior good is a net substitute for the other goods, while the others are all net complements to each other. Additional restrictions on the demand functions, due mainly to Samuelson and Houthakker, are left as exercises at the end of Chap. 11.

Weak separability specifies utility as a function of categories of goods, e.g., food, clothing, etc., each of which in turn contain one or more individual goods. For example, in a four-good case, we might write $V(x_1, x_2, x_3, x_4) = U(f(x_1, x_2), g(x_3, x_4)) = U(z_1, z_2)$. Strong separability is a special case of this specification. Of course, as with strong separability, it is not necessarily the case that $\partial x_i^M / \partial p_j = 0$, for goods i and j in different categories. However, consider the marginal rate of substitution between any two goods in the same category, say x_1 and x_2:

$$-\frac{\partial V / \partial x_1}{\partial V / \partial x_2} = -\frac{U_1 f_1}{U_1 f_2} = -\frac{f_1(x_1, x_2)}{f_2(x_1, x_2)}$$

It is apparent that the marginal rate of substitution between any two goods in the same category is a function only of the goods in that category. If the total expenditure on x_1 and x_2 were known, this tangency condition plus the implied budget constraint for x_1 and x_2 could be solved for the Marshallian demand functions, which would then be a function only of the prices of x_1 and x_2 (i.e., the goods in that category), and the total expenditure on the goods in that category. In that case we could imagine a two-stage budgeting process, whereby the consumer first decides the expenditures on the categories food, clothing, shelter, etc., and then allocates his or her budgets within each of those groups of goods on the basis of only the prices of goods in that group. However, such a two-stage budgeting process is not implied by weak separability. The total expenditure on a given category, say food, in fact depends inexorably on the prices of all goods, not just the prices of the food items. Only with further very stringent conditions is such two-stage budgeting possible.[†] It is *not* the case, for example, that if the

---

[†] For a more formal development of the implications of separability, see Robert Pollak, "Conditional Demand Functions and the Implications of Separability," *The Southern Economic Journal*, **37**: 423–433, April 1971. The most complete analysis of separability is C. Blackorby, D. Primont, and R.R. Russell, *Duality, Separability and Functional Structure: Theory and Applications*, Elsevier, New York, 1978.

"subutility" functions f and g above are homothetic or homogeneous, that two-stage budgeting is possible. For example, consider the utility function

$$U = f(x_1, x_2) + g(x_3, x_4) = \left(\frac{x_1^2}{2} + x_1 x_2\right) + \left(\frac{x_3^2}{2} + x_3 x_4\right)$$

Clearly, f and g are both homogeneous of degree 2. We leave it to the reader to confirm that for $p_1 > p_2$, this function achieves a positive interior constrained maximum subject to a linear budget constraint, and that, for example, $\partial x_i^M / \partial p_j \neq 0$, $i = 1, 2$, $j = 3, 4$. Moreover, letting f^* be the utility-maximizing value of f, $\partial f^* / \partial p_j \neq 0$, $j = 3, 4$. Thus even with these restrictions on the utility function, the amount of "food" a consumer will purchase will depend on the individual prices of "clothing" items.

The Labor-Leisure Choice

The decision as to how many hours out of the day to devote to work is an important choice made by individuals. We model this choice by assuming that consumers desire leisure, L, as well as the consumption of goods. Rather than listing out the goods individually, we simplify the model by asserting that utility is a function of income, Y, and leisure: $U = U(Y, L)$. Income is produced by working $(24 - L)$ hours at wage w per hour. In addition, nonwage income Y^0 occurs independently of any choice made by the individual. Nonwage income can be negative, as in the case of contractual debt obligations. The utility maximum problem is therefore

maximize $\qquad\qquad U = U(Y, L)$

subject to $\qquad\qquad Y = w(24 - L) + Y^0$

This situation is pictured in Fig. 10-11. The individual is endowed with 24 hours of leisure and nonwage income, assumed positive, of Y^0. The budget line passes through the point $(24, Y^0)$, and has slope $-w$. The consumer maximizes utility at some point, A, where the indifference curves are tangent to the budget line. An increase in w is represented by rotating the budget line clockwise through the endowment point, resulting in a new maximum position, B, on a higher indifference curve.

The Lagrangian for this model is

$$\mathscr{L} = U(Y, L) + \lambda(Y^0 - Y + w(24 - L))$$

The first-order conditions are

$$U_Y - \lambda = 0 \qquad\qquad (10\text{-}65a)$$

$$U_L - \lambda w = 0 \qquad\qquad (10\text{-}65b)$$

and the constraint

$$Y^0 - Y + w(24 - L) = 0 \qquad\qquad (10\text{-}65c)$$

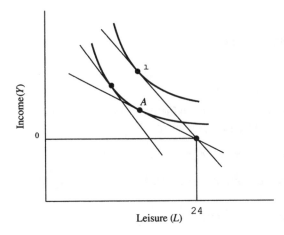

FIGURE 10-11
The Labor-Leisure Choice. A consumer is endowed with 24 hours of leisure and nonwage income Y^0. At some wage rate w, the utility maximum occurs at point A. An increase in w produces a pure substitution effect from A to C and an income effect from C to B. Assuming leisure is a normal good, the income effect acts in the *opposite* direction of the substitution effect, since the consumer *sells* leisure.

From (10-65a) and (10-65b), $U_L/U_Y = w$. This says that the marginal value of leisure, in terms of income forgone, is the wage rate. If a person can choose how many hours to work, then the decision not to work an additional hour entails giving up an hour's income, w.[†]

Assuming the sufficient second-order conditions hold, the Marshallian demand functions

$$L = L^M(w, Y^0) \tag{10-66a}$$

$$Y = Y^M(w, Y^0) \tag{10-66b}$$

and an expression for the Lagrange multiplier

$$\lambda = \lambda^M(w, Y^0) \tag{10-66c}$$

are implied. We can interpret λ^M as the marginal utility of nonwage income.

What is the effect on L and Y of an increase in the wage rate w? We already know that mathematically, no refutable implication is available. An increase in the wage rate raises the opportunity cost of leisure; we should expect on this account the individual to substitute away from leisure, i.e., toward more work. However, this is just the pure substitution effect. As the wage rate increases, income also increases. If leisure is a normal good, we should expect the person to consume more leisure, i.e., to work less. Let us derive the associated Slutsky equation.

The Hicksian, or utility-held-constant demand, functions for this model are derived from the expenditure minimization problem,

---

[†] Even though in the short run, hours per week may be fixed, in the long run, individuals make choices in jobs and careers for which that and other job characteristics are presumably variable.

minimize

$$Y^0 = Y - w(24 - L)$$

subject to

$$U(Y, L) = U^0$$

In this model, Y^0 is no longer a parameter; it is the value of the objective function. The utility level is now a parameter. The Lagrangian for this model is

$$\mathcal{L} = Y - w(24 - L) + \lambda(U^0 - U(Y, L))$$

Assuming the first and second-order conditions hold, the Hicksian demand functions

$$Y = Y^U(w, U^0) \tag{10-67a}$$

$$L = L^U(w, U^0) \tag{10-67b}$$

are implied. The associated expenditure function is derived by substituting these solutions into the objective function:

$$Y^*(w, U^0) = Y^U(w, U^0) - w[24 - L^U(w, U^0)] \tag{10-68}$$

The Hicksian and Marshallian demand functions for leisure are related to each other through the fundamental identity

$$L^U(w, U^0) \equiv L^M(w, Y^*(w, U^0)) \tag{10-69}$$

Differentiating both sides with respect to w,

$$\frac{\partial L^U}{\partial w} \equiv \frac{\partial L^M}{\partial w} + \left(\frac{\partial L^M}{\partial Y^0} \right) \left(\frac{\partial Y^*}{\partial w} \right) \tag{10-70}$$

Applying the envelope theorem to Eq. (10-68), $\partial Y^*/\partial w = -(24 - L^U)$. Thus, rearranging (10-70) slightly,

$$\frac{\partial L^M}{\partial w} \equiv \frac{\partial L^U}{\partial w} + (24 - L^U) \left(\frac{\partial L^M}{\partial Y^0} \right) \tag{10-71}$$

an equation analogous to the traditional Slutsky Eq. (10-34).

Notice in this case, however, the term multiplying the income effect is the amount of leisure "sold," $24 - L^U$, not the amount of some good purchased. When the consumer comes to the market with money income, which does not enter the utility function directly, and uses it to purchase goods that do enter the utility function, the income effect for normal (noninferior) goods reinforces the substitution effect. In this case, since the consumer is *selling* leisure, not buying it, the income effect acts in the opposite direction of the substitution effect, for normal goods. There is ample evidence that leisure is a normal good. (How does winning one of the various state lotteries now in existence affect the winner's time spent working?) Since $(24 - L^U)$ is positive, the income effect is positive, while the pure substitution effect $\partial L^U / \partial w$ is necessarily negative. Because of this, the slope of the Marshallian (uncompensated) demand for leisure, $\partial L^M / \partial w$ is less predictable than the slope of the Marshallian demands for ordinary goods and services.

A recurring public policy question concerns the effects of tax rates on work effort. The 1986 U.S. tax changes lowered the marginal rates on federal income taxation to 28 to 33 percent, from 50 percent. Some countries have tax rates in excess of 90 percent. It can be seen from the above analysis that lowering tax rates, which effectively raises the after-tax wage rate, does not have an implied effect on hours worked. Since the opportunity cost of leisure is now higher, the substitution effect produces less leisure. However, the individual is also wealthier; the income effect leads therefore to *more* leisure. The net effect is an empirical matter. (Of course, at a tax rate of 100 percent, no effort will be forthcoming (legally); the income effect of lowering taxes at that margin will certainly dominate, and induce greater effort.)

The preceding model of labor-leisure choice is a special case of a model that appears in the literature on general equilibrium. Assume that, instead of the consumer bringing an amount of money income M to the market to purchase goods and services, the consumer comes to the market with initial endowments of $n + 1$ goods $x_0^0, x_1^0, \ldots, x_n^0$. The market sets prices of $p_0, p_1, \ldots, p_n$ for these goods, and the consumer maximizes utility subject to the constraint that the value of the goods purchased equal the value of the initial endowment, i.e.,

maximize

$$U(x_0, x_1, \ldots, x_n)$$

subject to

$$p_0 x_0^0 + \cdots + p_n x_n^0 = p_0 x_0 + \cdots + p_n x_n$$

that is, subject to

$$\sum_{i=0}^{n} p_i x_i^0 = \sum_{i=0}^{n} p_i x_i$$

The first-order conditions are obtained by setting the partials of the Lagrangian equal to 0:

$$\mathcal{L} = U(x_0, \ldots, x_n) + \lambda \left(\sum p_i x_i^0 - \sum p_i x_i \right)$$

$$\mathcal{L}_0 = U_0 - \lambda p_0 = 0$$

$$\mathcal{L}_1 = U_1 - \lambda p_1 = 0$$

$$\vdots$$

$$\mathcal{L}_n = U_n - \lambda p_n = 0$$

$$\mathcal{L}_\lambda = \sum p_i^0 x_i^0 - \sum p_i x_i = 0$$

The first-order equations are solved for the demand functions:

$$x_i = x_i^M(p_0, \ldots, p_n, x_0^0, \ldots, x_n^0) \qquad i = 0, \ldots, n \qquad (10\text{-}72)$$

It is apparent, using reasoning similar to that used before, that these demand functions are homogeneous of degree zero in the $n + 1$ prices $p_0, \ldots, p_n$. It is customary to choose one commodity and set its price equal to one. This commodity, say x_0, is called the numéraire; it is the commodity in terms of which all prices are quoted. The situation being described is one of barter. If one of the goods is, say, gold, it may turn out that in addition to its amenity values (for which it enters the utility function, being useful in jewelry, dentistry, etc.), this commodity will also serve as a medium of exchange, being the commodity for which transactions costs are least. This model is incapable of predicting which commodity, if any, will be so chosen, but we can designate x_0 as that commodity which is the numéraire, and set $p_0 = 1$. The remaining prices $p_1, \ldots, p_n$ then become *relative* prices.

Similar results are obtained in this model as in the standard utility maximization problem. The endowment of the numéraire, x_0^0, serves the same function as M, the money income of the consumer. The compensated demand curves $x_i = x_i^U(p_1, \ldots, p_n, U^0)$ are derivable from

minimize

$$x_0^0 = \sum_{i=0}^{n} p_i x_i - \sum_{i=1}^{n} p_i x_i^0$$

subject to

$$U(x_0, \ldots, x_n) = U^0$$

Note that the implied compensated demand curves are *not* functions of the initial endowments, which enter the objective functions as constants and drop out upon differentiation. Once the utility level U^0 is specified, the original endowment is irrelevant—the demands are determined by tangency and the utility level U^0.

The indirect "endowment function" (formerly cost, or expenditure function) is given by

$$x_0 = x_0^*(p_1, \ldots, p_n, x_0^0, \ldots, x_n^0) = \sum_{i=0}^{n} p_i x_i^U - \sum_{i=1}^{n} p_i x_i^0 \qquad (10\text{-}73)$$

Thus, by the envelope theorem,

$$\frac{\partial x_0^*}{\partial p_i} \equiv (x_i^U - x_i^0) \qquad (10\text{-}74)$$

We can use these results to derive the implied Slutsky equation for this general equilibrium system. Proceeding as before, starting with the ordinary demand curves

$$x_i^M(p_1, \ldots, p_n, x_0^0, \ldots, x_n^0) \qquad i = 0, \ldots, n$$

define x_0^* to be the minimum x_0^0 to keep $U(x_0, \ldots, x_n) = U^0$. Then x_0^* is just the indirect function (10-73). Thus, by definition,

$$x_i^U(p_1, \ldots, p_n, x_0^0, \ldots, x_n^0) \equiv x_i^M(p_1, \ldots, p_n, x_0^*, x_1^0, \ldots, x_n^0)$$

Differentiating with respect to some p_j,

$$\frac{\partial x_i^U}{\partial p_j} \equiv \frac{\partial x_i^M}{\partial p_j} + \frac{\partial x_i^M}{\partial x_0^0} \frac{\partial x_0^*}{\partial p_j}$$

Using Eq. (10-74) and rearranging,

$$\frac{\partial x_i^M}{\partial p_j} = \frac{\partial x_i^U}{\partial p_j} + (x_j^0 - x_j^M)\frac{\partial x_i^M}{\partial x_0^0} \tag{10-75}$$

Thus, the Slutsky equation has the same form as previously, with the important exception that the *income* effect, $\partial x_i^M/\partial x_0^0$, is weighted by the *change* in the consumption of x_j, $(x_j^0 - x_j^M)$. If the amount of x_j was unchanged after going to the market, that is, $x_j^M = x_j^0$, there would be no income effect at all. Also, if, say, some price p_j goes up, then while formerly this acted as a decrease in real income, if the consumer is a net *seller* of x_j, this income effect is positive, i.e., it raises his or her real income.

Slutsky versus Hicks Compensations

Although we have been referring to Eq. (10-34) as the Slutsky equation, this version was in fact first introduced by J. R. Hicks in *Value and Capital* (1937), based on Pareto's discussion of the phenomenon. Slutsky compensated the consumer in a slightly different form: after a price change, instead of adjusting M to return the consumer to the original indifference curve, Slutsky gave the consumer enough income to purchase the original bundle of goods. This is in fact more than $M^*(p_1, \ldots, p_n, U^0)$, the minimum M to return the consumer to the original utility level. How does this affect the Slutsky equation? Surprisingly, not at all. In the limit (at the margin, that is), the Hicks and Slutsky compensations are identical.

Consider Fig. 10-12. The original tangency is at (x_1^0, x_2^0). Suppose p_1 is lowered. Then compensating à la Hicks leads to a new level of x_1, x_1^U, at a new tangency of the same indifference curve U^0, and a new budget line. Compensation according to Slutsky, however, places the new budget line through (x_1^0, x_2^0) at the new prices. Whether the prices are raised or lowered (the diagram is for p_1 lowered, relative to p_2), the consumer can achieve a higher level of utility, say U^s (for Slutsky). If x_1 is a normal good, this will raise the consumption of x_1. Hence, the Slutsky demand curve x_1^s, while equal to the Hicks curve at x_1^0, x_2^0, lies to the right of x_1^U for p_1 not equal to the original price. Assuming that $x_1^U(p_1, p_2, U^0)$ and $x_1^s(p_1, p_2, x_1^0, x_2^0)$ are both differentiable, the diagram clearly

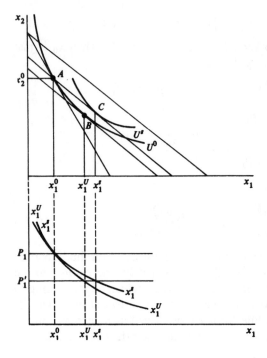

FIGURE 10-12
The Hicks and Slutsky Compensations. The consumer starts at point (x_1^0, x_2^0). When p_1 is lowered, compensating according to Hicks leads to the new tangency B where $x_1 = x_1^U$. If a Slutsky compensation is made through the original point A, a new tangency on a higher indifference level, at point C, is attained. If x_1 is a normal good, the Slutsky demand, x_1^s, is greater than x_1^U. The same situation $(x_1^s > x_1^U)$ occurs if the price change is in the other direction. The consumer can always achieve a higher indifference level by moving away, i.e., adjusting to the price change. Hence, $x_1^U = x_1^s$ at x_1^0, but $x_1^s > x_1^U$ everywhere else. Hence, x_1^s and x_1^U are tangent at x_1^0, i.e., they have the same slope there, or $\partial x_1^s / \partial p_1 = \partial x_1^U / \partial p_1$.

indicates that the two have a point of tangency at (x_1^0, x_2^0). But this says that the slopes of the two demand curves are equal there, or

$$\frac{\partial x_1^U}{\partial p_1} = \frac{\partial x_1^s}{\partial p_1}$$

This result is perfectly general; using similar reasoning,

$$\frac{\partial x_i^U}{\partial p_j} = \frac{\partial x_i^s}{\partial p_j}$$

If x_i is inferior rather than normal, a tangency still occurs, but with the Slutsky demand curve to the left of the Hicksian curve.

An algebraic proof follows trivially from the general equilibrium variant of the Slutsky Eq. (10-75),

$$\frac{\partial x_i^M}{\partial p_j} = \frac{\partial x_i^U}{\partial p_j} + (x_j^0 - x_j^M)\frac{\partial x_i^M}{\partial x_j^0}$$

A Slutsky compensation is equivalent to starting the consumer off at $x_i = x_i^0$, $i = 1, \ldots, n$. In this case, there is no income effect, and $\partial x_i^M/\partial p_j \equiv \partial x_i^s/\partial p_j$ by definition, and, hence, $\partial x_i^s/\partial p_j \equiv \partial x_i^U/\partial p_j$. Note, however, in the figure, that the Slutsky demand curve is more convex than the Hicks curve. The second derivatives are not equal, and, in fact, for normal goods, $\partial^2 x_i^s/\partial p_i^2 \geq \partial^2 x_i^U/\partial p_i^2$.

This was first brought out by A. Wald and J. Mosak, who resolved the conflict between the Hicks and Slutsky variants of compensation.[†] What Mosak showed was that if p_j changed by an amount Δp_j, the difference between the Hicksian demand and the Slutsky demand was of second-order smallness, i.e., it involved powers of Δp of order two and higher.

The importance of this result is that in general it will not matter much which type of compensation is used, if the price change is not too large. Although the Hicks compensation is probably neater from the standpoint of the mathematical theory, this compensation will not be easy to observe. The Slutsky compensation, on the other hand, is calculable on the basis of simple arithmetic. Using the Wald-Mosak result, we can be assured that the compensations will not be very different, and that the easily observed Slutsky compensation is a good approximation to the "ideal" compensation à la Hicks.

This issue comes into play in the definition of index numbers. The Laspeyres index, used by the United States and other countries to define the consumer price index, is essentially a Slutsky compensation. The price index indicates the amount of dollars needed in the current year to purchase *the original consumption bundle* in the base year. Substitution away from that original basket of goods is not considered (a feature that biases the CPI upward, i.e., it exaggerates the impact of price changes by not allowing the consumer to adjust to the change). However, for small relative price changes, the bias should not be much worse, since the Slutsky compensation is a good approximation to the Hicksian compensation, which a "true" price index would try to calculate.

The Division of Labor Is Limited by the Extent of the Market

We have thus far considered utility maximization subject to only a linear budget constraint. This specification of the constraint expresses a consumer's inability to affect prices by his or her consumption decisions. Suppose, however, that an individual engages in actual production of the goods consumed. In what ways would a consumer's choice of goods to consume be affected by the opportunity for exchange after production?

It is a familiar exercise in the theory of comparative advantage (demonstrated first, in virtually its current textbook form, by David Ricardo in his *Principles*)[‡] to show that if, say, Robinson Crusoe can either gather three coconuts or catch three fish (or any convex combination thereof) in a day, and Friday can either gather

---

[†] See J. Mosak, "On the Interpretation of the Fundamental Equation of Value Theory," in O. Lange et al. (eds.), *Studies in Mathematical Economics and Econometrics*, University of Chicago Press, Chicago, 1942.

[‡] David Ricardo, *The Principles of Political Economy and Taxation, Chapter VII*, 1817. The accessible publication is *The Works and Correspondence of David Ricardo*, P. Straffa (ed.), Cambridge University Press, Cambridge, England, 1966.

eight coconuts or catch four fish in a day, that mutual gains are possible if they specialize in their *comparative* advantages. In this case, Crusoe's marginal cost of producing fish is one coconut, whereas for Friday it is two coconuts; likewise, Friday's marginal cost of producing fish is half a coconut, whereas for Crusoe it is one coconut. Minimization of costs would therefore lead Crusoe to specialize in the production of fish, and Friday in coconuts. In that manner, they could share an output of eight coconuts and three fish, a consumption opportunity beyond their capabilities if specialization were not pursued. Since more is preferred to less, utility maximization would therefore tend to lead to such behavior.

Earlier, in an otherwise famous year, 1776, Adam Smith had outlined the benefits of specialization with a striking example of pin manufacturing:[†]

> A workman, not educated to this business (which the division of labor has rendered a distinct trade), nor acquainted with the use of the machinery employed in it (to the invention of which the same division of labor has probably given occasion), could scarce, perhaps, with his utmost industry, make one pin in a day, and could certainly not make twenty. But in the way in which this trade is now carried on, not only the whole work is a peculiar trade, but it is divided into a number of branches, of which the greater part are likewise peculiar trades. One man draws out the wire, another straightens it, a third cuts it, a fourth points it, a fifth grinds it at the top for receiving the head . . . [t]hose ten persons, therefore, could make among them upward of forty-eight thousand pins in a day . . . This great increase in the quantity of work . . . is owing to three circumstances; first to the increase in dexterity in every particular workman; secondly, to the saving of time which is commonly lost in passing from one species of work to another; and, lastly, to the invention of a great number of machines which facilitate labor and enable one man to do the work of many . . . It is naturally to be expected . . . that some one or other of those who are employed in each particular branch of labor should soon find out easier and readier methods of performing their particular work.

Since the incentives to specialize are derived from exchange, the extent to which exchange is available sets limits on specialization:

> But man has almost constant occasion for the help of his brethren . . . As it is by treaty, by barter, and by purchase that we obtain the greater part of those mutual good offices which we stand in need of, so it is this same trucking disposition which originally gives occasion to the division of labor . . . so the extent of this division must always be limited by the extent of that power or, in other words, by the extent of the market. When the market is small, no person can have any encouragement to dedicate himself entirely to one employment, for want of the power to exchange all that surplus part of the produce of his own labor, which is over and above his own consumption, for such parts of the produce of other men's labor as he has the occasion for.

[†] Adam Smith, *An Inquiry into the Nature and Causes of the Wealth of Nations.* Reprinted by Modern Library, New York.

Though it hardly does justice to Smith's and Ricardo's masterful analyses, we can depict this discussion mathematically by postulating a production frontier $g(x_1, x_2) = k$, representing the amounts of two goods an individual could produce with his or her own labor, and possibly other inputs. If the individual is unable to engage in trade, he or she will produce that bundle of goods that maximizes utility subject to that production constraint, i.e.,

maximize

$$U(x_1, x_2) = U$$

subject to

$$g(x_1, x_2) = k \qquad (10\text{-}76)$$

The Lagrangian for this problem is

$$\mathscr{L} = U(x_1, x_2) + \lambda(k - g(x_1, x_2))$$

producing the first-order conditions

$$\mathscr{L}_1 = U_1(x_1, x_2) - \lambda g_1(x_1, x_2) = 0$$

$$\mathscr{L}_2 = U_2(x_1, x_2) - \lambda g_2(x_1, x_2) = 0$$

$$\mathscr{L}_\lambda = k - g(x_1, x_2) = 0$$

The first two conditions imply $U_1/U_2 = g_1/g_2$; this plus the last condition (the constraint) indicates that the indifference curve must be tangent to the production frontier. This solution is shown as point A on Fig. 10-13.

In the preceding situation, the consumer must consume the identical bundle of goods he or she produces. This situation might have been approximated on the North American frontier in the nineteenth century, or perhaps in remote villages today. (The existence of itinerant traders in those locales is testimony to the advantages of specialization.) Suppose, however, there is a market for these

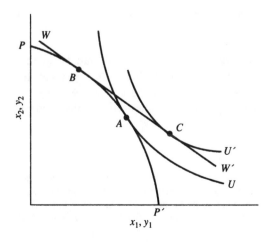

FIGURE 10-13

The Division of Labor Is Limited by the Extent of the Market. If trade is highly restricted, a consumer endowed with some production frontier PP' must consume largely what he or she produces. This utility maximum occurs at A. With efficient markets, the consumer can specialize in the production mix generating the highest wealth, B, and trade at market prices to achieve the higher utility level at C.

goods, so that once produced, the individual can trade these goods for some other, more preferred bundle. In this case, the consumer will produce that bundle of goods *with the highest market value,* which will not in general be the mix of goods desired in consumption, and will then trade these goods for the bundle that maximizes utility. With "extensive" markets, the consumer achieves point C in Fig. 10-13, on a utility level higher than when markets are so limited that no trade can take place. (Point C cannot be less preferred; the individual can always choose not to trade and remain on the production frontier.) By separating the problem of consumption from production, the consumer is able to exploit his or her comparative advantage, without having to worry whether he or she would like to consume only that bundle of goods produced.[†]

This model is formulated mathematically as follows. There are in fact 4 (i.e., $2n$) decision variables: the bundle produced, (y_1, y_2), and the bundle consumed, (x_1, x_2). The individual's problem is to
maximize

$$U(x_1, x_2) = U$$

subject to

$$g(y_1, y_2) = k$$
$$p_1 x_1 + p_2 x_2 = p_1 y_1 + p_2 y_2$$

where p_1 and p_2 are the market prices of the two goods. It is easier to analyze the problem by introducing a fifth variable, W, the total value of the individual's output (wealth). We can then state the model as

maximize

$$U(x_1, x_2) = U$$

subject to

$$p_1 x_1 + p_2 x_2 = W \qquad (10\text{-}77)$$
$$p_1 y_1 + p_2 y_2 = W$$
$$g(y_1, y_2) = k$$

It is clear from the last two constraints that for any y_1 and y_2 satisfying the production constraint, wealth W is determined. The problem then reduces to maximizing utility subject to the ordinary budget constraint $p_1 x_1 + p_2 x_2 = W$, where W is "conditional" on y_1 and y_2. However, assuming nonsatiation,

---

[†] This same idea was exploited by Irving Fisher, who explained that the existence of capital markets, in which individuals borrow and lend, allows individuals to first maximize wealth (the present value of all future income), and then rearrange consumption so as to maximize utility over time. This result is known as the "Fisher Separation Theorem." See Irving Fisher, *The Theory of Interest,* The Macmillan Company, New York, 1930. Reprinted by Augustus Kelley, New York, 1970.

increases in W will necessarily increase utility. It thus follows that in order to maximize utility, the consumer must first choose the output mix (y_1, y_2) that maximizes wealth; this occurs at point B on Fig. 10-13. The consumer then maximizes utility subject to the budget line WW' tangent to the production frontier at B, achieving consumption at point C. We leave it as an exercise to set this model up formally and derive the first- and second-order conditions. We note in passing, that as in all such utility maximization models, the prices appear in the constraints, making refutable comparative statics implications dependent upon further assumptions in the model.

Modern societies are characterized by a high degree of specialization. No one worries that they will have to consume what they produce; individual production is directed toward maximization of that individual's value of output. Adam Smith went on to say that

> As every individual direct[s] [his] industry that its produce may be of the greatest value, every individual necessarily labors to render the annual revenue of the society as great as he can. He generally, indeed, neither intends to promote the public interest nor knows how much he is promoting it . . . and he is in this, as in many other cases, led by an invisible hand to promote an end which was no part of his intention.

The maximization of *society's* total value of output depends upon further assumptions about property rights and one individual's effects on others.[†] We shall return to this issue in the chapter on welfare economics.

PROBLEMS

1. What is the difference, in a many-commodity model, between diminishing marginal rate of substitution between any pair of commodities, and quasi-concavity of the utility function? Which is the more restrictive concept?
2. Why does the proposition "More is preferred to less" imply downward-sloping indifference curves?
3. What dependence, if any, does the homogeneity of degree zero of the money-income-held-constant demand curves have on the homogeneity of the consumer's utility function?
4. Show that the marginal utility of money income, λ^M, is homogeneous of degree *minus one*.
5. Consider the utility functions of the form $U = x_1^{\alpha_1} x_2^{\alpha_2}$. Show that the implied demand curves are

$$x_1^M = \frac{\alpha_1}{(\alpha_1 + \alpha_2)} \frac{M}{p_1}$$

$$x_2^M = \frac{\alpha_2}{(\alpha_1 + \alpha_2)} \frac{M}{p_2}$$

Find λ^M and $U^*(x_1^M, x_2^M)$, and verify that $\lambda^M = \partial U^*/\partial M$.

6. Prove the elasticity formulas (10-53), (10-54), (10-59), (10-60), and (10-61) for the n commodity case.

7. Is it possible to define complements in consumer theory, by saying that the marginal utility of x_i increases when more x_j is consumed? (*Hint:* What mathematical term is being defined, and is it invariant to a monotonic transformation?)

8. Substitutes can be defined by the sign of the *gross* (including income effects) cross-effects of prices on quantities, or the *net* effect (i.e., *not* including income effects). That is, one may define "x_i is a substitute for x_j" if:

   (i) $\dfrac{\partial x_i^M}{\partial p_j} > 0$

   or

   (ii) $\dfrac{\partial x_i^U}{\partial p_j} > 0$

   (with the reverse sign on the inequality for "complements").
   (a) Which term is likely to be the more observable (empirically)?
   (b) Are these terms invariant to a monotonic transformation of the utility function?
   (c) According to the preceding definitions, if x_i is a substitute for x_j, is x_j necessarily a substitute for x_i?

9. Considering Hicks' "third law" and the preceding definition *(ii)* of substitutes and complements, show that there is a tendency toward substitution of commodities in the sense that

$$\sum_{i \neq j} p_i s_{ij} = \sum_{j \neq i} p_j s_{ij} > 0$$

10. Describe the effects of a monotonic transformation of the utility function on:
    (a) The rate of change of the marginal utility of one good with respect to a change in another good.
    (b) The law of diminishing marginal utility.
    (c) The slopes of demand curves.
    (d) The values of income elasticities.
    (e) The homogeneity of the demand functions.
    (f) The size and sign of the marginal utility of income.

11. For the utility maximization model, show that

$$\frac{\partial x_1^M}{\partial M} = \frac{-1}{\lambda^M}\left(\frac{\partial \lambda^M}{\partial p_1} + x_1^M \frac{\partial \lambda^M}{\partial M}\right)$$

where λ^M is the marginal utility of money income.

12. Suppose a consumer will have income x_1^0 this year and x_2^0 next year. He or she consumes x_1 this year and x_2 next year, being able to borrow and lend at interest rate r. Assume the consumer maximizes the utility of consumption over these two years.
    (a) Derive the comparative statics for this problem. Will an increase in this year's income necessarily lead to an increase in consumption this year?

(b) Prove that the consumer will be better off (worse off) if the interest rate rises if he or she was a net saver (dissaver) this year.

13. Consider the utility maximization problem, max $U(x_1,x_2)$ subject to $p_1x_1 + p_2x_2 = 1$, where prices have been "normalized" by setting $M = 1$. Let $U^*(p_1,p_2)$ be the indirect utility function, and λ be the Lagrange multiplier.
    (a) Show that $\lambda^M = (\partial U/\partial x_1)x_1^* + (\partial U/\partial x_2)x_2^*$
    (b) Show that $\partial U^*/\partial p_1 = -\lambda^M x_1^*$, $\partial U^*/\partial p_2 = -\lambda^M x_2^*$
    (c) Show that $\lambda^M = -[(\partial U^*/\partial p_1)p_1 + (\partial U^*/\partial p_2)p_2]$
    (d) Prove that if $U(x_1,x_2)$ is homogeneous of degree r in (x_1,x_2), then $U^*(p_1,p_2)$ is homogeneous of degree $-r$ in (p_1,p_2)

14. Consider the class of utility functions which are "additively separable," i.e., $U(x_1,x_2) \equiv U^1(x_1) + U^2(x_2)$.
    (a) Find the first- and second-order conditions for utility maximization for these utility functions. Show that diminishing marginal utility in at least one good is implied.
    (b) Show that if there is diminishing marginal utility in *each* good, then both goods are "normal," i.e., not inferior.
    (c) Show that this specification does not imply $\partial x_i^M/\partial p_j = 0, i \neq j$.
    (d) Show, however, that if $\partial x_i^M/\partial p_j \equiv \partial x_j^M/\partial p_i \equiv 0$, then $U(x_1,x_2) \equiv \alpha_1 \log x_1 + \alpha_2 \log x_2$.
    (e) Assume now that x_1 is a Giffen good, i.e., $\partial x_1^M/\partial p_1 > 0$. Prove that $\partial \lambda^M/\partial M > 0$.

15. Consider the two-good utility maximization model and assume x_1 is a Giffen good, i.e., $\partial x_1^M/\partial p_1 > 0$. Prove that $\partial x_2^M/\partial p_1$ and $\partial x_2^U/\partial p_1$ must be of opposite signs.

16. Derive an expression analogous to Eq. (10-42) for the difference between $\partial x_i^U/\partial p_j$ and $\partial x_i^s/\partial p_j, i \neq j$. Show that if x_i and x_j are either both net substitutes or both net complements of x_n, the Hicksian cross-elasticities of demand are numerically smaller in the long run than in the short run.

17. Let $U = f(x_1,x_2) + g(x_3,x_4) = (x_1^2/2 + x_1x_2) + (x_3^2/2 + x_3x_4)$. Show that if $p_1 > p_2$, this utility function achieves an interior constrained maximum subject to a linear budget constraint and that $\partial x_i^M/\partial p_j \neq 0$, $i = 1,2$, $j = 3,4$. Show also that if f^* is the utility-maximizing value of f, $\partial f^*/\partial p_j \neq 0$, $j = 3,4$. That is, strongly separable utility functions do not imply the possibility of "two-stage" budgeting.

18. The Hicksian "real income," or "utility held constant" demand curves are written
$$x_1 = x_1^U(p_1,p_2,U^0)$$
Suppose now, when p_1 changes, U^0 is also adjusted to that maximum amount achievable so as to keep money income M constant, i.e.,
$$U^0 = U^*(p_1,p_2,M)$$
is that functional relationship which keeps M constant by adjusting utility, when p_1 or p_2 changes. Thus, the money-income-held-constant demand curves can be written
$$x_1^M(p_1,p_2,M) \equiv x_1^U(p_1,p_2,U^*(p_1,p_2,M))$$
(a) Show that the income effect on x_1 is proportional to the "utility effect" on x_1, i.e., the change in x_1^U when U is changed, the factor of proportionality being the marginal utility of money income.

(b) Show that

$$\frac{\partial x_1^M}{\partial p_2} \equiv \frac{\partial x_1^U}{\partial p_2} - x_2 \frac{\partial x_1^M}{\partial M}$$

(This is an alternative derivation of the Slutsky equation to that given in the text.)

19. In a leading economics text, the following form of the "law of diminishing marginal rate of substitution" is given: The more of one good a consumer has, holding the *quantities* of all other goods constant, the smaller the marginal evaluation of that good becomes in terms of all other goods, i.e., the indifference curves become less steep. (Sketch this condition graphically.)

(a) This is a postulate about the slopes of indifference curves, i.e., about the term $(-U_1/U_2)$. What is the sign, according to this postulate, of $\partial(-U_1/U_2)/\partial x_1, \partial(-U_1/U_2)/\partial x_2$?

(b) Show that this postulate implies that the indifference curves are convex to the origin.

(c) Suppose this postulate is violated for good 2. Show that x_1 is an inferior good. Show that if the postulate is violated for good 1 also, then the indifference curves are *concave* to the origin.

(d) Show that the preceding postulate rules out inferior goods (for the two-good case).

(e) Show that in part (c), in which the indifference curves are still assumed to be convex to the origin, the marginal evaluation of x_2 *increases* the more it is consumed relative to x_1. Explain intuitively.

(f) Show that in a three-good world, the preceding postulate is insufficiently strong to imply indifference curves which are convex to the origin.

20. An historically important class of utility functions includes those functions which exhibit vertically parallel indifference curves, i.e., with x_1 on the horizontal axis and x_2 on the vertical axis, the slopes of *all* indifference curves are the same at any given level of x_1. For these utility functions:

(a) Prove graphically and algebraically that the income effect on x_1 equals 0.

(b) Show that the "ordinary" demand curve for x_1, $x_1^M(p_1, p_2, M)$ and the compensated demand curve for x_1, $x_1^U(p_1, p_2, U)$ are identical by showing that at any point, the slopes of x_1^M and x_1^U are the same, and that the shifts in x_1^M and x_1^U are the same with respect to a change in p_2, the price of the second good.

(c) Consider the utility function $U = x_2 + \log x_1$. Show that this function has vertically parallel indifference curves.

(d) For $U = x_2 + \log x_1$, show also that the price consumption paths with respect to changes in p_1 are horizontal, i.e., that the amount of x_2 consumed is independent of the price of good 1.

SELECTED REFERENCES

Alchian, A. A.: "The Meaning of Utility Measurement," *American Economic Review,* **43**:26–50, March 1953.

Becker, G. S.: "Irrational Behavior and Economic Theory," *Journal of Political Economy,* **70:** 1–13, 1962.

Debreu, G.: *Theory of Value,* Cowles Foundation Monograph 17, John Wiley & Sons, Inc., New York, 1959. The seminal work in the formal, abstract approach to economic theory. Get out your old topology notes first.

Friedman, M.: "The Marshallian Demand Curve," in *Essays in Positive Economics,* University of Chicago Press, Chicago, 1953. Debatable, to say the least, but important in terms of the issues analyzed.

Georgescu-Roegen, N.: "The Pure Theory of Consumer Behavior," *Quarterly Journal of Economics,* **50**:545–593, 1936.

Hicks, J. R.: *Value and Capital,* 2d ed., Oxford University Press, London, 1946.

———: *A Revision of Demand Theory,* Oxford University Press, London, 1956.

Marshall, A.: *Principles of Economics,* 8th ed., Macmillan & Co., Ltd., London, 1920.

Mosak, J. L: "On the Interpretation of the Fundamental Equation in Value Theory," in O. Lange, F. McIntyre, and T. O. Yntema (eds.), *Studies in Mathematical Economics and Econometrics in Memory of Henry Schultz,* University of Chicago Press, Chicago, 1942.

Pollak, R.: "Conditional Demand Functions and Consumption Theory," *Quarterly Journal of Economics,* **83**:60–78, February 1969.

Samuelson, P. A.: *Foundations of Economic Analysis,* Harvard University Press, Cambridge, Mass., 1947.

Slutsky, E.: "Sulla Teoria del Bilancio del Consumatore," *Giornale degli Economisti,* **51**:19–23, 1915. Translated as "On the Theory of the Budget of the Consumer," in G. Stigler and K. Boulding (eds.), *Readings in Price Theory,* Richard D. Irwin, Inc., Homewood, Ill., 1952.

Wold, H., and L. Jureen: *Demand Analysis,* John Wiley & Sons, Inc., New York, 1953.

CHAPTER
11

SPECIAL TOPICS IN CONSUMER THEORY

11.1 REVEALED PREFERENCE AND EXCHANGE

Any economic system solves, in some way, the problems of production and allocation of goods and resources. Starting with various factor endowments, resources are somehow organized and combined, and a certain set of finished goods emerges. All along the way, decisions are made concerning two fundamental problems:

1. What final set of goods shall be produced?
2. How shall factors of production be combined to produce those goods?

These problems are not independent. The choice of factors and their least-cost combinations vary depending on the level of demand for the goods. A person building a car in the back yard will use inputs different from those used by General Motors. These matters aside, how does it come to pass that producers of goods have any idea at all what to produce? What is it that guides these decision makers in selecting a certain, usually small, set of goods to produce, out of the vast array of conceivable alternative goods and services?

The problem is by no means trivial. Imagine yourself as the chief economic planner of a society in which it has been mandated by the ruling political party

362

that all goods are to be handed out free of charge. To make life easy for you, the government has provided you with a complete set of costs of producing all existing and potential goods. How much of each should you produce, assuming you had the best interests of the consumers in mind? To achieve your goal, you would need to know how much consumers valued the alternative goods. Without this information, a planner might decide to produce meat for a nation of vegetarians, or, on a less grandiose scale, too much wheat for people who would rather consume more rice or corn, or trains and buses for people who would rather drive their own cars. What mix of these goods and services should be produced?

The solution to this allocation problem in any economy depends upon the production of information concerning the valuation of goods by consumers and the ability of individuals to utilize that information. The latter problem has to do with the system of property rights developed in the nation in question. We shall not inquire into these matters here. Suffice it to say that a system that allows private ownership and free contracting between individuals will in all likelihood produce a different set of goods than a society where these rights are attenuated.

The former problem, how information is produced regarding consumers' valuations of goods, is the topic at hand here. Recall the definition of *value*. The value of goods (at the margin) is the amount of other goods consumers are willing to give up in order to consume an additional increment of the good in question. In most private exchanges, information about these marginal values is produced automatically by the willingness or reluctance of the participants to engage in trade. When a trade takes place, the value of the goods traded is revealed to the traders and other observers. Since, under the usual behavioral postulates of Chap. 10, individuals will purchase goods until the marginal value of those goods falls to the value of the next best alternative, *prices,* in a voluntary exchange economy, provide the information of consumers' *marginal* (though not total) value of each traded good. Any producer whose marginal costs of production are less than that price can benefit by producing more of that good and in so doing will be directing resources from low-valued to higher-valued uses. In this way the gains from trade will be further exhausted.

The value of goods will also be revealed, though not as precisely, when other means of allocation are used. When goods are price-controlled, e.g., gasoline in the winter of 1973–1974, waiting lines and other nonprice discrimination appeared. These phenomena provided evidence that the good was valued higher, at the margin, than the official controlled price. But exactly how much higher (a subject of intense debate at the time) was not known. The information on the precise marginal evaluation of gasoline during that time was never allowed to be produced. And, in the extreme case, where goods are handed out "free," very little information is produced concerning consumers' valuations of those goods.

In the usual case of so-called private goods in which congestion is so extreme that only one person can consume the item, preferences are revealed automatically through the act of exchange. Intensity of preference will be revealed through the level of purchase of goods and services. An important class of goods for which this does not easily occur is made up of the so-called public goods, in which congestion is absent, so that adding an additional consumer to the consumption of that service in no way diminishes the level of service provided the other consumers. The services national defense, lighthouses, or uncrowded freeways are classic examples of such goods. In some cases, the ability to *exclude* nonpayers from the benefits of these services would be difficult to arrange. (The right of exclusion, a fundamental part of property rights, is not peculiar to public goods, nor are all public goods incapable of having rights of exclusion cheaply enforced.) In the case of nonexclusive public goods, particularly, information concerning consumers' valuations of the good will be difficult to observe. Consumers will often have an incentive to understate the intensity of their preferences, and to "free-ride." Imagine how the production of such goods might be attempted: if the costs of production are to be assessed on the basis of the value of the service to the consumers, the consumers will tend to indicate how little they value the service (if at all), each hoping that enough others will indicate a high enough level of willingness to pay to make the project viable. The end result may be that the service is not produced at all, or that "too little" is produced. In these situations, coercive schemes such as government provision of the good through mandatory taxation or the formation of private clubs with assessment of dues are often resorted to as a means of lowering the contracting costs between consumers eager to exhaust the gains from exchange. But the preferences of individuals for these types of services will not be completely revealed, since individuals in the group will still, in all likelihood, have different marginal evaluations of the final level of public good produced.

Is it possible, given the nature of exchange explored above, to replace the utility maximization hypothesis with one based entirely on observable quantities? That is, can a behavioral postulate yielding refutable hypotheses be formulated in terms of exchanges? This question was initiated by Samuelson, Houthakker, and others in the 1930s and 1940s, resulting in what is known as the *theory of revealed preference*. It is intimately tied in with another classical question of the theory of the consumer, viz., whether the Slutsky relations of Chap. 10 constitute the entire range of implications of the utility maximization hypothesis. That is, is it possible, starting with a set of demand relations which obey symmetry and negative semidefiniteness of the pure substitution terms, to infer that there exists some utility function (together with all its monotonic transformations) from which those demand functions are derivable? This issue is known as the problem of *integrability*. A complete discussion of these issues is beyond the scope of this book, the integrability issue in particular being dependent upon subtle mathematical details. We shall, however, indicate the general nature of the problems.

Let us suppose that a consumer possesses a well-defined set of demand relations,

$$x_i = x_i^M(p_1, \ldots, p_n, M) \qquad i = 1, \ldots, n \tag{11-1}$$

At this point we need not even assume that these relations are single-valued; i.e., we allow, for the moment, that confronted with a set of prices $p_1, \ldots, p_n$

and a given money income M, the consumer might be willing to choose from more than one consumption bundle. Strictly speaking, then, the relations (11-1) are not functions, since single-valuedness of the dependent variable is part of the definition of a function; instead system (11-1) represents what are sometimes called *correspondences* or just simply *relations*. What is being insisted on here is that a consumer *will choose* some consumption bundle $\mathbf{x}^0 = (x_1^0, \ldots, x_n^0)$ when confronted with a price-income vector $(\mathbf{p}^0, M^0) = (p_1^0, \ldots, p_n^0, M^0)$. Let us also assert that the consumer, in so choosing, will spend his or her entire budget; i.e., the choice $\mathbf{x}^0$ will satisfy the budget relation $\sum p_i^0 x_i^0 = M^0$.

It will be much easier going if some elementary matrix and vector notation is used in the following discussion. Recall the definitions of vectors and matrix multiplication in Chap. 5. The scalar (or inner) product of two vectors $\mathbf{x} = (x_1, \ldots, x_n)$ and $\mathbf{y} = (y_1, \ldots, y_n)$ is defined as $\mathbf{xy} = \sum_{i=1}^{n} x_i y_i$. With this notation the budget equation $\sum p_i x_i = M$ is simply written $\mathbf{px} = M$. The set of differentials $dx_1, \ldots, dx_n$ is written simply $\mathbf{dx}$. The expression $\mathbf{p}$ $\mathbf{dx}$ means $\sum_{i=1}^{n} p_i dx_i$, etc. The entire set of demand relations (11-1) is written simply as $\mathbf{x} = \mathbf{x}^M(\mathbf{p}, M)$.

In Fig. 11-1, a consumer is faced with a price-income vector $(\mathbf{p}^0, M^0)$ and chooses the consumption bundle $\mathbf{x}^0$, where $\mathbf{p}^0 \mathbf{x}^0 = M^0$; that is, the budget equation is satisfied. In so doing, we shall say that the consumer reveals a preference for bundle $\mathbf{x}^0$ over some other bundle, say $\mathbf{x}^1$, which was not chosen. We say $\mathbf{x}^0$ is *revealed preferred* to $\mathbf{x}^1$. We cannot yet speak of the consumer being indifferent between $\mathbf{x}^0$ and $\mathbf{x}^1$, since indifference is a utility-related concept, which is not yet defined. The phrase "$\mathbf{x}^0$ revealed preferred to $\mathbf{x}^1$" simply means that where the consumer was confronted with two *affordable* consumption bundles $\mathbf{x}^0$ and $\mathbf{x}^1$, $\mathbf{x}^0$ was chosen and $\mathbf{x}^1$ not, although $\mathbf{x}^1$ was no more expensive than $\mathbf{x}^0$. It is not likely that we would be able to formulate a hypothesis about choices if the chosen bundle were less expensive than the nonchosen one; people choose Chevrolets instead of Cadillacs not necessarily because they prefer Chevrolets to Cadillacs but because the latter cost more. The statement that $\mathbf{x}^1$ is no more expensive than $\mathbf{x}^0$ is written $\mathbf{p}^0 \mathbf{x}^0 \geq \mathbf{p}^0 \mathbf{x}^1$.

Having so *defined* revealed preference, let us now assert something about behavior in terms of it.

The weak axiom of revealed preference. Assume that $\mathbf{x}^0$ is revealed preferred to $\mathbf{x}^1$, that is, at some price vector $\mathbf{p}^0$, $\mathbf{x}^0$ is chosen and $\mathbf{p}^0 \mathbf{x}^0 \geq \mathbf{p}^0 \mathbf{x}^1$, so that $\mathbf{x}^1$ could have been chosen but was not. Then $\mathbf{x}^1$ *will never be revealed preferred to* $\mathbf{x}^0$.

The weak axiom (we shall presently explain the reason for the adjective *weak*) does not say that $\mathbf{x}^1$ will never be chosen under any circumstances. The bundle $\mathbf{x}^1$ may very well be chosen at some price vector $\mathbf{p}^1$. What the weak axiom indicates is that if $\mathbf{x}^1$ is chosen at some price $\mathbf{p}^1$, then $\mathbf{x}^0$ will be more expensive than $\mathbf{x}^1$ at prices $\mathbf{p}^1$. Consider Fig. 11-1 again. At prices $\mathbf{p}^0$, the consumer chooses $\mathbf{x}^0$ even though $\mathbf{x}^1$ could have been chosen, since $\mathbf{x}^1$ lies below the implied budget line MM defined as $\mathbf{p}^0 \mathbf{x}^0 = M^0$. At some other set of prices $\mathbf{p}^1$, $\mathbf{x}^1$ might be the chosen bundle, forming a new budget equation $\mathbf{p}^1 \mathbf{x}^1 = M^1$. But note that at prices

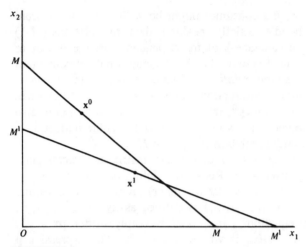

FIGURE 11-1
The weak axiom of revealed preference. At prices $\mathbf{p}^0$, the consumption bundle $\mathbf{x}^0$ is chosen, implying a budget line MM. The consumption bundle $\mathbf{x}^1$, since it lies interior to MM, could have been chosen but wasn't. Hence, $\mathbf{x}^0$ is said to be revealed preferred to $\mathbf{x}^1$. This does not mean that $\mathbf{x}^1$ will never be chosen. What it does mean is that when $\mathbf{x}^1$ is chosen, at some price vector $\mathbf{p}^1$, implying a budget line M^1M^1, $\mathbf{x}^0$ will be more expensive than $\mathbf{x}^1$ at those new prices. In other words, if $\mathbf{p}^0\mathbf{x}^0 \geq \mathbf{p}^0\mathbf{x}^1$, when $\mathbf{x}^1$ is chosen at $\mathbf{p}^1$, necessarily $\mathbf{p}^1\mathbf{x}^1 < \mathbf{p}^1\mathbf{x}^0$. This is illustrated in this diagram, since $\mathbf{x}^0$ lies outside the budget line M^1M^1.

$\mathbf{p}^1$, $\mathbf{x}^0$ is more expensive than $\mathbf{x}^1$, that is, $\mathbf{p}^1\mathbf{x}^0 > \mathbf{p}^1\mathbf{x}^1$. Hence, $\mathbf{x}^1$ is *not* revealed preferred to $\mathbf{x}^0$ merely because it was chosen, for the same reason that one would not want to infer that Chevrolets are preferred to Cadillacs. The bundle $\mathbf{x}^1$ is simply cheaper than $\mathbf{x}^0$ at prices $\mathbf{p}^1$; nothing can be inferred about the desirability of $\mathbf{x}^0$ and $\mathbf{x}^1$ from $\mathbf{p}^1\mathbf{x}^0 > \mathbf{p}^1\mathbf{x}^1$ alone.

Algebraically, then, the weak axiom of revealed preference says:

if

$$\mathbf{p}^0\mathbf{x}^0 \geq \mathbf{p}^0\mathbf{x}^1$$

then

$$\mathbf{p}^1\mathbf{x}^0 > \mathbf{p}^1\mathbf{x}^1 \tag{11-2}$$

where the consumption bundle chosen is the one whose superscript is the same as that on the price vector. Figure 11-2 shows a price consumption situation that would contradict the weak axiom. There, $\mathbf{x}^1$ is chosen at $\mathbf{p}^1$ when $\mathbf{x}^0$ could have been chosen; we have both $\mathbf{p}^0\mathbf{x}^0 \geq \mathbf{p}^0\mathbf{x}^1$ and $\mathbf{p}^1\mathbf{x}^1 \geq \mathbf{p}^1\mathbf{x}^0$. The weak axiom therefore does imply some restrictions in the range of observable behavior. What are they?

Proposition 1. The demand relations (11-1) are homogeneous of degree zero in all prices and money income; that is, $x_i^M(tp_1, \ldots, tp_n, tM) \equiv x_i^M(p_1, \ldots, p_n, M)$.

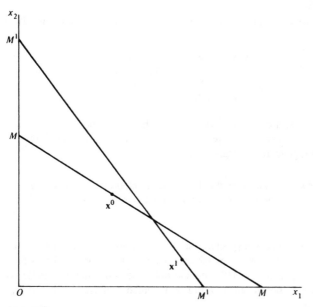

FIGURE 11-2
Violation of the weak axiom of revealed preference. In the initial situation at prices $\mathbf{p}^0$, $\mathbf{x}^0$ is chosen even though $\mathbf{x}^1$ could have been chosen. Hence, $\mathbf{x}^0$ is revealed preferred to $\mathbf{x}^1$. When $\mathbf{x}^1$ is chosen at prices $\mathbf{p}^1$, implying a budget line M^1M^1, $\mathbf{x}^0$ could still have been chosen and thus $\mathbf{x}^1$ would be revealed preferred to $\mathbf{x}^0$. This contradicts the weak axiom, which says that if $\mathbf{x}^0$ is revealed preferred to $\mathbf{x}^1$, then $\mathbf{x}^1$ will never be preferred to $\mathbf{x}^0$. Note that if one were to try to draw an indifference locus tangent to MM and M^1M^1 at $\mathbf{x}^0$ and $\mathbf{x}^1$, respectively, the locus would be concave to the origin. This behavior is ruled out by the weak axiom.

Proof. Let the consumption bundle $\mathbf{x}^0 = (x_1^0, \ldots, x_n^0)$ be chosen by the consumer when prices and income are $(\mathbf{p}^0, M^0) = (p_1^0, \ldots, p_n^0, M^0)$, and let $\mathbf{x}^1 = (x_1^1, \ldots, x_n^1)$ be chosen at prices and income $(\mathbf{p}^1, M^1) = (p_1^1, \ldots, p_n^1, M^1)$. By hypothesis, $\mathbf{p}^1 = t\mathbf{p}^0$, $M^1 = tM^0$. Assume now that $\mathbf{x}^1 \neq \mathbf{x}^0$, that is, that two distinct points are chosen in these situations. We shall show that a contradiction arises. Since $tM^0 = M^1$ and the consumer spends the entire budget,

$$t\mathbf{p}^0\mathbf{x}^0 = \mathbf{p}^1\mathbf{x}^1$$

However, $\mathbf{p}^1 = t\mathbf{p}^0$. Hence,

$$t\mathbf{p}^0\mathbf{x}^0 = t\mathbf{p}^0\mathbf{x}^1$$

or

$$\mathbf{p}^0\mathbf{x}^0 = \mathbf{p}^0\mathbf{x}^1 \tag{11-3}$$

Equation (11-3) says that $\mathbf{x}^0$ is revealed preferred to $\mathbf{x}^1$, since $\mathbf{x}^1$ could have been chosen and was not. Therefore, when $\mathbf{x}^1$ *is* chosen, $\mathbf{x}^0$ must be more expensive, i.e.,

$$\mathbf{p}^1\mathbf{x}^1 < \mathbf{p}^1\mathbf{x}^0 \tag{11-4}$$

by the weak axiom of revealed preference. However, $\mathbf{p}^1 = t\mathbf{p}^0$. Substituting this into (11-4) yields

$$t\mathbf{p}^0\mathbf{x}^1 < t\mathbf{p}^0\mathbf{x}^0$$

or

$$\mathbf{p}^0\mathbf{x}^1 < \mathbf{p}^0\mathbf{x}^0 \tag{11-5}$$

However, (11-5) and (11-3) are contradictory; hence, the assumption that $\mathbf{x}^1 \neq \mathbf{x}^0$ must be false, and the weak axiom of revealed preference implies that the demand relations (11-1) are homogeneous of degree zero.

Proposition 2. The weak axiom implies that the demand relations (11-1) are single-valued; i.e., for any price income vector $(\mathbf{p}, M)$ the consumer chooses a single point of consumption.

Proof. This proposition is actually a special case of proposition 1; simply let $t = 1$ in the above proof. Proposition 1 includes the case where $t = 1$ (since it holds for all $t > 0$), so when $\mathbf{p}^1 = \mathbf{p}^0$, $M^1 = M^0$, one and only one consumption bundle is chosen. If two points were chosen, each would be revealed preferred to the other, an obvious contradiction.

Thus, two properties of demand functions implied by utility analysis, single valuedness and homogeneity of degree zero, are also implied by the weak axiom of revealed preference. Most important, however, the axiom also implies the negativity of the Hicks-Slutsky type substitution terms $\partial x_i^M / \partial p_i + x_i \partial x_i^M / \partial M$. Let us define

$$s_{ij} = \frac{\partial x_i^M}{\partial p_j} + x_j \frac{\partial x_i^M}{\partial M} \tag{11-6}$$

We are not yet entitled to call these terms *pure-substitution effects,* or *compensated changes* because we have not yet shown (the weak axiom is insufficient for that purpose) that a utility function exists for this consumer. With utility as yet undefined, the concept of indifference or utility held constant has no meaning. However, we can show the following.

Proposition 3. The matrix of s_{ij}'s is negative semidefinite, under the assumption of the weak axiom of revealed preference.

Proof. Let us assume also that the demand functions (11-1), $\mathbf{x} = \mathbf{x}^M(\mathbf{p}, M)$, are differentiable. Let $\mathbf{p}^1 = \mathbf{p}^0 + \mathbf{dp}$, $\mathbf{x}^1 = \mathbf{x}^0 + \mathbf{dx}$, where the differentials indicate movements along the tangent planes. Then from the weak axiom,

$$\mathbf{p}^0\mathbf{x}^0 = \mathbf{p}^0\mathbf{x}^1 \quad \text{implies} \quad \mathbf{p}^1\mathbf{x}^1 < \mathbf{p}^1\mathbf{x}^0$$

With $\mathbf{p}^1$ and $\mathbf{x}^1$ defined as stated this becomes

$$\mathbf{p}^0\mathbf{x}^0 = \mathbf{p}^0(\mathbf{x}^0 + \mathbf{dx}) \tag{11-7}$$

implies

$$(\mathbf{p}^0 + \mathbf{dp})(\mathbf{x}^0 + \mathbf{dx}) < (\mathbf{p}^0 + \mathbf{dp})\mathbf{x}^0 \tag{11-8}$$

Equation (11-7) simplifies to $\mathbf{p}^0\mathbf{dx} = 0$, and (11-8) reduces to

$$(\mathbf{p}^0 + \mathbf{dp})\mathbf{x}^0 + (\mathbf{p}^0 + \mathbf{dp})\mathbf{dx} < (\mathbf{p}^0 + \mathbf{dp})\mathbf{x}^0$$

or

$$(\mathbf{p}^0 + \mathbf{dp})\mathbf{dx} < 0$$

Hence, for differentiable demand functions, the weak axiom can be stated as

$$\mathbf{dp}\ \mathbf{dx} \le 0 \tag{11-9}$$

whenever

$$\mathbf{p}\ \mathbf{dx} = 0 \tag{11-10}$$

That is, $\sum dp_i dx_i \le 0$ whenever $\sum p_i dx_i = 0$, where the equality holds in (11-9) only when all prices change in the same proportion; otherwise $\mathbf{dp}\ \mathbf{dx} < 0$. Now relate Eqs. (11-9) and (11-10) to Hicks-Slutsky terms, the s_{ij}'s defined in (11-6). For each demand function $x_i = x_i^M(p_1, \ldots, p_n, M)$,

$$dx_i = \sum_{j=1}^n \left(\frac{\partial x_i^M}{\partial p_j} dp_j \right) + \frac{\partial x_i^M}{\partial M} dM \tag{11-11}$$

However, when $\sum_{j=1}^n p_j dx_j = 0$,

$$dM = \sum_{j=1}^n x_j dp_j + \sum_{j=1}^n p_j dx_j = \sum_{j=1}^n x_j dp_j \tag{11-12}$$

Substituting (11-12) into (11-11) gives

$$dx_i = \sum_{j=1}^n \frac{\partial x_i^M}{\partial p_j} dp_j + \sum_{j=1}^n \frac{\partial x_i^M}{\partial M} x_j dp_j$$

or

$$dx_i = \sum_{j=1}^n \left(\frac{\partial x_i^M}{\partial p_j} + x_j \frac{\partial x_i^M}{\partial M} \right) dp_j = \sum_{j=1}^n s_{ij} dp_j \tag{11-13}$$

Applying Eq. (11-9) to (11-13) gives

$$\sum_{i=1}^n dx_i dp_i = \sum_{i=1}^n \sum_{j=1}^n s_{ij} dp_i dp_j \le 0 \tag{11-14}$$

where the equality holds when all prices change in the same proportion. Equation (11-14) says, by definition, that the matrix of Slutsky terms is negative semidefinite. As such, with the methods employed in deriving the conditions for maximization, $s_{ii} \le 0$ (usually $s_{ii} < 0$); that is, the pure substitution own effects are negative.

What is the meaning of (11-9) and (11-10)? The condition $\sum p_i dx_i = 0$ is precisely what is implied when, starting from the utility framework, utility is held constant. When $U(x_1, \ldots, x_n) = U^0$, a constant,

$$dU = \sum U_i dx_i = \lambda \sum p_i dx_i = 0$$

using the first-order equations for utility maximization subject to a budget constraint. Hence, in that case, assuming nonsatiation $(\lambda \neq 0), \sum p_i dx_i = 0$. Thus, the dx_i's would be interpretable as pure substitution movements. If only one price p_j is changed, that is, $dp_i = 0$, $i \neq j$, then Eq. (11-9) says that $dp_j dx_j < 0$, or that the own substitution effect is negative, as implied by utility analysis. But again, these are mere analogies at this point, since the existence of a utility function has not yet been shown.

The revealed preference approach to consumer theory was originally offered as an operational alternative to the sometimes vague and mysterious utility analysis. We see that, in fact, the weak axiom of revealed preference implies almost as much as utility analysis itself and hence is practically equivalent to it. The only result not implied by the weak axiom is the symmetry of the Slutsky terms; that is, $s_{ij} = s_{ji}$. Without this, a utility function cannot exist, since $s_{ij} = s_{ji}$ is a necessary consequence of utility theory. The question thus remains: Can the weak axiom of revealed preference be strengthened so that it implies symmetry and hence the possible equivalence of revealed-preference theory and utility analysis? The answer was provided by Houthakker in 1950, with results discussed in the next section.

11.2 THE STRONG AXIOM OF REVEALED PREFERENCE AND INTEGRABILITY

The inability to deduce the symmetry of Slutsky-type substitution terms from the weak axiom of revealed preference seems at first to be mainly an annoying detail. However, if a utility function does not exist for a given consumer, we should expect occasionally to observe behavior that most of us would regard as strange and not in conformity with the usual observations on consumer behavior. Let us see what type of behavior is *not* ruled out by the weak axiom.

Consider three consumption bundles, $\mathbf{x}^0$, $\mathbf{x}^1$, and $\mathbf{x}^2$, which the consumer purchases at price vectors $\mathbf{p}^0$, $\mathbf{p}^1$, and $\mathbf{p}^2$, respectively. Each bundle represents consumption levels of three separate goods. Let $\mathbf{x}^j = (x_1^j, x_2^j, x_3^j)$, $\mathbf{p}^j = (p_1^j, p_2^j, p_3^j)$, $j = 0, 1, 2$.

$$\mathbf{x}^0 = (2, 2, 2) \qquad \mathbf{p}^0 = (2, 2, 2)$$

$$\mathbf{x}^1 = (3, 1, 2) \qquad \mathbf{p}^1 = (1, 3, 2)$$

$$\mathbf{x}^2 = (4, 1, 1\tfrac{1}{2}) \qquad \mathbf{p}^2 = (2, 1\tfrac{1}{2}, 5)$$

In the initial situation, when each good is priced at $2, 2 units each are bought, for a total expenditure of $12. When p_1 is lowered from $2 to $1 and p_2 raised to

$3 from $2, to produce $\mathbf{p}^1 = (1,3,2)$, this consumer evidently increases consumption of the first good x_1 and lowers that of x_2. This is in accordance with substitution toward the lower-priced good. Similarly, when p_3 is raised from $2 to $5, among other changes, the consumer decreases consumption of x_3, from 2 units to $1\frac{1}{2}$ units. Although p_1 increases absolutely from $1 to $2, relative to the change in p_3, x_1 becomes relatively cheaper and consumption of x_1 increases. Hence, these consumption bundles and prices seem plausible enough.

They are even more plausible in that the weak axiom of revealed preference is satisfied for these points. In particular, we note

$$\mathbf{p}^0\mathbf{x}^0 = \mathbf{p}^0\mathbf{x}^1 = 12$$

and thus $\mathbf{x}^0$ is revealed preferred to $\mathbf{x}^1$. When $\mathbf{x}^1$ is in fact purchased, $\mathbf{x}^0$ is more expensive than $\mathbf{x}^1$:

$$\mathbf{p}^1\mathbf{x}^1 = 10 < \mathbf{p}^1\mathbf{x}^0 = 12$$

What is more, $\mathbf{x}^1$ is revealed preferred to $\mathbf{x}^2$:

$$\mathbf{p}^1\mathbf{x}^1 = \mathbf{p}^1\mathbf{x}^2 = 10$$

and when $\mathbf{x}^2$ is purchased, $\mathbf{x}^1$ is more expensive:

$$\mathbf{p}^2\mathbf{x}^2 = 17 < \mathbf{p}^2\mathbf{x}^1 = 17\frac{1}{2}$$

Now, however, something utterly revolting occurs: $\mathbf{x}^2$ is revealed preferred to $\mathbf{x}^0$.

$$\mathbf{p}^2\mathbf{x}^2 = \mathbf{p}^2\mathbf{x}^0 = 17$$

and, when $\mathbf{x}^0$ is purchased, $\mathbf{x}^2$ is more expensive:

$$\mathbf{p}^0\mathbf{x}^0 = 12 < \mathbf{p}^0\mathbf{x}^2 = 13$$

We see from this example that the weak axiom of revealed preference allows intransitivity of preferences to occur. If revealed preference is to be associated with the usual notions of consumers' preferences, we cannot allow the situation where $\mathbf{x}^0$ is preferred to $\mathbf{x}^1$ and $\mathbf{x}^1$ is preferred to $\mathbf{x}^2$ and then have $\mathbf{x}^2$ preferred to the original bundle $\mathbf{x}^0$. Such intransitivity could not occur under the usual assumptions of utility analysis—in particular, the assumption that indifference curves are nonintersecting. Yet this situation is precisely what occurs in the preceding example, an example in complete conformity with the weak axiom of revealed preference.

It is therefore not surprising that something less than what is implied by utility maximization is implied by the weak axiom. This took the form of allowing $s_{ij} \neq s_{ji}$. It is not obvious or easy to explain but nonetheless true that this asymmetry and the occurrence of nontransitive revealed preferences are equivalent in the sense that, together with the weak axiom, eliminating either one rules out the other also. In other words, if the weak axiom of revealed preference is strengthened to include the additional assertion that revealed preferences will not be nontransitive, i.e., that nontransitivity will not occur, then in fact it can be shown that a utility function exists for that consumer with the usual properties. These properties include the condition that $s_{ij} = s_{ji}, i, j = 1, \ldots, n$. Conversely, if, in addition to the weak axiom, it is also assumed that $s_{ij} = s_{ji}, i = 1, \ldots, n$, this too guarantees the existence of a utility function consistent with the observed behavior and hence nontransitivity of revealed preferences. This latter issue is the classic problem of integrability of the demand functions, i.e., the question of whether a given set of demand functions is capable of being generated by some utility function.

Let us formally state the strong axiom of revealed preferences, due to H. S. Houthakker.[†]

> **The strong axiom of revealed preference.** Let the bundle of goods purchased at price vector $\mathbf{p}^i$ be denoted $\mathbf{x}^i$. For any finite set of bundles $(\mathbf{x}^1, \ldots, \mathbf{x}^k)$, if $\mathbf{x}^1$ is revealed preferred to $\mathbf{x}^2$, $\mathbf{x}^2$ revealed preferred to $\mathbf{x}^3, \ldots, \mathbf{x}^{k-1}$ revealed preferred to $\mathbf{x}^k$, or algebraically, if $\mathbf{p}^1\mathbf{x}^1 \geq \mathbf{p}^1\mathbf{x}^2$, $\mathbf{p}^2\mathbf{x}^2 \geq \mathbf{p}^2\mathbf{x}^3, \ldots, \mathbf{p}^{k-1}\mathbf{x}^{k-1} \geq \mathbf{p}^{k-1}\mathbf{x}^k$, then $\mathbf{p}^k\mathbf{x}^k < \mathbf{p}^k\mathbf{x}^0$; that is, $\mathbf{x}^k$ is *not* revealed preferred to $\mathbf{x}^0$.

> **Theorem.** Individual demand functions $x_i = x_i^M(p_1, \ldots, p_n, M), i = 1, \ldots, n$, which are consistent with the strong axiom of revealed preference are derivable from utility analysis. That is, there exists a class of utility functions $F(U(x_1, \ldots, x_n))$, where F is any monotonic transformation, which, when maximized subject to the budget constraint $\sum p_i x_i = M$, results in those particular demand functions.

This "theorem" is subject to certain technical mathematical conditions concerning differentiability and other details (hence the quotation marks). In essence, however, the strong axiom is equivalent to the utility maximization hypothesis; either one implies the other. The proof of this theorem is unfortunately beyond the scope of this book. The interested reader should consult Houthakker's original paper and the later literature.

The strong axiom is a straightforward generalization of the weak axiom. It merely extends the notion of the weak axiom to a chain of more than two consumption bundles. In general, pairwise comparison of consumption points is too weak a basis for making statements about multidimensional curvature properties of functions. Suppose, for example, a consumer possesses well-defined indifference curves, all nonconcave, etc., for two commodities x_1 and x_2. Likewise, assume a similarly well-behaved indifference map between x_2 and some other good x_3 and another well-behaved set for x_3 and x_1. Are these separate indifference maps consistent with an overall utility function $U(x_1, x_2, x_3)$? Not necessarily. No such integral function need exist. The indifference maps may all be well-behaved taken alone, but they may be inconsistent with each other algebraically or they

---

[†]H. S. Houthakker, "Revealed Preference and the Utility Function," *Economica*, **17**:159–174, May 1950.

may allow the intransitivity demonstrated in the previous example. Suppose, for example, at a given point, this consumer's MRS of apples for oranges is three apples for one orange. And suppose the consumer will trade one orange for two pears and two pears for four apples. These marginal rates of substitution could not be generated by a three-dimensional utility function, for the consumer would spiral around the original point and wind up being indifferent between the original bundle of goods and one which had more of one good and the same amount of the others. Yet it is perfectly easy to draw these indifference curves in two-dimensional space.

In addition, the usual convexity of the separate two-dimensional curves is insufficient to guarantee usual convexity of the three-dimensional indifference surfaces, assuming it exists. If each two-dimensional curve is convex to the origin, the bordered Hessians of the form

$$H_2 = \begin{vmatrix} U_{ii} & U_{ij} & -p_i \\ U_{ji} & U_{jj} & -p_j \\ -p_i & -p_j & 0 \end{vmatrix}$$

are all nonnegative. However, even if they are all positive, the full bordered Hessian

$$H_3 = \begin{vmatrix} U_{11} & U_{12} & U_{13} & -p_1 \\ U_{21} & U_{22} & U_{23} & -p_2 \\ U_{31} & U_{32} & U_{33} & -p_3 \\ -p_1 & -p_2 & -p_3 & 0 \end{vmatrix}$$

need not have the appropriate sign (nonpositive). The resulting indifference surface can, at least locally, be concave to the origin at some point, even though all two-dimensional projections of that surface exhibit strict quasi-concavity. These are all subtle geometric issues. It is remarkable that as simple a statement as the strong axiom of revealed preference contains the same behavioral implications as the quasi-concavity of a multidimensional utility function.

Integrability

Suppose an econometrician estimates a set of demand relations $x_i = x_i^M(p_1, \ldots, p_n, M), i = 1, \ldots, n$, and asks you to check whether these estimated functions are capable of being derived by utility analysis. That is, is it possible (and if so, how) to determine that a given set of demand functions is consistent with standard utility analysis? Consider the two demand functions

$$x_1 = \frac{M}{2p_1} \qquad x_2 = \frac{M}{2p_2} \tag{11-15}$$

Let us make such a determination here (even though we know the answer, these demand functions having been derived in Chap. 10). Both functions are clearly homogeneous of degree zero in all prices and money income. Also,

$$p_1x_1 + p_2x_2 = \frac{M}{2} + \frac{M}{2} \equiv M$$

Thus, the budget constraint is satisfied identically. Let us calculate the matrix of Slutsky terms s_{ij} (remember, we cannot yet call these pure substitution effects, since that notion has not yet been established). We have

$$s_{11} = \frac{\partial x_1}{\partial p_1} + x_1\frac{\partial x_1}{\partial M} = -\frac{M}{2p_1^2} + \frac{M}{2p_1}\frac{1}{2p_1} = -\frac{M}{4p_1^2}$$

and hence $s_{11} < 0$ as needed. Similarly, $s_{22} = -M/4p_2^2 < 0$. For the cross-effects,

$$s_{12} = \frac{\partial x_1}{\partial p_2} + x_2\frac{\partial x_1}{\partial M} = 0 + \frac{M}{2p_2}\frac{1}{2p_1} = \frac{M}{4p_1p_2}$$

and

$$s_{21} = \frac{\partial x_2}{\partial p_1} + x_1\frac{\partial x_2}{\partial M} = 0 + \frac{M}{2p_1}\frac{1}{2p_2} = \frac{M}{4p_1p_2}$$

Thus, $s_{12} = s_{21}$, also as needed. The last requirement on these s_{ij}'s is that their matrix be negative semidefinite; that is, $s_{11}, s_{22} < 0$ (already shown) and $s_{11}s_{22} - s_{12}^2 = 0$. For the latter,

$$s_{11}s_{22} - s_{12}^2 = \left(-\frac{M}{4p_1^2}\right)\left(-\frac{M}{4p_2^2}\right) - \left(\frac{M}{4p_1p_2}\right)^2 \equiv 0$$

Thus these demand functions exhibit all the usual properties. But is that enough? How can we be sure that there are not other conditions that must be satisfied in order for a utility function to exist? Let us try to find a utility function (if it exists) that would generate these demand functions. Since the demand functions are solutions to first-order conditions (partial derivatives of a Lagrangian function), this problem is known as *integrating* back to the utility function. We proceed as follows. If a utility function $U(x_1, x_2)$ exists for these demand functions, then along any indifference curve

$$dU = U_1dx_1 + U_2dx_2 = 0$$

or

$$dx_1 + \frac{U_2}{U_1}dx_2 = 0 \tag{11-16}$$

This is equivalent to

$$\frac{dx_2}{dx_1} = -\frac{U_1}{U_2} \tag{11-17}$$

This is the familiar statement that at any point, the MRS between two goods equals the ratio of the marginal utilities of the two goods. However, at the chosen point, $U_1/U_2 = p_1/p_2$. For these demand functions, $p_1 = M/2x_1$, $p_2 = M/2x_2$. Hence,

$$\frac{U_1}{U_2} = \frac{p_1}{p_2} = \frac{x_2}{x_1}$$

The differential Eq. (11-17) then becomes

$$\frac{dx_2}{dx_1} = -\frac{x_2}{x_1} \tag{11-18}$$

This can be integrated by separating variables:

$$\frac{dx_2}{x_2} = -\frac{dx_1}{x_1}$$

Integrating gives

$$\log x_2 = -\log x_1 + \log F(U)$$

or

$$F(U) = x_1 x_2 \tag{11-19}$$

where the constant of integration $F(U)$ is the arbitrary indifference level chosen for the slope element dx_2/dx_1. This situation is depicted in Fig. 11-3.

Several things happened to go right in this puzzle. There was no problem expressing the slope element dx_2/dx_1 in terms of consumption variables x_1 and x_2 only, and the differential equation itself was easy to integrate. The resulting

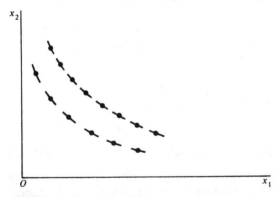

FIGURE 11-3

Integrability: the two-variable case. The differential Eq. (11-16) or (11-17) defines a direction at each point $(x_1 x_2)$ of the $x_1 x_2$ plane. These directional elements are depicted in the above graph as short line segments through each point. The problem of integrability is to find a function which links these directions up, for constant (the arbitrary constant of integration) levels of the functions. In utility analysis, these level-curve link-ups of the slope elements given by the differential equation (11-16) are the indifference curves. For two commodities, this integration is always possible.

utility function is that which was used in earlier chapters to derive the preceding demand functions. Let us investigate these matters more closely.

The first step was to express the slope element in terms of x_1 and x_2. This involved inverting the demand functions, which were originally functions of the prices and income, for functions of the quantities. In most cases, this can be done, with one qualification. The demand functions $x_i = x_i^M(p_1, , \ldots, p_n, M)$ are homogeneous of degree zero in prices and money income. Therefore, it is clearly *not* possible to write $p_i = p_i^*(x_1, \ldots, x_n)$, since any given consumption bundle is associated with an infinity of price vectors, all multiples of each other. However, we can expect to solve for the x_i's in terms of *relative* prices, or prices relative to income. Using the homogeneity property, we have

$$x_i^M(tp_1, \ldots, tp_n, tM) \equiv x_i^M(p_1, \ldots, p_n, M)$$

If we let $t = 1/M$, the demand function can be written

$$x_i^M(p_1, \ldots, p_n, M) \equiv x_i^M\left(\frac{p_1}{M}, \ldots, \frac{p_n}{M}, 1\right) \equiv g_i(r_1, \ldots, r_n) \qquad (11\text{-}20)$$

where $r_i = p_i/M$, $i = 1, \ldots, n$. The r_i's represent that fraction of a consumer's income necessary for the purchase of 1 unit of x_i. In general, we can expect the Jacobian matrix of the g_i relative price demand functions to have a nonzero determinant and to be able to solve for these relative prices in terms of the x_i's, or

$$r_i = h_i(x_1, \ldots, x_n) \qquad (11\text{-}21)$$

Then, since $p_i/p_j = r_i/r_j$, the slope elements $dx_i/dx_j = -p_j/p_i$ are expressible in terms of the quantity variables, using the inverted demand functions (11-21). This was accomplished in the above example, in the differential Eq. (11-18).

Having now found $r_i = h_i(x_1, \ldots, x_n)$ or, for the two-variable case, $r_1 = h_1(x_1, x_2)$, $r_2 = h_2(x_1, x_2)$, it remains to solve the differential Eq. (11-16) or (11-17),

$$\frac{dx_2}{dx_1} = -\frac{p_1}{p_2} = -\frac{h_1(x_1, x_2)}{h_2(x_1, x_2)}$$

or

$$h_1(x_1, x_2)dx_1 + h_2(x_1, x_2)dx_2 = 0 \qquad (11\text{-}22)$$

These differential equations are not, in general, easy to solve. However, for the *two-variable* case only, a solution is assured, by a well-known mathematical theorem.

How is Eq. (11-22) to be integrated, i.e., solved? Remember, this differential equation is supposed to represent the total differential of a utility function along an indifference curve; that is, $dU = 0$. Then for $U = U(x_1, x_2)$, from Eq. (11-16) we must have $U_1 = h_1$, $U_2 = h_2$. Moreover, since cross-partials are invariant to the order of differentiation, we must have $U_{12} = U_{21}$, or

$$\frac{\partial h_1}{\partial x_2} = \frac{\partial h_2}{\partial x_1} \tag{11-23}$$

This condition happened to be satisfied for the demand functions in the preceding example. There, $h_1 = 1/2x_1$, $h_2 = 1/2x_2$, $\partial h_1/\partial x_2 = \partial h_2/\partial x_1 = 0$. Whereas it is clear that $\partial h_1/\partial x_2 = \partial h_2/\partial x_1$ is a *necessary* condition that must exist if an integral function $U(x_1,x_2)$ is to exist, it is also the case that this condition is *sufficient* for the existence of such an integral function, by a well-known theorem of differential equations. Hence, since $\partial h_1/\partial x_2 = \partial h_2/\partial x_1$ in the preceding example, some integral utility function $U = U(x_1,x_2)$ necessarily existed, with $\partial U/\partial x_1 = h_1, \partial U/\partial x_2 = h_2$.

The point of the preceding discussion is that if one starts with an arbitrary set of demand functions $x_i = x_i^M(p_1, \dots, p_n, M), i = 1, \dots, n$, satisfying the usual budget and homogeneity conditions, it will be rather fortuitous if the resulting differential generalization of Eq. (11-16) has a solution:

$$h_1(x_1, \dots, x_n)dx_1 + \dots + h_n(x_1, \dots, x_n)dx_n = 0 \tag{11-24}$$

In general, a solution to this differential equation does not exist; i.e., there may be no utility function $U(x_1, \dots, x_n)$ such that $\partial U/\partial x_i = h_i, i = 1, \dots, n$. Special restrictions on the h_i's must be imposed in order to guarantee a solution.

Curiously enough, however, for the two-variable case, the differential Eq. (11-16) or (11-24) *always* has a solution. That is, starting with two demand functions $x_1 = x_1^M(p_1, p_2, M)$ and $x_2 = x_2^M(P_1, p_2, M)$ which satisfy the budget and homogeneity condition, the resulting $h_1(x_1, x_2)$ and $h_2(x_1, x_2)$ are always integrable. The resulting differential expression

$$h_1(x_1, x_2)dx_1 + h_2(x_1, x_2)dx_2 = 0$$

may not in fact exhibit $\partial h_1/\partial x_2 = \partial h_2/\partial x_1$. However, in this two-variable case, it happens that there will always be an *integrating factor* $G(x_1, x_2)$ such that

$$G(x_1, x_2)h_1(x_1, x_2)dx_1 + G(x_1, x_2)h_2(x_1, x_2)dx_2 = 0$$

is integrable, i.e., that $\partial(Gh_1)/\partial x_2 = \partial(Gh_2)/\partial x_1$. The proof of this nontrivial theorem is available in most calculus texts and will not be reproduced here. Notice, though, that $dx_2/dx_1 = -Gh_1/Gh_2 = -h_1/h_2$, and hence the G function corresponds to $F'(U)$, where $F(U)$ is any monotonic transformation of the utility function.

The reason the two-variable system is always integrable can be seen with the help of Fig. 11-3, and at the same time the relationship of integrability and revealed preference will be more clearly exhibited. The differential Eqs. (11-16) or (11-17) serve to define at each point (x_1, x_2) of the x_1, x_2 plane a slope element, or direction, $-h_1/h_2$. Every point has such a direction defined. Some of these are exhibited by the short line segments drawn through each point. The integral function $U(x_1, x_2)$ connects up these directional elements for constant functional values. Under some technical mathematical conditions, this can always be done, guaranteeing the existence of a solution to the differential Eq. (11-16) for the two-dimensional case.

In the three-good case, however, the story is different. In each of the x_1x_2, x_2x_3, and x_3x_1 planes, a slope element $dx_j/dx_i = -h_i/h_j$ will be defined. These will be the indifference elements described in the revealed preference section. However, there is no guarantee that these directional elements will all link up with each other; the possibility remains that a consumer can spiral around some point and reach a point that is indifferent to the original while having more of one good and not less of the others. The situation leaves open the possibility of the nontransitive behavior exhibited earlier. The force of the integrability condition $\partial h_i/\partial x_j = \partial h_j/\partial x_i$ is to guarantee that such behavior does not exist; like the strong axiom of revealed preference, integrability rules out nontransitive behavior by guaranteeing the existence of a utility function. This is illustrated in Fig. 11-4.

The consequences of this analysis with regard to revealed preference theory are that for the two-commodity case, the *weak* axiom is in fact sufficient to guarantee the existence of a utility function. The type of intransitive behavior exhibited earlier cannot occur with only two commodities if the weak axiom is satisfied. The fundamental difference between the two- and many-commodity

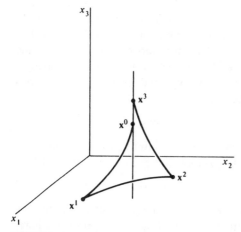

FIGURE 11-4

Integrability: the three-commodity case. Consider some point $\mathbf{x}^0 = (x_1^0, x_2^0, x_3^0)$. A slope element in the x_1x_3 direction, $-h_1/h_3$, is defined by the differential equation (11-24). Integrating in that plane, parallel to the x_1, x_3 axes, we come to some other point $\mathbf{x}^1$. At $\mathbf{x}^1$, a directional element $-h_1/h_2$ is defined in an x_1x_2 plane parallel to the x_1, x_2 axes. Integrating along some level curve there, we can get to another point $\mathbf{x}^2$ at which the original x_1 value is restored. At $\mathbf{x}^2$, a directional element $-h_3/h_2$ is defined in the x_2x_3 plane. Integrating along that level curve, we may get back to a point such as $\mathbf{x}^3$ which has the same level of x_1 and x_2 as $\mathbf{x}^1$ but has more of the third commodity x_3. This spiraling process is what is ruled out by the integrability conditions. In order for a well-defined indifference *surface* to exist, relating to a utility function $U(x_1, x_2, x_3)$, a point such as $\mathbf{x}^3$ cannot occur but must coincide with $\mathbf{x}^0$. Then the path $\mathbf{x}^0 \to \mathbf{x}^1 \to \mathbf{x}^2 \to \mathbf{x}^3$ represents a movement along one indifference surface. A path like $\mathbf{x}^0 \to \mathbf{x}^1 \to \mathbf{x}^2 \to \mathbf{x}^3$ in the diagram is what can occur if only the *weak* axiom of revealed preference is asserted. The numerical example illustrated this. The strong axiom, by asserting that the last point in the chain will not be revealed preferred to the first, effectively eliminates the situation depicted in the diagram.

situations is that for two commodities there is only one relative price. With only one price, the consumer cannot circle around the original point to a new position of greater commodity levels while remaining on the same indifference curve, as is possible in three dimensions if only the weak axiom is asserted.

What conditions on the demand functions themselves lead to integrability? Although it cannot be shown here, unfortunately, as advanced techniques are required, the symmetry of the Slutsky terms $s_{ij} = \partial x_i^M / \partial p_j + x_j \partial x_i^M / \partial M$ is sufficient to guarantee the existence of a utility function from which the demand curves are derived. Given this symmetry, the terms s_{ij} are interpretable as the slopes of compensated demand curves, i.e., the partial derivatives $\partial x_i^U(p_1, \ldots, p_n, U) / \partial p_j$. Since $\partial x_i^U / \partial p_j = \partial x_j^U / \partial p_i$, the differential expression $x_1^U dp_1 + \cdots + x_n^U dp_n$ is exact; i.e., it is integrable. Since by the envelope theorem we know that the expenditure, or cost, function $M^*(p_1, \ldots, p_n, U)$ has the property $\partial M^* / \partial p_j = x_j^U$, clearly, the above differential expression is simply

$$dM^* = \frac{\partial M^*}{\partial p_1} dp_1 + \cdots + \frac{\partial M^*}{\partial p_n} dp_n = x_1^U dp_1 + \cdots + x_n^U dp_n$$

Hence, $M^*(p_1, \ldots, p_n, U)$ is the integral of this expression and is known to exist since $\partial^2 M^* / \partial p_i \partial p_j = \partial x_i^U / \partial p_j = \partial x_j^U / \partial p_i = \partial^2 M^* / \partial p_j \partial p_i$. Thus, the expenditure function is well defined if the Slutsky terms are symmetrical. From the discussion in the previous chapter, the corresponding utility function must exist also.

Let us check that the two-variable case is always integrable. Consider two demand functions $x_1 = x_1^M(p_1, p_2, M)$ and $x_2 = x_2^M(p_1, p_2, M)$. Assume that

$$p_1 x_1^M + p_2 x_2^M \equiv M \tag{11-25}$$

and

$$x_i^M(tp_1, tp_2, tM) \equiv x_i^M(p_1, p_2, M) \quad i = 1, 2 \tag{11-26}$$

That is, the demand functions satisfy the budget and homogeneity conditions. If these demand curves are integrable, i.e., if there exists some utility function which generates these functions, then we should find $s_{12} = s_{21}$. Let us see if this is the case. Superscripts will be omitted to save notational clutter.

From homogeneity and (11-25), using Euler's theorem, we get

$$\frac{\partial x_1}{\partial p_1} p_1 + \frac{\partial x_1}{\partial p_2} p_2 + \frac{\partial x_1}{\partial M}(p_1 x_1 + p_2 x_2) \equiv 0$$

since $M = p_1 x_1 + p_2 x_2$. Collecting terms gives

$$p_1\left(\frac{\partial x_1}{\partial p_1} + x_1\frac{\partial x_1}{\partial M}\right) + p_2\left(\frac{\partial x_1}{\partial p_2} + x_2\frac{\partial x_1}{\partial M}\right) \equiv 0$$

or

$$p_1 s_{11} + p_2 s_{12} \equiv 0 \tag{11-27a}$$

In like fashion, applying Euler's theorem to $x_2(p_1, p_2, M)$ gives

$$p_1 s_{21} + p_2 s_{22} \equiv 0 \qquad (11\text{-}27b)$$

Equations (11-27) generalize to n commodities in a straightforward manner. In general,

$$\sum_{j=1}^{n} p_j s_{ij} \equiv 0, \quad i = 1, \ldots, n \qquad (11\text{-}28)$$

Now consider the budget relation (11-25). Differentiating with respect to p_1 yields

$$p_1 \frac{\partial x_1}{\partial p_1} + p_2 \frac{\partial x_2}{\partial p_1} \equiv -x_1$$

Differentiating (11-25) with respect to M yields

$$p_1 \frac{\partial x_1}{\partial M} + p_2 \frac{\partial x_2}{\partial M} \equiv 1$$

Multiplying this expression by $-x_1$ and substituting into the preceding equation leads to

$$p_1 \frac{\partial x_1}{\partial p_1} + p_2 \frac{\partial x_2}{\partial p_1} \equiv -p_1 x_1 \frac{\partial x_1}{\partial M} - p_2 x_1 \frac{\partial x_2}{\partial M}$$

Combining terms, we have

$$p_1 \left(\frac{\partial x_1}{\partial p_1} + x_1 \frac{\partial x_1}{\partial M} \right) + p_2 \left(\frac{\partial x_2}{\partial p_1} + x_1 \frac{\partial x_2}{\partial M} \right) \equiv 0$$

or

$$p_1 s_{11} + p_2 s_{21} \equiv 0 \qquad (11\text{-}29a)$$

In like fashion, by differentiating the budget relation with respect to p_2, one can derive

$$p_1 s_{12} + p_2 s_{22} \equiv 0 \qquad (11\text{-}29b)$$

In general, for n commodities,

$$\sum_{i=1}^{n} p_i s_{ij} \equiv 0 \qquad j = 1, \ldots, n \qquad (11\text{-}30)$$

Note that in Eq. (11-28) the sum runs over j, whereas in (11-30) it runs over i. These relations say that the weighted sum of the Slutsky terms for any good or for any price equals zero, where the weights are the prices. These relations were derived without any reference to utility theory; the only assumption was that the consumer had well-defined choice functions satisfying the budget and homogeneity conditions.

It is apparent from Eqs. (11-27*a*) and (11-29*a*) that for the two-commodity case, $s_{12} = s_{21}$. Hence, it is indeed always possible to find a utility function $U(x_1, x_2)$ which generates the money income demand curves $x_i = x_i^M(p_1, p_2, M), i = 1, 2$. If the additional property of negative semidefiniteness is imposed on the Slutsky terms, that is, $s_{11} < 0$, $s_{22} < 0, s_{11}s_{22} - s_{12}^2 = 0$ following from either Eqs. (11-27) or (11-29), then the utility function will have the usual convex indifference curves of consumer theory.

The importance of these results is that they demonstrate that negative semidefiniteness and symmetry of the Slutsky terms constitute all the implications of utility theory. Since it is possible to work backward from these assumptions and demonstrate the existence of quasi-concave utility functions, there can be no other independent results of utility theory. Any other results, e.g., Le Châtelier effects, can be derived from these assumptions as well as from utility theory. In addition, since the strong axiom of revealed preference also guarantees the existence of utility functions, these approaches are all equivalent aspects of consumer theory.

11.3 THE COMPOSITE COMMODITY THEOREM

One feature of economic systems is the interplay of a large number of variables. The number of commodities produced in a modern economy runs into the millions or billions; the variety of tasks, skills, and capital is enormous. Indeed, analysis of such systems would be impossible for most minds without some simplification or abstraction from reality. In the first chapter we discussed the role of assumptions in science, in particular the necessary simplification in order to make a theory tractable. In this section we shall investigate one aspect of this procedure, the lumping together of many commodities into one composite commodity.

Most textbooks and articles in economics generally reduce the world to two commodities or two factors of production, etc. One is usually the good under analysis, and the other is usually labeled "all other goods," or all other "closely related" goods. To what extent is this procedure justifiable? Under what circumstances can all other goods be treated as one good?

It might be appropriate at the start to recognize that what is in fact called a *commodity* is not a technological datum. Most commodities have several characteristics, each of which presumably generates utility to consumers. Yet usually, only one of these characteristics is used to label the commodity. Consider the example of eggs. Eggs come in various volumes, weights, colors, and degrees of firmness of yolk and white. The fact that egg sizes are by weight rather than volume is due to the relative ease, i.e., lower cost, of measuring that dimension than, say, volume. (The last characteristic, firmness, is the one used by the U.S. Department of Agriculture in grading. It is difficult to measure in a nondestructive manner.) Diamonds, on the other hand, are extensively measured. They are classified by color (white, blue-white, yellow, etc.), various degrees of departure from flawless crystal structure, shape of cut (round, marquise, emerald, etc.).

Each of these characteristics is carefully measured, and prices vary accordingly. Diamonds are so extensively measured and categorized because, given the "high" price of the basic material of diamonds, measurement is relatively cheap. Hence, a great deal of measuring is done on diamonds, and relatively less measuring is done on lower-valued commodities. As a last example, much produce is sold by the piece in season and by weight out of season. When the produce is in season, i.e., in relatively greater supply, its price is lower. The cost of measuring, e.g., weighing at the check-out counter, or bunching together uniform packages, is relatively high. Hence, less measuring is done, and consumers are left to do whatever measuring they please on their own. Thus, the units of the commodity are apt to be different at different times or even at different retail establishments, depending upon the level of retail services offered. The notion of a commodity is thus not a technological datum but dependent in large part on the economic costs of characterization of the good.

We shall ignore these matters, however, in the forthcoming discussion. Assume that there are n well-defined commodities, $x_1, \ldots, x_n$, which the consumer purchases in positive amounts, at prices $p_1, \ldots, p_n$, respectively. Suppose now that the prices of some subset of these commodities all change simultaneously in the same proportion. Mathematically, let $\mathbf{p}^0 = (p_1^0, \ldots, p_n^0)$ be the initial price vector. Suppose, by suitable relabeling of the commodities that $p_{k+1}, \ldots, p_n$ all vary in the same proportion; that is, $p_{k+1} = t p_{k+1}^0, \ldots, p_n = t p_n^0$, where initially $t = 1$. (If, for example, t became 2, then all prices would have doubled.) How would the consumer react to changes in t, that is, proportionate changes in $n - k$ of the prices?

As we have indicated in the previous sections, the behavioral implications of utility theory are summarized and exhausted in the statement that the compensated, or Slutsky, changes s_{ij} form a symmetric negative semidefinite matrix. These pure-substitution effects are derivable from the cost minimization problem:

minimize

$$\sum_{i=1}^{n} p_i x_i = M$$

subject to

$$U(x_1, \ldots, x_n) = U^0$$

The expenditure function $M^*(p_1, \ldots, p_n, U^0)$ has the property that $\partial M^* / \partial p_i = M_{p_i}^* = x_i^U(p_1, \ldots, p_n, U^0)$, $M_{p_i p_j}^* = \partial x_i^U / \partial p_j$. In the present problem, a new parameter t is introduced. To derive the compensated changes in the x_i's when t changes, one must consider the model:

minimize

$$M = \sum_{i=1}^{n} p_i x_i = \sum_{i=1}^{k} p_i x_i + \sum_{i=k+1}^{n} t p_i x_i \qquad (11\text{-}31)$$

subject to

$$U(x_1, \ldots, x_n) = U^0 \qquad (11\text{-}32)$$

The objective function (11-31) can be written:

minimize

$$M = \sum_{i=1}^{k} p_i x_i + ty \qquad (11\text{-}33)$$

where $y = \sum_{i=k+1}^{n} p_i x_i$, the total expenditure on commodities $k + 1$ through n, the ones whose prices are all changing proportionately. When $t = 1$, (11-33) is identical to (11-31); hence the same demand point results. We can thus analyze a change in t from 1 by use of the duality results of Chap. 7. Since $\partial M^*/\partial t = M_t^* = y^U = \sum_{i=k+1}^{n} p_i^0 x_i^U$,

$$M_{tp_j}^* = \frac{\partial y^U}{\partial p_j} \quad j = 1, \ldots, k$$

The $(k + 1) \times (k + 1)$ matrix of terms,

$$\mathbf{M}_{pt}^* = \begin{pmatrix} \dfrac{\partial x_1^U}{\partial p_1} & \cdots & \dfrac{\partial x_k^U}{\partial p_1} & \dfrac{\partial y^U}{\partial p_1} \\ \vdots & & & \\ \dfrac{\partial x_1^U}{\partial p_k} & & \dfrac{\partial x_k^U}{\partial p_k} & \dfrac{\partial y^U}{\partial p_k} \\ \dfrac{\partial x_1^U}{\partial t} & & \dfrac{\partial x_k^U}{\partial t} & \dfrac{\partial y^U}{\partial t} \end{pmatrix} \qquad (11\text{-}34)$$

must be negative semidefinite. The factor of proportion t enters this matrix exactly as do the prices $p_1, \ldots, p_k$, and total expenditure y^U on $x_{k+1}, \ldots, x_n$ enters just like any other quantity variable. Thus this system of compensated changes is no different from any other well-behaved set of $k + 1$ compensated demand functions. Therefore, when prices of several commodities vary simultaneously, in the same proportion, total expenditures on those commodities behave exactly like any other commodity. This new variable y is called a *composite commodity,* and was introduced first by John R. Hicks, in *Value and Capital.* The composite commodity is just like any other decision variable; e.g., the response to a change in its own "price" t is negative:

$$\frac{\partial y^U}{\partial t} < 0 \qquad (11\text{-}35)$$

Also, from the symmetry of the cross-partials in (11-34)

$$\frac{\partial y^U}{\partial p_i} = \frac{\partial x_i^U}{\partial t} \quad i = 1, \ldots, k \qquad (11\text{-}36)$$

in addition to the usual reciprocity conditions $\partial x_i^U/\partial p_j = \partial x_j^U/\partial p_i$.

This important theorem justifies the use of two-dimensional graphical analysis in much of economic theory. It is easy to imagine that in many empirically important cases where a single, outstanding price change takes place in the economy, variations in prices of a group of commodities will not vary significantly within the group. The group can thus be regarded as a single commodity. Since one price will have changed, say, this is equivalent, for relative price changes, to a proportionate change in all prices of goods within the group. Thus, the highly convenient simplification of economic analysis by considering the good in question vs. all other goods is at least consistent with utility theory and perhaps empirically sound in many instances.

Shipping the Good Apples Out

Consider now another type of simultaneous price change, that of adding a fixed amount to several prices. That is, consider the effects of changing a parameter t added to $p_1, \ldots, p_k$, yielding prices $p_1 + t, \ldots, p_k + t, p_{k+1}, \ldots, p_n$. Such a situation might occur if the first k goods are subject to the same tax or transportation charge. In this case, the composite good $z = \sum_{i=1}^{k} x_i$ acts as a single good.

Again, consider the relevant cost minimization problem:

minimize

$$M = \sum_{i=1}^{k} (p_i + t)x_i + \sum_{i=k+1}^{n} p_i x_i \tag{11-37}$$

subject to

$$U(x_1, \ldots, x_n) = U^0$$

from which the compensated demands

$$x_i = x_i^U(p_1, \ldots, p_n, t, U^0) \tag{11-38}$$

are derived. However, M is linear in the parameter t, and letting M^* denote the expenditure function $M^*(p_1, \ldots, p_n, t, U^0)$, we have

$$\frac{\partial M^*}{\partial t} = \sum_{i=1}^{k} x_i^U \equiv z^U(p_1, \ldots, p_n, t, U^0) \tag{11-39}$$

Hence, z^U exhibits the properties of any other good. The matrix of second partials of M^* with respect to just $p_1, \ldots, p_n$ and t is symmetric and negative semidefinite:

$$\mathbf{M}_{pt}^* = \begin{pmatrix} \dfrac{\partial x_1^U}{\partial p_1} & \cdots & \dfrac{\partial x_1^U}{\partial p_n} & \dfrac{\partial x_1^U}{\partial t} \\ \vdots & & & \\ \dfrac{\partial x_n^U}{\partial p_1} & & \dfrac{\partial x_n^U}{\partial p_n} & \dfrac{\partial x_n^U}{\partial t} \\ \dfrac{\partial z^U}{\partial p_1} & & \dfrac{\partial z^U}{\partial p_n} & \dfrac{\partial z^U}{\partial t} \end{pmatrix} \tag{11-40}$$

From the symmetry of this matrix,

$$\frac{\partial z^U}{\partial p_i} = \frac{\partial x_i^U}{\partial t} \tag{11-41}$$

From the definition of z^U, and the fact that $s_{ij} = s_{ji}$,

$$\frac{\partial x_i^U}{\partial t} = \sum_{j=1}^{k} \frac{\partial x_j^U}{\partial p_i} = \sum_{j=1}^{k} s_{ji} = \sum_{j=1}^{k} s_{ij} \tag{11-42}$$

The own effect of the composite commodity z^U is negative; i.e.,

$$\frac{\partial z^U}{\partial t} < 0 \tag{11-43}$$

This result is also derivable from the original substitution matrix. Letting $s_{ij} = \partial x_i^U / \partial p_j$, as before, with $s_{it} = \partial x_i^U / \partial t$, $s_{ti} = \partial z^U / \partial p_i$, by negative semidefiniteness we have

$$\sum_{i=1}^{n} \sum_{j=1}^{n} s_{ij} h_i h_j \leq 0 \tag{11-44}$$

where the equality holds when the h_i's are proportional to the prices. Let h_i, $h_j = 1$, $i = 1, \ldots, k$, and h_i, $h_j = 0$, $i, j = k + 1, \ldots, n$. Then (11-44) becomes

$$\sum_{i=1}^{k} \sum_{j=1}^{k} s_{ij} < 0$$

which is Eq. (11-43), assuming all prices are not the same number (all proportional to unity).

Let us now investigate the empirical effects of this type of price change more closely. Using the composite commodity theorem, we can consider a three-good world, x_1, x_2, x_3, where x_3 is the composite commodity of the previous section. Suppose goods 1 and 2 are transported from another location, with x_3 produced locally, producing a set of prices $p_1 + t$, $p_2 + t$, p_3, where p_1 and p_2 are the point of origin prices of x_1 and x_2, respectively.[†] The transportation charge is apt to produce a predictable change in the mix of goods consumed in the origin versus the destination of the goods. Consider the following complaint mailed into the "Troubleshooter" column of the *Seattle Times* by an irate consumer:[‡]

[†] This situation was first analyzed by A. Alchian and W. Allen in their principles texts, *University Economics*, and its condensation, *Exchange and Production*, Wadsworth Publishing Company, Inc., Belmont, CA, 1969.

[‡] *Seattle Times*, Sunday, October 19, 1975.

Why are Washington apples in local markets so small and old-looking? The dried-up stems might seem they were taken out of cold storage from some gathered last year.

Recently, some apple-picking friends brought some apples they had just picked, and they were at least four times the size of those available for sale here.

Where do these big Delicious apples go? Are they shipped to Europe, to the East or can they be bought here in Seattle?

M.W.P.

An answer from a trade representative allowed that "itinerant truckers" (price-cutters) were at fault:

The apples [she] is seeing in her local markets may have been some left from the 1974 crop, or could be lower-grade fruit sold store-to-store by itinerant truckers.

The textbook answer was supplied by this economist several days later:[†]

Comparing apples to apples

Regarding M.W.P.'s complaint (Sunday, October 19) that all the good apples were being shipped to the East, you might be interested to know that "shipping the good apples out" has been a favorite classroom and exam question in the economics department at U.W. for many years.

It is a real phenomenon, easily explained:

Suppose, for example, a "good" apple costs 10 cents and a "poor" apple 5 cents locally. Then, since the decision to eat one good apple costs the same as eating two poor apples, we can say that a good apple in essence "costs" two poor apples. Two good apples cost four poor apples.

Suppose now that it costs 5 cents per apple (any apple) to ship apples East. Then, in the East, good apples will cost 15 cents each and poor ones 10 cents each. But now eating two good apples will cost three—not four poor apples.

Though both prices are higher, good apples have become relatively cheaper, and a higher percentage of good apples will be consumed in the East than here.

It is no conspiracy—just the laws of supply and demand.

This appealing line of argument, though possibly empirically correct, was challenged by J. Gould and J. Segall, who pointed out that in a three-good world, interactions with the third good might destroy the effect.[‡]

[†] *Seattle Times,* Tuesday, October 28, 1975.

[‡] John Gould and Joel Segall. "The Substitution Effects of Transportation Costs," *Journal of Political Economy,* 130–137, 1968. Having to go to Maine to get a truly delectable lobster or having to drive out to the countryside to get truly fresh vegetables are not counterexamples of Alchian and Allen's hypothesis. If this occurs because of spoilage en route, this is an irrelevant consideration. More important, it doesn't matter if the lobsters are shipped to you or you are shipped to the lobsters. Going to Maine involves a transportation cost to people not from Maine. We should expect to observe, if Alchian and Allen's hypothesis is correct, that tourists in Maine consume a higher quality of lobster than the natives.

The problem with the textbook answer is that when t changes in a three-good world, more than one relative price change is involved: $p_1 + t$ and $p_2 + t$ both change relative to p_3. The law of demand strictly applies only to situations in which one and only one relative price in the system changes. Yet the argument seems empirically valid in a wide range of circumstances. Cheap French wines, sold in France in cans, are never exported to the United States. Surely there are French consumers irate about the best French wines being shipped out. Restaurants buy most of the U.S. Department of Agriculture prime beef because when the various amenities of restaurants, e.g., waiters and waitresses, cooks, fancy decor, etc., are added to the food costs, the higher-priced item becomes *relatively* cheaper. Houses situated on attractive (and thus expensive) sites will in general be more attractive houses than average.[†] Let us analyze the situation mathematically.

Alchian and Allen's thesis is that if x_1 is the premium quality good (higher-priced) and x_2 the inferior quality, then

$$\frac{\partial(x_1^U/x_2^U)}{\partial t} > 0 \qquad (11\text{-}45)$$

(Superscripts will now be dropped. The student must remember that these are all compensated changes. The introduction of income effects complicates the analysis in predictable ways; viz., income effects are always indeterminate.) Expanding the quotient in (11-45)[‡] gives

$$\frac{\partial(x_1/x_2)}{\partial t} = \left(x_2\frac{\partial x_1}{\partial t} - x_1\frac{\partial x_2}{\partial t}\right)\frac{1}{x_2^2}$$

From Eq. (11-42), $\partial x_1/\partial t = s_{11} + s_{12}$, $\partial x_2/\partial t = s_{21} + s_{22}$. Thus,

$$\frac{\partial(x_1/x_2)}{\partial t} = \frac{x_1}{x_2}\left(\frac{s_{11}}{x_1} + \frac{s_{12}}{x_1} - \frac{s_{21}}{x_2} - \frac{s_{22}}{x_2}\right)$$

Let us convert these terms to elasticities. Letting $\varepsilon_{ij} = (p_j/x_i)(\partial x_i/\partial p_j)$, we have

$$\frac{\partial(x_1/x_2)}{\partial t} = \frac{x_1}{x_2}\left(\frac{\varepsilon_{11}}{p_1} + \frac{\varepsilon_{12}}{p_2} - \frac{\varepsilon_{21}}{p_1} - \frac{\varepsilon_{22}}{p_2}\right)$$

[†] These last two examples are in fact suspect. The parameter t represents a charge for something that does not enter the consumer's utility function directly. The preceding (and ensuing) analysis cannot really be applied to "restaurant amenities" or the lot under a house, since these are really goods that enter the utility function, and which, in principle, could be purchased separately. In that case, the analysis boils down to the response to a change in the price of some third good, and would depend in the usual way on the signs of the substitution terms s_{ij}. The regularity appears strong, however. See John Umbeck, "Shipping the Good Apples Out: Some Ambiguities in the Interpretation of 'Fixed Charge'," *Journal of Political Economy*, **88**:199–207, February 1980. The resolution of the puzzle may lie in the economics of the way goods are bundled together.

[‡] The author is indebted to Thomas Borcherding for demonstrating this algebra.

However, from the homogeneity of the compensated demand, $\sum_{j=1}^{n} p_j s_{ij} = 0$ and hence by dividing by x_i yields

$$\varepsilon_{11} + \varepsilon_{12} + \varepsilon_{13} = 0$$

and

$$\varepsilon_{21} + \varepsilon_{22} + \varepsilon_{23} = 0$$

for this three-good model. Using these expressions to substitute for ε_{12} and ε_{22} in the preceding equation, we have

$$\frac{\partial(x_1/x_2)}{\partial t} = \frac{x_1}{x_2}\left[\frac{\varepsilon_{11}}{p_1} + \left(-\frac{\varepsilon_{11}}{p_2} - \frac{\varepsilon_{13}}{p_2}\right) - \frac{\varepsilon_{21}}{p_1} - \left(-\frac{\varepsilon_{21}}{p_2} - \frac{\varepsilon_{23}}{p_2}\right)\right]$$

or

$$\frac{\partial(x_1/x_2)}{\partial t} = \frac{x_1}{x_2}\left[(\varepsilon_{11} - \varepsilon_{21})\left(\frac{1}{p_1} - \frac{1}{p_2}\right) + (\varepsilon_{23} - \varepsilon_{13})\left(\frac{1}{p_2}\right)\right] \qquad (11\text{-}46)$$

Let us examine Eq. (11-46). Since x_1 is the higher quality good, $p_1 > p_2$, and thus $1/p_1 - 1/p_2 < 0$. Also, $\varepsilon_{11} < 0$ and $\varepsilon_{21} > 0$ since two qualities of the same good are presumably substitutes. Alchian and Allen's thesis is that $\partial(x_1/x_2)/\partial t > 0$; the first compound term in (11-46) confirms this. In a two-good world, this would be the entire expression, and then Alchian and Allen would be entirely correct. The last term, $\varepsilon_{23} - \varepsilon_{13}$, however, is indeterminate. If, however, we assume that the lower and higher quality good interact in the same manner with the composite good x_3, that is, that $\varepsilon_{13} = \varepsilon_{23}$, then the hypothesis will be valid. The hypothesis becomes invalid only in the asymmetrical case, where, say, the premium good is a much closer substitute for the third good than the inferior good ($\varepsilon_{13} > \varepsilon_{23}$). Then when p_1 and p_2 are both raised, say, to $p_1 + t$ and $p_2 + t$, respectively, the consumer substitutes x_3 for x_1 in greater proportion than x_3 for x_2, confounding the hypothesis. This asymmetry seems to be empirically insignificant to this casual observer.

A similar result can be derived for the *difference*, as opposed to the ratio of consumption of x_1 to x_2, when t changes. Letting $p_1 = p_2 + k$, $k > 0$, from homogeneity we get

$$(p_2 + k)s_{11} + p_2 s_{12} + p_3 s_{13} = 0$$

$$(p_2 + k)s_{21} + p_2 s_{22} + p_3 s_{23} = 0$$

Since $\partial x_1/\partial t = s_{1t} = s_{11} + s_{12}$ and $\partial x_2/\partial t = s_{2t} = s_{21} + s_{22}$,

$$p_2 s_{1t} + k s_{11} + p_3 s_{13} = 0$$

$$p_2 s_{2t} + k s_{21} + p_3 s_{23} = 0$$

Subtracting gives

$$p_2(s_{1t} - s_{2t}) = -k(s_{11} - s_{21}) + p_3(s_{23} - s_{13}) \qquad (11\text{-}47)$$

Assuming that the lower and higher quality goods are substitutes for each other (otherwise the whole exercise is meaningless), $s_{21} > 0$. Thus the first term on the right side of (11-47), $-k(s_{11} - s_{21})$, is positive. This tends to confirm the idea that an increase in transport cost will raise the absolute level of consumption of the premium good relative to the lower quality good. The validity of the inference in a three-good model boils down to the term $(s_{23} - s_{13})$, a term similar to that appearing in Eq. (11-46), dealing with the ratio x_1/x_2. If these interactions with the third good are similar, then the higher quality good will be shipped to distant places in greater amounts than the lower quality good.

It should be noted that a higher quality good and lower quality of the *same good* should be fairly close substitutes. Therefore, as an empirical matter one should expect relatively high absolute values of s_{11}, s_{12}, and s_{22}, or the corresponding elasticities. This will make the first term in Eqs. (11-46) and (11-47) relatively large. And if these goods are not closely related to the composite commodity, s_{13} and s_{23} should be fairly small, even if not approximately equal. Hence, as an empirical matter, the Alchian and Allen hypothesis that the higher quality good will tend to increase relative to the lower quality good when like transport (or other) costs are added to each item might be expected to be true for most commodities.

In general, simultaneous price changes of the form $p_i = p_i^0 + p_i(t), i = 1, \ldots, k$, $k < n$, with $p_i(0) = 0$ can be defined. These changes will in general not produce interesting comparative statics theorems. The resulting composite commodities will be complicated expressions involving the derivatives of $p_i(t)$. The empirical usefulness of such constructions is likely to be small.

11.4 HOUSEHOLD PRODUCTION FUNCTIONS

In 1965 and 1966, in two related articles, Gary Becker and Kelvin Lancaster introduced the concept of household production functions.[†] In these models, instead of receiving utility directly from goods purchased in the market, consumers derive utility from the attributes possessed by these goods, and then only after some transformation is performed on those market goods. For example, although consumers purchase raw foods in the market, utility is derived from consumption of the completed meal, which has been produced by combining the raw food with labor, time, and, perhaps, other inputs.

Many goods produced in a modern economy appear to serve similar purposes. For example, there are wide varieties and qualities of the same foods, and likewise for clothing, housing, etc. Consumers appear to select only one or

---

[†]Gary S. Becker, "A Theory of Allocation of Time," *Economic Journal,* **75**:493–517, September 1965, and Kelvin J. Lancaster, "A New Approach to Consumer Theory," *Journal of Political Economy,* **74**:132–57, April 1966.

a few of these different qualities, and forgo completely the consumption of the others. In the previous section, we analyzed the effects of adding a lump-sum tax or other cost to two different "qualities" of the same good. In fact, standard utility theory provides no mechanism for identifying two goods as different qualities of the same good, versus two separate goods altogether. The algebra of the previous section applies to any two goods, labeled "x_1" and "x_2." The analysis applies equally to apples and oranges, or for that matter, apples and typewriters, as to red and golden delicious apples. We seem to feel comfortable speaking of beef and pork as substitutes, and pencils and paper as complements; yet such pronouncements are based on the technology of using these particular goods, i.e., the way we combine these goods with other goods and inputs in order to produce utility. Standard utility theory provides no clues as to why food is different than clothing, shelter, etc.

In order to remedy this, Lancaster postulated that the vector of goods, x, purchased in the market at price vector p, are transformed by $z = g(x)$ into attributes z which produce utility. In a very general sense, therefore, the model is,

maximize

$$U = U(z)$$

subject to

$$z = g(x) \tag{11-48}$$

and

$$px = M$$

where M is the consumer's income. Combining the transformation function and the utility function,

maximize

$$U = U(g(x)) = V(x)$$

subject to

$$px = M \tag{11-49}$$

It is apparent that at this level of generality, the Lancaster model is equivalent to the standard utility model, assuming the $V(x)$ function exhibits the same curvature properties as utility functions. Assuming interior solutions to (11-49), the refutable implications will consist of the usual properties of the "compensated" demands $x = x^V(p, V^0)$, defined as the solutions to, minimize $M = px$ subject to $V(x) = V^0$, a constant. The partial derivatives of these demand functions are not really "pure substitution effects" in the traditional sense, since production changes (i.e., changes in the z's through $g(x)$) may take place as prices change. However, the statement that the matrix $(\partial x^V/\partial p)$ is negative semidefinite still comprises the complete set of refutable implications; thus at this level of generality, the model is indistinguishable from the standard theory.

In order to be useful, that is, to provide insights or propositions beyond that of ordinary utility analysis, some sort of *observable* structure must be imposed on the transformation function $g(x)$. Lancaster assumed that $g(x)$ is linear, i.e., $z = Bx$, where B is some matrix of (constant) technological coefficients. Lancaster further postulated that B was constant across consumers, i.e., the technology for converting market x's into attributes z is the same for all consumers. If the matrix B differs for each consumer, there is little likelihood that the model will be operational. To attain the utility-maximizing z, say z^*, the consumer would necessarily have to purchase the market x's that produced z^* at least cost, i.e., the consumer would have to solve the "linear programming problem," minimize px subject to $Bx \geq z^*$.

Linear models of this type will be analyzed in more detail in the chapter on linear programming. Suffice it to say here that the feasible region, i.e., the set of attainable z's, will now consist of a (n-dimensional) convex polyhedron, with many corners and faces, rather than the "flat" budget hyperplane. If changes in technology lowered the cost of producing some attribute z_i, a change to some new market good or goods would likely be the least-cost means of producing the utility-maximizing attributes. This seems in conformance with observation. Consider that as the prices of electronic calculators and computers have decreased, consumers have gradually shifted from hand calculations on simple calculators, to extensive calculations often made on sophisticated machines. The utility-producing attribute would be "calculations"; changes in the technology for producing calculations induce more calculations, on successively more powerful calculating machines. The idea of a "new commodity," always troublesome in traditional utility analysis, is also more easily accomplished with Lancaster's framework. In the traditional framework, a new utility function must be asserted. With Lancaster's model, the invention of new computers, for example, does not cause a rearrangement of preferences, but merely a new solution to a cost-minimizing problem involving the attribute "calculations."

All this being said and done, it still remains that empirical implementation of the Lancaster model in a truly observable manner is not straightforward. Identification and measurement of "attributes" may be more difficult than measurement of market goods. Even with relatively few variables, measurements and predictions of qualitative changes in the purchases of market goods, as the technological coefficients change, are apt to be quite difficult, as familiarity with the complex nature of solutions to just three linear equations in three unknowns would indicate. It remains the case that for "compensated" changes, $\partial x_i / \partial p_i \leq 0$; however, this is no improvement over traditional utility theory. The model has been most successful when applied to goods whose attributes are additive and nonconflicting, e.g., the nutrient values for foods.[†]

[†] This author showed that as incomes increase, the fraction of the food budget allocated to pure nutrition (as opposed to tastiness) falls, as diminishing marginal productivity of nutrition would suggest. See Eugene Silberberg, "Nutrition and the Demand for Tastes," *Journal of Political Economy*, **93**(5):881–900, October 1985.

   In his related article, Gary Becker sought to incorporate decisions concerning the use of time into the standard utility framework. By considering the cost
of time in terms of its foregone use in producing income, Becker provided a
basis for explaining some changes in consumption as wage income changes, in
terms of substitution effects, which have known sign, rather than through ad-hoc
income effects. If the increase in income is produced by an increase in wages,
this represents an increase in the marginal value of leisure. We should therefore
expect to see the consumer substituting away from time-intensive goods (goods
whose consumption involves relatively heavy use of time) and toward those goods
for which the time cost is relatively less. In this way, changes in consumption
that were once considered on an ad-hoc basis, by asserting a change in tastes or
a sign for an income effect, could be interpreted as consequences of the law of
demand.

   Like Lancaster, Becker assumes that utility is a function of a vector of
attributes z, i.e., $U = U(z)$. However, Becker adopts a very simple structure for
production of attributes. For each z_i,

$$T_i = t_i z_i \tag{11-50a}$$

$$x_i = b_i z_i \tag{11-50b}$$

where t_i is a parameter indicating the per-unit consumption of time for each z_i
consumed, so that the total time spent consuming some amount z_i is T_i, and b_i is
a parameter indicating the amount of market good x_i required per unit z_i. Those
attributes with relatively high values of t_i are called *time intensive*.

   Consumers are postulated to maximize utility of attributes consumed, subject
to a market budget constraint and a time constraint. Let T represent the total time
available for all activities (i.e., 24 hours per day), and let $T_w =$ amount of time
spent working at some constant wage rate w. Assume also that the individual has
available nonwage income in the amount Y. Then we can write

maximize

$$U = U(z_1, \ldots, z_n)$$

subject to

$$\sum p_i x_i = w T_w + Y$$

and

$$\sum T_i = T - T_w$$

However, since time and market goods are inextricably linked by the production
Eqs. (11-50), the two constraints can be combined. Replacing T_w in the income
constraint with $T - \sum T_i$ from the time constraint yields the single constraint

$$\sum p_i x_i = w(T - \sum T_i) + Y$$

or

$$\sum p_i x_i + \sum wT_i = wT + Y$$

Substituting $T_i = t_i z_i$ and $x_i = b_i z_i$ yields Becker's basic model

maximize

$$U(z_1, \ldots, z_n) = U$$

subject to

$$\sum (p_i b_i + wt_i) z_i = wT + Y \tag{11-51}$$

We can interpret the value $\pi_i = p_i b_i + wt_i$ as the "full price" of consuming z_i.[†]
When one unit of some attribute z_i is consumed, it entails the cash expenditure
of $p_i b_i$ (dollars) *plus* the time expenditure of t_i (hours). This time could have
been used to produce income in the amount wt_i, and so represents an opportunity
cost of consuming z_i. The sum of these full prices times quantities of attributes
consumed equals an individual's full income, consisting of nonwage income plus
the amount of income that would be earned if the entire day were spent at work.

In this model, idle time (and sleeping) are attributes, i.e., part of the set of
z_i's. They perhaps involve no cash expenditure, in which case b_i would be zero.
All of this time is valued at some constant wage rate w; thus it is assumed that
the individual has available as much work as he or she desires at that wage. The
total time spent consuming all attributes is $T_C = T - T_w = \sum T_i$.

Assuming the sufficient second-order conditions hold, the solutions to the
first-order equations yield the Marshallian demand functions

$$z_i = z_i^Y(\pi_1, \ldots, \pi_n, w, Y) = z_i^y(p, b, t, w, Y) \tag{11-52}$$

where p, b, and t are the vectors of prices, technological coefficients, and time
intensities, respectively. Using Eqs. (11-50), the demands for the market goods
x_i and time spent T_i on each attribute are immediately derivable.

Comparative Statics

The purpose of this model is to shed light on the use of time. In particular, we
are interested in characterizing consumers' responses to changing wage levels
and changing technological coefficients. As in the standard utility maximization

---

[†] The implicit price of any z_i is independent of the final choice of z_i's only because of special
assumptions regarding the technology of household production. Specifically, one must assume that
$z = g(x)$ exhibits constant returns to scale and no joint production. This is satisfied in Becker's
simple linear technology. See Robert A. Pollak and Michael L. Wachter, "The Relevance of the
Household Production Function and Its Implications for the Allocation of Time," *Journal of Political
Economy,* **88**(2):255–277, April 1975, for a more complete discussion of the theoretical limitations
of these models.

model, the parameters in the Becker model all enter the constraint, and thus, as usual, no refutable implications can be derived on the basis of the maximization hypothesis alone. We thus consider the pure substitution effects. The Hicksian demands are derived from the expenditure minimization model,

minimize

$$Y = \sum (p_i b_i + wt_i)z_i - wT$$

subject to

$$U(z_1, \ldots, z_n) = U^0$$

Assuming the first- and second-order conditions hold, the Hicksian demands are

$$z_i = z_i^u(\pi_1, \ldots, \pi_n, w, U^0) = z_i^U(p, b, t, w, U^0) \qquad (11\text{-}53)$$

The structure of this model in π_i and z_i is formally identical to the standard expenditure minimization model; thus $\partial z_i^u / \partial \pi_i < 0$ is implied. Also, since parametric changes in either p_i, b_i, or t_i increase π_i by a proportional amount, it follows that $\partial z_i^U / \partial p_i < 0$, $\partial z_i^U / \partial b_i < 0$ and $\partial z_i^U / \partial t_i < 0$ also. From the technological relations (11-50), and defining the Hicksian demands for the market goods and time spent on each good as x_i^U and T_i^U respectively, it follows that

$$\partial x_i^U / \partial p_i = b_i \partial z_i^U / \partial p_i < 0$$
$$\partial x_i^U / \partial t_i = b_i \partial z_i^U / \partial t_i < 0$$
$$\partial T_i^U / \partial p_i = t_i \partial z_i^U / \partial p_i < 0$$
$$\partial T_i^U / \partial b_i = t_i \partial z_i^U / \partial b_i < 0$$

The effects of changes in b_i on x_i, and t_i on T_i, are, however, ambiguous: $\partial x_i^U / \partial b_i = \partial(b_i z_i^U) / \partial b_i = b_i \partial z_i^U / \partial b_i + z_i^U = z_i^U(1 + \varepsilon_b)$, where ε_b is the elasticity of consumption of z_i with respect to changes in the coefficient b_i linking x_i with z_i. This elasticity is necessarily negative; however, the sign of the entire expression depends on its magnitude relative to unity. A similar expression holds for T_i: $\partial T_i^U / \partial t_i = T_i^U(1 + \varepsilon_t)$, where ε_t is the elasticity of consumption of z_i with respect to changes in the time coefficient t_i. We can understand these results as follows. Suppose some t_i increases. An increase in t_i means that consuming a given amount of z_i now requires greater time. This raises the full price of that z_i, which is therefore reduced in consumption. Only if the reduction in z_i is in greater proportion than the increase in t_i will the total amount of *time* spent on that attribute be reduced. However, since $x_i = b_i z_i$, a decrease in z_i must lead to less consumption of the market good x_i from which it derives.

The analysis of changes in wage rates is somewhat more problematic. The parameter w enters the full price of each and every z_i for which time is consumed. A change in w therefore necessarily changes many prices simultaneously, precluding application of the law of demand. That is, since w appears in many, if not all, first-order equations, a refutable hypothesis for the compensated demand functions concerning this important parameter is not possible even in this simple model. Becker argues that as the wage increases, consumption will in general switch to goods that are relatively less time-intensive. This seems plausible enough, but additional assumptions regarding the values of the various parameters in the model are required in order to rigorously derive such a result.

The pure substitution effect regarding the total number of hours worked, however, does have a determinate sign. Using the relation $\sum T_i = T - T_w$, we can express the expenditure minimization model in terms of the $n + 1$ variables $z_1, \ldots, z_n$ and T_w, and two constraints:

minimize

$$Y = \sum p_i b_i z_i - w T_w$$

subject to

$$U(z_1, \ldots, z_n) = U^0$$

and

$$\sum t_i z_i + T_w = T$$

Recall from the theorems on general methodology, as long as the first- and second-order conditions are assumed satisfied, the comparative statics theorems for parameters appearing in only the objective function are the same as for unconstrained models. Here, the parameter w does not appear in the constraints; it enters the objective function in the particularly simple form $-wT_w$, i.e., as a price of T_w. Since this is a minimization problem, the expenditure function is concave in $-w$, that is, $\partial(-T_w^U)/\partial w < 0$, or $\partial(T_w^U)/\partial w > 0$, where, of course, T_w^U denotes the compensated demand for hours worked. "Leisure" in this model really means the total time spent consuming the z_i's; thus $\partial T_C^U/\partial w = \partial(T - T_w^U)/\partial w < 0$. Thus, as in the simpler model of labor-leisure choice, a compensated increase in wages is an increase in the opportunity cost of leisure and leads to a decrease in leisure consumed, and a corresponding increase in the number of hours worked.

The theory of household production, as outlined here, concerns an important aspect of human behavior. The economic theories of family structure, birth rates, participation in the labor market, etc., proceed from this model. Higher market wages for women, for example, raise the opportunity cost of children and other homemaking tasks. Thus, even though "children" are most likely a noninferior good, higher incomes are associated with smaller families, if that income is derived from wages, as opposed to inheritance. The increased consumption of "convenience foods" by families with two wage-earners can be attributed to higher market wages of the homemaker in those families. Higher-wage families are predicted to purchase "higher quality" items, when the quality attribute reduces the amount of time required for repair, etc. The theory enables us to think more rigorously about some important choices, and provides a framework for replacing explanations based on tastes with explanations based on changing opportunities.

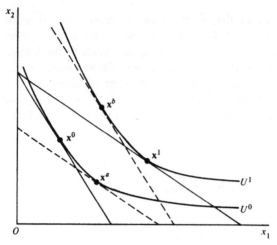

FIGURE 11-5

Two possible measures of the gains from exchange. Suppose the consumer is initially at point $\mathbf{x}^0$, at prices $\mathbf{p}^0 = (p_1^0, p_2^0)$. If p_1 is lowered to p_1^1, the consumer moves to point $\mathbf{x}^1$. The maximum amount this consumer would pay for the *right* to face this lower price is the amount of income M^{1a} that would shift the budget plane from $\mathbf{x}^1$ back to $\mathbf{x}^a$ which is on the original indifference surface U^0. This amount is known as the *compensating variation for a fall in price*. In that case, the consumer would be indifferent between consuming the original bundle $\mathbf{x}^0$ and facing the lower price but consuming bundle $\mathbf{x}^a$. Similarly, if the consumer already has the right, i.e., sufficient income, to consume $\mathbf{x}^1$, raising p_1 from p_1^1 to p_1^0 would move the consumer back to $\mathbf{x}^0$. The consumer will have to be paid at least the amount of income M^{0b} needed to shift the budget plane from $\mathbf{x}^0$ to $\mathbf{x}^b$ on U^1 in order to face the higher price of x_1 voluntarily. For then, the consumer will be no worse off than at $\mathbf{x}^1$. This amount of income is known as the *compensating variation to a rise in price*. These two measures of the gain in going from $\mathbf{x}^0$ to $\mathbf{x}^1$ will not in general be equal. If x_1 is a normal good, then $M^{1a} < M^{0b}$ (why?).

11.5   CONSUMER'S SURPLUS

One of the most vexing problems in the theory of exchange has been the measurement, in units of money income, of the gains from trade. Consider Fig. 11-5, in which the consumer is initially at point $\mathbf{x}^0 = (x_1^0, x_2^0)$ on indifference curve U^0, having faced prices of p_1^0, p_2^0 and money income M^0. Suppose that p_1 is now lowered to p_1^1, the consumer moving to point $\mathbf{x}^1 = (x_1^1, x_2^1)$ on indifference curve U^1. How much better off is the consumer at $\mathbf{x}^1$ compared with being back at $\mathbf{x}^0$? One answer might be to ask how much income can be taken away from the consumer and still leave him or her no worse off than before, at point $\mathbf{x}^0$. This represents a parallel shift of the budget line from $\mathbf{x}^1$ to a point $\mathbf{x}^a$ on the original indifference curve U^0. This amount of income is the maximum amount the consumer would be willing to pay for the right to face the lower price of x_1; it is called a *compensating variation*. Call this amount M^{1a}. Now consider another answer: How much income must this consumer be given at the original prices to be as well off as with the lowered price of x_1? This amount, call it M^{0b}, is the amount of income needed to shift the budget line parallel to itself from point $\mathbf{x}^0$ to a point $\mathbf{x}^b$ on U^1, since the consumer is indifferent between $\mathbf{x}^b$ and $\mathbf{x}^1$. This amount, M^{0b}, is the amount the consumer would have to be bribed to accept the higher price p_1^0 of x_1 voluntarily instead of the lower price. These are two plausible measures of the gains from going to $\mathbf{x}^1$ from $\mathbf{x}^0$. The problem arises because these two measures, M^{1a} and M^{0b} (and others that could be considered) are not in general equal. The consumer might be willing to pay $10 to face a lower price of some good; having achieved that point, however, the consumer might be unwilling to relinquish it for the original situation for any payment less than $15. Having achieved a higher indifference level (an increase in real income), if the good is not inferior, the consumer will value it more; hence, more will have to be paid to make the consumer give up the good than to get more units starting at the lower real income. (The reverse is true for inferior goods.) What to do?

The gains received by consumers, which are derived from the opportunity to purchase a good at its *marginal* rather than its average value, (in which case no gain could occur, since if we paid an average value per unit, our total payment for all units would, by definition, be the total value, leaving no gains), is termed *consumer's surplus*. If consumer's surplus is to be a useful construct, however, it must be capable, at least in principle, of being identified with some observable real-world problem or experiment. That is, knowledge of the value of consumer's surplus must imply something operational about the consumer's responses to price or quantity changes (or anything else affecting consumer welfare). Measures that correspond to no such operational experiment are useless.

The first systematic analysis of this problem, utilizing the modern concept of demand, was undertaken by Alfred Marshall, in his *Principles*. Marshall reasoned as follows. At any quantity consumed of some good, the height of the demand curve represents the consumer's marginal valuation of that good in terms of other goods forgone. Consider Fig. 11-6, showing the demand for tea, to use Marshall's example. At a price above, say, $10, the consumer purchases no tea at all, but when $p = $10, he or she (she, for convenience) purchases 1 pound. When the price is $9, she purchases 2 pounds, at $8, three pounds, etc. According to Marshall, this consumer is willing to pay $10 to obtain 1 pound, $9 to obtain a second pound, $8 to obtain the third pound, and so on down the demand curve (assumed linear in this discussion for computational ease.)[†]

If the market price of tea is $5, this consumer will purchase 6 pounds, at a total expenditure of $30. However, the total value of 6 lbs of tea to this consumer is evidently $10 + $9 + $8 + $7 + $6 + $5 = $45, the sum of the marginal evaluations of each succeeding pound. This total value is the area *under* the demand curve. Subtracting the rectangle representing the consumer's actual expenditure on the good leaves the triangular area *to the left* of the demand curve, above the market price, as the gain to the consumer from purchasing 6 lbs of tea at $5 each, rather than at her successive marginal evaluations. Marshall

---

[†]We ignore the errors associated with treating discrete purchases as a continuum.

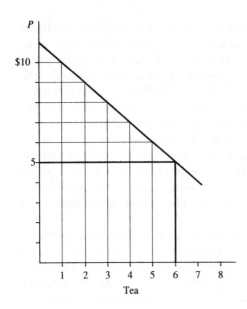

FIGURE 11-6
Marshallian Consumer's Surplus. If a consumer would pay $10 for one pound of tea, $9 for the next pound, and so on, he or she would pay 10 + 9 + 8 + 7 + 6 + 5 = $45 for 6 pounds, rather than go without any tea. Marshall concluded that the consumer's surplus was $15, since at price $5, 6 pounds would be purchased for only $30. This argument, however, ignores the income effects resulting from charging the consumer the intramarginal values for each successive unit.

called this area *consumer's surplus,* but added a *caveat.* In the text, he qualified his analysis as requiring one "to neglect for the moment the fact that the same sum of money represents a different amount of pleasure to different people." In the mathematical appendix (Note VI), Marshall identified the "total utility of the commodity" with the area under the demand curve, defined by an integral, and restated the above qualification by saying ". . . we assume that the marginal utility of money to the individual purchaser is the same throughout."[†]

The meaning of these phrases is anything but clear, and they have led to considerable confusion since publication. The text phrase seems to indicate that interpersonal comparisons of utility are a necessary prerequisite for the use of consumer's surplus; in the appendix, Marshall's concern is that as more of a commodity is purchased, money will yield less satisfaction to the consumer, destroying any linear relationship between money and utility. In 1942, Paul Samuelson further pointed out and analyzed the ambiguity surrounding the phrase, "constant marginal utility of money."[‡] To Marshall, money provided no direct utility to the consumer; it was a device solely for lowering the transactions cost of exchange. The concurrently developed general equilibrium theory of Walras, however, treated money as that one good which happened to have the additional property of serving as the medium of exchange, a *numéraire* commodity whose price was unity. Let us analyze these puzzles.

[†] Alfred Marshall, *Principles of Economics,* 8th ed., Macmillan, 1920, mathematical Note VI.

[‡] Paul A. Samuelson, "Constancy of the Marginal Utility of Money," *Studies in Mathematical Economics and Econometrics, in honor of Henry Schultz,* O. Lange et al. (eds.), University of Chicago Press, 1942.

Returning to Fig. 11-6, we did not specify exactly what kind of demand curve this is, i.e., what is being held constant as the price of tea changes. If $10 represents the maximum a consumer would pay for 1 lb of tea, *and she is in fact charged that entire amount for that unit,* then she must be no better or worse off having made the purchase. The *maximum* a consumer is willing to pay in order to acquire some good, is, by definition, the amount that leaves the consumer indifferent to the new versus the old situation, i.e., on the same indifference level. If a consumer is actually charged the maximum amounts she is willing to pay for succeeding units of a good, then these marginal values must represent points along a Hicksian, or compensated, utility-held-constant demand curve. These are the demand curves derived from minimize $M = \sum p_i x_i$ subject to $U(x_1, \ldots, x_n) = U^0$, where the associated expenditure function $M^*(p_1, \ldots, p_n, U^0) = \sum p_i x_i^U$ indicates the minimum cost of maintaining utility level U^0. Only for these demands is Marshall's reasoning appropriate.

Algebraically, the area to the left of a consumer's demand curve, for a reduction in price, is $-\int x_i dp_i$. The units of this integral are that of money income, being price times quantity. By the envelope theorem, the Hicksian demand functions are the first partials of the expenditure function. Therefore, the area to the left of these demand curves is simply a change in the value of the expenditure function:

$$-\int_{p^0}^{p^1} x_i^U dp_i = -\int_{p^0}^{p^1} \frac{\partial M^*}{\partial p_i} dp_i = M^*(p^0, U^0) - M^*(p^1, U^0) \qquad (11\text{-}54)$$

where p^0 and p^1 are the initial and final price vectors over which the integral is taken. The areas to the left of Hicksian demand functions therefore represent changes in expenditure holding utility constant. A moment's reflection reveals that these areas therefore indicate the amount a consumer would be willing to pay (or have to be paid) to willingly accept some change in property rights, e.g., a change in the purchase price of some good. If we interpret our numerical example as a Hicksian demand curve, the consumer would be willing to pay up to $15 to be able to purchase tea at $5 per lb, rather than be faced with a price in excess of $10. Similarly, she would be willing to pay $9 to face the price $5 rather than $7.

If more than one price were to change, the demand curve for any one good will start to shift, as the price of some other good changes. How could one calculate the amount a consumer would pay to have the prices of two interrelated goods, say, x_1, and x_2, each decrease by some amount? One could start by calculating the area to the left of the demand curve for x_1, holding p_2 constant. The demand for x_2 would then shift to some new position. Then, the area to the left of x_2 could be calculated and added to the previous area. Will this give us the desired answer? What if we had started by changing p_2, calculating the area to the left of the demand for x_2, allowing the demand for x_1 to shift, and then adding to that the area to the left of the resulting demand for x_1? Would we get the same answer?

For the case of the Hicksian, or compensated demands, we will get the same answer no matter what order or "path" of price changes we choose. For multiple price changes, letting p^0 represent the initial price vector and p^1 the final price vector, the sum of the areas to the left of the Hicksian demand functions is still simply the change in the value of the expenditure function between the initial and final prices:

$$-\sum \int_{p^0}^{p^1} x_i^u dp_i = -\int_{p^0}^{p^1} \sum (\partial M^*/\partial p_i) dp_i = -\int_{p^0}^{p^1} dM^*$$

$$= M^*(p^0, U^0) - M^*(p^1, U^0) \tag{11-55}$$

Equation (11-55) shows that the sum of all these areas is simply the difference in the minimum expenditures necessary to reach the indifference level U^0 at the alternative price levels. The difference in the value of the expenditure function at the final versus the initial prices indicates how much a consumer would be willing to pay (or have to be paid), to face the final, rather than the initial, prices.

To sum up, the areas to the left of the Hicksian demand functions are *always* interpretable as the amounts consumers would be willing to pay to face a lower price, or, if the price is to be raised, by how much they must be compensated in order to voluntarily accept the higher price. These amounts, often called *compensating variations,*[†] are always well defined, without the need for further assumptions about the shape or functional form of the utility function. These areas are geometric representations of changes in the value of the expenditure function, which is well defined for all utility functions satisfying the standard curvature properties, i.e., strictly increasing and quasi-concave.

The area to the left of a Marshallian demand function, however, has no such easy interpretation. Unlike the Hicksian demands, the Marshallian demand functions, derived from utility maximization subject to a budget constraint, are *not* in general the partial derivatives of some integral function, e.g., total expenditure or utility. Therefore, the integrals of the Marshallian demands are not expressible in terms of changes in some well-defined function of the initial and final prices and income levels.

From Roy's equality, the Marshallian demands are the first partials of the indirect utility function *divided by the marginal utility of income*. Thus,

$$-\int x_i^M dp_i = -\int \frac{1}{\lambda^M} (\lambda^M x_i^M) dp_i = \int \frac{1}{\lambda^M} \frac{\partial U^*}{\partial p_i} dp_i \tag{11-56}$$

Equation (11-56) says that the area to the left of a Marshallian demand curve is a sum (integral) of changes in utility $(\partial U^*/\partial p_i)$, as some price p_i changes,

---

[†] Following Hicks, for price *increases*, these areas are often referred to as *equivalent variations;* however, they are conceptually identical to the compensating variations.

multiplied by a factor, $1/\lambda^M$, that converts the change in utility into units of money. The conversion factor itself varies as p_i changes; that is, as price changes, a dollar, at the margin, is worth differing amounts of utiles. Although the integral in (11-56) takes on some value, it is not identifiable with any operational experiment concerning consumer behavior.

In the case of multiple price changes, the value of the integral depends on the order in which prices are changed. That is, even for specified initial and final price and income vectors, the value of the integral is not unique, but dependent on the path of prices between the initial and final values. Therefore, without further assumptions on the shape of the indifference curves, there is no obvious way to evaluate, in some useful sense, the gains or losses derived from one or more price changes, using the Marshallian demand functions alone.

If, however, the marginal utility of money term is "constant," it can be moved in front of the integral sign. This expression can then be integrated to yield a function of the endpoint prices (and money income):

$$-\int x_i^M dp_i = \frac{1}{\lambda^M} \int \frac{\partial U^*}{\partial p_i} dp_i = \frac{1}{\lambda^M} [U(p^1, M) - U(p^0, M)] \qquad (11\text{-}57)$$

In this case, the area to the left of the Marshallian demand function equals a change in utility divided by the marginal utility of money. Equation (11-57) in some sense rescues Marshall's claim that the area to the left of a demand curve is interpretable as a change in utility under the assumption of constant marginal utility of money, though how much of the preceding discussion he had in mind can easily be debated.

We have, however, glossed over the meaning of "constancy" of λ^M, the marginal utility of money. In fact, λ^M cannot literally be a "constant," i.e., some numerical value, say, 3 utiles per dollar, for all prices and income. Recall that λ^M is homogeneous of degree -1 in prices and money income. From Euler's theorem,

$$\sum \frac{\partial \lambda^M}{\partial p_i} p_i + \frac{\partial \lambda^M}{\partial M} M \equiv -\lambda^M$$

Therefore, λ^M cannot be independent of all its arguments; this would make the left-hand side of this expression vanish, while leaving the right-hand side at some nonzero, negative value. The marginal utility of income, λ^M, can, for example, be independent of all prices, but not income also, or it can be independent of money income and up to $n - 1$ prices.

What meaning, therefore, can be given to the concept, "constant marginal utility of money," and what implications does it have for the analysis of consumer's surplus? Since $\partial U^*/\partial p_i = -\lambda^M x_i^M$ and $\partial U^*/\partial M = \lambda^M$, applying Young's theorem on invariance of partial derivatives to the order of differentiation yields (omitting superscripts)

$$-\left[\lambda \frac{\partial x_i}{\partial M} + x_i \frac{\partial \lambda}{\partial M} \right] = \frac{\partial \lambda}{\partial p_i} \qquad (11\text{-}58)$$

Suppose $\partial \lambda^M / \partial p_i = 0, i = 1, \ldots, n$, in which case λ^M can be moved outside the integral, as in Eq. (11-57). Then $(M/x_i)(\partial x_i / \partial M) = -(M/\lambda)(\partial \lambda / \partial M)$ for $i = 1, \ldots, n$, i.e., the income elasticities are all equal (necessarily to unity, from the budget constraint); thus the utility function must be homothetic. Denoting the Marshallian area C, we have C $= (1/\lambda^M)[U^*(p^1, M) - U^*(p^0, M)]$. Thus for homothetic utility functions, where the indifference curves are all radial blowups of each other, the Marshallian area represents the unique monetary equivalent of a change in utility; the coefficient which converts utiles to money income is invariant over the price change.

Suppose now that λ^M is a function only of one price, say p_n. Then from Eq. (11-58), $\partial x_i^M / \partial M = 0$, $i = 1, \ldots, n - 1$. Since there is no income effect for goods 1 through $n - 1$, the Marshallian demands for goods 1 through $n - 1$ coincide with the Hicksian demands. This is the situation produced by "vertically parallel" indifference curves. (See problem 20, Chap. 10.) Therefore, the interpretation of the area to the left of any of these Marshallian demand curves is identical to the case of the Hicksian demands, i.e., the willingness to pay to face the lower price. The areas to the left of these Marshallian demand curves have meaning only because they are also the areas to the left of the Hicksian demands.

Example

Consider Fig. 11-7 in which various demand functions for some good, x, are displayed. At price OA, a consumer purchases $AB(=OB')$; the Marshallian demand curve for x passes through points B and D. The consumer attains some utility level U^0 at point B. The curve passing through B and E is the Hicksian demand for x, i.e., the demand for x derived from cost minimization, holding utility constant at $U = U^0$. When the price is lowered to OF, the consumer increases consumption of x to FD. The pure substitution effect of this price change is $B'E'$; the income effect (assumed positive) is ED $(=E'D')$. At point D, the consumer achieves utility $U^1 > U^0$. The curve passing through CD is the Hicksian demand for x holding utility constant at U^1.

Suppose now area $ABEF$ = $20, BDE = $5, and BCD = $5. Thus, between prices OA and OF, the area to the left of the Hicksian demand curve at the initial utility level U^0 is $20, the area to the left of the Marshallian demand curve is $25, and the area to the left of the Hicksian demand at the final utility level U^1 is $30. Here's the question: these values, $20, $25, and $30 are all well defined mathematically, but what are the questions they answer? That is, what operational, i.e., observable (even if hypothetical), experiments involving consumer behavior, are answered by these values?

The area to the left of x^{U^0}, $20, is the amount the consumer would be willing to pay in order to face price OF instead of OA. At OF, the consumer can attain utility U^0 with a total expenditure $20 less than at price OA. This would be indicated by the change in the value of the expenditure function between these two prices. Likewise, the area to the left of the Hicksian demand curve x^{U^1},

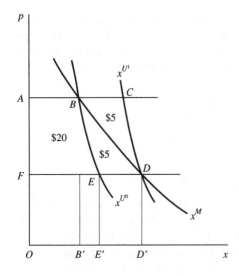

FIGURE 11-7
The Various Consumer's Surpluses. Initially, at price *OA*, the consumer purchases *AB*. When the price is lowered to *OF*, she moves down the Marshallian demand curve *BD* and purchases *FD*. *BE* is a section of the Hicksian (utility-held-constant) demand curve at the initial utility level; *CD* is a Hicksian demand curve at the level achieved when *FD* is purchased at price *OF*. Then *ABEF* is the amount the consumer would be willing to pay to face price *OF* instead of *OA*; *ACDF* is the amount the consumer would have to be paid to voluntarily accept the higher price *OA*, given the pre-existing right to face *OF*. The area to the left of the Marshallian demand curve, *ABDF*, has no operational meaning.

$30, is the amount the consumer would have to be paid, or compensated, in order to voluntarily accept the higher price *OA*. This higher value assumes that the consumer already has the right to face the lower price *OF*. As the diagram makes clear, with normal (noninferior) goods, the compensating variations are necessarily larger when the price is lowered to some new level, than when it is raised back up to the original level.

The amount $25, on the other hand, answers no operational question at all. That is, there is no finite experiment involving this consumer for which $25 represents some revealed value of an outcome. This area is best viewed as an approximation to the areas to the left of the compensated, or Hicksian demands; it has no other meaning.

Empirical Approximations

Although the areas to the left of the Marshallian and Hicksian demand curves are conceptually different, it is obvious that the extent to which such areas would differ from each other in practice depends mainly on the income elasticity of the good in question, and the size of the price change. If the Marshallian demand functions are more easily estimated in practice (since the Hicksian demands require that utility be held constant), it would be handy to be able to approximate the Hicksian areas from knowledge of the Marshallian demands. In 1976 Robert Willig presented some formulas in this regard.[†] Referring to Fig. 11-7, and using

---

[†] Robert D. Willig, "Consumer's Surplus Without Apology," *American Economic Review,* **66:** 589–597, September 1976.

Willig's notation, let E = area $ABEF$ (the compensating variation at the initial utility level), C = $ABDF$ (the Marshallian "surplus"), and A = $ACDF$, the compensating (or equivalent) variation at the final price level. Willig derived, using a Taylor series approach, the following approximation formulas:

$$\frac{\eta^0 |A|}{2M} \le \frac{C - A}{|A|} \le \frac{\eta^1 |A|}{2M}$$

and

$$\frac{\eta^0 |A|}{2M} \le \frac{A - E}{|A|} \le \frac{\eta^1 |A|}{2M}$$

where η^0 and η^1 are, respectively, the smallest and largest values of the income elasticity of the good in question within the region of the price change. If, for example, the income elasticities are near unity, and the area to the left of the Marshallian demand function is approximately 5 percent of money income M, then these areas are within a few percent of each other. If, however, one is estimating a "welfare loss" triangle, rather than the entire trapezoidal area to the left of a demand curve, the percent impact of the income effect might be much more significant, since the comparisons will be made among areas of similar magnitude.

It should also be noted that for price changes that are not small, the differences between the areas to the left of the Hicksian and Marshallian demands can get quite large. Consider, for example, the demand curves associated with the simple Cobb-Douglas utility function $U = x_1 x_2$. The Marshallian demand for x_1 is $x_1^M = M/2p_1$; the Hicksian demand is $x_1^U = (Up_2/p_1)^{(1/2)}$. Both of these demand curves are asymptotic to the vertical axis (p_1). However, above any arbitrary price p_1^0, the area to the left of the Marshallian demand curve tends to infinity, whereas the area to the left of the Hicksian curve is finite. That is, $\lim \int x_1^M dp_1 = \infty$, whereas $\lim \int x_1^U dp_1 = M^*(p_1^0, U)$. Thus, if one were interested in using these areas to measure the amount that consumers would be willing to pay in order to be able to consume x_1 at some price p_1^0, rather than not at all (the "all-or-none" situation), the difference between the Marshallian and Hicksian areas would, in this case, become unboundedly large. The area to the left of the Marshallian demand curve gradually loses all empirical meaning, as the initial or final price tends to infinity.

Finally, we note that since the Marshallian and the Hicksian demand functions are related by the Slutsky equation (or, more precisely, by the fundamental identity (10-35)), it is always possible, in principle at least, to calculate either demand function from the other. If, for example, a system of Marshallian demand functions has been empirically estimated, one could in principle integrate back to the utility function and then derive the Hicksian demands, using the expenditure minimization hypothesis. However, this procedure is apt to be intractable for even the simplest demand systems (though it was done earlier for the Cobb-Douglas case). A single linear demand equation in one price has been analyzed by Jerry Hausman, using the Roy identity.[†] However, it is clear that the task will in general be complex, though given the advances in computer technology, suitable approximation procedures may someday become available.

The phrase *consumer's surplus* is used in two contexts. As a tool of positive economic analysis, consumer's surplus is simply another term for the gains from trade. The law of demand implies that individuals participating in voluntary trade will always pay less for a total quantity of goods than they would if that quantity were offered on an all-or-none basis. It follows that individuals can be expected to devote some resources to enlarging this gain for themselves. The concept of consumer's surplus should therefore be the behaviorial basis for theories of the formation of monopolies and cartels and the political economy of legislation aimed at altering the terms of trade, i.e., the property rights, of the participants in exchange.

The most widespread use of an explicit concept of consumer's surplus, however, has been in the area of welfare economics and social policy. In this context, a function measuring the "welfare loss" due to, for example, a set of excise taxes is formulated to measure the costs, in terms of forgone opportunities to trade (sometimes called *deadweight loss*) of a given tax policy. This loss function is construed as a function of the deviations of prices p_i from marginal costs or, symbolically,

$$\mathcal{L} = f(p_1 - \mathrm{MC}_1, \ldots, p_n - \mathrm{MC}_n)$$

Similarly, the areas to the left of demand curves are used to measure the potential gains from erecting various public works, e.g., dams, to lower the marginal cost of some good.

It is now well established that the only meaningful measures of consumers' benefits are changes in the value of the expenditure function. Such calculations require no exotic assumptions about the utility function. Their shortcoming is that they depend on a single indifference curve, and thus do not measure "benefits" *per se*, but rather, amounts consumers would be willing to pay (or be paid) to face different constraints. Welfare loss functions such as the above represent attempts to generalize this concept to the case where marginal costs are not constant. They can be used to calculate (in principle) the amounts consumers would be willing to pay to avoid monopolies, distortionary taxes, or other policies that cause deviations from marginal cost pricing. We shall return to these matters in the chapter on welfare economics.

11.6 EMPIRICAL ESTIMATION AND FUNCTIONAL FORMS

In previous chapters we investigated the properties of the Cobb-Douglas and CES production functions and their associated cost functions. We also briefly

[†]Jerry Hausman, "Exact Consumer's Surplus and Deadweight Loss," *American Economic Review*, **71**(4):662–676, September 1981.

investigated the generalized Leontief cost function. These specifications have been useful in cost and production theory, and are also used in the empirical estimation of consumer demands. We shall now briefly analyze the CES and other functional forms that have been found to be useful in estimation of empirical demand relations.

Linear Expenditure System

The Linear Expenditure System (LES) is a generalization of the Cobb-Douglas utility function. It was developed by Klein and Rubin (1947–48) and Samuelson (1947–48) and investigated empirically by Stone (1954) and Geary (1950), and it is sometimes referred to as the Stone-Geary function. The function is basically the Cobb-Douglas function with the origin translated to a point (β_1, β_2) in the positive quadrant:

$$U(x_1, x_2) = \alpha_1 \log (x_1 - \beta_1) + \alpha_2 \log (x_2 - \beta_2) \tag{11-59}$$

where $x_i - \beta_i$ and α_i $(i = 1, 2)$ are positive and $\alpha_1 + \alpha_2 = 1$. Maximizing (11-59) subject to the budget constraint yields the first-order conditions:

$$\frac{\alpha_1}{x_1 - \beta_1} - \lambda p_1 = 0$$

$$\frac{\alpha_2}{x_2 - \beta_2} - \lambda p_2 = 0$$

$$M - p_1 x_1 - p_2 x_2 = 0$$

From the first two equations we get $p_i x_i = p_i \beta_i + \alpha_i/\lambda$, and substituting them into the third equation yields $\lambda = 1/(M - p_1\beta_1 - p_2\beta_2)$. Therefore the demand functions are

$$x_i^M = \beta_i + \frac{\alpha_i}{p_i}(M - p_1\beta_1 - p_2\beta_2), \quad i = 1, 2 \tag{11-60}$$

If we write the demand functions in expenditure form:

$$p_i x_i^M = p_i \beta_i + \alpha_i(M - p_1\beta_1 - p_2\beta_2), \quad i = 1, 2 \tag{11-61}$$

we see that the expenditure on each good is linear in all prices and in income—hence the name Linear Expenditure System.

The Cobb-Douglas utility function may be regarded as a special case of the LES, with all the β's equal to zero. In fact economists working with the LES often describe consumers as first buying subsistence quantities of each good (β_1, β_2), and then dividing the remaining expenditure among the goods in fixed proportions (α_1, α_2). Since the *marginal* budget shares are constant, the LES has linear Engel curves although preferences are not homothetic. These income-expenditure lines all pass through the point (β_1, β_2).

The indirect utility function corresponding to the LES can be derived by substituting the demand functions (11-60) into the direct utility function (11-59):

$$U^* = \alpha_1 \log \frac{\alpha_1}{p_1}(M - p_1\beta_1 - p_2\beta_2) + \alpha_2 \log \frac{\alpha_2}{p_2}(M - p_1\beta_1 - p_2\beta_2)$$

$$= \log \frac{\alpha_1^{\alpha_1}\alpha_2^{\alpha_2}(M - p_1\beta_1 - p_2\beta_2)^{\alpha_1 + \alpha_2}}{p_1^{\alpha_1}p_2^{\alpha_2}}$$

(11-62)

Since $\alpha_1 + \alpha_2 = 1$ and the indirect utility function is invariant to monotonic transformations, we can exponentiate (11-62) and delete the constant $\alpha_1^{\alpha_1}\alpha_2^{\alpha_2}$ from it. Such an operation yields

$$U^* = \frac{M - p_1\beta_1 - p_2\beta_2}{p_1^{\alpha_1}p_2^{\alpha_2}}$$

(11-63)

Equation (11-63) can be inverted to get the expenditure function:

$$M^* = U p_1^{\alpha_1} p_2^{\alpha_2} + p_1\beta_1 + p_2\beta_2$$

(11-64)

The Marshallian demand functions can be obtained by applying Roy's identity to (11-63); applying Shephard's lemma to (11-64) yields the Hicksian demands.

CES Utility Function

In direct analogy with production theory, the CES utility function (Arrow et al., 1961) has the form:

$$U(x_1, x_2) = (\alpha_1 x_1^\rho + \alpha_2 x_2^\rho)^{1/\rho} \qquad \rho \le 1$$

(11-65)

The first-order conditions for utility maximization are

$$\alpha_1 x_1^{\rho-1}(\alpha_1 x_1^\rho + \alpha_2 x_2^\rho)^{(1-\rho)/\rho} - \lambda p_1 = 0$$
$$\alpha_2 x_2^{\rho-1}(\alpha_1 x_1^\rho + \alpha_2 x_2^\rho)^{(1-\rho)/\rho} - \lambda p_2 = 0$$
$$M - p_1 x_1 - p_2 x_2 = 0$$

The first two equations can be combined to get

$$\frac{x_1}{x_2} = \left(\frac{\alpha_2 p_1}{\alpha_1 p_2}\right)^{1/(\rho-1)}$$

(11-66)

The elasticity of substitution, σ, is

$$\sigma = -\frac{\partial \log(x_1^*/x_2^*)}{\partial \log(p_1/p_2)} = \frac{1}{1-\rho}$$

(11-67)

The greater the value of the parameter ρ, the greater the degree of substitutability between the commodities.[†]

[†] When $\rho = 0$, the CES function becomes the Cobb-Douglas function.

The Marshallian demand functions corresponding to the CES utility function can be obtained by substituting (11-66) into the budget constraint, which gives

$$M - p_1(\frac{\alpha_2 p_1}{\alpha_1 p_2})^{-\sigma} x_2 - p_2 x_2 = 0$$

or,

$$M - \frac{(\alpha_1 p_2)^\sigma p_1 + (\alpha_2 p_1)^\sigma p_2}{(\alpha_2 p_1)^\sigma} x_2 = 0 \tag{11-68}$$

Thus,

$$x_1^M = \frac{(\alpha_1 p_2)^\sigma}{\alpha_1^\sigma p_1 p_2^\sigma + \alpha_2^\sigma p_2 p_1^\sigma} M$$

$$x_2^M = \frac{(\alpha_2 p_1)^\sigma}{\alpha_1^\sigma p_1 p_2^\sigma + \alpha_2^\sigma p_2 p_1^\sigma} M \tag{11-69}$$

Since the preferences represented by the CES utility function are homothetic, the Marshallian demand functions (11-69) are linear in income.

To derive the indirect utility function, substitute (11-69) into (11-66), and note that $\rho\sigma = \rho/(1 - \rho) = \sigma - 1$:

$$U^* = \left\{ \alpha_1 [\frac{(\alpha_1 p_2)^\sigma}{\alpha_1^\sigma p_1 p_2^\sigma + \alpha_2^\sigma p_2 p_1^\sigma} M]^\rho + \alpha_2 [\frac{(\alpha_2 p_1)^\sigma}{\alpha_1^\sigma p_1 p_2^\sigma + \alpha_2^\sigma p_2 p_1^\sigma} M]^\rho \right\}^{1/\rho}$$

$$= \left\{ (\alpha_1^{1+\rho\sigma} p_2^{\rho\sigma} + \alpha_2^{1+\rho\sigma} p_1^{\rho\sigma})(\frac{M}{\alpha_1^\sigma p_1 p_2^\sigma + \alpha_2^\sigma p_2 p_1^\sigma})^\rho \right\}^{1/\rho}$$

$$= (\alpha_1^\sigma p_2^{\sigma-1} + \alpha_2^\sigma p_1^{\sigma-1})^{1/\rho} \frac{M}{p_1 p_2 (\alpha_1^\sigma p_2^{\sigma-1} + \alpha_2^\sigma p_1^{\sigma-1})} \tag{11-70}$$

$$= \frac{M}{p_1 p_2} (\alpha_1^\sigma p_2^{\sigma-1} + \alpha_2^\sigma p_1^{\sigma-1})^{1/(\sigma-1)}$$

The expenditure function is obtained by inverting the indirect utility function:

$$M^* = U p_1 p_2 (\alpha_1^\sigma p_2^{\sigma-1} + \alpha_2^\sigma p_1^{\sigma-1})^{1/(1-\sigma)} \tag{11-71}$$

Indirect Addilog Utility Function

When a utility function is specified it is in principle possible to derive the commodity demand functions by maximizing the utility function subject to the budget constraint; however, a closed-form solution is not always available. Duality theory suggests that an alternative is to specify an indirect utility function. Any function that is (1) nondecreasing in income, (2) nonincreasing and quasi-convex in prices, and (3) continuous and homogeneous of degree zero in prices and income is a legitimate, indirect utility function that corresponds to some consumer preferences; and the commodity demand functions can be readily derived by using Roy's identity.

A useful functional form is the "addilog" indirect utility function introduced by Houthakker (1965):[†]

$$U^*(p_1, p_2, M) = \alpha_1 \left(\frac{M}{p_1}\right)^{\beta_1} + \alpha_2 \left(\frac{M}{p_2}\right)^{\beta_2} \tag{11-72}$$

The demand functions obtained from the addilog are

$$
\begin{aligned}
x_i^M &= \frac{-\partial U^*/\partial p_i}{\partial U^*/\partial M} \\
&= \frac{\alpha_i \beta_i p_i^{-\beta_i-1} M^{\beta_i}}{\alpha_1 \beta_1 p_1^{-\beta_1} M^{\beta_1-1} + \alpha_2 \beta_2 p_2^{-\beta_2} M^{\beta_2-1}}, \quad i = 1, 2
\end{aligned}
\tag{11-73}
$$

If we divide x_1^M by x_2^M the result will be log-linear in income and in the relative price of x_1 and x_2:

$$\log (x_1^M / x_2^M) = \log \frac{\alpha_1 \beta_1 p_1^{-\beta_1-1} M^{\beta_1}}{\alpha_2 \beta_2 p_2^{-\beta_2-1} M^{\beta_2}}$$

$$= \log (\alpha_1 \beta_1 / \alpha_2 \beta_2) - (\beta_1 + 1)\log p_1 + (\beta_2 + 1)\log p_2 + (\beta_1 - \beta_2)\log M \tag{11-74}$$

The parameters of the system of demand equations can therefore be estimated by the least-squares method.

Translog Specifications

The translog indirect utility function (Christensen, Jorgenson, and Lau 1971; 1975) has been one of the most widely used functional forms in empirical demand analysis. One advantage of the translog is that it is a flexible functional form: it can be a second-order local approximation to an arbitrary indirect utility function. The basic translog specification is given by

$$\log U^*(p_1, \ldots, p_n, M) = -\sum_j \alpha_j \log \frac{p_j}{M} - \frac{1}{2} \sum_k \sum_j \beta_{kj} \log \frac{p_k}{M} \log \frac{p_j}{M} \tag{11-75}$$

where $\sum_j \alpha_j = 1$ and $\beta_{kj} = \beta_{jk}$ for all k and j.

It is often more convenient to work with the expenditure share equations rather than the demand equations when using translog specifications. Note that

---

[†]The direct utility function and the cost function corresponding to the addilog have no closed-form solutions.

$$\frac{-\partial \log\ U^*/\partial \log\ p_i}{\partial \log\ U^*/\partial \log\ M} = \left(\frac{-\partial U^*/\partial p_i}{\partial U^*/\partial M}\right)\left(\frac{p_i/U^*}{M/U^*}\right) = \frac{p_i x_i^M}{M} \qquad (11\text{-}76)$$

Also, the translog specification can be alternatively written as

$$\log U^* = \log M - \sum_j \alpha_j \log p_j - \frac{1}{2}\sum_k \sum_j \beta_{kj}(\log p_k - \log M)(\log p_j - \log M)$$
$$(11\text{-}77)$$

Therefore the shares, ω_i, can be obtained upon logarithmic differentiation of (11-77):

$$
\begin{aligned}
\omega_i &= \frac{\alpha_i + \frac{1}{2}\sum_j \beta_{ij}\log (p_j/M) + \frac{1}{2}\sum_k \beta_{ki}\log (p_k/M)}{1 + \frac{1}{2}\sum_k \sum_j \beta_{kj}\log (p_j/M) + \frac{1}{2}\sum_k \sum_j \beta_{kj}\log (p_k/M)} \\[2mm]
&= \frac{\alpha_i + \sum_j \beta_{ij}\log (p_j/M)}{1 + \sum_k \sum_j \beta_{kj}\log (p_j/M)} \qquad i = 1, \ldots, n
\end{aligned}
$$
$$(11\text{-}78)$$

A special case of the basic translog is the homothetic translog, which is obtained by imposing the restrictions

$$\sum_j \beta_{kj} = 0, \qquad k = 1, \ldots, n$$

Given these n restrictions the indirect utility function and the share equations are

$$\log U^* = \log M - \sum_j \alpha_j \log p_j - \frac{1}{2}\sum_k \sum_j \beta_{kj}\log p_k \log p_j \qquad (11\text{-}79)$$

$$\omega_i = \alpha_i + \sum_j \beta_{ij}\log p_j, \ i = 1, \ldots, n \qquad (11\text{-}80)$$

Equations (11-80) show that the expenditure shares are independent of income, which confirms that preferences are homothetic. Also note that the indirect utility function (11-79) can be inverted to obtain the homothetic translog expenditure function:

$$\log M^*(p_1, \ldots, p_n, U) = \log U + \sum_j \alpha_j \log p_j + \frac{1}{2}\sum_k \sum_j \beta_{kj}\log p_k \log p_j$$
$$(11\text{-}81)$$

The expenditure function (11-81) is frequently used in empirical studies of production.[†] Interpreting M^* as total cost C^*, the factor share equations are readily obtained using Shephard's lemma:

[†]It is also possible to specify a translog profit function; but the translog profit function and the translog cost function will in general correspond to different technologies.

$$\omega_i = \frac{p_i x_i^*}{C^*} = \frac{\partial \log C^*}{\partial \log p_i} = \alpha_i + \sum_j \beta_{ij} \log p_j, \quad i = 1, \ldots, n \qquad (11\text{-}82)$$

Almost Ideal Demand System

A theoretically plausible system of demand equations may be derived from an expenditure function as long as the expenditure function is (1) continuous and nondecreasing in prices and utility, and (2) concave and homogeneous of degree one in prices. An example is the Almost Ideal Demand System (AIDS). It is obtained from the (logarithmic) cost function:

$$\log M^*(p_1, \ldots, p_n, U) = a(p_1, \ldots, p_n) + Ub(p_1, \ldots, p_n) \qquad (11\text{-}83)$$

where

$$a(\cdot) = \alpha_0 + \sum_j \alpha_j \log p_j + \frac{1}{2} \sum_k \sum_j \gamma_{kj} \log p_k \log p_j$$

$$b(\cdot) = \beta_0 \prod_j p_j^{\beta_j} \qquad (11\text{-}84)$$

$$\sum_j \alpha_j = 0$$

$$\sum_j \beta_j = 0$$

$$\sum_k \gamma_{kj} = 0$$

$$\gamma_{kj} = \gamma_{jk}$$

Using Shephard's lemma the share equations are

$$\omega_i = \frac{\partial \log M^*}{\partial \log p_i}$$

$$= \alpha_i + \sum_j \gamma_{ij} \log p_j + p_i U \frac{\beta_i}{p_i} b(\cdot)$$

$$= \alpha_i + \sum_j \gamma_{ij} \log p_j + p_i \frac{\log M - a(\cdot)}{b(\cdot)} \frac{\beta_i}{p_i} b(\cdot) \qquad (11\text{-}85)$$

$$= \alpha_i + \sum_j \gamma_{ij} \log p_j + \beta_i \log (M/P), \quad i = 1, \ldots, n$$

where $\log P = a(\cdot)$. Deaton and Muelbauer argue that P can be considered as a price index and it may be approximated by $\sum_j \omega_i \log p_i$. Given this approximation the system of demand equations are linear in the logarithm of prices and real income, and can be estimated easily.

PROBLEMS

1. Consider the class of utility functions which are *additively separable*, i.e.,

$$U(x_1, \ldots, x_n) \equiv U_1(x_1) + \cdots + U_n(x_n)$$

For this class of utility functions, show:

  (a) At most one good can exhibit increasing marginal utility and in that case *(i)* that good is normal whereas all remaining goods are inferior and *(ii)* that good is a *net* substitute $(\partial x_i^U / \partial p_j > 0)$ for the remaining goods whereas the remaining goods are all complementary to each other.

  (b) If all goods exhibit diminishing marginal utility, *(i)* all goods are normal, and *(ii)* all goods are net substitutes.

2. For demand functions derived from additively separable utility functions, show that

  (a) $\dfrac{\partial x_i / \partial p_k}{\partial x_j / \partial p_k} = \dfrac{\partial x_i / \partial M}{\partial x_j / \partial M}$

  (b) $s_{ij} = -k \dfrac{\partial x_i^M}{\partial M} \dfrac{\partial x_j^M}{\partial M}$ where $k = \dfrac{\lambda^M}{\partial \lambda^M / \partial M}$

3. Consider the indirect utility function $U^*(p_1, \ldots, p_n, M) \equiv U^*(p_1/M, \ldots, p_n/M, 1) \equiv V(r_1, \ldots, r_n)$, where $r_i = p_i/M$. Show that if V is additively separable in $r_1, \ldots, r_n$, then

$$\frac{\partial x_i^M / \partial p_k}{\partial x_j^M / \partial p_k} = \frac{x_i}{x_j}$$

4. Using the results of the previous two problems, show that if $U(\mathbf{x})$ and $V(\mathbf{r})$ are both additively separable, then $U(\mathbf{x})$ is homothetic.

5. Consider a set of demand functions $x_i = x_i^*(p_1, \ldots, p_n, M)$ whose only known properties are homogeneity and satisfying a budget constraint; i.e.,

$$\sum_{j=1}^{n} \frac{\partial x_i^*}{\partial p_j} p_j + \frac{\partial x_i^*}{\partial M} M \equiv 0 \qquad i = 1, \ldots, n \tag{1}$$

and

$$\sum_{i=1}^{n} p_i x_i^* \equiv M \tag{2}$$

Show that under (1) and (2) alone, Hicks' third law holds, i.e.,

$$\sum_{i=1}^{n} p_i s_{ij} = \sum_{j=1}^{n} p_j s_{ij} = 0 \qquad \text{where } s_{ij} = \frac{\partial x_i^*}{\partial p_j} + x_j \frac{\partial x_i^*}{\partial M}$$

6. Suppose a consumer's utility function is additively separable and, in addition, the marginal utility of money income is independent of prices. Show that the elasticity of each money-income demand curve is everywhere unity.

7. The development of utility theory can be regarded as the attempt to provide a theory that explains the phenomenon of downward-sloping demand curves. It was soon discovered that the Hicksian pure-substitution terms were symmetric, a result, said Samuelson, "which would not have been discovered without the use of mathematics."

    (a) Explain why it is something of a non sequitur to assert the symmetry of the substitution terms.

    (b) What behavioral differences are there, if any, in terms of observable price-quantity combinations, between a theory of the consumer that includes such symmetry and one that does not require such symmetry?

8. (A Yiddish parable, with love to Milt Gross.) Morty, de one in de schmatah beezness by Coney Highland (sotch a mensch), is exessparaded from de rise in de price from gebardins (is something tarrible), from $200 to $300 itch suit. Silskin cuts, denks Gut, is de same at $300. Voise, some doidy gonif didn't pay all de bills he chodged opp. Is diss a system? Meelton, dot spuxman from de right, lest year bought three of itch, for his trip witt spitches from China. Diss year, de books show one gebardin and four silskins. Leo, dot odder beeg shot, lest year bought four gebardins and three silskins, and diss year de books show five gebardins and two silskins. So, Nize Baby, I hesk you, who is de gonif?

9. Which of the following sets of observations of price-quantity data are consistent with utility maximization?

    (a) $\mathbf{p}^1 = (1, 2, 3)$ $\mathbf{x}^1 = (3, 2, 1)$
         $\mathbf{p}^2 = (2, 1, 2)$ $\mathbf{x}^2 = (2, 2, 1)$
         $\mathbf{p}^3 = (3, 5, 1)$ $\mathbf{x}^3 = (1, 2, 1)$
    (b) $\mathbf{p}^1 = (3, 4, 1)$ $\mathbf{x}^1 = (5, 1, 3)$
         $\mathbf{p}^2 = (2, 3, 2)$ $\mathbf{x}^2 = (3, 3, 3)$
         $\mathbf{p}^3 = (5, 3, 1)$ $\mathbf{x}^3 = (4, 2, 2)$
    (c) $\mathbf{p}^1 = (4, 3, 2)$ $\mathbf{x}^1 = (2, 2, 2)$
         $\mathbf{p}^2 = (5, 3, 3)$ $\mathbf{x}^2 = (1, 3, 3)$
         $\mathbf{p}^3 = (5, 2, 3)$ $\mathbf{x}^3 = (1, 3, 2)$

10. A certain consumer is observed to purchase bundles $\mathbf{x}^i$ at prices $\mathbf{p}^i$:

$$\mathbf{p}^1 = (4, 2, 3) \qquad \mathbf{x}^1 = (1, 3, 3)$$
$$\mathbf{p}^2 = (3, 2, 3) \qquad \mathbf{x}^2 = (2, 3, 2)$$
$$\mathbf{p}^3 = (2, 3, 3) \qquad \mathbf{x}^3 = (.5, 1, 5)$$

What is the sex of the consumer?

11. Consider the two demand functions

$$x_1 = \frac{p_2}{p_1} \qquad x_2 = \frac{M}{p_2} - 1 \qquad p_2 < M$$

Integrate these demand functions to find the class of utility functions from which they are derived.

12. Answer the previous question for the demand functions

$$x_1 = \frac{p_2 M}{p_1 p_2 + p_1^2}$$

$$x_2 = \frac{p_1 M}{p_1 p_2 + p_2^2}$$

13. A consumer faced with prices $p_1 = 9$, $p_2 = 12$ consumes at some point $\mathbf{x}^0$, where $x_1 = 4$, $x_2 = 7$, $U(\mathbf{x}^0) = 10$. When p_1 is lowered to $p_1 = 8$, the consumer would move to point $\mathbf{x}^1$, where $x_1 = 6$, $x_2 = 6$, $U(\mathbf{x}^1) = 15$. From these data, estimate the following values:

    (a) How much would the consumer be willing to pay to face the lower price of x_1?

(b) How much would a consumer initially at $\mathbf{x}^1$ have to be paid to accept the higher price of x_1 voluntarily?

(c) Are your answers to (a) and (b) exact calculations of these values, or are they approximations? If the latter, is the direction of bias predictable?

(d) How much better off is the consumer at $\mathbf{x}^1$ than at $\mathbf{x}^0$?

14. In his *Principles,* Marshall gave the following definition of consumer's surplus:

1. The amount a consumer would pay over which he does pay for a given amount of a good rather than none at all.

Several other consumer's surplus measures have been proposed, e.g.,

2. The amount the consumer would pay for the *right* to purchase the good at its market price rather than have no good at all.

3. The amount the consumer would have to be paid to voluntarily forgo entirely consumption of the good at its present level.

4. The monetary equivalent of the gain in utility that the consumer receives by being able to purchase the good at the market price rather than purchase none at some higher price.

5. The monetary equivalent of the fall in utility a consumer would experience if the right to purchase the good at the market price were taken away.

(a) Discuss the relationship, if any, between these measures.

(b) Show that measure 2 is greater than measure 1.

(c) Show that if the good is normal over the whole range of consumption, then measure 3 is greater than measure 2.

(d) Would knowledge of measures 1 to 3 enable one to determine which of two mutually exclusive projects would result in maximizing the consumer's utility?

15. Show that if a consumer's income consists of a numéraire commodity that enters the utility function, then the line integral generating consumer's surplus measures will be path-independent only if all nonnuméraire commodities have zero income elasticities.

REFERENCES ON THEORY

Barten, A. P.: "Consumer Demand Functions under Conditions of Almost Additive Preferences," *Econometrica,* **32**:1–38, 1964.

Becker, G. S.: "A Theory of the Allocation of Time," *Economic Journal,* **75**:493–517, September 1965.

Chipman, J. S., L. Hurwicz, M. K. Richter, and H. F. Sonnenschein (eds.): *Preferences, Utility, and Demand,* Harcourt Brace Jovanovich, New York, 1971.

Debreu, Gerard: *The Theory of Value,* John Wiley & Company, Inc., New York, 1959.

Georgescu-Roegen, N.: "The Pure Theory of Consumer Behavior," *Quarterly Journal of Economics,* **50**:545–593, 1936.

Hicks, J. R.: *Value and Capital,* 2d ed., Oxford University Press, London, 1946.

———: *A Revision of Demand Theory,* Oxford University Press, London, 1956.

Houthakker, H. S.: "Revealed Preference and the Utility Function," *Economica,* **17**:159–174, 1950. The original discussion of the strong axiom of revealed preference.

———: "Additive Preferences, *Econometrica,* **28**:244–257, 1960.

———: "The Present State of Consumption Theory," *Econometrica,* **29**:704–740, 1961.

Lancaster, K. J.: "A New Approach to Consumer Theory," *Journal of Political Economy,* **74**:132–157, April 1966.

Lau, L. J.: "Duality and the Structure of Utility Functions," *Journal of Economic Theory,* **1**:374–395, December 1969.

Morgan, J. N.: "The Measurement of Gains and Losses," *Quarterly Journal of Economics,* **62:** 287–308, February 1948.

Pollak, R. A., and M. L. Wachter: "The Relevance of the Household Production Function and Its Implications for the Allocation of Time," *Journal of Political Economy,* **83**(2):255–277, April 1975.

Samuelson, P. A.: *Foundations of Economic Analysis,* Harvard University Press, Cambridge, Mass., 1947.

———: "Consumption Theory in Terms of Revealed Preference," *Economica,* **15:**243–253, 1948.

———: "The Problem of Integrability in Utility Theory," *Economica,* **17:**355–385, 1950.

Silberberg, E.: "Duality and the Many Consumers' Surpluses," *American Economic Review,* **62:** 942–956, December 1972.

REFERENCES ON FUNCTIONAL FORMS

Arrow, Kenneth J., et al.: "Capital-Labor Substitution and Economic Efficiency," *Review of Economics and Statistics,* **43:**225–250, August 1961.

Christensen, Laurits R., Dale W. Jorgenson, and Lawrence J. Lau: "Conjugate Duality and the Transcendental Logarithmic Production Function," *Econometrica,* **39:**255–256, July 1971.

———: "Transcendental Logarithmic Utility Function," *American Economic Review,* **65:**367–383, June 1975.

Cobb, Charles W., and Paul H. Douglas: "A Theory of Production," *American Economic Review,* **18:**139–165, March 1928.

Deaton, Angus, and John Muelbauer: "An Almost Ideal Demand System," *American Economic Review,* **70:**312–326, June 1980.

Diewert, W. E.: "An Application of the Shephard Duality Theorem: A Generalized Leontief Production Function," *Journal of Political Economy,* **79:**481–507, June 1971.

———: "Duality Approaches to Microeconomic Theory," in Arrow, K. J., and M.D. Intrilligator (eds.), *Handbook of Mathematical Economics,* vol. II, North Holland, Amsterdam, 1982, pp. 535–599. A technical review of duality and functional forms.

Geary, R. C.: "A Note on 'A Constant Utility Index of the Cost of Living,'" *Review of Economic Studies,* **18**(2):65–66, 1950.

Houthakker, H. S.: "A Note on Self-Dual Preferences," *Econometrica,* **33:**797–801, October 1965.

Klein, L. R. and H. Rubin, "A Constant Utility Index of the Cost of Living," *Review of Economic Studies,* **15:**84–87, 1947-48.

Stone, Richard: "Linear Expenditure Systems and Demand Analysis: An Application to the Pattern of British Demand," *Economic Journal,* **64:**511–527, September 1954.

Samuelson, Paul A., "Some Implications of 'Linearity'" *Review of Economic Studies,* **15:**88–90, 1947-48.

CHAPTER
12

INTERTEMPORAL CHOICE

12.1 *n*-PERIOD UTILITY MAXIMIZATION

The analyses of previous chapters have all concerned choices among contemporaneous commodities. An important class of choices made by consumers, however, relates to consumption over time, that is, how one allocates income earned in different time periods to consumption. We notice, for example, that college students are in general poor, that earnings are highest during a person's middle age, and earnings fall after retirement; the typical response to this pattern of income is to borrow when one is young and lend (e.g., in the form of investing in a retirement fund) during middle age. It seems that when income is earned in an uneven pattern, individuals attempt to "smooth out" their consumption through borrowing and lending. In this way, people's consumption varies less than their income. Is there some systematic basis for this behavior?

We begin this discussion by considering consumption in just two time periods. Denote the present as period 1 and the future (next year) as period 2, and consumption in periods 1 and 2 as x_1 and x_2. Suppose a person earns x_1^0 in the present (this year) and x_2^0 in the future (next year). Suppose also that this individual can borrow and lend in the "capital market" at interest rate r. What this means is that any income y not spent this year can be loaned to others, in return for which the consumer receives some greater amount $y + ry = y(1 + r)$ next year. Alternatively, the consumer can increase present consumption by some amount y, and repay $y(1 + r)$ next year. The opportunity cost of consuming income y this year is thus forgoing consumption of $y(1 + r)$ next year. The *price* of present

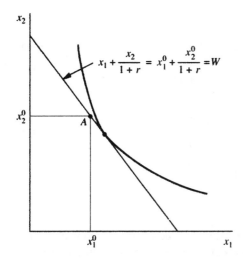

$$x_1 + \frac{x_2}{1+r} = x_1^0 + \frac{x_2^0}{1+r} = W$$

FIGURE 12-1
Maximization of Utility Subject to a Wealth Constraint. On a general level, utility maximization subject to a wealth constraint is structurally the same as any such problem in which endowments are brought to the market. In this diagram, the tangency occurs at a point of net borrowing, since $x_1^M > x_1^0$, $x_2^M < x_2^0$. Roy's identity states that $\partial U^*/\partial(1/(1+r)) = \lambda^M(x_2^0 - x_2^M)$. In this case, since an increase in the interest rate will rotate the budget line clockwise through A, the consumer will be worse off.

consumption is thus $(1 + r)$ units of future consumption; alternatively, the price of future consumption is $1/(1 + r)$ units of present consumption. We commonly say that the *present value* of \$$y$ one year from now is \$$y/(1 + r)$; this is merely the quantity, y, times its price in terms of present consumption. The interest rate, to quote Irving Fisher, is the *premium for earlier availability of goods.*[†]

Wealth, W, in the present, is defined as the present value of current and future income. The consumer's budget constraint is that he or she cannot spend more than his or her wealth, i.e.,

$$x_1 + \frac{x_2}{(1+r)} = x_1^0 + \frac{x_2^0}{(1+r)} = W \qquad (12\text{-}1)$$

The consumer maximizes $U(x_1, x_2)$ subject to (12-1). Though we are using "income" and "consumption" interchangeably as arguments in the utility function, it is well to remember, as pointed out by Fisher, that "income" really consists of *consuming* something. "Saving" (or dissaving) is just a way of rearranging consumption over time. Income is realized when it is consumed.

The model is depicted in Fig. 12-1. The budget line has slope $dx_2/dx_1 = -(1 + r)$, the price of x_1 in terms of x_2, and passes through the endowment point A, (x_1^0, x_2^0). An increase in the interest rate represents an increase in the price of present consumption, and has the effect of rotating the wealth constraint clockwise through A.

The Lagrangian for this problem is

$$\mathscr{L} = U(x_1, x_2) + \lambda \left[(x_1^0 - x_1) + \frac{(x_2^0 - x_2)}{(1+r)} \right] \qquad (12\text{-}2)$$

[†]Irving Fisher, *The Theory of Interest*, New York, August M. Kelley, 1970. (First Edition, The Macmillan Co., New York, 1930.)

producing the first-order conditions

$$\mathcal{L}_1 = U_1(x_1, x_2) \qquad - \lambda \qquad = 0 \tag{12-3a}$$

$$\mathcal{L}_2 = U_2(x_1, x_2) - \frac{\lambda}{(1+r)} = 0 \tag{12-3b}$$

and the constraint

$$\mathcal{L}_\lambda = (x_1^0 - x_1) + \frac{(x_2^0 - x_2)}{(1+r)} = 0 \tag{12-3c}$$

Combining (12-3a) and (12-3b) yields

$$\frac{U_1}{U_2} = 1 + r \tag{12-4}$$

Equation (12-4) says that the consumer's marginal value of present consumption, U_1/U_2, equals the opportunity cost of present consumption, in terms of future consumption forgone. It will simplify the algebra if we let $p = 1/(1+r)$, the price of future consumption. Assuming the sufficient second-order conditions hold, the first-order conditions can be solved for the Marshallian demand functions

$$x_i = x_i^M(p, x_1^0, x_2^0), \quad i = 1, 2 \tag{12-5}$$

It is apparent from the previous analyses of the demand for leisure and the "general equilibrium" demands that refutable implications cannot be derived from this model; like those other models, the parameters all enter the constraint. However, from the envelope theorem, $\partial U^*/\partial p = \lambda(x_2^0 - x_2^M)$. If the individual is a net borrower in the present, so that $x_1^0 - x_1^M < 0$ and thus $x_2^0 - x_2^M > 0$, then an increase in the interest rate (which decreases p) makes the individual worse off, since now a greater amount of future goods must be forgone in order to finance current consumption. Likewise, increases in the interest rate increase the achievable utility level for net lenders.

We can gain greater insight into the model by deriving the Slutsky equation, separating out the substitution effect and the wealth (income) effect.

The Hicksian demands can be derived minimizing the endowment in either period so as to achieve some arbitrary indifference level U^0. We can therefore state the model as

minimize

$$x_1^0 = x_1 + p(x_2 - x_2^0)$$

subject to

$$U(x_1, x_2) = U^0$$

The Lagrangian for this problem is then

$$\mathcal{L}' = x_1 + p(x_2 - x_2^0) + \lambda(U^0 - U(x_1, x_2)) \tag{12-6}$$

Assuming the first and sufficient second-order conditions hold, the implied first-order equations can be solved for the Hicksian demands

$$x_i = x_i^U(p, U^0) \tag{12-7}$$

Substituting these demands into the objective function produces a minimum "expenditure" type of function

$$x_1^*(p, U^0) = x_1^U + p(x_2^U - x_2^0) \tag{12-8}$$

The fundamental identity linking the Marshallian and Hicksian demands is therefore

$$x_i^U(p, U^0) \equiv x_i^M(p, x_1^*(p, U^0), x_2^0) \tag{12-9}$$

producing a Slutsky equation[†]

$$\frac{\partial x_i^M}{\partial p} \equiv \frac{\partial x_i^U}{\partial p} + (x_2^0 - x_2^U)\left(\frac{\partial x_i^M}{\partial x_1^0}\right) \tag{12-10}$$

If the interest rate increases, the price of future consumption, p, decreases. This produces a pure substitution effect toward less present and greater future consumption: $\partial x_2^U / \partial p < 0$. However, a change in the interest rate produces an attendant wealth effect. An increase in the endowment of present income is the same as an increase in wealth from any source, since income can be traded back and forth across time periods. Assume that consumption in both time periods enters the utility function as normal goods, so that $\partial x_i^M / \partial x_1^0 > 0$. The income, or, more properly, the wealth term on the right-hand side of the Slutsky equation, indicates that if, for example, the consumer is a net borrower in period 1, so that $(x_2^0 - x_2^U) < 0$, the substitution effect will be reinforced by the wealth effect. In this case, an increase in the interest rate, in addition to making present consumption relatively more expensive, also lowers the consumer's wealth, producing an additional reduction in present consumption. If the individual is a net lender in period 1, the wealth and substitution effects oppose one another: an increase in the interest rate raises present wealth and leads to greater present consumption.[‡]

Time Preference

The preceding discussion is formally identical to any utility maximization problem in which the consumer brings endowments to the market. What additional assumptions are appropriate if this is to be interpreted specifically as modeling consumption over time? We wrote utility as any well-behaved (strictly increasing and quasi-concave) function $U(x_1, x_2)$. However, suppose we wish to specify that the individual's tastes do not change over time. In that case, the trade-offs a consumer would be willing to make, with regard to present versus future con-

---

[†] See the derivation of Eq. (10-75).

[‡] However, if the interest rate has risen due to an increase in future prospects (see the next section), present consumption may rise due to the implied wealth effect.

sumption, should not depend on the *date,* i.e., the time identifier. That is, an individual's marginal willingness to sacrifice a unit of present consumption in return for some amount of future consumption should depend only on the levels of consumption in each time period, and not whether this evaluation is taking place in 1995, 2000, or 2005. We can incorporate this assumption by specifying the utility function as $V(x_1, x_2) = U(x_1) + U(x_2)$, with the same function U in each time period.[†] This utility function is *additively (or strongly) separable* in x_1 and x_2; moreover, the separate parts are functionally identical. This utility specification would rule out "becoming accustomed" to some level of, say, luxury. The utility received in any one time period is independent of either past history or future prospects.

Irving Fisher wrote that people were "impatient" (he in fact included it in the subtitle of his book), meaning they preferred present consumption to the same amount of future consumption. If wealth can be costlessly stored, it is of course always preferable to have wealth now, say, in the form of money, rather than in the future, simply as a consequence of more being preferred to less. If one has money now, one can always choose not to consume it for a while; the reverse is not true. The set of opportunities for consumption is necessarily larger if the money is in hand, as opposed to becoming available in the future, assuming there is no cost of insuring against theft, etc. *Impatience* means something else: it refers to *preferences,* not opportunities. Impatience means that a given level of income y will generate less utility if it is consumed in the future rather than in the present.

We can express impatience by writing the utility function as

$$V(x_1, x_2) = U(x_1) + \frac{U(x_2)}{(1 + \rho)} \qquad \rho \geq 0 \qquad (12\text{-}11)$$

For n time periods, this utility function is

$$\sum_{i=1}^{n} \frac{U(x_i)}{(1 + \rho)^{(i-1)}} \qquad (12\text{-}12)$$

Thus, consumption in the future is given less weight than consumption now, with proportionate decreases in weight, the further into the future the consumption takes place.

Though we tentatively allow for it, the existence of time preference is in fact controversial, and empirically unconfirmed. It implies a "myopia" concerning the future. If we know the future will arrive (and uncertainty about the future is assumed *not* to be the source of time preference), why should the future count for less than the present in our utility? Having shifted consumption earlier, will we not regret having done so when the future arrives, and can we not anticipate this regret?

[†] Of course, any monotonic transformation of this function would work as well. Note also that it would be incorrect to use the same symbol, U, to mean both a function of two variables and a function of one variable.

The general properties that are important in utility analysis, i.e., that $V(x)$ be strictly increasing and quasi-concave, allow an infinite variety of "discounting" schemes, by which the "goods" x_i are given successively less weight as i increases. However, we mean to interpret this function as the utility derived from consuming the *same* good, "consumption," in succeeding time periods. Robert Strotz argued compellingly that if, in some succeeding year, an individual could be predicted to change the weighting scheme for future years, then the original n-period utility function would essentially be inconsistent with itself and irrelevant.[†] Suppose, for example, an individual were to decide right now, in the present, that he or she would consume wealth evenly for two years, and then in year three, consume one half the remaining wealth, with constant consumption thereafter. Suppose two years pass, and year three is now "the present." Will the individual go forward with the original plan? Quasi-concavity of the utility function, by itself, does not rule out this behavior. However, such a consumption plan implies an inexplicable change in tastes. Suddenly, in a given year, the consumer is willing to sacrifice a much greater amount of future consumption than previously (or henceforth), in order to obtain a given amount of "present" consumption. It would be inconsistent with other applications of utility theory and the general paradigm of economics to allow such arbitrary taste changes over time. Therefore we would in general wish to impose this important property, commonly referred to as *dynamic consistency,* on intertemporal utility functions: specifically, that *the marginal value of consumption in period* i *in terms of forgone consumption in period* j *be independent of the date,* i.e., dependent only on the consumption levels in the two time periods.[‡]

The utility function (12-12) has this important property. The marginal rate of substitution (marginal value of x_i in terms of x_j) is

$$\frac{dx_j}{dx_i} = \frac{-V_i}{V_j} = \frac{-(1+\rho)^{(j-i)}U_i{}'(x_i)}{U_j{}'(x_j)} \tag{12-13}$$

Equation (12-13) says that the marginal value of consumption in period i, in terms of forgone consumption in period j, depends only on the *levels* of consumption in those two periods, and not *which* two time periods are involved, since the function $U(x_i)$ is the same for all $i = 1, \ldots, n$, and, moreover, only on the *number* of time periods separating the two periods, not *when* the time periods occur. Dynamic consistency is thus assured. This utility function is depicted, for two time periods, in Fig. 12-2. Along the 45° ray from the origin, $x_1 = x_2$, and thus all indifference curves cut through this line with slope $-(1 + \rho) \le -1$. That

---

[†]Robert Strotz, "Myopia and Inconsistency in Dynamic Utility Maximization," *Review of Economic Studies,* **23**(3):165–180, 1956.

[‡]Strotz went on to say that if such changes in marginal rates of substitution between two time periods were anticipated, a consumer might rationally plan ahead to prevent these changes in plans, by, for example, tying up his or her wealth in trusts containing penalties for changing the original consumption plan. We shall not explore this aspect of the problem here.

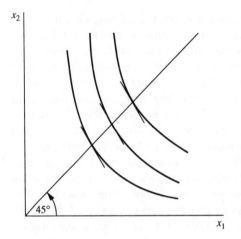

FIGURE 12-2
Indifference Curves for Additively Separable Utility Functions with Impatience. Indifference curves for $V(x_1, x_2) = U(x_1) + U(x_2)/(1 + \rho)$ are displayed, with $\rho > 0$. Along the 45° ray, where $x_1 = x_2$, the slopes are $-(1 + \rho) < -1$. Since the slope of the budget (wealth) line is $-(1 + r)$, $x_1^M > x_2^M$ if $\rho > r$.

is, the absolute slope is the rate of time preference $1 + \rho$, and is greater than or equal to unity. If no "impatience" is assumed, the indifference curves have slope -1 along the 45° ray.

Maximizing the utility function (12-12) subject to the wealth constraint

$$\sum \frac{x_i}{(1 + r)^{(i-1)}} = \sum \frac{x_i^0}{(1 + r)^{(i-1)}} \tag{12-14}$$

produces the tangency condition, for consecutive time periods i, j,

$$\frac{-(1 + \rho)U'(x_i)}{U'(x_j)} = -(1 + r)$$

or

$$\frac{U'(x_i)}{U'(x_j)} = \frac{(1 + r)}{(1 + \rho)} \tag{12-15}$$

From this condition we can see how consumption of income is affected by the relation between the consumer's *preference* for earlier availability, as measured by $1 + \rho$, and the market price of earlier availability, measured by $1 + r$. Suppose, initially, that the consumer is not impatient, so that $\rho = 0$. Then since we know the indifference curves have slope -1 along the 45° ray, and since the wealth constraint has the steeper slope $-(1 + r)$, it must be the case that the tangency lies above the 45° ray, so that $x_j^M > x_i^M$. Given no impatience and a positive premium for earlier availability of goods, the consumer shifts consumption to the future. If the rate of time preference ρ is positive, but less than the market premium for earlier availability r, then obviously the same result will occur: the consumer will consume more income in the future than in the present. If, however, the rate of time preference exceeds the interest rate, then consumption will be shifted forward to the present, and we will find $x_i^M > x_j^M$.

The sufficient second-order conditions for utility maximization include, for all consecutive time periods i and j, $j = 1 + i$, $-[(1 + \rho)/(1 + r)^2]U''(x_i) - U''(x_j) < 0$. If $x_i \neq x_j$ and $r \neq \rho$, these conditions do *not* imply diminishing marginal utility in each time period. Using the results of Chap. 11, Prob. 1, there can be (locally) increasing marginal utility in at most one time period, say period i. That is, there may be a convex portion of $U(x_i)$ occurring in a neighborhood of some particular consumption level x_i^*. In that case, an increase in wealth could, locally at least, produce an increase in consumption in period i and a decrease in consumption in all other time periods. Thus, using only the assumptions of quasi-concavity and strong separability, one could not rule out an individual spending an unexpected windfall entirely in the year it was received. Typically, $U'' < 0$ is asserted for all consumption levels, eliminating this possibility.

Since $V(x_1, \ldots, x_n)$ represents intertemporal utility, consumption takes place in the order x_1, x_2, $\ldots$ etc., unlike the model of contemporaneous consumption, where all goods are consumed together. With intertemporal utility, consumption levels in the past are fixed at whatever values were chosen. As time passes, additional x_i's become fixed. The Le Châtelier results for consumer models say that the Hicksian demand functions become more inelastic as additional "goods" are held fixed. The model predicts, therefore, that individuals become less responsive to changes in relative prices as they age. This perhaps confirms the casual empiricism that young people often regard their elders as rigid and conservative. (Of course, as we age, the payoff from experimenting with new procedures is less, due to the smaller number of years left to enjoy the possible benefits.)

Let us now explore the regularity stated at the beginning of this chapter, the tendency of consumers to even out the flow of consumption. Assume for the moment that the consumer's rate of impatience equals the market interest rate, i.e., $\rho = r$. In this case, from Eq. (12-15), $x_i^M = x_j^M$, i.e., consumption must be the same in any two adjacent time periods. Thus income will be consumed at a constant rate. There is no analogy to this result in the utility theory of consumption of contemporaneous goods; we never purport to demonstrate that $x_i^* = x_j^*$. The result appears here because of the additional structure imposed on the utility function; in particular, the assumptions of dynamic consistency.

The tendency to even out the flow of consumption is illustrated further in Fig. 12-3. Suppose, for convenience, that $\rho = r = 0$. The curve labeled x_1^U is the

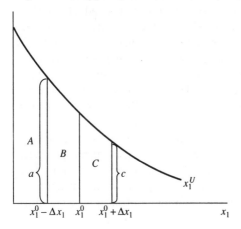

FIGURE 12-3
The Gain from Even Flows of Consumption. The total value of consumption, measured by the area under the compensated demand curve, is greatest when consumption is even. Neglecting interest and time preference, transferring a dollar of consumption from $x_1^0 + \Delta x$ to $x_1^0 - \Delta x$ increases total value by $a - c$. Alternatively, consuming x_1^0 twice yields total value $2(A + B) > 2A + B + C$, the amount the consumer would pay for the combination $(x_1^0 + \Delta x, x_1^0 - \Delta x)$.

Hicksian demand curve for present consumption; on the vertical axis is the "price" of that good. The height of the demand curve, as always, is the marginal value, in this case, of present consumption in terms of future consumption forgone; thus the subjective price of present consumption along the demand curve represents the amount of future consumption the individual is willing to trade in order to acquire an additional increment of present consumption.

Suppose the individual has the option of consuming x_1^0 in each of two time periods, versus consuming $x_1^0 + \Delta x$ in the first time period, and then $x_1^0 - \Delta x$ in the second period; i.e., let us compare the relative merits of steady consumption versus "feast and famine." During the time of feast, the marginal value of present consumption is some relatively low value, c; during famine, the marginal value of present consumption is relatively high, a. If the consumer can trade a unit of income from the time of feast to the time of famine, he or she will experience a net gain of $a - c$, by converting relatively low-valued consumption into higher-valued consumption. As such transfers of consumption take place, the respective marginal values converge on b, the marginal value of present consumption when consumption is steady. Recall that at maximum utility, the marginal values of goods are in proportion to their price. In this scenario, where $(1 + r)/(1 + \rho) = 1$, and the individual can rearrange consumption over time by either borrowing or lending, the gains will be a maximum when $x_1^U = x_2^U = x_1^0$.

Another way to view the gains from even consumption is to consider the "total" benefits of consuming various levels of present consumption. These total benefits are measured by the area under the compensated (Hicksian) demand curve. These areas represent the amounts of future income the consumer would be willing to pay to consume the specified level of present consumption. Denote the areas under the demand curve up to $x_1^0 - \Delta x$, between $x_1^0 - \Delta x$ and x_1^0, and between x_1^0 and $x_1^0 + \Delta x$ as A, B, and C, respectively. Then the total benefit from consuming x_1^0 for two years is $2A + 2B$. On the other hand, the total benefits from the feast/famine pattern are $(A + B + C) + A = 2A + B + C < 2A + 2B$, since $C < B$ due to the negative slope of the Hicksian demand curve. Thus income is valued more highly if it is consumed at an even rather than an uneven rate.

The analysis must be modified slightly if positive time preference or market interest rates are present and not equal to each other. Instead of constant consumption, consumption will either rise steadily or fall steadily at some rate given by the solution to Eq. (12-15). It is still the case that consumption will not be erratic, in the sense of varying up and down over time, but it will not be literally constant. If income is expected to be uneven, e.g., highest during a person's middle years, individuals will, even under these more general assumptions, endeavor to even out consumption by, in this case, borrowing when they are young and lending during middle age, in anticipation of retirement.

The increase in the value of goods resulting from even versus uneven consumption explains why resources are spent to store seasonably produced goods for future use. Although apples, for example, are all harvested in the fall, it is possible, through controlled climate storage, to spread their consumption throughout the year. Other procedures, such as canning and freezing, accomplish the same end. It is worthwhile for producers to engage in these costly activities only because consumers place a sufficiently higher value on these goods when they can be consumed over the entire year, rather than all at once. (Of course, storage encourages greater production for the same reasons.)

"Speculators" include people who purchase goods now for later resale. If the supply of oil, say, is interrupted, these individuals will purchase oil now for storage, further reducing the present supply and thus increasing the price above what would currently exist with this activity. The motives of the speculators are, of course, simply to buy low and sell high. However, an individual can only earn (produce) income in this manner if something of value is being produced for consumers. What is in fact being produced is the smoothing out of consumption. Although speculators always get a bad press regarding their withholding of goods from the market in the present, what is usually not noted is that when they inevitably resell those goods, the supply will be *greater,* and therefore the price lower, than if those goods had not been originally withdrawn. The price, and the flow of consumption, will be more even; it is this increase in the value of goods that speculators produce. It also follows that if an anticipated supply interruption does not materialize, then the preceding activity will not produce a valuable service for consumers, and at least some of the individuals engaging in this unproductive activity will suffer a loss in wealth.

The desire to even out consumption is the basis of the *permanent income hypothesis,* due to Milton Friedman,[†] and the *life cycle hypothesis,* developed by Franco Modigliani and others.[‡] If income can be costlessly traded across time at the prevailing interest rate, changes in income are identical to changes in wealth. Therefore, a temporary (one-period) increase in income is apt to have a relatively small effect on current consumption, since that wealth increase will be spread over all time periods. It would be odd if the utility function were such that the income (wealth) elasticity of current consumption were close to unity, and close to zero for future consumption. Of course, as one got older, leaving fewer years to consume income, changes in income could be expected to have relatively larger effects on current consumption. This result, however, depends upon an assumption that the utility of one's heirs is weighted less than one's own utility. If one derives utility from the anticipated future consumption of one's heirs equally to one's own utility, then there would be no effect of age on the propensity to consume increases in wealth.

Suppose, for example, in a given year, two individuals each have an income of $30,000, but individual A has this income every year, whereas individual B usually earns $20,000, but had unusually good fortune this year. Which individual

[†] Milton Friedman, *A Theory of the Consumption Function,* National Bureau of Economic Research, Princeton University Press, Princeton, N. J., 1957.

[‡] See, in particular, Franco Modigliani and R. Blumberg, "Utility Analysis and the Consumption Function: An Interpretation of Cross Section Data," in *Post Keynesian Economics,* K. Kurihara, ed., Rutgers University Press, New Brunswick, N. J., 1954, and Menahem Yaari, "On the Consumer's Lifetime Allocation Process, *International Economic Review,* 5:304–317, 1964.

is likely to save more (or dissave less)? Individual *B* has had a temporary increase in income. Assuming capital markets are available so that he or she is able to transfer this income to the future, this increase in wealth will be spread out over many time periods. The individual will do this by saving. Saving can take many forms, e.g., purchasing bonds, or perhaps purchasing consumer durables, such as a house or car, or investing in one's education. Thus we would expect persons with temporary increases in income to have greater savings rates than those consuming near their "permanent" or normal income.[†]

The Fisher Separation Theorem

In the preceding analysis we have treated the income received by an individual as exogenously fixed in each time period. Suppose now consumers can choose among alternative income plans, so that the income earned in a given year is part of the utility maximization decision. For example, individuals make career choices in which patterns of income often differ substantially. A person could enter the labor force right after high school and immediately start earning income in some trade. Alternatively, the individual can attend college and perhaps a graduate or professional school, e.g., law or medicine. In that case, income will be very low in the present, but eventually higher than that produced with no post-high school training. Or, several business investments might be possible, with varying "cash flows." What strategy is consistent with utility maximization?

Consider Fig. 12-4, in which a production possibilities frontier $g(x_1,x_2) = k$ is indicated. This function represents the locus of alternative income streams available to an individual. Whatever point the person chooses along this frontier, say point $A = (x_1^*,x_2^*)$, income can then be transferred across time by either borrowing or lending at the market interest rate r. Thus a wealth line $W = x_1^* + x_2^*/(1 + r)$ is implied, with slope $-(1 + r)$. The consumer chooses a point along this line which maximizes utility of consumption.

It is geometrically obvious that under these conditions (most crucially, the assumption of borrowing and lending at the same interest rate), *the consumer will achieve the highest indifference level by first choosing that income stream that maximizes wealth, and then rearranging consumption so as to maximize utility.* This famous result is known as the Fisher separation theorem, after Irving Fisher, who first propounded it.[‡] The algebraic analysis of this proposition is formally identical to that presented earlier, in Chap. 10, on Adam Smith's famous dictum, "the division of labor is limited by the extent of the market." This algebra therefore will not be repeated. With extensive markets, increases in income or

---

[†] Friedman never provided a precise conceptual definition of "permanent" income. M. J. Farrell defined "normal" income as that constant flow which had a present value equal to the individual's wealth. However, Friedman meant to allow the possibility that permanent income might rise (or, in general, change) over time. See M. J. Farrell, "The New Theories of the Consumption Function," *Economic Journal,* **69**(276):678–696, 1959.

[‡] See Fisher, *The Theory of Interest,* op. cit.

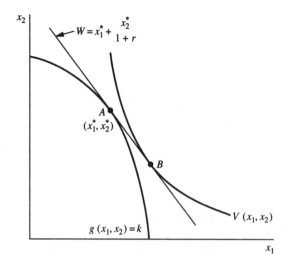

FIGURE 12-4
The Fisher Separation Theorem. Assume an individual can produce a combination of consumption points $g(x_1, x_2) = k$. With efficient capital markets, the bundle produced need not be the bundle consumed. The consumer maximizes utility by first maximizing wealth, and then by borrowing or lending (at some unique interest rate) moves along the budget (wealth) line to some point of tangency B.

wealth are always desirable. We must, however, assume that an individual does not have specific preferences with regard to the various investment or income streams available. In the case of career choice particularly, the theorem must be applied with caution, since individuals commonly are not indifferent to the nonpecuniary aspects of the various alternatives. However, the theorem still applies in a marginal sense: as the pecuniary wealth of some career increases relative to others, more individuals will be attracted to it.[†]

Lastly, the preceding argument assumes that the individual can borrow and lend at the same rate. Typically, however, individuals borrow at a higher rate of interest than that at which they lend. If the individual wishes to transfer income from the future to the present, he or she can do that at price $1 + r_b$ ("b" for borrowing); transfers of income from the present to the future are transacted at price $1 + r_l$ ("l" for lending). The effects of this are shown on Fig. 12-5. Point L on the production frontier is where the wealth line is tangent at the lending price $1 + r_l$. The individual can move "northwest" along the line LL', i.e., toward more future consumption and less present consumption. The extension of the line beyond the tangency point L is not available. Likewise, the consumer can transfer income to the present along the steeper line BB', but could not lend along the extension of this line beyond B. The set of feasible consumption points is that contained by the boundary $L'LBB'$.

It is obvious that without more detailed knowledge of the individual's utility function, in particular, knowledge of the marginal value of present consumption in the neighborhood of section LB of the production frontier, it is not possible

---

[†] Adam Smith first spoke of "compensating differentials" in wages to offset undesirable nonpecuniary aspects of jobs, and predicted that garbage collectors would likely be paid as well as teachers for that reason.

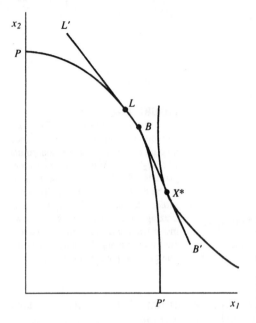

FIGURE 12-5
Utility Maximization When the Borrowing Rate Exceeds the Lending Rate. When the borrowing rate exceeds the lending rate, the Fisher separation theorem may not hold. Maximization of wealth may not lead to utility maximization.

to determine which segment of $L'LBB'$ the consumer will choose. As drawn, the utility maximum occurs at X^* along BB'; however, it could have as easily been drawn to occur along $L'L$. The individual's present wealth at X^*, evaluated using the higher interest rate r_b, is $W^* = x_1^* + x_2^*/(1 + r_b)$. This might in fact be a lower number than some point along $L'L$, where a higher price of future consumption, $(1 + r_l)$, prevails. Thus the exact correspondence of wealth and utility maximization is not present when borrowing and lending rates diverge.

Real versus Nominal Interest Rates

The previous discussion was entirely in terms of trading off one good for another, i.e., some real amount of consumption in one time period for some real amount of consumption in another time period. Most commonly, however, borrowing and lending contracts are stated in *nominal* terms, i.e., the monetary unit of account. Such contracts are of course always "forward-looking," meaning repayment of a loan will take place in the future, not in the past. If loan contracts are stated in dollars, say, the borrowers and lenders will attempt to incorporate into the contract any anticipated change in the value of dollars relative to goods. (If the contract were specified in any unit at all, say gold, the parties would attempt to build in anticipated changes in the price of that unit, i.e., gold.) We say *anticipated* changes, since when the contract is formed, the actual change in the value of the monetary unit is not known. The rate of interest fully adjusted for any changes in the unit of account of a loan contract is called the *real* rate of interest; it is what we have been dealing with thus far.

With continuous compounding of interest (see Chap. 2, Sec. 9), a loan of initial principal P, earning r percent per year, will have a future value after t

years of Pe^{rt}. However, suppose inflation is anticipated to occur at g percent per year. Any nominal amount P today would depreciate at that rate; in t years, its value would be Pe^{-gt}. The combined effect of real interest and inflation would produce a future value of $Pe^{rt}e^{-gt} = Pe^{(r-g)t}$. To offset the effect of anticipated inflation, interest would be set at $r + g$; in that case, the future value would be restored to Pe^{rt}, if the rate of inflation actually were g. The nominal rate of interest, i, is thus

$$i = r + \text{anticipated rate of inflation} \qquad (12\text{-}16)$$

Equation (12-16) is generally known as the Fisher equation. Letting p be the general price level, the anticipated rate of inflation is generally written $E[(1/p)(dp/dt)]$, where E is the mathematical expectation operator.[†] In terms of discrete time, Eq. (12-16) is only an approximation. The combined effect of the real interest rate r and anticipated inflation rate g would yield a nominal interest rate of $i = (1 + r)(1 + g) = 1 + r + g + rg$. However, for small values of r and g, the term rg is negligible, and Eq. (12-16) can be safely used. Estimation of the real rate of interest has been the subject of substantial research; it has been variously estimated in the 1 percent to 2 percent range, though the extent of its variation over time is the subject of debate.[‡]

Market rates of interest also incorporate a premium for the riskiness of the loan. Risk increases the variability of income; the previous analysis suggests that there should be such a risk premium in the market, to compensate for this lowering of the total value of consumption. The premium for risk is evident in the market for capital. For example, bonds issued by corporations promise higher interest than bonds issued by the U.S. government for the same time period. Corporate bonds are also rated by various rating services such as Moody's and Standard & Poor's; the interest that corporations must promise on their bonds generally increases as their ratings worsen, and the realized yields (lower than the promised yields, due to occasional defaults) are also higher to compensate for the greater variability in outcomes as risk increases. Lastly, the average long-term yield on equity capital, i.e., stocks, wherein dividends are contingent on the existence of corporate profits, is larger than the average long-term yields on bonds, reflecting the greater risk of stocks versus bonds. Thus we could write the Fisher equation as

$$i = r + E\left[\left(\frac{1}{p}\right)\left(\frac{dp}{dt}\right)\right] + \text{risk premium} \qquad (12\text{-}17)$$

The measurement of these quantities is the subject of much current research.[§]

[†] We will deal with uncertainty and mathematical expectation in the next chapter.

[‡] See, for example, *Ibbotson Associates, Stocks, Bonds, Bills and Inflation: 1987 [Annual] Yearbook,* Ibbotson Associates, Chicago, 1987.

[§] Most modern texts in corporate finance contain summaries and references to this research. See, for example, Richard A. Brealey and Stewart C. Myers, *Principles of Corporate Finance, 3rd Edition,* McGraw-Hill, New York, pp. 569–570, 1988.

12.2 THE DETERMINATION OF
THE INTEREST RATE

The rate of interest is a price that appears in the market. Probably no other price has engendered as much public and private hostility as this particular price, at which consumption is traded across time. Its persistence through history, in spite of religious and secular laws forbidding or restricting loans at interest, is testimony to the importance of its function.

It is perhaps best to first inquire as to why interest rates are positive, and whether they could reasonably be negative. Of course, the prospect of inflation and the presence of risk both increase the observed rates. We mean to inquire as to the existence of a positive *real* rate of interest. Following Fisher and Bohm-Bawerk, we shall consider, in turn, the effects of time preference, economic growth, and the conditions of production, i.e., the ability of society to increase future consumption by producing goods in the present which enhance future productivity.[†]

Consider first whether a negative real interest rate can prevail. Consider a pure trading economy, such as a World War II prisoner of war camp, in which no production takes place, and "income" arrives periodically in the form of Red Cross packages. Suppose, in addition, that it is impossible to store wealth for anything but a brief time period. The individuals in the camp will all attempt to even out their flow of consumption. Suppose now it becomes known that incomes will be declining in the future. In that case, each person would try to trade some present consumption for future consumption. Such trades could be made by sacrificing presently available goods in return for sharing the other person's Red Cross parcels in the future. In the absence of preference for earlier consumption, the simultaneous efforts of all individuals to transfer consumption to the future would lead to a negative interest rate. Crucial to this outcome is the assumption that wealth cannot be costlessly stored. If wealth can be costlessly stored, the real interest rate could never be negative. One would never in that case loan, say, $100 today in return for $95 next year; it would suffice simply to store the $100 for a year. Thus a negative real interest rate could only exist if sufficient individuals wished to shift income to the future, for example in anticipation of falling incomes, and if it is costly to store wealth over that time period.

Suppose, instead, that economic growth is taking place, so that individuals anticipate that future incomes will be higher than present income. In this case, the desire to even out consumption would lead individuals to contract with each other to shift future consumption to the present. Any one person can do this by promising to trade some amount of future income to another person, in return for receiving income in the present from that person. However, whereas it is possible for some of the individuals in the economy to accomplish this, it is impossible

---

[†]These three reasons for the existence of a positive interest rate can be found in Bohm-Bawerk's *Capital and Interest,* translated by William Smart as *The Positive Theory of Capital,* Books for Libraries Press, Freeport, N.Y., 1971.

for all to do so. Individuals are not really consuming next year's income; they are simply trading with other persons in the same economy. Next year's income cannot be consumed until it is produced. The simultaneous effort to transfer future income to the present will create a premium for sacrificing present consumption. As this premium increases, more individuals will be willing to make the sacrifice. Exhaustion of the gains from trade will lead to that premium, i.e., price of present consumption in terms of future consumption forgone, for which all individuals' marginal values of present consumption are the same.

Similar reasoning applies in the case where individuals have positive rates of time preference, so that the indifference curves cut through the 45° ray in Fig. 12-2 at a slope of $-(1 + \rho)$. This assumption is simply another reason why consumers would wish to transfer future income to the present. The same analysis as in the preceding paragraph applies; the simultaneous efforts to accomplish this will create a positive price for earlier availability of goods.

The foregoing analysis takes future income as exogenous; the individuals could do nothing to affect the levels of future income that would become available. Let us now incorporate this important aspect into the analysis. It is possible to increase future income by diverting present income to the production of "capital goods," which yield no consumption in and of themselves, but which increase the marginal product of other inputs in production, so that larger incomes can be produced in the future. Diverting resources into the production of tractors, computers, education, and the like costs society present consumption, but leads to higher future incomes. The ability to accomplish this "roundabout" production affects the rate of interest.

The simplest theoretical device along these lines is perhaps that used by the distinguished theorist Frank Knight. Knight contemplated Robinson Crusoe, stranded on an island, with a food supply consisting of an edible *Crusonia* bush, which grows exogenously at some constant rate, r, say 10 percent per year. It in fact grows at this constant rate no matter how small or large it is, that is, no matter how much of the bush Crusoe should partake at any given time. The situation is depicted in Fig. 12-6. Current consumption is plotted along the horizontal axis; future consumption is plotted vertically. The entire bush consists of a level of consumption C_1, which if consumed would lead to starvation, and if none is eaten, $C_2 = (1 + r)C_1$ in the next time period. In this case, Crusoe's budget constraint is the straight-line production frontier defined by the edible bush, with slope $-(1 + r)$. No matter what rate of time preference Crusoe might have, as long as his utility function is strictly increasing (Crusoe is not sated) and quasi-concave, and ruling out boundary solutions, at the utility maximum tangency point, his marginal value of present consumption must be $-(1 + r)$.[†] In this case, production conditions completely determine the real rate of interest. With pervasive technology of this sort, so that any number of individuals could trade

---

[†]If the bush in fact *shrank* at some rate s, and any part spoiled once removed from the bush, so that storage was impossible, Crusoe would face the negative real rate of interest s.

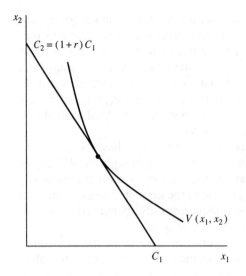

FIGURE 12-6
Intertemporal Consumption in a Crusoe Economy with Constant Marginal Cost of Present Consumption. If technology is such that one unit of present consumption can always be transformed into $(1 + r)$ units of future consumption, then the interest rate must be r, no matter what an individual's rate of time preference might be.

present for future consumption along this frontier, the rate of interest in a many-person economy would be the constant growth rate, r.

Assume now that production is such that current and future consumption can be produced along some concave frontier, as shown in Fig. 12-7. In a single-person economy, the rate of interest will be determined by the tangency representing the utility maximum subject to the production constraint. Both the rate of time preference, if present, and the (changing) marginal cost of transforming present consumption into future consumption determine the interest rate. In a many-person economy, the production frontier defines the marginal cost (supply) curve of present consumption in terms of future consumption forgone; the preferences of

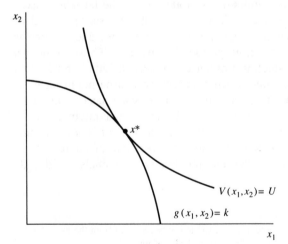

FIGURE 12-7
Market Determination of the Interest Rate. In a society where present consumption can be transformed into future consumption according to some concave production frontier, the market rate of interest will be determined where consumers' marginal value of present consumption equals the marginal opportunity cost of present consumption.

individuals would determine the demand for present consumption. Exhaustion of gains from exchange would lead to the establishment of a single market price such that for all participants in the market, the marginal subjective value of present consumption in terms of forgone future consumption would equal the marginal opportunity cost, in terms of future consumption forgone, of providing that level of present consumption.[†]

12.3 STOCKS AND FLOWS

For the most part, goods that provide income in the future are *durable*. Capital can consist of intermediate goods, which are used only once in some productive process, but interest rates and time preference are not directly relevant for such goods. Most interest (no pun intended) in capital goods focuses on those goods which last over several or many time periods. In that case we have to distinguish the physical item, called the *stock,* from the *flow* of service (per unit time) derived from the stock.

A convenient illustration of these concepts is the distinction between a house, and the flow of housing services we derive from owning or renting a house. When we rent housing, we purchase the service flow for periods of time. If we purchase the house itself, we are purchasing the stock. Owning the stock (the house) entitles you to consume the entire future service flow, for the duration of the existence of the stock, and also obligates you to pay any costs associated with ownership, e.g., property taxes, maintenance, and the like. The price of the stock is therefore the present value of the anticipated net rents (value of service flow, per unit time, net of costs) for the indefinite future. Let t = time, and suppose the stock lasts from $t = 0$ to $t = T$. If the net rental value is some constant R, the price of the stock is

$$P = \int_0^T Re^{-rt}dt = \left(\frac{1}{r}\right)R(1 - e^{-rT}) \qquad (12\text{-}18)$$

In general, R varies over time: $R = R(t)$. In that case, all anticipated net rents are incorporated into the price of the stock, P. With efficient markets, if some news occurs which changes the value of R at some future time, that news will quickly be "capitalized" into the price P.

In the case where $T \to \infty$,

$$P = \frac{R}{r} \qquad (12\text{-}19)$$

[†] In the second chapter on general equilibrium, we shall explore a model in which two factors, labor and capital, are used to produce two "goods," capital and a consumption good. In that case, the implied rental rate of capital, R, equals the marginal product of capital, $MP_{K'}$ times the price P of capital; by division, the interest rate $r = R/P = MP_K$. In that model, the interest rate is determined by the relative price of the capital and consumption goods, and the relative intensities of use of labor and capital in the production of those goods. See Chapter 16.

With, say, $1000 in hand and a permanent interest rate of .10, interest of $100 can be withdrawn every year. The opportunity cost of consuming the principal (the stock) is the forgone perpetual flow of $100 per year. Alternatively, the ("permanent") rental rate on some asset divided by the price of the asset is the implied interest rate: $r = R/P$.

In fact, the present value of rents beyond a generation or two is very small, for common levels of interest rates. The value of the stock, taken from $t = T$ to $t = \infty$, is

$$P = \int_T^\infty Re^{-rt}dt = \left(\frac{1}{r}\right)Re^{-rT} \tag{12-20}$$

If, for example, $T = 50$ and $r = .10$, less than 1 percent of the value of the asset is accounted for by the indefinite future past 50 years.[†] Thus it is often possible to approximate closely the present value of any long-lived asset with the simple formula (12-19), $P = R/r$. In present value calculations, the interest rate is often referred to as the *discount* rate, since using it has the effect of arithmetically lowering the nominal value of future income.

The proper interest rate to use in these formulas is the rate that reflects the opportunity cost of the funds in terms of their use either in alternative investment projects or in the production of present consumption. The risk associated with the level of future rents, based on actual uncertainty about the future, is part of the opportunity cost of using present funds to build capital which produces income in the future. Risk means that there is some chance that part or all of the current consumption sacrificed to build an asset may be for naught; the anticipated future income may never fully materialize. Thus the appropriate interest rate in these calculations would include the real rate plus the risk premium. The ratio of the price of publicly traded corporate stocks to current dividends is reported on the stock market tables as the "price-earnings" ratio. Typical numbers are 8 to 15; 5 is considered low, and 20 is high. If the current earnings are the expected average future earnings, the reciprocals of these numbers may approximate "rates of return on equity capital," i.e., the interest rate reflecting the opportunity cost of investing in those corporations, taking into account their riskiness.

Let us now investigate how the prices and quantities of stocks and flows, and the rate of investment, are affected by changes in interest rates.[‡] In Fig. 12-8, panel *(a)*, the supply and demand for *housing*, the service flow of shelter, is indicated. The supply curve is drawn vertically, to represent that the supply of

---

[†] The famous French mathematician Blaise Pascal once argued that, considering the infinity of afterlife, prudence dictated participation in religion. He neglected to take discounting to present value into account, which is why the young frequently ignore his advice and the old take it. See Azzi and Ehrenberg, *op. cit.*, Chap. 1.

[‡] This discussion is adapted from James Witte, Jr., "The Microfoundations of the Social Investment Function," *Journal of Political Economy*, 71:441–456, October 1963.

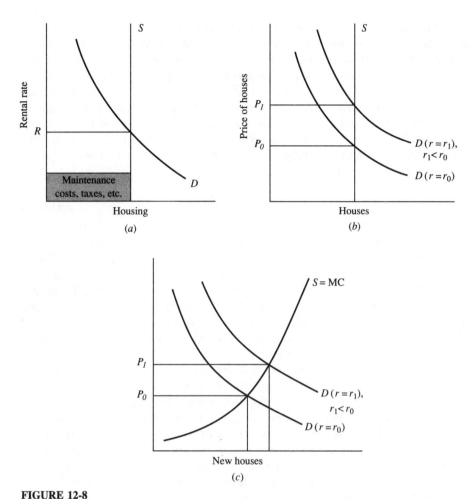

FIGURE 12-8
Stocks and Flows. Panel *(a)* shows the demand and supply for the *flow* of housing services; these curves are largely unaffected by changes in the interest rate. The demand for the *stock* of houses shifts up in panel *(b)* when the interest rate falls. The quantity of new houses supplied therefore increases due to the increase in the price of houses, as shown in panel *(c)*.

housing units is very large and cannot change a great deal in the short run. Of course, at any moment of time, some houses are being demolished and others are being built. For simplicity, assume that this supply curve represents a "steady state" of net housing supply. The demand for the service flow of housing is derived from utility maximization in the same way as the demand for any other good or service is derived. The fact that houses are sometimes rented and sometimes purchased has to do with minimizing the transactions costs associated with obtaining shelter in these various ways. A market rental price R of housing would be established.

Suppose now the real interest rate falls, from r_0 to r_1, due to some exogenous factor, say, lowered anticipated future economic growth or greater security regarding the existence of future income. Changes in the real interest rate would have no predictable effect on the demand for housing relative to other contemporaneous goods. A fall in the interest rate is a decrease in the price of present relative to future consumption; the *mix* of present goods, i.e., the amount of shelter versus food and clothing demanded, should not be affected in any particular way. Thus we would expect no change in the rental price R. In panel *(b)*, however, the demand and supply of *houses* is shown. The market price P is the present value of net rents:

$$P = \frac{(R - C)}{r} \qquad (12\text{-}21)$$

where C = annual obligations incurred by the owners of housing, such as maintenance costs and taxes. Costs C are represented by the shaded part of total annual rents in panel *(a)*. A fall in r means the premium for present consumption has fallen; future consumption is now relatively more highly valued. Therefore, any asset that generates future income is now more highly valued. The demand for owning such an asset therefore shifts out, as shown in panel *(b)*. The price P of the house (the stock), representing the present value of all anticipated future housing services, therefore increases.

An increase in the current price of houses has an obvious effect on the market for new houses. In panel *(c)*, the demand and supply of *new* houses is shown. When the interest rate falls, the demand for new houses shifts out, since owning an asset that provides income in the future is now relatively more valuable. Therefore, the prices of new (and old) houses increases; production will increase until the marginal cost of producing new houses equals consumers' marginal values of new houses. The housing stock will start to rise above its previous level. In the short run, there will be a negligible effect on rentals, as the housing stock is already very large. However, over time, the housing stock will increase above its former level, increasing the supply of housing services, and thereby lowering housing rental prices. If the new rate of interest is permanently lower, some new, larger, steady state stock of houses and housing supply will exist.

This analysis shows the futility of policies to "make housing more affordable" by attempting to lower the real interest rate. Even if the monetary authorities could actually do that (problematical, at best), the short-term effect is simply to raise the price of houses. Rental values are unaffected by such a policy; the only change will be in the mix of interest and principal in the mortgage payment. In the long run, when a larger housing stock prevails, some benefits might accrue to future home purchasers. However, if this result were achieved through the distortion of capital prices, i.e., if the price of present consumption were subsidized from other types of income, the economy as a whole would suffer some loss of efficiency, i.e., lost gains from trade. It is always possible to make certain individuals better off by subsidizing the interest *they* would have to pay on some loan contract, e.g., a home mortgage; enhancing everyone's wealth by such a procedure is another matter entirely.

Other questions can be addressed using the same framework. In 1978, voters in California passed the famous Proposition 13, which drastically lowered property taxes. It was sold to the public partly as a means to reduce rental prices. Of course, considering panel *(a)* above, it could do no such thing, at least in the short run, since neither the supply nor the demand for housing services was affected by the law. However, by lowering the costs C of housing ownership, net rents to property owners were increased. The price of houses would therefore rise, as shown by Eq. (12-21), producing increased new construction of houses. In the long run, rental prices would decrease, but only due to the larger supply of housing services resulting from the larger housing stock.[†]

PROBLEMS

1. Consider the utility functions

(a)
$$U(x) = \sum \left(\frac{1}{1+\rho} \right)^i \log x_i$$

(b)
$$U(x) = \sum \left(\frac{1}{1+\rho} \right)^i x_i^\alpha \qquad 0 < \alpha < 1$$

and assume an individual with these preferences and endowments $x_1^0, \ldots, x_n^0$ maximizes utility subject to the wealth constraint, with interest rate r. Prove that consumption in any time period (beyond the first) is a constant times consumption in the previous time period. Show that this constant is greater (less) than unity if $r > \rho$ $(r < \rho)$.

2. Suppose you own an apartment complex that generates R per year in rentals. It can be sold outright for some price P; alternatively, shares of ownership can be sold.

 (a) Plotting "present consumption" on the horizontal axis and "future consumption" (assumed infinite) on the vertical axis, indicate the feasible consumption points generated by selling ownership shares.

 (b) Suppose you hear that the value of the complex has fallen in half. This could be due to either a doubling of the interest rate or that half the complex has burned down. Under what conditions, if any, would you be indifferent to the cause of this wealth loss?[‡]

3. Currently, in the United States, interest on a home mortgage is deducted from income when calculating federal income taxes. How would the removal of this provision affect the wealth of

---

[†] On the other hand, many local property taxes are directly tied to local community services, such as schools. People move to certain cities and neighborhoods specifically to pay those taxes, i.e., to be able to consume the local services they provide. In that case, defeat, say, of a school levy might actually depress house prices, if the main purpose of moving to that locality was to consume the local school district.

[‡] Adapted from A. Alchian and W. Allen, *Exchange and Production*, 3d ed., Wadsworth, Belmont, Calif. 1983.

(a) Current home owners?

(b) Prospective home owners?

(c) People in the construction business?

4. Suppose sheep could reproduce so as to increase the stock of sheep 10 percent per year, forever. Would the real interest rate become 10 percent?

5. "Invest in land. Population grows steadily, and land is relatively fixed, so rentals will increase over time. Therefore, land will yield a profitable return." Evaluate. How does your answer depend, if at all, on the validity of the premises of population growth and fixed land?

6. Consider that current U.S. tax law requires corporations to value assets based on *historical* costs, not replacement value.

(a) How would inflation (on this account) affect the present value of future profits and the price of the stock?

(b) Consider that gold and owner-occupied houses are not depreciable for tax purposes under U.S. law. How would an unanticipated increase in inflation affect the price of these assets relative to others?

(c) "Capital gains" (increases in the value of some asset) are taxed on a nominal basis; inflation thus creates spurious taxable capital gains. Owner-occupied houses, however, are exempt if a new and more expensive house is purchased within a year. On this basis, how does (unanticipated?) inflation affect the relative price of these assets?

7. If home mortgages are based on fixed monthly payments, how does an increase in inflation affect the real burden of repayment over time? How might this affect a person's ability to secure such loans?

8. The voters in a certain urban area enact "greenbelt" legislation, which restricts development of surrounding rural land for housing development. What is the effect on

(a) Current and future rental rates?

(b) Current and future prices of houses?

9. Suppose cars are on average driven 10,000 miles per year, and gasoline retails at $1.00 per gallon. How much is it worth to consumers and to car manufacturers to increase the mileage of cars by 1 mile per gallon? Assume various initial mileages, e.g., 15 mpg, 20 mpg, 25 mpg.

SELECTED REFERENCES

Bohm-Bawerk, E.: *Capital and Interest,* translated by William Smart, as *The Positive Theory of Capital,* Books for Libraries Press, Freeport, N.Y., 1971.

Brealey, R. A., and S. C. Myers: *Principles of Corporate Finance, 3rd Edition,* McGraw-Hill, New York, 1988, pp. 569–570.

Fisher, I.: *The Theory of Interest,* August M. Kelley, New York, 1970. (First Edition, The MacMillan Co., New York, 1930.) This book is so clear, you may become convinced you knew this material all along, even if you didn't.

Friedman, M.: *A Theory of the Consumption Function,* National Bureau of Economic Research, Princeton University Press, Princeton, N. J., 1957.

Green, H. A. John: *Consumer Theory,* rev. ed., The MacMillan Co., London, 1976. Contains an excellent discussion of intertemporal choice and uncertainty.

Ibbotson Associates, *Stocks, Bonds, Bills and Inflation: 1987 [Annual] Yearbook,* Ibbotson Associates, Chicago, 1987.

Modigliani, F., and R. Blumberg: "Utility Analysis and the Consumption Function: An Interpretation of Cross Section Data," in *Post Keynesian Economics*, K. Kurihara, (ed.), Rutgers University Press, New Brunswick, N. J., 1954.

Olson, Mancur, and Martin J. Bailey: "Positive Time Preference," *Journal of Political Economy*, **89**(1):1–25, February 1981. A readable discussion of the issues surrounding the existence and evidence for positive time preference.

Strotz, R.: "Myopia and Inconsistency in Dynamic Utility Maximization," *Review of Economic Studies*, **23**(3):165–180, 1956.

Witte, J. Jr.: "The Microfoundations of the Social Investment Function," *Journal of Political Economy*, **71**:441–456, October 1963.

Yaari, M., "On the Consumer's Lifetime Allocation Process," *International Economic Review*, **5**: 304–317, 1964.

CHAPTER

13

BEHAVIOR UNDER UNCERTAINTY

13.1 UNCERTAINTY AND PROBABILITY

Uncertainty is a pervasive fact of life. A mathematical analysis of behavior under uncertainty requires use of the concept of probability. We first give three examples of how the probability of an event may be assigned.

1. There are two possible outcomes in a coin toss: a head or a tail. If it may be assumed that the two events are *equally likely* to occur, they must have the same probability. The probability of a head and the probability of a tail will each be 0.5.

2. In the United States roughly 8 out of every 1000 people die each year. We can say the probability that a person in the United States will die within one year is 0.008. Here the probability of an event is equal to the *relative frequency* with which the event occurs when the experiment is repeated a large number of times under similar conditions. Of course, people of different age, sex, or state of health represent dissimilar conditions. If we know that the person is, say, over 85 years old, the probability of death will become 0.14 because people in that age group die with that relative frequency.

3. When an entrepreneur introduces a new product into the market, the concepts of equally likely events and relative frequency are not very helpful. However, as long as a person's preferences for actions with uncertain outcomes satisfy some consistency conditions, his or her *subjective probabilities* of different possible events can be determined.[†] For example, the entrepreneur may assign a probability of, say, 0.71, that the new product is a flop and a probability of

---

[†]See L. J. Savage, *The Foundations of Statistics,* John Wiley & Sons, Inc., New York, 1954.

0.29 that it is a success. If we are interested in predicting behavior, it is these subjective probabilities that matter.

The preceding examples correspond to three different interpretations of probability. Regardless of which interpretation one adopts, the mathematical theory of probability is the same. Suppose S is the set of all possible outcomes and E is a subset of S. Denote the probability of event E by $Pr(E)$. A probability function is a function that assigns real numbers to subsets of S and that satisfies the following conditions:

1. For any event E, $Pr(E) > 0$.
2. $Pr(S) = 1$.
3. For any finite or infinite sequence of mutually exclusive events $E_1, E_2, \ldots$, $Pr(E_1 \cup E_2 \cup \cdots) = Pr(E_1) + Pr(E_2) \cdots$.

In this book space limitations dictate that we provide only the most cursory introduction to the concepts of probability, random variable, mean, and variance. The reader should consult any of the various textbooks on probability or mathematical statistics for a more detailed treatment of this important theory.

Random Variables and Probability Distributions

A random variable is a function that maps an outcome to a real variable. In a coin toss, for example, we can define a random variable X such that $X = 47$ if the coin lands on a head and $X = 35$ if it lands on a tail. Associated with each random variable X is a (cumulative) *distribution function F* such that

$$F(x) = \Pr[X \le x] \tag{13-1}$$

Continuing our example, if the coin is a fair coin, the distribution of X is given by

$$F(x) = \begin{cases} 1 & \text{for } x \ge 47 \\ 0.5 & \text{for } 47 > x \ge 35 \\ 0 & \text{for } x < 35 \end{cases} \tag{13-2}$$

Note that a distribution function must have the following properties:

1. $F(\infty) = 1$
2. $F(-\infty) = 0$
3. $F(x)$ is monotonically nondecreasing in x.

The distribution given in Eq. (13-2) obviously satisfies these conditions.

Random variables can be discrete or continuous. If a random variable X is discrete, it can only take on a finite or countably infinite number of values, say, $x_1, x_2, x_3, \ldots$. The *probability density function f* associated with X is

$$f(x) = \Pr[X = x] \tag{13-3}$$

Clearly, the probabilities must be nonnegative and sum to one. Therefore, we have:

1. $1 \geq f(x) \geq 0$
2. $\sum_x f(x) = 1$

When a random variable is continuous, the probability that it is (exactly) equal to a prespecified number is zero. We can nevertheless find the probability that the random variable lies in a small interval, $\Pr[x \leq X \leq x + h]$. Dividing this probability by the length of the interval and taking the limit as the length goes to zero, we obtain the *probability density function*:

$$f(x) = \lim_{h \to 0} \frac{\Pr[x \leq X \leq x + h]}{h}$$

$$= \lim_{h \to 0} \frac{F(x + h) - F(x)}{h} \qquad (13\text{-}4)$$

$$= F'(x)$$

The probability density function must also satisfy two conditions:

1. $f(x) \geq 0$
2. $\int_{-\infty}^{\infty} f(x)\,dx = 1$

Note that the value of $f(x)$ can be greater than 1 since it is not a probability.

Mean and Variance

A random variable can be completely characterized by its distribution function. However, it is often useful to summarize the central tendency or the average behavior of the random variable by a real number. The most important measure of central tendency is the *mean*. The mean or the expected value of a random variable x, denoted $E[x]$, is defined by

$$E[x] = \sum_x xf(x) \qquad \text{if } x \text{ is discrete}$$

$$E[x] = \int_{-\infty}^{\infty} xf(x)\,dx \qquad \text{if } x \text{ is continuous} \qquad (13\text{-}5)$$

Example. Consider the following gamble. A fair coin is flipped until a tail appears. You win \$1 if it appears on the first toss, \$2 if it appears on the second, \$4 if it appears on the third toss, and, in general, \$$2^{n-1}$ if it appears on the *n*th toss. Letting the random variable x denote your winnings, the probability of winning \$$2^{n-1}$ is $(\frac{1}{2})^n$. Thus, the expected value of x is

$$E[x] = \sum_n 2^{n-1}\left(\frac{1}{2}\right)^n$$

$$= \frac{1}{2} + \frac{1}{2} + \frac{1}{2} + \cdots \qquad (13\text{-}6)$$

$$= \infty$$

This gamble is known as the St. Petersburg paradox. It is a paradox because people do not seem willing to pay a large sum of money for the right to play this gamble, even though the expected value of the winnings is infinite. One way to reconcile this paradox is to propose that individuals are risk-averse. This is the approach taken by the eighteenth-century mathematician Daniel Bernoulli,[†] and we will discuss it in detail later. Another way is to suggest that your opponent does not have infinite wealth. Suppose your opponent possesses only the modest amount of one billion (10^9) dollars. If a tail appears at or before the 30th toss, your opponent will still be able to pay you the promised amount. After the 30th toss, he will only be able to pay you one billion dollars. The probability that you will get one billion dollars is $f(10^9) = \left(\frac{1}{2}\right)^{31} + \left(\frac{1}{2}\right)^{32} + \cdots = \left(\frac{1}{2}\right)^{30}$. The expected value of a St. Petersburg gamble given this wealth constraint is less than \$16:

$$
\begin{aligned}
E[x] &= \sum_{n=1}^{30} 2^{n-1}\left(\frac{1}{2}\right)^n + 10^9\left(\frac{1}{2}\right)^{30} \\
&= 30(0.5) + 10^9(9.3 \times 10^{-10}) \qquad (13\text{-}7) \\
&= 15.93
\end{aligned}
$$

The formula for expected value extends naturally for functions of random variables. If $u(x)$ is a function of random variable x, then $u(x)$ is itself a random variable and its expected value is given by

$$E[u(x)] = \sum_x u(x)f(x) \qquad \text{if } x \text{ is discrete}$$

$$E[u(x)] = \int_{-\infty}^{\infty} u(x)f(x)dx \qquad \text{if } x \text{ is continuous} \qquad (13\text{-}8)$$

In general, $E[u(x)] \neq u(E[x])$ unless u is linear in x. If $u = a + bx$, where a and b are constants,

$$E[a + bx] = a + bE[x] \qquad (13\text{-}9)$$

The linearity of expected value also applies to two or more random variables. Thus, for any two random variables x and y,

$$E[x + y] = E[x] + E[y] \qquad (13\text{-}10)$$

regardless of whether x and y are independent. Two random variables x and y are

---

[†] See Daniel Bernoulli, "Exposition of a New Theory on the Measurement of Risk," (1738), trans. by L. Sommer, *Econometrica*, **22**:23–36, 1954.

independent if and only if $\Pr[x \leq x^0, y \leq y^0] = \Pr[x \leq x^0] \Pr[y \leq y^0]$ for all x^0 and y^0. If x and y are independent, we also have

$$E[xy] = E[x]E[y] \tag{13-11}$$

Whereas the expected value of a random variable is a measure of its central tendency, the variance indicates the degree of variability of the random variable. The variance of a random variable x, denoted var$[x]$, is defined as

$$\text{var}[x] = E[(x - \mu)^2] \tag{13-12}$$

where $\mu = E[x]$. Equation (13-12) can also be expressed as

$$\begin{aligned}
\text{var}[x] &= E[x^2 - 2x\mu + \mu^2] \\
&= E[x^2] - 2\mu E[x] + \mu^2 \\
&= E[x^2] - 2\mu^2 + \mu^2 \\
&= E[x^2] - \mu^2
\end{aligned} \tag{13-13}$$

Two facts about the variance are worth mentioning. We will state them as two propositions and illustrate with an example.

Proposition 1. For any constants a and b,

$$\text{var}[a + bx] = b^2 \text{var}[x] \tag{13-14}$$

Proof. Let $\mu = E[x]$. Then

$$\begin{aligned}
\text{var}[a + bx] &= E[((a + bx) - (a + b\mu))^2] \\
&= E[b^2(x - \mu)^2] \\
&= b^2 E[(x - \mu)^2] \\
&= b^2 \text{var}[x]
\end{aligned}$$

Proposition 2. If $x_1, \ldots, x_n$ are independent random variables,

$$\text{var}[x_1 + \cdots + x_n] = \text{var}[x_1] + \cdots + \text{var}[x_n] \tag{13-15}$$

Proof. Let $\mu_i = E[x_i]$ for $i = 1, \ldots, n$. Then

$$\begin{aligned}
\text{var}[x_1 + \cdots + x_n] &= E[(x_1 + \cdots + x_n) - (\mu_1 + \cdots + \mu_n)]^2 \\
&= \sum_i (E[(x_i - \mu_i)^2] + 2\sum_{i>j} (E[x_i x_j] - \mu_i \mu_j)
\end{aligned}$$

If x_i and x_j are independent, the second sum is equal to zero and Eq. (13-15) follows.

$E[x_i x_j] - \mu_i \mu_j$ is equal to the covariance between x_i and x_j. Thus, in general,

$$\text{var}[x_1 + x_2] = \text{var}[x_1] + \text{var}[x_2] + 2\,\text{cov}[x_1, x_2] \tag{13-16}$$

Example. Let x be the value of one share of the stock in a firm. If σ^2 is the variance of x, an investment portfolio consisting of n shares in the firm will have a variance of $\text{var}[nx] = n^2\sigma^2$. On the other hand, suppose a person invests one share in n different stocks, $x_1, \ldots, x_n$, whose returns are independent. If each stock has a common variance of σ^2, the variance of the diversified portfolio is only $\text{var}[x_1 + \cdots + x_n] = n\sigma^2$.

13.2 SPECIFICATION OF PREFERENCES

State Preference Approach

Consumer theory as developed in earlier chapters can be readily generalized to cover behavior under uncertainty. Just as an apple consumed today is different from an apple consumed tomorrow, ice cream on a hot day is a different commodity from ice cream on a cold day. In intertemporal problems, the same physical good consumed at different dates is treated as different commodities. In problems related to uncertainty, we can treat the same physical good available at different states of the world as distinct commodities. Using such an approach, utility is defined as a function of *state-contingent commodities*. A state-contingent commodity is a good that can be consumed only if a specified state of the world obtains. An example is a contract that offers to deliver ice cream if the temperature is above 80° F (and nothing otherwise). Suppose there are only two possible states, and let W_1 and W_2 denote the amounts of commodities contingent upon state 1 and state 2, respectively. W_1 and W_2 can be vectors representing bundles of commodities, but very often they are simply scalars representing wealth or composite consumption. If the probabilities of state 1 and state 2 are π_1 and π_2, respectively ($\pi_1 + \pi_2 = 1$), a consumer's preferences can be represented by a utility function,

$$U(W_1, W_2; \pi_1, \pi_2) \tag{13-17}$$

Here utility is defined over the contingent consumption plan (W_1, W_2). The probabilities π_1 and π_2 are included as parameters of the utility function because the value of a state-contingent commodity depends on how likely the state is to occur. If there are complete markets where one can buy state-contingent commodities at exogenous prices, the analysis of consumer's choice under uncertainty is formally equivalent to the certainty case. The consumer will choose W_1 and W_2 so as to maximize utility subject to budget constraints. The resulting demand functions for state-contingent commodities will satisfy all the theorems about demand functions derived in earlier chapters. Whereas the state preference approach is very general, the requirement of complete markets in state-contingent commodities is hard to satisfy. If there are n different goods and s possible states of the world, there have to be ns separate markets. Arrow[†] has shown that trade

---

[†] See Kenneth J. Arrow, "The Role of Securities in the Optimal Allocation of Risk Bearing," *Review of Economic Studies*, **31**:91–96, 1964.

in state-contingent claims (i.e., financial contracts that yield different amounts of money under different states of the world) can be substituted for trade in state-contingent commodities. Then a complete set of markets requires only n goods markets plus s securities markets. It may well be the case that contingent markets are particularly costly to organize because specification and measurement of states are difficult. When state-contingent commodities are not traded in the market, the state preference approach is of limited empirical applicability.

The Expected Utility Hypothesis

The utility function shown in expression (13-17) is very general. It is possible to impose more structure on the utility function if preferences satisfy some additional axioms. Among the more important axioms are the following:

1. *State independence: An uncertain prospect consisting of x in state 1 and y in state 2 is equally preferred to a prospect of y in state 1 and x in state 2 if the probability of receiving x in both prospects is the same.* State-independence means that preferences depend on the probabilities of the states of the world but not on the states themselves. Whether this is reasonable is a matter of the context of the problem. In medical insurance problems, for example, preferences may depend on one's state of health even though all medical expenses are fully covered.

2. *Reduction of compound lotteries: If x is an uncertain prospect consisting of y and z with probabilities π and $1 - \pi$, then a prospect consisting of x and z with probabilities $\hat{\pi}$ and $1 - \hat{\pi}$ is equally preferred to a prospect of y and z with probabilities $\pi\hat{\pi}$ and $1 - \pi\hat{\pi}$.* This axiom asserts that a consumer's preferences for uncertain prospects depend only on the probabilities of receiving the various prizes, not on how these probabilities are formed. The axiom will be violated if, say, the consumer has a love for suspense.

3. *Continuity: If x is preferred to y and y is preferred to z, there exists some probability value π such that y is equally preferred to an uncertain prospect consisting of x and z, where x is realizable with probability π and z with probability $1 - \pi$.* It can be argued that the continuity axiom will not hold when x is two dollars, y is one dollar, and z is death. On the other hand, people do often take the risk of jaywalking to gain a few seconds.

4. *Independence of irrelevant alternativies: If x is preferred to y, then for any z an uncertain prospect consisting of x and z with probabilities π and $1 - \pi$ will be preferred to an uncertain prospect consisting of y and z with the same probabilities.* In the certainty case the independence axiom is a strong assertion, because there can be all sorts of complementarity and substitutability relationships between two goods when they are consumed simultaneously or in a temporal order. In the case of preferences for uncertain prospects, however, the individual will never get x and z together or y and z together. Thus, it is unlikely that the presence of z will affect the preferences for x and y.

Given these postulates it can be proven[†] that preferences for uncertain prospects can be expressed in terms of expected utility. If a prospect consists of prizes W_1 and W_2 with probabilities π_1 and π_2, respectively, we can find a utility function $u(\cdot)$ such that

$$U(W_1, W_2; \pi_1, \pi_2) = \pi_1 u(W_1) + \pi_2 u(W_2) \qquad (13\text{-}18)$$

The function $U(\cdot)$ is often called a *Von Neumann–Morgenstern utility function*, after their pioneering work on decision theory.[‡] Note that preferences are now expressed as the expected value of a utility function. This representation of preferences is simple because utility is additively separable in W_1 and W_2 and is linear in π_1 and π_2. Separability is a result of axiom 4, and linearity is a result of axiom 2. If preferences are not state-independent but the other axioms still hold, utility can be expressed as $U = \pi_1 u^1(W_1) + \pi_2 u^2(W_2)$, where u^1 and u^2 are different functions.

Cardinal and Ordinal Utility

As in the certainty case, the utility function for uncertain prospects is just a convenient way of representing preferences. If prospect x is preferred to or indifferent to prospect y whenever $U(x) \geq U(y)$, then $U(\cdot)$ is a valid utility function. Since $U(x) \geq U(y)$ implies $F(U(x)) \geq F(U(y))$ for any monotonically increasing transformation F, $F(U(\cdot))$ is also a valid utility function. In other words, utility is still an *ordinal* concept in the analysis of behavior under uncertainty.

Example. Let x be an uncertain prospect consisting of prizes W_1 and W_2 with respective probabilities π_1 and π_2. If preferences can be represented by the utility function

$$U(x) = \pi_1 \log W_1 + \pi_2 \log W_2 \qquad (13\text{-}19)$$

then

$$V(x) = e^{U(x)} = W_1^{\pi_1} W_2^{\pi_2} \qquad (13\text{-}20)$$

is also a valid utility function.

In this example, however, there is an important difference between Eqs. (13-19) and (13-20). If we let $u(W) = \log W$, Eq. (13-19) satisfies the expected utility property, whereas it is impossible to express (13-20) as the expected value of a utility function. In general, the expected utility property will not hold under an arbitrary monotonic transformation of the utility function. To preserve the expected utility property, the transformation has to be linear. This

---

[†] See R. D. Luce and H. Raiffa, *Games and Decisions*, John Wiley & Sons, Inc., New York, 1957.
[††] See J. Von Neumann and O. Morgenstern, *Theory of Games and Economic Behavior*, Princeton University Press, Princeton, N. J., 1944.

$a + b\pi_1 u(W_1) + b\pi_2 u(W_2)$

$pato \quad \pi_1 \pi_2 \quad \ell.$

claim is easily verified. Suppose $U = \pi_1 u(W_1) + \pi_2 u(W_2)$, and we subject it to a linear transformation $V = a + bU$ (with $b > 0$). Since $\pi_1 + \pi_2 = 1$, we get

$$V = a + b(\pi_1 u(W_1) + \pi_2 u(W_2))$$

$$= \pi_1(a + bu(W_1)) + \pi_2(a + bu(W_2)) \tag{13-21}$$

Equation (13-21) satisfies the expected utility property with the Von Neumann–Morgenstern utility function equal to $a + bU(\cdot)$. It is important to distinguish clearly between the utility function for an uncertain prospect, $U(x)$, and the Von Neumann–Morgenstern utility function, $u(W)$. Whereas any monotonic transformation of U is a valid utility function representing the same preferences for uncertain prospects, an arbitrary monotonic transformation of u will not necessarily produce a valid Von Neumann–Morgenstern utility function that represents the same preferences. Von Neumann–Morgenstern utility functions are unique only up to linear transformations.

> **Example.** Suppose preferences are represented by Eq. (13-19) in the previous example. The Von Neumann–Morgenstern utility function is $u(W) = \log W$. If we subject u to the monotonic transformation $v = e^u$ and treat v as a Von Neumann–Morgenstern utility function, then the preferences for uncertain prospects are given by
>
> $$V = \pi_1 W_1 + \pi_2 W_2 \tag{13-22}$$
>
> which is clearly different from the original preference structure shown in (13-19) or (13-20).

An index that is unique up to positive linear transformations is sometimes called a *cardinal* index. Once the origin and the interval of increments are determined, the cardinal index is uniquely determined. Temperature is an example of a cardinal scale; so is Von Neumann–Morgenstern utility. A function subject to a linear transformation has the property that the sign of its second derivative is unchanged. Suppose W stands for wealth and $u''(W)$ is negative, so that the marginal utility of wealth is decreasing. Since

$$\frac{d^2}{dW^2}\big(a + bu(W)\big) = bu''(W) \tag{13-23}$$

any increasing linear transformation of u will preserve the property of diminishing marginal utility of wealth. As we will see in the next section, whether the Von Neumann–Morgenstern utility function exhibits increasing or decreasing marginal utility has important implications for behavior toward risk. However, it cannot justify the claim that changes in the level of subjective satisfaction can be compared, because the Von Neumann–Morgenstern utility function is only one (convenient) way to represent consumer preferences.

13.3 RISK AVERSION

In the certainty case, convexity of preferences implies a preference for variety. Figure 13-1 shows the indifference curve for a consumer who is indifferent between *(a)* two apples and no orange and *(b)* no apple and two oranges. Since the indifference curve is convex to the origin, the combination of one apple and one orange is strictly preferred to options *(a)* and *(b)*. Similarly, in the theory of intertemporal consumption, convexity of indifference curves implies that a smooth path of consumption over time is preferred to an erratic path. When we analyze consumer behavior under uncertainty using the state preference approach, indifference curves can be drawn for state-contingent consumption. If we relabel the axes in Fig. 13-1 as "income in state 1" and "income in state 2," the diagram indicates that a sure income of one dollar in either state is preferred to an uncertain income prospect of two dollars in one state and nothing otherwise. In other words, the assumption of convex indifference curves implies that consumers are risk-averse.

Let us now consider the relationship between the convexity of indifference curves and the shape of the Von Neumann–Morgenstern utility function. Along an indifference curve, expected utility is constant. Thus, the indifference curve is defined by

$$\pi_1 u(W_1) + \pi_2 u(W_2(W_1)) \equiv U^0 \tag{13-24}$$

Differentiating (13-24) with respect to W_1, the slope of the indifference curve is

$$\frac{dW_2}{dW_1} = -\frac{\pi_1 u'(W_1)}{\pi_2 u'(W_2)} \tag{13-25}$$

$$\pi_1 \frac{\partial u(W_1)}{W_1} + \pi_2 \left[\frac{\partial u}{\partial W_2} \cdot \frac{\partial W_2}{\partial W_1} \right] = 0$$

$$\frac{\pi_1 u_1'(W_1)}{\pi_2 u_2'(W_2)} = \frac{\partial W_1}{\partial W_1}$$

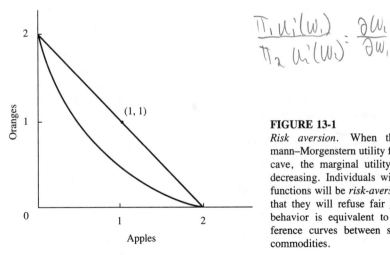

FIGURE 13-1

Risk aversion. When the Von Neumann–Morgenstern utility function is concave, the marginal utility of income is decreasing. Individuals with such utility functions will be *risk-averse*, in the sense that they will refuse fair gambles. Such behavior is equivalent to convex indifference curves between state-contingent commodities.

If indifference curves are convex everywhere, then the second derivative,

$$\frac{d^2 W_2}{dW_1^2} = -\frac{\pi_1 u''(W_1)(\pi_2 u'(W_2))^2 + \pi_2 u''(W_2)(\pi_1 u'(W_1))^2}{(\pi_2 u'(W_2))^3} \tag{13-26}$$

is positive for all W_1 and W_2. In particular, for $W_1 = W_2 = W$, the second derivative is

$$\frac{d^2 W_2}{dW_1^2} = -\frac{\pi_1 \pi_2(\pi_1 + \pi_2)u''(W)u'(W)^2}{(\pi_2 u'(W))^3} = -\frac{\pi_1 u''(W)}{\pi_2^2 u'(W)} \tag{13-27}$$

Expression (13-27) is positive if and only if $u''(W)$ is negative. The assumption that indifference curves are everywhere convex to the origin is equivalent to the assumption that the Von Neumann–Morgenstern utility function is concave.

When the Von Neumann-Morgenstern utility function is concave, marginal utility of income is decreasing. If an individual with a concave utility function is given a 50-50 chance of losing or winning one dollar, we can predict that the individual will not take the gamble. Loosely speaking, this is because the gain in utility as a result of winning one dollar is less than the utility loss from losing the gamble, although we cannot attribute any psychological significance to comparing changes in utility levels. In general, for any individual with a concave utility function, a sure income prospect is preferred to an uncertain income prospect with equal expected value. This is a consequence of *Jensen's inequality*, which states that for any random variable W and any strictly concave function $u(W)$,

$$E[u(W)] < u(E[W]) \tag{13-28}$$

Jensen's inequality is illustrated in Fig. 13-2. Expected utility is given by the height of the chord at $E[W]$, whereas the utility of expected wealth is given by the height of the arc at $E[W]$. On the other hand, if the utility function is convex, the chord will lie above the arc, and the individual will be risk-loving. An individual will be risk-neutral if and only if the utility function is linear in income.

Example. Suppose a person's utility function is $u(W) = \log W$. Since $u''(W) = -1/W^2 < 0$, the person is risk-averse. We have already seen in Sec. 13.1 that the expected value of a St. Petersburg gamble is infinite. However, the expected utility of such a gamble is finite when the person is risk-averse.

$$E[u(W)] = \sum_{n=1}^{\infty} \left(\frac{1}{2}\right)^n \log 2^{n-1}$$

$$= \log 2 \sum_{n=1}^{\infty} (n-1)\left(\frac{1}{2}\right)^n$$

$$= \log 2 \left(\sum_{2}^{\infty} \left(\frac{1}{2}\right)^n + \sum_{3}^{\infty} \left(\frac{1}{2}\right)^n + \sum_{4}^{\infty} \left(\frac{1}{2}\right)^n + \cdots \right)$$

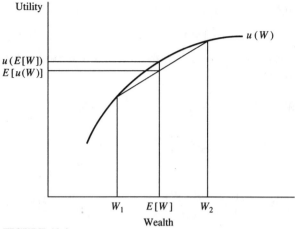

FIGURE 13-2

Jensen's inequality. For any concave (utility) function $u(W)$, $E[u(W)] \leq u[E(W)]$. Concave functions always lie above (or on) the chord joining any two points on the function. If, say, the random variable W varies between W_1 and W_2, the value of the function at the mean, $E[W]$, must be greater than (or equal to, for weak concavity) the expected value of utility, which lies along the chord joining $u(W_1)$ and $u(W_2)$.

$$= \log 2\left(\frac{1}{2} + \frac{1}{4} + \frac{1}{8} + \cdots\right)$$

$$= \log 2 \qquad\qquad (13\text{-}29)$$

In other words, if the person starts with no initial wealth, the certainty equivalent of a St. Petersburg gamble is worth two dollars.

Measures of Risk Aversion

We have seen that convex indifference curves imply risk aversion. A natural measure of the degree of risk aversion is therefore the degree of convexity of the indifference curves. In Eq. (13-27), the magnitude of the second derivative of the indifference curves along the 45° certainty line is proportional to $-u''(W)/u'(W)$. We call this quantity the *coefficient of absolute risk aversion* or the *Arrow-Pratt measure of absolute risk aversion,* after Kenneth Arrow[†] and John Pratt.[‡] The coefficient of absolute risk aversion has implications for the willingness of individuals to accept risk. Suppose an individual has initial wealth W. A risk-averse individual will not be willing to take a fair gamble. The risk premium, $P_x(W)$, is defined as the amount a person is willing to pay to avoid a

---

[†] See Kenneth J. Arrow, *Aspects of the Theory of Risk Bearing,* Yrjo Jahnssonin Saatio, Helsinki, 1965.

[‡] See John W. Pratt, "Risk Aversion in the Small and in the Large," *Econometrica,* **32**:122–136, 1964.

fair gamble x (*with mean* 0 *and variance* σ_x^2). Mathematically, we can write

$$u(W - P_x(W)) \equiv E[u(W + x)] \tag{13-30}$$

Taking a first-order Taylor series approximation on the left and a second-order approximation on the right, we obtain

$$u(W) - P_x(W)u'(W) \approx E\left[u(W) + xu'(W) + \frac{1}{2}x^2u''(W)\right]$$

$$\approx u(W) + \frac{1}{2}\sigma_x^2 u''(W)$$

and therefore

$$P_x(W) \approx \frac{1}{2}\sigma_x^2 \frac{-u''(W)}{u'(W)} \tag{13-31}$$

Thus, the higher the coefficient of absolute risk aversion, the higher the risk premium the individual is willing to pay.

A related measure of risk aversion is the coefficient of *relative* risk aversion, $-Wu''(W)/u'(W)$. Let $\hat{P}_x(W)$ be the proportional risk premium corresponding to a proportional risk x (with mean 0 and variance σ_x^2). Then $\hat{P}_x(W)$ is defined by the relation

$$u(W - W\hat{P}_x(W)) \equiv E[u(W + Wx)] \tag{13-32}$$

Taking Taylor approximations on both sides,

$$u(W) - W\hat{P}_x(W)u'(W) \approx E\left[u(W) + Wxu'(W) + \frac{1}{2}W^2x^2u''(W)\right]$$

and therefore

$$\hat{P}_x(W) \approx \frac{1}{2}\sigma_x^2 \frac{-Wu''(W)}{u'(W)} \tag{13-33}$$

Again, the relative risk premium is higher as the coefficient of relative risk aversion is higher.

Gambling, Insurance, and Diversification

In the absence of restrictions on the shape of the utility function, the expected utility hypothesis is consistent with both risk-taking and risk-avoiding behavior. Friedman and Savage[†] argue that if the utility function is shaped like the one shown in Fig. 13-3, an individual may buy insurance and lotteries at the same time. However, there are two problems with the theory that gambling is a result of nonconcavity of the utility function:

[†] See Milton Friedman and L. J. Savage, "The Utility Analysis of Choices Involving Risk," *Journal of Political Economy*, **56**:279–304, 1948.

1. Since it is relatively inexpensive to effect a gamble, any person with initial wealth falling into the nonconcave range of the utility function will take gambles to leave that range. In Fig. 13-3, an individual with initial wealth $E[W]$ will take even enormous gambles and end up at either W_1 or W_2. Enormous gambles are not common, and once people have taken such gambles they will behave as risk averters.

2. Most gambles have odds that are worse than fair. If gambling is for maximizing expected utility of wealth, the optimal strategy is to place the entire stake in one gamble. The observation that most people divide their stakes into small bets is consistent with the theory that people gamble because of its entertainment value.

When individuals have concave utility functions, they will take steps to reduce their exposure to risk. One approach is to buy market insurance. Suppose an individual has initial wealth W. There is a chance of losing x with probability π due to, say, theft. Assume the person can buy actuarily fair insurance at a premium of πQ dollars for Q dollars of coverage. He or she can choose the amount of coverage Q to maximize expected utility:

$$\max_{Q} \quad \pi u(W - x - \pi Q + Q) + (1 - \pi)u(W - \pi Q) \qquad (13\text{-}34)$$

The first-order condition is

$$\pi u'(W - x - \pi Q^* + Q^*)(1 - \pi) + (1 - \pi)u'(W - \pi Q^*)(-\pi) = 0 \qquad (13\text{-}35)$$

that is,

$$u'(W - x - \pi Q^* + Q^*) = u'(W - \pi Q^*) \qquad (13\text{-}36)$$

For $u(\cdot)$ strictly concave, (13-36) implies $W - x - \pi Q^* + Q^* = W - \pi Q^*$,

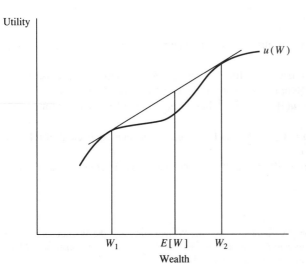

FIGURE 13-3

The Friedman-Savage proposition. In 1948, Milton Friedman and L. J. Savage proposed a utility function with a convex section to explain why an individual might buy insurance and lotteries at the same time. However, such an individual would take large gambles to leave the convex section and then behave as a risk averter. Gambling can be explained by its entertainment value, consistent with the observation that people divide their stakes into small bets.

or

$$Q^* = x \tag{13-37}$$

Thus, a risk-averse individual will buy full insurance if it is available at an actuarily fair premium. Very often, however, the probability and the amount of damage are not fixed. If efforts to reduce the chance and the extent of damage are costly to observe, buying insurance will reduce the individual's incentive to supply such efforts. This is known as *moral hazard*. Methods to mitigate moral hazard include coinsurance and deductibles, but these are beyond the scope of this chapter.[†]

Another way to reduce exposure to risk is diversification. If an individual invests in one risky project X, Eq. (13-31) shows that the risk premium is approximately $\frac{1}{2}\sigma_x^2 a$, where a is the coefficient of absolute risk aversion. On the other hand, if the individual invests in n different projects, with a $1/n$ share in each, the risk premium P for each project is given by

$$u(W - P) \equiv E\left[u\left(W + \frac{1}{n}x\right)\right] \tag{13-38}$$

Taking Taylor approximations on both sides and rearranging, we get

$$P \approx \frac{\frac{1}{2}\sigma_x^2}{n^2}a \tag{13-39}$$

If the returns to the n projects are independent, the total risk premium is

$$nP \approx \frac{1}{2}\frac{\sigma_x^2}{n}a, \tag{13-40}$$

which is only $1/n$ of the risk premium for the undiversified investment.

PROBLEMS

1. Show that the coefficient of absolute risk aversion is invariant to linear transformations of the utility function.
2. Let u and v be two utility functions, with $v(W) = f(u(W))$, where f is concave. Proof that the coefficient of absolute risk aversion for v is greater than that for u.
3. *(a)* Verify that the function $u(W) = -e^{-aW}$ has a constant coefficient of absolute risk aversion equal to a.
   (b) Verify that the function $u(W) = W^{1-a}/(1-a)$ has a constant coefficient of relative risk aversion equal to a.
   (c) Verify that the function $u(W) = \log W$ has a constant coefficient of relative risk aversion of 1.

[†]For further details, see, for example, Kenneth J. Arrow, "Uncertainty and the Welfare Economics of Medical Care," *American Economic Review*, **53**:941–973, 1963; and Bengt Holmstrom, "Moral Hazard and Observability," *Bell Journal of Economics*, **10**:74–91, 1979.

13.4 COMPARATIVE STATICS

Allocation of Wealth to Risky Assets

Most decisions are made under conditions of uncertainty. Economists postulate that individuals make choices so as to maximize expected utility. Let us begin with a problem in the allocation of wealth to risky and to safe assets. Suppose an individual has initial wealth W, which is to be divided between a safe asset (say, money) whose rate of return is zero and a risky asset whose rate of return is a random variable R. If he or she invests x dollars in the risky asset, final wealth will be $(W - x) + x(1 + R) = W + xR$. The individual chooses x so as to maximize expected utility of wealth:

$$\max_{x} E[u(W + xR)] \qquad (13\text{-}41)$$

When the utility function is well-behaved, we can differentiate inside the expectation sign[†] to get the first- and second-order conditions:

$$E[u'(W + xR)R] = 0$$
$$E[u''(W + xR)R^2] \leq 0 \qquad (13\text{-}42)$$

The assumption that the individual is risk-averse (i.e., $u'' < 0$) ensures that the second-order condition is satisfied. The first-order condition defines the amount of investment in the risky asset as a function of initial wealth, $x = x^*(W)$. Substituting $x^*(W)$ for x in the first-order condition and differentiating with respect to W, we obtain

$$E[u''(W + xR)(1 + Rx^{*\prime}(W))R] \equiv 0 \qquad (13\text{-}43)$$

Using the additive property of the expectation operator,

$$E[u''(W + xR)R] + E[u''(W + xR)R^2 x^{*\prime}(W)] \equiv 0$$

Therefore,

$$x^{*\prime}(W) = -\frac{E[u''(W + xR)R]}{E[u''(W + xR)R^2]} \qquad (13\text{-}44)$$

Since the denominator is negative, the sign of $x^{*\prime}(W)$ is the same as the sign of the numerator. It turns out that the numerator is positive if the coefficient of absolute risk aversion is decreasing in wealth. When absolute risk aversion is decreasing, we have

$$\frac{-u''(W + xR)}{u'(W + xR)} \leq \frac{-u''(W)}{u'(W)} \qquad \text{for } R \geq 0$$

$$\frac{-u''(W + xR)}{u'(W + xR)} \geq \frac{-u''(W)}{u'(W)} \qquad \text{for } R \leq 0 \qquad (13\text{-}45)$$

[†]Think of this as differentiating inside an integral sign.

Multiplying both sides by $-u'(W + xR)R$ (which is a negative number for the first inequality and a positive number for the second inequality), we get

$$u''(W + xR)R \geq \frac{u''(W)}{u'(W)} u'(W + xR)R \qquad \text{for all } R \qquad (13\text{-}46)$$

Taking expectations on both sides,

$$E[u''(W + xR)R] \geq \frac{u''(W)}{u'(W)} E[u'(W + xR)R] \qquad (13\text{-}47)$$

The left-hand side of the inequality is equal to zero by the first-order condition. Hence, $x^{*\prime}(W) \geq 0$. If absolute risk aversion is decreasing in wealth, a rise in wealth will lower the amount of investment in risky assets.

PROBLEMS

1. (a) Suppose the utility function is given by $u(W) = aW - bW^2$ (with a and b both positive). Does the function exhibit increasing or decreasing risk aversion?
   (b) If the rate of return on risky assets is a random variable R with mean $\overline{R} > 0$ and variance σ_R^2, and if the individual's initial wealth is W, what is the optimal amount of investment in risky assets?
   (c) Show that the optimal amount of risky investment is a decreasing function of wealth.
2. If the utility function is $u(W) = -e^{-aW}$, so that the absolute risk aversion is constant, show that the amount of investment in risky assets is independent of initial wealth.

Output Decisions under Price Uncertainty

In the previous example we derived a typical comparative statics result concerning the effect of a change in a nonrandom parameter. Under uncertainty, however, the exogenous factors affecting choice are often random. Instead of asking how changes in the *value* of a random variable will affect choice, we have to ask how changes in the *distribution* of the random variable affects behavior. We illustrate this with a model of the competitive firm under price uncertainty. Suppose a risk-averse, price-taking firm has to make output decisions before the price of the product is known. The objective of the firm is to maximize expected utility of profits:

$$\max_{y} E[u(py - c(y))] \qquad (13\text{-}48)$$

where p is a random variable denoting the price of the product, y is the output of the firm, and $c(y)$ is the cost function. Differentiating with respect to y, we obtain the conditions for a maximum:

$$E[u'(py - c(y))(p - c'(y))] = 0$$

$$D = E[u''(py - c(y))(p - c'(y))^2 - u'(py - c(y))c''(y)] < 0 \qquad (13\text{-}49)$$

As in the previous analyses, we assume the strict inequality for the second-order conditions.

It is instructive to compare the level of output under price uncertainty to the certainty case. Let $\bar{p}$ be the mean of the random variable p, and write the first-order condition as $E[u'(py-c(y))p] = E[u'(py-c(y))c'(y)]$. Then, subtracting $E[u'(py - c(y))\bar{p}]$ on both sides, we get

$$E[u'(py - c(y))(p - \bar{p})] = E[u'(py - c(y))(c'(y) - \bar{p})] \qquad (13\text{-}50)$$

The left-hand side of Eq. (13-50) is the covariance between price and marginal utility. When price is high, profits are high and (because of diminishing marginal utility) marginal utility is low. Similarly, marginal utility is high when price is low. The covariance term is thus negative. Consequently, the right-hand side of (13-50) is also negative, which implies

$$c'(y) \le \bar{p} \qquad (13\text{-}51)$$

In other words, output under price uncertainty is characterized by marginal cost being less than the expected price. If marginal cost is increasing in output, then for the same expected price, output under price uncertainty is lower than for the certainty case.

To derive comparative statics results, first note that output y^* is a function of the *distribution* of p. We cannot ask how y^* changes as p varies because p is itself a random variable. To do comparative statics we have to change the distribution or the parameters of the distribution of p. For example, since the mean of p is $\bar{p}$, we can write $p = \bar{p} + e$, where e is a random variable with mean zero. Then the first-order condition can be written as

$$E[u'((\bar{p} + e)y^*(\bar{p}) - c(y^*(\bar{p})))((\bar{p} + e) - c'(y^*(\bar{p})))] \equiv 0 \qquad (13\text{-}52)$$

Differentiating with respect to $\bar{p}$, we get

$$\frac{dy^*}{d\bar{p}} = \frac{yE[u''(py - c(y))(p - c'(y))]}{-D} + \frac{E[u'(py - c(y))]}{-D} \qquad (13\text{-}53)$$

The second term is clearly positive; it is the substitution effect. The sign of the first term depends on the degree of absolute risk aversion. Let x be the level of profits when $p = c'(y)$ (x is nonrandom). If absolute risk aversion is decreasing, then

$$\frac{-u''(py - c(y))}{u'(py - c(y))} \le \frac{-u''(x)}{u'(x)} \qquad \text{for } p \ge c'(y)$$

$$\frac{-u''(py - c(y))}{u'(py - c(y))} \ge \frac{-u''(x)}{u'(x)} \qquad \text{for } p \le c'(y) \qquad (13\text{-}54)$$

Multiplying both sides by $-u'(py - c(y))(p - c'(y))$, we have

$$u''(py - c(y))(p - c'(y)) \ge \frac{u''(x)}{u'(x)}u'(py - c(y))(p - c'(y)) \qquad \text{for all } p \qquad (13\text{-}55)$$

Taking expectations on Eq. (13-55), it can be seen from the first-order condition that the right-hand side has expected value zero. Thus, the first term of Eq. (13-53) is positive. That term represents the wealth effect. As expected price increases, wealth rises and (assuming decreasing risk aversion) the firm is willing to take greater risk by increasing production. The wealth effect reinforces the substitution effect to give a positive response of output to expected price.

Increases in Riskiness

In models of decision making under uncertainty, the choice variables are functions of the distribution of random variables. We have already seen how one can derive comparative statics results for changes in the mean of the distribution. Very often it is also interesting to analyze the change in behavior as the distribution becomes more "risky," with the mean remaining unchanged. One way to do this is to perform comparative statics for the scale parameter of the distribution. For example, if z is a random variable with mean $\bar{z}$ and standard deviation σ_z, we can let $z = \bar{z} + \sigma_z e$, with e being a random variable with zero mean and unit variance. Substituting $\bar{z} + \sigma_z e$ for z in the first-order condition for maximization, and differentiating with respect to σ_z, we obtain the optimal response to an increase in riskiness. An increase in the scale parameter is one way to increase the riskiness of the distribution of a random variable; it makes the probability distribution more "stretched" around a constant mean. A more general and more useful representation of increases in riskiness is "mean-preserving spreads."[†] If a random variable z is replaced by $z^+ = z + e$, where e is a random variable with conditional mean equal to zero, then z and z^+ have the same mean, and it is natural to say that z^+ is more risky than z. It turns out that adding noise to a random variable (i.e., replacing z with z^+) is equivalent to moving some of the probability mass from the center part of the density out to the tails. Figure 13-4 shows the probability density functions of z and z^+. The function z^+ is called *a mean-preserving spread of z*.

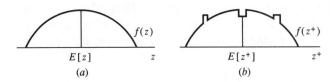

$E[z]$ z $E[z^+]$ z^+

(a)   (b)

FIGURE 13-4
Mean-preserving spread.   The density function shown in panel *(a)* is subjected to a mean-preserving spread, shown in panel *(b)*. The distributions have the same mean, but in panel *(b)* added weight is given to outcomes further from the mean.

[†]See Michael Rothschild and Joseph E. Stiglitz, "Increasing Risk: I. A Definition," *Journal of Economic Theory*, **2**:225–243, 1970.

The notion of mean-preserving spreads is useful because if z^+ is a mean-preserving spread of z, then for any concave function $u(\cdot)$,

$$E[u(z^+)] \leq E[u(z)] \tag{13-56}$$

Equation (13-56) follows from Jensen's inequality. Using the method of iterated expectation,

$$E[u(z + e)] = E[E[u(z + e)|z]]$$
$$\leq E[u(z + E[e|z])] = E[u(z)] \tag{13-57}$$

Thus, if an income prospect becomes more risky in the sense that its probability distribution undergoes a mean-preserving spread, the expected utility to a risk-averse individual will fall. Similarly, since $E[u(z^+)] > E[u(z)]$ for any convex function $u(\cdot)$, a risk-loving individual will prefer income prospects that are more risky. It is also convenient to do comparative statics using the concept of mean-preserving spreads. Suppose an individual chooses x to maximize the objective function $E[f(x,z)]$, where z is a random variable. The sufficient conditions for maximization are:

$$E[f_x(x,z)] = 0$$
$$E[f_{xx}(x,z)] < 0 \tag{13-58}$$

Now let α be a parameter that represents a mean-preserving spread to the distribution of z. The first-order condition defines a choice function $x = x^*(\alpha)$. A change in α will affect the value of x^* and the value of $E[f_x(x,z)]$ directly as well. Differentiating the first-order condition with respect to α, we get

$$\frac{\partial x^*}{\partial \alpha} E[f_{xx}(x,z)] + \frac{\partial}{\partial \alpha} E[f_x(x,z)] \equiv 0 \tag{13-59}$$

If $f_x(x,z)$ is a concave function in z, then $E[f_x(x,z)]$ will decrease as z undergoes a mean-preserving spread. Thus, the second term of (13-59) is negative. Since $E[f_{xx}(x,z)]$ is negative by the second-order condition, $\partial x^*/\partial \alpha < 0$. Similarly, $\partial x^*/\partial \alpha > 0$ if $f_x(x,z)$ is a convex function in z.

Let us illustrate the method with a simple model of investment under uncertainty. Suppose the production function is $f(K,L)$ where K is capital, L is labor, and f is homogeneous of degree one. For simplicity, assume that capital lasts only one period so that we do not have to consider the dynamic aspect of the problem. The producer has to choose K before output price is known. After K is chosen, output price is revealed, and the producer determines the number of workers to work with his capital. The wage rate for labor is w and the cost of capital is given by a convex function $c(K)$. We assume the producer is risk-neutral. For any given K, the producer will choose L so as to maximize profits. We can define the indirect profit function by

$$v(p,w,K) = \max_{L} pf(K,L) - wL \tag{13-60}$$

In earlier chapters we have shown that the indirect profit function is convex in p and w. It is linear in K if f is homogeneous of degree one. Thus, we can write $v(p, w, K) = K\hat{v}(p, w)$. Since the producer is risk-neutral, he or she will choose K to maximize expected profits:

$$\max_{K} E[K\hat{v}(p, w) - c(K)] \qquad (13\text{-}61)$$

The sufficient conditions are:

$$E[\hat{v}(p, w)] - c'(K) = 0$$

$$-c''(K) < 0 \qquad (13\text{-}62)$$

The assumption that marginal cost of capital is increasing ensures that the second-order condition is satisfied.

To see how the amount of investment will change as the distribution of output price becomes more variable, let α be a parameter that represents a mean-preserving spread to the distribution of p. Differentiating the first-order condition with respect to α, we get

$$\frac{\partial}{\partial \alpha} E[\hat{v}(p, w)] - c''(K)\frac{\partial K^*}{\partial \alpha} = 0 \qquad (13\text{-}63)$$

Since $\hat{v}(p, w)$ is convex, a mean-preserving spread will increase the value of $E[\hat{v}(p, w)]$. The first term of (13-63) is positive, and therefore $\partial K^*/\partial \alpha > 0$. If the amount of labor cannot be adjusted after output price is revealed, expected profits will be unaffected by changes in the price distribution as long as the mean price remains unchanged. In this model, however, the producer can hire more workers when output price is high. Consequently, the increase in profits will be more than proportional to the increase in price. On the other hand, when output price is low, the producer can reduce the number of workers so that the fall in profits will be less than proportional to the fall in price. As a result, the expected return to investment will be higher as output price becomes more variable, and the amount of investment will increase.

REFERENCES

Arrow, Kenneth J.: "Uncertainty and the Welfare Economics of Medical Care," *American Economic Review*, **53**:941–973, 1963.

———: "The Role of Securities in the Optimal Allocation of Risk Bearing," *Review of Economic Studies*, **31**:91–96, 1964.

———: *Aspects of the Theory of Risk Bearing*, Yrjo Jahnssonin Saatio, Helsinki, 1965.

Bernoulli, Daniel: "Exposition of a New Theory on the Measurement of Risk" (1738), (trans. by L. Sommer), *Econometrica*, **22**:23–36, 1954.

Friedman, Milton, and L. J. Savage: "The Utility Analysis of Choices Involving Risk," *Journal of Political Economy*, **56**:279–304, 1948.

Hartman, Richard: "The Effects of Price and Cost Uncertainty on Investment." *Journal of Economic Theory*, **5**:258–266, 1972.

Holmstrom, Bengt: "Moral Hazard and Observability," *Bell Journal of Economics*, **10**:74–91, 1979.

Luce, R. D., and H. Raiffa: *Games and Decisions*, John Wiley & Sons, Inc., New York, 1957.

Pope, R. D.: " The Generalized Envelope Theorem and Price Uncertainty," *International Economic Review,* **21:**75–86, 1980.

Pratt, J. W.: "Risk Aversion in the Small and in the Large," *Econometrica,* **32:**122–136, 1964.

Rothschild, Michael, and Joseph E. Stiglitz: "Increasing Risk: I. A Definition," *Journal of Economic Theory,* **2:**225–243, 1970.

Sandmo, Agnar: "On the Theory of the Competitive Firm Under Price Uncertainty," *American Economic Review,* **61:**65–73, 1971.

Savage, L. J.: *The Foundations of Statistics,* John Wiley & Sons, Inc., New York, 1954.

Von Neumann, J., and O. Morgenstern: *Theory of Games and Economic Behavior,* Princeton University Press, Princeton, N. J., 1944.

CHAPTER
14

MAXIMIZATION WITH INEQUALITY AND NONNEGATIVITY CONSTRAINTS

14.1 NONNEGATIVITY

In the previous pages we have largely ignored the issues raised by constraining the variables in a maximization model to be nonnegative. In the model of the firm, for example, we did not consider the possibility that simultaneous solution of the first-order equations might lead to negative values of one or more inputs. Such an occurrence would nullify the condition for profit maximization that wages be equal to marginal revenue product. In a more general sense, there are many factors of production which a firm chooses not to use at all. Similarly, consumers choose to consume only a small fraction of the myriad of consumer goods available. It is possible to characterize mathematically the conditions under which nonnegativity becomes a binding constraint. It might be remarked first, however, that since the refutable comparative-statics theorems are concerned with how choice variables change when parameters change, the comparative statics of variables *not* chosen is fairly trivial. In a local sense (the evaluation of the partial derivatives of the choice functions at a given point) these variables continue not to be chosen; that is, $\partial x_i^*/\partial \alpha_j = 0$ for these variables. In a global sense, e.g., price changes of finite magnitude, factors or goods previously not chosen may enter the relevant choice set. For these situations, more powerful assumptions must be made to yield refutable theorems than in our previous discussions, where strictly *local* phenomena were analyzed.

Consider the monopolist of the first chapter. A profit function of the type

$$\pi(x) = R(x) - C(x) \tag{14-1}$$

is asserted to be maximized, where $R(x)$ and $C(x)$ denote, respectively, the revenue and cost associated with a given level of output x. (We are ignoring the tax aspect of the model as it is not germane to this discussion.) The first-order conditions for a maximum of $\pi(x)$ are

$$\pi'(x) = R'(x) - C'(x) = 0 \tag{14-2}$$

However, this condition is meant to apply only to those situations where the solution to (14-2) is nonnegative. The firm might choose to produce zero output, however, if, for example, $R'(x) < C'(x)$ for all $x > 0$. In that case, where the marginal revenue is less than marginal cost, increasing output *reduces* profits $\pi(x)$. The existence of a *maximum* of profits (not necessarily *positive* profits, another issue entirely) at some *positive* level of output x^* presupposes that for some $0 \le x \le x^*, \mathrm{MR} > \mathrm{MC}$; that is, $R'(x) > C'(x)$ so that it "paid" for the firm to start operations in the first place. The only reason the profit *maximum* would occur at $x = 0$ is that $\mathrm{MR}(0) \le \mathrm{MC}(0)$. That is, *if* maximum π occurs at $x = 0$, then $\pi' = R'(x) - C'(x) \le 0$ at $x = 0$. The converse is not being asserted; it is in fact false. If $R'(x) - C'(x) < 0$ at $x = 0$, this does not imply that an interior maximum cannot occur at some x distant from the origin. Again, the only aspect of the firm's behavior under consideration here is the attainment of *maximum* profits, not whether the firm shall exist or not [presumably dependent upon $\pi(x) > 0$].

Let us summarize this condition for maximization of functions of one variable. Consider some function $y = f(x)$. Then the first-order condition for $f(x)$ to achieve a maximum *subject to the nonnegativity constraint $x \ge 0$*, is

$$f'(x) \le 0 \qquad \text{if } f'(x) < 0 \qquad \text{then } x = 0 \tag{14-3}$$

Alternatively, one can express the same idea as

$$f'(x) \le 0 \tag{14-4a}$$

$$xf'(x) = 0 \tag{14-4b}$$

Geometrically, the situation is as depicted in Fig. 14-1. In Fig. 14-1a the usual, *interior* maximum is illustrated. This solution is called an interior maximum because the value of x which maximizes $f(x)$ does not lie on the boundary of the set over which x is defined (here, the nonnegative real axis; its only boundary is the point $x = 0$). The set of positive real numbers is the *interior* of this domain of definition of x; hence the terminology. In Fig. 14-1b and c, corner solutions are depicted. That is, the maximum value of $f(x)$, for $x \ge 0$, occurs when $x = 0$. (The fact that the function in Fig. 14-1b achieves a regular maximum at a negative value of x is irrelevant.) When the maximum occurs at $x = 0$, it is impossible to have $f'(x) > 0$ there. If $f'(0) > 0$, increasing x would increase $f(x)$ and $f(0)$ could not be a maximum. However, it is possible that $f'(0) = 0$, as in Fig. 14-1c. There, the nonnegativity constraint is nonbinding. That is, the

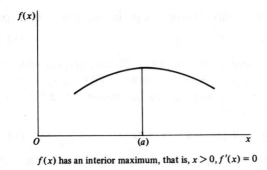

$f(x)$ has an interior maximum, that is, $x > 0, f'(x) = 0$

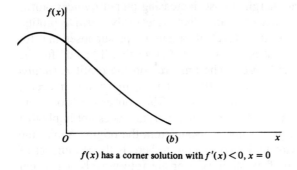

$f(x)$ has a corner solution with $f'(x) < 0, x = 0$

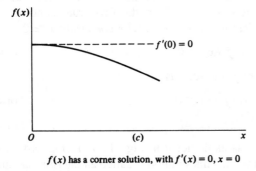

$f(x)$ has a corner solution, with $f'(x) = 0, x = 0$

FIGURE 14-1
(a) f(x) has an interior maximum;
that is, $x > 0, f'(x) = 0$. *(b) f(x)*
has a corner solution with $f'(x) < 0$.
(c) f(x) has a corner solution, with
$f'(x) = 0, x = 0$.

maximum $f(x)$ would occur at $x = 0$ anyway, even without the restriction $x \geq 0$. Thus, if a maximum occurs when $x > 0$, $f'(x) = 0$. If the maximum occurs when $x = 0$, then necessarily $f'(x) \leq 0$. This condition is expressed in relation (14-3) or, equivalently, (14-4).

These more general first-order conditions can be derived algebraically by the device known as adding a *slack variable*. The constraint $x \geq 0$ is an elementary form of the more general inequality constraint, $g(x) \geq 0$. By converting this inequality to an *equality constraint*, ordinary Lagrangian methods can be used to derive the first-order conditions.

The constraint $x \geq 0$ is equivalent to

$$x - s^2 = 0 \tag{14-5}$$

where s takes on any real value. When $s \neq 0$, an interior solution is implied, since $x = s^2 > 0$. When $s = 0$, a corner solution is present.

We can now state this as the constrained maximum problem:

maximize

$$y = f(x)$$

subject to

$$x - s^2 = 0$$

The Lagrangian for this problem is

$$\mathcal{L} = f(x) + \lambda(x - s^2) \tag{14-6}$$

Taking the first partials of $\mathcal{L}$ with respect to x, s, and λ gives

$$\mathcal{L}_x = f'(x) + \lambda = 0 \tag{14-7a}$$

$$\mathcal{L}_s = -2\lambda s = 0 \tag{14-7b}$$

$$\mathcal{L}_\lambda = x - s^2 = 0 \tag{14-7c}$$

From Eq.(14-7b) we see that if $s \neq 0$, that is, an *interior* solution is obtained, then $\lambda = 0$ and hence from (14-7a), $f'(x) = 0$. Thus, as expected, the usual condition $f'(x) = 0$ is obtained for noncorner solutions. Using the second-order conditions for constrained maximization, we can show that $\lambda \geq 0$. The second-order condition is that

$$\mathcal{L}_{xx}h_x^2 + 2\mathcal{L}_{xs}h_xh_s + \mathcal{L}_{ss}h_s^2 \leq 0 \tag{14-8}$$

for all h_x, h_s satisfying

$$g_x h_x + g_s h_s = 0 \tag{14-9}$$

where $g(x,s) = x - s^2$, the constraint. From the Lagrangian (14-6), $\mathcal{L}_{xx} = f''(x)$, $\mathcal{L}_{xs} = 0$, $\mathcal{L}_{ss} = -2\lambda$. From the constraint $g(x,s) = x - s^2$, $g_x = 1$, $g_s = -2s$. Hence, (14-8) and (14-9) become

$$f''(x)h_x^2 - 2\lambda h_s^2 \leq 0 \tag{14-10}$$

for all h_x, h_s satisfying

$$h_x - 2sh_s = 0 \tag{14-11}$$

We already know from Eq.(14-7b) that if $s \neq 0$, then $\lambda = 0$. Suppose now that $s = 0$. Then from Eq.(14-11), $h_x = 0$, but no restriction is placed on h_s. When we use $h_x = 0, h_s = $ anything, Eq. (14-10) becomes

$$-2\lambda h_s^2 \leq 0$$

implying, since $h_s^2 > 0$,

$$\lambda \geq 0 \tag{14-12}$$

We now have a complete statement of the first-order conditions for maximizing $f(x)$ subject to $x \geq 0$. From (14-7a), since $\lambda \geq 0$,

$$f'(x) \leq 0 \tag{14-13}$$

If $f'(x) < 0$, then $\lambda > 0$. From (14-7b) $s = 0$ and thus $x = 0$ from (14-7c). Therefore:

if

$$f'(x) < 0 \qquad x = 0 \tag{14-14}$$

Equations (14-13) and (14-14) are equivalent to

$$f'(x) \leq 0 \tag{14-15}$$

$$xf'(x) = 0 \tag{14-16}$$

commonly written

$$f'(x) \leq 0 \qquad \text{if} <, \ x = 0$$

Notice that if the maximum occurs at $x = 0$, no restrictions on $f''(0)$ are implied. In Fig. 14-1b, $f(x)$ could be either convex (as drawn) or concave, and the maximum would still occur at $x = 0$.

These conditions can also be derived using the determinantal conditions on the bordered Hessian of second partials of $\mathscr{L}$:

$$|\mathscr{L}| = \begin{vmatrix} \mathscr{L}_{xx} & \mathscr{L}_{xs} & g_x \\ \mathscr{L}_{sx} & \mathscr{L}_{ss} & g_s \\ g_x & g_s & 0 \end{vmatrix} > 0$$

Using the values previously calculated for these partials, we have

$$|\mathscr{L}| = \begin{vmatrix} f''(x) & 0 & 1 \\ 0 & -2\lambda & -2s \\ 1 & -2s & 0 \end{vmatrix} = -4s^2 f''(x) + 2\lambda \geq 0 \tag{14-17}$$

From (14-17), if $s = 0$ (corner solution), $2\lambda \geq 0$; hence $\lambda \geq 0$. Thus, from (14-7a), $f'(x) \leq 0$.

The first-order conditions for obtaining a *minimum* value of $f(x)$ subject to $x \geq 0$ are obtained in a similar manner. One quickly shows that these conditions are

$$f'(x) \geq 0 \qquad \text{if} >, \ x = 0 \tag{14-18}$$

That is, if a minimum occurs at $x = 0$, it must be the case that $f(x)$ is rising (or horizontal) at $x = 0$. Otherwise, i.e., if the function were falling at $x = 0$, making x positive would lower the value of $f(x)$ and $f(x)$ could not have a minimum at $x = 0$.

Functions of Two or More Variables

The principles just delineated for maximization of functions of one variable generalize in an obvious manner to functions of two or more variables. Consider the problem:

maximize

$$z = f(x_1, x_2)$$

subject to

$$x_1 \geq 0 \qquad x_2 \geq 0$$

Let us now add slack variables s_1^2, s_2^2 in the manner of the first example. The problem then becomes one of maximization subject to two *equality* constraints:

maximize

$$y = f(x_1, x_2)$$

subject to

$$g^1(x_1, s_1) = x_1 - s_1^2 = 0$$

$$g^2(x_2, s_2) = x_2 - s_2^2 = 0$$

The Lagrangian for this problem is

$$\mathcal{L} = f(x_1, x_2) + \lambda_1(x_1 - s_1^2) + \lambda_2(x_2 - s_2^2)$$

The first-order conditions for maximization are

$$\mathcal{L}_{x_1} = f_1 + \lambda_1 = 0 \qquad (14\text{-}19a)$$

$$\mathcal{L}_{x_2} = f_2 + \lambda_2 = 0 \qquad (14\text{-}19b)$$

$$\mathcal{L}_{s_1} = -2\lambda_1 s_1 = 0 \qquad (14\text{-}19c)$$

$$\mathcal{L}_{s_2} = -2\lambda_2 s_2 = 0 \qquad (14\text{-}19d)$$

$$\mathcal{L}_{\lambda_1} = x_1 - s_1^2 = 0 \qquad (14\text{-}19e)$$

$$\mathcal{L}_{\lambda_2} = x_2 - s_2^2 = 0 \qquad (14\text{-}19f)$$

From Eq.(14-19c) and (14-19d), if either constraint is nonbinding, i.e., if $s_1 \neq 0$ or $s_2 \neq 0$, then, respectively, $\lambda_1 = 0, \lambda_2 = 0$. In that case $(x_1 > 0, x_2 > 0)$, the ordinary first-order relations $f_1 = 0$, $f_2 = 0$ obtain.

We can show that $\lambda_1 \geq 0, \lambda_2 \geq 0$ by using the second-order conditions. For a constrained maximum,

$$\sum_{i=1}^{2}\sum_{j=1}^{2} \mathcal{L}_{x_i x_j} h_i h_j + 2\sum_{i=1}^{2}\sum_{j=1}^{2} \mathcal{L}_{x_i s_j} h_i k_j + \sum_{i=1}^{2}\sum_{j=1}^{2} \mathcal{L}_{s_i s_j} k_i k_j \leq 0 \qquad (14\text{-}20)$$

for all values h_1, h_2, k_1, k_2 such that

$$g^1_{x_1}h_1 + g^1_{s_1}k_1 = 0 \qquad (14\text{-}21a)$$

$$g^2_{x_2}h_2 + g^2_{s_2}k_2 = 0 \qquad (14\text{-}21b)$$

By inspection of the Lagrangian [or Eqs.(14-19)] we have

$$\mathscr{L}_{x_ix_j} = f_{ij} \qquad i,j = 1,2$$

$$\mathscr{L}_{x_is_j} = 0 \qquad i,j = 1,2$$

$$\mathscr{L}_{s_is_j} = \begin{cases} -2\lambda_i & \text{if } i = j \\ 0 & \text{if } i \neq j \end{cases}$$

$$g^i_{x_j} = \begin{cases} 1 & \text{if } i = j \\ 0 & \text{if } i \neq j \end{cases}$$

$$g^i_{s_j} = \begin{cases} -2s_i & \text{if } i = j \\ 0 & \text{if } i \neq j \end{cases}$$

Relations (14-20) and (14-21) therefore become

$$\sum_{i=1}^{2}\sum_{j=1}^{2} f_{ij}h_ih_j - 2\lambda_1k_1^2 - 2\lambda_2k_2^2 \leq 0 \qquad (14\text{-}22)$$

for all h_1, h_2, k_1, k_2 such that

$$h_1 - 2s_1k_1 = 0 \qquad (14\text{-}23a)$$

$$h_2 - 2s_2k_2 = 0 \qquad (14\text{-}23b)$$

We already know that if $s_i \neq 0$, then $\lambda_i = 0$. Suppose therefore that $s_i = 0$. Then from (14-23), $h_i = 0$. Then Eq.(14-22) becomes

$$-2\lambda_1k_1^2 - 2\lambda_2k_2^2 \leq 0$$

This must hold for all k_1, k_2. Setting $k_1 = 0, k_2 = 0$ in turn therefore yields

$$\lambda_1 \geq 0 \qquad (14\text{-}24a)$$

$$\lambda_2 \geq 0 \qquad (14\text{-}24b)$$

From the nonnegativity of the Lagrange multipliers, Eqs. (14-19a) and (14-19b) become

$$f_1 \leq 0 \qquad f_2 \leq 0$$

And if $f_i < 0$ (meaning $\lambda_i > 0$), then from (14-19c) and (14-19d), $s_i = 0$, and hence $x_i = 0$. Thus the first-order conditions for a maximum subject to nonnegativity constraints are

$$f_i \leq 0 \qquad \text{if } <, x_i = 0 \qquad i = 1,2 \qquad (14\text{-}25)$$

This reasoning generalizes to functions of n variables in a straightforward manner, yielding analogous results. The first-order conditions for:

maximize

$$z = f(x_1, \ldots, x_n)$$

subject to

$$x_i \geq 0 \qquad \text{some or all } i = 1, \ldots, n$$

are

$$f_i \leq 0 \qquad \text{if } <, \, x_i = 0 \qquad (14\text{-}26)$$

for variables constrained to be nonnegative, and simply

$$f_i = 0$$

for variables not constrained to be nonnegative.

Let us see what these conditions imply for the profit-maximizing firm. We previously considered the model:

maximize

$$\pi = pf(x_1, x_2) - w_1 x_1 - w_2 x_2$$

Let us now specify explicitly that the factors x_1 and x_2 can only be employed in positive amounts, as physical reality would dictate.[†] With $x_1, x_2 \geq 0$, the first-order conditions for profit maximization become

$$\pi_1 = pf_1 - w_1 \leq 0 \qquad \text{if } <, \, x_1 = 0$$
$$\pi_2 = pf_2 - w_2 \leq 0 \qquad \text{if } <, \, x_2 = 0 \qquad (14\text{-}27)$$

Equations (14-27) say that if the profit maximum occurs at zero input of some factor, then the value of the marginal product of that factor is less than its wage. This is in accord with intuition. If the marginal value product were initially greater than the wage of some factor, the firm could increase its profits by employing that factor in positive amounts.

Notice carefully the direction of implication intended by Eqs. (14-26) and, for the firm, (14-27). These relations do *not* say that if the marginal value product is initially, i.e., at $x_i = 0$, less than the wage of some factor, that factor will not be used. We might *initially* find $pf_i < w_i$, but, as x_i increased, f_i might increase and then decrease, yielding $pf_i = w_i$ at some finite, positive value of x_i.

[†] Some general mathematical treatments of the firm treat inputs as negative outputs. This type of black box approach to the theory of the firm generates a mathematical symmetry that is convenient in some analyses. Also, in more sophisticated models of the firm involving physical stocks of certain inputs, drawing down of some such stock (disinvestment) can be regarded as negative accumulation but probably still positive service flow from that stock.

The "law" of diminishing returns is in fact usually stated to allow this possibility; the usual assertion is that f_i declines after some level of use of x_i (holding the other factors constant). The preceding first-order equations say only that *if* the maximum of profits (or anything else) is observed to occur when $pf_i < w_i$, *then* it must be the case that that input is not used; that is, $x_i = 0$. The converse of this statement is *not* implied by this analysis and will in general be false. These are strictly local conditions around the maximum position.

To illustrate this important point, consider a farmer who has to decide which of two tractors, a large model x_L or a small one x_s, to purchase. Either one alone may yield positive profits, with a marginal value product initially greater than the rental wage. This particular farmer would never find it profitable to use two tractors. It turns out, say, that using only the smaller tractor yields the highest profits. At zero (or small) input levels of the other tractor, the marginal value product of either tractor is greater than the rental wage. But at *maximum* profits, $x_s > 0$, $x_L = 0$; at that point, $pf_{x_L} < w_L$. But the nonuse of some factor does *not* imply that the value of the marginal product of that factor is always less than its wage.

The generalized first-order conditions, while providing a conceptual generalization of the conditions for a maximum, are not useful for actually finding that maximum. As the previous paragraph indicates, these conditions describe the maximum position after the fact. They don't tell us in advance which variables will equal zero at the maximum position. Consider, for example, that firms usually employ only a few of the hundreds or thousands of potential factors of production available to them. Firms typically reject one type of machinery in favor of another, they set skill levels for employees, etc., rejecting certain factors outright. The preceding first-order conditions merely indicate that for the rejected factors, the marginal value product must have been less than the wage, even at zero input levels. But that is precious little to go on in predicting in advance exactly which factors will be employed and which factors will not.

More importantly, as indicated earlier, the only interesting refutable comparative-statics relations are those which predict a direction (or magnitude, if possible) of change in a choice variable as parameters change. The comparative statics of variables not chosen is rather elementary: $\partial x_i^*/\partial \alpha_j \equiv 0$ for all x_i not chosen, by definition. Hence the meaningful results that are forthcoming with mathematical model building will de facto be derived from the classical maximum conditions of first-order *equalities*. Models involving nonnegativity (or other inequality constraints) will in general require an *algorithm* for solution. That is, some iterative trial-and-error process will be required to see which, if any, constraints are in fact binding. In the chapter on linear programming, an example of such an algorithm will be presented.

14.2 INEQUALITY CONSTRAINTS

Let us now consider the imposition of an inequality constraint $g(x_1, x_2) \geq 0$ in addition to the nonnegativity constraints in a two-variable problem. That is, consider:

maximize

$$z = f(x_1, x_2)$$

subject to

$$g(x_1, x_2) \geq 0 \qquad \text{and} \qquad x_1 \geq 0, x_2 \geq 0$$

(No loss of generality is involved by writing the constraint as ≥ 0; multiplying the constraint by -1 reverses the sign.) Again, we first convert these inequalities to equalities, yielding the constrained maximum problem:

maximize

$$z = f(x_1, x_2)$$

subject to

$$g(x_1, x_2) - x_3^2 = 0$$

$$g^1(x_1, s_1) = x_1 - s_1^2 = 0 \qquad g^2(x_2, s_2) = x_2 - s_2^2 = 0$$

Here the slack variables are x_3, s_1, and s_2. The Lagrangian is

$$\mathscr{L} = f(x_1, x_2) + \lambda(g(x_1, x_2) - x_3^2) + \lambda_1(x_1 - s_1^2) + \lambda_2(x_2 - s_2^2) \qquad (14\text{-}28)$$

The first-order conditions for a maximum are thus

$$\mathscr{L}_{x_1} = f_1 + \lambda g_1 + \lambda_1 = 0 \qquad (14\text{-}29a)$$

$$\mathscr{L}_{x_2} = f_2 + \lambda g_2 + \lambda_2 = 0 \qquad (14\text{-}29b)$$

$$\mathscr{L}_{x_3} = -2\lambda x_3 = 0 \qquad (14\text{-}30a)$$

$$\mathscr{L}_{s_1} = -2\lambda_1 s_1 = 0 \qquad (14\text{-}30b)$$

$$\mathscr{L}_{s_2} = -2\lambda_2 s_2 = 0 \qquad (14\text{-}30c)$$

and the constraints

$$\mathscr{L}_\lambda = g(x_1, x_2) - x_3^2 = 0 \qquad (14\text{-}31a)$$

$$\mathscr{L}_{\lambda_1} = x_1 - s_1^2 = 0 \qquad (14\text{-}31b)$$

$$\mathscr{L}_{\lambda_2} = x_2 - s_2^2 = 0 \qquad (14\text{-}31c)$$

Using exactly the same reasoning as before, we note from Eqs.(14-30) that if any constraint is nonbinding (holds as a strict inequality), then the associated Lagrange multiplier is 0. Suppose, at the maximum point, $x_1, x_2 > 0$, and $g(x_1, x_2) > 0$; then all these constraints turn out to be completely irrelevant. From Eqs. (14-30), $\lambda = \lambda_1 = \lambda_2 = 0$, and Eqs. (14-29) become the ordinary equations for unconstrained maximum, $f_1 = f_2 = 0$. If in fact $g(x_1, x_2) = 0$, that is, the constraint is binding, and $x_1, x_2 > 0$, then Eqs.(14-29) give the ordinary first-order conditions for a constrained maximum, $\mathscr{L}_1 = f_1 + \lambda g_1 = 0, \mathscr{L}_2 = f_2 + \lambda g_2 = 0$.

It must also be the case that $\lambda, \lambda_1, \lambda_2 \geq 0$. The second-order conditions for constrained maximum are

$$\sum_{j=1}^{3}\sum_{i=1}^{3}\mathscr{L}_{x_ix_j}h_ih_j + 2\sum_{j=1}^{2}\sum_{i=1}^{3}\mathscr{L}_{x_is_j}h_ik_j + \sum_{j=1}^{2}\sum_{i=1}^{2}\mathscr{L}_{s_is_j}k_ik_j \le 0 \qquad (14\text{-}32)$$

for all h_1, h_2, h_3, k_1, k_2 satisfying

$$g_1h_1 + g_2h_2 + g_3h_3 = 0 \tag{14-33a}$$

$$g_{x_1}^1 h_1 + g_{s_1}^1 k_1 = 0 \tag{14-33b}$$

$$g_{x_2}^2 h_2 + g_{s_2}^2 k_2 = 0 \tag{14-33c}$$

Now

$$\mathscr{L}_{x_ix_j} = f_{ij} + \lambda g_{ij} = \mathscr{L}_{ij} \qquad \mathscr{L}_{x_is_j} = 0 \qquad \begin{array}{l} i = 1, 2, 3 \\ j = 1, 2 \end{array}$$

$$\mathscr{L}_{x_3x_3} = -2\lambda \qquad \mathscr{L}_{x_ix_3} = 0 \qquad \text{if } i \ne 3$$

$$\mathscr{L}_{s_is_j} = \begin{cases} -2\lambda_i & \text{if } i = j \\ 0 & \text{if } i \ne j \end{cases}$$

Then the relations (14-32) and (14-33) become

$$\sum_{j=1}^{2}\sum_{i=1}^{2}\mathscr{L}_{ij}h_ih_j - 2\lambda h_3^2 - 2\lambda_1 k_1^2 - 2\lambda_2 k_2^2 \le 0 \qquad (14\text{-}34)$$

for all h_1, h_2, h_3, k_1, k_2 such that

$$g_1h_1 + g_2h_2 - 2x_3h_3 = 0 \tag{14-35a}$$

$$h_1 - 2s_1k_1 = 0 \tag{14-35b}$$

$$h_2 - 2s_2k_2 = 0 \tag{14-35c}$$

Again, we already know that if $s_1, s_2 \ne 0$, then $\lambda_1, \lambda_2 = 0$, respectively. Also, if $x_3 \ne 0$, then $\lambda = 0$, from (14-30a). Therefore, suppose $s_1 = s_2 = 0$. Then, as before, from (14-35b) and (14-35c), $h_1 = h_2 = 0$. Then (14-34) becomes

$$-2\lambda h_3^2 - 2\lambda_1 k_1^2 - 2\lambda_2 k_2^2 \le 0$$

Letting any *two* of h_3, k_1, and $k_2 = 0$ [this is valid since (14-34) must hold for *all* h_i's and k_i's] yields

$$\lambda \ge 0 \qquad \lambda_1 \ge 0 \qquad \lambda_2 \ge 0$$

The first-order Eqs. (14-29) to (14-31) therefore can be stated as

$$\mathscr{L}_{x_i} = f_i + \lambda g_i \le 0 \qquad \text{if } <, x_i \lessapprox 0 \tag{14-36}$$

$$\mathscr{L}_\lambda = g(x_1, x_2) \ge 0 \qquad \text{if } >, \lambda = 0 \tag{14-37}$$

and we note that $\lambda \ge 0$.

These conditions generalize in a straightforward fashion to the case of n variables and m inequality constraints. In general, consider:

maximize

$$z = f(x_1, \ldots x_n)$$

subject to

$$g^1(x_1, \ldots, x_n) \geq 0$$

$$\vdots$$

$$g^m(x_1, \ldots, x_n) \geq 0$$

$$x_1, \ldots, x_n \geq 0$$

There is no a priori need to restrict m to be less than n (as might be the case with *equality* constraints) since some (or all) of these constraints may turn out to be nonbinding.

Define the Lagrangian

$$\mathcal{L} = f(x_1, \ldots, x_n) + \sum_{j=1}^{m} \lambda_j g^j(x_1, \ldots, x_n)$$

Then the first-order conditions for a maximum are

$$\mathcal{L}_{x_i} = f_i + \sum_{j=1}^{m} \lambda_j g_i^j \leq 0 \qquad \text{if} <, \; x_i = 0 \qquad (14\text{-}38)$$

$$\mathcal{L}_{\lambda_j} = g^j \geq 0 \qquad \text{if} >, \; \lambda_j = 0 \qquad (14\text{-}39)$$

These relations are known as the *Kuhn-Tucker* conditions for a maximum subject to inequality constraints.[†] Again, these conditions are not very useful for determining the actual solution of such a problem. They are descriptions of the maximum position, after the fact, so to speak. *If* it turns out that at the maximum position, $f_i + \lambda g_i < 0$, then $x_i = 0$. Nothing more is implied.

The conditions for a constrained *minimum* are similarly derived. Consider the problem:

minimize

$$z = f(x_1, \ldots, x_n)$$

subject to

$$g^j(x_1, \ldots, x_n) \leq 0 \qquad j = 1, \ldots, m$$

$$x_i \geq 0 \qquad i = 1, \ldots, n$$

The constraints are written as ≤ 0 to preserve symmetry. No loss of generality is involved; merely multiplying any constraint by -1 reverses the sign of any constraint. Again, the Lagrangian, as before, is

---

[†] The original paper is H. W. Kuhn and A. W. Tucker, "Nonlinear Programming," in J. Neyman (ed.), *Proceedings of the Second Berkeley Symposium on Mathematical Statistics and Probability,* University of California Press, Berkeley, 1951.

$$\mathcal{L} = f(x_1, \ldots, x_n) + \sum_{j=1}^{m} \lambda_j g^j(x_1, \ldots, x_n)$$

The first-order conditions are then

$$\mathcal{L}_{x_i} = f_i + \sum_{j=1}^{m} \lambda_j g_i^j \geq 0 \qquad \text{if} >, \ x_i = 0, \qquad i = 1, \ldots, n$$

$$\mathcal{L}_{\lambda_j} = g^j \geq 0 \qquad \text{if} >, \ \lambda_j = 0, \qquad j = 1, \ldots, m$$

Writing the constraints as $g^j \leq 0$ ensures that $\lambda_j \geq 0$.

Let us illustrate these Kuhn-Tucker conditions using the model of a consumer who maximizes his or her utility $U(x_1, x_2)$ subject to a budget constraint. Let us now assume that the consumer need not spend all of his or her money income. The model then becomes

maximize

$$U(x_1, x_2)$$

subject to

$$p_1 x_1 + p_2 x_2 \leq M \qquad x_1, x_2 \geq 0$$

The Lagrangian for this problem is

$$\mathcal{L} = U(x_1, x_2) + \lambda(M - p_1 x_1 - p_2 x_2)$$

The constraint has been incorporated in the Lagrangian in the form $M - p_1 x_1 - p_2 x_2 \geq 0$, conform with the previous analysis.

The first-order conditions are thus

$$\mathcal{L}_1 = U_1 - \lambda p_1 \leq 0 \qquad \text{if} <, \ x_1 = 0 \qquad (14\text{-}40a)$$

$$\mathcal{L}_2 = U_2 - \lambda p_2 \leq 0 \qquad \text{if} <, \ x_2 = 0 \qquad (14\text{-}40b)$$

$$\mathcal{L}_\lambda = M - p_1 x_1 - p_2 x_2 \geq 0 \qquad \text{if} >, \ \lambda = 0 \qquad (14\text{-}40c)$$

The Lagrange multiplier λ represents the consumer's marginal utility of money income. Briefly, suppose $x_1, x_2 > 0$. Then $U_1 = \lambda p_1, U_2 = \lambda p_2$, and

$$\lambda = \frac{U_1}{p_1} = \frac{U_2}{p_2}$$

The term U_1/p_1 represents the marginal utility, per dollar, of income spent on x_1. Likewise, U_2/p_2 represents the marginal utility of income spent on x_2. At a constrained maximum, these two ratios are equal, their common value being simply the marginal utility of money income.

Consider the last condition (14-40c). This can now be interpreted as saying that if the budget constraint is not binding, that is, $p_1 x_1 + p_2 x_2 < M$ (the consumer doesn't exhaust his or her income), then λ, the marginal utility of income, must be 0. The consumer is *satiated* in all commodities. This is confirmed by (14-40a) and (14-40b). If $\lambda = 0$, then $U_1 = U_2 = 0$; that is, the marginal utilities of both goods are 0. Hence, the consumer would not consume more of these goods even if they were given outright, i.e., free. This consumer is at a *bliss point.*

Now consider the situation where $\lambda > 0$ (the consumer would prefer to have more income) and $x_2 = x_2^* > 0$, but at the maximum point, $U_1 - \lambda p_1 < 0$, so that $x_1 = x_1^* = 0$. Assuming positive prices, we have at $x_1^* = 0$, $x_2^* > 0$,

$$\lambda = \frac{U_2}{p_2} > \frac{U_1}{p_1}$$

Rearranging terms gives

$$\frac{U_1}{U_2} < \frac{P_1}{P_2}$$

This situation is depicted in Fig. 14-2. At any point, the consumer's subjective marginal evaluation of x_1, in terms of the x_2 the consumer would willingly forgo to consume an extra unit of x_1, is given by U_1/U_2, the ratio of marginal utilities. This is the (negative) slope of the indifference curve at any point. If the consumer chooses to consume no x_1 at all at the utility maximum, then the consumer's subjective marginal evaluation must be less than the value the market places on

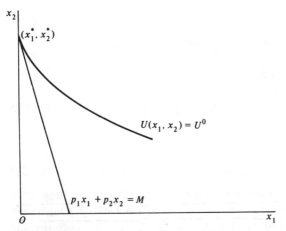

FIGURE 14-2
Maximization of utility at a corner. A consumer achieves maximum utility when $x_1^* = 0, x_2^* > 0$. The consumption of x_1 is 0 because $U_1 - \lambda p_1 < 0$. Assuming positive prices, this inequality is equivalent to $\lambda > U_1/p_1$, since x_2 is consumed in positive amounts. That is, for x_2, the marginal utility of income is the marginal utility per dollar spent on x_2. However, the marginal utility per dollar spent on x_1 is less than that spent on x_2 at the utility maximum; hence $x_1 = 0$. Combining these two relations gives $U_2/p_2 > U_1/p_1$ or $U_1/U_2 < p_1/p_2$, as exhibited in the above diagram, where U_1/U_2 represents the slope of an indifference curve (the consumer's marginal evaluation of x_1) and p_1/p_2 represents the market's evaluation of x_1. As depicted, with convexity, $U_1/U_2 < p_1/p_2$ all along the indifference surface. This consumer, no matter how little x_1 is consumed, always values x_1 less than the market does. Hence, no x_1 is consumed.

x_1. The market will exchange x_2 for x_1 at the ratio p_1/p_2. If, for example, $p_1 = \$6$ and $p_2 = \$2$, the market will exchange 3 units of x_2 for 1 unit of x_1. At zero x_1 consumption, a consumer valuing x_1 at only 2 units of x_2 would not be purchasing any x_1 at all at the utility maximum. In Fig. 14-2, this situation is represented by having the budget line cut the vertical x_2 axis at a steeper slope than the indifference curve $U(x_1, x_2) = U^0$, where U^0 is the maximum achievable utility. That is, $U_1/U_2 < p_1/p_2$ at $x_1^* = 0$, $x_2^* > 0$.

14.3   THE SADDLEPOINT THEOREM

Let us now return to the first-order conditions for the problem:

maximize

$$z = f(x_1, \ldots, x_n)$$

subject to

$$g^1(x_1, \ldots, x_n) \geq 0$$

$$\vdots$$

$$g^m(x_1, \ldots, x_n) \geq 0$$

$$x_1, \ldots, x_n \geq 0$$

For the Lagrangian

$$\mathcal{L} = f(x_1, \ldots, x_n) + \sum_{j=1}^{m} \lambda_j g^j(x_1, \ldots, x_n)$$

the Kuhn-Tucker conditions are, again,

$$\mathcal{L}_{x_i} = f_i + \sum_{j=1}^{m} \lambda_j g_i^j \leq 0 \qquad \text{if} <, \ x_i = 0 \tag{14-38}$$

and

$$\mathcal{L}_{\lambda_j} = g^j \geq 0 \qquad \text{if} >, \ \lambda_j = 0 \tag{14-39}$$

Noting the direction of the inequalities, we see that these conditions are suggestive of the *Lagrangian* function $\mathcal{L}(x_1, \ldots, x_n, \lambda_1, \ldots, \lambda_m)$ achieving a *maximum* in the x directions and a *minimum* in the λ directions. That is, consider the Lagrangian above as just some function of x_i's and λ_j's. If $\mathcal{L}$ achieved a *maximum* with regard to the x_i's, the first-order necessary conditions would be Eqs. (14-38). Likewise, if $\mathcal{L}$ achieved a *minimum* with respect to the λ_j's, the first-order necessary conditions would be precisely Eqs. (14-39).

A point on a function which is a maximum in some directions and a minimum in the others is called a *saddlepoint* of the function. The terminology is suggested by the shape of saddles: in the direction along the horse's backbone, the center of the saddle represents a minimum point, but going from one side of the horse to the other, the center of the saddle represents a maximum.

Consider a function $f(x_1, \ldots, x_n, y_1, \ldots, y_m)$, or, more briefly, $f(\mathbf{x}, \mathbf{y})$, where $\mathbf{x} = (x_1, \ldots, x_n)$, $\mathbf{y} = (y_1, \ldots, y_m)$. The point $(\mathbf{x}^0, \mathbf{y}^0)$ is said to be a saddlepoint of $f(\mathbf{x}, \mathbf{y})$ if

$$f(\mathbf{x}, \mathbf{y}^0) \leq f(\mathbf{x}^0, \mathbf{y}^0) \leq f(\mathbf{x}^0, \mathbf{y})$$

Let us now apply this concept to the Lagrangian above. If the Lagrangian $\mathcal{L} = f(x_1, \ldots, x_n) + \sum_{j=1}^{m} \lambda_j g^j(x_1, \ldots, x_n)$ has a saddlepoint at some values $x_i = x_i^*, i = 1, \ldots, n; \lambda_j = \lambda_j^*, j = 1, \ldots, m$ (briefly, at $\mathbf{x} = x^*, \boldsymbol{\lambda} = \boldsymbol{\lambda}^*$), then, as a necessary consequence, the relations (14-38) and (14-39) are implied. That is, *if*

$$\mathcal{L}(\mathbf{x}, \boldsymbol{\lambda}^*) \leq \mathcal{L}(\mathbf{x}^*, \boldsymbol{\lambda}^*) \leq \mathcal{L}(\mathbf{x}^*, \boldsymbol{\lambda}) \tag{14-41}$$

then it is being asserted that $\mathcal{L}(\mathbf{x}, \boldsymbol{\lambda})$ has a maximum in the $\mathbf{x}$ directions and a minimum in the $\boldsymbol{\lambda}$ directions. The first-order necessary conditions for such an extremum of $\mathcal{L}(\mathbf{x}, \boldsymbol{\lambda})$ are

$$\mathcal{L}_{x_i} \leq 0 \qquad \text{if } <, \ x_i = 0$$

and

$$\mathcal{L}_{\lambda_j} \geq 0 \qquad \text{if } >, \ \lambda_j = 0$$

However, the mere fact that two assertions [constrained maximum of $f(x_1, \ldots, x_n)$ and saddlepoint of $\mathcal{L}(\mathbf{x}, \boldsymbol{\lambda})$] imply the same conditions [Eq. (14-38) and (14-39)] does *not* imply that those two assertions are equivalent or that a particular one implies the other. It *is* the case, however, under fairly general mathematical conditions, that the saddlepoint criterion implies that $f(\mathbf{x})$ has a constrained maximum. The converse is *not* true, however, unless stronger conditions are attached. If it assumed, in addition, that (1) $f(\mathbf{x})$ and the $g^j(\mathbf{x})$'s are all concave functions and (2) there exists an $\mathbf{x}^0 > 0$ such that $g^j(\mathbf{x}^0) > 0$, $j = 1, \ldots, m$ (this condition is known as Slater's *constraint qualification*), then if $(\mathbf{x}^*, \boldsymbol{\lambda}^*)$ is a solution of the constrained maximum problem, $(\mathbf{x}^*, \boldsymbol{\lambda}^*)$ is also a saddlepoint of the Lagrangian function.

This theorem is known as the *Kuhn-Tucker saddlepoint theorem* (there are actually many variants of it). Part of the proof appears in the Appendix to this chapter. Vector notation will be used throughout.

Suppose $(\mathbf{x}^*, \boldsymbol{\lambda}^*)$ is in fact a saddlepoint of $\mathcal{L}(\mathbf{x}, \boldsymbol{\lambda})$. Then, by definition, for $\mathbf{x} \geq 0, \boldsymbol{\lambda} \geq 0$,

$$f(\mathbf{x}) + \boldsymbol{\lambda}^* g(\mathbf{x}) \leq f(\mathbf{x}^*) + \boldsymbol{\lambda}^* g(\mathbf{x}^*) \tag{14-42}$$

and

$$f(\mathbf{x}^*) + \boldsymbol{\lambda}^* g(\mathbf{x}^*) \leq f(\mathbf{x}^*) + \boldsymbol{\lambda} g(\mathbf{x}^*) \tag{14-43}$$

where $\boldsymbol{\lambda} g(\mathbf{x})$ means $\sum_{j=1}^{m} \lambda_j g^j(\mathbf{x})$, the inner product of the vectors $\boldsymbol{\lambda} = (\lambda_1, \ldots, \lambda_m)$ and $\mathbf{g}(\mathbf{x}) = (g^1(\mathbf{x}), \ldots, g^m(\mathbf{x}))$. From (14-43), after canceling $f(\mathbf{x}^*)$ from both sides and rearranging, we have

$$(\boldsymbol{\lambda} - \boldsymbol{\lambda}^*) g(\mathbf{x}^*) \geq 0 \tag{14-44}$$

Since (14-44) must hold for *any* λ, by hypothesis, for sufficiently large λ, $\lambda - \lambda^* \geq 0$ and hence

$$g(x^*) \geq 0 \tag{14-45}$$

Thus we have shown that x^* is *feasible;* i.e., it satisfies the constraints of the maximum problem. Moreover, we can set $\lambda = 0$ in (14-44) (again, since this must hold for *all* λ), obtaining, after multiplying by -1,

$$\lambda^* g(x^*) \leq 0 \tag{14-46}$$

However, $\lambda^* \geq 0, g(x^*) \geq 0$. Therefore, in order to satisfy (14-46), it must be that

$$\lambda^* g(x^*) = 0 \tag{14-47}$$

Now consider the first inequality, (14-42), which refers to the maximum in the x directions. When we use Eq. (14-47), (14-42) becomes

$$f(x^*) \geq f(x) + \lambda^* g(x) \tag{14-48}$$

However, $\lambda^* \geq 0$, and for any *feasible* x, that is, an x which satisfies the constraints, $g(x) \geq 0$. Therefore, $\lambda^* g(x) \geq 0$, and thus

$$f(x^*) \geq f(x) \tag{14-49}$$

for any feasible x. Therefore, x^* maximizes $f(x)$ subject to the constraints $g(x) \geq 0$. We have therefore shown that the saddlepoint condition implies that a constrained maximum exists.

To repeat, the converse of the preceding is in general false. If conditions 1 and 2 above are added, viz., that $f(x)$ and $g^j(x)$, $j = 1, \ldots, m$, are all concave and that there exists an x^0 such that $g^j(x^0) > 0$, $j = 1, \ldots, m$, then the "converse" follows. The proof of this proposition unfortunately requires more advanced methods of linear algebra dealing with convex sets. It is presented in the Appendix to the chapter. Note, however, that the right-hand part of the saddlepoint inequality follows readily from the assumption of a constrained maximum. If x^*, λ^* are the values that maximize $f(x)$ subject to $g(x) \geq 0$, then

$$\mathscr{L}(x^*, \lambda^*) = f(x^*) + \lambda^* g(x^*)$$

However, from the first-order conditions, $\lambda^* g(x^*) = 0$. Hence,

$$\mathscr{L}(x^*, \lambda^*) = f(x^*)$$

By definition

$$\mathscr{L}(x^*, \lambda) = f(x^*) + \lambda g(x^*)$$

But $g(x^*) \geq 0$, and $\lambda \geq 0$ by assumption; thus

$$\mathscr{L}(x^*, \lambda^*) = f(x^*) \leq f(x^*) + \lambda g(x^*) = \mathscr{L}(x^*, \lambda)$$

i.e., the right-hand part of the relation (14-41).

Example. We shall show by example that achieving a constrained maximum does not imply that the Lagrangian has a saddlepoint there. Consider a consumer who maximizes the utility function $U = x_1 x_2$ subject to the constraint $p_1 x_1 + p_2 x_2 \leq M$. Since the level (indifference) curves of the utility function, $x_1 x_2 = U^0$, never cross the axes and $U_1, U_2 > 0$ for all positive x, the consumer will in fact spend his or her entire income; that is $M - p_1 x_1 - p_2 x_2 = 0$. Thus, the problem is solved by formulating

$$\mathscr{L} = x_1 x_2 + \lambda(M - p_1 x_1 - p_2 x_2) \tag{14-50}$$

with first-order equations

$$\mathscr{L}_1 = x_2 - \lambda p_1 = 0$$
$$\mathscr{L}_2 = x_1 - \lambda p_2 = 0$$
$$\mathscr{L}_\lambda = M - p_1 x_1 - p_2 x_2 = 0 \tag{14-51}$$

The consumer's demand functions are found by first eliminating λ:

$$x_2 = \lambda p_1 \qquad x_1 = \lambda p_2$$

and thus

$$\frac{x_2}{x_1} = \frac{p_1}{p_2}$$

or

$$p_1 x_1 = p_2 x_2$$

Substituting this relation into the budget constraint ($\mathscr{L}_\lambda = 0$) gives

$$p_1 x_1 + p_1 x_1 = M$$

and thus

$$x_1^* = \frac{M}{2p_1} \tag{14-52a}$$

Similarly,

$$x_2^* = \frac{M}{2p_2} \tag{14-52b}$$

Also,

$$\lambda^* = \frac{x_2^*}{p_1} = \frac{x_1^*}{p_2} = \frac{M}{2p_1 p_2} \tag{14-53}$$

We therefore find

$$\mathscr{L}(\mathbf{x}^*, \lambda^*) = x_1^* x_2^* + \lambda^*(M - p_1 x_1^* - p_2 x_2^*) \tag{14-54}$$

However, the budget constraint is satisfied by x_1^*, x_2^*, and thus

$$\mathscr{L}(\mathbf{x}^*, \lambda^*) = \frac{M}{2p_1} \frac{M}{2p_2} = \frac{M^2}{4p_1 p_2} = U(x_1^*, x_2^*)$$

By definition

$$\mathscr{L}(\mathbf{x}^*, \lambda) = U(x_1^*, x_2^*) + \lambda(M - p_1 x_1^* - p_2 x_2^*)$$

Since the budget constraint is binding at x_1^*, x_2^*,

$$\mathcal{L}(\mathbf{x}^*, \lambda) = U(x_1^*, x_2^*) = \frac{M^2}{4p_1p_2} = \mathcal{L}(\mathbf{x}^*, \lambda^*)$$

Hence, the right-hand side of the saddlepoint is satisfied as an equality,

$$\mathcal{L}(\mathbf{x}^*, \lambda^*) = \mathcal{L}(\mathbf{x}^*, \lambda) \tag{14-55}$$

The left-hand side of the saddlepoint condition is *not* satisfied, however:

$$\mathcal{L}(\mathbf{x}, \lambda^*) = U(x_1, x_2) + \lambda^*(M - p_1x_1 - p_2x_2)$$

$$= x_1x_2 + \frac{M}{2p_1p_2}(M - p_1x_1 - p_2x_2)$$

If we let $x_1 = x_2 = 0$,

$$\mathcal{L}(\mathbf{x}, \lambda^*) = \frac{M^2}{2p_1p_2} > \frac{M^2}{4p_1p_2} = \mathcal{L}(\mathbf{x}^*, \lambda^*)$$

The saddlepoint condition is violated because although $U = x_1x_2$ is quasiconcave in x_1 and x_2, it is not *concave*. Thus the mere attainment of a constrained maximum is *not* sufficient for the Lagrangian to possess a saddlepoint at the maximum position.

14.4   NONLINEAR PROGRAMMING

The general class of problems involving maximization of a function subject to inequality and nonnegativity constraints is called *nonlinear programming problems*. These problems, of the form:

maximize

$$y = f(x_1, \ldots, x_n)$$

subject to

$$g^1(x_1, \ldots, x_n) \geq 0$$

$$\vdots$$

$$g^m(x_1, \ldots, x_n) \geq 0$$

$$x_1, \ldots, x_n \geq 0$$

do not contain specific enough structure to permit description of the solution. The determination of exactly which constraints will be binding and which will not makes this class of problems significantly more complex than the classical problem of maximizing a function subject to equality constraints with nonnegativity not imposed. Once it is shown which constraints are binding, the preceding problem reduces to a classical maximization problem, solvable (*in principle*—the equations may admit of no easily expressible solution) by standard Lagrangian techniques.

Solutions to nonlinear programming problems will be found only by some *iterative* procedure, i.e., an *algorithm* which leads one toward the maximum in a stepwise fashion. In general, such algorithms begin with an arbitrary *feasible* point, i.e., an $\mathbf{x} = (x_1, \ldots, x_n)$, which satisfies all the constraints, including nonnegativity. Then in the neighborhood of that point some evaluation is made of how $f(\mathbf{x})$ could be increased, e.g., by decreasing some x_i's and increasing others. When a new point is reached, the evaluation is repeated. A successful algorithm is one which leads to the maximum position in a finite (but not astronomically large) number of steps.

A number of algorithms have been developed, assuming various specific structures on the f and g^j functions. The most famous is the *simplex algorithm,* developed by George Dantzig in 1947 for solving the class of *linear* programming problems.[†] This type of problem results when f and the g^j's are all linear functions, or:

maximize

$$y = \sum_{i=1}^{n} p_i x_i$$

subject to

$$\sum_{j=1}^{n} a_{ij} x_j \leq b_i \qquad i = 1, \ldots, m$$

$$x_j \geq 0 \qquad j = 1, \ldots, n$$

This class of problems will be investigated in the chapter on linear general equilibrium models.

No general algorithm for all nonlinear programming problems exists. The specific algorithms that exist for some nonlinear problems are not of central interest to most economists and are outside the scope of this book. We shall only briefly indicate some structures for which algorithms have been more successful.

One of the central problems encountered in nonlinear programming problems is the determination of whether a *local* solution is in fact the *global* solution of the problem. That is, suppose $f(\mathbf{x}^*) \geq f(\mathbf{x})$ for all $\mathbf{x}$ in some neighborhood of $\mathbf{x}^*$. Then $\mathbf{x}^*$ is a *local* maximum. How can we be sure that $\mathbf{x}^*$ is the *global* solution, that is, $f(\mathbf{x}^*) \geq f(\mathbf{x})$, for all feasible $\mathbf{x}$? In general, of course, one can't be sure, but under certain structures local solutions are in fact global solutions. Let us explore these circumstances.

[†]G. Dantzig, 'Maximization of a Linear Function of Variables Subject to Linear Inequalities', in T.C. Koopmans (ed.), *Activity Analysis and Allocation, Cowles Commission Monograph* 13, John Wiley & Sons, Inc., New York, 1951.

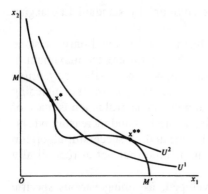

FIGURE 14-3

Utility maximization subject to nonlinear budget constraint. **x*** and **x**** are both *local* maxima of $U(x_1, x_2)$. However, **x**** is the *global* maximum point. The nonlinear budget constraint MM' produces a feasible set which is not convex. Under these circumstances, and with nonconcave objective functions, such nonglobal local maxima can occur. If the feasible set is convex and the objective function is a concave function, then any local maximum is the global maximum. The efficiency of solution algorithms can be vastly increased under those circumstances.

Consider Fig. 14-3, in which a consumer attempts to maximize some utility function $U(x_1, x_2)$ whose indifference curves, U^1 and U^2, are shown. Suppose, contrary to the usual assumptions, that the budget constraint is *not* the usual linear form, $p_1 x_1 + p_2 x_2 \leq M$, but the area bounded by the curved line MM'. Given this situation, *two* local constrained maxima exist: **x*** and **x****. At **x***, $U(\mathbf{x}^*) > U(\mathbf{x})$ for all **x** in *some* neighborhoods of **x***. An iterative procedure which led to **x*** as the solution to this problem might be insufficiently powerful to indicate that if the neighborhood is made large enough, some **x**'s will be found for which $U(\mathbf{x}) > U(\mathbf{x}^*)$. In the given example, **x**** is the *global* maximum, since clearly $U(\mathbf{x}^{**}) > U(\mathbf{x})$ for all other **x** in the budget set.

The problem of nonglobal maxima occurs here because points connecting **x*** and **x**** lie outside the *feasible region,* i.e., the set of all feasible **x**'s. That is, a straight line joining **x*** and **x**** contains points not admissible under the conditions of the model. A very important construct in analyses of nonlinear programming problems is therefore that of a *convex set.*

Definition. A set S is said to be convex if, for all $x^1 \in S, x^2 \in S$ (the symbol "$\in$" means "belonging to" or, "is an element of"), the points $x = kx^1 + (1-k)x^2$ belong to S, for all $0 \leq k \leq 1$.

Geometrically, a convex set is one such that all points along a straight line joining any two points in the set also belong to the set. The straight line joining any two points in the set never leaves the set. All squares, triangles, circles, spheres, and parallelograms are convex sets; sets like that depicted in Fig. 14-3, the points bounded by the axes and the curve MM', are nonconvex.

The principal result on local versus global maxima is, as indicated in the above discussion, the following theorem.

Theorem. Let $f(\mathbf{x}), \mathbf{x} = (x_1, \ldots, x_n)$ be a quasi-concave function defined over some convex set S. Then if $f(\mathbf{x}^*)$ is a unique local maximum in S, it is in fact the *global* maximum.

Proof. Suppose there exists an $\mathbf{x}^{**}$ such that $f(\mathbf{x}^{**}) > f(\mathbf{x}^*)$. Then, by quasi-concavity,

$$f(k\mathbf{x}^* + (1-k)\mathbf{x}^{**}) \geq f(\mathbf{x}^*) \qquad 0 \leq k \leq 1$$

By choosing k arbitrarily close to 1, the point $(k\mathbf{x}^* + (1-k)\mathbf{x}^{**})$ becomes arbitrarily close to $\mathbf{x}^*$; yet, the function has a value there greater than or equal to its value at $\mathbf{x}^*$, a unique local maximum. This contradiction demonstrates the result.

Heuristically, if $\mathbf{x}^*$ and $\mathbf{x}^{**}$ are any two finitely separated points of local maxima, the chord joining them must lie in the convex set S. The function evaluated along that chord must be at least as large as the smaller of $f(\mathbf{x}^*)$ and $f(\mathbf{x}^{**})$. If, say, $f(\mathbf{x}^*) > f(\mathbf{x}^{**})$, points $\mathbf{x}$ arbitrarily near $\mathbf{x}^{**}$ must also yield $f(\mathbf{x}^*) > f(\mathbf{x}^{**})$, contradicting the assumption that $\mathbf{x}^{**}$ is a local maximum. If $f(\mathbf{x}^*) = f(\mathbf{x}^{**})$, the function must be constant along the chord joining $\mathbf{x}^*$ and $\mathbf{x}^{**}$. It follows, therefore, that if a local maximum is unique, it is the global maximum over the convex set S.

Under what conditions will the set of variables over which a maximum problem is posed be convex? That is, under what conditions is the feasible region of a nonlinear programming problem a convex set? It is easy to show that if the constraints are all concave functions, the feasible region is in fact convex.

Consider the set S defined as the $\mathbf{x} = (x_1, \ldots, x_n)$ such that $g(\mathbf{x}) \geq a$, where a is any real number. Then S is convex; for consider any $\mathbf{x}^1, \mathbf{x}^2$ for which $g(\mathbf{x}^1) \geq a, g(\mathbf{x}^2) \geq a$. From concavity

$$g(k\mathbf{x}^1 + (1-k)\mathbf{x}^2) \geq kg(\mathbf{x}^1) + (1-k)g(\mathbf{x}^2) \geq ka + (1-k)a = a \qquad 0 \leq k \leq 1$$

Therefore the point $k\mathbf{x}^1 + (1-k)\mathbf{x}^2$ lies in the set, and S is convex. If some functions $g^1(\mathbf{x}), \ldots, g^m(\mathbf{x})$ are all concave, then the set of $\mathbf{x}$'s that satisfy

$$g^1(\mathbf{x}) \geq a_1$$
$$\vdots$$
$$g^m(\mathbf{x}) \geq a_m$$

simultaneously clearly also constitutes a convex set, as would be the case if non-negativity constraints are added. (The intersection of convex sets is a convex set.) Hence, if the constraints of a programming problem are all concave, the feasible region will be a convex set. If the objective function is also concave, we can be assured that any local maximum is the global maximum of the model.

The principal application of the above theorem, to be discussed in the next chapter, is in the theory of linear programming in which $f(\mathbf{x}), g^1(\mathbf{x}), \ldots, g^m(\mathbf{x})$ are all linear functions. In that case, the feasible region is convex, and an efficient algorithm for finding the solution to the problem has been developed.

14.5 AN "ADDING-UP" THEOREM

Many economic models have the general structure:

maximize

$$y = f(x_1, \ldots, x_n)$$

subject to

$$g^1(x_1, \ldots, x_n) \leq b_1$$

$$\vdots$$

$$g^m(x_1, \ldots, x_n) \leq b_m \quad x_1, \ldots, x_n \geq 0$$

Let us now assume that $f, g^1, \ldots, g^m$ are all homogeneous of the same degree r. Assume that the problem admits of a solution found by standard Lagrange-Kuhn-Tucker techniques. The Lagrangian is

$$\mathcal{L} = f(x_1, \ldots, x_n) + \sum_{j=1}^{m} \lambda_j^*(b_j - g^j(x_1, \ldots, x_n)) \tag{14-56}$$

The first-order conditions are therefore

$$f_i \leq \sum_{j=1}^{m} \lambda_j^* g_i^j \qquad \text{if } <, \; x_j = 0 \tag{14-57}$$

and

$$b_j - g^j \geq 0 \qquad \text{if } >, \; \lambda_j = 0 \tag{14-58}$$

Alternatively,

$$f_i x_i^* = \sum_{j=1}^{m} \lambda_j^* g_i^j x_i^* \tag{14-59}$$

and

$$b_j \lambda_j^* = g^j \lambda_j^* \tag{14-60}$$

Let us now sum (14-59) over i and (14-60) over j. This yields

$$\sum_{i=1}^{n} f_i x_i^* = \sum_{j=1}^{m} \lambda_j^* \sum_{i=1}^{n} g_i^j x_i^* \tag{14-61}$$

and

$$\sum_{j=1}^{m} b_j \lambda_j^* = \sum_{j=1}^{m} g^j \lambda_j^* \tag{14-62}$$

Now let us use Euler's theorem. Since f and $g^1, \ldots, g^m$ are all homogeneous of degree r, $\sum f_i x_i \equiv rf$, $\sum g_i^j x_i \equiv rg^j$, and hence from (14-61), letting $y^* = f(\mathbf{x}^*)$, we have

$$ry^* = rf(\mathbf{x}^*) = \sum_{j=1}^{m} \lambda_j^* rg^j(\mathbf{x}^*) = r \sum_{j=1}^{m} \lambda_j^* b_j$$

or

$$y^* = \sum_{j=1}^{m} \lambda_j^* b_j \tag{14-63}$$

Now from general envelope considerations,

$$\lambda_j^* = \frac{\partial y^*}{\partial b_j}$$

If the constraint $g^j(\mathbf{x}) \leq b_j$ is thought of as a *resource constraint,* wherein b_j represents the amount of some resource used by the economy, $\lambda_j^* = \partial y^*/\partial b_j$ represents the *imputed rent,* or shadow price, of that resource, measured in terms of y. In other words, $\lambda_j^* b_j$ can be thought of as the total factor cost of some factor associated with some resource allocation. Equation (14-63) then says that under these assumptions, the output being maximized can be allocated to each resource, with nothing left over on either side. This type of adding-up, or exhaustion-of-the-product, theorem appeared in the chapters on production and cost, when linear homogeneous production functions were involved. The preceding is a generalization of those results.

Moreover, consider the indirect objective function

$$\phi(b_1, \ldots, b_m) = f(x_1^*, \ldots, x_n^*) = y^*$$

Since $y^* \equiv \sum_{j=1}^{m} \lambda_j^* b_j$ and $\lambda_j^* = \partial y^*/\partial b_j = \partial \phi/\partial b_j$,

$$\phi(b_1, \ldots, b_m) \equiv \sum_{j=1}^{m} \frac{\partial \phi}{\partial b_j} b_j \tag{14-64}$$

Therefore, under these conditions, the indirect objective function is homogeneous of degree 1 in the parameters $b_1, \ldots, b_m$, from the converse of Euler's theorem.

PROBLEMS

1. Explain the error in the following statement: For a profit-maximizing firm, if the value of the marginal product of some factor is initially less than its wage, the factor will not be used. State the condition correctly.

2. Consider the constrained *minimum* problem:

   minimize

   $$z = f(x_1, x_2)$$

   subject to

   $$g(x_1, x_2) \leq 0 \qquad x_1, x_2 \geq 0$$

   Derive the Kuhn-Tucker first-order conditions for a minimum.

3. Consider the cost minimization problem:

   minimize

   $$C = w_1 x_1 + w_2 x_2$$

   subject to

   $$f(x_1, x_2) \geq y \qquad x_1, x_2 \geq 0$$

Derive and interpret the first-order conditions for a minimum. Under what conditions on the production function will the Lagrangian have a saddlepoint at the cost-minimizing solution?

4. Consider a consumer who maximizes the utility function $U = x_2 e^{x_1}$ subject to a budget constraint. Characterize the implied demand levels via the Kuhn-Tucker conditions, i.e., indicate when positive demand levels are present for both commodities, etc.

5. Consider the quadratic utility function, $U = ax_1^2 + 2bx_1x_2 + cx_2^2$. Discuss the nature of the implied consumer choices for this utility function in terms of the values a, b, and c.

6. Find the solution to the following nonlinear programming problem:

maximize

$$y = x_1 x_2$$

subject to

$$x_1 + x_2 \leq 10 \qquad x_1 + 2x_2 \leq 18 \qquad x_1, x_2 \geq 0$$

7. Consider the nonlinear programming problem:

maximize

$$y = x_1 x_2$$

subject to

$$x_1 + x_2 \leq 10 \qquad x_2 \leq k \qquad x_1, x_2 \geq 0$$

What is the maximum value of k for which that constraint is binding?

8. Solve:

minimize

$$y = x_1 + 2x_2$$

subject to

$$x_1 x_2 \geq 8 \qquad x_1 \geq 5 \qquad x_1, x_2 \geq 0$$

9. Solve the Prob. 8 with $x_1 \leq 5$ replacing $x_1 \geq 5$.

10. An individual has the utility function $U = x_1^{1/3} x_2^{2/3}$ for consumption in two time periods, with $x_1 = $ present consumption, $x_2 = $ next year's consumption. This person has an initial stock of capital of \$10, which can yield consumption along an "investment possibilities frontier," given by $2x_1^2 + x_2^2 = 200$. The person can, however, borrow and lend at some market rate of interest r to rearrange consumption. (a) Explain why maximization of utility requires a prior maximization of wealth W, where $W = x_1 + x_2/(1 + r)$. That is, explain why if W is not maximized, $U(x_1, x_2)$ cannot be maximized. (b) Suppose the consumer can borrow or lend at $r = 30$ percent. Find the utility maximizing consumption choices. Is the consumer a borrower or a lender? (c) Suppose the consumer can lend money at only 20 percent interest and can borrow at no less than 40 percent interest. What consumption plan maximizes utility, and what is the present value of that consumption?

The proof that if $f(\mathbf{x}), g^1(\mathbf{x}), \ldots, g^m(\mathbf{x})$ are all concave functions, then

$$\mathscr{L}(\mathbf{x}, \lambda^*) \le \mathscr{L}(\mathbf{x}^*, \lambda^*) = f(\mathbf{x}^*)$$

where $\mathbf{x}^*$ solves the maximum problem, is based on a famous theorem of convexset analysis. Consider two nonintersecting (disjoint) convex sets S_1 and S_2. It is geometrically obvious, though messy to prove, that a *hyperplane* (the generalization of a *line* in two dimensions, *plane* in three dimensions, etc.) can be passed between S_1 and S_2. This proposition is known as the *separating hyperplane theorem*. The theorem also holds if the sets are tangent at one point.

Consider Fig. 14-4; S_1 and S_2 are two convex sets that do not intersect. It is therefore possible to pass between them a line $p_1 x_1 + p_2 x_2 = k$ or, in vector notation, $\mathbf{px} = k$. Figure 14-5 shows why such may not be the case if the sets are nonconvex.

Since all the points in S_2 lie "above" the hyperplane, for all $\mathbf{x}^2 \in S_2, \mathbf{px}^2 \ge k$. (The weak inequality is used since the hyperplane might be tangent to S_2). Similarly, since S_1 lies "below" the hyperplane, for all $\mathbf{x}^1 \in S_1, \mathbf{px}^1 \le k$. Therefore, for any two disjoint convex sets S_1 and S_2, there exist scalars p_1, p_2 not both 0 such that

$$\mathbf{px}^1 \le \mathbf{px}^2$$

The direction of the inequality is actually arbitrary. Reversing the signs of p_1, p_2 changes the direction of the inequality. The theorem generalizes to n dimensions. If S_1 and S_2 are any two disjoint convex sets in euclidean n space, for any $\mathbf{x}^1 \in S_1, \mathbf{x}^2 \in S_2$, there exist scalars $p_1, \ldots, p_n$, not all zero, such that

$$\sum_{i=1}^{n} p_i x_i^1 \le \sum_{i=1}^{n} p_i x_i^2 \tag{14A-1}$$

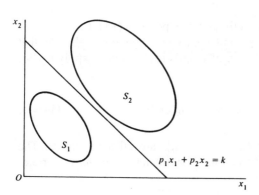

FIGURE 14-4

A *separating hyperplane*. Sets S_1 and S_2 are both convex, and they are *disjoint*; i.e., they have no point in common. Under these circumstances it is always possible to pass a hyperplane (in two dimensions, a straight line) between the two sets. The equation of this hyperplane, in two dimensions is $p_1 x_1 + p_2 x_2 = k$. Since S_2 lies above this plane, for all x_1^2, x_2^2 in $S_2, p_1 x_1^2 + p_2 x_2^2 \ge k$. Similarly, for all x_1^1, x_2^1 in $S_1, p_1 x_1^1 + p_2 x_2^1 \le k$. Hence, the separating hyperplane theorem says that if S_1 and S_2 are disjoint convex sets in n space, there exist scalars $p_1, \ldots, p_n$ not all 0, such that $\sum_{i}^{n} p_i x_i^1 \le \sum_{i=1}^{n} p_i x_i^2$, for all $\mathbf{x}^1$ in S_1 and $\mathbf{x}^2$ in S_2. The theorem also holds if the sets intersect at only one point, that is, S_1 and S_2 are tangent to each other.

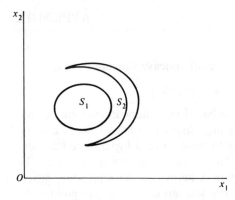

FIGURE 14-5
Nonconvex sets. It is not always possible to separate nonconvex sets with a hyperplane.

Let us return now to the saddlepoint problem. We are assuming that $\mathbf{x}^*$ maximizes $f(\mathbf{x})$ subject to $g^j(\mathbf{x}) \geq 0$, $j = 1, \ldots, m$, $\mathbf{x} \geq 0$. We shall also assume Slater's constraint qualification that there exists an $\mathbf{x}^0 \geq 0$ such that $g^j(\mathbf{x}^0) > 0$, $j = 1, \ldots, m$. For any given $\mathbf{x}$, there exist the $m + 1$ values $f(\mathbf{x})$, $g^1(\mathbf{x}), \ldots, g^m(\mathbf{x})$, an $(m + 1)$–dimensional vector.

1. Define the set S_1 as the vectors $\mathbf{U} = (U_0, U_1, \ldots, U_m)$ such that $U_0 \leq f(\mathbf{x})$, $U_j \leq g^j(\mathbf{x})$, $j = 1, \ldots, m$, for all feasible $\mathbf{x}$.
2. Define S_2 as the vectors $\mathbf{V} = (V_0, V_1, \ldots, V_m)$ such that $V_0 > f(\mathbf{x}^*)$, $V_j > 0, j = 1, \ldots, m$.

The sets S_1 and S_2 are convex, disjoint sets. S_1 is convex because $f, g^1, \ldots, g^m$ are all concave functions. The results at the end of Sec. 14.4 imply convexity for S_1; S_2 is convex because S_2 is essentially the positive quadrant in $m + 1$ space, except that the first coordinate, V_0, starts at $f(\mathbf{x}^*)$. Finally, since $f(\mathbf{x}^*) \geq f(\mathbf{x})$, and since $V_0 > f(\mathbf{x}^*)$, there can be no $\mathbf{V}$ vector which lies in S_1. The first coordinate, V_0, violates the definition of S_1.

Since S_1 and S_2 are disjoint convex sets, by the separating hyperplane theorem there exist scalars $\lambda_0, \lambda_1, \ldots, \lambda_m$ such that

$$\sum_{j=0}^{m} U_j \lambda_j \leq \sum_{j=0}^{m} V_j \lambda_j \tag{14A-2}$$

for all $\mathbf{U} \in S_1, \mathbf{V} \in S_2$. Moreover, although the point $(f(\mathbf{x}^*), 0, \ldots, 0)$ is not in S_2, it is on the boundary of S_2 and hence the theorem applies to that point as well. The point $(f(\mathbf{x}), g^1(\mathbf{x}), \ldots, g^m(\mathbf{x}))$ is in S_1. Hence, applying Eq. (14A-2) gives

$$\lambda_0 f(\mathbf{x}) + \sum_{j=1}^{m} \lambda_j g^j(\mathbf{x}) \leq \lambda_0 f(\mathbf{x}^*) \tag{14A-3}$$

It can be seen from Eq.(14A-2) that $\lambda_0, \lambda_1, \ldots, \lambda_m$ are all nonnegative. The vectors $\mathbf{U}$ include the entire negative "quadrant," or orthant of this $m + 1$ space.

Any of the U_j's can be made arbitrarily large, negatively. Note that $V_1, \ldots, V_m$ are all greater than 0. If any $\lambda_j, j = 1, \ldots, m$, were negative, making that U_j sufficiently negative would violate the inequality (14A-2). Lastly, since $f(\mathbf{x}^*)$ $\geq f(\mathbf{x})$, and since $\mathbf{x}^*$ maximizes $f(\mathbf{x})$, $\lambda_0 \geq 0$ for essentially the same reasons.

Therefore, all the λ's in (14A-3) are nonnegative. Moreover, given the constraint qualification, $\lambda_0 > 0$; for suppose $\lambda_0 = 0$; then (14A-3) says that

$$\sum \lambda_j g^j(\mathbf{x}) \leq 0$$

However, since the separating hyperplane theorem says that not all the λ_j's are 0 and the constraint qualification says that $g^j(\mathbf{x}^0) > 0, j = 1, \ldots, m$, it must be the case that at $\mathbf{x}^0$

$$\sum \lambda_j g^j(\mathbf{x}^0) > 0$$

contradicting the preceding. Hence, $\lambda_0 > 0$. We can therefore divide (14A-3) by λ_0, and if we define

$$\lambda_j^* = \frac{\lambda_j}{\lambda_0} \qquad j = 1, \ldots, m$$

Eq. (14A-3) becomes

$$f(\mathbf{x}) + \sum_{j=1}^m \lambda_j^* g^j(\mathbf{x}) \leq f(\mathbf{x}^*) \qquad (14A\text{-}4)$$

When $\mathbf{x} = \mathbf{x}^*$, (14A-4) yields

$$\sum \lambda_j^* g^j(\mathbf{x}^*) \leq 0$$

but since $\lambda_j^* \geq 0$, $g^j(\mathbf{x}^*) \geq 0$, $j = 1, \ldots, m$,

$$\sum \lambda_j^* g^j(\mathbf{x}^*) = 0$$

Defining the Lagrangian,

$$\mathscr{L}(\mathbf{x}, \boldsymbol{\lambda}) = f(\mathbf{x}) + \sum_{j=1}^m \lambda_j g^j(\mathbf{x})$$

we find, with $\mathbf{x} \geq \mathbf{0}, \boldsymbol{\lambda} \geq \mathbf{0}$,

$$\mathscr{L}(\mathbf{x}^*, \boldsymbol{\lambda}^*) = f(\mathbf{x}^*)$$

and therefore

$$\mathscr{L}(\mathbf{x}, \boldsymbol{\lambda}^*) = f(\mathbf{x}) + \sum_{j=1}^m \lambda_j^* g^j(\mathbf{x}) \leq f(\mathbf{x}^*) = \mathscr{L}(\mathbf{x}^*, \boldsymbol{\lambda}^*) \qquad (14A\text{-}5)$$

satisfying the saddlepoint criterion. We showed in the chapter proper that

$$\mathscr{L}(\mathbf{x}^*, \boldsymbol{\lambda}^*) \leq \mathscr{L}(\mathbf{x}^*, \boldsymbol{\lambda})$$

Hence, if $f(\mathbf{x}), g^1(\mathbf{x}), \ldots, g^m(\mathbf{x})$ are all concave, and if there exists an $\mathbf{x}^0$ such that $g^j(\mathbf{x}^0) > 0$, $j = 1, \ldots, m$, solving the constrained maximum problem implies that the saddlepoint condition will be satisfied.

BIBLIOGRAPHY

The following articles and books all require advanced mathematical training.

Arrow, K. J., and A. C. Enthoven: "Quasi-concave Programming," *Econometrica* **29**:779–800, 1961.

Arrow, K. J., A. C. Enthoven, L. Hurwicz, and H. Uzawa (eds.), *Studies in Linear and Nonlinear Programming,* Stanford University Press, Stanford, 1958.

Dantzig, G. B.: "Maximization of a Linear Function of Variables Subject to Linear Inequalities," in T. C. Koopmans (ed.) *Activity Analysis of Production and Allocation, Cowles Commission Monograph* 13, John Wiley & Sons, Inc., New York, 1951.

El Hodiri, M.: "Constrained Extrema: Introduction to the Differentiable Case, with Economic Application," *Lecture Notes in Operations Research and Mathematical Systems,* Vol. 56, Springer, 1970.

El Hodri, M. "The Math-Econ Trick," *Manifold,* **17**:8–15, Autumn 1975.

John, F.: "Extremum Problems with Inequalities as Subsidiary Conditions," in *Studies and Essays, Courant Anniversary Volume,* Interscience, New York, 1948.

Kuhn, H. W., and A. W. Tucker: "Nonlinear Programming" in J. Neyman (ed.), *Proceedings of the Second Berkeley Symposium on Mathematical Statistics and Probability,* University of California Press, Berkeley, 1951. The seminal work.

Rockafellar, R. T.: *Convex Analysis,* Princeton University Press, Princeton, NJ, 1970.

Valentine, F.: "The Problem of Lagrange with Differential Inequalities as Side Conditions," in *Contributions to the Calculus of Variations, 1933–1937,* University of Chicago Press, Chicago, 1937.

CHAPTER
15

GENERAL EQUILIBRIUM I: LINEAR MODELS

15.1 INTRODUCTION: FIXED-COEFFICIENT TECHNOLOGY

In the previous chapters, the models analyzed were derived from the Marshallian framework of partial equilibrium. That is, the models related to *one* firm or *one* individual, with the rest of the market taken as given. No attempt was made to consider the aggregate effects of the simultaneous actions of consumers or firms in response to some parameter change. The actions of each consumer or each firm by itself may in general have no significant impact on market prices or aggregate quantities. However, if all firms or consumers react to a given parameter change in the same direction, one would expect to observe changes in the aggregate levels of other variables formerly held constant in the analysis.

Consider, for example, the effects of an increase in the price of some final good, produced by a rightward shift of the demand curve for that good. Each firm in the industry will simultaneously attempt to increase its output of that good. If a competitive factor market is assumed, each firm takes factor prices as given. That is, individual adjustments of factor levels by a given firm are not expected to affect factor prices. However, if *all* firms simultaneously wish to employ more labor and capital, the prices of labor and capital can be expected to change. If this industry is a significant part of the economy, then whether or not factor prices rise or fall might not be determinable by considering this one industry alone. In a *closed economy,* an increase in the demand for this industry's output means a *decrease* in demand for some alternative commodity. If the labor and capital markets for the two industries are interrelated, i.e., resources can move from one industry to the other, the change in factor prices depends upon the relative intensity of factor use in each industry.

The preceding phenomena are usually labeled *general equilibrium problems.* The terms *partial equilibrium* and *general equilibrium* should not connote the superiority of one model over another. One model is not uniformly more general than the other. The differences between the models are best described as differences in test conditions. That is, different parameters are held fixed in the two classes of models. In the partial-equilibrium framework, in which one very small part of an economy is analyzed, prices of factors and goods in unrelated industries are assumed constant. Total quantities of goods and factors are generally considered variable. In the general-equilibrium models, as we shall see, total quantities of resources are usually assumed fixed, and the emphasis of the analysis is on interindustry reactions. The appropriateness of the model depends on the problem to be studied. Generality, while desirable *ceterus paribus,* is not necessarily to be preferred in all cases. Greater generality is usually accompanied by greater complexity. The proper trade-offs to be made for an efficient analysis of some problem cannot be assigned a priori.

This point was made earlier in Chap. 1, in the discussion of the realism of assumptions. To take a particular example, the analysis of price controls and rationing on one industry in the United States, even a large industry like the oil industry, is probably most easily handled by most economists within the standard Marshallian framework of partial equilibrium. Although large in absolute size, in relation to the rest of the economy, even the oil industry is comparatively small. On the other hand, the analysis of the introduction of, say, a national value-added tax to replace other economy-wide taxes would most likely require the general-equilibrium approach for empirically valid predictions. The selection of test conditions, i.e., the parameters to be held constant, is again a function of the problem at hand and not an a priori determinable procedure.

Let us now consider an economy in which n final goods, $y_1, \ldots, y_n$, are produced. These goods are produced using m factors of production, $x_1, \ldots, x_m$. The prices of the n final goods, $p_1, \ldots, p_n$, respectively, are assumed fixed by the world market. This is known as the *small country assumption.* This economy is sufficiently small in terms of the *world* economy for changes in its output levels not to affect world prices. (Shades of partial equilibrium analysis!) Let

x_{ij} = amount of factor i used in the production of good j

$$i = 1, \ldots, m \qquad j = 1, \ldots, n$$

The production function for good j is then written as

$$y_j = f^j(x_{1j}, \ldots, x_{mj})$$

The total resource levels of this economy are fixed at the levels $x_1, \ldots, x_m$. That is, the quantities $x_1, \ldots, x_m$ are not choice variables but parameters in this model. With competitive markets (or, more precisely, in the absence of transactions costs), the exhaustion of gains from trade implies that the value of total (final) output, or GNP (there are no depreciable assets here, hence no distinction between GNP and NNP) is maximized. Otherwise, some individual could gain by transferring a resource from a lower-valued use to a higher-valued use. In the words of Adam Smith,

> As every individual . . . endeavors as much as he can both to employ his capital in the support of domestic industry, and so to direct that industry that its produce may be of greatest value, every individual necessarily labors to render the annual revenue of the society as great as he can. . . . [He] is in this, as in many other cases, led by an invisible hand to promote an end which was no part of his intention.[†]

The assertion of exhaustion of gains from exchange subject to fixed resource constraints is stated mathematically as

maximize

$$z = \sum_{j=1}^{n} p_j y_j = \sum_{j=1}^{n} p_j f^j(x_{1j}, \ldots, x_{mj})$$

subject to

$$\sum_{j=1}^{n} x_{ij} \leq x_i \qquad i = 1, \ldots, m \tag{15-1}$$

We shall investigate this very general model in several stages of simplification. Consider first the model reduced to only *two* goods and *two* factors. Let us denote the factors labor L and capital K. Let the labor and capital allocated to industry j be denoted L_j and K_j, respectively. Then we can write this reduced model as follows:

maximize

$$p_1 f^1(L_1, K_1) + p_2 f^2(L_2, K_2)$$

subject to

$$L_1 + L_2 \leq L \qquad K_1 + K_2 \leq K \qquad L_1, \; L_2, \; K_1, \; K_2 \geq 0 \tag{15-2}$$

Here, L and K are, respectively, the parametrically "fixed" total resource endowments of labor and capital.

Of perhaps greater significance is another simplification commonly introduced into the analysis, viz., the assumption that $f^1(L_1, K_1)$ and $f^2(L_2, K_2)$ exhibit *constant returns to scale*. That is,

$$f^j(tL_j, \; tK_j) \equiv tf^j(L_j, \; K_j) = ty_j \qquad j = 1, 2$$

[†]Adam Smith, *Wealth of Nations*, Bk. IV, Chap. 2.

Since this relation holds for *all* t, let $t = 1/y_j$. Then the production relation becomes

$$1 = f^j\left(\frac{L_j}{y_j}, \frac{K_j}{y_j}\right)$$

If we let $a_{Lj} = L_j/y_j$ and $a_{Kj} = K_j/y_j$, the production functions become

$$f^j(a_{Lj}, a_{Kj}) = 1$$

This construction indicates that constant-returns-to-scale production functions are completely described by the knowledge of *one* isoquant, here, the unit isoquant, i.e., the isoquant representing 1 unit of output. This is as should be expected since the level curves of linear homogeneous functions are all radial blowups of each other.

The quantities a_{ij} represent the amount of resource i used to produce 1 unit of output j. They are often known as *input-output coefficients*. They are in general considered to be *variable*, changing continuously over a wide range (0 to $+\infty$ in the case of isoquants which are asymptotic to each axis).

When this formulation of the production functions is used, the model expressed in Eqs. (15-2) can be transformed into:

maximize

$$z = p_1 y_1 + p_2 y_2$$

subject to

$$a_{L1} y_1 + a_{L2} y_2 \leq L$$
$$a_{K1} y_1 + a_{K2} y_2 \leq K$$
$$f^1(a_{L1}, a_{K1}) = 1 \qquad\qquad (15\text{-}3)$$
$$f^2(a_{L2}, a_{K2}) = 1$$
$$y_1, \; y_2 \geq 0$$

In this form, the theorems of international trade theory (the factor price equalization, Stolper-Samuelson, and Rybczynski theorems) are derivable. We shall derive these theorems at this level of generality in the next chapter. In this chapter, however, we shall consider this model in a still simpler framework, that of fixed-coefficient technology. In so doing, we shall develop the body of analysis known as *linear programming* and illustrate its empirical usefulness. By fixed coefficients we mean the very special case where the a_{ij}'s are constants—fixed, as it were, by nature at preassigned values. In this case, the model described by Eqs. (15-3) becomes a *linear programming* problem:

maximize

$$z = p_1 y_1 + p_2 y_2$$

subject to

$$a_{L1}y_1 + a_{L2}y_2 \leq L$$

$$a_{K1}y_1 + a_{K2}y_2 \leq K \qquad y_1, \ y_2 \geq 0$$

Here, p_1, p_2, L, K, and all the a_{ij}'s are constants. The problem becomes one of maximizing a linear function subject to linear inequality constraints, hence, a *linear* programming problem. (In general, one could deal with several goods and factors.) Even in this highly restrictive form, the model is capable of yielding insights into the general equilibrium economy. This will be the object of this chapter. Let us first examine more closely the nature of fixed-coefficient technology.

Production functions of this type were discussed briefly in Chap. 10. They can be represented as

$$y_j = \min\left(\frac{L_j}{a_{Lj}}, \ \frac{K_j}{a_{Kj}}\right) \tag{15-4}$$

The isoquants of this production function (the term is applied loosely) are L-shaped, as depicted in Fig. 15-1. For example, consider the function $y = \min (L/1, K/2)$; 1 unit of output can be produced using 1 unit of labor and 2 units of capital. Thus, $a_{L1} = 1$, $a_{K1} = 2$. If either factor is increased, holding the other factor constant, output remains the same. For example, if L is increased to 2 units, holding K at 2, then

$$\min(\tfrac{2}{1}, \ \tfrac{2}{2}) = 1 \text{ unit of } y$$

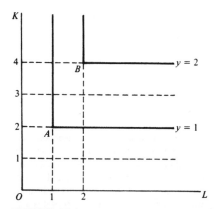

FIGURE 15-1
Fixed-coefficient production functions. The assumption that input-output coefficients of production are fixed leads to L-shaped isoquants. Production of 1 unit of output *requires* a certain amount of each factor. In the figure production of 1 unit of output requires 1 unit of labor and 2 units of capital. This input combination is labeled as point A. With 2 units of K available, no additional output occurs if more than 1 unit of labor is added. Thus, the isoquant is horizontal to the right of A, and $MP_L = 0$. Similarly, the isoquant is vertical above A, since $MP_K = 0$ for $L = 1, K > 2$. If both labor *and* capital are increased in the same proportion, then (since the input-output coefficients are constants) output will rise by the same proportion. Hence, this function is a special case of constant-returns-to-scale production functions. For example, in the figure when $L = 2, K = 4$, output is $y = 2$.

The marginal products of labor and capital are never simultaneously nonzero. For example, to the right of point A, $MP_L = 0$, since additional amounts of labor yield no increases in output. However, increases in capital will yield increases in output there, and hence $MP_K > 0$. At point A, the marginal products of labor and capital are undefined. Any movement at all to the right of A, no matter how small, will yield $MP_K > 0$. To the left of A, $MP_K = 0$; however, $MP_L > 0$. Thus, this production function yields discontinuous marginal product functions. The points of discontinuity are the corners of the isoquants, where the marginal technical rate of substitution, MP_L/MP_K is undefined, since no unique slope of the isoquant exists there.

Constancy of the a_{ij}'s is clearly a highly restrictive assumption about productive processes. It can be generalized somewhat by assuming that the firm is faced with not one but several (though finite) distinct production coefficient possibilities, called *activities*. That is, suppose, in addition to the input-output coefficients $(a_{L1},\ a_{K1}) = (1, 2)$ as in the example in Fig. 15-1, the firm could produce 1 unit of output with the coefficients $(b_{L1},\ b_{K1}) = (3, 1)$, or $(c_{L1}, c_{K1}) = (2, 3)$. This situation is depicted in Fig. 15-2. The three activities are denoted A,

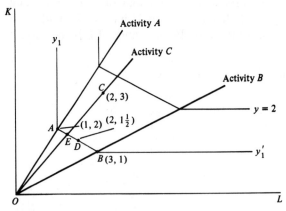

FIGURE 15-2
Several production activities. The firm has three distinct production activities, or technologies, available to it. The first, represented by point A, is the technology discussed in Fig. 15-1, wherein 1 unit of output requires 1 unit of labor L and 2 units of capital K. However, the firm can also produce 1 unit of output using 3 units of L and 1 unit of K (point B), or 2 units of L and 3 units of K (point C). In addition, the firm can use any *convex combination* of these processes. That is, any input combination whose coordinates lie along the straight line joining any two processes is also feasible. Thus, 1 unit of output can be produced by using 2 units of L and $1\frac{1}{2}$ units of K (point D). This is accomplished by using processes A and B simultaneously, at half the unit output rate each. If process A is used k percent and B is used $1 - k$ percent, the process $kA + (1 - k)B$ is generated, represented geometrically by the line segment AB.

It is clear that process C will never be used at positive factor prices. There is a process E utilizing activities A and B in some proportion (what proportions?) which yields 1 unit of output using less of *both* labor and capital than activity C. The unit isoquant for this firm is therefore a vertical line above A, the segment AB, and a horizontal line to the right of B. These points represent minimum combinations of L and K needed to produce 1 unit of output. Constant returns to scale imply that all other isoquants will have corners along the rays OA, OB.

B, and C, respectively. Let us now assume, in addition, that *the firm can choose to use one or more processes, or activities, simultaneously*. That is, assume that these activities are not mutually exclusive but can be used simultaneously side by side.

Suppose, for example, 1 unit of output was to be produced by producing $\frac{1}{2}$ unit using activity A and $\frac{1}{2}$ unit by activity B. To produce $\frac{1}{2}$ unit of output by A will require $\frac{1}{2}$ unit of labor and 1 unit of capital (halfway along the ray from the origin to point A). Similarly, using the B activity coefficients, producing $\frac{1}{2}$ unit of output will require $1\frac{1}{2}$ units of labor and $\frac{1}{2}$ unit of capital. Together, then, production of 1 unit of output using activities A and B together at equal (half) intensities will require 2 ($=\frac{1}{2} + 1\frac{1}{2}$) units of labor and $1\frac{1}{2}(=1 + \frac{1}{2})$ units of capital. Geometrically, this new composite activity $D = (d_{L1}, d_{K1}) = (2, 1\frac{1}{2})$ lies midway on the straight line joining points A and B. In fact, if each original activity can be used in any proportion with another, then 1 unit of output can be produced by the activities defined by the coordinates of all points lying on the straight line joining the original activity levels. Producing 1 unit by using A to produce $\frac{1}{4}$ unit and B $\frac{3}{4}$ unit will be represented by the point three-fourths of the way toward B on the line segment AB.

Algebraically, this is represented as follows. Suppose $A = (L^A, K^A)$ and $B = (L^B, K^B)$ are any two processes which yield 1 unit of output. Points A and B are two points on the unit isoquant. Under the assumptions of constant returns to scale and complete divisibility of these processes, 1 unit of output can be produced using any *weighted average* of processes A and B as long as the weights sum to unity. Thus, 1 unit of output can be produced using $\mathbf{x} = kA + (1 - k)B$, where $0 \leq k \leq 1$. That is, $L^{\mathbf{x}} = kL^A + (1 - k)L^B$, $K^{\mathbf{x}} = kK^A + (1 - k)K^B$. As k varies from 0 to 1, $\mathbf{x}$ traces out the points on the straight line joining A and B.

More generally, suppose that $\mathbf{x}^1, \ldots, \mathbf{x}^m$ represent m points in n space. The set of points $\mathbf{x} = \sum_{i=1}^{m} k_i \mathbf{x}^i$ such that $k_i \geq 0$, $\sum k_i = 1$, is called a *convex combination* of $\mathbf{x}^1, \ldots, \mathbf{x}^m$. The convex combination of points A, B, and C in Fig. 15-2 would be represented by all points within and on the boundary of a triangle formed by joining points A, B, and C. In linear models of this type the assumption is generally made that the convex combinations of unit processes are all alternative processes for the firm to consider.

It is clear from the geometry in Fig. 15-2, however, that the activity C will never be used by a cost-minimizing firm. Point E on the line AB, representing some mix of the activities A and B, leads to production of 1 unit of output using less of both labor and capital than point C. Activities A and B dominate activity C. Activity C becomes irrelevant because it will never be observed.

The unit isoquant for a firm endowed with activities A, B, and C is therefore the kinked line consisting of: (1) the vertical segment emanating from point A (designated Ay_1, though this line proceeds to infinity); (2) the line AB, and (3) a line horizontal from B, denoted By'_1. Since these production activities are linear homogeneous, isoquants for other levels of production will be radial blowups of this unit isoquant, with the kinks or corners along extensions of the rays OA,

OB. Most important, an isoquant map which is convex to the origin has been obtained.

Consider now the nature of a cost-minimizing solution, say for $y_1 = 1$ (perfectly representative, due to homotheticity), as depicted in Fig. 15-3. The slope of line segment *AB* is $-\frac{1}{2}$. Thus, along this segment the ratio of the marginal product of labor to that of capital is constant at $MP_L/MP_K = \frac{1}{2}$. Let

w be the wage rate of labor and *r* be the "rental" rate on capital

then the ordinary tangency condition for cost minimization is that $MP_L/MP_K = w/r$. Here, however, if the wage rate is ever so slightly more than half the rental rate, so that $w/r > \frac{1}{2}$, the cost-minimizing solution will occur at point *A*. This will be where an isocost line, *wr* in Fig. 15-3, just touches the isoquant $y_1 ABy_1'$. Only the relatively capital-intensive activity will be used. If the wage rate falls so that $w/r < \frac{1}{2}$, as depicted by the isocost segment $w'r'$, the cost-minimizing solution jumps to point *B*. With this shift in factor prices, only the labor-intensive activity, or process, will be used. We see that small changes in factor prices, from $\frac{1}{2} + \varepsilon$ to $\frac{1}{2} - \varepsilon$, where $\varepsilon > 0$ can be as small as one likes, can produce a substantial change in the factor mix. When $w/r = \frac{1}{2}$, the isocost line will be tangent to the isoquant along the whole segment *AB*, producing an infinite number of solutions.

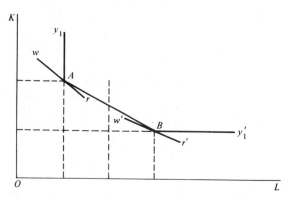

FIGURE 15-3

Cost minimization with linear segment isoquants. When isoquants consist of straight line segments with corners, as generated by constant-coefficient production functions with more than one technology, the cost-minimizing solution will not in general be the tangency condition $MP_L/MP_K = w/r$. This occurs simply because the isoquant will have only a finite number of slopes (above, only three: $-\infty, -\frac{1}{2}, 0$), whereas w/r can vary continuously from $+\infty$ to 0. For finite factor prices, only if $w/r = \frac{1}{2}$ will an actual tangency occur. If $w/r > \frac{1}{2}$, the cost-minimizing solution will be at point *A*. If $w/r < \frac{1}{2}$, the solution will be at point *B*. If $w/r = \frac{1}{2}$, all points along the line segment *AB* will be cost-minimizing solutions. Notice that changes in the factor-price ratio will often produce no change at all in the input combination. Only if in changing, w/r passes through the value of $\frac{1}{2}$ (even ever so slightly), will the input combination change. And any such small change around the value $\frac{1}{2}$ will produce a *discontinuous* change in the factor mix.

Let us formulate algebraically the problem of minimizing the cost of achieving some parametric level of output y^0, given the three possible activities above. The objective function is to minimize $z = wL + rK$, where w and r are parametric factor prices and L and K are the total amounts of labor and capital used. Labor and capital can be used in any of the three processes. Denote the amounts of labor allocated to processes A, B, and C as L_A, L_B, and L_C, respectively, and likewise K_A, K_B, and K_C for capital. Thus, $L = L_A + L_B + L_C$, and $K = K_A + K_B + K_C$.

If process A is used, with coefficients $(1, 2)$, then $L_A = K_A/2$, and $y_A = L_A$. Likewise for process B, $L_B = 3K_B$ and $y_B = L_B/3$. For process C, $L_C/2 = K_C/3$, and $y_C = L_C/2$. The problem can thus be posed as

minimize

$$w(L_A + L_B + L_C) + r\left(2L_A + \frac{L_B}{3} + \frac{3}{2}L_C\right)$$

subject to

$$L_A + \frac{L_B}{3} + \frac{L_C}{2} \geq y^0$$

and

$$L_A, L_B, L_C \geq 0 \tag{15-5}$$

Although the problem posed in (15-5) involves only simple linear equations, it is not at all trivial to solve. The Lagrangian is

$$\mathscr{L} = w(L_A + L_B + L_C) + r\left(2L_A + \frac{L_B}{3} + \frac{3}{2}L_C\right) + \lambda\left(y^0 - L_A - \frac{L_B}{3} - \frac{L_C}{2}\right)$$

producing the first-order relations

$$w + 2r - \lambda \geq 0 \qquad \text{if } >, L_A = 0$$

$$w + \frac{r}{3} - \frac{\lambda}{3} \geq 0 \qquad \text{if } >, L_B = 0$$

$$w + \frac{3}{2}r - \frac{\lambda}{2} \geq 0 \qquad \text{if } >, L_C = 0 \tag{15-6}$$

$$y^0 - L_A - \frac{L_B}{3} - \frac{L_C}{2} \leq 0 \qquad \text{if } <, \lambda = 0 \tag{15-7}$$

The Lagrange multiplier λ is interpretable as marginal cost as in the neoclassical case. Since MC $= w + 2r$ if process A is used, MC $= 3w + r$ if process B is used, and MC $= 2w + 3r$ if process C is used, relations (15-6) say that at the cost minimum point the only process that will be used is the process for which MC is minimized (unless several are equally minimal). Of course, for linear homogeneous production functions, of which this is a special case, MC $=$ AC, and thus this procedure minimizes total cost. But this does not help us much in actually *finding* the solution, i.e., finding which process or processes to use. Problems of this type require solution by *algorithm*. That is, some iterative procedure is required to approach the solution in a finite number of steps. This algorithm must be able to reveal which first-order conditions are in fact binding and which are to be ignored. This is not usually possible without some search procedure, in which changes in the variables which move the program closer to solution are revealed as the algorithm, or routine, is carried out.

The assumption of constant coefficients in any model of economic behavior can generally be counted on to be in violation of the facts over some finite time period. The assumption may nonetheless be useful, however, if it enlarges the tractability of the model. As pointed out in Chap. 1, assumptions are always simplifications of reality by definition and are incorporated into the analysis to improve the manageability of the model or theory. In the case of linear models, the benefit of this assumption is that a well-established, easy-to-use algorithm exists for finding the solution to the model. Reality of assumptions is traded off for tractability—in this case, actually obtaining solutions. We shall now investigate this class of models and their solution.

15.2 THE LINEAR ACTIVITY ANALYSIS MODEL: A SPECIFIC EXAMPLE

In this section we shall investigate a particular linear programming problem and use it to illustrate the general nature of such models. In the next section, the general theorems and methodology will be presented.

Consider a firm (or an economy made up of many such identical firms) which can produce two goods, food y_1 and clothing y_2. Let us now suppose that *three* inputs are used to produce these outputs: H, land; L, labor; and K, capital (to use an historically important but misleading taxonomy). These inputs must be combined in fixed proportions to produce 1 unit of either food or clothing. In particular, assume that to produce 1 unit of food requires 3 acres, 2 worker-hours, and 1 "machine" (unit of capital). To produce 1 unit of clothing requires 2 acres, 2 worker-hours, and 2 machines (the same machines as for food). This technology, or state of the art, is representable by the following input-output matrix **A**:

$$\mathbf{A} = \begin{pmatrix} 3 & 2 \\ 2 & 2 \\ 1 & 2 \end{pmatrix} \tag{15-8}$$

where a_{ij} = amount of factor i used to produce 1 unit of output j

$$i = H, L, K; \quad j = 1, 2$$

Since three factors and two outputs are involved, the resulting input-output matrix contains three rows and two columns. These coefficients are *fixed*, i.e., constant at their given values. No other processes or activities are available to this firm or economy.[†]

Let us assume now that this firm is endowed with 54 acres of land, 40 worker-hours, and 35 machines, representing the resource constraints. Further, assume that food sells for \$40 per unit and clothing for \$30 per unit; that is $p_1 = \$40, p_2 = \$30$.

We now assert that this firm or an economy made up of many such firms maximizes the total value of output of food and clothing, subject to the constraints imposed by the scarcity of resources (factors) and the nonnegativity of factors. The mathematical statement of this model is:

maximize

$$z = 40y_1 + 30y_2$$

subject to

$$3y_1 + 2y_2 \leq 54 \qquad \text{land constraint}$$

$$2y_1 + 2y_2 \leq 40 \qquad \text{labor constraint}$$

$$y_1 + 2y_2 \leq 35 \qquad \text{capital constraint} \qquad y_1, y_2 \geq 0 \qquad (15\text{-}9)$$

Mathematically, the problem is to maximize a linear function subject to linear inequality constraints and nonnegativity of the decision variables. The constraints in (15-9) say that no more than 54 acres, 40 worker-hours, and 35 machines may be used by this firm. However, it is possible to use *less* than these amounts. That is, the firm is not bound to use all its resources. And we can quickly see that it cannot be the case that all three factors will be fully utilized; in that case, the constraints in (15-9) would represent three independent equations in two unknowns, yielding no solution. How shall we discover which resources to utilize fully?

A graphical solution. The solution to this linear programming problem can be obtained graphically, since only two decision variables, y_1 and y_2, are present. In Fig. 15-4, coordinate axes have been drawn, with y_1 the abscissa and y_2

[†]More general models, called *Leontief input-output models,* after their inventor, Wassily Leontief, allow variables to be *both* the objects of final consumption (outputs) *and* inputs. For example, some food will likely be used in the production of clothing, and vice versa. The matrix of coefficients would have to be suitably expanded. If $\mathbf{B} = (b_{ij})$ represents the amount of outputs i used to produce 1 unit of output j, if $\mathbf{C} = (c_1, \ldots, c_n)$ represents a vector of final consumption of these outputs, and if $\mathbf{X} = (x_1, \ldots, x_n)$ represents total production of these goods, then, by arithmetic, $\sum_{j=1}^{n} b_{ij}x_j + c_i = x_i$, $i = 1, \ldots, n$. In matrix form, $\mathbf{BX} + \mathbf{C} = \mathbf{X}$, or $\mathbf{C} = (\mathbf{I} - \mathbf{B})\mathbf{X}$, where $\mathbf{I}$ represents the $n \times n$ identity matrix. The production $\mathbf{X}$ needed to sustain consumption $\mathbf{C}$ is $\mathbf{X} = (\mathbf{I} - \mathbf{B})^{-1}\mathbf{C}$. It can be shown that the inverse $(\mathbf{I} - \mathbf{B})^{-1}$ exists only if $(\mathbf{I} - \mathbf{B})^{-1} = \mathbf{I} + \mathbf{B} + \mathbf{B}^2 + \cdots$ is a convergent series, analogous to the sum of an infinite geometric series in ordinary algebra.

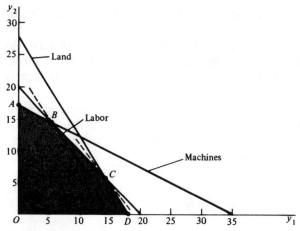

FIGURE 15-4

Graphical solution of a linear programming problem. The feasible region of a linear programming problem is the set of points that satisfy all the constraints (including nonnegativity) simultaneously. In the above model, this is represented by the region *OABCD*. Along *AB*, the capital, or machine, constraint $y_1 + 2y_2 = 35$ is binding, but the land and labor constraints are nonbinding. Those two constraints lie above and to the right (except at point *B*) of the capital constraint there. At point *B*, both the capital and labor constraints are binding, while along *BC* (excluding point *C*), only the labor constraint is binding, i.e., holds as an *equality*. Similarly, along *CD* (excluding *C*) only the land constraint holds as an equality. The feasible region is a *convex set*. If *any* two points in *OABCD* are selected, all points on the straight line joining those two points also lie in *OABCD*.

The (maximum) solution of the linear programming problem occurs where the isorevenue line $z = 40y_1 + 30y_2$ is shifted as far from the origin as is consistent with its remaining in contact with the feasible region *OABCD*. This occurs, for this problem, at point *C*, where the labor and land constraints are binding and the capital constraint is nonbinding. The slope of the isorevenue line is $p_1/p_2 = 40/30 = \frac{4}{3}$. This is *greater* than the slope of the production possibilities frontier along *BC* (1) and less than the slope along *CD* ($\frac{3}{2}$). No tangency (in the sense of equal slopes) occurs. Instead, the inequality conditions, that for each good, MR < MC for increases in output and MR > MC for decreases in output, hold at point *C*. The maximum is global because *OABCD* is a convex set. There are no corners jutting out at points removed from *C*.

the ordinate. Since outputs are constrained to be nonnegative, only the first (nonnegative) quadrant of Euclidean space is relevant. If all land were to be used, the combination of food and clothing that could be produced would satisfy $3y_1 + 2y_2 = 54$, a strict equality. This is the line denoted "land" in Fig. 15-4, having horizontal intercept 18, vertical intercept 27. However, the constraint says merely that *not more than 54* units of land may be used, and possibly less. Hence, the set of all output combinations possible under the land constraint is the triangular area bound by this line and the positive axes. It is not possible to obtain output combinations outside this triangle.

However, the preceding is only one of three constraints (aside from nonegativity). In addition, no more than 40 worker-hours are available. This implies that no output combinations are attainable which lie outside the line $2y_1 + 2y_2 = 40$ (denoted "labor" in Fig. 15-4). Output is further constrained to lie within (boundaries included) the triangle defined by this line and the nonnegative axes. Lastly, since only 35 machines are available, all output combinations must lie within the triangle whose boundaries are the nonnegative axes and the line $y_1 + 2y_2 = 35$.

The set of all output combinations that satisfy all the constraints (including nonnegativity) is called the *feasible region* for the problem. The feasible region for this problem is the shaded polygonal area $OABCD$ in Fig. 15-4. It is called the feasible region simply because this set of points represents all possible outputs, given the constraints imposed by scarcity of resources.

The feasible regions of all linear programming problems have the important property of being *convex sets*. Recall from the previous chapter that a convex set is one in which the straight line joining any two points in the set lies entirely in the set. The feasible region is convex here because the constraints, being linear, are therefore *concave* functions (though weakly so). As we saw in Chap. 14, if $g^j(x_1, \ldots, x_n)$ is a concave function, the area defined by $g^j \geq 0, j = 1, \ldots, m$ is a convex set. We shall show this again, in more detail, for linear functions in the next section. The objective function, also linear, is therefore also concave. Therefore, we know that if a *local* maximum of this function is achieved over the (convex) feasible region, it is also a *global* maximum. And if the maximum is not unique, there are an infinite number of local maxima, all equal, along the straight line joining any two maxima.

Let us now move on to the solution of the problem. The objective is to maximize the linear function $z = 40y_1 + 30y_2$ such that the point (y_1, y_2) lies in the feasible region $OABCD$. This isorevenue line (hyperplane, in more than three dimensions) achieves higher values the farther it is from the origin. This isorevenue line has a slope $= -\frac{4}{3}$. One such line is the dotted line through point B. It clearly is not the maximum z, which is in fact obtained when $z = 40y_1 + 30y_2$ passes through point C. At point C, only the land and labor constraints are binding. Point C lies wholly within the machine constraint, that is, $y_1 + 2y_2 < 35$. The solution values of y_1 and y_2 are thus obtained by solving simultaneously the land and labor constraints, *as equalities,* ignoring the machine constraint entirely. That is, point C is the intersection of

$$3y_1 + 2y_2 = 54 \quad \text{and} \quad 2y_1 + 2y_2 = 40 \quad (15\text{-}10)$$

Solving simultaneously quickly yields the solution values $y_1^* = 14$, $y_2^* = 6$, with $z^* = 40(14) + 30(6) = \$740$.

We can also determine the allocation of factor resources to each industry or final good. Since $y_1 = 14$, the amounts of land, labor, and capital used to produce food, y_1, are $a_{11}y_1, a_{21}y_1$, and $a_{31}y_1$, respectively, or 42 acres, 28 worker-hours, and 14 machines. For clothing, y_2, the resource requirements are $a_{12}y_2, a_{22}y_2$, and $a_{32}y_2$, respectively, or, since $y_2 = 6$, 12 acres, 12 worker-hours, and 12 machines. All together, $42 + 12 = 54$ acres, $28 + 12 = 40$ worker-hours, and $14 + 12 = 26$ machines are used. Land and labor are fully employed and machines are only partially employed, as indicated by the observation that the machine constraint is the only nonbinding constraint.

Geometrically, it is clear that point C provides the maximum value of z. It is also visually obvious for this problem that C is the *global* maximum of z. This latter statement is a consequence of $OABCD$ being a convex set, and $z = 40y_1 + 30y_2$ being a quasi-concave function. The impact of the theorem on maximization of such functions over convex sets is geometrically clear in this example. (Remember, of course, that one example proves little!)

That point C is the solution is clear from economic reasoning as well. The boundary of the feasible region, the broken line $ABCD$, is the production possibilities frontier for this firm or economy. The slope of this frontier represents the marginal cost of obtaining more y_1. Along line segment AB, this marginal cost is $\frac{1}{2}$ unit of y_2. The 5 units of y_1 produced at B are achieved at the expense of $2\frac{1}{2}$ units of y_2 ($17\frac{1}{2}$ at A minus 15 at B). However, the marginal *benefit* of producing y_1 is given by the slope of the isorevenue line, or $\frac{4}{3}$ unit of y_2. Since MR > MC for y_1, it pays to increase production of y_1. When point B is reached, the marginal cost changes discontinuously. Along the segment BC, marginal cost $= 1$. This is still less than marginal revenue, hence it pays to move all the way along BC to point C. However, it does not pay to move beyond point C. Along CD, MC of y_1 is $\frac{3}{2}$, which is greater than MR $= \frac{4}{3}$. There is no point on this frontier where MC = MR. However, there is a point C for which, in terms of y_1, MC < MR to the left of C and MC > MR to the right of C. That is, at point C, $y_1 = 14$. For $y_1 < 14$, MC < MR, whereas for $y_1 > 14$, MC > MR. (Marginal cost is undefined at $y_1 = 14$ since the frontier has a corner there, i.e., the frontier is nondifferentiable there). We can thus expect no marginal *equalities* as defining the extreme values of the objective functions, but we can expect a series of marginal *inequalities*, indicating that a move in any direction will leave the firm or economy in a lower-valued option.

There is one instance in which marginal equalities do occur. Suppose p_1 had been \$30 instead of \$40. Then the MR of y_1 would be unity. This is precisely MC all along segment BC. In this case there would not be one solution to the linear programming problem but an infinite number of solutions. The isorevenue line would be tangent to the feasible region at all points along BC; all those points would therefore be the solution of the problem. This is the situation where if two local maxima exist for a concave function defined over a convex set, all points along the straight line joining those maxima are also maxima.

To economists, the interest in this problem goes beyond the mere attainment of a solution. We have seen that in constrained maximization models, new variables, the Lagrange multipliers, imputed some sort of value to the constraint, e.g., the marginal utility of money income, or marginal cost of production with resources. These imputed values are present here also, though we have not yet expressly introduced them as Lagrange multipliers in the analysis.

Consider that since land is scarce, output is not as large as it otherwise would be. In particular, suppose this firm or economy possessed 55 acres of land instead of just 54. How would this affect the value of output? The maximum value of output would now occur at a new point C', the intersection of the constraint boundaries

$$3y_1 + 2y_2 = 55 \qquad \text{land}$$

$$2y_1 + 2y_2 = 40 \qquad \text{labor}$$

Solving, we get $y_1^* = 15$, $y_2^* = 5$. The value of total income, z^*, is now $z^* = 40(15) + 30(5) = \$750$, a gain of $\$10$.

The fact that income would grow by $\$10$ if one additional acre of land were available imputes a value, a *shadow price,* or *imputed rent* as it is called, to land. Clearly, the marginal value product of land is $\$10$. In a competitive economy, this land would rent for $\$10$ per acre. Moreover, the marginal value of land will remain constant as long as the maximum value of income is determined by the intersection of the land and labor constraints only.

Suppose land is increased to $54 + \Delta H$. Then the value of total income is determined using the solution of

$$3y_1 + 2y_2 = 54 + \Delta H \qquad 2y_1 + 2y_2 = 40 \qquad (15\text{-}11)$$

Thus

$$y_1^* = 14 + \Delta H \qquad y_2^* = 6 - \Delta H$$

Formerly, $z^* = 740$. The new value of z^* is

$$z^* + \Delta z^* = 40(14 + \Delta H) + 30(6 - \Delta H) = 740 + 10 \ \Delta H$$

Thus, $\Delta z^* = 10\Delta H$, or, taking limits,

$$\frac{\partial z^*}{\partial H} = 10 \qquad (15\text{-}12)$$

This is precisely the envelope theorem, which says that the rate of change of the objective function (here z^*) with respect to a parameter representing a resource constraint is the imputed value of that resource.

We shall denote this imputed value, or shadow price, of the first factor, land, as

$$u_1 = \frac{\partial z^*}{\partial H} = 10 \qquad (15\text{-}13a)$$

Note that u_1 is *constant* at $\$10$. It does not depend on the parametric values of either the land or labor resource constraints, 54 acres and 40 worker-hours, respectively. This result is the basis of what is known as the Stolper-Samuelson and factor price equalization theorems. In the next chapter we shall show that for the general case of linear homogeneous production functions (of which fixed coefficients are a special case), factor prices are functions of output prices only. Hence, the preceding result, that the factor price of land is constant (subject to the qualification below), independent of the resource endowments in some neighborhood of the initial solution.

We shall see more explicitly how the factor prices become Lagrange multipliers (called *dual variables* there) in the next section. Note, however, in the solution to Eq. (15-11), that ΔH must be less than 6; otherwise y_2 would become negative. The algebraic algorithm for solving these problems is vitally dependent on these changes. When ΔH becomes greater than 6, the solution will move to a new corner of the feasible region and the marginal valuation of resources will change. (In fact, the marginal value of land will fall to zero. Why?)

In a similar manner, we can determine the imputed wage rate in this "economy." If the amount of labor is increased by an amount ΔL, the new value of output is determined by

$$3y_1 + 2y_2 = 54 \qquad 2y_1 + 2y_2 = 40 + \Delta L$$

Thus

$$y_1^* = 14 - \Delta L \qquad y_2^* = 6 + \tfrac{3}{2}\Delta L$$

Therefore,

$$z^* + \Delta z^* = 40(14 - \Delta L) + 30(6 + \tfrac{3}{2}\Delta L) = 740 + 5\ \Delta L$$

Subtracting $z^* = 740$, we have $\Delta z^*/\Delta L = 5$, or, taking limits,

$$u_2 = \frac{\partial z^*}{\partial L} = 5 \qquad (15\text{-}13b)$$

The marginal value of labor is $5. A competitive economy would result in labor receiving this wage. Here, since $y_1^* = 14 - \Delta L$, $\Delta L \le 14$. If labor increased by more than 14 worker-hours, the marginal values of the factors would change since a new corner of the feasible region would be reached. (In fact, the marginal value of labor would fall to 0 if $\Delta L \ge 4.5$. Why?)

Lastly, consider what the effects on z^* would be if more machines ΔK were available. The machine constraint is already nonbinding. Only 26 machines are used, in spite of 35 being available. An additional machine would add nothing to income; its marginal value is 0. Machines, though limited, are not scarce. They are a free good, being available in greater supply than the quantity demanded at zero price. Thus,

$$u_3 = \frac{\partial z^*}{\partial K} = 0 \qquad (15\text{-}13c)$$

Do not assume that since the *marginal* evaluation of capital (machines) is 0 capital is redundant in this economy. In fact, 26 machines are used. Moreover, with fixed coefficients, production, by definition, is impossible without certain amounts of each factor. The *marginal* product of capital is 0 because the nine *extra* machines are incapable of being combined productively with the available land and labor. This is a feature of fixed-coefficient technology. The *total* product of capital is certainly not zero. Capital is merely redundant at the particular margin in question, where $y_1 = 14$, $y_2 = 6$.

GENERAL EQUILIBRIUM I: LINEAR MODELS **507**

The preceding phenomena are special cases of the factor price equalization theorem. With unchanging output prices, factor prices remain the same when endowments are changed. This holds until endowments change sufficiently to cause new factors to be brought in and one or more formerly positively used factors to fall from use.

15.3 THE RYBCZYNSKI THEOREM

Let us now consider the effects on output of changes in the land H and labor L endowments. We found $y_1^* = 14 + \Delta H$, $y_2^* = 6 - \Delta H$, and $y_1^* = 14 - \Delta L$, $y_2^* = 6 + \frac{3}{2} \Delta L$. Combining these into one total differential expression gives

$$dy_1^* = dH - dL \qquad dy_2^* = -dH + \frac{3}{2} dL$$

These results are examples of the *Rybczynski theorem*. This important theorem says that if the endowment of some resource increases, the industry that uses that resource most intensively will increase its output while the other industry will decrease its output. The relative factor intensity is measured by the ratio of factor use in each industry. For example, L_1/K_1, L_2/K_2, the labor-capital ratios in industry 1 and industry 2, are compared. The industry for which this ratio is higher is relatively labor-intensive; the other is relatively capital-intensive. However, note that

$$\frac{L_j}{K_j} = \frac{L_j/y_j}{K_j/y_j} = \frac{a_{Lj}}{a_{Kj}}$$

Hence, the factor intensities can also be determined by the ratios of the a_{ij}'s, in the appropriate manner.

In the present example, the only two factors relevant at the solution point are land and labor. The food industry y_1 is relatively *land*-intensive, since $a_{11}/a_{21} > a_{12}/a_{22}$, that is, $\frac{3}{2} > \frac{2}{2}$. Clothing y_2 is relatively *labor*-intensive. When the endowment of land *increases* by dH, food production is *increased* by dH while clothing production actually *decreases,* also by dH. On the other hand, if the endowment of labor were to *increase* by dL, the labor-intensive industry y_2 would *increase* by $\frac{3}{2} dL$, whereas food output would *decline* by dL. These results are shown graphically in Fig. 15-5.

Algebraically, the Rybczynski theorem results from the simple solution of simultaneous equations. In our example, the solution values of the model are determined by the land and labor constraints,

$$a_{11}y_1 + a_{12}y_2 = H \qquad \text{land} \tag{15-14a}$$

$$a_{21}y_1 + a_{22}y_2 = L \qquad \text{labor} \tag{15-14b}$$

Solving by Cramer's rule yields

$$y_1 = \frac{a_{22}H - a_{12}L}{a_{11}a_{22} - a_{12}a_{21}} \qquad y_2 = \frac{-a_{21}H + a_{11}L}{a_{11}a_{22} - a_{12}a_{21}} \tag{15-15}$$

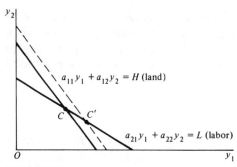

FIGURE 15-5
The Rybczynski theorem in a linear model, showing the land and labor constraints. The capital constraint, being nonbinding, is omitted. Maximum income occurs at point C. The slope of the land constraint is $-a_{11}/a_{12} = -\frac{3}{2}$ in our model. The slope of the labor constraint is $-a_{21}/a_{22} = -1$. Since $a_{11}/a_{12} > a_{21}/a_{22}$, $a_{11}/a_{21} > a_{12}/a_{22}$, or industry 1, food, is *land*-intensive. Industry 2, clothing, is labor-intensive. Notice how the solution to the problem changes when the amount of land H is increased. The land constraint shifts to the right, producing a new output mix designated by point C'. At C', output of y_1, the land-intensive good, is increased, while the output of the labor-intensive good decreases.

The factor intensities determine the sign of the denominator. If say, the food (y_1) industry is relatively *land*-intensive, then $H_1/L_1 > H_2/L_2$. This is equivalent to $a_{11}/a_{21} > a_{12}/a_{22}$ or $a_{11}a_{22} - a_{12}a_{21} > 0$. (It is clearly critical that $a_{11}a_{22} - a_{12}a_{21} \neq 0$. Otherwise, with equal factor intensities, the constraints determining the solution would be parallel to each other, i.e., linearly dependent. In that case, no solution to the model in its present form could exist; one constraint would have to be discarded as nonbinding.) If the denominator is positive, then by simple differentiation,

$$\frac{\partial y_1}{\partial H} = \frac{a_{22}}{(+)} > 0 \qquad \frac{\partial y_1}{\partial L} = -\frac{a_{12}}{(+)} < 0$$

$$\frac{\partial y_2}{\partial H} = -\frac{a_{21}}{(+)} < 0 \qquad \frac{\partial y_2}{\partial L} = \frac{a_{11}}{(+)} > 0 \qquad (15\text{-}16)$$

the Rybczynski results. Moreover, when some factor endowment changes, the output that is intensive in that factor will change in *greater* absolute proportion than the parameter change. For example,

$$y_1 = k_1 H + k_2 L$$

where

$$k_1 = \frac{a_{22}}{a_{11}a_{22} - a_{12}a_{21}}$$

$$k_2 = \frac{-a_{12}}{a_{11}a_{22} - a_{12}a_{21}}$$

Thus

$$\frac{\Delta y_1/y_1}{\Delta H/H} = \frac{H}{y_1}\frac{\partial y_1}{\partial H} = \frac{H}{y_1}k_1 = \frac{k_1 H}{k_1 H + k_2 L}$$

Since

$$k_2 < 0, \qquad k_1 H > k_1 H + k_2 L$$

hence

$$\frac{H}{y_1}\frac{\partial y_1}{\partial H} > 1$$

The same result obtains for the change in y_2 with respect to a change in L. Outputs respond *elastically* (absolute elasticity greater than unity) to change in resource endowments in which they are intensive.

15.4 THE STOLPER-SAMUELSON THEOREM

The solution to this linear model will remain at point C in Fig. 15-4 as long as p_1/p_2, the ratio of output prices, is less than $\frac{3}{2}$ and greater than 1. In our present example, $p_1/p_2 = \frac{40}{30} = \frac{4}{3}$. Let us calculate the effect on factor prices produced by an increase in the price of clothing, say, to $p_2 = 33$, i.e., by 10 percent.

The new shadow factor prices can be calculated as before. However, consider the unit factor cost of y_1 and y_2. The first column of the (a_{ij}) matrix gives the amounts of land, labor, and capital needed to produce 1 unit of y_1. The unit factor cost of y_1 is therefore

$$a_{11}u_1 + a_{21}u_2 + a_{31}u_3 = 3(10) + 2(5) + 1(0) = \$40 = p_1 \qquad (15\text{-}17a)$$

Similarly, the second column of a_{ij}'s gives the amounts of land, labor, and capital needed to produce 1 unit of y_2. The unit factor cost of y_2 is therefore

$$a_{12}u_1 + a_{22}u_2 + a_{32}u_3 = 2(10) + 2(5) + 2(0) = \$30 = p_2 \qquad (15\text{-}17b)$$

Unit factor cost equals output price. Equations (15-17) represent zero-profit conditions. Since the production function here exhibits constant returns to scale, zero profits are to be expected. Since in this example $u_3 = 0$ (the marginal product of capital is 0) at point C, the zero-profit conditions are

$$a_{11}u_1 + a_{21}u_2 = p_1$$

$$a_{12}u_1 + a_{22}u_2 = p_2 \qquad (15\text{-}18)$$

These are two equations in two unknowns, from which we can solve for u_1 and u_2 in terms of p_1 and p_2, using our data about the a_{ij}'s. [Remember, though, that these equations apply only when the solution is at point C. If the solution were at point B, u_1 would be 0 and Eqs. (15-8) would involve the coefficients a_{31} and a_{32}.] Most importantly, note that the coefficients of these equations are the transpose of the coefficients in Eqs. (15-14). The only difference is that a_{12}

and a_{21} are interchanged. The algebra of the relations between factor and output prices is therefore virtually identical to the relations between physical outputs and resource endowments.

Solving Eqs. (15-18) by Cramer's rule gives

$$u_1 = \frac{a_{22}p_1 - a_{21}p_2}{a_{11}a_{22} - a_{12}a_{21}} = \frac{2p_1 - 2p_2}{2} = p_1 - p_2 \tag{15-19a}$$

$$u_2 = \frac{a_{11}p_2 - a_{12}p_1}{a_{11}a_{22} - a_{12}a_{21}} = \frac{3p_2 - 2p_1}{2} = \frac{3}{2}p_2 - p_1 \tag{15-19b}$$

Notice the direction of change: if p_1 increases (in price of the land-intensive good increases), then the price of land u_1 increases while the price of labor decreases. Likewise, if the price of the labor-intensive good y_2 increases, land decreases in price while labor increases in price. With $p_1 = 40$, $p_2 = 30$, we derived $u_1 = 10$, $u_2 = 5$, in accordance with Eqs. (15-13). With, say, $p_1 = 40$, $p_2 = 33$, we find $u_1 = 7$, $u_2 = 9.5$. With the price of the labor-intensive good rising by 10 percent, the price of land falls by 30 percent, whereas the price of labor nearly doubles. These results are known as the *Stolper-Samuelson theorem*.

The Stolper-Samuelson theorem states that if, say, the price of the labor-intensive good *rises,* the price of labor will not only *rise* but will rise in greater proportion to the output price increase. The price of the other factor *falls*, not necessarily in greater proportion to the rise in output price. The same elastic response that was observed for the physical quantities occurs for prices. This duality is apparent from the similar structures of Eqs. (15-14) and (15-19). Since the algebra is identical (save for interchanging a_{12} and a_{21}), we shall not repeat it.

The direction of change of factor prices can be seen geometrically in Fig. 15-6. There, the zero-profit Eqs. (15-17) are plotted in the $u_1 u_2$ plane. The steeper line is Eq. (15-17a). The slope of this line is $-a_{11}/a_{21} = -\frac{3}{2}$. The less steep line is Eq. (15-17b), which has slope $-a_{12}/a_{22} = -1$. The intersection, point P, represents the solution values of u_2 and u_1. Suppose now that p_2 increases. This is represented geometrically by a parallel shift in (15-17b), as shown by the dotted line. The new intersection is at P'. At P', u_2 has increased and u_1 has decreased. Again, an increase in the price of the labor-intensive good will raise the price of labor and lower the price of the other factor, in this instance land.

15.5 THE DUAL PROBLEM

Let us summarize the analysis of the problem just solved. The problem, again, was to:

maximize

$$z = 40y_1 + 30y_2$$

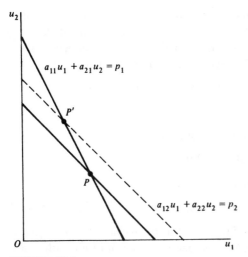

FIGURE 15-6
The Stolper-Samuelson theorem in a linear model, showing plot of the two zero-profit conditions (15-17). Capital is nonscarce, with $u_3 = 0$, and is thus omitted from the diagram. The slopes of the two lines depend on the factor intensities. For y_1, the slope of the zero-profit equation is $-a_{11}/a_{21}$. For y_2, the slope is $-a_{12}/a_{22}$. Given the numbers in our example, $a_{11}/a_{21} = \frac{3}{2}$, $a_{12}/a_{22} = 1$, and hence y_1, food, is *land*-intensive, whereas y_2, clothing, is labor-intensive. Under these conditions, and increase in p_2, which causes a parallel shift in (15-17*b*), produces a new solution at P'. This lowers u_1 and raises u_2. In words, if the price of say, the labor-intensive good rises, the price of labor will rise while the price of the other factor (here, land) will fall.

subject to

$$3y_1 + 2y_2 \leq 54 \qquad \text{land constraint}$$

$$2y_1 + 2y_2 \leq 40 \qquad \text{labor constraint}$$

$$y_1 + 2y_2 \leq 35 \qquad \text{capital constraint}$$

$$y_1, \ y_2 \geq 0 \qquad\qquad\qquad\qquad (15\text{-}9)$$

The coefficients in the constraints, the a_{ij}'s, represent the (constant) amounts of factor i used in the production of 1 unit of output j. The solution to this particular linear programming problem is $y_1^* = 14$, $y_2^* = 6$. At that point, the land and labor constraints are binding, but the capital constraint is nonbinding. That is,

$$3y_1^* + 2y_2^* = 54 \qquad 2y_1^* + 2y_2^* = 40 \qquad y_1^* + 2y_2^* < 35$$

By considering how much income would change if factor endowments were altered incrementally, marginal evaluations, or shadow prices, were imputed to the three factors. Letting u_1, u_2, and u_3 represent the shadow factor prices of land, labor, and capital, respectively, we found, at point C, where total income was maximized,

$$u_1 = \$10 \qquad u_2 = \$5 \qquad u_3 = 0$$

We also found that the unit factor costs of y_1 and y_2 equaled the output prices, \$40 and \$30, respectively. For food, y_1, the first column of the (a_{ij}) matrix gives the amounts of land, labor, and capital needed to produce a unit of y_1. Thus, the unit cost of y_1 given the preceding shadow factor prices is

$$u_1 a_{11} + u_2 a_{21} + u_3 a_{31} = 10(3) + 5(2) + 0(1) = \$40 = p_1$$

Likewise, for y_2, total unit factor cost is

$$u_1 a_{12} + u_2 a_{22} + u_3 a_{32} = 10(2) + 5(2) + 0(3) = \$30 = p_2$$

The linear model implies the zero-profit conditions:

$$a_{11} u_1 + a_{21} u_2 + a_{31} u_3 = p_1$$

$$a_{12} u_1 + a_{22} u_2 + a_{32} u_3 = p_2 \qquad (15\text{-}17)$$

In general, we would expect the unit factor cost to be *greater than or equal to the price* of that good. If unit cost were *less* than the price, no finite solution to the linear programming problem could exist; increasing the output of such a good would lead to ever-increasing total revenues. It might be the case, however, that unit factor cost *exceeded* price in a finite solution. Then we should expect the output of that good to be zero (negative outputs are not admissible).

There is a symmetry, or duality, in the preceding analysis. In the original model, in which income (revenue) was maximized, the constraints were statements of limited resource endowments. When these constraints held as equalities, a nonnegative, generally positive new variable, a shadow factor price, appeared. This "price" was 0 when the constraint was nonbinding, i.e., when a strict inequality appeared, as in the capital constraint above.

However, achieving an actual maximum of revenue also implies that unit costs will be at least as great as output prices,

$$a_{1j} u_1 + a_{2j} u_2 + a_{3j} u_3 \geq p_j \qquad \text{for all } j \qquad (15\text{-}20)$$

Moreover, revenue maximization implies that if this relation holds as a strict *inequality*, output y_j will be zero. Otherwise, $y_j \geq 0$ (with $y_j > 0$ expected). This is the same "algebra" as when the constraints were the original resource constraints involving y_1 and y_2 and the new, dual variables were the shadow prices u_1, u_2, and u_3. The preceding symmetry, or duality, occurs because the u_i's are the Lagrange multipliers for the original, primal problem, whereas the outputs y_1 and y_2 are Lagrange multipliers for an associated constrained minimization problem. It is an example of the Kuhn-Tucker saddlepoint theorem. Let us see how this occurs.

Denote the original revenue maximization problem (15-9) as the primal problem. When we let u_1, u_2, and u_3 represent the Lagrange multipliers associated with the three resource constraints, the Lagrangian for this problem is

$$\mathcal{L} = p_1 y_1 + p_2 y_2 + u_1(H - a_{11} y_1 - a_{12} y_2)$$

$$+ u_2(L - a_{21} y_1 - a_{22} y_2) + u_3(K - a_{31} y_1 - a_{32} y_2) \qquad (15\text{-}21)$$

Among the Kuhn-Tucker first-order conditions for a maximum are that the first partials of $\mathcal{L}$ with respect to y_1 and y_2 be nonpositive, and if $\partial\mathcal{L}/\partial y_j < 0$,

$y_j = 0$. At an interior solution, $\partial \mathcal{L} / \partial y_j = 0$. If a maximum should occur at $y_j = 0$, some j, this must happen because the Lagrangian would become larger if *smaller*, i.e., negative, values of y_j were allowed. Hence, it must be that if a maximum occurs at $y_j = 0$, $\partial \mathcal{L} / \partial y_j \leq 0$ there. Applying these conditions to the Lagrangian (15-21), we have

$$\frac{\partial \mathcal{L}}{\partial y_1} = p_1 - a_{11}u_1 - a_{21}u_2 - a_{31}u_3 \leq 0 \qquad \text{if} <, \ y_1 = 0 \quad (15\text{-}22a)$$

$$\frac{\partial \mathcal{L}}{\partial y_2} = p_2 - a_{12}u_1 - a_{22}u_2 - a_{32}u_3 \leq 0 \qquad \text{if} <, \ y_2 = 0 \quad (15\text{-}22b)$$

These first-order conditions are precisely the nonpositive profit conditions (15-20) just discussed. The remaining first-order conditions are, of course, the inequality constraints, obtained by differentiation with respect to the Lagrange multipliers, here u_1, u_2, and u_3:

$$\frac{\partial \mathcal{L}}{\partial u_1} = H - a_{11}y_1 - a_{12}y_2 \geq 0 \qquad \text{if} >, \ u_1 = 0$$

$$\frac{\partial \mathcal{L}}{\partial u_2} = L - a_{21}y_1 - a_{22}y_2 \geq 0 \qquad \text{if} >, \ u_2 = 0$$

$$\frac{\partial \mathcal{L}}{\partial u_3} = K - a_{31}y_1 - a_{32}y_2 \geq 0 \qquad \text{if} >, \ u_3 = 0$$

These are precisely the resource constraints with the added stipulation that if the resource constraint is nonbinding, the imputed shadow price of that factor is 0, in accordance with our previous reasoning and results.

There is more to the Lagrangian (15-21) than first meets the eye. Let us rearrange the terms of (15-21) as follows:

$$\mathcal{L} = Hu_1 + Lu_2 + Ku_3 + y_1(p_1 - a_{11}u_1 - a_{21}u_2 - a_{31}u_3)$$
$$+ y_2(p_2 - a_{12}u_1 - a_{22}u_2 - a_{32}u_3) \qquad (15\text{-}23)$$

This functional form can be interpreted as a Lagrangian for an extremum problem with choice variables u_1, u_2, and u_3 whose objective function is $w = Hu_1 + Lu_2 + Ku_3$, the total value of the resource endowment. The outputs y_1 and y_2 appear in the position of Lagrange multipliers for profit constraints.

A competitive economy can be expected to utilize its resources efficiently. We should expect in this model that revenue maximization implies, and is implied by, *minimization of the total value of resources*, subject to the constraints that profits are nonpositive. The Lagrangian (15-23), if *minimized* with respect to u_1, u_2, and u_3, yields the following first-order inequality conditions:

$$\frac{\partial \mathcal{L}}{\partial u_1} = H - a_{11}y_1 - a_{12}y_2 \geq 0 \qquad \text{if} >, \ u_1 = 0 \quad (15\text{-}24a)$$

$$\frac{\partial \mathcal{L}}{\partial u_2} = L - a_{21}y_1 - a_{22}y_2 \geq 0 \qquad \text{if} >, \ u_2 = 0 \quad (15\text{-}24b)$$

$$\frac{\partial \mathcal{L}}{\partial u_3} = K - a_{31}y_1 - a_{32}y_2 \geq 0 \qquad \text{if} >, u_3 = 0 \qquad (15\text{-}24c)$$

and

$$\frac{\partial \mathcal{L}}{\partial y_1} = p_1 - a_{11}u_1 - a_{21}u_2 - a_{31}u_3 \leq 0 \qquad \text{if} <, y_1 = 0 \quad (15\text{-}25a)$$

$$\frac{\partial \mathcal{L}}{\partial y_2} = p_2 - a_{12}u_1 - a_{22}u_2 - a_{32}u_3 \leq 0 \qquad \text{if} <, y_2 = 0 \quad (15\text{-}25b)$$

exactly the same resource and nonpositive profit conditions derived from the primal problem.

Thus, the following two problems yield the same first-order conditions:

1. The primal problem:

maximize

$$z = p_1 y_1 + p_2 y_2$$

subject to

$$a_{11}y_1 + a_{12}y_2 \leq H$$
$$a_{21}y_1 + a_{22}y_2 \leq L$$
$$a_{31}y_1 + a_{32}y_2 \leq K \qquad y_1, \ y_2 \geq 0$$

2. The dual problem:

minimize

$$w = Hu_1 + Lu_2 + Ku_3$$

subject to

$$a_{11}u_1 + a_{21}u_2 + a_{31}u_3 \geq p_1$$
$$a_{12}u_1 + a_{22}u_2 + a_{32}u_3 \geq p_2 \qquad u_1, \ u_2, \ u_3 \geq 0$$

Moreover, the values of the objective functions of these two problems are identical when the solutions are obtained. In this model, this is a statement that the total value of output equals the total value of resource endowment when resources are used efficiently. In the preceding example, the maximum value of output was

$$z^* = p_1 y_1^* + p_2 y_2^* = 40(14) + 30(6) = \$740$$

as computed earlier. The total value of the resource endowment at that point is

$$w^* = Hu_1^* + Lu_2^* + Ku_3^* = 54(10) + 40(5) + 35(0) = \$740$$

the same as for the primal problem.

This adding-up or exhaustion-of-product theorem is a consequence of the homogeneity of the objective and constraint functions. As we showed in Chap.

14, when the objective and constraint functions in a maximum problem are all homogeneous of the same degree [the constraints appearing as $g^j(x_1, \ldots, x_n) \leq k^j$], then the indirect objective function $\phi(k^1, \ldots, k^m)$ is homogeneous of degree 1 in the k^j's. Hence, by Euler's theorem,

$$z^* \equiv \frac{\partial z^*}{\partial H}H + \frac{\partial z^*}{\partial L}L + \frac{\partial z^*}{\partial K}K = u_1^* H + u_2^* L + u_3^* K = w^*$$

where w^* is the minimum value of the dual objective function (total factor cost) and the u_i^*'s are the u_i's that achieve that minimum.

This remarkable duality was first noted and explored by Koopmans and others.[†] They converted a purely mathematical puzzle into an interesting (albeit highly restrictive) economic model.

In general, consider the linear programming problem:

maximize

$$z = \sum_{j=1}^{n} p_j x_j$$

subject to

$$\sum_{j=1}^{n} a_{ij}x_j \leq b_j \qquad i = 1, \ldots, m \qquad (15\text{-}26)$$

$$x_j \geq 0, \qquad j = 1, \ldots, n$$

There is no need for m, the number of constraints, to be less than the number of decision variables, since these are *inequality* constraints. Some of these constraints will in general be nonbinding, though it is not easy to discover which ones will be binding. In fact, finding the solution to this problem consists precisely of discovering which constraints are binding and which are not. (The algorithm for doing so will be presented in the next section.)

The preceding problem can be written using matrix notation. Denote the column vector of x_j's as

$$\mathbf{x} = \begin{pmatrix} x_1 \\ \vdots \\ x_n \end{pmatrix}$$

the objective coefficient matrix of p_j's as

$$\mathbf{p} = \begin{pmatrix} p_1 \\ \vdots \\ p_n \end{pmatrix}$$

[†]*Activity Analysis of Production and Allocation, Cowles Commission Monograph* 13, John Wiley & Sons, Inc., New York, 1951.

and the right-hand side coefficients, the b_i's, as

$$\mathbf{b} = \begin{pmatrix} b_1 \\ \vdots \\ b_m \end{pmatrix}$$

Denote the matrix of technical coefficients, the a_{ij}'s, as $\mathbf{A}$:

$$\mathbf{A} = \begin{pmatrix} a_{11} & \cdots & a_{1n} \\ \vdots & & \\ a_{m1} & & a_{mn} \end{pmatrix}$$

Let $\mathbf{x} \geq \mathbf{0}$ mean $x_j \geq 0$, $j = 1, \ldots, n$. The prime denotes the transpose of a matrix.

The general linear programming problem can then be written:

maximize

$$z = \mathbf{p}'\mathbf{x}$$

subject to

$$\mathbf{A}\mathbf{x} \leq \mathbf{b} \quad \mathbf{x} \geq \mathbf{0} \tag{15-27}$$

Associated with the linear programming problem is a dual problem:

minimize

$$w = \mathbf{b}'\mathbf{u}$$

subject to

$$\mathbf{A}'\mathbf{u} \geq \mathbf{p} \quad \mathbf{u} \geq \mathbf{0} \tag{15-28}$$

where

$$\mathbf{u} = \begin{pmatrix} u_1 \\ \vdots \\ u_m \end{pmatrix}$$

is a new vector of decision variables, the *dual variables*.

Note that the primal problem involves n decision variables and m linear inequality constraints. The dual problem involves m decision variables and n linear inequality constraints. The coefficient matrix of the constraints of the dual problem is simply the transpose of the coefficient matrix of the primal problem. The right-hand-side coefficients of one problem appear as the objective function coefficients of the other. *These problems are self-dual;* i.e., the dual problem of the dual problem is the original primal problem. In fact, either problem can be considered the primal problem.

We shall now state and briefly discuss the fundamental theorem of linear programming.

Theorem. Suppose there exists an $\mathbf{x}^0 \geq \mathbf{0}$ which satisfies the constraints of the primal problem, that is, $\mathbf{Ax}^0 \leq \mathbf{b}$ ($\mathbf{x}^0$ is a *feasible* solution) and a $\mathbf{u}^0 \geq \mathbf{0}$ which satisfies the constraints of the dual problem; that is, $\mathbf{A'u}^0 \geq \mathbf{p}$ ($\mathbf{u}^0$ is a solution of the dual problem). *Then both problems possess an optimal solution,* i.e., a finite solution to the problem posed, *and these two solution values are in fact identical.* That is, suppose $\mathbf{x}^* \geq \mathbf{0}$ is that $\mathbf{x}$ vector which maximizes $z = \mathbf{p'x}$ subject to $\mathbf{Ax} \leq \mathbf{b}$. The maximum value of $\mathbf{p'x}$ is $z^* = \mathbf{p'x}^*$. Similarly, let $\mathbf{u}^* \geq \mathbf{0}$ be the $\mathbf{u}$ vector for which $w = \mathbf{b'u}$ is a minimum, and let $w^* = \mathbf{b'u}^*$. Then $z^* = w^*$.

Discussion. It is easy to show that $z^* \leq w^*$. The constraints of the primal problem are

$$\sum_{j=1}^{n} a_{ij}x_j \leq b_i \qquad i = 1, \ldots, m$$

Multiply each constraint by $u_i \geq 0$ and add:

$$\sum_{i=1}^{m} \sum_{j=1}^{n} u_i a_{ij} x_j \leq \sum_{i=1}^{m} b_i u_i = w$$

In matrix notation, this is simply premultiplying $\mathbf{Ax} \leq \mathbf{b}$ by the vector $\mathbf{u'}$, yielding

$$\mathbf{u'Ax} \leq \mathbf{u'b} = w \qquad (15\text{-}29)$$

(Note that the term $\mathbf{u'Ax}$ is the product of matrices of respective size $1 \times m$, $m \times n$, and $n \times 1$. Hence, $\mathbf{u'Ax}$ has size (1×1); that is, it is a simple number, or scalar.)

Now consider the constraints of the dual problem,

$$\sum_{i=1}^{m} a_{ij}u_i \geq p_j \qquad j = 1, \ldots, n$$

Multiply each constraint by $x_j \geq 0$ and add:

$$\sum_{j=1}^{n} \sum_{i=1}^{m} x_j a_{ij} u_i \geq \sum_{j=1}^{n} p_j x_j = z$$

Again, in matrix terms, this is simply multiplying, on the right, $\mathbf{u'A} \geq \mathbf{p'}$ by the vector $\mathbf{x}$, yielding

$$\mathbf{u'Ax} \geq \mathbf{p'x} = z \qquad (15\text{-}30)$$

From (15-29) and (15-30)

$$z \leq \mathbf{u'Ax} \leq w \qquad (15\text{-}31)$$

Since this holds for *all* feasible $\mathbf{u}$ and $\mathbf{x}$ vectors (including $\mathbf{u}^*$ and $\mathbf{x}^*$),

$$z^* \leq w^* \qquad (15\text{-}32)$$

Consider now the statement of the preceding fundamental theorem. Suppose $\mathbf{x}^0$ and $\mathbf{u}^0$ are (finite) feasible solutions to the primal and dual problems, respectively. Then from (15-31),

$$\mathbf{p}'\mathbf{x}^0 \leq \mathbf{u}^{0'}\mathbf{b}$$

This relation implies that a finite maximum exists for the primal problem and a finite minimum exists for the dual problem. For consider that

$$\mathbf{p}'\mathbf{x}^0 \leq \mathbf{p}'\mathbf{x}^* \leq \mathbf{u}^{*'}\mathbf{b} \leq \mathbf{u}^{0'}\mathbf{b} \qquad (15\text{-}33)$$

by the definition of the optimality of $\mathbf{x}^*$ and $\mathbf{u}^*$ and Eq. (15-31). But since $\mathbf{u}^{0'}\mathbf{b}$ and $\mathbf{p}'\mathbf{x}^0$ are finite numbers, $\mathbf{p}'\mathbf{x}^*$, the maximum, or optimal, value of $z = \mathbf{p}'\mathbf{x}$, is bounded from above by $\mathbf{u}^{0'}\mathbf{b}$. Likewise, $\mathbf{u}^{*'}\mathbf{b}$ is bounded from below by $\mathbf{p}'\mathbf{x}^0$. Therefore, if *feasible* solutions exist to both the primal and dual problems, finite *optimal* solutions must exist for each problem.

That $z^* = \mathbf{p}'\mathbf{x}^* = \mathbf{u}^{*'}\mathbf{b} = w^*$ at this optimum is a consequence of the Kuhn-Tucker saddlepoint theorem. Since the objective and constraint functions are all linear, they are all concave. Therefore, the existence of a solution $\mathbf{x}^*$ to the maximum (primal) problem implies and is implied by the Lagrangian of the primal problem having a saddlepoint.

Write the constraints of the primal problem as

$$b_i - \sum_{j=1}^{n} a_{ij}x_j \geq 0 \qquad i = 1, \ldots, m$$

Multiply each constraint by a Lagrange multiplier u_i and add. This yields the Lagrangian

$$\mathcal{L} = \sum_{j=1}^{n} p_j x_j + \sum_{i=1}^{m} u_i \left(b_i - \sum_{j=1}^{n} a_{ij}x_j \right)$$

In matrix notation this Lagrangian is

$$\mathcal{L}(\mathbf{x}, \mathbf{u}) = \mathbf{p}'\mathbf{x} + \mathbf{u}'(\mathbf{b} - A\mathbf{x}) \qquad (15\text{-}34)$$

The saddlepoint theorem says that if $\mathbf{x}^*$ is the solution to the primal problem, there exists a $\mathbf{u}^* \geq 0$ such that

$$\mathcal{L}(\mathbf{x}, \mathbf{u}^*) \leq \mathcal{L}(\mathbf{x}^*, \mathbf{u}^*) \leq \mathcal{L}(\mathbf{x}^*, \mathbf{u}) \qquad (15\text{-}35)$$

However, $\mathcal{L}(\mathbf{x}, \mathbf{u})$ can be rewritten

$$\mathcal{L}(\mathbf{x}, \mathbf{u}) = \mathbf{u}'\mathbf{b} + (\mathbf{p}' - \mathbf{u}'A)\mathbf{x} \qquad (15\text{-}36)$$

Define $M(\mathbf{u}, \mathbf{x}) \equiv -\mathcal{L}(\mathbf{x}, \mathbf{u}) = -\mathbf{u}'\mathbf{b} + (\mathbf{u}'A - \mathbf{p}')\mathbf{x}$. Then, from (15-35),

$$M(\mathbf{u}, \mathbf{x}^*) \leq M(\mathbf{u}^*, \mathbf{x}^*) \leq M(\mathbf{u}^*, \mathbf{x}) \qquad (15\text{-}37)$$

Since $M(\mathbf{u}, \mathbf{x})$ has a saddlepoint at $(\mathbf{u}^*, \mathbf{x}^*)$, $\mathbf{u}^*$ maximizes

$$-w = -\mathbf{u}'\mathbf{b} = -\sum_{i=1}^{m} b_i u_i$$

subject to

$$\mathbf{u}'\mathbf{A} - \mathbf{p}' \geq \mathbf{0}$$

or

$$\sum_{i=1}^{m} a_{ij}u_i \geq p_j \qquad j = 1, \ldots, n$$

This is precisely the dual problem (15-28). (Of course, minimizing $\sum b_i u_i$ is equivalent to maximizing $-\sum b_i u_i$.)

From the first-order conditions for maximizing $\mathcal{L}$ with respect to $\mathbf{x}$,

$$\mathcal{L}_\mathbf{x} = \mathbf{p}' - \mathbf{u}'\mathbf{A} \leq \mathbf{0} \qquad \text{if } <, \quad \mathbf{x} = \mathbf{0} \tag{15-38a}$$

$$\mathcal{L}_\mathbf{u} = \mathbf{b} - \mathbf{A}\mathbf{x} \geq \mathbf{0} \qquad \text{if } >, \quad \mathbf{u} = \mathbf{0} \tag{15-38b}$$

where $\mathcal{L}_\mathbf{x}$ simply means the whole vector of $\mathcal{L}_{x_j}$'s, $j = 1, \ldots, n$, etc. Equivalently, from (15-38a),

$$(\mathbf{p}' - \mathbf{u}'*\mathbf{A})\mathbf{x}^* = \mathbf{0} \tag{15-39a}$$

and from (15-38b),

$$\mathbf{u}^{*'}(\mathbf{b} - \mathbf{A}\mathbf{x}^*) = \mathbf{0} \tag{15-39b}$$

Hence, at $\mathbf{x}^*$, $\mathbf{u}^*$, the Lagrangian has the common value

$$\mathcal{L}(\mathbf{x}^*, \mathbf{u}^*) = \mathbf{p}'\mathbf{x}^* + \mathbf{u}^{*'}(\mathbf{b} - \mathbf{A}\mathbf{x}^*) = \mathbf{p}'\mathbf{x}^* = z^*$$

and

$$\mathcal{L}(\mathbf{x}^*, \mathbf{u}^*) = \mathbf{u}^{*'}\mathbf{b} + (\mathbf{p}' - \mathbf{u}^{*'}\mathbf{A})\mathbf{x}^* = \mathbf{u}^{*'}\mathbf{b} = w^*$$

Therefore, $z^* = w^*$ at the saddlepoint, which represents the *maximum* in the $\mathbf{x}$ directions (the solution to the primal problem) and a *minimum* in the $\mathbf{u}$ directions (representing the solution to the dual problem).

As a final note, from the envelope theorem,

$$u_i^* = \frac{\partial z^*}{\partial b_i}$$

We showed in Chap. 14 that when the objective and constraint functions $f(\mathbf{x})$ and $g(\mathbf{x})$ [the constraints being $g(\mathbf{x}) \leq \mathbf{b}$] are all homogeneous of the same degree, then $z^* = \phi(b_1, \ldots, b_m)$ is homogeneous of degree 1 in the b_i's. Therefore, by the converse of Euler's theorem,

$$w^* = \sum_{i=1}^{m} b_i u_i^* = \sum_{i=1}^{m} \frac{\partial z^*}{\partial b_i} b_i \equiv z^*$$

Equivalently,

$$x_j^* = \frac{\partial w^*}{\partial p_j}$$

and therefore

$$z^* = \sum p_j x_j^* = \sum \frac{\partial w^*}{\partial p_j} p_j \equiv w^*$$

15.6 THE SIMPLEX ALGORITHM[†]

In the previous sections we discussed some of the economic aspects of the solutions to linear programming problems. In particular, we have shown that there is often an interesting dual problem associated with any linear maximization model. The primary reason for considering as restrictive a model as that of constant coefficients, however, is the trade-off in terms of ease of empirical solution. In fact, a relatively simple, easily programmable (in the computer sense) algorithm, or routine, exists for finding the solution to linear programming problems. Let us explore this aspect of these models now, and then apply it to the earlier example of maximization of total revenue, or income.

Mathematical Prerequisites

Consider the general linear programming problem:

maximize

$$z = \sum_{j=1}^{r} p_j x_j \tag{15-40}$$

subject to

$$a_{11} x_1 + \cdots + a_{1r} x_r \le b_1$$
$$\vdots$$
$$a_{m1} x_1 + \cdots + a_{mr} x_r \le b_m$$
$$x_1, \ldots, x_r \ge 0 \tag{15-41}$$

Here, we have r decision variables and m linear inequality constraints.

The first step in solving such a problem is to convert the *inequality* constraints to *equalities* (which are easier to deal with) through the introduction of *slack variables*. The constraints (15-41) are replaced by the set

$$a_{11} x_1 + \cdots + a_{1r} x_r + x_{r+1} = b_1$$
$$a_{21} x_1 + \cdots + a_{2r} x_r + x_{r+2} = b_2$$
$$\vdots$$
$$a_{m1} x_1 + \cdots + a_{mr} x_r + x_{r+m} = b_m \tag{15-42}$$
$$x_1, \ldots, x_{r+m} \ge 0$$

[†]This section uses concepts developed in the Appendix to Chap. 5.

Since the slack variables $x_{r+1}, \ldots, x_{r+m}$ are constrained to be nonnegative, the equalities (15-42) define the same feasible region as the inequalities (15-41). We see, therefore, that no generality is lost by considering a linear programming problem in which a linear function is maximized subject to linear *equality* constraints, plus nonnegativity. If the constraints are of the form $\sum_j a_{ij}x_j \geq b_i$, however, the slack variable must enter with a *negative* sign, to preserve the meaning of the inequality. Thus, if the constraint were $x_1 + x_2 \geq 10$, the relevant equality constraint would be $x_1 + x_2 - x_3 = 10$, x_1, x_2, $x_3 \geq 0$.

Thus, the problem we shall attempt to solve is:

maximize

$$z = \sum_{i=1}^{n} p_i x_i$$

subject to

$$\sum_{j=1}^{n} a_{ij}x_j = b_i \qquad i = 1, \ldots, m$$

$$x_j \geq 0 \qquad j = 1, \ldots, n$$

In matrix notation, this problem can be written:

maximize

$$\mathbf{p'x}$$

subject to

$$\mathbf{Ax = b} \qquad \mathbf{x \geq 0}$$

where $\mathbf{p}, \mathbf{x} = n \times 1$ matrices, or *column vectors*
$\quad\mathbf{A} = m \times n$ matrix of coefficients
$\quad\mathbf{b} = m \times 1$ column vector

No generality is lost if we assume that these m constraints are all *independent*, i.e., that it is not possible to derive any constraint by combining the remaining $m - 1$. Mathematically, we say that the matrix $\mathbf{A}$ has *rank m*.

Example. Consider the constraints

$$x_1 + 2x_2 + x_4 = 2$$

$$2x_1 - 2x_2 + x_3 = 3$$

$$4x_1 + 2x_2 + x_3 + 2x_4 = 6$$

If the first equation is multiplied by 2 and added to the second equation, the resulting equation is

$$4x_1 + 2x_2 + x_3 + 2x_4 = 7$$

The left-hand side is identical to the third constraint above. The three constraints are obviously inconsistent with each other, since $6 \neq 7$. If the 6 had been a 7 in the original third constraint, that constraint could have been ignored, since it would be redundant. We could then simply consider this a two-constraint system.

Denote the rows of the matrix $\mathbf{A}$ by $\mathbf{A}_1, \ldots, \mathbf{A}_m$, respectively. The matrix $\mathbf{A}$ has rank m if there do not exist scalars $k_1, \ldots, k_m$ such that

$$\mathbf{A}_j = \sum_{\substack{i=1 \\ i \neq j}}^{m} k_i \mathbf{A}_i$$

That is, $\mathbf{A}$ has rank m if no row is a linear combination of the remaining rows. This ensures that any $m \times m$ determinant formed from $\mathbf{A}$ will be nonzero. The number of decision variables n must be greater than the number of constraints m to have any meaningful problem. If $m = n$, a unique solution of the constraints exists; the feasible region consists of that one point, and hence, the maximization part of the problem is trivial. If $m > n$, the feasible region is void.

With m independent equations, it is possible to solve for any m x_j's uniquely, in terms of the remaining $n - m$. If these remaining $n - m$ x_j's are set equal to 0, a *basic feasible* solution results (assuming that nonnegativity, as always, holds as well). That is, a *basic feasible* solution is a feasible solution in which $n - m$ of the x_j's equal 0, or the number of positive x_j's is no greater than the number of constraints. The m x_j's in the basic feasible solution are called the *basis*.

Geometrically, the set of basic feasible solutions corresponds to the *corners* of the feasible region, e.g., the origin and points A, B, C, and D in Fig. 15-4. We can see this as follows. A corner is a point that does *not* lie between two other points in the feasible region. Suppose $\mathbf{y} = (y_1, \ldots, y_m, 0, \ldots, 0)$ is a basic feasible solution, that is, $\mathbf{A}\mathbf{y} = \mathbf{b}$, $\mathbf{y} \geq \mathbf{0}$, where the coordinates have been numbered so that the last $n - m$ y_j's are zero. If $\mathbf{y}$ is not on a corner of the feasible region, then there exist two other feasible solutions, $\mathbf{u}$ and $\mathbf{v}$, such that $\mathbf{y}$ lies on the straight line joining $\mathbf{u}$ and $\mathbf{v}$, that is,

$$\mathbf{y} = k\mathbf{u} + (1 - k)\mathbf{v} \qquad 0 < k < 1$$

For the last $n - m$ components of $\mathbf{u}$ and $\mathbf{v}$,

$$0 = ku_j + (1 - k)v_j \qquad j = m + 1, \ldots, n$$

Since $u_j \geq 0$ and $v_j \geq 0$, this can happen only if $u_j = v_j = 0$, $j = m + 1, \ldots, n$. Thus, $\mathbf{u}$ and $\mathbf{v}$ are also basic feasible solutions. However, $\mathbf{y}$, $\mathbf{u}$, and $\mathbf{v}$ must all be the same point. With the last $n - m$ components of each vector equal to zero, the matrix equation of constraints, $\mathbf{A}\mathbf{x} = \mathbf{b}$, reduces to

$$\sum_{j=1}^{m} a_{ij} y_j = b_i \qquad i = 1, \ldots, m$$

$$\sum_{j=1}^{m} a_{ij}u_j = b_i \qquad i = 1, \ldots, m$$

$$\sum_{j=1}^{m} a_{ij}v_j = b_i \qquad i = 1, \ldots, m$$

These are the same m equations in m unknowns. The equations are all linearly independent by assumption. Hence, there is a unique solution; that is, $\mathbf{y} = \mathbf{u} = \mathbf{v}$. This contradicts the assumption that $\mathbf{y}$ lies *between* two other feasible solutions. Hence, the set of *basic feasible* solutions is the corners of the feasible region.

As indicated earlier, the feasible region is always a *convex set* for linear programming problems. This was illustrated earlier. The proof is quite simple and follows from more general considerations since the constraints are all concave functions. Suppose $\mathbf{u}$ and $\mathbf{v}$ are any two feasible solutions, that is, $\mathbf{Au} = \mathbf{b}$, $\mathbf{Av} = \mathbf{b}$, $\mathbf{u}, \mathbf{v} \geq \mathbf{0}$. Then any point $\mathbf{y} = k\mathbf{u} + (1 - k)\mathbf{v}$, $0 \leq k \leq 1$ is also a feasible solution:

$$\mathbf{Ay} = \mathbf{A}(k\mathbf{u} + (1 - k)\mathbf{v}) = k\mathbf{Au} + (1 - k)\mathbf{Av} = k\mathbf{b} + (1 - k)\mathbf{b} = \mathbf{b}$$

Hence, $\mathbf{Ay} = \mathbf{b}$. Clearly, $\mathbf{y} \geq \mathbf{0}$, since $\mathbf{u}, \mathbf{v} \geq \mathbf{0}$, and the scalar $k \geq 0$. Hence, $\mathbf{y}$, which represents all points on the straight line joining $\mathbf{u}$ and $\mathbf{v}$, is feasible whenever $\mathbf{u}$ and $\mathbf{v}$ are, and thus by definition the feasible region is convex.

The importance of these results is that they tell us that any local maximum must be the global maximum (though not necessarily unique) of the problem. There can be no "hills further on" with higher maxima than the given one.

It is geometrically obvious from Fig. 15-4 that in general the maximum, or *optimal solution* as it is usually called, *will be at a corner of the feasible region.* We shall not prove this important theorem, as it depends upon more advanced techniques of linear algebra. It may be the case that there are an infinite number of solutions. This occurs when the objective hyperplane is parallel to a flat portion of the feasible region at the maximum position. In the example in Sec. 15.2, if $p_1 = p_2$, so that $p_1/p_2 = 1$, for example, the maximum will occur at all points along the line segment BC in Fig. 15-4. However, the *basic* feasible solutions B and C will still be optimal. *In any linear programming problem in which a finite optimum exists, there exists an optimal solution that is a basic feasible solution. If the optimal solution is unique, it is a basic feasible solution.*

These results drastically reduce the number of points over which we have to search for the optimal solution. One approach to the problem would be simply to program a computer to search all the corners, evaluate $z = \mathbf{p}'\mathbf{x}$ at each one, and pick the largest. However, vastly more efficient routines are available. The number of corners can be quite large; e.g., a model with 10 equations and 20 variables may contain

$$\binom{20}{10} = \frac{20!}{10!10!} = 184,756$$

basic feasible solutions.

The Simplex Algorithm: Example

We shall now illustrate the simplex algorithm for solving linear programming models by using the algorithm on the three-factor, two-good model analyzed in Sec. 15.2. The problem, again, is:

maximize

$$z = 40y_1 + 30y_2$$

subject to

$$3y_1 + 2y_2 \le 54$$

$$2y_1 + 2y_2 \le 40$$

$$y_1 + 2y_2 \le 35 \qquad y_1, \ y_2 \ge 0$$

The first step is to convert the constraints to equalities, by adding slack variables:

maximize

$$z = 40y_1 + 30y_2 \tag{15-43}$$

subject to

$$3y_1 + 2y_2 + y_3 = 54 \tag{15-44a}$$

$$2y_1 + 2y_2 + y_4 = 40 \tag{15-44b}$$

$$y_1 + 2y_2 + y_5 = 35 \tag{15-44c}$$

$$y_1, \ y_2, \ y_3, \ y_4, \ y_5 \ge 0$$

We now have three independent constraints in five variables. A basic feasible solution is a vector $\mathbf{y} = (y_1, \ldots, y_5)$ such that any *two* ($= 5 - 3$) y_j's are set equal to 0, and the remaining y_j's are nonnegative and satisfy the preceding constraints. Let us arbitrarily set $y_4 = y_5 = 0$ and see if this yields a basic feasible solution. However, let us keep y_4 and y_5 in the equations and *solve for* y_1, y_2, and y_3 *in terms of* y_4 *and* y_5.

Subtracting (15-44c) from (15-44b) and rearranging terms gives

$$y_1 = 5 - y_4 + y_5 \tag{15-45a}$$

Substituting this into (15-44c) and solving for y_2, we have

$$2y_2 = 35 - y_5 - (5 - y_4 + y_5)$$

or

$$y_2 = 15 + 0.5y_4 - y_5 \tag{15-45b}$$

Lastly, we substitute (15-45a) and (15-45b) into (15-44a) to solve for y_3:

$$y_3 = 54 - 3(5 - y_4 + y_5) - 2(15 + 0.5y_4 - y_5)$$

or

$$y_3 = 9 + 2y_4 - y_5 \qquad (15\text{-}45c)$$

Consider this solution, Eqs. (15-45). Setting $y_4 = y_5 = 0$, we get $y_1 = 5$, $y_2 = 15$, $y_3 = 9$. This is a basic *feasible* solution since $y_1, y_2, y_3 \geq 0$. It corresponds to point B in Fig. 15-4. Notice that the slack variable y_3 is positive. Hence, the first (land) constraint is nonbinding, but with $y_4 = y_5 = 0$, the labor and capital constraints are binding.

However, is this solution optimal; i.e., does it maximize the objective function? Let us substitute these values of y_1 and y_2 into the objective function [y_3 does not appear in (15-43)], carrying y_4 and y_5 along:

$$z = 40(5 - y_4 + y_5) + 30(15 + 0.5y_4 - y_5)$$

$$z = 650 - 25y_4 + 10y_5 \qquad (15\text{-}46)$$

Equation (15-46) is the indirect objective function for this solution vector. It quickly reveals that the solution $y_1 = 5$, $y_2 = 15$, $y_3 = 9$ just obtained is *not* optimal. Using the envelope theorem, we get

$$\frac{\partial z}{\partial y_5} = 10 > 0 \qquad (15\text{-}47)$$

This relation says that the value of the objective function z can be increased by increasing the variable y_5. In fact, z will increase by a factor of 10 for each unit increase in y_5.

Thus, we should seek to make y_5 as large as possible. How large is "possible"? We have to make sure that the remaining variables remain nonnegative. Consider Eqs. (15-45) again. We know we have to bring y_5 into the basis, but which variable, y_1, y_2, or y_3, shall we take out to leave only three basic variables? There is no reason, from Eq. (15-45a), why y_5 cannot be increased indefinitely (along with y_1). However, (15-45b) tells us, for example, that y_5 cannot be made larger than 15. Ignoring y_4 (which remains at 0), nonnegativity and Eqs. (15-45) mean that we must satisfy, simultaneously,

$$y_1 = 5 + y_5 \geq 0$$

$$y_2 = 15 - y_5 \geq 0$$

$$y_3 = 9 - y_5 \geq 0$$

In fact, the last inequality indicates that $y_5 \leq 9$ is required for nonnegativity. This relation tells us both that "as large as possible" for y_5 is in fact $y_5 = 9$ and that y_3 is the variable that comes out of the basis.

The new basis is therefore y_1, y_2, and y_5. We must now solve for these variables and in the same manner check whether this solution is optimal. We know it will be an improvement, since $\partial z / \partial y_5 > 0$. In fact, we know (since $\partial z / \partial y_5 = 10$ and $y_5 = 9$) that z will increase by $10(9) = 90$, yielding $z = 650 + 90 = 740$. Let us proceed.

From (15-45c),

$$y_5 = 9 + 2y_4 - y_3 \qquad (15\text{-}48a)$$

Substituting this into (15-45a) yields

$$y_1 = 5 - y_4 + (9 + 2y_4 - y_3)$$

or

$$y_1 = 14 - y_3 + y_4 \qquad (15\text{-}48b)$$

Substituting (15-48a) into (15-45b) gives

$$y_2 = 15 + 0.5y_4 - (9 + 2y_4 - y_3)$$

or

$$y_2 = 6 + y_3 - 1.5y_4 \qquad (15\text{-}48c)$$

Equations (15-48) are the new basic feasible solution. Setting $y_3 = y_4 = 0$, we get $y_1 = 14$, $y_2 = 6$, $y_5 = 9$, and $z = 40(14) + 30(6) = 740$, as expected. This is point C in Fig. 15-4.

   Is this solution optimal? Using (15-48b) and (15-48c), we get

$$z = 40(14 - y_3 + y_4) + 30(6 + y_3 - 1.5y_4)$$

or

$$z = 740 - 10y_3 - 5y_4 \qquad (15\text{-}49)$$

Equation (15-49), the indirect objective function for this solution, tells us that this is indeed the optimal solution. This relation implies that $\partial z/\partial y_3 < 0$, $\partial z/\partial y_4 < 0$. Bringing in either of the nonbasic variables will only *reduce* the value of the objective function. Moreover, this solution is *globally* optimal. Convexity of the feasible region and concavity of the objective function (weak concavity here; the objective function is linear) tell us that any local maximum must be a global maximum. We have thus found the maximum solution in one easy iteration, a combination of luck and the efficiency of the simplex algorithm.

   To summarize, the simplex algorithm consists of first finding some basic feasible solution by rote, if necessary. The basic variables are solved in terms of the nonbasic variables. These values are then substituted into the objective function, a procedure by which the objective function becomes expressed in terms of the nonbasic variables only. If $\partial z/\partial y_j > 0$ for any nonbasic variable, the original solution is not optimal. Suppose one or more y_j is such that $\partial z/\partial y_j > 0$. Pick one of them (perhaps the one for which $\partial z/\partial y_j$ is largest, though this will not ensure that the optimal solution will be reached the fastest). Use the previously obtained solutions to determine how large that nonbasic variable can be made and which previously basic variable must be set equal to zero, i.e., taken out of the basis. Solve for the new basic feasible solution. Repeat this process until $\partial z/\partial y_j \leq 0$ for all nonbasic variables. When this condition holds, the solution is optimal, since bringing new variables into the basis will not increase z.

Remark 1. If $\partial z/\partial y_j = 0$ for some nonbasic variable, bringing that y_j into the basis will neither increase nor decrease z. If this occurs at an optimal solution, multiple optima are indicated.

Remark 2. For a *minimization* problem, the criterion that must be satisfied is $\partial z/\partial y_j \geq 0$ for all nonbasic y_j. For minimization problems, the optimal solution is characterized by having the nonbasic variables *increase* the objective function if they are introduced.

Example. Let us consider the following minimization problem, stripped of any economic content, for the purposes of exhibiting the simplex algorithm once more:

minimize

$$z = 2x_1 + x_2 + 2x_3$$

subject to

$$x_1 - 2x_2 + x_3 \geq 16$$
$$2x_2 + x_3 \leq 10$$
$$x_3 \leq 6 \qquad x_1,\ x_2,\ x_3 \geq 0$$

The first step is to add slack variables to convert the constraints into equalities. Note the direction of the inequalities:

minimize

$$z = 2x_1 + x_2 + 2x_3$$

subject to

$$x_1 - 2x_2 + x_3 - x_4 = 16$$
$$2x_2 + x_3 + x_5 = 10$$
$$x_3 + x_6 = 6 \qquad x_1,\ x_2,\ x_3,\ x_4,\ x_5,\ x_6 \geq 0$$

Let us choose x_1, x_2, and x_3 as a basis. Solving for these variables in terms of the remaining ones yields (the student should work through this algebra):

$$x_3 = 6 - x_6$$
$$x_2 = 2 - 0.5x_5 + 0.5x_6$$
$$x_1 = 14 + x_4 - x_5 + 2x_6$$

Computing z, we get

$$z = 2(14 + x_4 - x_5 + 2x_6) + (2 - 0.5x_5 + 0.5x_6) + 2(6 - x_6)$$

or

$$z = 42 + 2x_4 - 2.5x_5 + 2.5x_6$$

We see that $\partial z/\partial x_5 < 0$; bringing x_5 into the basis will decrease z. Hence, this solution is not optimal. How large can we make x_5? From the preceding solution, to ensure nonnegativity of x_1, x_2, and x_3, we must have (ignoring x_4 and x_6, which remain at 0)

$$x_2 = 2 - 0.5x_5 \geq 0 \qquad x_1 = 14 - x_5 \geq 0$$

Since these must both be satisfied, we cannot increase x_5 beyond 4. Hence, x_2 comes out of the basis. The new basis is x_1, x_3, and x_5. Solving for these variables yields

$$x_3 = 6 - x_6$$

$$x_5 = 4 - 2x_2 + x_6$$

$$x_1 = 10 + 2x_2 + x_4 + x_6$$

Computing the new z [we expect this z to be less than the old z by $2.5(4) = 10$] gives

$$z = 2(10 + 2x_2 + x_4 + x_6) + x_2 + 2(6 - x_6)$$

or

$$z = 32 + 5x_2 + 2x_4$$

Notice that $\partial z/\partial x_2 > 0$, $\partial z/\partial x_4 > 0$ but that $\partial z/\partial x_6 = 0$. This solution is optimal, since there is no variable to be brought in which would *lower* z. However, this is not the only solution. Bringing x_6 into the basis will keep z the same. There are an infinite number of solutions along the line segment between this solution ($x_1 = 10$, $x_5 = 4$, $x_3 = 6$) and the one which results from bringing x_6 in. The remainder of this problem is left as an exercise for the student.

PROBLEMS

1. Consider an economy made up of many identical fixed-coefficient firms, each of which produces food y_1 and clothing y_2. There are three inputs: land, labor, and capital, inputs 1, 2, and 3, respectively. The matrix of technological coefficients is

$$A = \begin{pmatrix} 1 & 1 \\ 1 & 2 \\ 1 & 4 \end{pmatrix}$$

Each firm has available to it 30 units of land, 40 units of labor, and 72 units of capital. Prices are \$20 per unit for food and \$30 per unit for clothing.
   (a) Find the production plan that maximizes the value of output.
   (b) Find the shadow prices of land, labor, and capital.
   (c) Write down the dual problem and interpret it.
   (d) Solve the dual problem and verify that the optimal value of its objective function equals the maximum value of output.
   (e) From the factor intensities of the goods at the optimum, predict the changes in output levels that would occur if an additional unit of labor were available. Check by actual solution.
   (f) From the factor intensities, predict the change in factor prices if p_1 rises to 21. Check by actual solution.
   (g) What effect does a small increase in factor endowments have on factor prices?
2. Answer the same questions as in Prob. 1 for an economy made up of firms with coefficient matrix

$$A = \begin{pmatrix} 2 & 1 \\ 1 & 1 \\ 1 & 0 \end{pmatrix}$$

endowments of

$$\mathbf{b} = \begin{pmatrix} 40 \\ 30 \\ 15 \end{pmatrix}$$

and prices $p_1 = 15$, $p_2 = 10$. For part (f), suppose here that p_2 rises to 11.

3. Solve the following linear programming problem:

minimize

$$z = 4x_1 + 5x_2 + x_3$$

subject to

$$x_1 + x_2 \geq 9$$

$$x_1 + x_3 \leq 8 \qquad x_1, \ x_2, \ x_3 \geq 0$$

$$2x_2 - x_3 \geq 5$$

Start with x_1, x_2, x_3 as a basis.

4. A firm makes banjos (x_1), guitars (x_2), and mandolins (x_3). It uses three inputs: wood, labor, and brass, inputs 1, 2, and 3, respectively. Let

$$a_{ij} = \text{amount of } i\text{th input used in production of 1 unit of product } j$$

The matrix of these technological coefficients is

$$\begin{pmatrix} 1 & 1 & 1 \\ 2 & 2 & 1 \\ 1 & 2 & 1 \end{pmatrix}$$

The firm has available to it 50 units of wood, 60 units of labor, and 55 units of brass. The firm sells banjos for $200, guitars for $175, and mandolins for $125.

(a) Find the production plan that maximizes the total value of output. Start with x_1, x_2, x_3 as your first basis.

(b) Formulate the dual for this problem and explain its economic interpretation. Solve the dual problem using, if you wish, whatever information about its solution you can glean from the solution of the primal problem. How much would the firm be willing to pay for an additional unit of wood, labor, and brass?

5. *The Diet Problem.* Suppose a consumer has available n foods, $x_1, \ldots, x_n$. Each food contains a certain amount of nutrients (vitamins, minerals, etc.). Let a_{ij} = amount of nutrient i in food j. If the foods x_i cost p_i per unit, and the consumer wishes to obtain a minimum daily requirement (MDR) b_j of nutrient j, what diet should be consumed?

(a) Formulate this problem as a linear programming problem. What assumptions about how nutrients are combined is needed?

(b) Formulate and interpret the dual problem.

(c) Suppose there are only three nutrients to consider, A, B, and C, with MDRs of 34, 32, and 50, respectively. There are three foods, x_1, x_2, and x_3 with prices $p_1 = 1$, $p_2 = 3$, $p_3 = 2$. The matrix of nutrient contents of the foods is

$$\mathbf{A} = \begin{pmatrix} 1 & 2 & 1 \\ 2 & 1 & 3 \\ 2 & 3 & 1 \end{pmatrix}$$

Find the diet that minimizes the cost of satisfying the MDRs of each nutrient. Check by solving the dual problem also.

6. Complete the discussion of the linear programming problem presented in the text preceding the problems. Bring x_6 into the basis and show that the maximum value of z is unchanged. Formulate and solve the dual problem and verify that its objective function has as its solution the same value as z^*.

BIBLIOGRAPHY

Dantzig, G. B.: "Maximization of a Linear Function of Variables Subject to Linear Inequalities," in T. C. Koopmans (ed.), *Activity Analysis of Production and Allocation, Cowles Commission Monograph* 13, John Wiley & Sons, Inc., New York, 1951.

Dorfman, R., P. A. Samuelson, and R. M. Solow: *Linear Programming and Economic Analysis,* McGraw-Hill Book Company, New York, 1958.

Gale, D.: *The Theory of Linear Economic Models,* McGraw-Hill Book Company, New York, 1960.

Hadley, G.: *Linear Programming,* Addison-Wesley Publishing Company, Inc., Reading MA, 1962.

Jones, R. W.: "Duality in International Trade: A Geometrical Note," *Canadian Journal of Economics and Political Science,* **31**:390–393, 1965.

Jones, R. W.: "The Structure of Simple General Equilibrium Models," *Journal of Political Economy,* **73**:557–572, 1965.

Koopmans, T. C. (ed.): *Activity Analysis of Production and Allocation, Cowles Commission Monograph* 13, John Wiley & Sons, Inc., New York, 1951.

Koopmans, T. C.: *Three Essays on the State of Economic Science,* McGraw-Hill Book Company, New York, 1957.

Leontief, W. W., et al.: *Studies in the Structure of the American Economy,* Oxford University Press, New York, 1953.

Rybczynski, T. M.: "Factor Endowment and Relative Commodity Prices," *Econometrica,* **22**:336–341, 1955.

Samuelson, P. A.: "Frank Knight's Theorem in Linear Programming," RAND Corp., Santa Monica, CA, 1950; reprinted in J. Stiglitz (ed.), *The Collected Scientific Papers of Paul A. Samuelson,* MIT Press, Cambridge, MA, 1966.

Stigler, G. J.: "The Cost of Subsistence," *Journal of Farm Economics,* **27**:303–314, 1945.

Stolper, W. F., and P. A. Samuelson: "Protection and Real Wages," *Review of Economic Studies,* **9**:58–73, 1941.

Von Neumann, J.: "A Model of General Equilibrium," *Review of Economic Studies,* **13**:1–9, 1945.

Walras, L.: *Elements of Pure Economics,* trans. W. Jaffe, Richard D. Irwin, Inc., Homewood, IL, 1954.

CHAPTER 16

GENERAL EQUILIBRIUM II: NONLINEAR MODELS

16.1 TANGENCY CONDITIONS

In this chapter, the more plausible model of general equilibrium based on *variable* coefficients of production will be investigated. The bulk of the chapter will be concerned with the derivation of the Stolper-Samuelson and Rybczynski theorems in this more general context. It is a rather remarkable feature of these models that when the production functions are assumed merely to be *linear homogeneous,* the comparative statics of the model yield the same implications as in the case of fixed-coefficient technology (indeed, the algebra is identical).

The most general model to be considered here is the one in which n final goods, $y_1, \ldots, y_n$, are produced using m factors of production, $x_1, \ldots, x_m$. The economy faces world output prices, $p_1, \ldots, p_n$. If we let

$$x_{ij} = \text{amount of factor } i \text{ used in} \\ \text{production of good } j$$

the production function for y_j is

$$y_j = f^j(x_{1j}, \ldots, x_{mj}) \qquad j = 1, \ldots, n \tag{16-1}$$

We assert that an invisible hand leads the economy to:

maximize

$$z = \sum_{j=1}^{n} p_j y_j = \sum_{j=1}^{n} p_j f^j(x_{1j}, \ldots, x_{mj}) \tag{16-2}$$

subject to

$$\sum_{j=1}^{n} x_{ij} \leq x_i \qquad i = 1, \ldots, m \tag{16-3}$$

$$x_{ij} \geq 0 \qquad \text{all } i, j$$

The model, at this point, is a general nonlinear programming problem. Without the knowledge of the specific functional forms for the production functions (16-1), no solution algorithm is available (as opposed to the linear model of the previous chapter). We shall therefore concentrate on the *comparative statics* of the model, assuming that the x_{ij}'s are the ones that the economy uses in positive amounts. In that case, the Kuhn-Tucker first-order conditions become the classical Lagrangian techniques.

All the comparative statics results that are forthcoming in this general model can be adequately indicated by reducing the model to two goods and two factors, since we shall not be concerned with which factors are present in the first place. Let us therefore change notation to conform with the previous analysis and consider *two* factors, L, labor, and K, capital. Let L_j and K_j represent the amounts of labor and capital, respectively, which are used in the production of good j. The production functions for each of the two goods are

$$y_j = f^j(L_j, K_j) \qquad j = 1, 2$$

The model thus becomes

maximize

$$z = p_1 f^1(L_1, K_1) + p_2 f^2(L_2, K_2) \tag{16-4}$$

subject to

$$L_1 + L_2 = L \tag{16-5a}$$

$$K_1 + K_2 = K \tag{16-5b}$$

We are assuming that we shall find L_1, L_2, K_1, and K_2 all positive and fully employed at the parametrically fixed levels L and K, respectively. The Lagrangian for this model is

$$\mathscr{L} = p_1 f^1(L_1, K_1) + p_2 f^2(L_2, K_2) + \lambda_L(L - L_1 - L_2) + \lambda_K(K - K_1 - K_2) \tag{16-6}$$

The first-order equations for constrained maximum are obtained by differentiating $\mathscr{L}$ with respect to the four choice variables, L_1, L_2, K_1, K_2, and the two Lagrange multipliers. When we let

$$f^j_L = \frac{\partial f^j}{\partial L_j} = \frac{\partial y_j}{\partial L_j} \qquad f^j_K = \frac{\partial f^j}{\partial K_j} = \frac{\partial y_j}{\partial K_j}$$

these first-order conditions are

$$p_1 f^1_L - \lambda_L = 0 \tag{16-7a}$$

$$p_1 f^1_K - \lambda_K = 0 \tag{16-7b}$$

$$p_2 f^2_L - \lambda_L = 0 \tag{16-7c}$$

$$p_2 f^2_K - \lambda_K = 0 \tag{16-7d}$$

$$L - L_1 - L_2 = 0 \tag{16-8a}$$

$$K - K_1 - K_2 = 0 \tag{16-8b}$$

The second-order conditions consist of restrictions on the border-preserving principal minors of the border Hessian determinant formed by differentiating Eqs. (16-7) and (16-8) again with respect to the L_i's, K_i's, and λ's. Letting $f^j_{LL} = \partial^2 f^j/(\partial L_j \partial L_j)$, etc., we have

$$H = \begin{vmatrix} p_1 f^1_{LL} & p_1 f^1_{LK} & 0 & 0 & -1 & 0 \\ p_1 f^1_{KL} & p_1 f^1_{KK} & 0 & 0 & 0 & -1 \\ 0 & 0 & p_2 f^2_{LL} & p_2 f^2_{LK} & -1 & 0 \\ 0 & 0 & p_2 f^2_{KL} & p_2 f^2_{KK} & 0 & -1 \\ -1 & 0 & -1 & 0 & 0 & 0 \\ 0 & -1 & 0 & -1 & 0 & 0 \end{vmatrix} \tag{16-9}$$

Specifically, the border-preserving principal minors of order k alternate in sign, the whole determinant H having sign $+1$.

Assuming the sufficient second-order conditions hold, Eqs. (16-7) and (16-8) can be solved for the explicit choice functions

$$L_i = L^*_i(p_1, p_2, L, K) \qquad i = 1, 2 \tag{16-10a}$$

$$K_i = K^*_i(p_1, p_2, L, K) \qquad i = 1, 2 \tag{16–10b}$$

and

$$\lambda_L = \lambda^*_L(p_1, p_2, L, K) \tag{16-11a}$$

$$\lambda_K = \lambda^*_K(p_1, p_2, L, K) \tag{16-11b}$$

Equations (16-10) show the quantities of each factor that will be used by each industry at given output prices and total resource constraints. They are in fact neither factor supply nor factor demand equations, since they are not functions of factor prices. The factor supply curves to the whole economy are vertical lines at L and K, respectively. Equations (16-10) represent the solutions to the allocation problem wherein each factor is demanded by two industries.

As in the linear model of the previous chapter, the role of factor prices is filled by the Lagrange multipliers λ_L and λ_K. Substituting the L^*_i's and K^*_i's into the objective function z yields

$$z^* = \phi(p_1, p_2, L, K) = p_1 f^1(L_1^*, K_1^*) + p_2 f^2(L_2^*, K_2^*) \tag{16-12}$$

Using the envelope theorem, we get

$$\frac{\partial z^*}{\partial L} = \frac{\partial \phi}{\partial L} = \frac{\partial \mathscr{L}}{\partial L} = \lambda_L^*(p_1, p_2, L, K) \tag{16-13a}$$

$$\frac{\partial z^*}{\partial K} = \frac{\partial \phi}{\partial K} = \frac{\partial \mathscr{L}}{\partial K} = \lambda_K^*(p_1, p_2, L, K) \tag{16-13b}$$

That is, λ_L^* is the rate of change of maximum NNP with respect to a change in the resource endowment of labor, with a similar interpretation for λ_K^*. These multipliers are the incremental increases in income that would result if an additional increment of labor or capital were available. In a competitive economy, these are the marginal revenue products of labor and capital, respectively. They indicate what labor and capital would be paid in a competitive economy. Hence, the Lagrange multipliers represent the imputed values, or shadow prices, of resources in this model. They are not exogenous, as in the previous partial equilibrium treatments of the firm, but endogenous, appearing as part of the solution to the model.

Let us in fact designate the wage rate w as $w \equiv \lambda_L$ and the flow price of capital as $r \equiv \lambda_K$. The symbol r does *not* represent an interest rate. It is the rate at which capital is *rented,* analogous to the rate w at which labor is rented. Capital is treated as a service flow, as is labor, and not as a stock that is purchased outright, with r the wage of capital.

Industry supply curves can be defined in this model by substituting the L_i^*'s and K_i^*'s into the production function, yielding

$$y_1 = f^1(L_1^*, K_1^*) = y_1^*(p_1, p_2, L, K) \tag{16-14a}$$

$$y_2 = f^2(L_2^*, K_2^*) = y_2^*(p_1, p_2, L, K) \tag{16-14b}$$

These are the industry supply curves because they indicate how much output will be produced for a given price of output, price of the other good, and resource constraints. The demand curves for each industry are the horizontal price lines at the levels p_1 and p_2, respectively, reflecting competitive output markets.

The supply curves (16-14) are homogeneous of degree zero in output prices. Increasing both prices by the same proportion leaves output unchanged, or

$$y_j^*(tp_1, tp_2, L, K) \equiv y_j^*(p_1, p_2, L, K) \qquad j = 1, 2 \tag{16-15}$$

This is easily seen from the objective function (16-4), $z = p_1 y_1 + p_2 y_2$. If both prices are increased by the factor t, $z = t(p_1 y_1 + p_2 y_2)$, a simple monotonic (linear, in fact) transformation of the original function. The values of the factors that maximize $p_1 y_1 + p_2 y_2$ also maximize $t p_1 y_1 + t p_2 y_2$. The solutions (16-10), $L_i = L_i^*(p_1, p_2, L, K)$, etc., are thus homogeneous of degree zero in p_1 and p_2, and thus so must be $y_1^* = f^1(L_1^*, K_1^*)$ and $y_2^* = f^2(L_2^*, K_2^*)$.

The production possibilities frontier for this economy is defined as the locus of points (y_1, y_2) such that for any given y_2, the maximum y_1 is obtained, or vice versa. It can be obtained by eliminating the prices from Eqs. (16-14a) and (16-14b). In Eq. (16-15), let $t = 1/p_2$, $p = p_1/p_2$. The variable p represents the *relative* price of output y_1 (in terms of units of y_2). Then we obtain

$$y_1^*(p_1, p_2, L, K) = y_1^*\!\left(\frac{p_1}{p_2}, 1, L, K\right) = Y_1^*(p, L, K) \qquad (16\text{-}16a)$$

and

$$y_2^*(p_1, p_2, L, K) = y_2^*\!\left(\frac{p_1}{p_2}, 1, L, K\right) = Y_2^*(p, L, K) \qquad (16\text{-}16b)$$

Assuming $\partial Y_j^*/\partial p \neq 0$, $j = 1,2$, the variable p, relative output price, can be eliminated from these two equations, leaving

$$G(y_1^*, y_2^*, L, K) = 0 \qquad (16\text{-}17)$$

or, in explicit form,

$$y_2^* = g(y_1^*; L, K) \qquad (16\text{-}18)$$

The typical assumed shape of this function is concave to the origin, as depicted in Fig. 16-1. We shall see presently how this shape is implied by the sufficient second-order equations for this model. As drawn, $\partial y_2^*/\partial y_1^* < 0$, and $\partial^2 y_2^*/\partial y_1^{*2} < 0$.

Before analyzing the comparative statics of this model, let us investigate the first-order marginal relations (16-7). As we have indicated, $w(=\lambda_L)$ and $r(=\lambda_K)$ are the imputed marginal revenue products of labor and capital, respectively. From Eqs. (16-7a) and (16-7c), we see that the marginal revenue product of labor must be the same in both industries. Likewise, from (16-7b)

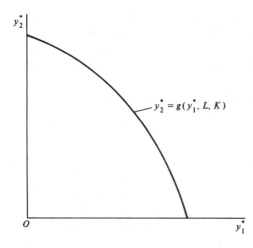

y_2^*

$y_2^* = g(y_1^*, L, K)$

O

y_1^*

FIGURE 16-1
The production possibilities frontier indicates the maximum amount of one output that is attainable for given amounts of the other. In order for the economy to achieve maximum NNP for given resource constraints, a point on this frontier must be reached. Otherwise, increasing both y_1 and y_2 will increase NNP $= p_1 y_1 + p_2 y_2$. The second-order conditions for the maximization of NNP model imply that $\partial y_2^*/\partial y_1^* < 0, \partial^2 y_1^*/\partial y_1^{*2} < 0$, as drawn above. However, this is not implied by simply maximizing y_2 for given y_1, L, and K unless additional restrictions are placed on the production functions. (See Prob. 5.)

and (16-7*d*), the marginal revenue product of capital must be the same in both industries. One would expect this on the basis of intuitive reasoning. If labor, say, were more productive, i.e., yielded more output at the margin, in industry 1 than in industry 2, the owners of labor would find competitive bids for their services more attractive in the first industry. Labor will leave industry 2 and enter industry 1. In so doing, the marginal product of labor will rise in industry 2 and fall in industry 1. This process will continue until the bids for labor (or capital) are the same in both industries. It is this process of competitive bidding, with owners of labor and capital seeking their highest valued employment, that is the essence of Adam Smith's invisible hand mechanism, in which the value of total output is maximized.

Combining Eqs. (16-7*a*) and (16-7*b*) gives

$$\frac{f_L^1}{f_K^1} = \frac{w}{r} \tag{16-19a}$$

Likewise, from (16-7*c*) and (16-7*d*) we have

$$\frac{f_L^2}{f_K^2} = \frac{w}{r} \tag{16-19b}$$

These last two equations say that the ratio of the marginal products of labor and capital, for each industry, is equal to the ratio of the (imputed) factor prices. This is analogous to the partial equilibrium tangency condition for profit maximization or cost minimization, in which the isoquants are tangent to the isocost line, with common slope equal to the ratio of wage rates.

In the present model, however, this imputed ratio of wage rates or relative factor costs is common to both industries. From Eq. (16-19),

$$\frac{f_L^1}{f_K^1} = \frac{w}{r} = \frac{f_L^2}{f_K^2} \tag{16-20}$$

At the wealth-maximizing input combination, the slopes of the isoquants in each industry are the same. Again, if they were different, one factor would be more productive (at the margin) in one industry than the other (the reverse holding for the other factor). In that case, factors would move from the relatively low-valued use to the high-valued use, increasing both the return to that factor and the NNP of the economy.

This situation is commonly depicted in an Edgeworth-Bowley box diagram. In Fig. 16-2, industry 1 is depicted in the usual manner, with origin O_1 at the lower left, or southwest, corner of the box. The isoquants of industry 1 are the curves convex to that origin. The axes are finite, however, and extend only to the limits of resource endowments. In the horizontal direction, labor is plotted up to the parametric value L. Likewise, in the vertical direction, units of capital are plotted until the parametric value K is reached. At these limits, a rectangle is formed, yielding another origin O_2. The production function $f^2(L_2, K_2)$ is plotted upside down, starting at O_2, with increased labor plotted in a westerly direction, increased capital in the southerly direction. Various isoquants

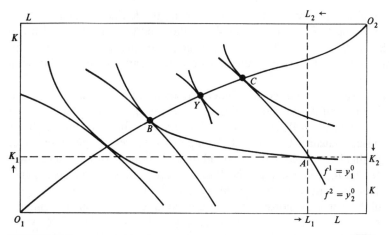

FIGURE 16-2
Edgeworth-Bowley box diagram for factor utilization. This famous diagram, attributed to F. Y. Edgeworth and A. L. Bowley, depicts the set of factor allocations in an economy in which all gains from trade are exhausted. The dimensions of the box are the total endowments of labor (plotted horizontally) and capital (plotted vertically). The labor L_1, used by industry 1, at some point, say A, is the horizontal distance from A to the vertical axis emanating from origin O_1. Likewise, the vertical distance from the labor axis to A is the capital K_1 used by industry 1. Continuing to the right from A to the right-hand extremity of the box is the remaining labor L_2 in the economy, which is used by industry 2. Likewise, the vertical distance above A to the top horizontal axis is the amount of capital K_2 used by industry 2. Since $L_1 + L_2 = L$ and $K_1 + K_2 = K$, where L and K are constants, a rectangle is depicted such that any point inside it defines an allocation of factors to each industry.

With this in mind, the production function $f^1(L_1, K_1)$ can be plotted with respect to the origin defined by the southwest corner of the box, and $f^2(L_2, K_2)$ can be plotted with respect to the origin defined by the northeast corner of the box. Industry 2's production function $f^2(L_2, K_2)$, however, is plotted negatively. *Increasing L_2 is a leftward movement since it represents decreasing L_1. Likewise, increasing K_2 is a downward movement since it represents decreasing K_1. Hence, while the isoquants of f^1 appear normally, the isoquants of f^2 appear concave to O_1. Actually, though, they are to be interpreted as convex to O_2, the appropriate origin from which $f^2(L_2, K_2)$ is plotted.

The efficient factor allocations, i.e., those which result in output levels on the production frontier, are those input combinations at which the slopes of the isoquants are equal, in accordance with Eq. (16-20). At such points, each industry values the inputs identically. If industry 1 were willing to give up 3 units of capital for 1 unit of labor and industry 2 were willing to give up 1 unit of labor for 1 unit of capital, both industries could experience an increase in output by, say, industry 2 exchanging only 2 units of capital and getting 1 unit of labor from industry 1 in return. Such mutually advantageous reallocations are possible as long as the slopes of the isoquants for the two industries are different. The locus of points at which those slopes are identical, indicating exhaustion of gains from exchange of factors, is the curve line between O_1 and O_2, known as the *contract curve* or *efficiency locus*. In the absence of transactions costs, some point on the contract curve must be achieved. If the initial point is A, say, in this diagram, then *voluntary* exchange will lead to an allocation of factors on the contract curve.

of $f^2(L_2, K_2)$ are plotted in Fig. 16-2. These curves are concave to O_1 but convex to O_2, the origin from which they are plotted.

Any point in the box represents an allocation of factors to each industry. For example, at point A, L_1 units of labor are allocated to industry 1 and L_2 to industry 2. As at all interior points, $L_1 + L_2 = L$, the horizontal dimension of the box. Likewise at A, K_1 units of capital are allocated to industry 1 and K_2 to industry 2. Since $K_1 + K_2 = K$, the vertical height of the box at all values of L_1, the entire amount of capital available to the economy is allocated between the two industries.

Point A, however, cannot be an efficient allocation, i.e., one in which NNP is maximized. At point A, the slope of industry 1's isoquant is flatter than that of industry 2. Industry 1 will be bidding relatively low for labor and high for capital. Likewise, industry 2, which at A employs relatively large amounts of capital (though this is not necessary), will bid higher amounts for labor and lower amounts for capital than industry 1. The slopes of each industry's isoquants at A indicate that labor is valued more to industry 2 than to industry 1 while capital is relatively high-valued to industry 1. The competitive mechanism will induce labor to move to industry 2 and capital to industry 1. In terms of the Edgeworth diagram, the allocation point will move to the contract curve. Eventually, some point will be reached, such as point Y, at which the slopes of industry 1's and industry 2's isoquants are identical, in accordance with Eq. (16-20). At such a point, the isoquants for the two industries will be tangent to each other. The locus of all such points of tangency within the Edgeworth box is called the *contract curve*. In the absence of transactions costs, a competitive economy must always be at some point on the contract curve. To be otherwise would deny the postulate that more is preferred to less. Individual self-seeking will force the economy to some point along the contract curve at which all gains from trade are exhausted.

One more tangency, which is not depicted but nonetheless is implied, is the response of consumers to this situation. All consumers in this economy face the prices p_1 and p_2 for the output of these industries. Utility-maximizing consumers will consume these goods where their subjective marginal valuation of the goods equals the price ratio, i.e., the relative costs to the consumers. The slope of the consumers' indifference curves, their marginal rate of substitution, will equal the price ratio, or the slope of the production possibility frontier at the final output point.

Any point on the production possibility frontier depicted in Fig. 16-1 corresponds to some point on the contract curve of Fig. 16-2, since only at efficient factor utilization can the maximum output of one good be obtained for a given amount of the other. Any factor allocation not on the contract curve of Fig. 16-2 will result in an output point inside the production frontier depicted in Fig. 16-1. In the literature, two kinds of efficiency are usually defined. If the production point achieved is perceived to be on the production possibilities frontier, then the economy is said to be *efficient in production*. However, due to, for example, monopolies in the economy, the marginal rates of substitution of consumers may not equal the relative cost of production. In that case, gains from exchange could occur, using the reasoning just described, that would allow all consumers to gain. When the MRS of all consumers equals the relative marginal costs of production, the economy is said to be *efficient in consumption*. These welfare-type considerations were first enunciated by V. Pareto. An economy in which all the gains from exchange are exhausted is called *Pareto-optimal* or *Pareto-efficient*. We shall delve into this in more detail in the next chapter.

The student should be warned that efficiency is an essentially unobservable condition. In the absence of transactions costs, all gains from exchange must at all times be exhausted, and hence efficiency follows tautologically. If an economy is asserted to be at an inefficient, or non-Pareto, point, the implied losses to consumers must be reconciled with the consumers' preferences for more rather than less. That is, some observable cost of trading, perhaps embodied in some institutional restriction on open markets, must be identified to make the theory internally consistent. (A deeper analysis would in fact have to explain why consumers sometimes get together and enact laws resulting in lost gains from trade.)

16.2 GENERAL COMPARATIVE STATICS RESULTS

As we have repeatedly emphasized, the potentially observable, refutable hypotheses generated by a model are the goals of theory. The first-order conditions (16-7) and (16-8) are nonobservable in the absence of knowledge of the specific functional forms. The refutable hypotheses of this model are the restrictions in sign of the various partial derivatives of the explicit choice functions, Eqs. (16-10a) and (16-10b), that are implied by the maximization hypothesis. Additional refutable hypotheses, derived from the preceding, are the possible restrictions in sign of the output supply functions (16-14). Let us investigate these comparative statics relations using the envelope analysis of Chap. 7.

The indirect national income function, defined in Eq. (16-12), is the maximum value of NNP for given output prices and resource endowments. It is found by substituting the explicit choice functions (16-10) into the objective function defining NNP, or

$$z^* = \text{NNP}^* = \phi(p_1, p_2, L, K) = p_1 f^1(L_1^*, K_1^*) + p_2 f^2(L_2^*, K_2^*)$$

Since this is the maximum value of NNP for given parameter values, $\text{NNP} - \text{NNP}^* \leq 0$, with $\text{NNP} - \text{NNP}^* = 0$ when $L_i = L_i^*, K_i = K_i^*, i = 1, 2$. Thus, the function

$$F(L_1, L_2, K_1, K_2, p_1, p_2, L, K) = \text{NNP}(L_1, L_2, K_1, K_2, p_1, p_2, L, K)$$
$$- \text{NNP}^*(p_1, p_2, L, K)$$

has a constrained maximum (of 0) at $L_i = L_i^*, K_i = K_i^*, i = 1, 2$. The Lagrangian for this primal-dual problem is

$$\mathcal{L} = \text{NNP} - \text{NNP}^* + w(L - L_1 - L_2) + r(K - K_1 - K_2)$$

The comparative-statics sign restrictions are derived from the bordered Hessian of second partials of $\mathcal{L}$ with respect to the parameters p_1, p_2, L, and K. The first partials of $\mathcal{L}$ with respect to these parameters are the envelope relations

$$\frac{\partial \mathcal{L}}{\partial p_1} = y_1 - y_1^* = 0 \tag{16-21a}$$

$$\frac{\partial \mathcal{L}}{\partial p_2} = y_2 - y_2^* = 0 \tag{16-21b}$$

$$\frac{\partial \mathcal{L}}{\partial L} = -w^* + w = 0 \tag{16-21c}$$

$$\frac{\partial \mathcal{L}}{\partial K} = -r^* + r = 0 \tag{16-21d}$$

The constraints are the first partials of $\mathcal{L}$ with respect to w and r, set equal to 0:

$$\frac{\partial \mathcal{L}}{\partial w} = L - L_1 - L_2 = 0 \tag{16-22a}$$

$$\frac{\partial \mathcal{L}}{\partial r} = K - K_1 - K_2 = 0 \tag{16-22b}$$

The relevant bordered Hessian is formed from the second partials of $\mathcal{L}$ with respect to $p_1, p_2, L, K, w,$ and r. These second partials are the first partials of Eqs. (16-21) and (16-22) with respect to those variables, since those equations are the first partials of $\mathcal{L}$ with respect to those variables. The bordered Hessian is thus

$$|\mathcal{L}_{\alpha\alpha}| = \begin{vmatrix} -\dfrac{\partial y_1^*}{\partial p_1} & -\dfrac{\partial y_1^*}{\partial p_2} & -\dfrac{\partial y_1^*}{\partial L} & -\dfrac{\partial y_1^*}{\partial K} & 0 & 0 \\[2mm] -\dfrac{\partial y_2^*}{\partial p_1} & -\dfrac{\partial y_2^*}{\partial p_2} & -\dfrac{\partial y_2^*}{\partial L} & -\dfrac{\partial y_2^*}{\partial K} & 0 & 0 \\[2mm] -\dfrac{\partial w^*}{\partial p_1} & -\dfrac{\partial w^*}{\partial p_2} & -\dfrac{\partial w^*}{\partial L} & -\dfrac{\partial w^*}{\partial K} & 1 & 0 \\[2mm] -\dfrac{\partial r^*}{\partial p_1} & -\dfrac{\partial r^*}{\partial p_2} & -\dfrac{\partial r^*}{\partial L} & -\dfrac{\partial r^*}{\partial K} & 0 & 1 \\[2mm] 0 & 0 & 1 & 0 & 0 & 0 \\[1mm] 0 & 0 & 0 & 1 & 0 & 0 \end{vmatrix} \tag{16-23}$$

The first comparative statics relations that appear are the reciprocity conditions, derived from the symmetry of $\mathcal{L}_{\alpha\alpha}$. We note

$$\frac{\partial y_1^*}{\partial p_2} = \frac{\partial y_2^*}{\partial p_1} \tag{16-24}$$

$$\frac{\partial y_i^*}{\partial L} = \frac{\partial w^*}{\partial p_i} \qquad i = 1, 2 \tag{16-25a}$$

$$\frac{\partial y_i^*}{\partial K} = \frac{\partial r^*}{\partial p_i} \qquad i = 1, 2 \tag{16-25b}$$

Also

$$\frac{\partial w^*}{\partial K} = \frac{\partial r^*}{\partial L} \tag{16-26}$$

Equation (16-24) says that if the output price of y_1 is raised, say, the effect on industry 2's output is exactly the same as the effect on industry 1's output of an increase in p_2. Equations (16-25) indicate, for example, that if the resource endowment of labor is increased, the effect on the ith industry's output will be the same as the effect of an increase in the price of the ith industry's output on the imputed wage or shadow price of labor. Equations (16-24) to (16-26) demonstrate a duality of prices and quantities in this model. All the relations that are valid for quantities are also valid for prices. The reciprocity relations (16-26) are exact analogs of (16-24) with the prices of the goods or factors replacing the respective physical quantities and vice versa.

Equations (16-24) to (16-26) generalize in a straightforward manner to the case of n goods and m factors. When we let $\lambda_1, \ldots, \lambda_m$ represent the shadow factor prices of factors $x_1, \ldots, x_m$, these equations become, respectively,

$$\frac{\partial y_i^*}{\partial p_j} = \frac{\partial y_j^*}{\partial p_i} \qquad i, j = 1, \ldots, n$$

$$\frac{\partial y_j^*}{\partial x_i} = \frac{\partial \lambda_i^*}{\partial p_j} \qquad i = 1, \ldots, m; \quad j = 1, \ldots, n$$

$$\frac{\partial \lambda_i}{\partial x_j} = \frac{\partial \lambda_j}{\partial x_i} \qquad i, j = 1, \ldots, m$$

Thus far, however, we have not placed any sign restrictions on these partial derivatives. At this level of generality, it is not possible to say whether an increase in the endowment of labor will increase or decrease the output of either industry. (It can be shown, as one would expect with positive marginal products, that an increase in labor or capital cannot lead to a decrease in output of *both* industries.) The effect on the imputed wages of changes in output prices is likewise indeterminate. The only comparative statics sign restrictions that are derivable at this level of generality relate to the supply of output functions $y_i = y_i^*(p_1, p_2, L, K)$. These curves must be upward-sloping in their own prices, assuming the sufficient second-order conditions. The parameters in this model are partitionable into two distinct sets, p_1 and p_2, which appear only in the objective function, and L and K, which appear only in the constraints. No signed comparative statics relations can appear for these latter parameters, as the analysis of Chap. 7 makes clear. In the case of p_1 and p_2, the associated decision variables y_1^* and y_2^* behave the same as in an unconstrained model. Since this is a maximum problem, the diagonal elements $-\partial y_1^*/\partial p_1$ and $-\partial y_2^*/\partial p_2$ must be negative.

Thus,

$$\frac{\partial y_i^*}{\partial p_i} > 0 \qquad i = 1, 2 \tag{16-27}$$

The output supply curves are thus upward-sloping. Again, the analogous assertions for $-\partial w^*/\partial L$, $-\partial r^*/\partial K$ are *not* valid, since L and K are parameters that appear in the constraints. It is *not* possible to say at this level of generality that, for example, an increase in the amount of labor in the economy will depress the wage rate of labor. Plausible as that result sounds, it is not implied by the preceding model. However, if the production functions are concave, for example, if they are homogeneous of degree $s \leq 1$, then the entire objective function (16-2) or (16-4) is concave. By the theorem at the end of Sec. 7.4, it must then be the case that $\partial w^*/\partial L \leq 0$ and $\partial r^*/\partial K \leq 0$, with the strict inequality holding if the production functions are strictly concave, e.g., $s < 1$. If the production functions exhibit constant-returns-to-scale, the wage rates are *independent* of the resource endowments. We shall explore these issues in the next section.

Let us now consider the implied properties of the production transformation frontier, defined in Eq. (16-17) and depicted in Fig. 16-1. The factor choice equations are, again,

$$L_i = L_i^*(p_1, p_2, L, K) \qquad K_i = K_i^*(p_1, p_2, L, K)$$

Since these equations are homogeneous of degree zero in p_1, p_2, they can be expressed in terms of the price ratio $p = p_1/p_2$. We shall suppress the parameters L and K in the following discussion for notational ease; these parameters are not relevant to this discussion. Writing $L_i = L_i^*(p)$, $K_i = K_i^*(p)$, we define Eq. (16-14) again as

$$y_1^*(p) = f^1(L_1^*(p), K_1^*(p)) \tag{16-28a}$$

and

$$y_2^*(p) = f^2(L_2^*(p), K_2^*(p)) \tag{16-28b}$$

Assuming these functions are invertible, the functional dependence

$$y_2^* = y_2^*(p(y_1^*)) = y_2^*(y_1^*) \tag{16-29}$$

is valid. From the chain rule,

$$\frac{\partial y_2^*}{\partial y_1^*} = \frac{\partial y_2^*/\partial p}{\partial y_1^*/\partial p} \tag{16-30}$$

When Eqs. (16-28) are used, Eq. (16-30) becomes

$$\frac{\partial y_2^*}{\partial y_1^*} = \frac{f_L^2(\partial L_2^*/\partial p) + f_K^2(\partial K_2^*/\partial p)}{f_L^1(\partial L_1^*/\partial p) + f_K^1(\partial K_1^*/\partial p)}$$

Using the first-order conditions $p_1 f_L^1 = p_2 f_L^2 = w$, $p_1 f_K^1 = p_2 f_K^2 = r$, we have

$$\frac{\partial y_2^*}{\partial y_1^*} = \frac{(1/p_2)[w(\partial L_2^*/\partial p) + r(\partial K_2^*/\partial p)]}{(1/p_1)[w(\partial L_1^*/\partial p) + r(\partial K_1^*/\partial p)]}$$

However, since $L_1^*(p) + L_2^*(p) \equiv L,\ K_1^*(p) + K_2^*(p) \equiv K,$

$$\frac{\partial L_1^*}{\partial p} \equiv -\frac{\partial L_2^*}{\partial p} \qquad \frac{\partial K_1^*}{\partial p} \equiv -\frac{\partial K_2^*}{\partial p}$$

The numerator (excluding the price term) is thus exactly the negative of the denominator, or

$$\frac{\partial y_2^*}{\partial y_1^*} = \frac{p_1}{p_2}(-1) = -p = -p(y_1^*) \tag{16-31}$$

Equation (16-31) asserts that when NNP is maximized, the production possibilities frontier will be tangent to an *isorevenue* (same revenue) line. NNP is given as a linear function of output levels,

$$NNP = p_1 y_1 + p_2 y_2$$

The values of y_1 and y_2 which maximize NNP, that is, those values that allow this line to move farthest from the origin in the output space, are those values where the production frontier has the same slope as the isorevenue line, $-p = -p_1/p_2$. This situation is depicted in Fig. 16-3. As drawn there, the production possibilities frontier is concave to the origin. This is verified mathematically by differentiating both sides of the identity (16-31) with respect to y_1^*:

$$\frac{\partial^2 y_2^*}{\partial y_1^{*2}} = -\frac{\partial p}{\partial y_1^*} = \frac{-1}{\partial y_1^*/\partial p} = \frac{-p_2}{\partial y_1^*/\partial p_1} < 0 \tag{16-32}$$

Equations (16-31) and (16-32) assert that this economy is characterized by positive and increasing marginal costs of production in the neighborhood of the wealth-maximizing output choices. The fact that $\partial y_2^*/\partial y_1^*$ is negative means that if more y_1 is desired, some y_2 will have to be forgone. The partial derivative $\partial y_2^*/\partial y_1^*$ measures the rate at which y_2^* must be sacrificed in order to get more y_1. Therefore, $\partial y_2^*/\partial y_1^*$ is the (negative) marginal opportunity cost of obtaining more y_1^*. Since $\partial(\partial y_2^*/\partial y_1^*)/\partial y_1^* = \partial^2 y_2^*/\partial y_1^{*2} < 0$, the marginal cost of y_1 must be increasing. As y_1 increases, the slope, or marginal cost $\partial y_2^*/\partial y_1^*$ of y_1 becomes more negative. Hence, the more y_1 the economy produces the more y_2 must be forgone to obtain additional units of y_1. This situation is depicted in Fig. 16-3. As y_1 increases from y_1^1 to y_1^2 to y_1^3, the marginal cost of these increments, measured by the vertical declines in y_2 produced ($y_2^1 - y_2^2$ and $y_2^2 - y_2^3$), increases.

Given the interpretation of $\partial y_2^*/\partial y_1^*$ as the marginal cost of y_1, Eq. (16-31) becomes the familiar condition for maximizing behavior so that marginal costs equal marginal benefits, i.e., here, marginal revenue. The world market is willing to exchange y_2 for additional units of y_1 at the rate $p = p_1/p_2$. NNP will be maximized when, at the margin, the cost of y_1 in terms of y_2 forgone is just equal to the additional revenue produced by the increased y_1 and decreased

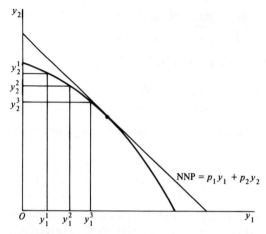

FIGURE 16-3

Maximization of NNP $=p_1y_1 + p_2y_2$. An interior maximization of NNP subject to resource constraints implies a production possibilities frontier that is concave to the origin. This feature is visually obvious in the above diagram. If the frontier were convex to the origin, maximum NNP, where the line NNP $=p_1y_1 + p_2y_2$ was as far from the origin as possible, would occur at a corner, implying production of one good only. The interior maximum above occurs at a point where the consumers' marginal evaluations of the two goods (measured by the slope $-p_1/p_2$ of the isorevenue line NNP $=p_1y_1 + p_2y_2$) equals the marginal production trade-off of y_2 for y_1. This latter trade-off is the marginal cost of y_1 measured by the ordinary slope of the production frontier. The concavity of this frontier is indicative of increasing marginal costs of production. As output of y_1 increases from y_1^1 to y_1^2, the *cost* of this increased output is measured by the *decrease* in y_2 available, $y_2^1 - y_2^2$. Increasing y_1 by the same increment, to y_1^3, leads to the *larger* sacrifice of y_2, measured by the vertical distance $y_2^2 - y_2^3$. In the limit, for small changes in y_1, the marginal cost of y_1 in terms of the rate at which y_2 must be forgone is the slope of the production possibilities frontier. The increasing (in absolute value) slope as y_1 increases indicates increasing marginal cost of y_1. The same situation obtains for y_2: the reciprocal slope measures the marginal cost of y_2 and increases with increasing y_2.

y_2 production, measured by the price ratio $p = p_1/p_2$. Equation (16-32) is the statement that at a *maximum* position, marginal costs must be rising. Of course, all this analysis can be done with the axes interchanged, i.e., in terms of marginal costs and benefits for y_2 rather than y_1. The model is perfectly symmetric in y_1 and y_2; valid results are obtainable by interchanging y_1 and y_2, and likewise labor and capital.

We note in passing that in the two-good case, since $\partial y_1^*/\partial p_1, \partial y_2^*/\partial p_2 > 0$, it must be that $\partial y_2^*/\partial p_1 = \partial y_1^*/\partial p_2 < 0$. This follows from the homogeneity of the output supply functions and is left as a problem for the student. In the n-good case, however, no sign is implied for the off-diagonal terms $\partial y_i^*/\partial p_j, i \neq j$.

16.3 THE FACTOR PRICE EQUALIZATION AND RELATED THEOREMS

Let us now move on to the analysis of the classic theorems of international trade: the factor price equalization, Stolper-Samuelson, and Rybczynski theorems. These results were presented for the special case of fixed-coefficient technology in the previous chapter. To derive these results for the case of variable proportions, the assumption of linear homogeneous industry production functions must be added.

We have not been specific about the nature of the firms in this model, as it was not germane to the results. Let us now assume, however, that each industry is composed of many "identical" firms. They may differ in scale, but the underlying production function for each firm in a given industry must be the same. Under these conditions, an industry production function can be well defined. That is, if all firms are identical in the preceding sense, the aggregate output of the industry is expressible as a well-defined (single-valued) function of the total labor and capital inputs. Moreover, this aggregate production function will be linear homogeneous. Consider a 10 percent increase in the demand for the industry's output. With constant factor prices, the long-run effects will be merely to increase the number of firms in the industry by 10 percent (if the scale of each firm is the same). These new firms, being identical to the preexisting firms in the industry, will hire like proportions of labor and capital. Hence, 10 percent more labor and 10 percent more capital will be used to produce the 10 percent increase in output. Since this will occur for any initial input combination, the industry, or aggregate production, function can be characterized as having constant returns to scale.

Example. Consider two firms *in the same industry*, with production functions

$$y_1 = f^1(L_1, K_1) = L_1^{1/3}K_1^{2/3}$$

$$y_2 = f^2(L_2, K_2) = L_2^{2/3}K_2^{1/3}$$

The industry output y by definition is $y \equiv y_1 + y_2$. (Remember, this is for *one good*, not the previous model for two goods.) Total factor usage for these two firms is $L \equiv L_1 + L_2$, $K \equiv K_1 + K_2$. Is it possible to define a function $y = f(L, K)$, that is, aggregate output, as a function of aggregate factor inputs? The answer is readily seen to be in the negative. Students can convince themselves of this by trying to do so. For example,

$$y = L_1^{1/3}K_1^{2/3} + L_2^{2/3}K_2^{1/3} = L_1^{1/3}K_1^{2/3} + (L - L_1)^{2/3}(K - K_1)^{1/3}$$

There is no way to eliminate L_1 and K_1 from this equation. Output y will always depend on the allocation of labor and capital between the two firms. That is, if a unit of labor and/or capital is moved from firm 1 to firm 2, then even though aggregate labor and capital remain the same, total output will change, since the firms' production functions are different. Hence, *industry* output, under these circumstances, is *not* a (single-valued) function of *total* resource utilization.

We shall therefore make the assumption that there are two industries, each consisting of many identical "small" firms. Then, although factor prices are endogenously determined in the model, each firm can be perceived as taking factor prices as given. That is, the actions of any one firm cannot affect in any substantial way either factor or output prices. The simultaneous (and identical, since all firms are identical) actions of all firms together do affect prices, but these effects are beyond the control of any given firm. Most importantly, the *industry* production functions can be assumed to be linear homogeneous, i.e., exhibiting constant returns to scale. Let us characterize this linear homogeneity as follows. By definition,

$$f^j(tL_j, tK_j) \equiv tf^j(L_j, K_j) \equiv ty_j \qquad j = 1, 2$$

Since this holds for all t, let $t = 1/y_j$. Then

$$f^j\left(\frac{L_j}{y_j}, \frac{K_j}{y_j}\right) \equiv f^j(a_{Lj}, a_{Kj}) \equiv 1 \qquad j = 1, 2 \qquad (16\text{-}33)$$

Equation (16-33) defines the production function in terms of the input-output coefficients. These a_{ij}'s were utilized in the linear model of the previous chapter. There, they were considered to be constants. Here, they are variable, changing continuously along the firm's *unit isoquant*. Equation (16-33) says that for constant-returns-to-scale production functions, the function is completely described by the unit isoquant. This occurs since all other isoquants are linear radial blowups or contractions of the unit (or any other) isoquant.

We shall use Eqs. (16-33) explicitly as constraints in the problem. In inequality form, we shall presume that inputs are combined such that

$$f^j(a_{Lj}, a_{Kj}) \geq 1$$

The resource constraints can also be expressed in terms of the a_{ij}'s. By simple arithmetic,

$$L_1 + L_2 = \frac{L_1}{y_1}y_1 + \frac{L_2}{y_2}y_2 = L$$

or

$$a_{L1}y_1 + a_{L2}y_2 = L \qquad (16\text{-}34a)$$

Similarly, the capital constraint is

$$a_{K1}y_1 + a_{K2}y_2 = K \qquad (16\text{-}34b)$$

The model of revenue (income) maximization subject to resource constraints can therefore be written

maximize

$$z = p_1y_1 + p_2y_2$$

subject to

$$a_{L1}y_1 + a_{L2}y_2 \leq L \qquad a_{K1}y_1 + a_{K2}y_2 \leq K$$

$$f^1(a_{L1}, a_{K1}) \geq 1 \qquad f^2(a_{L2}, a_{K2}) \geq 1 \qquad (16\text{-}35)$$

The decision variables are the *six* variables $y_1, y_2, a_{L1}, a_{K1}, a_{L2}, a_{K2}$. Remember, the a_{ij}'s are not constants, as in the linear programming model. They represent input combinations that are jointly determined with outputs.

The Lagrangian for the problem posed in (16-35) is

$$\mathcal{L} = p_1 y_1 + p_2 y_2 + w(L - a_{L1}y_1 - a_{L2}y_2)$$
$$+ r(K - a_{K1}y_1 - a_{K2}y_2)$$
$$+ \lambda_1(f^1(a_{L1}, a_{K1}) - 1) + \lambda_2(f^2(a_{L2}, a_{K2}) - 1) \qquad (16\text{-}36)$$

The Lagrange multipliers w and r represent the imputed wages, or rental values, of labor and capital, as before. The Kuhn-Tucker first-order conditions are thus

$$\frac{\partial \mathcal{L}}{\partial y_1} = p_1 - a_{L1}w - a_{K1}r \leq 0 \qquad \text{if } <, \ y_1 = 0 \qquad (16\text{-}37a)$$

$$\frac{\partial \mathcal{L}}{\partial y_2} = p_2 - a_{L2}w - a_{K2}r \leq 0 \qquad \text{if } <, \ y_2 = 0 \qquad (16\text{-}37b)$$

$$\frac{\partial \mathcal{L}}{\partial a_{L1}} = -wy_1 + \lambda_1 \frac{\partial f^1}{\partial a_{L1}} \leq 0 \qquad \text{if } <, \ a_{L1} = 0 \qquad (16\text{-}38a)$$

$$\frac{\partial \mathcal{L}}{\partial a_{K1}} = -ry_1 + \lambda_1 \frac{\partial f^1}{\partial a_{K1}} \leq 0 \qquad \text{if } <, \ a_{K1} = 0 \qquad (16\text{-}38b)$$

$$\frac{\partial \mathcal{L}}{\partial a_{L2}} = -wy_2 + \lambda_2 \frac{\partial f^2}{\partial a_{L2}} \leq 0 \qquad \text{if } <, \ a_{L2} = 0 \qquad (16\text{-}38c)$$

$$\frac{\partial \mathcal{L}}{\partial a_{K2}} = -ry_2 + \lambda_2 \frac{\partial f^2}{\partial a_{K2}} \leq 0 \qquad \text{if } <, \ a_{K2} = 0 \qquad (16\text{-}38d)$$

and the constraints

$$\frac{\partial \mathcal{L}}{\partial w} = L - a_{L1}y_1 - a_{L2}y_2 \geq 0 \qquad \text{if } >, \ w = 0 \qquad (16\text{-}39a)$$

$$\frac{\partial \mathcal{L}}{\partial r} = K - a_{K1}y_1 - a_{K2}y_2 \geq 0 \qquad \text{if } >, \ r = 0 \qquad (16\text{-}39b)$$

$$\frac{\partial \mathcal{L}}{\partial \lambda_1} = f^1(a_{L1}, a_{K1}) - 1 \geq 0 \qquad \text{if } >, \ \lambda_1 = 0 \qquad (16\text{-}40a)$$

$$\frac{\partial \mathcal{L}}{\partial \lambda_2} = f^2(a_{L2}, a_{K2}) - 1 \geq 0 \qquad \text{if } >, \ \lambda_2 = 0 \qquad (16\text{-}40b)$$

Notice the relations (16-37). These are precisely the nonpositive profit conditions which formed the constraints of the dual linear programming problem of the previous chapter. They say that if the maximum position occurs such that "profits" are negative for either good, then the output of that good will be 0.

The relations (16-38) are the marginal conditions for factor utilization, with the units adjusted to reflect the constraint of being on the unit isoquant. Since $f^j(L_j, K_j)$ is homogeneous of degree 1, f^j_L is homogeneous of degree zero. Thus

$$f_L^j(L_j, K_j) \equiv f_L^j\left(\frac{L_j}{K_j}\right) \equiv f_{a_{Lj}}^j\left(\frac{a_{Lj}}{a_{Kj}}\right)$$

Dividing Eqs. (16-38) by y_j gives

$$\frac{\lambda_j}{y_j}\frac{\partial f^j}{\partial a_{Lj}} - w \leq 0$$

etc., or

$$\frac{\lambda_j}{y_j}\frac{\partial f^j}{\partial L_j} - w \leq 0 \qquad \text{if } <, \ L_j = 0 \qquad (16\text{-}41a)$$

with a similar relation with respect to capital:

$$\frac{\lambda_j}{y_j}\frac{\partial f^j}{\partial K_j} - r \leq 0 \qquad \text{if } <, \ K_j = 0 \qquad (16\text{-}41b)$$

Equations (16-41) are equivalent to Eqs. (16-38). They are the usual marginal conditions for factor utilization if one interprets (λ_j/y_j) as marginal cost of y_j. Equations (16-38) or (16-41) say that if the maximum position occurs where the value of the marginal product of any factor is less than its wage (or rental price), it will not be used. Otherwise, the value of the marginal product equals the wage.

Consider again the maximum problem posed in (16-35) and the associated Lagrangian (16-36). This maximization takes place at six margins, i.e., for six choice variables, $y_1, y_2, a_{L1}, a_{K1}, a_{L2}$, and a_{K2}. It is possible to conceive of this maximization as taking place in two stages. Recall that the assertion that profits are maximized carries with it the implication that the total cost of that level of output must be minimized. The maximization can be achieved by first minimizing cost for *any* output level; then, with costs minimized, that output level which maximizes profits can be determined as the second part of a two-stage maximization procedure.

In the present model, the hypothesis that total revenue is maximized (subject to resource constraints) can be regarded as occurring in two stages also. First, the "correct" input combinations *along the unit isoquant* can be found. That is, holding $y_j = 1, j = 1,2$, we select the a_{ij}'s so as to minimize total factor cost for each industry. This results in having the marginal technical rate of substitution between the factors equal the factor price ratio. Then, given this tangency condition, outputs are varied along the expansion path [in this case, along a ray through the point (a_{Lj}^*, a_{Kj}^*) on the unit isoquant] until the y_j^*'s are found.

This process can be seen algebraically by rearranging the terms in the Lagrangian (16-36) as follows:

$$\begin{aligned}
\mathcal{L} = \ & p_1 y_1 + p_2 y_2 + wL + rK \\
& - [y_1(a_{L1}w + a_{K1}r) + \lambda_1(1 - f^1(a_{L1}, a_{K1}))] \\
& - [y_2(a_{L2}w + a_{K2}r) + \lambda_2(1 - f^2(a_{L2}, a_{K2}))] \qquad (16\text{-}42)
\end{aligned}$$

The maximum value of $\mathcal{L}$ is NNP* $= p_1 y_1^* + p_2 y_2^*$. Let us maximize $\mathcal{L}$ by first *minimizing* the two square-bracketed terms (which enter negatively) with respect to the a_{ij}'s, treating y_1 and y_2 as parametric. This is equivalent to two separate *minimizations:*

minimize

$$y_1(a_{L1}w + a_{K1}r)$$

subject to

$$f^1(a_{L1}, a_{K1}) = 1 \qquad (16\text{-}43a)$$

and minimize

$$y_2(a_{L2}w + a_{K2}r)$$

subject to

$$f^2(a_{L2}, a_{K2}) = 1 \qquad (16\text{-}43b)$$

The Lagrangians for these two problems are exactly the square-bracketed terms in the Lagrangian (16-42). Moreover, these minimization problems are equivalent to the standard cost minimization formats: multiply the objective functions through by y_1 or y_2 as indicated in (16-43). Since $y_1 a_{L1} = L_1$, etc., and $y_j f^j(a_{Lj}, a_{Kj}) \equiv f^j(y_j a_{Lj}, y_j a_{Kj}) \equiv f^j(L_j, K_j)$ by linear homogeneity, these square-bracketed terms are respectively equivalent to

$$(wL_1 + rK_1) + \lambda_1(y_1 - f^1(L_1, K_1)) \qquad (16\text{-}44a)$$

and

$$(wL_2 + rK_2) + \lambda_2(y_2 - f^2(L_2, K_2)) \qquad (16\text{-}44b)$$

[Again, from homogeneity, $f^1(a_{L1}, a_{K1}) = 1$ is equivalent to $f^1(L_1, K_1) = y_1$, etc.] The Lagrangian expressions (16-44) are exactly those which result from the problems:

minimize

$$wL_1 + rK_1 = C_1$$

subject to

$$f^1(L_1, K_1) = y_1 \qquad (16\text{-}45a)$$

and minimize

$$wL_2 + rK_2 = C_2$$

subject to

$$f^2(L_2, K_2) = y_2 \qquad (16\text{-}45b)$$

where y_1 and y_2 are at this point parametric. Problems (16-43) and (16-45) are thus equivalent. The setup (16-45) is the classical problem of minimizing the cost of achieving some output y_j. The objective function C_j is the total cost of achieving that output level, *and λ_j is the marginal cost of that output.* The λ_j's are *not* the same, however, in (16-45) and (16-43), because the units of the constraints are different.

The Lagrangian associated with the submodel (16-43a) is

$$\mathcal{L} = y_1(wa_{L1} + ra_{K1}) + \lambda_1(1 - f^1(a_{L1}, a_{K1})) \qquad (16\text{-}46a)$$

Note that since y_1 is treated as a constant here, minimizing $y_1(wa_{L1} + ra_{K1})$ yields the same solution and comparative statics results as minimizing $wa_{L1} + ra_{K1}$. The first-order conditions obtained from (16-46a) are

$$\frac{\partial \mathcal{L}}{\partial a_{L1}} = y_1 w - \lambda_1 \frac{\partial f^1}{\partial a_{L1}} = 0 \qquad (16\text{-}47a)$$

$$\frac{\partial \mathcal{L}}{\partial a_{K1}} = y_1 r - \lambda_1 \frac{\partial f^1}{\partial a_{K1}} = 0 \qquad (16\text{-}47b)$$

$$\frac{\partial \mathcal{L}}{\partial \lambda_1} = 1 - f^1(a_{L1}, a_{K1}) = 0 \qquad (16\text{-}47c)$$

Equations (16-47) are precisely the relations (16-38a), (16-38b), and (16-40a), respectively (ignoring the possibility of corner solutions).

A similar set of results follows from the submodel (16-43b). The Lagrangian for industry 2 is

$$\mathcal{L} = y_2(a_{L2}w + a_{K2}r) + \lambda_2(1 - f^2(a_{L2}, a_{K2})) \qquad (16\text{-}46b)$$

producing the first-order conditions

$$y_2 w - \lambda_2 \frac{\partial f^2}{\partial a_{L2}} = 0 \qquad (16\text{-}48a)$$

$$y_2 r - \lambda_2 \frac{\partial f^2}{\partial a_{K2}} = 0 \qquad (16\text{-}48b)$$

$$1 - f^2(a_{L2}, a_{K2}) = 0 \qquad (16\text{-}48c)$$

These equations are, respectively, the same as relations (16-38c), (16-38d), and (16-40b). *Hence, the two suboptimizations account for six out of the ten first-order equations of the whole model.* These six equations determine the cost-minimizing input combinations $(a_{L1}^*, a_{K1}^*), (a_{L2}^*, a_{K2}^*)$ along the unit isoquants of each industry and the two industry marginal cost functions (λ_1^*/y_1^*) and (λ_2^*/y_2^*). The remaining four variables to be determined are y_1^*, y_2^*, w, and r.

The Four-Equation Model

Let us "solve" the systems (16-47), (16-48) for the a_{ij}^*'s. Dividing (16-47a) by (16-47b) and (16-48a) by (16-48b) yields

$$\frac{\partial f^1/\partial a_{L1}}{\partial f^1/\partial a_{K1}} = \frac{w}{r} \qquad (16\text{-}49a)$$

and

$$\frac{\partial f^2/\partial a_{L2}}{\partial f^2/\partial a_{K2}} = \frac{w}{r} \qquad (16\text{-}49b)$$

Equations (16-49a) and (16-47c) represent two equations in the two unknowns, a_{L1}, a_{k1}, and the variable w/r. Likewise, (16-49b) and (16-48c) represent two equations in the two unknowns a_{L2}, a_{K2}, and the same variable w/r. Thus, we can write the solution of the equation systems (16-47) and (16-48) as

$$a_{ij} = a_{ij}^* \left(\frac{w}{r}\right) \qquad i = L, K; \qquad j = 1, 2 \qquad (16\text{-}50)$$

and

$$\lambda_j/y_j = (\lambda_j^*/y_j^*)(w, r) \qquad j = 1, 2 \qquad (16\text{-}51)$$

These equations are a very important feature of this model. They say that the input-output coefficients are functions of the *factor price ratio only*. In particular, the a_{ij}^*'s are *not* functions of the endowments of either factor. Second, the marginal cost functions (16-51) are not functions of output levels but only of factor prices. This all occurs because of the linear homogeneity of the production functions. The independence of marginal cost from output level was shown in Chap. 9 on cost functions. There, we showed that if $y = f(x_1, x_2)$ was linear homogeneous, the cost function could be written $C^* = yA(w_1, w_2)$. Consequently, $\partial C^*/\partial y = A(w_1, w_2)$, which is Eqs. (16-51). Equations (16-50) occur because for linear homogeneous functions, any level curve describes the whole function. Whatever occurs at any output level y_j^0 is simply a magnification or contraction of what occurs at $y_j = 1$.

It is apparent from general comparative statics theory that

$$\frac{\partial a_{Lj}^*}{\partial w} < 0 \qquad (16\text{-}52a)$$

and

$$\frac{\partial a_{Kj}^*}{\partial r} < 0 \qquad (16\text{-}52b)$$

The unit input-output factor levels are downward-sloping in their own price. It is also apparent that $a_{ij}^*(w/r)$ is homogeneous of degree zero in w and r, since a_{ij}^* is a function of the ratio w/r. From Euler's theorem,

$$\frac{\partial a_{Lj}^*}{\partial w} w + \frac{\partial a_{Lj}^*}{\partial r} r \equiv 0$$

Since $\partial a_{Lj}^*/\partial w < 0$,

$$\frac{\partial a_{Lj}^*}{\partial r} > 0 \qquad (16\text{-}52c)$$

Similarly, it can be shown that

$$\frac{\partial a_{Kj}^*}{\partial w} > 0 \tag{16-52d}$$

We shall use these results later.

If we use these solutions to the *six* Eqs. (16-47) and (16-48), the entire ten-equation model (the ten first-order conditions) can be reduced to four equations in the four unknowns y_1, y_2, w, and r. The remaining equations of the original ten are (16-37a), (16-37b), (16-39a), and (16-39b). Substituting the solution values (16-50) back into these equations (again, we ignore the possibility of corner solutions) yields

$$a_{L1}^* w + a_{K1}^* r = p_1 \tag{16-53a}$$

$$a_{L2}^* w + a_{K2}^* r = p_2 \tag{16-53b}$$

and

$$a_{L1}^* y_1 + a_{L2}^* y_2 = L \tag{16-54a}$$

$$a_{K1}^* y_1 + a_{K2}^* y_2 = K \tag{16-54b}$$

The entire model has been compressed to four equations. *Moreover, these are precisely the same four relations as were derived for the linear programming model, two zero-profit conditions Eqs. (16-53) and two resource constraints* (16-54). Here, however, the a_{ij}^*'s are not constants. They are functions of the factor price ratio w/r, as indicated by Eqs. (16-50).

Although the preceding are four equations in four unknowns, these equations have a very special structure. The variables w and r and the parameters p_1 and p_2 appear only in the first two Eqs. (16-53). And the variables y_1 and y_2 and the parameters L and K appear only in the second set of Eqs. (16-54). Thus, these equations are actually decomposable, or separable, into two sets of two equations in two unknowns. Just as in the linear model, the coefficient matrix of a_{ij}^*'s for the first set [Eqs. (16-53a) and (16-53b)] is the transpose of the coefficient matrix of the second set [Eqs. (16-54)].

As a consequence of this separability, Eqs. (16-53) can be "solved" independently of (16-54), since the a_{ij}^*'s are functions of w/r only:

$$w = w^*(p_1, p_2) \tag{16-55a}$$

$$r = r^*(p_1, p_2) \tag{16-55b}$$

On the other hand, although Eqs. (16-54) can be solved for y_1 and y_2 in terms of L and K, these solutions will involve the a_{ij}^*'s, which are functions of w/r and hence p_1 and p_2 through (16-55). Thus, solving Eqs. (16-54) and using (16-55) leads to the output supply functions

$$y_1 = y_1^*(p_1, p_2, L, K) \tag{16-56a}$$

$$y_2 = y_2^*(p_1, p_2, L, K) \qquad (16\text{-}56b)$$

just as in the original model without the homogeneity conditions. As before, the results $\partial y_1^*/\partial p_1, \partial y_2^*/\partial p_2 > 0$ are still valid; the supply curves of each industry are upward-sloping.

The Factor Price Equalization Theorem

Equations (16-55) are the basis of what is known as the *factor price equalization theorem*, a fundamental result in the theory of international trade. Consider the case of two countries, each producing the same two commodities and engaging in trade with one another. In the pretrade, or *autarky,* situation, output prices in the two countries will in general differ, given different marginal costs of production, i.e., different production possibility frontiers, for the two countries. (Of course, consumers' tastes might differ systematically in the two countries, producing different output prices even if the marginal cost functions for the two countries were identical.) However, with the opening up of trade, which will occur precisely because output prices (and hence consumers' marginal evaluations of the goods) are different, the output prices will tend toward equality. With no transportation or other transactions costs of trading, the gains from trade will be exhausted only when output prices are identical in the two countries, i.e., when each country's consumers face the same set of output prices. Given the postulate of "more preferred to less," this outcome is implied.

A less obvious question is the effect on *factor* prices of this tending to equality of output prices. If factors were freely mobile between the two countries at zero cost, clearly, factor prices in the two countries would also have to be identical. Factors would simply move to the higher-paying country, depressing wages or rentals there and raising them in the former location. But what if factors *cannot* move from one country to another? That is, suppose goods can move costlessly from one country to the other but factors can never emigrate. What will happen to factor prices then, when output prices converge?

Equations (16-55) say that under certain conditions, factor prices will also be equal, in the two countries, when output prices are the same for both countries, in spite of factor immobility. This surprising result, known as the *factor price equalization theorem,* depends upon the form of Eqs. (16-55). Those equations indicate that factor prices are functions of *output prices only.* Factor endowments do not enter the right-hand side of these equations and hence are irrelevant in determining factor prices. However, the specific functional form of $w^*(p_1, p_2)$ and $r^*(p_1, p_2)$ will depend upon the underlying production functions in the economy. If the production technology, i.e., the underlying production functions, *is the same in both countries,* i.e., trade is taking place because of different endowments of factors or differences in consumers' tastes (or both) between the two countries, then the functional form of Eqs. (16-55) will be the same for the two countries. In that case, the factor prices will be the same in both countries, since they will depend in identical fashion upon the output prices, which are the same for both countries. An additional qualification, relating to differing relative factor intensities in the two countries, will be explored presently. Notice, too, that the result depends critically on the assumption of linear homogeneous industry production functions. It is that assumption which permits the formulation of the first-order conditions in terms of the factor intensity variables, the a_{ij}'s, which, in turn, allows solution of these a_{ij}'s in terms of the relative price ratio w/r alone. It is the dependence of relative factor intensities on factor prices alone which makes Eqs. (16-53), the zero-profit conditions, soluble for factor prices solely in terms of output prices. Without constant returns to scale in each industry, the preceding procedure cannot be carried out.

The Stolper-Samuelson Theorems

Let us now investigate the effects of changes in output prices on factor prices. Since Eqs. (16-53) are the sole determinants of factor prices, the comparative statics of this part of the model is accomplished by differentiating Eqs. (16-53) with respect to output prices. Let us differentiate these equations with respect to p_1, remembering that the "solutions" $w = w^*(p_1, p_2), r = r^*(p_1, p_2)$ have been substituted into these equations for w and r, respectively, and that the a_{ij}^*'s, being functions of factor prices, are thereby also functions of the output prices. Hence, upon differentiation of (16-53a),

$$a_{L1}^* \frac{\partial w^*}{\partial p_1} + w^* \frac{\partial a_{L1}^*}{\partial p_1} + a_{K1}^* \frac{\partial r^*}{\partial p_1} + r^* \frac{\partial a_{K1}^*}{\partial p_1} \equiv 1$$

or

$$a_{L1}^* \frac{\partial w^*}{\partial p_1} + a_{K1}^* \frac{\partial r^*}{\partial p_1} \equiv 1 - w^* \frac{\partial a_{L1}^*}{\partial p_1} - r^* \frac{\partial a_{K1}^*}{\partial p_1} \qquad (16\text{-}57a)$$

Similarly differentiating (16-53b) gives

$$a_{L2}^* \frac{\partial w}{\partial p_1} + a_{K2}^* \frac{\partial r^*}{\partial p_1} \equiv -w^* \frac{\partial a_{L2}^*}{\partial p_1} - r^* \frac{\partial a_{K2}^*}{\partial p_1} \qquad (16\text{-}57b)$$

However, the last two terms on the right-hand side of (16-57a) and (16-57b) sum to zero: consider the production function $f^1(a_{L1}^*, a_{K1}^*) \equiv 1$. Differentiating this identity with respect to p_1 gives

$$\frac{\partial f^1}{\partial a_{L1}} \frac{\partial a_{L1}^*}{\partial p_1} + \frac{\partial f^1}{\partial a_{K1}} \frac{\partial a_{K1}^*}{\partial p_1} \equiv 0 \qquad (16\text{-}58)$$

Using the first-order conditions $\partial f^1/\partial a_{L1} = y_1 w/\lambda_1, \partial f^1/\partial a_{K1} = y_1 r/\lambda_1$, and eliminating the factor y_1/λ_1 in each term, we get

$$w^* \frac{\partial a_{L1}^*}{\partial p_1} + r^* \frac{\partial a_{K1}^*}{\partial p_1} \equiv 0 \qquad (16\text{-}59a)$$

A similar procedure shows that

$$w^* \frac{\partial a_{L2}^*}{\partial p_1} + r^* \frac{\partial a_{K2}^*}{\partial p_1} \equiv 0 \qquad (16\text{-}59b)$$

Therefore, the comparative statics Eqs. (16-57) reduce to the simple form

$$a_{L1}^* \frac{\partial w^*}{\partial p_1} + a_{K1}^* \frac{\partial r^*}{\partial p_1} \equiv 1 \qquad (16\text{-}60a)$$

$$a_{L2}^* \frac{\partial w^*}{\partial p_1} + a_{K2}^* \frac{\partial r^*}{\partial p_1} \equiv 0 \qquad (16\text{-}60b)$$

Equations (16-60), which give the changes in factor prices caused by changes in output prices, *have exactly the same structure as the equations that determined these variables in the linear models.* [In the case of constant a_{ij}'s, the differential form (16-60) is directly equivalent to the undifferentiated form (16-53).] Therefore, the analysis of this model is identical, in regard to these variables, to the linear model. Proceeding as before, let

$$A = \begin{vmatrix} a_{L1}^* & a_{K1}^* \\ a_{L2}^* & a_{K2}^* \end{vmatrix}$$

Solving for $\partial w^*/\partial p_1, \partial r^*/\partial p_1$ by Cramer's rule, we have

$$\frac{\partial w^*}{\partial p_1} = \frac{a_{K2}^*}{A} \qquad (16\text{-}61a)$$

and

$$\frac{\partial r^*}{\partial p_1} = -\frac{a_{L2}^*}{A} \qquad (16\text{-}61b)$$

In like fashion, if Eqs. (16-53) are differentiated with respect to p_2, one gets

$$\frac{\partial w^*}{\partial p_2} = -\frac{a_{K1}^*}{A} \qquad (16\text{-}61c)$$

$$\frac{\partial r^*}{\partial p_2} = \frac{a_{L1}^*}{A} \qquad (16\text{-}61d)$$

Let us investigate these relationships. In the first place, these solutions are valid only if $A \neq 0$. This is in fact the sufficient condition of the implicit function theorem that the equations $w = w^*(p_1, p_2), r = r^*(p_1, p_2)$ are locally well defined. Hence, this condition is also required for the factor price equalization theorem. The determinant A will be nonzero, in this two-factor, two-good case, if either

$$\frac{a_{L1}^*}{a_{K1}^*} > \frac{a_{L2}^*}{a_{K2}^*} \qquad (16\text{-}62a)$$

or

$$\frac{a^*_{L1}}{a^*_{K1}} < \frac{a^*_{L2}}{a^*_{K2}} \tag{16-62b}$$

These equations are equivalent to

$$\frac{L^*_1}{K^*_1} > \frac{L^*_2}{K^*_2} \tag{16-63a}$$

or

$$\frac{L^*_1}{K^*_1} < \frac{L^*_2}{K^*_2} \tag{16-63b}$$

In other words, if one industry is more labor-intensive than the other, i.e., its capital labor ratio is lower than that ratio in the other industry, then the equations defining factor prices as functions of output prices only will be well defined. Also, the comparative statics relations (16-61) indicating the response of factor prices to changes in output prices will be well defined.

With regard to the comparative statics relations (16-61), the condition that one industry be more labor-intensive is a strictly *local* condition. All comparative statics equations, despite the name which connotes comparing separate equilibria, are in fact simply partial derivatives evaluated at a certain point. The functions defining the choice relations need only be well-behaved around that one point; i.e., they must have the various properties of differentiability, nonzero Jacobian determinant, etc., to allow a solution for a choice function at a given point.

For purposes of asserting factor price equalization, however, the *local* condition that $L_1/K_1 \neq L_2/K_2$ is insufficiently strong. The factor price equalization theorem is an essentially *global* assertion. That is, it asserts that, starting at finitely different output prices in two countries, as output prices converge, factor prices will converge also. But this is supposed to take place over a whole path of prices. Therefore, a strictly local condition on factor intensities cannot be enough to guarantee the convergence of factor prices. If factor prices are to converge *for any initial output prices* and for any endowments, then one industry will *always* have to be more labor- (or capital-) intensive than the other. That is, we must have $L_i/K_i > L_j/K_j$ for *all* output prices. If industry 1 is initially the more labor-intensive industry, as output prices change, that industry must remain the more labor-intensive. Should one industry switch from being relatively labor- to relatively capital-intensive, the direction of movement of factor prices with regard to output price changes will reverse. In Eqs. (16-61), the denominators will all change sign. This means that if, say, industry 1 is labor-intensive at some output prices, wages and rents will move in one direction as output prices converge. However, for different endowments or if output prices are such that industry 1 is *capital*-intensive, factor prices will move in the opposite direction as output prices converge in the two countries. What is therefore needed, in order to assert factor price equalization (aside from the other assumptions such as linear homogeneity, etc.) is the *global* condition that $L_i/K_i > L_j/K_j$ for *all* possible output or output price combinations along the production frontier. Strictly local conditions are insufficiently strong.

If the production functions in each sector are homothetic (e.g., linear homogeneous), this "switching" of factor intensities cannot occur. Switching implies that the contract curve depicted in Fig. 16-4 would cross the diagonal line connecting the two origins, O_1 and O_2. But then the diagonal would have to be the expansion paths of each production function; the contract curve would have to be the diagonal itself. This situation occurs when the factor intensities are constant and identical, e.g., if the production functions in each industry are identical Cobb-Douglas functions.

Suppose now that industry 1 is the more labor-intensive industry, i.e., that $a_{L1}/a_{K1} > a_{L2}/a_{K2}$. (To save notational clutter, the asterisks will now be dropped.) Then $A > 0$ and, from Eqs. (16-61a) and (16-61b),

$$\frac{\partial w}{\partial p_1} > 0 \qquad\qquad (16\text{-}64a)$$

and

$$\frac{\partial r}{\partial p_1} < 0 \qquad\qquad (16\text{-}64b)$$

These results are the general Stolper-Samuelson theorem. They say, again, that if the price of the labor-intensive industry is increased, nominal wage rates will rise, whereas capital rental rates will fall. If p_1 rises, then we know that y_1 increases and y_2 decreases, that is, $\partial y_1/\partial p_1 > 0, \partial y_2/\partial p_1 < 0$, as the economy moves along the production possibilities frontier. Hence, in this case, the labor-intensive industry is expanding whereas the capital-intensive industry is contracting. This results in a net increase in the aggregate demand for labor and a decrease in aggregate demand for capital. Hence, the factor price of labor rises while that of capital falls. In general, the price of a factor of production will rise if the price of the industry in which that factor is most intensively used rises; it will fall if the industry which is less intensive in that factor experiences an output price increase.

The preceding analysis, however, pertains to *nominal* price changes only. If p_1 and w *both* rise, as in the preceding example, will "real" wages in fact have risen? That is, will the owners of labor be able to purchase more goods at the higher wages after these two price changes? Clearly, the owners of capital, whose money price has fallen, are worse off in real as well as money terms.

The *real* income of the owners of labor will also rise if the wage rate increases. Wages will increase at a higher percentage rate than the output price, i.e.,

$$\lim\frac{\Delta w/w}{\Delta p_1/p_1} = \frac{\partial w}{\partial p_1}\frac{p_1}{w} > 1 \qquad\qquad (16\text{-}65)$$

If the owners of labor consume the output of industry 1 only, then Eq. (16-65)

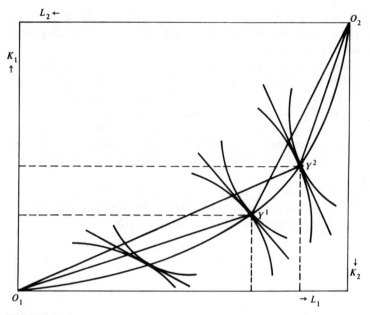

FIGURE 16-4

Diagrammatic exposition of the Stolper-Samuelson theorem: variable proportions. Consider an Edgeworth-type diagram as in Fig. 16-2, with labor plotted along the horizontal axes and capital plotted vertically. A contract curve O_1O_2 connecting the two origins has been drawn. It has a special shape: it is convex to the labor axis from O_1; that is, the contract curve rises toward O_2 at an increasing rate. It is this shape that guarantees that industry 1 will always be more labor-intensive than industry 2. Consider point Y^1 along O_1O_2. The slope of the chord O_1Y^1 is K_1/L_1. The slope of the chord connecting Y^1 and O_2, Y^1O_2, is K_2/L_2. As drawn, $K_1/L_1 < K_2/L_2$, or $L_1/K_1 > L_2/K_2$. Moreover, this is true along any point of the contract curve. Industry 1 is always more labor-intensive than industry 2.

Consider now the slopes of the isoquants as they cross the contract curve. Near O_1, where the contract curve is close to the labor axis, the isoquants are quite flat; i.e., they have a low absolute slope. As one moves along O_1O_2 toward O_2, the isoquants cut the curve at increasing slopes, as depicted at points Y^1 and Y^2. The slope of the isoquants is w/r, the ratio of wages to rental rates. Thus, with industry 1 always the more relatively intensive, as output y_1 expands, in response to increases in p_1, wage rates rise relative to rental rates. This is in accordance with Eqs. (16-61) and the subsequent analysis. The increase in *real* wages is not easily depicted geometrically, however. Notice, too, that as p_1 and thus y_1 increase, *both* industries become less labor-intensive (though industry 1 remains more so than industry 2). As output moves from Y^1 to Y^2, for example, the capital-labor ratio, measured for industry 1 by the slope of the chord O_1Y^2 and for industry 2 by the slope of Y^2O_2, increases. That is, the labor-capital ratio decreases, or both industries become less labor-intensive. This can be viewed as a response to the increase in real wage rates and the fall of real capital rental rates.

guarantees greater purchasing power. If the owners of labor consume some y_2 also, then since the price of y_2 hasn't changed, (16-65) represents an even greater increase in real income. (In the limit, if *only* y_2 were consumed, then *any* increase in w would be an increase in real income, since p_2 is constant here.)

From Eq. (16-61a), again,

$$\frac{\partial w}{\partial p_1} = \frac{a_{K2}}{A} > 0$$

From the zero-profit first-order relation (16-53a),

$$p_1 = a_{L1}w + a_{K1}r$$

or

$$\frac{p_1}{w} = a_{L1} + a_{K1}\frac{r}{w}$$

Thus,

$$\frac{p_1}{w}\frac{\partial w}{\partial p_1} = \frac{a_{K2}a_{L1} + (r/w)a_{K1}a_{K2}}{a_{K2}a_{L1} - a_{K1}a_{L2}} > 1 \qquad (16\text{-}65a)$$

just as in the case of fixed coefficients. The same procedure shows that

$$\frac{p_2}{r}\frac{\partial r}{\partial p_2} > 1 \qquad (16\text{-}65b)$$

That is, since industry 2 is capital-intensive, an increase in p_2 will not only increase nominal rental rates on capital but real rates also.†

Another set of results coming under the heading of the Stolper-Samuelson theorem are the effects on factor intensities of changes in output prices. That is, consider how the labor-capital ratio varies in each industry when, say, p_1 is increased. Assume as before that industry 1 is labor-intensive. The labor-capital ratio in industry j is $L_j/K_j = a_{Lj}/a_{Kj}$. Specifically, the a_{ij}'s are functions of the factor prices w and r, which are in turn functions of output prices, or

$$\frac{a_{Lj}}{a_{Kj}} = g(w^*(p_1,p_2), r^*(p_1,p_2))$$

Using the quotient rule with the chain rule gives

$$(a_{Kj})^2\frac{\partial(a_{Lj}/a_{Kj})}{\partial p_1} = a_{Kj}\left(\frac{\partial a_{Lj}}{\partial w}\frac{\partial w}{\partial p_1} + \frac{\partial a_{Lj}}{\partial r}\frac{\partial r}{\partial p_1}\right)$$

$$-a_{Lj}\left(\frac{\partial a_{Kj}}{\partial w}\frac{\partial w}{\partial p_1} + \frac{\partial a_{Kj}}{\partial r}\frac{\partial r}{\partial p_1}\right)$$

Rearranging terms gives

---

† In the first edition, I mistakenly asserted that the cross-effects also exhibited this elasticity, e.g., $(p_1/r)(\partial r/\partial p_1) < -1$, along with the analogous Rybczynski expressions.

$$(a_{Kj})^2 \frac{\partial (a_{Lj}/a_{Kj})}{\partial p_1} = \left(a_{Kj} \frac{\partial a_{Lj}}{\partial w} - a_{Lj} \frac{\partial a_{Kj}}{\partial w} \right) \frac{\partial w}{\partial p_1}$$

$$+ \left(a_{Kj} \frac{\partial a_{Lj}}{\partial r} - a_{Lj} \frac{\partial a_{Kj}}{\partial r} \right) \frac{\partial r}{\partial p_1} < 0 \qquad (16\text{-}66a)$$

This result follows from the comparative-statics relations derived for the cost minimization submodels (16-43). The comparative statics of those models yielded the results, *for both industries,*

$$\frac{\partial a_{Lj}}{\partial w} < 0 \qquad j = 1, 2 \qquad (16\text{-}52a)$$

$$\frac{\partial a_{Kj}}{\partial r} < 0 \qquad j = 1, 2 \qquad (16\text{-}52b)$$

$$\frac{\partial a_{Lj}}{\partial r} > 0 \qquad j = 1, 2 \qquad (16\text{-}52c)$$

$$\frac{\partial a_{Kj}}{\partial w} > 0 \qquad j = 1, 2 \qquad (16\text{-}52d)$$

Inserting these sign values and also Eqs. (16-64), that is, $\partial w/\partial p_1 > 0$, $\partial r/\partial p_1 < 0$, into (16-66a) immediately shows that

$$\frac{\partial (a_{Lj}/a_{Kj})}{\partial p_1} < 0 \qquad j = 1, 2$$

when y_1 is labor-intensive.

Similarly, with regard to changes in p_2, we have

$$(a_{Kj})^2 \frac{\partial (a_{Lj}/a_{Kj})}{\partial p_2} = \left(a_{Kj} \frac{\partial a_{Lj}}{\partial w} - a_{Lj} \frac{\partial a_{Kj}}{\partial w} \right) \frac{\partial w}{\partial p_2}$$

$$+ \left(a_{Kj} \frac{\partial a_{Lj}}{\partial r} - a_{Lj} \frac{\partial a_{Kj}}{\partial r} \right) \frac{\partial r}{\partial p_2} > 0 \qquad (16\text{-}66b)$$

The only differences between (16-66b) and (16-66a) are the terms $\partial w/\partial p_2$, $\partial r/\partial p_2$ instead of $\partial w/\partial p_1$ and $\partial r/\partial p_1$. Since these latter two terms have the opposite sign of the first two, respectively,

$$\frac{\partial (a_{Lj}/a_{Kj})}{\partial p_2} > 0 \qquad j = 1, 2$$

Note that Eqs. (16-66) say that if the price of the labor-intensive good (y_1 here) rises, then the labor-capital ratio will fall *in both industries*. With the rise in p_1, more of the labor-intensive good will be produced and less of the capital-intensive good. This results in a net increase in the demand for labor. However, total labor to the economy is fixed. The economy responds to this increase in demand in two ways: the price of labor w rises, and the rental price of capital falls, in accordance with Eqs. (16-64). To economize on the now higher-priced labor, *both* industries reduce the ratio of labor to capital utilized in production. (It may be a surprising piece of arithmetic that this is possible.) This situation is illustrated in Fig. 16-4. These results cannot be observed in the model with fixed-coefficient technology. There, the a_{ij}'s are constant and hence unchanged by output prices.

The Rybczynski Theorem

Let us now turn to the comparative statics of this two-factor, two-good variable-proportions model with respect to changes in endowments. Under the hypotheses of the factor price equalization theorem, which includes the assumption that one industry is always more labor-intensive than the other, a change in the resource endowment of either labor or capital (or both) will have *no effect* on factor prices. Again [Eqs. (16-50)] $a_{ij} = a_{ij}^*(w/r)$, and Eqs. (16-53) imply that factor prices are functions of *output prices only* [Eqs. (16-55)]. Thus, the first result is

$$\frac{\partial w}{\partial L} = \frac{\partial w}{\partial K} = \frac{\partial r}{\partial L} = \frac{\partial r}{\partial K} = 0 \qquad (16\text{-}67)$$

Do not forget that in these relations, output *prices* are being held fixed. Only resource endowments are changing. As endowments shift, the NNP plane $p_1 y_1 + p_2 y_2$ depicted in Fig. 16-3 shifts *parallel* to itself and becomes tangent to a new production frontier (not depicted) at the same output prices. Since output prices remain the same, factor prices are unchanged, given our assumptions.

Let us now consider the effects of changing the endowment of labor, say, on output levels. Since Eqs. (16-53) involve prices only, the comparative statics relations are derivable from Eqs. (16-54) alone, repeated here:

$$a_{L1}^* y_1 + a_{L2}^* y_2 = L \qquad (16\text{-}54a)$$

$$a_{K1}^* y_1 + a_{K2}^* y_2 = K \qquad (16\text{-}54b)$$

These two identities are the original resource constraints of the model, with the important added condition that the linear homogeneity assumption for the production function has been used to express the a_{ij}'s as functions of factor prices w and r (in particular w/r) only. If now either L or K changes, the a_{ij}'s remain constant, since $\partial a_{ij}^*/\partial L = [\partial a_{ij}^*/\partial(w/r)][\partial(w/r)/\partial L] = 0$, since the latter term is 0, from the preceding discussion. Hence, for the comparative statics of this model *with regard to changes in endowments, the a_{ij}^*'s can be treated as constants, even in this variable proportions model!*

Let us then differentiate Eqs. (16-54), partially of course, with respect to L. (Again, the asterisks will be dropped to save clutter. But do not forget the assumptions needed to perform these operations.) Differentiating gives

$$a_{L1}\frac{\partial y_1}{\partial L} + a_{L2}\frac{\partial y_2}{\partial L} \equiv 1$$

$$a_{K1}\frac{\partial y_1}{\partial L} + a_{K2}\frac{\partial y_2}{\partial L} \equiv 0$$

Thus, using Cramer's rule, we find, as in the linear programming model,

$$\frac{\partial y_1}{\partial L} \equiv \frac{a_{K2}}{A} = \frac{a_{K2}}{a_{L1}a_{K2} - a_{L2}a_{K1}} \tag{16-68a}$$

$$\frac{\partial y_2}{\partial L} \equiv -\frac{a_{K1}}{A} = \frac{-a_{K1}}{a_{L1}a_{K2} - a_{L2}a_{K1}} \tag{16-68b}$$

Under the assumption that industry 1 is labor-intensive, $A > 0$, and thus $\partial y_1/\partial L > 0, \partial y_2/\partial L < 0$. Differentiation of (16-54) with respect to K yields

$$\frac{\partial y_1}{\partial K} \equiv -\frac{a_{L2}}{A} = \frac{-a_{L2}}{a_{L1}a_{K2} - a_{L2}a_{K1}} \tag{16-68c}$$

$$\frac{\partial y_2}{\partial K} \equiv \frac{a_{L1}}{A} = \frac{a_{L1}}{a_{L1}a_{K2} - a_{L2}a_{K1}} \tag{16-68d}$$

Again, assuming industry 1 is labor-intensive, (16-68c) says that $\partial y_1/\partial K < 0$, and (16-68d) shows that $\partial y_2/\partial K > 0$.

These results, known as the *Rybczynski theorem,* state that under the hypotheses of the factor price equalization theorem, an increase, say, in the endowment of labor (holding output prices constant) will increase the output of the labor-intensive industry and decrease the output of the capital-intensive industry. Likewise, an increase in the endowment of capital, *ceteris paribus,* will increase the output of the capital-intensive industry and decrease the output of the labor-intensive industry. Again, under our strong assumptions, all these repercussions will leave factor *prices* unchanged. These results were illustrated for the linear models in Fig. 15-5.

Equations (16-68) are in fact derivable from earlier results. Recall the reciprocity conditions (16-25a) and (16-25b), which were derived from the general model, without the homogeneity restrictions:

$$\frac{\partial y_1}{\partial L} = \frac{\partial w}{\partial p_1} \qquad \frac{\partial y_2}{\partial L} = \frac{\partial w}{\partial p_2} \tag{16-25a}$$

and

$$\frac{\partial y_1}{\partial K} = \frac{\partial r}{\partial p_1} \qquad \frac{\partial y_2}{\partial K} = \frac{\partial r}{\partial p_2} \tag{16-25b}$$

Inspection of Eqs. (16-61) and (16-68) confirms these reciprocity conditions. For example, from (16-61a) and (16-68a),

$$\frac{\partial w}{\partial p_1} = \frac{a_{K2}}{A} = \frac{\partial y_1}{\partial L}$$

The Rybczynski theorems are in fact merely the dual relationships of the Stolper-Samuelson theorems. The relations between factor and output *prices* are identical to the relations between *physical* factors and outputs. All the results for factor prices have exact analogs for the factors themselves and vice versa.

In particular, the elasticity relationships (16-65) for real factor price changes have corresponding results for the factors themselves. The algebra is identical, since the comparative statics formulas (16-61) and (16-68) are identical. For example, suppose the endowment of labor increases, again assuming that industry 1 is labor-intensive. Then the output of industry 1 will not only increase but will increase at a faster rate than the increase in labor, i.e.,

$$\frac{L}{y_1}\frac{\partial y_1}{\partial L} > 1$$

As before, since $L = a_{L1}y_1 + a_{L2}y_2$, $L/y_1 = a_{L1} + a_{L2}(y_2/y_1)$. Thus

$$\frac{L}{y_1}\frac{\partial y_1}{\partial L} = \frac{a_{K2}a_{L1} + a_{K2}a_{L2}(y_2/y_1)}{a_{K2}a_{L1} - a_{K1}a_{L2}} > 1 \qquad (16\text{-}69a)$$

A similar procedure shows

$$\frac{K}{y_2}\frac{\partial y_2}{\partial K} > 1 \qquad (16\text{-}69b)$$

in perfect analogy with Eqs. (16-65).

16.4 APPLICATIONS OF THE TWO-GOOD, TWO-FACTOR MODEL

The Stolper-Samuelson theorem can be used to determine the effects of tax policies on income distribution. Consider an economy characterized by all the assumptions underlying the theorem. Assume the economy is trading freely with the rest of the world, i.e., with no policy restrictions on the flow of commodities. Assume the size of the economy is small so that it is a price-taker, and that transport costs are small. Denote the exogenously given world prices of goods 1 and 2 by p_1^0 and p_2^0, respectively. Assume that under free trade, good 1, the labor-intensive good, is imported, and the capital-intensive good 2 is exported by the economy.

Suppose now the government imposes a tariff on the imported foreign good. Denote the *ad valorem* tariff rate by t. The domestic prices become

$$p_1 = (1 + t)p_1^0 \qquad (16\text{-}70a)$$

$$p_2 = p_2^0 \qquad (16\text{-}70b)$$

These two equations show that as a result of the tariff, the price of good 1

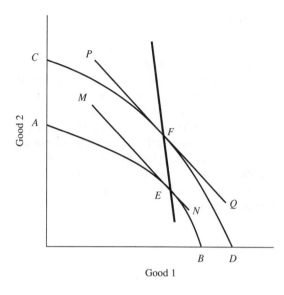

FIGURE 16-5

As a country accumulates capital, its production frontier shifts out. Letting good 1 be labor-intensive, at constant world prices (indicated by the slope of *MN* and *PQ*), output of good 1 expands, while output of good 2 contracts. The locus of production points *EF* is linear, since the input-output coefficients are functions of output prices only.

increases relative to that of good 2. Since good 1 is labor-intensive, by the Stolper-Samuelson theorem, the real wage rate (in terms of either good) increases while the real rental rate decreases. Thus, we have the following result: A tariff will benefit the factor that is used more intensively in the importable sector and will hurt the other factor.

Two simple applications of the Rybczynski theorem will now be introduced. First, consider again the small open economy just discussed. The production possibility frontier of the economy is represented by the curve *AB* in Fig. 16-5. Firms in the economy face exogenously given world prices of p_1^0 and p_2^0; *MN* represents the world price line whose slope equals $-p_1^0/p_2^0$. As shown in Fig. 16-3, the production point occurs at the point of tangency, point *E*, between curve *AB* and price line *MN*. Suppose now that through accumulation, the capital endowment of the economy increases while the labor endowment remains unchanged. With more capital endowment and factor substitution in both industries, more of either good can be produced when the production of the other good is fixed. The production possibility frontier with more capital endowment therefore shifts out to curve *CD* in Fig. 16-5. The new production point occurs at the point of tangency, point *F*, between curve *CD* and a new world price line, *PQ*, whose slope is $-p_1^0/p_2^0$. Because the economy is small, world prices are not disturbed by the capital accumulation in the economy, meaning line *PQ* is parallel to line *MN*.

By the Rybczynski theorem, production of the capital-intensive good 2 must thereby increase while that of labor-intensive good 1 must decrease. This means that point *F* is to the northwest of point *E*. Line *EF* is the locus of the production points as the capital stock grows. It is, in fact, linear. To see this, note that the rate of change of good 2 output with respect to good 1 output is given as dy_2/dy_1. Using Eqs. (16-68*c*) and (16-68*d*),

$$\frac{dy_2}{dy_1} = \frac{\partial y_2 / \partial K}{\partial y_1 / \partial K} = -\frac{a_{L1}}{a_{L2}} \qquad (16\text{-}71a)$$

Since the a_{ij}'s are functions of the output prices only, the slope of the locus is constant (and negative). Since point F must be above the price line MN, EF must be steeper than MN. The locus EF is sometimes called the Rybczynski line (for capital).

The preceding analysis can be similarly used to show the production effects of an increase in labor endowment. The Rybczynski line for labor has a slope of

$$\frac{dy_2}{dy_1} = \frac{\partial y_2 / \partial L}{\partial y_1 / \partial L} = -\frac{a_{K1}}{a_{K2}} \qquad (16\text{-}71b)$$

Because industry 2 is capital intensive,

$$\frac{a_{L1}}{a_{L2}} > \frac{a_{K1}}{a_{K2}}$$

This implies that the Rybczynski line for capital is steeper than the Rybczynski line for labor. In fact, the Rybczynski line for labor is less steep than the price line MN.

The Rybczynski theorem can also be used to prove the Heckscher-Ohlin theorem, which is widely used in the theory of international trade to explain the patterns of trade of two trading partners. Consider two countries, A and B, and denote the endowments of capital and labor in the two countries by K^i and L^i, $i = A, B$. Country B is said to be capital abundant (or labor scarce) relative to country A if and only if

$$\frac{K^B}{L^B} > \frac{K^A}{L^A}$$

The Heckscher-Ohlin theorem is as follows. Assume:

a. There are two tradeable goods, 1 and 2, and two factors, labor and capital.

b. The technologies are identical across countries in the sense that the production function of a sector is the same in both countries.

c. The countries have identical and homothetic preferences, which are represented by a quasi-concave, increasing (social) utility function.

d. The production function of each sector exhibits constant returns to scale.

e. The factors are perfectly mobile across sectors but immobile across countries.

f. All markets are perfectly competitive.

g. There is no factor intensity reversal in the sense that sector 1 is labor intensive relative to sector 2 at all factor prices.

Then each country will export the good that uses its abundant factor more intensively.

The theorem is proved as follows. Assume for the moment that the countries are exactly identical, with identical technologies, preferences, and factor endowments. Then the production possibility frontiers of both countries are identical and can be represented by curve AA' in Fig. 16-6. The self-sufficient, or autarky, equilibrium point, P, of each country is depicted as the point of tangency between the production frontier AA' and an indifference curve. The slope of the tangent to curve AA' at P equals the autarky relative price of good 1. Obviously, under these conditions, the two countries have no incentive to trade.

Suppose now that country B has more capital, implying that country B is capital abundant and country A is labor abundant. Suppose further that the relative price in country B remains unchanged. Then by the Rybczynski theorem, the production point will shift to point Q, which is above and to the left of point P. Country B's production possibility frontier is represented by curve BB'. As explained previously, curve BB' is entirely beyond curve AA'. Because of homothetic preferences, the consumption point will shift to point C, the point of intersection between the tangent to curve BB' at point Q and a ray from the origin through point P. As a result, at the original price ratio, an excess demand for good 1 and an excess supply of good 2 are created in country B. This means that under autarky, the relative price of good 1 is higher in country B, or the relative price of good 2 is higher in country A. Because of the difference in the autarky prices, it is sometimes said that country A has a comparative advantage in good 1 and a comparative disadvantage in good 2 relative to country B.

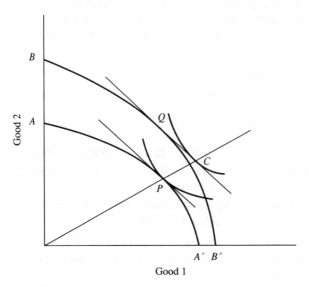

FIGURE 16-6

The Heckscher-Ohlin Theorem. Assume two initially identical countries, A and B, and let B then accumulate capital. Country A's production frontier is AA'; B's is BB'. Under autarky, the relative price of the labor-intensive good, y_1, would rise in country B and fall in A. With trade, each country would export the good with the lowest (internal) relative price; thus, B would export the capital intensive good y_2. Thus (under the assumptions of the theorem), each country will export the good that uses its abundant factor more intensively.

Now allow trade between the countries. Each country will export the good that is cheaper under autarky. This means that country A will export good 1 while country B will export good 2. Thus, we have proved the theorem: the capital-abundant country exports the capital-intensive good while the labor-abundant country exports the labor-intensive good. Although the proof assumes that country B has more capital but the same amount of labor as country A, this assumption is not necessary for the theorem. As long as country B is capital abundant, the production point Q must be to the left of the consumption point C, and an excess demand for good 1 and an excess supply of good 2 will be created under autarky and at the original price.

As our last application of this model, consider an economy that uses labor L and capital K to produce a universal consumption good C, *and more capital, K.* The production functions are, respectively, $C = f^C(L_C, K_C)$, $K = f^K(L_K, K_K)$. Assuming exogenously determined prices p_C and p_K for the consumption good and capital, the first-order conditions for maximization of the value of output include

$$\lambda_K = \text{Rental rate on capital} = p_K \frac{\partial f^K}{\partial K_K} = p_C \frac{\partial f^C}{\partial K_C}$$

Assuming the capital lasts forever, the interest rate equals the rental rate of capital divided by the price of capital:

$$i = \frac{p_K \partial f^K / \partial K_K}{p_K} = \partial f^K / \partial K_K$$

That is, the interest rate in this model is the marginal product of capital in producing more capital. (The letter "r" is commonly used in some models to mean the real interest rate; in others, it means the rental rate on capital. Do not confuse these different concepts!) In this model, the interest rate is determined by (among other things, perhaps, depending on the other assumptions in the model) the relative price of capital versus the consumption good. Assume for the moment that the capital goods industry is relatively capital-intensive. Then an exogenous increase in the price of capital increases the rental rate on capital by a greater proportion. In order to maintain the first-order condition, therefore, the marginal product of capital must rise, producing a higher real interest rate. However, the interest rate will fall if it is the consumption good industry that is capital intensive. Thus we see that in such a two-sector model, the determination of the interest rate is a somewhat complicated process, depending in part on the relative capital intensities of the capital and consumer goods industries.

16.5 SUMMARY AND CONCLUSIONS

Let us now briefly summarize the results and the underlying assumptions of the two-good, two-factor model. The fundamental hypothesis is that in a competitive economy, the owners of factors will contract with each other in such a way as to maximize the value of national income. This invisible hand process is not the intention of any person in the economy. Self-seeking owners of resources, in trying to maximize the return of such ownership, can be expected if transactions costs are 0, to combine in a way that all gains from trade are exhausted. This must place the economy on the production frontier and at that point on that frontier where the marginal evaluations by consumers of each good, in terms of forgone consumption of the other good, equals the marginal cost of production of each good, measured in terms of forgone production of the other good. This occurs at a point of tangency of the line, or plane, defining NNP, $z = p_1 y_1 + p_2 y_2$, and the production possibilities frontier.

Since factors are completely mobile between the two industries, factor prices must be the same in both industries. Factor prices emerge as the Lagrange multipliers associated with the resource constraints. Although the wage and capital rental rates are determined endogenously by the model, these factor prices are taken exogenously by the relatively "small," identical firms that make up each industry. It is the simultaneous actions of each firm that change factor prices and aggregate output levels.

Under these general conditions, it is possible to show that the supply of output curves, $y_j = y_j^*(p_1, p_2)$, are upward-sloping in their own price. This is a direct consequence of the concavity of the production possibilities frontier with respect to the origin. This shape of the production frontier is indicative of increasing marginal costs (hence, upward-sloping supply curves) for each industry. These matters are discussed in Sec. 16.2.

Lastly, for the general model, certain reciprocity conditions appear, Eqs. (16-24) to (16-26). These relations indicate a duality between physical quantities and their respective prices. The relation of outputs to resource endowments is the same as the relation of resource *prices* to output *prices*. These results are independent of any homogeneity assumptions concerning the production functions.

In Sec. 16.3, the assumption that each industry is characterized by constant returns to scale is added to the model. This permits representation of the production function in terms of the unit isoquant only (since all isoquants are radial blowups or contractions of that or any other isoquant). Mathematically, letting a_{ij} = the amount of input i used to produce 1 unit of output j, where $i = L, K, j = 1, 2$, the production relations become $f^1(a_{L1}, a_{K1}) = 1$ and $f^2(a_{L2}, a_{K2}) = 1$. These a_{ij}'s are the fundamental quantities in this more restricted model. When we use the preceding production relations and the first-order marginal relations (16-38), the a_{ij}'s are shown to depend only on the factor prices, the Lagrange multipliers, w and r; in particular, $a_{ij} = a_{ij}^*(w/r)$. This critical step allows the model to be defined by two independent sets of two equations each, Eqs. (16-53) and (16-54). The former indicate that profits are zero in each industry, i.e., that the amount of labor used to produce 1 unit of y_1, times the price of labor plus the amount of capital used to produce 1 unit of y_1 times the unit price of capital exactly equals the price of 1 unit of y_1. Similarly, the total unit factor cost of y_2 equals the unit price of y_2. The second set of equations constitutes the original resource constraints, with the added feature that the a_{ij}'s are functions of w/r only. Because of the dependence of the a_{ij}'s on w/r only, the comparative statics of this model is the same as in the case where the a_{ij}'s are technologically fixed. The variable proportions model (including the assumption of linear homogeneous production functions) yields the same comparative statics results as the fixed proportions linear programming model.

Equations (16-53), dealing with prices, yield as solutions Eqs. (16-55), factor prices expressed as functions of *output prices only*. This result yields the factor price equalization theorem, under the global assumption that in each country, one industry is always more labor-intensive than the other. This theorem then indicates that if two countries trade with each other, then as output prices converge in the two countries, the factor prices in each country will be functions of output prices only and not dependent in any way on resource endowments. If the production functions are the same in the two countries, the functional relationship $w = w^*(p_1, p_2)$, $r = r^*(p_1, p_2)$ will be the same for both countries. Then, since with free trade both countries will face the same output prices, factor prices will also equalize in both countries even though factors are immobile between countries.

Differentiation of Eqs. (16-53), dealing with prices only, yields the set of results known as the Stolper-Samuelson theorem. It is shown in Eqs. (16-61) and (16-65) that if the price of the, say, labor-intensive industry rises (inducing an expansion of that industry), nominal *and* real wages will rise and capital rental rates will fall. Likewise, if the price of the capital-intensive industry rises, the capital-goods industry expands, the labor-intensive industry contracts, and thus rental rates rise, in real as well as nominal terms, and the wage rate falls. Also, if the price of the labor-intensive industry rises, *both* industries become less labor-intensive, with similar results holding if the price of the capital-intensive good rises.

Analogous results for the physical quantities are known as the Rybczynski theorem. By using the reciprocity conditions (16-24) to (16-26), the algebra of the Rybczynski theorem is shown to be the same as that used in the Stolper-Samuelson theorem. Alternatively, these results are derivable from the second set of two equations defining the model [Eqs. (16-54)], the resource constraints. In Eqs. (16-68) and (16-69), it is shown that if, say, the amount of labor available to the whole economy increases, the output of the labor-intensive industry will not only expand but will expand in greater proportion to the increase in labor. Analogous results hold for an autonomous increase in capital.

This completes our discussion of the two-good, two-factor model. Let us briefly comment on the many-good, many-factor generalization of this model. This generalization is in fact exceedingly complex and beyond the scope of this book. The general model of maximization of NNP subject to resource constraints proceeds in an obvious way, with no difficulty. One derives the upward slope of the supply functions and the reciprocity conditions analogous to (16-24) to (16-26) in the same manner. The difficulty begins with trying to generalize the factor-price equalization, Stolper-Samuelson, and Rybczynski-type theorems. In general, if the number of goods exceeds the number of factors, certain goods, not determinable without an algorithmic process, will not be produced. Similarly, if the number of factors exceeds the number of goods in these models, certain factors will not be used and their associated Lagrange multiplier shadow prices will equal 0. The relation of factor price to output price changes is much more complex than a simple dependence upon factor intensities, since higher-order determinants are involved. Under restricted conditions, however, the factor price equalization theorem is valid. However, no easy or intuitive factor intensity rules can be stated to give the results analogous to those derived in Sec. 16.3.

PROBLEMS

1. In the n-good, m-factor model, with y_1^* the output of the ith industry, show that $\sum_{j=1}^{n} \varepsilon_{ij} = 0$, where $\varepsilon_{ij} = (p_j/y_i^*)(\partial y_i^*/\partial p_j)$. Show therefore in the two-good model that $\partial y_1^*/\partial p_2 > 0$.

2. Show that with linear homogeneous production functions, the model with n goods and m factors has the property that the (maximum) total value of output equals total factor cost.

3. Explain why it is critical, from the standpoint of deriving the Stolper-Samuelson and Rybczynski theorems, for the technological coefficients a_{ij} to be dependent on factor prices only and not the factor endowments. Explain what assumptions in the model produce this result.

4. Explain the assumptions needed to yield the result that factor prices are dependent on output prices only. Does it follow from this alone that if two countries engage in costless trade, factor prices will be the same in both countries? Why or why not?

5. The production possibilities frontier is derivable by treating one output level, say y_1, as fixed (parametric) and then using the resources to maximize the output level of y_2. As y_1 is varied parametrically, the production possibilities locus will be traced out.
   (a) Set up this problem for two goods and two factors and interpret the (three) Lagrange multipliers.
   (b) Show that the production frontier is not necessarily concave in this formulation. What distinguishes these assumptions from the ones used in the text, in which concavity of the production frontier is implied?
   (c) Show that if both production functions are concave, the production possibilities frontier is concave.

6. Consider the maximization of NNP model with $y_1 = L_1^{1/3}K_1^{2/3}$, $y_2 = L_2^{2/3}K_2^{1/3}$.
   (a) Show that the capital-labor ratio in industry 1 will always be 4 times the capital-labor ratio in industry 2.
   (b) Derive Eqs. (16-50) for this specification; i.e., verify for this model that each a_{ij}^* is a function of the factor price ratio only.
   (c) Show that $\partial a_{Lj}^*/\partial w_j < 0$, $\partial a_{Kj}^*/\partial r < 0$ directly from the equations for a_{ij}^*.
   (d) On the basis of the factor intensities in each industry, which factor price would you expect to increase and which to decrease when p_1 increases?
   (e) Find the explicit functions $w = w^*(p_1,p_2)$ and $r = r^*(p_1,p_2)$ and verify the predictions in part (d).
   (f) On the basis of factor intensities, which industry will increase output and which will decrease output when the endowment of labor increases?
   (g) Verify this result by applying Eqs. (16-54) for this model.

7. Derive the Rybczynski theorem from the Stolper-Samuelson theorem using the reciprocity relations present in the two-good, two-factor model.

8. Suppose that the NNP function of an economy is given as

$$(a_1p_1 + a_2p_2 + b\frac{p_1^2}{2p_2})(\alpha_L L + \alpha_K K) + (c_L L + c_K K + d\frac{L^2}{2K})(\beta_1 p_1 + \beta_2 p_2)$$

    (a) Show that the NNP function is linear homogeneous in p_1 and p_2 and linear homogeneous in L and K.

    (b) If it is required that the NNP function is a convex function of p_1 and p_2 and a concave function of L and K, what restrictions on the sign of b and d are needed?

    (c) Derive the supply functions of goods 1 and 2. Show that these functions are homogeneous of degree zero in prices and linear homogenous in factor endowments.

    (d) Derive the shadow prices of L and K. Show that these functions are linear homogeneous in prices and homogeneous of degree zero in factor endowments.

9. Define the unit cost function of sector i as

$$c^i(w,r) = \min \ \{wa_{Li} + ra_{Ki}: \ f^i(a_{Li}, a_{Ki}) \geq 1\}$$

where a_{Li} and a_{Ki} are the labor and capital inputs, respectively. Show that the following function is equivalent to the NNP function defined in the text.

$$g(p_1, p_2, L, K) = \min \ \{wL + rK: \ c^1(w,r) \geq p_1 \ \text{and} \ c^2(w,r) \geq p_2\}$$

10. By using the NNP function defined in Prob. 9, show that

$$w = p_1\frac{\partial y_1}{\partial L} + p_2\frac{\partial y_2}{\partial L}$$

$$r = p_1\frac{\partial y_1}{\partial K} + p_2\frac{\partial y_2}{\partial K}$$

11. "International trade necessarily lowers the real wage of the relatively scarce factor expressed in terms of any good." Comment.

BIBLIOGRAPHY

Arrow, K. J.: "Economic Equilibrium," *International Encyclopedia of the Social Sciences*, **4:** 376–388. The Macmillan Company and the Free Press, New York, 1968.

Debreu, G.: "Theory of Value," *Cowles Foundation Monograph* 17, John Wiley & Sons, Inc., New York, 1959.

Dorfman, R., P. A. Samuelson, and R. M. Solow: *Linear Programming and Economic Analysis*, McGraw-Hill Book Company, New York, 1958.

Edgeworth, F. Y.: *Mathematical Psychics*, Routledge & Kegan Paul, Ltd., London, 1881.

Hicks, J. R.: *Value and Capital,* 2d ed., Oxford University Press, New York, 1946.

Jones, R. W.: "Duality in International Trade: A Geometrical Note," *Canadian Journal of Economics and Political Science,* **31:**390–393, 1965.

Jones, R. W.: "The Structure of Simple General Equilibrium Models," *Journal of Political Economy,* **73:**557–572, 1965.

Koopmans, T. C., ed.: "Activity Analysis of Production and Allocation," *Cowles Commission Monograph* 13, John Wiley & Sons, Inc., New York, 1951.

Koopmans, T. C., ed.: *Three Essays on the State of Economic Science,* McGraw-Hill Book Company, New York, 1957.

Patinkin, D.: *Money, Interest, and Prices,* 2d ed., Harper & Row, Publishers, New York, 1965.

Quirk, J., and R. Saposnik: *Introduction to General Equilibrium Theory and Welfare Economics,* McGraw-Hill Book Company, New York, 1968.

Rybczynski, T. M.: "Factor Endowment and Relative Commodity Prices," *Econometrica,* **22:** 336–341, 1955.

Samuelson, P. A.: "Prices of Factors and Goods in General Equilibrium," *Review of Economic Studies,* **21:**1–20, 1953–1954.

Walras, L.: *Elements of Pure Economics,* trans. W. Jaffe, Richard D. Irwin, Inc., Homewood, IL, 1954.

CHAPTER
17

WELFARE
ECONOMICS

17.1 SOCIAL WELFARE FUNCTIONS

Throughout this book it has been stressed repeatedly that the goal of any empirical science is the development of refutable propositions about some set of observable phenomena. Refutable propositions that survive repeated testing form the important principles on which the science is based. (It is easy, of course, to state refutable hypotheses that are in fact refuted.)

Parallel to the development of economics along the preceding lines has arisen a discipline called *welfare economics,* which seeks not to explain observable events but to *evaluate* the desirability of alternative institutions and the supposed resulting economic choices. For example, it is commonly alleged that "too many" fish are being caught in the oceans, that tariffs and other specific excise taxes cause an "inefficient" allocation of resources ("too little" production of the taxed item), that "too much" pollution and congestion occur in metropolitan areas, and the like. In this chapter we shall investigate the basis of these assertions and comment on the empirical content of such pronouncements.

It was common for classical economists to speak of "the benefits to society," the interest of the "working class," and other such phrases that implied a sufficient harmony of interests between members of the relevant class to permit speaking of them as a group. Today, we often hear of individuals representing "the interests of consumers" or of someone taking the position of "big business."

A difficulty in the concept of group preferences, or interests, was pointed out by Kenneth Arrow in his classic paper, "A Difficulty in the Concept of Social Welfare."[†] The use of such phrases implies that there is a well-defined function of individual preferences, or utility functions, representing the utility, or "welfare," of the group. Such a function was first posed explicitly by A. Bergson in 1938.[‡] The social welfare function posited by Bergson had the form

$$W = f(U^1, \ldots, U^m) \tag{17-1}$$

where $U^1, \ldots, U^m$ were the utility functions of the m individuals in the group being considered, perhaps the whole economy. Bergson considered various first-order marginal conditions for the maximization of W subject to the resource constraints of the economy.

Arrow's discussion of these matters began with a 200-year-old example of the problem of construction of a group preference function. The example was based upon majority voting. Voting is a very common way for groups to reach decisions. Suppose one were to attempt to define collective preferences on the basis of what a majority of the community would vote for. Suppose there are three alternatives, **a**, **b**, and **c**, and three individuals in the group. Let P represent "is preferred to," so that **a**P**b** means that **a** is preferred to **b**.

Suppose now that the three individuals have the following preferences:

Individual 1: **a**P**b**, **b**P**c**
Individual 2: **b**P**c**, **c**P**a**
Individual 3: **c**P**a**, **a**P**b**

Assume, in accordance with ordinary utility theory, that these consumers' preferences are *transitive*. That is, for individual 1, **a**P**b** and **b**P**c**, means that **a**P**c**, etc. Then it can be quickly seen that a majority-rule social welfare function will have the unsatisfactory property of being *intransitive*. Consider, for example, alternative **a**. A majority of voters, namely voters 2 and 3, prefer **c** to **a**. Likewise, a majority of voters (1 and 3) prefer **a** to **b**, and another, different majority (1 and 2) prefer **b** to **c**. Whichever alternative is selected, a majority of voters will prefer some other alternative. Thus, the social welfare function

---

[†]*The Journal of Political Economy*, **58**, 328–46, 1950. This paper was part of a larger study, *Social Choice and Individual Values*, 2d ed., *Cowles Commission Monograph* 12, John Wiley & Sons, Inc., New York, 1963.

[‡]Abram Bergson, "A Reformulation of Certain Aspects of Welfare Economics," *Quarterly Journal of Economics*, **52**:310–334, 1938.

based on what the majority wishes will exhibit the properties **a**P**b**, **b**P**c** *and* **c**P**a**.[†]

Let us now summarize Arrow's theorem about social welfare functions. Arrow uses a weaker form of the preference relation: let **a**R_i**b** represent the statement, "**a** is *preferred or indifferent* to **b**, according to individual i." Suppose there are n individuals in this society. Then, by a *social welfare function,* in this terminology, we mean a relation R that corresponds to the individual orderings, $R_1, \ldots, R_n$, of all social states by the n individuals in the society. That is, given the preference orderings of all people in the polity, there exists some social ordering R which denotes "society's" values and rankings of the alternatives being considered.

Arrow proceeded to list five conditions which he felt almost any reasonable social welfare function ought to contain. The first of these is that the social welfare function is in fact defined for all sets of individual orderings that obey some set of individualistic hypotheses about behavior, e.g., the usual economic postulates of convex indifference curves and the like.

Condition 1. The social welfare function is defined for every admissible pair of individual orderings R_1, R_2.

Second, the social ordering should describe welfare and not, in Arrow's word, "illfare." The social welfare function should react in the same direction, or at least not oppositely to, alterations in individual values.

Condition 2. If a social state **a** rises or does not fall in the ordering of each individual without any other change in those orderings, and if **a**R**b** before the change, for any other alternative **b**, then **a**R**b** after the change in individual orderings.

[†]This voting paradox illustrates one of the outstanding differences between *market* choices and *political* choices. In the former, the consumer has the option of expressing the *intensity* of a preference by the simple act of choosing to purchase differing amounts of goods. In political choice, however, ordinary voters get one and only one vote. The consumer under these circumstances is unable to express intensity of preference. In the above example, the three alternatives were merely *ranked*. The voters were not able to say, for example, that they preferred **a** a great deal more than **b** and **b** only slightly more than **c**. In legislative bodies, in which there are relatively few voters, the individuals can *trade* votes on successive issues. Suppose, for example, individual 1 has the above-stated intensities of preferences and individual 2 was almost indifferent between **a**, **b**, and **c**. Then voter 1 could make a contract or a deal to vote for some other issue which voter 2 felt strongly about (and which voter 1 had no strong preferences about) in exchange for an agreement from voter 2 to vote for alternative **a** in the text example. The paradox would be resolved through trade. However, more trade is not necessarily preferred to less trade for individuals, and voter 3 might end up worse off for such political trading. It is for these reasons that many people believe that special-interest legislation is more apt to be enacted by legislative bodies than by referendum vote. But such vote trading also protects minorities who feel intensely about some issue from the "tyranny of the majority." The gains-from-trade aspect of political trading is emphasized in James Buchanan and Gordon Tullock, *The Calculus of Consent,* University of Michigan Press, Ann Arbor, 1963.

The most controversial of Arrow's conditions is the third, the *independence of irrelevant alternatives*. Consider an election in which three candidates, **a**, **b**, and **c**, are running. Suppose an individual's preferences are $\mathbf{a}R_i\mathbf{b}R_i\mathbf{c}$. Suppose, before the election, candidate **b** dies. Then we would expect to observe $\mathbf{a}R_i\mathbf{c}$. In like manner, we expect the social welfare function's ranking of any two alternatives to be unaffected by the addition or removal of some other alternative.

Condition 3. Let R_1, R_2, and R'_1, R'_2 be two sets of individual orderings. Let S be the entire set of alternatives. Suppose, for both individuals and all alternatives **a**, **b** in S, that $\mathbf{a}R_i\mathbf{b}$ if and only if $\mathbf{a}R'_i\mathbf{b}$. Then the social choice made from S is the same whether the individual orderings are R_1 and R_2 or R'_1 and R'_2.

Conditions 4 and 5 imposed by Arrow amount to assertions that individual preferences *matter*. That is, individual values are to "count," in determining the social welfare function. Conditions 4 and 5 say that the social welfare function is not to be either *imposed* or *dictatorial*. A social welfare function is said to be *imposed* if, for some pair of alternatives **a** and **b**, $\mathbf{a}R\mathbf{b}$ for any set of individual orderings R_1, R_2, that is, irrespective of the individual orderings R_1, R_2, where R is the social ordering corresponding to R_1, R_2. Likewise, a social welfare function is said to be *dictatorial* if there exists an individual i such that for all **a** and **b**, $\mathbf{a}R_i\mathbf{b}$ implies $\mathbf{a}R\mathbf{b}$ regardless of the orderings of all individuals other than i, where R is the social preference ordering corresponding to the R_i's.

Condition 4. The social welfare function is not to be imposed.

Condition 5. The social welfare function is to be nondictatorial.

Arrow succeeded in showing that these five conditions could not all hold simultaneously. In particular, he showed that any social welfare function that satisfied the first three conditions was either imposed or dictatorial. This very strong result is called the *possibility theorem*.[†] It says that no matter how complicated a scheme might be constructed for determining a set of social preferences, social ordering R cannot meet all conditions 1 to 5. It will be impossible to construct *any* welfare function of the type described in Eq. (17-1), $W = f(U^1, \ldots, U^m)$, that is, some function of individual utility levels, obeying the preceding conditions.

Another interpretation of the possibility theorem is that interpersonal comparisons of social utility are ruled out. It is impossible to say that taking a dollar away from a rich person and giving it to a poor person will make society better off, in some nondictatorial or nonimposed sense. The problem of interpersonal comparisons of utility was a vehicle by which ordinal utility replaced the older cardinal utility idea.

[†] The author would have called it the impossibility theorem.

On a less rigorous but more intuitive basis, the reason sensible social welfare functions cannot exist is that they conflict in a fundamental way with the notion that more is preferred to less. At any given moment, there is a frontier of possibilities for the consumers in any society. Any movement *along* this frontier involves gains for some individuals and losses for others. Without a measure for comparing these gains and losses between individuals, there is no sense to the phrase social welfare. (We shall explore these matters in more detail in Sec. 17.3.)

A rigorous proof of the possibility theorem is beyond the scope of this book. It can be found in the reference cited. We conclude this section by noting that in spite of this theorem, hundreds, perhaps thousands of articles have been written in economics journals using social welfare functions. Indeed, a whole new area of mathematical theology has arisen. However, to quote Samuelson,[†] "the theorems enunciated under the heading of welfare economics are not meaningful propositions of hypotheses in the technical sense. For they represent the deductive implications of assumptions which are not themselves meaningful refutable hypotheses about reality."

17.2 THE PARETO CONDITIONS

Faced with the impossibility of constructing a meaningful social welfare function, economists have opted for a weaker criterion by which to evaluate alternative situations. This criterion, known as the *Pareto condition,* after the Italian economist Vilfredo Pareto, states that a social state **a** is to be preferred to **b** if there is at least one person better off in **a** than in **b**, and no one is worse off in **a** than in **b**. This is a weaker value judgment only in the sense that more people would probably accept this judgment over more specific types of social orderings wherein some individuals lose and others gain. A state **a** that is preferred to **b** in the paretian senses is said to be *Pareto-superior* to **b**. One can imagine some sort of frontier of possible states of the economy such that there are no Pareto-superior points. That is, along this frontier, any movement entails a loss for at least one individual. The points for which no Pareto-superior states exist are called *Pareto-optimal.*

In general, we shall find that the set of Pareto-optimal points is quite large. Whether or not these points are a useful guide to policy is debatable. Even so, to say that the economy *ought* to be at a Pareto-optimal state is a value judgment and therefore a part of moral philosophy and not part of the empirical science of economics. We can, however, as economists, investigate the conditions under which various ideal Pareto-optimal states will be obtained. In this section we shall investigate certain famous conditions that achieve Pareto optimality. It is useful, in these discussions, to maintain the perspective indicated in the preceding quotation from Samuelson.

[†] *Foundations of Economic Analysis,* pp. 220–221, Harvard University Press, Cambridge, MA, 1947.

Pure Exchange

Consider an economy containing two individuals who consume two commodities, x and y. Let x_i, y_i denote the amounts of x and y consumed by the ith person, whose utility function is $U^i(x_i, y_i)$. Suppose that the total amounts of x and y are fixed, that is, $x_1 + x_2 = x$, $y_1 + y_2 = y$, where x and y are constants. Under what circumstances will the allocation of x and y between the two individuals be Pareto-optimal?

This problem can be formulated mathematically as follows:

maximize

$$U^2(x_2, y_2)$$

subject to

$$U^1(x_1, y_1) = U_0^1$$

$$x_1 + x_2 = x \qquad y_1 + y_2 = y \tag{17-2}$$

It is meaningless to attempt to maximize both individual's utilities simultaneously.[†] Instead, we first fix either individual's utility at some arbitrary level; then, the other person's utility is maximized. In this way, a position is attained in which neither party can be made better off without lowering the other person's utility.

The Lagrangian for the preceding problem is

$$\mathcal{L} = U^2(x_2, y_2) + \lambda(U_0^1 - U^1(x_1, y_1)) + \lambda_x(x - x_1 - x_2) + \lambda_y(y - y_1 - y_2) \tag{17-3}$$

Differentiating with respect to x_1, y_1, x_2, y_2 and the Lagrange multipliers yields

$$\mathcal{L}_{x_2} = U_x^2 - \lambda_x = 0 \tag{17-4a}$$

$$\mathcal{L}_{y_2} = U_y^2 - \lambda_y = 0 \tag{17-4b}$$

$$\mathcal{L}_{x_1} = -\lambda U_x^1 - \lambda_x = 0 \tag{17-4c}$$

$$\mathcal{L}_{y_1} = -\lambda U_y^1 - \lambda_y = 0 \tag{17-4d}$$

and

$$\mathcal{L}_\lambda = U_0^1 - U^1(x_1, y_1) = 0 \tag{17-5a}$$

$$\mathcal{L}_{\lambda_x} = x - x_1 - x_2 = 0 \tag{17-5b}$$

$$\mathcal{L}_{\lambda_y} = y - y_1 - y_2 = 0 \tag{17-5c}$$

[†]We leave such constructions to those who aspire to find that economic system which seeks "the greatest good for the greatest number of people."

where $U_x^i = \partial U^i / \partial x_i$, etc. Combining Eqs. (17-4) gives

$$\frac{U_x^1}{U_y^1} = \frac{\lambda_x}{\lambda_y} = \frac{U_x^2}{U_y^2} \qquad (17\text{-}6)$$

Equation (17-6) is the tangency condition that the consumers' indifference curves have the same slope. The marginal rate of substitution of x for y must be the same for both consumers. This is the familiar condition which must hold if the gains from trade are to be exhausted. The set of all points that satisfy (17-6) (and the constraints) is called the *contract curve* as depicted in Fig. 17-1. This diagram is the Edgeworth box diagram first shown in the chapter on general-equilibrium theory. (There, though, the axes were quantities of factors of production, not final goods as is the case here. The mathematics is, of course, formally identical.)

The set of Pareto-optimal points is the set of allocations for which the gains from exchange are exhausted. If the consumers were presented a different allocation, e.g., point A in Fig. 17-1, then with no cost of trading we should expect them to move to some point on the contract curve O_1O_2. If the trade is voluntary, the final allocation must lie between (or on) the two original indifference curves, i.e., some point on the segment BC of the contract curve. Without a further specification of the constraints of the bargaining process, the theory is inadequate to determine the actual final point. But in the absence of transactions costs and coercion self-seeking maximizers must wind up at *some* point along BC.

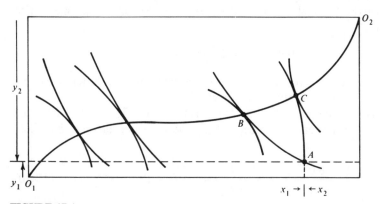

FIGURE 17-1
The Edgeworth box diagram is useful for depicting the set of Pareto-optimal points in a pure trade, zero transaction cost world. The dimensions of the box are the total amounts of each good available, x and y. Any point, such as A in the interior of the box, represents an allocation of x and y to the two individuals. Individual 1's utility function is plotted in the usual direction from the origin marked O_1. Individual 2's utility function is plotted opposite (right to left and down) from origin O_2. The set of points for which the slopes of U^1 and U^2 are identical at the same point, i.e., a level curve of U^1 is tangent to a level curve of U^2, is called the *contract curve,* designated O_1O_2. This curve represents the set of points for which the gains from trade are exhausted. It is occasionally referred to as the *conflict curve* because movements *along* O_1O_2 represent conflicts of interest: one individual gains and the other loses. For that reason, it is the set of Pareto-optimal points in this economy.

The problem as posed in (17-2) does not actually start at some particular point such as A and then move to the contract curve. As formulated in (17-2), the indifference level of individual 1 is fixed, say at the level that goes through point A. The resulting solution of the problem, i.e., solution to Eqs. (17-4) and (17-5), would place the economy at point B, where person 2 achieves maximum utility, leaving person 1 on the original indifference curve. Hence, the problem posed in (17-2) admits of a unique answer, even if a bargaining process that starts *both* individuals at A is unspecified.

The indirect utility function for individual 2 is obtained first by solving Eqs. (17-4) and (17-5) and substituting the chosen values of x_2 and y_2 into $U^2(x_2, y_2)$. Let the solutions to (17-4) and (17-5) be designated

$$x_i = x_i^*(U_0^1, x, y) \qquad y_i = y_i^*(U_0^1, x, y) \tag{17-7}$$

and likewise for the Lagrange multipliers:

$$\lambda = \lambda^*(U_0^1, x, y)$$

$$\lambda_x = \lambda_x^*(U_0^1, x, y) \qquad \lambda_y = \lambda_y^*(U_0^1, x, y) \tag{17-8}$$

Then

$$U^{2*} = U^2(x_2^*, y_2^*) = f(U_0^1, x, y) \tag{17-9}$$

Holding constant x and y, the total amounts of the goods, one can imagine a utility frontier, defined by Eq. (17-9). Starting with $U_0^1 = 0$, the maximum level of utility for person 2 is that which is achieved when person 2 consumes all of both goods, i.e.,

$$f(0, x, y) \equiv U^{2*}(x, y)$$

Likewise some maximum level of U^1 exists, represented by the indifference curve for person 1 which passes through O_2, for which $U^2 = 0$.

This utility frontier is plotted as the curve UU in Fig. 17-2, where the subscript 0 on U^1 has been suppressed. Using the envelope theorem and Eqs. (17-4) leads to

$$\frac{\partial U^{2*}}{\partial U^1} = \lambda = -\frac{U_x^2}{U_x^1} = -\frac{U_y^2}{U_y^1} < 0 \tag{17-10}$$

Assuming the tangencies defining the contract curve take place at positive marginal utilities (downward-sloping indifference curves), $\partial U^{2*}/\partial U^1 < 0$, as indicated. The Pareto frontier could not very well exhibit $\partial U^{2*}/\partial U^1 > 0$, since then movements along it in the northeast direction would imply gains for *both* individuals, contradicting the notion of Pareto optimality. It is *not* possible to infer that the Pareto frontier UU is concave to the origin; this follows from the ordinal nature of utility. A monotonic transformation of $U^1(x_1, y_1)$, say, could bend the frontier as desired, though keeping it downward-sloping.

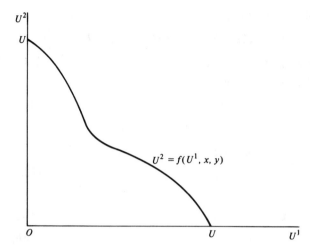

FIGURE 17-2
The utility frontier for given total quantities of goods. For any given amount of the goods x and y there exist a whole set of points for which neither individual can gain without the other person's losing. This Pareto frontier consists of reading off the (ordinal) utility levels for each person at every point along the contract curve O_1O_2. The frontier is necessarily downward-sloping, by definition of Pareto optimality.

Production

Suppose now we generalize the preceding discussion to the case where x and y are produced using two (or more) factors of production. In the preceding chapter on general equilibrium, an Edgeworth box diagram was constructed for the two-factor case. In order for consumers to be on the Pareto frontier in consumption, the goods must be produced efficiently. That is, a production point interior to the production possibilities frontier cannot result in a Pareto-optimal state for consumers. The consumers could both (or all, in the n-person case) have more of all goods and hence higher utility if production were moved to the production possibilities frontier in the appropriate manner. Hence, the problem of defining the Pareto frontier for consumers in the case in which x and y are *produced,* and not fixed constants, begins with the problem of defining the production possibilities frontier. Points on the production frontier are called *efficient in production.*

The mathematics for the production case is formally identical to the preceding analysis of final goods. Let there be two factors of production, L and K, and let L_x denote the amount of labor used in producing x, etc. Then the problem of efficient production can be stated:

maximize

$$y = f(L_y, K_y)$$

subject to

$$g(L_x, K_x) = x$$

$$L_x + L_y = L \qquad K_x + K_y = K \qquad (17\text{-}11)$$

where $f(L_y, K_y)$ and $g(L_x, K_x)$ are the production functions of y and x, respectively. The value x is taken as a parameter; it is *not* a decision variable.

The Lagrangian for the problem (17-11) is

$$\mathcal{L} = f(L_y, K_y) + \lambda(x - g(L_x, K_x)) + \lambda_L(L - L_x - L_y)$$
$$+ \lambda_K(K - K_x - K_y) \qquad (17\text{-}12)$$

The resulting first-order relations are

$$f_L - \lambda_L = 0 \qquad (17\text{-}13a)$$
$$f_K - \lambda_K = 0 \qquad (17\text{-}13b)$$
$$-\lambda g_L - \lambda_L = 0 \qquad (17\text{-}13c)$$
$$-\lambda g_K - \lambda_K = 0 \qquad (17\text{-}13d)$$

and the constraints

$$x - g(L_x, K_x) = 0 \qquad (17\text{-}14a)$$
$$L - L_x - L_y = 0 \qquad (17\text{-}14b)$$
$$K - K_x - K_y = 0 \qquad (17\text{-}14c)$$

From Eqs. (17-13),

$$\frac{f_L}{f_K} = \frac{\lambda_L}{\lambda_K} = \frac{g_L}{g_K} \qquad (17\text{-}15)$$

The ratio of marginal products must be equal for both goods along the production contract curve. This is the tangency condition illustrated in Fig. 16-2. Solving Eqs. (17-13) and (17-14) simultaneously gives

$$L_y = L_y^*(x, L, K) \qquad (17\text{-}16a)$$
$$K_y = K_y^*(x, L, K) \qquad (17\text{-}16b)$$
$$L_x = L_x^*(x, L, K) \qquad (17\text{-}16c)$$
$$K_x = K_x^*(x, L, K) \qquad (17\text{-}16d)$$

and

$$\lambda = \lambda^*(x, L, K) \qquad (17\text{-}17a)$$
$$\lambda_L = \lambda_L^*(x, L, K) \qquad (17\text{-}17b)$$
$$\lambda_K = \lambda_K^*(x, L, K) \qquad (17\text{-}17c)$$

Equations (17-16) give the chosen values of labor and capital in both industries. Substituting these values into the objective function gives the maximum y, y^* for any value of x:

$$y^* = f(L_y^*, K_y^*) = y^*(x, L, K) \qquad (17\text{-}18)$$

Using the envelope theorem, we have

$$\frac{\partial y^*}{\partial x} = \frac{\partial \mathcal{L}}{\partial x} = \lambda^* \qquad (17\text{-}19)$$

Hence, λ^* has the interpretation of the *marginal cost of x*, since it shows how much y^* must be given up in order to get an additional unit of x. The multiplier λ^* is the slope of the production possibility frontier by definition, since $\lambda^* = \partial y^*/\partial x$. Assuming the marginal products of the factors are positive, $\lambda^* < 0$, i.e., the production frontier is negatively sloped. As before, from Eqs. (17-13),

$$\lambda^* = -\frac{\lambda^*_L}{g_L} = -\frac{f_L}{g_L} = -\frac{f_K}{g_K} = -\frac{\lambda^*_K}{g_K} < 0 \qquad (17\text{-}20)$$

This equation has the interesting interpretation that the marginal cost of x is the same if only labor is varied (the ratio f_L/g_L) or if only capital is varied (f_K/g_K) or both are varied. In the partial-equilibrium framework this phenomenon was encountered in the formula

$$\text{MC} = \frac{w_L}{f_L} = \frac{w_K}{f_K} \qquad (17\text{-}21)$$

where the w's were the respective factor prices. Here, of course, λ_L and λ_K are the factor prices, *measured in terms of the physical output y*, i.e.,

$$\lambda^*_L = \frac{\partial y^*}{\partial L} \qquad (17\text{-}22a)$$

$$\lambda^*_K = \frac{\partial y^*}{\partial K} \qquad (17\text{-}22b)$$

This interpretation of λ_L and λ_K makes (17-21) and (17-20) equivalent except for units.

The production possibilities curve yields the set of "efficient" production plans. A necessary condition for overall Pareto optimality is to be on this frontier. However, that in itself is not sufficient. To exhaust all the gains from trade, the goods produced must be allocated to the consumers in an efficient manner. This requires at least that the previous analysis of the *consumer's* Edgeworth box diagram apply, i.e., the consumers must be on their contract curve, for any production levels (x, y). However, one more tangency condition must also apply: for each consumer, the marginal rates of substitution of x for y, that is, the marginal evaluation of x in terms of y forgone, must equal the marginal cost of producing x (in terms of y forgone). This condition implies that the consumers are on their contract curve, since *each* consumer's marginal evaluation of x must equal the marginal cost of x. Let us see how this last condition is derived.

The only difference between this last, and most general problem and the first one posed in (17-2) is that instead of x and y being fixed, they are determined by the production possibilities frontier derived in the production model as Eq. (17-18). Thus, the locus of overall efficient (Pareto-optimal) points is defined by:

maximize

$$U^2(x_2, y_2)$$

subject to

$$U^1(x_1, y_1) = U_0^1 \qquad x_1 + x_2 = x$$

$$y_1 + y_2 = y \qquad y = y^*(x, L, K) \qquad (17\text{-}23)$$

It will simplify the algebra to combine the last three constraints into one. These three equations define the production possibility curve, written in implicit form, as

$$h(x, y) = h(x_1 + x_2, y_1 + y_2) = 0$$

where the parameters L and K have been suppressed because they will not be used. The problem is then simply:

maximize

$$U^2(x_2, y_2)$$

subject to

$$U^1(x_1, y_1) = U_0^1$$

$$h(x_1 + x_2, y_1 + y_2) = 0 \qquad (17\text{-}24)$$

The Lagrangian for (17-24) is

$$\mathscr{L} = U^2(x_2, y_2) + \lambda_1(U_0^1 - U^1(x_1, y_1)) + \lambda h(x, y) \qquad (17\text{-}25)$$

Noting that $\partial h / \partial x_i = (\partial h / \partial x)(\partial x / \partial x_i) = \partial h / \partial x$, etc., we see that the first-order conditions are

$$U_x^2 + \lambda h_x = 0 \qquad (17\text{-}26a)$$

$$U_y^2 + \lambda h_y = 0 \qquad (17\text{-}26b)$$

$$-\lambda_1 U_x^1 + \lambda h_x = 0 \qquad (17\text{-}26c)$$

$$-\lambda_1 U_y^1 + \lambda h_y = 0 \qquad (17\text{-}26d)$$

and the two constraints

$$U_0^1 - U^1(x_1, y_1) = 0 \qquad (17\text{-}27a)$$

$$h(x, y) = 0 \qquad (17\text{-}27b)$$

Eliminating the Lagrange multipliers from Eqs. (17-26), we find

$$\frac{U_x^1}{U_y^1} = \frac{U_x^2}{U_y^2} = \frac{h_x}{h_y} \qquad (17\text{-}28)$$

The quantity h_x / h_y is the absolute slope of the production possibilities frontier; i.e., in explicit form, by the chain rule,

$$\frac{\partial y}{\partial x} = -\frac{h_x}{h_y}$$

Hence, Eq. (17-28) gives the marginal condition stated above: *for overall (production and consumption) Pareto optimality, the marginal evaluation of each commodity must be the same for all individuals, and that common marginal evaluation must equal the marginal cost of producing that good.* (The words *all* and *each* have been used instead of *both*. The generalization of these results to n goods and m consumers is straightforward.)

The overall utility frontier is found by solving Eqs. (17-26) and (17-27) for $x_i = x_i^*(U_0^1)$, $y_i = y_i^*(U_0^1)$. Substituting these values into the objective function, we derive

$$U^2 = U^2(x_2^*, y_2^*) = U^{2*}(U_0^1) \tag{17-29}$$

This situation is shown geometrically in Fig. 17-3. The curve PP represents the production possibilities frontier for given resource endowments. At any point, say A, the slope of this frontier is the marginal cost of x. From this point, which represents a certain total amount of x and y, an Edgeworth box diagram is constructed. The points in the interior of the box represent the allocations of x and y to the two consumers. The curve OA represents the implied contract curve for the consumers. At some point (or points) along OA, say, A', the marginal evaluations of x (the marginal rates of substitution) will equal the slope of the tangent line at A, the marginal cost of x. This is an overall Pareto-optimal allocation, i.e., efficient in production and consumption. The point A' represents one particular point on the implied *utility* frontier, as depicted in Fig. 17-2. It is a special point, however, in that marginal cost equals marginal benefits there.

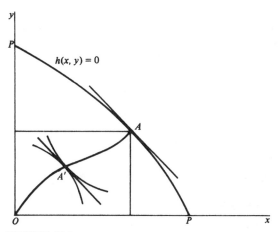

FIGURE 17-3

Overall Pareto optimality. The curve PP represents the *production* possibilities frontier of the economy for given resource endowments. The slope of this frontier is the marginal cost of producing x, in terms of y forgone. At any point, say A, along the frontier, an Edgeworth box can be constructed as shown. The points in the box represent allocations of x and y to the two consumers. These consumers will presumably trade to the contract curve OA. At some point or points on OA, the slopes of the indifference curves will equal the slope of the transformation curve at A. This is an overall Pareto efficient point, since the MRSs of each consumer are equal and equal to marginal cost.

At each point along the *production* possibilities frontier, an Edgeworth box can be drawn and the overall efficient allocation(s) can be determined. In Fig. 17-4 the utility frontiers for several production points are drawn. The *envelope* curve for all these partial frontiers is Eq. (17-29), $U^2 = U^{2*}(U_0^1, x, y)$. The partial frontiers are those for specific values of x and y, that is, holding x and y constant. From general envelope considerations

$$\frac{\partial U^{2*}}{\partial U_0^1} = \left(\frac{\partial U^{2*}}{\partial U_0^1}\right)_{x,y} \tag{17-30}$$

That is, along the overall frontier, the slope of the frontier at any point is the same if x and y are held constant or allowed to vary.

The grand utility frontier UU represents the complete set of Pareto-optimal, or efficient, productions and distributions of the goods x and y. The choice of *which* Pareto-optimal point is somehow "best for society" is a value judgment and outside the scope of positive economics. If some social welfare function is posited (social welfare functions can exist, but not with all the properties outlined by Arrow), its indifference curves can be plotted in Fig. 17-4, and some optimal point along the frontier UU will be selected. There are some who believe that governments consciously seek some overall optimum as just described. It is difficult to explain political behavior with such a model.

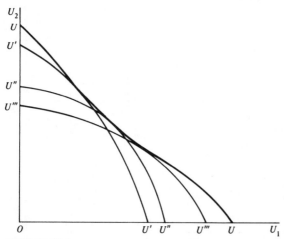

FIGURE 17-4
Partial and overall utility frontiers. For any given x and y, that is, for some particular point on the production possibilities curve, some *utility* frontier is implied. Several of these are drawn: $U'U'$, $U''U''$, and $U'''U'''$. The *envelope* curve for all these partial frontiers is the overall, or *grand,* utility frontier UU. The frontier UU represents the maximum utility any one consumer can achieve for given level of the other person's utility. Each point on UU represents, in general, a different production point, though there is no reason why some partial frontier could not be tangent to UU at more than one point.

17.3 THE CLASSICAL "THEOREMS" OF WELFARE ECONOMICS

In this section we shall present the classical "theorems" of welfare economics. The quotation marks are used because the propositions derived in what follows are not in fact refutable theorems. They represent generally unobservable first-order conditions for maximization, i.e., statements that at an optimum, marginal benefits equal marginal costs. As was indicated in the quotation from Samuelson's *Foundations of Economic Analysis,* these propositions represent the logical implications of propositions which are not themselves refutable.

The first theorem is that *perfect competition leads to a Pareto-optimal allocation of goods and services.* This proposition holds only under certain restrictive conditions. Specifically, the formulation of the problems posed in the previous section ruled out two major classes of phenomena: interdependence of the consumer's utility functions, and interdependence of the production functions. In the preceding presentation, there were no *externalities,* or side effects, present between any of the maximizing agents. Such interdependence would be indicated by writing, say,

$$y = f(L_y, K_y, x) \tag{17-31a}$$

or

$$U^2 = U^2(x_2, y_2, U^1) \tag{17-31b}$$

In the case of (17-31a), the output of y depends not only on the labor and capital inputs in the production function for y but also the level of x produced. In a later section we shall consider a particular example of this, where the output of a farm depends in part on a neighboring rancher's output of cattle, who trample some of the farmer's output. Similarly, (17-31b) indicates that another person's happiness is an influence on one's own utility.

In the absence of occurrences (17-31a) and (17-31b) and in the absence of monopoly, the prices of goods and services offered in the economy will equal their respective marginal costs of production. The condition for profit maximization under competitive factor and output markets yields, for each industry h,

$$p_h f_i^k - w_i = 0 \qquad i = 1, \ldots, n \tag{17-32}$$

where

$$f^k(x_1, \ldots, x_n) = k\text{th firm's production function}$$

$$w_i = \text{wage of } x_i$$

$$p_h = \text{output price}$$

Suppose there are m firms. The supply function of the firms is the solution of

$$p_h - \frac{\partial C_k^*}{\partial y_k} = 0 \tag{17-33}$$

where $C_k^*(y_k, w_1, \ldots, w_n)$ is the firm's total cost function. From (17-32),

$$\frac{w_i}{w_j} = \frac{f_i^k}{f_j^k} \qquad k = 1, \ldots, m \qquad (17\text{-}34)$$

This is precisely the condition that the economy be on the production possibilities frontier: the ratio of marginal products for all pairs of factors is the same for all firms, equal to the ratio of factor prices.

Moreover, utility-maximizing consumers with utility functions $U^k(y_1, \ldots, y_n)$ in the n output goods will set the ratios of marginal utilities equal to the price ratios; i.e.,

$$\frac{U_i^k}{U_j^k} = \frac{p_i}{p_j} \qquad \text{for all } i, j, k \qquad (17\text{-}35)$$

Since all consumers will face the same prices, Eq. (17-35) says that all consumers' marginal evaluations of the good will be identical, the condition for efficient consumption for given outputs. Lastly, using Eq. (17-33),

$$\frac{U_i^k}{U_j^k} = \frac{p_i}{p_j} = \frac{MC_i}{MC_j} \qquad \text{for all } i, j, k \qquad (17\text{-}36)$$

Hence, not only are all consumers' marginal evaluations equal, they are equal to the ratio of marginal costs of those goods, expressed in money terms. This ratio of money marginal costs is precisely the marginal cost of good i, in terms of good j forgone. That is, converting to units of good j makes $MC_j \equiv 1$. [Note that the units of MC_i/MC_j are $(\$y_i) \div (\$y_j) = y_j/y_i$, the amount of y_j forgone to produce another increment of y_i, or the *real* marginal cost of y_i.]

Thus, under perfect competition with no side effects (externalities), the Pareto conditions for overall efficiency hold. Therefore, in such a perfectly competitive economy, no individual will be able to improve himself or herself without making someone else worse off.

It does *not* follow from the preceding that it is desirable for the economy to be perfectly competitive. Consider Fig. 17-5, where the grand utility frontier *UU* has been plotted. Suppose, somehow, the economy has situated the two individuals at point *A*, a nonparetian allocation. Any movement to the right or upward from *A*, resulting in a point on the utility frontier along the segment *BC*, is clearly Pareto-superior to *A*. However, a movement to *D*, a Pareto-optimal point, leaves consumer 2 worse off; it is not an improvement from consumer 2's standpoint. Hence, aside from being a value judgment, a move to the Pareto frontier may involve losses.

The second "theorem" of classical welfare economics is the statement that there is an allocation under perfect competition for any overall Pareto optimum. That is, starting now with a point on the Pareto frontier, there exists a competitive solution which achieves that optimum. The proof of this proposition, for general functional forms of utility and production functions, is a formidable mathematical

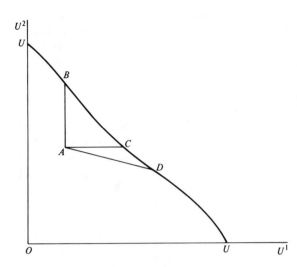

FIGURE 17-5
A non-Pareto move. Suppose the economy is at point *A*. Then any move northeast will be to a Pareto-superior position: each consumer will gain. Any point along the segment *BC* of the Pareto frontier *UU* is Pareto-superior to *A*. However, not every point along *UU* is Pareto-superior to *A*. Point *D*, for example, leaves consumer 1 better off and consumer 2 worse off than at *A*. Consumer 2 will not advocate economic efficiency if it results in the economy's moving to point *D*. It is not possible to argue, even with the weak Paretian value judgment, that the economy "ought" to be at a Pareto-optimal point.

problem, which has been analyzed by K. Arrow,[†] G. Debreu,[‡] L. Hurwicz,[§] and others. A rigorous discussion is considerably beyond the scope of this book.

Note what this second "theorem" does *not* say: it does not say that in order to achieve a Pareto position the economy must be competitive. An omniscient dictator could mandate the correct prices and quantities so that the economy would reach the same position as a competitive economy would.

Two of the outstanding reasons why an economy might not be on the overall Pareto frontier are (1) excise taxes and (2) monopolistic raising of price over marginal cost. With regard to the latter, a *perfectly discriminating monopolist,* who extracts all the gains from trade via some sort of all-or-nothing pricing, does *not* disturb the Pareto conditions. The reason, fundamentally, is that all the gains from trade are exhausted. The only difference is that only the perfectly discriminating monopolist gains whereas with open markets the buyers and sellers both gain. But as long as all the gains from trade are exhausted, there can be no Pareto-*superior* moves.

17.4 A "NONTHEOREM" ABOUT TAXATION

A commonly stated proposition is that to raise any given amount of tax revenue it is best, from the standpoint of consumers' achieving the highest possible indiffer-

---

[†] The principal investigation of both the above theorems is in K. Arrow, "An Extension of the Basic Theorems of Classical Welfare Economics," in J. Neyman (ed.), *Proceedings of the Second Berkeley Symposium on Mathematical Statistics and Probability,* University of California Press, Berkeley, 1951.

[‡] Gerard Debreu, *Theory of Value,* John Wiley & Sons, Inc., New York, 1959.

[§] Leonid Hurwicz, "Optimality and Informational Efficiency in Resource Allocation Processes, " in *Mathematical Methods in the Social Sciences 1959,* Stanford University Press, Stanford, CA, 1960.

ence curve, to collect those taxes via proportional excise taxes or income taxes. (With no savings in the economy, these taxes are equivalent.) The argument is loosely based on the observation that the Pareto conditions $p_j/p_i = \mathrm{MRS}^k = \mathrm{MC}_j/\mathrm{MC}_i$ would not be disturbed if $p_j = (1 + t)\mathrm{MC}_j$, where the tax rate t is constant across all commodities. This, however, is a logical error, since these first-order marginal conditions for Pareto optimality, while necessary, are not sufficient. Other criteria may lead to the same conditions.

The "theorem" has been criticized on the empirical grounds that not all goods are easily taxed. A person's labor-leisure choice is affected by any tax on income. The price of leisure is the forgone wage; a tax on that wage income is a *subsidy* on leisure. In addition, many commodities, for more or less technological reasons, may be difficult to tax, e.g., services one provides for oneself or family. Under these conditions, a proportional tax on all taxable items is not a proportional tax on all items.

These empirical matters aside, however, a correct theorem is difficult to state. Even if one could tax all goods and services proportionately, this would not in general lead to a Pareto allocation, as we shall presently see. The most famous "proof" of this nontheorem was presented by Harold Hotelling in 1938.[†] Hotelling's proof went essentially as follows. Suppose a consumer currently consumes n goods, $q_i, i = 1, \ldots, n$, at prices $p_i = \mathrm{MC}_i$. The consumer's *income* is taxed, however, and money income after taxes is $m = \sum p_i q_i$. Since the commodity bundle $\mathbf{q} = (q_1, \ldots, q_n)$ was chosen at prices $\mathbf{p} = (p_1, \ldots, p_n)$ and income m, any other bundle of goods $\mathbf{q}' = \mathbf{q} + \Delta \mathbf{q}$ which the consumer *could* have chosen must be inferior. Hotelling was asserting (without using the phraseology, which was not yet invented) that $\mathbf{q}$ was *revealed preferred* to $\mathbf{q}'$ if

$$\sum p_i q_i \geq \sum p_i q_i'$$

or

$$\sum p_i \Delta q_i \leq 0 \tag{17-37}$$

Now suppose prices are changed by amounts Δp_i, representing excise taxes but money income (tax) is also changed so that the consumer can have the same opportunities to purchase goods as before. By definition,

$$m + \Delta m = \sum (p_i + \Delta p_i)(q_i + \Delta q_i)$$

Subtracting $m = \sum p_i q_i$ gives

$$\Delta m = \sum p_i \Delta q_i + \sum \Delta p_i (q_i + \Delta q_i)$$

Rearranging terms, we have

[†] H. Hotelling, "The General Welfare in Relation to Problems of Taxation and of Railway and Utility Rates," *Econometrica*, **6**, 242–269, 1938; reprinted in *A.E.A. Readings in Welfare Economics*, Richard D. Irwin, Homewood, IL, 1969.

$$\sum p_i \Delta q_i = \Delta m - \sum \Delta p_i (q_i + \Delta q_i) \qquad (17\text{-}38)$$

Consider this last equation. The term $q_i + \Delta q_i$ represents the q_i's sold if taxed; hence, the last term represents the total tax revenue from the excise taxes, $\Delta p_i, i = 1, \ldots, n$. The term Δm represents the change in income taxes. Therefore, this expression says that if the change in excise taxes results in revenue absolutely greater than or equal to the income tax change, $\sum p_i \Delta q_i \leq 0$. In this case, it is argued, that since prices were set at marginal costs, replacing income taxes by excise taxes leads the consumer to purchase some bundle q' which was shown to be revealed inferior to q. Hence, to quote Hotelling,

> If government revenue is produced by any system of excise taxes there exists a possible distribution of personal levies among the individuals of the community such that the abolition of the excise taxes and their replacement by these levies will yield the same revenue while leaving each person in a state more satisfactory to himself than before.[†]

This "proof," however, seems to be merely a theorem about revealed *preferences*. Starting at *any* set of prices whatsoever, making the just stated changes in prices and income will leave the consumer worse off. Nowhere is the condition $p_i = MC_i$ used in this "proof." That marginal condition is irrelevant to the argument. No assumptions about *production* are contained in the argument; only assumptions concerning *preferences* are used. The same "proof" follows if initially $p_i \neq MC_i$ and the Δp_i's and m are changed so as to make $p_i = MC_i$ in the final position.

17.5 THE THEORY OF THE SECOND BEST[‡]

The problem of optimal excise taxation cannot be handled without considering the ends of this taxation. Suppose there are *three* goods—two private goods, x and y, and government services, z. If these government services are services for which normal pricing is possible, e.g., postal services, the optimal taxes are zero. The government merely sells its services at marginal cost, which, together with selling x and y at their respective marginal costs, will yield a Pareto optimum. The question of optimal taxation makes sense only in the context that some good, say the services of the government, is not, for some reason, to be sold at marginal cost. In some cases, e.g., national defense, it would be difficult to do so. Also, an important class of goods exists, e.g., the so-called *public goods* discussed

---

[†] Italics in the original. There is no apparent distinction in Hotelling's paper between income tax, proportional excise tax, and lump-sum or personal-levy tax.

[‡] R. G. Lipsey and K. Lancaster, "The General Theory of the Second Best," *Review of Economic Studies,* **24**, 11–32, 1956.

in the next section, for which marginal costs are less than average costs—the declining-AC industries. It is impossible to sell these goods at marginal cost without subsidies raised via taxation. The question thus becomes: Suppose some good z is not sold at marginal cost. Is it possible to infer that consumers will be on the highest indifference curves if the remaining goods are sold at prices proportional to their marginal costs, e.g., by proportional excise or income taxes? The answer is no, as the following argument shows.

Consider the simplest case of one consumer. The consumer maximizes utility subject to the production possibilities frontier, or:

maximize

$$U(x,y,z)$$

subject to

$$g(x,y,z) = 0$$

The Lagrangian is

$$\mathcal{L} = U(x,y,z) + \lambda g(x,y,z)$$

producing the first-order conditions

$$U_x + \lambda g_x = 0 \qquad U_y + \lambda g_y = 0 \qquad U_z + \lambda g_z = 0$$

or

$$\frac{U_x}{U_y} = \frac{g_x}{g_y} \qquad \frac{U_z}{U_y} = \frac{g_z}{g_y} \tag{17-39}$$

The marginal rates of substitution equal the respective marginal costs. Suppose now that z is not sold at MC. A simple constraint which expresses this is $U_z = kg_z$, where $k \neq U_y/g_y$. Let us now maximize $U(x,y,z)$ subject to this new constraint also, in addition to the resource constraint $g(x,y,z) = 0$. The Lagrangian for this problem is

$$\mathcal{L} = U(x,y,z) + \lambda g(x,y,z) + \mu(U_z - kg_z)$$

The first-order conditions for this maximization are (excluding the constraints)

$$\mathcal{L}_x = U_x + \lambda g_x + \mu(U_{zx} - kg_{zx}) = 0$$
$$\mathcal{L}_y = U_y + \lambda g_y + \mu(U_{zy} - kg_{zy}) = 0$$
$$\mathcal{L}_z = U_z + \lambda g_z + \mu(U_{zz} - kg_{zz}) = 0$$

Since the constraint $U_z - kg_z$ is assumed to be binding, $\mu \neq 0$. Solving for the marginal rates of substitution,

$$\frac{U_x}{U_y} = \frac{-\lambda g_x - \mu(U_{zx} - kg_{zx})}{-\lambda g_y - \mu(U_{zy} - kg_{zy})} \tag{17-40}$$

with a similar expression for U_x/U_z or U_y/U_z.

The left-hand side of Eq. (17-40) is the MRS between x and y. It cannot be inferred that this MRS should be equal to $MC_x/MC_y = g_x/g_y$. For arbitrary values of the cross-partials U_{zx}, g_{zx}, U_{zy}, and g_{zy}, *nonproportional* excise taxes on x and y will in general satisfy (17-40). It might be noted that if these cross-partials are all 0, Hotelling's "theorem" holds, but this is a special case.

In general, therefore, it cannot be argued that if some distortion, that is, $p_j \neq MC_j$, is removed in the economy, consumers will move closer to the Pareto frontier if other distortions are present. If the industries involved are unrelated, a case might be made that the above cross-partials are 0. In that case, a more efficient allocation is implied by removal of the distortion.

Hotelling correctly argued for a nondistorting, or lump-sum, tax. As previously mentioned, an income tax is a subsidy on leisure and hence distorts the labor-leisure choice. A poll tax is cited as an example of a lump-sum tax. More precisely, an existence tax is advocated. Even with this type of tax, however, we shall find, in the long run, less existence, i.e., fewer children, less spent on lifesaving devices, etc. For all practical purposes, it is probably safe to conclude that there is no such thing as a lump-sum tax.

17.6 PUBLIC GOODS

There is an important class of goods which have the characteristic of being *jointly consumed* by more than one individual. These goods, known as *public goods,* are goods for which there is *no congestion.* Ordinary private goods are goods for which congestion is so severe that only one person can consume the good.

The most famous example of a public good is perhaps the service national defense. The protection afforded any individual by the nation's foreign policy and military prowess is substantially unaffected if additional recipients are added to that service flow. Similarly, driving on an uncrowded freeway, watching a movie or play in an uncrowded theater, or watching a television program are services for which the marginal cost, in terms of resources used up, of accommodating an additional consumer is essentially 0. These goods are the polar case of goods for which average costs are forever declining.

The problem such goods raise for welfare economic considerations is that the Pareto frontier is reached only if all goods and services are sold at their marginal cost of production. If public goods are sold at marginal cost, no revenues will be generated to finance the production of those goods. If production of the public good is financed by revenues derived from taxation of other goods, these other goods will be sold to consumers at prices other than marginal cost, thereby moving the economy off the Pareto frontier. The problems of second best, just discussed, apply to these goods.

Matters of financing aside, assuming that the public good is to be sold at marginal cost, that is, 0, what level of the good is to be produced in the first place, i.e., how many uncrowded highways, open-air concerts, etc., are to be produced? The *production* of public goods is not free; these goods are "free" only in the sense that the marginal cost of having an additional individual consume the good, once produced, is 0. In the case of private goods, this problem does not arise (except in the case of declining average costs). The goods are produced by profit-maximizing firms and sold at marginal cost. No private firm, however, could produce a public good and satisfy the Pareto condition $p = MC = 0$.

Suppose there are two consumers with utility functions $U^1(x_1, y_1)$ and $U^2(x_2, y_2)$, where x is the public good and y is the ordinary private good. By definition of a public good, both consumers consume the total amount x of the good produced. Hence,

$$x_1 = x_2 = x \tag{17-41}$$

For the private good, as before, $y_1 + y_2 = y$. Suppose there is a transformation surface $g(x, y)$ defining the production possibilities frontier for the economy. The Pareto optimum is achieved by solving:

maximize

$$U^2(x, y_2)$$

subject to

$$U^1(x, y_1) = U_0^1 \qquad g(x, y) = 0 \tag{17-42}$$

with $y = y_1 + y_2$. The Lagrangian is

$$\mathcal{L} = U^2(x, y_2) + \lambda_1(U_0^1 - U^1(x, y_1)) + \lambda g(x, y) \tag{17-43}$$

Differentiating $\mathcal{L}$ with respect to x, y_1, y_2 and the multipliers, noting that $g_{y_i} = g_y(\partial y/\partial y_i) = g_y, i = 1, 2$, we have, denoting $U_{x_j}^j = U_x^j$, etc.

$$\mathcal{L}_x = U_x^2 - \lambda_1 U_x^1 + \lambda g_x = 0 \tag{17-44a}$$

$$\mathcal{L}_{y_1} = -\lambda_1 U_y^1 + \lambda g_y = 0 \tag{17-44b}$$

$$\mathcal{L}_{y_2} = U_y^2 + \lambda g_y = 0 \tag{17-44c}$$

with the constraints

$$\mathcal{L}_{\lambda_1} = U_0^1 - U^1(x, y_1) = 0 \tag{17-45a}$$

$$\mathcal{L}_\lambda = g(x, y) = 0 \tag{17-45b}$$

From (17-44c), $\lambda = -U_y^2/g_y$. Substituting this in (17-44b) gives $\lambda_1 = -U_y^2/U_y^1$. Using these two expressions in (17-44a) leads to

$$U_x^2 + \frac{U_y^2}{U_y^1}U_x^1 - \frac{U_y^2}{g_y}g_x = 0 \tag{17-46}$$

Dividing through by U_y^2 yields

$$\frac{U_x^2}{U_y^2} + \frac{U_x^1}{U_y^1} = \frac{g_x}{g_y} \tag{17-47}$$

Equation (17-47) admits of an interesting interpretation. U_x^1/U_y^1 and U_x^2/U_y^2 are, respectively, the marginal rates of substitutions, or the marginal evaluations, of the public good x. The expression g_x/g_y is the marginal rate of transformation of y into x or the marginal cost of the public good in terms of private good forgone. Since both consumers consume the *total* amount of x produced, the marginal benefits to society of the public good are the *sum* of each consumer's marginal benefits. Equation (17-47) therefore says that when the Pareto frontier is achieved, the total consumers' marginal benefits equal marginal cost. The usual reasoning of equating benefits and costs at the margin is preserved. The rule is adapted for goods with the characteristic of joint consumption.

Equation (17-47) says that to find the market demand curve for a public good, the individual demand curves are to be added *vertically,* as shown in Fig. 17-6. The market demand for ordinary goods is, of course, the *horizontal* sum of individual demands, because each consumer consumes a part of the total. For public goods, each consumer jointly consumes the total. The height of the individual demand curves, D^1 and D^2 in Fig. 17-6, are the marginal evaluations of the public good x.[†] The curve D^T is the vertical sum of D^1 and D^2, representing the benefits of x at the margin to both consumers jointly. The quantity x^* where D^T intersects the marginal cost curve of producing x is the point which satisfies the Pareto conditions for production of a public good.

The preceding analysis generalizes in a straightforward manner to the case of K consumers. In that case, the Pareto conditions for public good production become

$$\sum_{i=1}^{K} \text{MRS}^i = \text{MC} \qquad (17\text{-}48)$$

The problem of private production of public goods is that the ordinary market transactions are not likely to yield the Pareto allocation. In order to arrive at production of x at the level x^* where $\sum \text{MRS} = \text{MC}$, each consumer's differing marginal evaluations would have to be known. However, consumers will have no occasion to reveal these preferences. With private goods, consumers reveal their preferences by their choices in the market, purchasing additional units of a good until the marginal evaluation falls to the market price. There is no comparable mechanism for public goods. Each consumer consumes the total amount produced, and each has in general a different marginal evaluation of that good. Moreover, since the good is to be dispersed in total, it will pay consumers to understate their evaluation of the benefits of the good, lest the government attempt to allocate the good on the basis of fees based on each consumer's personal evaluations of benefits. Lastly, a fee charged for per unit use of the public good will result in "too little" consumption of the good. Consider the case of an uncrowded bridge. When a toll is charged, consumers will not cross the bridge if their marginal evaluation of the benefits is greater than 0 but less than the toll. But since the resource cost to society for the consumer's use of the bridge

---

[†] The income being held constant in these demand curves is the total value of x and y given by the transformation surface $g(x, y) = 0$.

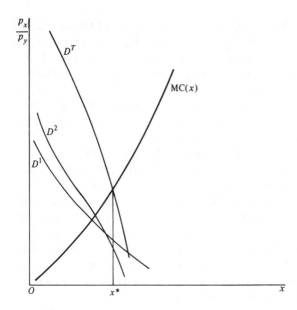

FIGURE 17-6
Market demand for public good. If D^1 and D^2 are the two individual demand curves for the public good, the total demand D^T is the *vertical* sum of D^1 and D^2. That is, D^T represents the sum of each consumer's marginal evaluation of the public good. This vertical summation occurs because both consumers consume the total quantity of public good produced. The output x^* at which D^T intersects the marginal cost curve for producing x yields consumption on the Pareto frontier.

is 0, the ideal Pareto optimum cannot be achieved. Thus, the ordinary contracting in the marketplace for public goods production is not likely to lead to an efficient allocation of resources in terms of the Pareto ideal.

17.7 CONSUMER'S SURPLUS AS A MEASURE OF WELFARE GAINS AND LOSSES

We have previously investigated the problems associated with defining, in units of money income, the gains from trade. One of the most prominent uses of these measures is the evaluation of costs and benefits of alternative tax schemes or the benefits of public-good production. Let us briefly recapitulate these issues and apply the analysis to the problem of public good production.

Since the publication of Marshall's *Principles,* economists have attempted to measure the benefits of consumption by some sort of calculation based on the area beneath a consumer's demand curve. In Fig. 17-7, the height of the consumer's demand curve at each point represents the consumer's marginal evaluation of the good in terms of other goods forgone, measured in terms of money. It is therefore tempting to integrate, or add up, these marginal gains to arrive at the total gain received from consuming some positive level of the good rather than none at all. However, we have seen in Chap. 11 that this is not possible. If the demand curve in Fig. 17-7 is a Hicksian, or *utility-held-constant* demand curve, the area *OACD* represents the maximum dollar amount a consumer would pay to have *OD* units of x rather than none at all. It likewise follows that for these demand curves, *ABC* represents the maximum amount a consumer would pay for the *right* to consume x at unit price *OB*. If the license fee is actually paid, *OD* will be purchased

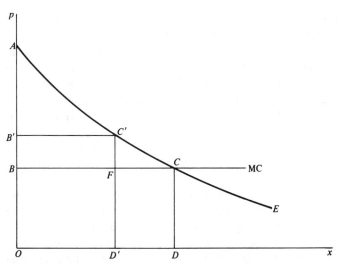

FIGURE 17-7
The attempt to measure welfare losses by consumer's surplus. The analysis of welfare losses is an attempt to have a money measure of the loss in utility incurred from selling commodities at prices other than marginal cost. Let OB = MC of x, and suppose $OD' = B'C'$ of x is sold at OB'. The traditional analysis asserts that the benefits from consuming OD is the trapezoidal area $OACD$. At price OB', total benefits are supposed to be $OAC'D'$. The difference, $D'C'CD$, is partitioned into $FC'C$ and $D'FCD$. The latter area is an amount of income spent on other commodities, presumed to be sold at marginal cost. The remaining area $FC'C$ is called *deadweight loss,* a money measure of the loss due to the price distortion BB'. This distortion is commonly attributed to excise taxation or monopolistic sale of x. If AE is a *real-income,* or *utility-held-constant,* demand curve, then although these areas represent well-defined measures of willingness to pay to face different prices, since these measures hold utility *constant,* they cannot very well measure utility *changes.*

and the consumer will remain on the same indifference level before and after the purchase, by definition of ABC as the *maximum* license fee the consumer would pay. This measure has the desirable property of being well defined and at least in principle observable.

If, on the other hand, the demand curve in Fig. 17-7 is a *money-income*-held-constant demand curve, the area ABC does *not* represent an observable quantity. The monetary value of gain in utility associated with the terminal prices OA and OB is generated by a line integral which is generally path dependent; different adjustments of prices leading to the same initial and final price income vectors will generally lead to different monetary evaluations of the consumer's gain in utility. This is an inescapable index number problem for nonhomothetic utility functions. Only in the case of homothetic utility functions are changes in utility proportional to changes in income for any set of initial prices.

The quantity OD is special in the sense that the marginal benefits to consumers from x exactly equal the consumer's evaluation of the resources used to produce x in producing something else—the marginal opportunity cost of x. If there are no "distortions" of prices from marginal costs elsewhere in the economy, this occurrence is part of the Pareto conditions. However, if there are other goods whose prices differ from MC so that such efficient consumption levels do not occur, then, again, it is not possible to conclude that selling this good x at MC will lead the economy closer to the Pareto frontier. In general, if one good is sold at some price other than MC, say due to an excise tax on that good, then the set of excise taxes $(t_1, \ldots, t_n)$ on the n commodities in the economy which will lead to the Pareto frontier will not consist of zero tax rates on the other commodities, nor will they all necessarily be proportional to their respective marginal costs. The specification of such an optimal set of taxes $(t_1^*, \ldots, t_n^*)$, which leads the economy to the Pareto frontier for given deviations from MC of certain goods or for the purpose of financing government services, is too protracted a discussion to consider here.

Following the early French economist Dupuit, and stimulated greatly by Marshall's discussion of consumer's surplus, the monetary evaluation of the welfare loss associated with consuming OD' instead of OD units of x is usually given as the triangular area $FC'C$, in Fig. 17-7. The total benefits of consuming x are reduced by the trapezoidal area $D'C'CD$. However, the rectangular area $D'FCD$ represents income spent on other goods, *presumably at the marginal cost of those other goods,* eliminating this area as a part of welfare loss. The only remaining deadweight loss of the sale of x at price $OB' > $ MC is the area $FC'C$. Summing these areas over all commodities is commonly used to measure the welfare loss associated with a set of departures of price from marginal cost.

The compensating variation

$$M^*(\mathbf{p}, u) = -\int_{p_i + t_i}^{p_i} \sum x_i(\mathbf{p}, U) dp_i \qquad (17\text{-}49)$$

represents the amount of money income *the consumer would be willing to pay* to face the prices p_i instead of $p_i + t_i$, $i = 1, \ldots, n$. (If some $t_i < 0$ and $M^* < 0$, M^* represents the amount a consumer *would have to be paid* to accept $p_i + t_i$ voluntarily instead of p_i, $i = 1, \ldots, n$.) The problem of using M^* as a measure of the benefits from increased utility is that M^* *depends only on one indifference level.* Utility is held constant in the integral (17-49). This may lead to inappropriate welfare rankings.

In Fig. 17-8, we set $p_y = 1$ arbitrarily. Since the vertical intercepts are $M/p_y = M$ in this case, changes in income can be read directly off the vertical axis. The consumer initially faces price p_x for x, producing the budget line emanating from A, with income OA. From the graph, the consumer is willing to pay an amount AB to have the price of x reduced to p_x' and willing to pay AC to have the price of x reduced to p_x''. Suppose $AB = \$10$ and $AC = \$20$. Suppose the consumer is actually going to have to pay $\$5$ (AB') to have p_x reduced to p_x' or is actually going to pay $\$14$ (AC') to have p_x reduced to p_x''. Suppose AB' and AC' represent the cost of two alternative, mutually exclusive public works projects. Are these data sufficient to evaluate these projects in terms of answering which will place this consumer on a higher indifference level? Although the gain measured by the compensating variation minus the cost is greater for the second project, one *cannot* conclude that the consumer would be better off with it. With the first project, lowering p_x to p'_x, the consumer will wind up at some point P' on the budget line emanating from B' with slope p'_x. For the second project, the consumer will be at some point P'' on the budget line emanating from C' with slope p''_x. Now within a broad range of price changes, there is no way to determine whether P' is more preferred or less preferred than P''. The reason is that nothing has been said of the properties of this consumer's utility function other than the one indifference curve $U = U^0$ from which all the compensating variations are derived. One must therefore conclude that integrals of the form (17-49) may not be reliable measures of gains from trade; they hold utility constant throughout.

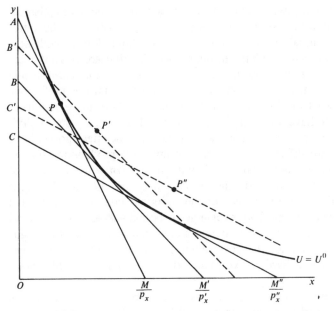

FIGURE 17-8
Measuring gains from trade by compensating variations in income. The consumer has income M and faces prices p_x, $p_y = 1$. Money income is therefore measurable as distances along the vertical axis since the budget line intercepts that axis at $M/p_y = M$. At price p_x, the consumer consumes at point P on utility level U^0. The consumer is willing, according to this diagram, to pay amounts AB, AC to face the lower prices p'_x, p''_x, respectively. Suppose the consumer only *has* to pay AB', AC' to face those lower prices. Suppose the differences between what the consumer is *willing* to pay and what is actually paid, that is, BB' and CC', are not equal; e.g., suppose $BB' < CC'$. Can one infer that the second situation leaves the consumer on a higher indifference curve? Alas, no. For the first case, the consumer faces price p'_x with income OB', winding up at some point P'. In the second situation, the consumer faces price p''_x and income OC', winding up at some point P''. There is no way in general to tell which if either of P' and P'' is on a higher indifference level. The only indifference curve specified is $U = U^0$; no information is provided (except convexity) about where preferred indifference levels lie. Hence, the differences between compensating variations and actual costs of, say, two mutually exclusive projects may be unreliable measures of their ultimate benefits for consumers.

17.8 PROPERTY RIGHTS AND TRANSACTIONS COSTS

The analysis of the Pareto conditions for economic efficiency has been presented in the absence of any institutional framework. We have assumed that production, exchange, and consumption take place without conflict. In actuality, production and exchange based on mutual benefit is not a universally admired principle; in many parts of the world such activities are severely proscribed by government edict. No society allows literally any mutually advantageous trade; but more importantly, the ability, or *cost* of engaging in trade can vary substantially from good to good, and from nation to nation. The extent to which trade takes place depends on the rights individuals have over the use of resources and the costs of exchange.

Robinson Crusoe will always achieve an efficient outcome given his preferences; he maximizes utility subject to his production constraint. The introduction of another individual, Friday, presents Crusoe (and Friday) with several more "margins" to consider. Gains through specialization are possible, but specialization requires agreement as to the terms of trade, and *enforcement* of the contract: Trade almost always involves "asymmetric information"; one usually knows better what one is giving up than what is about to be received. Crusoe and Friday will have to worry a bit about whether the other individual is living up to the terms of the contract. In modern societies, goods have many dimensions and are difficult to measure completely; production and exchange may involve many individuals, each with their own self-interest, and intruders, who would steal some of the goods, may be present. Whereas it is probably a useful first step to lay out the marginal conditions that must be satisfied in order for all gains from exchange to be exhausted, the empirical realization of such gains is subject to a society's laws and institutions that regulate commerce, and the transactions costs attendant upon production and exchange. Specialization could hardly take place, if, for example, stealing were rampant.

In recent years economists have taken renewed interest in the relationships between property rights and economic activity. While the Pareto conditions are generally unobservable, it is possible to show that certain institutions, or lack thereof, would make the achievement of the Pareto frontier very unlikely. The study of transactions costs, and how the structure of contracts changes to accommodate the realization of gains from trade under varying constraints, is an important new area of economics. Transactions costs are not the same as, say, a tax, which can be analyzed in the usual way by shifting a supply curve by the amount of the tax. Transactions costs are the lost gains from trade, due to imperfect monitoring of exchange, caused by the uncertainty of receiving what is bargained for. As yet, the subject has largely eluded successful mathematical analysis.[†]

[†] Analyses that begin with "Let t be transactions costs . . . " are doomed to failure.

A resource is "private" if it has three essential attributes:[†]

1. *Exclusivity*—an individual has the right to exclude others from use.
2. *Ownership of income*—an individual may derive (and keep) the income produced by the resource.
3. *Transferability*—an individual may transfer the resource to others at some mutually agreed upon price.

In modern societies, these rights may be varyingly enforced (and attenuated) by the government. These rights are almost never complete. Most land in the United States not held by the government is private in the preceding sense, but, for example, use and transferability may be restricted by zoning laws, rights to remove underground minerals may be restricted, etc. When the American west was settled in the nineteenth century, the "homestead acts" gave land title to individuals, but those individuals had to work that land themselves, and could not resell the land, usually for about 10 years. Pollution from a factory is an attenuation of our right to breathe fresh air; rowdy neighbors infringe on our ability to enjoy the income produced by our homes, thus reducing the degree to which our homes are "private." Economic activity varies in important ways as the enforcement of private property varies.

An important polar case occurs when the right to exclude is completely absent. In that case, no one owns the resource; it is called "common property." A prominent instance is provided by deep-sea fishing. Outside a country's territorial limits, varying from 3 to 200 miles offshore, unless covered by specific treaty, ocean resources, and specifically fish, are often not subject to effective ownership. Even when treaties are present, the ability to police limits on catches of fish in, say, the Pacific Ocean may be severely limited. In some countries, private land ownership is severely restricted or forbidden. In such cases we can usually predict the resource will be utilized beyond the level implied by the Pareto conditions.

Suppose the daily production of food takes place by combining labor, L, and land, K, according to some well-behaved production function $y = f(L,K)$; output y is sold competitively at price p. In Fig. 17-9, the (value of the) marginal and average product curves of labor are shown. Assume workers are available at daily wage w, and that this wage represents the opportunity cost of labor in food production. That is, workers could produce nonagricultural output valued at w per day; for each worker in agriculture, nonagricultural output in the amount w is foregone per day.

[†]This categorization of private property, to my knowledge, was first developed by Steven N. S. Cheung, in "A Theory of Price Control," *Journal of Law and Economics,* **17**(1): 53–72, April 1974. It is similar to the analysis presented in the first edition of Armen Alchian and William Allen's *Exchange and Production,* Wadsworth, 1964.

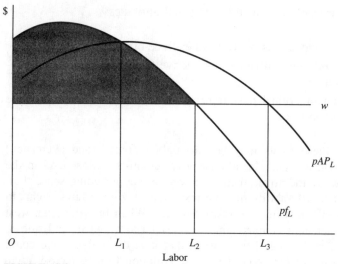

FIGURE 17-9

Allocation of resources under private and common property. Faced with an opportunity cost of labor of w, a private owner of some resource, say land, will hire L_2 workers, where $pf_L = w$. This is an efficient allocation since the marginal value of goods produced in this firm equals the marginal value of labor elsewhere; no reallocation of labor could increase output. Under common property, workers crowd onto the land until *their* own return, which includes some share of the rents on the land, equals their opportunity cost elsewhere. Under this system, L_3 workers, where $pAP_L = w$ will work the land. This is an inefficient allocation since workers add only pf_L on the farm, less than their opportunity cost elsewhere.

Consider now two "stylized" systems of property rights.

PRIVATE PROPERTY. Suppose a fixed plot of land is privately owned by an individual. A private owner maximizes the rents on the land, i.e.,

maximize
  L

$$R = pf(L, K) - wL$$

The first-order conditions for rent maximization are

$$pf_L = w$$

or input L_2 in Fig. 17-9. Since the area under the marginal product schedule is total product, the shaded area under pf_L and over the wage line w represents the maximum daily rent on the land.

The important aspect of this outcome is that the Pareto conditions are satisfied: the gains from trade are exhausted. For labor inputs $0 \le L \le L_2, pf_L \ge w$, thus the additional agricultural output generated exceeds the output lost in the other sector of the economy. Beyond L_2, the forgone nonagricultural output exceeds what the economy is getting in the way of food. No further mutual benefits can be realized by applying more workers to the land. The "invisible hand" is working: private ownership leads to the greatest output gain to society, though the owner of this land neither knows nor intends that outcome.

COMMON PROPERTY. Suppose now access to the land is unrestricted: anyone can become a "squatter" on the land. For example, suppose agriculture is organized into "communes," with unrestricted entry. Anyone can join the commune and share equally in the output produced.[†] Since workers share equally in output, each receives the value of *average product*. In making their choice as to whether to join the commune, workers compare their alternative earnings, w, with their average product on the farm. At labor input levels less than L_3, workers earn more on the farm. This extra income derives from ownership of the land rents acquired when workers join the commune. With unrestricted entry, however, the rent on the land is *nonexclusive income*. Workers will compete with each other for ownership of this income, until, at the margin, it no longer exists (or exceeds the cost of acquiring it). In this example, workers will continue to join the commune until the marginal gain from joining (the average product), equals their alternative earnings, w. When $pAP_L = w$, total product $= wL =$ total factor cost. The rents are *dissipated*.

This outcome is inefficient, i.e., further gains from trade are possible. At labor inputs greater than L_2, the marginal contribution to output when workers engage in farming, pf_L, is less than what workers could produce elsewhere, w. Resources are being directed to activities that lower, rather than increase, total output. If these extra workers could be induced to leave the farm, the resulting increment in output could in principle be shared, making everyone better off.[‡] Nothing in the preceding argument depends on exhaustion of the land, as might especially be the case with ocean fish (though the problem exists with land also). In the case of deep sea fishing, for example, preservation of the stock of fish for future harvest is an important margin. Increasing the catch this year may reduce the future stock of fish, raising the marginal cost of catching fish in the future. This is a separate and important issue. Under common property, valuable species may be depleted, perhaps to extinction, because no individual owns the right to any *future* income derived from preserving the resource. In that case, wealth maximization leads to shifting consumption to the present to a level where consumers' marginal value of present consumption of that good is less than its opportunity cost, in terms of the present value of future consumption forgone.

Freeway congestion is another common property problem. As was shown in Chap. 8 (Sec. 8.4), with no restrictions on access, cars enter the freeway until the average time cost equals the marginal (and average, if the "bad" roads are

---

[†] We ignore the problem of "shirking," which is perhaps the main reason this type of firm is not prevalent.

[‡] Other types of legal ownership can lead to different misallocations. For example, "socialist cooperative" firms, in which workers currently employed decide the labor input, and share, say, equally in the output, will maximize average product, (at L_1 in Fig. 17-9), leading to *too little* agriculture production.

never congested) cost on the sidestreets. However, each car slows all the others; thus the sum of marginal time costs to all drivers will exceed the gain to any one driver who enters the freeway. As drivers compete for the rents received by access to the freeway (in terms of time saved), those rents are dissipated as all traffic slows down. Resources would be saved if some cars took the sidestreets. Under private ownership, a toll will be charged leading to the efficient outcome; under common property, the freeway is "overutilized."

Price controls typically create nonexclusive income. Suppose the market price of gasoline would be $1.50 per gallon, but, in an attempt to transfer rents to consumers, the government fixes the price at $1.00. If gas tanks hold 10 gallons, say, the price control would grant each driver a gift of $5.00 per fill-up. However, this income is nonexclusive; it can be acquired only by the act of filling up one's gas tank. Car owners will compete for this gift. Though the exact form this competition will take depends upon the additional legal and economic restrictions attendant on the price control, the typical response, such as occurred in the 1970s (apart from some minor violence), is for drivers to compete by waiting in line for purchase. In so doing, the $5.00 gain is at least partially dissipated by having to forego alternative, utility-increasing activities (including, perhaps, leisure). If consumers have identical alternative costs of time, given, say, by a marginal wage rate of $5.00 per hour, the line will be 1 hour long, and the rent will be completely dissipated. The dissipation can be prevented by the issuance of freely tradeable ration coupons; in that case, the price of gasoline would again be $1.50, $1.00 in cash plus $.50 foregone by not selling the coupon to someone else. By giving exclusive title to the $.50 gain, the rents can actually be transferred to consumers.[†]

The Coase Theorem

The first systematic discussion of the role of transaction costs in relation to the allocation of resources was Ronald Coase's pathbreaking article, "The Problem of Social Cost."[‡] The context of the misallocations were various "technological externalities"—the situation where production of one good was, in this case, a negative input in the production of some other good. The example first cited was the historically important case of straying cattle: a rancher-producer raises cattle who invariably trample some of a neighboring farmer's crop.

The classical welfare economic treatment of this problem, in the tradition of A. C. Pigou, took place as follows. Consider Fig. 17-10. The marginal private cost of cattle, disregarding the trampled crops, is labeled MC^p. This curve describes all the usual forgone opportunities of production, expressed in terms of

---

[†] A less expensive procedure, however, is to simply tax the gasoline $.50 per gallon, and return the receipts to consumers through some lump-sum tax not related to consumers' own purchases.

[‡] Ronald Coase, "The Problem of Social Cost," *Journal of Law and Economics,* pp. 1–44, October 1960.

costs of feed, land, shelter, fences, etc. However, an additional cost of production is also incurred by society. Each additional steer raised tramples some crops, lowering output of the adjacent farmer. With this damage treated as a cost of producing cattle, a marginal social cost curve MC^s is drawn, the difference $MC^s(x) - MC^p(x)$ being the marginal damage to the farmer's crops.

Suppose the price of cattle is OA. Traditional (Pigovian) welfare analysis held that unless the rancher were somehow made liable for the crop damage, the rancher would have no occasion to consider marginal *social* costs; cattle would be produced in the amount x^p, where $p = MC^p$. There would be a misallocation of resources in that too many cattle (and too little food) would be produced. The marginal conditions for Pareto optimality require that output x^s, where $p = MC^s$, be produced, since MC^s represents the actual marginal cost function for producing cattle.

If x^p is produced, the total private cost is the area OCx^p, the total damage to crops is the area between the two marginal cost curves OEC, and thus the total cost of production is the area OEx^p. At this level of output, resources are misallocated: at output greater than x^s, the marginal opportunity cost of producing cattle is greater than the marginal benefits to consumers, measured by the price

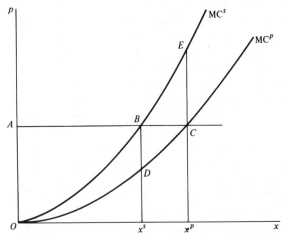

FIGURE 17-10

Private and social marginal costs. Diagrams of this type have been used to indicate the difference between social and private costs. The curve MC^p misspecifies the marginal cost of producing cattle in the present example by excluding the cost of destroyed crops. The marginal destruction of crops, the side effect, or externality, is represented by the vertical difference between MC^s, social, i.e., actual marginal cost, and MC^p. It was formerly alleged that if the rancher was not legally liable for damaged crops, x^p would be produced. This analysis never came to grips with why individual maximizers would not reach the contract curve. In order to analyze where production will take place, the cost of contracting, i.e., the constraints on the rancher and farmer, must be specified. If these transactions costs are 0, the rancher and farmer are essentially one person. They will never allow x^p to be produced instead of x^s since the additional net profits gained BCD are less than the crop damage $BECD$. If the rancher is not liable for damage done to crops, the farmer will contract to pay the rancher more than BCD (but less than $BECD$) for the rancher to produce x^s instead of x^p. Since both parties will gain, such a contract is implied.

OA. Producing x^p instead of x^s results in a deadweight loss in the amount of BEC.

Coase's contribution was to point out that the preceding argument could be valid only if the rancher and the farmer were somehow prevented from further contracting with each other. A misallocation of resources means that some mutual gains from trade or transacting are being lost. *If* the cost of transacting is 0 (and no specific mention of transactions costs was presented), it cannot be that individual maximizers would arrive at some point *off* the contract curve. It would be a denial that more is preferred to less for two people to agree to a non-Pareto allocation or misallocation, of resources.

The assignment of legal liability for the wandering cattle constitutes a specification of *endowments* only. Any rancher who does not have to pay damages for trampled crops will be wealthier. It is an expansion of the rancher's property rights and an attenuation of the farmer's property rights. Likewise, a court ruling that the rancher *is* liable for crop damage is a transfer of assets only, from the rancher to the farmer, not a change in production possibilities or preferences. There is no reason why a change in endowments should foreclose a movement to the contract curve, i.e., the Pareto frontier. The classical theorems of welfare economics indicate that individuals will move to the contract curve irrespective of where the endowment point is placed in the Edgeworth box.

The error of assuming a non-Pareto solution hinged upon a failure to consider the range of contracting possibilities available to individuals, e.g., the rancher and farmer in the preceding case. If the rancher is liable for crop damage, no further contracting is necessary; the state enforces the contract that the rancher pay the farmer for damage. If the rancher is *not* liable, however, there are still options to consider. The farmer can contract with the rancher to reduce cattle production for some fee. Consider Fig. 17-10. The damage to the farmer's crops caused by producing x^p instead of x^s is the area $DBEC$. However, the net profit to the rancher derived from this extra production is only part of that area, DBC. Since the damage to the farmer is greater by the amount BEC than the gain to the rancher from producing x^p instead of x^s, the farmer will be able to offer the rancher more than DBC, the rancher's gain, but less than $DBEC$ to induce the rancher to reduce production to x^s. With no transactions cost, this contract is implied, since both the farmer and the rancher are better off. At any level of production beyond x^s, the damages to the farmer exceed the incremental gains to the rancher; both parties will gain by a contract wherein the farmer pays the rancher something in between these two amounts to reduce cattle production to x^s.

If transactions costs are not 0, forgone gains from trade may exist. To point this out, however, is to only begin the problem. The parties involved still have an incentive to consider various contracts to extract some of the mutual benefits. Different contracts have different negotiation and enforcement costs associated with them. Merger or outright purchase of one firm by another can be used to internalize side effects such as trampled crops. With merger or outright purchase, the rancher will produce x^s cattle, since it will now be the rancher's crops that are being trampled. We should expect to see individuals devising contracts that lead to the greatest extraction of mutual gains from exchange. In fact, this hypothesis is the basis for an emerging theory of contracts, based on maximizing behavior.[†]

The Theory of Share Tenancy: An Application of the Coase Theorem

Perhaps the first empirical application of Coase's analysis was the analysis of sharecropping by Steven N. S. Cheung.[‡] Sharecropping is a form of rent payment in agriculture in which the landlord takes some share of the output, specified in advance, instead of a fixed amount, as payment for the use of the land (rent). This form of contract is somehow less enthusiastically regarded by many social reformers than the fixed-rent contract.

Sharecropping as a contractual form of rent payment came under attack by various economists on the grounds that it misallocated resources relative to the fixed-rent contract. In its neoclassical formulation, the rental share paid to the landlord was regarded as equivalent to an excise tax on the sharecropper's efforts, inducing sharecroppers to reduce output below the level where the marginal value product of the sharecropper equaled their alternative wage.

Consider Fig. 17-11. The top curve is the marginal product of labor. Under a fixed-rent or fixed-wage contract, labor input L_2 would be hired, where the marginal product of labor equals its alternative wage OM. Suppose, however, the tenant has contracted to pay r percent of the output to the landlord as payment for rent. Then the lower curve $(1 - r)\text{MP}_L$ represents the tenant's marginal product curve net of rental payments. It is tempting to conclude that the tenant, under these conditions, will produce at input level L_1, an inefficient point since there the true marginal product of labor is higher than its next best use, measured by the wage line w.[§]

The argument is correct up to this point. A *tax* on labor of r percent of the tenant's output would indeed lead the tenant to produce at L_1. The mistake is

---

[†] Coase also showed that when transactions costs were not 0, it is not possible to deduce a priori which assignment of liability would reduce misallocation more. Consider the famous case of a railroad that occasionally sets fire to fields adjacent to the tracks because of sparks from the locomotive. If the railroad is made liable for all damage, the farmers lose an incentive to reduce the damage by not planting flammable crops too close to the tracks. The land close to the tracks may have as its highest value use a repository for sparks. On the other hand, if the railroad is not liable, it may run too many trains, i.e., produce beyond where $\text{MC}^s = p$. One form of contract which may emerge is for the railroad to purchase land near the tracks, eliminating most, if not all, of the problems.

[‡] Steven N. S. Cheung, *The Theory of Share Tenancy*, University of Chicago Press, Chicago, 1969.

[§] Curiously enough, much social criticism of sharecropping appears to be based upon the landlord's working his tenants to an undue degree, perhaps, as we shall see, a more astute observation than the above economic argument.

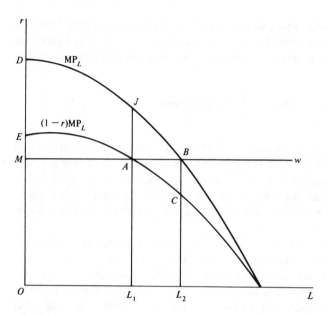

FIGURE 17-11

The tax-equivalent approach to sharecropping. This diagram has been used to show that sharecropping is an inefficient contract. Using a tax analogy, if MP_L is the marginal product of labor, and if r percent of the tenant's output is collected as rent, the net marginal product to the tenant is $(1 - r)MP_L$. With such a tax, the tenant would produce at L_1, where the actual marginal benefits MP_L exceed the opportunity cost of labor measured by its wage OM. This argument, while correct with regard to an excise tax on labor, cannot easily be extended to the case of sharecropping. In a share *contract*, many more variables are specified than the share itself. Farm size, nonlabor inputs in general, and labor inputs are negotiable. Under the postulate that the landlord maximizes the rent on the land subject to the constraint of competing for labor at labor's alternative cost, the Pareto condition $MP_L = w$ is implied. (From S.N.S. Cheung, *The Theory of Share Tenancy,* University of Chicago Press, Chicago, 1969, p. 43.

to apply this tax analysis to sharecropping, a situation in which a landlord and tenant voluntarily *contract* with each other. Again, the fundamental issue raised by Coase is invoked: Why would utility maximizers get together and *not* exhaust the gains from trade? If L_1 instead of L_2 is used, the total output lost is L_1JBL_2, whereas the alternative cost to society of this labor differential, $L_2 - L_1$, is L_1ABL_2. Hence, mutual gains *JAB* are lost. Why should the landlord be willing to forgo this additional rental value on the land?

Applying the tax analysis to sharecropping amounts to assuming that the only variable that can be specified is the rental share or the wage rate. A contract, however, need not contain only one clause. It is possible to specify more than one variable in a contract. (Indeed, why else would contracts exist?) Even in the normal wage contract, often an informal agreement between employer and employee, the hourly wage is not the only thing specified. The employer expects the employee to show up on time, work a certain number of hours at some minimum level of intensity, etc. If only the wage were specified, maximizing behavior indicates that workers would show up and do no work at all. Real-world share contracts specify such things as amount of land to be cultivated, nonlabor inputs to be supplied by the tenant, "the droppings [of water buffalo] go to the [landowner's] soil," etc.[†] Under these conditions, the tax analysis is simply inapplicable. The test conditions of the experiment are entirely different.

That sharecropping as a contractual form is consistent with the Pareto conditions is shown by the following argument. Suppose the landlord owns an amount of land (capital) K. Labor is available at wage rate w, representing the alternative value of labor. The landlord can subdivide his land into m tenant farms, *where m is a choice variable*. Similarly, *the rental share r going to the landlord is not fixed but is also a choice variable*. Let the amount of labor supplied to each tenant farm be L. The amount of land supplied to each farm is $k = K/m$. The tenant's production function can therefore be written

$$y = f(L,k) = f\left(L, \frac{K}{m}\right)$$

The landlord will seek to maximize the rent on the land, $R = mry$. However, this is not an unconstrained maximization. Landlords must compete for tenants. Under this constraint of competition, the wage share to the tenant cannot be lower than the tenant's alternative earnings in wage labor. The model thus becomes

maximize
m, r, L
$$R = mrf(L,k)$$

subject to
$$wL = (1 - r)f(L,k) \tag{17-50}$$

From the constraint,
$$rf(L,k) = f(L,k) - wL$$

Hence, the problem can be posed in the unconstrained form when the variable r has been eliminated:

maximize
m, L
$$R = m[f(L,k) - wL] \tag{17-51}$$

Differentiating and remembering that $k = K/m$, we have

$$\frac{\partial R}{\partial m} = m\frac{\partial f}{\partial k}\left(-\frac{K}{m^2}\right) + [f(L,k) - wL] = 0 \tag{17-52a}$$

$$\frac{\partial R}{\partial L} = m\frac{\partial f}{\partial L} - mw = 0 \tag{17-52b}$$

[†] Cheung, op. cit.

From Eq. (17-52b), we immediately see that the landlord will contract with the tenant so as to set the (value of the) marginal product of labor equal to the alternative cost of labor. Thus, the labor input in Fig. 17-11 will be L_2, *not* L_1. The Pareto conditions will be satisfied. Substituting $w = \partial f/\partial L$ into Eq. (17-52a) and rearranging leads to

$$\frac{\partial f}{\partial k}k + \frac{\partial f}{\partial L}L = f(L,k) \tag{17-53}$$

Equation (17-53) is a statement of product exhaustion (*not* the Euler expression, which is an *identity*). The imputed value of land (capital) measured by its marginal product times the land input plus the same expression for labor equals the total output of the farm.

The share of output going to the landlord, $rf(L,k)$, from the original constraint in (17-50) and (17-53),

$$rf(L,k) = f(L,k) - \frac{\partial f}{\partial L}L = \frac{\partial f}{\partial k}k \tag{17-54}$$

The landlord's share is precisely the imputed land value of the farm. In Fig. 17-11 this is the area *MDB*. *When r is chosen so as to maximize the rent of the land,* the landlord's share is also represented by the area *EDBC = MDB*. However, *EDBC* is not the landlord's share for *any* arbitrary r, only for the rent-maximizing r. This rent-maximizing share, from (17-54), is

$$r^* = \frac{f_k k}{y}$$

This share is not determined by custom or tradition; it is a *contracted* amount. It varies with the fertility of the land, the cost of labor, and other variables specified in the share contract.

Showing that sharecropping is consistent with the Pareto conditions, however, is to merely state a normative condition. The interesting question of *positive* economic analysis is why the form of contract varies, i.e., why is it sometimes a fixed rent and other times a share contract? The reader is referred to Cheung for detailed answers to this question. We shall merely indicate here that some answers lie in the area of contracting cost and risk aversion. Share contracting is likely to be a more costly contract to enforce. However, to cite one example from agriculture, if the variance in output, due, say, to weather, is high, the landlord and tenant may *share the risk* of uncertain output by using a share contract. Indeed, empirical evidence from Taiwan indicates that share contracting is more prevalent in wheat than rice farming, wheat having a much higher coefficient of variation of output than rice. Other tests of these hypotheses are available.

It is generally uninteresting merely to pronounce some economic activity inefficient. The normative statements of welfare analysis are perhaps most useful if they are used to investigate why it is that certain ideal marginal conditions are being violated. The analysis then becomes positive rather than normative. Instead of labeling certain actions as irrational or inefficient, one asserts that the participants will seek to contract with each other to further exhaust the mutual gains from trade and one derives refutable propositions therefrom.

PROBLEMS

1. Explain why it is nonsense to seek the greatest good for the greatest number of people.
2. Suppose two consumers have the utility functions $U^1 = x_1^{1/3} y_1^{2/3}$, $U^2 = x_2^{2/3} y_2^{1/3}$. Suppose $x = x_1 + x_2$, $y = y_1 + y_2$ represent the total amount of goods available. Find the equation representing the contract curve for these consumers.
3. Suppose there are two goods, x and y, which are *both* public goods. There are two individuals whose entire consumption is made up of these two goods. There is a production possibilities frontier given by $g(x, y) = 0$. Find the marginal conditions for production levels of x and y which satisfy the Pareto conditions.
4. Suppose all firms except one in an economy are perfect competitors, the remaining firm being a perfectly discriminating monopolist. Explain why the Pareto conditions will still be satisfied. What differences in allocation and distribution of income result from that firm's not being a perfect competitor also?
5. Two farmers, A and B, live 8 and 12 miles, respectively, from a river and are separated by 15 miles along the river. The river is their only source of water. Pumphouses cost P dollars each and must be located on the river. Laying pipe costs $100 per mile. Once the pipe is laid and pumphouses installed, the water is available at no extra cost.
   (a) Do farmers have an incentive to minimize the total (to both farmers) cost of obtaining water?
   (b) If one pumphouse is used to supply both farmers, show that it will be located 6 miles from the point on the river closest to farm A. (Use either calculus or similar triangles). What will the cost of water be for each farmer and totally in terms of P?
   (c) Suppose the farmers build their own pumps. What will the cost to each be and the total cost?
   (d) Show that in a certain range of pumphouse costs, one farmer will induce the other to share a pumphouse if transactions costs are low enough. (Assume for simplicity that pumphouse cost is shared equally. Then relax that assumption.)
6. Explain why the utility frontier must be downward-sloping and why it is not necessarily concave to the origin on the basis of the elementary properties of utility functions.
7. "Interdependencies in individuals' utility functions or in production functions will lead to non-Pareto allocations of resources." Evaluate.
8. The cases where markets allocate resources less efficiently than the Pareto ideal is often called *market failure*.
   (a) Why isn't the case where governments allocate resources less than the Pareto ideal called *government failure?*
   (b) Under what conditions will there be market failure?
   (c) Suppose, to cite a famous example, that in a certain region there is apple growing and beekeeping and that bees feed on apple blossoms. If the apple farmers increase their production of apples, they will allegedly increase honey production. The apple farmers acting alone will not, it is said, perceive the true marginal product of apple trees and hence will misallocate resources. Devise a model for this problem.

Would the existence of actual contracts between beekeepers and apple farmers affect your conclusions as to whether market failure is a necessary consequence of production externalities, or interdependencies?

BIBLIOGRAPHY

Arrow, K. J.: "An Extension of the Basic Theorems of Classical Welfare Economics," in J. Neyman (ed.), *Proceedings of the Second Berkeley Symposium on Mathematical Statistics and Probability*, University of California Press, Berkeley, 1951.

— — —: *Social Choice and Individual Values*, 2d ed., Cowles Foundation Monograph 12, John Wiley & Sons, Inc., New York, 1963.

Bator, F.: "The Simple Analytics of Welfare Maximization," *American Economic Review*, **47**:22–59, 1957.

— — —: "The Anatomy of Market Failure," *Quarterly Journal of Economics*, **72**:351–379, 1958.

Bergson, A.: "A Reformulation of Certain Aspects of Welfare Economics," *Quarterly Journal of Economics*, **52**:310–334, February 1938; reprinted in K. Arrow and T. Scitovsky (eds.), *Readings in Welfare Economics*, Richard D. Irwin, Homewood, IL, 1969.

Buchanan, J., and G. Tullock: *The Calculus of Consent*, University of Michigan Press, Ann Arbor, 1963.

Cheung, S. N. S.: "A Theory of Price Control," *Journal of Law and Economics*, **17**(1):53–72, April 1974.

— — —: *The Theory of Share Tenancy*, University of Chicago Press, Chicago, 1969.

— — —: "The Fables of the Bees: An Economic Investigation," *Journal of Law and Economics*, **16**:11–33, April 1973.

Coase, R. H.: "The Problem of Social Cost," *Journal of Law and Economics*, **3**:1–44, October 1960.

Davis, Otto A., and Andrew B. Whinston: "Welfare Economics and the Theory of Second Best," *Review of Economic Studies*, **32**:1–14, 1965.

Demestz, H.: "Information and Efficiency, Another Viewpoint," *Journal of Law and Economics*, **12**:1–22, April 1969.

Gordon, H. Scott: "The Economic Theory of a Common Property Resource: The Fishery," *Journal of Political Economy*, **52**:124–142, April 1954.

Harberger, A. C.: "Monopoly and Resource Allocation," *American Economic Review Proceedings*, **44**:77–87, May 1954.

— — —: "Taxation, Resource Allocation and Welfare," in *The Role of Direct and Indirect Taxes in the Federal Revenue System*, Princeton University Press, Princeton, NJ, 1964.

— — —: "Three Basic Postulates for Applied Welfare Economics: An Interpretive Essay," *Journal of Economic Literature*, **9**:785–797, September 1971.

Hotelling, H.: "The General Welfare in Relation to Problems of Taxation and Railway and Utility Rates," *Econometrica*, **6**:242–269, 1938.

Lerner, A. P.: *The Economics of Control*, The Macmillan Company, New York, 1944.

Lipsey, R. G., and K. Lancaster: "The General Theory of the Second Best," *Review of Economic Studies*, **24**:11–32, 1956.

Little, L. M. D.: *A Critique of Welfare Economics*, 2d ed., The Clarendon Press, Oxford, 1957.

Mishan, E. J.: *Welfare Economics*, Random House, Inc., New York, 1964.

Quirk, J., and R. Saposnik: *Introduction to General Equilibrium Theory and Welfare Economics*, McGraw-Hill Book Company, New York, 1968.

Samuelson, P. A.: *Foundations of Economic Analysis*, Harvard University Press, Cambridge, MA, 1947.

— — —: "The Pure Theory of Public Expenditure," *Review of Economics and Statistics*, **36**:387–390, 1954.

— — —: "Diagrammatic Exposition of a Theory of Public Expenditure," *Review of Economics and Statistics*, **37**:350–356, 1955.

Silberberg, E.: "Duality and the Many Consumers' Surpluses," *American Economic Review*, **62**:942–956, December 1972.

CHAPTER

18

RESOURCE ALLOCATION OVER TIME: OPTIMAL CONTROL THEORY

18.1 THE MEANING OF DYNAMICS

The theory of comparative statics concerns the instantaneous rates of change of choice variables as the parameters (constraints) faced by the decision maker change. In many cases (most, perhaps), this provides an acceptable basis for stating refutable hypotheses, by extrapolating these instantaneous changes over a finite interval. Thus, for example, even though the mathematical derivation of the law of demand for compensated price changes is, strictly speaking, a statement about the demand function at a single price and income vector, the additional assumption that the underlying curvature properties hold over an interval of values allows us to state the law of demand in its useful empirical form.

In certain problems, however, the mere statement of the instantaneous movements in choice variables is inadequate. The problem is most apparent in capital theory, where the important quantity — capital — is typically durable, and where an important decision concerns the changing level of service flow to be provided over time. Moreover, it is precisely the changes in the rate of utilization of resources over time that are of interest, rather than the mere specification of the initial direction of change. Such decisions are inherently *dynamic;* the entire future time path of the choice variables changes as decisions are made in the present. The fundamental property of dynamic models is that decisions made in the present affect decisions in the future.

Some of the most important applications of dynamic analysis have been in the area of natural resource utilization. The issue of efficient (long-run wealth maximization) use of some resource, such as fish, which may be depleted through extensive harvest, is a prominent example. For this reason, and because it allows us to illustrate clearly the prominent issues involved in these types of problems, we will use this as our prototype model of resource utilization over time.

In Chap. 2, we briefly analyzed the Fisherian investment problem of maximizing the present value of some resource, say, trees, with growth function $g(t)$, where $t = $ time. The objective function is $P = g(t)e^{-rt}$; the problem concerns the length of time the resource should be left to grow. Maximizing P with respect to t yields the first-order condition $r = g'/g$; the trees are left to grow until the increase in the value of the stock each year falls to the alternative value of capital, given by the interest rate, r. Although this is a problem of maximization "over time," it is not really a dynamic problem. There is only one decision to be made, and there is no linkage of that decision with any other choice (there are none, in fact) to be made at some later date.

Even the case of repeated plantings (the so-called Faustmann solution), where an additional opportunity cost is added, that of repeated use of the land through replanting, is essentially a static problem. The solution of this problem, however, is suggestive of the general approach to dynamic problems. After the initial harvest, with value $g(t)e^{-rt}$, the "optimal" policy is to repeat the earlier decision. Thus, the objective function becomes

$$P = g(t)e^{-rt} + Pe^{-rt}$$

or

$$P = \frac{g(t)e^{-rt}}{(1 - e^{-rt})}$$

Solving for the wealth-maximizing time of harvest (see Chap. 2, Sec. 2.9) yields a shorter growth period than when the opportunity cost of the land after harvest is zero, as in Fisher's original model. Put somewhat more generally, the policy that maximizes the value (in this case, wealth) today of some extended (perhaps infinite) flow of income must, after the first harvest, be a policy that maximizes wealth from that point on as well. Ignoring, for the moment, exactly how one arrives at the point of the first and succeeding harvests, the entire path cannot be "optimal" (wealth-maximizing, in this case) unless the future after that harvest is optimally timed as well. Otherwise, the entire decision from the initial time forward can be improved simply by replacing the old path after the first harvest with the new. This reasoning was first enunciated by the mathematician Richard Bellman in the 1950s and is known as the *principle of optimality*. This insight has been used extensively in past decades to analyze problems where decisions are linked, that is, where a decision in one time period affects the level of some relevant variable in the future. In that case, simple replication of past decisions will not be optimal; each decision imposes an "externality" on the future. It is only then that a problem becomes truly dynamic.

To illustrate these issues more concretely, consider a privately owned lake that contains an initial stock of fish, x_0. Assume that the only value of this lake is the value of the stock of fish in it. In general, as fish are harvested over time, the size of the stock of fish will change, and the value of the resource will vary correspondingly. Moreover, it is often the case that the greater the number of fish in the lake, the easier it is to catch them; for this reason, harvest decisions in the present may have an additional effect on the marginal cost of fishing in the future and, thus, the present value of the resource. Since the present price of the entire resource is the capitalized value of all future benefits less costs, decisions made "today" that affect the cost of fishing "tomorrow" are reflected in the present value of the resource. An owner who disregarded the future cost of decisions made in the present would not likely use the resource in a wealth-maximizing manner. The situation is directly analogous to Coase's example of the cattle who wander onto a neighboring farmer's land and destroy some crops. Choosing the number of cattle to raise without regard to the cost imposed on farmland will lead to an allocation with less value to all resources (farm and cattle production together) than if those "external" costs are considered. In the instant case, the external costs are those imposed in the future, perhaps on the same owner as in the present.

Let us use the variable $x(t)$ to denote the stock of fish in the lake at any time t, where, initially, $x_0 = x(t_0)$. Fish are harvested at some rate $u(t)$, to be chosen by the owner of the resource. The variable $u(t)$ is called the *control;* it is the path of decisions made (with regard to the harvesting of fish, in this case). We make the simplifying assumption that the fish are sold in the world market at price p, assumed constant now and into the future. The amount of fish harvested depends on the stock of fish and the input of labor and other factors. We assume a well-defined cost function with the usual properties; $c = c(x, u, w)$ is defined, where w is a vector of factor prices. For the moment, assume a finite planning horizon, so that the owner of the lake maximizes the value of the fish between times t_0 and t_1.

The hypothesis of maximization of the present value of the resource (wealth) is thus

$$\underset{u(t)}{\text{maximize}} \quad \int_{t_0}^{t_1} [pu(t) - c(u(t), x(t), w)]e^{-rt}dt \qquad (18\text{-}1a)$$

However, the model is not yet complete because the dependence of the stock of fish in the future on the present rate of harvest has not been specified. Since $x(t)$ is the stock of fish at any time, its derivative, $x'(t)$, is the stock's rate of growth or decline at time t. In general, the rate of change of the stock of fish depends on some biological rate of growth of the stock, $G(x)$, and the rate of harvest:

$$x'(t) = G(x(t)) - u(t) \tag{18-1b}$$

In addition, restrictions on the values of the control variable must be specified, e.g., $u(t) \geq 0$. We say in general that $u(t)$ must belong to some control set U. Lastly, some endpoint conditions must be specified, e.g., the initial stock of capital (the initial stock of fish, in this example), $x(t_0) = x_0$, and perhaps a terminal condition on the stock, $x(t_1) = x_1$.

Equation (18-1b) defines the dynamics of this and similar models. It is called the *state equation*; $x(t)$ is the *state* variable. The variable $u(t)$ is called the *control* variable; it is analogous to the decision variables of static theory. This is the variable the decision maker chooses, or controls (e.g., the rate of harvest, the rate of investment in new capital, or any other flow that affects the size of the stock of some resource). The state variable, $x(t)$, represents the size of the stock of some resource at time t. The stock that exists at time t_1, of course, depends on the initial stock and the path of decisions $u(t)$ regarding harvest rates for $t \leq t_1$. (We usually think of choices about u affecting the level of x, although it is possible, in principle, assuming suitable invertibility of the functions, to imagine choosing the stock x at each time and inferring the flow u that must be implied to achieve that stock.) Equations (18-1), plus the endpoint conditions and some specified control set U, are prototypic of problems in dynamic optimization.

The general form of control theory problems is

maximize
$u(t)$
$$\int_{t_0}^{t_1} f(x(t), u(t), t) dt \tag{18-2a}$$

subject to
$$x'(t) = g(x(t), u(t), t) \tag{18-2b}$$

with endpoint conditions

$$x(t_0) = x_0, \quad x(t_1) = x_1 \quad \text{(or } x(t_1) \text{ "free")}$$

and some specified control set $U(t) \in U$. The time period (t_0, t_1) is called the planning period. In many important problems, $t_1 \to +\infty$, so that the planning horizon is infinite. Endpoint conditions vary. Typically the initial stock of the state variable is fixed, although the final stock may not be. In addition, there may be restrictions on the variables, such as nonnegativity, and perhaps inequality bounds on the control. We will not cover these more advanced situations.

Problems of the type just outlined are fundamentally different from those encountered in traditional comparative statics analysis. In the so-called static theory, maximizing behavior consists of finding values of the independent variables that maximize functions with specified curvature properties. Although the directions of change of the choice variables with respect to changes in the constraints may sometimes be derived, the empirical properties of the static models do not include specification of the time rates of change of those variables. In dynamic models, the "solution" consists not merely of finding the maximum value of some function, but rather of finding *the actual function* that provides a time path of values of the economic variables so that some value function, specified over an interval of time, is maximized (or minimized). For this reason, the integrand f in (18-2*a*) is often referred to as a *functional,* being a function of *functions* $x(t)$ and $u(t)$.

Brief History[†]

The mathematical problem of finding a function that minimizes or maximizes some integral was first posed by Johann Bernoulli in 1696. Bernoulli challenged his colleagues (and particularly his older brother Jacob, whom he publicly derided as an incompetent) to find the shape of a frictionless wire such that a bead sliding down it would move between two points (not vertically aligned) in the least time. Mathematicians immediately realized the different nature of the problem and set about its solution. Bernoulli's solution was specific to this problem and provided little in the way of generality. (The shape involved is an inverted "cycloid," the path generated by a point on the rim of a coin as it is rolled on a plane.) The first systematic solution was derived in the early eighteenth century by Euler and Lagrange, who provided the general differential equation to be solved for such problems. This result will be discussed shortly. In its original form, this mathematics is called *the calculus of variations*.

In the 1950s, the theory was generalized by L. S. Pontryagin and his colleagues in the Soviet Union and by Richard Bellman and others in the United States. Pontryagin's work was motivated by problems in the physical sciences; Bellman's orientation was generally in the direction of economics and management science. The classical calculus of variations can be considered a special case of control theory; however, the older techniques are still simplest for some problems, although they are usually harder to interpret in terms of economic theory.

18.2 SOLUTION TO THE PROBLEM

We shall exploit the reasoning behind Bellman's principle of optimality to develop a heuristic solution to the control problem. The conceptual "trick" is to divide the entire time period into just two periods: the "present," which lasts only an instant (or some brief time), from some t to $t + \Delta t$, $\Delta t > 0$; and the "future," consisting of the rest of the planning period, from $t + \Delta t$ to t_1. Let us interpret the control problem in terms of maximizing the present value of the fish in a lake, as previously described. The integrand in (18-2), $f(x(t), u(t), t)$, represents the instantaneous net benefits from fishing at the rate $u(t)$. When a decision is made

---

[†] Adapted from Richard Courant and Herbert Robbins, *What Is Mathematics,* Oxford University Press, New York, 1941.

to harvest fish, this produces a flow of net benefits right now, in the present, in the amount of $f\Delta t$. In this short period of time, the stock changes little. If the fish in the lake were common property, an individual fishing would maximize short-term profits by setting $\partial f/\partial u = 0$, as in the static framework. (Typically, this would consist of some first-order condition such as $p = \text{MC}$.) Under these circumstances, fishermen would have no incentive to incorporate the effects of their present actions on the future, e.g., on the stock of fish available and the attendant effect on the marginal cost of fishing. With no ownership of the future stock of fish, there is no personal gain from curtailing present profits to achieve what might in principle be even larger future gains, since these future benefits will likely be captured by someone else.

As fishing proceeds, however, the stock of fish and, thus, the value of ownership of the stock begin to change. In a competitive market, assuming the fish in this lake make up only a negligible part of the entire market, the value of the stock in the lake at any time would be $(p\text{–MC})\,x(t)$, assuming for convenience, constant marginal cost of fishing through time. Even without reference to a market, however, there is an *imputed* value of the stock, given by the product of the stock, x, times the net marginal value of fish. The net marginal value of fish is the increase in the value of the stock if, somehow, an extra fish were placed in the lake. This present increment in the stock might have complicated long-term implications for the future stock, as determined by the biological growth function and harvesting rate.

Let us ignore for the moment exactly how the control problem (18-2) is solved, but assume that a finite interior solution $(u^*(t), x^*(t))$ does indeed exist. The values $(u^*(t), x^*(t))$ represent the "optimal" time paths of the control variables (harvest rate, in this example) and the state variable (the stock of fish). Although we are suppressing it in the notation, x^* and u^* in fact depend on the parameters x_0, t_0, etc. Denote the resulting value of the objective functional as $V(x_0, t_0)$, that is,

$$V(x_0, t_0) \equiv \int_{t_0}^{t_1} f(x^*(t), u^*(t), t)\,dt \qquad (18\text{-}3)$$

The function $V(x_0, t_0)$ is directly analogous to the indirect objective functions of comparative statics; it is called the *optimal value function*. Although (18-2) requires us to find an actual path, or function, that maximizes an integral, that function, once found, results in some ordinary maximum value function of the parameters of the model (we suppress t_1 as not germane to the discussion). The marginal value of an increment in the initial stock of fish is simply $\partial V(x_0, t_0)/\partial x_0$. More generally, $V_x(x(t), t)$ represents the marginal value of the resource at time t if the state variable x is increased exogenously at time t, and the optimal path of values $(x(t), u(t))$ is carried forward from that time until the end of the planning period.

Given x_0, a marginal value of the stock exists for any time t between the initial time t_0 and the terminal time t_1. Denote this imputed value $\lambda(t) = V_x(x^*(t), t)$. The marginal value of the stock, $\lambda(t)$, is often referred to as the *costate* or *adjoint* variable. The change in the value of the stock of fish caused by fishing is $d[\lambda(t)x(t)]/dt = \lambda x' + x\lambda'$. The true net benefit of fishing at some rate $u(t)$ is the sum of the benefits in the present, $f(x, u, t)$, and the change in the maximum value of the stock caused by taking that action in the present. The optimum (wealth-maximizing, for example) path is obtained by always setting the true (present plus future) marginal net benefits equal to zero along the entire optimal path of values $(u^*(t), x^*(t))$. Thus, we can characterize the solution to the control problem as requiring, at each $t, t_0 \le t \le t_1$:

$$\text{maximize} \atop u, x \qquad\qquad f(x, u, t) + \lambda x' + x\lambda' \qquad\qquad (18\text{-}4)$$

Using the state Eq. (18-2b), this becomes

$$\text{maximize} \atop u, x \qquad\qquad f(x, u, t) + \lambda g(x, u, t) + x\lambda' \qquad\qquad (18\text{-}5)$$

We suppress the dependence on t at this point because we have not yet found the functions $(u^*(t), x^*(t))$ and expressed them as functions of t. Differentiating with respect to the control u and the state variable x yields

$$f_u + \lambda g_u = 0 \qquad\qquad (18\text{-}6)$$

$$f_x + \lambda g_x + \lambda' = 0 \qquad\qquad (18\text{-}7)$$

Equation (18-6) is called the *maximum principle;* (18-7) is called the *costate* or *adjoint* equation. These two conditions plus the state equation

$$x' = g(x, u, t) \qquad\qquad (18\text{-}8)$$

are the necessary conditions for an optimal path $(u^*(t), x^*(t))$ of control and state variables over the planning period. Also determined is the path of marginal values of the stock, $\lambda(t)$.

These equations, however, are not simple equations in x, u and λ, in which case ordinary algebraic or comparative statics techniques would apply. The adjoint Eq. (18-7) and the state equation are *differential equations;* they are, in general, difficult to solve.

Equations (18-6) and (18-7) are generally expressed in terms of the expression $H = f + \lambda g$, called a *Hamiltonian*. The maximum principle is $\partial H/\partial u = 0$ (assuming an interior solution to the problem); the adjoint equation is $\partial H/\partial x = -\lambda'$. In the original problem, given the initial value of the stock, x_0, choosing $u(t)$ determines $x'(t)$ and thus $x(t)$, through the state equation. Thus, there is really only one "independent variable," u. However, the introduction of the new variable $\lambda(t)$ adds another degree of freedom; as in static lagrangian analysis, we "pretend" the problem has one more dimension than it actually has.

Using the maximum principle, Eq. (18-6), which is not a differential equation, and invoking the implicit function theorem, we can "solve" for u: $u = k(x, \lambda, t)$. Substituting this into the adjoint and state equations produces two first-order differential equations

$$x' = g(x, k(x, \lambda, t), t) \tag{18-9}$$

and

$$\lambda' = -f_x(x, k(x, \lambda, t), t) - \lambda g_x(x, k(x, \lambda, t), t) \tag{18-10}$$

Solving these differential equations (and using the relevant endpoint conditions to evaluate the constants of integration) yields the optimum path of x and λ. Using the solutions to these equations yields the optimum path of the control variable, u, by substituting into $k(x, \lambda, t)$.

Somewhat more formally, consider any point (x_0, t_0), not necessarily the initial point, along the optimum path. The maximum (or minimum, but we proceed in the maximization format) value of the objective integral is some function $V(x_0, t_0)$. As we proceed along some specified path $(x(t), u(t))$ for some small interval of time Δt, immediate "net benefits" of $f(x, u, t)\Delta t$ are realized. At that point, the function V is dependent on the new coordinates $(x_0 + \Delta x, t_0 + \Delta t)$ and the path chosen between $t_0 + \Delta t$ and t_1, the end of the planning period. Since $V(x_0, t_0)$ is the value of the objective integral when the optimal path is chosen, for arbitrary initial choices,

$$V(x_0, t_0) \geq f(x, u, t)\Delta t + V(x_0 + \Delta x, t_0 + \Delta t) \tag{18-11}$$

Applying the mean value theorem (or, alternatively, a Taylor series expansion) to the last term, we have, approximately,

$$V(x_0 + \Delta x, t_0 + \Delta t) = V(x_0, t_0) + V_x \Delta x + V_t \Delta t$$

Substituting this expression in the right-hand side of (18-11) and canceling $V(x_0, t_0)$ from both sides yields

$$f(x, u, t)\Delta t + V_x \Delta x + V_t \Delta t \leq 0$$

Dividing by Δt and taking limits, and using the state equation $dx/dt = x' = g(x, u, t)$ yields

$$f(x, u, t) + V_x(x, t)g(x, u, t) + V_t(x, t) \leq 0 \tag{18-12}$$

Along the *optimal* path, (18-12) holds as an equality; in that form, the equation is known as the *Hamilton-Jacobi* equation:

$$f(x^*, u^*, t) + V_x(x^*, t)g(x^*, u^*, t) + V_t(x^*, t) = 0 \tag{18-13}$$

Recall that $\lambda(t) = V_x(x, t)$. Making this substitution in (18-12) yields

$$f(x, u, t) + \lambda(t)g(x, u, t) + V_t(x, t) \leq 0 \tag{18-14}$$

Again, this expression holds as an equality along the optimal path $(x^*(t), u^*(t))$:

$$f(x^*, u^*, t) + \lambda^*(t)g(x^*, u^*, t) + V_t(x^*, t) = 0 \tag{18-15}$$

The last term, V_t, the rate of change of the objective functional with respect to time, is a function only of x and t; it is independent of u. Therefore, for given x, the optimal path requires maximization of $H = f(x, u, t) + \lambda(t)g(x, u, t)$ with respect to u along the optimal path. This is the maximum condition (18-6).

The adjoint equation is also derivable from (18-13). This relation is an identity in time and the parameters of the system, in particular x_0, when the optimal paths are substituted back into it, as indicated. Differentiating with respect to x_0 (suppressing the *'s),

$$f_x(\partial x/\partial x_0) + f_u(\partial u/\partial x_0) + V_x(x, t)[g_x(\partial x/\partial x_0) + g_u(\partial u/\partial x_0)]$$
$$+ gV_{xx}(\partial x/\partial x_0) + V_{tx}(\partial x/\partial x_0) \equiv 0$$

Collecting terms,

$$[f_x + V_x(x, t)g_x + V_{xx}g + V_{tx}](\partial x/\partial x_0)$$
$$+ [f_u + V_x(x, t)g_u](\partial u/\partial x_0) \equiv 0 \qquad (18\text{-}16)$$

However, the last bracketed term is zero, by the maximum condition (18-6), remembering that $\lambda(t) = V_x(x, t)$. Also, differentiating $V_x(x, t)$ with respect to t,

$$\lambda'(t) = V_{xx}x' + V_{xt} = V_{xx}g + V_{tx}$$

constituting the last two terms in the first set of brackets. Assuming $\partial x/\partial x_0 \neq 0$ (the capital stock is not redundantly abundant, i.e., having more of it would affect the level of the stock later on), Eq. (18-15) thus implies the adjoint equation $f_x + \lambda g_x + \lambda' = 0$.

Equation (18-15) yields an interpretation of the Hamiltonian, which is the sum of the first two terms. The last term, V_t, indicates by how much the maximum value of the objective integral will change after an instant of time has passed, holding the stock, x, constant. Therefore, the Hamiltonian equals the (negative) net effect of starting the process a bit later.

Example. Consider the optimal control problem:

maximize

$$\int_0^1 (-x - \tfrac{1}{2}\alpha u^2)\,dt$$

subject to

$$x' = u$$

$$x(0) = x_0, \qquad x(1) = x_1$$

where $\alpha > 0$ is a parameter for this problem. The Hamiltonian for this problem is

$$H(x, u, \lambda) = -x - \tfrac{1}{2}\alpha u^2 + \lambda u$$

Assuming an interior solution, the necessary conditions are

$$\frac{\partial H}{\partial u} = -\alpha u + \lambda = 0$$

$$\frac{\partial^2 H}{\partial u^2} = -\alpha \leq 0$$

By assumption $\alpha > 0$, so $\partial^2 H/\partial u^2 < 0$. Solving $\partial H/\partial u = 0$ for u gives $u = \lambda/\alpha$. The other necessary conditions are the state and adjoint equations

$$x' = \frac{\partial H}{\partial \lambda} = u$$

$$\lambda' = -\frac{\partial H}{\partial x} = 1$$

Using $u = \lambda/\alpha$ in these equations yields

$$x' = \lambda/\alpha, \qquad x(0) = x_0, \qquad x(1) = x_1$$
$$\lambda' = 1$$

Integrating $\lambda' = 1$ directly gives $\lambda^*(t) = t + c_1$, where c_1 is an unknown (as of yet) constant of integration. Substitute $\lambda^*(t)$ in $x' = \lambda/\alpha$ to get $x' = (t + c_1)/\alpha$. Integrating this equation yields $x^*(t) = t^2/2\alpha + c_1 t/\alpha + c_2$, where c_2 is another constant of integration. The constants of integration c_1 and c_2 are determined by using the initial and terminal conditions $x(0) = x_0$ and $x(1) = x_1$, respectively. Use $x(0) = x_0$ in $x^*(t)$ to get $x^*(0) = c_2 = x_0$. Now use $x(1) = x_1$ to obtain the value of c_1: $x^*(1) = \frac{1}{2\alpha} + c_1/\alpha + x_0 = x_1$; thus, $c_1 = \alpha(x_1 - x_0) - \frac{1}{2}$. These constants of integration are then substituted in (x^*, λ^*) to yield their optimal paths, and then λ^* is substituted into $u = \lambda/\alpha$ to give the control's optimal time path. Doing this gives

$$x^*(t; \alpha, x_0, x_1) = \frac{t^2}{2\alpha} + [(x_1 - x_0) - \frac{1}{2\alpha}]t + x_0$$

$$\lambda^*(t; \alpha, x_0, x_1) = t + \alpha(x_1 - x_0) - \frac{1}{2}$$

$$u^*(t; \alpha, x_0, x_1) = \frac{t}{\alpha} + (x_1 - x_0) - \frac{1}{2\alpha}$$

The Calculus of Variations

The original formulation of the problem of determining an optimal path is to find some function $x(t)$ that solves

maximize $\qquad \displaystyle\int_{t_0}^{t_1} f(x, x', t)\,dt$

This is in fact a special case of the control problem, where $x' = g(x, u, t) = u$. That is, the time rate of change of the stock is identically the control variable, rather than some more general function that might also include the stock itself and time. Substituting the state equation $u = x'$ into the integrand in (18-2a) yields this specification.

In this case, the necessary conditions for a maximum (or minimum) are as follows. The maximum principle is

$$H_u = H_{x'} = f_{x'} + \lambda g_{x'} = 0$$

However, $g_{x'} = g_u \equiv 1$, so this condition becomes

$$f_{x'} = -\lambda \tag{18-17}$$

The adjoint or costate equation is

$$H_x = f_x + \lambda g_x = f_x = -\lambda' \tag{18-18}$$

since $g_x \equiv 0$. Since the right-hand side of (18-18) is the time derivative of the right-hand side of (18-17), these equations can be combined into

$$\frac{d}{dt} f_{x'} = \frac{\partial f}{\partial x} \tag{18-19}$$

Carrying out the differentiation in (18-19) results in the equivalent expression

$$f_x = f_{x't} + f_{x'x}x' + f_{x'x'}x'' \tag{18-19'}$$

Equation (18-19) is the classic Euler-Lagrange relation defining the necessary condition for an optimal path. Application of (18-19) (except for special cases) results in a second-order differential equation, whereas the necessary conditions of control theory result in the simultaneous first-order differential Eqs. (18-9) and (18-10). There is no uniform computational advantage to one approach over the other; however, the Euler-Lagrange equation is difficult to interpret, and the control theory equations often provide useful characterizations of the dynamics of economic models.

The solution to the Euler-Lagrange equation may be obscure. In special cases, however, certain procedures may be of assistance.[†] In particular, if the objective functional is a function of x and x' only, i.e., not including t explicitly, the Euler-Lagrange equation is

$$f_x = \frac{df_{x'}(x,x')}{dt} = f_{x'x}x' + f_{x'x'}x''$$

or

$$f_x - f_{x'x}x' - f_{x'x'}x'' = 0$$

[†] See M. I. Kamien and N. L. Schwartz, *Dynamic Optimization: The Calculus of Variations and Optimal Control in Economics and Management*, North Holland, New York, 1981, p. I.5.

As expected, this is a second-order differential equation. It turns out, however, that x' is an integrating factor for this expression: multiplying through by x' yields

$$x'(f_x - f_{x'x}x' - f_{x'x'}x'') = \frac{d(f - x'f_{x'})}{dt} = 0$$

Thus, in this case the Euler-Lagrange equation implies

$$f - x'f_{x'} = k$$

where k is the constant of integration. This equation may (but not always) be easier to solve than the Euler-Lagrange condition in its original form.

> **Example.** Let us prove algebraically a result everyone knows intuitively: The shortest distance between two points on a plane is a straight line. The two points will be designated (t_0, x_0) and (t_1, x_1). Recalling Pythagoras's theorem, starting at some point and making small movements dt in the t direction and dx in the x direction, the distance traveled is the length of the hypotenuse:
>
> $$ds = [(dt)^2 + (dx)^2]^{1/2} = [1 + x'(t)^2]^{1/2} dt$$
>
> We seek to minimize the sum of these little segments, or
>
> minimize $$\int_{t_0}^{t_1} [1 + x'(t)^2]^{1/2} dt$$
>
> This is a special case: The integrand depends only on x'. Applying the Euler equation in the form (18-19'),
>
> $$f_{x'x'}x'' = 0$$
>
> Thus, either $x'' = 0$ or $f_{x'x'} = 0$. Here $f = [1 + x'(t)^2]^{1/2}$; thus, $f_{x'x'} \neq 0$. Therefore, $x'' = 0$. This simple differential equation has the solution $x = c_1 t + c_2$, confirming the result. Using the coordinates of the endpoints to evaluate the constants of integration yields
>
> $$c_1 = \frac{(x_1 - x_0)}{(t_1 - t_0)}, \qquad c_2 = \frac{(x_0 t_1 - x_1 t_0)}{(t_1 - t_0)}$$

Endpoint (Transversality) Conditions

Up to this point, we have been imprecise as to the effects of assumptions regarding the initial and final values of the optimal path. Endpoint conditions are not generally an issue in comparative statics analysis, since the solutions are assumed to occur at interior points. In dynamic analysis, the path may depend critically on the assumption made regarding initial and final values. The solution to optimal control problems involves solving a second-order differential equation (or, equivalently, two simultaneous first-order equations). In either case, two arbitrary constants of integration appear. For these parameters to be evaluated, additional assumptions must be made about the optimal paths.

Consider the fishing problem. If the model is stated as a maximization problem between time t_0 and finite time t_1, the model essentially assumes there is "no time" after t_1; that is, in essence, the world comes to an end at t_1. (A slightly more general class of models appends a salvage value $S[x(t_1), t_1]$ to the maximization problem.) If, somehow, the stock of fish is simply specified in terms of some initial and final values $x(t_0) = x_0$ and $x(t_1) = x_1$, there is no further issue; these values will be used to evaluate the arbitrary constants that appear in the solution to the differential equation defining the optimal path. If, however, a positive stock of fish were to exist at t_1 (the end of the world), it surely could have no value. Therefore, necessarily, if $x(t_1) > 0$, $\lambda(t_1) = 0$. (With positive salvage values, $\lambda(t_1) = \partial S/\partial x_1$.) In many cases, however, the final value of the stock of fish is not specified *a priori;* it is to be determined by the maximization hypothesis. The same reasoning would then suggest that, since additional stock would have zero value in terms of the objective function f, if $x(t_1)$ is taken to be "free" (i.e., not specified in advance), then $\lambda(t_1) = 0$. Such conditions are known as *transversality conditions;* they are the additional conditions needed in order to evaluate the constants of integration in optimal control problems. For maximization problems, if $x(t_1) \geq 0$ is the constraint on the terminal stock, the transversality conditions can be stated as

$$\lambda(t_1) \geq 0, \qquad x(t_1) \geq 0, \qquad \lambda(t_1)x(t_1) = 0 \qquad (18\text{-}20)$$

In addition, in some problems, the final time itself, t_1, is taken as free. In this case the activity, say, fishing, would cease when prolonging it would have no value, i.e., would add nothing to the value $V(x, t)$ of the objective integral. From the Hamilton-Jacobi Eq. (18-15), at t_1

$$-V_t = f(x^*, u^*, t) + \lambda^*(t)g(x^*, u^*, t) = 0 \qquad (18\text{-}21)$$

if t_1 is free. These conditions must be modified for more complex models, e.g., those involving inequality constraints and salvage values; the modifications in general resemble the Kuhn-Tucker restrictions in static maximization.[†]

Autonomous Problems

In the general control problem framework, the variable t can enter the objective function and the state equation directly. The general specification

maximize $$\int_{t_0}^{t_1} f(x, u, t)\,dt$$

subject to $$x' = g(x, u, t), \qquad x(t_0) = x_0$$

where t enters f and g directly, means *the date matters.* That is, the cost or revenue generated by the activity $u(t)$ depends not only on the level of extraction

---

[†] See Kamien and Schwartz, *op. cit.,* p. II.7.

and stock of a resource, or utilization of capital (i.e., on the level of the control and state variables), but also on exactly when this activity is taking place. In many (most, perhaps) economic models, however, such dependence on the date is incorporated only in the term e^{-rt}, used to discount future income to the present, t_0.

Models in which t is absent from the objective and state equations, i.e.,

maximize $$\int_{t_0}^{t_1} f(x,u)dt$$

subject to $$x' = g(x,u), \qquad x(t_0) = x_0 \qquad (18\text{-}22)$$

are called *autonomous*. In this case, the maximum condition $H_u = f_u + \lambda g_u = 0$, the state equation $x' = g(x,u)$, and the adjoint equation $f_x + \lambda g_x + \lambda' = 0$ result in differential equations in x' and λ' that do not involve t explicitly. These equations are much easier to solve than those in which t appears explicitly. For practical reasons as well, therefore, this modification is important.

Models in which time enters explicitly only as part of the discount factor e^{-rt} are generally referred to as autonomous as well, as the time dependence is easily eliminated. That is, consider models of the form

maximize $$\int_{t_0}^{t_1} f(x,u)e^{-rt}dt$$

subject to $$x' = g(x,u), \qquad x(t_0) = x_0 \qquad (18\text{-}23)$$

By replacing time t with the variable $s = e^{-rt}$ and defining the initial and terminal times in terms of s, the problem immediately becomes autonomous.

In models of the form (18-23), the costate variable $\lambda(t)$ is the *present value* (i.e., at time t_0) of the marginal value of an increment of capital at time t. It is sometimes more convenient to solve these problems using a "current value multiplier," $m(t)$, where

$$e^{-rt}m(t) = \lambda(t) \qquad (18\text{-}24)$$

The necessary conditions for optimality are, again,

$$H_u = e^{-rt}f_u + \lambda g_u = 0 \qquad (18\text{-}25)$$

and

$$H_x = e^{-rt}f_x + \lambda g_x = -\lambda' \qquad (18\text{-}26)$$

Using (18-24), however,

$$e^{-rt}m'(t) - re^{-rt}m(t) = \lambda'(t)$$

If we now write the Hamiltonian in current value form as

$$\mathcal{H} = e^{rt}H = f + e^{rt}\lambda g = f + mg$$

the first-order conditions are equivalent to

$$\mathcal{H}_u = f_u + mg_u = 0 \qquad (18\text{-}27)$$

and

$$\mathcal{H}_x = f_x + mg_x = rm - m'(t) \qquad (18\text{-}28)$$

after canceling e^{-rt} from each term. Equations (18-27) and (18-28) are autonomous differential equations; that is, the independent variable t does not enter explicitly as a separate argument. The system is usually more easily solved in this form.

Sufficient Conditions

The Euler-Lagrange equation, or the control theory variant, Eqs. (18-6) and (18-7), plus the state eq. (18-8) and transversality conditions are first-order necessary conditions for either a maximum or minimum. Sufficient conditions analogous to those in static theory are as follows:

If $f(x, u, t)$ and $g(x, u, t)$ are both everywhere concave in x and u for all t, if $g(x, u, t)$ is nonlinear in x or u, if $\lambda(t) \geq 0$, and if the first-order necessary conditions are satisfied, the solution represents a maximum.

Likewise, if $f(x, u, t)$ and $g(x, u, t)$ are both everywhere convex, then the solution represents a minimum.

Under these conditions, the Hamiltonian will be concave (or convex, for minimum problems). Since the expression

$$H + \lambda'x = f(x, u, t) + \lambda g(x, u, t) + \lambda'x$$

is maximized (minimized) at every point along the optimal path, these conditions are intuitively plausible. Note that if $g(x, u, t)$ is linear in x and u, then concavity of this expression will be independent of g and, thus, the sign of $\lambda(t)$. For classical calculus of variations problems, i.e.,

maximize $\qquad \displaystyle\int_{t_0}^{t_1} F(x, x', t)\,dt$

the sufficient condition is that the integrand $F(x, x', t)$ be concave in x and x' for all t. For minimum problems, F must be convex in x and x' for all t. This condition can be applied in control problems if the control variable can be eliminated through substitution, converting the problem to one in the calculus of variations. It is important to note that the preceding sufficient condition requires *global* concavity (or convexity) of f and g (or F); hence, the solution (if one exists) to the first-order necessary conditions yields the global optimum. A weaker condition, $F_{x'x'} \leq 0$ along the optimal path (≥ 0 for minimum problems), is known as the Legendre condition, and is a *local* curvature property. It is *necessarily* implied by maximization (note the weak inequality). As in static optimization problems, these conditions are often the basis for comparative statics or comparative dynamics results in dynamic problems.

18.3 SOLUTIONS TO DIFFERENTIAL EQUATIONS

Through the use of techniques analogous to comparative statics, the effects of changes in the parameters on the optimal path or on steady-state values are sometimes available. However, in order to be more tractable and useful, many models incorporate simplifying assumptions. Many control problems of interest assume specific functional forms in the objective and state equations. The maximum and adjoint equations then result in specific differential equations whose solution is of interest. To that end, we investigate briefly the nature of these solutions.

In general, differential equations are difficult to solve, and some innocent-looking equations are in fact intractable. Certain standard procedures are useful; we review them briefly here.[†] As shown in Chap. 2, some differential equations can be solved by separation of the variables: to solve $y' = dy/dt = y/t$, we write

$$\frac{dy}{y} = \frac{dt}{t}$$

Integrating both sides yields

$$\log y = \log t + \log k$$

where the arbitrary constant of integration is denoted $\log k$ for convenience. Thus, the general solution can be written

$$y(t) = kt$$

If it is specified that the curve must pass through some particular point (t_0, y_0), the constant of integration can be evaluated. Differential equations that can be solved in this manner are the easiest to work with.

Consider now the class of *linear* first-order differential equations

$$y'(t) + b(t)y(t) = c(t) \tag{18-29}$$

This equation is called *linear* because there are no terms of the form $(y')^2, yy'$,

---

[†]The student is cautioned against reinventing the wheel in these procedures but it is only through practice that skill is acquired.

etc. By a *solution* to this equation, we mean a function $y = s(t)$ such that when this function is substituted into this equation, an identity results. The fundamental theorem identifying the nature of these solutions is as follows. Consider Eq. (18-29) without the right-hand side:

$$y' + b(t)y(t) = 0 \qquad (18\text{-}30)$$

This is called the *reduced* equation. (When there is no right-hand-side function, a differential equation is called *homogeneous*.) This equation is usually much easier to solve than (18-29), assuming a solution exists. The solutions to differential equations, of course, involve arbitrary constants. *However, if any* particular *solution can be found for* (18-29), *the* general *solution to* (18-29) *is the sum of that particular solution plus the general solution to the reduced* Eq. (18-30).

Let us first investigate these equations when b and c are constants, as opposed to being functions of t. Equation (18-29) is then called a first-order differential equation with constant coefficients. In that case, the solution to Eq. (18-30) can always be found by multiplying through by e^{bt}. Note that

$$e^{bt}(y' + by) = \frac{d(e^{bt}y(t))}{dt} = 0$$

Thus, the general solution to the reduced equation is $e^{bt}y(t) = K$, where K is an arbitrary constant, or

$$y(t) = Ke^{-bt}$$

By inspection, a *particular* solution to (18-29) is $y = c/b$ (note that $y' = 0$). The *general* solution to (18-29) is therefore

$$y(t) = Ke^{-bt} + \frac{c}{b}$$

Substituting this expression into (18-30) confirms that it is indeed a solution.

Example. Consider the differential equation

$$y' + y = t + 1$$

A particular solution of the unreduced equation is $y = t$; the general solution, since $b = 1$, is therefore

$$y = Ke^{-t} + t$$

In the more general case where $b = b(t)$ and $c = c(t)$, finding a particular solution may not be easy. However, by proceeding in a manner similar to the case of constant coefficients, the general solution to the reduced equation is always of the form

$$y(t) = Ke^{-\int b(t)dt}$$

Adding a particular solution of (18-29) to this yields the general solution.

The same procedures apply to second-order linear differential equations; however, the algebra is more complex. General solutions of

$$y'' + by' + cy = d \tag{18-31}$$

consist of the sum of a particular solution to the entire equation plus the general solution to the reduced (homogeneous) equation

$$y'' + by' + cy = 0 \tag{18-32}$$

To solve (18-32), we "try" a solution of the form $y = e^{rx}$. Substituting this into (18-32) yields

$$e^{rx}(r^2 + br + c) = 0$$

This equation will be satisfied for solutions to the quadratic equation, called the *characteristic equation*,

$$r^2 + br + c = 0$$

Using the quadratic formula, the roots are

$$r_1, r_2 = \frac{-b}{2} \pm \frac{(b^2 - 4c)^{1/2}}{2} \tag{18-33}$$

There are several cases to explore.

1. If $b^2 - 4c > 0$, the roots are real and distinct; in that case the solution to (18-32) is

$$y(t) = c_1 e^{r_1 t} + c_2 e^{r_2 t} \tag{18-34}$$

where c_1 and c_2 are the arbitrary constants of integration. Note that if both roots are negative, $y(t) \to 0$ as $t \to \infty$. Control theory problems with this type of solution converge asymptotically toward some "steady state"; if one or both roots are positive and the attached constant(s) are not zero, the path will diverge.

2. If $b^2 - 4c = 0$, the roots are identical: $r_1 = r_2 = r$; the solution to (18-32) is then

$$y(t) = (c_1 + c_2 t)e^{rt} \tag{18-35}$$

3. If $b^2 - 4c < 0$, the roots are imaginary, i.e., they involve $i = \sqrt{-1}$. The solution is again of the form (18-34) since the roots are distinct; however, (18-34) is not a convenient expression. For this reason, we make use of the well-known identity

$$e^{it} = \cos t + i \sin t$$

The real and imaginary parts of the roots to the characteristic equation are defined, respectively, by $p = -b/2$, $q = (b^2 - 4c)^{1/2}/2$. The solution to (18-32) is then

$$y(t) = e^{pt}(c_1 \cos(qt) + c_2 \sin(qt)) \qquad (18\text{-}36)$$

where, again, c_1 and c_2 are arbitrary constants. Note that if the real part of the roots p is negative, the solution $y(t)$ will oscillate around zero, converging to zero as $t \to \infty$.

Simultaneous Differential Equations

The control theory format results in simultaneous differential equations—typically, one for the state variable, $x(t)$, and one for the costate variable, $\lambda(t)$. These are generally of lower order than the single differential equation resulting from the Euler-Lagrange equation of the calculus of variations. The two, however, are equivalent.

We consider only the linear first-order case:

$$x' = a_1 x(t) + b_1 y(t) + f(t)$$

$$y' = a_2 x(t) + b_2 y(t) + g(t) \qquad (18\text{-}37)$$

As in the case of single differential equations, solutions to (18-37) consist of the sum of a particular solution to the complete system and the general solution to the reduced (homogeneous) system

$$x' = a_1 x(t) + b_1 y(t)$$

$$y' = a_2 x(t) + b_2 y(t) \qquad (18\text{-}38)$$

We consider only the solution of the homogeneous system, (18-38). Differentiating the first equation with respect to t and substituting for x' and y' in (18-38) yields the equivalent *second-order* differential equation:

$$x'' - (a_1 + b_2)x' + (a_1 b_2 - b_1 a_2)x = 0 \qquad (18\text{-}39)$$

This can be solved using the previously discussed methods. However, we can proceed directly with (18-38) and try solutions of the form $x(t) = Ae^{rt}, y(t) = Be^{rt}$. Substituting into (18-38) and canceling e^{rt} from each term yields the matrix equation

$$\begin{pmatrix} a_1 - r & b_1 \\ a_2 & b_2 - r \end{pmatrix} \begin{pmatrix} A \\ B \end{pmatrix} = \begin{pmatrix} 0 \\ 0 \end{pmatrix}$$

This equation has a nontrivial solution only if its determinant is zero:

$$\begin{vmatrix} a_1 - r & b_1 \\ a_2 & b_2 - r \end{vmatrix} = 0 \qquad (18\text{-}40)$$

Expanding (18-40) yields the characteristic equation

$$r^2 - (a_1 + b_2)r + (a_1 b_2 - b_1 a_2) = 0 \qquad (18\text{-}41)$$

It is apparent that this is the characteristic equation associated with the equivalent second-order Eq. (18-39). The solution thus follows as before. Letting r_1 and r_2

be the roots (solutions) of (18-41), if, for example, $r_1 \neq r_2$, the solutions to the homogeneous simultaneous differential Eqs. (18-38) are

$$x(t) = A_1 e^{r_1 t} + A_2 e^{r_2 t}$$

$$y(t) = B_1 e^{r_1 t} + B_2 e^{r_2 t} \tag{18-42}$$

For autonomous infinite-horizon problems, i.e., where the upper limit on the objective functional is ∞, and time t enters directly only in the discount factor, if at all, it is often of concern whether the solution to the control problem converges to some steady state path (usually involving the solution to the nonhomogeneous part of (18-37)). If the roots are negative, or if the real parts of the complex roots are negative, this outcome is assured since $e^{rt} \to 0$ as $t \to \infty$ in those cases. If one root is negative and the other positive, the system is said to have a saddlepoint. If, for example, $r_1 > 0$, the solution will converge to the steady state if A_1 and $B_1 = 0$.

18.4 INTERPRETATIONS AND SOLUTIONS

Intertemporal Choice

Let us consider first the continuous analogue of the model of intertemporal choice investigated in Chap. 12. Assume a consumer has a utility function $U(C(t))$, where $C(t)$ is a flow of consumption. We assume $U' > 0$ and $U'' < 0$, as in static theory. The individual is endowed with an initial stock of capital K_0. The individual's income is the flow iK earned from the capital stock, where i is the market interest rate. In addition, the individual can, by selling capital (we normalize its price to unity), consume the capital stock as well at any time. Finally, assume that the consumer is "impatient," i.e., he or she has a time rate of preference ρ. The model of intertemporal utility maximization can then be stated as

maximize $\qquad \displaystyle\int_0^T U(C)e^{-\rho t}\,dt$

subject to $\qquad K' = iK - C, \qquad K(0) = K_0, \qquad K(T) \geq 0$

The state variable is the capital stock; the control is the flow of consumption, $C(t)$, the consumer chooses. The state equation (constraint) says that the change in the capital stock ("savings" when positive and "dissavings" when negative) equals the difference between the income earned by the stock, iK, and consumption, C. We assume, of course, that $C(t) > 0$ and $K(t) > 0$ for all t.

The Hamiltonian is

$$H = U(C)e^{-\rho t} + \lambda(iK - C)$$

which yields the maximum and adjoint equations

$$H_C = U'(C)e^{-\rho t} - \lambda = 0 \qquad (18\text{-}43)$$

$$H_K = i\lambda = -\lambda' \qquad (18\text{-}44)$$

Note that the integrand is concave in C, due to the assumption of diminishing marginal utility ($U'' < 0$); the constraint is linear in C and K. Thus, the Hamiltonian is concave in C and K, assuring us that solutions to the first-order equations represent maximum values.

Equation (18-43) says that at every point along the optimal consumption path, the discounted marginal utility of consumption equals the present value (i.e., the value at time $t = 0$) of an extra unit of capital. Differentiating (18-43) with respect to t yields

$$U''(C)C'e^{-\rho t} - \rho U'(C)e^{-\rho t} = \lambda'$$

From (18-44), $\lambda' = -i\lambda = -iU'(C)e^{-\rho t}$, using (18-43). Using this in the right-hand side of the above equation yields, after canceling the $e^{-\rho t}$ terms,

$$\frac{(-U''C')}{U'} = i - \rho \qquad (18\text{-}45)$$

The left-hand side of (18-45) is the proportionate change, with respect to time, in the individual's marginal utility of consumption. This represents the marginal benefits of increasing consumption at any point in time. This equation thus says that along the optimal consumption path, these marginal benefits equal the marginal opportunity cost of increasing consumption, the "net" interest rate, i.e., the market (real) yield less the rate of impatience.

Note now the implications of (18-45) for observable behavior. Since $U' > 0$ and $U'' < 0$, $C'(t)$ has the same sign as $i - \rho$. Thus, if $i = \rho$, that is, if the rate of interest equals the rate of impatience, then, as in the static models, the consumer chooses constant consumption. Likewise, if the market opportunity cost of consumption exceeds the individual's rate of impatience, consumption rises over time, and vice versa. If the interest rate should rise at some point t, the consumer will accelerate the flow of consumption, thus shifting consumption to the present at a greater rate. Note also that (18-44) is a simple linear homogeneous differential equation; its solution is

$$\lambda(t) = \lambda_0 e^{-it} \qquad (18\text{-}46)$$

where $\lambda_0 > 0$ is the constant of integration. The present value of the marginal value of capital thus decreases over time; its current value, $e^{it}\lambda(t)$ remains constant at λ_0. Combining this equation with (18-43) yields

$$U'(C(t)) = \lambda_0 e^{(\rho - i)t} \qquad (18\text{-}47)$$

Consider now what must happen at the end of the planning period. Recall that the transversality condition (18-20), which is a result of the nonnegativity restriction on the terminal capital stock, requires that $\lambda(T)K(T) = 0$. Either capital must be exhausted, $K(T) = 0$, or its marginal value must fall to zero at the terminal date. The only reason capital would *not* be completely used up is if the additional consumption it afforded had no value, i.e., if the consumer had already been sated so that more income was no longer preferred to less at that margin. If, as we have assumed, $U'(C) > 0$ for any level of consumption, it must be the case that at $t = T$, $K(T) = 0$. Thus, assuming more is always preferred to less, capital will be exhausted at the end of the planning period.

Equations (18-45) through (18-47) characterize the solution to this model. In order to derive actual paths of consumption and capital utilization, we would need to assume a specific functional form for the utility function. To illustrate the solution to control models, let us assume that $U(C) = \log C$. In that case, (18-45) becomes

$$\frac{C'}{C} = \left(\frac{1}{C}\right)\frac{dC}{dt} = i - \rho$$

Separating variables and integrating,

$$C(t) = C_0 e^{(i-\rho)t} \tag{18-48}$$

Equation (18-48) is the path of the control variable $C(t)$. To derive the path of the state variable K, recall the state equation (the constraint):

$$K' - iK = -C = -C_0 e^{(i-\rho)t}$$

This can be integrated using the integrating factor e^{-it}:

$$e^{-it}(K' - iK) = \frac{d(e^{-it}K)}{dt} = -C_0 e^{-\rho t}$$

Integrating both sides yields

$$e^{-it}K(t) = \left(\frac{C_0}{\rho}\right)e^{-\rho t} + A \tag{18-49}$$

where A is the arbitrary constant of integration. At $t = 0$, $K(0) = K_0$; thus,

$$A = K_0 - \frac{C_0}{\rho}$$

Likewise, using $K(T) = 0$,

$$0 = \left(\frac{C_0}{\rho}\right)e^{-\rho T} + A \text{ or } A = \frac{-C_0}{\rho}e^{-\rho T}$$

and thus,

$$A = \frac{-K_0 e^{-\rho T}}{1 - e^{-\rho T}}, \qquad C_0 = \frac{\rho K_0}{(1 - e^{-\rho T})}$$

The solution to (18-49) is thus

$$K(t) = K_0 e^{it}\left[\frac{e^{-\rho t} - e^{-\rho T}}{1 - e^{-\rho T}}\right]$$

$$C(t) = \frac{\rho K_0 e^{(i-\rho)t}}{(1 - e^{-\rho T})}$$

Harvesting a Renewable Resource

A closely related problem to the preceding one has been applied to the problem of harvesting some renewable resource, such as fish.[†] We assume the same objective function, except that for this example, we take the time horizon to be infinite. Most importantly, we assume that, left alone, the stock of fish would grow at some rate to some maximum size; and, if the stock were somehow larger, the fish would on net balance die off, reducing the stock to its steady state size. We formulate the model as

maximize $\qquad\qquad \displaystyle\int_0^\infty U(C)e^{-\rho t}\,dt$

subject to $\qquad\qquad K' = g(K) - C, \qquad K(0) = K_0 \qquad\qquad$ (18-50)

where K represents the stock of the renewable resource (in this case, fish). The function $g(K)$ represents the biological growth of the stock; it is depicted in Fig. 18-1. With zero stock ($K = 0$), there is no reproduction, and K remains at zero. Left alone, for positive K, the stock would grow at some rate given by $K' = g(K)$. For many species in given environments, a "maximum sustained yield" K_{msy} exists, where $g'(K) = 0$. We assume that $g'(K) > 0$ for $K < K_{msy}$

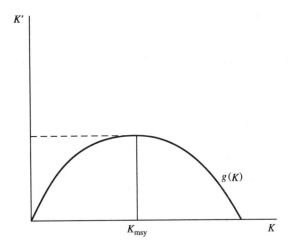

FIGURE 18-1
The function $K' = g(K)$ shows the rate of change of the stock of fish (capital stock) when no harvesting takes place. For $K < K_{msy}$, the stock of fish grows; when $K > K_{msy}$, K shrinks. Left alone, some maximum sustained yield (maximum value of K') occurs at K_{msy}. However, this harvest rate is not in general efficient.

[†]See, e.g., C. G. Plourde, "A Simple Model of Replenishable Natural Resource Exploitation," *American Economic Review*, **60**:518–522, June 1970.

and $g'(K) < 0$ for $K > K_{msy}$; thus, $g''(K) < 0$. Therefore, if K_{msy} were the current stock of fish, it would be possible to consume $K' = g(K_{msy})$ forever. It sounds plausible that this is an efficient (utility-maximizing) level of consumption. However, consideration of the dynamic aspects of the model, in particular the possibilities of time preference and the effect of the size of the fish stock on the marginal cost of fishing, changes that view.

The *current-value* Hamiltonian for (18-50) is

$$\mathcal{H} = U(C) + m(g(K) - C) \tag{18-51}$$

The maximum and adjoint equations are

$$\mathcal{H}_C = U'(C) - m = 0 \tag{18-52}$$

and

$$\mathcal{H}_K = mg'(K) = \rho m - m' \tag{18-53}$$

Note that the preceding assumptions concerning the shapes of $U(C)$ and $g(K)$, and the fact that the current marginal value of the stock is positive, guarantee the concavity of the Hamiltonian in C and K; thus, solutions to the first-order equations are paths that maximize the objective integral. As in the previous model, the maximum equation (18-52) says that along the optimal path, the current marginal imputed value of the stock of capital—in this case fish—equals the marginal utility of consumption of fish. Equation (18-53) can be rewritten

$$g'(K) = \rho - \left(\frac{m'}{m}\right) \tag{18-54}$$

The term $g'(K)$ specifies the rate of growth of the stock of fish; it is the benefit of waiting, or delaying consumption an increment of time. In a nondynamic model, wealth or utility maximization would require this marginal benefit to equal the opportunity cost of capital, which in this case is given by the consumer's rate of impatience, ρ. However, decisions in the present affect the future; consumption of fish affects the percent rate of change of the marginal value of fish. This additional cost, the capital loss, $-m'/m$, must be added to the direct cost of waiting. (Of course, $-m'/m$ might be negative, thus offsetting the impatience rate.)

Without specific functions for $U(C)$ and $g(K)$, an analytical solution of the model is impossible. However, for autonomous models such as these, an analytic device known as a *phase diagram* can be used to characterize the solution and to derive comparative statics results.

From the maximum condition (18-52), $U'(C) = m$. Since $U'' < 0$, this is a monotonic function; it can be inverted, using a global version of the implicit function theorem, yielding $C = c(m)$. Using this in the state equation (the constraint) yields two differential equations determining the motion of the model:

$$K' = g(K) - c(m), \qquad K(0) = K_0 \tag{18-55}$$

$$m' = \rho m - mg'(K) \tag{18-56}$$

A steady, or stationary, state occurs when the values of the variables remain constant over time. These values are therefore determined by setting $K' = m' = 0$ in the preceding equations, resulting in

$$g(K) - c(m) = 0 \tag{18-57}$$

$$\rho - g'(K) = 0 \tag{18-58}$$

These two equations are plotted in Fig. 18-2. Denote the steady state values of K and m as K^* and m^*. Consider the locus where $K' = 0$, Eq. (18-57), first. Since $U'(C) > 0$ and $U''(C) < 0$, $c'(m) = 1/U'' < 0$. By assumption, $g(K)$ first rises and then, after K_{msy}, falls. Therefore, $c(m)$ must rise and then fall to maintain the equality in (18-57). Since $c'(m) < 0$, as K increases from the origin, m itself must fall and then rise, reaching its minimum value where $g(K)$ is largest, at K_{msy}. Thus, the locus of (K, m) where $K' = 0$ is the U-shaped curve depicted. On the other hand, for $m' = 0$, Eq. (18-58) is simply a vertical line, at $K = K^*$. But note that since $g'(K) = 0$ at $K = K_{msy}$ and $g'(K^*) = \rho > 0$, K^* is to the left of K_{msy}. With positive time preference, steady state consumption is shifted toward the present. Moreover, as the rate of time preference (or the market interest rate, in an equivalent model) increases, the steady state capital stock and $m(t)$ fall, since, to the left of K_{msy}, $g'(K) > 0$ and $g''(K) < 0$.

We have not shown, however, that for some arbitrary K_0, the optimal path will actually tend toward the steady state. Consider how the values of K and m will change in the four areas of the phase plane between the curves $K' = 0$ and $m' = 0$. At all points above the U-shaped locus defined by $K' = 0$, $K' > 0$; below it, $K' < 0$. Likewise, to the left of the vertical line $m' = 0$, $m' < 0$; to the right of this line, $m' > 0$. Thus, if K and m take on values other than (K^*, m^*), they will move in the directions indicated by the signs of K' and m'. These directions are indicated by the arrows in Fig. 18-2. At points A and C,

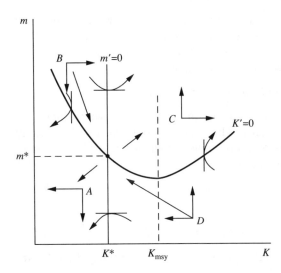

FIGURE 18-2
Phase Diagram Showing Saddlepoint Stability. The optimal (utility-maximizing) harvest rate occurs at K^*, where $g'(K) = \rho > 0$, i.e., to the left of K_{msy}. The steady state occurs at the intersection of the $K' = 0$ and $m' = 0$ loci. Above $K' = 0$, K increases over time; below it, K decreases. Similarly, to the left of $m' = 0$, the current value of the stock, m, decreases; to the right, m increases. At points such as A and C, the paths diverge from the steady state; at points such as B and D, they converge to the steady state.

the path moves *away* from the steady state. From points such as B and D, the path converges toward (K^*, m^*). This stationary point is thus a saddlepoint. The characteristic equation determining the solution to the control problem contains one positive and one negative root. The optimal solution is obtained when the constant of integration attached to the positive root is set equal to zero.

It is important to note that this procedure is valid only because the system is autonomous. If time entered Eq. (18-55) or (18-56) directly, i.e., *if the date mattered,* then merely knowing K and m would not be sufficient to determine the movement of the variables. The date, i.e., if the value of t, would also have to be specified.

That the steady state is the optimal path is often an assertion. It can sometimes be justified by appeal to the curvature properties of the functions in the model. In this case, for example, if we assume that as $C \to 0, U'(C) \to \infty$, and that as $C \to \infty$, $U'(C) \to 0$, then paths that converged to zero consumption, for example, could not be optimal; the marginal value of an increment of consumption at small values of C will exceed the full marginal cost of harvest. Likewise, paths that diverged to infinity could not be optimal with positive marginal costs of fishing.

An alternative justification for the interest in a steady state solution is that stable rather than explosive behavior seems to be empirically more relevant. The world does not seem to provide examples of divergence of capital to infinity, and extinction of resources is uncommon with well-defined property rights.

A related model of renewable resource extraction formulates the objective functional in terms of wealth maximization, as introduced earlier in this chapter:

maximize
$$\int_0^\infty [pu - c(K, u)]e^{-rt}dt$$

subject to $\qquad K' = g(K) - u, \qquad K(0) = K_0 \qquad (18\text{-}59)$

In this model, fish are harvested and sold at the rate $u(t)$ at some constant price p; the cost function depends on the stock as well as the rate of extraction. (Note that the symbol c denotes "cost" in this formulation, not "consumption," as in the previous model.) The current-value Hamiltonian is

$$\mathcal{H} = pu - c(K, u) + m(g(K) - u)$$

We assume the cost function is strictly convex in K and u, and we maintain the concavity assumption concerning $g(K)$. Thus, the Hamiltonian itself is strictly concave, and the first-order necessary conditions are sufficient for a maximum. The maximum and adjoint equations are

$$\mathcal{H}_u = p - c_u - m = 0 \qquad (18\text{-}52')$$

and

$$\mathcal{H}_K = -c_K + mg'(K) = rm - m' \qquad (18\text{-}53')$$

Equation (18-52') is equivalent to (18-52) in the sense of defining the ordinary conditions for maximization; here the marginal current value of the stock, m, equals the net current benefits of fish extraction, price minus marginal cost. In static models, this condition would simply be price equals marginal cost; in dynamic models, the opportunity cost of future events are capitalized into present decisions. Rearranging (18-53'), we have

$$g'(K) = r - \frac{m'}{m} + \frac{c_K}{m} \tag{18-54'}$$

This equation is similar to (18-54) except that an additional term, c_K/m, is present. Recall that in the earlier analysis, the steady state, derived by setting $m' = K' = 0$, occurred where $g'(K) = r$ (or the rate of impatience, ρ). Since r (or ρ) is assumed positive, $K^* < K_{msy}$. However, in Eq. (18-54'), we have the extra term c_K/m, the sign of which is an empirical matter. (We, of course, assume $m > 0$; the capital stock never has negative marginal value.) This term indicates the effect on the cost of fishing of an increase in the stock of fish. It is easy to imagine (and empirically likely) that a larger stock of fish lowers the marginal and total costs of fishing, for any level of activity. In that case $c_K < 0$, and it is possible for K^* to occur where $g'(K) < 0$, implying $K^* > K_{msy}$. It is possible that *delaying* harvesting and waiting for the stock to build up can produce a sufficiently large gain in the future to offset the opportunity cost of funds, by lowering the cost of harvesting.

Capital Utilization

Let us now consider a model of capital utilization with a somewhat more general objective function. Imagine a stock of capital $x(t)$ at time t, that enables a firm (or person—perhaps this is human capital) to earn a stream of rents $R(x)$. Subsumed into this function, for simplicity, is some behavior in which the person or firm combines some other inputs (e.g., labor) with the capital stock in some presumably cost-minimizing manner. Assume that capital depreciates (or "evaporates") at a linear rate bx and that the cost of investing in new capital is given by $c(u)$. The firm wishes to utilize and acquire capital so as to maximize wealth over an infinite horizon. The model is

maximize $\qquad \displaystyle\int_0^\infty [R(x(t)) - c(u(t))]e^{-rt}\,dt$

subject to $\qquad x'(t) = u(t) - bx(t), \qquad x(0) = x_0 > 0 \tag{18-60}$

We assume an interior solution exists, with $u(t) > 0$, and that $x(t) > 0$ throughout. The state equation $x' = u - bx$ defines, as always, the dynamics of the model; it says that the rate of change in the capital stock equals the rate of acquisition of new capital minus the evaporation at time t. The control variable is the acquisition rate of capital, i.e., the investment rate. The objective function is again autonomous (in the sense that time enters only in the discount function), and the state and control variables are functionally separated. These simplifying assumptions, though limiting in terms of their theoretical application, provide substantial increases in tractability. We shall assume that $R(x)$ is concave and $c(u)$ is convex (and, thus, $-c(u)$ is concave), so that a maximum is assured if the first-order necessary conditions are satisfied. Note that the state equation is linear, so that it has no effect on the sufficient conditions.

The current-value Hamiltonian is

$$\mathcal{H} = R(x) - c(u) + m(u - bx)$$

producing the maximum and adjoint equations

$$\mathcal{H}_u = -c'(u) + m = 0 \tag{18-61}$$

and

$$\mathcal{H}_x = R'(x) - bm = rm - m' \tag{18-62}$$

along with the state equation

$$x'(t) = u(t) - bx(t) \tag{18-63}$$

Equation (18-61) says, as in the previous models, that the current marginal value of the capital stock, $m(t)$, equals the current value of marginal costs of investing in new capital, $c'(u)$. The adjoint Eq. (18-62) is easiest to interpret by writing it as

$$R'(x) + m' = (b + r)m$$

The right-hand side is the opportunity cost of funds, consisting of rate of depreciation of *value* of the capital stock x at time t plus the alternative investment yield, r. Along a wealth-maximizing path, this marginal opportunity cost must equal the marginal rate at which benefits are being produced. These marginal benefits derive from two sources: the instantaneous (marginal) profits from an additional increment of capital, $R'(x)$, plus the capital gain, $m'(t)$ (i.e., the rate of change in the marginal value of the capital occurring at time t, which derives from future wealth-maximizing use of the capital stock). As in all dynamic processes (and this is what makes them dynamic), the value of actions taken in the present have *two* components: some immediate net benefits plus the sum of the future net benefits.

Equation (18-62) can be further interpreted in this manner by multiplying through by $e^{-(b+r)t}$ and writing it as

$$e^{-(r+b)t}[m' - (b + r)m] = -e^{-(r+b)t}R'(x)$$

Integrating both sides and assuming $R'(x)$ is bounded from above, so that the integral function evaluated at the upper limit is zero,

$$e^{-(r+b)t}m = \int_t^\infty e^{-(r+b)s}R'(x(s))ds$$

or, multiplying through by $e^{(r+b)t}$,

$$m(t) = \int_t^\infty e^{-(r+b)(s-t)} R'(x(s)) ds \qquad (18\text{-}64)$$

Equation (18-64) says that the current (at time t) marginal value of capital is the future net marginal profits discounted back to time t, where the interest rate used for discounting is the sum of the real interest rate, r, and the depreciation rate, b, reflecting the true opportunity cost of using this particular capital. Lastly, combining this equation with Eq. (18-61) says that marginal costs equal these marginal benefits:

$$c'(u(t)) = \int_t^\infty e^{-(r+b)(s-t)} R'(x(s)) ds \qquad (18\text{-}65)$$

Let us now "solve" this problem, in the sense of investigating whether some steady state solution exists and what its properties are. We use a diagrammatic analysis similar to that used previously and investigate paths in the (x, m) phase plane that satisfy the first-order conditions.

Since marginal cost is strictly increasing ($c'' > 0$), we eliminate the control variable u by inverting $c'(u) = m$; thus, $u = h(m)$, where $h'(m) = 1/c'' > 0$. Substituting this into the state equation gives

$$x' = h(m) - bx \qquad (18\text{-}66)$$

Equation (18-66) and the adjoint equation, (18-62)

$$R'(x) + m' = (b + r)m \qquad (18\text{-}62)$$

constitute two differential equations in x and m. The steady state occurs where $x' = m' = 0$:

$$h(m) = bx \qquad (18\text{-}67)$$

$$R'(x) = (b + r)m \qquad (18\text{-}68)$$

These equations are sketched in Fig. 18-3. Since $c'(0) = 0$ and $c'' > 0$, Eq. (18-67) passes through the origin and is positively sloped. The intersection of the two curves is the steady state and is denoted S; let x^* and m^* be the steady state values of x and m.

We next ask if paths exist that are consistent with the first-order equations and that approach S asymptotically. Since $h(m)$ is increasing in m, at points above the line, $x' = h(m) - bx > 0$; likewise, $x' < 0$ below the line. Also, since $R''(x) < 0$, $R'(x)$ is decreasing in x; thus, Eq. (18-68) is negatively sloped in the phase plane. Above this curve, $m' = (b + r)m - R'(x) > 0$; thus, m is increasing above the curve and decreasing below the curve.

The combined effect of these movements is indicated by the directions indicated by the arrows in Fig. 18-3. Paths converging to the steady state exist starting either to the "northwest" (but below $m' = 0$) or to the "southeast" (but above $m' = 0$) of S. The other indicated paths are unstable, i.e., they diverge to

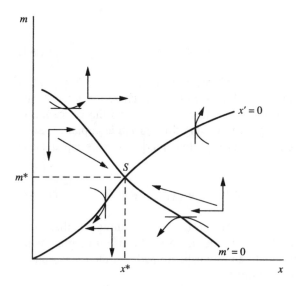

FIGURE 18-3
Phase Diagram Showing Saddle-point Stability for the Capital Utilization Model. The steady state S occurs at the intersection of the $x' = 0$ and $m' = 0$ loci. Above $x' = 0$, x is increasing; below it, x is decreasing. Also, above $m' = 0$, m is increasing; below it, m is decreasing. The combined effects are shown by the arrows. Some paths starting from the "northwest" and "southeast" of S converge to the steady state. An increase in r leaves the $x' = 0$ locus unaffected but shifts the $m' = 0$ locus toward the origin. Therefore, increases in the interest rate lower both the steady state capital stock x^* and current marginal value m^*.

infinity or zero. The steady state is a saddlepoint. We reject the divergent paths as empirically unobserved or ruled out by the curvature properties of $R(x)$ and $c(u)$, e.g., $R'(x) \to \infty$ as $x \to 0$, etc.

A common algebraic procedure used to confirm the properties of the steady state, when the defining equations are nonlinear (as in this example), is to linearly approximate the x' and m' differential equations around the steady state, using the first-order terms of a Taylor series. Performing this operation,

$$x' = -b(x - x^*) + h'(m)(m - m^*)$$

$$m' = -R''(x^*)(x - x^*) + (r + b)(m - m^*)$$

The characteristic roots are (see Eq. (18-33))

$$k_1, k_2 = \frac{1}{2}\{r \pm [(r + 2b)^2 - 4h'(m^*)R''(x^*)]^{1/2}\}$$

Since $h' > 0$ and $R'' < 0$, the roots are real, and since the term in the radical is larger than r, the roots are of opposite sign, with the absolute smaller root negative. Thus, the steady state is a saddlepoint within some neighborhood.

It has been stressed throughout this book that the goal of mathematical modeling is to derive refutable hypotheses, and that such propositions generally take the form of statements about the directions of responses of the decision variables to changes in the constraints. In dynamic models, such questions can be posed, for example, about the effect on the steady state values of the capital stock as various parameters change. These are termed comparative statics questions, as in static models. A more difficult inquiry concerns the effect of a change in a parameter on the entire path of either the control or the state variable; these questions are termed *comparative dynamics*. We briefly illustrate this analysis using the present example.

It is clear from Eqs. (18-67) and (18-68) that an increase in the interest rate leaves the first equation ($x' = 0$) unaffected, but shifts the second ($m' = 0$) locus toward the origin. As a result, the steady state capital stock is lowered, i.e., $\partial x^*/\partial r < 0$. From the positive slope of the $x' = 0$ locus, $\partial m^*/\partial r < 0$ as well, and from the maximum condition $c'(u) = m$, $\partial u^*/\partial r < 0$. We expect these results. If the opportunity cost of funds for use in the present increases, deferring consumption to the future (by investing in new capital) should decrease, resulting in a smaller final capital stock. An increase in the depreciation rate, b, produces somewhat more ambiguous changes; b enters Eq. (18-68) ($m' = 0$) in the same manner as does r, but it also enters Eq. (18-67) ($x' = 0$). Since $h'(m) > 0$, an increase in b shifts the $x' = 0$ locus up. As a result, x^* must clearly fall, but the change in m^* (and, thus, u^*) is ambiguous.

Although general comparative statics theorems of this type are difficult to state, a result is available for the effects of changes in the interest rate (or rate of time preference) on the steady state capital stock, for "autonomous" models.

Caputo's Theorem.[†] Consider a general autonomous optimal control model with infinite horizon,

maximize
$$\int_{t_0}^{\infty} f(x, u, \alpha) e^{-rt} dt$$

subject to
$$x' = g(x, u), \qquad x(0) = x_0, \qquad u \in U$$

where U is the control set and $\alpha > 0$ is a time-independent parameter. Assume an optimal solution exists that converges to the saddlepoint steady state of the model. Let $(x^*(\alpha, r), u^*(\alpha, r))$ denote this steady state, with the *'s on the functions used to indicate that they are evaluated at the steady state values.

1. The response of $x^*(\alpha, r)$ and $u^*(\alpha, r)$ to a change in the interest rate, r, is given by

$$\text{sgn}\left(\frac{\partial x^*}{\partial r}\right) = \text{sgn}(f_u^* g_u^*) \tag{18-69a}$$

$$\text{sgn}\left(\frac{\partial u^*}{\partial r}\right) = -\text{sgn}(f_u^* g_x^*) \tag{18-69b}$$

2. If the parameter α enters f such that it is attached to x only, that is, $f_{u\alpha} \equiv 0$, then the effect of change in α is given by

---

[†] See Michael R. Caputo, "The Qualitative Content of Simple Dynamic Optimization Models," unpublished Ph.D. dissertation, University of Washington, 1987.

$$\text{sgn}\left(\frac{\partial x^*}{\partial \alpha}\right) = \text{sgn}(f^*_{x\alpha}) \tag{18-70a}$$

$$\text{sgn}\left(\frac{\partial u^*}{\partial \alpha}\right) = -\text{sgn}(g^*_u g^*_x f^*_{x\alpha}) \tag{18-70b}$$

3. If the parameter α enters f such that it is attached to u only, that is, $f_{x\alpha} \equiv 0$, then the effect of change in α is given by

$$\text{sgn}\left(\frac{\partial x^*}{\partial \alpha}\right) = \text{sgn}(f^*_{u\alpha}(r - g^*_x)g^*_u) \tag{18-71a}$$

$$\text{sgn}\left(\frac{\partial u^*}{\partial \alpha}\right) = -\text{sgn}(f^*_{u\alpha}(r - g^*_x)g^*_x) \tag{18-71b}$$

Results 2 and 3 are "conjugate pairs" theorems, analogous to those derived earlier in the static models. It can be shown that g^*_x appears in all the steady state comparative statics results for $u^*(\alpha, r)$. Thus, if $g^*_x = 0$ (or if $g_x \equiv 0$), that is, if the state equation is independent of the state variable at the steady state (or globally), then the steady state value of the control variable is independent of α and the discount rate r.

In the preceding example, $f_u = -c'(u) < 0$ and $g_u = 1$; thus, $\partial x^*/\partial r < 0$, as derived directly. The theorem has wide applicability in resource extraction models. The signs of these partials are often apparent. Typically, the integrand function $f(x, u)$ measures some sort of net benefits (or negative values of costs) which are increasing in u, so typically $f_u > 0$ and the state equation has the form $x' = h(x) - u$, so that $g_u < 0$ (see, e.g., the models in the section on harvesting a renewable resource). Thus, in those models, we will generally find $\partial x^*/\partial r < 0$.

Comparative dynamics concerns the responses of the entire paths $x(t)$, $u(t)$ and $\lambda(t)$ (or $m(t)$) as the parameters of the model change. The procedure is similar to that used in comparative statics in that the "solutions," $x(t, r, b)$, $m(t, rb)$ are substituted into the simultaneous differential equations defining the paths of x and m ((18-62) and (18-66) in this model). These simultaneous equations are then differentiated with respect to some parameter, producing what is called a *variational differential equation system*. It is sometimes possible to determine the shift in the path, based on the curvature properties of the functions in the model. With more than one state variable, however, two-dimensional graphical analysis is impossible. Such material is beyond the scope of this text; the references at the end of the chapter contain discussions of this problem.

PROBLEMS

1. Solve the optimal control problem

maximize $\qquad\qquad \displaystyle\int_0^1 -u^2 \, dt$

subject to $\qquad x' = x + u, \qquad x(0) = 1, \qquad x(1) = 0$

2. Solve the optimal control problem

maximize
$$\int_1^2 (x + tu - u^2)\,dt$$

subject to $\qquad x' = u, \qquad x(1) = 3, \qquad x(2) = 4$

3. Solve the optimal control problem

maximize
$$\int_0^1 \left(\alpha tu - \frac{u^2}{2} \right) dt$$

subject to $\qquad x' = u - x, \qquad x(0) = x_0, \qquad x(1) = 0$

4. In the section entitled "Capital Utilization," let $R(x) = ax - x^2/2$ and $c(u) = cu^2$. Solve the model explicitly, and relate your solution to the analysis in the chapter.

5. Consider a mine containing some amount X of some mineral resource. Let $x(t)$ represent the cumulative amount mined at time t, so that $u = x'(t)$ is the rate of extraction. Suppose the current rate of profits of the mine is given by $P(u)$, where $P' > 0$, $P'' < 0$. Assume the owner of the mine maximizes wealth over the period $[0, T]$ and that there is no salvage value after T. Assume a fixed market interest rate, r,
   (a) Show that the present value of marginal profits is constant over $[0, T]$. Explain.
   (b) Show that the extraction rate declines over time.
   (c) Suppose the current rate of profits of the mine is given by $\log u$. Find the actual wealth-maximizing path of resource extraction, where $x(0) = 0$, $x(T) = X$.
   (d) How is the exploitation of the resource affected by changes in the interest rate, r?

6. Resolve the renewable resource model, (18-50), using a phase diagram in (K,C) phase space. Hint: Differentiate the maximum condition with respect to time, then use the adjoint and maximum equations to eliminate m and m'.

7. Solve the optimal control problem

maximize
$$\int_0^2 (2x - 3u - \alpha u^2)\,dt$$

subject to
$$x' = x + u$$

$$x(0) = 5, \quad x(2) \text{ free}$$

SELECTED REFERENCES

Bellman, R., *Dynamic Programming,* Princeton University Press, Princeton, N. J., 1957. The seminal work on D.P.

Caputo, M. R.: "How to Do Comparative Dynamics on the Back of an Envelope in Optimal Control Theory," *Journal of Economic Dynamics and Control,* 1990. Generalizes the primal-dual methodology to optimal control problems.

Caputo, M. R.: "The Qualitative Content of Renewable Resource Models," *Natural Resource Modeling,* 3:241–259. This paper uses a Taylor series approach to study the comparative static and comparative dynamic properties of a general renewable resource model.

Clark, C. W.: *Mathematical Bioeconomics: The Optimal Management of Renewable Resources,* John Wiley and Sons, Inc., New York, 1976. Complete coverage of renewable resource management using variational calculus and optimal control theory.

Dorfman, R.: "An Economic Interpretation of Optimal Control Theory," *American Economic Review,* **59:**817–831, 1969. An heuristic proof and economic interpretation of the necessary conditions of optimal control theory.

Epstein, L. G.: "The Le Chatelier Principle in Optimal Control Problems," *Journal of Economic Theory,* **19:**103–122, 1978.

Hadley, G., and M. C. Kemp: *Variational Methods in Economics,* American Elsevier Publishing Co., Inc., New York, 1971. Requires solid knowledge of static optimization theory, linear algebra, and ordinary differential equations.

Intriligator, M. D.: *Mathematical Optimization and Economic Theory,* Prentice-Hall, Inc., Englewood Cliffs, N. J., 1971. Covers both static and dynamic optimization techniques relatively briefly but at an intermediate level.

Kamien, M. I., and N. L. Schwartz: *Dynamic Optimization: The Calculus of Variations and Optimal Control in Economics and Management,* Elsevier Science Publishing Co., Inc., New York, 1981. A self-contained readable introduction to dynamic optimization theory.

CHAPTER
19

EQUILIBRIUM, DISEQUILIBRIUM, AND THE STABILITY OF MARKETS

19.1 THREE SOURCES OF REFUTABLE HYPOTHESES

In the past chapters, the choice functions of comparative statics were derived from a specific behavioral assertion of maximizing behavior. The first-order necessary conditions for a maximum or a minimum served to define what is commonly called the *equilibrium position* of the model. Specifically, these equations indicate the choices made by economic agents for various parameter values. They are the logical deductions of the behavioral hypothesis and assumed functional forms of the model.

The simultaneous solution of the first-order equations for the decision variables in terms of the parameters produces the explicit choice functions

$$\mathbf{x} = \mathbf{x}^*(\boldsymbol{\alpha}) \qquad (19\text{-}1)$$

The refutable theorems generated by models like these consist of restrictions of the signs of the various partial derivatives of (19-1). That is, consider the $n \times m$ matrix in terms of $\partial x_i / \partial \alpha_j$. If certain restrictions in sign are deducible from the maximization hypothesis and the specific functional forms, e.g., for three choice variables and four parameters,

$$\begin{pmatrix} - & ? & ? & + \\ ? & + & ? & ? \\ + & ? & ? & ? \end{pmatrix}$$

then meaningful theorems or refutable hypotheses are implied. We showed earlier that if parameters entered one and only one first-order relation (but not the constraints), certain sign patterns were implied; in particular, for $\mathcal{L}_{x_i \alpha_i} > 0$,

$$\frac{\partial x_i^*}{\partial \alpha_i} > 0$$

The signs of these diagonal terms are in fact the only qualitative comparative-statics implications of the general maximizing models formulated above in which the only functional restriction is that a given parameter enter one and only one first-order equation. These sign restrictions are deducible from the sufficient second-order conditions for a maximum.

The assertion of maximization of some objective function is a fundamental part of many economic models. In past chapters we have been concerned principally with the implications of such models. In general, there are two other categories of hypotheses used to specify economic models. Thus, in addition to the hypothesis:

1. Some objective function $f(\mathbf{x}, \boldsymbol{\alpha})$ is maximized, possibly subject to other, constraint functions.

one may consider the alternative or additional hypotheses:

2. The parameters and functions in the model take on certain values or specific forms, e.g., assumptions of linearity in the parameters, linear overall, Cobb-Douglas production functions, etc.
3. The equations defining the choice variables in terms of the parameters (the equilibrium equations) exhibit some sort of dynamic stability which restricts the values of certain $\partial x_i^*/\partial \alpha_j$'s.

This taxonomy was first presented by Samuelson in *Foundations of Economic Analysis*.

In certain models, no explicit maximization hypothesis is used. Instead, a system of n equations is postulated to represent the equilibrium position or the choice equations. That is, one may simply consider the system

$$f^1(\mathbf{x}, \boldsymbol{\alpha}) = 0$$
$$\vdots$$
$$f^n(\mathbf{x}, \boldsymbol{\alpha}) = 0 \tag{19-2}$$

where $\mathbf{x} = (x_1, \ldots, x_n)$ are choice variables and $\boldsymbol{\alpha} = (\alpha_1, \ldots, a_m)$ are parameters. Here, f^i is *not* postulated to be the partial derivative of some objective function. Assuming the Jacobian determinant of terms $\partial f^i/\partial x_j$ is not 0, the implicit-function theorem allows solution of (19-2) for the explicit choice function, as before:

$$\mathbf{x} = \mathbf{x}^*(\boldsymbol{\alpha}) \tag{19-3}$$

It is still possible to inquire about the partial derivatives of these functions, i.e., the terms in the $n \times m$ matrix $(\partial x_i / \partial \alpha_j)$. However, the information about the sign of the determinant of the Jacobian matrix and its principal minors is no longer present. There are no curvature properties of an objective function to be assumed here; hence, there is less information. In this case, some other type of information about the $f^i(\mathbf{x}, \boldsymbol{\alpha})$'s must be incorporated into the model to make it possible to derive refutable implications.

For example, recall the two-factor, two-good general-equilibrium model of Chap. 16. This model was reduced to the following equations:

$$a_{L1}^* w + a_{K1}^* r = p_1 \qquad a_{L2}^* w + a_{K2}^* r = p_2$$

$$a_{L1}^* y_1 + a_{L2}^* y_2 = L \qquad a_{K1}^* y_1 + a_{K2}^* y_2 = K$$

where, in general, $a_{ij}^* = a_{ij}^*(w/r)$. These equations are *not* (except for linear models) the first-order conditions for any objective function (although a maximization hypothesis is used earlier). The determination of comparative-statics results was dependent upon specific *assumptions* about the a_{ij}'s, for example, $a_{L1}^*/a_{K1}^* > a_{L2}^*/a_{K2}^*$, or the reverse. Invoking linear homogeneity and restricting the values of certain variables led to refutable propositions.

A class of models for which no explicit objective function is generally postulated is the various models of macroeconomics. To cite a famous example, consider the three-sector macromodel commonly found in intermediate textbooks. Let C, I, Y, P denote, respectively, *nominal* consumption, investment, income, and the price level. Let lowercase letters represent the corresponding *real* quantities, i.e., nominal, or money, values divided by the price level. Let i denote the nominal (market) interest rate, and assume the following functional dependence between the above variables:

$$c = \frac{C}{P} = a + b\frac{Y}{P} = a + by \tag{19-4}$$

$$z = \frac{I}{P} = \alpha + \beta i \tag{19-5}$$

$$y = c + z \tag{19-6}$$

These three equations can be combined into one expression by eliminating the terms z and c. The resulting equation gives the values of i and y which are consistent with the above equations. This new relation is called the *IS* curve:

$$y = \frac{1}{(1-b)}(a + \alpha + \beta i) \tag{19-7}$$

In addition to this output-sector relation, the monetary sector is governed by the intersection of the monetary supply and demand equations. Let $L(i, Y/P)$ denote the demand for *real* cash balances (nominal demand divided by the price level, P), and let $(1/P)h(i)$ denote the supply curve of money, as determined by the monetary authorities. The monetary sector is then

$$L(i,y) - \frac{1}{P}h(i) = 0 \tag{19-8}$$

Finally, a factor market must be described. The simplest assumption is that resources are fully employed, and thus

$$y = y_f = \text{constant} \tag{19-9}$$

(The fact that this assumption negates the one reason macroeconomics is studied at all will be ignored here.)

Equations (19-7) to (19-9) represent three equations in the "unknowns" y, i, and P. [Consumption c is determined from (19-4) once y is known. Likewise, z is determined from (19-5).] One can use these equations to drive the implications of autonomous increases in the marginal propensity to consume, b, or a shift in the consumption function itself, a, or like parameters in the system. Suppose the parameter a increased. Substitute (19-9) into (19-7) and (19-8) to reduce the system to two equations. Differentiating with respect to a, noting that $\partial y/\partial a = 0$, we have, since $y = y_f$,

$$\frac{1}{1-b} + \frac{1}{1-b}\beta\frac{\partial i}{\partial a} = 0 \tag{19-10}$$

$$L_i\frac{\partial i}{\partial a} - \frac{1}{P}h'(i)\frac{\partial i}{\partial a} + \frac{1}{P^2}h(i)\frac{\partial P}{\partial a} = 0 \tag{19-11}$$

From (19-10), if $b \neq 1$,

$$\frac{\partial i}{\partial a} = -\frac{1}{\beta} \tag{19-12}$$

Substituting this value into (19-11) yields, after some manipulation,

$$\frac{\partial P}{\partial a} = \frac{1}{\beta L(i,y)}[PL_i - h'(i)] \tag{19-13}$$

The determination of the sign of these partial derivatives depends upon assumptions about the signs of the parameter β and the slopes of the liquidity-preference function L_i and the supply-of-money function $h'(i)$. If the investment function is downward-sloping ($\beta < 0$), if the demand for cash balances is negatively sloping ($L_i < 0$), and if $h'(i) \geq 0$, then an autonomous increase in the consumption function will raise the interest rate (thereby lowering real investment, z), thus increasing real consumption, c. The price level will also increase, there being no automatic offsetting downward shift in the propensity to invest in this simple model.

Thus, there are important economic models whose choice functions, or equilibrium equations, are not the first-order equations of some objective function.

This being the case, criterion 1 above for deriving refutable hypotheses is irrelevant. Refutable hypotheses will be forthcoming only via explicit assumptions about the functional forms or parameter values or an assertion about the stability of the model.

19.2 EQUILIBRIUM AND STABILITY

The reader will probably have noticed by now that we have largely eschewed the term *equilibrium* in the preceding chapters. The reason for this is twofold. First, by so doing, the choice-theoretic foundations of economic theory are emphasized. Instead of labeling the functional relations between decision variables and parameters *equilibrium conditions,* the name *choice functions* has been used. The reason is that these equations in fact state what values of the x_i's, the choice variables, will be *chosen* for given parameter values. The term *choice function* is simply more descriptive.

A second and more fundamental reason for not using the term *equilibrium* is that in the context of models with a specific behavioral assertion, it is at best redundant and at worst misleading. Consider one of the first models studied, that of a firm with the profit function $\pi = pf(x_1, x_2) - w_1 x_1 - w_2 x_2$. If we *assert* that the firm maximizes π with respect to x_1 and x_2, then the conditions $pf_1 = w_1$, $pf_2 = w_2$ are *implied*. These are not equilibrium conditions. To call these marginal relations *equilibrium conditions* is to imply that some sort of disequilibrium can exist; otherwise the term *equilibrium* is redundant. But such disequilibrium, i.e., the situation where $pf_i \neq w_i$, for some i, constitutes a denial of the original hypothesis. If $pf_i \neq w_i$ is observed, it is not disequilibrium *but a refutation of the asserted theory.*

In general, if some behavioral postulate is asserted, the logical deductions of that assertion, e.g., the first-order conditions for maximization, define the choices that will be made in the system either explicitly by individuals or as a result of the simultaneous interaction of individual choices. These deductions, which we have called *choice functions,* are commonly referred to as *equilibrium conditions.* However, since they are the logical implications of the behavioral postulate, no disequilibrium can exist without denying the theory. To imply that the reason events predicted by the theory do not occur is due to disequilibrium is to assert two sets of conflicting hypotheses.

We now briefly indicate the nature of dynamic-stability analysis. Consider a single, isolated market for one good, x. Let the demand and supply curves for x be denoted, respectively, by

$$x_D = D(p, M) \quad \text{and} \quad x_S = S(p) \tag{19-14}$$

where M is money income. Let us begin by assuming that there exists some price p^e for which $x_S = x_D$; that is,

$$D(p^e, M) - S(p^e) = 0 \tag{19-15}$$

Here we are not asserting that this relation holds all the time. It is merely being asserted that *there exists some price p^e for which it holds*. This price p^e is called the *equilibrium price*.

Walrasian Stability

Instead of making specific assertions about the slopes of these functions, let us instead postulate a mechanism by which prices change. Specifically, suppose that the rate of change of price moves directly with excess demand, $E(p) = D(p,M) - S(p)$, or

$$p' = \frac{dp}{dt} = g(D(p,M) - S(p)) = g(E(p)) \qquad (19\text{-}16)$$

where $g' > 0$. This relation attempts to capture the notion that if the quantity demanded exceeds the quantity supplied at some price, the sellers of the good will find it to their advantage to raise the price. This price-adjustment hypothesis was first explored by Walras and formulated mathematically by Samuelson. Walras considered the process one of *tâtonnement,* or groping, for an equilibrium. An auctioneer was imagined who called out successive prices and received bids to buy and sell. The price called would be adjusted upward or downward in accordance with the sign of excess demand. No trade would be allowed until the equilibrium-price vector was found [otherwise some sort of nonprice rationing would have to be used, generating in the process income effects which would shift the demand functions $D(p,M)$]. When p^e was located, trade would take place.

Let us make the basic behavioral postulate that this *tâtonnement* process will be successful; i.e., at least for prices "near" p^e, mechanism (19-16) will generate a path of prices which will approach p^e as t increases. That is, we *assert*

$$\lim_{t \to \infty} p(t) = p^e \qquad (19\text{-}17)$$

Relation (19-17) is called *stability*. Although there is an extensive taxonomy of stability concepts, only two will be considered here. If (19-17) holds for *any* initial price p, then the system is called *globally stable*, assuming p^e is unique. (If there is more than one equilibrium-price vector, then if $p(t)$ approaches any of the p^e's, the model is called *system-stable*.) Global stability requires very strong mathematical properties on the functions and is a difficult problem to analyze for general functions. For that reason, the more limited, but vastly more tractable, concept of *local* stability is considered. A model is *locally stable* if (19-17) holds for all prices p *in some neighborhood of p^e*.

Let us now refine the assertion made above to mean local stability. What refutable hypotheses emerge from this assertion? At prices "close" to p^e, the function $g(E(p))$ can be represented by a Taylor series expansion. Neglecting terms of order 2 and above (the critical feature of *local* stability), relation (19-16) becomes

$$\frac{dp}{dt} = g(E(p^e)) + g'E'(p^e)(p - p^e) + \cdots \qquad (19\text{-}18)$$

As long as only *local* stability is considered, the higher-order terms are negligible in comparison with the first-order term above and hence can be ignored. Since $E(p^e) = 0$ by definition of $E(p)$, the adjustment mechanism becomes the differential equation

$$\frac{dp}{dt} = (g'E')(p - p^e) \qquad (19\text{-}19)$$

The solution of this differential equation, as can be verified by direct substitution, is[†]

$$p(t) = p^e + (p^0 - p^e)e^{(g'E')t} \qquad (19\text{-}20)$$

where the initial price p^0 is the arbitrary constant of integration (presumably the old equilibrium).

The assertion of stability requires that the exponential term approach zero as $t \to \infty$. This will occur if the exponent $g'E' < 0$. Since $g' > 0$, the consequence of asserting Walrasian local stability is the assertion that in some neighborhood of p^e

$$E' = D_p(p, M) - S_p(p) < 0 \qquad (19\text{-}21)$$

Equation (19-21) is *not*, however, a refutable proposition about observable behavior. These supply and demand functions are themselves unobservable. Prices and quantities are observable, not these functions. The meaningful theorems are the answers to the question: Suppose some parameter (money income, here) changes; in what direction will price and quantity change?

Consider the behavior of the *equilibrium* price, as defined by (19-15), when M changes. Assuming a functional dependence $p^e = p^e(M)$, defined by solution of (19-15), differentiation of (19-15) with respect to p^e yields

$$D_p\frac{\partial p^e}{\partial M} + D_M - S_p\frac{\partial p^e}{\partial M} = 0$$

$$\frac{\partial p^e}{\partial M} = -\frac{D_M}{D_p - S_p} \qquad (19\text{-}22)$$

If the good x is asserted to be normal, i.e., not inferior, so that $D_M > 0$, Eq. (19-22) indicates that $\partial p^e/\partial M > 0$, at least locally, using the assertion of local stability (19-21). More precisely, suppose initially that $p = p^e$. If M, say, increases, the demand curve shifts to the right. The new equilibrium price, according to (19-22), will be higher than before. It is the stability hypothesis (19-17) that $\lim p(t) = p^e$ which guarantees that in the transitional period (which is actually infinitely long in this specification) price will actually tend toward the new equilibrium.

[†]When we let $p^* = p - p^e$, the deviation of price from its equilibrium value, Eq. (19-19) becomes $dp^*/dt = kp^*$, with $k = g'E'$; note that $dp^e/dt = 0$ since p^e is constant.

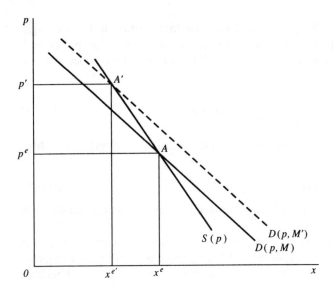

FIGURE 19-1

Walrasian stability. The supply and demand curves are *both* downward-sloping, although the supply curve is more so. This system is Walrasian-stable. Suppose the demand curve shifts to $D(p, M')$, the dotted curve. At old equilibrium price p^e there is now positive excess demand; that is, $E(p^e, M') > 0$. The Walrasian adjustment mechanism says that p must rise. In so doing, the price will move toward point A', the new equilibrium, defined by $E(p^{e'}, M') = 0$. Here however, the new equilibrium quantity is *less* than the previous one.

The implication of stability in one market, as given by (19-21), is that the demand curve has a lower slope than the supply curve. This is satisfied in the usual case, where $D_p < 0$, $S_p > 0$. However, it is also satisfied, for example, where $D_p < 0$ and $S_p < 0$, with $|S_p| < |D_p|$, as depicted in Fig. 19-1. (Remember that the dependent variable is on the *horizontal* axis.) If the demand curve shifts to $D(p, M')$, the new equilibrium price $p^{e'}$ will indeed be higher, in accordance with Eq. (19-22). However, the new equilibrium *quantity* $x^{e'} = D(p^{e'}, M') = S(p^{e'})$ will be *lower* than previously, unlike the case where the supply curve is positively sloped. Hence, we should expect this Walrasian-stability mechanism to be insufficiently strong to assert a sign for $\partial x^e / \partial M$. Using the supply identity $x^e = S(p^e)$ leads to $\partial x^e / \partial M = S_p \partial p^e / \partial M$, or

$$\frac{\partial x^e}{\partial M} = \frac{-D_M S_p}{D_p - S_p} \tag{19-23}$$

From the stability hypothesis, the denominator $D_p - S_p < 0$. Hence (with $D_M > 0$), $\partial x^e / \partial M \gtrless 0$, as $S_p \gtrless 0$. Since the sign of S_p is not implied by the Walrasian dynamic-stability hypothesis, no refutable hypothesis about quantity changes is forthcoming in this elementary model.

Marshallian Stability

An alternative stability mechanism is the one proposed by Alfred Marshall, who treated prices as functions of quantities. At any given quantity, the *height* of the demand curve was called the *demand price* and the height of the supply curve the *supply price*. (In more modern terminology, these values are, of course, the marginal rate of substitution and marginal cost, respectively.) Marshall postulated that whenever demand price exceeded supply price, the *quantity* offered for sale would increase. Likewise, if supply price exceeded demand price, quantity would decrease. This mechanism can be formulated mathematically as

$$x' = \frac{dx}{dt} = g(D^*(x,M) - S^*(x)) = g(E^*(x)) \tag{19-24}$$

where $g(0) = 0$, $g' > 0$ and $p = D^*(x,M)$ and $p = S^*(x)$ are the inverted demand and supply functions, respectively. As before, let us postulate that there exists an equilibrium price and quantity (p^e, x^e) such that

$$p^e = D^*(x^e, M) = S^*(x^e) \tag{19-25}$$

Proceeding as before, Marshallian stability implies

$$E^{*'} = D_x^* - S_x^* < 0 \tag{19-26}$$

Also,

$$\frac{\partial x^e}{\partial M} = -\frac{D_M^*}{D_x^* - S_x^*} \tag{19-27}$$

Using the assertion of Marshallian stability, (19-26), we get $\partial x^e/\partial M > 0$. The new equilibrium quantity sold must be larger than previously. However, in addition to determining a sign for $\partial x^e/\partial M$, the stability condition $\lim x(t) = x^e$ is the guarantee that the new equilibrium will actually be approached. Thus, the derivation of refutable comparative-statics propositions in this model are, as in the Walrasian case, dependent upon the assertion of some *dynamic*-stability hypothesis.

Although the Marshallian dynamic mechanism implies a sign for *quantity* changes, no refutable proposition emerges for *price* changes. From $p^e = S^*(x^e)$, $\partial p^e/\partial M = S_x^* \partial x^e/\partial M$, or

$$\frac{\partial p^e}{\partial M} = -\frac{D_M^* S_x^*}{D_x^* - S_x^*} \tag{19-28}$$

Since $S_x^* \gtrless 0$, $\partial p^e/\partial M \gtrless 0$ as $S_x^* \gtrless 0$. Whereas the Walrasian dynamic-adjustment mechanism implies a definitive direction for *price* changes (but not quantity changes), the Marshallian mechanism implies a definitive sign for *quantity* changes (but not price changes). In the usual case of downward-sloping demand curves and upward-sloping supply curves, *both* adjustment mechanisms imply the expected changes: an increase in money income (for a normal good) implies an increase in both price and quantity. But this result is dependent upon the

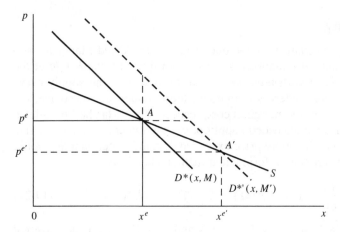

FIGURE 19-2
Marshallian stability. In this model, while the supply and demand curves are both downward-sloping, the demand curve is more so. Equilibrium is defined as $E^*(x, M) = 0$, where E^* is the excess of demand *price* (marginal value) over supply *price* (marginal cost). The *Marshallian* adjustment mechanism postulates that *quantity* will change in the same direction as E^*. Suppose the demand curve shifts *up* to $D^{*'}(x, M')$. (Remember that price is the dependent variable here.) Then at x^e, there is now an excess of demand price over supply price. According to the dynamic postulate, quantity will increase, thereby moving the system toward the new equilibrium A'.

Note that this model is *not* Walrasian-stable. At the old equilibrium price, p^e, there is now positive excess demand. The Walrasian mechanism says that price will increase. But this leads the system *away* from the new equilibrium. Check your understanding of these mechanisms by showing that in Fig. 19-1 the model is not *Marshallian*-stable. In the usual case of downward-sloping demand and upward-sloping supply curves, the system is both Walrasian-stable and Marshallian-stable.

additional assertion of the slopes of each of these curves. In Fig. 19-2, an example of a system which is Marshallian-stable but not Walrasian-stable is shown.

There is a formal *mathematical* similarity between the Marshallian and Walrasian adjustment mechanisms. It would be unwise to conclude from this, however, that the analyses of price adjustments and quantity adjustments are identical. In the real world, changing quantities is a rather different order of business from changing prices. The latter can be changed with no great resource cost: one simply posts a different price. Changing *quantities,* on the other hand, means employing different amounts of resources—hardly a costless mechanism. The problem stems from the assertion of ad hoc adjustment mechanisms not clearly related to utility or wealth maximization.

19.3 MULTIMARKET EQUILIBRIUM AND STABILITY

The previous discussions of stability related to one isolated market. The analysis of interrelated markets proceeds along similar lines but is mathematically more complex. We shall only briefly indicate the results of extending the discussion of stability to multiple markets.

Open Systems: Stability

Suppose first that there are only two interrelated goods, x_1 and x_2, which are transacted at prices p_1 and p_2, respectively. Assume that the demand functions for x_1 and x_2 are functions of both prices. We shall assume income constant in this discussion and thus suppress that argument in the demand functions. These two goods are *not* the entire set of goods produced; hence, this market is called an *open* economy.

The demand functions are thus

$$x_1 = x_1^D(p_1, p_2) \quad x_2 = x_2^D(p_1, p_2) \tag{19-29}$$

Let us suppose that the supply functions are functions of the good's own price only (though this assumption is nowhere critical):

$$x_1 = x_1^S(p_1) \quad x_2 = x_2^S(p_1) \tag{19-30}$$

Assume as before that an equilibrium-price vector exists, i.e., there is some p_1^e, p_2^e (not necessarily unique) such that

$$E_1(p_1^e, p_2^e) = x_1^D(p_1^e, p_2^e) - x_1^S(p_1^e) = 0$$
$$E_2(p_1^e, p_2^e) = x_2^D(p_1^e, p_2^e) - x_2^S(p_2^e) = 0 \tag{19-31}$$

The excess demand functions E_1 and E_2 are functions of both prices, a feature of some mathematical consequence. Equations (19-31) merely define the *equilibrium* position; however, prices and quantities are allowed to take on other values. For nonequilibrium prices, the behavioral relations defining the system are

$$\frac{dp_1}{dt} = g_1(E_1(p_1, p_2)) \quad \frac{dp_2}{dt} = g_2(E_2(p_1, p_2)) \tag{19-32}$$

with $g_i(0) = 0$, $g_i'(E_i) > 0$. That is, in each market, positive excess demand will tend to raise the price in that market, with the rate of price change positively related to the excess demand in that market. The dynamic relations (19-32) include the equilibrium relations (19-31) as long as an equilibrium point exists.

Proceeding as before, each relation in (19-32) is approximated by the first-order terms in a Taylor series expansion. Since the E_i are functions of two variables, this yields

$$\frac{dp_1}{dt} = g_1'(E_{11}(p_1 - p_1^e) + E_{12}(p_2 - p_2^e))$$

$$\frac{dp_2}{dt} = g_2'(E_{21}(p_1 - p_1^e) + E_{22}(p_2 - p_2^e)) \tag{19-33}$$

where $E_{ij} = \partial E_i / \partial p_j$. No conceptual generality is lost by letting g_1' and g_2' be constant; for ease of exposition let $g_1' = k_1$, $g_2' = k_2$. These k_1 and k_2 values are regarded as *speeds of adjustment*. The solution to the simultaneous system of differential equations (19-33) proceeds first by defining new variables $p_1^* = p_1 - p_1^e$, $p_2^* = p_2 - p_2^e$, that is, the deviations of each price from the equilibrium price.

Since p_1^e, p_2^e are constant, $dp_i^e/dt = 0$ and hence $dp_i^*/dt = dp_i/dt$. Therefore, (19-33) becomes

$$\frac{dp_1^*}{dt} = k_1 E_{11} p_1^* + k_1 E_{12} p_2^*$$

$$\frac{dp_2^*}{dt} = k_2 E_{21} p_1^* + k_2 E_{22} p_2^* \qquad (19\text{-}34)$$

To find the general solution to these simultaneous linear differential equations, let

$$p_i^* = A_i e^{\lambda t} \qquad (19\text{-}35)$$

Substituting (19-35) into (19-34), noting that $dp_i^*/dt = \lambda A_i e^{\lambda t} = \lambda p_i^*$, yields

$$\lambda p_1^* = k_1 E_{11} p_1^* + k_1 E_{12} p_2^*$$

$$\lambda p_2^* = k_2 E_{21} p_1^* + k_2 E_{22} p_2^*$$

These equations can be written in matrix form as

$$\begin{pmatrix} k_1 E_{11} - \lambda & k_1 E_{12} \\ k_2 E_{21} & k_2 E_{22} - \lambda \end{pmatrix} \begin{pmatrix} p_1^* \\ p_2^* \end{pmatrix} = \begin{pmatrix} 0 \\ 0 \end{pmatrix} \qquad (19\text{-}36)$$

Equations (19-36) are two linear equations in two "unknowns," p_1^* and p_2^*. Since the right-hand side of these equations is 0, the solution of these two equations can exist only if the determinant of the left-hand matrix equals 0:

$$\begin{vmatrix} k_1 E_{11} - \lambda & k_1 E_{12} \\ k_2 E_{21} & k_2 E_{22} - \lambda \end{vmatrix} = 0 \qquad (19\text{-}37)$$

Equations of the form (19-37) are called the *characteristic equations* or *eigenvalue equations* of a matrix. The values of λ that satisfy this equation are called *eigenvalues* or *characteristic values*. There is an extensive literature on the eigenvalue problem as it relates to many important problems of maxima and minima and stability analysis, as in this application. Equation (19-37) is the quadratic equation

$$(k_1 E_{11} - \lambda)(k_2 E_{22} - \lambda) - k_1 k_2 E_{12} E_{21} = 0$$

or

$$\lambda^2 - (k_1 E_{11} + k_2 E_{22})\lambda + k_1 k_2 (E_{11} E_{22} - E_{12} E_{21}) = 0 \qquad (19\text{-}38)$$

The two values of λ that satisfy this equation can be obtained by use of the quadratic formula. If the solution consists of two complex numbers, these numbers are *complex conjugates*, i.e.,

$$\lambda_1 = a + bi \qquad \lambda_2 = a - bi \qquad (19\text{-}39)$$

If the roots λ_1 and λ_2 of (19-38) are not equal, the general solution of the differential Eq. (19-34) is

$$p_i^*(t) = A_{i1} e^{\lambda_1 t} + B_{i2} e^{\lambda_2 t} \qquad i = 1, 2$$

Under what conditions will stability result, that is, $\lim p(t) = p^e$ or, equivalently, $\lim p^*(t) = 0$? If λ_1 and λ_2 are real numbers, stability requires $\lambda_1 < 0$, $\lambda_2 < 0$; that is, both roots of the quadratic Eq. (19-38) must be negative. If λ_1 and λ_2 are complex and have the form given by (19-39), oscillatory paths of prices will be generated. However, these paths will converge to the equilibrium price *if the real part of λ_1 and λ_2 is negative*; that is, $a < 0$ in (19-39).

The generalization of this analysis to n goods proceeds along similar lines. Let $E_i(\mathbf{p})$ represent the excess demand function of good i, with $\mathbf{p} = (p_1, \ldots, p_n)$. Assume there exists a $\mathbf{p}^e$ such that $E_i(\mathbf{p}^e) = 0$, $i = 1, \ldots, n$. The equations defining the paths of prices are

$$\frac{dp_i}{dt} = k_i E_i(\mathbf{p}) \quad i = 1, \ldots, n \tag{19-40}$$

By using a Taylor series expansion of $E_i(\mathbf{p})$ and letting $p_i^* = p_i - p_i^e$, Eqs. (19-40) can be approximated by the n equations

$$\frac{dp_i^*}{dt} = k_i \sum_{j=1}^{n} E_{ij} p_j^* \tag{19-41}$$

Upon letting $p_i^* = A_i e^{\lambda t}$, the simultaneous Eqs. (19-41) reduce to the matrix equation

$$
\begin{pmatrix}
k_1 E_{11} - \lambda & k_1 E_{12} & \cdots & k_1 E_{1n} \\
k_2 E_{21} & k_2 E_{22} - \lambda & \cdots & k_2 E_{2n} \\
\cdots\cdots\cdots\cdots\cdots\cdots\cdots\cdots \\
k_n E_{n1} & k_n E_{n2} & \cdots & k_n E_{nn} - \lambda
\end{pmatrix}
\begin{pmatrix}
p_1^* \\
p_2^* \\
\cdot \\
p_n^*
\end{pmatrix}
=
\begin{pmatrix}
0 \\
0 \\
\cdot \\
0
\end{pmatrix}
\tag{19-42}
$$

These equations have a solution only if the characteristic equation of the E_{ij} matrix is satisfied, i.e., for values of λ that satisfy

$$
\begin{vmatrix}
k_1 E_{11} - \lambda & k_1 E_{12} & \cdots & k_1 E_{1n} \\
k_2 E_{21} & k_2 E_{22} - \lambda & \cdots & k_2 E_{2n} \\
\cdots & \cdots & \cdots & \cdots \\
k_n E_{n1} & k_n E_{n2} & \cdots & k_n E_{nn} - \lambda
\end{vmatrix}
= 0 \tag{19-43}
$$

This is the characteristic equation of the matrix $\mathbf{KE}$, where $\mathbf{K}$ is a diagonal matrix of speeds of adjustment and $\mathbf{E}$ is the matrix of terms $E_{ij} = \partial E_i / \partial p_j$.

Equation (19-43) is an nth-order polynomial; it can be represented as

$$\lambda^n + b_1 \lambda^{n-1} + b_2 \lambda^{n-2} + \cdots + b_n = 0 \tag{19-44}$$

By a famous theorem in algebra, $b_i = (-1)^i$ times the sum of the ith-order principal minors of the matrix $\mathbf{KE}$. If all the characteristic roots λ are unequal, the solution to the set of simultaneous differential Eqs. (19-41) is given by

$$p_i^*(t) = \sum_{j=1}^{n} A_{ij} e^{\lambda_j t} \tag{19-45}$$

where $\lambda_1, \ldots, \lambda_n$ are the n distinct characteristic roots. If a root is repeated r times, the solution to (19-41) is given by

$$p_i^*(t) = \sum_{j=1}^{n-r} (B_{i1} + B_{i2}t + \cdots + B_{i,\,r-1}t^{r-1})e^{\lambda_{jt}} \qquad (19\text{-}46)$$

In either case, the condition that $\lim p_i^*(t) = 0$ implies that the real parts of the characteristic roots $\lambda_1, \ldots, \lambda_n$ (even if some are repeated) are all negative. A matrix whose characteristic roots are all negative is therefore called a *stable matrix*.

The preceding theorems are not much help in determining the quantitative properties of the E_{ij} matrix that leads to stability of the system. Further help is provided by the following well-known theorems.

Theorem 1.[†] If a matrix $\mathbf{A}$ is symmetric, that is, $a_{ij} = a_{ji}$, then the eigenvalues are all real.

Theorem 2.[‡] If a matrix $\mathbf{A}$ is symmetric and stable, $\mathbf{A}$ is necessarily negative definite.

Theorem 3.   (Routh-Hurwitz)[§] Let $b_i = (-1)^i$ times the sum of all ith-order principal minors of a real $n \times n$ matrix $\mathbf{A}$. Then $\mathbf{A}$ is stable if and only if

1. $b_i > 0$, $i = 1, \ldots, n$

2.

$$\begin{vmatrix} b_1 & b_3 \\ 1 & b_2 \end{vmatrix} > 0 \qquad \begin{vmatrix} b_1 & b_3 & b_5 \\ 1 & b_2 & b_4 \\ 0 & b_1 & b_3 \end{vmatrix} > 0$$

and so forth, where $b_i = 0$ if $i > n$.

Theorem 4.   (Lyapunov)[‖] A real matrix $\mathbf{A}$ is stable if and only if there exists a symmetric positive definite matrix $\mathbf{B}$ such that $\mathbf{BA} + \mathbf{A}'\mathbf{B}$ is negative definite (where $\mathbf{A}'$ is the transpose of $\mathbf{A}$). (Of course, $\mathbf{B}$ may be a positive diagonal matrix, such as the speed-of-adjustment matrix $\mathbf{K}$ above.)

A complete discussion of the known implications of these and other theorems related to matrix stability is beyond the scope of this book.[#] Let us briefly

[†] See, for example, G. Hadley, *Linear Algebra,* Addison-Wesley Publishing Company, Inc., Reading, Mass., 1961.

[‡] Ibid.

[§] See F. R. Gantmacher, *The Theory of Matrices,* vol. II, Chelsea Publishing Company, New York, 1960.

[‖] Ibid.

[#] See, for example, J. Quirk and R. Saposnik, *Introduction to General Equilibrium Theory and Welfare Economics,* McGraw-Hill, New York, 1968.

note the following, however. For 2×2 matrices, the Routh-Hurwitz theorem implies that the *sum* of the diagonal elements is negative and the whole determinant is positive if the matrix is stable. Consider then the two-equation system (19-31) and (19-32). Suppose an equilibrium position is disturbed a slight amount (within the region of local stability) by, say, a shift in the excess demand curve of the first good. We have

$$E_1(p_1^e, p_2^e, \alpha_1) = 0 \quad E_2(p_1^e, p_2^e, \alpha_2) = 0$$

Differentiating with respect to α_1 and solving gives

$$\frac{\partial p_1^e}{\partial \alpha_1} = \frac{-E_{1\alpha}E_{22}}{E_{11}E_{22} - E_{12}E_{21}} \tag{19-47}$$

$$\frac{\partial p_2^e}{\partial \alpha_1} = \frac{E_{1\alpha}E_{21}}{E_{11}E_{22} - E_{12}E_{21}} \tag{19-48}$$

Unfortunately, local stability alone is not sufficiently powerful to sign these expressions. [Of course, (19-48) would be unsignable even under a maximization hypothesis.] By the Routh-Hurwitz theorem, the denominators are positive. But that theorem merely implies that $E_{11} + E_{22} < 0$, *not* that both $E_{11} < 0$ and $E_{22} < 0$, as in the case of maximization models. We *can* infer that at least one of $\partial p_i^e / \partial \alpha_i > 0$ (assuming $E_{i\alpha_i} > 0$), but not *necessarily* both. Thus, local dynamic stability is a rather weak behavioral postulate when taken alone; it is, for example, insufficiently powerful to derive the law of demand in multimarket equilibrium.

Closed Economies

When combined with other hypotheses, local dynamic stability can imply some refutable hypotheses. Consider a pure-trade model with $n + 1$ commodities. That is, suppose there are fixed stocks of the $n + 1$ goods, $x_0^0, x_1^0, \ldots, x_n^0$ available. Consumers own these stocks in varying amounts and trade them in the marketplace at prices $p_0, p_1, \ldots, p_n$, respectively. In the aggregate, if the total amount purchased equals the amount sold, then

$$\sum_{i=0}^{n} p_i x_i^D(p) = \sum_{i=0}^{n} p_i x_i^0 \tag{19-49}$$

When we let the aggregate demand $E_i(p) = x_i^D - x_i^0$, Eq. (19-49) becomes

$$\sum_{i=0}^{n} p_i E_i = 0 \tag{19-50}$$

known as *Walras' law*. The total value of excess demand in a closed economy equals 0, *even at nonequilibrium prices*. Suppose now that n of these $n + 1$

markets, say, goods 1 to n, are in equilibrium. Then, by definition, $E_i(p_i^e) = 0$, $i = 1, \ldots, n$. Then, assuming $p_0 \neq 0$, necessarily, $E_0(p_0) = 0$; that is, $p_0 = p_0^e$. The $(n + 1)$th market must also be in equilibrium. This system therefore reduces to an n-equation system. If the demand curves (and hence the excess demands) are assumed homogeneous of degree zero, then one price, say, p_0, can arbitrarily be set equal to unity. Good x_0 becomes the numéraire commodity, and the system reduces to

$$E_i(p_1^e, \ldots, p_n^e) = 0 \quad i = 1, \ldots, n \tag{19-51}$$

as before, in the open economy.

With fixed initial endowments, $\partial E_i / \partial p_j = \partial x_i^D / \partial p_j$. If these are the demand curves of utility-maximizing consumers, $\partial x_i^D / \partial p_j = (\partial x_i^D / \partial p_j)_U + (x_i^D - x_i^0) \times (\partial x_i^D / \partial M)$, the Slutsky equation for trading models. If the income effects are all symmetric, so that $\partial x_i^D / \partial p_j = \partial x_j^D / \partial p_i$, then the matrix $\mathbf{E} = (E_{ij})$ is symmetric. If it is also stable, then by theorem 2 above, the principal minors of E alternate in sign; in particular, the $(n - 1)$th- and nth-order principal minors are of opposite sign. In this case, the comparative statics of this model follows exactly that of the corresponding maximization models. An outward shift in any demand function will cause an increase in the price of that good.

19.4 GAME THEORY

We see that stability mechanisms predicated on price versus quantity adjustments lead to different restrictions on the behavior of markets. The ambiguities present are due to the fundamentally ad hoc nature of the analysis. Clearly, some constraints on the traders have not been fully specified; something is missing. Market stability is imposed on the combined effects of individuals seeking their own maximum positions without any specification of the costs or other constraints facing these traders in the market. In fact, as was first pointed out by Kenneth Arrow in 1959, in competitive markets, all individuals are supposed to be "price takers"—none can affect the market price by their own actions.[†] How then can prices ever change? Who changes prices in competitive markets?

In recent years, interest in game theory has been renewed in an attempt to model in a more specific way the interactions of competing utility or wealth maximizers. The term *game theory* refers to models in which specific strategies of competing players are modeled. In ordinary supply and demand analysis, we of course refer to the competing actions of consumers and suppliers. However, we typically assume that in a market, consumers are price takers and suppliers, even if they possess some price-making ability, choose some price structure and then sell to specific buyers at those prices. Actual interaction, such as haggling over the price, is not as frequently modeled.

[†] Kenneth Arrow, "Toward a Theory of Price Adjustment," in *The Allocation of Resources*, Moses Abromovitz (ed.), Stanford University Press, Stanford, Calif., 1959, pp. 41–51.

The theory of games was started in its modern form by the mathematician John Von Neumann and the economist Oskar Morgenstern in their 1944 volume, *Theory of Games and Economic Behavior.*[†] A type of game that we shall not analyze is called *zero sum*; in such models, one person's gain is exactly the other person's loss. Lotteries, poker games, etc. are zero sum. Economics, however, is fundamentally about *mutually advantageous* trades; zero sum transactions are necessarily coercive (although agreeing to play such a game, e.g., poker, may be voluntary).

Perhaps the first instance of modeling actual interaction by market participants is Cournot's analysis of a *duopoly*, that is, a market in which exactly two suppliers produce identical goods.[‡] Let x_i be output of firm i ($i = 1, 2$), let $C_i(x_i)$ be that firm's cost function, and let $p(x)$ represent the (industry) demand curve, where $x = x_1 + x_2$. We assume, of course, that $p'(x) < 0$. If the firms were able to collude perfectly, that is, together act as a monopolist, they would achieve maximum joint profits by setting $MR(x) = xp'(x) + p = C_1'(x_1) = C_2'(x_2)$. Cournot considered the case where such collusion was impossible. He postulated that, at any moment, each firm would maximize firm profits assuming the other firm's output as given. The firms then continually adjust their outputs until each firm has no further incentive to do so. For firm 1, therefore, the objective function would be

$$\underset{x_1}{\text{maximize}} \qquad \pi = p(x_1 + x_2)x_1 - C_1(x_1)$$

with a similar expression for firm 2. The other firm's output is taken as parametric. The first-order conditions are

$$\pi_1 = x_1 p'(x_1 + x_2) + p - C_1'(x_1) = 0 \qquad (19\text{-}52a)$$

$$\pi_2 = x_2 p'(x_1 + x_2) + p - C_2'(x_2) = 0 \qquad (19\text{-}52b)$$

Solving each equation in terms of the other firm's output yields the *reaction functions*

$$x_1 = x_1^*(x_2) \qquad (19\text{-}53a)$$

$$x_2 = x_2^*(x_1) \qquad (19\text{-}53b)$$

These reaction functions are depicted in Fig. 19-3. Note that the intersections of these curves with the axes produce, where the other firm's output is zero, the simple monopoly solutions x_i^M. Cournot postulated an equilibrium where, given the observed output of the other firm, neither firm wished to change its output.

[†] John Von Neumann and Oskar Morgenstern, *Theory of Games and Economic Behavior,*

[‡] A. Cournot, *Researches into the Mathematical Principles of the Theory of Wealth,* trans. Nathaniel T. Bacon, The Macmillan Company, New York, 1897 (first published in French in 1838).

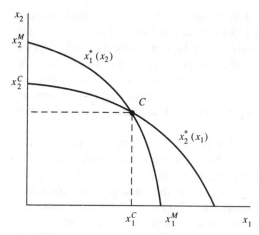

FIGURE 19-3
Nash Equilibrium in a Cournot Duopoly. The functions $x_1^*(x_2)$ and $x_2^*(x_1)$ are the reaction functions of each firm. They indicate the profit-maximizing output of each firm, for parametric values of the other firm's output. The intersection of these curves, point C, is the Cournot solution to the duopoly problem. It is a Nash equilibrium, since neither firm will change its decision, under the assumed behavior. However, it is not a Pareto solution, since further gains from trade could exist with a lower price. For that reason, each firm has a wealth-maximizing incentive to cheat on this arrangement.

This outcome occurs at the simultaneous solution to (19-53), the point C in Fig. 19-3, at outputs (x_1^C, x_2^C).

Although these reaction functions have been drawn as downward sloping and intersecting at only one point, that situation is not implied by profit maximization alone. For example, substituting (19-53a) into (19-52a),

$$\pi_1(x_1^*(x_2), x_2) \equiv 0$$

Differentiating implicitly with respect to x_2,

$$\frac{dx_1^*}{dx_2} = \frac{-\pi_{12}}{\pi_{11}} = \frac{-MR_1'}{(MR_1' - MC_1')}$$

where MR_1 means the marginal revenue of firm 1 when firm 2's output is held fixed. Although $MR_1' < 0$ might reasonably be assumed, it is not implied by a downward-sloping demand curve or by profit maximization. The denominator, however, is negative, from the second-order conditions. A similar expression of course holds for dx_2^*/dx_1.

The first-order conditions for either firm can be written

$$\frac{p(x) - MC_i(x_i)}{p(x)} = -\frac{dp}{dx} \frac{x_i}{p} \frac{x}{x} = \frac{s_i}{\epsilon}$$

where s_i is the ith firm's market share and $-\epsilon$ is the elasticity of demand at the Cournot equilibrium. This expression can be interpreted to mean that the "markup" above marginal cost varies inversely with the elasticity of demand, as one might expect in any non-perfectly competitive market. Also,

$$s_i = \frac{p(x) - \mathrm{MC}_i(x_i)}{p(x)} \epsilon$$

This expression indicates that firms with lower marginal costs will have larger market shares. Note also that under Cournot's behavioral hypothesis, the relatively high-marginal-cost firm is not altogether driven out of the market, even if that marginal cost is higher for all relevant output levels. Rearranging again,

$$p = \mathrm{MC}_i \frac{\epsilon}{\epsilon - s_i}$$

This expression indicates that the Cournot price is less than the pure-monopoly price, where $s_i = 1$.

The solution proposed by Cournot to the duopoly problem is an example of what is now referred to as a *Nash equilibrium,* after the mathematician John Nash, who first proposed it. A Nash equilibrium is a situation where all players in a game choose not to alter their decisions; it is a "no regret" situation. The equilibrium depends on the assumed strategies of the other players. In the Cournot duopoly model, the strategy of the other player is assumed fixed and known to the other firm. Under these assumptions, once the simultaneous solution of the response functions is found, there is "no regret" on either player's (firm's) part. The concept of a Nash equilibrium has become a fundamental aspect of modern game theory.

The Cournot solution, however, is not the only Nash equilibrium for duopoly models. Cournot's work was criticized by Joseph Bertrand in 1883,[†] who argued that firms would use prices rather than quantities as their decision variables. That is, each firm chooses a price, assuming the other firm's *price* will not change. Under this hypothesis, the model becomes, for each firm,

$$\underset{p_i}{\text{maximize}} \qquad \pi^i(p_1, p_2) = (p_i - \mathrm{MC}_i)x_i(p_1, p_2)$$

where, for simplicity, we assume each firm has constant marginal cost MC_i. Since we are assuming both firms produce the same product, the demand curve facing each firm, $x_i(p_1, p_2)$, consists of either the entire demand if $p_i < p_j$ half the demand, presumably, if $p_i = p_j$, and 0 if $p_i > p_j$.

It is easy to see that under the Bertrand hypothesis, the Nash equilibrium is where the low-cost firm serves the entire market, at the higher of the two marginal costs. Suppose, for example, $\mathrm{MC}_1 > \mathrm{MC}_2$. If the firms charge some price $p > \mathrm{MC}_1$ and share the market, either firm can approximately double profits by lowering the price just a bit and capturing the entire market. However, only the low-cost firm can price slightly below MC_1, and thus firm 2 can ultimately capture the entire market. If $\mathrm{MC}_1 = \mathrm{MC}_2$, then both firms sell at the same price, equal to the common marginal cost. In that case, the Nash equilibrium is the competitive equilibrium, since output is sold where price equals marginal cost.

[†] *Journal des Savants*, September 1883.

A third hypothesis, called *Stackelberg behavior,* proposes that one firm, say firm 2, assumes that firm 1 will react in a Cournot manner to firm 2's output decision, according to the reaction function $x_1 = x_1^*(x_2)$. Firm 2 then chooses output assuming the above relation for x_1; that is, it does not assume, as in the Cournot model, that firm 1's output will be fixed. Firm 2 is the "Stackelberg leader"; firm 1 is the "follower." Depending on the cost functions, different solutions emerge. Both firms could choose to be leaders, resulting in "Stackelberg warfare."

All the preceding models suffer the important flaw of being ad hoc. Firms maximize wealth. If collusion were costless, the monopoly solution would occur. These other outcomes have been proposed because collusion is apparently not costless. Although the concept of a "no regret" Nash equilibrium sounds appealing, the relevant question is: Under what conditions of coordinating and policing noncompetitive equilibria are any of these behavioral hypotheses and Nash equilibria consistent with wealth maximization? In the Cournot solution, either firm, by lowering the price just a bit, can capture the entire market by cheating on the arrangement. All collusive solutions depend for their existence on policing the arrangements. We see in the real world, as in the case of the so-called OPEC oil cartel, that policing is not a simple affair. Each participant can profit at the expense of the others by lowering price. Output quotas are very difficult to maintain for that reason.

Game theory coupled with a more complete specification of transactions and policing costs perhaps offers the most promising framework for the study of nonperfectly competitive behavior. A significant issue in this literature is the problem of *asymmetric information.* In this situation, one party to an exchange (usually the seller) has more information about the item to be traded than does the other. This is a prominent feature of the market for used cars. However, buyers are aware that many sellers of used cars are selling because their car is a "lemon." Therefore, they are not willing to pay as much for the car because measuring the quality of the car is costly; it is cheaper simply to offer a lower amount. Thus, the price of used cars reflects the presence of lemons in that market. However, some individuals sell cars for other reasons, e.g., they are transferred or get divorced. These sellers often pay a penalty because they may be unable to convince the buyer that their car is not a lemon.

The problem of asymmetric information also figures prominently in the theory of mergers. Vertical integration is a way of reducing the transactions costs associated with this problem. By merging two firms, the incentives for one party to withhold valuable information are reduced, since joint wealth maximization may more likely be the mutual interest of both former owners. Game theory is being increasingly utilized in the analysis of industrial organization.

19.5 OVERVIEW AND CONCLUSIONS

The purpose of this chapter has been to evaluate the concepts of equilibrium, disequilibrium, and stability. Not analyzed at all was the existence of an equilibrium price vector in the first place. It is very easy to draw supply and demand curves that never intersect, or indifference curves in an Edgeworth box diagram that have no tangency at a positive price; students can practice this artwork for themselves. A vast, highly mathematical literature has arisen specifying the conditions under which "equilibrium" exists.

It is important, of course, to check the logical consistency of economic models. A model that purports to explain how equilibrium prices or quantities vary would be empty unless it were possible for equilibrium to exist. However, the claim of logical consistency is vastly weaker than the assertion that *any* functions with some elementary properties *must* intersect at a positive price. Much effort has been directed at identifying the topological properties needed to make these existence proofs work. Consistency, on the other hand, can be demonstrated by providing an example, e.g., with a simple supply-and-demand diagram. Prices exist when property rights are well defined and when consumers are willing to pay more for some good than the alternative value of the resources utilized. More productive than finding minimal topological conditions under which competitive equilibria must exist, therefore, is the modeling of the empirical features that impede the consummation of mutually beneficial transactions.

In addition, the literature in existence has focused on achieving some solution to a system of equations in terms of *prices* only. Real-world contracts, however, allow for much more complicated transactions, e.g., contracts specifying quantity, quality, and date of delivery, in addition to price. (Indeed, as was mentioned earlier, why else would contracts exist?) As we saw in the section on sharecropping in Chap. 17, individuals may specify many variables in a contract in order to extract gains from trade. Lastly, one must ask what events in the real world are described by nonexistent equilibrium. The object of science, after all, is to explain these events.

We began this book with a discussion of the structure of theories. Recall that a theory consists of three conceptually different parts. A set of behavioral postulates A (assertions, axioms) is *asserted*. These generally universal-type statements define the basic paradigm of the science. These assertions A imply that under certain observable test conditions C, various observable events E will occur. In symbols, $A \cdot C \rightarrow E$. In economics, the assertions A include statements such as "individuals prefer more goods to less" and "marginal rates of substitution diminish." These assertions form the first class of postulates that Samuelson outlined under which meaningful theorems were derived: maximizing behavior. The second such category of empirical input in economic theories, as mentioned in Sec. 19.1, is the direct *assumption* of functional forms, parameter values, etc. These are assumptions about test conditions, i.e., about the particular nature of the problem at hand. Economists will frequently *assume* that regression equations are linear, that production functions are Cobb-Douglas, etc., in an attempt to simplify the economic paradigm and thus render it tractable. Hence, some input under category 2 is necessary in empirical science.

Samuelson's third hypothesis, that equilibrium is stable, is an attempt to replace the explicit assertions of maximizing behavior with a weaker statement of how markets operate. This methodology is a departure from the explicitly choice-theoretic microeconomic paradigm. Without the unifying hypothesis of maximizing behavior, models that merely assert some mystical stability properties tend to be ad hoc, i.e., contrived to meet a specific problem. They are not easily made consistent with wealth maximization.

In the static models, i.e., ones for which an explicit time path of variable changes is not predicted, the events E *are* the comparative-statics theorems concerning instantaneous rates of change of variables with respect to parameter changes, i.e., changes in some constraints C. These events E are often termed *equilibrium positions*. However, as discussed previously, there can be no disequilibrium in these models. The disequilibrium events "not E" are in fact refutations of either the asserted axioms A or the empirical validity of the test conditions, or assumptions, C (or both). Dynamic stability in these models is a *deus ex machina,* an additional assertion that may very well be in conflict with the postulates of maximizing behavior, e.g., if noninstantaneous adjustment is postulated in a world of utility or wealth maximizers with no costs of transacting. Thus, the law of demand for factors of production for static profit-maximizing firms or for income-compensated consumer demand curves is in no way dependent upon a dynamic-adjustment mechanism. The assertions of profit or utility maximization are sufficient to imply these results.

In the explicitly dynamic models, equilibrium is most commonly defined as that subset of the events for which the variables take on stationary values, that is, $\mathbf{dx}/dt = 0$, where $\mathbf{x}$ is the vector of choice variables. However, equilibrium is also used, for example, in some growth models to refer to the whole time path of predicted values. Again, the events "not E" are time paths that refute the theory. In the market equilibrium models discussed above, equilibrium is defined as $E_i = D_i - S_i = 0$. Not surprisingly, if some parameter changes, this theory as it stands is too weak (in fact, nothing at all has been asserted about behavior) to derive refutable hypotheses. The postulate of dynamic stability is merely one way of making the set of assertions A sufficiently powerful to derive a refutable hypothesis. It is not more fundamental than the assertions of maximizing behavior contained in Samuelson's category 1. It is simply that arbitrarily defining the solution to some equations as representing equilibrium is merely definitional. It is impossible to derive refutable theorems from definitions without adding *some* behavior, whether it is utility maximization or some more vague hypothesis leading to stability. But it is the adequate vs. inadequate specification of models, not statics vs. dynamics, that is at issue.

The confusion of these issues has produced what this author considers to be methodologically strange theorems. One of the most famous theorems of multimarket equilibrium is the statement that if all goods in a general-equilibrium pure-trade model are gross substitutes, that is, $\partial E_i/\partial p_j = \partial x_i^D/\partial p_j > 0$, $i \neq j$, then the equilibrium defined by $E_i = 0$, $i = 1, \ldots, n$, is stable. ($E_{ii} < 0$ is also assumed.)[†] The purpose of asserting *nonobservable* hypotheses such as *utility*

[†] See Quirk and Saposnik, op. cit.

maximization or *stability* of markets is to derive refutable propositions such as, "if some price p_j increases, the consumption of some good x_i will increase." This statement represents (potentially) observable events. The preceding theorem uses the observable events, the goals of theory, to assert something nonobservable— stability! Of what use is such a theorem? If behavior is sufficiently well specified to imply the choice functions known as demand functions in a pure-trade situation, and if it is already known that an increase in some price will reduce the demand for that good and increase it for all other goods, what else is there left to specify? Some price changes are implied. A dynamic specification of the variables is merely a prediction in *greater detail* than the comparative-statics predictions of the response of variables to parameter changes. If the dynamic time path is inconsistent with the comparative-statics theorems, then one or more of these predictions is simply wrong: i.e., the theory is internally inconsistent.

It may very well be that the variables in question may temporarily move opposite to the directions predicted by the comparative-statics theorems. For example, a sustained expansion of the rate of growth of money (from a previously nonnegative amount) may, as its *first* impact, reduce market interest rates. Eventually, if inflation occurs, inflationary expectations will *raise* interest rates above their previous level. A simple comparative-statics model might predict this increase in interest rates and miss entirely the transitional period of depressed interest rates (perhaps the crucial period). In this case, the dynamic model is not inconsistent with the static model; it merely provides a more detailed prediction of the events E. The comparative-statics result of increased interest rates with increased monetary growth suffers from being incomplete and perhaps misleading. But dynamics and comparative statics must be consistent if the model is to make any sense.

PROBLEMS

1. Suppose the market for one good, in terms of its own price, is both Marshallian- and Walrasian-stable. Show that the demand curve must be downward-sloping and the supply curve upward-sloping.
2. How do we know whether markets are stable or not?
3. Prove that in a pure-trade world, with utility-maximizing consumers, if there is no trade at equilibrium, then the equilibrium is locally stable for all speeds of adjustment of prices.
4. Suppose in an open economy, the demands and supplies of two goods are given by:
   (a) $x_i^D = M/2p_i$, $X_i^S = x_i^0$, $i = 1, 2$
   (b) $x_i^D = p_2/p_1$, $x_2^D = (M/p_2) - 1$, $x_i^S = x_i^0$, $i = 1, 2$
   Show explicitly for these systems that $\lim_{t \to \infty} p_i(t) \to p_i^e$ for any equilibrium prices p_i^e.

BIBLIOGRAPHY

Arrow, K. J.: "Economic Equilibrium," in *International Encyclopedia of the Social Sciences*, **4:** 376–388. The Macmillan Company and the Free Press, New York, 1968.

————: "Toward a Theory of Price Adjustment," in *The Allocation of Resources*, Moses Abromovitz (ed.), Stanford University Press, Stanford, Calif., 1959, pp. 41–51.

————, J. D. Block, and L. Hurwicz: "On the Stability of Competitive Equilibrium, II," *Econometrica*, **27**:82–109, 1959.

————and G. Debreu: "Existence of an Equilibrium for a Competitive Economy," *Econometrica*, **22**:265–290, 1954.

————and L. Hurwicz: "On the Stability of Competitive Equilibrium, I, *Econometrica*, **26**:522–552, 1958.

Cournot, Augustin: *Researches into the Mathematical Principles of the Theory of Wealth*, trans. by Nathaniel T. Bacon, The Macmillan Company, New York, 1897.

Goldberg, S.: *Introduction to Difference Equations*, John Wiley & Sons, Inc., New York, 1958.

Hahn, F.: "On the Stability of a Pure Exchange Equilibrium," *International Economic Review*, **3**:206–213, 1962.

Hicks, J. R.: *Value and Capital*, 2d ed., Clarendon Press, Oxford, 1946.

Quirk, James, and Rubin Saposnik: *Introduction to General Equilibrium Theory and Welfare Economics*, McGraw-Hill Book Company, New York, 1968.

Samuelson, Paul A.: *Foundations of Economic Analysis*, Harvard University Press, Cambridge, Mass., 1948.

Walras, L.: *Elements of Pure Economics*, trans. W. Jaffe, Richard D. Irwin, Inc., Homewood, Ill., 1954.

HINTS AND ANSWERS

CHAPTER 1

1. The law of demand asserts that the quantity demanded will fall when the price is raised, *holding various other things constant*. In particular, tastes are assumed constant. In this scenario, tastes change as the price changes.

3. Follows from the law of demand.

6. Yes; the human mind is incapable of dealing with *all* aspects of a given situation.

7. No; not very.

8. (a) $a, b, k \geq 0$. (b) $x^*(t) = [(a/b) - t]/[(2/b) + 2k]$. (c) $-2/b - 2k < 0$; weaker (less restrictive on the values of a, b, k; since b may be negative, this expression is *not* equivalent to $bk > -1$. (e) Differentiate $x^*(t)$ directly.

9. Let $R(x) = px$, where p, output-price, is parametric.

11. Since $dx^*/dt < 0$ is implied here, no amount of data relating to *changes* in quantities sold and *changes* in tax rates will ever distinguish this theory from the others.

12. Substitute $y^*(t)$ into the gross and net functions, and differentiate with respect to t. Use the first-order conditions to cancel out some terms, and remember this when you get to Chap. 7.

13. This problem is most tractable as a cost (physical amount of metal used) minimization problem. When the corners are wasted, the ends use D^2 each, and the sides use $\pi D h$. The volume of one can is $(\pi D^2/4)h$. Use this to eliminate h and minimize with respect to D. The waste per can is $2k(D^2 - \pi D^2/4)$. Subtract this from the original objective function, and see how h^*/D^* varies with k.

CHAPTER 2

Section 2.1

1. (b) Suppose $x_0 > 0$. Then $1/x - 1/x_0 = (x_0 - x)/xx_0$. For x "near" x_0, $xx_0 > M$, some finite M. Let $\delta = \epsilon/M$. Then for any x such that $|x - x_0| < \delta$, $|1/x - 1/x_0| = |x - x_0|/xx_0 < \delta/M = \epsilon$, for any $\epsilon > 0$. Hence, $f(x)$ is continuous at any positive x_0. Similar reasoning holds for $x_0 < 0$.

3. No.

4. Unity.

Section 2.2

1. (a) $6x$, (b) $3x^2$, (c) m, (d) $-x^{-2}$.

4. Let A = area, C = circumference. Since $A = \pi r^2$, $dA/dr = 2\pi r = C$. The area can be thought of as being built up from concentric rings.

Section 2.3

1. (a) $\Delta y - dy = 3x(\Delta x)^2 + (\Delta x)^3$. (c) $\Delta y - dy = (2/x^2)\Delta x^2 - (3!/x^3)\Delta x^3 + \cdots$.

Section 2.8

1. (a) $x = \frac{3}{4}$, min. (c) All real x; both a min and a max. (d) No max or min for real values of x.

2. Length: $P/2$, width: $P/4$

3. MR $= 0$ at midpoint.

4. $x = 33.3$, $p = 133.3$, $\pi = 3333.3$, $\varepsilon = -2$.

5. (c) $t = 100$.

6. Differentiating Eq. (2-13), we have $M'(x) = 2A'(x) + xA''(x)$. At min AC, $A'(x) = 0$. Can $A''(x)$ be negative at min AC?

Section 2.9

2. (b) $dy/dx = \log x$. (c) $dy/dx = xe^x + e^x$. (f) $dy/dx = 2/x$. (g) $dy/dx = (2/x)\log x$. (h) $dy/dx = 1/x \log x$.

4. Equation (2-19) differs from Eq. (2-18) by a positive term. If $g'(t) > 0$, $g''(t) < 0$; then if replanting is impossible, $g'(t)$ must be smaller. This must occur when crops are left to grow longer.

6. The actual formula would be $69.3/r$ percent, for continuous compounding. Look up the natural logarithm of 2.

Section 2.12

1. (c) $e^{x^n} n + C$; (d) $-x^2/4 + (x^2/2)\log x + C$; (e) use the rules of logarithms.

2. 1.172, .586.

4. 11,000; AC $= 10 + x$, AC has half the slope of MC.

Section 2.13

1. $y = (2x^2 + C)^{1/2}$.

3. $y = (C - 2x)^{1/2}$; may not have solution in real values.

6. $\log y = e^x + C$.

8. $\log y = \int \log x \, dx \cdots$.

CHAPTER 3

Section 3.4

1. (c) $f_{11} = -x_2/x_1^2$, $f_{12} = f_{21} = 1/x_1$, $f_{22} = 0$. (e) Let $y = x_1^{x_2}$. Then $\log y = x_2 \log x_1$.

$(1/y)f_1 = x_2/x_1$, or $f_1 = (x_2/x_1)y = (x_2/x_1)f(x_1, x_2)$. Similarly, $(1/y)f_2 = \log x_1$, or $f_2 = (\log x_1)f(x_1, x_2)$. Now take second partials using the product rule.

3. $dy - \Delta y = (\Delta x_1)^2 + \Delta x_1 \Delta x_2 - (\Delta x_2)^2$.
4. 1.965; 1.952; no.
5. (b) $dy/y = \alpha(dL/L) + (1 - \alpha)(dK/K)$.

Section 3.6

1. (b) $U_{12} = U_{21} = 1$; $V_{12} = V_{21} = 4x_1 x_2$, $W_{12} = W_{21} = 0$. (c) MRS $= -x_2/x_1$ for U, V, W. (d) The MRSs.
3. (a) $MP_L = \alpha(K/L)^{1-\alpha}$, $MP_K = (1 - \alpha)(L/K)^\alpha$. (c) Yes.
6. $dy/dt = [\alpha n + (1 - \alpha)m] L_0^\alpha K_0^{1-\alpha} e^{[\alpha n + (1-\alpha)m]t}$.
7. (a) Follows from $V_i = F'(U)U_i$. (b) Use product rule on above; $V_{ij} = F'U_{ij} + F''U_i U_j$. Although $F' > 0$ is stipulated. F'' can have either sign.
8. $\partial U/\partial p_1 = -\frac{1}{9}(x_2/x_1)^{2/3}(M/p_1^2) < 0$; yes
   $\partial U/\partial p_2 = -\frac{4}{9}(x_1/x_2)^{1/3}(M/p_2^2) < 0$; yes
   $\partial U/\partial M = \frac{1}{9}(x_2/x_1)^{2/3}(1/p_1) + \frac{4}{9}(x_1/x_2)^{1/3}(1/p_2) > 0$; yes

Section 3.7

2. (a) $y = \log(x_1 x_2)$; $x_1 x_2$ is homogeneous. (c) $y = F(z) = z^2 - z$, where $z = x_1 x_2$, a homogeneous function.
4. Note that $f_i = F'h_i$; slopes of level curves are f_i/f_j; result follows.
5. Apply Euler's theorem to f_1.
6. Follow proof in text.

CHAPTER 4

Section 4.2

1. (a) The origin; saddlepoint; (b) $(\frac{22}{7}, \frac{16}{7})$; minimum; (c) (4,2); maximum.
3. When $\alpha + \beta = 1$, $L^\alpha K^\beta$ is (weakly) concave.
5. $g_i = F'f_i$; since at a stationary value $f_i = g_i = 0$, $g_{ij} = F'f_{ij}$, result follows by applying second-order conditions.

Section 4.6

1. Since the term f_{12} enters the expressions for $\partial x_1^*/\partial p$ and $\partial x_2^*/\partial p$, these partials are indeterminate in sign. If one assumes, however, that both are negative, then after eliminating the positive term in the denominators, a contradiction of the second-order conditions occurs after a little manipulation.
2. Since $y^* = f(x_1^*, x_2^*)$, $\partial y^*/\partial w_1 = f_1(\partial x_1^*/\partial w_1) + f_2(\partial x_2^*/\partial w_1)$. Applying Eqs. (4-20) gives the negative of the expression for $\partial x_1^*/\partial p$. The same analysis follows for $\partial y^*/\partial w_2$.
3. Assuming $\alpha_1 + \alpha_2 < 1$ (otherwise the second-order conditions for profit-maximization are violated), the factor demand for x_1, letting $\beta = \alpha_1 + \alpha_2 - 1$ (note $\beta < 0$) is

$$x_1^* = \alpha_1^{(\alpha_2-1)/\beta} \alpha_2^{-\alpha_2/\beta} p^{-1/\beta} w_1^{(1-\alpha_2)/\beta} w_2^{\alpha_2/\beta}$$

Since the exponent of w_1 is negative, $\partial x_1^*/\partial w_1 < 0$. To find the factor demand for x_2, interchange all the 1s and 2s.

4. (a) Follows from $f_{12} = f_{21}$, $\partial x_1^*/\partial w_2 = \partial x_2^*/\partial w_1$. (b) Follows from Eqs. (4-20b) and (4-20c). (c) They aren't; $\partial x_i^*/\partial w_j$ involves more than simply f_{ij}. Other second partials will be present.

5. (a) $\partial y_1^*/\partial t = \pi_{22}/(\pi_{11}\pi_{22} - \pi_{12}^2) < 0$; (b) nothing; $\pi_{12} = C''(y)$ has either sign.

7. (a) $\partial y^*/\partial t < 0$; $\partial y_i^*/\partial t \gtrless 0$, $i = 1, 2$. (b) $(dy_1/dt)_{y_2} < 0$.

8. There are no observable differences unless the cost and revenue functions can be measured. Both yield $\partial x_1^*/\partial t < 0$; $\partial x_2^*/\partial t \gtrless 0$ (prove).

9. The cost of hiring x_2 is now $w_2 x_2 + t w_2 x_2 = (1 + t)w_2 x_2$. The factor demands are still homogeneous of degree 0 in all prices. Increasing t clearly has the same effect of the firm as increasing w_2; thus, the qualitative comparative statics results are the same.

10. (a) The factor demands are not homogeneous of any degree. Doubling both factor prices leaving the demand function unchanged would certainly change factor demand. Show this algebraically by trying to duplicate the proof in the text for the competitive case. (b) Proceed as before, differentiating with respect to w_1. (c) Define $R^*(w_1, w_2)$ as $R(x_1^*, x_2^*)$; differentiate with respect to w_1. Answer: No.

11. (a) Nothing. (b) $\partial y_2^*/\partial t < 0$. (c) No differences except that now $\partial y_1^*/\partial t = 0$. (d) Yes. This part is really like two separate firms; there is no interaction term. (e) No. Is the price a parameter, or is it endogenously determined by the maximization hypothesis? (f) No differences. (g) Same as earlier exercises.

CHAPTER 5

Text

1. (a) -1. (b) 2. (c) -2 (short cut: add row 3 to row 1). (d) 2.

3. Apply Cramer's rule.

APPENDIX

1. rank $\mathbf{A} = 1$, rank $\mathbf{B} = 2$, rank $\mathbf{C} = 3$; $|\mathbf{C}| \neq 0$.

3. $\mathbf{A}^{-1}(\mathbf{A}^{-1})^{-1} = \mathbf{I}$ by definition. However, $\mathbf{A}^{-1}\mathbf{A} = \mathbf{I}$. Since inverses are unique, $\mathbf{A} = (\mathbf{A}^{-1})^{-1}$.

6. Let h_i, $h_j = 0$, $i, j = 2, \ldots, n$. Then $\mathbf{h'Ah} = a_{11}h_1^2 < 0$; hence $a_{11} < 0$. A similar procedure shows $a_{ii} < 0$, $i = 1, \ldots, n$.

7. Apply the definition of orthogonal matrices.

CHAPTER 6

3. Convexity of indifference curves means $-U_{11}p_2^2 + 2U_{12}p_1p_2 - U_{22}p_1^2 > 0$. This neither implies nor is implied by $U_{11} < 0$, $U_{22} < 0$ because of the U_{12} term.

4. (a) $x_1^* = 1$, $x_2^* = 1$; max. (b) $x_1^* = 1$, $x_2^* = 1$; min. (c) $x_1^* = M/2p_1$, $x_2^* = M/2p_2$; max. (d) $x_1^* = (p_2 U^0/p_1)^{1/2}$, $x_2^* = (p_1 U^0/p_2)^{1/2}$; min.

6. (a) For α, your right-hand-side column matrix in the comparative statics system should be $(-1,0,0)'$, yielding $\partial x_1^*/\partial \alpha = -H_{11}/H > 0$. For β, the cofactors are all off-diagonal. (b) Find expressions for the component parts of these expressions and combine.

7. (a) This is really a special case of 6(b) above. (b) The objective function in Prob. 6 produces this result.

8. This says firms will hire inputs until wage equals the value of marginal product; however, VMP $= pf_i = $ AC$^*f_i$. (c) The right-hand-side column is *not* $(1,0)'$ or $(0,1)'$; don't forget w_i is part of AC*. You can multiply through by y^*; terms in the left-hand-side matrix are then $-$AC$^*f_{ij}$. (d) This is an identity in w_1 and w_2, *not* in x_1 and x_2.

9. (a) By an increase in k_1. (b) Yes; find $\partial x_1^* \partial k_1$. (c) Can go either way. (d) Wages are not parameters here; one cannot write $x_i = x_i^*(w_1, w_2, p)$, as in the competitive case. (e) Essentially the same analysis as the competitive case.

CHAPTER 7

Section 7.4

1. This problem follows the text presentation and is intended as a review. The only difference is the special form of the constraint. Compare your results with those derived by the traditional methodology in Chap. 6, Prob. 7. (f) This result shows that the marginal increase in the value of the (indirect) objective function when the resource is increased is the Lagrange multiplier λ. This important concept originated in economics in the theory of linear programming. Of course, $\partial \lambda^* / \partial k \gtrless 0$.

3. It was this problem that led me to the primal-dual analysis. Compare with the traditional methodology, as outlined in Chap. 6, Prob. 8. (b) AC is linear in w_1; since AC* is *minimum* AC, it must lie below AC (except at x_1^*, x_2^*) and is therefore concave. (c) x_1^*/y^*. (g) When the output price is continuously adjusted to the minimum average cost of the (identical) firms in an industry, the short-run demand functions become the long-run demands, by definition. (h) Differentiate with respect to w_1. Use the reciprocity condition for $\partial x_1^p / \partial p$ first derived in Chap. 4.

4. The Lagrangian for the "short-run" model is $\mathcal{L} = pf(x_1, x_2) - w_1 x_1 - w_2 x_2 + \lambda(k - w_1 x_1 - w_2 x_2)$, but at the profit maximum, the constraint is "just binding," so that $\lambda^* = 0$. However, $\partial \lambda^* / \partial w_1 \neq 0$. Develop a reciprocity condition for $\partial \lambda^* / \partial w_1$. Use this with the tangency condition

$$\pi_{w_1}^* = \pi_{w_1}^s \qquad \pi_{w_1 w_1}^* \geq \pi_{w_1 w_1}^s$$

Alternatively, define the conditional demand for x_1^*: $x_1^*(w_1, w_2, p) \equiv x_1^s(w_1, w_2, p, k^*(w_1, w_2, p))$; differentiate with respect to w_1, and use the homogeneity of x_1^s in evaluating $\partial k^* / \partial w_1$.

CHAPTER 8

3. The factor demands derived in this chapter are functions of factor prices and output level. Previously, they were functions of factor prices and output-*price*. They are different functions. They are both, however, downward-sloping in their own price, perhaps the only property useful for deriving refutable hypotheses.

4. For two factors (i) and (ii) are equivalent (see Prob. 4, Sec. 4.6), whereas by (iii), the factors are always substitutes. For more than two factors, knowledge that two factors are substitutes (or complements) by any one or two definitions provides no information about the sign of the third type of expression.

7. (a) Apply Euler's theorem to f_L, f_K. (d) Follows from $dK/dL = -f_L/f_K$. (f) Apply the formulas in (a) by multiplying row 1 by L, row 2 by K, and adding one row to the other. Repeat for columns. What effects do these manipulations have on H?

CHAPTER 9

1. Returns to scale is a broader concept than homogeneity.
2. $C = w_1 x_1 + w_2 x_2 = pf_1 x_1 + pf_2 x_2 = rpy = rTR$. This model does not specify the recipient of these rents. (Indeed, there is no explanation of who it is that is maximizing profits.) Entry will always exist, driving firm size, output-price, and profits to 0.
3. (a) $y = \log 4x_1 x_2$.
4. Suppose x_1 is held fixed. Then from Euler's theorem, $\sum_{i=1}^{n} f_i x_i = ry$ and $\sum_{i=2}^{n} f_i x_i = sy$. Combine and integrate, remembering that the arbitrary constant of integration is a function of the variables held fixed in partial differentiation. Apply to each x_i in turn.
6. Since for homothetic functions, $C = J(y)A(w_1, w_2)$, $MC = J'(y)A(w_1, w_2)$ and $AC = [J(y)/y]A(w_1, w_2)$. At min AC, AC = MC, or $J' = J/y$. Integration yields, for min AC outputs only, $J(y) = ky$, an equation in y only.

CHAPTER 10

1. Diminishing MRS is a two-dimensional concept; quasi-concavity is a much stronger restriction of the curvature of the utility function.
3. None.
7. No. If $U(x_1, \ldots, x_n)$ is a utility function and $V = F(U)$, $F'(U) > 0$, V_{ij} and U_{ij} need not have the same sign.
8. (a) (i). (b) Yes. (c) For (ii) yes; for (i) no, because of the possibility of asymmetrical income effects.
10. (a) Can change its size and sign. (b) No such law. (c) No effect. (d) No effect. (e) No effect. (f) Size can change; not the sign, however.
12. (a) Not necessarily. (b) Intuitively, if a person is a net saver this year, an increase in the interest rate will provide a larger income next year, and vice versa.
18. (a) Differentiate the identity with respect to M, noting that $\lambda^M = \partial U*/\partial M$. (b) Differentiate the identity with respect to p_2, using the above and Roy's identity.
20. (a) *Vertically parallel* means $\partial(U_1/U_2)/\partial x_2 = 0$. Use the quotient rule on this expression; the numerator is proportional to D_{31}, the relevant cofactor in the expression for $\partial x_1^M/\partial M$. (b) Follows from part (a) and the Slutsky equation. (c) Note that $U_1/U_2 = 1/x_1$, a function of x_1 only. Hence, U_1/U_2 is independent of x_2. (d) Show that $\partial x_2^M/\partial p_1 = 0$.

CHAPTER 11

1. The border-preserving principal minors of order 2 are all positive; in the case of separable utility functions, this condition implies $-U_i'' p_j^2 - U_j'' p_i^2 > 0$, all i, j, $i \neq j$. Hence, there cannot be *two* U_i'''s that are both positive; otherwise one of the above conditions would be violated.

We have $U_i'(x_i^M) = \lambda^M p_i$. Differentiating with respect to M gives $U_i''(\partial x_i^M/\partial M) = p_i \partial \lambda^M/\partial M$, from which parts (i) of (a) and (b) follow. For the compensated demands, $\lambda^U U_i'(x_i) = p_i$. Differentiate with respect to p_j, noting that $\partial \lambda^U/\partial p_j = \partial x_i^U/\partial U^0$. Can inferiority or superiority be defined in terms of the sign of $\partial x_i^U/\partial U^0$?

2. Use the same hints.
3. From envelope considerations, one gets *Roy's equality*, $U_{p_i}^* = -\lambda x_i^M$. Differentiate with respect to p_k, noting that $U_{p_i p_k}^* = 0$. Do the same for $U_{p_j}^*$. Note that $U_{p_i}^* = V_{r_i}^*(1/M)$.
4. Use Prob. 3 and part (*a*) of Prob. 2.
6. $U_i'(x_i) = \lambda^M p_i$. Therefore, $U_i''(\partial x_i^M/\partial p_j) = p_i(\partial \lambda^M/\partial p_j) = 0$. Therefore, $\partial x_i^M/\partial p_j = 0$, $i, j = 1, \ldots, n$, $j \neq i$. Result follows from budget equation.
7. (*a*) A theory, utility maximization, was invented because it implied (under certain restrictions) downward-sloping demand curves. The theory also implied other things, e.g., symmetry of the substitution terms, but those properties do not follow from the assertion of downward-sloping demand functions. See the reference by El Hodiri in Chap. 14 for an amusing exposition of this point.
8. At the very least, Leo is retrading coats for the people up north.
9. (*a*) Consistent, (*b*) inconsistent, (*c*) consistent.
10. I wouldn't touch this one with a 10-foot pole. Strange behavior.
11. $U = F(x_2 + \log x_1)$
13. (*a*) At least \$4. (*b*) Less than \$6. (*c*) Approximations; bias indicated. (*d*) Not answerable.

CHAPTER 12

1. Construct the ratio of marginal utilities in consecutive time periods.
2. (*b*) If you had no heirs and you were going to die tomorrow.
3. (*a*) Once-and-for-all loss of wealth. (*b*) Price decreases by present value of tax savings for the marginal buyer. (*c*) Bad news.
4. Assuming diminishing marginal value of wool and mutton, no.
5. This is all capitalized into the present price.
6. (*a*) Lower both. (*b*) With greater inflation, this feature raises the relative value of holding these assets, increasing their price relative to depreciable assets.
7. This shifts the real burden of repayment to the present, possibly imposing liquidity constraints.
9. It is interesting that the annual amount saved varies dramatically with the initial mileage assumed. Calculate the present value of these savings.

CHAPTER 13

Section 13.3

1. Let $v = a + bu$. Then $v' = bu'$ and $v'' = bu''$. The coefficient of absolute risk aversion for v is $-bu''/bu' = -u''/u'$.
2. $v' = f'u'$, $v'' = f''u'^2 + f'u''$, $-v''/v' = -(f''u'^2 + f'u'')/f'u' = -u''/u' - f''u'/f' > -u''/u'$ since $f'' < 0$.
3. (*a*) $u' = ae^{-aW}$, $u'' = -a^2 e^{-aW}$, $-u''/u' = a^2 e^{-aW}/ae^{-aW} = a$.
   (*b*) $u' = W^{-a}$, $u'' = -aW^{-a-1}$, $-Wu''/u' = aW^{-a}/W^{-a} = a$.
   (*c*) $u' = 1/W$, $u'' = -1/W^2$, $-Wu''/u' = (1/W)/(1/W) = 1$.

Section 13.4

1. (a) $u' = a - 2bW$, $u'' = -2b$, $-u''/u' = 2b/(a - 2bW)$. As W increases, the denominator decreases so that the coefficient of absolute risk aversion rises.
(b) Let x be the amount invested in risky assets. The choice problem is:

$$\max E[a(W + xR) - b(W + xR)^2]$$

The first-order condition is

$$E[aR - 2bR(W + x*R)] = 0$$

That is, $a\bar{R} - 2bW\bar{R} - 2bx*(\bar{R} + \sigma_R^2) = 0$. This gives

$$x* = \frac{(a - 2bW)\bar{R}}{2b(\bar{R} + \sigma_R^2)}$$

(c) $x*'(W) = -\bar{R}/(\bar{R} + \sigma_R^2) < 0$.

2. $\max E[-e^{-a(W + xR)}]$. FOC: $E[aRe^{-a(W + xR)}] = 0$; i.e., $ae^{-aW}E[Re^{-axR}] = 0$; i.e., $E[Re^{-axR}] = 0$.
The first-order condition for x does not involve W. Therefore, the amount of investment in risky assets is not a function of initial wealth.

CHAPTER 14

1. The Kuhn-Tucker conditions specify *necessary* conditions for a corner solution, not *sufficient* conditions. At some point, MP_i may be greater than w_i even if at $x_i = 0$, $MP_i < w_i$.
3. $f(x_1, x_2)$ has to be concave to achieve a saddlepoint solution.
6. $x_1 = 5$, $x_2 = 5$.
7. $k = 5$.
8. $x_1 = 5$, $x_2 = \frac{8}{5}$.
10. (a) This is the *Fisher Separation Theorem* (see Chap. 12). If the consumer can borrow and lend, maximizing wealth leads to the largest opportunity set. Consumers can then rearrange consumption in accordance with their preferences by borrowing or lending. But don't take my word for it; read Fisher. (b) $x_1 = 4.93$, $x_2 = 12.82$; consumer is lender in period 1, PV $= 14.78$. (c) $x_1 = 5.15$, $x_2 = 12.36$, PV $= 15.45$.

CHAPTER 15

1. (a) $z* = 700$. (b) $u_1 = 10$, $u_2 = 10$, $u_3 = 0$. (e) Industry 1 is relatively land-intensive. Therefore, if an additional unit of labor were available, industry 1 would expand and industry 2 would contract. (f) If the price of the land-intensive industry rises, the shadow price of land u_1 must rise in greater proportion than the rise in p_1 (5 percent). The shadow price of labor must fall. (g) None.
3. $z* = 37$.
4. $z* = \$7000$.

CHAPTER 16

1. The output-supply functions are homogeneous of degree zero in output prices. The result follows from the application of Euler's theorem to these functions.

2. This is a direct application of the adding-up theorem of Sec. 14.5.

3. This allows analysis of the four-equation model [Eqs. (16-53) and (16-54)] consisting of two zero-profit conditions and two resource constraints as two separate parts, with endowments appearing in only the latter two. With respect to endowment changes, the a_{ij}s are constant, and hence this part of the model behaves like the linear models of Chap. 15 for that reason. From cost-minimization considerations, the a_{ij}s behave as though they were constants in the first two equations dealing with output-price changes.

5. (b) This production frontier is not necessarily concave because no matter what the production functions themselves are—e.g., there may be extreme increasing returns to scale—as long as marginal products are finite and resources are limited, there must be some finite maximum production of either good for fixed amounts of the other good. Thus, the only curvature properties needed for this problem are convex (to the origin) isoquants, i.e., quasi-concavity. The production frontier may therefore be convex to the origin, e.g., if both production functions exhibit rapidly increasing returns to scale, and the maximum value of output may very well occur along either axis, i.e., for positive output of only one good.

8. (c) and (d) Use the envelope theorem.

10. With linear homogeneous production functions, total factor cost equals total output, i.e.,

$$w(p_1, p_2)L + r(p_1, p_2)K \equiv p_1 y_1(p_1, p_2, L, K) + p_2 y_2(p_1, p_2, L, K)$$

Differentiate this identity.

11. The statement is valid if the conditions for the Stolper-Samuelson *and* the Hecksher-Ohlin theorems are valid.

CHAPTER 17

1. With finite resources and unlimited wants, a Pareto frontier of allocations exists along which any greater good for one person means lesser good for some other person.

2. $4y/y_1 - x/x_1 = 3$.

4. A perfectly discriminating monopolist will product output as long as some consumer will pay at least MC. Hence, the Pareto condition $p = $ MC will be satisfied, except that the monopolist will be the sole gainer from the trade. If the monopolist's income elasticities differ from other consumers, overall production will change due to the redistribution of income only.

5. (a) Yes, if transactions costs are low. (b) $1000 + \frac{1}{2}P$ to A, $1500 + \frac{1}{2}P$ to B, $2500 + P$ total. (c) $800 + P$ to A, $1200 + P$ to B, $2000 + 2P$ total. (d) If $500 < P < 600$, A's gain from sharing a pump will be greater than B's loss from so doing. With zero contracting costs, A and B will contract to share the overall gain and will thus share.

6. The curvature of the utility frontier is sensitive to the (ordinal) units of utility. Its negative slope is a consequence of scarcity.

7. Depends on transactions costs.

8. (a) Curious. (b) Generally, when property rights are costly to define or enforce. (c) See several articles on this subject in the April 1973 issue of the *Journal of Law and Economics*.

CHAPTER 18

1. $x^*(t) = -e^2k(-t) + k(t)$; $\lambda^*(t) = 4e^2k(-t)$; $u^*(t) = 2e^2k(-t)$, where $k(t) = [e^t/(1 - e^2)]$.

2. $x^*(t) = t + 2$; $u^*(t) = 1$; $\lambda^*(t) = -t + 2$.

3. $x^*(t, \alpha, x_0) = \alpha(t - 1) + (x_0 + \alpha)k(t) - e^2(x_0 + \alpha)k(-t)$; $\lambda^*(t, \alpha, x_0) = 2(x_0 + \alpha)k(t)$; $u^*(t, \alpha, x_0) = \alpha t + 2(x_0 + \alpha)k(t)$, where $k(t) = [e^t/(1 - e^2)]$.

7. $x^*(t, \alpha) = (e^2/2\alpha)e^{-t} + (1/2\alpha) + [(10\alpha - e^2 - 1)/2\alpha]e^t$; $\lambda^*(t, \alpha) = 2(1 - e^{2-t})$; $u^*(t, \alpha) = (e^{2-t} - 1)/\alpha$.

CHAPTER 19

2. We do not *know* that markets are stable. Like profit maximization, stability is a behavioral postulate which is *asserted*, with the ultimate aim of deriving refutable hypotheses from it.

3. This result follows from the elementary properties of the substitution matrix.

INDEX

Adding-up theorem, 483–485
Adjoint equation, 619
Adjoint variable, 618–619
Alchian and Allen substitution theorem, 384–389
Arrow, Kenneth J., 446n, 451n, 574n, 662, 662n
Arrow impossibility theorem, 574–577
Assertions, 10
  vs. assumptions, 10
Assumptions, 10
  realism of, 11
Autonomous problems in control theory, 625
Average cost:
  definition, 227
  envelope results, 264
  relation to marginal cost, 229–230
Azzi, Corry, 434n

Becker, Gary S., 389n
Bellman, Richard, 614, 617
Bernoulli, Daniel, 443n
  (See also St. Petersburg paradox)
Bernoulli, Johann, 617
Bertrand equilibrium, 665
Blumberg, R., 425n
Bohm-Bawerk, 430n
Bordered hessian, 175
  (See also Maximization, constrained)

Border-preserving principal minor, 175–176, 183

Calculus of variations, 622–624
Capital utilization, 639–644
Caputo, Michael R., 643n
Caputo's theorem, 643
CES production function:
  derivation, 291–293
  factor demands for, 294–295
Chain rule:
  monotonic transformations, 82–84
  one variable, 36, 79–80
  second derivatives, 84–86
  several variables, 80–82
Cheung, Steven N. S., 607
Coase, Ronald, 604n
Coase theorem, 604–607
Cobb-Douglas production function, 93, 94–95, 99
  unitary elasticity of substitution, 286–287, 292–293
Common property, 603–604
Comparative statics:
  analysis under risk, 455–460
  definition of, 15–16
  traditional methodology, 180–187
  two variables, 158–160
  using duality, 195–202, 210–222

Composite commodity theorem, 381–384
  and "shipping the good apples out,"
    384–389
Concave functions:
  one variable, 57
  several variables, 132–133
Conditional demands:
  addition of a new commodity, 335–336
  cost minimization model, 254–255
  Hicksian demand functions, 333–334
  Marshallian demand functions, 334–334
  profit maximization, 126–127
    (*See also* Le Châtelier principle)
  relation of profit maximization and cost
    minimization factor demands, 256–258
  short- and long-run competitive equilibrium,
    268–269
Conjugate pairs theorem, 160, 197
Constant returns to scale, 93
  (*See also* Homogeneous functions)
Consumer theory (*see* Utility)
Consumer's surplus:
  compensating variation, 396
  constancy of the marginal utility of money,
    398, 401–402
  defined as changes in the expenditure
    function, 399–400
  empirical approximations, 403–405
  measure of welfare loss, 596–599
Continuity, 28
Control theory:
  adjoint, or costate, equation, 619
  adjoint, or costate, variable, 618–619
  autonomous problems, 625–627
  and calculus of variations, 622–624
  capital utilization, 639–644
  control variable, 616
  endpoint (transversality) conditions,
    624–625
  general problem, 616
  Hamiltonian, 619
  harvesting a renewable resource, 635–639
  intertemporal choice, 632–635
  maximum principle, 619
  principle of optimality, 614
  state equation, 619
  state variable, 616
  sufficient conditions, 627–628
Control variable (*see* Control theory)
Convex function, 57
  (*See also* Concave functions)
  one variable, 57
Convex set, 177–178, 482, 487
  in linear programming models, 503, 523

Cost function:
  definition, 225
  duality with production functions, 281–285
  generalized Leontief, 297
  homogeneity of, 275–276
    functional form of, 278
  for homogeneous production functions,
    278
  for homothetic productions functions,
    279–281
    functional form of, 279–281
Cost minimization:
  comparative statics
    reciprocity conditions, 250–252
    traditional methodology, 241–249
    using duality theory, 249–252
  factor demand functions
    defined, 237
    elasticity formulas, 261–262
    homogeneity of, 259
    output elasticities, 262–263
    relation to demand functions derived from
      profit maximization, 256–258
    short vs. long run, 254–255
  interpretation of first- and second-order
    conditions, 230–236
  interpretation of Lagrange multiplier as
    marginal cost, 237–241
Costate equation, 619
Costate variable, 618–619
Cournot duopoly solution, 663–665

Demand function (consumer):
  (*See also* Cost, minimization, Profit
    maximization)
  with endowments, 349–351
  Hicks vs. Slutsky compensations, 351–353
  Hicksian
    conditional demands, 333–334
    elasticity formulas, 341–344
    and expenditure minimization, 319–320
    homogeneity of, 341–342
    relation to Marshallian, 329–331
  labor-leisure choice, 346–349
  Marshallian
    conditional demands, 334–335
    defined, 308–309
    elasticity formulas, 339–340
    homogeneity, 313
    relation to Hicksian, 329–331
Derivatives:
  one variable, 31
  partial, 70–76

Determinants:
  Cramer's rule, 143
  expansion by alien cofactors, 142–143
  use in second-order conditions, 160–163,
      175–176
  (*See also* comparative statics)
Diewert, Erwin, 297
Differential:
  one variable, 34
  several variables, 76–78
Differential equations, 65–66, 628–632
Diversification, 452–454
Division of labor, 353–357
Duality theory:
  constrained maximization models, 198–207
  cost and production functions, 281–285
  unconstrained maximization models,
      195–198
Dupuit, Jules, 598
Dynamics, meaning of, 613–615

Edgeworth-Bowley box diagram, 537
Efficiency:
  and common property, 603
  in production, 581
  in production and consumption, 585
  and share cropping, 607–611
Ehrenberg, Ron, 434n
Elasticity, 40
  definition, 40
  relation to marginal revenue, 41
Elasticity of substitution:
  for Cobb-Douglas production function, 287,
      293, 294
  definition of, 287–288
  derivation of CES production function,
      291–293
  relation to cross-elasticities, 289
Envelope theorem:
  history, 190–191
  unconstrained models, 192, 196
  graphical depiction of, 196
Equilibrium:
  Bertrand, 665
  Marshallian stability, 655–656
  Nash, 665
  Walrasian stability, 652–654, 656–662
Euler-Lagrange equation, 623–624
Euler's theorem, 98
  (*See also* Homogeneous functions)
  converse of, 100
e^x, 46
  relation to compound interest, 46–49

Expected utility hypothesis, 446–448
Expenditure function, 330

Factor demands (*see* Cost minimization; Profit
      maximization)
Factor price equalization:
  in linear models, 505
  in nonlinear models, 553–554
Faustmann solution, 50, 614
Fisher, Irving, 49, 417, 420, 426, 429
Fisher separation theorem, 426
Fisherian investment, 49
Freeway congestion, 230
Friedman, Milton, 425n, 452n
Function:
  one variable, 26
  several variables, 68

Game theory, 662–666
Generalized Leontief production function, 297
Gould, John, 386n

Hamiltonian, 619
  interpretation of,, 621
Hamilton-Jacobi equation, 620
Harvesting a renewable resource, 635–639
Hausman Jerry, 405n
Heckscher-Ohlin theorem, 565–567
Homogeneous functions:
  constant returns to scale, 93
  definition, 93
  Euler's theorem, 98
  exhaustion of the product, 92–93
  relation to homotheticity, 96
  relation to "stages of production,"
      99–100
Homothetic functions, 97
  (*See also* Homogeneous functions)
Hotelling, Harold, 590n
Hotelling taxation theorem, 589–591
Household production functions, 389–396
  comparative statics, 393–395

Implicit function theorem, 144–148
Implicit functions, 39
Indirect objective function, 192
Inequality constraints, 470–476
  (*See also* Kuhn-Tucker conditions)
Input-output models, 501n
Insurance, 452–454

Integral, 58–64
  area under a curve, 60–64
Integration by parts, 63–64
Interest rate:
  determination, 430–433
    crusonia bush, 431
  premium for earlier availability, 417
  real vs. nominal, 428–429
  vs. time preference, 420, 422
Intertemporal choice, in control theory,
      632–635

Kamien, Morton I., 413, 624n, 625n
Knight, Frank, 230, 431
Koopmans, T.C., 515
Kuhn, H. W., 473n
Kuhn-Tucker conditions, 473

Labor-leisure choice, 346–349
Lagrange multiplier:
  definition, 169
  interpretation as an imputed shadow price,
      204–205
  interpretation of, 184
Lagrangian (See Maximization, constrained)
Lancaster, Kelvin J., 389n, 591n
Le Châterlier principle:
  general results, 216–222
  in profit maximization model, 124–127
  (See also Conditional demands)
Leontief, Wassily, 501n
  generalized Leontief cost function, 297
Level curves:
  convexity of, 89–91
  negative slope of, 86–89
Life-cycle hypothesis, 425–426
Limits, 28
Linear programming, 494–530
  activities, 496
  dual problem, 514
  feasible region, 503, 518
  fundamental theorem of, 517
  graphical solution, 501–504
  input-output coefficient, 494
  simplex algorithm, 520–530
Lipsey, Richard G., 591n
Log x, 50
Long-run competitive equilibrium:
  adjustment of firms, 265–267
  relation of factor demands to short-run profit
      maximization, 268–269
Lyapunov theorem, 660

Marginal cost:
  definition, 226
  relation to average cost, 229–230
Marshall, Alfred, 398n
Matrix (matrices):
  associative law, 150
  distributive law, 150
  inverse, 153–154
  orthogonality, 154–155
  rank, 151–152
Maximization:
  constrained
    geometry of, 176–180
    more than one constraint, first-order
        conditions, 171–173
    n variables, second-order conditions,
        175–176
    two variables, second-order conditions,
        173–175
  unconstrained
    n variables, 160–163, 166–170
    one variable, 41–42, 56, 58
    two variables, 108–112
Maximum principle, 619
Mean, 442
Mean value theorem, 53
Modigliani, Franco, 425n
Monotonic transformations, 82–84
  invariance of Marshallian demands, 311
Morgenstern Oskar, 447n, 663, 663n
Mosak, Jacob, 353

Nonlinear programming:
  saddlepoint theorem, 476–478, 487–490
  Slater constraint qualification, 477, 488
Nonnegativity constraints, 462–470
  (See also Kuhn-Tucker conditions)

Pareto conditions:
  competitive equilibrium, 587–589
  in economies with production, 581–586
  optimality, 577, 585, 610
  public goods, 595
  in pure exchange economy, 579
  taxation, 589–591
  transactions costs, 600–611
Partial derivatives:
  definition, 71
  invariance to order of differentiation (Young's
      theorem), 73–76
Pascal, Blaise, 434n
Peano, 114

Permanent income hypothesis, 425–426
Pollak, Robert, 126n, 393n
  (*See also* conditional demands)
Pontryagin, L. S., 617
Pratt, John W., 451n
Present value, 417
Principal minor, 162
Principle of optimality, 614
Probability, 440
Product Rule, 38
Production functions:
  (*See also* Elasticity of substitution)
  Cobb-Douglas, 93, 94–95, 99
  constant elasticity of substitution (CES), 293
Production possibilities frontier, 535
Profit function, 192
  graph of, 194
Profit maximization:
  analysis of finite changes, 130–131
  elasticity formulas, 123–124
  and law of diminishing marginal product,
    115–117
  two factors
    comparative statics, 117–122
    definition of factor demand functions, 117
    definition of supply function, 121
    homogeneity of the demand functions,
      122–123
    long-run vs. short-run demands, 124–127
    (*See also* Le Châtelier principle)
  using determinants, 156–158, 163–166
Public goods, 593–596
Pure exchange economy, 578–580

Quasi-concavity, 177–178
Quotient rule, 39

Reciprocity conditions:
  cost minimization, 250–252
  general relations, 198, 214
  profit maximization, 120
Refutable proposition:
  definition of, 12–14
  three sources of, 648
Revealed preference, 362–381
  equivalence to utility theory, 373–381
  and intransitivity, 370–371
  strong axiom, 372
    and integrability, 373–381
  weak axiom, 365
Risk, measures of, 458–459
Risk aversion, 449–452

Risk aversion *(Cont.)*
  Arrow-Pratt measure of, 451
  relative risk aversion, 452
Routh-Hurwitz theorem, 660, 661
Roy's identity, 315
Rybczynski theorem:
  linear models, 507–509
  nonlinear models, 561–563
  use in Heckscher-Ohlin theorem, 564–567

Saddlepoint, 476
Saddlepoint theorem:
  in linear programming models, 518
  in nonlinear programming models, 476–478
St. Petersburg paradox, 442–443
Samuelson, Paul, 398n
Savage, L. J., 452n
Schwartz, Nancy L., 624n, 625n
Second best, 591–593
Second-order smallness, 35
Segall, Joel, 386n
Separating hyperplane, 487–488
Sharecropping, 607–611
Shipping the good apples out, 384–389
Silberberg, Eugene, 391n
Slater constraint qualification, 477, 488
Slutsky equation (*see* Utility; Demand functions)
Smith, Adam, 353–357, 493n
Social welfare function, 574–577
Stability (*see* Equilibrium)
State equation (*see* Control theory)
State preference,, 445
Stocks and flows, 433–437
Stolper-Samuelson theorem:
  application to effects of taxes, 563–564
  linear models, 509–510
  nonlinear models, 554–561
Sufficient conditions in control theory,
    627–628

Tastes, 4–9
Tatonnement process, 652
Taylor series:
  one variable, 54
  several variables, 131–132
    derivation of first- and second-order
      conditions, 132–133
Theories:
  vs. models, 14–16
  structure of, 10–12
Time preference, 419–421
  Strotz criticism, 421

Transactions costs, 600–611
    Coase theorem, 604–607
    sharecropping, 607–611
Transversality conditions, 624–625
Tucker, A. W., 473 n

Umbeck, John, 387 n
Utility:
    cardinal vs. ordinal, 301
        and monotonic transformations, 82–83,
            86, 302–303
    maximization of
        basic postulates, 304–308
        Hicksian demands, 341–344
        indirect utility function, 310
        interpretation of Lagrange multiplier,
            313–315
        invariance of demands to monotonic
            transformation, 311
        Marshallian demands, 308–309, 313
        over time, 416–437
        relation to cost minimization,
            319–323
    Roy's identity, 315
    Slutsky equation, 329, 329–331,
        346–351

Utility *(Cont.)*
    specific functional forms, 405–411
        almost ideal demand system, 411
        constant elasticity of substitution (CES)
            utility, 407–408
        indirect addilog, 408–409
        linear expenditure system, 406–407
        translog, 409–411

Variance, 444
Viner, Jacob, 191
Viner-Wong diagram, 191
Von Neumann, John, 447 n, 663
Von Neumann-Morgenstern utility, 447
Voting paradox, 574

Wachter, Michael, 393 n
Wald, Abraham, 353
Walras *(see* Equilibrium)
Walras' Law, 661
Willig, Robert, 403 n
Witte, James, Jr., 434 n

Young's theorem, 74